General Paper 1 Casebook

16th edition

Part I Tort edited by E D Pitchfork
BSc, PhD, CChem, FRSC, Cert Ed (F & HE), Barrister-at-Law
Course Supervisor, LLB Courses, Holborn College

Part II Criminal Law edited by Michael T Molan
BA, LLM (Lond), Barrister
Head of Law, South Bank University

HLT Publications

HLT PUBLICATIONS
200 Greyhound Road, London W14 9RY

First published 1979
16th edition 1996

© The HLT Group Ltd 1996

All HLT publications enjoy copyright protection and the copyright belongs to The HLT Group Ltd.

All rights reserved. No part of this publication may be reproduced or transmitted in any form or by any means, electronic, mechanical, photocopying, recording or otherwise, or stored in any retrieval system of any nature without either the written permission of the copyright holder, application for which should be made to The HLT Group Ltd, or a licence permitting restricted copying in the United Kingdom issued by the Copyright Licensing Agency.

Any person who infringes the above in relation to this publication may be liable to criminal prosecution and civil claims for damages.

ISBN 0 7510 0677 7

British Library Cataloguing-in-Publication.
A CIP Catalogue record for this book is available from the British Library.

Acknowledgement

The publishers and author would like to thank the Incorporated Council of Law Reporting for England and Wales for kind permission to reproduce extracts from the Weekly Law Reports, and Butterworths for their kind permission to reproduce extracts from the All England Law Reports.

Printed and bound in Great Britain

Contents

Preface *v*

Table of Main Cases *vii*
    The Law of Tort *vii*
    Criminal Law *xv*

The Law of Tort

1 Joint and Several Tortfeasors *3*
2 Vicarious Liability *5*
3 Liability for Independent Contractors *16*
4 Negligence: The Duty of Care *20*
5 Negligence: Breach of the Duty *76*
6 Negligence: Causation *92*
7 Negligence: Remoteness of Damage *101*
8 Contributory Negligence *112*
9 Volenti Non Fit Injuria *118*
10 Breach of Statutory Duty *122*
11 Employers' Liability *130*
12 Product Liability *137*
13 Occupiers' Liability *139*
14 Private Nuisance *156*
15 Public Nuisance *172*
16 The Rule in *Rylands* v *Fletcher* *177*
17 Remedies *187*
18 Miscellaneous Defences and Limitation *214*
19 Torts to Chattels *221*

Criminal Law

20 Attempts *235*

21 Criminal Damage *236*

22 Non-Fatal Offences against the Person I *241*

23 Non-Fatal Offences against the Person II *255*

24 Homicide I *278*

25 Homicide II: Voluntary Manslaughter *292*

26 Homicide III: Involuntary Manslaughter *313*

27 Participation *328*

28 Inchoate Offences I *349*

29 Inchoate Offences II *372*

30 Defences I *382*

31 Defences II *418*

32 Defences III *445*

33 Introduction to Theft – The Actus Reus of Theft *463*

34 Appropriation *474*

35 The Mens Rea of Theft *492*

36 Sections 8, 9 and 10 Theft Act 1968 *502*

37 Sections 21 and 25 Theft Act 1968 *512*

38 Sections 15 and 16 Theft Act 1968 *521*

39 The Theft Act 1978 *541*

40 Handling Stolen Goods *547*

41 Accomplices *562*

Preface

This HLT casebook can be used as a companion volume to the Textbook but also comprises an invaluable reference tool in itself. Its aim is to supplement and enhance students' understanding and interpretation of these particular areas of the law, and to provide essential background reading.

This year, as well as being updated, the *General Paper I Casebook* has been revised to better reflect the contents of the Textbook, and consequently the Bar syllabus.

There have been a number of important and interesting developments in the Law of Tort. In particular, the House of Lords has on three occasions examined the scope of *Hedley Byrne* in *Henderson v Merrett Syndicates Ltd* [1994] 3 WLR 761, *Spring v Guardian Assurance plc* [1994] 3 WLR 354 and *White v Jones* [1995] NLJ 251, and it now seems clear that the scope of *Hedley Byrne* is not limited to negligent misstatements but covers negligent acts and omissions. As *Hedley Byrne* is the one secure cause of action in which pure economic loss can be recovered, it seems certain that more litigation will emerge in this area. The High Court has also held that an employer's duty to provide a safe system of work includes a duty not to cause foreseeable psychiatric damage to an employee due to the stress and pressures of his workload: *Walker v Northumberland County Council* [1994] NLJ 1659. This, too, could prove to be a rich vein for further working.

The House of Lords has reviewed and stated the law on breach of statutory duty, negligence in the exercise of a statutory power and the co-existence of a common law duty of care in *X v Bedfordshire County Council* [1995] 3 WLR 152. Although the House did not add to the law as regards the first cause of action, the speech of Lord Browne-Wilkinson on the latter two areas, and the relationship between private and public law, will repay much study.

The Court of Appeal in *Hunter v Canary Wharf* [1995] NLJ 1645 has continued to hold that the classic interest in land described in *Malone v Laskey* [1907] 2 KB 141 is no longer a prerequisite to suing in nuisance.

The law is stated on the basis of materials available as of 1 January 1996.

In relation to Criminal Law, key decisions of the House of Lords and Privy Council new to this edition include *R v Adomako*, which sees the re-establishment of killing by gross negligence; *R v Kingston* which examines the scope for a defence of disinhibition, based on intoxication; *R v Morhall* on the characteristics to be taken into account when formulating the defence of provocation; *C v DPP* which reasserts the defence of infancy for defendants between the ages of 10 and 14; and the *Meridian Global Funds* case, which suggests a new approach to the problem of locating corporate criminal liability.

The law is stated as of 1 January 1996.

Table of Main Cases: The Law of Tort

AB v South West Water Services Ltd [1993] 2 WLR 507   *187*
Adams v Ursell [1913] 1 Ch 269   *156*
Admiralty Commissioners v Volute (Owners), The Volute [1922] 1 AC 129   *112*
Afzal v Ford Motor Co Ltd [1994] 4 All ER 720   *20*
Airedale NHS Trust v Bland [1993] 2 WLR 316   *76*
Al-Kandari v J R Brown & Co [1988] 2 WLR 671   *21*
Alcock v Chief Constable of the South Yorkshire Police [1991] 3 WLR 1057   *21*
Alcock v Wraith (1991) The Times 23 December   *16*
Alexandrou v Oxford [1993] 4 All ER 328   *24*
Allen v Gulf Oil Refining Ltd [1981] AC 1001; [1981] 2 WLR 188   *156*
Alliance & Leicester Building Society v Edgestop [1993] 1 WLR 1462   *112*
Allied Maples Group Ltd v Simmons & Simmons [1995] 1 WLR 1602   *92*
American Cyanamid Co v Ethicon [1975] AC 396; [1975] 2 WLR 316   *189*
Ancell v McDermott [1993] 4 All ER 355   *24*
Andrews v Schooling [1991] 1 WLR 783   *139*
Anns v Merton London Borough Council [1978] AC 728   *25*
Antonelli v Wade Gery Farr (1992) The Times 29 December   *26*
Armory v Delamirie (1722) 1 Stra 505   *221*
Atkinson v Newcastle Waterworks Co (1877) 2 Ex D 441   *122*
Attia v British Gas plc [1987] 3 WLR 1101   *27*
Attorney-General v PYA Quarries Ltd [1957] 2 QB 169; [1957] 2 WLR 770   *172*

Baker v Willoughby [1970] AC 467; [1970] 2 WLR 50   *92*
Balfour v Barty-King [1957] 1 QB 496; [1957] 2 WLR 84   *16*
Banque Bruxelles Lambert SA v Eagle Star Insurance Co Ltd [1995] 2 WLR 607   *189*
Barkway v South Wales Transport Co Ltd [1950] AC 185   *77*
Barnett v Chelsea & Kensington Hospital Management Committee [1969] 1 QB 428; [1968] 2 WLR 422   *93*
Bayley v Manchester, Sheffield and Lincolnshire Rail Co (1873) LR 8 CP 148   *5*
BBMB Finance (Hong Kong) Ltd v Eda Holdings Ltd (1990) The Times 12 February   *190*
Bhoomidas v Port of Singapore Authority [1978] 1 All ER 956   *5*
Billings (AC) & Sons Ltd v Riden [1958] AC 240; [1957] 3 WLR 496   *139*
Blyth v Birmingham Waterworks Co (1856) 11 Exch 781   *77*
Bolam v Friern Hospital Management Committee [1957] 1 WLR 582   *78*
Bolton v Stone [1951] AC 850   *78*
Bourhill (or Hay) v Young [1943] AC 92   *27*
Bowater v Rowley Regis Corporation [1944] KB 476   *118*
Bradburn v Great Western Rail Co (1874) LR 10 Ex 1   *190*
Bradford v Robinson Rentals [1967] 1 WLR 337   *101*
Bridges v Hawkesworth (1851) LJ QB 75   *221*
Bridlington Relay Ltd v Yorkshire Electricity Board [1965] Ch 436; [1965] 2 WLR 349   *157*
British Celanese Ltd v A H Hunt (Capacitors) Ltd [1969] 1 WLR 959   *157*

British Railways Board v Herrington [1972] AC 877; [1972] 2 WLR 537   *140*
British Transport Commission v Gourley [1956] AC 185; [1956] 2 WLR 41   *190*
Broadley v Guy Clapham & Co [1994] 4 All ER 439   *214*
Brooke v Bool [1928] 2 KB 578   *3*
Brunsden v Humphrey (1884) 14 QBD 141   *191*
Burton v Winters [1993] 1 WLR 1077   *191*
Bute (Marquess) v Barclays Bank Ltd [1955] 1 QB 202   *222*

Calveley v Chief Constable of Merseyside [1989] 2 WLR 624   *28*
Cambridge Water Company v Eastern Counties Leather plc [1994] 2 WLR 53   *177*
Candlewood Navigation Corp Ltd v Mitsui Osk Lines Ltd, The Mineral Transporter [1986] AC 1; [1985] 3 WLR 381   *29*
Caparo Industries plc v Dickman [1990] 2 WLR 358   *30*
Carslogie Steamship Co Ltd v Royal Norwegian Government, The Carslogie [1952] AC 292   *101*
CBS Songs Ltd v Amstrad Consumer Electronics plc [1988] AC 1013   *31, 122*
Century Insurance Co Ltd v Northern Ireland Road Transport Board [1942] AC 509   *6*
Chadwick v British Transport Commission [1967] 1 WLR 912   *32*
Christie v Davey [1893] 1 Ch 316   *158*
Colledge v Bass Mitchells & Butlers Ltd [1988] 1 All ER 536   *191*
Coltman v Bibby Tankers Ltd, The Derbyshire [1987] 3 WLR 1181   *130*
Condon v Basi [1985] 1 WLR 866   *79*
Cook v Square D Ltd [1992] IRLR 34   *130*
Cookson v Knowles [1979] AC 556; [1978] 2 WLR 978   *192*
Cork v Kirby Maclean Ltd [1952] 2 All ER 402   *93*
Cresswell v Eaton [1991] 1 WLR 1113   *192*
Cunningham v Reading Football Club Ltd [1992] PIQR 141   *141*
Cutler v United Dairies (London) Ltd [1933] 2 KB 297   *118*
Cutler v Vauxhall Motors Ltd [1971] 1 QB 418   *94*
Cutler v Wandsworth Stadium Ltd [1949] AC 398   *124*

D & F Estates Ltd v Church Commissioners for England [1988] 3 WLR 368   *32*
Dann v Hamilton [1939] 1 KB 509   *119*
Darbishire v Warran [1963] 1 WLR 1067   *193*
Davey v Harrow Corporation [1958] 1 QB 60; [1957] 2 WLR 941   *159*
Davis v Radcliffe [1990] 1 WLR 821   *34*
Department of Environment v Thomas Bates & Son Ltd [1990] 3 WLR 457   *35*
Derbyshire, The see Coltman v Bibby Tankers Ltd
Dobbie v Medway Health Authority [1994] 4 All ER 450   *214*
Dodd Properties (Kent) Ltd v Canterbury City Council [1980] 1 WLR 433   *193*
Doleman v Deakin (1990) The Times 30 January   *194*
Dominion Mosaics and Tile Co Ltd v Trafalgar Trucking Co Ltd [1990] 2 All ER 246   *194*
Donoghue (or McAlister) v Stevenson [1932] AC 562   *36*
Donovan v Gwentoys Ltd [1990] 1 WLR 472   *215*
Doughty v Turner Manufacturing Co Ltd [1964] 1 QB 518; [1964] 2 WLR 240   *101*
Dulieu v White & Sons [1901] 2 KB 669   *36*

East Suffolk Rivers Catchment Board v Kent [1941] AC 74   *37*
Edison, The [1933] AC 449   *102*
Emeh v Kensington and Chelsea and Westminster Area Health Authority [1985] 2 WLR 233   *37*

Esso Petroleum Co Ltd *v* Mardon [1976] 1 QB 801; [1976] 2 WLR 583   *38*
Evans *v* Triplex Safety Glass Co Ltd [1936] 1 All ER 283   *137*

Ferguson *v* Welsh [1987] 1 WLR 1553   *142*
Fetter *v* Beale *see* Fitter *v* Veal
Fitter *v* Veal (1701) 12 Mod Rep 542   *195*
Fitzgerald *v* Lane [1989] AC 328   *113*
Froom *v* Butcher [1975] 3 WLR 379   *114*

Galoo Ltd *v* Bright Graham Murray [1994] 1 WLR 1360   *94*
Gammell *v* Wilson [1982] AC 27; [1980] 3 WLR 591   *196*
General Cleaning Contractors Ltd *v* Christmas [1953] AC 180; [1953] 2 WLR 6   *131*
General Engineering Services Ltd *v* Kingston and St Andrew Corp [1989] 1 WLR 69   *6*
Gillingham Borough Council *v* Medway (Chatham) Dock Co Ltd [1993] QB 343   *172*
Gitsham *v* C H Pearce & Sons plc [1992] PIQR 57   *143*
Glasgow Corporation *v* Muir [1943] 2 AC 448   *79*
Glasgow Corporation *v* Taylor [1922] 1 AC 44   *143*
Gorris *v* Scott (1874) LR 9 Exch 125   *125*
Gough *v* Thorne [1966] 1 WLR 1387   *114*
Gran Gelato Ltd *v* Richcliff (Group) Ltd [1992] 1 All ER 865   *38*
Grant *v* Australian Knitting Mills Ltd [1936] AC 85   *137*
Green *v* Chelsea Waterworks Co (1894) 70 LT 547   *180*
Greenwood *v* Bennett [1973] QB 195   *223*
Groves *v* Lord Wimborne [1898] 2 QB 402   *125*

Hale *v* Jennings Bros [1938] 1 All ER 579   *181*
Haley *v* London Electricity Board [1965] AC 778; [1964] 3 WLR 479   *80*
Hallam-Eames *v* Merrett (1995) The Times 25 January   *215*
Halsey *v* Esso Petroleum Co Ltd [1961] 1 WLR 683   *159*
Hannah *v* Peel [1945] KB 509   *224*
Harris *v* Birkenhead Corporation [1976] 1 WLR 279   *143*
Harris *v* Wyre Forest District Council *see* Smith *v* Eric S Bush
Harrison *v* British Railways Board [1981] 3 All ER 679   *115*
Harrison *v* Southwark and Vauxhall Water Co [1891] 2 Ch 409   *159*
Hayden *v* Hayden [1992] 1 WLR 986   *196*
Heasmans *v* Clarity Cleaning Co Ltd [1987] ICR 949   *7*
Hedley Byrne & Co Ltd *v* Heller & Partners [1964] AC 465; [1963] 3 WLR 101   *39*
Hemmens *v* Wilson Browne [1993] 4 All ER 826   *40*
Henderson *v* Henry E Jenkins & Sons [1970] AC 282; [1969] 3 WLR 732   *81*
Henderson *v* Merrett Syndicates Ltd [1994] 3 WLR 761   *40*
Hewett *v* Alf Brown's Transport Ltd (1992) The Times 4 February   *131*
Hicks *v* Chief Constable of the South Yorkshire Police [1992] 2 All ER 65   *197*
Hill *v* Chief Constable of West Yorkshire [1989] AC 53   *41*
Hoare & Co Ltd *v* Sir Robert McAlpine, Sons & Co [1923] 1 Ch 167   *160*
Hodgson *v* Trapp [1988] 3 WLR 1281   *198*
Holliday *v* National Telephone Co [1899] 2 QB 392   *17*
Hollywood Silver Fox Farm Ltd *v* Emmett [1936] 2 KB 468   *160*
Holt *v* Payne Skillington (1995) The Times 22 December   *42*
Home Office *v* Dorset Yacht Co Ltd [1970] AC 1004; [1970] 2 WLR 1140   *43*

Honeywill & Stein Ltd v Larkin Brothers (London's Commercial Photographers) Ltd [1934] 1 KB 191   17
Hotson v East Berkshire Area Health Authority [1987] AC 50; [1987] 3 WLR 232   95
Housecroft v Burnett [1986] 1 All ER 332   200
Hudson v Ridge Manufacturing Co Ltd [1957] 2 QB 348; [1957] 2 WLR 948   132
Hughes v Lord Advocate [1963] AC 837; [1963] 2 WLR 779   103
Hughes v National Union of Mineworkers [1991] 4 All ER 278   43
Hunt v Severs [1994] 2 All ER 385   200
Hunter v Canary Wharf Ltd [1995] NLJ 1645   161
Hussain v New Taplow Paper Mills Ltd [1988] 2 WLR 266   201

International Factors Ltd v Rodriguez [1979] 1 QB 351   225

James McNaughton Papers Group Ltd v Hicks Anderson & Co [1991] 2 WLR 641   44
Jefford v Gee [1970] 2 QB 130; [1970] 2 WLR 702   202
Jerome v Bentley & Co [1952] 2 All ER 114   226
Jobling v Associated Dairies Ltd [1982] AC 794; [1981] 3 WLR 155   95
Jones v Boyce (1816) 1 Stark 493   104
Jones v Department of Employment [1988] 2 WLR 493   45
Jones v Jones [1985] 2 QB 704   202
Jones v Livox Quarries Ltd [1952] 2 QB 608   115
Junior Books Ltd v Veitchi Co Ltd [1983] 1 AC 520; [1982] 3 WLR 477   45

K v P [1993] 1 All ER 521   216
Kay v Ayrshire and Arran Health Board [1987] 2 All ER 417   96
Kelly v Dawes (1990) The Times 27 September   202
Kennaway v Thompson [1981] QB 88; [1980] 3 WLR 361   161
Khorasandjian v Bush [1993] 3 WLR 476   162
King v Liverpool City Council [1986] 1 WLR 890   46
Kirkham v Chief Constable of the Greater Manchester Police [1990] 2 WLR 987   47
Knightley v Johns [1982] 1 WLR 349   104
Knowles v Liverpool City Council [1993] 4 All ER 321   132
Koursk, The [1924] P 140   3
Kowal v Ellis (1977) 76 DLR (3d) 546   226

Lamb v Camden London Borough Council [1981] QB 625; [1981] 2 WLR 1038   47
Lancashire & Cheshire Association of Baptist Churches v Howard & Seddon Partnership [1993] 3 All ER 467   48
Latimer v AEC Ltd [1953] 2 AC 643   81
Laws v Florinplace Ltd [1981] 1 All ER 659   163
Leakey v National Trust for Places of Historic Interest or Natural Beauty [1980] QB 485; [1980] 2 WLR 65   164
Lemmon v Webb [1895] AC 1   161
Liesbosch Dredger v SS Edison see Edison, The
Lim Poh Choo v Camden and Islington AHA [1980] AC 174; [1979] 3 WLR 44   203
Limpus v London General Omnibus Co (1892) 1 H & C 526   8
Lister v Romford Ice & Cold Storage Co Ltd [1957] AC 555; [1957] 2 WLR 158   8
Littler v Liverpool Corporation [1968] 2 All ER 343   173
Lloyd v Grace, Smith & Co [1912] AC 716   8

Lonrho Ltd v Shell Petroleum Co Ltd [1982] AC 173; [1981] 3 WLR 33   *126*
Lord v Pacific Steam Navigation Co Ltd, The Oropesa [1943] P 32   *105*
Luxmore-May v Messenger May Baverstock [1990] 1 WLR 1009   *82*
Lyons, Sons & Co v Gulliver [1914] 1 Ch 631   *174*

McAuley v Bristol City Council [1992] 1 All ER 749   *144*
McCall v Abelesz [1976] QB 585; [1976] 2 WLR 151   *127*
McCamley v Cammell Laird Shipbuilders Ltd [1990] 1 WLR 963   *204*
McDermid v Nash Dredging and Reclamation Co Ltd [1987] AC 906   *133*
McFarlane v EE Caledonia Ltd [1994] 2 All ER 1   *48*
McGeown v Northern Ireland Housing Executive [1994] 3 All ER 53   *145*
McGhee v National Coal Board [1973] 1 WLR 1   *97*
McHale v Watson [1966] ALR 513   *82*
McKew v Holland & Hannen & Cubitts (Scotland) Ltd [1969] 3 All ER 1621   *106*
McLeish v Amoo-Gottfried & Co (1993) The Times 13 October   *205*
McLoughlin v O'Brian [1983] AC 410; [1982] 2 WLR 982   *49*
McWilliams (or Cummings) v Sir William Arrol & Co Ltd [1962] 1 WLR 295   *97*
Malone v Laskey [1907] 2 KB 141   *165*
Manders v Williams (1849) 4 Ex 339   *227*
Mariola Marine Corporation v Lloyd's Register of Shipping, The Morning Watch [1990] 1 Lloyd's Rep 547   *51*
Mason v Levy Auto Parts of England Ltd [1967] 2 QB 530; [1967] 2 WLR 1384   *181*
Matania v The National Provincial Bank Ltd [1936] 2 All ER 633   *166*
Mattocks v Mann (1992) The Times 19 June   *98*
Maynard v West Midlands Regional Health Authority [1984] 1 WLR 634   *83*
Meah v McCreamer [1985] 1 All ER 367   *205*
Mersey Docks & Harbour Board v Coggins & Griffith (Liverpool) Ltd [1947] AC 1   *9*
Miller v Jackson [1977] QB 96; [1977] 3 WLR 20   *166*
Mineral Transporter, The *see* Candlewood Navigation Corp Ltd v Mitsui Osk Lines Ltd
Mint v Good [1951] 1 KB 517   *174*
Moffatt v Kazana [1969] 2 WLR 71   *228*
Moore (DW) & Co Ltd v Ferrier [1988] 1 WLR 267   *217*
Morales v Eccleston [1991] RTR 151   *116*
Morgan Crucible Co plc v Hill Samuel Bank Ltd [1991] 2 WLR 655   *52*
Morgan v Incorporated Central Council of the Girls' Friendly Society [1936] 1 All ER 404   *18*
Morgans v Launchbury [1973] AC 127; [1972] 2 WLR 1217   *9*
Morning Watch, The *see* Mariola Marine Corporation v Lloyd's Register of Shipping
Morrell v Owen (1993) The Times 14 December   *52*
Morris v CW Martin & Sons Ltd [1966] 1 QB 716; [1965] 3 WLR 276   *10*
Morris v Murray [1991] 2 WLR 195   *120*
Morris v Redland Bricks Ltd *see* Redland Bricks Ltd v Morris
Muirhead v Industrial Tank Specialities Ltd [1985] 3 WLR 993   *53*
Murphy v Bradford Metropolitan Council [1992] PIQR 68   *146*
Murphy v Brentwood District Council [1990] 3 WLR 414   *54*
Mutual Life and Citizens' Assurance Co Ltd v Evatt [1971] AC 793; [1971] 2 WLR 23   *55*

Nance v British Columbia Electric Railway Co Ltd [1951] AC 601   *116*
Nettleship v Weston [1971] 2 QB 691; [1971] 3 WLR 370   *83*
Nichols v Marsland (1876) 2 Ex D 1   *182*

Nitrigin Eireann Teoranta v Inco Alloys Ltd [1992] 1 WLR 498   *56*
Nocton v Lord Ashburton [1914] AC 932   *56*
North-Western Utilities Ltd v London Guarantee and Accident Co Ltd [1936] AC 108   *182*

O'Connell v Jackson [1972] 1 QB 270; [1971] 3 WLR 463   *117*
O'Kelly v Trusthouse Forte plc [1984] QB 90   *10*
Ogwo v Taylor [1987] 3 WLR 1145   *146*
Ormrod v Crossville Motor Services Ltd [1953] 1 WLR 1120   *11*
Oropesa, The see Lord v Pacific Steam Navigation Co Ltd
Osman v Ferguson [1993] 4 All ER 344   *57*
Overseas Tankship (UK) Ltd v The Miller Steamship Pty Ltd, (The Wagon Mound No 2) [1967] 1 AC 617; [1966] 3 WLR 498   *106*
Overseas Tankship (UK) Ltd v Morts Dock & Engineering Co Ltd (The Wagon Mound No 1) [1961] AC 388; [1961] 2 WLR 126   *107*
Owens v Brimmell [1977] QB 859; [1977] 3 WLR 943   *117*

Page v Smith [1995] 2 WLR 644   *57*
Pape v Cumbria County Council [1992] ICR 132   *134*
Paris v Stepney Borough Council [1951] AC 367   *84*
Parker v British Airways Board [1982] 1 QB 1004   *228*
Parry v Cleaver [1970] AC 1; [1969] 2 WLR 821   *206*
Partington v Wandsworth London Borough Council (1989) The Independent 8 November   *58*
Performance Cars Ltd v Abraham [1962] 1 QB 33; [1961] 3 WLR 749   *98*
Perl (P) (Exporters) Ltd v Camden London Borough Council [1984] QB 342; [1983] 3 WLR 769   *58*
Perry v Kendricks Transport Ltd [1956] 1 WLR 85   *183*
Perry (Howard E) & Co Ltd v British Railways Board [1980] 1 WLR 1375   *229*
Petch v Commissioners of Customs and Excise (1993) The Times 4 March   *59*
Phipps v Rochester Corporation [1955] 1 QB 450; [1955] 2 WLR 23   *147*
Pickett v British Rail Engineering Ltd [1980] AC 136; [1978] 3 WLR 955   *206*
Pidduck v Eastern Scottish Omnibuses Ltd [1990] 1 WLR 993   *207*
Pitts v Hunt [1990] 3 WLR 542   *120*
Poland v John Parr and Sons [1927] 1 KB 236   *12*
Polemis and Furness, Withy & Co Ltd, Re [1921] 3 KB 560   *108*
Ponting v Noakes [1894] 2 QB 281   *183*
Pritchard v J H Cobden Ltd [1988] Fam 22   *207*

R v Shorrock [1993] 3 WLR 698   *175*
Racz v Home Office [1993] 2 WLR 23   *12*
Read v J Lyons & Co Ltd [1947] AC 156   *184*
Ready Mixed Concrete (South East) Ltd v Minister of Pensions and National Insurance [1968] 2 QB 497; [1968] 2 WLR 775   *12*
Redland Bricks Ltd v Morris [1969] 2 WLR 1437   *208*
Reid v Rush & Tompkins Group plc [1990] 1 WLR 212   *60*
Revill v Newberry (1995) The Independent 10 November   *148*
Richardson v Pitt-Stanley [1995] 2 WLR 26   *127*
Rickards v Lothian [1913] AC 263   *184*
Rigby v Chief Constable of Northamptonshire [1985] 1 WLR 1242   *217*
Robinson v Kilvert (1889) 41 Ch D 888   *166*
Robinson v The Post Office [1974] 1 WLR 1176   *109*

Table of Main Cases: The Law of Tort xiii

Robson v Hallett [1967] 2 QB 393; [1967] 3 WLR 28   *148*
Roe v Ministry of Health [1954] 2 QB 66; [1954] 2 WLR 915   *84*
Roles v Nathan [1963] 1 WLR 1117   *149*
Rondel v Worsley [1969] 1 AC 191; [1967] 3 WLR 1666   *60*
Rose v Miles (1815) 4 M & S 101   *175*
Rose v Plenty [1976] 1 WLR 141   *13*
Ross v Caunters [1980] Ch 297; [1979] 3 WLR 605   *61*
Rouse v Squires [1973] QB 889; [1973] 2 WLR 925   *109*
Rowling v Takaro Properties Ltd [1988] 2 WLR 418   *61*
Rylands v Fletcher (1868) LR 3 HL 330   *185*

Saif Ali v Sydney Mitchell and Co [1980] AC 198; [1978] 3 WLR 849   *63*
St Helen's Smelting Co v Tipping (1865) 11 HL Cas 642   *167*
Salmon v Seafarer Restaurants Ltd [1983] 1 WLR 1264   *149*
Salsbury v Woodland [1970] 1 QB 324   *18*
Scott v London & St Katherine Docks Co (1865) 3 H & C 596   *85*
Scott v Shepherd (1733) 2 Wm Bl 892   *110*
Sedleigh-Denfield v O'Callaghan [1940] AC 880   *167*
Shelfer v City of London Electric Lighting Co [1895] 1 Ch 287   *168*
Sheppard v Glossop Corporation [1921] 3 KB 132   *64*
Shiffman v The Grand Priory in the British Realm of the Venerable Order of the Hospital of St John of Jerusalem [1936] 1 All ER 557   *186*
Sidaway v Bethlem Royal Hospital Governors [1985] AC 871   *85*
Simaan General Contracting Co v Pilkington Glass Ltd (No 2) [1988] 2 WLR 761   *65*
Simkiss v Rhondda Borough Council (1983) 81 LGR 460   *150*
Simms v Leigh Rugby Football Club Ltd [1969] 2 All ER 923   *151*
Smith v Eric S Bush; Harris v Wyre Valley District Council [1989] 2 WLR 790   *66*
Smith v Leech Brain & Co Ltd [1962] 2 QB 405; [1962] 2 WLR 148   *110*
Smith v Littlewoods Organisation Ltd [1987] 2 WLR 480   *67*
Smith v *Marchioness/Bowbelle* [1993] NLJ 813   *209*
Smith v Stages [1989] 2 WLR 529   *13*
Smoker v London Fire and Civil Defence Authority [1991] 2 WLR 1052   *209*
Somasundaram v M Julius Melchior & Co [1988] 1 WLR 1394   *68*
South Staffordshire Water Co v Sharman [1896] 2 QB 44   *230*
Southern Portland Cement Ltd v Cooper [1974] AC 623; [1974] 2 WLR 152   *151*
Spartan Steel and Alloys Ltd v Martin & Co (Contractors) Ltd [1973] 1 QB 27; [1972] 3 WLR 502   *69*
Spring v Guardian Assurance plc [1994] 3 WLR 354   *70*
Stanley v Saddique [1991] 2 WLR 459   *210*
Stansbie v Troman [1948] 2 KB 48   *111*
Staples v West Dorset District Council (1995) The Times 28 April   *152*
Stone v Taffe [1974] 1 WLR 1575   *153*
Stubbings v Webb [1993] 2 WLR 120   *218*
Sturges v Bridgman (1879) 11 Ch D 852   *169*

Targett v Torfaen Borough Council [1991] NPC 126   *153*
Tarry v Ashton (1876) 1 QBD 314   *175*
Tetley v Chitty [1986] 1 All ER 663   *169*
Thomas v National Union of Mineworkers (South Wales Area) [1985] 2 WLR 1081   *176*

Thornton v Kirklees Metropolitan Borough Council [1979] QB 626; [1979] 3 WLR 1   *128*
Tinsley v Milligan [1993] 3 WLR 126   *219*
Topp v London Country Bus (South West) Ltd [1993] 3 All ER 448   *71, 99*
Twine v Bean's Express Ltd (1946) 175 LT 131   *14*

Union Transport Finance v British Car Auctions Ltd [1978] 2 All ER 385   *231*

Van Oppen v Clerk to the Bedford Charity Trustees [1990] 1 WLR 235   *71*
Volute, The *see* Admiralty Commissioners v Volute (Owners)

Walker v Northumberland County Council [1994] NLJ 1659   *135*
Walpole v Partridge and Wilson [1993] 3 WLR 1093   *72*
Ward v Tesco Stores Ltd [1976] 1 WLR 810   *86*
Warren v Henlys Ltd [1948] 2 All ER 935   *15*
Watson v Willmot [1990] 3 WLR 1103   *210*
Watt v Hertfordshire County Council [1954] 1 WLR 835   *86*
Waverley Borough Council v Fletcher [1995] 3 WLR 772   *231*
Welsh v Chief Constable of the Merseyside Police [1993] 1 All ER 692   *87*
Wheat v E Lacon & Co Ltd [1966] AC 552; [1966] 2 WLR 581   *154*
Wheeler v J J Saunders [1995] 3 WLR 466   *170*
White v Blackmore [1972] 2 QB 651; [1972] 3 WLR 296   *154*
White v Jones [1995] 2 WLR 481   *73*
White v St Albans City and District Council (1990) The Times 12 March   *155*
Whitehouse v Jordan [1981] 1 WLR 246   *89*
Wieland v Cyril Lord Carpets Ltd [1969] 3 All ER 1006   *111*
Wigg v British Railways Board (1986) The Times 4 February   *74*
Wilks v The Cheltenham Home Guard Motor Cycle and Light Car Club [1971] 1 WLR 668   *89*
Willson v Ministry of Defence [1991] 1 All ER 638   *211*
Wilsher v Essex Area Health Authority [1988] 2 WLR 557   *99*
Wilson v Lombank Ltd [1963] 1 WLR 1294   *232*
Wood v British Coal Corp [1991] 2 WLR 1052 *see* Smoker v London Fire and Civil Defence Authority
Wooldridge v Sumner [1963] 2 QB 43; [1963] 3 WLR 616   *90*
Woollins v British Celanese Ltd (1966) 110 SJ 686   *155*
Wright v British Railways Board [1983] 2 AC 773; [1983] 3 WLR 211   *212*
Wright v Lodge [1993] 4 All ER 299   *99*
Wringe v Cohen [1940] 1 KB 229   *170*

X v Bedfordshire County Council; M v Newham London Borough Council; E v Dorset County Council; Christmas v Hampshire County Council; Keating v Bromley London Borough Council [1995] 3 WLR 152   *128*

Yuen Kun-yeu v Attorney-General of Hong Kong [1987] 3 WLR 776   *74*

Table of Main Cases: Criminal Law

Abbot *v* R [1977] AC 755   *418*
Anderton *v* Ryan [1985] AC 560; [1985] 2 WLR 968   *372*
Attorney-General for Northern Ireland *v* Gallagher [1963] AC 349   *382*
Attorney-General's Reference (No 1 of 1975) [1975] 3 WLR 11   *329, 562*
Attorney-General's Reference (No 6 of 1980) [1981] QB 715   *243*
Attorney-General's Reference (No 1 of 1983) [1984] 3 WLR 686   *463*
Attorney-General's Reference (No 1 of 1992) (1993) 96 Cr App R 298   *372*
Attorney-General's Reference (No 2 of 1992) [1993] 3 WLR 982   *384*
Attorney-General's Reference (No 3 of 1992) [1994] 1 WLR 409   *373*

Beckford *v* R [1987] 3 WLR 611   *418, 445*
Bedder *v* DPP [1954] 2 All ER 801   *292*
Bratty *v* Attorney-General for Northern Ireland [1963] AC 386   *388*

C (A Minor) *v* DPP [1995] 2 WLR 383   *447*
Chan Man-Sin *v* R [1988] 1 WLR 196   *475*
Chan Wing-Siu *v* R [1984] 3 WLR; [1985] AC 168   *336, 564*
Commissioner of Police of the Metropolis *v* Caldwell [1982] AC 341   *236, 393*
Commissioner of Police for the Metropolis *v* Charles [1977] AC 177   *522*

DPP *v* Beard [1920] AC 479   *396*
DPP *v* Camplin [1978] AC 705   *294*
DPP *v* Daley and McGhie [1980] AC 237   *283*
DPP *v* Majewski [1977] AC 142   *396*
DPP *v* Morgan [1976] AC 182   *450*
DPP *v* Newbury and Jones [1976] AC 500   *320*
DPP *v* Nock [1978] AC 979   *353*
DPP *v* Ray [1974] AC 370   *526*
DPP *v* Taylor; DPP *v* Little [1992] 1 QB 645   *251*
DPP for Northern Ireland *v* Maxwell [1978] 1 WLR 1350   *566*

Halstead *v* Patel [1972] 1 WLR 661   *530*
Hills *v* Ellis [1983] QB 680; [1983] 1 All ER 667   *252*
Hui Chi-ming *v* R [1991] 3 WLR 495   *567*

Jaggard *v* Dickinson [1981] 2 WLR 118   *238, 453*
Johnson *v* Youden [1950] 1 KB 544   *345, 571*

Lawrence *v* Metropolitan Police Commissioner [1972] AC 626   *488*

Moynes *v* Cooper [1956] 1 QB 439   *472*

Table of Main Cases: Criminal Law

National Coal Board v Gamble [1958] 3 WLR 434   *572*

Palmer v R [1971] AC 814   *439*

R v Adomako [1994] 3 WLR 288   *313*
R v Aitken and Others [1992] 1 WLR 1066   *241*
R v Allen [1985] AC 1029   *541*
R v Anderson [1986] AC 27   *349*
R v Anderson and Morris [1966] 2 QB 110   *328, 562*
R v Atakpu; R v Abrahams [1993] 3 WLR 812   *474*
R v Bailey [1983] 1 WLR 760   *386*
R v Bainbridge [1959] 3 WLR 356   *331, 563*
R v Baldessare (1930) 22 Cr App R 70   *333*
R v Betts and Ridley (1930) 22 Cr App R 148   *334*
R v Blaue [1975] 1 WLR 1411   *255, 278*
R v Bloxham [1983] 1 AC 109   *547*
R v Bourne [1939] 1 KB 687   *418*
R v Bourne (1952) 36 Cr App R 125   *563*
R v Brown [1970] 1 QB 105   *549*
R v Brown [1993] 2 WLR 556   *244*
R v Bundy [1977] 1 WLR 914   *512*
R v Burgess [1991] 2 WLR 1206   *319*
R v Byrne [1960] 2 QB 396   *292*
R v Calhaem [1985] QB 808; [1985] Crim LR 303   *355, 564*
R v Callender [1992] 3 WLR 501   *521*
R v Cato [1976] 1 WLR 110   *255, 315*
R v Chan-Fook [1994] 1 WLR 689   *249*
R v Cheshire [1991] 1 WLR 844   *280*
R v Church [1966] 1 QB 59   *316*
R v Clarence (1888) 22 QBD 23   *255*
R v Clarkson [1971] 1 WLR 1402   *337, 565*
R v Clegg [1995] 2 WLR 80   *418*
R v Cogan and Leak [1975] 3 WLR 316; [1976] QB 217   *256, 338, 565*
R v Collins [1972] 3 WLR 243   *502*
R v Coney (1882) 8 QBD 534   *566*
R v Cooke [1986] AC 909   *513*
R v Court [1988] 2 WLR 1071   *256*
R v Curr [1968] 2 QB 944   *351*
R v Dalby [1982] 1 WLR 425   *317*
R v Dawson [1908] 2 KB 454   *284*
R v Dawson (1976) 64 Cr App R 170   *505*
R v Dawson (1985) 81 Cr App R 150   *317*
R v Doukas [1978] 1 WLR 372   *515, 526*
R v Dudley and Stephens (1884) 14 QBD 273   *420*
R v Dunnington [1984] QB 472   *340*
R v Duru (1973) 58 Cr App R 151   *492*
R v Ellames [1974] 1 WLR 1391   *516*
R v Firth (1990) 91 Cr App R 127   *543*
R v Fitzmaurice [1983] 2 WLR 227   *356*

Table of Main Cases: Criminal Law xvii

R v Fitzpatrick [1977] NI 20   *421*
R v Garwood [1987] 1 WLR 319   *517*
R v George [1956] Crim LR 52   *258*
R v Ghosh [1982] 3 WLR 110   *492*
R v Gilks [1972] 1 WLR 1341   *465*
R v Gomez [1992] 3 WLR 1067   *478*
R v Goodfellow (1986) 83 Cr App R 23   *321*
R v Gotts [1992] 2 AC 412   *424*
R v Governor of Pentonville Prison, ex parte Osman [1990] 1 WLR 277   *485*
R v Graham [1982] 1 WLR 294   *429*
R v Grainge [1974] 1 WLR 619   *551*
R v Griffiths (1974) 60 Cr App R 14   *553*
R v Hale (1978) 68 Cr App R 415   *488, 506*
R v Hall [1973] 1 QB 126   *467*
R v Hardie [1985] 1 WLR 64   *400*
R v Harvey and Others (1980) 72 Cr App R 139   *519*
R v Hennessy [1989] 1 WLR 287   *403*
R v Hill; R v Hall (1988) 89 Cr App R 74   *236*
R v Hollinshead [1985] AC 978   *358*
R v Holt and Lee [1981] 1 WLR 1000   *544*
R v Howe [1987] AC 417   *342, 430*
R v Hudson and Taylor [1971] 2 QB 202   *436*
R v Hyde [1990] 3 WLR 1115   *342, 569*
R v Jefferson [1994] 1 All ER 270   *571*
R v Johnson [1989] 1 WLR 740   *297*
R v Jones (1990) 91 Cr App R 351   *235*
R v Jones (John) and Smith (Christopher) [1976] 1 WLR 672   *508*
R v Kanwar [1982] 1 WLR 845   *557*
R v Kemp [1957] 1 QB 399   *405*
R v Khan and Others [1990] 1 WLR 813   *258*
R v Kimber [1983] 1 WLR 1118   *253*
R v King; R v Stockwell [1987] 2 WLR 746   *532*
R v Kingston [1994] 3 WLR 519   *406*
R v Lambie [1982] AC 449   *534, 546*
R v Linekar [1995] 2 WLR 237   *261*
R v Lipman [1970] 1 QB 152   *410*
R v Lloyd [1985] 3 WLR 30   *498*
R v McDonough (1962) 47 Cr App R 37   *360*
R v McInnes [1971] 1 WLR 1600   *437*
R v McIvor [1982] 1 WLR 409   *501*
R v Malcherek; R v Steel [1981] 1 WLR 690   *285*
R v Mandair [1994] 2 WLR 700   *265*
R v Martin (1989) 88 Cr App R 343   *438*
R v Meech [1973] 3 WLR 507   *469*
R v Miller [1954] 2 QB 282   *266*
R v Mitchell [1983] 2 WLR 938   *323*
R v Morhall [1995] 3 WLR 330   *298*
R v Mowatt [1968] 1 QB 421   *267*

R v Navvabi [1986] 1 WLR 1311   489
R v O'Grady [1987] 3 WLR 321   453
R v Olugboja [1981] 3 WLR 585   267
R v Pagett (1983) 76 Cr App R 279   287
R v Pitchley (1973) 57 Cr App R 30   559
R v Pitham and Hehl (1976) 65 Cr App R 45   491, 560
R v Quick [1973] QB 910   411
R v Richards [1973] 3 WLR 888   572
R v Roberts [1993] 1 All ER 583   573
R v Rook [1993] 1 WLR 1005   346, 574
R v Sanders (1991) 93 Cr App R 245   301
R v Sanderson (1994) 98 Cr App R 325   304
R v Saunders and Archer (1573) 2 Plowd 473   348
R v Savage; R v Parmenter [1991] 3 WLR 914   268
R v Seers (1984) 79 Cr App R 261   306
R v Shepherd (1988) 86 Cr App R 47   441
R v Shivpuri [1986] 2 WLR 988   235, 374
R v Siracusa (1990) 90 Cr App R 340   361
R v Sirat (1985) 83 Cr App R 41   364
R v Slack [1989] 3 WLR 513   573
R v Smith [1974] QB 354   239, 455
R v Smith [1988] Crim LR 616   576
R v Spratt [1990] 1 WLR 1073   273
R v Steer [1987] 3 WLR 205   240
R v Sullivan [1984] AC 156   413
R v Tandy [1989] 1 WLR 350   309
R v Thompson [1984] 1 WLR 962   537
R v Tolson (1889) 23 QBD 168   456
R v Turner (No 2) [1971] 1 WLR 901   473
R v Venna [1975] 3 WLR 737   253, 276
R v Walker and Hayles (1990) 90 Cr App R 226   378
R v Walkington [1979] 1 WLR 1169   509
R v Warner (1970) 55 Cr App R 93   501
R v Watson [1989] 1 WLR 684   326
R v Whitefield [1984] Crim LR 97   577
R v Williams (Gladstone) (1984) 78 Cr App R 276   444, 458
R v Williams; R v Davis [1992] 1 WLR 380   290
R v Wilson [1983] 3 WLR 686   276, 511
R v Windle [1952] 2 QB 826   416
R v Woods (1981) 74 Cr App R 312   460

Wai Yu-Tsang v R [1991] 3 WLR 1006   365

Yip Chiu-Cheung v R [1994] 3 WLR 514   370

THE LAW OF TORT

1 Joint and Several Tortfeasors

Brooke* v *Bool [1928] 2 KB 578 High Court (Salter and Talbot JJ)

Joint tortfeasors

Facts
The plaintiff tenant of a lock-up shop had asked her landlord, who lived in adjoining premises, to visit the shop occasionally at night to see that everything was secure. When the defendant landlord's lodger complained of a smell of gas from the shop, both went to investigate. Both used naked lights, but the lodger's caused an explosion and the plaintiff sought damages from the defendant in respect of damage to her goods.

Held
The plaintiff's action should succeed. The lodger was the defendant's agent, the defendant had been in control of the proceedings and they had been engaged in a joint tortious enterprise.

Commentary
Applied: *The Koursk* [1924] P 140.
   Approved and applied in *Honeywill & Stein Ltd v Larkin Bros (London's Commercial Photographers) Ltd* [1934] 1 KB 191.

Koursk, The [1924] P 140 Court of Appeal (Bankes, Scrutton and Sargant LJJ)

Joint tortfeasors?

Facts
Some ships, including the Itria, the Clan Chisholm and the Koursk, were in convoy. Due to K's negligent navigation, it threatened to run into the C and, although C took avoiding action, a collision took place. As a result of attempting to avoid the collision, C ran into the I. C's navigation had also been negligent. I sued C, but the amount recovered was insufficient to cover I's loss. I then sued K.

Held
I's second action was not barred as the two negligences had been separate and independent and not committed in concert or as part of a common plan.

Bankes LJ:

'It is easy to put instances the mere mention of which indicates that the law must require something more than the single damnum to convert two quite separate and distinct torts into a joint tort. For instance, A, who wishes to approach B's house in order to commit a burglary trespass on his land and crosses a brook by an already damaged bridge, which he seriously weakens by his weight. Next day, C, wishing to approach the same house, mistaking it for that of a friend, trespasses on B's land, and in crossing the same bridge, breaks it completely down by his weight. Can it possibly be said that the damage to the bridge was caused by a joint tort, or that A and C are joint tortfeasors? I think not, and if this view is correct it follows that in order to constitute a joint tort there must be some connection between the act of the one alleged tortfeasor and that of the other. It would be unwise to attempt to define the necessary amount of connection. Each case must depend upon its own circumstances.'

Commentary
Applied in *Brooke* v *Bool* [1928] 2 KB 578.

2 Vicarious Liability

Bayley* v *Manchester, Sheffield and Lincolnshire Rail Co (1873) LR 8 CP 148 Court of Exchequer Chamber (Kelly CB, Martin, Cleasby and Pigott BB, Blackburn, Mellor and Lush JJ)

Scope of porter's authority

Facts
The plaintiff was violently pulled from one of the defendants' carriages by one of the defendants' porters, just after the train had started: the porter had erroneously believed that the plaintiff was travelling in the wrong train. The plaintiff fell and suffered injuries. While it was part of porters' duties to prevent passengers going by wrong trains so far as they were able to do so, the defendants' byelaws expressly provided that they (passengers) were not to be removed.

Held
The defendants were liable as the porter had acted within the scope of his authority.

Kelly CB:

> 'When we look for the principle which governs all the cases, the result is that, where a servant, acting within the scope of his authority, does even that which he is told not to do, his master, who gave him the general authority, is responsible. The defendants had given a general authority to their servants to prevent passengers from travelling in wrong carriages as far as possible; and it was the duty of each servant to act on this general authority and to prevent travellers from so travelling accordingly. It could not be said that a servant was not acting within the scope of his authority when, in order to prevent this, he pulled a passenger out of a carriage by force; for there might be circumstances – where a carriage is too full for instance – in which a porter might really think it is his duty to use force. The cases in which the servant has been held not to have acted within the scope of his authority are cases where the act complained of was an isolated act, done in disobedience of an express or implied injunction, and are on that ground distinguishable from the present case. There is, indeed, here a statement in byelaw 6 that it is not the duty of the porters to remove passengers from wrong trains or carriages; but where a porter finds inconsistent directions, such as this and the other to do his best to prevent persons from travelling in wrong carriages, he may well follow one and disregard the other. This porter was interfering in a state of things in which, acting on the discretion which the defendants had given him, it was his duty to interfere. Consequently, the defendants are responsible for what he did.'

Bhoomidas* v *Port of Singapore Authority [1978] 1 All ER 956 Privy Council (Lord Simon of Glaisdale, Lord Salmon, Lord Keith of Kinkel, Sir Garfield Barwick and Sir Richard Wild)

Vicarious liability – loan of employee

Facts
A gang of stevedores was employed by the respondents who engaged them, paid them, prescribed the jobs they were to undertake and alone had power to dismiss them. While loading a cargo of timber, due to the negligence of a member, or members, of the gang, another member was fatally injured. Harbour by-laws provided that 'labourers employed in ... loading vessels should be under the superintendence of the ship's officers; the [respondents] undertake no responsibility as stevedores'.

Held
The by-law did not exclude the respondents' liability.

Lord Salmon:

> 'Their Lordships consider that this byelaw falls far short of putting the servants of the respondent under the entire and absolute control of the ship. It does not seem to their Lordships in the least inconsistent with their being the servants of the respondent, and not the servants of the shipowners. It throws no light on the extent of the superintendence of the ship's officers. Superintendence is a somewhat loose and ambiguous word. For example a building owner's architect superintends on behalf of the building owner the work of the building contractor's workmen, but this does not make them the building owner's servants. The ship's officers no doubt have the right to superintend the loading by directing into which holds the cargo is to be loaded and the order in which it is to be loaded but this in no way puts the servants of the respondent so completely and entirely under the control and at the disposition of the ship's officers as to make them the servants of the shipowners, who neither pay them, nor select them, nor could discharge them.'

Commentary
Applied: *Mersey Docks and Harbour Board* v *Coggins & Griffiths (Liverpool) Ltd* [1947] AC 1.

Century Insurance Co Ltd v *Northern Ireland Road Transport Board* [1942] AC 509 House of Lords (Viscount Simon LC, Lord Wright, Lord Romer, Lord Porter)

Vicarious liability – course of employment

Facts
The defendants' employee, a petrol tanker driver, was waiting by his tanker whilst the tanks of a petrol station were being filled. He lit a cigarette and threw the match on the ground, causing an explosion and fire. The plaintiffs, the defendants' insurers, argued that the negligent act of the driver was not done in the course of his employment so as to make the defendants vicariously liable for him.

Held
The driver's act in lighting a cigarette was not done for his employers' benefit but for his own convenience. That does not matter: it was one and indivisible from the carrying out of his work and was within the scope of his employment.

General Engineering Services Ltd v *Kingston and Saint Andrew Corp* [1989] 1 WLR 69 Privy Council (Lord Bridge of Harwick, Lord Templeman, Lord Ackner, Lord Oliver of Aylmerton and Sir John Stephenson)

Intentional wrongful acts

Facts
The plaintiffs' property was completely destroyed by fire and the damage was increased by the fact that the firemen who answered the plaintiffs' emergency call were involved in a 'go-slow' in support of a pay claim and took 17 minutes rather than three and a half minutes to reach the plaintiffs' property. The plaintiffs alleged that the defendants, who were the employers of the firemen, were vicariously liable for the acts of the firemen.

Held
This was not the case.

Lord Ackner:

> 'It is, of course, common ground that a master is not responsible for a wrongful act done by his servant unless it is done in the course of his employment. Further, it is well established that the act is deemed to be so done if it is either (1) a wrongful act authorised by the master, or (2) a wrongful and unauthorised mode of doing some act authorised by the master ...
>
> Their Lordships have no hesitation in agreeing ... that the members of the fire brigade were not acting in the course of their employment when they, by their conduct ..., permitted the destruction of the building and its contents. Their unauthorised and wrongful act was so to prolong the time taken by the journey to the scene of the fire, as to ensure that they did not arrive in time to extinguish it, before the building and its contents were destroyed. Their mode and manner of driving, the slow progression of stopping and starting, was not so connected with the authorised act, that is driving to the scene of the fire as expeditiously as reasonably possible, as to be a mode of performing that act ...
>
> Here the unauthorised and wrongful act by the firemen was a wrongful repudiation of an essential obligation of their contract of employment, namely the decision and its implementation not to arrive at the scene of the fire in time to save the building and its contents. This decision was not in furtherance of their employers' business. It was in furtherance of their industrial dispute, designed to bring pressure on their employers to satisfy their demands, by not extinguishing fires until it was too late to save the property.
>
> Such conduct was the very negation of carrying out some act authorised by the employer, albeit in a wrongful and unauthorised mode. Indeed in preventing the provision of an essential service, members of the fire brigade were ... guilty of a criminal offence.'

Heasmans v *Clarity Cleaning Co Ltd* [1987] ICR 949 Court of Appeal (Purchas and Nourse LJJ)

Vicarious liability – conversion

Facts
An office cleaning contractor company employed a cleaning lady whose task it was to go into offices after hours and clean the offices. Whilst in the office she used the telephone to make personal calls (adding up to £1,500 in total). The plaintiffs, the owner of the office, sued the defendant, the contractor, as being vicariously liable for the conversion of the cleaning lady.

Held
The defendants were not vicariously liable for the cleaning lady's phone calls. They were not made in the course of employment, as phoning was not part of her duties, though cleaning the phone was.

Limpus v *London General Omnibus Co* (1892) 1 H & C 526 Court of Exchequer Chamber (Wightman, Williams, Crompton, Willes, Byles and Blackburn JJ)

Vicarious liability – course of employment

Facts
The defendant's drivers were expressly forbidden to obstruct or race with other buses. S did so and caused damage to P.

Held
S's act was done for defendants' purposes not his own and defendants were vicariously liable.

Commentary
Distinguished in *Conway* v *George Wimpey & Co Ltd* [1951] 2 KB 266.

Lister v *Romford Ice & Cold Storage Co Ltd* [1957] 2 WLR 158 House of Lords (Viscount Simonds, Lord Morton of Henryton, Lord Ratcliffe, Lord Tucker and Lord Somervell of Harrow)

Vicarious liability – injury to fellow workman

Facts
The appellant, a lorry driver employed by the respondents, was backing his lorry and negligently ran into and injured his father, another of the respondents' employees. The respondents being vicariously liable, the father obtained judgment against them. The respondents sought to recover this amount from the appellant.

Held
They should succeed as the appellant had been in breach of his duty to them to take due care.

Lloyd v *Grace, Smith & Co* [1912] AC 716 House of Lords (Lord Loreburn LC, Earl of Halsbury, Lord Macnaghten, Lord Atkinson, Lord Shaw and Lord Robson)

Vicarious liability – employee's fraud

Facts
Authorised to undertake conveyancing matters on the firm's behalf, a managing clerk defrauded a client in the course of a conveyancing transaction. The client sued the solicitors, the clerk's employers.

Held
Although the solicitors were innocent of the fraud and it was committed for the clerk's, not their, benefit, they were liable as it had been committed in the course of the clerk's employment.

Commentary
Applied in *Morris* v *C W Martin & Sons Ltd* [1965] 3 WLR 276.

Mersey Docks & Harbour Board v *Coggins & Griffith (Liverpool) Ltd* [1947] AC 1 House of Lords (Viscount Simon, Lord Macmillan, Lord Porter, Lord Simonds and Lord Uthwatt)

Vicarious liability – employee on loan

Facts
M1 hired to M2 a crane and driver. Whilst on hire, M1 was responsible for paying the driver and could dismiss him, but the hire agreement declared the driver to be M2's employee. Due to the driver's negligence in operating the crane, one of M2's employees was injured. Was M1 or M2 vicariously liable?

Held
M1, being the permanent employer, retained control over the driver and was vicariously liable.

Lord Porter:

> 'Many factors are relevant, but in such a case as the present, particular importance may be attached to who may give orders as to how the work was to be done. If this power to control the method of performing the work is transferred from the general employer (M1) to the temporary employer (M2) then the latter may be liable. But, this is not so here.'

Viscount Simon:

> 'The permanent employer carries the burden of proving responsibility for the servant has shifted to the temporary employer ... I see the test as being – who had the authority to direct or delegate to the workman the manner in which the vehicle was driven? Here, in operating the crane the driver was using his own discretion which had been delegated to him by his regular employers. If he made a mistake in operating the crane, this was nothing to do with the hirers.'

Commentary
Applied in *Bhoomidas v Port of Singapore Authority* [1978] 1 All ER 956.

Morgans v *Launchbury* [1972] 2 WLR 1217 House of Lords (Lord Wilberforce, Viscount Dilhorne, Lord Pearson, Lord Cross of Chelsea and Lord Salmon)

Vicarious liability – negligent driving of agent

Facts
The respondents were passengers in a car owned by the appellant and driven by C. They were injured in an accident in which C and the appellant's husband, who was also in the car, were killed, due to C's negligent driving. The car was used jointly by the appellant and her husband. On the day of the accident, the appellant's husband went drinking with friends and, finding himself unfit to drive, he asked C to drive, having on several occasions previously promised his wife that if he drank too much, he would ask someone else to drive. At the time of the accident, C was not driving the appellant's husband straight back home, but was on the way to a restaurant. The respondents alleged that the appellant was vicariously liable for C, who at the time was acting as her agent.

Held
The appellant was not liable. When the husband asked C to drive that did not suffice to make C the appellant's agent.

Lord Wilberforce:

'I regard it as clear that in order to fix vicarious liability on the owner of a car in such a case as the present, it must be shown that the driver was using it for the owner's purposes, under delegation of a task or duty. The substitution for this clear conception of a vague test based on "interest" or "concern" has nothing in reason or authority to commend it. Every man who gives permission for the use of his chattel may be said to have an interest or concern in its being carefully used, and, in most cases if it is a car, to have an interest or concern in the safety of the driver, but it has never been held that mere permission is enough to establish vicarious liability.'

Commentary
Distinguished: *Ormrod v Crosville Motor Services Ltd* [1953] 1 WLR 1120.

Morris v *CW Martin & Sons Ltd* [1965] 3 WLR 276 Court of Appeal (Lord Denning MR, Diplock and Salmon LJJ)

Vicarious liability for criminal act

Facts
The plaintiff gave her fur coat to be cleaned by the defendants and it was stolen by one of their employees. The plaintiff sought to hold the defendants vicariously liable.

Held
The plaintiff's claim would succeed.

Lord Denning MR:

'When can a servant's fraud or dishonesty done for his own benefit, be said to be in the course of his employment? ... The essential point in the present case is that the defendants were bailees of the coat and thus they owed the plaintiff a duty of care with regard to its safekeeping. If they entrust this duty to their servant, they remain under a duty – they cannot delegate it.'

Diplock LJ:

'The defendants were bailees for reward and the servant who had stolen it was acting as their agent, entrusted with the duty of cleaning it. This act was therefore done within the course of his employment and the defendants were vicariously liable. Had the coat been stolen by some other employee, the result might be different.'

Salmon LJ:

'A bailee for reward is not answerable for the theft by any of his servants: only of the person to whom he has delegated the duty because that person alone can be said to act within the scope of his employment.'

Commentary
Overruled: *Cheshire v Bailey* [1905] 1 KB 237.
   Applied: *Lloyd v Grace, Smith & Co* [1912] AC 716.
   Approved in *Port Swettenham Authority v T W Wu & Co (M) Sdn Bhd* [1978] 3 WLR 530.

O'Kelly v *Trusthouse Forte plc* [1984] QB 90 Court of Appeal (Sir John Donaldson MR, Ackner and Fox LJJ)

Distinction between contract of service and contract for services

Facts
The applicants were 'regular casual' banqueting staff at the employers' hotel, ie, they were engaged on a regular basis to such an extent that some regular casuals had no other regular work. After seeking recognition as permanent employees working under contracts of employment, the applicants were dismissed. Were they working under contracts of employment and therefore entitled to complain of unfair dismissal?

Held
No. There was no overall contract between the parties and the applicants were in business on their own account as independent contractors supplying services.

Ackner LJ:

> 'The following factors were considered by the industrial tribunal to be *inconsistent* with a contract of employment: (n) the engagement was terminable without notice on either side. (o) The respondents had the right to decide whether or not to accept work, although whether or not it would be in their interest to exercise the right to refuse work is another matter. (p) The employers had no obligation to provide any work. (q) During the subsistence of the relationship it was the parties' view that casual workers were independent contractors engaged under successive contracts for services. (r) It is the recognised custom and practice of the industry that casual workers are engaged under a contract for services.'

Commentary
Considered: *Young & Woods Ltd* v *West* [1980] IRLR 201.

Ormrod v *Crosville Motor Services Ltd* [1953] 1 WLR 1120 Court of Appeal (Singleton, Denning and Morris LJJ)

Vicarious liability – car driven by friend

Facts
A friend agreed to drive the owner's car from Birkenhead to Monte Carlo. He was to take a suitcase for the owner and, after meeting up in Monte Carlo, they were to go on holiday together, with the car, in Switzerland. While driving through France the car was in collision with a coach.

Held
In so far as the friend was guilty of negligence, the owner was vicariously liable.

Denning LJ:

> 'The law puts an especial responsibility on the owner of a vehicle who allows it to go on the road in charge of someone else, no matter whether it is his servant, his friend, or anyone else. If it is being used wholly or partly on the owner's business or for the owner's purposes, the owner is liable for any negligence on the part of the driver. The owner only escapes liability when he lends it or hires it to a third person to be used for purposes in which the owner has no interest or concern ... That is not this case.'

Commentary
Distinguished in *Morgans* v *Launchbury* [1972] 2 WLR 1217.

Poland v John Parr and Sons [1927] 1 KB 236 Court of Appeal (Bankes, Scrutton and Atkins LJJ)

Vicarious liability – defence of employer's property

Facts
A carter, the defendant's employee, honestly and reasonably thought that the plaintiff, a boy aged 12, was pilfering, or about to pilfer, some sugar. He struck the boy on the back of the neck. The boy fell forward, one of the wagon's wheels went over his foot and the boy's leg had to be amputated in consequence.

Held
The defendants were liable. The carter had implied authority to make reasonable efforts to protect their property and the force used was not so excessive as to take his act – the striking of the boy – outside the scope of that authority.

Commentary
Considered in *Warren* v *Henlys Ltd* [1948] 2 All ER 935.

Racz v Home Office [1993] 2 WLR 23 House of Lords (Lord Templeman, Lord Goff, Lord Jauncey, Lord Browne-Wilkinson and Lord Mustill)

Misfeasance in public office – whether Home Office vicariously liable

Facts
The plaintiff, a remand prisoner, alleged that he had been ill-treated by prison officers and brought an action against the Home Office for damages in assault, misfeasance in public office and false imprisonment. The defendants sought to strike out the plaintiff's claim relating to misfeasance in public office: this application was granted by Ebsworth J and upheld by the Court of Appeal. The plaintiff appealed to the House of Lords.

Held
The House of Lords allowed the plaintiff's appeal and held that the Home Office could be vicariously liable for acts of prison officers that amounted to misfeasance in public office. The plaintiff's allegations of misfeasance in public office could only be struck out where it inevitably followed that if the allegations were true, that the unauthorised act of the prison officers had been so unconnected with their authorised duties as to be independent of and outside them, which was a question of fact and degree that should go to trial.

Commentary
Distinguished: *R* v *Deputy Governor of Parkhurst Prison, ex parte Hague* [1992] 1 AC 58.

Ready Mixed Concrete (South East) Ltd v Minister of Pensions and National Insurance [1968] 2 WLR 775 High Court (MacKenna J)

Employee or independent contractor?

Facts
The plaintiff company devised a scheme whereby concrete was to be delivered to its customers ready-

mixed. L entered into a contract with the company to deliver such concrete on a daily basis. L was to buy, run, maintain, repair, insure and drive his own lorry. He was paid by the company on a mileage plus bonus basis. He was subject to all the rules and regulations of the company which had a high degree of control over him and his work. Was L an employee or an independent contractor?

Held
He was an independent contractor as the provisions of his contract were inconsistent with its being a contract of service.

MacKenna J:
A contract of service exists if the following three conditions are fulfilled:

> '(i) The servant agrees that in consideration of a wage or other remuneration he will provide his own work and skill in the performance of some service for his master. (ii) He agrees, expressly or impliedly, that in the performance of that service he will be subject to the other's control in a sufficient degree to make that other master. (ii) The other provisions of the contract are consistent with its being a contract of service.'

Rose v Plenty [1976] 1 WLR 141 Court of Appeal (Lord Denning MR, Lawton and Scarman LJJ)

Vicarious liability – prohibited act

Facts
Contrary to his employers' orders, the first defendant, a milkman, took with him on his milk-round the plaintiff, a boy aged thirteen, to help with the work. Due to the milkman's negligent driving of the float, the boy was injured. Were the milkman's employers vicariously liable?

Held
Yes, as the milkman's employment of the boy was within the scope of his own employment and had been for the purpose of his employers' business.

Lord Denning MR:

> 'An employer's prohibition of the doing of an act is not necessarily such as to exempt the employer from liability, provided the act is done not for the employee's own purposes, but in the course of his service and for his employer's benefit.'

Commentary
Applied: *Limpus v London General Omnibus Co* (1862) 1 H & C 526.
    Distinguished: *Twine v Bean's Express Ltd* (1946) 175 LT 131 and *Conway v George Wimpey & Co Ltd* [1951] 2 KB 266.

Smith v Stages [1989] 2 WLR 529 House of Lords (Lord Keith of Kinkel, Lord Brandon of Oakbrook, Lord Griffiths, Lord Goff of Chieveley and Lord Lowry)

Different place of work

Facts
Two peripatetic laggers were working on a power station in the Midlands when they were sent to carry out urgent work in Wales. No stipulation was made as to the mode of travel, but they were paid for the

travelling time and the equivalent of the rail fare. They travelled in the car of one of the laggers, the first defendant, and the other lagger was injured on the return journey when, as a result of the first defendant's negligence, his car crashed through a brick wall. The first defendant was uninsured: were the employers, the second defendants, also liable?

Held
They were as the laggers had been travelling in their (the employers') time.

Lord Lowry:

'The paramount rule is that an employee travelling on the highway will be acting in the course of his employment if, and only if, he is at the material time going about his employer's business. One must not confuse the duty to turn up for one's work with the concept of already being "on duty" while travelling to it.

It is impossible to provide for every eventuality and foolish, without the benefit of argument, to make the attempt, but some prima facie propositions may be stated with reasonable confidence. (1) An employee travelling from his ordinary residence to his regular place of work, whatever the means of transport and even if it is provided by the employer, is not on duty and is not acting in the course of his employment, but, if he is obliged by his contract of service to use the employer's transport, he will normally, in the absence of an express condition to the contrary, be regarded as acting in the course of his employment while doing so. (2) Travelling in the employer's time between workplaces (one of which may be the regular workplace) or in the course of a peripatetic occupation, whether accompanied by goods or tools or simply in order to reach a succession of workplaces (as an inspector of gas meters might do), will be in the course of the employment. (3) Receipt of wages (though not receipt of a travelling allowance) will indicate that the employee is travelling in the employer's time and for his benefit and is acting in the course of his employment, and in such a case the fact that the employee may have discretion as to the mode and time of travelling will not take the journey out of the course of his employment. (4) An employee travelling in the employer's time from his ordinary residence to a workplace other than this regular workplace or in the course of a peripatetic occupation or to the scene of an emergency (such as a fire, an accident or a mechanical breakdown of plant) will be acting in the course of his employment. (5) A deviation from or interruption of a journey undertaken in the course of employment (unless the deviation or interruption is merely incidental to the journey) will for the time being (which may include an overnight interruption) take the employee out of the course of his employment. (6) Return journeys are to be treated on the same footing as outward journeys.

All the foregoing propositions are subject to any express arrangements between the employer and the employee or those representing his interests. They are not, I would add, intended to define the position of salaried employees, with regard to whom the touchstone of payment made in the employer's time is not generally significant.'

Commentary
Applied: *Canadian Pacific Railway Co* v *Lockhart* [1942] AC 591.
  Approved: *Vandyke* v *Fender* [1970] 2 WLR 929.

Twine v Bean's Express Ltd (1946) 175 LT 131 Court of Appeal (Lord Greene MR, Morton and Tucker LJJ)

Vicarious liability – unauthorised passenger

Facts
The plaintiff's husband was killed when the van in which he was being carried was involved in an accident due to the negligence of the driver, the defendants' servant. The deceased and the driver knew that the giving of lifts to unauthorised persons was forbidden.

Held
The plaintiff's claim would fail as the driver was acting outside the scope of his employment.

Lord Greene MR:

> 'The deceased had no right to be in the van and the driver had no right to give him a lift: the deceased was therefore a trespasser and was owed no duty of care by the employers of the driver ... The driver, in giving a lift to the deceased, was clearly acting outside the scope of his employment. He had no right whatsoever to do such a thing and in this respect, he was on a frolic of his own.'

Commentary
Applied in *Conway* v *George Wimpey & Co Ltd* [1951] 2 KB 266.

Warren v *Henlys Ltd* [1948] 2 All ER 935 High Court (Hilbery J)

Vicarious liability – assault on customer

Facts
Mistakenly believing that the plaintiff had tried to drive away without paying for his petrol, the pump attendant had used violent language when calling on him to stop. The plaintiff told the attendant that he would report him to his employers (the defendants) and the attendant 'gave him one on the chin to get on with'.

Held
The defendants were not liable as the act – the assault – was one of personal vengeance and not in the course of the attendant's employment.

Commentary
Considered: *Poland* v *John Parr & Sons* [1927] 1 KB 243.

3 Liability for Independent Contractors

Alcock* v *Wraith (1991) The Times 23 December Court of Appeal (Neill LJ and Cazalet J)

Liability for independent contractor

Facts

Mr and Mrs Swinhoe engaged Mr Wraith to re-roof their terraced house. Some months later the plaintiff noticed damp in his adjoining property and, Mr Wraith having been adjudged bankrupt, the county court judge upheld the plaintiff's claim for damages and held that Mr and Mrs Swinhoe were liable to him in trespass, in nuisance and in negligence. Mr and Mrs Swinhoe appealed.

Held

Their appeal would be dismissed. Neill LJ affirmed that where someone employs an independent contractor to do work on his behalf he is not in the ordinary way responsible for any tort committed by the contractor in the course of the execution of the work. However, there are exceptions to that general rule which include cases which involve the withdrawal of support from neighbouring land and cases which involve extra-hazardous acts. Both the general rule and the exceptions apply whether an action has been framed in negligence or nuisance and no different approach is adopted in an action for trespass. It is not possible to provide a list of activities which would be regarded as 'extra-hazardous' so as to fall within the exception of liability where a contractor was employed to carry out a task which was extra-hazardous, but it is clear that the activity has to involve some special risk of damage or that it has to be work which from its very nature is likely to cause danger or, more appropriately, damage.

His Lordship said that the crucial questions were:

i) Did the work involve some special risk or was it from its very nature likely to cause damage?
ii) Could one apply by analogy the exception to the general rule which could be relied upon in cases which involved party walls?

The fact that the work necessarily, because they were terraced properties, involved the creation of a fresh joint between the adjoining roofs made the case similar to a party-wall case. The true basis for the exception in the party-wall cases was that where the law conferred a right to carry out work on a wall or other division between two properties, and that work involved a risk of damage to the adjoining property, the law also imposed a duty on the party carrying out the work to ensure that it was carried out carefully. Mr and Mrs Swinhoe had the right to interfere with the joint between the two roofs but if they exercised that right, they were under a duty to see that reasonable skill and care was used in the operation. That duty could not be delegated to an independent contractor.

Balfour* v *Barty-King [1957] 2 WLR 84 Court of Appeal (Lord Goddard CJ, Morris LJ, Vaisey J)

Escape of fire – negligence of independent contractor

Facts
The defendant and plaintiff owned adjacent properties. The defendant employed an independent contractor to thaw frozen pipes in a loft which contained large amounts of combustible material. He used a blowlamp which ignited the lagging, the loft and eventually P's premises.

Held
D was liable for such an escape of fire when it resulted from a dangerous object being brought onto his premises at his invitation.

Commentary
Applied: *Musgrove* v *Pandelis* [1919] 2 KB 43.
Applied in *Emanuel (H & N) Ltd* v *Greater London Council* [1971] 2 All ER 835.

Holliday v *National Telephone Co* [1899] 2 QB 392 Court of Appeal (Earl of Halsbury LC, A L Smith and Vaughan Williams LJJ)

Negligence – independent contractor

Facts
When laying telephone wires in trenches under a highway, the defendants engaged a plumber – an independent contractor – to carry out some aspects of the work. Due to the negligence of the plumber's employee, there was an explosion and molten solder flew out and injured the plaintiff who was passing along the footway.

Held
The defendants were liable.

A L Smith LJ:

> 'Where a person is executing work upon a public highway, he cannot escape liability by employing an independent contractor, because there is a duty cast upon him to see that the work upon the highway is so carried out as not to injure persons who are using the highway.'

Honeywill & Stein Ltd v *Larkin Bros (London's Commercial Photographers) Ltd* [1934] 1 KB 191 Court of Appeal (Lord Hewart CJ, Lord Wright and Slessor LJ)

Independent contractor – negligence

Facts
After they had installed sound reproduction apparatus in a cinema, the plaintiffs employed the defendants to take photographs of the cinema's interior. The defendants negligently set light to the cinema's curtains and the plaintiffs sought to recover from the defendants the compensation which they (the plaintiffs) had paid to the cinema's owners.

Held
They should succeed as they were themselves liable to the cinema owners for the defendants' negligence.

General Paper I: The Law of Tort

Slessor LJ:

> 'To take a photograph in the cinema with a flashlight was, on the evidence stated above, a dangerous operation in its intrinsic nature, involving the creation of fire and explosion on another person's premises, that is, in the cinema, the property of the cinema company. The plaintiffs, in procuring this work to be performed by their contractors, the defendants, assumed an obligation to the cinema company which was, as we think, absolute, but which was at least an obligation to use reasonable precautions to see that no damage resulted to the cinema company from those dangerous operations. That obligation they could not delegate by employing the defendants as independent contractors, but they were liable in this regard for the defendants' acts. For the damage actually caused the plaintiffs were, accordingly, liable in law to the cinema company, and are entitled to claim and recover from the defendants damages for their breach of contract or negligence in performing their contract to take photographs.'

Commentary
Approved and applied: *Brooke* v *Bool* [1928] 2 KB 578.

Morgan v *Incorporated Central Council of the Girls' Friendly Society* [1936] 1 All ER 404 High Court (Horridge J)

Negligence – independent contractor

Facts
On his way to an office in the defendants' building, seeing the lift door partially open the plaintiff stepped through it. The lift was not there: the plaintiff fell down the shaft and was injured. The defendants had contracted with the Express Lift Co for the lift's maintenance and they – the independent contractors – had been guilty of negligence.

Held
The defendants were not liable for the plaintiff's injuries.

Horridge J:

> 'I am satisfied that the Express Lift Co were independent contractors, and that it was their duty to have discovered this defect. If they were independent contractors, the relationship of master and servant does not exist between defendants and themselves, and therefore the defendants are not liable for the acts of the contractors unless they can bring themselves within any known exceptions ... This case is an ordinary case of an independent contractor. The negligence was that of the independent contractor. Notwithstanding that, the defendants may be liable on other grounds. First it is said that they ought to have found the defect out. I do not agree. They employed people who knew better than they about lifts. I do not think the defendants were guilty of any default.'

Salsbury v *Woodland* [1970] 1 QB 324 Court of Appeal (Harman, Sachs and Widgery LJJ)

Independent contractor – negligence

Facts
Defendant one, the occupier of a house, employed defendant two, an apparently competent tree-feller, to cut down a large tree in the front garden. D2 did so negligently so that the tree brought down some telephone wires which fell onto the road. P, who lived opposite, went to remove the wires from the road

and was struck by a car driven negligently by D3. All three defendants were held liable. D1 appealed on the grounds that he was not vicariously liable for the negligence of his independent contractor, D2.

Held
The appeal would be allowed. as the work involved was not inherently dangerous. An employer is only liable for the torts of an independent contractor in limited circumstances where the employer himself is under a direct duty to see that care is taken throughout the operation.

4 Negligence: The Duty of Care

Afzal* v *Ford Motor Co Ltd [1994] 4 All ER 720 Court of Appeal (Neill, Beldam and Steyn LJJ)

Small personal injury claims – whether arbitration or trial in court

Facts
In a number of actions the plaintiff employees brought claims against their employers for damages in respect of minor personal injuries sustained in the workplace. Mostly the claims did not exceed £1,000 and under CCR O.19 r3 such claims would be automatically referred for arbitration by a district judge, unless he was satisfied that he should order a court trial on the grounds, inter alia, that a difficult question of law and a question of fact of exceptional complexity was involved (r3(2)(a)) or that it would be unreasonable for the claim to proceed to arbitration having regard to its subject matter, the size of any counterclaim, the circumstances of the parties or the interests of any other person likely to be affected by the award (r3(2)(2)). The plaintiffs applied for the reference to arbitration to be rescinded, contending that compulsory arbitration was unsuitable for personal injury claims, particularly in cases involving employers' liability, since the issues involved were too complex for summary judgment. In addition, the costs recoverable in arbitrated claims were limited so trade unions would be deterred from assisting claimants, who would then be at a serious disadvantage. The judge granted the employees' applications on the basis of O.19 r3(2)(d) and ordered that all the claims should be tried in court in view of the subject matter and the circumstances of the parties and, in particular, the fact that the employees could not be expected to present their own cases where breaches of statutory duty, medical evidence and discovery might play a large part without legal representation. The defendant appealed, on the grounds that the judge had applied the wrong test as he had not shown, pursuant to r3(2(d) that it was unreasonable for the claims as a class to be referred to arbitration and that, while a reference to arbitration could be rescinded after r3(2)(a) if the case raised difficult problems of law or fact, no such considerations arose in the instant cases.

Held
The appeals were allowed. The court should not rescind an automatic reference to arbitration under O.19 r3(1) merely because a question of law was involved or the facts were complex, since r3(2)(a) made it clear that a question of law had to be difficult or a question of fact exceptionally complex for a claim to be tried in court. The law applicable to employers' liability claims was often straightforward, and although the facts could be complex, in most instances the question was whether the employer had taken reasonable care and the medical issues were unlikely to be complex where the amount involved was less than £1,000. Further, the hardship of an employee representing himself against a legally represented employer was one faced in all cases where the financial resources of the parties were unequal. Thus it was wrong to approach employers' liability claims involving amounts below £1,000 as a class of case which was, in general, unsuited to arbitration.

The court also held that the intentional overstatement of a claim to avoid automatic reference to arbitration was a clear misuse of process.

Commentary

As a result of this decision the Lord Chancellor announced that he did not intend to take any further action on his proposals regarding small personal injury claims.

Al-Kandari v *J R Brown & Co* [1988] 2 WLR 671 Court of Appeal (Lord Donaldson of Lymington MR, Dillon and Bingham LJJ)

Negligence – solicitor's duty of care

Facts

The plaintiff was married to a Kuwaiti national and their two children were included on his passport. In 1981 the couple separated and the husband abducted the children to Kuwait. He was persuaded to return with them: the wife was given custody, care and control of the children and the husband undertook to deposit his passport with his solicitors, the defendants. Wishing to return to Kuwait, the husband wanted to have the children's names removed from it. To this end, the defendants forwarded the passport to London agents with instructions to take it to the Kuwait embassy. While it was there, the husband persuaded the embassy to release it to him. He then arranged for the plaintiff to be kidnapped and he used the passport to take the children to Kuwait. The plaintiff claimed damages for, inter alia, negligence.

Held

She was entitled to succeed. The defendants owed the plaintiff a duty to take reasonable care to keep the passport in their possession and they had been in breach of that duty. The damage suffered by the plaintiff had been a natural and probable consequence of the breach of duty.

Bingham LJ:

> 'The judge found against the plaintiff on the ground that it was not reasonably foreseeable that Mr Al-Kandari would be given any opportunity to abduct the children. The correct approach is to consider the breach of duty which has been proved and to ask whether an ordinarily competent solicitor in the defendants' position would have foreseen damage of the kind which actually occurred as a not unlikely result of that breach ... In my judgment such a solicitor would have foreseen the damage which the plaintiff has in fact suffered as a possible and by no means fanciful consequence of the breach of duty established. I would not, therefore, agree with the judge that this damage was too remote to be recoverable in law.'

Alcock v *Chief Constable of the South Yorkshire Police* [1991] 3 WLR 1057 House of Lords (Lord Keith of Kinkel, Lord Ackner, Lord Oliver of Aylmerton, Lord Jauncey of Tullichettle and Lord Lowry)

Persons entitled to damages for nervous shock

Facts

The defendant admitted liability in negligence in respect of the 95 deaths and over 400 physical injuries in the Hillsborough Stadium disaster. Scenes from the ground were broadcast live on television from time to time and later on television news. News of the disaster was also broadcast over the radio. None of the television broadcasts depicted the suffering or dying of recognisable individuals. Sixteen persons, some of whom were at the match but not in the area where the disaster occurred, and all of whom were relatives, or in one case the fiance, of persons who were in that area, brought actions against the defendant claiming damages for nervous shock resulting in psychiatric illness alleged to have been caused by seeing or hearing news of the disaster. The question of law having been tried as a preliminary issue and the Court of Appeal having decided against them, ten of the plaintiffs made a final appeal.

Held

Their appeals would be dismissed, either because the plaintiffs had not been at the match or their relationship to a victim had not been sufficiently close.

Lord Keith of Kinkel:

> 'The question of liability in negligence for what is commonly, if inaccurately, described as "nervous shock" has only twice been considered by this House, in *Hay (or Bourhill)* v *Young* [1943] AC 92 and in *McLoughlin* v *O'Brian* [1983] 1 AC 410. In the latter case ... Lord Wilberforce ... expressed the opinion that foreseeability did not of itself and automatically give rise to a duty of care owed to a person or class of persons and that considerations of policy entered into the conclusion that such a duty existed. He then considered the arguments on policy which had led the Court of Appeal to reject the plaintiff's claim, and concluded that they were not of great force. ...
>
> Lord Bridge of Harwich, with whom Lord Scarman agreed ... appears to have rested his finding of liability simply on the test of reasonable foreseeability of psychiatric illness affecting the plaintiff as a result of the consequences of the road accident ... Lord Edmund-Davies and Lord Russell of Killowen both considered the policy arguments which had led the Court of Appeal to dismiss the plaintiff's claim to be unsound ... Neither speech contained anything inconsistent with that of Lord Wilberforce.
>
> It was argued for the appellants in the present case that reasonable foreseeability of the risk of injury to them in the particular form of psychiatric illness was all that was required to bring home liability to the respondent. In the ordinary case of direct physical injury suffered in an accident at work or elsewhere, reasonable foreseeability of the risk is indeed the only test that need be applied to determine liability. But injury by psychiatric illness is more subtle, as Lord Macmillan observed in *Bourhill* v *Young*. In the present type of case it is a secondary sort of injury brought about by the infliction of physical injury, or the risk of physical injury, upon another person. That can affect those closely connected with that person in various ways. One way is by subjecting a close relative to the stress and strain of caring for the injured person over a prolonged period, but psychiatric illness due to such stress and strain has not so far been treated as founding a claim in damages. So I am of the opinion that in addition to reasonable foreseeability liability for injury in the particular form of psychiatric illness must depend in addition upon a requisite relationship of proximity between the claimant and the party said to owe the duty. Lord Atkin in *M'Alister (or Donoghue)* v *Stevenson* [1932] AC 562 at 580, described those to whom a duty of care is owed as being –
>
>> "persons who are so closely and directly affected by my act that I ought reasonably to have them in contemplation as being so affected when I am directing my mind to the acts or omissions which are called in question."
>
> The concept of a person being closely and directly affected has been conveniently labelled "proximity", and this concept has been applied in certain categories of cases, particularly those concerned with pure economic loss, to limit and control the consequences as regards liability which would follow if reasonable foreseeability were the sole criterion.
>
> As regards the class of persons to whom a duty may be owed to take reasonable care to avoid inflicting psychiatric illness through nervous shock sustained by reason of physical injury or peril to another, I think it sufficient that reasonable foreseeability should be the guide. I would not seek to limit the class by reference to particular relationships such as husband and wife or parent and child. The kinds of relationship which may involve close ties of love and affection are numerous, and it is the existence of such ties which leads to mental disturbance when the loved one suffers a catastrophe. They may be present in family relationships or those of close friendship, and may be stronger in the case of engaged couples than in that of persons who have been married to each other for many years. It is common knowledge that such ties exist, and reasonably foreseeable that those bound by them may in certain

circumstances be at real risk of psychiatric illness if the loved one is injured or put in peril. The closeness of the tie would, however, require to be proved by a plaintiff, though no doubt being capable of being presumed in appropriate cases. The case of a bystander unconnected with the victims of an accident is difficult. Psychiatric injury to him would not ordinarily, in my view, be within the range of reasonable foreseeability but could not perhaps be entirely excluded from it if the circumstances of a catastrophe occurring very close to him were particularly horrific.

In the case of those within the sphere of reasonable foreseeability the proximity factors mentioned by Lord Wilberforce in *McLoughlin* v *O'Brian* must, however, be taken into account in judging whether a duty of care exists. The first of these is proximity of the plaintiff to the accident in time and space. For this purpose the accident is to be taken to include its immediate aftermath, which in *McLoughlin*'s case was held to cover the scene at the hospital which was experienced by the plaintiff some two hours after the accident. In *Jaensch* v *Coffey* (1984) 54 ALR 417 the plaintiff saw her injured husband at the hospital to which he had been taken in severe pain before and between his undergoing a series of emergency operations, and the next day stayed with him in the intensive care unit and thought he was going to die. She was held entitled to recover damages for the psychiatric illness she suffered as a result. Deane J said:

> "... the aftermath of the accident extended to the hospital to which the injured person was taken and persisted for so long as he remained in the state produced by the accident up to and including immediate post-accident treatment ... Her psychiatric injuries were the result of the impact upon her of the facts of the accident itself and its aftermath while she was present at the aftermath of the accident at the hospital."

As regards the means by which the shock is suffered, Lord Wilberforce said in *McLoughlin*'s case that it must come through sight or hearing of the event or of its immediate aftermath. He also said that it was surely right that the law should not compensate shock brought about by communication by a third party. On that basis it is open to serious doubt whether *Hevican* v *Ruane* [1991] 3 All ER 65 and *Ravenscroft* v *Rederiaktiebolaget Transatlantic* [1991] 3 All ER 73 were correctly decided, since in both of these cases the effective cause of the psychiatric illness would appear to have been the fact of a son's death and the news of it.

Of the present appellants two, Brian Harrison and Robert Alcock, were present at the Hillsborough ground, both of them in the West Stand, from which they witnessed the scenes in pens 3 and 4. Brian Harrison lost two brothers, while Robert Alcock lost a brother-in-law and identified the body at the mortuary at midnight. In neither of these cases was there any evidence of particularly close ties of love or affection with the brothers or brother-in-law. In my opinion the mere fact of the particular relationship was insufficient to place the plaintiff within the class of persons to whom a duty of care could be owed by the defendant as being foreseeably at risk of psychiatric illness by reason of injury or peril to the individuals concerned. The same is true of other plaintiffs who were not present at the ground and who lost brothers, or in one case a grandson. I would, however, place in the category of members to which risk of psychiatric illness was reasonable foreseeable Mr and Mrs Copoc, whose son was killed, and Alexandra Penk, who lost her fiance. In each of these cases the closest ties of love and affection fall to be presumed from the fact of the particular relationship, and there is no suggestion of anything which might tend to rebut that presumption. These three all watched scenes from Hillsborough on television, but none of these depicted suffering of recognisable individuals, such being excluded by the broadcasting code of ethics, a position known to the defendant. In my opinion the viewing of these scenes cannot be equiparated with the viewer being within "sight or hearing of the event or of its immediate aftermath", to use the words of Lord Wilberforce in *McLoughlin* v *O'Brian*, nor can the scenes reasonably be regarded as giving rise to shock, in the sense of a sudden assault on the nervous system. They were capable of giving rise to anxiety for the safety of relatives known or believed to be present in the area affected by the crush, and undoubtedly did so, but that is very different from seeing the fate of the relative or his condition shortly after the event. The viewing of the television scenes did not create the necessary degree of proximity.'

Commentary

See also *Ravenscroft* v *Rederiaktiebolaget Transatlantic* [1992] 2 All ER 470n.

Alexandrou v *Oxford* [1993] 4 All ER 328 Court of Appeal (Slade, Parker and Glidewell LJJ)

Duty of care owed by police to victim of a crime

Facts
The plaintiff's shop was burgled, and an alarm was activated at both the shop and the local police station. Two police officers checked the premises but failed to inspect the rear of the shop where the burglars had forced entry. Some hours later a substantial amount of goods was removed from the shop. The plaintiff sued the chief constable alleging that the police had been negligent in failing to take adequate precautions to discover why the alarm had been activated and in assuming that it was a false alarm. The trial judge found as a fact that the theft would have been prevented had the police officers properly inspected the rear of the building and were thus in breach of the duty of care they owed to the plaintiff. The chief constable appealed.

Held
A plaintiff who alleged that a defendant owed him a duty to take reasonable care to prevent loss caused by the actions of a third party had to prove not only that loss was foreseeable if the defendant did not exercise reasonable care, but also that he stood in a special relationship to the defendant from which the duty of care arose. In the present case there was no such special relationship between the plaintiff and the police because the call to the police was an emergency call which did not differ from an emergency call by a member of the public. If a duty of care was owed to the plaintiff that duty would be owed to all members of the public, and on the principle in *Hill* v *Chief Constable of West Yorkshire* [1988] 2 All ER 238 such a duty did not exist.

Further, it would not be in the public interest to impose such a duty of care on the police as it would not promote a higher standard of care but would result in a significant diversion of resources from the suppression of crime.

Ancell v *McDermott* [1993] 4 All ER 355 Court of Appeal (Norse and Beldam LJJ, Sir John Megaw)

Duty of care owed by police to road users

Facts
The first defendant drove over an obstruction in the road, rupturing his fuel tank. He continued to drive without stopping to see whether his car had suffered any damage, leaving a trail of diesel fuel on the road. Some officers of Hertfordshire police noticed the diesel fuel and notified Bedfordshire police of the spillage. Some 20 minutes after the spillage commenced an officer of Bedfordshire police noticed the spillage and reported it to Bedfordshire highways department. Ten minutes later a car skidded on the diesel fuel and was involved in a collision. The passengers and husband of the driver who was killed as a result sued (inter alia) the Hertfordshire and Bedfordshire chief constables. The chief constables applied to strike out the claims against them, but this was refused by the judge on the grounds that whether a duty of care existed depended on the precise circumstances, including the nature of the hazard, the extent of the danger created and the likelihood of injury, and that those matters could only be determined at trial. The chief constables appealed.

Held
The police were under no duty of care to protect road users from, or to warn them of, hazards discovered

by the police on the highway. There was no special relationship between the plaintiffs and the police giving rise to an exceptional duty to prevent harm from dangers created by another. The extreme width and scope of such a duty would impose on the police a potential liability of almost unlimited scope, which would be against public policy because it would divert extensive police resources and manpower from, and hamper the performance of, ordinary police duties. Hence the police did not owe a duty of care in the circumstances.

Anns v *Merton London Borough Council* [1978] AC 728 House of Lords (Lord Wilberforce, Lord Diplock, Lord Simon of Glaisdale, Lord Salmon and Lord Russell of Killowen)

Duty of care

Facts

The plaintiffs were lessees and occupiers of flats in a block built in 1962 by a private builder and developer. Some of the plaintiffs had taken their leases in 1962, others had acquired them subsequently by assignment from original lessees. In 1970, the building began to suffer damage, eg cracks in the walls, due to the movement of the foundations. Under by-laws made pursuant to the Public Health Act 1936, the local authority – the defendants – had a power (but no duty) to inspect the foundations of new buildings. The most likely cause of the movement was inadequate (too shallow) foundations. Assuming this to be so, and assuming that the local authority had carried out an inspection pursuant to its powers, but had done so negligently, it owed a duty of care to subsequent occupiers.

Held

Both a statutory power and a statutory duty could give rise to a duty of care and if there had been a negligent exercise by the council of their power to inspect the foundations, they would be liable to the plaintiffs.

Obiter: the builder may also be liable, either under *Donoghue* v *Stevenson* or for breach of his statutory duty to comply with the relevant bye-laws.

Lord Wilberforce:

'Through the trilogy of cases in this House, *Donoghue* v *Stevenson, Hedley Byrne & Co Ltd* v *Heller & Partners* and *Home Office* v *Dorset Yacht,* the position has now been reached that in order to establish that a duty of care arises in a particular situation, it is not necessary to bring the facts of that situation within those of previous situations in which a duty of care has been held to exist. Rather, the question has to be approached in two stages. First, one has to ask whether, as between the alleged wrongdoer and the person who has suffered damage there is a sufficient relationship of proximity or neighbourhood such that, in the reasonable contemplation of the former, carelessness on his part may be likely to cause damage to the latter, in which case a prima facie duty of care arises. Secondly, if the first question is answered affirmatively, it is necessary to consider whether there are any considerations which ought to negate, or to reduce or limit the scope of the duty of the class of person to whom it is owed, or the damages to which a breach of it may give rise ... Examples of this are *Hedley Byrne* ... where the class of potential plaintiffs was reduced to those shown to have relied on the correctness of statements made and *Weller & Co* v *Foot & Mouth Disease Research Institute* ... and cases about 'economic loss' where a duty having been held to exist, the nature of the recoverable damages was limited (see *SCM* v *Whittall, Spartan Steel* v *Martin*).'

It was also contended on behalf of the council that the plaintiffs do not even allege that they relied on the inspection of the foundations by the council. Nor they did, and I daresay they never even knew about it. This, however, is irrelevant. I think that the noble Lords who decided *Hedley Byrne & Co Ltd* v *Heller*

& Partners Ltd would have been very surprised that what they said about reliance in that case would one day be cited as relevant to a case such as the present. There are a wide variety of instances in which a statement is negligently made by a professional man which he knows will be relied on by many people besides his client, eg a well-known firm of accountants certifies in a prospectus the annual profits of the company issuing it and unfortunately due to negligence on the part of the accountants, the profits are seriously overstated. Those persons who invested in the company in reliance on the accuracy of the accountants' certificate would have a claim for damages against the accountants for any money they might have lost as a result of the accountants' negligence: see the *Hedley Byrne* case.

In the present case, however, the loss is caused not by any reliance placed by the plaintiffs on the council or the building inspector, but by the fact that if the inspection had been carefully made, the defects in the foundations would have been rectified before the erection of the building was begun. The categories of negligence, as Lord Macmillan said, are never closed and there are now a great many of them. In a few, reliance is of importance. In the present case, reliance is not even remotely relevant.'

If there was at one time a supposed rule that the doctrine of *Donoghue* v *Stevenson* did not apply to realty, there is no doubt under modern authority that a builder of defective premises may be liable in negligence to persons who thereby suffer injury. (The authorities) expressly leave open the question whether the immunity against action of builder-owners, established by older authorities *Bottomley* v *Bannister*) still survives ... I am unable to understand why this principle or proposition should prevent recovery in a suitable case, by a person who has subsequently acquired the house, on the principle of *Donoghue* v *Stevenson* the same rules should apply to all careless acts of a builder: whether he happens to own the land or not ...'

Commentary
Applied: *Home Office* v *Dorset Yacht Co Ltd* [1970] 2 WLR 1140.

Distinguished: *East Suffolk Rivers Catchment Board* v *Kent* [1941] AC 74.

Disapproved: *Bottomley* v *Bannister* [1932] 1 KB 458.

Explained in *Peabody Donation Fund (Governors)* v *Sir Lindsay Parkinson & Co Ltd* [1984] 3 WLR 953.

In *Murphy* v *Brentwood District Council* [1990] 3 WLR 414, the House of Lords said that *Anns* had been wrongly decided as regards the scope of any private law duty of care resting on local authorities in relation to their function of taking steps to secure compliance with building bye-laws or regulations.

Antonelli v *Wade Gery Farr* (1992) The Times 29 December High Court (Turner J)

Liability of counsel regarding conduct of trial

Facts
Counsel had wasted the court's time in that her submissions had been rambling with many embarrassing pauses and she had failed to prepare written submissions when requested by the judge.

Held
That where time had been wasted by counsel during the conduct of proceedings, and the court was satisfied that counsel had acted negligently, unreasonably or improperly, the court could make an order for wasted costs against counsel. Section 51(6) of the Supreme Court Act 1981 (as modified by s4 Courts and Legal Services Act 1990) removed the immunity of counsel from liability for the conduct of proceedings in that it allowed an order for wasted costs to be made against counsel.

Attia v *British Gas plc* [1987] 3 WLR 1101 Court of Appeal (Dillon, Woolf and Bingham LJJ)

Negligence – nervous shock

Facts
While installing central heating in the plaintiff's house, the defendants negligently caused it to catch fire. The plaintiff was out at the time and she returned home to see smoke pouring from the loft. She claimed damages, inter alia, for nervous shock and psychological reaction caused by seeing her house on fire.

Held
Whether the plaintiff's psychiatric damage was a reasonably foreseeable consequence of the defendants' negligence was a question of fact to be decided at the trial.

Bingham LJ:

'Since the defendants were working in the house where the plaintiff lived, it must have been obvious to them that she would be so closely and directly affected by their performance of their work that they ought reasonably to have had her in contemplation as being so affected when they carried out the work. It is not, I think, contested that the defendants owed her a duty to take reasonable care to carry out the work so as to avoid damaging her home and property. But it is said that the defendants owed her no duty to take reasonable care to carry out the work so as to avoid causing her psychiatric damage. This analytical approach cannot, I think, be said to be wrong, but it seems to me to be preferable, where a duty of care undeniably exists, to treat the question as one of remoteness and ask whether the plaintiff's psychiatric damage is too remote to be recoverable because it was not reasonably foreseeable as a consequence of the defendants' careless conduct. The test of reasonable foreseeability is, as I understand it, the same in both contexts, and the result should be the same on either approach. So the question in any case such as this, applying the ordinary test of remoteness in tort, is whether the defendant should reasonably have contemplated psychiatric damage to the plaintiff as a real, even if unlikely, result of careless conduct on his part.'

Commentary
Considered: *Hay (or Bourhill)* v *Young* [1943] AC 92 and *McLoughlin* v *O'Brian* [1982] 2 WLR 982.

Bourhill (or Hay) v *Young* [1943] AC 92 House of Lords (Lord Thankerton, Lord Russell of Killowen, Lord Macmillan, Lord Wright and Lord Porter)

Negligence – shock

Facts
The appellant claimed damages against the estate of the respondent, now deceased, who due to his negligent riding of a motor-cycle was involved in a collision with a motor car. The appellant was getting off a tram when she heard the sound of the collision some fifty feet away. Shortly after she saw blood on the road. She sustained nervous shock and had a miscarriage. At no time was there any danger of physical injury to the appellant herself, who brought an action in negligence.

Held
The cyclist owed no duty of care to the appellant as he could not have reasonably foreseen the likelihood that the appellant, placed as she was, could be affected by his negligent act.

Lord Thankerton:

'Clearly (the duty of the motor-cyclist) is to drive the cycle with such reasonable care as will avoid the risk of injury to such persons as he can reasonably foresee might be injured by failure to exercise such reasonable care. It is now settled that such injury includes injury by shock although no direct physical impact or lesion occurs. If then the test of proximity or remoteness is to be applied, I am of the opinion that such a test involves that injury must be within that which the cyclist ought reasonably to have contemplated as the area of potential danger which would arise as the result of his negligence and the question in the present case is whether the appellant was within that area. I am clearly of the opinion that she was not ...'

Lord Wright:

'The general concept of reasonable foresight as the criterion of negligence or breach of duty ... may be criticised as too vague; but negligence is a fluid principle, which has to be applied to the most diverse conditions and problems of human life. It is a concrete, not an abstract idea. It has to be fitted to the facts of the particular case ... It is also always relative to the individual affected. This raises a serious additional difficulty in the cases where it has to be determined not merely whether the act itself is negligent against someone, but whether it is negligent vis-a-vis the plaintiff. This is a crucial point in cases of nervous shock. Thus, in the present case, John Young was certainly negligent in an issue between himself and the owner of the car which he ran into, but it is another question whether he was negligent vis-a-vis the appellant ...

I cannot accept that Young could reasonably have foreseen, or more correctly the reasonable hypothetical observer could reasonably have foreseen, the likelihood that anyone placed as the appellant was, could be affected in the manner in which she was.'

Lord Porter:

'The duty (of care) is not owed to the world at large ... In order to establish a duty towards herself, the pursuer must show that the cyclist should reasonably have foreseen emotional injury to her as a result of his negligent driving and I do not think she has done so ... The driver of a car or vehicle, even though careless, is entitled to assume that the ordinary frequenter of the streets has sufficient fortitude to endure such incidents as may from time to time occur in them, including the noise of a collision and the sight of injury to others and is not to be considered negligent towards one who does not possess the customary phlegm...'

Commentary
Applied in *King* v *Phillips* [1953] 2 WLR 526.

Calveley* v *Chief Constable of Merseyside [1989] 2 WLR 624 House of Lords (Lord Bridge of Harwich, Lord Ackner, Lord Oliver of Aylmerton, Lord Goff of Chieveley and Lord Lowry)

Police disciplinary proceedings

Facts
Following complaints, the plaintiff police officers had been suspended on full pay and allowances pending the outcome of investigations. In disciplinary proceedings the complaints had either been dismissed, quashed on appeal or discontinued, but the plaintiffs now sought general damages for anxiety, vexation and loss of reputation and special damages for loss of overtime pay, alleging, inter alia, that the investigating officer had been in breach of duty at common law in failing to proceed expeditiously.

Held
Their claims could not succeed.

Lord Bridge of Harwich:

> 'Leading counsel for the plaintiffs submitted that a police officer investigating any crime suspected to have been committed, whether by a civilian or by a member of a police force, owes to the suspect a duty of care at common law. It follows, he submits, that the like duty is owed by an officer investigating a suspected offence against discipline by a fellow officer. It seems to me that this startling proposition founders on the rocks of elementary principle. The first question that arises is: what injury to the suspect ought reasonably to be foreseen by the investigator as likely to be suffered by the suspect if the investigation is not conducted with due care which is sufficient to establish the relationship of legal neighbourhood or proximity in the sense explained by Lord Atkin in *Donoghue (or M'Alister) v Stevenson* [1932] AC 562 at 580-582 as the essential foundation of the tort of negligence? The submission that anxiety, vexation and injury to reputation may constitute such an injury needs only to be stated to be seen to be unsustainable. Likewise, it is not reasonably foreseeable that the negligent conduct of a criminal investigation would cause injury to the health of the suspect, whether in the form of depressive illness or otherwise. If the allegedly negligent investigation is followed by the suspect's conviction, it is obvious that an indirect challenge to that conviction by an action for damages for negligent conduct of the investigation cannot be permitted. One must therefore ask the question whether foreseeable injury to the suspect may be caused on the hypothesis either that he has never been charged or, if charged, that he has been acquitted at trial or on appeal, or that his conviction has been quashed on an application for judicial review. It is, I accept, foreseeable that in these situations the suspect may be put to expense, or may conceivably suffer some other economic loss, which might have been avoided had a more careful investigation established his innocence at some earlier stage. However, any suggestion that there should be liability in negligence in such circumstances runs up against the formidable obstacles in the way of liability in negligence for purely economic loss. Where no action for malicious prosecution would lie, it would be strange indeed if an acquitted defendant could recover damages for negligent investigation. Finally, all other considerations apart,it would plainly be contrary to public policy, in my opinion, to prejudice the fearless and efficient discharge by police officers of their vitally important public duty of investigating crime by requiring them to act under the shadow of a potential action for damages for negligence by the suspect.
>
> If no duty of care is owed by a police officer investigating a suspected crime to a civilian suspect, it is difficult to see any conceivable reason why a police officer who is subject to investigation ... should be in any better position. Junior counsel for the plaintiffs, following, put the case in negligence on a very much narrower basis. He submitted that in the case of a police officer subject to investigation a specific duty of care is owed to him to avoid any unnecessary delay in the investigation precisely because the officer is, or is liable to be, suspended from duty until the investigation is concluded. The short answer to this submission is that suspension from duty is not in itself and does not involve any foreseeable injury of a kind capable of sustaining a cause of action in negligence ... In the light of the provision made by the relevant regulations suspension is not a foreseeable cause of even economic loss.'

Candlewood Navigation Corp Ltd v *Mitsui Osk Lines Ltd, The Mineral Transporter* [1985] 3 WLR 381 Privy Council (Lord Fraser of Tullybelton, Lord Roskill, Lord Brandon of Oakbrook, Lord Templeman and Lord Griffiths)

Negligence – title to sue

Facts
The first plaintiff was the owner of vessel IM, which he hired to the second plaintiff (the bareboat charterer) so that the latter took complete control over her and effectively became her owner during the period of hire. The second plaintiff then rehired the vessel to the first plaintiff for a set period of time

(time charter). This gave the first plaintiff the exclusive right to use the vessel during this period. The vessel MT collided with the vessel IM whilst the latter was still at anchor, thereby causing damage under the bareboat charter; the second plaintiff had agreed to pay the cost of any repairs resulting from collision. Under the time charter the first plaintiff was liable for a reduced rate of hire whilst the necessary repairs were being carried out. The plaintiffs claimed damages against the defendant.

Held
The first plaintiff was not entitled to recover damages. He was suing only in his capacity as time charterer. As such he did not have a proprietary or a possessory right in the chartered vessel (even though he was, in another capacity, the owner of that vessel). The time charterer had only a contractual interest in the vessel which had been damaged by the defendants. His contractual use of the vessel was made less profitable as a result of their negligence. This was not recoverable from the defendants but simply irrecoverable pure economic loss. However, the losses incurred by the bareboat charterer (the second plaintiff) would be recoverable. These included the amount by which the hire had been reduced in consequence of the negligence including delays occasioned by a union ban, requiring final repair to be carried out in Japan. There was no ground to distinguish between industrial strikes and strikes which are essentially political in nature as submitted by the defendants. Such a distinction would be unrealistic especially since many strikes have both political and industrial objectives.

Commentary
Applied: *Cattle* v *Stockton Waterworks Co* (1875) LR 10 QB 453.

Caparo Industries plc v *Dickman* [1990] 2 WLR 358 House of Lords (Lord Bridge of Harwich, Lord Roskill, Lord Ackner, Lord Oliver of Aylmerton and Lord Jauncey of Tullichettle)

Auditor – duty of care

Facts
The plaintiff shareholder in Fidelity plc received the accounts audited by the defendants and at first purchased more shares and then made a successful takeover bid. The plaintiffs alleged that the accounts had been inaccurate and misleading: instead of showing a pre-tax profit for the year of some £1.2m, they should have revealed a loss of over £400,000. Had the defendants owed the plaintiffs a duty of care?

Held
They had not, either as shareholders or potential investors.

Lord Jauncey of Tullichettle:

> ' ... the purpose of annual accounts, so far as members are concerned, is to enable them to question the past management of the company, to exercise their voting rights, if so advised, and to influence future policy and management. Advice to individual shareholders in relation to present or future investment in the company is not part of the statutory purpose of the preparation and distribution of the accounts ...
>
> If the statutory accounts are prepared and distributed for certain limited purposes, can there nevertheless be imposed on auditors an additional common law duty to individual shareholders who choose to use them for another purpose without the prior knowledge of the auditors? The answer must be No. Use for that other purpose would no longer be ... use for the "very transaction" which Denning LJ in *Candler* v *Crane Christmas & Co* [1951] 2 KB 164 at 183 regarded as determinative of the scope of any duty of care. Only where the auditor was aware that the individual shareholder was likely to rely on the accounts for a

particular purpose such as his present or future investment in or lending to the company would a duty of care arise. Such a situation does not obtain in the present case.

... it was argued that the relationship of the unwelcome bidder in a potential takeover situation was nearly as proximate to the auditor as was the relationship of a shareholder to whom the report was directed. Since I have concluded that the auditor owed no duty to an individual shareholder, it follows that this argument must also fail. The fact that a company may at a time when the auditor is preparing his report be vulnerable to a takeover bid cannot per se create a relationship of proximity between the auditor and the ultimate successful bidder. Not only is the auditor under no statutory duty to such a bidder but he will have reason at the material time to know neither of his identity nor of the terms of his bid. In this context the recent case of *Al Saudi Banque* v *Clark Pixley* [1990] 2 WLR 344 is in point. There Millett J held that the auditors of a company owed no duty of care to a bank which lent money to the company, regardless of whether the bank was an existing creditor or a potential one, because no sufficient proximity of relationship existed in either case between the auditor and the bank. I have no doubt that this case was correctly decided ...'

Commentary

See also *Mariola Marine Corporation* v *Lloyd's Register of Shipping, The Morning Watch* [1990] 1 Lloyd's Rep 547 and *Punjab National Bank* v *de Boinville* [1992] 1 WLR 1138.

CBS Songs Ltd v *Amstrad Consumer Electronics plc* [1988] AC 1013 House of Lords (Lord Keith of Kinkel, Lord Templeman, Lord Griffiths, Lord Oliver of Aylmerton and Lord Jauncey of Tullichettle)

Infringement of copyright – negligence

Facts

(See Chapter 10 – Breach of Statutory Duty)

Held

The plaintiffs' appeal would be dismissed.

Lord Templeman:

'Finally, [the plaintiffs] submit that Amstrad committed the tort of negligence, that Amstrad owes to all owners of copyright a duty to take care not to cause or permit purchasers to infringe copyright or, alternatively, that Amstrad owes a duty to take care not to facilitate by the sale of their models or by their advertisement the infringement of copyright. My Lords, it is always easy to draft a proposition which is tailor-made to produce the desired result. Since *Anns* v *Merton London Borough Council* [1978] AC 728 put the floodgates on the jar, a fashionable plaintiff alleges negligence. The pleading assumes that we are all neighbours now, Pharisees and Samaritans alike, that foreseeability is a reflection of hindsight and that for every mischance in an accident-prone world someone solvent must be liable in damages. In *Governors of the Peabody Donation Fund* v *Sir Lindsay Parkinson & Co Ltd* [1985] AC 210 the plaintiffs were the authors of their own misfortune but sought to make the local authority liable for the consequences. In *Yuen Kun-yeu* v *A-G of Hong Kong* [1988] AC 175 the plaintiff chose to invest in a deposit-taking company which went into liquidation; the plaintiff sought to recover his deposit from the commissioner charged with the public duty of registering deposit-taking companies. In *Rowling* v *Takaro Properties Ltd* [1988] 2 WLR 418 a claim for damages in negligence was made against a minister of the Crown for declining in good faith to exercise in favour of the plaintiff a statutory discretion vested in the minister in the public interest. In *Hill* v *Chief Constable of West Yorkshire* [1988] 2 WLR 1049 damages against a police force were sought on behalf of the victim of a criminal. In the present proceedings damages and an injunction for negligence are sought against Amstrad for a breach of statutory duty which Amstrad did not commit and in which Amstrad did not participate. The rights of [the plaintiffs] are to be found in the 1956 Act and nowhere else. Under and by virtue of that Act Amstrad owed a duty not to infringe copyright and not to authorise an infringement of copyright. They did not owe a duty to prevent or discourage or warn against infringement.'

Chadwick v *British Transport Commission* [1967] 1 WLR 912 High Court (Waller J)

Negligence – nervous shock

Facts
Due to the horrific scenes which he witnessed while giving assistance to the victims of the Lewisham rail disaster, the plaintiff's husband (now deceased) suffered severe nervous shock. The disaster had occurred as a result of negligence for which the defendants were legally responsible.

Held
The test of liability is whether injury by nervous shock was reasonably foreseeable. The defendants having been negligent vis-a-vis the dead and injured passengers, they should have foreseen the likelihood of someone trying to rescue them. In the circumstances, it was clearly foreseeable that such a rescuer might be shocked by what he saw and the plaintiff should succeed.

D & F Estates Ltd v *Church Commissioners for England* [1988] 3 WLR 368 House of Lords (Lord Bridge of Harwich, Lord Templeman, Lord Ackner, Lord Oliver of Aylmerton and Lord Jauncey of Tullichettle)

Negligence – extent of duty – economic loss

Facts
The third defendants (Wates) were the main contractors for the construction of a block of flats (Chelwood House) owned by the first defendants: they engaged a sub-contractor, whom they reasonably believed to be skilled and competent, to carry out the plastering, but he did the work negligently. Some 15 years after construction, and again some three years later, the plaintiffs, lessees and occupiers of one of the flats, found that the plaster in their flat was loose: they sued, inter alia, Wates, claiming the cost of remedial work already carried out and the estimated cost of future remedial work.

Held
Their claim could not succeed as (a) it was for pure economic loss and (b) Wates' only duty was to engage a competent contractor which they had done.

Lord Bridge of Harwich:

'In relation to both issues, it is instructive and, I think, necessary to consider two developments of the law in relation to a builder's liability in tort for defective premises which have been effected on the one hand by statute and on the other by judicial development of the law by the adaptation and application of common law principles to situations to which they had not previously been applied. Both these developments have taken place since 1970. Both have effected far-reaching changes in the law, at all events as it had been supposed to be before 1970. But the two developments have been markedly different in their scope and effect. The statutory development enacted by the Defective Premises Act 1972 effected clear and precise changes in the law imposing certain specific statutory duties subject to carefully defined limitations and exceptions. This change did not, of course, operate retrospectively. The common law developments have effected changes in the law which inevitably lack the kind of precision attainable by statute though limits have had to be and are still being worked out by decisions of the courts in a spate of ensuing litigation, including the instant case, and since our jurisprudence knows nothing of the American doctrine of "prospective overruling" and the law once pronounced authoritatively by the courts here is deemed always to have been the law, the changes have full retrospective operation ...

In the instant case the only hidden defect was in the plaster. The only item pleaded as damage to other property was "cost of cleaning carpets and other possessions damaged or dirtied by falling plaster; £50". Once it appeared that the plaster was loose, any danger of personal injury or of further injury to other property could have been simply avoided by the timely removal of the defective plaster.

It seems to me clear that the cost of replacing the defective plaster itself, either as carried out ... or as intended to be carried out in future, was not an item of damage for which the builder of Chelwood House could possibly be made liable in negligence under the principle of *Donoghue* v *Stevenson* [1932] AC 562 or any legitimate development of that principle To make him so liable would be to impose on him for the benefit of those with whom he had no contractual relationship the obligation of one who warranted the quality of the plaster as regards materials, workmanship and fitness for purpose. I am glad to reach the conclusion that this is not the law, if only for the reason that a conclusion to the opposite effect would mean that the courts, in developing the common law, had gone much farther than the legislature were prepared to go in 1972 ... in making builders liable for defects in the quality of their work to all who subsequently acquire interests in buildings they have erected. The statutory duty imposed by the 1972 Act was confined to dwelling houses and limited to defects appearing within six years. The common law duty, if it existed, could not be so confined or so limited. I cannot help feeling that consumer protection is an area of law where legislation is much better left to the legislators ...

The submission in support of the appeal was put in three ways which amount, as it seems to me, to three alternative formulations of what is, in essence, the same proposition of law. Expressed in summary form the three formulations are (i) that Wates were vicariously liable for the negligence of their sub-contractor; (ii) that Wates as main contractors responsible for building Chelwood House owed a duty to future lessees and occupiers of flats to take reasonable care that the building should contain no hidden defects of the kind which might cause injury to persons or property and that this duty could not be delegated; (iii) that Wates as main contractors owed a duty of care to future lessees and occupiers of flats to supervise their sub-contractors to ensure that the sub-contracted work was not negligently performed so as to cause such defects.

It is trite law that the employer of an independent contractor is, in general, not liable for the negligence or other torts committed by the contractor in the course of the execution of the work. To this general rule there are certain well-established exceptions or apparent exceptions. Without enumerating them it is sufficient to say that it was accepted by counsel for the plaintiffs that the instant case could not be accommodated within any of the recognised and established categories by which the exceptions are classified ... If Wates are to be held liable for the negligent workmanship of their sub-contractors (assumed for this purpose to result in dangerously defective work) it must first be shown that in the circumstances that they had assumed a personal duty to all the world to ensure that Chelwood House should be free of dangerous defects. This was the assumption on which the judge proceeded when he said: 'The duty of care itself is of course not delegable.' Whence does this non-delegable duty arise? Counsel for the plaintiffs submits that it is a duty undertaken by any main contractor in the building industry who contracts to erect an entire building. I cannot agree because I cannot recognise any legal principle to which an assumption of duty can be related. Just as I may employ a building contractor to build me a house, so may the building contractor, subject to the terms of my contract with him, in turn employ another to undertake part of the work. If the mere fact of employing a contractor to undertake building work automatically involved the assumption by the employer of a duty of care to any person who may be injured by a dangerous defect in the work caused by the negligence of the contractor, this would obviously lead to absurd results. If the fact of employing a contractor does not involve the assumption of any such duty by the employer, then one who has himself contracted to erect a building assumes no such liability when he employs an apparently competent independent sub-contractor to carry out part of the work for him. The main contractor may, in the interests of the proper discharge for his own contractual obligations, exercise a greater or lesser degree of supervision over the work done by the sub-contractor. If in the course of supervision the main contractor in fact comes to know that the sub-contractor's work is being done in a defective and foreseeably dangerous way and if he condones that negligence on the part of the sub-contractor, he will no doubt make himself potentially liable for the consequences as a joint tortfeasor. But the judge made no finding against Wates of actual knowledge ...

The conclusion I reach is that Wates were under no liability to the plaintiffs for damage attributable to the negligence of their plastering sub-contractor in failing to follow the instructions of the manufacturer of the plaster they were using, but that in any event such damage could not have included the cost of renewing the plaster.'

Commentary
Not followed: *Anns* v *Merton London Borough Council* [1978] AC 728 and *Junior Books Ltd* v *Veitchi Co Ltd* [1983] AC 520.

Doubted: *Batty* v *Metropolitan Property Realizations Ltd* [1978] QB 554.

Followed in *Department of the Environment* v *Thomas Bates & Son* [1990] 3 WLR 457 and *Nitrigin Eireann Teoranta* v *Inco Alloys Ltd* [1992] 2 WLR 407.

Davis v *Radcliffe* [1990] 1 WLR 821 Privy Council (Lord Keith of Kinkel, Lord Brandon of Oakbrook, Lord Templeman, Lord Goff of Chieveley and Lord Lowry)

Licensing of banks – duty of care

Facts
By statute, and subject to the directions of the Isle of Man Finance Board, the Treasurer had power to issue, revoke and suspend banking licences: he issued such a licence to Savings and Investment Bank Ltd (SIB) with which the plaintiffs deposited money. SIB was wound up and it appeared that the plaintiffs would receive no more than a small dividend from the liquidator. The plaintiffs sued the Treasurer and the Board alleging negligence and/or breach of statutory duty: their claim was struck out: they appealed.

Held
Their appeal would be dismissed as the defendants had not owed them a duty of care.

Lord Goff of Chieveley:

'Their Lordships feel great sympathy for those who, like the [plaintiffs], have deposited substantial sums of money with a bank in the confident expectation that a bank is a safe place for their money, only to find that the bank has become insolvent and that the most they can expect to receive is a small dividend payable in its winding up. But, when it is sought to make some third person responsible in negligence for the loss suffered through the bank's default, the question whether that third person owes a duty of care to the depositor has to be decided in accordance with the established principles of the law of negligence. In the present case the [judge], having reviewed the authorities with care, concluded that neither the members of the Finance Board nor the Treasurer owed any such duty to the [plaintiffs], and so struck out their statement of case as disclosing no reasonable cause of action. Their Lordships are in no doubt that [he] was right to reach that conclusion, substantially for the reasons given by him. Indeed they are in agreement with him that the present case is, for all practical purposes, indistinguishable from the decision of their Lordships' Board in *Yuen Kun-yeu* v *A-G of Hong Kong* [1987] 3 WLR 776 ... The [judge] also dismissed, in a terse paragraph, an alternative plea based on breach of statutory duty, on the principle set out in *Cutler* v *Wandsworth Stadium Ltd* [1949] AC 398. Their Lordships entirely agree with [his] conclusion on this point, which was plainly right.'

Department of the Environment* v *Thomas Bates & Son Ltd [1990] 3 WLR 457
House of Lords (Lord Keith of Kinkel, Lord Brandon of Oakbrook, Lord Ackner, Lord Oliver of Aylmerton and Lord Jauncey of Tullichettle)

Negligence – economic loss

Facts
The plaintiffs were underlessees of the upper storeys of an office block built by the defendants in 1970 and 1971. In 1981 and 1982 it was discovered that low-strength concrete had been used in the pillars which, although they could support the existing load, could not support the design load safely. The plaintiffs strengthened the pillars and sought to recover the cost from the defendants; the trial judge found, inter alia, that there had been no imminent danger to the health or safety of the plaintiffs' employees or the public.

Held
The plaintiffs could not succeed as the cost of the remedial work was purely economic loss.

Lord Keith of Kinkel:

> 'The foundation of the plaintiffs' case is *Anns* v *Merton London Borough* [1977] 2 WLR 1024 ... It has been held by this House in *Murphy* v *Brentwood DC* [1990] 3 WLR 414 that *Anns* was wrongly decided and should be departed from, by reason of the erroneous views there expressed as to the scope of any duty of care owed to purchasers of houses by local authorities when exercising the powers conferred on them for the purpose of securing compliance with building regulations. The process of reasoning by which the House reached its conclusion necessarily included close examination of the position of the builder who was primarily responsible, through lack of care in the construction process, for the presence of defects in the building. It was the unanimous view that, while the builder would be liable under the principle of *Donoghue* v *Stevenson* [1932] AC 562 in the event of the defect, before it had been discovered, causing physical injury to persons or damage to property other than the building itself, there was no sound basis in principle for holding him liable for the pure economic loss suffered by a purchaser who discovered the defect, however such discovery might come about, and who was required to expend money in order to make the building safe and suitable for its intended purpose.
>
> In the present case it is clear that the loss suffered by the plaintiffs is pure economic loss. At the time the plaintiffs carried out the remedial work on the concrete pilars the building was not unsafe by reason of the defective construction of these pillars. It did, however, suffer from a defect of quality which made the plaintiffs' lease less valuable than it would otherwise have been, in respect the the building could not be loaded up to its design capacity unless any occupier who wished so to load it had incurred the expenditure necessary for the strengthening of the pillars. It was wholly uncertain whether during the currency of their lease the plaintiffs themselves would ever be likely to require to load the building up to its design capacity, but a purchaser from them might well have wanted to do so. Such a purchaser, faced with the need to strengthen the pillars, would obviously have paid less for the lease than if they had been sound. This underlines the purely economic character of the plaintiffs' loss. To hold in favour of the plaintiffs would involve a very significant extension of the doctrine of *Anns* so as to cover the situation where there existed no damage to the building and no imminent danger to personal safety or health. If *Anns* was correctly decided, such an extension could reasonably be regarded as entirely logical. The undesirability of such an extension, for the reasons stated in in *Murphy*, formed an important part of the grounds which led to the conclusion that *Anns* was not correctly decided. That conclusion must lead inevitably to the result that the plaintiffs' claim fails.'

Donoghue (or McAlister) v *Stevenson* [1932] AC 562 House of Lords (Lord Buckmaster, Lord Atkin, Lord Tomlin, Lord Thankerton and Lord Macmillan)

Negligence – duty of care

Facts
The appellant went, together with her friend, to a cafe, where the friend purchased a bottle of ginger beer which was sealed and in opaque glass. Both drank from the ginger beer before realising that it contained a dead snail. The appellant suffered gastro-enteritis and shock as a result and sued the manufacturer of the ginger beer for damages on the ground that he had been negligent in the production of the product. The only question before the House of Lords was whether the respondent (manufacturer) owed a duty of care to the appellant.

Held (Lord Buckmaster and Lord Tomlin dissenting)
The respondent owed the appellant a duty of care, although he did not know the product to be dangerous and no contractual relationship existed between the parties. On proof of the facts the appellant would be entitled to damages.

Lord Atkin:

> 'You must take reasonable care to avoid acts or omissions which you can reasonably foresee would be likely to injure your neighbour. Who then, in law, is my neighbour? The answer seems to be – persons who are so closely and directly affected by my act that I ought reasonably to have them in contemplation as being so affected when I am directing my mind to the acts or omissions which are called in question.'

Lord Macmillan:

> 'In the daily contacts of social and business life, human beings are thrown into, or place themselves in, an infinite variety of relations with their fellows; and the law can refer only to the standards of the reasonable man in order to determine whether any particular relation gives rise to a duty to take care, as between those who stand in that relation to each other. The grounds of action may be as various and manifold as human errancy; and the conception of legal responsibility may develop in adaptation to altering social conditions and standards. The criterion of judgment must adjust and adapt itself to the changing circumstances of life. The categories of negligence are never closed.'

Dulieu v *White & Sons* [1901] 2 KB 669 High Court (Kennedy and Phillimore JJ)

Negligence – nervous shock

Facts
The plaintiff was standing behind the bar of her husband's public house when the defendant's employee negligently drove his van through the wall. The plaintiff suffered nervous shock with a resultant miscarriage.

Held
The plaintiff had a good cause of action as a plaintiff is entitled to recover if the nervous shock is caused by being put in fear of immediate physical injury to himself, due to the negligence of the defendant.

Commentary
Applied in *Janvier* v *Sweeney* [1919] 2 KB 316.

East Suffolk Rivers Catchment Board v *Kent* [1941] AC 74 House of Lords (Viscount Simon LC, Lord Atkin, Lord Thankerton, Lord Romer and Lord Porter)

Negligence – repair of sea-wall

Facts
The respondent's low-lying land was flooded when high tides caused breaches of a sea-wall which the appellant Board had power to repair under statute, but no duty to do so. The Board did attempt repairs, but so inefficiently that it took far longer than it should have done had they acted with reasonable efficiency.

Held (Lord Atkin dissenting)
The respondent's claim was ill-founded.

Lord Romer:

> 'Where a statutory authority is entrusted with a mere power, it cannot be made liable for any damage sustained by a member of the public by reason of a failure to exercise that power. If, in the exercise of that discretion, they embark upon an execution of that power, the only duty they owe to any member of the public is not thereby to add to the damages which he would have suffered if they had done nothing.'

Commentary
Distinguished in *Dutton* v *Bognor Regis Urban District Council* [1972] 2 WLR 299.

Emeh v *Kensington and Chelsea and Westminster Area Health Authority* [1985] 2 WLR 233 Court of Appeal (Waller, Slade and Purchas LJJ)

Negligence – unwanted pregnancy

Facts
At the same time as she was having an abortion, the plaintiff, a mother of three normal children, was sterilised to prevent further pregnancies. The sterilisation was performed negligently and she became pregnant again, a fact that she did not discover until she was some 20 weeks into the pregnancy. As she did not want any more operations she decided against another abortion and she gave birth to a child which was congenitally abnormal. The appeal concerned the damages to which the plaintiff was entitled.

Held
The plaintiff's entitlement extended to any reasonably foreseeable financial loss directly caused by her unexpected pregnancy. Accordingly, she was entitled to damages for loss of future earnings, maintenance of the child up to trial, maintenance of the child in the future, the plaintiff's pain and suffering up to the time of the trial and future loss of amenity and pain and suffering, including the extra care that the child would require. The plaintiff's decision not to have an abortion was not a novus actus interveniens or a failure to mitigate damage, because the health authority, by the negligence for which it was itself responsible, had confronted the plaintiff with the very dilemma of whether to have the child or an abortion which she had sought to avoid by having herself sterilised. Furthermore, there was no rule of public policy which prevented the plaintiff from recovering in full the financial damage sustained by her as the result of the negligent failure to perform the sterilisation operation properly, regardless of whether the child was healthy or abnormal.

Commentary
Doubted: *Udale v Bloomsbury Area Health Authority* [1983] 1 WLR 1098.
  Applied in *Allen v Bloomsbury Health Authority* [1993] 1 All ER 651, above.

Esso Petroleum Co Ltd v *Mardon* [1976] 2 WLR 583 Court of Appeal (Lord Denning MR, Ormrod and Shaw LJJ)

Negligence – pre-contract negotiations

Facts
The defendant took a lease of a petrol filling-station from the plaintiffs, relying on the plaintiffs' representations as to the expected turnover. These representations turned out to be grossly inaccurate and the defendant suffered loss.

Held
The plaintiffs' statements were, inter alia, a negligent misrepresentation for which the defendant could recover damages in tort. The plaintiffs, though not in the business of giving advice, were possessed of the special knowledge or expertise necessary to give the information requested.

Ormrod LJ:

> 'There is no magic in the phrase "special relationship". It means no more than a relationship, the nature of which is such that one party, for a variety of reasons, will be regarded by the law as under a duty of care to another.'

Commentary
Applied: *Hedley Byrne & Co Ltd v Heller and Partners Ltd* [1963] 3 WLR 101.
  Applied in *Batty v Metropolitan Property Realizations Ltd* [1978] 2 WLR 500.

Gran Gelato Ltd v *Richcliff (Group) Ltd* [1992] 1 All ER 865 High Court Sir Donald Nicholls V-C

Whether solicitor acting for seller owes a duty of care when answering preliminary inquiries

Facts
The plaintiffs acquired an underlease from Richcliff which was expressed to be for 10 years. The plaintiffs sent pre-contract enquiries to Richcliff's solicitors, the second defendants, which, inter alia, asked whether there were any 'rights affecting the ... superior leasehold titles which would ... in any way inhibit the enjoyment of the property by the tenant in accordance with the terms of the present draft lease'. The second defendants replied 'Not to the lessor's knowledge'. In fact the head leases contained redevelopment break clauses which, when exercised, had the effect of reducing the term of the underlease to five years. The head lessors later exercised the break clause and the plaintiffs brought a claim for damages for misrepresentation against Richcliff and their solicitors.

Held
The plaintiffs had established a good cause of action for damages against Richcliff under s2(1) of the Misrepresentation Act 1967 but the claim against the solicitors would be dismissed. Sir Donald Nicholls V-C said that the foreseeability requirement was satisfied and that there was a close and direct relationship between the plaintiffs and the second defendants. But a vital factor in persuading his

Lordship to conclude that the second defendants did not owe a duty of care to the plaintiffs was that in making the representations the second defendants were acting as agents for Richcliff. This was not, however, enough in itself to displace the existence of a duty of care because the fact that the person making the representation was acting for a known principal does not necessarily negative the existence of a duty of care. A further vital factor which persuaded him to conclude that no duty of care was owed was that the second defendants were solicitors. He held that in 'normal conveyancing transactions solicitors who are acting for a seller do not in general owe to the would-be buyer a duty of care when answering enquiries before contract or the like'. His Lordship identified three factors to support his conclusion. The first was the context in which the representations were made (a contract for the sale of an interest in land). The second was that the buyer has a remedy against the seller in respect of any misrepresentations in the answers given by his solicitors. The third was that to impose a duty of care upon the solicitors would be to expose them to conflicting duties: one owed to their client and the other to his contracting party. His Lordship did not accept this argument in its entirety but concluded that 'in general, in a case where the principal himself owes a duty of care to the third party, the existence of a further duty of care, owed by the agent to the third party, is not necessary for the reasonable protection of the latter'. It was true that this conclusion might lead to a buyer being left without a remedy in the situation where the seller becomes insolvent but the risk of insolvency is 'an ordinary risk of everyday living'.

Sir Donald Nicholls V-C added two caveats to his judgment. The first was that there will be special cases where the general rule does not apply and a duty of care will be owed by a solicitor to a buyer, for example where the solicitor steps outside his normal role and assumes a responsibility towards the buyer (see *Al-Kandari* v *JR Brown* [1988] QB 655). The second was that a solicitor does owe a duty to his own client when answering enquiries before contract and, if the client is exposed to a claim for damages as a result of his carelessness, the solicitor will be liable to indemnify his client on well-established principles.

Harris v *Wyre Forest District Council* see *Smith* v *Eric S Bush*

Hedley Byrne & Co Ltd v *Heller & Partners* [1963] 3 WLR 101 House of Lords (Lord Reid, Lord Morris of Borth-y-Gest, Lord Hodson, Lord Devlin and Lord Pearce)

Negligence – duty of care in relation to information or advice

Facts
The appellants, an advertising agency, wished to make enquiries about the financial reliability of one of their customers, Easipower Ltd. Their bankers made enquiries of the respondents, Easipower's bankers. The respondents replied, first orally then in writing, stating that Easipower Ltd was financially sound, although this information was given 'without responsibility'. The appellants relied on this advice which proved to be inaccurate and they suffered considerable losses when Easipower went into liquidation.

Held
A duty of care in making statements may arise when the parties are in a 'special relationship'. But the appeal was dismissed because the respondents had excluded their responsibility.

Lord Hodson:

> '... if in a sphere where a person is so placed that others could reasonably rely on his judgment or on his skill or on his ability to make careful enquiry, such person takes it on himself to give information or advice to, or allows his information or advice to be passed on to, another person who, as he knows or should know, will place reliance on it, then a duty of care will arise.'

Lord Devlin:

'A defendant who is given a car to overhaul and repair if necessary is liable to the injured driver if (a) he overhauls and repairs it negligently and tells the driver that it is safe when it is not; (b) he overhauls it and negligently finds it not to be in need of repair and tells the driver that it is safe when it is not; (c) he negligently omits to overhaul it at all and tells the driver that it is safe when it is not. It would be absurd in any of these cases to argue that the proximate cause of the driver's injury was not what the defendant did or failed to do, but his negligent statement on the faith of which the driver drove the car and for which he could not recover.'

Lord Pearce:

'The reason for some divergence between the law of negligence in word and that of negligence in act is clear. Negligence in word creates problems different from those of negligence in act. Words are more volatile than deeds. They travel fast and far afield. They are used without being expended and take effect in combination with innumerable facts and other words ... Damage by negligent acts to persons or property on the other hand is more visible and obvious, its limits are more easily defined ...'

Commentary
Distinguished in *Dutton* v *Bognor Regis Urban District Council* [1972] 2 WLR 299.

Hemmens v *Wilson Browne* [1993] 4 All ER 826 High Court (Judge Moseley QC)

Applicability of *Ross* v *Caunters* where testator or donor still alive

Facts
P instructed a solicitor to draft a document giving the plaintiff the right to call on P at any time in the future to pay her £110,000. The document as drafted did not confer any enforceable rights on the plaintiff. Some weeks later the plaintiff called upon P to fulfil his promise and he refused. The plaintiff sued the solicitor claiming (inter alia) that he owed her a duty of care and was in breach of that duty.

Held
Although the solicitor's carelessness had resulted in a document being drafted which gave the plaintiff no enforceable rights, and it was reasonably foreseeable that the plaintiff would suffer damage from such carelessness and there was a sufficient degree of proximity between the solicitor and the plaintiff, it would not be fair, just or reasonable for a duty of care to be imposed because P was still alive and could rectify the situation and could also sue the solicitor. Hence it was not necessary for the law to give the plaintiff a remedy as it was in *Ross* v *Caunters*.

Henderson v *Merrett Syndicates Ltd* [1994] 3 WLR 761 House of Lords (Lords Keith, Goff, Browne-Wilkinson, Mustill and Nolan)

Liability for pure economic loss – co-existence of tort and contract

Facts
The plaintiffs, who were underwriting members ('Names') at Lloyds, brought proceedings against the defendant underwriting agents, alleging that the defendants had been negligent in their conduct of the Names' business and were also in breach of contract. In fact, the House in *Henderson* decided some five appeals with slightly differing factual situations, but made several clear statements of the law.

Held

The House of Lords held that a duty of care was owed by the underwriting agents to the Names, and that the existence of such a duty was not excluded by the existence of a contractual relationship.

Lord Goff:

> 'From ... *Hedley Byrne*, we can derive some understanding of the breadth of the principle underlying the case. We can see that it rests upon a relationship between the parties, which may be general or specific to the particular transaction, and which may or may not be contractual in nature. All of their Lordships spoke in terms of one party having assumed or undertaken a responsibility towards the other. ...
>
> In subsequent cases concerned with liability under the *Hedley Byrne* principle in respect of negligent misstatements, the question has frequently arisen whether the plaintiff falls within the category of persons to whom the maker of the statement owes a duty of care. In seeking to contain that category of persons within reasonable bounds, there has been some tendency on the part of the courts to criticise the concept of "assumption of responsibility" as being "unlikely to be a helpful or realistic test in most cases" (see *Smith* v *Eric S Bush* [1990] 1 AC 831, 864, 865, per Lord Griffiths; and see also *Caparo Industries plc* v *Dickman* [1990] 2 AC 605, 628, per Lord Roskill). However, at least in cases such as the present, in which the same problem does not arise, there seems to be no reason why recourse should not be had to the concept, which appears after all to have been adopted, in one form or another, by all of their Lordships in *Hedley Byrne* [1964] AC 465 ...
>
> Approached as a matter of principle, therefore, it is right to attribute to that assumption of responsibility, together with its concomitant reliance, a tortious liability, and then to inquire whether or not that liability is excluded by the contract because the latter is inconsistent with it. This is the reasoning which Oliver J, as I understand it, found implicit, where not explicit, in the speeches in *Hedley Byrne*. With his conclusion I respectfully agree. But even if I am wrong in this, I am of the opinion that this House should now, if necessary, develop the principle of assumption of responsibility as stated in *Hedley Byrne* to its logical conclusion so as to make it clear that a tortious duty of care may arise not only in cases where the relevant services are rendered gratuitously, but also where they are rendered under a contract.'

Hill v *Chief Constable of West Yorkshire* [1989] AC 53 House of Lords (Lord Keith of Kinkel, Lord Brandon of Oakbrook, Lord Templeman, Lord Oliver of Aylmerton and Lord Goff of Chieveley)

Negligence – duty of care

Facts

A claim brought on behalf of the estate of Jacqueline Hill for damages under the Law Reform (Miscellaneous Provisions) Act 1934, against the Chief Constable of an area where the 'Yorkshire Ripper' had murdered many women, Jacqueline Hill being his last victim. The Chief Constable sought to strike out the claim on the ground that the statement of claim did not disclose a cause of action and the trial judge decided in his favour.

Held

The proceedings had been properly struck out.

Lord Keith of Kinkel:

> 'It has been said almost too frequently to require repetition that foreseeability of likely harm is not in itself a sufficient test of liability in negligence. Some further ingredient is invariably needed to establish the requisite proximity of relationship between the plaintiff and defendant, and all the circumstances of the case must be carefully considered and analysed in order to ascertain whether such an ingredient is present. The nature of the ingredient will be found to vary in a number of different categories of decided cases ...

It is plain that vital characteristics which were present in the *Dorset Yacht* case and which led to the imposition of liability are here lacking. Sutcliffe was never in the custody of the police force. Miss Hill was one of a vast number of the female general public who might be at risk from his activities but was at no special distinctive risk in relation to them, unlike the owners of yachts moored off Brownsea Island in relation to the foreseeable conduct of the borstal boys. It appears from the ... speech of Lord Diplock in the *Dorset Yacht* case that in his view no liability would rest on a prison authority, which carelessly allowed the escape of an habitual criminal, for damage which he subsequently caused, not in the course of attempting to make good his getaway, to persons at special risk, but in further pursuance of his general criminal career to the person or property of members of the general public. The same rule must apply as regards failure to recapture the criminal before he had time to resume his career. In the case of an escaped criminal his identity and description are known. In the instant case the identity of the wanted criminal was at the material time unknown and it is not averred that any full or clear description of him was ever available. The alleged negligence of the police consists in a failure to discover his identity. But, if there is no general duty of care owed to individual members of the public by the responsible authorities to prevent the escape of a known criminal or to recapture him, there cannot reasonably be imposed on any police force a duty of care similarly owed to identify and apprehend an unknown one. Miss Hill cannot for this purpose be regarded as a person at special risk simply because she was young and female. Where the class of potential victims of a particular habitual criminal is a large one the precise size of it cannot in principle affect the issue. All householders are potential victims of a habitual burglar, and all females those of a habitual rapist. The conclusion must be that although there existed reasonable foreseeability of likely harm to such as Miss Hill if Sutcliffe were not identified and apprehended, there is absent from the case any such ingredient or characteristic as led to the liability of the Home Office in the *Dorset Yacht* case. Nor is there present any additional characteristic such as might make up the deficiency. The circumstances of the case are therefore not capable of establishing a duty of care owed towards Miss Hill by the West Yorkshire police.

That is sufficient for the disposal of the appeal. But in my opinion there is another reason why an action for damages in negligence should not lie against the police in circumstances such as those of the present case, and that is public policy ... I consider that ... the police were immune from an action of this kind on grounds similar to those which in *Rondel* v *Worsley* were held to render a barrister immune from actions for negligence in his conduct of proceedings in court.'

Commentary
Applied: *Rondel* v *Worlsey* [1969] 1 AC 191.

Applied in *Clough* v *Bussan* [1990] 1 All ER 431, *Hughes* v *National Union of Mineworkers* [1991] 4 All ER 278 and *Alexandrou* v *Oxford* [1993] 4 All ER 328.

Distinguished: *Home Office* v *Dorset Yacht Co Ltd* [1970] 2 WLR 1140.

Holt v *Payne Skillington* (1995) The Times 22 December Court of Appeal (Hirst and Peter Gibson LJJ, Forbes J)

Duty of care arising between parties to a contract – wider obligations possible in tortious duty

Facts
The plaintiffs purchased a property, and the first defendants acted as solicitors and the second defendants as estate agents in respect of the purchase. The plaintiffs alleged that both defendants were in breach of duty in both contract and tort. At first instance the judge held (inter alia) that the plaintiffs could not succeed against the second defendants in contract but could succeed in tort. The second defendants appealed.

Held
That where a duty of care in tort arose between parties to a contract, wider obligations could be imposed by the duty of care in tort than those arising under the contract. There was no reason in principle why a *Hedley Byrne* type of duty could not arise where the same parties entered into a contractual relationship involving more limited obligations that those imposed by the tortious duty of care.

Commentary
In *Aiken* v *Stewart Wrightson Members Agency Ltd* [1995] 1 WLR 1281 it was held that a concurrent duty of care in tort could fall short of a duty imposed by the express terms of a contract.

Home Office v *Dorset Yacht Co Ltd* [1970] 2 WLR 1140 House of Lords (Lord Reid, Lord Morris of Borth-y-Gest, Viscount Dilhorne, Lord Pearson and Lord Diplock)

Negligence – escape of trainees

Facts
The appellants were responsible for the operation and running of a Borstal institution. Several inmates were on a training exercise under the supervision of three Borstal officers when they escaped one night and damaged the respondents' yacht which was moored nearby. Did the appellants owe any duty of care to the yacht owners?

Held (Viscount Dilhorne dissenting)
Yes. The appellants should reasonably have foreseen that if they failed to exercise reasonable care in controlling and supervising the boys in their charge, damage of the kind which occurred was likely to be caused. There was no ground in public policy for granting the appellants immunity from liability in negligence.

Commentary
Applied in *Anns* v *Merton London Brough Council* [1978] AC 728.
    See also *Peabody Donation Fund (Governors)* v *Sir Lindsay Parkinson & Co Ltd* [1984] 3 WLR 953.

Hughes v *National Union of Mineworkers* [1991] 4 All ER 278 High Court (May J)

Negligence – duty of care

Facts
On duty at a colliery during a strike, the plaintiff police officer sustained injuries when the police were attacked by some 4,000 mineworkers. The plaintiff alleged that the officer in charge had been negligent in the deployment of the police, but the chief constable sought to have his action struck out on the ground that he had not owed the plaintiff a duty of care.

Held
The plaintiff's claim was bound to fail and it would be struck out.

May J:

> 'The plaintiff was one of a number of police officers deployed to control serious public disorder by a vast number of picketing miners. He was injured by some of those disorderly miners. Having considered *Hill* v *Chief Constable of West Yorkshire* [1988] 2 All ER 238 on the one hand and *Knightley* v *Johns*

[1982] 1 All ER 851 and *Rigby* v *Chief Constable of Northamptonshire* [1985] 2 All ER 985 on the other, in my judgment, as a matter of public policy, if senior police officers charged with the task of deploying what may or may not be an adequate force of officers to control serious public disorder are to be potentially liable to individual officers under their command if those individuals are injured by attacks from rioters, that would be significantly detrimental to the control of public order.

It will no doubt often happen that in such circumstances critical decisions have to be made with little or no time for considered thought and where many individual officers may be in some danger of physical injury of one kind or another. It is not, I consider, in the public interest that those decisions should generally be the potential target of a negligence claim if rioters do injure an individual officer, since the fear of such a claim would be likely to affect the decisions to the prejudice of the very task which the decisions are intended to advance. Accordingly, in my judgment, public policy requires that senior police officers should not generally be liable to their subordinates who may be injured by rioters or the like for on the spot operational decisions taken in the course of attempts to control serious public disorder. That, in my judgment, should be the general rule in cases of policing serious public disorders. There may be exceptions where the plaintiff's injuries arise, as in *Knightley* v *Johns*, from specifically identified antecedent negligence or specific breach of identified regulations, orders or instructions by a particular senior officer. There is no such specific allegation in the statement of claim in this case and none has been suggested in argument. It follows that the plaintiff's claim against the [chief constable] taken at its pleaded highest is bound to fail and that the claim should be struck out.'

James McNaughton Papers Group Ltd v *Hicks Anderson & Co* [1991] 2 WLR 641
Court of Appeal (Neill, Nourse and Balcombe LJJ)

Negligence – accountants' duty of care

Facts
The plaintiffs were negotiating an agreed takeover of a rival company which was in financial difficulty. The chairman of the target company had asked the defendants, the target company's accountants, to prepare draft accounts as quickly as possible so that they could be used in the negotiations for the takeover. After the takeover had been completed, the plaintiffs alleged that they had relied on the draft accounts (which, they said, contained certain discrepancies) and also upon a statement made by a representative of the defendants at a meeting with the plaintiffs to the effect that, as a result of rationalisation, the target company was breaking even or doing a little worse.

Held
The plaintiffs' action for damages for negligence could not succeed. On the facts no duty of care was owed by the defendants because: (i) the accounts were produced only for the vendor; (ii) the accounts were in draft form; (ii) the defendants were not participants in the negotiating process; (iv) the target company was, to the knowledge of the plaintiffs, in poor financial health; (v) the parties were experienced businessmen and, in particular, the plaintiffs had their own independent advisers; and (vi) the statement of the representative of the defendants at the meeting with the plaintiffs was a very general one and the defendants could not have known that the plaintiffs would rely on the statement without making further inquiry or seeking further advice.

In deciding whether or not a duty of care arose in a case in which a plaintiff has suffered economic loss as a result of reliance upon a negligent statement Neill LJ identified the following relevant factors: (i) the precise purpose for which the statement was made; (ii) the purpose for which the statement was communicated; (iii) the relationship between the adviser, advisee and any relevant third party; (iv) the size of any class to which the advisee belongs; (v) the state of knowledge of the adviser; and (vi) the reliance by the advisee (including whether the advisee was entitled to rely on the statement, whether he did so rely, whether he should have relied upon his own judgment and whether he should have sought and obtained independent advice). Two further points are worthy of note. The first is that this case underlines the unwillingness of the courts to extend the scope of liability beyond the person directly intended by the maker of the statement to act upon it. The second is that Neill LJ stated that *Caparo Industries plc* v *Dickman*, above, had not been affected by anything said by their Lordships in *Murphy* v *Brentwood District Council*, below.

Jones v *Department of Employment* [1988] 2 WLR 493 Court of Appeal (Slade, Glidewell LJJ and Caulfield J)

Adjudication officer's alleged negligence

Facts
The plaintiff's claim for unemployment benefit was disallowed by the adjudication officer but allowed by the appeal tribunal. The plaintiff sought damages alleging negligence on the part of the adjudication officer.

Held
His action could not succeed as, inter alia, the adjudication officer had not owed the plaintiff a duty of care.

Glidewell LJ:

> 'The question ... is whether, taking all [the] circumstances into account, it is just and reasonable that the adjudication officer should be under a duty of care at common law to the claimant to benefit. Having regard to the non-judicial nature of the adjudication officer's responsibilities, and in particular to the fact that the statutory framework provides a right of appeal which, if a point of law arises, can eventually bring the matter to this court, it is my view that the adjudication officer is not under any common law duty of care. In other words ... his decision is not susceptible of challenge at common law unless it be shown that he is guilty of misfeasance.
>
> Indeed, in my view, it is a general principle that, if a government department or officer, charged with the making of decisions whether certain payments should be made, is subject to a statutory right of appeal against his decisions, he owed no duty of care in private law. Misfeasance apart, he is only susceptible in public law to judicial review or to the right of appeal provided by the statute under which he makes his decision.'

Junior Books Ltd v *Veitchi Co Ltd* [1982] 3 WLR 477 House of Lords (Lord Fraser of Tullybelton, Lord Russell of Killowen, Lord Keith of Kinkel, Lord Roskill and Lord Brandon of Oakbrook)

Duty of care: proximity

Facts
The plaintiff engaged building contractors to build a factory at Grangemouth. The defendant was a specialist company engaged by the main contractors to lay composition flooring in the factory. P claimed that D was negligent in laying the floor with the result that it was defective and had to be replaced. There was no contractual relationship between P and D and P claimed damages in negligence against D, the damages consisting mainly of the direct and indirect cost of replacing the floor. Assuming D had been negligent in laying a defective floor, was D liable for economic loss caused to P which was not related to any injury to P's person or property?

Held
The economic loss would be recoverable, notwithstanding that it was 'pure' economic loss, unrelated to injury to the person or to property.

Lord Roskill:

> 'I therefore ask first whether there was the requisite degree of proximity so as to give rise to the relevant duty of care ... I regard the following facts as of crucial importance in requiring an affirmative answer to that question (1) the appellants were nominated sub-contractors; (2) the appellants were specialists in flooring; (3) the appellants knew what products were required by the respondents and their main contractors and specialised in the production of those products; (4) the appellants alone were responsible for the composition and construction of the flooring; (5) the respondents relied on the appellants' skill and experience; (6) the appellants as nominated sub-contractors must have known that the respondents relied on their skill and experience; (7) the relationship between the parties was as close as it could be short of actual privity of contract; (8) the appellants must be taken to have known that if they did the work negligently (as it must be assumed that they did) the resulting defects would at some time require remedying by the respondents expending money on the remedial measures as a consequence of which the respondents would suffer financial or economic loss ... On the facts I have just stated, I see nothing whatever to restrict the duty of care arising from the proximity of which I have spoken ... I see no reason why what was called during the argument "damage to the pocket" simpliciter should be disallowed when "damage to the pocket" coupled with physical damage has hitherto always been allowed. I do not think that this development, if development it may be, will lead to untoward consequences.'

Commentary
Applied: *Anns* v *Merton London Borough Council* [1977] 2 WLR 1024; *Home Office* v *Dorset Yacht Co Ltd* [1970] 2 WLR 1140.

Distinguished in *Nitrigin Eireann Teoranta* v *Inco Alloys Ltd* [1992] 2 WLR 407.

King v *Liverpool City Council* [1986] 1 WLR 890 Court of Appeal (Purchas and Nicholls LJJ and Caulfield J)

Negligence – act of third party

Facts
Liverpool City Council were the owners of a flat occupied by the plaintiff. She informed the council of the fact that the flat immediately above her own was vacant and requested it be secured against trespassers. Trespassers entered the flat and damaged the pipes causing the plaintiff's property to be flooded. The plaintiff claimed damages in nuisance and negligence against the council.

Held
The duty of care which was owed to the plaintiff had to be assessed by reference to the individual circumstances of the case. Even if the flat had been secured it would not have been possible to prevent damage by flooding. The water supply could not be cut off without affecting the other flats. Therefore there was no effective measure which the council could have taken to prevent damage of this kind. The council did not therefore owe a duty to prevent trespassers from entering the premises and doing this kind of damage.

Commentary
Followed: *P Perl (Exporters) Ltd* v *Camden London Borough Council* [1983] 3 WLR 769.

Kirkham v *Chief Constable of the Greater Manchester Police* [1990] 2 WLR 987 Court of Appeal (Lloyd, Farquharson LJJ and Sir Denys Buckley)

Prisoner's suicide – duty of care

Facts
When a man was arrested, his wife, the plaintiff, told the police that he had recently attempted to commit suicide. At the police station, appropriate precautions were taken but, when the man was remanded, the police failed to inform the prison authorities of his suicidal tendencies. At the remand centre he was treated like a normal prisoner: he hanged himself in his cell: the plaintiff claimed damages.

Held
She was entitled to succeed as the police, by failing to pass on the relevant information, had been in breach of their duty of care. The maxims volenti non fit injuria and ex turpi causa non oritur actio did not afford the police a good defence.

Lamb v *Camden London Borough Council* [1981] 2 WLR 1038 Court of Appeal (Lord Denning MR, Oliver and Watkins LJJ)

Damage – foreseeability

Facts
In 1972, the plaintiff let her house while she spent some time abroad. In 1973 an employee of the defendants negligently fractured a water main outside her house which flooded the foundations and caused the house to subside. The tenants consequently moved out and squatters moved in during 1974, though they were subsequently evicted. In 1975, there was a second 'invasion' by squatters who ripped out fixtures in the house and the central heating. The plaintiff brought an action against the defendant council for negligence, including a claim for the damage which had been caused to the house by the squatters.

Held
The plaintiff could not recover damages for the actions of the squatters, since they were not reasonably foreseeable.

Oliver LJ:

> 'Few things are less certainly predictable than human behaviour, and if one is asked whether in any given situation a human being may behave idiotically, irrationally or even criminally the answer must always be that that is a possibility, for every society has its proportion of idiots and criminals. It cannot be said that you cannot foresee the possibility that people will do stupid or criminal acts, because people are constantly doing stupid or criminal acts. But the question is not what is foreseeable merely as a possibility but what would the reasonable man actually foresee if he thought about it ... If the instant case is approached as a case of negligence and one asks the question, did the defendants owe a duty not to break a water pipe so as to cause the plaintiff's house to be invaded by squatters a year later, the tenuousness of the linkage between act and result becomes apparent. I confess that I find it inconceivable that the reasonable man, wielding his pick in the road in 1973, could be said reasonably to foresee that his puncturing of a water main would fill the plaintiff's house with uninvited guests in 1974.'

Lancashire & Cheshire Association of Baptist Churches v Howard & Seddon Partnership [1993] 3 All ER 467 High Court (Judge Michael Kershaw QC)

Co-existence of tort and contract – pure economic loss

Facts

The plaintiffs wished to build a new sanctuary for their church and contracted with the defendant firm of architects to design the sanctuary and supervise its building. The plaintiffs alleged that the completed sanctuary contained defects in design as regards ventilation and condensation, and claimed damages for breach of contract and negligence. At the date of issue of the writ the plaintiffs' claim in contract was statute-barred, but the plaintiffs claimed that the damage had occurred within the limitation period for tort. The defendants contended that where there was a contract between the parties, or at least where there was a contract for professional services, there could not, as a matter of law, be a duty in tort.

Held

The High Court held that a duty of care could exist where the parties were in a contractual professional relationship, as it was illogical that a contracting party could not sue in respect of a negligent act, whereas a non-contracting party could. The principle that the law of tort could not alter the contractual rights existing between parties applied only to rights created by the terms of the contract and not to rights in respect of the limitation period. Thus a duty in tort did exist and the extent of this duty was regulated by the express and implied terms of the contract.

Unfortunately for the plaintiffs, however, the Court went on to hold that when the defendants submitted designs for the sanctuary they made no express statement as to its technical qualities. Thus in the absence of actual damage to the person or to property the cost of putting right the defects was pure economic loss and the defendants owed no duty of care to prevent such loss.

The defendants relied on *Tai Hing Cotton Mill* v *Liu Chong Hing Bank* [1985] 2 All ER 947, a Privy Council decision, where Lord Scarman said at p957: 'Their Lordships do not believe that there is anything to the advantage of the law's development in searching for a liability in tort where the parties are in a contractual relationship. This is particularly so in a commercial relationship.' The plaintiffs relied, of course, on the decision of Oliver J in *Midland Bank Trust* v *Hett Stubbs & Kemp* [1978] 3 All ER 571 where the duty of care was held to co-exist with the contractual duty.

The High Court decided to follow the *Midland Bank* decision rather than the obiter dictum in *Tai Hing*, encouraged by the speech of Lord Bridge in *Caparo* v *Dickman* [1990] 1 All ER 568 where he expressly recognised the co-existence of duties in tort and contract.

McFarlane v EE Caledonia Ltd [1994] 2 All ER 1 Court of Appeal (Ralph Gibson, Stuart-Smith and McCowan LJJ)

Duty owed to bystander at a horrific event

Facts

The plaintiff was employed on the Piper Alpha oil rig in the North Sea. He was off duty on a support vessel some 550 metres from the rig when a series of massive explosions and a fire engulfed the rig. For an hour and three quarters the plaintiff witnessed the explosions and destruction of the rig which caused the death of 164 men, and he came within 100 metres of the fire. The plaintiff suffered psychiatric illness as a result of witnessing these events and sued the defendants, the owners and operators of the rig. In the High Court it was held that the plaintiff succeeded as he was reasonably in fear of his life and safety and the fear had caused the shock which led to his injury and he was therefore a participant in the event. The judge found that the plaintiff was not a rescuer, and expressed no opinion on the submission that the plaintiff could recover even if he was only a bystander at an event if it was so horrendous that it was reasonably foreseeable that it would cause psychiatric injury to a bystander. The defendants appealed.

Held

The Court of Appeal found as a fact that the plaintiff was not genuinely in fear for his safety, and agreed with the trial judge's finding that the plaintiff was not a rescuer.

In *Alcock* v *Chief Constable of South Yorkshire* [1991] 4 All ER 907 three Law Lords (Keith, Ackner and Oliver) thought that a mere bystander could recover if the circumstances of an accident occurring close to him were particularly horrific. Despite these dicta the Court of Appeal held that as the whole basis of the decision in *Alcock* is that reasonable foreseeability is not enough, there must additionally be a sufficiently close tie of love and affection between the plaintiff and the victim.

Stuart-Smith LJ:

> 'The whole basis of the decision in Alcock's case is that where the shock is caused by fear of injury to others as opposed to fear of injury to the participant, the test of proximity is not simply reasonable foreseability. There must be a sufficiently close tie of love and affection between the plaintiff and the victim. To extend the duty to those who have no such connection, is to base the test purely on reasonable foreseeability.'

McLoughlin v *O'Brian* [1982] 2 WLR 982 House of Lords (Lord Wilberforce, Lord Edmund-Davies, Lord Russell of Killowen, Lord Scarman and Lord Bridge of Harwich)

Negligence – foreseeable harm

Facts

The plaintiff's husband and three young children were involved in a serious road accident caused by the negligence of the defendant. The plaintiff's husband and two of her children were very badly injured. The other child was killed. At the time that the accident occurred, the plaintiff was at home two miles away. She was informed of the accident by a neighbour and was taken to the hospital where she saw the extent of the injuries of her family and was told of her daughter's death. In consequence of seeing and hearing the results of the accident, the plaintiff suffered severe and persistent nervous shock. The plaintiff claimed damages against the defendant for nervous shock, distress and injury to health caused by the negligence of the defendant.

Held

The test of liability for damages for nervous shock was simply reasonable foreseeability of the plaintiff being injured by the defendant's negligent act or omission. Applying this test, the plaintiff was entitled to recover damages because even though the plaintiff was not at or near the scene of the accident, either at the time or shortly afterwards, the nervous shock suffered by the plaintiff was a reasonably foreseeable consequence of the defendant's negligence.

Lord Wilberforce:

> ' ... Although we continue to use the hallowed expression "nervous shock", English law, and common understanding, have moved some distance since recognition was given to this symptom as a basis for liability. Whatever is unknown about the mind-body relationship (and the area of ignorance seems to expand with that of knowledge), it is now accepted by medical science that recognisable and severe

physical damage to the human body and system may be caused by the impact, through the senses, of external events on the mind. There may thus be produced what is as identifiable an illness as any that may be caused by direct physical impact. It is safe to say that this, in general terms, is understood by the ordinary man or woman who is hypothesised by the courts in situations where claims for negligence are made. Although in the only case which has reached this House (*Hay (or Bourhill) v Young* [1943] AC 92), a claim for damages in respect of "nervous shock" was rejected on its facts, the House gave clear recognition to the legitimacy, in principle, of claims of that character. As the result of that and other cases, assuming that they are accepted as correct, the following position has been reached:

1. While damages cannot, at common law, be awarded for grief and sorrow, a claim for damages for "nervous shock" caused by negligence can be made without the necessity of showing direct impact or fear of immediate personal injuries for oneself ...

2. A plaintiff may recover damages for "nervous shock" brought on by injury caused not to him or herself but to a near relative, or by the fear of such injury ...

3. Subject to the next paragraph, there is no English case in which a plaintiff has been able to recover nervous shock damages where the injury to the near relative occurred out of sight and earshot of the plaintiff. In *Hambrook* v *Stokes Bros* an express distinction was made between shock caused by what the mother saw with her own eyes and what she might have been told by bystanders, liability being excluded in the latter case.

4. An exception from, or I would prefer to call it an extension of, the latter case has been made where the plaintiff does not see or hear the incident but comes on its immediate aftermath ...

5. A remedy on account of nervous shock has been given to a man who came on a serious accident involving people immediately thereafter and acted as a rescuer of those involved (*Chadwick* v *British Transport Commission* [1967] 1 WLR 912). 'Shock' was caused neither by fear for himself nor by fear or horror on account of a near relative. The principle of 'rescuer' cases was not challenged by the respondents and ought, in my opinion, to be accepted. But we have to consider whether, and how far, it can be applied to such cases as the present.

If one continues to follow the process of logical progression it is hard to see why the present plaintiff also should not succeed. She was not present at the accident, but she came very soon after on its aftermath. If, from a distance of some 100 yards she had found her family by the roadside, she would have come within principle 4 above. Can it make any difference that she comes on them in an ambulance, or, as here, in a nearby hospital, when as the evidence shows, they were in the same condition, covered with oil and mud, and distraught with pain? If Mr Chadwick can recover when, acting in accordance with normal and irresistable human instinct, and indeed moral compulsion, he goes to the scene of an accident, may not a mother recover if, acting under the same motives, she goes to where her family can be found? ... To argue from one factual situation to another and to decide by analogy is a natural tendency of the human and legal mind. But the lawyer still has to inquire whether, in so doing, he has crossed some critical line behind which he ought to stop ... Foreseeability which involves a hypothetical person, looking with hindsight at an event which has occurred, is a formula adopted by English law, not merely for defining, but also for limiting the persons to whom duty may be owed, and the consequences for which an actor may be held responsible. It is not merely an issue of fact to be left to be found as such. When it is said to result in a duty of care being owed to a person or a class, the statement that there is a "duty of care" denotes a conclusion into the forming of which considerations of policy have entered. That foreseeability does not of itself and automatically lead to a duty of care is, I think, clear ... cases of "nervous shock" and the possibility of claiming damages for it are not necessarily confined to those arising out of accidents in public roads. To state, therefore, a rule that recoverable damages must be confined to persons on or near the highway is to state not a principle in itself but only an example of a more general rule that recoverable damages must be confined to those within sight and sound of an event caused by negligence or, at least, to those in close, or very close, proximity to such a situation.

The policy arguments against a wider extension can be stated under four heads. First, it may be said that such extension may lead to a proliferation of claims, and possibily fraudulent claims, to the establishment of an industry of lawyers and psychiatrists who will formulate a claim for nervous shock damages, including what in America is called the customary miscarriage, for all, or many road accidents and industrial accidents. Second, it may be claimed that an extension of liability would be unfair to defendants, as imposing damages out of proportion to the negligent conduct complained of. In so far as such defendants are insured, a large additional burden will be placed on insurers, and ultimately on the class of persons insured: road users or employers. Third, to extend liability beyond the most direct and plain cases would greatly increase evidentiary difficulties and tend to lengthen litigation. Fourth, it may be said (and the Court of Appeal agreed with this) that an extension of the scope of liability ought only to be made by the legislature, after careful research. This is the course which has been taken in New South Wales and the Australian Capital Territory ... In *Hambrook* v *Stokes Bros* [1924] All ER 110, indeed it was said that liability would not arise in such a case, and this is surely right. It was so decided in *Abramzik* v *Brenner* (1967) 65 DLR (2d) 651. The shock must come through sight or hearing of the event or of its immediate aftermath. Whether some equivalent of sight or hearing, eg through simultaneous television, would suffice may have to be considered.

My Lords, I believe that these indications, imperfectly sketched, and certainly to be applied with common sense to individual situations in their entirety, represent either the existing law, or the existing law with only such circumstantial extension as the common law process may legitimately make. They do not introduce a new principle. Nor do I see any reason why the law should retreat behind the lines already drawn. I find on this appeal that the appellant's case falls within the boundaries of the law so drawn. I would allow her appeal.'

Commentary
Applied: *Alcock* v *Chief Constable of the South Yorkshire Police* [1991] 3 WLR 1057.

Mariola Marine Corporation v *Lloyd's Register of Shipping, The Morning Watch*
[1990] 1 Lloyd's Rep 547 High Court (Phillips J)

Purchaser of vessel – duty of care

Facts
Shortly after *The Morning Watch* had been examined by a Lloyd's surveyor and given a clean bill of health, the plaintiffs purchased it. The plaintiffs now alleged that the vessel had serious defects and was in fact unseaworthy: in their action for damages for negligence they maintained that the alleged defects should have been detected had the survey been properly conducted.

Held
The plaintiffs' claim would be dismissed. Phillips J said that the plaintiffs had established that it was reasonably foreseeable to Lloyd's that Mariola might rely on the survey result. But that was not in itself enough to establish a duty of care in a case of economic loss. There must also be a sufficient degree of proximity between plaintiff and defendant and it must be just and reasonable to impose on the defendant a duty of care to the plaintiff. There was no universal test to determine whether the necessary proximity existed. After referring to the decision of the Court of Appeal in *Caparo Industries plc* v *Dickman* [1989] 2 WLR 316, he said that in the present case there was no statutory scheme and no relationship akin to contract. There was no more a voluntary assumption by Lloyd's of responsibility to purchasers, than there was a voluntary assumption by auditors of responsibility to potential purchasers of shares. Nor was the case analogous with *Smith* v *Eric S Bush* [1989] 2 WLR 790 where the court had found a relationship akin to contract and the valuer had assumed responsibility to the purchaser. The House of Lords had since reversed the decision of the Court of Appeal in *Caparo Industries plc* v *Dickman* [1990] 2 WLR 358 and nothing in their Lordships' speeches had altered his view of the present case.

Morgan Crucible Co plc v Hill Samuel Bank Ltd [1991] 2 WLR 655 Court of Appeal (Slade, Mustill and Nicholls LJJ)

Negligence – duty of care to takeover bidder

Facts
This case arose out of a contested takeover bid and the plaintiffs' action was brought against the directors, bank and accountants of the target company. The directors responded to the plaintiffs' bid by issuing circulars to the shareholders advising them to reject the offer and stating, inter alia, that the profits of the company were forecast to increase by 38 per cent. The latter circular was accompanied by a statement by the company's accountants that the forecast had been prepared in accordance with the company's accounting procedures and a statement by their bank stating that, in their opinion, the forecast had been made after due and careful inquiry. As a result of such circulars the plaintiffs increased their bid for the company and it was accepted. The plaintiffs subsequently alleged that the pre-bid financial statements and the profit forecast were negligently misleading and that, had they known the true situation, they would never have bid for the company. All three defendants alleged that the plaintiffs' statement of claim, as amended, disclosed no cause of action.

Held
The plaintiffs had an arguable case and their claim would not be struck out. The point of distinction between this case and *Caparo* was that the statements relied upon were made *after* the plaintiffs had made their bid and not before (it was conceded that no duty was owed before the initial bid was made). Slade LJ noted the six factors identified by Neill LJ in *McNaughton* (above) and stated that they were neither 'conclusive or exhaustive'. In the present case the directors were aware that the plaintiffs would rely upon the circulars and *they intended that they should rely upon them*. It was also arguable that, for the same reasons, the bank and the accountants owed a duty of care to the plaintiffs.

Commentary
Distinguished: *Caparo Industries plc v Dickman* [1990] 2 WLR 358.

Morrell v Owen (1993) The Times 14 December High Court (Mitchell J)

Duty of care owed by organiser and coaches of a disabled persons' sporting event to the disabled participant

Facts
The plaintiff, who was disabled, was taking part in an archery contest for disabled persons when she was injured by a participant in another disabled sporting event, a discus-throwing contest taking place in the same arena. The plaintiff sued, inter alia, the archery coach and the discus coach of the event in question.

Held
The court found that these defendants were in breach of their duty by failing to provide safety instructions and precautions. Mitchell J held that the misthrow which caused the plaintiff's injuries was entirely foreseeable as was the actual accident. The judge added that organisers and coaches of a disabled persons' sporting event owed a greater duty of care to participants than would have been owed had the participants been able-bodied.

Commentary

While a final evaluation of the judgment in *Morrell* must await a full report of the case, the statement as reported must be regarded as inaccurate. English law has never accepted the concept of a variable duty of care in these circumstances: see for example *Ogwo v Taylor* [1987] 3 All ER 961 (House of Lords) for a rejection of this concept. The *duty* of care owed to disabled and able-bodied athletes by the organisers of a sporting event is identical, namely to take reasonable steps to ensure that the participants do not suffer any reasonably foreseeable injury. However, the actions that might constitute a *breach* of this duty will differ in the case of disabled and able-bodied athletes – precautions that are sufficient for the latter may well be insufficient for the former. The fact that different actions may constitute a breach of duty does not mean that a different duty is owed in each case.

Muirhead v *Industrial Tank Specialities Ltd* [1985] 3 WLR 993 Court of Appeal (O'Connor, Robert Goff and Nourse LJJ)

Negligence – economic loss

Facts

The plaintiff was a wholesale fish merchant. The first defendant was required to install a tank to store lobsters. The second defendants supplied the pumps for the tank. The third defendants manufactured and supplied the motors for the pumps. The plaintiff's entire lobster stock died when the motors cut out as they were unsuited to UK voltage. The plaintiff claimed inter alia, and in particular, against the third defendant, damages for the loss of the lobsters and consequential economic loss thereupon, including loss of profit which the plaintiff could have made by keeping the lobsters and selling them at Christmas.

Held

The third defendant was liable for the physical damage suffered to the plaintiff's lobster stock and loss of profit in consequence of the physical damage as such damage was of the type reasonably foreseeable by the third defendant. However, the plaintiff could not recover his whole economic loss.

Nourse LJ:

> 'In his analysis of *Junior Books Ltd* v *Veitchi Co Ltd* Robert Goff LJ has identified the three features of that case on which the decision that the nominated sub-contractor had voluntarily assumed a direct responsibility to the building owner was founded. The first two of these were very close proximity between the sub-contractor and the building owner and reliance by the building owner on the sub-contractor. Having been so decided, that case cannot, in my respectful opinion, be taken to be authority for the proposition that where those features are absent a defendant is liable in tort in respect of economic loss which is not consequent on physical damage to the person or property of the plaintiff. Where those features are absent, I agree with O'Connor LJ that we remain bound by the decision of this court in *Spartan Steel and Alloys Ltd* v *Martin & Co (Contractors) Ltd*. I too regard the recent observations of the Privy Council in *Candlewood Navigation Corp Ltd* v *Mitsui Osk Lines Ltd, The Mineral Transporter, The Ibaraki Mar* was being significant in this respect.
>
> In the present case there was no very close proximity between the manufacturers and the plaintiff. Contractually they were several stages removed from each other. More important, there was no reliance by the plaintiff on the manufacturers in the sense in which that concept was applied in *Junior Book*. The people on whom the plaintiff relied to install the system and to get the right equipment, including pumps with electric motors which worked, were ITS. They were the people who stood in the same factual relationship with the plaintiff as the sub-contractor did with the building owner in *Junior Books*. The two features of very close proximity and reliance having been absent, it is unnecessary to look further in the present case. The plaintiff's claim in respect of pure economic loss must fail. I therefore agree that the appeal should be allowed to that extent.'

Commentary
Applied: *Spartan Steel and Alloys Ltd* v *Martin & Co (Contractors) Ltd* [1972] 2 WLR 649.

Murphy v *Brentwood District Council* [1990] 3 WLR 414 House of Lords (Lord Mackay of Clashfern LC, Lord Keith of Kinkel, Lord Bridge of Harwich, Lord Brandon of Oakbrook, Lord Ackner, Lord Oliver of Aylmerton and Lord Jauncey of Tullichettle)

Negligence – economic loss

Facts
The plaintiff purchased a house in 1970 from builders who had constructed it in 1969. The house was built upon a single concrete raft foundation because the site had been filled and levelled. The foundation raft was designed by a firm of civil engineers but its design was inadequate and differential settlement of the ground beneath the raft caused it to distort and caused cracks to appear in the building. When the plaintiff discovered the extent of the damage to the house he decided that it was impractical to have the necessary remedial work performed himself and so he sold it, at a price considerably below the market price of a house which was sound, to a builder who knew the cause of the damage. The plaintiff then brought an action against the local authority alleging that they had been negligent in passing plans which were inadequate. The defendants had in fact referred the plans to an independent firm of consulting engineers and, in reliance upon their report, had passed the plans. The Court of Appeal ([1990] 2 WLR 944) concluded, being bound by the decision of the House of Lords in *Anns* v *Merton London Borough Council* [1978] AC 728, that the local authority did owe a duty of care to the plaintiff as an innocent purchaser who had bought the house from the builder who was in breach of the building regulations. It was further held that the duty owed by the council was a non-delegable one so that they could not discharge their duty simply by entrusting the work to an apparently competent form of consultant engineers. The court held that, on the facts, the plaintiff was entitled to recover damages measured by the diminution in value on resale caused by the defects up to an amount which did not exceed the cost of eliminating the danger. On appeal to the House of Lords:

Held
The appeal would be allowed.

Lord Bridge of Harwich:

> '... these considerations lead inevitably to the conclusion that a building owner can only recover the cost of repairing a defective building on the ground of the authority's negligence in performing its statutory function of approving plans or inspecting buildings in the course of construction if the scope of the authority's duty of care is wide enough to embrace purely economic loss. The House has already held in *D & F Estates* that a builder, in the absence of any contractual duty or of a special relationship of proximity introducing the *Hedley Byrne* principle of reliance, owes no duty of care in tort in respect of the quality of his work. As I pointed out in *D & F Estates*, to hold that the builder owed such a duty of care to any person acquiring an interest in the product of the builder's work would be to impose on him the obligations of an indefinitely transmissible warranty of quality.
>
> By s1 of the Defective Premises Act 1972 Parliament has in fact imposed on builders and others undertaking work in the provision of dwellings the obligations of a transmissible warranty of the quality of their work and of the fitness for habitation of the completed dwelling. But, besides being limited to dwellings, liability under that Act is subject to a limitation period of six years from the completion of the work and to the exclusion provided for by s2. It would be remarkable to find that similar obligations in the nature of a transmissible warranty of quality, applicable to buildings of every kind and subject to no such

limitations or exclusions as are imposed by the 1972 Act, could be derived from the builder's common law duty of care or from the duty imposed by building byelaws or regulations. In *Anns* Lord Wilberforce expressed the opinion that a builder could be held liable for a breach of statutory duty in respect of buildings which do not comply with the byelaws. But he cannot, I think, have meant that the statutory obligation to build in conformity with the byelaws by itself gives rise to obligations in the nature of transmissible warranties of quality. If he did meant that, I must respectfully disagree. I find it impossible to suppose that anything less than clear express language such as is used in s1 of the 1972 Act would suffice to impose such a statutory obligation.

As I have already said, since the function of a local authority in approving plans or inspecting buildings in the course of construction is directed to ensuring that the builder complies with building byelaws or regulations, I cannot see how, in principle, the scope of the liability of the authority for a negligent failure to ensure compliance can exceed that of the liability of the builder for his negligent failure to comply.

There may, of course, be situations where, even in the absence of contract, there is a special relationship of proximity between builder and building owner which is sufficiently akin to contract to introduce the element of reliance so that the scope of the duty of care owed by the builder to the owner is wide enough to embrace purely economic loss. The decision in *Junior Books Ltd v Veitchi Co Ltd* [1983] 1 AC 520 can, I believe, only be understood on this basis.

In *Sutherland Shire Council* v *Heyman* (1985) 60 ALR 1 the critical role of the reliance principle as an element in the cause of action which the plaintiff sought to establish is the subject of close examination, particularly in the judgment of Mason J. The central theme of his judgment, and a subordinate theme in the judgments of Brennan and Dean JJ, who together with Mason J formed the majority rejecting the *Anns* doctrine, is that a duty of care of a scope sufficient to make the authority liable for damage of the kind suffered can only be based on the principle of reliance and that there is nothing in the ordinary relationship of a local authority, as statutory supervisor of building operations, and the purchaser of a defective building capable of giving rise to such a duty. I agree with these judgments. It cannot, I think, be suggested, nor do I understand *Anns* or the cases which have followed *Anns* in Canada and New Zealand to be in fact suggesting, that the approval of plans or the inspection of a building in the course of construction by the local authority in performance of their statutory function and a subsequent purchase of the building by the plaintiff are circumstances in themselves sufficient to introduce the principle of reliance which is the foundation of a duty of care of the kind identified in *Hedley Byrne*.'

Commentary
Applied in *Department of the Environment* v *Thomas Bates & Son Ltd* [1990] 3 WLR 457.

Mutual Life & Citizens' Assurance Co Ltd v *Evatt* [1971] 2 WLR 23 (Privy Council) Lord Reid, Lord Morris of Borth-y-Gest, Lord Hodson, Lord Guest and Lord Diplock)

Negligence – advice

Facts
The plaintiff was a policyholder in the defendant company. Wishing to make some investments in P Ltd, with whom the defendants had close connections, the plaintiff asked for the defendants' advice. The advice was negligently given and the plaintiff, who had relied upon it, lost his investments.

Held (Lord Reid and Lord Morris of Borth-y-Gest dissenting)
The defendants were neither in the business of giving advice, nor held themselves out as having the skill to do so, and thus owed no duty to the plaintiff.

Lord Diplock:

'The carrying on of a business or profession which involves the giving of advice of a kind which calls for special skill and competence is the normal way in which a person lets it be known to the recipient of the advice that he claims to possess that degree of skill and competence and is willing to exercise that degree of diligence which is generally possessed and exercised by persons who carry on the business or profession of giving advice of the kind sought ...'

Commentary
Distinguished: *Hedley Byrne & Co Ltd* v *Heller & Partners Ltd* [1963] 3 WLR 101.

Nitrigin Eireann Teoranta v *Inco Alloys Ltd* [1992] 1 WLR 498 High Court (May J)

Negligence – economic loss and physical damage

Facts
The defendants had supplied steel alloy tubing for the plaintiffs' chemical plant. An allegedly defective pipe was supplied in summer 1981. In 1983 the plaintiffs discovered that it was damaged by cracking. They were unable to find the cause but repaired the pipe. On 27 June 1984 the pipe burst and there was an explosion which caused damage to the structure of the plant around the pipe. A writ alleging negligent manufacture was issued on 21 June 1990 and the plaintiffs alleged it was issued within six years of the accrual of their cause of action in negligence. Did the plaintiffs have a cause of action in negligence and, if they did, was it statute-barred?

Held
They did have a cause of action which was not statute-barred.

May J accepted the plaintiffs' argument, on the basis of *D & F Estates* v *Church Commissioners* [1989] AC 177, that cracking in the pipe in 1983 was a defect in the quality of the pipe itself which did not cause personal injury or damage to other property, so they had no cause of action in 1983 for that pure economic loss. By contrast, the 1984 explosion did cause damage to other property and a cause of action then arose which was not statute-barred. His Lordship declined to apply *Junior Books Ltd* v *Veitchi Co Ltd* [1983] 1 AC 520, which was a unique case depending on there being a special relationship between plaintiff and defendant amounting to reliance. There was no such relationship in the present case.

Nocton v *Lord Ashburton* [1914] AC 932 House of Lords (Viscount Haldane LC, Lord Dunedin, Lord Atkinson, Lord Shaw and Lord Parmoor)

Misrepresentation – liability of adviser

Facts
The respondent alleged that his solicitor, the appellant, had improperly advised and induced him to advance £65,000 upon a mortgage by other clients of the solicitor, a transaction out of which the solicitor was said to have gained advantage for himself. Charges of fraud were not made out.

Held
The solicitor had been in a fiduciary position towards the respondent and he was therefore under a duty to make a full, and not a misleading, disclosure of facts known to him when advising the respondent. For any loss caused by a breach of this duty the respondent was entitled to compensation.

Lord Shaw:

'The principle to be found running through this branch of the law is, in my opinion, this. Once the relations of parties have been ascertained to be those in which a duty is laid upon one person of giving information or advice to another upon which that other is entitled to rely as the basis of a transaction, responsibility for error amounting to misrepresentation in any statement made will attach to the adviser or informer, although the information and advice have been given, not fraudulently, but in good faith. It is admitted in the present case that misrepresentations were made; that they were material; that they were the cause of loss; that they were made by a solicitor to his client in a situation in which the client was entitled to rely, and did rely, upon the information received. I, accordingly, think that the situation is plainly open for the application of the principle of liability to which I have referred – namely, liability for the consequences of a failure of duty in circumstances in which it was a matter equivalent to contract between the parties that that duty should be fulfilled.'

Osman v *Ferguson* [1993] 4 All ER 344 Court of Appeal (McCowan, Beldam and Simon Brown LJJ)

Duty of care owed by police to victim of crime

Facts

P, a schoolteacher, formed an unhealthy attachment to a 15-year-old male pupil and harassed him. In May 1987 he damaged property belonging to the boy's father. In mid-1987 P was dismissed from the school but continued the harassment. The police were aware of these facts and in late 1987 P told a police officer that the loss of his job was distressing and he feared he would do something criminally insane. In December 1987 P deliberately rammed a vehicle in which the boy was a passenger. The police laid an information against P in January 1988 alleging driving without due care and attention but it was not served. In March 1988 P shot and severely injured the boy and killed his father. The mother, as administratix of the father's estate, and the boy sued the police alleging negligence in that although the police had been aware of P's activities since May 1987 they had failed to apprehend or interview him, search his home or charge him with a more serious offence before March 1988. The police's action to strike out the statement of claim was dismissed and the police appealed.

Held

As the boy and his family had been exposed to a risk over and above that suffered by members of the public, there was an arguable case that there was a very close degree of proximity amounting to a special relationship between the plaintiff's family and the investigating police officers. However, the general duty of the police to suppress crime did not carry with it liability to individuals for damage caused to them by criminals the police had failed to apprehend when it was possible to do so. Applying *Hill* and *Alexandrou* the Court held it would be against public policy to impose such a duty for the reasons stated in *Alexandrou*.

Page v *Smith* [1995] 2 WLR 644 House of Lords (Lords Keith, Ackner, Jauncey, Browne-Wilkinson and Lloyd)

Nervous shock – no personal injury caused to primary victim

Facts

The plaintiff's car was involved in a collision with the defendant's car in which the plaintiff suffered no physical injury. For 20 years prior to the accident the plaintiff had suffered from ME (myalgic encephalomyelitis) which had manifested itself from time to time with different degrees of severity. The plaintiff claimed damages for personal injuries, alleging that as a result of the accident his condition had become chronic and permanent. At first instance the High Court found for the plaintiff, and an appeal to the Court of Appeal allowed the defendant's appeal on the grounds that the plaintiff's injury was not foreseeable. The plaintiff appealed to the House of Lords.

Held
(Lords Keith and Jauncey dissenting) the appeal would be allowed. Once it was established that the defendant was under a duty of care to avoid causing personal injury to the plaintiff, it was immaterial whether the injury sustained was physical, psychiatric or both. Thus the question is whether the defendant should have reasonably foreseen that the plaintiff might suffer personal injury as a result of his negligence. It was unnecessary to ask whether the defendant should have reasonably foreseen injury by shock. It was also irrelevant that the plaintiff did not sustain external physical injury.

The House also stated that in cases of nervous shock it was essential to distinguish between primary victims and secondary victims. In the case of secondary victims, the law insists on certain control mechanisms to limit the number of potential claimants. Where the plaintiff is the primary victim, these control mechanisms have no place.

Partington v *Wandsworth London Borough Council* (1989) The Independent 8 November High Court (Schiemann J)

Handicapped person – duty of care

Facts
The plaintiff suffered injury when she was pushed to the ground by a mentally handicapped 17 year old girl who was, at the time of the incident, in the care of the defendants and was being accompanied by a supervisor.

Held
The plaintiff's claim could not succeed. Although the defendants had been under a duty to take reasonable care to prevent the girl from inflicting injury upon others, the difficulty lay in whether or not that duty had been breached. Schiemann J said that the court must seek to balance what was best for the handicapped person against what was best for the rest of the world. There was no need to keep an autistic girl locked up, nor was it necessary to keep a physical hold of her while out on walks. In the light of these considerations, it had not been proved that the defendants had breached their duty of care because, although the autistic girl had acted in an anti-social manner from time to time, no one knew when she would so act and, in particular, it was not known that she would attack the plaintiff.

Perl (P) (Exporters) Ltd v *Camden London Borough Council* [1983] 3 WLR 769 Court of Appeal (Waller, Oliver and Robert Goff LJJ)

Negligence – duty to adjacent occupier

Facts
The appellant local authority owned a block of flats which included an unoccupied basement flat, which shared a common wall with the basement of the respondent company's neighbouring flat. The appellants' flat was not secured against admission by intruders and they did nothing to improve security despite the fact that there had been burglaries in other flats in the block and there had been complaints. Thieves

entered the unoccupied flat and knocked a hole in the common wall, thereby gaining access to the respondents' flat, and stole a large amount of their property. At the trial, the judge held that Camden LBC should have foreseen that damage to property would ensure from their failure to keep their property secure; there had been an absence of reasonable care and he therefore awarded damages to the respondent company.

Held
The appeal would be allowed. In the absence of any special relationship of control existing between the occupier of premises and a third party, the occupier did not owe a duty of care to an occupier of neighbouring premises to protect his own premises so as to prevent a third party gaining access to them and from there gaining access to the adjoining premises and damaging the neighbour's property.

Oliver LJ:

'What gave rise to the duty in the *Dorset Yacht* case was the special relationship which existed between the defendant and the third person who inflicted the damage, in as much as the defendants had both the statutory right and the statutory duty to exercise control over those persons.'

Waller LJ:

'... no case has been cited to us where a party has been held liable for the acts of a third party when there was no element of control over the third party. While I do not take the view that there can never be such a case I do take the view that the absence of control must make the court approach the suggestion that there is liability for a third party who was not under the control of the defendant with caution.'

Commentary
Followed in *King* v *Liverpool City Council* [1986] 1 WLR 890.
    Distinguished in *Topp* v *London Country Bus (South West) Ltd* (1993) The Times 15 February.

Petch v *Commissioners of Customs and Excise* (1993) The Times 4 March Court of Appeal (Dillon, Beldam and Roch LJJ)

Duty of care owed to subject of statement

Facts
The plaintiff, who was employed by the defendants, was retired from the Civil Service on medical grounds. The plaintiff claimed injury benefit under the Civil Service pension scheme which was administered by the Treasury, and the Treasury requested certain information from the defendants. The plaintiff alleged that the defendants had negligently furnished inaccurate written information to the Treasury as regards the plaintiff's work record, and at first instance the High Court held that a duty of care was imposed on the defendants in respect of this information. The defendants appealed.

Held
The Court of Appeal upheld the appeal and held that an employer answering queries from pension scheme trustees regarding a former employee's work record owed no duty of care to the employee. The majority of the Court (Dillon and Beldam LJJ) could see no difference between the present case and *Spring* (below), while Roch LJ concurring in the decision left open the question whether an employer or former employer owed an employee or former employee a duty to take care in providing factual information at the request of a third party that the information provided was correct where the employer or former employer knew that the third party would use such information to determine the employee's or former employee's entitlement to financial payments from the third party.

Reid v Rush & Tompkins Group plc [1990] 1 WLR 212 Court of Appeal (May, Neill and Ralph Gibson LJJ)

Employer – duty of care to employee

Facts

The plaintiff was seriously injured in a road accident in Ethiopia while working for the defendants. The other driver's negligence was the sole cause of the accident, but his identity was unknown: there was no compulsory third party insurance or scheme to cover uninsured third parties. The plaintiff alleged that the defendants had been in breach of their duty of care as employers in failing either to insure him against such accidents or to advise him to effect such cover himself.

Held

No reasonable cause of action had been disclosed and the plaintiff's claim had therefore been properly struck out.

May LJ:

' ... the ordinary duty of care owed by a master to his servant arises both in contract and in tort. I agree that it is impossible to imply any term into the plaintiff's contract of service with the defendants in the instant case of which, on the facts alleged in the statement of claim, a breach would entitle the plaintiff to recover by way of damages compensation for the loss he has sustained. This being so, then I also agree that it is not open to us to extend the duty of care owed by the defendants to the plaintiff by imposing a duty in tort which is not contained in any express or implied term of the contract.'

Rondel v Worsley [1967] 3 WLR 1666 House of Lords (Lord Reid, Lord Morris of Borth-y-Gest, Lord Pearce, Lord Upjohn and Lord Pearson)

Negligence – barrister's immunity

Facts

Facing a charge of causing grievous bodily harm, the appellant obtained the services of the respondent as counsel to defend him on a dock brief. The appellant was convicted and, nearly six years later, he issued a writ alleging, in effect, negligence on the part of the respondent in the conduct of his defence.

Held

Even if the respondent had been guilty of negligence, an action did not lie at the suit of the appellant.

Lord Morris of Borth-y-Gest:

'Though in most cases, by reason of the special and distinctive features of the work of advocates in which personal discretion is so much involved, assertions of negligence could readily be repelled, a cause of action alleging professional negligence could nevertheless always be framed. Is it, then, desirable in the public interest, while rejecting the wide immunity which has hitherto been proclaimed, to retain an immunity relating only to the limited field of the conduct and management of a case in court? Is it, as a matter of public policy, expedient that actions which involve a searching review almost amounting to a re-trial in different actions of previous actions or cases already concluded should not be allowed? Is the administration of justice (which is so much the concern of the community) better promoted if such actions are not countenanced? If it is recognised that there could be some cases where negligence (as opposed to errors of judgment) could be established, is it nevertheless on a balance of desirabilities wise to disallow the bringing of such cases? In my view, the answer to these questions is that it is in the public interest that such actions should not be brought.'

Commentary
Applied in *Hill* v *Chief Constable of West Yorkshire* [1989] AC 53

Ross v *Caunters* [1979] 3 WLR 605 High Court (Sir Robert Megarry V-C)

Duty of care – solicitors

Facts
A testator instructed the defendant solicitors to draw up his will under which the plaintiff was a beneficiary. Due to the defendants' negligence, the will was invalid and the gift to the plaintiff failed and she brought an action to recover her loss.

Held
The plaintiff was entitled to succeed. The defendants owed her a duty of care because she was within their direct contemplation as a person so closely and directly affected by their acts and omissions that they could reasonably foresee she would be injured by those acts or omissions.

Sir Robert Megarry V-C:

'*Hedley Byrne* is important, of course, as opening the door to the recovery of damages for negligence to at least some cases where the negligence has caused purely financial loss, without any injury to person or property; to that I shall come under the second main head of counsel for the defendants. But, for present purposes, its importance is that the House of Lords rejected pure *Donoghue* v *Stevenson* principles as forming the basis of liability for negligent misstatements and instead based liability on the plaintiff having trusted the defendant to exercise due care in giving information on a matter in which the defendant had a special skill and knew, or ought to have known, of the plaintiff's reliance on his skill and judgment. In this type of case, reliance forms part of the test of liability, as well as part of the chain of causation: and the effect of such a test of liability is to confine the extent of liability far more closely than would an application of pure *Donoghue* v *Stevenson* principles. If liability for negligently putting into circulation some innocent misrepresentation were to be imposed on the same basis as negligently putting into circulation some dangerous chattel, the resulting liability might be for enormous sums to a great multiplicity of plaintiffs. One way of preventing any such liability being imposed is to make the test of liability more strict: and that was the way adopted in *Hedley Byrne*. But, that does not affect those cases in which the principles of *Donoghue* v *Stevenson* apply. If I am right in thinking that the case before me falls within those principles, then there is no need to consider questions of reliance.

There are at least two ways in which *Hedley Byrne* may be regarded. First, it may be regarded as establishing a special category of case in which alone, by way of exception from the general rule, purely financial loss may be recovered in an action for negligence. Second, it may alternatively be regarded as establishing that there is no longer any general rule (if there ever was one) that purely financial loss is irrecoverable in negligence. Instead, such loss may be recovered in those classes of case in which there are no sufficient grounds for denying recovery and, in particular, no danger of exposing the defendant to a degree of liability that is unreasonable in its extent.'

Commentary
See *White* v *Jones* [1995] 2 WLR 187.

Rowling v *Takaro Properties Ltd* [1988] 2 WLR 418 Privy Council (Lord Mackay of Clashfern LC, Lord Keith of Kinkel, Lord Brandon of Oakbrook, Lord Templeman and Lord Goff of Chieveley)

Negligence – minister's duty of care

Facts
Rush, a United States' citizen, established a high class travel lodge in New Zealand, but it incurred heavy losses. A rescue package needed the approval of the Minister of Finance: he refused his consent, the rescue collapsed and a receiver was appointed for Rush's company. Both Rush and the company sought damages against the minister, alleging that he had been negligent in the exercise of his statutory powers arising out of his negligent construction of the regulations under which he had refused to approve the rescue scheme.

Held
Even if the minister had owed a duty of care to construe the relevant legislation correctly, he had not been in breach of that duty as, inter alia, his view had been tenable and he had not been unreasonable or negligent in holding it.

Lord Keith of Kinkel:

'Their Lordships wish to refer in particular to certain matters which they consider to be of importance. The first is that the only effect of a negligent decision, such as is here alleged to have been made, is delay. This is because the processes of judicial review are available to the aggrieved party; and, assuming that the alleged error of law is so serious that it can properly be described as negligent, the decision will assuredly be quashed by a process which, in New Zealand as in the United Kingdom, will normally be carried out with promptitude.

The second is that, in the nature of things, it is likely to be very rare indeed that an error of law of this kind by a minister or other public authority can properly be categorised as negligent. As is well known, anybody, even a judge, can be capable of misconstruing a statute; and such misconstruction, when it occurs, can be severely criticised without attracting the epithet 'negligent'. Obviously, this simple fact points rather to the extreme unlikelihood of a breach of duty being established in these cases ... but it is nevertheless a relevant factor to be taken into account when considering whether liability in negligence should properly be imposed.

The third is the danger of overkill. It is to be hoped that, as a general rule, imposition of liability in negligence will lead to a higher standard of care in the performance of the relevant type of act; but sometimes not only may this not be so, but the imposition of liability may even lead to harmful consequences. In other words, the cure may be worse than the disease. There are reasons for believing that this may be so in cases where liability is imposed on local authorities whose building inspectors have been negligent in relation to the inspection of foundations, as in [*Anns* v *Merton London Borough Council*], because there is a danger that the building inspectors of some local authorities may react to that decision by simply increasing, unnecessarily, the requisite depth of foundations, thereby imposing a very substantial and unnecessary financial burden on members of the community. A comparable danger may exist in cases such as the present, because, once it became known that liability in negligence may be imposed on the ground that a minister has misconstrued a statute and so acted ultra vires, the cautious civil servant may go to extreme lengths in ensuring that legal advice, or even the opinion of the court, is obtained before decisions are taken, thereby leading to unnecessary delay in a considerable number of cases.

Fourth, it is very difficult to identify any particular case in which it can properly be said that a minister is under a duty to seek legal advice. It cannot, their Lordships consider, reasonably be said that a minister is under a duty to seek legal advice in every case in which he is called on to exercise a discretionary power conferred on him by legislation; and their Lordships find it difficult to see how cases in which a duty to seek legal advice should be imposed should be segregated from those in which it should not. In any event, the officers of the relevant department will be involved; the matter will be processed and presented to the minister for decision in the usual way, and by this means his mind will be focused on the relevant issue. Again, it is not to be forgotten that the minister, in exercising his statutory discretion, is acting essentially as a guardian of the public interest; in the present case, for example, he was acting under legislation enacted not for the benefit of applicants for consent to share issues but for the protection of the community as a whole. Furthermore, he is, so far as their Lordships are aware, normally under no duty to exercise his discretion within any particular time; and if, through a mistaken construction of the statute, he acts ultra vires and delay thereby occurs before he makes an intra vires decision, he will have in any event to exercise his discretion anew and, if his discretion is then exercised in the plaintiff's favour, the effect of the delay will only be to postpone the receipt by the plaintiff of a benefit which he had no absolute right to receive.

No doubt there may be possible answers to some of these points, taken individually. But, if the matter is looked at as a whole, it cannot be said to be free from difficulty ... In all the circumstances, it must be a serious question for consideration whether it would be appropriate to impose liability in negligence in these cases, or whether it would not rather be in the public interest that citizens should be confined to their remedy, as at present, in those cases where the minister or public authority has acted in bad faith.'

Saif Ali v *Sydney Mitchell & Co* [1978] 3 WLR 849 House of Lords (Lord Wilberforce, Lord Diplock, Lord Salmon, Lord Russell of Killowen and Lord Keith of Kinkel)

Negligence – barrister's immunity

Facts
The plaintiff was injured in a car accident and was advised to institute proceedings against the owner of the vehicle involved. Counsel negligently failed to advise suing the driver of the vehicle so that the plaintiff was eventually left without remedy. Was counsel immune from proceedings for professional negligence?

Held (Lord Russell of Killowen and Lord Keith of Kinkel dissenting)
No, because a barrister's immunity extends only to those matters of pre-trial work which are so intimately connected with the conduct of the cause in court that they could fairly be said to be preliminary decisions affecting the cause's conduct at the hearing.

Lord Salmon:

'Unless what seems to me to be an untenable proposition is accepted, namely that public policy always requires that a barrister should be immune from liability for his neglect or incompetence in respect of all paperwork, he is rightly in no better position than any other professional man who is sued for negligence. The normal rule applied by the law is that, if anyone holding himself out as possessing reasonable competence in his avocation undertakes to advise or to settle a document, he owes a duty to advise or settle the document with reasonable competence and care. This duty is owed to anyone he should foresee may suffer loss if the duty is breached.

If in breach of that duty he fails to exercise reasonable competence or care and as a result the person to whom the duty was owed suffers damage, he is liable to compensate that person for the damage he has suffered. The law requires the damage to be borne by the person whose breach of duty has caused it, rather than by the innocent person who has suffered it.

I am far from saying that if the advice or document turns out to be wrong, it necessarily follows that he who gave or drew it is liable for the loss caused by its imperfection. The barrister is under no duty to be right; he is only under a duty to exercise reasonable care and competence. Lawyers are often faced with finely balanced problems. Diametrically opposite views may and not infrequently are taken by barristers and indeed by judges, each of whom has exercised reasonable, and sometimes far more than reasonable, care and competence. The fact that one of them turns out to be wrong certainly does not mean that he has been negligent. In my opinion, however, it can only be in the rarest of cases that the law confers any immunity on a barrister against a claim for negligence in respect of any work he has done out of court; and this case is certainly not amongst them.

I ought to add that when *Rondel* v *Worsley* came to the Court of Appeal, I felt bound ... to deal with points which I considered to be wholly irrelevant to anything we had to decide. I may have put the case too high if I used words which might give the impression that counsel's immunity always extended to the drafting of pleadings and to advising on evidence. I should have said that the immunity might *sometimes* extend to drafting pleadings and advising on evidence. If in an advice on evidence counsel states that he will not call Y as a witness whom he believes his client wishes to call solely to prejudice his opponent, counsel is immune on grounds of public policy from being sued in negligence by his client for advising that Y must not be called or for refusing to call him. In such a case the advice would be so closely connected with the conduct of the case in court that it should be covered by the same immunity. It would be absurd if counsel who is immune from an action in negligence for refusing in court to call a witness could be sued in negligence for advising out of court that the witness should not be called. If he could be sued for giving such advice it would make a travesty of the general immunity from suit for anything said or done in court and it is well settled that any device to circumvent this immunity cannot succeed ... The advice given made it impossible for the plaintiff's unanswerable case to be heard in court. It was not even remotely connected with counsel's duty to the court or with public policy.'

Commentary
But see *Antonelli* v *Wade Gery Farr* (1992) The Times 29 December.

Sheppard v *Glossop Corporation* [1921] 3 KB 132 Court of Appeal (Bankes, Scrutton and Atkin LJJ)

Negligence – exercise of statutory discretion

Facts
Under the Public Health Act 1875, the defendants could light their district but they had no obligation to do so. One Christmas night the defendants turned off a particular gas lamp at 9 pm. In the dark, the plaintiff fell and injured himself. The judge found that the accident would not have happened if the lamp had remained alight.

Held
The defendants were not liable.

Atkin LJ:

'It appears to me that if a local authority having statutory powers decides to exercise those powers, then in doing that which it so decides to do it is under a duty to persons interested to take reasonable care not to cause damage so far as the avoidance of damage is consistent with the exercise of the statutory powers. On the other hand, it is under no legal duty to act reasonably in deciding whether it shall exercise its statutory powers or not, or in deciding to what extent those powers shall be exercised – for example, over what area or for what time. Thus, it appears to me that, if it decides to light any area, its lamps and appliances must be placed and maintained with reasonable care so as to avoid danger to wayfarers or owners or occupiers of adjoining property. If gas or electricity is conducted to the lamps, reasonable care must be taken that the gas or electricity do not escape so as to cause damage. There is no duty to exercise the power of lighting at all, nor, if the local authorities do light, are they obliged to light the whole of their urban district or any particular part of it. They are under no duty to light all dangerous places or any dangerous particular place, and, if they do light a dangerous place for some of the time, they are under no duty to light it for all the time. In the present case the local authority did not cause the danger. The danger was in existence, because there was a steep place adjoining a highway over which a wayfarer at night might easily fall in the dark. The real complaint of the plaintiff is not that the local authority caused the danger, but that, the danger being there, if they had lighted the place, he would have seen the danger and avoided it. As I have said, in my opinion, there was no duty upon the local authority to light that dangerous place. Putting it in another way, during the hours of 6 to 9 pm, while, in pursuance with their decision, they were lighting the entrance to Dun Lane, they were under a duty to exercise reasonable care in the way I have mentioned; but after nine o'clock, when they had decided not to light the place, they were under no duty to light it at all.'

Simaan General Contracting Co v *Pilkington Glass Ltd (No 2)* [1988] 2 WLR 761
Court of Appeal (Lord Donaldson of Lymington MR, Dillon and Bingham LJJ)

Negligence – duty of care – economic loss

Facts
The plaintiffs were the main contractors for a building to be erected in Abu Dhabi and the defendants' double glazed units of green glass were specified. A subcontractor duly ordered the glass, but the glass supplied was not of a uniform colour and the building owner withheld payment from the plaintiffs until the glass was replaced. The plaintiffs sued the defendants for the economic loss caused by the withholding of payment.

Held
In the absence of a contract between the parties or damage to property owned by the plaintiffs, the plaintiffs could not bring a direct claim against the defendants for economic loss alone.

Dillon LJ:

'In my judgment there are at least two reasons (there may well be more) why the submissions of counsel for Simaan cannot be accepted and Simaan's direct claim for economic loss against Pilkington must fail.

(1) It is clear, as Lord Keith point out in *Yuen Kun-yeu* v *A-G of Hong Kong* [1987] 3 WLR 776 at 783 that foreseeability of harm or loss does not of itself and automatically lead to a duty of care. Foreseeability of harm is a necessary ingredient of a relationship in which a duty of care will arise, but not the only ingredient. Foreseeability of harm does not become enough to make the harm recoverable by the plaintiff just because what was foreseeable was harm to the plaintiff as an individual rather than as a member of a general and unascertained class ...

If, however, foreseeability does not automatically lead to a duty of care, the duty in a *Hedley Byrne* type of case must depend on the voluntary assumption of responsibility towards a particular party giving rise to a special relationship, as Lord Keith held in *Yuen Kun-yeu* v *A-G of Hong Kong* ... that *Hedley Byrne & Co Ltd* v *Heller & Partners Ltd* [1963] 3 WLR 101 was concerned with the assumption of responsibility ...

But in the present case I can see nothing whatever to justify a finding that Pilkington had voluntarily assumed a direct responsibility to Simaan for the colour and quality of Pilkington's glass panels. On the contrary, all the indications are the other way and show that a chain of contractual relationships was deliberately arranged the way it was without any direct relationship between Simaan and Pilkington.

(2) The approach of the law to awarding damages for economic loss on the grounds of negligence where there has been no injury to the person or property has throughout been greatly affected by pragmatic considerations ...

It might at first glance seem reasonable that, if Simaan have a right of action in contract against Feal [the subcontractors] and Feal have in respect of the same general factual matters a claim in contract, albeit a different contract, against Pilkington, Simaan should be allowed a direct claim against Pilkington. But in truth to allow Simaan a direct claim against Pilkington where there is no contract between them would give rise to formidable difficulties.

If Simaan have a direct claim against Pilkington, so equally or a fortiori has the sheikh [the building owner]. Feal have their claim in contract also. All three claims should be raised in separate proceedings, whether by way of arbitration or litigation, and possibly in separate jurisdictions. The difficulties of awarding damages to any one claimant would be formidable, in view of the differing amounts of retentions by the sheikh against Simaan and by Simaan against Feal and other possibilities of set-off, and in view, even more, of the fact that none of the parties have yet actually incurred the major cost of replacing Pilkington's (assumedly) defective glass panels with new panels of the correct colour. It would not be practicable, in my view, for the court to award damages against Pilkingtons in a global sum for all possible claimants and for the court subsequently to apportion that fund between all claimants and administer it accordingly.

Moreover, if in principle it were to be established in this case that a main contractor or an owner has a direct claim in tort against the nominated supplier to a sub-contractor for economic loss occasioned by defects in the quality of the goods supplied, the formidable question would arise, in future cases if not in this case, as to how far exempting clauses in the contract between the nominated supplier and the sub-contractor were to be imported into the supposed duty in tort owed by the supplier to those higher up the chain ...

If, by contrast, the court does not extend, and in my judgment it would be an extension, the principle of *Hedley Byrne* to cover a direct claim by Simaan against Pilkington, no party will be left without a remedy, by English law at any rate, which is the only system of law we have been asked to consider. There will be the normal chain of liability ... in that the sheikh can sue Simaan on the main building contract, Simaan can sue Feal on the sub-contract and Feal can sue Pilkington. Each liability would be determined in the light of such exemptions as applied contractually at that stage. There is thus no warrant for extending the law of negligence to impose direct liability on Pilkington in favour of Simaan.'

Commentary

Considered: *Junior Books Ltd* v *Veitchi Co Ltd* [1982] 3 WLR 477, in relation to which Dillon LJ said:

'My own view of *Junior Books* is that the speeches of their Lordships have been the subject of so much analysis and discussion with differing explanations of the basis of the case that the case cannot now be regarded as a useful pointer to any development of the law, whatever Lord Roskill may have had in mind when he delivered his speech. Indeed I find it difficult to see that future citation from *Junior Books* can ever serve any useful purpose.'

Smith v *Eric S Bush, Harris* v *Wyre Forest District Council* [1989] 2 WLR 790 House of Lords (Lord Keith of Kinkel, Lord Brandon of Oakbrook, Lord Templeman, Lord Griffiths and Lord Jauncey of Tullichettle)

Valuation – duty of care

Facts
In *Smith*, wishing to buy a terraced house at the lower end of the housing market, the plaintiff applied to the Abbey National Building Society for a mortgage. She paid an inspection fee and signed an application form which stated that she would receive a copy of the survey report and mortgage valuation; the form also contained a disclaimer of responsibility for the contents of the report and valuation. The society instructed the defendant surveyors to carry out the inspection: the plaintiff duly received a copy of their report and valuation which also included a disclaimer. On the strength of the report, which stated that no essential repairs were required, the plaintiff purchased the house, but the defendants had carried out their work negligently, overlooking a serious defect. Eighteen months later, as a result of that defect, some flues collapsed and caused substantial damage. The facts of *Harris* were essentially the same except that the inspection was carried out by their own surveyor.

Held
The defendants were liable: they had owed the plaintiff in tort a duty to exercise reasonable skill and care, they had been in breach of that duty and the disclaimer clauses were ineffective.

Lord Templeman said that in each case the valuer knew that the purchaser was providing the money for the valuation, that the purchaser would only contract to purchase the house if the valuation was satisfactory and that the purchaser might suffer injury or damage or both if the valuer did not exercise reasonable skill and care. In those circumstances his Lordship would expect the law to impose on the valuer a duty owed to the purchaser to exercise reasonable skill and care in carrying out the valuation. The considerations referred to by Denning LJ in *Candler v Crane, Christmas & Co* [1951] 2 KB 164, 176-181, whose dissenting judgment was subsequently approved by the House of Lords in *Hedley Byrne & Co Ltd v Heller & Partners Ltd* [1964] AC 465, applied to the valuers in the present appeals. The statutory duty of the council to value the house did not prevent the council coming under a contractual or tortious duty to the plaintiffs who in *Harris* were informed of the valuation and relied on it.

The contractual duty of a valuer to value a house for the Abbey National did not prevent the valuer coming under a tortious duty to Mrs Smith who was furnished with a report of the valuation and relied on it. In general, his Lordship was of the opinion that in the absence of a disclaimer of liability the valuer who valued a house for the purpose of a mortgage, knowing that the mortgagee would, and the mortgagor would probably rely on the valuation, knowing that the purchaser mortgagor had in effect paid for the valuation, was under a duty to exercise reasonable skill and care, and that duty was owed to both parties to the mortgage for which the valuation was made. Indeed, in both appeals the existence of such a dual duty was tacitly accepted and acknowledged because notices excluding liability for breach of the duty owed to the purchaser were drafted by the mortgagee and imposed on the purchaser. In those circumstances it was necessary to consider the second question which arose in the appeals, namely, whether the disclaimers of liability were notices which fell within the Unfair Contract Terms Act 1977. In his Lordship's opinion, both ss11(3) and 13(1) supported the view that the 1977 Act required that all exclusion notices which would at common law provide a defence to an action for negligence must satisfy the requirement of reasonableness. Here, they did not and the evidence and findings of Mr Justice Park in *Yianni v Edwin Evans & Sons* [1982] QB 438, supported the view that it was unfair and unreasonable for a valuer to rely on an exclusion clause directed against a purchaser in the circumstances of the present appeals.

Lord Griffiths, concurring, said that it had to be remembered that each of the appeals concerned a dwelling house of modest value in which it was widely recognised by valuers that purchasers were in fact relying on their care and skill. It would obviously be of general application in broadly similar circumstances. But his Lordship expressly reserved his position in respect of valuations of quite different types of property for mortgage purposes, such as industrial property, large blocks of flats or very expensive houses. In such cases it might well be that the general expectation of the behaviour of the purchaser was quite different. With very large sums of money at stake prudence would demand that the purchaser obtain his own structural survey to guide him in his purchase and, in such circumstances, with such large sums of money at stake, it might be reasonable for the valuers acting on behalf of the mortgagees to exclude or limit their liability to the purchaser.

Smith v *Littlewoods Organisation Ltd* [1987] 2 WLR 480 House of Lords (Lord Keith of Kinkel, Lord Brandon of Oakbrook, Lord Griffiths, Lord Mackay of Clashfern and Lord Goff of Chieveley)

Negligence – act of third party

Facts
The defendants purchased a cinema in Dunfermline with a view to demolishing it and building a supermarket on the site. From June 1976 the site was empty and unattended. Vandals broke into the old cinema and attempted to set fire to the building. On 5 July 1976 a fire was started in the building and spread to neighbouring properties, including the plaintiffs' property. The plaintiffs sued the defendants in negligence, alleging that they had failed to take reasonable steps to prevent damage.

Held
The defendants were not liable. An occupier was under a general duty to exercise reasonable care in order to ensure that the condition of his premises was not a source of danger to neighbouring properties. Although it was expressly found that the damage by fire was foreseeable, the defendants had done all that a reasonable owner of the property could do in boarding up the cinema. There was no duty to patrol the premises all the time to keep vandals away.

Lord Griffiths:

> 'The fire in this case was caused by the criminal activity of third parties on Littlewoods' premises. I do not say that there will never be circumstances in which the law will require an occupier of premises to take special precautions against such a contingency but they would surely have to be extreme indeed. It is common ground that only a 24-hour guard on these premises would have been likely to prevent this fire, and even that cannot be certain, such is the determination and ingenuity of young vandals.
>
> There was nothing of an inherently dangerous nature stored in the premises, nor can I regard an empty cinema stripped of its equipment as likely to be any more alluring to vandals than any other recently vacated premises in the centre of a town. No message was received by Littlewoods from the local police, fire brigade or any neighbour that vandals were creating any danger on the premises. In short, so far as Littlewoods knew, there was nothing significantly different about these empty premises from the tens of thousands of such premises up and down the country. People do not mount 24-hour guards on empty properties and the law would impose an intolerable burden if it required them to do so save in the most exceptional circumstances. I find no such exceptional circumstances in this case ...
>
> I doubt myself if any search will reveal a touchstone that can be applied as a universal test to decide when an occupier is to be held liable for a danger created on his property by the act of a trespasser for whom he is not responsible. I agree that mere foreseeability of damage is certainly not a sufficient basis to found liability. But with this warning I doubt that more can be done than to leave it to the good sense of the judges to apply realistic standards in conformity with generally accepted patterns of behaviour to determine whether in the particular circumstances of a given case there has been a breach of duty sounding in negligence.'

Commentary
Applied in *Topp* v *London Country Bus (South West) Ltd* [1993] 3 All ER 448.

NB: distinguished in *Walpole* v *Partridge and Wilson* [1994] 1 All ER 385 (CA).

Somasundaram v *M Julius Melchior & Co* [1988] 1 WLR 1394 Court of Appeal (May, Stocker and Stuart-Smith LJJ)

Lawyers' immunity

Facts
Charged with offences relating to the stabbing of his wife, the appellant at first instructed his solicitors, the respondents, that he intended to plead guilty, but then changed his mind. The respondents arranged a conference with counsel who advised the appellant to plead guilty: he did, but the sentence was reduced on appeal. The appellant alleged that the respondents had overpersuaded him to change his story and now claimed damages for negligence. His action was struck out.

Held
His appeal against this decision would be dismissed as, on the facts, his action had no reasonable chance of success. Additionally, it had been an abuse of the process of the court for the appellant to bring an action which necessarily involved an attack on the conviction and sentence imposed by the Crown Court and upheld in the Court of Appeal, subject to the reduction of sentence.

May LJ:

'The remaining ground on which counsel for the respondents submits that the action should be struck out is on the ground that the respondents are immune from suit in respect of the allegations in the statement of claim and the action is therefore bound to fail. This submission was supported by counsel as amicus curiae. Both counsel submit, rightly in our judgment, that advice as to a plea is something which is so intimately connected with the conduct of the cause in court that it can fairly be said to be a preliminary decision affecting the way that the cause is to be conducted when it comes to a hearing, within the test ... approved by the House of Lords in *Saif Ali's* case [1980] AC 198. Indeed it is difficult to think of any decision more closely so connected. Counsel submitted that such immunity must therefore extend to solicitors and he relied on passages in the speeches of their Lordships in *Rondel* v *Worsley* [1969] 1 AC 191 to this effect. But to our minds it is clear that in extending the immunity to solicitors, their Lordships limited it to the occasions when they were acting as advocates, as of course they frequently do in the magistrates' courts and county courts and occasionally in those Crown Courts where they have rights of audience ...

Counsel as amicus curiae submitted that in a case where there was both solicitor and barrister, it would be anomalous if the immunity in relation to advising on plea extended to the barrister, but not to the solicitor. That may be so; but we would not be willing to extend the immunity that protects barristers and solicitors qua advocates any further than is necessary in the interests of justice and public policy. Thus we are not persuaded in this case that the action should be struck out on the grounds of immunity from suit ...

In practice of course it makes no difference, because in a criminal case advice on plea is likely to result in a decision of the court, which would first have to be upset by the proper appeal process before any action for damages could be sustained. Moreover where, as here, the advice as to plea was later confirmed by counsel, any action against the solicitor would almost certainly be bound to fail either on the ground that the solicitor has also been advised by counsel and was not negligent or, as a matter of causation, counsel's intervention broke any link between the solicitor's advice and the eventual plea.'

Spartan Steel & Alloys Ltd v *Martin & Co (Contractors) Ltd* [1972] 3 WLR 502
Court of Appeal (Lord Denning MR, Edmund-Davies and Lawton LJJ)

Negligence – economic loss

Facts
Due to the negligence of the defendants' servants who were carrying out roadworks, an electricity supply cable was damaged. This caused a loss of power for about 14 hours which meant that the plaintiffs' smelting works a quarter of a mile away had to be shut down. The result was that the molten metal ('melt') which was in the furnace had to be drawn out to avoid the danger of it solidifying and causing damage to the mould. The plaintiffs claimed damages as follows:

a) Actual physical damage to furnace: £368;
b) Loss of profit on the melt which could not be properly completed: £400;
c) Loss of profit due to being unable to process further melts for 14 hours: £1,767.

Held (Edmund-Davies LJ dissenting):
The plaintiffs could recover (a). They could also recover (b) because it was truly consequential upon (a). But (c) was not recoverable as it was economic loss independent of the physical damage.

Lord Denning MR:

'At bottom I think the question of recovering economic loss is one of policy. Whenever the courts draw a line to mark out the bounds of duty, they do it as a matter of policy so as to limit the responsibility of the defendant. Wherever courts set bounds to the damages recoverable – saying that they are, or are not, too remote – they do it as a matter of policy so as to limit the liability of the defendant.'

Commentary
Applied in *Muirhead* v *Industrial Tank Specialities Ltd* [1985] 3 WLR 993.

Spring v *Guardian Assurance plc* [1994] 3 WLR 354 House of Lords (Lord Keith, Lord Goff, Lord Lowry, Lord Slynn and Lord Woolf)

Duty of care owed to subject of reference

Facts
The plaintiff, who was employed by the defendants, was dismissed and sought employment with a competitor of the defendants. The competitors were obliged by the LAUTRO rules to obtain a reference from the plaintiff's previous employer, and received such a bad reference from the defendants that they refused to employ the plaintiff. The plaintiff sued the defendants in negligence claiming damages for the loss caused by the reference. At first instance the judge found that the defendants owed a duty of care to the plaintiff as regards the reference, that they had been negligent in preparing the reference and that the plaintiff was entitled to damages. The defendants appealed to the Court of Appeal who allowed the appeal and held that no duty of care existed. The plaintiff appealed to the House of Lords.

Held
The appeal was allowed. An employer who gives a reference in respect of a former employee owes that employee a duty to take reasonable care in its preparation. The imposition of such a duty was not contrary to public policy on the ground that it might inhibit the giving of full and frank references, and the fact that in an action for defamation or injurious falsehood the employer would have a defence of qualified privilege did not bar an action in negligence where no such defence was available.

Lord Slynn and Lord Woolf also held that it was an implied term of the contract between the employer and employee that the employer would take reasonable care in compiling and giving a reference, and that the employers were in breach of this implied term.

Lord Goff:

> 'In my opinion, the source of duty of care lies in the principle derived from *Hedley Byrne & Co Ltd* v *Heller & Partners Ltd* [1964] AC 465, viz an assumption of responsibility by those companies to the plaintiff in respect of the reference, and reliance by the plaintiff upon the exercise by them of due care and skill in respect of its preparation.
>
> The wide scope of the principle recognised in *Hedley Byrne* is reflected in the broad statements of principle which I have quoted. All the members of the Appellate Committee in this case spoke in terms of the principle resting upon an assumption or undertaking of responsibility by the defendant towards the plaintiff, coupled with reliance by the plaintiff on the exercise by the defendant of due care and skill. Lord Devlin, in particular, stressed that the principle rested upon an assumption of responsibility when he said, at p531, that "the essence of the matter in the present case and in others of the same type is the acceptance of responsibility". For the purpose of the case now before your Lordships it is, I consider, legitimate to proceed on the same basis. Furthermore, although *Hedley Byrne* itself was concerned with the provision of information and advice, it is clear that the principle in the case is not so limited and extends to include the performance of other services, as for example the professional services rendered by a solicitor to his client (see in particular, Lord Devlin, at pp529, 530). Accordingly, where the plaintiff entrusts the defendant with the conduct of his affairs, in general or in particular, the defendant may be held to have assumed responsibility to the plaintiff, and the plaintiff to have relied on the defendant to exercise due skill and care, in respect of such conduct.'

Lord Lowry:

'I also agree with my noble and learned friend Lord Goff's interpretation of *Hedley Byrne*.'

Commentary

Henderson and *Spring* are important in that in both cases the House of Lords, and Lord Goff in particular, held that *Hedley Byrne* is not limited to cases of negligent misstatement, but can cover the performance of services where there is a voluntary assumption of responsibility by the defendant or where the special relationship exists. This is particularly important since *Hedley Byrne* is the one course of action in which recovery for pure economic loss is unquestioned.

Topp v *London Country Bus (South West) Ltd* [1993] 3 All ER 448 Court of Appeal (Dillon, Rose LJJ and Peter Gibson J)

Duty of care – action of a third party

Facts

The defendants' minibus had been stolen from outside a public house by an unknown person who had, while driving the minibus, shortly afterwards knocked down and killed the plaintiff's wife. The vehicle had been left unattended with the ignition key in the lock. May J dismissed the plaintiff's claim in negligence.

Held

The plaintiff's appeal would be dismissed.

Dillon LJ said that the plaintiff's claim was founded in negligence on the basis that the defendant, knowing that the bus might be stolen and driven dangerously, was in breach of duty in failing to collect the bus or to render it incapable of being driven away by unauthorised persons. In so far as the case was put on the basis that leaving the bus with the key in the ignition switch was to create a special risk, it was pertinent to refer to *P Perl (Exporters) Ltd* v *Camden London Borough Council* [1984] QB 342. The cases referred to in that case were far different from the present. There was no evidence in the instant case that the malefactor had been frequenting the public house, nor was there any presumption that persons frequenting the public house were likely to steal vehicles. There was no valid distinction between the present case and *Denton* v *United Counties Omnibus Co* (1986) The Times 6 May where a bus was unlawfully taken by an unknown person from a bus station and driven about and it collided with a parked motor car. The bus company owed no duty of care to the plaintiff owner of the car and his claim failed.

All such cases, continued Dillon LJ, in a sense depended on their own facts, but it was inevitable to consider what valid distinctions there could be between them. There were none between the present case and *Denton's* case. It did not matter that in the present case the bus was parked on the highway. His Lordship recalled that in *Smith* v *Littlewoods Organisation Ltd* [1987] AC 41 Lord Mackay of Clashfern LC had pointed out that the determination of the question whether there was a duty to protect against the wrongful act of a third party was a matter for the judges of fact. There was no basis for interfering with the judge's decision in the present case.

Van Oppen v *Clerk to the Bedford Charity Trustees* [1990] 1 WLR 235 Court of Appeal (O'Connor, Croom-Johnson and Balcombe LJJ)

School – duty of care

Facts

The plaintiff, when aged sixteen and a half, suffered injury at the defendant school during an inter-house rugby match. He sued for damages on two distinct bases: (1) an allegation that the school was negligent in failing to take reasonable care for his safety on the rugby field, by failing to coach or instruct him in proper tackling techniques (the rugby claim); and (2) an allegation that the school was negligent in (a) failing to inform or advise his father (i) of the inherent risk of serious injury in the game of rugby, (ii) of the consequent need for personal accident insurance, and (iii) that the school had not arranged such insurance for him; and (b) in default of such information or advice failing itself to ensure that he was covered by personal accident insurance (the insurance claim). The trial judge dismissed both claims ([1989] 1 All ER 272); the plaintiff appealed in respect of the insurance claim.

Held

The appeal would be dismissed.

O'Connor LJ:

> 'There is no dispute that had a personal accident policy been in position the plaintiff would have received the appropriate payment as a result of his injury. It is the plaintiff's case that he has suffered this loss as a result of the negligence of the school and that although it is pure economic loss it is recoverable.
>
> Counsel for the plaintiff accepts that there is no duty on parents to take out personal accident insurance policies in favour of their children. He accepts that there is no general duty on schools to take out personal accident policies in favour of their pupils and quite plainly it is no part of a school's function to advise parents or anybody else on insurance matters.
>
> The next matter which is of importance is that it is not suggested that the school was negligent in allowing the plaintiff to play rugby knowing that there was no personal accident policy in position. I am satisfied that the plaintiff's "insurance claim" cannot be brought within the scope of the duty owed by school to pupil arising out of the relationship which existed between them.
>
> When one considers the duty owed by a school to its pupils one finds first of all the duties which the law imposes on all schools because they are schools. These duties are of general application whether the school be provided by the state, or privately, and regardless of whether it be fee-paying or free. Next one must look at the individual school to see whether it owes some additional duty to its pupils. On analysis such may be no more than a special standard of care to discharge the general duties, for example a school for the blind. The terms on which the school accepts pupils may show that it would be fair and reasonable to impose some additional duty on the school. Personal accident insurance is a very good example of such a term. If a school decides that all pupils are to be covered by personal accident insurance under a block policy taken out by the school and the school negligently fails to renew the policy, then in my judgment an injured pupil would have a good claim against the school.
>
> However, I can see no justification for the court to write in such a term for a period before the school has introduced it, whether by agreement with the parents or unilaterally.
>
> It is said that knowledge reaching the school ... on the rugby injury/personal accident insurance topic put them under a duty ... to warn parents of the desirability of taking out personal accident insurance. I do not think that the facts support this contention.'

Walpole v *Partridge and Wilson* [1993] 3 WLR 1093 Court of Appeal (Ralph Gibson, Beldam and Peter Gibson LJJ)

Use of negligence as a challenge to a court decision

Facts

Solicitor acting for the plaintiff failed, in breach of duty, to advance an appeal on a point of law which would probably have been successful. At first instance the judge struck out the plaintiff's claim as an abuse of process within *Hunter* v *Chief Constable of West Midlands Police* [1982] AC 529.

Held
Allowing the appeal, that although proceedings which amounted to a collateral attack on a final decision of a court, which the plaintiff had had a full opportunity to contest, might be an abuse of the process of the court, an action in which the plaintiff alleged that his legal advisers had failed in breach of duty to advance an appeal on a point of law which might have been decided in favour of the plaintiff was not an abuse. The fresh proceedings did not amount to relitigation of an issue decided in the earlier proceedings. The point of law in question was arguable and the defendants had failed to show that the decision of the Crown Court was a final decision. It would thus be manifestly unfair to deny the plaintiff an opportunity to have his case tried on its merits.

White v *Jones* [1995] 2 WLR 481 House of Lords (Lord Keith, Lord Goff, Lord Browne-Wilkinson, Lord Mustill and Lord Nolan)
Validity of *Ross* v *Caunters*

Facts
A testator quarrelled with his two daughters and instructed his solicitor, the defendants, to prepare a will cutting his daughters out of his estate. After this was done the testator became reconciled with his daughters and instructed the defendants to prepare a fresh will leaving £9,000 to each daughter. The defendants did nothing for a month and then began preparation of the new will. They arranged to visit the testator one month later, but unfortunately the testator died three days before the meeting. The distribution of the estate was governed by the old will, and so the daughters lost their bequests of £9,000 each. They sued the defendants, alleging that they had been negligent in the preparation of the new will and claimed £9,000 each by way of damages. The trial judge held that the defendants owed no duty of care to the plaintiffs and dismissed the action.

Held
The Court of Appeal held that *Ross* v *Caunters* [1979] 3 All ER 580 was still good law and that each plaintiff was entitled to damages of £9,000. The court held that in these circumstances liability arose because:
1. it was foreseeable that the disappointed beneficiary would suffer financial loss;
2. there was a sufficient degree of proximity between the solicitor and the intended beneficiary; and
3. it was fair, just and reasonable that liability should be imposed in negligence on the solicitor to compensate the intended beneficiary where the solicitor was in breach of his professional duty, but there was no remedy in contract and no effective remedy for the client's estate. Had damages been paid to the estate they would have passed under the original will and so would not have been received by the plaintiffs. Thus if no liability had been imposed, the only person with a valid claim (the estate) had suffered no loss, and the only person who suffered a loss (the plaintiffs) would have had no valid claim.

The House of Lords dismissed the appeal by a bare majority on the ground that the assumption of responsibility by a solicitor to his client, who had given instructions for the drawing up of a will, extended to an intended beneficiary under that will where the solicitor could reasonably foresee that his negligence might result in the loss of the intended legacy without either the testator or his estate having a remedy against him.

Lord Goff:

'For the reasons I have already given, an ordinary action in tortious negligence on the lines proposed by Sir Robert Megarry V-C in *Ross* v *Caunters* [1980] Ch 297 must, with the greatest respect, be regarded as inappropriate, because it does not meet any of the conceptual problems which have been raised. Furthermore, for the reasons I have previously given, the *Hedley Byrne* [1964] AC 465 principle cannot, in the absence of special circumstances, give rise on ordinary principles to an assumption of responsibility by the testator's solicitor towards an intended beneficiary. Even so it seems to me that it is open to your Lordships' House ... to fashion a remedy to fill a lacuna in the law and so prevent the injustice which would otherwise occur on the facts of cases such as the present. ... In my opinion, therefore, your Lordships' House should in cases such as these extend to the intended beneficiary a remedy under the *Hedley Byrne* principle by holding that the assumption of responsibility by the solicitor towards his client should be held in law to extend to the intended beneficiary who (as the solicitor can reasonably foresee) may, as a result of the solicitor's negligence, be deprived of his intended legacy in circumstances in which neither the testator nor his estate will have a remedy against the solicitor. Such liability will not of course arise in cases in which the defect in the will comes to light before the death of the testator, and the testator either leaves the will as it is or otherwise continues to exclude the previously intended beneficiary from the relevant benefit. I only wish to add that, with the benefit of experience during the 15 years in which *Ross* v *Caunters* has been regularly applied, we can say with some confidence that a direct remedy by the intended beneficiary against the solicitor appears to create no problems in practice. That is therefore the solution which I would recommend to your Lordships.'

Wigg v *British Railways Board* (1986) The Times 4 February High Court (Tucker J)

Negligence – nervous shock

Facts
The plaintiff was a train driver of 20 years' standing. On the occasion in question he started the train having received a signal from the guard that it was safe to do so. In fact a person had been attempting to board the train as it pulled away and he was pulled under the train. The plaintiff attempted to comfort the victim on realising what had happened. He remained with him for ten minutes and suffered nervous shock. This was aggravated by the fact that he had encountered two previous incidents of this nature in the recent years.

Held
The guard had been negligent in failing to notice that the carriage door was open and therefore in allowing the train to start. British Rail were therefore vicariously liable for his negligence. It was a reasonably foreseeable consequence of that negligence that the plaintiff might suffer nervous shock since he was in sufficient proximity to the accident by hearing it and seeing the aftermath. The plaintiff was entitled to damages.

Yuen Kun-yeu v *Attorney-General of Hong Kong* [1987] 3 WLR 776 Privy Council (Lord Keith of Kinkel, Lord Templeman, Lord Griffiths, Lord Oliver of Aylmerton and Sir Robert Megarry)

Negligence – test for establishing whether duty of care exists

Facts
The Commissioner of Deposit-taking Companies in Hong Kong had a wide statutory discretion as to

the registration of deposit-taking businesses. The appellants made substantial deposits with a registered deposit-taking company: subsequently it went into liquidation and they lost their money. The appellants alleged negligence by the commissioner in the discharge of his functions and sought an award of damages.

Held
They should not succeed as there was no special relationship between the commissioner and the company, or between the commissioner and would-be depositors, capable of giving rise to a duty of care.

Lord Keith:

> 'In their Lordships' opinion the circumstance that the commissioner had, on the appellants' averments, cogent reason to suspect that the company's business was being carried on fraudulently and improvidently did not create a special relationship between the commissioner and the company of the nature described in the authorities. They are also of opinion that no special relationship existed between the commissioner and those unascertained members of the public who might in future become exposed to the risk of financial loss through depositing money with the company. Accordingly, their Lordships do not consider that the commissioner owed to the appellants any duty of care on the principle which formed the ratio of the *Dorset Yacht* case. To hark back to Lord Atkin's words, there were not such close and direct relations between the commissioner and the appellants as to give rise to the duty of care desiderated.
>
> The appellants, however, advanced an argument based on their averment of having relied on the registration of the company when they deposited their money with it. It was said that registration amounted to a seal of approval of the company, and that by registering the company and allowing the registration to stand the commissioner made a continuing representation that the company was creditworthy. In the light of the information in the commissioner's possession that representation was made negligently and led to the appellant's loss ... While the investing public might reasonably feel some confidence that the provisions of the ordinance as a whole went a long way to protect their interests, reliance on the fact of registration as a guarantee of the soundness of the particular company would be neither reasonable nor justifiable, nor should the commissioner reasonable be expected to know of such reliance, if it existed. Accordingly their Lordships are unable to accept the appellants' arguments about reliance as apt, in all the circumstances, to establish a special relationship between them and the commissioner such as to give rise to a duty of care.'

Commentary
Followed in *Davis* v *Radcliffe* [1990] 1 WLR 821 and *Clough* v *Bussan* [1990] 1 All ER 431.

5 Negligence: Breach of the Duty

Airedale NHS Trust* v *Bland [1993] 2 WLR 316 House of Lords (Lord Keith of Kinkel, Lord Goff of Chievely, Lord Lowry, Lord Browne-Wilkinson and Lord Mustill)

Withdrawal of treatment – breach of duty of care?

Facts
When aged 17$^1/_2$ Anthony Bland was crushed in the 1989 Hillsborough football disaster. He had since then been in a persistent vegetative state, without hope of recovery or improvement of any kind. The plaintiffs now sought a declaration that they could lawfully discontinue all life-sustaining treatment.

Held
The declaration had been properly granted.

Lord Browne-Wilkinson:

'... this House in *F* v *West Berkshire Health Authority* [1989] 2 WLR 1025 developed and laid down a principle, based on concepts of necessity, under which a doctor can lawfully treat a patient who cannot consent to such treatment if it is in the best interests of the patient to receive such treatment. In my view, the correct answer to the present case depends on the extent of the right to continue lawfully to invade the bodily integrity of Anthony Bland without his consent. If in the circumstances they have no right to continue artificial feeding, they cannot be in breach of any duty by ceasing to provide such feeding.

What then is the extent of the right to treat Anthony Bland which can be deduced from *F* v *West Berkshire Health Authority*? Both Lord Brandon of Oakbrook and Lord Goff make it clear that the right to administer invasive medical care is wholly dependent upon such care being in the best interests of the patient ... Moreover, a doctor's decision whether invasive care is in the best interests of the patient falls to be assessed by reference to the test laid down in *Bolam* v *Friern Hospital Management Committee* [1957] 1 WLR 582, viz is the decision in accordance with a practice accepted at the time by a responsible body of medical opinion? ... In my judgment it must follow from this that, if there comes a stage where the responsible doctor comes to the reasonable conclusion (which accords with the views of a responsible body of medical opinion) that further continuance of an intrusive life support system is not in the best interests of the patient, he can no longer lawfully continue that life support system: to do so would constitute the crime of battery and the tort of trespass to the person. Therefore he cannot be in breach of any duty to maintain the patient's life. Therefore he is not guilty of murder by omission ...

Finally, the conclusion I have reached will appear to some to be almost irrational. How can it be lawful to allow a patient to die slowly, though painlessly, over a period of weeks from lack of food but unlawful to produce his immediate death by a lethal injection, thereby saving his family from yet another ordeal to add to the tragedy that has already struck them? I find it difficult to find a moral answer to that question. But it is undoubtedly the law and nothing I have said casts doubt on the proposition that the doing of a positive act with the intention of ending life is and remains murder.'

Barkway* v *South Wales Transport Co Ltd [1950] AC 185 House of Lords (Lord Porter, Lord Normand, Lord Morton of Henryton, Lord Reid and Lord Radcliffe)

Negligence – accident due to burst tyre

Facts
The offside front tyre of the respondents' bus burst and the vehicle veered across the road and fell over an embankment. The appellant's husband, a passenger in the bus, was killed. The tyre had been defective.

Held
The appellant should succeed as the defect in the tyre might have been discovered if the respondents had exercised due diligence.

Lord Ratcliffe:

> 'I do not think that the appellant was entitled to judgment in the action because of any special virtue in the maxim *res ipsa loquitur*. I find nothing more in that maxim than a rule of evidence, of which the essence is that an event which in the ordinary course of things is more likely than not to have been caused by negligence is by itself evidence of negligence. In this action much more is known than the bare fact that the omnibus mounted the pavement and fell down the bank. The true question is not whether the appellant adduced some evidence of negligence, but whether on all the evidence she proved that the respondents had been guilty of negligence in a relevant particular. In my view, the important thing is that the tyre on the respondents' omnibus was defective.'

Blyth* v *Birmingham Waterworks Co (1856) 11 Exch 781 Court of Exchequer (Alderson, Martin and Bramwell BB)

Negligence – frost of exceptional severity

Facts
In pursuance of statutory powers, the defendants laid down water pipes. During 'one of the severest frosts on record', a plug failed to work correctly and a large quantity of water escaped into the plaintiff's house.

Held
On the facts, the defendants were not liable.

Alderson B:

> 'The case turns upon the question whether the facts proved show that the defendants were guilty of negligence. Negligence is the omission to do something which a reasonable man, guided upon those considerations which ordinarily regulate the conduct of human affairs, would do, or doing something which a prudent and reasonable man would not do. The defendants might have been liable for negligence, if, unintentionally, they omitted to do that which a reasonable person would have done, or did that which a person taking reasonable precautions would not have done. A reasonable man would act with reference to the average circumstances of the temperature in ordinary years. The defendants had provided against such frosts as experience would have led men, acting prudently, to provide against; and they are not guilty of negligence, because their precautions proved insufficient against the effects of the extreme severity of the frost of 1855, which penetrated to a greater depth than any which ordinarily occurs south of the polar regions. Such a state of circumstances constitutes a contingency against which no reasonable man can provide. The result was an accident, for which the defendants cannot be held liable.'

Bolam v Friern Hospital Management Committee [1957] 1 WLR 582 High Court (McNair J)

Negligence – two schools of thought

Facts
Suffering from mental illness, the plaintiff agreed to undergo electro-convulsive therapy. The method of treatment adopted was favoured by one body of medical opinion, but another preferred a different approach. The plaintiff suffered injury in the course of his treatment and he sought damages for negligence.

Held
His action failed.

McNair J:

'I must explain what in law we mean by "negligence". In the ordinary case which does not involve any special skill, negligence in law means this: some failure to do some act which a reasonable man in the circumstances would do, or doing some act which a reasonable man in the circumstances would not do; and if that failure or doing of that act results in injury, then there is a cause of action. How do you test whether this act or failure is negligent? In an ordinary case it is generally said, that you judge that by the action of the man in the street. He is the ordinary man. In one case it has been said that you judge it by the conduct of the man on the top of a Clapham omnibus. He is the ordinary man. But where you get a situation which involves the use of some special skill or competence, then the test whether there has been negligence or not is not the test of the man on the top of a Clapham omnibus, because he has not got this special skill. The test is the standard of the ordinary skilled man exercising and professing to have that special skill. A man need not possess the highest expert skill at the risk of being found negligent. It is well-established law that it is sufficient if he exercises the ordinary skill of an ordinary competent man exercising that particular art. I do not think that I quarrel much with any of the submissions in law which have been put before you by counsel. Counsel for the plaintiff put it in this way, that in the case of a medical man negligence means failure to act in accordance with the standards of reasonably competent medical men at the time. That is a perfectly accurate statement, as long as it is remembered that there may be one or more perfectly proper standards; and if a medical man conforms with one of those proper standards then he is not negligent. Counsel for the plaintiff was also right, in my judgment, in saying: that a mere personal belief that a particular technique is best is no defence unless that belief is based on reasonable grounds. That again is unexceptionable.'

Commentary
Applied in *Clark* v *MacLennan* [1983] 1 All ER 416 and *Airedale NHS Trust* v *Bland* [1993] 2 WLR 316.
See also *Whitehouse* v *Jordan* [1981] 1 WLR 246 and *F* v *West Berskhire Health Authority* [1989] 2 All ER 545.

Bolton v Stone [1951] AC 850 House of Lords (Lord Porter, Lord Normand, Lord Oaksey, Lord Reid and Lord Radcliffe)

Negligence – injury from cricket ball

Facts
The plaintiff was standing on the highway when she was hit by a cricket ball which had been struck from the defendant's adjoining cricket ground. The evidence showed that, in the many years that cricket

had been played on the ground, only very occasionally had the ball been hit so far. The ball had travelled over 100 yards after being hit and had cleared a seven foot boundary fence. The plaintiff sued in, inter alia, negligence. In the House of Lords it was conceded that, in the circumstances, nuisance could not be established unless negligence was proved.

Held
The defendants were not negligent in failing to take steps to guard against such a small risk: such an injury would not have been anticipated by a reasonable man.

Lord Oaksey:

> 'An ordinary, careful man does not take precautions against every foreseeable risk. He can, of course, foresee the possibility of many risks, but life would be almost impossible if he were to attempt to take precautions against every risk which he can foresee. He takes precautions against risks which are reasonably likely to happen.'

Lord Reid:

> 'In the crowded conditions of modern life, even the most careful person cannot avoid creating some risks and accepting others. What a man must not do ... is to create a risk which is substantial.'

Commentary
Distinguished in *Overseas Tankship (UK) Ltd* v *The Miller Steamship Co Pty Ltd (The Wagon Mound No 2)* [1966] 3 WLR 498.

Condon v *Basi* [1985] 1 WLR 866 Court of Appeal (Sir John Donaldson MR, Stephen Brown LJ and Glidewell J)

Negligence – injury during football match

Facts
The plaintiff and defendant were playing on opposite sides in a football match, and the defendant made a foul tackle on the plaintiff resulting in breaking the plaintiff's leg. The plaintiff claimed damages for negligence and assault.

Held
His claim should succeed. The duty of care between sports players is a duty to take reasonable care in the light of the circumstances in which they are playing. A player is negligent if he fails to exercise reasonable care *or* if he acts in a way to which another player cannot be expected to consent. On the facts of the case, there had been, in the words of the county court judge, 'serious and dangerous foul play which showed a reckless disregard of the plaintiff's safety'.

Glasgow Corporation v *Muir* [1943] 2 AC 448 House of Lords (Lord Thankerton, Lord Macmillan, Lord Wright, Lord Romer and Lord Clauson)

Negligence – danger reasonably foreseeable?

Facts
The defendants owned a tea-room in Glasgow run by a manageress, a Mrs Alexander. On the day in question, a party of children were in the room. The manageress gave permission for a church party to

use the room to eat their sandwiches. The latter group made their tea in an urn and were carrying it along a narrow passage into the tea-room itself when it was accidentally dropped. Scalding-hot tea injured six of the children in the tea-room. An action was brought on behalf of the children alleging negligence against the manageress.

Held
The plaintiffs' claim would fail as the manageress had not acted in a way which amounted to negligence.

Lord Macmillan:

'The standard of foresight of the reasonable man is in one sense an impersonal test. It eliminates the personal equation and is independent of the idiosyncracies of the particular person whose conduct is in question. Some persons are, by nature, unduly timorous and imagine every path beset with lions; others, of more robust temperament, fail to foresee or nonchalantly disregard even the most obvious dangers. The reasonable man is presumed to be free both from over-apprehension and from over-confidence. But, there is a sense in which the standard of care of the reasonable man involves in its application a subjective element. It is still left to the judge to decide what, in the circumstances of the particular case, the reasonable man would have had in contemplation and what accordingly the party sought to be made liable ought to have foreseen. Here there is room for diversity of view, as indeed is well illustrated in the present case. What to one judge may seem far-fetched may seem to another both natural and probable.'

Lord Wright:

'In the present case, as I have stated, as the permitted operation was intrinsically innocuous, I do not think any obligation rested on Mrs Alexander to attempt to supervise how it was carried out. As a reasonable person, not having any ground for anticipating harm, she was entitled to go on with her proper work and leave the church party to do what was proper. There might, of course, be circumstances in which, because there was an obvious risk, a duty might rest on the occupier to supervise how the operation was actually conducted, if the permission was given. I do not see what Mrs Alexander could have done in that respect, unless she had seen that all the children were removed from the passage when the urn was being carried through. That might be her obligation if the operation she permitted had been intrinsically dangerous, but it was not so in the circumstances as I apprehended them. No doubt some difficult questions of fact may arise in these cases. In the present case, however, as I think that there was no reasonably foreseeable danger to the children from the use of the premises which the appellants permitted to be made, I think the respondent's claim cannot be supported.'

Commentary
Distinguished in *Hughes* v *Lord Advocate* [1963] 2 WLR 779.

Haley v *London Electricity Board* [1964] 3 WLR 479 House of Lords (Lord Reid, Lord Morton of Henryton, Lord Evershed, Lord Hodson and Lord Guest)

Negligence – street works

Facts
The Board's workmen dug a hole in the pavement and left it guarded by a wooden handle resting some nine inches above the ground. The plaintiff, a blind man accustomed to the stretch of pavement, was unable to detect the barrier with his stick and tripped over it, causing himself injuries.

Held
The Board were liable as they had been guilty of negligence. They owed a duty of care, not only to

able-bodied pedestrians, but also to the blind or infirm as it was reasonably foreseeable that the latter might use the pavement.

Lord Morton of Henryton:

> '(The Board's) duty is to take reasonable care not to act in a way likely to endanger other persons who may reasonably be expected to walk along the pavement. That duty is owed to blind persons if the operators foresee or ought to have foreseen that blind persons may walk along the pavement and is in no way different from the duty owed to persons with sight, though the carrying out of the duty may involve extra precautions in the case of blind pedestrians. I think that everyone living in Greater London must have seen blind persons walking slowly along on the pavement and waving a white stick in front of them so as to touch any distraction which may be in their way and I think that the respondent's workmen ought to have foreseen that a blind person might well come along the pavement in question.'

Henderson v *Henry E Jenkins & Sons* [1969] 3 WLR 732 House of Lords (Lord Reid, Lord Guest, Viscount Dilhorne, Lord Donovan and Lord Pearson)

Negligence – burden of proof

Facts
While the respondents' five year old lorry was descending a steep hill, its brakes failed: the lorry struck and killed a van driver. A hole had developed in the brake fluid pipe, a very uncommon fault of which the lorry driver would have had no warning.

Held (Lord Guest and Viscount Dilhorne dissenting)
It was for the respondents to prove that, in all the circumstances which they knew or ought to have known, they took all proper steps to avoid danger. As they had failed to do this, the van driver's estate was entitled to damages.

Lord Pearson:

> '... it seems to me clear, as a prima facie inference, that the accident must have been due to default of the respondents in respect of inspection or maintenance or both. Unless they had a satisfactory answer, sufficient to displace the inference, they should have been held liable.'

Latimer v *AEC Ltd* [1953] 2 AC 643 House of Lords (Lord Porter, Lord Oaksey, Lord Reid, Lord Tucker and Lord Asquith of Bishopstone)

Negligence – slippery factory floor

Facts
A sudden rainstorm caused flooding in the defendants' factory and resulted in the floor becoming slippery. Sawdust was spread over the floor, but they did not have sufficient quantities to cope with the extreme situation. The plaintiff, an employee, slipped on a part of the floor which had not been covered in sawdust and was injured.

Held
There was no negligence on the part of the defendants. They had acted reasonably when faced with an extreme situation and had taken prompt action to make the floor as safe as they could. The only other thing would have been to shut down the factory altogether, but the risk was not of such gravity as to compel any reasonable, prudent employer to do this.

Luxmoore-May* v *Messenger May Baverstock [1990] 1 WLR 1009 Court of Appeal (Slade, Mann LJJ and Sir David Croom-Johnson)

Auctioneer – standard of care

Facts
The plaintiffs owned two paintings of foxhounds and they asked the defendant provincial auctioneers to look at them: their representative, Mrs Zarek, thought they were worth about £30 but took them away 'for research'. The defendants offered expert advice by a Mr Thomas, an independent contractor. He valued them at £30 to £50. Shortly before the sale, Mrs Zarek took the paintings to Christie's of London but they made no favourable comment about them. The paintings were sold at auction for £840: five months later they were sold at Sotheby's for £88,000: the plaintiffs sued for the difference.

Held
Their claim could not succeed as the defendants had not been guilty of negligence.

Slade LJ:

> ' ... I am of the opinion that the judge ... demanded too high a standard of skill on the part of the defendants and of Mr Thomas, in concluding that no competent valuer could have missed the signs of Stubbs [a noted 18th century sporting artist] potential. In my judgment, the question whether the foxhound pictures had Stubbs potential ... was one which competent valuers, and indeed competent dealers, could have held widely differing views. It has not been argued that a valuation of £30 to £40 would have been too low if these pictures were simply to be regarded as objects to be hung on a wall *without* Stubbs potential. For these reasons, I am of the opinion that negligence on the part of Mr Thomas has not been established, and accordingly that negligence on the part of the defendants would not have been established, even if Mrs Zarek, after taking Mr Thomas's advice, had taken no further advice in relation to the pictures.'

Commentary
Applied: *Maynard* v *West Midlands Regional Health Authority* [1984] 1 WLR 634.

McHale* v *Watson [1966] ALR 513 High Court of Australia (McTiernan ACJ, Kitto, Menzies and Owen JJ)

Negligence – standard of care

Facts
The plaintiff girl was injured when a steel spike thrown by the defendant, a boy of 12, glanced off a post at which he was aiming and hit the plaintiff in the eye. The plaintiff had been standing about five feet to the left of the post.

Held
The defendant had not been negligent.

Kitto J:

> 'To expect a boy of that age to consider before throwing the spike whether the timber was hard or soft, to weigh the chances of being able to make the spike stick in the post and to foresee that it might glance off and hit the girl, would be, I think, to expect a degree of sense and circumspection which nature ordinarily withholds till life has become less rosy.'

Maynard v *West Midlands Regional Health Authority* [1984] 1 WLR 634 House of Lords (Lord Fraser of Tullybelton, Lord Elwyn-Jones, Lord Scarman, Lord Roskill and Lord Templeman)

Negligence – conflicting medical opinion

Facts
A consultant physician and a surgeon thought that the plaintiff in this case was probably suffering from tuberculosis when they made a diagnosis, but also thought it might be Hodgkin's disease, carcinoma or sarcoidosis. Hodgkin's disease can be fatal unless treated early so they carried out an operation which carried with it a risk of damage to a nerve of the larynx, even if carried out correctly. The operation was carefully performed, but damage was caused to the patient's nerve. The disease was eventually found to be TB and there was conflicting medical opinion at the trial to the effect that the TB was diagnosable as such at that early stage on the one hand, and that the defendants' course of action was approved on the other hand.

Held
The plaintiff's action for negligence would fail. In the medical profession, there was room for differences of opinion and practice and it was insufficient to prove negligence by showing merely that a body of competent professional opinion considered the decision in question wrong, if another body thought that what the defendant did was reasonable.

Commentary
Applied in *Luxmoore-May* v *Messenger May Baverstock* [1990] 1 All ER 1067.

Nettleship v *Weston* [1971] 3 WLR 370 Court of Appeal (Lord Denning MR, Salmon and Megaw LJJ)

Negligence – duty to passenger in car

Facts
The plaintiff took the defendant for driving lessons in a car belonging to the defendant's husband. The plaintiff had first checked to satisfy himself that he would be covered by the defendant's insurance in the event of an accident. During one of the lessons an accident occurred when the defendant, having taken a corner, failed to straighten the car up and crashed into a lamp-post despite the plaintiff's own attempts to stop the car. The plaintiff was injured and claimed damages from the defendant.

Held
The plaintiff should succeed. The standard of care which the law expects of a learner driver is the same as that of any other reasonably competent driver. There can be no such thing as a varying standard of care. However, the damages awarded were reduced by 50 per cent: if the plaintiff had acted more quickly the accident would have been avoided.

Lord Denning MR:

> 'In all that I have said, I have treated Mrs Weston as the driver who was herself in control of the car. On that footing, she is plainly liable for the damage done to the lamp-post. She is equally liable for the injury done to Mr Nettleship. She owed a duty of care to each. The standard of care is the same in either case. It is measured objectively by the care to be expected of an experienced skilled and careful driver.

Mr Nettleship is not defeated by the maxim volenti non fit injuria. He did not agree, expressly or impliedly, to waive any claim for damages owing to her failure to measure up to the standard. But his damages may fall to be reduced owing to his failure to correct her error quick enough. Although the judge dismissed the claim, he did (in case he was wrong) apportion responsibility. He thought it would be just and equitable to regard them equally to blame. I would accept this apportionment.'

Commentary
Applied: *Dann* v *Hamilton* [1939] 1 KB 509 and *Wooldridge* v *Sumner* [1962] 3 WLR 616.

Paris v *Stepney Borough Council* [1951] AC 367 House of Lords (Lord Simonds, Lord Normand, Lord Oaksey, Lord Morton of Henryton and Lord MacDermott)

Negligence – employers' liability

Facts
The plaintiff, who had lost the sight in one eye, was employed by the defendants who knew of his condition. One day, when he was repairing a vehicle, he hit a bolt with a hammer to release it. The impact caused a piece of metal to fly off and enter his other eye, causing total loss of sight. He alleged his employers had been negligent in failing to supply him with protective goggles.

Held (Lord Simonds and Lord Morton of Henryton dissenting)
The plaintiff's claim succeeded. In assessing what a reasonable employer would do to ensure the safety of his employees, it is necessary to take into account not only the likelihood of the accident occuring, but also the gravity of its consequences. The employer's duty is owed to each individual workman and account must be taken of the relative gravity as regards each.

Lord Oaksey:

'In the present case the question is whether an ordinarily prudent employer would supply goggles to a one-eyed workman whose job was to knock bolts out of a chassis with a steel hammer while the chassis was elevated on a ramp so that the workman's eye was close to and under the bolt. In my opinion, Lynskey J was entitled to hold that an ordinarily prudent employer would take that precaution. The question was not whether the precaution ought to have been taken with ordinary two-eyed workmen.'

Roe v *Ministry of Health* [1954] 2 WLR 915 Court of Appeal (Somervell, Denning and Morris LJJ)

Negligence – liability for staff

Facts
The plaintiff underwent a minor operation in hospital. He was given an anaesthetic injected into the spine. The anaesthetic was kept in glass ampoules which were stored in a jar containing phenol (carbolic acid) to prevent infection. Unknown to anyone, tiny cracks were present in the ampoules and some of the phenol had seeped in and contaminated the anaesthetic. This resulted in the plaintiff being permanently paralysed. He brought a claim against the Ministry (the owner of the hospital) and the anaesthetist who worked at the hospital part-time.

Held
The plaintiff's claim should fail as, having regard to the standard of knowledge at the time, the anaesthetist had not been guilty of negligence.

Denning LJ:

'The hospital authorities are responsible for the whole of their staff, not only for the nurses and doctors, but also for the anaesthetists and the surgeons. It does not matter whether they are permanent or temporary, resident or visiting, whole-time or part-time. The hospital authorities are responsible for all of them. The reason is because, even if they are not servants, they are the agents of the hospital to give the treatment. The only exception is the case of consultants or anaesthetists selected and employed by the patient himself ... (see) *Cassidy* v *Ministry of Health* [1951] 2 KB 343 ...'

Scott v *London & St Katherine Docks Co* (1865) 3 H & C 596 Court of Exchequer Chamber (Erle CJ, Crompton, Byles, Blackburn, Keating and Mellor JJ)

Negligence – res ipsa loquitur

Facts
The plaintiff was passing the defendants' warehouse, where bags of sugar were being lowered by a crane, when he was struck and injured by a bag which apparently had fallen off the crane. The plaintiff relied on this fact alone as establishing negligence on the part of the defendants or their servants.

Held
There should be a new trial as there was evidence of negligence by the defendants' servants.

Erle CJ:

'The majority of the court have come to the following conclusion. There must be reasonable evidence of negligence, but, where the thing is shown to be under the management of the defendant, or his servants, and the accident is such as, in the ordinary course of things, does not happen if those who have the management of the machinery use proper care, it affords reasonable evidence, in the absence of explanation by the defendant, that the accident arose from want of care.'

Sidaway v *Bethlem Royal Hospital Governors* [1985] AC 871 House of Lords (Lord Scarman, Lord Diplock, Lord Keith of Kinkel, Lord Bridge of Harwich and Lord Templeman)

Negligence – risk of misfortune

Facts
The plaintiff underwent an operation on the spinal cord to relieve neck pain, and was told by the surgeon of the possibility of disturbing a nerve root and the consequences of that, but not of the possibility of danger to the spinal cord. As a result of the operation, the plaintiff was severely disabled. In the plaintiff's action for damage to her spinal cord, based on an alleged breach of duty to warn her of the risks involved, it was found that there was a 1 – 2 per cent risk of damage to nerve roots and an even lower percentage of risk of damage to the spinal cord.

Held (Lord Scarman dissenting)
The plaintiff's action would fail. The test was whether the surgeon had acted in accordance with a practice accepted at the time as proper by a responsible body of medical opinion.

Lord Bridge:

'I can see no reasonable ground on which the judge could properly reject the conclusion to which the unchallenged medical evidence led in the application of the *Bolam* test. The trial judge's assessment of the risk at 1 per cent or 2 per cent covered both nerve root and spinal cord damage and covered a spectrum of possible ill-effects 'ranging from the mild to the catastrophic'. In so far as it is possible and appropriate to measure such risks in percentage terms (some of the expert medical witnesses called expressed a marked and understandable reluctance to do so), the risk of damage to the spinal cord of such severity as the appellant in fact suffered was, it would appear, certainly less than 1 per cent. But there is no yardstick either in the judge's findings or in the evidence to measure what fraction of 1 per cent that risk represented. In these circumstances, the appellant's expert witness's agreement that the non-disclosure complained of accorded with a practice accepted as proper by a responsible body of neuro-surgical opinion afforded the respondents a complete defence to the appellant's claim.'

Ward v *Tesco Stores Ltd* [1976] 1 WLR 810 Court of Appeal (Megaw, Lawton and Ormrod LJJ)

Negligence – burden of proof

Facts
The plaintiff was shopping in the defendants' supermarket when she slipped on some yoghurt which had been spilt on the floor. The evidence was that the floor was swept some six times a day and in addition, staff were instructed to deal promptly with spillages, which were a common occurence. The plaintiff was unable to say how long the yoghurt had been on the floor on the day she fell, but said that on a subsequent visit she had seen a spillage remain uncleared for some time. The plaintiff alleged the defendants were negligent in their maintenance of the floor.

Held (Ormrod LJ dissenting)
The plaintiff should succeed. She had made out a prima facie case which the defendant had not rebutted.

Megaw LJ:

> 'It is for the plaintiff to show that there has occurred an event which is unusual and which, in the absence of explanation, is more consistent with fault on the part of the defendants than the absence of fault; and to my mind the learned judge was wholly right in taking that view of the presence of this slippery liquid on the floor of the supermarket in the circumstances of this case: that is that the defendants knew or should have known that it was a not uncommon occurrence; and that if it should happen, and should not be promptly attended to, it created a serious risk that customers would fall and injure themselves. When the plaintiff has established that, the defendants can still escape from liability. They could escape from liability if they could show that the accident must have happened, or even on balance of probability would have been likely to have happened, irrespective of the existence of a proper and adequate system, in relation to the circumstances, to provide for the safety of customers. But, if the defendants wish to put forward such a case, it is for them to show that, on balance of probability, either by evidence or by inference from the evidence that is given or is not given, this accident would have been at least equally likely to have happened despite a proper system designed to give reasonable protection to customers. That, in this case, they wholly failed to do.'

Watt v *Hertfordshire County Council* [1954] 1 WLR 835 Court of Appeal (Singleton, Denning and Morris LJJ)

Negligence – liability of fire authority

Facts
The plaintiff, a fireman, was on duty when an emergency call was received to free a woman who was

trapped under a heavy vehicle. Those on duty were given instructions to load a jack onto a lorry and proceed to the scene. The jack could not be properly secured on this particular vehicle (a specially fitted vehicle was properly on duty elsewhere) and the plaintiff and two others rode on the back of the lorry to hold it. In the course of the journey, the driver was forced to brake suddenly and the jack fell over, injuring the plaintiff.

Held
The plaintiff was not entitled to damages as his employers had not been guilty of negligence.

Denning LJ:

> 'It is well settled that in measuring due care one must balance the risk against the measures necessary to eliminate the risk ... In this case the risk in sending out the lorry was not so great as to prohibit the attempt to save life ... It is always a question of balancing the risk against the end.'

Welsh v *Chief Constable of the Merseyside Police* [1993] 1 All ER 692 High Court (Tudor Evans J)

Negligence – immunity of Crown Prosecution Service

Facts
The plaintiff alleged that the Crown Prosecution Service (CPS) had negligently failed to inform a magistrates' court, from which he had been bailed on charges of theft, that those offences had subsequently been taken into consideration at the Crown Court, and that, as a result of that failure, he had been arrested and detained and thereby suffered loss, damage and distress. The registrar struck out the plaintiff's claim.

Held
The claim would be reinstated.

Tudor Evans J:

> 'It is not necessary to go further than ... *Saif Ali* v *Sydney Mitchell & Co* [1978] 3 All ER 1033 ... If ... a solicitor acting on behalf of the [CPS] failed as an advocate in court to inform the court that the offences had been taken into consideration, the [CPS] and the solicitor would be immune from any action based on that failure.
>
> I am therefore solely concerned with the question whether the [CPS] owed the plaintiff a duty of care apart from [such a failure].
>
> Counsel [for the plaintiff] formulated the following proposition as containing the criteria by which it is necessary to decide whether a duty of care is owed to a particular plaintiff: first, it is necessary to consider the principle of reasonable foreseeability of loss and damage and, in so far as different factors may be involved, the question of proximity. It is then necessary to consider whether it would be fair, just and reasonable to hold such a duty to exist and finally the question has to be answered whether there is any ground of public policy for excluding a duty.
>
> I have been referred to a large number of authorities in support of this proposition, but I need only list them since [counsel for the CPS] accepted the proposition as I have stated it. The authorities to which I referred are *Anns* v *Merton London Borough* [1977] 2 All ER 492, *Governors of the Peabody Donation Fund* v *Sir Lindsay Parkinson & Co Ltd* [1984] 3 All ER 529, *Yuen Kun-yeu* v *A-G of Hong Kong* [1987] 2 All ER 705, *Davis* v *Radcliffe* [1990] 2 All ER 536, *Caparo Industries plc* v *Dickman* [1990] 1 All ER 568, *James McNaughton Papers Group Ltd* v *Hicks Anderson & Co (a firm)* [1991] 1 All ER 134 and *Morgan Crucible Co plc* v *Hill Samuel Bank Ltd* [1991] 1 All ER 148 ...
>
> I think it appropriate ... to consider the proposition agreed between the parties as containing the test by which to decide whether a duty of care exists. First, [counsel for the CPS] accepted that it was

reasonably foreseeable by the [CPS] that the plaintiff would suffer loss if the magistrates' court were not informed that the offences had been taken into consideration but he qualified this concession by submitting that the plaintiff was represented by solicitors and that the [CPS] would therefore contemplate that the plaintiff's solicitors would inform the court. In my view that is an argument based on causation, that is that the effective cause of the damage was the failure of the plaintiff's solicitors to inform the court. Causation is not an argument available at this stage. Then [he] submitted that the parties were not proximate. He contended that they could not be neighbours bearing in mind that they were antagonists in adversarial litigation. Counsel relied on the decision of Scott J in *Business Computers International Ltd v Registrar of Companies* [1987] 3 All ER 465 and *Al-Kandari v J R Brown & Co (a firm)* [1988] 1 All ER 833 ...

Both of these cases were concerned with civil litigation. I think that it is highly arguable that the CPS, responsible for the preparation and presentation of criminal charges of many types and of varying gravity is not in the same position as a solicitor acting at arm's length in adversarial civil litigation. The traditions which govern the attitude of a prosecutor in criminal cases in this country suggest otherwise. The Code for Prosecutors issued under the powers conferred by s10 of the [Prosecution of Offences Act] 1985 ... stating, for example in para 8, the factors to be taken into consideration when deciding whether to prosecute in cases where a conviction might otherwise be secured is another example which emphasises the difference. There are many other instances: for example, the duty to make available to the defence witnesses who can give material evidence and whom the prosecution do not intend to call and also the obligation to inform the defence of any previous convictions of a prosecution witness. All these practices are alien to civil litigation.

Apart from [counsel for the plaintiff's] other submissions on proximity, the question of proximity is raised by the plaintiff as arising from [the fact that the CPS's] "solicitor for Ormskirk" approved of the offences being taken into consideration and, by reasonable inference, he agreed to note the file. The plaintiff relies in this context on *Kirkham v Chief Constable of the Greater Manchester Police* [1990] 3 All ER 246 at 250 where Lloyd LJ said:

> "The question depends in each case on whether, having regard to the particular relationship between the parties, the defendant has assumed a responsibility towards the plaintiff, and whether the plaintiff has relied on that assumption of responsibility."

In my view the solicitor for Ormskirk assumed responsibility towards the plaintiff ... or at least it is highly arguable that he did. Moreover, the assumed facts show that the plaintiff was relying on that responsibility. He did not expect to have to answer to his bail ...

Next, in my view it is fair, just and reasonable to hold that a duty of care exists on the assumed facts of this case. [Counsel for the CPS] submitted that it would be wrong to look at this aspect of the question of duty within the narrow confines of this case. There may be cases, he contended, in which there are a very large number of offences taken into consideration and the burden on the [CPS] would be such that it would not be fair or just or reasonable to cast a duty. I do not agree.

Finally, is there any ground of public policy for excluding a duty? To hold that a duty exists does not impugn the decision of the magistrates' court. It does not infringe any of the immunities which arise from the conduct of cases or from the evidence of witnesses. In *Business Computers International Ltd v Registrar of Companies* [1987] 3 All ER 465 Scott J, in rejecting the existence of a duty of care in the circumstances of that case, was influenced by the existence of safeguards against impropriety which are to be found in the rules and procedure that controlled the litigation. There are none such on the facts of the present case. I can find no reason for excluding a duty on the grounds of public policy.

It follows that in my view, by every one of the agreed tokens by which to test the existence of a duty, a duty is found to exist. [Counsel for the CPS] has not produced an authority which unambiguously states that proof of malice is an integral part in an action which touches on a judicial process. No authority has been produced to show that a duty of care cannot exist at stages anterior to litigation or resumed litigation. In these circumstances ... I would decline to strike out this action.'

Whitehouse v *Jordan* [1981] 1 WLR 246 House of Lords (Lord Wilberforce, Lord Edmund-Davies, Lord Fraser of Tullybelton, Lord Russell of Killowen and Lord Bridge of Harwich)

Negligence – error of judgment

Facts
The defendant, a senior hospital registrar, delivered the plaintiff baby. The birth was a difficult one and the defendant decided to use forceps, but after pulling five or six times, he delivered the baby by Caesarean section. The prolonged use of the forceps resulted in brain damage to the plaintiff, who sued the defendant in negligence.

Held
Even if the defendant had pulled too hard and too long (which was not shown by the evidence to be the case), this did not here amount to legal negligence.

Lord Edmund-Davies:

'To say that a surgeon committed an error of clinical judgment is wholly ambiguous, for, while some such errors may be completely consistent with the due exercise of professional skill, other acts or omissions in the course of exercising "clinical judgment" may be so glaringly below proper standards as to make a finding of negligence inevitable. Indeed, I should have regarded this as a truism were it not that, despite the exposure of the "false antithesis" by Donaldson LJ in his dissenting judgment in the Court of Appeal, counsel for the defendants adhered to it before your Lordships. But doctors and surgeons fall into no special category, and, to avoid any future disputation of a similar kind, I would have it accepted that the true doctrine was enunciated, and by no means for the first time, by McNair J in *Bolam* v *Friern Hospital Management Committee* [1957] 1 WLR 582 at 586 in the following words:

" ... where you get a situation which involves the use of some special skill or competence, then the test as to whether there has been negligence or not is not the test of the man on the top of a Clapham omnibus because he has not got this special skill. The test is the standard of the ordinary skilled man exercising and professing to have that special skill."

If a surgeon fails to measure up to that standard in any respect ("clinical judgment" or otherwise), he has been negligent and should be so adjudged.'

Commentary
Applied in *Clark* v *MacLennan* [1983] 1 All ER 416.

Wilks v *The Cheltenham Home Guard Motor Cycle and Light Car Club* [1971] 1 WLR 668 Court of Appeal (Lord Denning MR, Edmund-Davies and Phillimore LJJ)

Negligence – duty of care to spectators

Facts
Spectators at a motor cycle scramble, the plaintiffs were lined against the 'spectators' rope'. Ten feet beyond there was a 'wrecking rope'. During a race, the second defendant's machine suddenly veered to one side, crossed the ropes and landed amongst the spectators, injuring the plaintiffs. There was no explanation of how the accident had, or could have, occurred.

Held
The plaintiffs were not entitled to damages: there was no evidence of negligence and a slip or misjudgment not amounting to negligence could have accounted for the accident.

Lord Denning MR:

'This result may indicate that the club, the first defendants, ought to have been made liable. They ought to have provided safety precautions which are sufficient to protect spectators from harm owing to a motor cycle running off the course. But they gave evidence which persuaded the judge that they had done all that was reasonable. They had erected the 'wrecking rope' and the 'spectators' rope' in accordance with the requirements of the Auto-Cycle Union. They had driven the stakes in well at the correct intervals and had kept the ropes taut. There is no appeal from the judge's finding in their favour. So we must accept it as correct. On that footing there is only one conclusion possible, and that is that this was one of those rare accidents which do occur from time to time when nobody is at fault. No doubt, in consequence of it, stricter precautions will be taken in future. The world gets wiser as it gets older. But it does not mean that there was negligence on the first happening.'

Wooldridge v *Sumner* [1963] 3 WLR 616 Court of Appeal (Sellers, Danckwerts and Diplock LJJ)

Negligence – injury to spectator

Facts
The plaintiff, a photographer, was attending a horse show and was standing on the edge of the arena. One of the horses, owned by the defendant, suddenly panicked on one of the corners and began to gallop towards where the plaintiff was standing. In his attempt to move out of the way, the plaintiff was struck and injured by the horse.

Held
There was no breach of duty by the defendant and the plaintiff's claim failed.

Diplock LJ:

'A person attending a game or competition takes the risk of any damage caused to him by any act of a participant done in the course of and for the purposes of the game or competition, notwithstanding that such an act may involve an error of judgment or lapse of skill, unless the participant's conduct is such as to evince a reckless disregard of the spectator's safety.

The spectator takes the risk because such an act involves no breach of the duty of care owed by the participant to him. He does not take the risk by virtue of the doctrine expressed or obscured by the maxim volenti non fit injuria. The maxim states a principle of estoppel applicable originally to a Roman citizen who consented to being sold as a slave. Although pleaded and argued below, it was only faintly relied on by counsel for the first defendant in this court. In my view, the maxim, in the absence of express contract, has no application to negligence simpliciter where the duty of care is based solely on proximity or 'neighbourship' in the Atkinian sense. The maxim in English law presupposes a tortious act by the defendant. The consent that is relevant is not consent to the risk of injury, but consent to the lack of reasonable care that may produce that risk and requires on the part of the plaintiff at the time at which he gives his consent full knowledge of the nature and extent of the risk that he ran. In *Dann* v *Hamilton*, Asquith J expressed doubts whether the maxim ever could apply to license in advance a subsequent act of negligence, for if the consent precedes the act of negligence, the plaintiff cannot at that time have full knowledge of the extent as well as the nature of the risk which he will run. Asquith J, however, suggested that the maxim might, nevertheless, be applicable to cases where a dangerous physical condition had been brought about by the negligence of the defendant and the plaintiff with full knowledge of the existing danger elected to run the risk thereof. With the development of the law of negligence in the last twenty years, a more consistent explanation of this type of case is that the test of liability on the part of the person creating the dangerous physical condition is whether it was reasonably foreseeable by him that the defendant would so act in relation to it as to endanger himself. This is the principle which has been applied in the rescue cases (see *Cutler v United Dairies (London) Ltd* and contrast *Haynes v Harwood*) and the part of Asquith J's judgment in *Dann v Hamilton* dealing with the possible application of the maxim to the law of negligence was not approved by the Court of Appeal in *Ward v TE Hopkins & Son Ltd; Baker v Same*. In the type of case envisaged by Asquith J, if I may adapt the words of Morris LJ in *Ward v Hopkinn*, the plaintiff could not have agreed to run the risk that the defendant might be negligent, for the plaintiff would only play his part after the defendant had been negligent.'

Commentary
Applied in *Nettleship* v *Weston* [1971] 3 WLR 370 and *White* v *Blackmore* [1972] 3 WLR 296.

6 Negligence: Causation

Allied Maples Group Ltd* v *Simmons & Simmons [1995] 1 WLR 1602 Court of Appeal (Stuart-Smith, Hobhouse and Millett LJJ)

Causation – loss of a chance

Facts
The plaintiffs wished to purchase certain properties from G. Four of these properties could not be conveyed to the plaintiffs because there were conditions against alienation or planning consents which were personal to G's subsidiary, K Ltd, in which the properties were vested. The plaintiffs, on the advice of the defendant solicitors, acquired all the shares in K Ltd, intending to sell the unwanted properties of K and keep the four desired. However, some of the properties owned by K had liabilities which, after the acquisition, resulted in claims against K, and hence the plaintiffs. The plaintiffs sued the defendants to recover their losses. In the High Court it was held that the plaintiffs were entitled to succeed because if the defendants had given the advice on liability which they ought to have given, the plaintiffs would have taken steps to obtain a warranty from G or to protect themselves in some other way. The defendants appealed to the Court of Appeal.

Held
Where the plaintiff's loss depends on the hypothetical action of a third party, the plaintiff can succeed if he shows that he had a substantial chance rather than a speculative one. He does not have to prove on the balance of probabilities that the third party would have acted so as to confer a benefit or avoid the risk to the plaintiff. If he proves as a matter of causation that he has a real or substantial chance as opposed to a speculative one, the evaluation of the chance is part of the assessment of the quantum of damage, the range lying somewhere between something that just qualifies as real or substantial on the one hand, and near certainty on the other.

Baker* v *Willoughby [1970] 2 WLR 50 House of Lords (Lord Reid, Lord Guest, Viscount Dilhorne, Lord Donovan and Lord Pearson)

Damages – subsequent further injury

Facts
The plaintiff was knocked down by the defendant whilst crossing the road. The effect of the injuries was to reduce the movement in his left leg so that he could no longer carry on with his previous employment. Shortly afterwards, the plaintiff was shot in the leg by robbers and had to have his left leg amputated. What was the extent of the defendant's liability?

Held
The second injury was irrelevant for the purpose of assessing the damages to which the plaintiff was entitled in respect of the first injury.

Lord Reid:

> 'A man is not compensated for the physical injury; he is compensated for the loss which he suffers as a result of that injury. His loss is not in having a staff leg; it is in his inability to lead a full life, his inability to enjoy those amenities which depend on freedom of movement and his inability to earn as much as he used to earn or could have earned if there had been no accident. In this case, the second injury did not diminish any of these. So why should it be regarded as having obliterated or superseded them?'

Commentary
Doubted and not followed in *Jobling* v *Associated Dairies Ltd* [1981] 3 WLR 155.

Barnett v *Chelsea & Kensington Hospital Management Committee* [1968] 2 WLR 422 High Court (Nield J)

Negligence – cause of death

Facts
The plaintiff's husband went to the casualty department of the defendants' hospital complaining of stomach pains and vomiting after drinking tea. A doctor was contacted, but did not come to examine the husband and sent a message that he should go home to bed and call his own doctor. The plaintiff's husband died shortly after from arsenic poisoning.

Held
Although the doctor was negligent in failing to examine the deceased, the defendants were not liable because this was not the cause of his death.

Nield J:

> 'It remains to consider whether it is shown that the deceased's death was caused by this negligence or whether, as the defendants have said, the deceased must have died in any event. In his concluding submission counsel for the plaintiff submitted that Dr Banerjee should have examined the deceased and, had he done so, he would have caused tests to be made which would have indicated the treatment required and that, since the defendants were at fault in these respects, therefore the onus of proof passed to the defendants to show that the appropriate treatment would have failed, and authorities were cited to me. I find myself unable to accept this argument and I am of the view that the onus of proof remains on the plaintiff ... However, were it otherwise and the onus did pass to the defendants, then I would find that they have discharged it.'

Cork v *Kirby Maclean Ltd* [1952] 2 All ER 402 Court of Appeal (Singleton, Denning and Romer LJJ)

Negligence – cause of accident

Facts
A painter entered the defendants' employment without telling them that he was subject to epileptic fits and that his doctor had forbidden him to work at heights. While working on a platform, which did not comply with statutory requirements, he had a fit, fell to the ground, and was killed.

Held
Both the defendants and the painter had been at fault and the damages recoverable by his estate would therefore be reduced by one half.

Denning LJ:

'Subject to the question of remoteness, causation is, I think, a question of fact. If you can say that the damage would not have happened but for a particular fault, then that fault is in fact a cause of the damage; but if you can say that the damage would have happened just the same, fault or no fault, then the fault is not a cause of the damage. It often happens that each of the parties at fault can truly say to the other: "But for your fault, it would not have happened." In such a case both faults are in fact causes of the damage.

In this case, on the facts, I am clearly of opinion that both faults were causes of the damage. The man's fault (in not telling his employers he was forbidden to work at heights) was clearly one of the causes of his death. But for that fault on his part, he would never have been on this platform at all and would never have fallen. The employers' fault (in not providing a guard-rail or toe-boards) is more doubtful a cause. One cannot say that but for that fault the accident *would* not have happened. All that can be said is that it *might* not have happened. A guard-rail and toe-boards *might* have saved him from falling. If this was a very remote possibility, it could not be said to be a cause at all. But the judge did not so regard it. He thought that it probably would have saved him. On that view the employers' fault was also one of the causes of the man's death.'

Cutler v *Vauxhall Motors Ltd* [1971] 1 QB 418 Court of Appeal (Russell, Edmund-Davies and Karminski LJJ)

Negligence – operation inevitable at future date

Facts
An accident at work (for which D was liable) aggravated P's pre-existing varicose condition and necessitated an operation.

Held (Russell LJ dissenting)
The plaintiff could not recover losses due to the operation as his condition would anyway have required surgery in the near future.

Galoo Ltd v *Bright Grahame Murray* [1994] 1 WLR 1360 Court of Appeal (Glidewell, Evans and Waite LJJ)

Negligence – causation

Facts
The plaintiffs claimed that they incurred trading losses as a result of relying on the defendants' negligent auditing and thus continued to trade when they otherwise would not have done, and that these trading losses were caused by the defendants' breach of duty.

Held
In considering whether a breach of duty, whether the duty was imposed by contract or in tort in a situation analogous to contract, was the cause of the loss or merely the occasion for the loss, the court had to arrive at a decision on the basis of the application of common sense. The 'but for' test of causation was not sufficient.

Hotson v *East Berkshire Area Health Authority* [1987] 3 WLR 232 House of Lords (Lord Bridge of Harwich, Lord Brandon of Oakbrook, Lord Mackay of Clashfern, Lord Ackner and Lord Goff of Chieveley)

Negligence – causation

Facts
A boy aged 13, the plaintiff, injured his hip in a fall. He was taken to the defendants' hospital; the injury was not correctly diagnosed and he was sent home. Even if a correct diagnosis had been made, there was a 75 per cent risk that the boy's disability would have developed, but the medical staff's breach of duty had turned the risk into an inevitability.

Held
The boy was without a remedy.

Lord Ackner:

> '... the plaintiff was not entitled to any damages in respect of the deformed hip because the judge had decided that this was not caused by the admitted breach by the authority of their duty of care but was caused ... when he fell some 12 feet from a rope on which he had been swinging.'

Jobling v *Associated Dairies Ltd* [1981] 3 WLR 155 House of Lords (Lord Wilberforce, Lord Edmund-Davies, Lord Russell of Killowen, Lord Keith of Kinkel and Lord Bridge of Harwich)

Injury – subsequent further injury

Facts
In 1973 P slipped and fell in the course of his employment as a result of a breach of statutory duty by his employer, D. His back was injured and in consequence his earning capacity was reduced by 50 per cent. In 1976 P was found to be suffering from spondylotic myelopathy, a spinal disease which was unrelated to the accident but which made him totally unfit to work. The trial of his claim against D took place in 1979.

Held
In a case where a supervening illness was apparent and known of before the trial, the court had to take it into account in order to prevent P from being overcompensated. However, the question was left open whether the same principle would apply where the supervening disability was the result of a tortious act by a second tortfeasor as opposed to a natural illness or purely accidental injury.

Lord Wilberforce:

> "We do not live in a world governed by the pure common law and its logical rules. We live in a mixed world where a man is protected against injury and misfortune by a whole web of rules and dispositions with a number of timid legislative interventions. To attempt to compensate him on the basis of selected rules without regard to the whole must lead either to logical inconsistencies or to over or under-compensation. As my noble and learned friend Lord Edmund-Davies has pointed out, no account was taken in *Baker* v *Willoughby* of the very real possibility that the plaintiff might obtain compensation from the Criminal Injuries Compensation Board. If he did in fact obtain this compensation he would, on the ultimate decision, be over-compensated.
>
> In the present case, and in other industrial injury cases, there seems to me no justification for

disregarding the fact that the injured man's employer is insured (indeed since 1972 compulsorily insured) against liability to his employees. The state has decided, in other words, on a spreading of risk. There seems to me no more justification for disregarding the fact that the plaintiff (presumably; we have not been told otherwise) is entitled to sickness and invalidity benefit in respect of his myelopathy, the amount of which may depend on his contribution record, which in turn may have been affected by his accident. So we have no means of knowing whether the plaintiff would be over-compensated if he were, in addition, to receive the assessed damages from his employer, or whether he would be under-compensated if left to his benefit. It is not easy to accept a solution by which a partially incapacitated man becomes worse off in terms of damages and benefit through a greater degree of incapacity. Many other ingredients, of weight in either direction, may enter into individual cases. Without any satisfaction I draw from this the conclusion that no general, logical or universally fair rules can be stated which will cover, in a manner consistent with justice, cases of supervening events, whether due to tortious, partially tortious, non-culpable or wholly accidental events.

If rationalisation is needed, I am willing to accept the "vicissitudes" argument as the best available. I should be more firmly convinced of the merits of the conclusion if the whole pattern of benefits had been considered, in however general a way. The result of the present case may be lacking in precision and rational justification, but so long as we are content to live in a mansion of so many different architectures this is inevitable.'

Commentary
Doubted and not followed: *Baker* v *Willoughby* [1970] 2 WLR 50.

Kay v *Ayrshire and Arran Health Board* [1987] 2 All ER 417 House of Lords (Lord Keith of Kinkel, Lord Brandon of Oakbrook, Lord Griffiths, Lord Mackay of Clashfern and Lord Ackner)

Negligence – causation

Facts
A boy suffering from pneumococcal meningitis was negligently given an overdose of penicillin. After recovering from the meningitis he was found to be suffering from deafness. Expert evidence on behalf of the hospital was to the effect that there was no recorded case of a penicillin overdose having caused deafness, although it was a common sequela of meningitis.

Held
Where there were two competing causes of damage, the law could not presume that the tortious cause was responsible if it was not first proved that it was an accepted fact that the tortious cause was capable of causing or aggravating such damage. Accordingly, in the light of the evidence, the deafness had to be regarded as resulting solely from the meningitis and the boy's claim therefore failed.

Lord Ackner:

'[the boy] can derive no assistance from your Lordships' decision in *McGhee* v *National Coal Board*. In *McGhee's* case the absence of washing facilities was known to be a factor which increased the risk of dermatitis arising from the circumstances in which the pursuer worked. In this case, as previously stated, there is no evidence to incriminate the overdose of intrathecal penicillin. Moreover, if, contrary to the view which I have expressed, the decision in *McGhee's* case can be used to transfer to the respondents the onus of establishing that the excessive injection of penicillin did not cause the deafness, then in my judgment they have discharged that onus.'

Commentary
Distinguished: *McGhee v National Coal Board* [1973] 1 WLR 1.

McGhee v *National Coal Board* [1973] 1 WLR 1 House of Lords (Lord Reid, Lord Wilberforce, Lord Simon of Glaisdale, Lord Kilbrandon and Lord Salmon)

Negligence – causation

Facts
The respondent employers sent the appellant to clean out brick kilns, but they negligently failed to provide him with adequate washing facilities. In consequence, he cycled home, continuing to exert himself, covered in sweat and grime. He was found to be suffering from dermatitis caused by working conditions in the brick kilns, but his journeys home had added materially to the risk that he might develop the disease.

Held
The respondents were liable.

Lord Salmon:

'I would suggest that the true view is that, as a rule, when it is proved, on a balance of probabilities, that an employer has been negligent and that his negligence has materially increased the risk of his employee contracting an industrial disease, then he is liable in damages to that employee if he contracts the disease notwithstanding that the employer is not responsible for other factors which have materially contributed to the disease.

... In the circumstances of the present case, the possibility of a distinction existing between (a) having materially increased the risk of contracting the disease, and (b) having materially contributed to causing the disease may no doubt be a fruitful source of interesting academic discussions between students of philosophy. Such a distinction is, however, far too unreal to be recognised by the common law.'

Commentary
Distinguished in *Kay v Ayrshire and Arran Health Board* [1987] 2 All ER 417.

McWilliams (or Cummings) v *Sir William Arrol & Co Ltd* [1962] 1 WLR 295 House of Lords (Viscount Kilmuir LC, Viscount Simonds, Lord Reid, Lord Morris of Borth-y-Gest and Lord Devlin)

Negligence – causation

Facts
The plaintiff was the widow of a steel erector who was employed by the defendants. On one occasion when he was erecting a steel tower some seventy feet from the ground, he slipped and fell to his death. His widow alleged the defendants were at fault in not providing safety belts, an item which clearly would have saved the deceased. The defendants alleged that, although such belts were customary, even if they had provided one, there was a high degree of probability that the deceased would not have worn it and that, therefore, any breach of duty on their part was not the cause of the deceased's death.

Held
The plaintiff's claim failed as the defendants' breach of duty (if there was one) was not the cause of the

accident since (a) on the evidence the deceased would not have worn a safety belt if it had been provided and (b) there was no duty on the defendants to instruct or exhort the deceased to wear a safety belt.

Mattocks v *Mann* (1992) The Times 19 June Court of Appeal (Nourse, Stocker and Beldam LJJ)

Negligence – plaintiff's impecuniosity

Facts
The plaintiff's car was damaged in an accident that was caused by the admitted negligence of the defendant. The only issue before the court concerned damages and (inter alia) whether the plaintiff could recover for the hire period between completion of the repairs to her car and the release of payment by the defendant's insurers of the cost of repairs. The defendant claimed that under the principle in *The Liesbosch* [1933] AC 449 that it was the plaintiff's impecuniosity that led to her inability to provide resources to pay the repair bill and that was the effective cause of the additional hire period.

Held
The plaintiff could recover the hire charges for this period.

Beldam LJ:

> '... the law of damages had not stood still since 1933 and in *Perry* v *Sidney Phillips & Son* [1982] 1 WLR 1297, 1307 Lord Justice Kerr had said that the authority of what Lord Wright said in *The Liesbosch* was consistently being attenuated in more recent decisions.
>
> In the varied web of affairs after an accident, only in exceptional circumstances was it possible or correct to isolate impecuniosity of a plaintiff as a separate cause and as terminating the consequences of a defendant's wrong.'

Performance Cars Ltd v *Abraham* [1961] 3 WLR 749 Court of Appeal (Lord Evershed MR, Harman and Donovan LJJ)

Negligence – successive torts

Facts
The plaintiffs' car was damaged in an accident and the respraying of the lower part of its body was necessary as a result. Two weeks later, and before the car had been resprayed, it was involved in a collision with the defendant's car. The defendant admitted liability and respraying of the lower part of the car was again required. Could the plaintiffs recover the cost of this respraying from the defendant?

Held
No, because that damage did not flow from the defendant's wrongful act.

Lord Evershed MR:

> 'In my judgment in the present case the defendant should be taken to have injured a motor car that was already injured in certain respects, that is, in respect of the need for respraying; and the result is that to the extent of that need or injury the damage claimed did not flow from the defendant's wrongdoing. It may no doubt be unfortunate for the plaintiffs that the collisions took place in the order in which they did. Had the first collision been that brought about by the defendant and had they recovered the £75 now in question from him, they could not clearly have recovered the same sum again from the other wrongdoer.

It is, however, in my view irrelevant (if unfortunate for the plaintiffs) that the judgment obtained against the other wrongdoer has turned out to be worthless.'

Topp v *London Country Bus (South West) Ltd* [1993] 3 All ER 448 Court of Appeal (Dillon and Rose LJJ and Peter Gibson J)

Causation – intervening act of the third party

Facts
The defendants' minibus was parked with the key in the ignition switch, unlocked and unattended, at a bus stop at a lay-by outside a public house. Some nine hours later, while being driven without authority on a public road by an unidentified third party, the bus was involved in an accident in which the plaintiff's wife was killed. The plaintiff sued the defendants in negligence and his claim was dismissed in the High Court. The plaintiff appealed.

Held
That even if the defendants had been at fault in leaving the bus unlocked on the highway, near a public house and with the key in the ignition, they were not responsible in law for the injury caused by a voluntary act of the third party since he was a complete stranger to them. The majority of the Court of Appeal also doubted whether there was a relationship of proximity between the defendants and the plaintiff's wife.

Wilsher v *Essex Area Health Authority* [1988] 2 WLR 557 House of Lords (Lord Bridge of Harwich, Lord Fraser of Tullybelton, Lord Lowry, Lord Griffiths and Lord Ackner)

Negligence – causation – burden of proof

Facts
The plaintiff was an infant who had been born prematurely. He was being kept on life support system and being looked after by a team of doctor and nurses. A junior doctor, whilst checking on the plaintiff, inserted a catheter into a vein, instead of an artery. The doctor asked a registrar to ensure that the catheter had been put in correctly. The registrar failed to do so, and indeed repeated the error later. The plaintiff as a result received too much oxygen and it was alleged that this had caused him brain damage. The plaintiff sued the Area Health Authority.

Held
As the plaintiff's condition could have been caused by any one of a number of different agents and it had not been proved that it was caused by excess oxygen, the plaintiff had not discharged the burden of proof as to causation. There was no presumption that the defendants' negligence had caused the injury. Accordingly, there must be a retrial.

Wright v *Lodge* [1993] 4 All ER 299 Court of Appeal (Parker, Woolf and Staughton LJJ)

Causation – negligent and reckless acts

Facts
A Mini driven by the respondent, Miss Shepherd, broke down on an unlit dual carriageway at night when

visibility was very poor owing to fog. The car came to a stop in the nearside lane of the carriageway and while the respondent was attempting to start it a Scania articulated container lorry driven by the appellant, Mr Lodge, crashed into the back of it, causing a passenger in the rear seat of the Mini to be seriously injured. The lorry then veered out of control across the central reservation and came to rest on its side in the opposite westbound carriageway where it was struck by three cars and a lorry. The driver of one of the cars was killed and another driver was injured. At the time of the collision the appellant's lorry was travelling at 60mph. The injured driver and the personal representatives of the dead driver sued the appellant and the respondent while the injured passenger in the respondent's car sued the appellant who joined the respondent as a third party. The appellant admitted liability but claimed contribution from the respondent. Hobhouse J found that the appellant was driving recklessly and ordered that the respondent should contribute 10 per cent in respect of the claim by her passenger but dismissed the contribution claims relating to the injured and dead drivers. The appellant appealed contending that the judge should have ordered a 10 per cent contribution in respect of those claims.

Held

The driver of a motor vehicle could owe different duties of care to different road users since different questions of foreseeability, causation and remoteness could arise in respect of different road users affected by his negligence. Thus, if his vehicle was involved in a collision with another vehicle partly as a result of his own negligence, he was not necessarily responsible for subsequent events which occurred as the result of another driver's reckless driving which caused damage which would not have occurred if that driver had merely been driving negligently, since reckless driving was in a different category from negligent driving and an obstruction on the highway which was a danger only to a reckless driver was not necessarily a relevant danger in considering the liability of the person who negligently caused the obstruction to be present. On the facts, although the respondent had been negligent in not removing her car from the carriageway onto the verge, the sole cause of the lorry ending up on the westbound carriageway and the drivers' consequent death and injuries was the appellant's reckless driving, which was the only relevant legal cause of that event. The judge had accordingly been correct to find that the respondent was not liable to make a contribution in respect of the appellant's liability in regard to the dead and injured drivers' claims. The appeal would therefore be dismissed.

Parker LJ:

> 'In any event approaching the matter as if he [the trial judge] were a jury and taking a common sense view, he was, as we are, clearly entitled to conclude that the presence of the Scania in the westbound carriageway was wholly attributable to Mr Lodge's reckless driving. It was unwarranted and unreasonable. It was the violence of the swerve and braking which sent his lorry out of control. Such violence was due to the reckless manner in which he was driving and it was his reckless speed which resulted in the swerve, loss of control and headlong career onto, and overturn on, the westbound carriageway. It is true that it would not have been there had the Mini not obstructed the nearside lane of the eastbound carriageway but the passages which I have cited show clearly that this is not enough. It does not thereby necessarily become a legally operative cause. The subsequent conduct of Mr Lodge was such that any judge or jury could in my judgment exclude Miss Shepherd's conduct as being causative of the subsequent accident. The judge did exclude it and in my judgment he was right to do so.'

7 Negligence: Remoteness of Damage

Bradford v *Robinson Rentals Ltd* [1967] 1 WLR 337 High Court (Rees J)
Negligence – foreseeability of damage

Facts
The plaintiff was employed by the defendants as a service engineer which involved a considerable amount of travel by road. In the extraordinarily severe winter of 1963, the defendants ordered him to undertake a journey of some 450 miles. On the day in question, conditions were especially bad due to heavy snow and ice. Due to the poor state of the vehicle provided for him and in particular the absence of a working heater, the plaintiff sustained severe frostbite.

Held
The plaintiff was entitled to damages as the injury which he suffered was of the kind that was foreseeable. It was not necessary for the precise nature of the injury to be reasonably foreseeable before liability resulted.

Commentary
Applied: *Hughes* v *Lord Advocate* [1963] 2 WLR 779.
    Distinguished in *Tremain* v *Pike* [1969] 1 WLR 1556.

Carslogie Steamship Co Ltd v *Royal Norwegian Government, The Carslogie* [1952] AC 292 House of Lords (Viscount Jowitt, Lord Normand, Lord Morton of Henryton, Lord Tucker and Lord Asquith of Bishopstone)
Negligence – damage

Facts
The plaintiffs' ship was damaged by the defendants' negligence and had to undergo a voyage to a shipyard for repairs. En route, it was further damaged by a severe storm.

Held
The defendants were not liable for damage by the storm which was an unforeseeable novus actus unconnected with their negligence.

Doughty v *Turner Manufacturing Co Ltd* [1964] 2 WLR 240 Court of Appeal (Lord Pearce, Harman and Diplock LJJ)
Negligence – foreseeability

Facts

A fellow workman inadvertently knocked an asbestos cement cover into a cauldron of extremely hot molten liquid. The extreme heat caused the abestos cement to undergo a chemical change creating or releasing water: the water turned to steam which, a minute or two later, caused an eruption of the molten liquid from the cauldron. The plaintiff was injured by some of this liquid. Until the accident had been investigated, no one knew or suspected that heat would cause the chemical change which had taken place.

Held

The employers were not liable as the eruption had been unforeseeable by a reasonable man. Although risk by splashing was foreseeable, the accident which had occurred was of an entirely different kind.

Harman LJ:

> 'We ought, in my opinion, to start with the premise that the criterion in English law is foreseeability. I take it that whether *The Wagon Mound* is or is not binding on this court we ought to treat it as the law. Our inquiry must, therefore, be whether the result of this hard-board cover slipping into the cauldron, which we know now to be inevitably an explosion, was a thing reasonably foreseeable at the time when it happened. It is acknowledged by the plaintiff that no one in the employer's service knew of the likelihood of such an event, and it is clear that no one in the room at the time thought of any dangerous result. There was a striking piece of evidence of the two men who went and looked over the edge of the cauldron to see where the piece of board had gone. Neither they, nor anyone else, thought that they were doing anything risky.
>
> The plaintiff's argument most persuasively urged by Mr James rested, as I understood it, on admissions made that, if this lid had been dropped into the cauldron with sufficient force to cause the molten material to splash over the edge, that would have been an act of negligence or carelessness for which the employers might be vicariously responsible. Reliance was put on *Hughes v Lord Advocate* where the exact consequences of the lamp overturning were not foreseen, but it was foreseeable that if the manhole were left unguarded boys would enter and tamper with the lamp and it was not unlikely that serious burns might ensue for the boy. Their lordships' House distinguished *The Wagon Mound* on the ground that the damage which ensued though differing in degree was the same in kind as that which was foreseeable. So it is said here that a splash causing burns was foreseeable and that this explosion was really only a magnified splash which also caused burns and that, therefore, we ought to follow *Hughes v Lord Advocate* and hold the defendants liable. I cannot accept this. In my opinion, the damage here was of an entirely different kind from the foreseeable splash. Indeed, the evidence showed that any disturbance of the material resulting from the immersion of the hard-board was over an appreciable time before the explosion happened. This latter was caused by the distintegration of the hard-board under the great heat to which it was subjected and the consequent release of the moisture enclosed within it. This had nothing to do with the agitation caused by the dropping of the board into the cyanide. I am of opinion that it would be wrong on these facts to make another inroad on the doctrine of foreseeability which seems to me to be a satisfactory solvent of this type of difficulty.'

Commentary

Applied: *Overseas Tankship (UK) Ltd v Morts Dock & Engineering Co Ltd (The Wagon Mound)* [1961] 2 WLR 126.
 Distinguished: *Hughes v Lord Advocate* [1963] 2 WLR 779.

Edison, The [1933] AC 449 House of Lords (Lord Buckmaster, Lord Warrington, Lord Tomlin, Lord Russell of Killowen and Lord Wright)

Negligence – measure of damages

Facts
The Edison, in leaving the port of Patras, caught the anchor ropes of *The Liesbosch* and dragged *The Liesbosch* out to sea where it sank. The plaintiffs were using *The Liesbosch* to dredge; they could not afford to buy another dredger so they had to hire one at a high rate. How should their damage be assessed?

Held
The plaintiffs were entitled to the market price of a dredger comparable to *The Liesbosch,* the cost of adapting a new vessel and transporting it to the port in question and insuring it for the voyage, and compensation for their loss in respect of their inability to carry out their contract between the sinking of *The Liesbosch* and the date on which the new dredger could reasonably have been available. Interest on this sum would run from the date of the loss. No account would be taken of any special loss due to the financial position of the owners of *The Liesbosch* as their impecuniosity was not traceable to the acts of the owners of *The Edison*.

Commentary
Distinguished in *Martindale v Duncan* [1973] 1 WLR 574 and *Dodd Properties (Kent) Ltd v Canterbury City Council* [1980] 1 WLR 433.

Hughes v *Lord Advocate* [1963] 2 WLR 779 House of Lords (Lord Reid, Lord Jenkins, Lord Morris of Borth-y-Gest, Lord Guest and Lord Pearce)

Negligence – foreseeability of damage

Facts
Post Office employees had opened a manhole in order to carry out repairs on the highway. A tent was placed over the open manhole and there were paraffin lamps around the tent. The entrance to the tent was blocked by a ladder and a tarpaulin. In the absence of the employees, the plaintiff, aged ten, went into the tent with a paraffin lamp. He fell and dropped the lamp into the hole. An explosion resulted and he was severely burned.

Held
The plaintiff's injuries were of the same kind as those which were reasonably foreseeable and thus not too remote: he could recover damages for negligence.

Lord Pearce:

> 'The dangerous allurement was left unguarded in a public highway in the heart of Edinburgh. It was for the respondent to show by evidence that, although this was a public street, the presence of children there was so little to be expected that a reasonable man might leave the allurement unguarded. But in my opinion their evidence fell short of that ...
>
> The defenders are therefore liable for all the foreseeable consequences of their neglect. When an accident is of a different type and kind from anything that a defender could have foreseen he is not liable for it ... But to demand too great precision in the test of foreseeability would be unfair to the pursuer since the facets of misadventure are innumerable ... In the case of an allurement to children it is particularly hard to foresee with precision the exact shape of the disaster that will arise. The allurement in this case was the combination of a red paraffin lamp, a ladder, a partially closed tent, and a cavernous hole within it, a setting well-fitted to inspire some juvenile adventure that might end in calamity. The obvious risks were burning and conflagration and a fall. All these in fact occurred, but unexpectedly the mishandled lamp instead of causing an ordinary conflagration produced a violent explosion. Did the explosion create an accident and damage of a different type from the misadventure and damage that could be foreseen? In my judgment it did

not. The accident was but a variant of the foreseeable ... No unforeseeable extraneous, initial occurrence fired the train. The children's entry into the tent with the ladder, the descent into the hole, the mishandling of the lamp, were all foreseeable. The greater part of the path to injury had thus been trodden, and the mishandled lamp was quite likely at that stage to spill and cause a conflagration. Instead, by some curious chance of combustion, it exploded and no conflagration occurred, it would seem, until after the explosion. There was thus an unexpected manifestation of the apprehended physical dangers. But it would be, I think, too narrow a view to hold that those who created the risk of fire are excused from the liability for the damage by fire, because it came by way of explosive combustion. The resulting damage, though severe, was not greater than or different in kind from that which might have been produced had the lamp spilled and produced a more normal conflagration in the hole.'

Lord Reid:

'The cause of the accident – the lamp – was a known source of danger, but the way in which it behaved was unforeseeable. This does not absolve the defendant because the accident was caused by a known danger, but caused in a way which could not have been foreseen. That is no defence.'

Commentary
Applied in *Bradford* v *Robinson Rentals Ltd* [1967] 1 WLR 337 and *Doughty* v *Turner Manufacturing Co Ltd* [1964] 2 WLR 240.
Distinguished: *Glasgow Corporation* v *Muir* [1943] AC 448.

Jones v *Boyce* (1816) 1 Stark 493 Court of King's Bench (Lord Ellenborough CJ)

Negligence – alarm and apprehension

Facts
The plaintiff was a passenger on the defendant's coach. Due to a defective coupling, one of the reins broke, the wheel came off the coach and it veered to the side of the road. The plaintiff, who was on the outside of the coach, feared it was about to overturn and jumped off, severely injuring his leg. In the event, the driver managed to bring the coach to a halt. The defendant alleged that as there had been no need for the plaintiff to jump off, his own action was the main cause of his injury and his claim should fail.

Held
The plaintiff succeeded.

Lord Ellenborough CJ:

'If I place a man in such a situation that he must adopt a perilous alternative, I am responsible for the consequences.'

Knightley v *Johns* [1982] 1 WLR 349 Court of Appeal (Stephenson and Dunn LJJ and Sir David Cairns)

Negligence – remoteness of damage

Facts
A serious road accident had occurred near the exit of a tunnel which carried one-way traffic. The accident had been caused by the negligence of the first defendant. The police inspector in charge at the scene realised that he had forgotten to close the tunnel to oncoming traffic. This was particularly important as

there was a sharp bend in the middle of the tunnel which obscured the exit, as well as the site of the first defendant's accident, to drivers entering the tunnel. The police inspector ordered two officers on motor cycles to go back and close off the tunnel. The two officers, one of whom was the plaintiff, rode into the tunnel against the oncoming traffic. Near the tunnel entrance the plaintiff collided with a motorist who, on the facts, was held not to have been negligent. Both the inspector in giving the order and the plaintiff in obeying the order were acting contrary to Standing Orders. The plaintiff claimed damages from, inter alia, the first defendant.

Held
The inspector had been guilty of negligence and this had been the real cause of the plaintiff's injuries. It was also a new cause, disturbing and interrupting the sequence of events between the first defendant's accident and that of the plaintiff. The inspector (and his chief constable) were liable in respect of the plaintiff's injuries; the first defendant was not.

Stephenson LJ:

> 'In the long run the question is ... one of remoteness of damage, to be answered, as has so often been stated, not by the logic of philosophers but by the common sense of plain men ... In my judgment, too much happened here, too much went wrong, the chapter of accidents and mistakes was too long and varied, to impose on [the first defendant] liability for what happened to the plaintiff in discharging his duty as a police officer, although it would not have happened had not [the first defendant] negligently overturned his car. The ordinary course of things took an extraordinary course.'

Liesbosch Dredger v SS Edison see Edison, The

Lord v Pacific Steam Navigation Co Ltd, The Oropesa [1943] P 32 Court of Appeal (Lord Wright, Scott and MacKinnon LJJ)

Negligence – chain of causation

Facts
Due to the negligence of *The Oropesa,* the ship collided with *The Manchester Regiment* and caused it serious damage. Most of the crew of the latter took to the lifeboats and the captain decided to go to *The Oropesa* in one of them in the hope of obtaining assistance of various kinds. This lifeboat capsized and nine of the crew lost their lives.

Held
The owners of *The Oropesa* were liable in respect of this loss of life as there had been no break in the chain of causation.

Lord Wright:

> 'In all these cases the question is not whether there was what one may call negligence or not. Negligence involves a breach of duty as between the plaintiff and the defendant. The captain or Lord, or whoever was deciding what to do, were not then owing a duty to anybody except, possibly, a duty to minimise damage so far as they could; but that is not a point which is relevant here. They were acting in an emergency. If they did something which was outside the exigencies of the emergency, whether it was from miscalculation or from error, or, if you like, from mere wilfulness, they would be debarred from saying that there had not intervened a new cause. The question is not whether there was new negligence, but whether there was a new cause ... It must always be shown that there is something which I will call ultroneous, something unwarrantable, a new cause coming in disturbing the sequence of events, something

that can be described as either unreasonable or extraneous or extrinsic. I doubt very much whether the law can be stated more precisely than that ...

The real difficulty here is the application of the principle, which is a question of fact ... I am not prepared to say, and I do not say in this case that the fact that Lord's death was due in the circumstances to his leaving the ship in a boat, and to the unexpected and very unfortunate capsizing of that boat, prevented his death being a direct consequence of the casualty. It was a risk, no doubt; but a boat would not generally capsize in those circumstances; and I cannot think that that prevents it being held that his death was a direct consequence of the casualty.'

McKew v Holland & Hannen & Cubitts (Scotland) Ltd [1969] 3 All ER 1621 House of Lords (Lord Reid, Lord Hodson, Lord Guest, Viscount Dilhorne and Lord Upjohn)

Damages – subsequent further injury

Facts
Due to the defendants' negligence, the plaintiff's leg was injured. As a result, he occasionally lost the control of his left leg and it 'buckled'. Before the trial, the plaintiff went to visit a flat and while descending a steep staircase, his leg gave way; he attempted to avoid falling head-first and jumped, landing on his right leg and breaking it. The plaintiff claimed in respect of both injuries.

Held
The injuries from the second incident were the result of a novus actus interveniens (the attempt to descend a steep staircase without a handrail or adult assistance) and, therefore, too remote.

Lord Guest:

> 'The appellant was still convalescent from his first accident when the second accident occurred. He was limping. He had the experience of his leg giving way. Yet he chose without assistance, without hanging on to the wall, to commence to descend those steep stairs holding his young daughter by the hand. Like the Lord Justice-Clerk I could not characterise such conduct as other than unreasonable in the circumstances. If this be so, then the chain of causation between the first and second accident is broken and the appellant must fail.'

Oropesa, The see *Lord v Pacific Steam Navigation Co Ltd, The Oropesa*

Overseas Tankship (UK) Limited v The Miller Steamship Pty Ltd (The Wagon Mound No 2) [1966] 3 WLR 498 Privy Council (Lord Reid, Lord Morris of Borth-y-Gest, Lord Pearce, Lord Wilberforce and Lord Pearson)

Negligence – foreseeability of damage

Facts
On October 30 1951 the defendants' ship, the *Wagon Mound,* was loading oil in Sydney Harbour. Due to the negligence of the ship's engineers, a large quantity of the oil was spilt and floated on the surface of the water. The plaintiffs' vessels were being repaired at a wharf some 200 yds away, and oil began to accumulate there. The wharf owners were using welding equipment and, fearing the danger of fire, their manager made enquiries and was told it was safe to continue. On November 1, the oil ignited and both the plaintiffs' ship and the wharf were severely damaged by fire. The plaintiffs claimed damages in negligence and nuisance: the central issue was whether the risk of fire was foreseeable.

Held
The defendants were liable in negligence as a reasonable man in the position of the engineers would have thought that there was a real risk of fire and that it was not justifiable to neglect to take steps to eliminate that risk.

Lord Reid:

> '... a person must be regarded as negligent if he does not take steps to eliminate a risk which he knows or ought to know is a real risk and not a mere possibility which could never influence the mind of a reasonable man ... it is justifiable not to take steps to eliminate a real risk if it is small and if the circumstances are such that a reasonable man, careful of the safety of his neighbour, would think it right to neglect it.'

Commentary
Distinguished: *Overseas Tankship (UK) Ltd v Mort Docks & Engineering Co Ltd (The Wagon Mound No 1)* [1961] 2 WLR 126 and *Bolton v Stone* [1951] AC 850.

Overseas Tankship (UK) Ltd v Morts Dock & Engineering Co Ltd (The Wagon Mound No 1) [1961] 2 WLR 126 Privy Council (Viscount Simonds, Lord Reid, Lord Radcliffe, Lord Tucker and Lord Morris of Borth-y-Gest)

Negligence – remoteness of damages

Facts
For the facts of this case see *The Wagon Mound No 2*, above. The present case concerned the claim by the wharf-owners, whose wharf was also destroyed by fire. The evidence in the present case differed in two material respects from that in *The Wagon Mound No 2*:

a) Some damage to the wharf-owners' property was reasonably foreseeable from the fouling of their slipways through oil;
b) It was *not* reasonably foreseeable that the oil on the water would catch fire.

The defendants here contended, inter alia, that the plaintiffs' damage was too remote.

Held
The defendants were not liable. as a man is only liable for those consequences of his negligent act which a reasonable man would have foreseen.

Viscount Simonds:

> 'It is a principle of civil liability, subject only to qualifications which have no present relevance, that a man must be considered to be responsible for the probable consequences of his act. To demand more of him is too harsh a rule; to demand less is to ignore that civilised order requires the observance of a minimum standard of behaviour. This concept, applied to the slowly developing law of negligence, has led to a great variety of expressions which can, as it appears to their Lordships, be harmonised with little difficulty with the single exception of the so-called rule *Polemis*. For, if it is asked why a man should be responsible for the natural or necessary or probable consequences of his act (or any other similar description of them) the answer is that it is not because they are natural or necessary or probable, but because since they have this quality, it is judged by the standard of the reasonable man, that he ought to have foreseen them. Thus, it is that, over and over again, it has happened that in different judgments in the case and sometimes in a single judgment, liability for a consequence has been imposed on the ground that it was reasonably foreseeable, or alternatively on the ground that it was natural or necessary or probable. The two

grounds have been treated as coterminous and so they largely are. But, where they are not, the question arises to which the wrong answer was given in *Polemis*. For, if some limitation must be imposed on the consequences for which the negligent actor is to be held responsible – and all are agreed that some limitation there must be – why should that test (reasonable foreseeability) be rejected which, since he is judged by what the reasonable man ought to foresee, corresponds with the common conscience of mankind and a test (the 'direct' consequence) be substituted which leads to nowhere but the never ending and insoluble problems of causation.'

Commentary

Disapproved: *Re Polemis and Furness, Withy & Co Ltd* [1921] 3 KB 560.

Applied in *Doughty* v *Turner Manufacturing Co Ltd* [1964] 2 WLR 240.

Distinguished in *Overseas Tankship (UK) Ltd* v *The Miller Steamship Co Pty Ltd (The Wagon Mound No 2)* [1966] 3 WLR 498.

Polemis and Furness, Withy & Co Ltd, Re [1921] 3 KB 560 Court of Appeal (Bankes, Warrington and Scrutton LJJ)

Negligence – consequences of negligent act

Facts

The plaintiffs were the owners of a ship under charter to the defendants. After the cargo of petrol had been unloaded, the defendants' servants, stevedores, negligently caused a wooden plank to drop into the hold of the ship. This caused a spark and, due to the presence of inflammable vapour in the hold, an explosion ensued and the ship was destroyed by fire. It was found as a fact that although the dropping of the plank was likely to cause some damage to the ship, the spark and explosion were not foreseeable.

Held

The defendants were liable for the loss of the ship. If a reasonable man would have foreseen any damage as likely to result from his breach of duty, he is liable for all the direct consequences whether foreseeable or not.

Scrutton LJ:

'The second defence is that the damage is too remote from the negligence, as it could not be reasonably foreseen as a consequence. On this head we were referred to a number of well-known cases in which vague language, which I cannot think to be really helpful, has been used in an attempt to define the point at which damage becomes too remote from, or not sufficiently directly caused by, the breach of duty, which is the original cause of action, to be recoverable. For instance, I cannot think it useful to say the damage must be the natural and probable result. This suggests that there are results which are natural but not probable, and other results which are probable but not natural. I am not sure what either adjective means in this connection; if they mean the same thing, two need not be used; if they mean different things, the difference between them should be defined. And as to many cases of fact in which the distinction has been drawn, it is difficult to see why one case should be decided one way and one another ... In this case, however, the problem is simpler. To determine whether an act is negligent, it is relevant to determine whether any reasonable person would foresee that the act would cause damage; if he would not, the act is not negligent. But if the act would or might probably cause damage, the fact that the damage it in fact causes is not the exact kind of damage one would expect is immaterial, so long as the damage is in fact caused sufficiently directly by the negligent act, and not by the operation of independent causes having no connection with the negligent act, except that they could not avoid its results. Once the act is negligent, the fact that its exact operation was not foreseen is immaterial ... In the present case it was negligent in discharging cargo to knock down the planks of the temporary staging, for they might easily cause some damage either to workmen, or cargo, or the ship. The fact that they did directly produce an unexpected result, a spark in an atmosphere of petrol vapour which caused a fire, does not relieve the person who was negligent from the damage which his negligent act directly caused.'

Commentary
Disapproved in *Overseas Tankship (UK) Ltd v Morts Docks and Engineering Co Ltd (The Wagon Mound No 1)* [1961] 2 WLR 126.

Robinson v *The Post Office* [1974] 1 WLR 1176 Court of Appeal (Davies, Buckley and Orr LJJ)

Negligence – remoteness of damages

Facts
Due to Ds' negligence, P cut his leg at work. At hospital, P was given an anti-tetanus injection by Dr X without first being tested for allergy. In fact, P was allergic and suffered brain damage. A test would not have revealed the allergy.

Held
The defendants were liable for all P's damage – they must take P as they find him, including allergy. Dr X was also negligent, but this was not a cause of P's injury.

Commentary
Applied: *Smith* v *Leech Brain & Co Ltd* [1962] 2 WLR 148.

Rouse v *Squires* [1973] 2 WLR 925 Court of Appeal (Buckley and Cairns LJJ and MacKenna J)

Negligence – causation – contributory negligence

Facts
Due to the negligence of Allen, his lorry 'jack-knifed' on a motorway on a frosty night. Rouse was one of those who stopped to assist. Five or ten minutes later, Squires negligently collided with another lorry which had stopped to help and this lorry knocked down and killed Rouse. Rouse's widow was awarded damages against Squires: could Squires obtain contributions from Allen and the owners of the 'jack-knifed' lorry?

Held
He could and 25 per cent of the blame was attributed to them. There was no breach in the chain of causation between the original negligent driving and the killing of Mr Rouse.

Cairns LJ:

'If a driver so negligently manages his vehicles as to cause it to obstruct the highway and constitute a danger to other road users, including those who are driving too fast or not keeping a proper look-out, but not those who deliberately or recklessly drive into the obstruction, then the first driver's negligence may be held to have contributed to the causation of an accident of which the immediate cause was the negligent driving of the vehicle which because of the presence of the obstruction collides with it or with some other vehicle or some other person. Accordingly, I would hold in this case that Mr Allen's negligence did contribute to the death of Mr Rouse.'

Commentary
Distinguished: *Dymond* v *Pearce* [1972] 2 WLR 633.

Scott v *Shepherd* (1773) 2 Wm Bl 892 Court of Common Pleas (De Grey CJ, Nares, Blackstone and Gould JJ)

Squib – chain of causation

Facts
The defendant threw a lighted squib into a covered market: it fell on Yates's gingerbread stall and to save himself and the wares Willis picked it up and threw it across the market house. It landed on Ryal's stall and he, to save his goods, threw it away: it struck the plaintiff in the face, exploded and put out one of his eyes. The plaintiff sought damages for trespass and assault.

Held (Blackstone J dissenting)
His action would be successful.

Nares J:

> 'I am of opinion that trespass would well lie in the present case. The natural and probable consequence of the act done by the defendant was injury to somebody, and, therefore, the act was illegal at common law ... Being, therefore, unlawful, the defendant was liable to answer for the consequences, be the injury mediate or immediately ... malus animus is not necessary to constitute a trespass ... The principle I go on is ... that if the act in the first instance be unlawful, trespass will lie. Wherever, therefore, an act is unlawful at first, trespass will lie for the consequences of it ... I do not think it necessary, to maintain trespass, that the defendant should personally touch the plaintiff; if he does it by a mean it is sufficient. Qui facit per aliud facit per se. He is the person who, in the present case, gave the mischievous faculty to the squib. That mischievous faculty remained in it until the explosion. No new power of doing mischief was communicated to it by Willis or Ryal. It is like the case of a mad ox turned loose in a crowd. The person who turns him loose is answerable in trespass for whatever mischief he may do. The intermediate acts of Willis and Ryal will not purge the original tort in the defendant. But he who does the first wrong is answerable for all the consequential damages ...'

Smith v *Leech Brain & Co Ltd* [1962] 2 WLR 148 High Court (Lord Parker CJ)

Negligence – remoteness of damages

Facts
Due to the failure of the defendant employers to provide a safe system of working, the plaintiff's husband was burnt on the lip by a piece of molten metal. Soon after, the lip began to swell and cancer was diagnosed. Despite treatment, the plaintiff's husband died of the cancer some three years later. The evidence showed that the deceased had a pre-malignant condition, promoted into cancer by the burn.

Held
The plaintiff's claim against the defendants in respect of her husband's death succeeded.

Lord Parker CJ:

> 'The test is not whether these defendants could reasonably have foreseen that a burn would cause cancer and that Mr Smith would die. The question is whether these defendants could reasonably foresee the

type of injury which he suffered, namely, the burn. What, in the particular case, is the amount of damage which he suffers as a result of that burn, depends on the characteristics and constitution of the victim.'

Commentary
Applied in *Robinson* v *The Post Office* [1974] 1 WLR 1176.

Stansbie v *Troman* [1948] 2 KB 48 Court of Appeal (Tucker and Somervell LJJ and Roxburgh J)

Negligence – duty of care

Facts
The plaintiff, a painter and decorator, was working on the defendant's premises. One day when the house was unoccupied, the plaintiff left to buy some more wallpaper, leaving the front door unlocked. In his absence, a thief entered and stole some of the defendant's property. On a claim by the plaintiff for work done, the defendant counter-claimed alleging negligence.

Held
The theft was not too remote a consequence of the plaintiff's negligence in leaving the house unlocked. The entry of the thief was a direct result of his negligence and not a novus actus interveniens.

Wieland v *Cyril Lord Carpets Ltd* [1969] 3 All ER 1006 High Court (Eveleigh J)

Negligence – remoteness of damage

Facts
The plaintiff injured her neck due to the defendants' negligence and had to wear a neck-collar: this made it difficult to use her bi-focal spectacles. Next day, she fell down steps.

Held
The defendants were liable for the second injury also. The plaintiff was not acting unreasonably so soon after the first accident and the chain of causation had not been broken.

8 Contributory Negligence

Admiralty Commissioners* v *Volute (Owners), The Volute [1922] 1 AC 129 House of Lords (Viscount Birkenhead LC, Viscount Cave, Viscount Finlay, Lord Shaw and Lord Phillimore)

Negligence – contributory negligence

Facts
There was a collision between HMS Radstock, a destroyer, and the Volute, an oil tanker. If the Volute had signalled, there would have been no collision: similarly if, in its position of danger brought about by the Volute, the Radstock had not gone full steam ahead, a collision would have been avoided.

Held
The Volute was partly to blame for the collision.

Viscount Birkenhead LC:

'Upon the whole I think that this question of contributory negligence must be dealt with somewhat broadly and upon common-sense principles as a jury would probably deal with it. While, no doubt, where a clear line can be drawn, the subsequent negligence is the only one to look to, there are cases in which the two acts come so closely together, and the second act of negligence is so much mixed up with the state of things brought about by the first act that the party secondly negligent, while not held free from blame ... might, on the other hand, invoke the prior negligence as being part of the cause of the collision so as to make it a case of contribution.'

Alliance & Leicester Building Society* v *Edgestop [1993] 1 WLR 1462 High Court (Mummery J)

Availability of defence in action for deceit

Facts
A private unlimited company of estate agents were sued by the plaintiff building society claiming that the estate agents were vicariously liable for the deceit of one of its former employees. The estate agents pleaded contributory negligence to claims in deceit. The question arose on a striking out application as to whether in law it was entitled to plead such a defence to a claim in deceit. The master held that this was not possible, and the plaintiffs appealed.

Held
That a person liable for deceit, whether personally or vicariously, was not entitled either at common law or under the Law Reform (Contributory Negligence) Act 1945 to plead as a defence that his victim was guilty of contributory negligence.

Fitzgerald v *Lane* [1989] AC 328 House of Lords (Lord Bridge of Harwich, Lord Brandon of Oakbrook, Lord Templeman, Lord Ackner and Lord Oliver of Aylmerton)

Contributory negligence – apportionment

Facts
Although the lights were green to traffic and red against pedestrians, the plaintiff walked on to a pelican crossing. He was struck by the first defendant's car and thrown across the road where he was struck by the second defendant's car travelling in the opposite direction. As a result of these collisions he suffered multiple injuries.

Held
As the plaintiff's responsibility for his injuries had been at least as great as that of the defendants jointly, he was entitled to no more than 50 per cent of his claim, the amount awarded by the Court of Appeal.

Lord Ackner:

> *'The correct approach to the determination of contributory negligence, apportionment and contribution*
> It is axiomatic that, whether the plaintiff is suing one or more defendants for damages for personal injuries, the first question which the judge has to determine is whether the plaintiff has established liability against one or other or all the defendants, ie that they, or one or more of them, were negligent (or in breach of statutory duty) and that that negligence (or breach of statutory duty) caused or materially contributed to his injuries. The next step, of course liability has been established, is to assess what is the total of the damage that the plaintiff has sustained as a result of the established negligence. It is only after these two decisions have been made that the next question arises, namely whether the defendant or defendants have established (for the onus is on them) that the plaintiff, by his own negligence, contributed to the damage which he suffered. If, and only if, contributory negligence is established does the court then have to decide, pursuant to s1 of the Law Reform (Contributory Negligence) Act 1945, to what extent it is just and equitable to reduce the damages which would otherwise be recoverable by the plaintiff, having regard to his "share in the responsibility for the damage".
>
> All the decisions referred to above are made in the main action. Apportionment of liability in a case of contributory negligence between plaintiff and defendants must be kept separate from apportionment of *contribution between the defendants inter se*. Although the defendants are each liable to the plaintiff for the whole amount for which he has obtained judgment, the proportions in which, as between themselves, the defendants must meet the plaintiff's claim do not have any direct relationship to the extent to which the total damages have been reduced by the contributory negligence, although the facts of any given case may justify the proportions being the same.
>
> Once the questions referred to above in the main action have been determined in favour of the plaintiff to the extent that he has obtained a judgment against two or more defendants, then and only then should the court focus its attention on the claims which may be made between those defendants for contribution pursuant to the Civil Liability (Contribution) Act 1978, re-enacting and extending the court's powers under s6 of the Law Reform (Married Women and Tortfeasors) Act 1935. In the contribution proceedings, whether or not they are heard during the trial of the main action or by separate proceedings, the court is concerned to discover what contribution is just and equitable, having regard to the responsibility between the tortfeasors inter se, for the damage which the plaintiff has been adjudged entitled to recover. That damage may, of course, have been subject to a reduction as a result of the decision in the main action that the plaintiff, by his own negligence, contributed to the damage which he sustained.
>
> Thus, where the plaintiff successfully sues more than one defendant for damages for personal injuries and there is a claim between co-defendants for contribution, there are two distinct and different stages in the decision-making process, the one in the main action and the other in the contribution proceedings.'

Froom v Butcher [1975] 3 WLR 379 Court of Appeal (Lord Denning MR, Lawton and Scarman LJJ)

Negligence – contributory negligence

Facts
Due to the negligent driving of the defendant, he collided with the plaintiff's car. At the time of the accident, the plaintiff was not wearing a seat-belt. Had he done so, most of his injuries, which were largely to the head and chest, would have been avoided.

Held
The plaintiff's damages would be reduced by 25 per cent for contributory negligence.

Lord Denning MR:

> 'The question is not what was the cause of the accident. It is rather what was the cause of the damage. In most accidents on the road the bad driving which causes the accident also causes the ensuing damage. But, in seat-belt cases, the cause of the accident is one thing. The cause of the damage is another. The accident is caused by the bad driving. The damage is caused in part by the bad driving of the defendant and in part by the failure of the plaintiff to wear a seat belt. If the plaintiff was to blame in not wearing a seat-belt, the damage is in part the result of his own fault. He must bear some share in the responsibility for the damage and his damages fall to be reduced to such extent as the court thinks just and equitable.'

Commentary
Applied in *Eastman* v *South West Thames Health Authority* (1991) The Times 22 July

Gough v Thorne [1966] 1 WLR 1387 Court of Appeal (Lord Denning MR, Danckwerts and Salmon LJJ)

Negligence – contributory negligence – child

Facts
The plaintiff, aged 13, was waiting to cross the road. A lorry which was about to turn stopped, and the driver beckoned her to cross the road. As she did so, a 'bubble car' drove through a small gap between the lorry and a bollard in the centre of the road and collided with the plaintiff, causing her serious injuries. The trial judge found the car-driver to blame, but reduced the plaintiff's damages by 33 per cent finding that she was contributorily negligent in not stopping to look for other traffic after passing the lorry.

Held
The plaintiff had not been negligent in relying entirely on the lorry driver's signal and the finding of contributory negligence could not therefore be upheld.

Lord Denning MR:

> 'A very young child cannot be guilty of contributory negligence. An older child may be; but, it depends on the circumstances. A judge should only find a child guilty of contributory negligence if he or she is of such an age as reasonably to be expected to take precautions for his or her own safety; and then he or she is only to be found guilty if blame should be attached to him or her.'

Harrison v *British Railways Board* [1981] 3 All ER 679 High Court (Boreham J)

Negligence – injury to rescuer

Facts
The plaintiff was a guard on a passenger train. The second defendant, a Mr Howard, attempted to board the train while it was moving out of the station. The plaintiff gave an incorrect signal to the driver of the train to stop; the train kept accelerating. The plaintiff then attempted to grab the second defendant and pull him onto the train; in consequence, the second defendant fell off the train pulling the plaintiff with him. The plaintiff suffered injuries and brought an action in negligence against, amongst others, the second defendant. The second defendant argued that he was not liable on the ground that a person being rescued owed no duty to his rescuer, or, if he did owe the plaintiff a duty, the plaintiff had been contributorily negligent in giving the wrong signal to the driver to stop or failing to apply the emergency brake himself.

Held
The plaintiff would succeed, but his damages would be reduced by 20 per cent.

Boreham J:

> 'Thus, two questions arise: had the second defendant, Mr Howard, by a lack of reasonable care for his own safety, created a situation of danger? I have no doubt that he had. The second question: ought he, as a reasonable man, to have foreseen that the plaintiff might very well come to his aid? I have said enough already to indicate that in my view he should have foreseen, and he probably did foresee, the probability of the plaintiff's intervention. In these circumstances I hold that the second defendant is liable in negligence to the plaintiff ... It was the plaintiff's duty, according to the rules, to apply the brake in an emergency; he knew it and I think he was negligent in not doing so. Had he done so, the speed of the train would have been reduced. He should have known it was his duty, and I believe he did know it. As it was, he gave (no doubt in the heat of the moment) a meaningless signal and the train continued to accelerate. In these circumstances, I have come to the conclusion that had he acted as he should have done it is probable, though not certain, that both the chance of his being injured at all and the severity of his injuries would have been reduced. He should, therefore, bear some of the blame for those injuries.
>
> One has a feeling of distaste about finding a rescuer guilty of contributory negligence. It can rarely be appropriate to do so, in my judgment. Here, however, the contributory negligence which is alleged does not relate to anything done in the course of the actual rescue. What is alleged is the failure by the man in authority to reduce the danger by doing what he was duty-bound to do. The major responsibility must, of course, be borne by the second defendant. I assess the plaintiff's share at 20 per cent.'

Commentary
Applied: *Videan* v *British Transport Commission* [1963] 3 WLR 374.

Jones v *Livox Quarries Ltd* [1952] 2 QB 608 Court of Appeal (Singleton, Denning and Hodson LJJ)

Negligence – contributory negligence

Facts
The plaintiff was riding on the back of his employers' traxcavator (a slow-speed tracked excavator) when, due to the negligence of another employee, it was struck in the rear by another vehicle. The plaintiff sued the defendants, his employers, as being vicariously liable for the negligence of the second driver.

Held
Although the defendants were liable, the plaintiff's damages would be reduced by 20 per cent for contributory negligence.

Denning LJ:

> 'A person is guilty of contributory negligence if he ought reasonably to have foreseen that, if he did not act as a reasonable, prudent man, he might be hurt himself; and in his reckonings he must take into account the possibility of others being careless.'

Morales v *Eccleston* [1991] RTR 151 Court of Appeal (Staughton and McCowan LJJ and Sir John Megaw)

Contributory negligence – child

Facts
An 11-year-old boy, who ran into the road without looking to retrieve a ball, was struck by a car. At trial it was accepted that there was some degree of contributory negligence.

Held
That the child's contributory negligence would be assessed at 75 per cent.

Nance v *British Columbia Electric Railway Co Ltd* [1951] AC 601 Privy Council (Viscount Simon, Lord Porter, Lord Morton of Henryton, Lord Reid and Lord Asquith of Bishopstone)

Negligence – contributory negligence

Facts
Late at night the appellant and her husband were crossing a road. The respondents' street-car, having stopped to pick up passengers, restarted without warning and knocked down and killed the appellant's husband. The respondents pleaded contributory negligence.

Held
The respondents were solely to blame.

Viscount Simon:

> 'The statement that, when negligence is alleged as the basis of an actionable wrong, a necessary ingredient in the conception is the existence of a duty owed by the defendants to the plaintiff to take due care, is, of course, indubitably correct. But when contributory negligence is set up as a defence, its existence does not depend on any duty owed by the injured party to the party sued and all that is necessary to establish such a defence is to prove to the satisfaction of the jury that the injured party did not in his own interest take reasonable care of himself and contributed, by this want of care, to his own injury. For when contributory negligence is set up as a shield against the obligation to satisfy the whole of the plaintiff's claim, the principle involved is that, where a man is part author of his own injury, he cannot call on the other party to compensate him in full.'

Commentary
Applied: *Davies* v *Swan Motor Co (Swansea) Ltd* [1949] 2 KB 291.

O'Connell v *Jackson* [1971] 3 WLR 463 Court of Appeal (Russell, Edmund-Davies and Cairns LJJ)

Negligence – contributory negligence – failure to wear crash helmet

Facts

The plaintiff's moped collided with the defendant's motor car. The defendant admitted negligence: had the plaintiff been guilty of contributory negligence because, at the time of the accident, he had not been wearing a crash helmet?

Held

He had and his damages would be reduced by 15 per cent.

Edmund-Davies LJ:

> ' ... in the present case the probable effectiveness of crash helmets in reducing the risk of a serious head injury was solidly established. It is true that no use has yet been made of the power conferred by s41 of the Road Traffic Act 1962 to make regulations requiring the wearing of protective headgear in such cases as the present. We would welcome such a regulation if economic considerations permit, for the possibility of serious injury resulting from failure to do so is manifest. More to the point, the evidence of the plaintiff himself in the present case establishes that he was alive to this risk and had only himself to blame for failing to remedy the omission. In these circumstances, we respectfully dissent from the judge's complete exculpation of the plaintiff, and we hold that he should bear part of the responsibility for the severe consequences of the accident.'

Owens v *Brimmell* [1977] 3 WLR 943 High Court (Tasker Watkins J)

Negligence – contributory negligence

Facts

The plaintiff and the defendant went out for an evening's drinking in the defendant's car. They visited several public houses and consumed a considerable amount of beer. On the return journey, due to the defendant's admitted negligence, there was an accident in which the plaintiff was severely injured. At the time of the accident, the plaintiff was not wearing a seat-belt, although given the severity of the impact, he would still have been injured even if he had worn one. The plaintiff claimed damages and the defendant pleaded contributory negligence.

Held

The plaintiff's damages would be reduced by 20 per cent for his contributory negligence in travelling with a driver whom he knew to be under the influence of alcohol. He was aware of the amount consumed and must have realised it was likely substantially to impair the defendant's driving ability. However, there would be no reduction for the plaintiff's failure to wear a seat-belt. Much of his injuries were to the head and face, but there are several ways in which these could have been sustained: it could have been that the plaintiff was thrown forward onto the fascia, in which case the belt might have restrained him. It is just as possible that the fascia was pushed back into him by the force of the impact, in which case the belt would have been of little, if any, assistance. If a defendant raises the defence of contributory negligence, the burden is upon him to prove, by evidence, that the plaintiff's act was a cause of his injury. This the defendant has not done.

9 Volenti Non Fit Injuria

Bowater* v *Rowley Regis Corporation [1944] KB 476 Court of Appeal (Scott, Goddard and du Parcq LJJ)

Negligence – volenti non fit injuria

Facts
The plaintiff rubbish collector was provided by his employers, the defendants, with a horse and cart. He was ordered to take a horse which was known to be restive and to have run away on previous occasions. He protested, but eventually obeyed. The horse ran away and the plaintiff was thrown from the cart and injured.

Held
The plaintiff was entitled to damages as the defendants had been guilty of negligence. He had not been contributorily negligent and, as it was not part of his employment to manage unruly horses, he had not accepted the risk.

Goddard LJ:

'The maxim volenti non fit injuria is one which in the case of master and servant is to be applied with extreme caution. Indeed, I would say that it can hardly ever be applicable where the act to which the plaintiff is said to be "volens" arises out of his ordinary duty, unless the work for which the plaintiff is engaged is one in which danger is necessarily involved. Thus a man in an explosives factory must take the risk of an explosion occurring in spite of the observance and provision of all statutory regulations and safeguards. A horse-breaker must take the risk of being thrown or injured by a restive or unbroken horse; it is an ordinary risk of his employment. But a man whose occupation is not one of a nature inherently dangerous but who is asked or required to undertake a risky operation is in a different position. To rely on this doctrine the master must show that the workman undertook that the risk should be on him. It is not enough that, whether under protest or not, he obeyed an order or complied with a request which he might have declined as one which he was not bound either to obey or to comply with. It must be shown that he agreed that what risk there was should lie on him. I do not mean that it must necessarily be shown that he contracted to take the risk, as that would involve consideration, though a simple case of showing that a workman did take a risk upon himself would be that he was paid extra for so doing, and in some occupations "danger money" is often paid ...

For this maxim or doctrine to apply it must be shown that a servant who is asked or required to use dangerous plant is a volunteer in the fullest sense; that, knowing of the danger, he expressly or impliedly said that he would do the job at his own risk and not at that of his master. The evidence in this case fell far short of that and, in my opinion, the plaintiff was entitled to recover.'

Cutler* v *United Dairies (London) Ltd [1933] 2 KB 297 Court of Appeal (Scrutton and Slesser LJJ and Eve J)

Negligence – volenti non fit injuria

Facts

The defendants' milkman left his horse and cart unattended. The horse bolted and ran off down a country road. The plaintiff was injured whilst trying to catch and control the horse.

Held

The plaintiff's action was unnecessary; his assistance had not been requested; there was no danger to others; volenti non fit injuria barred his claim.

Commentary

Distinguished: *Haynes* v *G Harwood & Son* [1935] 1 KB 146.

Dann v *Hamilton* [1939] 1 KB 509 High Court (Asquith J)

Negligence – volenti non fit injuria – intoxicated driver

Facts

The defendant's husband drove the plaintiff and her mother out for the evening. A considerable amount of alcohol was drunk and on the return, another passenger, T, was given a lift. When T was let out of the car, he commented on the bad state of the defendant's husband's driving and said to the plaintiff and her mother, 'You two have more pluck than I have'. The plaintiff replied, 'You should be like me. If anything is going to happen, it will happen.' A few minutes later, an accident occurred in which the defendant's husband and the plaintiff's mother were killed and the plaintiff herself injured. The plaintiff brought this action against the defendant representing the estate. Negligence was admitted and the defence of volenti non fit injuria relied upon.

Held

The plaintiff would be awarded damages. For the defence to succeed, there must be not only complete knowledge of the danger, but also consent: the maxim says volenti not scienti and knowledge does not necessarily imply consent.

Asquith J:

> 'I find it difficult to believe, although I know of no authority directly in point, that a person who voluntarily travels as a passenger in a vehicle driven by a driver who is known by the passenger to have driven negligently in the past is *volens* as to future negligent acts of such driver, even though he could have chosen some other form of transport if he had wished. Then, to take the last step, suppose that such a driver is likely to drive negligently on the material occasion, not because he is known to the plaintiff to have driven negligently in the past, but because he is known to the plaintiff to be under the influence of drink. That is the present case. Ought the result to be any different? After much debate, I have come to the conclusion that it should not, and that the plaintiff, by embarking in the car, or re-entering it, with knowledge that through drink the driver had materially reduced his capacity for driving safely, did not impliedly consent to, or absolve the driver from liability for, any subsequent negligence on his part whereby the plaintiff might suffer harm.
>
> There may be cases in which the drunkenness of the driver at the material time is so extreme and so glaring that to accept a lift from him is like engaging in an intrinsically and obviously dangerous occupation, inter-meddling with an unexploded bomb or walking on the edge of an unfenced cliff. It is not necessary to decide whether in such a case the maxim *volenti non fit injuria* would apply, for in the present case I find as a fact that the driver's degree of intoxication fell short of this degree. I therefore conclude that the defence fails, and the claim succeeds.'

Commentary
Applied in *Nettleship* v *Weston* [1971] 3 WLR 370.

Morris v *Murray* [1991] 2 WLR 195 Court of Appeal (Fox, Stocker LJJ and Sir George Waller)

Volenti non fit injuria – aircraft joyride

Facts
The plaintiff was a passenger in an aeroplane which crashed because the pilot was drunk. The plaintiff had, in fact, been out drinking with the pilot, had driven to the airport with him and had assisted in the preparations for the flight. The plaintiff brought a claim against the estate of the deceased pilot claiming damages for personal injury. An autopsy on the pilot showed that he had consumed the equivalent of 17 whiskies. The trial judge gave judgment for the plaintiff; he held that the defence of volenti could not succeed, although he did reduce the damages payable by 20 per cent because of the plaintiff's contributory negligence in participating in this enterprise.

Held
The defendant's appeal would be allowed on the ground that the plaintiff was volens. The present case was distinguishable from *Dann* v *Hamilton* [1939] 1 All ER 59 on the very inception (which was not the case in *Dann* because there the driver did not get drunk until a late stage in the social outing at a time when it might not have been very easy for the plaintiff 'to extricate herself without giving offence'). Sir George Waller was also of the opinion that there was a fundamental difference between driving a car and piloting an aeroplane; the latter being more risky and requiring greater accuracy of control than the former. Nor was the plaintiff so drunk that he was incapable of appreciating the risks involved in the enterprise. He was sufficiently aware of what was going on that he drove the car to the airport and assisted in the preparations for the flight.

Pitts v *Hunt* [1990] 3 WLR 542 Court of Appeal (Dillon, Balcombe and Beldam LJJ)

Negligence – joint illegal enterprise

Facts
The plaintiff was 18 and his friend Mark 16. Mark owned a motor cycle which he used as a trail bike, but he was not, as the plaintiff was aware, insured to use it on a road and he did not have a licence. After spending the evening drinking, they set off for home on Mark's bike with the plaintiff on the pillion. Encouraged by the plaintiff, Mark rode in a fast, reckless and hazardous manner, intending to frighten members of the public. They collided with a car; the plaintiff was severely injured and Mark (more than twice over the legal limit) was killed. The plaintiff claimed damages in negligence against, inter alia, Mark's personal representative. The judge held that the claim was barred by the maxim ex turpi causa non oritur actio and public policy; he also decided that volenti non fit injuria would have defeated the claim, but for s148(3) of the Road Traffic Act 1972, and that in any case the plaintiff had been 100 per cent contributorily negligent. The plaintiff appealed.

Held
The appeal would be dismissed on grounds of public policy and the application of the maxim ex turpi causa non oritur actio and because the circumstances precluded the court from finding that Mark had owed the plaintiff a duty of care.

Beldam LJ:

'On the facts found by the judge in this case the plaintiff was playing a full and active part in encouraging the young rider to commit offences which, if a death other than that of the young rider himself had occurred, would have amounted to manslaughter. And not just manslaughter by gross negligence on the judge's findings. It would have been manslaugther by the commission of a dangerous act either done with the intention of frightening other road users or when both the plaintiff and the young rider were aware or but for self-induced intoxication would have been aware that it was likely to do so and nevertheless they went on and did the act regardless of the consequences. Thus on the findings made by the judge in this case I would hold that the plaintiff is precluded on grounds of public policy from recovering compensation for the injuries which he sustained in the course of the very serious offences in which he was participating.'

Dillon LJ:

'I feel unable to draw any valid distinction between the reckless riding of the motor cycle in the present case by the deceased boy, Hunt, and the plaintiff under the influence of drink, and the reckless driving of the cars, albeit stolen, in *Smith v Jenkins and Bondarenko v Sommers* (1968) 69 SR(NSW) 269. The words of Barwick CJ in *Smith v Jenkins* (1970) 119 CLR 397 at 399-400:

> "The driving of the car by the appellant, the manner of which is the basis of the respondent's complaint, was in the circumstances as much a use of the car by the respondent as it was a use by the appellant. That use was their joint enterprise of the moment."

apply with equal force to the riding of the motor cycle in the present case. This is a case in which ... the plaintiff's action in truth arises directly ex turpi causa.'

Balcombe LJ:

'In a case of this kind I find the ritual incantation of the maxim ex turpi causa non oritur actio more likely to confuse than to illuminate. I prefer to adopt the approach of the majority of the High Court of Australia in the most recent of the several Australian cases to which we were referred, *Jackson v Harrison* (1978) 138 CLR 438. That is to consider that what would have been the cause of action had there been no joint illegal enterprise, that is the tort of negligence based on the breach of a duty of care owed by the deceased to the plaintiff, and then to consider whether the circumstances of the particular case are such as to preclude the existence of that cause of action ... I prefer to found my judgment on the simple basis that the circumstances of this particular case were such as to preclude the court from finding that the deceased owed a duty of care to the plaintiff.

I agree ... that s148(3) of the Road Traffic Act 1972 does not affect the position under this head ...

Counsel for the first defendant sought to persuade us that the application of the volenti doctrine is to extinguish liability and, if liability has already been extinguished, there is nothing on which s148(3) of the Road Traffic Act 1972 can bite. As Dillon LJ says, if this argument were to be accepted, it would mean that s148(3) could never apply to a normal case of volenti, although that was clearly its intention ... I agree that the effect of s148(3) is to exclude any defence of volenti which might otherwise be available. On this issue I agree with the judge below that Ewbank J's decision in *Ashton v Turner* [1981] QB 137 at 148 was incorrect ...

I agree that the judge's finding that the plaintiff was 100 per cent contributorily negligent is logically unsupportable and, to use his own words, "defies common sense". Such a finding is equivalent to saying that the plaintiff was solely responsible for his own injuries, which he clearly was not.'

Commentary

Section 148(3) of the Road Traffic Act 1972 has been replaced by s149 of the Road Traffic Act 1988 but its effect is unchanged.

10 Breach of Statutory Duty

Atkinson* v *Newcastle Waterworks Co (1877) 2 Ex D 441 Court of Appeal (Lord Cairns LC, Cockburn CJ and Brett LJ)

Breach of statutory duty – civil action

Facts
The plaintiff's house, timber yard and saw mills caught fire and were burnt down. By statute, the defendants were obliged to supply water and keep the mains charged to a prescribed pressure: on the occasion in question they had failed to do so: for this the Act provided penalties.

Held
No action for damages lay for the defendants' breach of statutory duty.

Lord Cairns LC:

'The proposition a priori appears to be somewhat startling that a company supplying a town with water – although they are willing to be put under obligation to keep up the pressure, and to be subject to penalties if they fail to do so – should further be willing to assume, or that Parliament should think it necessary to subject them to liability to individual actions by any householder who could make out a case. In the one case they are merely under liability to penalties if they neglect to perform their duty, in the other case they are practically insurers, so far as water can produce safety from damage by fire. It is necessary to look at the provisions of s43 [of the Waterworks Clauses Act 1847]. Four cases are there specified, which cover all the duty imposed by the former sections, and for neglect of any one of these duties, there is a penalty of £10. For neglect of two of them, viz, to furnish to the town commissioners a sufficient supply of water for public purposes, and to furnish a supply of water to the owner or occupier, there is a further penalty of 40s a day, payable to every person who has paid or tendered the rate, for as long as such neglect or refusal continues after notice in writing has been given of the want of supply. It is not material to say, but it is possible that it might be held that neglect or refusal to fix fire-plugs would also subject the company to the 40s penalty. If so that penalty would be applicable in three cases out of the four. We have to consider why in some cases the penalty should go into the pocket of the individuals injured, and not in others. In the case of the obligation to keep the pipes charged, and allow all persons to use the water for the purpose of extinguishing fires, the provision is for the benefit of the public, and not of any individual specially, and the guarantee for the performance of the obligation is the liability to the public penalty of £10.'

CBS Songs Ltd* v *Amstrad Consumer Electronics plc [1988] AC 1013 House of Lords (Lord Keith of Kinkel, Lord Templeman, Lord Griffiths, Lord Oliver of Aylmerton and Lord Jauncey of Tullichettle)

Breach of copyright? – injunction

Facts

The first and second defendants made and sold respectively tape recording machines with a 'tape-to-tape' facility which were advertised in a manner likely to encourage home taping and copying of copyright material. The plaintiff record companies and copyright owners sought an injunction and the judge allowed them to amend their statement of claim to allege that the selling and advertising were an unlawful incitement to members of the public to commit an offence under s21(3) of the Copyright Act 1956. This decision was reversed on appeal: the plaintiffs appealed.

Held

The appeal would be dismissed.

Lord Templeman:

'BPI's [the plaintiff's] initial submissions are that Amstrad "authorised" infringement and that Amstrad is a joint infringer together with any person who uses an Amstrad machine for the purpose of making an infringing reproduction of a recording in which copyright subsists ... No manufacturer and no machine confers on the purchaser authority to copy unlawfully. The purchaser or other operator of the recorder determines whether he shall copy and what he shall copy. By selling the recorder Amstrad may facilitate copying in breach of copyright but do not authorise it.

BPI's next submission is that Amstrad by their advertisement authorise the purchaser of an Amstrad model to copy records in which copyright subsists. Amstrad's advertisement drew attention to the advantages of their models and to the fact that the recorder incorporated in the model could be employed in the copying of modern records. But the advertisement did not authorise the unlawful copying of records; on the contrary, the footnote warned that some copying required permission and made it clear that Amstrad had no authority to grant that permission ... The Amstrad advertisement is open to serve criticism but no purchaser of an Amstrad model could reasonably deduce from the facilities incorporated in the model or from Amstrad's advertisement that Amstrad possessed or purported to possess the authority to grant any required permission for a record to be copied ...

In the present case, Amstrad did not sanction, approve or countenance an infringing use of their model and ... in the context of the Copyright Act 1956 an authorisation means a grant or purported grant, which may be express or implied, of the right to do the act complained of ... Amstrad conferred on the purchaser the power to copy but did not grant or purport to grant the right to copy ...

BPI next submitted that Amstrad were joint infringers; they became joint infringers if and as soon as a purchaser decided to copy a record in which copyright subsisted; Amstrad could become a joint infringer not only with the immediate purchaser of an Amstrad model but also with anyone else who at any time in the future used the model to copy records. My Lords, Amstrad sells models which include facilities for receiving and recording broadcasts, disc records and taped records. All these facilities are lawful although the recording device is capable of being used for unlawful purposes. Once a model is sold Amstrad had no control over or interest in its use. In these circumstances the allegation that Amstrad is a joint infringer is untenable ...

My Lords, joint infringers are two or more persons who act in concert with one another pursuant to a common design in the infringement. In the present case there was no common design. Amstrad sold a machine and the purchaser or the operator of the machine decided the purpose for which the machine should from time to time be used. The machine was capable of being used for lawful or unlawful purposes. All recording machines and many other machines are capable of being used for unlawful purposes but manufacturers and retailers are not joint infringers if purchasers choose to break the law. Since Amstrad did not make or authorise other persons to make a record embodying a recording in which copyright subsisted, Amstrad did not entrench on the exclusive rights granted by the 1956 Act to copyright owners and Amstrad was not in breach of the duties imposed by the Act.

BPI submit, however, that, if the 1956 Act is defective to protect them, they are entitled to the protection of the common law ... in *Macmillan & Co Ltd* v *K & J Cooper* (1923) LR 51 Ind App 109 at 118, Lord

Atkinson said that an infringer of copyright disobeyed the injunction, "Thou shalt not steal." My Lords, these considerations cannot enhance the rights of owners of copyright or extend the ambit of infringement. The rights of BPI are derived from statute and not from the Ten Commandments. Those rights are defined by Parliament, not by the clergy or the judiciary. The rights of BPI conferred by the 1956 Act are in no way superior or inferior to any other legal rights; if BPI prove that on the true construction of the Act Amstrad and Dixons have infringed the rights conferred on BPI by the Act, the court will grant appropriate and effective reliefs and remedies. But the court will not invent additional rights or impose fresh burdens.

On behalf of BPI it was submitted that even if Amstrad did not authorise infringement and were not themselves infringers, nevertheless the activities of Amstrad in the sale and advertisement of Amstrad's models constitute a common law tort. The suggested torts were three in number, namely incitement to commit a tort, incitement to commit a criminal offence and negligence ...

My Lords, I accept that a defendant who procures a breach of copyright is liable jointly and severally with the infringer for the damages suffered by the plaintiff as a result of the infringement. The defendant is a joint infringer; he intends and procures and shares a common design that infringement shall take place. A defendant may procure an infringement by inducement, incitement or persuasion. But in the present case Amstrad does not procure infringement by offering for sale a machine which may be used for lawful or unlawful copying and it does not procure infringement by advertising the attractions of its machine to any purchaser who may decide to copy unlawfully. Amstrad is not concerned to procure and cannot procure unlawful copying ...

The next tort suggested by BPI was incitement to commit a criminal offence ... It is said that when a purchaser of an Amstrad model has in his possession a record in which copyright subsists that record becomes a "plate" and the purchaser commits an offence under s21(3) [of the 1956 Act] as soon as he forms the intention of copying that record.

There are two answers to this submission. First, as a matter of construction a record is not a plate but the product of the master recording which is a plate and from which the record is derived. Second, it is a mistake to compare crime and tort. If three persons are incited by a fourth to break into a house and cause damage each will be guilty of a crime and will receive separate punishment. The inciter will be guilty of the criminal offence of inciting others to commit crime. The other three will be guilty of the crime of breaking in. If the damage caused amounts to £5,000 then in a civil action the three who caused the damage will be jointly and severally liable for £5,000 and no more. The inciter will also be jointly and severally liable for the damage if he procures the commission of the tort and is a joint tortfeasor.'

Commentary
The Copyright Act 1956 has been repealed and replaced by the Copyright, Designs and Patents Act 1988 from various appointed days.

Cutler v *Wandsworth Stadium Ltd* [1949] AC 398 House of Lords (Lord Simonds, Lord du Parcq, Lord Normand, Lord Morton of Henryton and Lord Reid

Breach of statutory duty – civil action

Facts
By statute, so long as a totalisator was in operation, space had to be made available for bookmakers at dog racing tracks. A bookmaker brought an action for an alleged breach of this obligation.

Held
As the statutory provision was intended to benefit the public as opposed to bookmakers, a breach of it was a public and not a private wrong. The bookmaker therefore had no right of civil action against the occupier.

Lord Reid:

'The occupier is required to take such steps as are necessary to secure "that there is available for bookmakers space on the track where they can conveniently carry on bookmaking". This cannot mean that space must be provided on every occasion for as many bookmakers as wish to carry on business on that occasion. It cannot mean that, after the allotted space is fully occupied, an individual bookmaker who cannot find room there can demand further space where he can conveniently carry on business. The occupier must provide a space which is adequate in all the circumstances and which is in a convenient situation, but if he does that he has fulfilled his statutory obligation. He is not required by anything in the Act to find a place for each bookmaker who presents himself. If the Act does not give to an individual bookmaker a right to demand a place for himself, I find nothing to suggest that it gives him any other right enforceable by civil action. The sanction of prosecution appears to me to be appropriate and sufficient for the general obligation imposed by the sub-section.'

Commentary

Applied in *Thornton* v *Kirklees Metropolitan Borough Council* [1979] 3 WLR 1 and *Davis* v *Radcliffe* [1990] 1 WLR 821.

Gorris v *Scott* (1874) LR 9 Exch 125 Court of Exchequer (Kelly CB, Pigott and Pollock BB)

Breach of statutory duty – civil action

Facts

Contrary to their statutory obligation, the defendants, shipowners and carriers, did not provide separate pens for cattle and sheep which they were transporting. The object of this requirement was to prevent the spread of disease amongst the animals. The plaintiff's sheep were swept overboard by high seas and he claimed damages on the defendants' breach of statutory duty.

Held

The plaintiff's damage was entirely different from that which the statute sought to prevent: its object was to prevent disease, not accidents such as that which had occurred. The plaintiff's claim therefore failed.

Groves v *Lord Wimborne* [1898] 2 QB 402 Court of Appeal (A L Smith, Rigby and Vaughan Williams LJJ)

Breach of statutory duty – civil action

Facts

The plaintiff employee was injured by reason of the defendant factory owner's failure to fence machinery in accordance with statutory regulations made under the Factories Acts. For this breach, the defendant was fined the statutory £100.

Held

The plaintiff could recover damages for his personal injuries.

A L Smith LJ:

'... unless it can be found from the whole purview of the Act that the legislature intended that the only remedy for a breach of the duty created by the Act should be the infliction of a fine upon the master, it seems clear to me that upon proof of such a breach of duty and of an injury done to the workman, a cause of action is given to the workman against the master.'

Lonrho Ltd v *Shell Petroleum Co Ltd* [1981] 3 WLR 33 House of Lords (Lord Diplock, Lord Edmund-Davies, Lord Keith of Kinkel, Lord Scarman and Lord Bridge of Harwich)

Breach of statutory duty – conspiracy

Facts
Lonrho owned an oil pipeline from Beira to Umtali and Shell and BP used it. After UDI, by statute the United Kingdom prohibited the supply of oil to Rhodesia, as it then was. Lonrho alleged that, before UDI, Shell and BP had assured the illegal Rhodesian regime that it would continue to be supplied with oil and that this had influenced the decision to declare independence and prevented the sanctions from being effective.

Held
Contravention of the sanctions order did not give Lonrho a right to recover in tort any loss caused by it. Further, Lonrho could not claim in conspiracy as any agreement to contravene the sanctions would have been to further the commercial interests of Shell and BP, not to injure Lonrho.

Lord Diplock:

> 'The sanctions order thus creates a statutory prohibition on the doing of certain classes of acts and provides the means of enforcing the prohibition by prosecution for a criminal offence which is subject to heavy penalties including imprisonment. So one starts with the presumption laid down originally by Lord Tenterden CJ in *Doe d Bishop of Rochester* v *Bridges* (1831) 1 B & Ad 847, where he spoke of the "general rule" that "where an Act creates an obligation, and enforces the performance in a specified manner ... that performance cannot be enforced in any other manner", a statement that has frequently been cited with approval ever since, including on several occasions in speeches in this House. Where the only manner of enforcing performance for which the Act provides is prosecution for the criminal offence of failure to perform the statutory obligation or for contravening the statutory prohibition which the Act creates, there are two classes of exception to this general rule.
>
> The first is where on the true construction of the Act is apparent that the obligation or prohibition was imposed for the benefit or protection of a particular class of individuals, as in the case of the Factories Acts and similar legislation.
>
> ... The second exception is where the statute creates a public right (ie a right to be enjoyed by all those of Her Majesty's subjects who wish to avail themselves of it) and a particular member of the public suffers what Brett J in *Benjamin* v *Storr* (1874) LR 9 CP 400 described as "particular, direct and substantial" damage "other and different from that which was common to all the rest of the public".
>
> ... My Lords, it has been the unanimous opinion of the arbitrators with the concurrence of the umpire, of Parker J and of each of the three members of the Court of Appeal that the sanctions orders made pursuant to the Southern Rhodesia Act 1965 fell within neither of these two exceptions. Clearly they were not within the first category of exception. They were not imposed for the *benefit* or *protection* of a particular class of individuals who were engaged in supplying or delivering crude oil or petroleum products to Southern Rhodesia. They were intended to put an end to such transactions. Equally plainly they did not create any public right to be enjoyed by all those of Her Majesty's subjects who wished to avail themselves of it. On the contrary, what they did was to withdraw a previously existing right of citizens of, and companies incorporated in, the United Kingdom to trade with Southern Rhodesia in crude oil and petroleum products.
>
> ... In agreement with all those present and former members of the judiciary who have considered the

matter I can see no ground on which contraventions by Shell and BP of the sanctions orders, though not amounting to any breach of their contract with Lonrho, nevertheless constituted a tort for which Lonrho could recover in a civil suit any loss caused to them by such contraventions ...

This House, in my view, has an unfettered choice whether to confine the civil action of conspiracy to the narrow field to which alone it has an established claim or whether to extend this already anomalous tort beyond those narrow limits that are all that common sense and the application of the legal logic of the decided cases require.

My Lords, my choice is unhesitatingly the same as that of Parker J and all three members of the Court of Appeal. I am against extending the scope of the civil tort of conspiracy beyond acts done in execution of an agreement entered into by two or more persons for the purpose not of protecting their own interests but of injuring the interests of the plaintiff.'

Commentary
Applied in *RCA Corp* v *Pollard* [1982] 3 WLR 1007.
Explained in *Lonrho plc* v *Fayed* [1991] 3 WLR 188.

McCall v *Abelesz* [1976] 2 WLR 151 Court of Appeal (Lord Denning MR, Ormrod and Shaw LJJ)

Breach of statutory duty – civil liability

Facts
The plaintiff was tenant of a room in the defendant's house. At times, the gas, electricity and water supplies were cut off. The plaintiff sought damages for breach of the defendants' statutory duty not to harass him.

Held
His claim would fail as the relevant statutory duty did not give rise to a civil remedy in addition to imposing a criminal sanction.

Richardson v *Pitt-Stanley* [1995] 2 WLR 26 Court of Appeal (Russell and Stuart-Smith LJJ and Sir John Megaw)

Whether breach of Employers' Liability (Compulsory Insurance) Act 1969 gives right of action to injured worker

Facts
The plaintiff was severely injured during the course of his employment. The company had not taken out insurance as required by s1 Employers' Liability (Compulsory Insurance) Act 1969. The plaintiff successfully sued the company, but the company went into liquidation with no assets to satisfy the judgment. The plaintiff then brought an action against the company's directors and secretary claiming, inter alia, that they had committed an offence under s5 of the 1969 Act by having knowingly consented to or connived at the failure to insure, and the plaintiff had suffered loss equivalent to the sum he would have recovered had the company been properly insured. The master struck this out but the judge allowed the appeal, holding that the 1969 Act created a civil liability upon directors and officers not to consent to or connive at a breach of duty to insure.

Held
The appeal would be allowed (Sir John Megaw dissenting). Whether a breach of statutory duty which involved criminal liability also gave rise to a civil cause of action was a question of construction as to whether the relevant statutory provision as a whole, by express provision or by necessary implication, created such a civil liability. There was no express provision in the 1969 Act creating civil liability and the Act was intended to lie within the criminal law. Hence no civil liability could attach to the company or its directors or officers.

Per Sir John Megaw: The obligation on an employer to insure against injury sustained by its employees was imposed by Parliament to give protection to a particular class of individuals, the employees, to eliminate or reduce the risk to an injured employee of finding that he was deprived of his lawful compensation because of the financial position of the employer. Failure to perform this obligation should give rise to civil liability.

Commentary
Although the leading judgments in this case involve detailed consideration of the law, there is much force in Sir John Megaw's dissenting judgment. In it he noted that the statute in question imposed a criminal penalty and that under Lord Diplock's general rule in *Lonrho* v *Shell Petroleum* [1982] AC 173 performance could not be enforced in any other manner. Lord Diplock went on to say that there was an exception to this general rule where the obligation was imposed for the benefit or protection of a particular class of individuals. Sir John Megaw thought that this exception 'undoubtedly' applied in the present case.

Thornton v *Kirklees Metropolitan Borough Council* [1979] 3 WLR 1 Court of Appeal (Megaw and Roskill LJJ)

Breach of statutory duty – civil action

Facts
The plaintiff alleged that the defendant housing authority was in breach of its duty under the Housing (Homeless Persons) Act 1977 and claimed damages for the distress and inconvenience which he alleged he had suffered.

Held
Such an action – which would be treated as an action in tort – would lie. The Act had imposed a duty on the housing authority for the benefit of a specified category of persons, but it had prescribed no special remedy for breach of that duty.

Commentary
Applied: *Cutler* v *Wandsworth Stadium Ltd* [1949] AC 398.

X v *Bedfordshire County Council*; *M* v *Newham London Borough Council*; *E* v *Dorset County Council*; *Christmas* v *Hampshire County Council*; *Keating* v *Bromley London Borough Council* [1995] 3 WLR 152 House of Lords (Lord Jauncey, Lord Lane, Lord Ackner, Lord Browne-Wilkinson and Lord Nolan)

Breach of statutory duty

Facts
This case concerns five appeals to the House of Lords regarding breach of statutory duty, negligence in the exercise of a statutory power and the co-existence of a common law duty of care.

Held
1. 'That a breach of statutory duty did not, by itself, give rise to any private law cause of action, but such a right might arise where, on its true construction, the statute imposed a duty for the limited class of the public and there was a clear parliamentary intention to confer a private right of action for breach on members of that class; that there was no general rule for ascertaining whether a statute conferred such a right of action, but the absence of another remedy for breach and a clear intention to protect the limited class, were indications that a private right of action existed, and the mere existence of some other remedy was not necessarily decisive that no private right existed.'
2. 'That a plaintiff basing his claim on a careless exercise of a statutory duty had to show the existence of circumstances giving rise to a duty of care at common law.'
3. 'That in the performance of statutory functions a common law duty of care might arise, but the manner in which a discretion was exercised had to be distinguished from the implementation of the discretionary decision in practice; that where a statutory discretion was conferred on a public authority nothing done by the authority within the ambit of the discretion was actionable at common law, but where the decision complained of fell outside the statutory discretion it could give rise to common law liability; that the court could not adjudicate on the factors relevant to the exercise of the discretion in so far as they included matters of policy; that where such matters were justiciable the ordinary principles of negligence applied, but that a common law duty could not be imposed if it was inconsistent with, or had a tendency to discourage, the due performance of a statutory duty; and that, even where the defendant's servant was not alleged to owe a separate duty to the plaintiff, his negligent acts could constitute a breach of the duty of care, if any, owed directly by the defendant to the plaintiff.'

Commentary
This is now the leading case in this area. It is a long case (some 54 pages) and factually complex, involving as it does five appeals. However, that part of the speech of Lord Browne-Wilkinson in which he discusses the law is admirably lucid and concise for such a wide-ranging review and should be studied.

11 Employers' Liability

Coltman* v *Bibby Tankers Ltd, The Derbyshire [1987] 3 WLR 1181 House of Lords (Lord Keith of Kinkel, Lord Roskill, Lord Griffiths, Lord Oliver of Aylmerton and Lord Goff of Chieveley)

Employers' liability – defective equipment

Facts
A 90,000 ton bulk carrier owned by the defendants sank off the coast of Japan with the loss of all hands. The plaintiffs, personal representatives of a crew member, alleged that the ship had been unseaworthy because of defects in its hull and that the ship was defective 'equipment' within s1 of the Employer's Liability (Defective Equipment) Act 1969.

Held
The ship was 'equipment' in this sense, regardless of its size. Accordingly, where a seaman suffered in consequence of the unseaworthiness of a ship its owner was liable in negligence for that injury or loss of life.

Lord Oliver:

'My Lords, it is common ground that the 1969 Act was introduced with a view to rectifying what was felt to be the possible hardship to an employee resulting from the decision of this House in *Davie* v *New Merton Board Mills Ltd* [1959] 2 WLR 331. In that case an employee was injured by a defective drift supplied to him by his employers for the purpose of his work. The defect resulted from a fault in manufacture but the article had been purchased by the employers without knowledge of the defect from a reputable supplier and without any negligence on their part. It was held that the employers' duty was only to take reasonable care to provide a reasonably safe tool and that that duty had been discharged by purchasing from a reputable source an article whose latent defect they had no means of discovering. Thus the action against them failed although judgment was recovered against the manufacturer. Clearly this opened the door to the possibility that an employee required to work with, on or in equipment furnished by his employer and injured as a result of some negligent failure in design or manufacture might find himself without remedy in a case where the manufacturer and the employer were, to use the words of Viscount Simonds, "divided in time and space by decades and continents" so that the person actually responsible was no longer traceable or, perhaps, was insolvent or had ceased to carry on business ... Parliament accordingly met this by imposing on employers a vicarious liability and providing, in a case where injury was due to a defect caused by the fault of the third party, that the employer should, regardless of his own conduct, be liable to his employee as if he had been responsible for the defect, leaving it to him to pursue against the third party such remedies as he might have whether original or by way of contribution.'

Cook* v *Square D Ltd [1992] IRLR 34 Court of Appeal (Mustill, Mann and Farquharson LJJ)

Delegation of employer's duty to provide safe system of work

Facts
The plaintiff was sent by the defendants, his employers, to work as a computer consultant in Saudi Arabia. While working there he slipped into a small hole in the tiled floor of the control room and suffered injury. The plaintiff argued that the duty to provide a safe system of work was non-delegable, that the defendants were in breach of it and that the facts were analogous to those in *McDermid* v *Nash Dredging and Reclamation Co Ltd* [1987] AC 906 where the plaintiff's claim had succeeded.

Held
Rejecting the analogy, there had been no breach of duty by the defendants: the site was some 8,000 miles away and both the site occupiers and the general contractors were reliable companies who were aware of their responsibility for the safety of workers on site. However, there was not ruled out the possibility that circumstances might require employers in the UK to take steps to satisfy themselves as to the safety of foreign sites, for example where a number of their employees were going to work on a foreign site or where one or two employees were going to work there for a considerable period of time.

General Cleaning Contractors Ltd v *Christmas* [1953] 2 WLR 6 House of Lords (Earl Jowitt, Lord Oaksey, Lord Reid and Lord Tucker)

Employers' liability – safe system of working

Facts
The plaintiff, a window-cleaner for twenty years, was employed as such by the defendants. In cleaning sash windows, he followed the usual practice of standing on the outside sill and cleaning first the top half: this was then pushed up so as to leave just enough hand-hold while cleaning the bottom half. On one occasion the sash fell shut, dislodging the plaintiff's hand and causing him to fall. He sued his employers in negligence.

Held
The plaintiff's claim would succeed. The method of cleaning windows, although customary, was known to be dangerous and the employers were under a duty to devise a safer system.

Lord Reid:

> 'It is the duty of the employer to consider the situation, to devise a suitable system, to instruct his men what they must do, and to supply any implements that may be required such as in this case wedges or objects to be put on the window sill to prevent the window from closing. No doubt, he cannot be certain that his men will do as they are told when they are working alone. But, if he does all that is reasonable to ensure that his safety system is operated, he will have done what he is bound to do. In this case the appellants do not appear to have done anything as they thought they were entitled to leave the taking of precautions to the discretion of each of their men. In this I think that they were in fault, and I think that this accident need not have happened if the appellants had done as I hold they ought to have done.'

Commentary
Applied in *Pape* v *Cumbria County Council* [1992] 2 All ER 211.

Hewett v *Alf Brown's Transport Ltd* (1992) The Times 4 February Court of Appeal (Nourse, Taylor and Scott LJJ)

Lead poisoning from spouse's overalls – liability of spouse's employer

Facts
The plaintiff suffered lead poisoning as a result of coming into contact with lead oxide powder while washing her husband's overalls. Her husband worked for the defendants and his job required him to drive a lorry containing waste, including lead oxide, from a large gasworks which was being dismantled to a tip. However, her husband's exposure to lead was no more than one hour a day.

Held
There was such a low level of exposure to lead that no duty of care to the husband arose, nor was there any duty to provide washing facilities or to warn him of the risk of taking his overalls and boots home with him. Given that the exposure of the husband was minimal, the exposure of the plaintiff was also minimal and there had therefore been no breach by the defendants of their statutory obligations or of their common law duty to her. However, the court did accept that an employer owed a duty of care to members of an employee's family in respect of foreseeeable risk.

Hudson v *Ridge Manufacturing Co Ltd* [1957] 2 WLR 948 High Court (Streatfield J)

Employers' liability – competent staff

Facts
Over the years, Chadwick had indulged in horseplay at the expense of his fellow employees. The defendant employers were aware of this and had frequently issued reprimands and warnings. On the occasion in question Chadwick's prank caused the plaintiff a fractured wrist.

Held
The employers were liable as they had been in breach of their duty at common law to provide competent staff.

Streatfield J:

> 'It is really unarguable that here is a case where there did exist, as it were in the system of work, a source of danger, through the conduct of one of the employers' workmen, of which the employers knew: repeated conduct which went on over a long space of time, and which they did nothing whatever to remove, except to reprimand and go on reprimanding to no effect whatever ... whatever steps were taken, it was the duty of the employers to put a stop to such conduct. By that time they must have known that one day there might be injury if Mr Chadwick went on with this sort of conduct. He had done it before, he went on doing it and still he was allowed to remain in their employment and was not removed from it. In my judgment, therefore, the injury was sustained as a result of the employers' failure to take proper steps to put an end to that conduct, to see that it would not happen again and, if it did happen again, to remove the source of it. It was for that reason that this injury resulted. In those circumstances, although it is an unusual type of case, I have come to the conclusion that counsel for the plaintiff is right in his contention and that the employers are liable for the plaintiff's injuries.'

Knowles v *Liverpool City Council* [1993] 4 All ER 321 House of Lords (Lord Keith, Lord Templeman, Lord Jauncey, Lord Browne-Wilkinson and Lord Mustill)

Whether flagstones equipment

Facts
The plaintiff, who was employed by the defendant council to lay flagstones, was injured when a flagstone he was handling broke. He claimed damages for his injury alleging, inter alia, that the council had been

negligent under s1 Employers' Liability (Defective Equipment) Act 1969 in providing him with equipment in a defective condition. The recorder held that the flagstone was 'equipment' within the meaning of the Act, and the Court of Appeal dismissed the appeal. The council appealed to the House of Lords.

Held
That the purpose of the 1969 Act was to protect employees where the employer, despite having exercised all proper care and relying on a reputable supplier, had exposed his employee to dangerous material. It was thus consistent with the purpose of the Act to construe the word 'equipment' widely so that it included every article provided by an employer to an employee for the purpose of the employer's business. The House applied its earlier wide approach in *Coltman* v *Bibby Tankers* [1988] AC 276.

McDermid v *Nash Dredging and Reclamation Co Ltd* [1987] AC 906 House of Lords (Lord Hailsham of St Marylebone LC, Lord Bridge of Harwich, Lord Brandon of Oakbrook, Lord Mackay of Clashfern and Lord Ackner)

Employers' liability – duty of care

Facts
The defendants employed the plaintiff as a deckhand for dredging operations carried out by the defendants and their parent company. Working on a tug which was owned by the parent company and controlled by one of their employees, the tug-master, the plaintiff suffered serious injuries. The accident had been caused by the tug-master's negligence.

Held
The defendants were liable as their duty of care was personal or non-delegable, but they had delegated both their duty of devising a safe system of work, and its operation, to the tug-master.

Lord Hailsham of St Marylebone LC:

> 'The plaintiff's claim in the proceedings was based on the allegation inter alia, of a "non-delegable" duty resting on his employers to take reasonable care to provide a "safe system of work" ... The defendants did not, and could not, dispute the existence of such a duty of care, nor that it was 'non-delegable' in the special sense in which the phrase is used in this connection. This special sense does not involve the proposition that the duty cannot be delegated in the sense that it is incapable of being the subject of delegation, but only that the employer cannot escape liability if the duty has been delegated and then not properly performed. Equally the defendants could not and did not attempt to dispute that it would be a central and crucial feature of any safe system on the instant facts that it would prevent so far as possible the occurrence of such an accident as actually happened, viz injury to the plaintiff as the result of the use of Ina's engine so as to move the Ina before both the ropes were clear of the dredger and stowed safely in board and the plaintiff was in a position of safety.
>
> Since such a system could easily have been designed and put in operation at the time of the accident in about half a dozen different ways, and since it is quite obvious that such a system would have prevented the accident had it been in operation, and since the duty to provide it was "non-delegable" in the sense that the defendants cannot escape liability by claiming to have delegated performance of their duty, it is a little difficult to see what possible defence there could ever have been to these proceedings.'

Lord Brandon:

'A statement of the relevant principle of law can be divided into three parts. First, an employer owes to his employee a duty to exercise reasonable care to ensure that the system of work provided for him is a safe one. Second, the provision of a safe system of work has two aspects: (a) the devising of such a system and (b) the operation of it. Third, the duty concerned has been described alternatively as either personal or non-delegable. The meaning of these expressions is not self-evident and needs explaining. The essential characteristic of the duty is that, if it is not performed, it is no defence for the employer to show that he delegated its performance to a person, whether his servant or not his servant, whom he reasonably believed to be competent to perform it. Despite such delegation the employer is liable for the non-performance of the duty.'

Pape v *Cumbria County Council* [1992] ICR 132 High Court (Waite J)

Employer's liability – duty to warn of dangers

Facts

The plaintiff aged 57 was employed as a part-time cleaner by the defendants and was required to use various detergents and chemical cleaning products in the course of her employment. The defendants supplied the plaintiff with gloves, which she used occasionally, but they did not warn her of the dangers of irritant dermatitis from sustained exposure of skin to cleaning products. The plaintiff later began to suffer from irritated skin on her hands and wrists, which developed into acute dermatitis affecting her entire skin, and she claimed damages for personal injuries.

Held

Her action would be successful as the defendants had been under a duty to warn her of the dangers and, as no attempt had been made to give her any such warning, the defendants had been in breach of their duty of care.

Waite J:

[Counsel] are both satisfied that there is no English authority precisely on this point. I do not think there is any difficulty about tackling this case from first principles. The question to be answered here is the same as the question that was exposed by the House of Lords in *General Cleaning Contractors Ltd* v *Christmas* [1953] AC 180 at 193, namely, reading from the speech of Lord Reid, the following:

"... whether it is the duty of the appellants to instruct their servants what precautions they ought to take, and to take reasonable steps to see that those instructions are carried out."

The House held in that case in the context of a claim against a window cleaning company that it had a duty not only to provide a safe system of work but to instruct employees in the use of it. The answer to that question was Yes. So it is in my judgment in the present case. The dangers of dermatitis or acute eczema from the sustained exposure of unprotected skin to chemical cleansing agents is well known, well enough known to make it the duty of a reasonable employer to appreciate the risks it presents to members of his cleaning staff but at the same time not so well known as to make it obvious to his staff without any necessity for warning or instruction.

There was a duty on the defendants to warn their cleaners of the dangers of handling chemical cleaning materials with unprotected hands and to instruct them as to the need to wear gloves at all times. It is common ground that no such warning or instruction was given and that is sufficient to place the defendants in breach of their duty of care. Since that is enough to establish liability I think it undesirable that I should attempt to answer the question, to which any reply would perforce be obiter in the present case, as to whether the placing of rubber gloves in the cleaning cupboard with a facility for replacement on demand was sufficient to discharge the defendants' further duty of care to ensure that any warning and instruction had it been given was observed and carried out ...

It remains to deal with damages. Counsel have already been able to agree a formula for the assessment of special damages ... subject to only one outstanding issue, namely the multiplier to be applied to the figure which is the already agreed multiplicand for lost future earnings ... The plaintiff enjoyed her work and apart from her eczema is in basic good health. She might reasonably have expected had it not been for the defendants' breach of duty to carry on working for someone, even if retired from the defendants' employment at 60, in a job for which there always seems to be a demand whatever the fortunes of the economy as a whole. All in all I consider that the multiplier of five would be appropriate.

As for general damages, pain and suffering and loss of amenity, counsel are once again agreed that there is no reported decision on facts sufficiently similar to provide an analogy for the instant case. Dealing with the matter at large, therefore, and remembering this is a case where the plaintiff's pain, embarrassment and discomfort were of a severe order when at their height and her symptoms will to some extent at least as regards her hands remain with her for ever, I have decided an appropriate figure to award under this head would be £22,000.'

Walker v *Northumberland County Council* [1994] NLJ 1659 High Court (Colman J)
Safe system of work – duty not to cause psychiatric damage

Facts
The plaintiff was employed by the defendant council as an area social services officer, responsible for managing four teams of social workers in an area with a high proportion of child-care problems. In 1986, the plaintiff suffered a nervous breakdown because of the stress and pressure of work, and was off work for three months. Before he returned to work it was agreed assistance would be provided to lessen his work burden, but in the event only limited assistance was provided. Six months later the plaintiff suffered a second breakdown and was forced to cease work permanently. The plaintiff sued his employer claiming damages for breach of its duty of care to take reasonable steps to avoid exposing him to a health-endangering work-load.

Held
Where it is reasonably foreseeable to an employer that an employee might suffer a nervous breakdown because of the stress and pressures of his work-load, the employer is under a duty of care, as part of his duty to provide a safe system of work, not to cause the employee psychiatric damage by the volume and character of the work which the employee is required to perform.

Colman J:

> 'In the present case, the mental illness and the lasting impairment of his personality which Mr Walker sustained in consequence of the 1987 breakdown was so substantial and damaging that the magnitude of the risk to which he was exposed must be regarded as relatively large. Moreover, there can, in my judgment, be no doubt on the evidence that by 1985 at the latest, it was reasonably foreseeable to Mr Davison [the plaintiff's superior], given the information which I have held that he then had, that by reason of stress of work there was in general *some* risk that Mr Walker might sustain a mental breakdown of some sort in consequence of his work. ...
>
> I have no doubt that it ought to have been foreseen by Mr Davison that if Mr Walker was again exposed to the same work-load as he had been handling at the time of his breakdown in October 1986 there was risk that he would once again succumb to mental illness and that such illness would be likely to end his career as an area manager and perhaps his career in the social services ... In my judgment [Mr Davison] should have appreciated that Mr Walker was a man distinctly more vulnerable to psychiatric damage than he had appeared to be in 1986 ... In my judgment, once [support staff were] not fully available to assist Mr Walker, it was quite likely, if not inevitable, that he would again break down. I find that the failure ... to provide continuous and effective back-up for Mr Walker was fatal to Mr Walker's ability to

survive ... In the result, it is established that by April 1987 Mr Walker was exposed in his job to a reasonably foreseeable risk to his mental health which materially exceeded the risk to be anticipated in the ordinary course of an area officer's job. Was it in those circumstances reasonable for the council to take action to alleviate or remove that risk? In my view, the only course which would have had a reasonable probability of preventing another mental breakdown was the provision of continuous or at least substantial back-up for Mr Walker ... Having regard to the reasonably foreseeable size of the risk of repetition of Mr Walker's illness if his duties were not alleviated by effective additional assistance and to the reasonably foreseeable gravity of the mental breakdown which might result if nothing were done, I have come to the conclusion that the standard of care to be expected of a reasonable local authority required that in March 1987 such additional assistance should be provided ... In the event, there will be judgment for the plaintiff on liability with damages yet to be assessed.'

12 Product Liability

Evans v *Triplex Safety Glass Co Ltd* [1936] 1 All ER 283 High Court (Porter J)
Negligence – liability of manufacturer

Facts
The plaintiff was injured when, for no apparent reason, his car windscreen shattered. He had had the car over a year and the windscreen had been fitted by the car-makers. The plaintiff sued the manufacturers of the windscreen.

Held
The plaintiff's claim would fail as, in the circumstances, it could not be presumed that the manufacturers had been at fault.

Grant v *Australian Knitting Mills Ltd* [1936] AC 85 Privy Council (Lord Hailsham LC, Lord Blanesburgh, Lord Macmillan, Lord Wright and Sir Lancelot Sanderson)
Negligence – liability of manufacturer

Facts
The plaintiff contracted a skin disease after wearing underpants manufactured by the defendants. The disease was due to an excess of chemical left in the garment during manufacture.

Held
The defendants were liable to the plaintiff on the principle of *Donoghue (or McAlister)* v *Stevenson*.

Lord Wright:

'The presence of the deleterious chemical in the pants, due to negligence in manufacture, was a hidden and latent defect, just as much as were the remains of the snail in the opaque bottle : it could not be detected by any examination that could reasonably be made. Nothing happened between the making of the garments and their being worn to change their condition. The garments were made by the manufacturers for the purpose of being worn exactly as they were worn in fact by the appellant: it was not contemplated that they should be first washed. It is immaterial that the appellant has a claim in contract against the retailers, because that is a quite independent cause of action, based on different considerations, even though the damage may be the same. Equally irrelevant is any question of liability between the retailers and the manufacturers on the contract of sale between them. The tort liability is independent of any question of contract.

It was argued, but not perhaps very strongly, that *Donoghue's* case was a case of food or drink to be consumed internally, whereas the pants here were to be worn externally. No distinction, however, can be logically drawn for this purpose between a noxious thing taken internally and a noxious thing applied externally: the garments were made to be worn next the skin: indeed Lord Atkin specifically puts as examples of what is covered by the principle he is enunciating things operating externally, such as "an ointment, a soap, a cleaning fluid, or cleaning powder" ... The decision in *Donoghue's* case did not depend on the bottle being stoppered and sealed; the essential point in this regard was that the article should reach the consumer or user subject to the same defect as it had when it left the manufacturer. That this was true of the garments is in their Lordships' opinion beyond question. At most there might in other cases be a greater difficulty of proof of that fact.'

13 Occupiers' Liability

Andrews* v *Schooling [1991] 1 WLR 783 Court of Appeal (Balcombe and Beldam LJJ and Sir Denys Buckley)

Section 1 of the Defective Premises Act 1972

Facts
The third defendants granted the plaintiffs a 199 year lease of a ground floor flat including a cellar. Extensive work had been done to the flat itself but the only work which had been done in the cellar was the painting of the walls. The plaintiff later discovered that the flat suffered from penetrating dampness which she alleged emanated from the cellar. She claimed damages from the defendants, alleging, inter alia, that the defendants were in breach of the duty which they owed to her under s1 of the 1972 Act. The defendants argued that they were not liable because they had not done any relevant work on the flat so that it could not be said that they had taken on work in relation to the cellar. Thus they argued that the Act applied only to cases of misfeasance and not to non-feasance.

Held
This argument would be rejected and the plaintiff awarded damages. A dwelling was unfit for habitation when it was without some essential attribute when the works were completed, even though the problems arising therefrom had not then been patent.

Beldam LJ:

'In my view, s1 of the Defective Premises Act 1972 applies to the failure to carry out necessary work as well as carrying it out badly. The evidence before the court establishes that the plaintiff's flat was not fit for habitation. That was due to the manner in which the work undertaken by the defendants for or in connection with the provision of the flat had been carried out.'

Billings (AC) & Sons Ltd* v *Riden [1957] 3 WLR 496 House of Lords (Viscount Simonds, Lord Reid, Lord Cohen, Lord Keith of Avonholm and Lord Somervell of Harrow)

Occupier's liability – independent contractor

Facts
The appellants had been employed by the occupier of a house to reconstruct the front pathway. In the course of carrying out this work, they laid a foundation of stones, bordered by a muddy area. On this was laid a plank which, for the time being, was the only means of access to the house. This plank passed alongside some railings which guarded it from a sunken basement next door. The appellants removed these railings also. One night the respondent, a lawful visitor to the premises, fell into the basement and was injured. She claimed against the appellants.

Held

The appellants, who were independent contractors of the occupier, owed a duty to take reasonable care for the safety of visitors. They had been in breach of this duty as they had made the route to the house unsafe: they were therefore liable. Her damages were reduced by 50 per cent for contributory negligence: she knew the path was dangerous, but refused assistance and did not have a torch, despite the fact that it was dark.

Commentary

Overruled: *Malone* v *Laskey* [1907] 2 KB 141 so far as it dealt with negligence.

British Railways Board v *Herrington* [1972] 2 WLR 537 House of Lords (Lord Reid, Lord Morris of Borth-y-Gest, Lord Wilberforce, Lord Pearson and Lord Diplock)

Negligence – duty owed to trespasser

Facts

The respondent, a six year old boy, was playing in a field beside which ran the appellants' railway line. The fence between the field and the line was in a bad state of repair and in fact, people often broke through it to cross the railway line. Some weeks before the appellants had been told of the presence of children on the line. The respondent passed through the fence and was electrocuted on the live rail.

Held

The appellants owed the respondent a duty of common humanity and though he was a trespasser, he was entitled to recover damages.

Lord Reid:

> 'So the question whether an occupier is liable in respect of an accident to a trespasser on his land would depend on whether a conscientious humane man with his knowledge, skill and resources could reasonably have been expected to have done or refrained from doing before the accident something which would have avoided it. If he knew before the accident that there was a substantial probability that trespassers would come, I think that most people would regard as culpable failure to give any thought to their safety. He might often reasonably think, weighing the seriousness of the danger and the degree of likelihood of trespassers coming against the burden he would have to incur in preventing their entry or making his premises safe, or curtailing his own activities on his land, that he could not fairly be expected to do anything. But, if he could at small trouble and expense take some effective action, again I think that most people would think it inhumane and culpable not to do that. If some such principle is adopted, there will no longer be any need to strive to imply a fictitious licence. It would follow that an impecunious occupier with little assistance at hand would often be excused from doing something which a large organisation with ample staff would be expected to do.'

Lord Morris of Borth-y-Gest:

> 'The duty that lay on the appellants was a limited one. There was no duty to ensure that no trespasser could enter on the land. And, certainly, an occupier owes no duty to make his land fit for trespassers to trespass in. Nor need he make surveys of his land in order to decide whether dangers exist of which he is unaware. The general law remains that one who trespasses does so at his peril. But, in the present case, there were a number of special circumstances: (a) the place where the fence was faulty was near to a public path and public ground; (b) a child might easily pass through the fence; (c) if a child did pass through and go on to the track, he would be in grave danger of death or serious bodily harm; (d) a child might not realise the risk involved in touching the live rail or being in a place where a train might pass at speed. Because

of these circumstances (all of them well known and obvious) there was, in my view, a duty which, while not amounting to the duty of care which an occupier owes to a visitor, would be a duty to take such steps as common sense or common humanity would dictate; they would be steps calculated to exclude or to warn or otherwise within reasonable and practicable limits to reduce or avert danger.'

Lord Diplock:

'I would then seek to summarise the characteristics of an occupier's duty to trespassers ... First, the duty does not arise until the occupier has actual knowledge either of the presence of the trespasser on his land or of facts which make it likely that the trespasser will come on to his land; and has also actual knowledge of facts as to the condition of his land or of activities carried out on it which are likely to cause personal injury to a trespasser who is unaware of the danger. He is under no duty to the trespasser to make any enquiry or inspection to ascertain whether or not such facts do exist. His liability does not arise until he actually knows of them.

Secondly, once the occupier has actual knowledge of such facts, his own failure to appreciate the likelihood of the trespasser's presence or the risk to him involved, does not absolve the occupier from his duty to the trespasser if a reasonable man possessed of the actual knowledge of the occupier would recognise that likelihood and that risk.

Thirdly, the duty when it arises is limited to taking reasonable steps to enable the trespasser to avoid the danger. Where the likely trespasser is a child too young to understand or heed a written or a previous oral warning, this may involve providing reasonable physical obstacles to keep the child away from the danger.

Fourthly, the relevant likelihood to be considered is of the trespasser's presence at the actual time and place of danger to him. The degree of likelihood needed to give rise to the duty cannot, I think be more closely defined than as being such as would compel a man of ordinary humane feelings to take some steps to mitigate the risk of injury to the trespasser to which the particular danger exposes him. It will thus depend on all the circumstances of the case: the permanent or intermittent character of the danger; the severity of the injuries which it is likely to cause; in the case of children, the attractiveness to them of that which constitutes the dangerous object or condition of the land; the expense involved in giving effective warning of it to the kind of trespasser likely to be injured, in relation to the occupier's resources in money or in labour.'

Commentary

Distinguished: *Edwards v Railway Executive* [1952] AC 737.
   Not followed: *Addie (R) & Sons (Collieries) Ltd v Dumbreck* [1929] AC 358.
   Applied in *Pannett v P McGuinness & Co Ltd* [1972] 3 WLR 386.

Cunningham v Reading Football Club Ltd [1991] PIQR 141 High Court (Drake J)

Football club – duty to visitor policeman

Facts

As the defendants were aware, at a match on their ground only four months earlier spectators had loosened concrete by kicking and jumping on it and had then thrown concrete missiles at the police. After that match no measures had been taken to make it more difficult to loosen the concrete. On this occasion, the plaintiff police officers had all been struck by pieces of concrete loosened from the terraces and thrown at them by spectators. The defendants had known in advance that crowd trouble might well occur.

Held

The plaintiffs were entitled to damages for personal injury caused by the defendants' negligence and breach of statutory duty under the Occupiers' Liability Act 1957. Drake J said that, given the appallingly dilapidated state of the ground, the conduct of the spectators was easily foreseeable by the defendants and was a strong probability. A reasonably prudent occupier would have realised the concrete in the ground was dangerous, because it might supply a source of missiles, and would have taken steps to remove or minimise the risk.

Ferguson v *Welsh* [1987] 1 WLR 1553 House of Lords (Lord Keith of Kinkel, Lord Brandon of Oakbrook, Lord Griffiths, Lord Oliver of Aylmerton and Lord Goff of Chieveley)

Occupier's liability – duty to contractor's employee

Facts
As part of a council's sheltered housing scheme, it was necessary to demolish a building and Spence's tender for this aspect of the work was accepted on condition, amongst others, that the council's approval must be obtained before subcontractors were employed on the site. Without obtaining such approval, Spence subcontracted the work to the Welsh brothers and, as they adopted an unsafe system of work, the appellant, their employee, was injured. The judge held that the Welsh brothers were liable and the Court of Appeal ordered a new trial against Spence. Were the council also liable?

Held
No, because the appellant had been unable to show that the council knew or ought to have known that Spence would subcontract the work without authority to persons who would employ an unsafe system of work. The council had not been in breach of the common duty of care owed to visitors under s2(2) of the Occupiers' Liability Act 1957 or the ordinary common law duty of care.

Lord Keith of Kinkel:

> 'It would not ordinarily be reasonable to expect an occupier of premises having engaged a contractor whom he has reasonable grounds for regarding as competent, to supervise the contractor's activities in order to ensure that he was discharging his duty to his employees to observe a safe system of work. In special circumstances, on the other hand, where the occupier knows or has reason to suspect that the contractor is using an unsafe system of work, it might well be reasonable for the occupier to take steps to see that the system was made safe.
>
> The crux of the present case therefore, is whether the council knew or had reason to suspect that Mr Spence, in contravention of the terms of his contract, was bringing in cowboy operators who would proceed to demolish the building in a thoroughly unsafe way. The thrust of the affidavit evidence admitted by the Court of Appeal was that Mr Spence had long been in the habit of sub-contracting his demolition work to persons who proceeded to execute it by the unsafe method of working from the bottom up. If the evidence went the length of indicating that the council knew or ought to have known that this was Mr Spence's usual practice, there would be much to be said for the view that they should be liable to Mr Ferguson. No responsible council should countenance the unsafe working methods of cowboy operators. It should be clearly foreseeable that such methods exposed the employees of such operators to very serious dangers. It is entirely reasonable that a council occupying premises where demolition work is to be executed should take steps to see that the work is carried out by reputable and careful contractors. Here, however, the council did contract with Mr Spence subject to the condition that sub-contracting without their consent was prohibited. The fresh evidence sought to be adduced by Mr Ferguson does not go the length of supporting any inference that the council or their responsible officers knew or ought to have known that Mr Spence was likely to contravene this prohibition.'

Gitsham v *C H Pearce & Sons plc* [1992] PIQR 57 Court of Appeal (Glidewell and Stocker LJJ)

Occupier's liability – snow on factory road

Facts

The plaintiff fell outside his place of work on a roadway which was covered with ice and snow. He brought an action against his employers alleging that they were in breach of their statutory duty (under s29 of the Factories Act 1961) in failing to ensure that all means of access to his place of work had been gritted by the start of the working day.

Held

The plaintiff's appeal would be dismissed as the employers had an extensive procedure for clearing snow and ice which was being properly carried out on the morning of the accident and the defendants had done all that was reasonably practicable in the severe weather conditions to ensure that the access roads were safe. Glidewell LJ said that even if the particular area had not been gritted, on the evidence, particularly the severity of the weather, it had been open to the judge to conclude that the employers were not in breach of their statutory duty.

Glasgow Corporation v *Taylor* [1922] 1 AC 44 House of Lords (Lord Buckmaster, Lord Atkinson, Lord Shaw, Lord Sumner and Lord Wrenbury)

Occupier's liability – children

Facts

A boy of seven went with some other children to the defendant's recreation ground where, easily accessible, were shrubs with poisonous berries looking like grapes or cherries. The boy ate some – and died as a result.

Held

If the basic facts were proved, the defendants would be guilty of negligence.

Lord Atkinson:

> 'The liability of defendants in cases of this kind rests, I think, in the last resort upon their knowledge that by their action they may bring children of tender years, unable to take care of themselves, yet inquisitive and easily tempted, into contact, in a place in which they, the children, have a right to be, with things alluring or tempting to them, and possibly in appearance harmless, but which, unknown to them and well known to the defendants, are hurtful or dangerous if meddled with... I think, in the latter case, as much as in the former, the defendant would be bound, by notice or warning or some other adequate method, to protect the children from injury. In this case the averments are that the appellants did nothing of the kind. If that be true they were in my view guilty of negligence, giving the plaintiff a right of action.'

Harris v *Birkenhead Corporation* [1976] 1 WLR 279 Court of Appeal (Megaw, Lawton and Ormrod LJJ)

Negligence – occupation or control

Facts

The defendants acquired X's house by compulsory purchase order which stated that within a specified time they would enter and take possession. X vacated the house, but did not inform the defendants of the date of her departure. The defendants knew that property in the area was likely to be vandalised if left vacant and although they generally boarded up empty houses, they did not do so to X's house. The house was left empty by the defendants for three months, during which time it was ruined by vandals. The plaintiff, aged four and a half, wandered into the house from a nearby playground and was severely injured when she fell from a window.

Held

The defendants were occupiers of the premises and liable because they had been in breach of their duty to the plaintiff.

Ormrod LJ:

> 'The only question on the first part of this case is whether the corporation is properly regarded in law as a person occupying or in control of the premises in which the accident happened... there is, in my judgment, only one possible answer to that question. They were at all material times the persons with the right to control that property. It would have been almost absurd to suggest that, in the circumstances of this case, the second defendant [the previous owner] could have been expected by the law to go to expense in securing these premises against the damage which was inevitable and was bound to happen to them immediately or very soon after the tenant had vacated them. In those circumstances it would be a disastrous injustice to her to hold her liable for this appalling accident.'

Lawton LJ:

> '... a man cannot claim that he has no knowledge when he has shut his eyes to the obvious.'

McAuley v *Bristol City Council* [1992] 1 All ER 749 Court of Appeal (Neill and Ralph Gibson LJJ)

Landlord's duty under Defective Premises Act 1972

Facts

The plaintiff and her husband were weekly tenants of a house owned by the defendants. The tenancy agreement required the defendants to keep the structure and exterior of the property in good repair while the plaintiffs were required to keep the premises, including the garden, in a clean and orderly condition. Under condition 6(c) of the agreement the plaintiffs were required to give the defendants access 'for any purpose which may from time to time be required ...' The plaintiff fell and sustained injury because a concrete garden step was unstable and, in an action for damages, she alleged, inter alia, that the defendants had been in breach of the duty of care imposed by s4(1) of the Defective Premises Act 1972.

Held

Her action would be successful.

Ralph Gibson LJ:

> 'Section 4(1) [of the 1972 Act] applies where the landlord is under an obligation to repair. A duty of care is imposed upon the landlord, assuming proof of knowledge or means of knowledge under subs(2) in respect of a "relevant defect", that is to say a defect which constitutes a failure to carry out the repairing obligation. Subsection (4) extends the basis of liability by treating the landlord as being under an

obligation to repair, when in fact he is not. The extension is made when the landlord is given a right to enter "to carry out any description of maintenance or repair" but the extension of liability is not general. The landlord, when he is given a right to enter to carry out "any description of maintenance or repair" is to be treated as if he were under an obligation to the tenant "for that description of maintenance or repair", not all and any description of maintenance or repair.

Thus, in this case, assuming that there was no actual obligation, contractual or statutory, to repair the garden step, the plaintiff, to succeed under s4, must show that the defect in the garden step was a "relevant defect", ie that it was a defect in the state of the premises which constituted a failure by the council to carry out repair of a description for which the council had a right to enter the premises.

There is, I think, no warrant for a wide construction of the words of the section. They apply to all landlords, and not merely to local authorities, and can operate so as to impose a substantial burden upon a landlord in respect of premises under the immediate control of the tenant and in respect of which the landlord has assumed no contractual obligation.

Condition 6(c) applies to "any purpose which may from time to time be required by the council"; it does not say "for any purpose for which the council may be required to enter". I do not accept that the right of entry is limited to entry for the purpose of discharging the obligations of the council. The words are not, I think, perfectly drafted but the meaning seems to me to be clear, namely "any purpose for which from time to time entry may be required by the council" ...

In imposing the obligations stated in s4 of the 1972 Act where there is no obligation to repair, whether contractual or statutory, Parliament required proof of a tenancy which "expressly or impliedly gives the landlord the right to enter the premises to carry out any description of maintenance or repair". If such a right is proved, the landlord is, if the other conditions are satisfied, to be treated as under an obligation to the tenant for that description of repair. Parliament thus legislated by reference to the common law. If the common law says that the right to repair is implied, the statute imposes the obligation. The provisions apply to any tenancy agreement. The fact that, for this purpose, it would suit the tenants very well to have implied against them a right in favour of the landlord enforceable against the tenants does not, in my judgment, enable the court to imply such a right in circumstances where it could not properly do so upon the relevant principles ...

The decisive question in this case, therefore, is whether the court can properly hold that the council impliedly reserved a right against the tenant to carry out repair to the garden ... After some hesitation, I have reached the conclusion that the necessary reservation should be implied in restricted terms. The defect in the step exposed the tenants and visitors to the premises to the risk of injury. In this case ... the basis of the agreement was that the premises would be kept in reasonable and habitable condition and that, apart from interior decorative work and work to keep the garden in a clean and orderly condition, the work would be done by the council. The council had expressly reserved the right to enter "for any purpose for which from time to time entry may be required", if I have correctly construed the term, and the agreement did not expressly identify those purposes. If there should be a defect in the garden which exposed the tenants and lawful visitors to the premises to significant risk of injury, then I think that, to give business efficacy to the agreement ... a right should be implied in the council to carry out repairs for the removal of that risk of injury. A reasonable tenant could not sensibly object to such a right. If the council became aware of a dangerous defect in the steps of a steep garden, as in this case, and asked the tenant for access to repair it, in the interest of all persons who might be expected to be affected by the defect, the court could, in my judgment, properly require the tenant to allow such access upon the basis of an implied right in the council to do the work. So limited, I would hold that the implied right to enter to do the necessary repair was proved and the [defendants'] appeal should be dismissed.'

McGeown v *Northern Ireland Housing Executive* [1994] 3 All ER 53 House of Lords (Lords Keith, Goff, Browne-Wilkinson, Mustill and Lloyd)

Liability of owner of land to persons using right of way

Facts

The appellant was using a public right of way when she tripped in a hole and was injured. She sued the owner of the land over which the right of way ran. The trial judge and Court of Appeal in Northern Ireland dismissed her action and she appealed to the House of Lords claiming (a) that the rule that the owner of land over which a public right of way ran was under no liability for negligent nonfeasance towards members of the public using it was no longer good law and (b) that the appellant was not merely a member of the public but a visitor to whom a duty was owed under s2 Occupiers' Liability Act (Northern Ireland) 1957 (which is identical to s2 Occupiers' Liability Act 1957).

Held

The rule that the owner of the land over which a public right of way passed was under no liability for negligent nonfeasance towards members of the public was good law. Rights of way passed over many different types of terrain and it would be unreasonable if landowners were to owe a duty of care to members of the public, who needed no permission of the owner to use the right of way, to maintain the rights in good condition.

Furthermore, a person using a public right of way was neither the licensee nor invitee of the occupier, and any licence to use the way formerly granted by the owner before it became subject to the right of way was merged in the right of way and extinguished, because once a public right of way had been established there was no question of permission being granted and users used it as of right and not by virtue of any licence or invitation. Hence the appellant could not succeed at either common law or under the 1957 Act.

Murphy v Bradford Metropolitan Council [1992] PIQR 68 Court of Appeal (Glidewell and Stocker LJJ)

Occupier's liability – snow on school path

Facts

The plaintiff teacher fell on a path leading to a school run by the council and she suffered injury. The path was notoriously slippery but on the morning of the accident the school caretaker had cleared the path of snow at 6.20 am and treated it with rock salt and had done so again at 8 am, on being told that the path was still slippery. Despite these efforts the plaintiff still slipped on the path half an hour later.

Held

The defendants had not discharged their duty under s2(2) of the Occupiers' Liability Act 1957 because the path was a likely place for an accident to occur and they had failed to lay grit and cinders on it. Stocker LJ said that the trial judge had considered all the relevant facts and there was ample evidence on which he could conclude that the plaintiff's injuries from her fall were a result of the council's failure to take reasonable care to see that she would be reasonably safe when using the path in the school grounds.

Ogwo v Taylor [1987] 3 WLR 1145 House of Lords (Lord Mackay of Clashfern LC, Lord Bridge of Harwich, Lord Elwyn-Jones, Lord Templeman and Lord Ackner)

Negligence – duty of care to fireman

Facts

The defendant negligently set the roof of his house on fire whilst trying to burn off old paintwork on the eaves and guttering with a blow-lamp. The plaintiff, a fireman, came to put out the fire and whilst doing so he entered the loft of the house with a water hose. The intense heat in the confined loftspace caused much steam and afterwards the plaintiff discovered that he had suffered severe steam burns. The question was whether the defendant was liable for the plaintiff's burns, and whether a person who negligently starts a fire owes a duty of care to the firemen who come to put it out.

Held
The plaintiff should succeed as the defendant had been in breach of his duty of care.

Lord Bridge:

'Of course, I accept that not everybody, whether professional fireman or layman, who is injured in a fire negligently started will *necessarily* recover damages from the tortfeasor. The chain of causation between the negligence and the injury must be established by the plaintiff and may be broken in a number of ways. The most obvious would be where the plaintiff's injuries were sustained by his foolhardy exposure to an unnecessary risk either of his own volition or acting under the orders of a senior fire officer. But, subject to this, I can see no basis of principle which would justify denying a remedy in damages against the tortfeasor responsible for starting a fire to a professional fireman doing no more and no less than his proper duty and acting with skill and efficiency in fighting an ordinary fire who is injured by one of the risks to which the particular circumstances of the fire give rise. Fire out of control is inherently dangerous. If not brought under control, it may, in most urban situations, cause untold damage to property and possible danger to life. The duty of professional firemen is to use their best endeavours to extinguish fires and it is obvious that, even making full use of all their skills, training and specialist equipment, they will sometimes be exposed to unavoidable risks of injury, whether the fire is described as "ordinary" or "exceptional". If they are not to be met by the doctrine of volenti, which would be utterly repugnant to our contemporary notions of justice, I can see no reason whatever why they should be held at a disadvantage as compared to the layman entitled to invoke the principle of the so-called "rescue" cases.

Counsel for the defendant suggested it would be anomalous that a fireman should recover damages for injuries sustained in fighting a fire caused by negligence when his colleague who suffers similar injuries in fighting another fire of which the cause is unknown has no such remedy. If this be an anomaly, it is one which is common to most, if not all, injuries sustained by accident and is inevitable under a system which requires proof of fault as the basis of liability. The existence of the suggested anomaly is the strongest argument advanced by those who support the introduction of a "no fault" system of compensation. But it has no special application to the case of firemen.

At the end of the day I am happy to find my views in full accord with those expressed in the latest authority directly in point, which is the decision at first instance of Woolf J in *Salmon v Seafarer Restaurants Ltd*.'

Commentary
Approved: *Salmon v Seafarer Restaurants Ltd* [1983] 1 WLR 1264.

Phipps v Rochester Corporation [1955] 2 WLR 23 High Court (Devlin J)
Occupier's liability to child

Facts
The plaintiff, aged five, and his sister, aged seven, crossed the defendants' land, having implied permission to do so. The land was being developed for house building and in one place a deep trench had been dug. The plaintiff fell in and was injured.

Held
To a young child, the trench was a concealed danger, but his claim failed as the defendants had not been in breach of their duty towards him.

Devlin J:

> '... the responsibility for the safety of little children must rest primarily upon the parents; it is their duty to see that such children are not allowed to wander about by themselves, or at least to satisfy themselves that the places to which they do allow their children to go unaccompanied are safe for them to go to. It would not be socially desirable if parents were, as a matter of course, able to shift the burden of looking after their children from their own shoulders to those of persons who happen to have accessible bits of land. Different considerations may well apply to public parks or to recognised playing grounds where parents allow their children to go unaccompanied in the reasonable belief that they are safe.'

Revill v *Newbury* (1995) The Independent 10 November Court of Appeal (Neill, Evans and Millett LJJ)

Occupiers' liability – duty of care owed to a trespasser

Facts
The plaintiff attempted to break into the defendant's property. The defendant loaded a shotgun, poked the barrel through a small hole in the door, and fired and hit the plaintiff at a range of around five feet. The plaintiff pleaded guilty to the relevant criminal offences, and claimed against the defendant under s1 Occupiers' Liability Act (OLA) 1984 and in negligence. At first instance the plaintiff succeeded, the judge rejecting the defences of ex turpi causa non omitar acto, accident and self-defence. The defendant appealed to the Court of Appeal.

Held
The appeal failed. On the facts, the negligence issue was identical to the issue of a breach of duty under s1 OLA 1984. Section 1 shows that an occupier cannot treat a burglar as an outlaw and defines the scope of the duty owed in s1(4). There was no room for a two-stage determination in first considering whether there had been a breach of duty, and second whether, despite this breach, the plaintiff was barred from recovering. The question at both common law and under s1(3)(b) OLA 1984 was: did the defendant have reasonable grounds to believe that the plaintiff was in the vicinity of the danger? On the facts the judge was entitled to treat the gunshot not as merely a warning shot but as a shot likely to strike anyone in the vicinity of the door. If the ex turpi defence applied, any claim by a trespasser would be barred, no matter how excessive or unreasonable the force used against him.

Note: a high level of contributory negligence was found on the part of the plaintiff.

Robson v *Hallett* [1967] 3 WLR 28 High Court (Lord Parker CJ, Diplock LJ and Ashworth J)

Police – trespassers

Facts
Three police officers without warrant were making inquiries at Ds' house. D1 ordered them to leave and as one PC was departing, he was leapt upon and assaulted by D2. D2 claimed that this assault was lawful because the police officer was trespassing.

Held
When a licence is revoked, a reasonable time must be given for the person requested to leave. Here, that time had not been allowed and the assault was therefore unlawful.

Roles v *Nathan* [1963] 1 WLR 1117 Court of Appeal (Lord Denning MR, Harman and Pearson LJJ)

Occupier's liability – warnings disregarded

Facts
The plaintiffs were the widows of two chimney-sweeps who had been called in by the defendant occupier to service and clean a central heating boiler and who were overcome by fumes whilst working in the boiler-room. They had been advised not to enter or remain in the room when the boiler was alight, but had disregarded this advice and a warning about the dangers of carbon monoxide.

Held (Pearson LJ dissenting)
The defendant was not in breach of his duty of care, by virtue of s2(4)(a) of the Occupiers' Liability Act 1957, and he was not therefore liable.

Lord Denning MR:

> 'When a householder calls in a specialist to deal with a defective installation on his premises, he can reasonably expect the specialist to appreciate and guard against the dangers arising from the defect. The householder is not bound to watch over him to see that he comes to no harm. I would hold, therefore, that the occupier here was under no duty of care to these sweeps. At any rate, in regard to the dangers which caused their deaths. If it had been a different danger, as for instance if the stairs leading to the celler had given way, the occupier might no doubt be responsible, but not for these risks which were special risks ordinarily incidental to their calling.
>
> We all know the reason for this subsection. It was inserted so as to clear up the unsatisfactory state of the law as it had been left by the decision of the House of Lords in *London Graving Dock Co* v *Horton* [1951] AC 737. That case was commonly supposed to have decided that, when a person comes onto premises as an invitee and is injured by the defective or dangerous condition of the premises (due to the default of the occupier) it is nevertheless a complete defence for the occupier to prove that the invitee knew of the danger, or had been warned of it. Suppose, for instance, that there was only one way of getting into and out of premises and it was by a footbridge over a stream which was rotten and dangerous. According to *Horton's* case, the occupier could escape all liability to any visitor by putting up a notice: "this bridge is dangerous", even though there was no other way by which the visitor could get in or out; and he had no option but to go over the bridge. In such a case, s2(4) makes it clear that the occupier would nowadays be liable. But, if there were two footbridges, one of which was rotten and the other safe, a hundred yards away, the occupier could still escape liability, even today, by putting up a notice: "Do not use this footbridge. It is dangerous. There is a safe one further upstream". Such a warning is sufficient because it does enable the visitor to be reasonably safe.'

Salmon v *Seafarer Restaurants Ltd* [1983] 1 WLR 1264 High Court (Woolf J)

Occupier's liability to fireman

Facts
The plaintiff, a fireman, was injured by an explosion on premises occupied by the defendants as a fish and chip shop when a fire in the premises melted a seal on a gas meter thus allowing gas to escape. The fire

was caused by the negligence of an employee of the defendants. P contended that because the fire had been started negligently he was entitled to recover damages from the Ds. The defendants, however, argued that the occupier's duty of care to firemen attending his premises in the course of their work was limited to protecting the fireman from any special or exceptional risks over and above the ordinary risks necessarily incidental to a fireman's job and did not extend to protecting firemen from such ordinary risks which included an explosion of the kind which had taken place on the Ds' premises.

Held

The defendants were liable to P. An occupier of premises owes the same duty of care to a fireman attending his premises to extinguish a fire as he owed to other visitors under s2 of the Occupiers' Liability Act 1957, subject to the fact that in determining whether the occupier was in breach of that duty a fireman was expected to exercise those skills which could be expected to be shown by firemen. Negligence was the cause of the fire in this case and since it was reasonably foreseeable that firemen would attend the fire and that an explosion of the kind which occurred might result from the fire, the Ds were liable to P for his consequent injury. The Ds' third party action against the British Gas Corporation was dropped for lack of evidence of any negligence against the latter.

Woolf J:

> 'Having found nothing in the authorities to which I was referred which is inconsistent with the ordinary approach to liability in these circumstances, I go on to consider, in the absence of authority, whether there is any basis for limiting the duty which is owed to firemen. It is true that their very occupation is one where they are specially trained to deal with the dangers inherent in any outbreak of fire. However, it seems to me that their consequent special skills should not change the normal approach to the establishing of liability. It is only a factor to take into account in seeing whether a liability is established and their calling is not in itself a defence. In deciding whether the negligent act could foreseeably cause injury to a fireman, it is necessary to take into account the skills that are ordinarily expected to be shown by firemen. To decide whether there has been any breach of the duty, which in my view undoubtedly exists, in certain cases it will be very relevant to consider whether or not the danger to the fireman requires the taking of precautions. Here again it is proper to take into account the special skills of the fireman. Where it can be foreseen that the fire which was negligently started is of the type which could, first of all, require firemen to attend to extinguish that fire, and where, because of the very nature of the fire, when they attend they will be at risk even though they exercise all the skill of their calling, there seems no reason why a fireman should be at any disadvantage when the question of compensation for his injuries arises.
>
> I make the remarks which I have made, with regard to the position of firemen, because it was submitted by counsel on behalf of the defendants, in his very careful and helpful submissions, that in the case of firemen there were good public policy reasons why there should be a restriction on the extent of the duty owed to them, and that they should be treated differently from other "rescuers" (I here use the expression to identify the category of cases which I have in mind). Notwithstanding the submissions of counsel for the defendants, I find no principle of public policy which requires the ordinary rules to be limited, and it seems to me that the same principles disclosed by the "rescue" cases should be applied to firemen, though taking into account, of course, in the way I have already indicated, the special skills of firemen.'

Commentary

Approved in *Ogwo* v *Taylor* [1987] 3 WLR 1145.

Simkiss v *Rhondda Borough Council* (1983) 81 LGR 460 Court of Appeal (Waller, Dunn and Slade LJJ)

Occupier's liability – failure to fence

Facts
A seven-year-old girl, the plaintiff, lived opposite a mountain with a bluff abutting the road. She tried to slide down the bluff on a blanket and sustained severe injuries as a result. The land was occupied by the defendants and they had not fenced it. The girl alleged that they had been negligent.

Held
The defendants were not liable. Although an occupier had to be prepared for children to be less careful than an adult, the defendants did not have a higher duty of care than a reasonably prudent parent. They were entitled to assume that parents would warn their children and would not allow them to play there unless they appreciated the danger.

Simms v *Leigh Rugby Football Club Ltd* [1969] 2 All ER 923 High Court (Wrangham J)

Occupier's liability – injury to visiting player

Facts
During a rugby match, a visiting player was tackled and thrown towards a concrete wall 7 feet 3 inches from the touchline. Rugby Football League byelaws said that the distance had to be at least 7 feet. The player suffered a broken leg, but there was no evidence of a previous serious injury of this type. Was the club liable?

Held
No. On the balance of probabilities the injury had not arisen from contact with the concrete wall and having a leg broken in a tackle is one of rugby's accepted risks. Even if there had been contact with the wall, and the club owed the player the common duty of care under s2(1) of the Occupiers' Liability Act 1957, the injury, although foreseeable, was so improbable that it was not necessary to guard against it. Further, the club would have been saved by s2(5) of the 1957 Act.

Southern Portland Cement Ltd v *Cooper* [1974] 2 WLR 152 Privy Council (Lord Reid, Lord Morris of Borth-y-Gest, Lord Wilberforce, Lord Simon of Glaisdale and Lord Salmon)

Occupier's liability to trespasser

Facts
The defendants allowed a mound of waste from their limestone quarry so to grow that a high tension cable was within reach from the top of it. Children were in the habit of playing on adjoining land: they had been warned off the defendants' land and there had not been much trespassing, at least during working hours. One Sunday afternoon the plaintiff, aged 13, was playing on the mound: his arm came into contact with the electric cable and he suffered severe injuries.

Held
The defendants owed the plaintiff a duty to take steps to prevent the development of this dangerous situation and, as they were in breach of this duty, they were liable in respect of his injuries.

Lord Reid:

'The rights and interests of the occupier must have full consideration. No unreasonable burden must be put on him. With regard to dangers which have arisen on his land without his knowledge he can have no obligation to make enquiries or inspection. With regard to dangers of which he has knowledge but which he did not create he cannot be required to incur what for him would be large expense.

If the occupier creates the danger when he knows that there is a chance that trespassers will come that way and will not see or realise the danger he may have to do more. There may be difficult cases where the occupier will be hampered in the conduct of his own affairs if he has to take elaborate precautions. But in the present case it would have been easy to prevent the development of the dangerous situation which caused the plaintiff's injuries. The more serious the danger the greater is the obligation to avoid it. And if the dangerous thing or something near it is an allurement to children that may greatly increase the chance that children will come there.

Next comes the question to whom does the occupier owes a duty. Their Lordships have already rejected the view that no duty is owed unless the advent of a trespasser is extremely probable. It was argued that the duty could be limited to cases where the coming of trespassers is more probable than not. Their Lordships can find neither principle nor authority nor any practical reason to justify such a limitation. The only rational or practical answer would seem to be that the occupier is entitled to neglect a bare possibility that trespassers may come to a particular place on his land but is bound at least to give consideration to the matter when he knows facts which shew a substantial chance that they may come there.

Such consideration should be all-embracing. On the one hand the occupier is entitled to put in the scales every kind of disadvantage to him if he takes or refrains from action for the benefit of trespassers. On the other hand he must consider the degree of likelihood of trespassers coming and the degree of hidden or unexpected danger to which they may be exposed if they come. He may have to give more weight to these factors if the potential trespassers are children because generally mere warning is of little value to protect children.

It is easy to be wise after an accident has occurred. In considering whether the occupier did all that he ought to have done before the accident the court or jury must endeavour to put itself back in the situation which confronted the occupier before the trespassers arrived. It is not enough to consider the point where the accident occurred if there are other danger points which the occupier would also have had to protect.

The problem then is to determine what would have been the decision of a humane man with the financial and other limitations of the occupier. Would he have done something which would or might have prevented the accident, or would he, regretfully it may be, have decided that he could not reasonably be expected to do anything... Once it is accepted that the nature of this duty cannot be determined without reference to such all embracing considerations as their Lordships have mentioned, the need for the imposition of two separate parallel duties disappears. Their Lordships believe that the above reformulation of the law would achieve results not substantially different from those achieved by recent decisions of the High Court. They believe moreover that it is substantially in line with the development in England law as expressed by the House of Lords in *British Railways Board* v *Herrington*.'

Commentary
Explained: *Commissioner for Railways* v *Quinlan* [1964] 2 WLR 817.
Not followed: *Addie (R) and Sons (Collieries) Ltd* v *Dumbreck* [1929] AC 358.

Staples v West Dorset District Council (1995) The Times 28 April Court of Appeal (Nourse, Kennedy and Evans LJJ)

Occupiers' liability – breach of duty of care

Facts
The plaintiff, a visitor to the defendants, slipped on some visible algae that was an obvious danger and was injured. The plaintiff succeeded against the defendants in the High Court. On appeal to the Court of Appeal:

Held
The defendants owed the plaintiff a duty of care under s2(2) Occupiers' Liability Act 1957, but were not in breach of this duty. The plaintiff saw the algae before the accident and knew that it might well be slippery. He was well able to evaluate the danger and needed no warning.

Stone v *Taffe* [1974] 1 WLR 1575 Court of Appeal (Megaw, Stephenson LJJ and Sir Seymour Karminski)

Occupier's liability – duty to visitors

Facts
The second defendants were owners of public house run by the first defendant who, contrary to his employers' instructions, allowed guests to remain drinking after hours. The plaintiff left the pub at 1.00 am, fell on unlit stairs and was killed.

Held
At the time of the accident, the plaintiff was not a trespasser, but a lawful visitor, as no indication that his licence to be on the premises was withdrawn had been given. D1 was in breach of his duty under the Occupiers' Liability Act 1957 by failing to ensure the stairs were illuminated and D2 was vicariously liable.

Targett v *Torfaen Borough Council* [1991] NPC 126 Court of Appeal (Sir Donald Nicholls VC, Russell and Leggatt LJJ)

Negligence – personal injury – liability of landlord

Facts
The plaintiff was injured when he fell down stairs outside his council house. The house had been designed and built by the defendant council. There was no handrail for the lower steps, nor was there any lighting in the immediate vicinity of the steps. The recorder held that the council was liable for the plaintiff's injuries, although he reduced the damages payable by 25 per cent on the ground that the plaintiff had been guilty of contributory negligence. The council appealed. The difficulty facing them was that the Court of Appeal in *Rimmer* v *Liverpool City Council* [1984] 1 All ER 930 had held that a landowner, who designs or builds a house, is no more immune from personal responsibility for faults of construction than a building contractor, or from personal responsibility for faults of design than an architect, simply on the ground that he has disposed of the house by selling it or letting it. The defendant sought to get round *Rimmer* on two grounds. The first was that there was no defect in manufacture because the lack of a handrail or of lighting did not render the steps of faulty manufacture. The second ground was that *Rimmer* could no longer be regarded as good law in the light of the decision of the House of Lords in *Murphy* v *Brentwood District Council* [1991] 1 AC 398.

Held
Both arguments would be rejected and the appeal dismissed. The first argument was rejected because the lack of a handrail and lighting constituted manufacturing and design defects respectively, the second because *Murphy* was a case in which the plaintiffs had suffered *economic* loss and it did not overrule cases in which plaintiffs had suffered personal injury as a result of the negligence of the defendant.

Wheat v E Lacon & Co Ltd [1966] 2 WLR 581 House of Lords (Viscount Dilhorne, Lord Denning, Lord Morris of Borth-y-Gest, Lord Pearce and Lord Pearson)

Negligence – occupation or control

Facts
The respondent brewery company owned a public house, the first floor of which was the living quarters of the resident manager and his wife, who occasionally took in paying guests. The appellant and her husband took a room there. At about 9.00 pm one evening, the appellant's husband slipped and fell down the stairs from the first floor and was killed. The cause of the accident was found to be a) that the handrail did not go right to the bottom of the stairs, and b) the light at the top of the stairs was missing. The appellant sued the respondents, alleging they were in breach of their common duty of care under the Occupiers' Liability Act 1957.

Held
The respondents, together with the manager and his wife, were occupiers of the premises and owed a duty of care to all lawful visitors. However, the facts disclosed no breach of duty so the appeal was dismissed.

Lord Denning:

> '... wherever a person has a sufficient degree of control over premises that he ought to realise that any failure to use care of his part may result in injury to a person coming lawfully there, then he is an "occupier" and the persons coming there are his "visitors"; and the "occupier" is under a duty to the "visitor" to use reasonable care. In order to be an occupier, it is not necessary for a person to have entire control over the premises. He need not have exclusive occupation. Suffice it that he has some degree of control. He may share control with others. Two or more may be occupiers. And, whenever this happens, each is under a duty to use care towards persons coming lawfully on the premises, dependent on his degree of control... any degree of control over the state of the premises may be enough (to make a person an occupier).'

Commentary
Applied in *Emanuel (H & N) Ltd v Greater London Council* [1971] 2 All ER 835.

White v Blackmore [1972] 3 WLR 296 Court of Appeal (Lord Denning MR, Buckley and Roskill LJJ)

Occupier's liability – exclusion

Facts
The plaintiff's husband entered as a competitor in a jalopy-race and took his wife as a spectator. At the entrance to the course were several notices stating 'Warning to the Public: Motor racing is dangerous' and exempting all persons involved in the racing from liability for loss or injuries however caused. Whilst standing by a safety rope watching the race, the plaintiff's husband received fatal injuries when a wheel of a competitor's car became tangled with the rope and caused the rope to spring forward, catapulting her husband some distance. The plaintiff sued, inter alia, the organisers of the race.

Held (Lord Denning MR dissenting)
The plaintiff's claim would fail, although the defendants had been negligent, because they had excluded their liability, as they were entitled to do under s2(1) of the Occupiers' Liability Act 1957. All the

judges agreed that the maxim volenti non fit injuria did not apply here because the deceased could not have known the nature or extent of the risk created by the defendants' negligence.

Commentary
Applied: *Wooldridge* v *Sumner* [1962] 3 WLR 616 and *Ashdown* v *Samuel Williams & Sons Ltd* [1956] 3 WLR 1104.

White v *St Albans City and District Council* (1990) The Times 12 March Court of Appeal (Neill, Nicholls and Bingham LJJ)

Duty to trespasser under 1984 Act

Facts
The plaintiff, a trespasser, sustained injuries when he fell into a 12ft trench when walking across the defendants' fenced-off property while taking a short cut to a car park.

Held
The trial judge's rejection of the claim would be upheld as there was no evidence that people tended to use the land as a short cut.

Neill LJ said that the question for consideration under s1(3)(b) of the Occupiers' Liability Act 1984 had to be answered by looking at the actual state of affairs on the ground when the injury was met with and asking: had the occupiers reasonable grounds for believing someone would come into the vicinity of the danger? In the instant case the accident occurred on private land surrounded by a fence, which was insufficient to stop all but the elderly and disabled from entering the land. Nevertheless, the judge had been wholly justified in holding that the council had no reason to believe that the appellant would be in the vicinity of the trench.

Woollins v *British Celanese Ltd* (1966) 110 SJ 686 Court of Appeal (Lord Denning MR, Danckwerts and Salmon LJJ)

Occupier's liability – warning

Facts
The plaintiff was doing constructional work at a factory and he fell while on a roof. A warning that the roofing was unsafe without special caution had been put in the vicinity by the defendants, but it had been placed behind a door where it was not to be expected.

Held
The defendants had been in breach of s2 of the Occupiers' Liability Act 1957, although the plaintiff had been contributorily negligent.

Lord Denning MR:

> 'The defendants should have taken what care was reasonable in the circumstances. As they had put up a warning, but in the wrong place, they foresaw the risk and should have foreseen the accident. The risk was not a special risk ordinarily incident to the plaintiff's employment. It was a risk incident to the premises. Section 2(3)(b) did not apply to a place or means of access to a place, like this roofing, on to which a workman might clamber.'

14 Private Nuisance

Adams v *Ursell* [1913] 1 Ch 269 High Court (Swinfen Eady J)
Nuisance – smells

Facts
Using 'the most approved appliances', the defendant established a fried fish shop in a working-class district but next to the plaintiff's house which was rather superior.

Held
The plaintiff was entitled to an injunction to restrain the nuisance caused by odour and vapour from the defendant's premises.

Swinfen Eady J:

> 'It does not follow that because a fried fish shop is a nuisance in one place it is a nuisance in another.'

Allen v *Gulf Oil Refining Ltd* [1981] 2 WLR 188 House of Lords (Lord Wilberforce, Lord Diplock, Lord Edmund-Davies, Lord Keith of Kinkel and Lord Roskill)
Nuisance – statutory authority

Facts
The Gulf Oil Refining company wished to construct an oil refinery at Milford Haven. They were given wide authority under the provisions of the Gulf Oil Refining Act 1965 to undertake all necessary preliminaries to the creation of the refinery, including compulsory purchase. The plaintiff, who lived in the vicinity of the refinery, brought an action against Gulf Oil claiming damages or compensation, alleging that the operation of the refinery was a nuisance, or, in the alternative, that Gulf Oil were guilty of negligence in the method of construction and operation of the refinery. Gulf Oil defended the claim by a plea of statutory authority. On a preliminary issue, the judge ordered that Gulf Oil could rely on the 1965 Act as having authorised the construction of the oil refinery. The plaintiff appealed to the Court of Appeal which reversed the judge's ruling. Gulf Oil appealed to the House of Lords.

Held (Lord Keith dissenting)
The 1965 Act bestowed a wide authority upon Gulf Oil to construct a refinery, and to take all necessary preliminary steps necessary for that construction. Accordingly, Gulf Oil were entitled to statutory immunity in respect of any nuisance which was an inevitable result of the constructing and operating of the refinery which conformed with the intention of Parliament. The fact that the nuisance was an inevitable result of a refinery on that site was, as a matter of defence, for Gulf Oil to prove. However, to the extent that the actual nuisance caused by the refinery exceeded the nuisance which inevitably resulted from any refinery on that site, the statutory immunity would not apply and Gulf Oil would be liable to the plaintiff. Appeal allowed.

Lord Wilberforce:

'We are here in the well-charted field of statutory authority. It is now well settled that where Parliament by express direction or by necessary implication has authorised the construction and use of an undertaking or works, that carries with it an authority to do what is authorised with immunity from any action based on nuisance. The right of action is taken away .. To this there is made the qualification, or condition, that the statutory powers are exercised without 'negligence', that word here being used in a special sense so as to require the undertaker, as a condition of obtaining immunity from action, to carry out the work and conduct the operation with all reasonable regard and care for the interests of other persons .. It is within the same principle that immunity from action is withheld where the terms of the statute are permissive only, in which case the powers conferred must be exercised in strict conformity with private rights.'

Bridlington Relay Ltd v *Yorkshire Electricity Board* [1965] 2 WLR 349 High Court (Buckley J)

Nuisance – electrical interference

Facts
The plaintiffs operated a TV relay system and erected a mast on their own land for that purpose. A year later, the defendants proceeded to erect an overhead power line placing two pylons within 250 yards of Ps' mast. Ps sought a quia timet injunction to restrain the erection in so far as it interfered with Ps' reception and transmission.

Held
The injunction would not be granted as the defendants were already willing to do their best to suppress the interference.

Buckley J:

'On the evidence the interference was caused by defects in the power lines which could be remedied. If this was not the case, the plaintiffs were, in any event, only entitled to the same immunity from interference as a domestic user ... For myself, however, I do not think that it can at present be said that the ability to receive television free from occasional, even if recurrent and severe, electrical interference is so important a part of an ordinary householder's enjoyment of his property that such interference should be regarded as a legal nuisance, particularly perhaps if such interference affects only one of the suitable alternative programmes.'

Commentary
Applied: *Hunt* v *Canary Wharf Ltd* (1995) NLJ 1645.

British Celanese Ltd v *A H Hunt (Capacitors) Ltd* [1969] 1 WLR 959 High Court (Lawton J)

Nuisance – escape of metal foil

Facts
The defendants were manufacturers of electrical components and had on their land strips of metal foil. The plaintiffs were manufacturers of yarn whose premises were 150 yards from Ds' on the same industrial estate. Electricity on the estate came from a sub-station nearby. Some of the strips of metal foil were blown from Ds' land to this sub-station, where they hit the bus-bars and caused a power

failure. A similar, though less serious, occurrence had taken place some three and a half years previously. The plaintiffs lost time, profits, etc; material solidified in machines and they had to be cleared. The Ps sued under three heads:

a) *Rylands* v *Fletcher*;
b) negligence;
c) nuisance.

Held
a) There was no special use of the property and hence no liability under *Rylands* v *Fletcher*;
b) the defendants were liable in negligence, and the damage was not too remote to be recovered;
c) the defendants were liable in nuisance and damages could be recovered. Ds' method of storing metal foil amounted to an interference with Ps' use of their property.

Lawton J:

'Most nuisances do arise from a long continued condition and many isolated happenings do not constitute a nuisance. It is, however, clear from the authorities that an isolated happening by itself can create an actionable nuisance.'

Commentary
Followed: *Midwood & Co Ltd* v *Manchester Corporation* [1905] 2 KB 597.
    Distinguished: *Cattle* v *Stockton Waterworks Co* (1875) LR 10 QB 453.
    Approved in *SCM (UK) Ltd* v *WJ Whittall & Son Ltd* [1970] 1 WLR 1017.
    But see *Cambridge Water Company* v *Eastern Counties Leather plc* [1994] 2 WLR 53 regarding liability in *Rylands* v *Fletcher*.

Christie v *Davey* [1893] 1 Ch 316 High Court (North J)

Nuisance – 'retaliation'

Facts
The plaintiff was a music teacher living with her husband, daughter (who studied at the Royal Academy of Music and was also a teacher) and a lodger friend of the daughter with like qualifications. The son of the house played the cello (badly!). The defendant lived next door and wrote to P, requesting that the amount of music played be curbed. When he received no reply, D commenced 'retaliation' by shrieking, banging and howling. This disrupted P's professional music lessons and she sued for an injunction, claiming the retaliation amounted to nuisance.

Held
While the playing of music was not here a nuisance, the defendant's behaviour did amount to a nuisance and it would be restrained by injunction.

North J:

'If what has taken place had occurred between two sets of persons both perfectly innocent, I should have taken an entirely different view of the case. But, I am persuaded that what was done by D was done solely for the purpose of annoyance and, in any view, it was not a legitimate use of D's house.'

Davey v *Harrow Corporation* [1957] 2 WLR 941 Court of Appeal (Lord Goddard CJ, Jenkins and Morris LJJ)

Nuisance – roots of trees

Facts
Roots of the defendants' trees penetrated into the plaintiff's land and caused subsidence to his house.

Held
The defendants were liable and it was immaterial whether the trees were planted or self-sown.

Lord Goddard CJ:

> ' .. it must be taken to be established law that, if trees encroach whether by branches or roots and cause damage, an action for nuisance will lie.'

Commentary
Approved in *Leakey* v *National Trust for Places of Historic Interest or Natural Beauty* [1980] 2 WLR 265.

Halsey v *Esso Petroleum Co Ltd* [1961] 1 WLR 683 High Court (Veale J)

Nuisance – oil depot

Facts
The plaintiff lived in Fulham in an area zoned for residential purposes. The defendants operated an oil distribution depot nearby in an industrial zone. They worked day and night in a boiler house with chimneys. The plaintiff claimed for the following: (i) Acid smuts came from chimney and damaged clothes and car paint on highway. (ii) A pungent/nauseating smell was emitted. (iii) Noise throughout night shook windows. (iv) Noise from tankers leaving and arriving throughout night on the road outside.

Held
The defendants were: (i) liable in damages for: (a) escape of harmful substances under *Rylands* v *Fletcher*; (b) as a private nuisance for damage to clothing; (c) as a public nuisance for damage to car; (ii) liable in damages for private nuisance; (iii) liable in damages for private nuisance and liable in damage for public nuisance; (iv) liable in damages for private nuisance.

Harrison v *Southwark and Vauxhall Water Co* [1891] 2 Ch 409 High Court (Vaughan Williams J)

Nuisance – noise and vibration

Facts
The defendants in the exercise of statutory powers sank a shaft beneath land adjacent to the plaintiff's house and employed lift pumps. The plaintiff commenced an action for nuisance based on noise and vibration from these pumps. The defendants then installed new centrifugal pumps and the nuisance was abated.

Held
The defendants were not liable in nuisance as they had used reasonable skill and care in the exercise of their statutory powers.

Vaughan Williams J:

'It frequently happens that the owners or occupiers of land cause in the execution of lawful works in the ordinary user of land a considerable amount of temporary annoyance to their neighbours, but they are not necessarily on that account held to be guilty of causing an unlawful nuisance. The business of life could not be carried on if it were so .. a man who pulls down his house for the purpose of building a new one no doubt causes considerable inconvenience to his next door neighbours during the process of demolition, but he is not responsible as for a nuisance if he uses all reasonable care and skill to avoid annoyance. This is so even though the noise and dust and consequent annoyance be such as would constitute a nuisance if the same, instead of being created for the purpose of the demolition, had been created .. in the execution of works for a purpose involving the permanent continuance of the noise and dust.'

Hoare & Co Ltd v *Sir Robert McAlpine, Sons & Co* [1923] 1 Ch 167 High Court (Astbury J)

Nuisance – vibration

Facts
The defendants prepared a city centre site for a large building. They drove heavy piles into the soil which caused serious structural damage to an old house owned by the plaintiffs. The plaintiffs sued in nuisance and under the principle in *Rylands* v *Fletcher*.

Held
The defendants were liable under *Rylands* v *Fletcher* for the escape of vibrations. They were also liable in nuisance because the instability of the house was not so great as to be abnormal.

Astbury J:

'In my judgment, *Rylands* v *Fletcher* applies in this case, though I do not wish to be understood as indicating that the law as to legal nuisance does not also apply. The plaintiffs' proposition was – a man cannot limit the operation of his neighbour on his own land, or increase his neighbour's liability by putting his own property into a structural condition in which it is more than ordinarily liable to be affected by legitimate operations. In some cases, this may be accurate.'

Hollywood Silver Fox Farm Ltd v *Emmett* [1936] 2 KB 468 High Court (Macnaghten J)

Nuisance – unreasonable acts

Facts
The plaintiff purchased land next to the defendant's in order to breed silver foxes. He erected a sign saying 'Hollywood Silver Fox Farm' which was visible both from D's field and from the road which bounded them both. D was developing his land as a building estate and objected to the sign. P refused to remove it and D, knowing that silver foxes are unusually sensitive to noise during the breeding season, threatened to fire a shot gun near to P's pens and prevent the foxes breeding. D's son carried out the threat and it was at least in part successful. The plaintiff sued in nuisance for the damage the farm had suffered.

Held
The firing was a nuisance for which the defendant was liable in damages and an injunction was granted restraining firing or other noises during the breeding season.

Hunter v *Canary Wharf Ltd* [1995] NLJ 1645 Court of Appeal (Neill, Waite and Pill LJJ)

Nuisance – interference with television reception – interest required to sue in nuisance

Facts
The defendants built a large tower in East London. The plaintiffs claimed damages for interference with their television reception which they claimed was caused by the tower. At first instance it was held that this was capable of constituting a nuisance. The defendants appealed to the Court of Appeal.

Held
That although television plays an important part in the lives of very many people, interference with television reception did not constitute an actionable nuisance, either private or public. The plaintiffs relied on the dicta of Buckley J in *Bridlington Relay Ltd* v *Yorkshire Electricity Board* [1965] 1 All ER 264 where, although holding that interference with television reception did not constitute a nuisance, he stated:

> 'I do not think that it can at present be said that the ability to receive television free from ... interference is so important a part of an ordinary householder's enjoyment of his property that such interference should be regarded as a legal nuisance ...!

The plaintiffs argued that in 1995 the ability to receive interference-free television did play an important part in people's lives, as was held in the Canadian case of *Nor-Video Services Ltd* v *Ontario Hydro* (1978) 84 DLR (3d) 231. However the Court of Appeal held that the presence of a high building between a television transmitter and a property leading to loss of quality of reception was analogous to loss of prospect or view and was hence not actionable.

Interestingly, however, the court held that the defence of statutory authority would not have protected the defendants if a nuisance had been established.

The court went on to consider whether an interest in property was necessary to claim in private nuisance. Following *Khorasandjian* v *Bush* [1993] 3 All ER 669 the court held that a proprietary or possessory interest in land was no longer necessary, but that a substantial link between the person enjoying the land and the land in question was required. Mere occupation of the property was insufficient, but occupation of the property as a home was sufficient.

Kennaway v *Thompson* [1980] 3 WLR 361 Court of Appeal (Lawton and Waller LJJ and Sir David Cairns)

Nuisance – private against public interest

Facts
The plaintiff built a house on land where the defendant club organised motor boat races and water skiing. When she began to build, she felt that the club's activities would not interfere with her enjoyment of her new house, but those activities developed and boats became more powerful and noisy.

Held
Despite the public interest in the club's activities, an injunction would be granted restricting the club's racing and the noise level of boats at other times.

Lawton J:

'The principles enunciated in *Shelfer's* case, which is binding on us, have been applied time and time again during the past 85 years. The only case which raises a doubt about the application of the *Shelfer* principles to all cases is *Miller* v *Jackson*, a decision of this court. The majority, Geoffrey Lane and Cumming-Bruce LJJ, Lord Denning MR dissenting, adjudged that the activities of an old-established cricket club which had been going for over seventy years, had been a nuisance to the plaintiffs by reason of cricket balls landing on their garden. The question then was whether the plaintiffs should be granted an injunction. Geoffrey Lane LJ was of the opinion that one should be granted. Lord Denning MR and Cumming-Bruce LJ though otherwise. Lord Denning MR said that the public interest should prevail over the private interest. Cumming-Bruce LJ stated that a factor to be taken into account when exercising the judicial discretion whether to grant an injunction was that the plaintiffs had bought their house knowing that it was next to the cricket ground. He thought that there were special circumstances which should inhibit a court of equity from granting the injunction claimed. The statement of Lord Denning MR that the public interest should prevail over the private interest runs counter to the principles enunciated in *Shelfer's* case and does not accord with the reason of Cumming-Bruce LJ for refusing an injunction. We are of the opinion that there is nothing in *Miller* v *Jackson*, binding on us, which qualifies what was decided in *Shelfer*. Any decisions before *Shelfer's* case (and there were some at first instance as counsel for the defendants pointed out) which give support for the proposition that the public interest should prevail over the private interest must be read subject to the decision in *Shelfer's* case.

It follows that the plaintiff was entitled to an injunction .. But she was only entitled to an injunction restraining the club from activities which caused a nuisance, and not all of their activities did.'

Commentary
Distinguished in *Tetley* v *Chitty* [1986] 1 All ER 663.
    Applied: *Shelfer* v *City of London Electric Lighting Co* [1895] 1 Ch 287.

Khorasandjian v *Bush* [1993] 3 WLR 476 Court of Appeal (Dillon and Rose LJJ and Peter Gibson J)

Whether interest in land required to sustain an action in nuisance

Facts
The plaintiff, whose friendship with the defendant had broken down, claimed relief in respect of her complaints that the defendant had, inter alia, pestered her with unwanted telephone calls to her parents' home. An injunction was granted to restrain this activity at first instance, and the defendant appealed on the grounds that as the plaintiff had no interest in the land affected she could not maintain an action based on private nuisance.

Held
That harassment by unwanted telephone calls amounting to interference with the ordinary and reasonable enjoyment of property which the recipient of the calls had a right to occupy was actionable as a private nuisance, notwithstanding that she had no proprietary interest in the property. The Court refused to be bound by its earlier decision in *Malone* v *Laskey* [1907] 2 KB 141, and adopted instead the reasoning of the Appellate Division of the Alberta Supreme Court in *Motherwell* v *Motherwell* (1976) 73 DLR (3d) 62.

Dillon LJ:

'That a legal owner of property can obtain an injunction, on the ground of private nuisance, to restrain persistent harassment by unwanted telephone calls to his home was decided by the Appellate Division of the Alberta Supreme Court in *Motherwell* v *Motherwell* (1976) 73 DLR (3d) 62. The court there rejected, by reference to English authority, a submission, at p67:

> "that the common law does not have within itself the resources to recognise invasion of privacy as either included in an existing category or as a new category of nuisance, and that it has lost its original power, by which indeed it created itself, to note new ills arising in a growing and changing society and pragmatically to establish a principle to meet the need for control and remedy; and then by categories to develop the principle as the interests of justice make themselves sufficiently apparent."

Consequently, notwithstanding *Malone* v *Laskey*, the court held that the wife of the owner had also the right to restrain harassing telephone calls to the matrimonial home. Clement JA who delivered the judgment of the court said, at p78:

> "Here we have a wife harassed in the matrimonial home. She has a status, a right to live there with her husband and children. I find it absurd to say that her occupancy of the matrimonial home is insufficient to found an action in nuisance. In my opinion she is entitled to the same relief as is her husband, the brother."

I respectfully agree, and in my judgment this court is entitled to adopt the same approach.'

Laws v *Florinplace Ltd* [1981] 1 All ER 659 High Court (Vinelott J)

Nuisance – sex shop

Facts

The defendants purchased a shop in Longmore Street, Pimlico. They proceeded to convert the shop into a 'sex centre', for the sale of pornographic magazines and films; they also installed seating for the purpose of enabling customers to view pornographic films. They advertised the enterprise with a large illuminated sign, warning that explicit sex acts were to be shown on the premises. The plaintiffs, being a small residential association led by Mr Laws, a barrister, sought an injunction and damages; they further sought interlocutory relief pending trial. The defendants argued that the centre would not harm the vicinity, and alleged that on the contrary it would have a therapeutic effect. The plaintiffs contended that the existence of the centre would adversely affect property prices in the area, and would attract undesirables to the area who might make indecent suggestions to young girls living in the area.

Held

It was established law that cases of nuisance were not confined to cases where there was some physical emanation of a damaging kind from the defendants' premises which had happened, or was reasonably feared but included cases where the use made by the defendant of his property was such that, while not necessarily criminal, was such as to affront ordinary reasonably people. In the circumstances of the case it was not possible to say that there was not at least a triable issue whether the existence of the centre was not a nuisance independently of any risk of undesirables being attracted to the area. The fact that the centre was proposing to sell hard core pornography and would thus be a business repugnant to the sensibilities of ordinary men and women could not be disregarded. Since the danger that might be suffered by the defendants upon grant of interlocutory relief which was afterwards found to be unjustified was quantifiable, and since there were strong factors which favoured the grant of interlocutory relief, not least of which was the fact that the centre would be operating near the boundary of the criminal law, the balance of convenience lay in favour of granting the interim relief sought by the plaintiffs.

Leakey v National Trust for Places of Historic Interest or Natural Beauty [1980] 2 WLR 65 Court of Appeal (Megaw, Shaw and Cumming-Bruce LJJ)

Nuisance – national process

Facts
The defendants owned and occupied a parcel of land consisting of a conical shaped hill 'Burrow Hump' next to P's houses which were situated effectively at the base of the hill being separated from it only by a narrow strip of land. The hill was composed of keaper marl which made it prone to cracking and slipping. In the past weathering had caused soil slides onto P's property. After the long drought in 1976, a large crack appeared. The plaintiff notified Ds of this and Ds, having taken legal advice, refused to act. A large slide of earth onto P's property then occurred, the soil in fact reaching P's houses. The plaintiff sued for a mandatory injunction to get it removed. Pursuant to this, Ds spent £2,000 removing the material. The action then proceeded to trial and before O'Connor J P succeeded in establishing nuisance. Between the first instance decision and the Court of Appeal hearing, Ds spent a further £4,000 on protective works. The purpose of the appeal was to establish whether the case of *Goldman* v *Hargrave* represented the law of England.

Held
a) There is a general duty imposed on occupiers in relation to hazards occurring on their land whether natural or man-made. A person on whose land a natural hazard develops which threatens to encroach on another's land must do all that is reasonable to prevent it;
b) this was properly described as a claim in nuisance;
c) the defendants were liable for nominal damages.

Megaw LJ:

'In my judgment, there is, in the scope of the duty as explained in *Goldman* v *Hargrave*, a removal, or at least a powerful amelioration, of the injustice which might otherwise be caused in such a case by the recognition of the duty of care. Because of that limitation on the scope of the duty, I would say that, as a matter of policy, the law ought to recognise such a duty of care.

This leads on to the question of the scope of the duty. This is discussed, and the nature and extent of the duty is explained, in the judgment in *Goldman* v *Hargrave*. The duty is a duty to do that which is reasonable in all the circumstances, and no more than what, if anything, is reasonable, to prevent or minimise the known risk of damage or injury to one's neighbour or to his property. The considerations with which the law is familiar are all to be taken into account in deciding whether there has been a breach of duty, and, if so, what that breach is, and whether it is causative of the damage in respect of which the claim is made. Thus, there will fall to be considered the extent of the risk. What, so far as reasonably can be foreseen, are the chances that anything untoward will happen or that any damage will be caused? What is to be foreseen as to the possible extent of the damage if the risk becomes a reality? Is it practicable to prevent, or to minimise, the happening of any damage? If it is practicable, how simple or how difficult are the measures which could be taken, how much and how lengthy work do they involve, and what is the probable cost of such works? Was there sufficient time for preventive action to have been taken, by persons acting reasonably in relation to the known risk, between the time when it became known to, or should have been realised by, the defendant, and the time when the damage occurred? Factors such as these, so far as they apply in a particular case, fall to be weighed in deciding whether the defendant's duty of care requires, or required, him to do anything, and, if so, what.'

Commentary
Applied: *Goldman* v *Hargrave* [1966] 3 WLR 513 and *Sedleigh-Denfield* v *O'Callagan* [1940] AC 880.

Approved: *Davey v Harrow Corporation* [1957] 2 WLR 941.
Distinguished: *Rylands v Fletcher* (1868) LR 3 HL 330.
Overruled: *Giles v Walker* (1890) 24 QBD 656 and *Pontardawe Rural District Council v Moore-Gwyn* [1929] 1 Ch 656.
Applied in *Home Brewery plc v William Davis & Co (Loughborough) Ltd* [1987] 2 WLR 117.

Lemmon v *Webb* [1895] AC 1 House of Lords (Lord Herschell LC, Lord Macnaghten and Lord Davey)

Nuisance – overhanging trees

Facts
The plaintiff had trees growing on his land, the branches of which overhung the defendant's property. The defendant, without notice to P, cut these branches off at the boundary, alleging they were a nuisance. P claimed: (i) a declaration that D could not cut the branches except for any recent growth; (ii) an injunction restraining D from cutting any more; (iii) damages.

Held
Providing there was no trespass on the neighbour's land, D could cut the branches without notice to P because they constituted a nuisance.

Malone v *Laskey* [1907] 2 KB 141 Court of Appeal (Sir Gorell Barnes P, Fletcher Moulton and Kennedy LJJ)

Nuisance – vibration

Facts
The defendants were trustees of a building society which owned a great deal of property. X was a sub-tenant of one of Ds' properties. On their property next door, Ds placed machinery for the purpose of generating electricity to light their premises. This machinery caused much vibration which in turn caused a water tank in the lavatory of X's premises to become insecure. This tank fell on X's wife and seriously injured her. She sued Ds in nuisance.

Held
She had no cause of action against Ds on the ground of nuisance because she had no interest in the premises or any right of occupation. On the evidence Ds were not liable in negligence.

Sir Gorell Barnes P:

> 'Many cases were cited in the course of the argument in which it had been held that actions for nuisance could be maintained where a person's rights of property had been affected by the nuisance, but no authority was cited nor, in my opinion, could any principle of law be formulated to the effect that a person who has no interest in property, no right of occupation in the proper sense of the term can maintain an action in nuisance.'

Commentary
Overruled in *Billings (AC) & Sons Ltd v Riden* [1957] 3 WLR 496 in so far as it deals with negligence.
See *Khorasandjian v Bush* [1993] 3 WLR 476 regarding the requirements for an interest in land in nuisance actions.

Matania v *The National Provincial Bank Ltd* [1936] 2 All ER 633 Court of Appeal (Slesser and Romer LJJ and Finlay J)

Nuisance – building operations

Facts
Premises were demised to the defendant bank, who let the second and third floors to the plaintiffs. They then let the first floor to the defendant syndicate. The latter wished to make extensive alterations and obtained the permission of the bank for this purpose. The plaintiffs suffered greatly from dust and noise caused by the contractors employed.

Held
Although the defendant syndicate had employed independent contractors to carry out the work, they were liable for damages in nuisance.

Slesser LJ:

> 'We are not here concerned with danger, such as might found an action for negligence; we are here concerned with danger such as might found an action for nuisance, but the principles are in my view the same .. that is to say that if the act done is one in its very nature that involves a special danger of nuisance being complained of then it is one which falls within the exception for which the employer of the contractor will be responsible.
>
> It seems to me that in the present case, looking at all the facts of the case, it is not possible to say that here (the builders) did use all reasonable care and skill.'

Miller v *Jackson* [1977] 3 WLR 20 Court of Appeal (Lord Denning MR, Geoffrey Lane and Cumming-Bruce LJJ)

Nuisance – village cricket club

Facts
Cricket was played on a village ground since 1905. In 1970 houses were built in such a place that cricket balls would inevitably be hit into their gardens. The plaintiff, who bought one of the houses in 1972, sued the members of the cricket club for damages for negligence and nuisance, on the basis of incidents causing physical damage to the house and apprehension of personal injury.

Held
(1) The defendants were guilty of negligence, since the risk of injury was both foreseeable and foreseen. (2) The playing of cricket in the circumstances constituted an unreasonable interference with the plaintiff's enjoyment of land, and therefore a nuisance, since there was a real risk of serious injury. It was no defence that the plaintiff brought trouble on his own head by coming to live in the house. (3) By reason of special circumstances, namely the plaintiff's knowledge when he bought his house that cricket was played nearby, and the interest of the village as a whole in the existence of a cricket ground, no injunction should be granted to restrain the playing of cricket, and the plaintiff's only remedy was in damages.

Robinson v *Kilvert* (1889) 41 Ch D 888 Court of Appeal (Cotton, Lindley and Lopes LJJ)

Nuisance – heat-sensitive paper

Facts
The defendant owned a warehouse. He let a floor to the plaintiff for the latter to store paper. D later started a process of manufacturing paper boxes on the ground floor. This heated the first floor to 80CC. The plaintiff sued in nuisance on the grounds that this dried his brown paper. Evidence at trial showed that neither P's workforce nor normal paper was affected by the heat. Also, that D did not know at the time of letting that P would store heat-sensitive paper.

Held
There was no nuisance to P on these facts.

Cotton LJ:

> 'It would, in my opinion, be wrong to say that the doing of something not in itself noxious is a nuisance because it does harm to a particular trade in the adjoining property, although it would not prejudice or affect any adjoining trade carried on in the property and does not interfere with the ordinary enjoyment of life.'

St Helen's Smelting Co v *Tipping* (1865) 11 HL Cas 642 House of Lords (Lord Westbury LC, Lord Cranworth and Lord Wensleydale)

Nuisance – injurious vapour

Facts
The plaintiff bought an estate consisting of about 1,300 acres near to the defendants' copper smelting works. The vapour from the work proved injurious to the plaintiff's trees and crops and he claimed to be entitled to damages.

Held
The plaintiff would succeed. The jury was correctly directed that an actionable injury was one producing sensible discomfort and that every man, unless enjoying rights obtained by prescription or agreement, was bound to use his property in such a way as not to injure that of his neighbour. The law was not concerned with trifling inconvenience and everything had to be considered from a reasonable point of view. In this case the jury was asked to consider whether the injury was such as visibly diminished the value of the property and the comfort and enjoyment of it. Time and locality were factors to be taken into account.

Sedleigh-Denfield v *O'Callaghan* [1940] AC 880 House of Lords (Viscount Maugham, Lord Atkin, Lord Wright, Lord Romer and Lord Porter)

Nuisance by flooding

Facts
The plaintiff's land was next to defendants'. A ditch ran between their land and the end of his garden. Owners of other land agreed with the County Council that a pipe or culvert be put in. A grating should have been placed near the opening to prevent blockage. Instead, it was placed on top of the culvert. The opening was on defendants' land, although they had never given permission for the installation. However, their servants did clean it out bi-annually. In a heavy rainstorm, the pipe was blocked and plaintiff's land flooded.

Held

The defendants must be taken to have some knowledge of the existence of the pipe on their land and, consequently, they were liable for all damage caused.

Lord Wright:

> 'I do not attempt any exhaustive definition of that cause of action (nuisance) but it has never lost its essential character which was derived from its prototype, the Assize of Nuisance, and was maintained under the form of action on the case of Nuisance. The Assize of Nuisance was a real action supplementary to the Assize of Novel disseisin. The latter (ie Assize of Novel Disseisin) was devised to protect the plaintiff's seisin of his land, and the former (ie the Assize of Nuisance) aimed at vindicating the plaintiff's right to the use and enjoyment of his land. The Assize became .. superseded by the less formal procedure of an action on the case for Nuisance which lay for damages. This action was less limited in its scope for whereas the Assize was by a freeholder against a freeholder, the action lay also between possessors and occupiers of land. With possibly certain anomalous exceptions not here, material possession or occupation is still the test.
>
> The forms which Nuisance may take are protean. Certain classifications are possible, but many reported cases are no more than illustrations of particular matters of fact that have been held to be Nuisances.
>
> The liability for a nuisance is not, at least in modern law, a strict or absolute liability... it has, I think, been rightly established in the Court of Appeal that an occupier is not prima facie responsible for a nuisance created without his knowledge or consent. If he is to be liable, a further condition is necessary, namely that he had knowledge or means of knowledge, that he knew or should have known of the nuisance in time to correct it and obviate its mischievous effects.'

Commentary

Applied in *Leakey* v *National Trust* [1980] 2 WLR 65.
    Distinguished in *Mint* v *Good* [1951] 1 KB 517.

Shelfer v *City of London Electric Lighting Co* [1895] 1 Ch 287 Court of Appeal (Lord Halsbury LC, Lindley and A L Smith LJJ)

Nuisance – injunction

Facts

The defendant electricity company erected powerful engines and other works on land near to the house which the plaintiff had leased from a brewery. Both the brewery and the plaintiff sued the defendants. The brewery sued for physical damage to the house and thus to their reversion. The plaintiff sued for annoyance by noise. Before Kekewich J, both claims succeeded as to damages, but not as to an injunction.

Held

The claim for an injunction must also succeed.

A L Smith LJ:

> 'In my opinion, it may be stated as a good working rule that: (i) if the injury to the P's legal rights is small; (ii) and is one which is capable of being estimated in money; (iii) and is one which can be adequately compensated by a small money payment; (iv) and the case is one in which it would be oppressive to D to grant an injunction; then damages may be given in substitution for an injunction.'

Commentary
Applied in *Kennaway v Thompson* [1980] 3 WLR 361.

Sturges v Bridgman (1879) 11 Ch D 852 Court of Appeal (Thesiger, James and Baggallay LJJ)
Nuisance – doctor's consulting room

Facts
The plaintiff was a doctor who bought premises in Wimpole Street. The defendant had a confectionery business in Wigmore Street, which runs at right angles to Wimpole Street. The defendant's kitchen abutted part of P's garden. In the kitchen, against the abutting wall, D had two mortars for pounding loaf sugar and meat: he had used them there for more than 20 years. Some eight years after he moved in, P built a consulting room on the abutting wall. He alleged that the noise from the mortars then became a nuisance to him and he sought an injunction.

Held
The injunction would be granted. The defendant was not protected by prescription as until the consulting room was built there was no actionable nuisance.

Thesiger LJ:

> 'Whether anything is a nuisance or not is a question to be determined not merely by an abstract consideration of the thing itself, but with reference to its circumstances; what would be a nuisance in Belgrave Square would not necessarily be so in Bermondsey or where a locality is devoted to a particular trade or manufacture carried on by the traders in a particular or established manner not constituting a public(?) nuisance. Judges and juries would be justified in finding and may be trusted to find, that the trade or manufacture so carried on in that locality is not a private or actionable wrong .. It would be on the one hand in a very high degree unreasonable and undesirable that there should be a right of action for acts which are not (in the present condition of the adjoining land) and perhaps never will be any inconvenience or annoyance and it would be on the other hand in an equal degree unjust that the use and value of the adjoining land should for all time and in all circumstances be diminished by reason of the continuance of acts incapable of physical interruption and which the law gives no power to prevent.'

Tetley v Chitty [1986] 1 All ER 663 High Court (McNeill J)
Nuisance – landlord's liability

Facts
The Medway Borough Council (the second defendants) leased to the Medway Kart Club premises to be used as a go-kart track. Local residents brought an action against the council and the first defendant, representing the club, and claimed damage for noise resulting from nuisance and an injunction restraining the operation of the track. The noise created varied according to the number of karts in operation, speed alterations and the direction of the wind, and technical evidence supported the assertion that the noise was excessive.

Held
The second defendants were liable in nuisance because the noise was an ordinary and necessary consequence, or a natural and necessary consequence, of the operation of go-karts on their land, and they as landlords had given express or at least implied consent to the nuisance on their land.

Commentary
Applied: *Harris* v *James* (1876) 45 LJQB 545.
　Distinguished: *Kennaway* v *Thompson* [1980] 3 WLR 361.

Wheeler v *JJ Saunders* [1995] 3 WLR 466 Court of Appeal (Staughton and Peter Gibson LJJ and Sir John May)

Nuisance – effect of planning permission

Facts
The plaintiffs and the defendants were neighbours. The defendants obtained planning permission to build two pig houses close to the plaintiffs' land, resulting in strong smells affecting the plaintiffs' property. The plaintiffs claimed that the defendants were liable in nuisance in respect of these odours. At first instance it was held that the smells amounted to an actionable nuisance. The defendants appealed.

Held
That the smells did amount to a nuisance. Although statutory authorisation for a development could confer immunity in respect of a nuisance inevitably arising from it, a planning authority could not authorise a nuisance other than by permitting a change in the character of the neighbourhood, which might render lawful activities that would have previously constituted a nuisance. Thus, although the smells were an inevitable result of the planning permission, that permission did not allow a change in character of the neighbourhood and thus the planning permission did not afford a defence.

Commentary
Compare this case with *Gillingham Borough Council* v *Medway (Chatham) Dock Co Ltd* [1993] QB 343. There the grant of planning permission did alter the character of the neighbourhood, and thus provided a defence, as the alleged nuisance had to be considered in the light of the change in character of the neighbourhood brought about by the planning permission.

Wringe v *Cohen* [1940] 1 KB 229 Court of Appeal (Slesser and Luxmoore LJJ and Atkinson J)

Nuisance – owner's liability

Facts
The plaintiff owned a lock-up shop in Sheffield. The defendant owned a house next door. D let the house to X some two years before. When one night in a storm the gable end of D's house fell through the roof of P's shop, P sued for repair cost in: (i) negligence; (ii) nuisance. There had been a bulge in the wall due to defective repair, especially poor pointing and collaring. Repairs were D's obligation under the lease. He said in defence that he did not appreciate the danger.

Held
This provided no defence to the action and D was liable.

Atkinson J:

'In our judgment if owing to want of repair premises on a highway become dangerous and therefore a nuisance and a passer-by or an adjoining owner suffers damage by their collapse, the occupier or owner who has undertaken the duty of repair is answerable whether he knew or ought to have known of the danger or not .. On the other hand, if the nuisance is created not by want of repair, but, for example, by the act of a trespasser or by a secret and unobservable operation of nature such as a subsidence under or near the foundation of the premises, neither an occupier nor an owner responsible for repair is answerable unless with knowledge or means of knowledge he allows the danger to continue.'

Commentary
Applied in *Mint* v *Good* [1951] 1 KB 517.

15 Public Nuisance

Attorney-General v *PYA Quarries Ltd* [1957] 2 WLR 770 Court of Appeal (Denning, Romer and Parker LJJ)

Public nuisance – definition

Facts
The Attorney General on the relation of a county council alleged that the defendants were committing a public nuisance at their quarries. Their system of blasting caused stones, splinters, dust and vibration. The plaintiffs got an injunction restraining Ds: (1) from causing stones and splinters to leave the quarry confines; and (2) from causing a nuisance to HM's subjects by dust/vibration. The defendants prevented stones leaving the quarry and appealed against (2) on the grounds that at most there was a private, not a public nuisance. There were two highways and 30 or so houses close to the quarry. Oliver J described these as 'a little colony'.

Held
There was a public nuisance and the injunction had been rightly granted.

Romer LJ:

'It is, however, clear in my opinion that any nuisance is public which materially affects the reasonable comfort and convenience of a class of Her Majesty's subjects. The sphere of nuisance may be described generally as "the neighbourhood", but the question whether the local community within that sphere comprises a sufficient number of persons to constitute a "class of the public" is a question of fact in every case. It is not necessary in any judgment to prove that every member of the class has been injuriously affected; it is sufficient to show that a representative cross-section of the class has been so affected.'

Denning LJ:

'So I here declined to answer the question how many people are necessary to make up Her Majesty's subjects generally. I prefer to look to the reason of the thing and say that a public nuisance is a nuisance which is so widespread in its range or so indiscriminate in its effect that it would not be reasonable to expect one person to take proceedings on his own responsibility to put a stop to it, but that it should be taken on the responsibility of the community as a whole.'

Gillingham Borough Council v *Medway (Chatham) Dock Co Ltd* [1993] QB 343 High Court (Buckley J)

Public nuisance – effect of planning permission

Facts
The defendants were lessees of a port. The plaintiffs alleged that the use of the roads around the port at night by numerous heavy goods vehicles (HGVs) constituted a public nuisance. The evidence established that in 1988 there were approximately 750 HGV 'movements' every night and that the sleep and comfort

of the residents in the vicinity of the port were disturbed. The defendants conceded that these conditions constituted a substantial interference with the residents' enjoyment of their property up to June 1990 and that, subject to defences, enough residents were affected to constitute a public nuisance. However the defendants argued that they had been given planning permission to operate a commercial port, that such a port could operate viably only on a 24-hour basis, that no limits had been placed on the volume of traffic in the vicinity when they had been granted planning permission and that their estimate of the likely throughput of traffic had been remarkably accurate.

Held
The plaintiffs' action would not succeed.

Buckley J noted that planning legislation had been enacted by Parliament in an effort to balance the interests of the community and the interests of individuals likely to be adversely affected by the plans being put forward. He then asked himself the question whether residents could defeat the planning legislation by bringing an action in nuisance. His conclusion was that 'where planning consent is given for a development or change of use, the question of nuisance will thereafter fall to be decided by reference to a neighbourhood with that development or use and not as it was previously'. So planning permission was not, of itself, a defence to a nuisance action but it was a factor to be taken into account in identifying the character of the neighbourhood. So, on the facts, account had to be taken of the fact that planning permission had been given to use the dockyard as a commercial port. In the light of this fact, in his Lordship's view the disturbance experienced by the residents of the area was not an actionable nuisance.

Littler v *Liverpool Corporation* [1968] 2 All ER 343 High Court (Cumming-Bruce J)

Highway repairs – statutory duty

Facts
On his way to a shop carrying two empty lemonade bottles, a young man tripped on the paving stones, fell and suffered injury.

Held
His claim for damages could not succeed.

Cumming-Bruce J:

> 'The test in relation to a length of pavement is reasonable foreseeability of danger. A length of pavement is only dangerous if, in the ordinary course of human affairs, danger may reasonably be anticipated from its continued use by the public who usually pass over it. It is a mistake to isolate and emphasise a particular difference in levels between flagstones unless that difference is such that a reasonable person who noticed and considered it would regard it as presenting a real source of danger. Uneven surfaces and differences in level between flagstones of about an inch may cause a pedestrian temporarily off balance to trip and stumble, but such characteristics have to be accepted. A highway is not to be criticised by the standards of a bowling green.
>
> In the present case the only significant defect in the pavement was the small triangular gap which at its deepest presented a trip of half-an-inch. This is the kind of imperfection which has to be accepted in a pavement used by children and adults. Its presence would not make a reasonable person ... think injury would ensue unless it was repaired ... it is important that all concerned in litigation should realise that there is not a cause of action whenever someone trips over an uneven pavement or as a result of a fractional difference in levels between flagstones.'

Lyons, Sons & Co v *Gulliver* [1914] 1 Ch 631 Court of Appeal (Cozens-Hardy MR, Swinfen Eady and Phillimore LJJ)

Nuisance – theatre crowd

Facts
Persons waiting for admission to the defendants' theatre formed a queue outside the plaintiffs' shop.

Held (Phillimore LJ dissenting)
This amounted to an actionable nuisance.

Swinfen Eady LJ:

> 'In my opinion, there can be no question about the law applicable to the present case. Collecting together a crowd of people to the annoyance of one's neighbours may be a nuisance ... If the natural and probable consequence of what the defendant is doing is to collect a crowd so as to obstruct the highway, that may be an indictable nuisance, and if damage is occasioned to an individual, he may have a right of action in respect of it.'

Mint v *Good* [1951] 1 KB 517 Court of Appeal (Somervell, Denning and Birkett LJJ)

Nuisance – premises adjoining highway

Facts
A wall in front of two houses which were let to weekly tenants collapsed on the public footpath and injured the plaintiff. The danger could have been ascertained by inspection. No express agreement existed between the landlord and his tenants as to liability to repair and no right of entry to carry out repairs had been reserved to him.

Held
The landlord was liable for the plaintiff's injuries as there was an implied term that he would keep the premises in a reasonable and habitable condition.

Lord Denning LJ:

> 'The law of England has always take particular care to protect those who use a highway. It puts on the occupier of adjoining premises a special responsibility for the structures which he keeps beside the highway. If those structures fall into disrepair so as to be a potential danger to passers-by, they become a nuisance, and, what is more, a public nuisance, and the occupier is liable to anyone using the highway who is injured by reason of the disrepair. It is no answer for him to say that he and his servants took reasonable care, for even if he has employed a competent independent contractor to repair the structure, and has every reason for supposing it to be safe, the occupier is still liable if the independent contractor did the work badly: see *Tarry* v *Ashton*. The occupier's duty to passers-by is to see that the structure is as safe as reasonable care can make it – a duty which is as high as the duty which an occupier owes to people who pay to come on his premises. He is not liable for latent defects which could not be discovered by reasonable care on the part of anyone nor for acts of trespassers of which he neither knew nor ought to have known ... but he is liable when structures fall into dangerous disrepair, because there must be some fault on the part of someone for that to happen and he is responsible for it to persons using the highway, even though he was not actually at fault himself. That principle was laid down in this court in *Wringe* v *Cohen,* where it is to be noted that the principle is confined to "premises on a highway".'

Commentary
Applied: *Wringe* v *Cohen* [1940] 1 KB 229.
    Distinguished: *Sedleigh-Denfield* v *O'Callaghan* [1940] AC 880.

R v *Shorrock* [1993] 3 WLR 698 Court of Appeal (Simon Brown LJ, Popplewell and Rattee JJ)

Public nuisance – mental element

Facts
The defendant granted a licence for the use of a field on which loud music was played, causing noise and disturbance to local residents. The question arose as to the necessary mental element required for public nuisance.

Held
That the mental element of the crime of public nuisance was the same as that of the tort of private and public nuisance, namely that liability would arise where the person knew or ought to have known, because the means of knowledge were available to him, that there was a real risk of a nuisance arising.

Commentary
Sedleigh-Denfield v *O'Callaghan* [1940] AC 880 applied.

Rose v *Miles* (1815) 4 M & S 101 Court of King's Bench (Lord Ellenborough CJ, Bayley and Dampier JJ)

Public nuisance – private injury

Facts
Wrongfully intending to injure the plaintiff, the defendant moored a barge across a creek of a public navigable river. As a result, the plaintiff had to carry the merchandise from his barges 'a great distance over land'.

Held
The plaintiff was entitled to damages.

Lord Ellenborough CJ:

> 'The is something substantially more injurious to this person, than to the public at large, who might only have it in contemplation to use [the river]. And he has been impeded in his progress by the defendants' wrongfully mooring their barge across and has been compelled to unload and to carry his goods over land, by which he has incurred expense, and that expense caused by the act of the defendants. If a man's time or his money are of any value, it seems to me that this plaintiff has shown a particular damage.'

Tarry v *Ashton* (1876) 1 QBD 314 High Court (Blackburn, Quain and Lush JJ)

Nuisance – negligent independent contractor

Facts
The defendant moved into a house which had a heavy lamp projecting from the front wall. After moving

in, D employed an experienced gas fitter, an independent contractor, to mend the lamp. Some months later, the lamp fell on and injured the plaintiff as she was walking along the pavement.

Held

D was liable for the plaintiff's injuries.

Lush J:

'The question is what is the duty of a person in the position of the defendant? Is it his duty to maintain his premises in good repair, or only to employ a competent person in the work of maintaining them? I think the mere statement of the case suggests its answer. A person who keeps a lamp of this kind puts the public in peril. He cannot get rid of his duty to put the public out of peril by employing another person to take the necessary steps for doing so.'

Thomas v *National Union of Mineworkers (South Wales Area)* [1985] 2 WLR 1081
High Court (Scott J)

Nuisance – obstruction of highway

Facts

During a strike, the plaintiffs decided to return to work, but 60-70 pickets outside the colliery gates sought to deter them by using abusive and violent language. The plaintiffs sought interlocutory injunctions.

Held

On the facts, and in the light of the relevant law, the injunctions would not be granted.

Scott J:

'The working miners are entitled to use the highway for the purpose of entering and leaving their respective places of work. In the exercise of that right they are at present having to suffer the presence and behaviour of the pickets and demonstrators. The law has long recognised that unreasonable interference with the rights of others is actionable in tort ... It is, however, not every act of interference with the enjoyment by an individual of his property rights that will be actionable in nuisance. The law must strike a balance between conflicting rights and interests ...

Nuisance is strictly concerned with, and may be regarded as confined to, activity which unduly interferes with the use or enjoyment of land or of easements. But there is no reason why the law should not protect on a similar basis the enjoyment of other rights. All citizens have the right to use the public highway. Suppose an individual were persistently to follow another on a public highway, making rude gestures or remarks in order to annoy or vex. If continuance of such conduct were threatened no one can doubt but that a civil court would, at the suit of the victim, restrain by an injunction the continuance of the conduct. The tort might be described as a species of private nuisance, namely unreasonable inference with the victim's rights to use the highway. But the label for the tort does not, in my view, matter.

In the present case, the working miners have the right to use the highway for the purpose of going to work. They are, in my judgment, entitled under the general law to exercise that right without unreasonable harassment by others. Unreasonable harassment of them in their exercise of that right would, in my judgment, be tortious.

A decision whether in this, or in any other similar case, the presence or conduct of pickets represents a tortious interference with the right of those who wish to go to work to do so without harassment must depend on the particular circumstances of the particular case. The balance to which I have earlier referred must be struck between the rights of those going to work and the rights of the pickets.'

16 The Rule in *Rylands* v *Fletcher*

Cambridge Water Company v *Eastern Counties Leather plc* [1994] 2 WLR 53 House of Lords (Lord Templeman, Lord Goff, Lord Jauncey, Lord Lowry and Lord Woolf)

Need for foreseeability of damage

Facts
The defendants used a chlorinated solvent at their tannery which was situated some 1.3 miles from the plaintiff's borehole where water was abstracted for domestic purposes. This water became unfit for human consumption by solvent contamination when the solvent seeped into the ground below the defendants' premises and then percolated into the borehole. The plaintiffs brought an action in, inter alia, *Rylands*. In the High Court this action was dismissed on the grounds that the defendants had not made a non-natural user of their land, which was situated in an industrial village. On appeal, the Court of Appeal declined to determine the matter on the basis of *Rylands* but imposed liability on other grounds. The defendants appealed.

Held
That foreseeability of harm of the relevant type by the defendants was required to recover damages under the rule in *Rylands* v *Fletcher* (and also in nuisance). The House of Lords also held, contrary to the finding at first instance, that the defendants had made a non-natural user of their land. However, on the facts of the case the contamination was not foreseeable and the appeal was allowed.

Lord Goff, with whose speech the other law Lords agreed, also briefly considered the meaning of the phrase 'natural use of the land', and doubted whether the storage of substantial quantities of chemicals on industrial premises could ever be a natural user. Lord Goff pointed out that now foreseeability of damage was an essential ingredient of the tort, courts might feel less inclined to extend the concept of natural use to circumstances such as those in the present case.

Lord Goff:

Foreseeability of damage under the rule in Rylands v Fletcher
'I start with the judgment of Blackburn J in *Fletcher* v *Rylands* (1866) LR 1 Ex 265 itself. His celebrated statement of the law is to be found at pp279–280, where he said:

"We think that the true rule of law is, that the person who for his own purposes brings on his lands and collects and keeps there anything likely to do mischief if it escapes, must keep it in at his peril, and, if he does not do so, is prima facie answerable for all the damage which is the natural consequence of its escape. He can excuse himself by showing that the escape was owing to the plaintiff's default; or perhaps that the escape was the consequence of vis major, or the act of God; but as nothing of this sort exists here, it is unnecessary to inquire what excuse would be sufficient. The general rule, as above stated, seems on principle just. The person whose grass or corn is eaten down by the escaping cattle of his neighbour, or whose mine is flooded by the water from his neighbour's reservoir, or whose cellar is invaded by the filth of his neighbour's privy, or whose habitation is made unhealthy by the fumes and noisome vapours of his neighbour's alkali works, is damnified without any fault of his own; and it seems but reasonable and just that the neighbour, who has brought something on his own property which was not naturally there, harmless to others so long as it is confined to his own property, but which he knows to be mischievous if it gets on his neighbour's, should be obliged to make good the damage which ensues if he does not succeed in confining it to his own property. But for his act in bringing it there no mischief could have accrued, and it seems but just that he should at his peril keep it there so that no mischief may accrue, or answer for the natural and anticipated consequences. And upon authority, this we think is established to be the law whether the things so brought be beasts, or water, or filth, or stenches."

In that passage, Blackburn J spoke of "anything *likely* to do mischief if it escapes"; and later he spoke of something "which he *knows* to be mischievous if it gets on his neighbour's [property]", and the liability to "answer for the natural *and anticipated* consequences". Furthermore, time and again he spoke of the strict liability imposed upon the defendant as being that he must keep the thing in at his peril; and, when referring to liability in actions for damage occasioned by animals, he referred, at p282, to the established principle that "it is quite immaterial whether the escape is by negligence or not". The general tenor of his statement of principle is therefore that knowledge, or at least foreseeability of the risk, is a prerequisite of the recovery of damages under the principle; but that the principle is one of strict liability in the sense that the defendant may be held liable notwithstanding that he has exercised all due care to prevent the escape from occurring.

There are however early authorities in which foreseeability of damage does not appear to have been regarded as necessary: see, eg, *Humphries* v *Cousins* (1877) 2 CPD 239. Moreover, it was submitted by Mr Ashworth for CWC that the requirement of foreseeability of damage was negatived in two particular cases, the decision of the Court of Appeal in *West* v *Bristol Tramways Co* [1908] 2 KB 14, and the decision of this House in *Rainham Chemical Works Ltd* v *Belvedere Fish Guano Co Ltd* [1921] 2 AC 465.

In *West* v *Bristol Tramways Co* the defendant tramway company was held liable for damage to the plaintiff's plants and shrubs in his nursery garden adjoining a road where the defendant's tramline ran, the damage being caused by fumes from creosoted wooden blocks laid by the defendants between the rails of the tramline. The defendants were so held liable under the rule in *Rylands* v *Fletcher*, notwithstanding that they were exonerated from negligence, having no knowledge of the possibility of such damage; indeed the evidence was that creosoted wood had been in use for several years as wood paving, and no mischief had ever been known to arise from it. The argument that no liability arose in such circumstances under the rule in *Rylands* v *Fletcher* was given short shrift, both in the Divisional Court and in the Court of Appeal. For the Divisional Court, it was enough that the creosote had been found to be dangerous by the jury, Phillimore J holding that creosote was like the wild animals in the old cases. The Court of Appeal did not call upon the plaintiffs, and dismissed the appeal in unreserved judgments. Lord Alverstone CJ relied upon a passage from *Garrett on the Law of Nuisances*, 2nd ed (1897), p129, and rejected a contention by the defendant that, in the case of non-natural use of land, the defendant will not be liable unless the thing introduced onto the land was, to the knowledge of the defendant, likely to escape and cause damage. It was however suggested, both by Lord Alverstone CJ (with whom Sir Gorell Barnes P agreed) and by Farwell LJ that, by analogy with cases concerning liability for animals, the defendant might escape liability if he could show that, according to the common experience of mankind, the thing introduced onto the land had proved not to be dangerous.

The *Rainham Chemical* case [1921] 2 AC 465 arose out of a catastrophic explosion at a factory involved in the manufacture of high explosive during the First World War, with considerable loss of life and damage to neighbouring property. It was held that the company carrying on the business at the premises was liable for the damage to neighbouring property under the rule in *Rylands* v *Fletcher*; but the great question in the case, at least so far as the appellate courts were concerned, was whether two individuals, who were shareholders in and directors of the company, could be held personally responsible on the same principle.

However, this House dismissed their appeal on a point of some technicality, viz that their Lordships could not satisfy themselves that the two individuals had sufficiently divested themselves of the occupation of the premises, so as to substitute the occupation of the company in the place of their own – notwithstanding that the company itself was also in occupation: see [1921] 2 AC 465, 478-479, per Lord

Buckmaster; pp480, 483-484, per Lord Sumner; p491, per Lord Parmoor; and pp492, 493-494, per Lord Carson.

I feel bound to say that these two cases provide a very fragile base for any firm conclusion that foreseeability of damage has been authoritatively rejected as a prerequisite of the recovery of damages under the rule in *Rylands* v *Fletcher*. Certainly, the point was not considered by this House in the *Rainham Chemical* case. In my opinion, the matter is open for consideration by your Lordships in the present case, and, despite recent dicta to the contrary (see, eg *Leakey* v *National Trust for Places of Historic Interest or Natural Beauty* [1980] QB 485, 519, per Megaw LJ), should be considered as a matter of principle. Little guidance can be derived from either of the two cases in question, save that it seems to have been assumed that the strict liability arising under the rule precluded reliance by the plaintiff on lack of knowledge or the means of knowledge of the relevant danger.

The point is one on which academic opinion appears to be divided: cf *Salmond & Heuston on the Law of Torts*, 20th ed (1992), pp324-325, which favours the prerequisite of foreseeability, and *Clerk & Lindsell on Torts*, 16th ed (1989), p1429, para 25.09, which takes a different view. However, quite apart from the indications to be derived from the judgment of Blackburn J in *Fletcher* v *Rylands*, LR 1 Ex 265 itself, to which I have already referred, the historical connection with the law of nuisance must now be regarded as pointing towards the conclusion that foreseeability of damage is a prerequisite of the recovery of damages under the rule. I have already referred to the fact that Blackburn J himself did not regard his statement of principle as having broken new ground; furthermore, Professor Newark has convincingly shown that the rule in *Rylands* v *Fletcher* was essentially concerned with an extension of the law of nuisance to cases of isolated escape. Accordingly since, following the observations of Lord Reid when delivering the advice of the Privy Council in *The Wagon Mound (No 2)* [1967] 1 AC 617, 640, the recovery of damages in private nuisance depends on foreseeability by the defendant of the relevant type of damage, it would appear logical to extend the same requirement to liability under the rule in *Rylands* v *Fletcher*.

Natural use of land

I turn to the question whether the use by ECL of its land in the present case constituted a natural use, with the result that ECL cannot be held liable under the rule in *Rylands* v *Fletcher*. In view of my conclusion on the issue of foreseeability, I can deal with this point shortly.

The judge held that it was a natural use. He said:

"In my judgment, in considering whether the storage of organochlorines as an adjunct to a manufacturing process is a non-natural use of land, I must consider whether that storage created special risks for adjacent occupiers and whether the activity was for the general benefit of the community. It seems to me inevitable that I must consider the magnitude of the storage and the geographical area in which it takes place in answering the question. Sawston is properly described as an industrial village, and the creation of employment is clearly for the benefit of that community. I do not believe that I can enter upon an assessment of the point on a scale of desirability that the manufacture of wash leathers comes, and I content myself with holdings that this storage in this place is a natural use of land."

It is commonplace that this particular exception to liability under the rule has developed and changed over the years. It seems clear that, in *Fletcher* v *Rylands*, LR 1 Ex 265 itself, Blackburn J's statement of the law was limited to things which are brought by the defendant onto his land, and so did not apply to things that were naturally upon the land. Furthermore, it is doubtful whether in the House of Lords in the same case Lord Cairns, to whom we owe the expression "non-natural use" of the land, was intending to expand the concept of natural use beyond that envisaged by Blackburn J. Even so, the law has long since departed from any such simple idea, redolent of a different age; and, at least since the advice of the Privy Council delivered by Lord Moulton in *Rickards* v *Lothian* [1913] AC 263, 280, natural use has been extended to embrace the ordinary use of land. I ask to be forgiven if I again quote Lord Moulton's statement of the law which has lain at the heart of the subsequent development of this exception:

"It is not every use to which land is put that brings into play at that principle. It must be some special use bringing with it increased danger to others, and must not merely be the ordinary use of the land or such a use as is proper for the general benefit of the community."

Rickards v *Lothian* itself was concerned with a use of a domestic kind, viz the overflow of water from a basin whose runaway had become blocked. But over the years the concept of natural use, in the sense of ordinary use, has been extended to embrace a wide variety of uses, including not only domestic uses but also recreational uses and even some industrial uses.

It is obvious that the expression "ordinary use of the land" in Lord Moulton's statement of the law is one which is lacking in precision. There are some writers who welcome the flexibility which has thus been introduced into this branch of the law, on the ground that it enables judges to mould and adapt the principle of strict liability to the changing needs of society; whereas others regret the perceived absence of principle in so vague a concept, and fear that the whole idea of strict liability may as a result be undermined. A particular doubt is introduced by Lord Moulton's alternative criterion – "or such a use as is proper for the general benefit of the community". If these words are understood to refer to a local community, they can be given some content as intended to refer to such matters as, for example, the provision of services; indeed the same idea can, without too much difficulty, be extended to, for example, the provision of services to industrial premises, as in a business park or an industrial estate. But if the words are extended to embrace the wider interests of the local community or the general benefit of the community at large, it is difficult to see how the exception can be kept within reasonable bounds. A notable extension was considered in your Lordships' House in *Read* v *J Lyons & Co Ltd* [1947] AC 156, 169-170, per Viscount Simon, and p174, per Lord Macmillan, where it was suggested that, in time of war, the manufacture of explosives might be held to constitute a natural use of land, apparently on the basis that, in a country in which the greater part of the population was involved in the war effort, many otherwise exceptional uses might become "ordinary" for the duration of the war. It is however unnecessary to consider so wide an extension as that in a case such as the present. Even so, we can see the introduction of another extension in the present case, when the judge invoked the creation of employment as clearly for the benefit of the local community, viz "the industrial village" at Sawston. I myself, however, do not feel able to accept that the creation of employment as such, even in a small industrial complex, is sufficient of itself to establish a particular use as constituting a natural or ordinary use of land.

Fortunately, I do not think it is necessary for the purposes of the present case to attempt any redefinition of the concept of natural or ordinary use. This is because I am satisfied that the storage of chemicals in substantial quantities, and their use in the manner employed at ECL's premises, cannot fall within the exception. ... Indeed I feel bound to say that the storage of substantial quantities of chemicals on industrial premises should be regarded as an almost classic case of non-natural use; and I find it very difficult to think that it should be thought objectionable to impose strict liability for damage caused in the event of their escape. It may well be that, now that it is recognised that foreseeability of harm of the relevant type is a prerequisite of liability in damages under the rule, the courts may feel less pressure to extend the concept of natural use to circumstances such as those in the present case; and in due course it may become easier to control this exception, and to ensure that it has a more recognisable basis of principle. For these reasons, I would not hold that ECL should be exempt from liability on the basis of the exception of natural use.

However, for the reasons I have already given, I would allow ECL's appeal with costs before your Lordships' House and in the courts below.'

Green v Chelsea Waterworks Co (1894) 70 LT 547 Court of Appeal (Lindley, Kay and A L Smith LJJ)

Statutory authority – burst water pipe

Facts
Acting under statutory powers, the defendants laid a main water pipe in a street near the plaintiffs' premises. Without negligence on the defendants' part, the pipe burst and water flowed into the plaintiffs' premises and damaged their stock.

Held
The defendants were not liable.

Lindley LJ:

> 'So far as the action is based on negligence it is not maintainable, because the jury have found that there was no negligence. Then on what principle can the defendants be held liable except negligence? It was argued that they were liable by reason of the doctrine in *Rylands* v *Fletcher*, and it was said that this was like the case of a landowner who stores water on his land so as to become a source of danger to his neighbours, and that, consequently, the defendants were bound to show that they were relieved by the Acts of Parliament under which they were constituted from the duty of keeping the water in their pipes. The fault of that argument is in the major proposition. *Rylands* v *Fletcher* was not a case of a company authorised to lay down water pipes by Act of Parliament. It was a case of a private individual storing water on his own land for his own purposes. There was no negligence on his part ... That case is not to be extended beyond the legitimate principle on which the House of Lords decided it. If it were extended as far as strict logic might require, it would be a very oppressive decision. Here the defendants were only doing what they were authorised to do by their Act, and, as they were not guilty of negligence, they are not liable for damage.'

Commentary
Distinguished: *Rylands* v *Fletcher* (1868) LR 3 HL 330.

Hale v *Jennings Brothers* [1938] 1 All ER 579 Court of Appeal (Slessor, Scott and Clauson LJJ)

Chair-o-plane injury

Facts
The defendants were the proprietors of a fairground. One of their attractions was a roundabout with planes on, which revolved at high speed. The plaintiff ran a stall as a tenant of the defendants. One of the planes came away and caused considerable injury to the plaintiff.

Held
The defendants were liable without proof of negligence under the *Rylands* v *Fletcher* principle.

Mason v *Levy Auto Parts of England Ltd* [1967] 2 WLR 1384 High Court (MacKenna J)

Escape of fire

Facts
The defendants' yard contained machinery, which was greased and stacked in wooden cases pending sale. There was also other inflammable material there. The defendants had installed fire-fighting equipment on the advice of the local fire brigade because of the considerable fire-risk. After a period of very dry weather, fire broke out in the yard; despite immediate steps taken to put the blaze out, it spread to the plaintiff's adjoining property where it destroyed trees and plants in his garden. The cause of the fire was unknown, but was probably caused by a workman's cigarette. The defendants disclaimed liability, inter alia, on the ground that the fire had 'accidentally begun' within s86 of the Fires Prevention (Metropolis) Act 1774.

Held
The defendants were liable under the principle in *Rylands* v *Fletcher*, because their use of the yard was non-natural user of the land, having regard to the material they had brought on to it, the manner in which it was stored and the character of the neighbourhood. As far as the statutory protection went, the defendants were not under any burden of disproving negligence when seeking its protection.

Nichols v *Marsland* (1876) 2 Ex D 1 Court of Appeal (Cockburn CJ, Mellish and James LJJ, Baggallay JA and Archibald J)

Flooding – Act of God

Facts
On the defendant's land were artificial pools containing large quantities of water connected by weirs. This was achieved by damming a stream and allowing the water to return to it further down its course. After a very heavy rain storm, the pools flooded and damaged the plaintiff's property.

Held
The rainstorm was an Act of God and the defendant was not liable.

Mellish LJ:

> 'The present case is distinguished from *Rylands* v *Fletcher* in that it is not the act of the defendants in keeping this reservoir, an act in itself lawful, which alone leads to the escape of the water, and so renders wrongful that which but for such escape would have been lawful. It is the supervening "vis major" of the water caused by the flood, superadded to the water in the reservoir, which of itself would have been innocuous, caused the disaster. A person cannot, in our opinion, be properly said to have caused or allowed the water to escape, if the act of God or the Queen's enemies was the real cause of its escaping without any fault on the part of the defendant. If a reservoir was destroyed by an earthquake, or the Queen's enemies destroyed it in conducting some warlike operation, it would be contrary to all reason and justice to hold the owner of the reservoir liable for any damage that might be done by the escape of the water. We are of opinion, therefore, that the defendant was entitled to excuse herself by proving that the water escaped through the act of God.'

North-Western Utilities Ltd v *London Guarantee and Accident Co Ltd* [1936] AC 108 Privy Council (Lord Hailsham LC, Lord Blanesburgh and Lord Wright)

Escape of gas – fire

Facts
The appellants laid gas pipes under a street in Edmonton. Eight years later the local authority constructed a storm sewer beneath the gas main. The following year gas escaped into a hotel where it ignited: the hotel was burned down. The gas had escaped because of a break in a welded joint which had occurred because of the local authority's sewer operations.

Held
The appellants were liable as their failure to know of the local authority's operations was not consistent with due care on their part.

Lord Wright:

> 'That gas is a dangerous thing within the rules applicable to things dangerous in themselves is beyond question. Thus the appellants, who are carrying in their mains the inflammable and explosive gas, are

prima facie within the principle of *Rylands* v *Fletcher*; that is to say, that, though they are doing nothing wrongful in carrying the dangerous thing so long as they keep it in their pipes, they come prima facie within the rule of strict liability if the gas escapes; the gas constitutes an extraordinary danger created by the appellants for their own purposes, and the rule established by *Rylands* v *Fletcher* requires that they act at their peril and must pay for damage caused by the gas if it escapes, even without any negligence on their part. The rule is not limited to cases where the defendant has been carrying or accumulating the dangerous thing on his own land; it applies equally in a case like the present where the appellants were carrying the gas in mains laid in the property of the city – that is, in the subsoil – in exercise of a franchise to do so ...

This form of liability is in many ways analogous to a liability for nuisance, though nuisance is not only different in its historical origin, but in its legal character and many of its incidents and applications. But the two causes of action often overlap, and in respect of each of these causes of action the rule of strict liability has been modified by admitting as a defence that what was being done was properly done in pursuance of statutory powers, and the mischief that has happened has not been brought about by any negligence on the part of the undertakers ...

By the same reasoning the rule has been held inapplicable where the casualty is due to the act of God; or to the independent or conscious volition of a third party ... and not to any negligence of the defendants.'

Perry v *Kendricks Transport Ltd* [1956] 1 WLR 85 Court of Appeal (Singleton, Jenkins and Parker LJJ)

Explosion caused by strangers

Facts
The plaintiff (a boy of ten) was seriously injured in the defendants' coach park when he approached two other boys who were near a coach, who jumped away having thrown a match into an empty petrol tank causing an explosion. The P sued the Ds on the grounds that the coach was a dangerous thing within *Rylands* v *Fletcher*.

Held
The defendants were not liable.

Singleton LJ:

> 'The principle laid down may cease to be applicable if the harm done was due to the act of a stranger. If the mischievous, deliberate and conscious act of a stranger causes the damage, the occupier can escape liability ... I am prepared to accept this position: if the person who interferes with something of the Ds' is a person whom they might expect to be upon their ground and the character of the interference is something they ought to anticipate, then they do owe some duty.'

Commentary
Applied: *Rickards* v *Lothian* [1913] AC 263.

Ponting v *Noakes* [1894] 2 QB 281 High Court (Charles and Henn Collins JJ)

Liability for horse's death

Facts
A yew tree grew on the defendants' land adjoining the plaintiff's field. The tree did not overhang the field, but the plaintiff's colt had reached its branches from the field, eaten some of its leaves – and died. The plaintiff sued to recover the colt's value.

Held
His action could not succeed.

Charles J:

> 'The poisonous tree was admitted to be wholly on the defendants' land, but, inasmuch as it was so near to the boundary that an animal could easily reach the branches, it was contended that the principle of *Rylands* v *Fletcher* was applicable. But this argument appears to me to rest on a misconception of what that case really decided. The decision only refers to the escape from a defendant's land of something which he has brought there, and which is likely to do mischief if it escapes ... The rule of law enunciated in *Rylands* v *Fletcher* I think therefore has no application ... The hurt which the animal received was due to his wrongful intrusion. He had no right to be there, and his owner therefore has no right to complain.'

Read v *J Lyons & Co Ltd* [1947] AC 156 House of Lords (Viscount Simon, Lord Macmillan, Lord Porter, Lord Simonds, and Lord Uthwatt)

Explosion – escape

Facts
The defendants manufactured high explosive shells for the Government and occupied factory premises as agents of the Minister for the purpose. The plaintiff was employed by the Ds at this factory as a supervisor in the shell-filling shop. While she was there, an explosion occured which injured her. She could prove no negligence and sued on the principle in *Rylands* v *Fletcher*.

Held
The defendants were not liable because there was no 'escape' of any dangerous thing from their premises.

Viscount Simon:

> 'It seems better therefore when a plaintiff relies on *Rylands* v *Fletcher* to take the conditions declared by this House to be essential for liability in that case and to ascertain whether these conditions exist in the actual case.
>
> Now the strict liability recognised by this House to exist in *Rylands* v *Fletcher* is conditioned by two elements which I may call the condition of "escape" from the land of something likely to do mischief if it escapes and the condition of "non-natural use" of the land.'

Rickards v *Lothian* [1913] AC 263 Privy Council (Viscount Haldane LC, Lord Macnaghten, Lord Atkinson and Lord Moulton)

Overflow – act of third party

Facts
D was the tenant of a building. P was a sub-tenant of the second floor and various other of D's tenants occupied the floors above him. Someone on the floor above turned on a wash basin tap and plugged the sink so that water left the over-flow pipe and soaked into the second floor wall, damaging P's stock-in-trade.

Held
D was not liable either for negligence or nuisance.

Lord Moulton:

'The legal principle which underlies the decision in *Fletcher* v *Rylands* was well known in English law from a very early period, but it was explained and formulated in a strikingly clear and authoritative manner in that case and, therefore, is usually referred to by that name. It is nothing other than an application of the old maxim, sic utere tuo at aberum non laedas.

It is not every use to which land is put which brings into play that principle [in *Rylands* v *Fletcher*]. It must be some special use bringing with it increased danger to others and must not merely be the ordinary use of the land or such a use as is proper for the general benefit of the community ... The provision of a proper supply of water to the various parts of a house is not only reasonable, but has become in accordance with modern sanitary views, an almost necessity. It is recognised as being so desirable in the interests of the community that in some form or other it is usually made obligatory in civilized nations. Such a supply cannot be installed without causing some concurrent danger of leakage or overflow. It would be unreasonable for the law to regard those who instal or maintain such a system of supply as doing so at their own peril with an absolute liability for any damage resulting from its presence, even if there has been no negligence.'

Commentary
Applied in *Perry* v *Kendricks Transport Ltd* [1956] 1 WLR 85.

Rylands v *Fletcher* (1868) LR 3 HL 330 House of Lords (Lord Cairns LC and Lord Cranworth)

Escape of dangerous things

Facts
The plaintiff built a colliery on his land. One shaft was extended to join up with some old shafts which had been excavated under land adjacent to the plaintiff's. Using competent but, on this occasion, negligent independent contractors, the defendants constructed a reservoir on nearby land under which some of the old mine shafts were situated. When they filled the reservoir, the water entered the old shafts and, by that route, flooded the plaintiff's mine. The defendants themselves had not been negligent.

Held
The defendants were liable for the damage caused. Their Lordships approved the judgment of Blackburn J in the Court of Exchequer Chamber in which he said:

'The question therefore arises what is the obligation which the law casts upon a person who, like the defendants, lawfully brings onto his land something which though harmless while it remains there, will do mischief if it escapes ...

We think the true rule of law is that the person who for his own purposes brings onto his lands and collects and keeps there anything likely to do mischief if it escapes, must keep it in at his peril and if he does not do so, is prima facie liable for all the damage which is the natural consequence of its escape. He can excuse himself by showing that the escape was owing to the plaintiffs' default or, perhaps, that the escape was the consequence of vis major or Act-of-God but as nothing of this sort exists here, it is unnecessary to inquire what excuse would be sufficient.

The general rule as stated above, seems on principle just. The person whose grass or corn is eaten down by the escaping cattle of his neighbour or whose mine is flooded by water from his neighbour's reservoir or whose cellar is invaded by the filth of his neighbour's privy or whose habitat is made unhealthy by the fumes and noisome vapours of his neighbour's alkali works, is dominified without any fault of his own and it seems but reasonable and just that the neighbour who has brought something on his own property which was not naturally there, harmless to others so far as it is confined to his own property but which he knows will be mischievous if it gets on his neighbour's, should be obliged to make good the damage which ensues if he does not succeed in confining it to his own property.

... And upon authority this we think is established to be the law whether the things so brought be beasts or water or filth or stenches.'

Lord Cairns LC:

'... if the defendants not stopping at the natural use of their close (land) had desired to use it for any purpose which I may term non-natural use for the purpose of introducing into the close that which in its natural use was not in or upon it ... then it appears to me that that which the defendants were doing they were doing at their own peril.'

Commentary
Approved in *Leakey* v *National Trust* [1980] 2 WLR 65.

Distinguished in *Noble* v *Harrison* [1926] 2 KB 332 and *Green* v *Chelsea Waterworks Co* (1894) 70 LT 547.

Shiffman v *The Grand Priory in the British Realm of the Venerable Order of the Hospital of St John of Jerusalem* [1936] 1 All ER 557 (Atkinson J)

Flag pole accident

Facts
Here the defendants, at the request of the police, erected a casualty tent to cope with an anticipated public crowd. They also erected a flag pole, supported by four guy ropes. Children kept playing on this and, despite attempts to prevent them, they pulled it down onto the plaintiff.

Held
On the facts, the defendants had been negligent. Seemingly, the flag pole was within *Rylands* v *Fletcher* and was erected at the defendants' peril.

17 Remedies

AB v ***South West Water Services Ltd*** [1993] 2 WLR 507 Court of Appeal (Sir Thomas Bingham MR, Stuart-Smith and Simon Brown LJJ)

Nuisance – exemplary and aggravated damages

Facts
Drinking water supplied by the defendants had been accidentally polluted by aluminium sulphate and the plaintiffs suffered ill effects in respect of which they sought damages for personal injuries. The defendants admitted liability for compensatory damages for breach of statutory duty but the judge refused to strike out the plaintiffs' claim for exemplary and/or aggravated damages for the tort of nuisance.

Held
This claim would be struck out.

Sir Thomas Bingham MR:

'A defendant accused of crime may ordinarily be ordered (if convicted) to pay a financial penalty. In such a case he will enjoy the constitutional safeguards afforded to defendants in criminal cases, which may include trial by jury, and the sum he is ordered to pay is received by the state, not (even in the case of a private prosecution) by the prosecutor. In a civil case, arising out of a civil wrong (whether or not it is also a crime), the defendant may be ordered to pay damages. In the ordinary way, damages bear no resemblance to a criminal penalty. The damages awarded to a plaintiff will be such as will compensate him for the loss he has suffered as a result of the wrong, so far as money can. The court looks to the extent of the plaintiff's loss not to the quality of the defendant's conduct. Since the damages are awarded to compensate the plaintiff they are of course paid to him.

Exemplary (or, as they were once revealingly called, punitive) damages cut across this simple distinction. They are awarded in civil cases, so that the defendant does not enjoy the safeguards afforded to defendants in criminal cases including, save in a small minority of cases, trial by jury. They are paid to the plaintiff, not the state. But they are not paid to compensate the plaintiff, who will be fully compensated by the ordinary measure of damages. They are paid to punish or deter the defendant, to mark the disapproval which his conduct has provoked. For the plaintiff such damages represent a bonus, an addition to the sum needed to compensate him fully for the loss he has suffered as a result of the wrong done to him.

In his leading speech on this topic of *Rookes* v *Barnard* [1964] AC 1129 Lord Devlin recognised the law on exemplary damages as anomalous. But he (and the other members of the House, all of whom agreed with him) did not think it open to them to refuse to recognise the exemplary principle and in any event held that there were certain classes of case in which it served a valuable purpose. So the House ruled that awards of exemplary damages should not be abolished but should be curtailed or restricted ... It is the extent of that curtailment or restriction which raises the first, and major, issue in this appeal.

In his speech Lord Devlin was not, as I understand him, concerned to identify certain causes of action which could and others which could not properly ground claims for exemplary damages. His focus was not on causes of action at all. Rather, his concern was to identify those elements which had been present in claims which had led to awards of exemplary damages in the past and which served to justify retention of the principle. Statute apart, he identified two such elements giving rise to two categories or classes of case.

In the first category there had been what he variously described as an "arbitrary and outrageous use of executive power" and "oppressive, arbitrary or unconstitutional action by the servants of the government" ... there can be no doubt what Lord Devlin was speaking about. It was gross misuse of power, involving tortious conduct, by agents of government ...

The second category covered cases in which the defendant had acted tortiously on a calculation that the economic benefits to him of his unlawful conduct would outweigh any compensation he might be liable to pay the injured party. The rationale underlying this category was clearly stated: "Exemplary damages can properly be awarded whenever it is necessary to teach a wrongdoer that tort does not pay." This again suggests that it was the quality of the conduct complained of rather than the cause of action pleaded which governed the right to claim exemplary damages.

Lord Devlin's speech in *Rookes* v *Barnard* was the subject of detailed exegesis by an enlarged Appellate Committee of the House of Lords in *Cassell & Co Ltd* v *Broome* [1972] AC 1027 ... I cannot pretend to find the answer at all clear, but I incline to think that a majority of the House regarded an award of exemplary damages as permissible only where (a) a case fell within one or other of Lord Devlin's categories and (b) was founded on a tort for which exemplary damages had been awarded before *Rookes* v *Barnard*. This may involve a misreading of their Lordships' speeches in *Cassell & Co Ltd* v *Broome*, but I think it is the basis upon which the Court of Appeal should, until corrected, proceed.

If it is correct to import a cause of action test, this court is bound to hold that the plaintiffs' claims in negligence cannot found a claim for exemplary damages even if they fall within one or other of Lord Devlin's categories. Our attention has been drawn to no negligence claim leading to such an award before 1964 (or, I think, since). By contrast, I understand *Bell* v *Midland Rly Co* (1861) 10 CBNS 287, in which damages described as exemplary were awarded, to have been founded in private nuisance, possibly in addition to other causes of action. More recently, in *Guppys (Bridport) Ltd* v *Brookling*, *Guppys (Bridport) Ltd* v *James* (1983) 14 HLR 1 the Court of Appeal upheld an award of damages for private nuisance, although the present issue was not raised or addressed.

It does not, however, appear that there has ever, before *Rookes* v *Barnard* or since, been an award of exemplary damages for public nuisance. In one sense, public nuisance is private nuisance writ large. But there are significant differences. First, the causing of a public nuisance in a number of its forms is a crime (and a crime for which, in this case, the defendants were prosecuted) which a private nuisance will rarely, if ever, be. I describe this difference as significant because Lord Devlin in *Rookes* v *Barnard* regarded conduct falling within his two categories as not ordinarily falling within the criminal law. He would plainly have regarded the award of exemplary damages as even more anomalous in cases where the conduct in question already attracted the sanctions of the criminal law. Secondly, a public nuisance may lead to numerous complainants, which a private nuisance will not. I describe this difference as significant because it highlights an obvious and intractable difficulty: in the case of a public nuisance affecting hundreds or even thousands of plaintiffs, how can the court assess the sum of exemplary damages to be awarded to any one of them to punish or deter the defendant without knowing at the outset the number of successful plaintiffs and the approximate size of the total bill for exemplary damages which the defendant must meet? If, as I think, a claim in public nuisance falls foul of the cause of action test, assuming there is one, these seem to me good reasons for holding that it will not support an award of exemplary damages.

It is, however, necessary to consider whether the plaintiffs' claims for exemplary damages, if otherwise good on the facts as pleaded, fall within one or other or both of Lord Devlin's two categories ... If the defendants' conduct was as pleaded, as we must for present purposes assume, it was highly reprehensible, but the conduct complained of was quite unlike the abuses of power which Lord Devlin had in mind and I cannot regard the defendants, for any purposes relevant to these claims, as wielding executive or governmental power. They were a publicly owned utility acting as monopoly supplier of a necessary commodity, enjoying certain statutory powers and subject to certain obligations, but they were not acting as an instrument or agent of government. I regard this case as falling well outside the first category.

The plaintiffs have not in my opinion pleaded a claim arguably falling within the second category either. It is true that the defendants' conduct is said ... to have been "calculated by them to make a profit for themselves which may well exceed that payable to the plaintiffs". This is plainly directed towards establishing a second category claim. But [the statement of claim does] ... not in my opinion contain facts from which the necessary inference could be drawn. The plaintiffs say that when they obtain discovery they will either obtain material to support the allegation or they will drop it. That is not in my view a correct approach. Unless the plaintiffs already have enough material to plead a plausible (even if incomplete) case, the pleading should not be allowed to stand. It is not permissible to plead a bare assertion in the hope that material to support it will turn up on discovery.

I turn, lastly, to the claim ... for aggravated damages. The plaintiffs are of course entitled to be fully compensated for all they suffered as a direct result of the defendants' admitted breach of duty. The ordinary measure of compensatory damages will cover all they have suffered as a result of that breach, physically, psychologically and mentally. Full account will be taken of the distress and anxiety which such an event necessarily causes. To the extent that any of these effects was magnified or exacerbated by the defendants' conduct, the ordinary measure of damages will compensate. The question is whether, in addition to that full compensatory measure, the plaintiffs have pleaded a sustainable claim for additional compensation by way of aggravated damages. This is claimed ... on the basis that the plaintiffs' feelings of indignation were aroused by the defendants' high-handed way of dealing with the incident. I know of no precedent for awarding damages for indignation aroused by a defendant's conduct. Defamation cases in which a plaintiff's damages are increased by the defendant's conduct of the litigation (as by aggressive cross-examination of the plaintiff or persistence in a groundless plea of justification) are not in my view a true exception, since injury to the plaintiff's feelings and self-esteem is an important part of the damage for which compensation is awarded. In very many other tort actions (and, for that matter, actions in contract, boundary disputes, partnership actions and other disputes) the plaintiff is indignant at the conduct of the defendant (or his insurers). An award of damages does not follow; nor, in my judgment should it, since this is not damage directly caused by the defendant's tortious conduct and this is not damage which the law has ever recognised.'

American Cyanamid Co v *Ethicon Ltd* [1975] 2 WLR 316 House of Lords (Lord Diplock, Viscount Dilhorne, Lord Cross of Chelsea, Lord Salmon and Lord Edmund-Davies)

Interlocutory injunctions

Facts
The appellants registered a patent in relation to surgical sutures and alleged that the respondents were proposing to introduce a product which would infringe it. The appellants sought an injunction.

Held
The injunction would be granted. There were serious questions to be tried and the balance of convenience favoured it.

Banque Bruxelles Lambert SA v *Eagle Star Insurance Co Ltd* [1995] 2 WLR 607 Court of Appeal (Sir Thomas Bingham MR, Rose and Morritt LJJ)

Damages – measure of damages

Facts
The plaintiff mortgagees claimed damages against the defendants, who had acted as valuers. The

plaintiffs alleged that the property had been negligently over-valued, and that but for that valuation they would not have entered into the transaction with the borrower. Following a general fall in the property market the borrowers defaulted, and so on possession and sale the plaintiffs obtained much less than the figure at which the property had been valued. In their claim for damages the plaintiffs included a sum in respect of the loss due to the market fall between the date of valuation and date of realisation. At first instance the judge refused to award a sum arising from the market fall. The plaintiffs appealed to the Court of Appeal.

Held
Where a lender would not, but for the negligent valuation, have entered into the transaction with the borrower, that negligence was the cause of the plaintiff's loss. A fall in the market was foreseeable and was not to be treated as a new intervening cause breaking the link between the valuer's negligence and the loss sustained. Thus the lenders could recover damages for the loss they had sustained due to the market fall.

BBMB Finance (Hong Kong) Ltd v *Eda Holdings Ltd* (1990) The Times 12 February Privy Council (Lord Bridge of Harwich, Lord Templeman, Lord Griffiths, Lord Goff of Chieveley and Lord Lowry)

Damages – conversion

Facts
Certain shares had been converted and the judge had awarded the value of the shares at the date of conversion less the value of replacement shares at the date of replacement.

Held
His decision had been correct. When property is irreversibly converted, damages are measured by the value of the property at the date of conversion.

Bradburn v *Great Western Rail Co* (1874) LR 10 Ex 1 Exchequer Division (Bramwell, Pigott and Amphlett BB)

Damages – insurance monies

Facts
The plaintiff passenger was injured on the defendants' railway in consequence of the negligence of the defendants' servants. The plaintiff was insured against such accidents and he received compensation of £31 from the insurers in respect of his injuries.

Held
The amount so received should not be deducted from the damages payable by the defendants.

British Transport Commission v *Gourley* [1956] 2 WLR 41 House of Lords (Earl Jowitt, Lord Goddard, Lord Reid, Lord Radcliffe, Lord Tucker, Lord Keith of Avonholm and Lord Somervell of Harrow)

Damages – income tax

Facts
The plaintiff was injured as a result of the defendant's negligence. The trial judge awarded him £37,720 damages in respect of loss of earnings (actual and prospective) paying no regard to the tax and surtax he would have had to pay if he had not been injured. This tax would have reduced the earnings award to £6,695.

Held (Lord Keith of Avonholm dissenting)
The judge ought to have taken the tax position into account. The award in respect of lost earnings should be reduced to £6,695.

Brunsden v *Humphrey* (1884) 14 QBD 141 Court of Appeal (Lord Coleridge CJ, Sir Baliol Brett MR and Bowen LJ)

Damages – different causes of action

Facts
The plaintiff sued the defendant for damage to his cab and was awarded damages. Afterwards, he sued for damages for personal injury suffered in the same collision.

Held (Lord Coleridge dissenting on the facts)
There were two distinct causes of action and the second proceedings were not barred by the first.

Burton v *Winters* [1993] 1 WLR 1077 Court of Appeal (Lloyd LJ and Connell J)

Right of self-help

Facts
In an action for trespass and nuisance, the plaintiff sought an injunction requiring the defendants to remove a portion of a garage which encroached on her land. A declaration was granted that part of the garage was on the plaintiff's land, but no injunction was granted. Some time afterwards the defendants were granted an injunction restraining the plaintiff from trespassing onto and from interfering with their property. The plaintiff appealed, and the question arose as to whether she was entitled to exercise the right of self-help.

Held
That the right of self-help for trespass by encroachment was a summary remedy which was justified only in clear and simple cases or in an emergency. In the present case there was no emergency, some difficult issues were raised and the disproportionate consequences of self-help, namely the demolition of the garage, made the case unsuitable for the remedy of self-help.

Colledge v *Bass Mitchells & Butlers Ltd* [1988] 1 All ER 536 Court of Appeal (Sir John Donaldson MR, Glidwell LJ and Sir Denys Buckley)

Damages – redundancy payment

Facts
The plaintiff severely injured his back at work and he sued his employers alleging negligence. Before

the action was heard he was offered and he accepted voluntary redundancy and he received a payment of £9,000. The trial judge held that the employers were liable, but he refused to deduct the £9,000 from the damages awarded. The employers appealed as to the amount of damages.

Held
The appeal would be allowed as the redundancy payment should have been deducted.

Sir John Donaldson MR:

'In my judgment the starting point is Lord Reid's classic judgment in *Parry* v *Cleaver* [1970] AC 1 at 13. In effect Lord Reid states an equation "a-b=c", where "a" represents the sums which the plaintiff would have received but for the accident, but which by reason of the accident he can no longer get, "b" represents the sums which he did in fact receive as a result of the accident, but which he would not have received if there had been no accident, and "c" represents the compensation to which he is entitled.

On the judge's findings, but for the accident the plaintiff would have been unlikely ever to have been made redundant and would have worked for the defendants until his retirement. Whilst the judge did say that if the plaintiff's employment by the defendants ended prematurely, he would have been able to obtain other employment, he did not suggest that such a change would have benefited the plaintiff by enabling him to take a redundancy payment and immediately obtain other employment without loss of wages. Prima facie, therefore, the £9,000 is part of "b", but no part of "a" and accordingly falls to be deducted.'

Cookson v *Knowles* [1978] 2 WLR 978 House of Lords (Lord Diplock, Viscount Dilhorne, Lord Salmon, Lord Fraser of Tullybelton and Lord Scarman)

Damages – calculation

Facts
In December 1973 plaintiff's husband was killed in a motor accident caused negligently by the defendant. At death, H was 49, in steady employment as machinist. The trial was in May 1976. The trial judge awarded dependency at £2,250 x 11 (the multiplier) = £24,750 and awarded interest at 9 per cent on the whole amount from death to judgment.

Held
1. Because of the current financial climate, the more reliable assessment of a dependant's loss in fatal accidents would be best achieved by splitting the award into two parts: a) the pecuniary loss from death to trial (pre trial loss) and b) the pecuniary loss which it is estimated would be suffered from trial onwards (future loss), for which the proper multiplicand was the figure to which it was estimated the annual dependency would have amounted by the date of trial, and damages should in general be assessed in this way in all such cases.
2. No additional allowance should be made for inflation because this would be taken care of in the higher interest rates. Interest on pre trial loss should be at half the short term rates current during that period. No interest should be awarded on future loss.

Commentary
Applied in *Auty* v *National Coal Board* [1985] 1 WLR 784.

Cresswell v *Eaton* [1991] 1 WLR 1113 High Court (Simon Brown J)

Damages – death of mother

Facts
A mother of three young children was killed while crossing the road as a result of the defendant's negligent driving. She had recently divorced her husband and she was in full-time employment. The children went to live with grandmother and, after grandmother's death, with an aunt (with two children of her own) who gave up her job to care for them. The children sought damages under the Fatal Accidents Act 1976 for loss of dependency, including compensation for the aunt's loss of salary.

Held
As it had been entirely reasonable for the aunt to give up work and to remain unemployed to care for the children on a full-time basis, damages for loss of services would be calculated by reference to a notional housekeeping wage during the short period of the grandmother's care, discounted by 30 per cent to reflect the part-time nature of the mother's care, and by reference to the aunt's net earnings loss projected over the remaining period of dependency for each child, again discounted by 15 per cent to reflect the mother's part-time care, the discounts also being intended to take into account the children's broadly diminishing need for care and the loss of the special qualitative factor of maternal care.

Darbishire v *Warran* [1963] 1 WLR 1067 Court of Appeal (Harman and Pearson LJJ and Pennycuick J)

Damages – mitigation of loss

Facts
The plaintiff's Lea Francis shooting brake collided with the defendant's car: the accident was entirely the defendant's fault. Although he could have brought a similar Lea Francis for £85-£100, the plaintiff did not attempt to find one: instead, he had his repaired at a cost of £192. The plaintiff sought to recover the difference between the amount received from his insurance company (£80) and the repair costs.

Held
His claim would fail as he had not taken all reasonable steps to mitigate the damage, ie, bought a replacement vehicle.

Dodd Properties (Kent) Ltd v *Canterbury City Council* [1980] 1 WLR 433 Court of Appeal (Megaw, Browne and Donaldson LJJ)

Damages – assessment

Facts
In 1968 the plaintiffs' building was damaged by the defendants' pile-driving operations on an adjoining site. Shortly before the hearing in 1978 the defendants admitted liability and the question arose as to the date at which damages should be assessed.

Held
The cost of repairs was to be assessed at the earliest date when, having regard to all the circumstances, they could reasonably be undertaken. Taking due account of, inter alia, the plaintiffs' financial stringency in 1970 (the earliest date when it would have been physically possible to put the work in hand), the fact that it made commercial sense to postpone the repairs until the outcome of the action and the defendants' wrongful denial of liability, the cost of the repairs should be assessed at the date of the action, ie 1978.

Megaw LJ:

'The general principle, referred to in many authorities, ... [is] that "as a general rule in English law damages for tort or for breach of contract are assessed as at the date of the breach". But ... it is stressed that it is not a universal rule. That it is subject to many exceptions and qualifications is clear. ... Indeed, where, as in the present case, there is serious structural damage to a building, it would be patently absurd, and contrary to the general principle on which damages fall to be assessed, that a plaintiff, in a time of rising prices, should be limited to recovery on the basis of the prices of repair at the time of the wrongdoing, on the facts here, being two years, at least, before the time when, acting with all reasonable speed, he could first have been able to put the repairs in hand. Once that is accepted, as it must be, little of practical reality remains in postulating that, in a tort such as this, the 'general rule' is applicable. The damages are not required by English law to be assessed as at the date of breach. The true rule is that, where there is a material difference between the cost of repair at the date of the wrongful act and the cost of repair when the repairs can, having regard to all the relevant circumstances, first reasonably be undertaken, it is the latter time by reference to which the cost of repairs is to be taken in assessing the damages.'

Commentary
Distinguished: *The Edison* [1933] AC 449.

Doleman v *Deakin* (1990) The Times 30 January Court of Appeal (Dillon, Ralph Gibson and Stuart-Smith LJJ)

Bereavement damages

Facts
The deceased was unmarried and under 18 years of age when he suffered injuries, from which he died, as a result of the defendant's negligence. However, he did not die until after his 18th birthday: were his parents entitled to bereavement damages under s1(A) of the Fatal Accidents Act 1976?

Held
They were not as the cause of action had accrued at the date of death and on that date their son was not a minor.

Dominion Mosaics and Tile Co Ltd v *Trafalgar Trucking Co Ltd* [1990] 2 All ER 246 Court of Appeal (Fox, Stocker and Taylor LJJ)

Measure of damages

Facts
The plaintiffs sold part of their freehold premises to the local authority, the second defendants, who engaged the first defendants to demolish the buildings on the part sold. As a result of the first defendants' negligence, the buildings retained by the plaintiffs were severely damaged by fire. The premises' diminution in value was about £60,000, rebuilding would have cost £570,000 and loss of profits during the rebuilding period would have been £300,000 a year. In view of these factors, the plaintiffs purchased the lease of other premises (with 20 per cent more floor space) at Waterden Road for £390,000 and then the freehold for £60,000. On moving again, they resold this freehold for £690,000. Amongst other things, the fire destroyed 11 carpet-holding machines which the plaintiffs had recently purchased at a special sale price of £13,500: replacement new machines would have cost £65,000, but they had not in fact been replaced. The plaintiffs claimed the cost of the lease (£390,000) and the cost of new machines (£65,000).

Held
They were entitled to succeed.

Taylor LJ:

'There was no suggestion that the [plaintiffs] could have availed themselves of premises in which to resume business anywhere else, or any quicker than they did. In as much as they were remiss in failing to resume their retail trade at Waterden Road as soon as they might, they conceded they could claim only a limited period for lost profits. Although the ground area was somewhat greater at Waterden Road than their original premises, I consider that this falls within the sort of betterment for which no reduction should be made. It is not a case, as this court instanced in the *Harbutt's Plasticine Ltd* case, of a rebuilding deliberately incorporating enlargement, improvement or added facilities. Here it was a question of finding some existing premises which most nearly matched the [plaintiffs'] requirements. Against the extra floor space there would have to be considered the saving in lost profits of obtaining Waterden Road quickly, and the need to adapt and modernise premises not purpose-built for the [plaintiffs].

But then counsel for the [defendants] sought to bring later dealings into account. The [defendants], by the comparatively modest expenditure of £60,000 in 1986, acquired the freehold of Waterden Road and were then able to sell it for £690,000 in April 1987. It is argued that, since all of this happened before trial, it should all be brought into account in the [defendants'] favour. There should, up to the trial, be in effect a running account between the parties so that any gain to the [plaintiffs] from whatever cause in regard to their property or its proceeds can be used by the [defendants] to diminish their liability.

The judge rejected this argument on the practical ground that the gains made by the [plaintiffs] were attributable simply to the inflationary rise in the value of real property during the relevant period. I agree with him; but further, as a matter of principle, I do not accept that a defendant is entitled to the benefit of any successful dealing which the plaintiff may have had up to trial ...

[As to the machines,] counsel's arguments ... were based solely on the alternative awards of £13,500 or £65,000. No intermediate figure was canvassed. It was not suggested by the [defendants], either in evidence or by submission, that there was any secondhand source of paternoster machines. The [plaintiffs'] evidence was that no such source existed to their knowledge. Where this is the case and the only way the owner of destroyed chattels can replace them is by buying new ones, the measure of damages is the cost of doing that, unless the result would be absurd ...

Accordingly the proper figure here was prima facie £65,000 ... That figure could not, in regard to such recently new machines, be called absurd ...

Had it been argued that in fairness to the [defendants] some discount from £65,000 should have been allowed to reflect the depreciation of the machines in their few months of service, the point would have merited consideration. But no such submission was made, nor was there any evidence on which to base an assessment of an appropriate discount. In these circumstances I consider that, of the two alternatives contended for, £65,000 was the proper sum.'

Commentary
Applied: *Harbutt's Plasticine Ltd* v *Wayne Tank and Pump Co Ltd* [1970] 2 WLR 198.

Fetter v *Beale* see *Fitter* v *Veal*

Fitter v *Veal* (1701) 12 Mod Rep 542 Court of King's Bench (Holt CJ)

Damages – further surgery

Facts
The plaintiff was assaulted by the defendant and he sued and recovered damages. Long after the award, P discovered that he would require further surgery. As a result, P sought to bring a further action.

Held
Damages are recoverable once only for the same injury. Accordingly, P was not entitled to bring a second action.

Gammell v *Wilson* [1980] 3 WLR 591 House of Lords (Lord Diplock, Lord Edmund-Davies, Lord Fraser of Tullybelton, Lord Russell of Killowen and Lord Scarman)

Damages – lost years

Facts
The plaintiff's 15-year-old son was killed in a road accident. The defendants admitted liability and the damages awarded included a sum in respect of loss of future earnings during the boy's lost years.

Held
The award would not be disturbed.

Lord Edmund-Davies:

> ' ... the assessment of compensation for the "lost years" rests on no special basis of its own and it proceeds on no peculiar principle. It may present unusual difficulties, but the task itself is the ordinary one of arriving at a fair figure to compensate the estate of the deceased for a loss of a particular kind sustained by him in his lifetime at the hands of the defendant.'

Commentary
Applied: *Pickett* v *British Rail Engineering Ltd* [1978] 3 WLR 955.

Hayden v *Hayden* [1992] 1 WLR 986 Court of Appeal (Parker, McCowan LJJ and Sir David Croom-Johnson)

Damages – death of mother – father caring for child

Facts
The infant plaintiff's mother was killed when a car driven by the defendant father overturned. The father admitted liability and he sought to replace the mother's lost services by giving up his job and caring for the plaintiff himself.

Held (McCowan LJ dissenting)
Section 4 of the Fatal Accidents Act 1976 did not apply (the father's services were not a benefit which had accrued as a result of the death) and the value of the father's services should be taken into account in assessing the plaintiff's damages.

Parker LJ:

> 'It was long ago established that a dependant child could recover under the Fatal Accidents Act damages for the loss of the gratuitous services of a deceased mother who had been killed due to the negligence of a tortfeasor. In such cases, even without complications, the court is faced with the task of quantifying in money that which cannot in reality be so quantified. This is difficult enough but the facts of this case are such that the difficulties of reaching a just solution are greatly increased.
>
> The essential facts are that the infant plaintiff (Danielle) who was aged four at the time of the accident lost her mother's services, that in order himself to replace such services her father, whose negligence had

caused her mother's death, gave up his employment to look after her and that his remuneration from his former employment had been £15,000 pa.

For the defendant it is submitted that the value of his services should be taken into account, ie set against the value of the mother's lost services in arriving at her loss and for the plaintiff that the father's services must be wholly disregarded by reason of the provisions of s4 of the Fatal Accidents Act 1976 as amended by the Administration of Justice Act 1982 ...

With conflicting decisions on the point whether the gratuitous services of a relative do or do not result from the death of the mother I for my part have no hesitation in following *Hay* v *Hughes* [1975] 2 WLR 34 rather than *Stanley* v *Saddique* [1991] 2 WLR 459 and if this is right s4 of the 1976 Act does not apply. This however does not dispose of the matter because in *Hay* v *Hughes* the benefit of such gratuitous services was excluded, quite apart from any relevant statutory exclusion, on the grounds that they did not result from the death. That decision was considered to be the result of s2 of the 1846 Act and the common law.

Section 2 of the 1846 Act has now been replaced by s3 of the Fatal Accidents Act 1976 as substituted by s3(1) of the Administration of Justice Act 1982 ... There is no material difference between this provision and s2 of the 1846 Act. The reference to the jury is dropped but this is immaterial. Damages remain a "jury question", albeit now decided by a judge. This is plain from *Hay* v *Hughes* itself ...

If then it is a jury question, would a jury be likely to say that the tortfeasor who had provided the services and given up his job so to do must nevertheless pay what it would cost to provide the services which he himself has provided? That a jury could conceivably come to the conclusion must I suppose be accepted but if it reached the opposite conclusion it could not in my view be held to have reached an unreasonable verdict. Suppose for example that the deceased mother was hopelessly inadequate, that the tortfeasor was a trained nanny and, appalled by what she had done, gave up her job and provided the child with services infinitely better than those provided by the deceased mother. Can it possibly be the law that she must then pay the cost of employing another nanny? I think not and, if it were, I would regard it as regrettable.

What then has the judge done in this case? He had before him a figure of £48,000 as being the full cost of a nanny until Danielle was 11 and half such cost from 11 to 15. He then, without giving specific reasons concluded that an appropriate figure would be £20,000, apportioned £15,000 to date of trial and £5,000 thereafter. I do not consider that we have before us material to enable us to interfere with this award, which if I am right as to the approach, appears to me to be an entirely reasonable award and to do justice between the parties ...

I would add by way of postscript that, where the provider of the replacement services is the tortfeasor, arguments successfully advanced in earlier cases that it would be unjust if the tortfeasor were to benefit from the generosity of a third party cannot apply.'

Hicks v *Chief Constable of the South Yorkshire Police* [1992] 2 All ER 65 House of Lords (Lord Templeman, Lord Bridge of Harwich, Lord Griffiths, Lord Goff of Chieveley and Lord Browne-Wilkinson)

Damages – fear of impending death

Facts
The plaintiffs, parents of two girls who were crushed to death in the Hillsborough disaster, as joint administrators of the girls' estates claimed damages for the benefit of each estate under s1(1) of the Law Reform (Miscellaneous Provisions) Act 1934 and s1(1)(b) of the Administration of Justice Act 1982. The trial judge dismissed the action on the ground that the plaintiffs had failed to prove that the girls had suffered any recoverable damage for pre-death pain and suffering and the Court of Appeal adopted a similar approach.

Held
The plaintiffs' further appeal would be dismissed as it was impossible to say that the courts below had been clearly wrong to conclude that no physical injury had been suffered by the girls prior to the fatal crushing injuries.

Lord Bridge of Harwich:

> 'The evidence here showed that both girls died from traumatic asphyxia. They were in the pens at one end of the Hillsborough Stadium to which access was through a tunnel some 23 metres in length. When the pens were already seriously overcrowded a great number of additional spectators, anxious to see the football match which was about to start, were admitted through the turnstiles and surged through the tunnel causing the dreadful crush in the pens in which 95 people died. Medical evidence which the judge accepted was to the effect that in cases of death from traumatic asphyxia caused by crushing the victim would lose consciousness within a matter of seconds from the crushing of the chest which cut off the ability to breathe and would die within five minutes ... Hidden J was not satisfied that any physical injury had been sustained before what he described as the "swift and sudden [death] as shown by the medical evidence". Unless the law were to distinguish between death within seconds of injury and unconsciousness within seconds of injury followed by death within minutes, which I do not understand to be suggested, these findings, as Hidden J himself said "with regret", made it impossible for him to award any damages ... I do not intend myself to embark on a detailed review of the evidence. In the circumstances I think it sufficient to say that, in my opinion, the conclusion of fact reached by Hidden J and the Court of Appeal was fairly open to them and it is impossible to say that they were wrong ...
>
> It is perfectly clear law that fear by itself, of whatever degree, is a normal humane motion for which no damages can be awarded. Those trapped in the crush at Hillsborough who were fortunate enough to escape without injury have no claim in respect of the distress they suffered in what must have been a truly terrifying experience. It follows that fear of impending death felt by the victim of a fatal injury before that injury is inflicted cannot by itself give rise to a cause of action which survives for the benefit of the victim's estate.'

Hodgson v *Trapp* [1988] 3 WLR 1281 House of Lords (Lord Mackay of Clashfern LC, Lord Bridge of Harwich, Lord Brandon of Oakbrook, Lord Oliver of Aylmerton and Lord Goff of Chieveley)

Damages – deduction of allowances

Facts
The plaintiff was almost totally physically and mentally incapacitated as the result of an accident caused by the negligence of the defendant. The trial judge awarded the plaintiff damages of £431,840 and refused to make any deduction in respect of the attendance and mobility allowances payable to the plaintiff under ss35(1) of the Social Security Act 1975 and he also increased the multipliers for future cost and future loss of earnings to take account of the higher rates of tax payable on the interest from the award of damages.

Held
The deduction should have been made but the multiplier should not have been increased.

Lord Bridge of Harwich:

> 'In the end the issue in these cases is not so much one of statutory construction as of public policy. If we have regard to the realities, awards of damages for personal injuries are met from the insurance premiums payable by motorists, employers, occupiers of property, professional men and others. Statutory benefits payable to those in need by reason of impecuniosity or disability are met by the taxpayer. In this context to ask whether the taxpayer, as the "benevolent donor", intends to benefit "the wrongdoer", as represented

by the insurer who meets the claim at the expense of the appropriate class of policy holders, seems to me entirely artificial. There could hardly be a clearer case than that of the attendance allowance payable under s35 of the 1975 Act where the statutory benefit and the special damages claimed for cost of care are designed to meet the identical expenses. To allow double recovery in such a case at the expense of both taxpayers and insurers seems to me incapable of justification on any rational ground. It could only add to the enormous disparity, to which the advocates of a "no-fault" system of compensation constantly draw attention, between the position of those who are able to establish a third party's fault as the cause of their injury and the position of those who are not.

A separate and subordinate point was raised on behalf of the plaintiff in relation to mobility allowance ... I see no reason why the whole of the mobility allowance should not be regarded, just as the attendance allowance, as available to meet the cost of her care generally and thus as mitigating the damages recoverable in respect of the cost of that care.'

Lord Oliver of Aylmerton:

'The second ground of appeal raises a quite distinct issue which arises in this way. It was agreed at the trial before Taylor J that the plaintiff had suffered a continuing loss of salary of £3,267.77 per annum and there was, in addition, an assessed loss of £3,000 per annum in respect of freelance work in which the plaintiff had engaged prior to the accident. To these multiplicands Taylor J applied a multiplier of 11, which is not challenged. That figure, however, he increased to 12 in order to take account of the fact that the income likely to be produced from conventional investment of the sums awarded would attract income tax at the higher rate ... Similarly in relation to the prospective cost of nursing care and attendance, the judge adopted a multiplicand of £11,000 to which he applied a multiplier of 13, which again is not challenged. To that, however, he again added a further one year in order to take account of the incidence of taxation at the higher rates. The defendants do not challenge the general proposition that the prospective incidence of higher-rate income tax may, in exceptional circumstances, be a factor which can legitimately tip the scales in favour of selecting a multiplier at the higher end of the conventional scale. They do, however, challenge the correctness of an approach which involves, after the calculation of the appropriate multiplier in accordance with the conventional scale, the making of a specific addition to the multiplier in order to take account, as a separate and individual feature, of the higher taxation rates which may be attracted by the income likely to be produced by the investment of a very substantial award ...

I am, as I have said, content to deal with the question raised on the footing that the answer is not already subsumed in the answer given by this House in *Lim Poh Choo* v *Camden and Islington Area Health Authority* [1980] AC 174 to the allied question of whether specific allowance should be made for inflation. The principle, however, appears to me to be much the same. That tax will be levied is, no doubt, as Benjamin Franklin observed, one of the two certainties of life, but the extent and manner of its exaction in the future can only be guessed at. It is as much an imponderable as any of the other uncertainties which are embraced in the exercise of making a just assessment of damages for future loss. The system of multipliers and multiplicands conventionally employed in the assessment takes account of a variety of factors, none of which is or, indeed, is capable of being worked out scientifically, but which are catered for by allowing a reasonably generous margin in the assumed rate of interest on which the multiplier is based. There is, in my judgment, no self-evident justification for singling out this particular factor and making for it an allowance which is not to be made for the equally imponderable factor of inflation...

In my opinion, the incidence of taxation in the future should ordinarily be assumed to be satisfactorily taken care of in the assumption of an interest rate applicable to a stable currency and the selection of a multiplier appropriate to that rate.'

Commentary

Followed in *McCamley* v *Cammell Laird Shipbuilders Ltd* [1990] 1 All ER 854.
   Overruled: *Thomas* v *Wignall* [1987] 2 WLR 930.

Housecroft v *Burnett* [1986] 1 All ER 332 Court of Appeal (O'Connor, Slade LJJ and Bristow J)

Damages – personal injury

Facts
When she was aged 16, the plaintiff suffered severe injuries resulting in tetraplegia. The defendant admitted liability and the plaintiff appealed against the amount awarded as damages.

Held
In April 1985, the average award in such a case for pain, suffering and loss of amenity should be £75,000. Where the plaintiff is to be looked after under the National Health Service, a nil award should be made in respect of nursing care. Where care is provided by a relative out of love, a capital sum should be included in the award and it should be sufficient to enable the plaintiff to make reasonable recompense to the relative. Where a relative gives up work, the court should award sufficient to ensure that he or she does not lose as a result; the ceiling would be the commercial rate.

Commentary
Applied: *Donnelly* v *Joyce* [1973] 3 WLR 514.

Hunt v *Severs* [1994] 2 All ER 385 House of Lords (Lord Keith, Lord Bridge, Lord Jauncey, Lord Browne-Wilkinson and Lord Nolan)

Plaintiff cared for by the tortfeasor – whether value of these services recoverable

Facts
The plaintiff was seriously injured whilst riding as a pillion passenger on the defendant's motor cycle. She later married the defendant who assisted in her care. Liability was admitted but the defendant disputed, inter alia, claims for the value of the services rendered by him to the plaintiff. Recovery was allowed at first instance and upheld on appeal to the Court of Appeal. The defendant appealed to the House of Lords.

Held
The appeal would be allowed. Where services in the form of care and assistance were gratuitously rendered by a defendant tortfeasor, the plaintiff could not recover the cost of these services via damages. The object of an award for voluntary care received by the plaintiff was compensation for the voluntary carer, and where the tortfeasor had rendered services there was no ground for requiring the tortfeasor to pay to the plaintiff a sum of money which the plaintiff then had to repay to him.

The House also held that an injured plaintiff who recovers damages as recompense for services rendered by a voluntary carer holds them on trust for the voluntary carer, upholding the dictum of Lord Denning in *Cunningham* v *Harrison* [1973] 3 All ER 463. The criticism of *Cunningham* in *Housecroft* v *Burnett* [1986] 1 All ER 332 must now be regarded as invalid.

Lord Bridge:

> 'The law with respect to the services of a third party who provides voluntary care for a tortiously injured plaintiff has developed somewhat erratically in England. The voluntary carer has no cause of action of his own against the tortfeasor. The justice of allowing the injured plaintiff to recover the value of the services so that he may recompensate the voluntary carer has been generally recognised, but there has been

difficulty in articulating a consistent juridical principle to justify this result ... But it is nevertheless important to recognise that the underlying rationale of the English law, as all the cases before *Donnelly* v *Joyce* demonstrate, is to enable the voluntary carer to receive proper recompense for his or her services and I would think it appropriate for the House to take the opportunity so far as possible to bring the law of the two countries [England and Scotland] into accord by adopting the view of Lord Denning MR in *Cunningham* v *Harrison* that in England the injured plaintiff who recovers damages under this head should hold them on trust for the voluntary carer.'

Hussain v *New Taplow Paper Mills Ltd* [1988] 2 WLR 266 House of Lords (Lord Bridge of Harwich, Lord Havers, Lord Ackner, Lord Oliver of Aylmerton and Lord Goff of Chieveley)

Damages – deduction of sickness benefit

Facts
The appellant sustained an injury in the course of his employment by the respondents which necessitated the amputation of his left arm below the elbow. Under his contract of employment, he received full pay for 13 weeks and thereafter 50 per cent of his pre-accident earnings by way of long-term sickness benefit payable under an insurance scheme run by the defendants who had covered this liability by means of an insurance policy entirely at their own expense. Under the plaintiff's contract of employment such long-term benefit was a continuation of earnings and taxable: there was no evidence that his wages would have been any higher if the defendants had not operated the insurance scheme.

Held
The benefit should be brought into account and deducted from the damages awarded to the plaintiff for pre-trial and future loss of earnings.

Lord Bridge of Harwich:

> 'Counsel for the plaintiff seeks to apply by analogy a principle said to be established by *Parry* v *Cleaver* in support of the argument that all payments to an employee enjoying the benefit of the defendants' permanent health insurance scheme are effectively in the nature of the fruits of insurance accruing to the benefit of the employee in consideration of the contributions he has made by his work for the defendants prior to incapacity. Much emphasis was laid on the long-term nature of the scheme payments to which the plaintiff has become entitled and it was submitted that they are strictly comparable to a disability pension. Both these arguments fall to the ground, as it seems to me, in the light of the concession rightly made at an early stage that the nature of payments under the scheme is unaffected by the duration of the incapacity which determines the period for which payments will continue to be made. The question whether the scheme payments are or are not deductible in assessing damages for loss of earnings must be answered in the same way whether, after the first 13 weeks of incapacity, the payments fall to be made for a few weeks or for the rest of an employee's working life. Looking at the payments made under the scheme by the defendants in the first weeks after the expiry of the period of 13 weeks of continuous incapacity, they seem to me indistinguishable in character from the sick pay which the employee receives during the first 13 weeks. They are payable under a term of the employee's contract by the defendants to the employee qua employee as a partial substitute for earnings and are the very antithesis of a pension, which is payable only after employment ceases. The fact that the defendants happen to have insured their liability to meet these contractual commitments as they arise cannot affect the issue in any way.'

Commentary
Distinguished in *McCamley* v *Cammell Laird Shipbuilders Ltd* [1990] 1 All ER 854.

Jefford v *Gee* [1970] 2 WLR 702 Court of Appeal (Lord Denning MR, Davies and Salmon LJJ)

Damages – interest

Facts
The defendant knocked the plaintiff off his motor scooter. P had many broken bones and lost teeth for which he had to stay off work for a long time. Waller J gave £5,631 damages, including £2,131 special damages; he awarded interest under s3 of the Law Reform (Miscellaneous Provisions) Act 1934 at 6.5 per cent of general damages of £3,560 from date of trial. He allowed no interest on the special damages.

D appealed and P cross-appealed on interest. He argued that on the basis of s22(1) of the Administration of Justice Act 1969 (amending s3 of the 1934 Act), obliging the court to award interest on damages, this meant on all damages after 1 January 1970.

Held
Interest should be awarded where P had been 'kept out of his money'. The appropriate rate is that payable on money in court on short investment account taken as an average over the period of the award. In general, interest should be granted on special damages from date of accident until trial at half the appropriate rate. No interest should be awarded on damages in respect of loss of future earnings and interest should be awarded on pain and suffering and loss of amenities from date of writ to trial.

Accordingly, the order was varied to give 3 per cent interest on the special damages from accident to trial; and on the £2,500 – that part of the general damages which related to pain and suffering and loss of amenities at 6 per cent pa from date of accident to date of trial.

Jones v *Jones* [1985] 2 QB 704 Court of Appeal (Stephenson, Dunn and Robert Goff LJJ)

Damages – divorce

Facts
The plaintiff, in an accident, sustained severe personal injuries and suffered permanent brain damage, which in turn caused the breakdown of his marriage. By a court order, the plaintiff was required to make periodical payments to his wife in the sum of £2,445 per annum (less tax) and to his children, payments of £64 per month; he was further ordered to pay a lump sum of £25,000 to enable his wife to buy a house for herself and the children, and claimed damages for his injuries including the payments he had to make to his family.

Held
The plaintiff was entitled to recover damages to compensate him for having to make financial provision for his family.

Commentary
Applied: *McLoughlin* v *O'Brian* [1982] 2 WLR 982.
    Not followed in *Pritchard* v *J H Cobden Ltd* [1987] 2 WLR 627.

Kelly v *Dawes* (1990) The Times 27 September Queen's Bench Division (Potter J)

Damages – structured settlement – tax implications

Facts
The first plaintiff had suffered serious injury in a road accident in which her husband was killed. The second plaintiff was her father and next friend, and also sued as administrator of the deceased's estate.

Held
The parties to a personal injury action were entitled to enter into what is known as a 'structured settlement' under which the defendant's insurers invested a part of the sum payable to the plaintiff in the purchase of an annuity which would provide the plaintiff with an index-linked annual sum for the rest of his life, thus providing the plaintiff with a greater degree of security than could be obtained under the lump sum system. This type of settlement also has advantages for defendants because it yields tax advantages for the plaintiff and Potter J held that this tax advantage could be reflected by the payment of a smaller sum than would have been paid under the lump sum system. Under a structured settlement damages would commonly be divided into two parts: the first part relating to financial losses to the date of settlement, which would be paid by means of a lump sum, and the second part, relating to future losses, would be covered by the annuity. The court also laid down various guidelines for future applications for the approval by the court of structured settlement agreements. See also *Practice Direction* [1992] 1 All ER 862.

Lim Poh Choo v *Camden and Islington Area Health Authority* [1979] 3 WLR 44
House of Lords (Lord Diplock, Viscount Dilhorne, Lord Simon of Glaisdale and Lord Scarman)

Personal injury – damages

Facts
The plaintiff was admitted to hospital, aged 36, for minor surgery. She was reasonably healthy and worked as a senior psychiatric registrar. She suffered a cardiac arrest and irreparable brain damage due to the negligence of a member of the defendants' staff. She had no dependants. Her only relatives were an elderly mother in Penang and a sister. Her life expectancy was 37 years. If she had not suffered the injuries, she would have become a consultant by 1978. She would require care permanently for the rest of her life. She had no sensation of what had happened to her. She would eventually have to live in an institution. The trial judge awarded a total sum of £254,765 damages (the breakdown of which appears in the summary below). The defendants appealed on quantum, having admitted liability.

Held
Lord Scarman:

> '1. *Pain, suffering and loss of amenity*
> The judge awarded £20,000 for this which we uphold on the basis that this award was made on the fact that the plaintiff had lost most of her amenities and the sum should not be varied, on the basis of *Wise* v *Kay* and *H West & Son Ltd* v *Shephard*, where even though the injured person was not aware of the deprivation of amenities, nevertheless they could recover a full award for loss under this head. The reversal of these cases would cause widespread injustice. The sum is certainly not too high nor should it be increased: in the context of current money values, it is still substantial. [Distinguished: *Benham* v *Gambling* [1941] AC 157.]
>
> 2. *Loss of earnings*
> The plaintiff is entitled to substantial damages for loss of earnings despite the fact that she will never be in a position to enjoy them. However, there should not be any duplication of damages, nor should P receive

an award which is above what she could have earned. Accordingly, the expenses which she would have incurred in earning the money must be deducted and so should her future living expenses be. In the case of a plaintiff who was permenantly incapacitated but whose life expectancy has not been shortened, any duplication between damages for loss of earnings and damages for cost of care can be remedied by deducting P's future living expenses from the damages awarded for the cost of care. The judge's award of lost future earnings at £92,000 (including pension) was correct. [Applied: *Pickett* v *British Rail Engineering Ltd* [1978] 3 WLR 955.]

3. *Cost of future care*
This should be awarded and on the basis that capital as well as income was to be used to meet the cost and, therefore, any award is to be calculated on an annuity basis. Future living expenses should also be deducted from the award. In all the circumstances, the multiplier should be 12 which will give £76,800 (as opposed to £105,500 at trial).

4. *Effect of future inflation*
In *Cookson* v *Knowles*, Lord Diplock's remark that future inflation is taken care of in a rough way because the multiplier only assumes interest at 4-5%, whereas in reality it is much higher and, therefore, the plaintiff gains approximately 8-13% per annum. No allowance should be made for inflation: (1) because it is pure speculation and (2) it is best left to be dealt with by an investment policy. [Applied: *Taylor* v *O'Connor* [1970] 2 WLR 472.]

5. *The total award*
The total award was not excessive merely because of its size and should not be reduced because of its size. The amended total is, therefore, £229,298.64.'

Commentary
Applied in *Auty* v *National Coal Board* [1985] 1 WLR 784.

McCamley v *Cammell Laird Shipbuilders Ltd* [1990] 1 WLR 963 Court of Appeal (O'Connor, Croom-Johnson and Balcombe LJJ)

Damages – deduction of insurance moneys

Facts
The defendant employers admitted liability for the serious injuries suffered by the plaintiff in the course of his employment and the judge awarded £387,790 by way of damages. The defendants ('the insured') had a personal accident group insurance policy for the benefit of their employees ('the insured persons'). The plaintiff had not contributed to this policy and, before his accident, he had not been aware of it. He received £45,630 under the policy and also attendance and mobility allowances: were these sums, or any of them, to be taken into account in assessing damages?

Held
The allowances were deductible but the payment under the policy would be disregarded.

O'Connor LJ:

' ... the payment to the plaintiff was a payment by way of benevolence, even though the mechanics required the use of an insurance policy. The payment was not an ex gratia act where the accident had already happened, but the whole idea of the policy, covering all the many employees ... was clearly to make the benefit payable as an act of benevolence whenever a qualifying injury took place. It was a lump sum payable regardless of fault or whether the employers or anyone else were liable, and it was not a method of advancing sick pay covered by a contractual scheme such as existed in *Hussain's* case ... That the arrangement was made before the accident is immaterial. The act of benevolence was to happen contingently on an event and was prepared for in advance. To refer to Lord Bridge's speech in *Hussain's* case this payment was one analogous to "one of the two classic exceptions" to the rule that there should be no double recovery.

The point was well made on behalf of the plaintiff that this sum was not to be payable in respect of any particular head of damage suffered by him and was not an advance in respect of anything at all. To say that does not mean that in an appropriate case there may not be a general payment or an advance to cover a number of different heads of damage. The importance in the present case is that the sum was quantified before there had been an accident at all and when it could not have been foreseen what damages might be sustained when one did take place.'

Commentary
Followed: *Hodgson* v *Trapp* [1988] 3 WLR 1281.
    Distinguished: *Hussain* v *New Taplow Paper Mills Ltd* [1988] 2 WLR 266.
    As to the deduction of social security benefits from tort damages, see now s82 Social Security Administration Act 1992.

McLeish v *Amoo-Gottfried & Co* (1993) The Times 13 October High Court (Scott Baker J)

Facts
The plaintiff was wrongly convicted of a criminal offence due to his solicitor's admitted negligence. The plaintiff claimed damages for distress and mental anxiety and injury to reputation.

Held
The plaintiff could recover damages for distress and mental anxiety. No award for injury to reputation had ever been made in a case of negligence, although it was a possible head of damages in other torts. The court held that damages for loss of reputation could not be recovered in the instant case as a separate head of damage, but that in so far as any loss of reputation was an integral part of the plaintiff's distress it could enhance his award for distress and mental anxiety.

Meah v *McCreamer* [1985] 1 All ER 367 High Court (Woolf J)

Damages – sexual assaults

Facts
The plaintiff sustained serious head injuries and brain damage in a car accident which was caused by the defendant's negligence. He underwent a personality change and attacked and sexually assaulted three women. As a result he was sentenced to life imprisonment.

Held
Although the plaintiff had suffered no financial loss as a result of being sent to prison, his damages would take account of his imprisonment, using, as a guideline, awards for wrongful imprisonment. An overall sum of £60,000 was awarded.

Morris v *Redland Bricks Ltd* see *Redland Bricks Ltd* v *Morris*

Parry* v *Cleaver [1969] 2 WLR 821 House of Lords (Lord Reid, Lord Morris of Borth-y-Gest, Lord Pearce, Lord Wilberforce and Lord Pearson)

Damages – deductions

Facts
The appellant police constable was injured, as a result of the respondent's negligence, whilst he was directing traffic. In the following year he was discharged from the force and granted a police ill-health award for life.

Held (Lord Morris of Borth-y-Gest and Lord Pearson dissenting)
In computing damages, the ill-health award was not deductible in assessing the amount payable for loss of earnings, although it would have to be brought into account in respect of his loss of retirement pension.

Lord Reid:

> 'It would be revolting to the ordinary man's sense of justice, and therefore contrary to public policy, that the sufferer should have his damages reduced so that he would gain nothing from the benevolence of his friends or relations or of the public at large, and that the only gainer would be the wrongdoer. We do not have to decide in this case whether these considerations also apply to public benevolence in the shape of various unconvenanted benefits from the welfare state, but it may be thought that Parliament did not intend them to be for the benefit of the wrongdoer.
>
> As regards moneys coming to the plaintiff under a contract of insurance, I think that the real and substantial reason for disregarding them is that the plaintiff has bought them and that it would be unjust and unreasonable to hold that the money which he prudently spent on premiums and the benefit from it should enure to the benefit of the tortfeasor. Here again I think that the explanation that this is too remote is artificial and unreal. Why should the plaintiff be left worse off than if he had never insured? In that case he would have got the benefit of the premium money; if he had not spent it he would have had it in his possession at the time of the accident grossed up at compound interest ... Then I ask – why should it make any difference that he insured by arrangement with his employer rather than with an insurance company? In the course of the argument the distinction came down to be as narrow as this: if the employer says nothing or merely advises the man to insure and he does so, then the insurance money will not be deductible; but if the employer makes it a term of the contract of employment that he shall insure himself and he does so, then the insurance money will be deductible. There must be something wrong with an argument which drives us to so unreasonable a conclusion.'

Commentary
See also *Colledge* v *Bass Mitchells & Butlers Ltd* [1988] 1 All ER 536.
Applied in *Smoker* v *London Fire and Civil Defence Authority* [1991] 2 WLR 1052.

Pickett* v *British Rail Engineering Ltd [1978] 3 WLR 955 House of Lords (Lord Wilberforce, Lord Salmon, Lord Edmund-Davies, Lord Russell of Killowen and Lord Scarman)

Damages – loss of future earnings

Facts
The plaintiff, the widow of H, appealed to the House of Lords on quantum. He had been a fit man until he was 53, working for the defendants, but he contracted asbestosis and his life expectancy was reduced to one year instead of the 12 which he could have expected. The Court of Appeal refused to award any

sum for earnings during the lost years. The Court of Appeal had increased general damages from £7,000 to £10,000.

Held (Lord Russell of Killowen dissenting)
Where P's life expectancy was diminished as a result of D's negligence, P's future earnings were an asset of value of which he had been deprived and which could be assessed in money terms and were not merely an intangible prospect to be disregarded. He or his wife/widow had been deprived of the money over and above that which he would have spent on himself. Accordingly, this head of loss of earnings for the lost years forms a separate head and should *not* form part of the 'loss of expectation of life' head. The judge's general damages award was restored.

Commentary
Applied in *Lim Poh Choo* v *Camden and Islington Area Health Authority* [1979] 3 WLR 44 and *Gammell* v *Wilson* [1980] 3 WLR 591.
 Overruled: *Oliver* v *Ashman* [1961] 3 WLR 669.

Pidduck v *Eastern Scottish Omnibuses Ltd* [1990] 1 WLR 993 Court of Appeal (Purchas, Glidewell LJJ and Sir Roger Ormrod)

Damages – widow's allowance

Facts
The plaintiff received a pension from her late husband's former employers, the Bank of England. The pension fund also made provision for the payment of certain allowances should the pensioner die within five years of retirement. The plaintiff's husband was killed within that period as a result of the defendant's negligence: she was awarded damages under s3(1) of the Fatal Accidents Act 1976: should the amount of her allowance be deducted?

Held
It should not.

Sir Roger Ormrod:

 '... as I understood the argument of counsel for the defendants, he founded primarily on s3(1) of the Fatal Accidents Act 1976 (as amended). By applying, in its simplest form, Lord Reid's test in *Parry* v *Cleaver* [1970] AC 1, ie by comparing the plaintiff's position "before and after", he contends that the widow has suffered no loss and hence no "injury" because, whereas "before" she was supported by the Bank of England Pension's Fund via her husband, "after" she was supported by the same fund via the widow's allowance and there is no significant difference in the amounts involved.
 This argument goes too far. If it is right, it would pre-empt the express provisions of s4 of the 1976 Act and emasculate it in many cases because it would apply to all pension fund cases where the deceased was living on a pension and the scheme included a widow's benefit. In my judgment, the "injury" suffered by the widow is the loss of her dependency on her deceased husband. The value of this loss is to be quantified in accordance with the provisions of s4. The widow's allowance is, therefore, to be disregarded in the calculation.'

Pritchard v *J H Cobden Ltd* [1988] Fam 22 Court of Appeal (O'Connor, Croom-Johnson LJJ and Sir Roger Ormrod)

Damages – divorce

Facts
In 1976 the plaintiff was injured in a motor accident caused by the defendant's negligence. The plaintiff as a result suffered a character change and he and his wife divorced in 1984. This cost him £53,000 in settlement to his wife. The trial judge added this sum to the damages that he recovered from the defendant.

Held
Owing to the special nature of matrimonial proceedings, generally it would be very difficult to calculate what the plaintiff would have to pay to his wife. As such the damage would be too remote. Generally it was undesirable to bring family matters into personal injury litigation.

Commentary
Not followed: *Jones v Jones* [1984] 3 WLR 862.

Redland Bricks Ltd v Morris [1969] 2 WLR 1437 House of Lords (Lord Reid, Lord Morris of Borth-y-Gest, Lord Hodson, Lord Upjohn and Lord Diplock)

Damages – mandatory injunction

Facts
Due to lack of support, some of the respondents' market garden slipped into the appellants' clay quarry. The judge, inter alia, granted a mandatory injunction requiring the appellants to 'take all necessary steps to restore the support to the [respondents'] land within a period of six months'.

Held
Although there was a strong probability of further slippage, the injunction would be discharged as it did not inform the appellants exactly what they had to do.

Lord Upjohn:

> '1. A mandatory injunction can only be granted where the plaintiff shows a very strong probability on the facts that grave damage will accrue to him in the future ... It is a jurisdiction to be exercised sparingly and with caution but, in the proper case, unhesitatingly.
> 2. Damages will not be a sufficient or adequate remedy if such damage does happen. This is only the application of a general principle of equity ...
> 3. Unlike the case where a negative injunction is granted to prevent the continuance or recurrence of a wrongful act the question of the cost to the defendant to do works to prevent or lessen the likelihood of a future apprehended wrong must be an element to be taken into account: (a) where the defendant has acted without regard to his neighbour's rights, or has tried to steal a march on him or has tried to evade the jurisdiction of the court or, to sum it up, has acted wantonly and quite unreasonably in relation to his neighbour he may be ordered to repair his wanton and unreasonable acts by doing positive work to restore the status quo even if the expense to him is out of all proportion to the advantage thereby accruing to the plaintiff ... (b) but where the defendant has acted reasonably, although in the event wrongly, the cost of remedying by positive action his earlier activities is most important for two reasons. First, because no legal wrong has yet occurred (for which he has not been recompensed at law and in equity) and, in spite of gloomy expert opinion, may never occur or possibly only on a much smaller scale than anticipated. Secondly, because if ultimately heavy damage does occur the plaintiff is in no way prejudiced for he has his action at law and all his consequential remedies in equity.'

Smith v *Marchioness/Bowbelle* [1993] NLJ 813 High Court (Master Topley)

Dependants and dependency

Facts
The plaintiff was the mother of a young woman who was drowned in an accident. Liability was admitted and the plaintiff claimed, inter alia, on behalf of herself and the deceased's maternal and paternal grandparents as dependants under the Fatal Accidents Act 1976.

Held
The court found that the plaintiff had lost a contribution to the household of £25 per week for shopping and £5 per week for chores. The court also found that the deceased gave her grandparents birthday and Christmas presents valued at £300 for each grandmother and received gifts from her grandparents valued at £30, making a net claim of £270 for each grandmother. These amounts, multiplied by the appropriate multiplier, were awarded, inter alia, under the 1976 Act.

Commentary
The definition of dependants, under s1(3) of the Fatal Accidents Act 1976, is wide. This case takes a wide approach to the question of whether a person who comes within s1(3) is financially dependent on the deceased.

Smoker v *London Fire and Civil Defence Authority, Wood* v *British Coal Corp* [1991] 2 WLR 1052 House of Lords (Lord Mackay of Clachfern LC, Lord Bridge of Harwich, Lord Brandon of Oakbrook, Lord Templeman and Lord Lowry)

Damages – pension deductible?

Facts
In the first case, the plaintiff fireman was disabled and his employers were liable in respect of his injuries. In relation to his claim for loss of earnings, the question arose whether there should be deducted from the amount of damages the amount that he had received by way of ill-health and injury pension and gratuity under a compulsory pension scheme to which he had contributed 10.75 per cent of his wages and his employer twice that amount.

The same question as to deductibility from loss of earnings damages arose in the second case where the injured former employee had received an incapacity retirement pension under a scheme to which he had contributed 5.14 per cent of his pay and the employer a like amount.

Held
In neither case were the pensions deductible.

Lord Templeman:

> 'The [former employers] claim that there has been a change of circumstance in that it can be shown that *Parry* v *Cleaver* [1970] AC 1 introduced uncertainty in the law and that since 1970 there has been a clear trend at common law against double recovery. But *Parry* v *Cleaver* established clearly that pension benefits are not deductible and that double recovery is not involved. The cases on which the appellants rely are mainly those in which the courts have decided that payments which correspond to wages must be taken into account when assessing loss of wages. Thus unemployment benefit (*Nabi* v *British Leyland* [1980] 1 All ER 667), family income supplement (*Gaskill* v *Preston* [1981] 3 All ER 427), supplementary benefit (*Lincoln* v *Hayman* [1982] 2 All ER 819), payments under job release schemes and student

maintenance grants are statutory wages which reduce the loss of contractual wages resulting from the tort. In *Hussain* v *New Taplow Paper Mills Ltd* [1988] 1 All ER 541 at 547 the plaintiff was entitled to receive full-scale pay over 13 weeks and thereafter half his pre-accident earnings, and the House held that these payments were deductible because, in the words of Lord Bridge of Harwich:

> " ... it has always been assumed as axiomatic that an employee who receives under the terms of his contract of employment either the whole or part of his salary or wages during a period when he is incapacitated for work cannot claim damages for a loss which he has not sustained ..." ...

I can find nothing in the authorities which casts doubt over the effect or logic of this House in *Parry* v *Cleaver*.

The appellants relied on s22 of the Social Security Act 1989 and Sch 4 to that Act. These provisions direct that social security benefits shall not be deducted in the assessment of damages for tort but that the tortfeasor shall repay to the state out of the damages thus assessed the amount of the social security benefits provided by the state for the benefit of the victim. These provisions, far from assisting the appellants, only demonstrate that Parliament is quite capable of legislating in this field but has not legislated to reduce the damages payable to the tortfeasor.'

Commentary
Applied: *Parry* v *Cleaver* [1970] AC 1.

Stanley v *Saddique* [1991] 2 WLR 459 Court of Appeal (Purchas, Ralph Gibson LJJ and Sir David Croom-Johnson)

Benefit should be disregarded?

Facts
A minor's mother had been killed in a road accident as a result of the defendant's negligence. On the hearing of a claim under s4 of the Fatal Accidents Act 1976, as amended by s3(1) of the Administration of Justice Act 1982, it appeared that the minor's father had since married Tracy and the judge found that Tracy was providing excellent motherly services to the minor which were of a higher quality than could foreseeably be expected to have been provided by the minor's mother. In the light of this finding it was contended that as the minor was better off in the home provided by his father and Tracy than he would ever have been with his mother there was no loss of dependency and, therefore, no damages to be awarded under the Act.

Held
This contention had properly been rejected: the benefits accruing to the minor as a result of his absorption into the family unit consisting of his father and stepmother and siblings should be wholly disregarded in assessing damages. However, the deceased mother's shortcomings was a matter which should have been taken into account when calculating the damages for loss of dependency.

Commentary
See also *Hayden* v *Hayden* [1992] 1 WLR 986, above.

Watson v *Willmott* [1990] 3 WLR 1103 High Court (Garland J)

Damages – effect of adoption

Facts
The plaintiff's mother was killed in an accident caused by the negligence of the defendant and, some months later, his father committed suicide as a result of the depression caused by the death of his wife. The plaintiff was looked after by his aunt and uncle who later adopted him. The defendants argued that the effect of the adoption was to preclude the recovery of any loss of dependency after the date of the adoption because from that date the child was treated in law as if he had been born as a child of the adoptive parents. The plaintiff, on the other hand, argued that the adoption had no effect on his claim because his cause of action accrued as at the dates of death of his parents and it could not be abrogated or extinguished by his subsequent adoption.

Held
Both arguments would be rejected and, drawing an analogy with the 'stepfather' cases, the adoption would be taken into account in the *quantification* of the dependency. In the case of the loss of the plaintiff's father, the loss of dependency was to be calculated by comparing the plaintiff in the position he would have been in had his father lived with his position with his adoptive father; therefore the sum to be awarded was the plaintiff's loss of dependency on his father less his dependency on his adoptive father. But, in so far as his dependency on his mother was concerned, the adoption replaced his non-pecuniary dependency on his deceased mother and therefore the non-pecuniary dependency on his mother was to be passed only up to the date of his adoption.

Willson v *Ministry of Defence* [1991] 1 All ER 638 High Court (Scott Baker J)

Provisional damages – 'chance' of 'serious deterioration'

Facts
The plaintiff injured his ankle at work and he was left with continuing disability and pain. In an action against his former employers, he applied for an award of provisional damages under s32A of the Supreme Court Act 1981. Medical reports stated that there would be degeneration of the ankle joint, that he would remain prone to further injuries and that there was a possibility that he would develop arthritis.

Held
The application for an award of provisional damages would fail and damages would be awarded on a lump sum basis.

Scott Baker J:

> 'A "chance" ... is not defined in s32A ... It seems to me that the legislature has used a wide word here and used it deliberately. I think [counsel for the defendants] is right when he points out that it can cover a wide range between, on the one hand, something that is de minimis and, on the other hand, something that is a probability. In my view, to qualify as a chance it must be measurable rather than fanciful. There is certainly, in my judgment, in this case a chance of osteoarthritis developing and a chance of the plaintiff suffering further traumatic injury. I think that there is a chance that he will develop arthritis to the extent that he requires surgery. I think that there is a chance that he will develop arthritis to the extent that he has to change his employment and I think there is a chance that he will suffer further injury in the nature of further damage to his ankle or elsewhere. However slim those chances may be, I think that they are measurable within the meaning of this section ...
>
> The second question turns on the words "serious deterioration in his physical condition". It is clear that, as drafted, the word "serious" appears to qualify the words "deterioration in his physical condition". There is a question of how "serious" should be interpreted in the light of this section. On one view,

"serious" could cover a wide range of circumstances from something not far beyond the trivial at the bottom end of the scale to something approaching the catastrophic at the top end of the scale.

In my judgment, what is envisaged here is something beyond ordinary deterioration. Whether deterioration is serious in any particular case seems to me to be a question of fact depending on the circumstances of that case, including the effect of the deterioration upon the plaintiff. For example, where a plaintiff suffers a hand injury and there is a deterioration it may be a matter of great gravity for a concert pianist but a matter of rather less importance for somebody else ... I am not ... satisfied that it is established that there is a chance of *serious* – and I emphasise that word – deterioration in this case. That is not a matter that I have found entirely easy ...

When the criteria set out in s32A(1) are all met the court then has to exercise a discretion whether or not to make an order for provisional damages. This is clear from the use of the word "may" in RSC Ord 37 r8(1), as opposed to the word "shall".

The question then arises as to which cases are appropriate for a provisional damages award and which are not. I deal with this because, although I formed the view that there was no serious deterioration envisaged, that was not a matter that I found entirely easy and indeed there are some matters that may more properly be dealt with under the heading of "discretion" rather than taking into account the circumstances of the case in looking at whether or not the section was complied with.

The general rule in English law is that damages are assessed on a once-and-for-all basis. Section 32A of the 1981 Act creates a valuable statutory exception. In my judgment, the section envisages a clear and severable risk rather than a continuing deterioration, as is the typical osteoarthritic picture.

In my judgment, many disabilities follow a developing pattern in which the precise results cannot be foreseen. Within a general band this or that may or may not occur. Such are not the cases for provisional damages. The courts have to do their best to make an award in the light of a broad medical prognosis.

In my judgment, there should be some clear-cut event which, if it occurs, triggers an entitlement to further compensation ...

It seems to me that the case falls within the general run of cases where there are uncertainties as to the future. Nobody can look into a crystal ball and see precisely how the plaintiff's ankle will develop, but I think that the uncertainties are such that they can all properly be taken into account in making a once-and-for-all assessment of damages today. My conclusion therefore is that this is not an appropriate case in which to exercise discretion in favour of a provisional damages order.'

Wood v British Coal Corp see Smoker v London Fire and Civil Defence Authority

Wright v British Railways Board [1983] 3 WLR 211 House of Lords (Lord Diplock, Lord Fraser of Tullybelton, Lord Scarman, Lord Bridge of Harwich and Lord Brandon of Oakbrook)

Damages – interest

Facts
The plaintiff guard was awarded damages, inter alia, for pain, suffering and loss of amenity against his employers, the defendants. The question arose as to the rate of interest to be paid.

Held
It should be 2 per cent from the date of service of the writ to the date of judgment.

Lord Diplock:

'As regards the fixing of the conventional rate of interest to be applied to the conventional figure at which damages for non-economic loss have been assessed, the rate of 2% adopted and recommended as a guideline by the Court of Appeal in *Birkett* v *Hayes* [1982] 1 WLR 816 covered a period during which inflation was proceeding at a very rapid rate ... I see no ground that would justify this House in holding that guideline to have been wrong, or to overrule the trial judge's application of it to the instant case. Although the rate of inflation has slowed, at least temporarily, since the period in respect of which the 2% guideline in *Birkett* v *Hayes* was laid down, no one yet knows what the long-term future of the phenomenon of inflation will be; and the guideline, if it is to serve its purpose in promoting predictability and so facilitating settlements and eliminating the expense of regularly calling expert economic evidence at trials of personal injury actions, should continue to be followed for the time being at any rate, until the long-term trend of future inflation has become predictable with much more confidence. When that state of affairs is reached, and it would be unrealistic to suppose that it will be in the immediate future, it may be that the 2% guideline will call for examination afresh in the light of fresh expert economic evidence, which may show that assumptions that could validly be made at the time of *Birkett* v *Hayes* as to what was the current rate of interest obtainable in the market that was attributable to forgoing the use of money will have ceased to hold good. But there is no material before your Lordships to suggest that the time is yet ripe for this.'

18 Miscellaneous Defences and Limitation

Broadley* v *Guy Clapham & Co [1994] 4 All ER 439 Court of Appeal (Balcombe, Leggatt, Hoffmann LJJ)

Limitation period for personal injury – date of plaintiff's knowledge for s11 and s14 Limitation Act 1980

Facts
In 1980 the plaintiff underwent a knee operation. Her condition did not improve and subsequent examinations revealed that she had left foot drop. In 1983 the plaintiff instructed the defendant solicitors who took few steps to prosecute the action. In August 1990 the plaintiff sued the defendants alleging that they had failed to take any adequate action, and as a result her claim for medical negligence had become time-barred under the Limitation Act 1980.

The question arose for determination as a preliminary issue as to whether the plaintiff's date of knowledge of her cause of action was before or after August 1981. At first instance it was held that the plaintiff knew before this date that her injury was significant, although she did not have knowledge of its cause or pathology, and while such knowledge did not satisfy s14(1) it was sufficient to fix the plaintiff with constructive knowledge under s14(3)(b), namely knowledge that the operation had in some way caused her injury. The plaintiff appealed.

Held
The appeal was dismissed. A person who alleged that medical negligence had occurred during a surgical operation was fixed with a cause of action for the purposes of s14(3) of the 1980 Act when he knew, or could have known with the help of medical advice reasonably obtainable, that his injury had been caused by damage resulting from an act or omission by the surgeon during the operation. Knowledge which was detailed enough to enable the plaintiff's advisers to draft a statement of claim was not required before time began to run.

Dobbie* v *Medway Health Authority [1994] 4 All ER 450 Court of Appeal (Sir Thomas Bingham MR, Beldam and Steyn LJJ

Limitation period for personal injury – date of plaintiff's knowledge

Facts
In 1973 the plaintiff was admitted to hospital for the removal of a lump from her breast. During the operation, the surgeon considered the lump to be cancerous and performed a mastectomy. Subsequent examination showed that the growth was benign. In 1988 the plaintiff heard of a similar case and realised, for the first time, that her breast need not have been removed until the lump had to be examined and found to be malignant. In 1989 she issued proceedings in negligence. The defendant contended that the claim was time-barred under s11(4)(b) and s14(1) of the Limitation Act 1980 as the time limit for actions for personal injuries was three years from the date of knowledge of the person injured which was defined

as the date on which the plaintiff first had knowledge (a) that the injury was significant and (b) that it was attributable in whole or part to the act or omission which was alleged to constitute negligence. At first instance it was held that the action was statute-barred. The plaintiff appealed.

Held
The appeal was dismissed. Time started to run against a claimant for the purposes of s14(1) when he knew that the injury on which he founded his claim was capable of being attributed to an act or omission of the defendant, irrespective of whether at that point he knew that the act or omission was actionable or tortious. It thus followed that the plaintiff's cause of action was time-barred since she knew within the limitation period that she had suffered a significant injury which was attributable to the defendant's act or omission, even though she had not been aware until after this period that the conduct might be actionable.

Commentary
It would seem from *Broadley* and *Dobbie* that very little knowledge indeed is necessary to cause time to run under s14 of the Limitation Act 1980. But see *Hallam-Eames* v *Merrett* (below).

Donovan v *Gwentoys Ltd* [1990] 1 WLR 472 House of Lords (Lord Bridge of Harwich, Lord Templeman, Lord Griffiths, Lord Oliver of Aylmerton and Lord Lowry)

Limitation period – discretion

Facts
In 1979 the plaintiff, then aged 16, fell at work: she strained a wrist and aggravated a knee condition. She received industrial injury benefit for the wrist but made no mention of the knee: she left the defendants' employment in 1980. Shortly before any action became statute-barred by virtue of ss11 and 28 of the Limitation Act 1980, the plaintiff consulted solicitors: they applied for legal aid but failed to issue a writ to protect her position. A writ was issued in October 1984 (5 1/2 months after the expiration of the limitation period) but the defendants did not receive full information regarding the plaintiff's claim for injury to her knee, alleging negligence and breach of statutory duty, until June 1987. The defendants contended that the action was statute-barred: the plaintiff sought to rely on s33 of the 1980 Act. The trial judge decided in favour of the plaintiff, confining himself to a consideration of the prejudice to the defendants resulting from the 5 1/2 months' delay: the Court of Appeal upheld this decision: the defendants appealed.

Held
The appeal would be allowed. The judge's discretion under s33(1) of the 1980 Act had been unfettered, especially in relation to s33(3). He should not have confined himself to the 5 1/2 months period, but considered all the circumstances, in particular the fact that it was 5 years before the defendants had been notified of a claim. The balance of prejudice was heavily in favour of the defendants, especially as the plaintiff had a strong claim against her solicitors for failing to issue a protective writ.

Hallam-Eames v *Merrett* (1995) The Times 25 January Court of Appeal (Sir Thomas Bingham MR, Hoffman and Saville LJJ)

Limitation period – date of plaintiff's knowledge

Facts
This case involved various insurance matters, and the question arose as to whether the claims were statute-barred. The plaintiffs sought to rely on s14A Limitation Act 1980 and the relevant part of s14A(8)(a) reads 'that the damage was attributable in whole or in part to the act or omission which is alleged to constitute negligence'. This mirrors the language of s14(1)(b) and thus the court considered the authorities on the latter provision.

Held
The judge at first instance had interpreted *Broadley* v *Guy Clapham & Co* (above) and *Dobbie* v *Medway Health Authority* (above) to mean that a plaintiff need only have known that his damage had been caused by an act of omission or the defendant.

Hoffman LJ found that this was an over-simplification of the reasoning in the two cases. The statute referred to damage being attributable to 'the act or omission which is alleged to cause negligence', ie, the act or omission of which the plaintiff had to have knowledge had to be the one which was causally relevant for the purposes of an allegation of negligence. The plaintiff did not have to know that he had a cause of action or that the defendant's acts could be characterised in law as negligence or as falling short of some standard of professional or other behaviour. The words 'which is alleged to constitute negligence' identify the facts of which the plaintiff must have knowledge.

Commentary
Both *Broadley* v *Guy Clapham & Co* (above) and *Dobbie* v *Medway Health Authority* (above) must be read in the light of this case. It will certainly be relied on by future plaintiffs, and it is hoped that future decisions will elucidate its ratio decidendi.

K v *P* [1993] 1 All ER 521 High Court (Ferris J)

Extent of the ex turpi causa defence

Facts
The plaintiffs sued various defendants, alleging fraud and conspiracy to defraud. One defendant issued a third party notice against the plaintiffs' accountant under s1(1) of the Civil Liability (Contribution) Act 1978 claiming an indemnity against any damages payable to the plaintiffs on the grounds that the accountant had acted in breach of contract or negligently. The question arose as to whether a party who was held to be merely negligent could be required to contribute to damages payable by a party who had been guilty of fraud, and whether the maxim ex turpi causa non oritur actio afforded a defence under the 1978 Act.

Held
The ex turpi causa defence was not available to a claim for contribution under the 1978 Act, since the specific purpose of that Act was to enable claims to be made between parties who had no claim under the general law. The only necessary ingredient for an action under the Act was that the plaintiffs had a cause of action against a third party as regards the same damage that gave rise to the plaintiffs' cause of action against the defendants. To permit the ex turpi causa defence to be relied on would substantially narrow the deliberately wide wording of s6(1) of the Act. Thus it was irrelevant that the plaintiffs' cause of action against the defendants arose out of fraud while their cause of action against the third party arose from breach of contractual or tortious duty of care. Additionally, under s2(1) and s2(2) of the 1978 Act all of the factors which were relevant to the ex turpi causa defence could be taken into account when assessing the amount of contribution, and could result in a nil contribution.

Moore (DW) & Co Ltd v Ferrier [1988] 1 WLR 267 Court of Appeal (Kerr, Neill and Bingham LJJ)

Negligence – limitation of action

Facts
Having agreed in 1971 and 1975 to issue shares in the company to Fenton, an employee and director of the company, subject to his entering into a covenant against setting up as an insurance broker if he left the company, the plaintiff insurance brokers consulted the defendant solicitors who drew up agreements containing a restrictive covenant which would apply if Fenton ceased 'to be a member of the company'. In 1980 Fenton decided to set up business in a way which appeared to breach the covenant: he resigned as an employee and director but remained a shareholder and it was then discovered that the covenant was effective only if he ceased to be a shareholder. In consequence, the plaintiffs were unable to enforce the covenant and in 1985 they sued the defendants alleging negligence in drafting the covenant.

Held
The plaintiffs' cause of action had accrued more than six years before they brought their action and it was therefore time-barred.

Bingham LJ:

> 'The limitation of tort actions in negligence is, and has for many years been, governed by two main rules: first, that time runs against the claimant from the date when his cause of action accrues; and second, that his cause of action accrues when he suffers damage caused by the negligence complained of.
>
> In the great majority of cases these rules work well, because the claimant knows of his injury or damage at about the time he suffers it, and if he does not take action within the generous time limits provided he has only himself to blame. But difficulty has arisen in the minority of cases where a claimant does not know that he has suffered injury or damage, so that time begins to run, and may even expire, before he is aware of the damage or injury, or of his right to complain against its author ... [The Limitation Acts passed in 1963 and 1975 were] only concerned with personal injuries and the problem was not confined to that field. Architects and engineers designing or supervising the construction of buildings or other structures, barristers and solicitors and accountants giving advice and settling documents, may all make negligent mistakes in circumstances where the mistake may not become apparent for many years. Following the 24th Report of the Law Reform Committee (Latent Damage) (Cmnd 9390) this problem also was the subject of legislative intervention, in the Latent Damage Act 1986. But that Act does not affect this action, which is subject to the law which governed negligence actions not involving personal injury before it was passed. Under that law, in the absence of fraud, concealment or mistake (which are not suggested here), time runs for the date of damage whether the claimant knows of the damage or not.
>
> So the crucial question here is when the plaintiffs suffered damage ... It seems to me clear beyond argument that from the moment of executing each agreement the plaintiffs suffered damage because instead of receiving a potentially valuable chose in action they received one that was valueless.'

Rigby v Chief Constable of Northamptonshire [1985] 1 WLR 1242 High Court (Taylor J)

Necessity as a defence to trespass

Facts
The police fired a canister of CS gas into the plaintiff's shop in an effort to flush out a dangerous

psychopath who had broken into it. The canister set the shop ablaze and the plaintiff sued the police (inter alia) in trespass.

Held
That the defence of necessity was available in an action for trespass.

Stubbings v *Webb* [1993] 2 WLR 120 House of Lords (Lord Templeman, Lord Bridge of Harwich, Lord Griffiths, Lord Ackner and Lord Slynn of Hadley)

Trespass to the person – limitation period

Facts
In August 1987 the respondent issued a writ claiming damages for personal injuries arising out of alleged sexual and physical abuse by the appellants between December 1959 and January 1971. The alleged abuse was said to have taken place when the respondent was between the ages of 2 and 14.

Held
The claim was within s2 (as opposed to s11) of the Limitation Act 1980 and it was therefore time-barred.

Lord Griffiths:

'I accept that *Letang* v *Cooper* [1964] 3 WLR 573 was correctly decided in so far as it held that negligent driving is a cause of action falling within s2(1) of the Law Reform (Limitation of Actions etc) Act 1954. But I cannot agree that the words "breach of duty" have the effect of including within the scope of the section all actions in which damages for personal injuries are claimed which is the other ground upon which the Court of Appeal decided *Letang* v *Cooper*. If that had been the intention of the draftsman it would have been easy enough to say so in the section. On the contrary the draftsman has used words of limitation; he has limited the section to actions for negligence, nuisance and breach of duty and the reason he did so was to give effect to the recommendation of the Tucker Committee that the three-year period should not apply to a number of causes of action in which damages for personal injury might be claimed, namely damages for trespass to the person, false imprisonment, malicious prosecution or defamation. There can be no doubt that rape and indecent assault fell within the category of trespass to the person.

Lord Denning MR in *Letang* v *Cooper* was not prepared to assume that Parliament did intend to give effect to the Tucker Committee's recommendations, but we can now look at Hansard and can see that it was the express intention of Parliament to do so. The proposer of the Bill ... in moving the second reading said:

> "In its main provisions the Bill follows precisely the recommendations of the committee which sat under the chairmanship of the then Lord Justice Tucker. There is only one comparatively minor point upon which the provisions vary from the recommendations of the Tucker committee."

The minor point I have already identified: it was to substitute a fixed period of three years for a two-year period which might be extended to six years ...

Even without reference to Hansard I should not myself have construed "breach of duty" as including a deliberate assault. The phrase lying in juxtaposition with "negligence" and "nuisance" carries with it the implication of a breach of duty of care not to cause personal injury, rather than an obligation not to infringe any legal right of another person. If I invite a lady to my house one would naturally think of a duty to take care that the house is safe but would one really be thinking of a duty not to rape her. But, however this may be, the terms in which this Bill was introduced to my mind make it clear beyond peradventure that the intention was to give effect to the Tucker recommendation that the limitation period in respect of trespass to the person was not to be reduced to three years but should remain at six years. The language of s2(1) of the 1954 Act is in my view apt to give effect to that intention, and cases of deliberate assault such as we are concerned with in this case are not actions for breach of duty within the meaning of s11(1) of the 1980 Act.

The language of s2(1) of the 1954 Act was carried without alteration into the 1975 Act and then into s11(1) of the 1980 Act where it must bear the same meaning as it had in the 1954 Act.

It thus follows that the respondent's causes of action against both appellants were subject to a six-year limitation period. This period was suspended during her infancy but commenced to run when she attained her majority: see s28 of the 1980 Act. This period expired many years before she issued her writ in these proceedings. There are no provisions for extending this period and her actions are therefore statute-barred and cannot proceed.'

Tinsley v *Milligan* [1993] 3 WLR 126 House of Lords (Lord Keith, Lord Goff, Lord Jauncey, Lord Lowry and Lord Browne-Wilkinson)

Extent of ex turpi causa defence

Facts
The plaintiff and defendant formed a joint business venture to run lodging houses. Using funds generated by the business they purchased a house in which they lived together and which was vested in the sole name of the plaintiff, on the understanding that they were the joint beneficial owners of the property. The purpose of this arrangement was to perpetrate a fraud on the Department of Social Security, and over a number of years both the plaintiff and the defendant made false benefit claims on the Department. The plaintiff brought proceedings against the defendant claiming sole ownership of the property and the defendant counterclaimed for a declaration that the property was held by the plaintiff on trust for the parties in equal shares. The judge dismissed the plaintiff's claim and allowed the counterclaim. The plaintiff appealed to the Court of Appeal who dismissed the appeal, and thence to the House of Lords.

Held
The appeal was dismissed on the grounds that a claimant to an interest in property, whether based on a legal or equitable title, was entitled to recover if he was not forced to plead or rely on illegality, even though the title on which he relied was acquired via an illegal transaction. In the circumstances, by showing that she had contributed to the purchase price of the property and that there was a common understanding between the parties that they owned the property equally, the defendant had established a resulting trust. There was no necessity to prove the reason for the conveyance into the plaintiff's sole name, which was irrelevant to the defendant's claim, and since there was no evidence to rebut the presumption of a resulting trust the defendant's counterclaim succeeded.

Note that the House rejected the 'public conscience' test used by the Court of Appeal.

Lord Goff:

'Finally, I wish to revert to the public conscience test favoured by Nicholls LJ in the Court of Appeal. Despite the fact that I have concluded that on the authorities it was not open to the Court of Appeal to apply the public conscience test to a case such as the present, I have considered whether it is open to your Lordships' House to do so and, if so, whether it would be desirable to take this course. Among the authorities cited to your Lordships, there was no decision of this House; technically, therefore, it may be said that this House is free to depart from the line of authority to which I have referred. But the fact remains that the principle invoked by the appellant has been consistently applied for about two centuries. Furthermore the adoption of the public conscience test, as stated by Nicholls LJ, would constitute a revolution in this branch of the law, under which what is in effect a discretion would become vested in the court to deal with the matter by the process of a balancing operation, in place of a system of rules, ultimately derived from the principle of public policy enunciated by Lord Mansfield CJ in *Holman* v *Johnson*, 1 Cowp 341, which lies at the root of the law relating to claims which are, in one way or another, tainted by illegality. Furthermore, the principle of public policy so stated by Lord Mansfield cannot be disregarded as having no basis in principle. In his dissenting judgment in the present case Ralph Gibson LJ pointed out [1992] Ch 310, 334:

> "In so far as the basis of the ex turpi causa defence, as founded on public policy, is directed at deterrence it seems to me that the force of the deterrent effect is in the existence of the known rule and in its stern application. Lawyers have long known of the rule and must have advised many people of its existence. It does not stop people making arrangements to defraud creditors, or the revenue, or the DSS. Such arrangements as are under consideration in this case are usually made between married couples as in *Tinker* v *Tinker*, or between unmarried lovers as in this case or in *Cantor* v *Cox*, 239 EG 121. If they do not fall out, no one will know. If they do fall out, one side may reveal the fraud. It is an ugly situation when that is done. I think that the law has upheld the principle on the simple ground that, ugly though its working may be, it is better than permitting the fraudulent an avenue of escape if the fraud is revealed."

I recognise, of course, the hardship which the application of the present law imposes upon the respondent in this case; and I do not disguise my own unhappiness at the result. But, bearing in mind the passage from the judgment of Ralph Gibson LJ which I have just quoted, I have to say that it is by no means self-evident that the public conscience text is preferable to the present strict rules. Certainly, I do not feel able to say that it would be appropriate for your Lordships' House, in the face of a long line of unbroken authority stretching back over 200 years, now by judicial decision to replace the principles established in those authorities by a wholly different discretionary system.'

19 Torts to Chattels

Armory v *Delamirie* (1722) 1 Stra 505 Court of Kings Bench (Sir John Pratt CJ)

Boy finds jewel – was he entitled to it?

Facts
A chimney sweeper's boy found a jewel set in a socket and took it to a goldsmith 'to know what it was'. The goldsmith returned the socket but retained the jewel so the boy sued for its recovery.

Held
His action would be successful

Sir John Pratt CJ:

> 'the finder of a jewel, though he does not by such finding acquire an absolute property or ownership, yet he has such a property as will enable him to keep it against all but the rightful owner, and consequently may maintain trover ...' As to the value of the jewel, several of the trade were examined to prove what a jewel of the finest water that would fit the socket would be worth; and Sir John Pratt CJ, directed the jury that, unless the defendant did produce the jewel and show it not to be of the finest water, they should presume the strongest against him and make the value of the best jewels the measure of their damages, which they accordingly did.

Commentary
Applied in *Bridges* v *Hawkesworth* (1851) 21 LJQB 75 and *Parker* v *British Airways Board* [1982] 1 All ER 834.

Bridges v *Hawkesworth* (1851) LJ QB 75 Court of Queen's Bench (Pattison and Wightman JJ)

Parcel found in shop – who should have it?

Facts
The plaintiff traveller, having visited the defendant's shop on business, noticed a parcel on the floor: the parcel contained bank-notes. The plaintiff asked the defendant to keep the notes until they were claimed by their owner. After three years, the notes having not been claimed, the plaintiff asked the defendant to return them to him; he refused. In an action in the county court it was found that when the plaintiff passed the notes to the defendant he (the plaintiff) had not intended to give up any title to them that he might possess.

Held
The plaintiff was entitled to the notes as against the defendant.

Pattison J:

'The notes which are the subject of this action were dropped by mere accident in the defendant's shop by the owner of them. The facts do not warrant the supposition that they had been deposited there intentionally, nor has the case been put at all upon that ground. The plaintiff found them on the floor, they being manifestly lost by someone. The general right of the finder to any article which has been lost as against all the world except the true owner, was established in *Armory* v *Delamirie* (1722) 1 Stra 505, which has never been disputed. This right would clearly have accrued to the plaintiff had the notes been picked up by him outside the shop of the defendant; and if he once had the right, the case finds that he did not intend by delivering the notes to the defendant, to waive the title (if any) which he had to them, but they were handed to the defendant merely for the purpose of delivering them to the owner, should he appear.

Nothing that was done afterwards has altered the state of things ... The case, therefore, resolves itself to the single point on which it appears that the judge decided it, namely, whether the circumstance of the notes being found in the defendant's shop gives him, the defendant, authority in our law to be found directly in point... The notes never were in the custody of the defendant, nor within the protection of his house, before they were found, as they would have been had they been intentionally deposited there ... We find, therefore, no circumstances to take this case out of the general rule of law that the finder of a lost article is entitled to it as against all persons, except the real owner; and we think that that rule must prevail, and that the judge was mistaken in holding that the place in which they were found makes any legal difference.'

Commentary
Followed in *Hannah* v *Peel* [1945] KB 509 and *Parker* v *British Airways Board* [1982] 1 All ER 834.
Distinguished in *South Staffordshire Water Co* v *Sharman* [1896] 2 QB 44.

Bute (Marquess) v *Barclays Bank Ltd* [1955] 1 QB 202 High Court (McNair J)

Crossed warrants – conversion?

Facts
A Mr McGaw managed the plaintiff's sheep farms. Under the terms of his contract of employment, all sums received by him in respect of the farms had to be taken to the estate office for payment into the plaintiff's farm account. In January, in accordance with his duty, he applied for sheep subsidy; he resigned in April and left the plaintiff's service in May. Later that year, McGaw received three crossed warrants in satisfaction of the January claim: they were drawn in his favour '(for Marquess of Bute)'. McGaw opened an account with the defendant bank and paid in the warrants which were specially crossed by a rubber stamp bearing the defendants' name and forwarded by them for payment. The plaintiff sued for the amount of the warrants, inter alia, as damages for conversion.

Held
His action would be successful as he had been entitled to immediate possession of the property converted.

McNair J:

'In substance, three grounds of defence were taken by the bank. First, it was said that McGaw was at all material times the true owner of the warrants and their proceeds, though he was accountable to the plaintiff, that the plaintiff was not the true owner and that, accordingly, the plaintiff is not entitled to sue either in conversion ...

As to the first ground, the short answer, in my judgment, is that, in order to claim in conversion, it is not necessary for the plaintiff to establish that he is the true owner of the property alleged to have been converted. It is sufficient if he can prove that at the time of the alleged conversion he was entitled to immediate possession. McGaw's employment was terminated not later than May 9, 1949, and thereafter the plaintiff was clearly entitled, if he so wished, to require McGaw to deliver the warrants to him when they were received, since McGaw's only title to receive them stemmed from his appointment as manager; and thus, I think, it is clear that at the date of the alleged conversion in September 1949, the plaintiff was entitled to immediate possession and, accordingly, was entitled to sue in conversion. I have no doubt that, if the plaintiff had known the true facts in September 1949, before McGaw approached the bank, he could successfully have applied for an injunction to restrain McGaw from dealing with the warrants otherwise than by handing them over to him...

Counsel for the defendants, rightly as I consider, submitted that the test in this case was to be found in the intention of the drawer as expressed in the document. Though it was argued that, as a matter of construction, the words "for Marquess of Bute" were merely inserted for the information of McGaw, I consider that these words, particularly having regard to their position on the warrants, form an essential part of the description of the drawee. On this view the warrants contain a promise to pay A for B ... Having regard ... to the fact that the warrants on their face purported to be payments in respect of hill sheep subsidy, which, to the knowledge of the drawers, was due to the plaintiff and not to McGaw, it seems to me to be plain that the intention of the drawers, as evidenced by the warrants, must be taken to have been that the plaintiff should be the true owner of the warrants and their proceeds and not that the true owner should be McGaw, and McGaw should be merely accountable to the plaintiff ... Accordingly, quite apart from the fact that at the material time McGaw's authority had been terminated, I consider that at all times, including the date of the conversion, the plaintiff was the true owner and not McGaw.'

Greenwood v *Bennett* [1973] QB 195 Court of Appeal (Lord Denning MR, Phillimore and Cairns LJJ)

Stolen car – cost of repair

Facts

A Mr Searle stole a Jaguar car from a garage of which Mr Bennett was manager. Searle involved the car in a collision with another vehicle and, in its damaged state, sold it to a Mr Harper who bought it in good faith for £75. Harper repaired the car at a cost of £226 and then sold it to a finance company which let it on hire purchase to a Mr Prattle for £450. The police recovered the vehicle and Mr Greenwood, the chief constable, asked the court to whom they should return it. Harper accepted the county court judge's ruling that Bennett was entitled to possession, but appealed against his decision that Bennett was not obliged to reimburse the amount that he (Harper) had expended on repairs.

Held

The appeal would be allowed.

Lord Denning MR:

'To decide this case, I think it helpful to consider the legal position as if the police had not taken possession of the car, but it had remained in Mr Prattle's possession. In the first place, if Mr Bennett's company had brought an action against Mr Harper for conversion of the car (relying on his purchase of it from Mr Searle for £75 as the act of conversion) then the damages would be £75 as its value at that time; whereas, if they had brought an action for conversion (relying on his sale of it to the finance company as the act of conversion) the damages would be its improved value at the time of sale, but Mr Bennett's company would have to give credit for the work which Mr Harper had done on it: see *Munro* v *Willmott* [1949] 1 KB 295 ... if Mr Bennett's company had brought an action against Mr Prattle for specific delivery of the car, it is very unlikely that an order for specific delivery of the car would be made. But if it had been, no court would order its delivery unless compensation was made for the improvements ... I should have thought that the county court judge here should have imposed a condition on Mr Bennett's company. He should have required them to pay Mr Harper the £226 as a condition of being given delivery of the car. But the judge did not impose such a condition. They have regained the car, and sold it. What then is to be done? It seems to me that we must order them to pay Mr Harper the £226 for that is the only way of putting the position right.

On what principle is this to be done? Counsel for Mr Bennett has referred us to the familiar cases which say that a man is not entitled to compensation for work done on the goods or property of another unless there is a contract express or implied to pay for it... That is undoubtedly the law when the person who does the work knows, or ought to know, that the property does not belong to him. He takes the risk of not being paid for his work on it. But it is very different when he honestly believes himself to be the owner of the property and does the work in that belief ... Here we have an innocent purchaser who bought the car in good faith and without notice of any defect in the title to it. He did work on it to the value of £226. The law is hard enough to him when it makes him give up the car itself. It would be most unjust if Mr Bennett's company could not only take the car from him, but also the value of the improvements he has done to it – without paying for them. There is a principle at hand to meet the case. It derives from the law of restitution. Mr Bennett's company should not be allowed unjustly to enrich themselves at his expense. The court will order them, if they recover the car, or its improved value, to recompense the innocent purchaser for the work he had done on it. No matter whether they recover it with the aid of the courts, or without it, the innocent purchaser will recover the value of the improvements he has done to it.'

Hannah v Peel [1945] KB 509 High Court (Birkett J)

Brooch found in house owner had never occupied

Facts

A house was conveyed to the defendant in 1938 but he had never actually occupied it. War broke out, the house was requisitioned and the plaintiff soldier found a brooch there. The real owner of the brooch not having been traced, the plaintiff claimed it as the finder.

Held

His action would be successful.

Birkett J:

'I think it is fairly clear from the authorities that this proposition would not be doubted, *viz*, that a man possesses everything which is attached to or under his land. Secondly, it would appear to be the law from the authorities I have cited, and particularly *Bridges v Hawkesworth* (1851) 21 LJ QB 75 that a man does not necessarily possess a thing which is lying unattached on the surface of his land even though the thing is not possessed by someone else. But the difficulty arises because the rule which governs things an occupier possesses as against those which he does not has never been very clearly formulated in our law. He may possess everything upon the land from which he intends to exclude others ... or, he may possess those things over which he has a *de facto* control ... These things are not clearly laid down in cases. That is all that I think I can usefully say about the authorities. Neither do I think that a discussion of the merits helps at all.

There is no doubt that the brooch was lost in the ordinary connotation of that term, and from the appearance of the brooch when found, *ie*, the dirt and cobwebs, it had apparently been lost for a very considerable time ...

It is clear that the defendant, as I gather from the agreed statement of facts, was never physically in possession of these premises at any time. It is clear the brooch was never his in the ordinary acceptation of the term, in that he had the prior possession. He had no knowledge of it until it was brought to his knowledge by the finder. As I say, a discussion of the merits does not seem to help a great deal, but it is clear on the facts (i) that the brooch was lost in the ordinary meaning of words, (ii) it appears to me clear that the brooch was found by the plaintiff in the ordinary meaning of words, and (iii) it is clear that the true owner of the brooch has never been found. The defendant was the owner of the premises and had his notice drawn to this matter by the plaintiff who found the brooch. In all those circumstances I asked for a little time in order that I might consider these authorities which are very difficult to reconcile. The conclusion to which I have come is that I propose to follow the decision in *Bridges* v *Hawkesworth* and I propose to give judgment in this case for the plaintiff.'

International Factors Ltd v *Rodriguez* [1979] 1 QB 351 Court of Appeal (Buckley, Bridge LJJ and Sir David Cairns)

Factoring agreement – right to possession of cheques

Facts
The plaintiffs entered into a factoring agreement with a company: the company's book debts were assigned to the plaintiffs for 98.5 per cent of their full value. Four cheques were sent to the company and, knowing that it was in breach of the factoring agreement, the defendant director paid them into the company' account. The plaintiffs sued for conversion.

Held
They were entitled to succeed as the agreement gave them a right to immediate possession of the cheques.

Sir David Cairns (Bridge LJ agreeing):

'It is clear law that a contractual right to have goods handed to him by another person is not in itself sufficient to clothe the person who has that right with power to sue in conversion ...

In my view, however, there was here something more than a contractual right ... the agreement provided both that the supplier was to hold any debt paid direct to the supplier in trust for the factor, that is, the company was to hold in trust for the plaintiffs, and immediately after receipt of a cheque, in the case of payment by cheque, to hand over that cheque to the company. Taking together the trust which was thereby set up and the obligation immediately on receipt to hand over the cheque to the plaintiffs, I am satisfied that the plaintiffs had here a sufficient proprietary right to sue in conversion.'

Buckley LJ:

'...whether or not an enforceable trust would attach immediately on the payment of any debt direct to the company by cheque, whether or not an immediate trust would attach to such a cheque, I think that there is a contractual right here for the plaintiffs to demand immediate delivery of the cheque to them, and that that is a sufficient right to possession to give them a status to sue in conversion. On the findings of the learned judge the defendant was personally responsible for the payment of each of the four cheques to which this case relates into the company's account, and in those circumstances the right conclusion appears to me to be that it was the defendant who misapplied the cheque and who is liable for conversion. Counsel for the defendant has suggested that he could only be made liable in conversion if the company itself was guilty of conversion and so he, as an officer of the company, could be made vicariously responsible for conversion. In my view that is the wrong approach; the cheque was physically in the possession or under the control of the defendant, it was he who applied it wrongly in a manner in conflict with the right of the plaintiffs, and in my judgment it was he who was guilty of conversion as a primary participant and not merely as a secondary participant in the transaction.'

Jerome v *Bentley & Co* [1952] 2 All ER 114 High Court (Donovan J)

Conversion – sale to third party

Facts
Believing that he would try to sell a diamond ring for him, the plaintiff dealer allowed Major Tatham to take the ring. It was arranged that, if he sold the ring, Tatham would give the plaintiff £550 and keep any surplus; if the ring was not sold within seven days, it was to be returned to the plaintiff. After the seven days had expired Tatham, representing that he was the owner of the ring, sold it for £175 to the defendants who bought it in good faith and re-sold it. The plaintiff claimed damages for wrongful conversion.

Held
He was entitled to succeed.

Donovan J:

> 'That brings me to the circumstances in which Major Tatham sold the ring ... his sole duty was to hand the ring back to the plaintiff, and he had no authority to deal with it in any way except for the purpose of its safe custody. He has admitted that he stole the ring as a bailee. In other words, when he entered the shop he intended fraudulently to convert the ring to his own use, and he accomplished that purpose. He then became a thief of the ring ... No one represented Major Tatham to the defendants as the plaintiff's agent with authority to sell the ring. The defendants knew nothing of the plaintiff. In fact, they made Major Tatham show his identity card and sign a declaration that the ring was his. So they dealt with him on the footing of a principal selling his own property...
>
> The plaintiff here did nothing which misled the defendants. Is the circumstances I hold that no property in this ring passed to the defendants and there is nothing to prevent the plaintiff from setting up his title as against them. Therefore, I decide in his favour. On the evidence before me I value the ring at £250, and I give judgment for the plaintiff in that amount.'

Kowal v *Ellis* (1977) 76 DLR (3d) 546 Manitoba Court of Appeal

Abandoned pump – finder could keep it?

Facts
Driving across the defendant's land, with the defendant's permission, the plaintiff saw an abandoned pump.

Held
The plaintiff's claim to the pump prevailed over that of the defendant.

O'Sullivan JA:

> 'One can imagine cases where a chattel is abandoned by its true owner and may then become the property of someone else, perhaps a land-owner who exercises control and dominion over it. In such a case, the land-owner would assert a claim against the finder, not by virtue of his right as owner of land, but by virtue of his right as owner of the chattel. In the case before us, however, the defendant asserts no such right of ownership. The pump in question appears to have been cached rather than abandoned. So this is a case where the defendant does not even assert that he is the owner of the chattel in question; that being so, the defendant can succeed only by showing that he himself was in possession of the pump at the time of the finding in such a way that he, the defendant, had already constituted himself a bailee for the true owner. I know there have been weighty opinions expressed in favour of the proposition that the possessor of land

possesses all that is on the land, and there is a sense in which that may be so, but to oust the claim of a bailee by finding it is not enough to establish some kind of metaphysical possession. What must be shown is that the land-owner claimant, who has not acquired ownership of a chattel, is a prior bailee of the chattel with all the rights, but also with all the obligations, of a bailee. I am sure that no one would be more surprised that the defendant if, prior to the finding by the plaintiff, the true owner had come along and asserted that the defendant land-owner owed him any duty either to take care of the pump or to seek out the owner of it. The reality is that the defendant, not even being aware of the existence of the pump, owed no duty with respect to it to its true owner. He was not a bailee of the pump and consequently has no claim to possession which can prevail over the special property which the plaintiff has by virtue of his having become a bailee by finding.'

Commentary
Applied in *Parker* v *British Airways Board* [1982] 1 All ER 834.

Manders v *Williams* (1849) 4 Ex 339 Court of Exchequer (Parke, Alderson and Platt BB)
Empty casks – customer bailee

Facts
The plaintiffs were merchants in Dublin and they sent porter in casks to John David, a customer in Wales. Empty casks were to be returned to them within six months at David's expense or paid for by him. The defendant sheriff seized and sold, under a writ of execution against David, 300 of the casks which were lying empty in his cellar. The plaintiffs sued for trover in respect of these casks: did they have sufficient possession of the casks to maintain this action?

Held
They did and they would be awarded the price of the casks.

Parke B:

'The true construction of the contract is to give David an interest only until the casks were empty. I agree ... that, in this contract, every stipulation is for the benefit of the vendors, not the vendee. The latter is to incur all risk; he is under the obligation of sending the empty casks to Dublin at his own expense and before the end of six months from the date of the contract; if not, there is an option for the benefit of the vendors of calling on him to purchase the casks at a fixed price. Those stipulations show that the interest of the vendee was never meant to extend beyond the right to keep the casks until the porter was consumed. Possibly, he might within the six months have transferred the porter in the casks to a sub-vendee, but as soon as the casks were emptied the right to them reverted to the vendors. According to the true construction of this contract, I am satisfied that it was never intended that David should have the casks for any other purpose than keeping the porter. Indeed, I do not see what advantage there could be in his right of possession continuing after the casks were empty; for, during the residue of the six months, he could neither let them to anyone else nor make any further use of himself without being a wrongdoer and, at the end of the six months, he was bound to return them.

So soon as the casks were empty, the right of property and the right of possession reverted to the plaintiffs, and David was in the situation of a mere bailee during pleasure. No proposition can be more clear than that either the bailor or the bailee of a chattel may maintain an action in respect of it against a wrongdoer; the latter by virtue of his possession, the former by reason of his property.'

Moffatt v *Kazana* [1969] 2 WLR 71 High Court (Wrangham J)

Hidden bank-notes – who owns them?

Facts

A man (Mr Russell) hid some bank-notes in a tin box which he placed in the roof of his house. The house was sold to the defendant, one of whose employees found the money. Meanwhile, Mr Russell had died; his executors sued to recover the cash.

Held

Their action would be successful.

Wrangham J:

> 'It is clear therefore that in the existing authorities there is an implication at least from the language in which the judgments are expressed that the true owner of a chattel found on land has a title superior to that of anybody else. Accordingly, having disposed of the authorities in that way, counsel on behalf of the plaintiffs was able to say that the plaintiffs are, as representatives of Mr Russell, the true owners of this money and they must be held to remain the true owners of the money unless they or Mr Russell had divested himself or themselves of the ownership by one of the recognised methods, abandonment, gift or sale. Abandonment is not suggested. One does not abandon property merely because one has forgotten where one put it. Gift is not suggested. There remains only sale ...
>
> I am content to ground my judgment on this, that the conveyance itself, in view of the language of s62 [of the Law of Property Act 1925], cannot be said to have transferred the ownership of these £1 notes from Mr Russell to the defendant and that there is no other way in which it is even suggested that the ownership of these notes could have been transferred from Mr Russell to the defendant. If Mr Russell never got rid of the notes, that is to say, never got rid of the ownership of the notes, he continued to be the owner of them and, if he continued to be the owner of them, he had a title to those notes which nobody else, whether the owner of the land on which they were found, or the finders, or anybody else would have.'

Parker v *British Airways Board* [1982] 1 QB 1004 Court of Appeal (Eveleigh, Donaldson LJJ and Sir David Cairns)

Finders keepers?

Facts

A passenger found a gold bracelet in the British Airways executive lounge at Heathrow. He handed it to an employee, asking that it should be returned to him if it was not claimed. The owner never claimed the bracelet; the airline sold it and kept the proceeds; the passenger sued for its value.

Held

He was entitled to succeed.

Donaldson LJ:

> 'Mr Parker was not a trespasser in the executive lounge and, in taking the bracelet into his care and control, he was acting with obvious honesty. Prima facie, therefore, he had a full finder's right and obligations. He in fact discharged those obligations by handing the bracelet to an official of British Airways, although he could equally have done so by handing the bracelet to the police or in other ways such as informing the police of the find and himself caring for the bracelet.
>
> Mr Parker's prima facie entitlement to a finder's rights was not displaced in favour of an employer or principal. There is no evidence that he was in the executive lounge in the course of any employment or

agency and, if he was, the finding of the bracelet was quite clearly collateral thereto. The position would have been otherwise in the case of most or perhaps all of British Airways' employees.

British Airways, for their part, cannot assert any title to the bracelet based on the rights of an occupier over chattels attached to a building. The bracelet was lying loose on the floor. Their claim must, on my view of the law, be based on a manifest intention to exercise control over the lounge and all things which might be in it. The evidence is that they claimed the right to decide who should and who should not be permitted to enter and use the lounge, but their control was in general exercised on the basis of classes or categories of user and the availability of the lounge in the light of the need to clean and maintain it. I do not doubt that they also claimed the right to exclude individual undesirables, such as drunks, and specific types of chattels such as guns and bombs. But this control has no real relevance to a manifest intention to assert custody and control over lost articles. There was no evidence that they searched for such articles regularly or at all.

Evidence was given of staff instructions which govern the action to be taken by employees of British Airways if they found lost articles or lost chattels were handed to them. But these instructions were not published to users of the lounge and in any event I think that they were intended to do no more than instruct the staff on how they were to act in the course of their employment.

It was suggested in argument that in some circumstances the intention of the occupier to assert control over articles lost on his premises speaks for itself. I think that this is right. If a bank manager saw fit to show me round a vault containing safe deposit boxes and I found a gold bracelet on the floor, I should have no doubt that the bank had a better title than I, and the reason is the manifest intention to exercise a very high degree of control. At the other extreme is the park to which the public has unrestricted access during daylight hours. During those hours there is no manifest intention to exercise any such control. In between these extremes are the forecourts of petrol filling stations, unfenced front gardens of private houses, the public parts of shops and supermarkets as part of an almost infinite variety of land, premises and circumstances.

This lounge is in the middle band and in my judgment, on the evidence available, there was no sufficient manifestation of any intention to exercise control over lost property before it was found such as would give British Airways a right superior to that of Mr Parker or indeed any right over the bracelet. As the true owner has never come forward, it is a case of "finders keepers".'

Commentary
Applied: *Armory* v *Delamine* (1722) 5 Stra 505, *Bridges* v *Hawkesworth* (1851) 21 LJQB 75 and *Kowal* v *Ellis* (1977) 76 DLR (3d) 546.

Perry (Howard E) & Co Ltd v *British Railways Board* [1980] 1 WLR 1375 High Court (Sir Robert Megarry V-C)

Strike – wrongful interference with goods

Facts
Steelworkers were on strike; to assist them, the National Union of Railwaymen refused to transport steel. Fearing escalation of the dispute, the defendants refused to deliver the plaintiff stockholders' steel or to allow the plaintiffs to collect it from their (the defendants') depots. The plaintiffs sought an order under the Torts (Interference with Goods) Act 1977 that they be allowed to collect the steel.

Held
They were entitled to succeed.

Sir Robert Megarry V-C:

> 'What I have to consider here is a case in which the defendants are in effect saying to the plaintiffs: "We admit that the steel is yours and that you are entitled to possession of it. Yet because we fear that industrial action may be taken against us if we permit you to remove it, we have refused to allow you to collect it for some weeks now, despite your demands, and we will continue to refuse to allow you to collect it until our fears have been removed." Looking at the matter as one of principle, I would conclude that this is a clear case of conversion. The defendants are denying the plaintiffs most of the rights of ownership, including the right to possession, for a period which plainly is indefinite. It may be short, or it may be long; but it is clearly uncertain. I do not think that a period which will not end until the defendants reach the conclusion that their fears no longer justify the withholding of the steel can very well be called "definite". There is a detention of the steel which is consciously adverse to the plaintiffs' rights, and this seems to me to be of the essence of at least one form of conversion. A denial of possession to the plaintiffs does not cease to be a denial by being accompanied by a statement that the plaintiffs are entitled to the possession that is being denied to them ... For the defendants to withhold the steel from the plaintiffs is a wrongful interference with goods within the 1977 Act unless the reason for the withholding provides a justification. I cannot see that it does. This is no brief withholding made merely in order that the defendants may verify the plaintiffs' title to the steel, or for some other purpose to confirm that the delivery of the steel would be proper. This is a withholding despite the plain right of the plaintiff's to the ownership and possession of the steel, on the ground that the defendants fear unpleasant consequences if they do not deny the plaintiffs what they are entitled to.'

South Staffordshire Water Co v *Sharman* [1896] 2 QB 44 High Court (Lord Russell of Killowen CJ and Wills J)

Rings found in pool

Facts

The plaintiff freeholders of a pool employed the defendant, amongst others, to clean it out. In the course of this work the defendant found two gold rings: the plaintiffs sued to recover them.

Held

They were entitled to succeed.

Lord Russell of Killowen CJ:

> '*Bridges* v *Hawkesworth* (1851) 21 LJQB 75 really stands by itself and on its own special grounds, and, standing on its own grounds, I think the decision was perfectly right. There a person had dropped a bundle of bank notes in a public shop, public, that is to say, in the sense that it was open to the public. A customer came in and picked up the bundle of notes and showed it to the shopman, and afterwards gave it to the shopkeeper in order that he might advertise it. The owner was not found, and the shopkeeper afterwards refused to give up the notes to the customer who had found them. The customer then brought an action against the shopkeeper for the notes, and it was held that he was justified in demanding the notes, and the true ground of that decision is stated by PATTESON J, where he says:
>
>> "The notes never were in the custody of the defendant, nor within the protection of his house before they were found."
>
> The general principle within which the case falls seems to me to be that where there is possession of a house or land, with a manifest intention to exercise control over it, and the things in or upon it, and with control over that particular locus in quo, then if something is found on it by a person who is either a stranger or a servant, the presumption is that the possession of the thing so found is in the owner of that locus in quo. For these reasons I think judgment must be for the plaintiffs.'

Union Transport Finance Ltd v *British Car Auctions Ltd* [1978] 2 All ER 385 Court of Appeal (Cairns, Roskill and Bridge LJJ)

Termination of bailment – right to sue

Facts
The plaintiffs bought an Audi motor car and let it on hire purchase to a Mr Smith (or Smithers). In breach of the agreement, Smith altered the car's registration number and, without disclosing the agreement, instructed the defendant auctioneers to sell it, later receiving the net proceeds of sale. Unaware of any of this, when instalments were overdue the plaintiffs served notice to terminate the agreement. When they discovered what had happened, they sued for conversion and the defendants argued it, inter alia, that the plaintiffs had not been entitled to immediate possession at the time of the sale.

Held
This was not the case and the plaintiffs were entitled to judgment.

Roskill LJ:

> 'It seems to me that there is no room for doubt that the position at common law is this: if the bailee acts in a way which, to use the phrase used in argument, destroys the basis of the contract of bailment, the bailor becomes entitled at once to bring that contract to an end, and thus at once acquires the right to immediate possession of the article bailed ...
>
> In those circumstances, it seems to me that the only question that remains for consideration is whether the provisions of the present contract affect the basic common law position. Counsel for the defendants strenuously argued that they do. He contends that because there is this express contractual right to bring this contract to an end only after notice of termination, there is no room for the survival as between the plaintiffs and Mr Smith of the basic common law rule ... I think, with respect, that this argument is misconceived for a number of reasons. When one looks at these clauses one can see why they are there. They give a modicum of protection to the hirer but they also give certain specific contractual rights to the bailor in the happening of certain events. They give him the right to bring the contract to an end and to re-take possession in the event of certain things happening. But they do not expressly deprive the bailor of any other rights that he may have at common law; and still less, in my view, do these clauses, either expressly or impliedly, confer any right, possessory or otherwise, on the bailee which would lead to a conclusion different from that which would follow at common law if the bailee deliberately, as happened here, tears up the contract of bailment by fraudulently selling the car through an auctioneer, to an innocent third party. Therefore, it seems to me, following the reasoning in *North Central Wagon and Finance Co Ltd* v *Graham* [1950] 1 All ER 780, that even if there be room in principle for the existence of a contract which may contract out of the basic common law rule, it would require very clear language to deprive the bailor, of his common law rights in circumstances such as these. In the case of the present contract the language used is nothing like strong enough to achieve that result.'

Waverley Borough Council v Fletcher [1995] 3 WLR 772 Court of Appeal (Sir Thomas Bingham MR, Auld and Ward LJJ)

Ownership of chattels found on land

Facts
The plaintiff council were owners of a park and the defendant, whilst in the park, used a metal detector to locate a mediaeval gold brooch buried in the ground. He excavated the soil to a depth of nine inches and recovered the brooch, and the question arose as to whether the plaintiff or the defendant had the better title to the brooch.

Held
Where an object is found in or attached to land, the owner or lawful possessor of the land had a better title to the object than the finder; where the object was unattached on land the owner or lawful possessor only had a better title than the finder where he had exercised such manifest control over the land as to indicate an intention to control it and anything found on it.

Wilson v *Lombank Ltd* [1963] 1 WLR 1294 High Court (Hinchcliffe J)
Trespass to goods – car taken from garage

Facts
The plaintiff motor car dealer bought a car from a man who had no title to sell. As the car needed repair, the plaintiff took it to his regular garage; after completion of the work the car was placed on the garage forecourt. Believing – mistakenly – that they had a legal right to do so, the defendants took the car away. On discovering that the true owner was a finance company, the defendants returned the car to them. The plaintiff claimed damages for alleged trespass.

Held
He was entitled to succeed and to recover the value of the car and the full cost of the repair.

Hinchcliffe J:

> '... in my judgment the plaintiff was in possession of the car; not only did he have the right to immediate possession, but I do not think that, in the circumstances of this case, the plaintiff ever lost possession of the car. In my view, the plaintiff at all times could have demanded the return of the car ... I do not think that there was a lien on the motor car, having regard to the course of dealing between the plaintiff and the Haven Garage over a period of eight years, during which time there existed this monthly credit. On the view which I have formed, that the plaintiff never lost possession of the motor car, it seems to me that the defendants wrongfully took the car and that the plaintiff is entitled to recover damages.'

CRIMINAL LAW

20 Attempts

R v Jones (1990) 91 Cr App R 351 Court of Appeal (Criminal Division) (Taylor LJ, Mars-Jones and Waite JJ)

Attempted murder?

Facts
The appellant had pointed a sawn-off shotgun at his victim with the safety catch on. The victim was unclear whether the appellant's finger was ever on the trigger. The trial judge had rejected a submission that since the appellant would have had to perform at least three more acts before the full offence could have been completed, that is, remove the safety catch, put his finger on the trigger and pull it, the evidence was insufficient to support the charge of attempted murder.

Held
The appeal against conviction would be rejected. Taylor LJ said that the Criminal Attempts Act 1981 was a codifying statute: it amended and set out completely the law relating to attempts and conspiracies. The correct approach was to look first at the natural meaning of the statutory words, not to turn back to the earlier case law and seek to fit some previous test to the words of s1(1). The question for the judge in the present case was whether there was evidence from which a reasonable jury properly directed could conclude that the appellant had done acts which were more than merely preparatory. Once the appellant had pointed the loaded gun at the victim with the intention of killing him there was sufficient evidence to go before the jury on the attempted murder charge. It was a matter for them to decide whether they were sure those acts were more than merely preparatory.

R v Shivpuri [1986] 2 WLR 988

See Chapter 29.

21 Criminal Damage

Commissioner of Police of the Metropolis* v *Caldwell [1982] AC 341
See Chapter 30.

R* v *Hill; R* v *Hall (1988) 89 Cr App R 74 Court of Appeal (Criminal Division) (Lord Lane CJ, McCullough J, and Kennedy J)
Criminal damage – defence of lawful excuse

Facts
Both defendants were convicted of possession of an article with intent to damage property, contrary to section 3 of the Criminal damage Act 1971. The article in question in each case was a hacksaw blade. Each defendant had intended to use such a blade to damage the perimeter fences of airforce bases, as part of a larger campaign of protest at the presence of nuclear missiles on British soil. Both defendants sought to rely on the 'lawful excuse' defence provided by section 5(2) of the 1971 Act, which provides inter alia:

> 'A person charged with an offence to which this section applies shall, whether or not he would be treated for the purposes of this Act as having a lawful excuse apart from this subsection, be treated for those purposes as having a lawful excuse ... (b) if he ... intended to use or cause or permit the use of something to destroy or damage [the property], in order to protect property belonging to himself or another or a right or interest in property which was or which he believed to be vested in himself or another, and at the time of the act or acts alleged to constitute the offence he believed (i) that the property, right or interest was in immediate need of protection ...' Subsection (3) reads: 'For the purposes of this section it is immaterial whether belief is justified or not if it is honestly held.'

The Lord Chief Justice summarised the nature of the defendants' 'excuse' in referring to the case of Valerie Hill:

> '[She] believed that the purpose of [the airbase] base was to monitor the movements of Soviet submarines, that in the event of hostilities breaking out between the United States and the Soviets or the Soviets and ourselves, the base would be the subject of a nuclear strike with devastation in that area. She lived about 40 miles away from the base. Consequently her property and the property of friends and neighbours of hers in Pembrokeshire would be put at risk, to say the least, should there be any such nuclear strike. There was an alternative limb to this particular argument, and that was this that the Soviets might select the site at Brawdy as a target for a sudden nuclear strike in order to indicate that they, the Soviets, did not want all-out nuclear war, but were in a position to protect their submarines in the Atlantic if they so wished, and so to maintain the nuclear threat which those submarines posed to the United States. That latter limb, so to speak, was the subject of evidence by a gentleman called Dr Cox, whose qualifications seemed to us, if we may say so respectfully, to fall far short of entitling him to speak about these matters as an expert which he purported to be. However that may be, the way in which the matter presented itself to Valerie Hill was this, that if enough people took a hacksaw blade and did as she intended to do, namely cut a strand of the perimeter wire, the Americans might come to the conclusion that it was no longer possible to

maintain the safety and integrity of their base: it would be too insecure to be maintained. They accordingly might remove their base. Thereby they would have removed the reason for any nuclear attack to be made by the Soviet forces; or else possibly the United Kingdom government would take steps to remove the need for such places by abandoning the idea of nuclear defence. Thus, goes the reasoning that at the end of these hypothetical events, the property, whether it was her own property or the property of neighbours in Pembrokeshire, would avoid destruction. It seems that this was part of a concerted campaign by the Campaign for Nuclear Disarmament. Broadly speaking that was the background to these two cases.'

The defendants now appealed against the trial judge's directions to the jury in relation to subsections 5(2) and (3).

Held

The appeals would be dismissed.

Lord Lane CJ said in the course of his judgment:

'The learned judge, as I have already indicated, directed the jury to convict on two bases. The first basis was this, that what the applicant did or proposed to do could not, viewed objectively, be said to have been done to protect her own or anyone else's property under section 5(2)(b) which I have just read. It is simply, he concluded, part of a political campaign aimed at drawing attention to the base and to the risks as she described them raised by the presence of the base in Pembrokeshire. It aimed further at having the base removed. He came to the conclusion that the causative relationship between the acts which she intended to perform and the alleged protection was so tenuous, so nebulous, that the acts could not be said to be done to protect viewed objectively. The second ground was with reference to the provision that the lawful excuse must be based upon an immediate need for protection. In each case the judge came to the same conclusion that on the applicant's own evidence the applicant could not be said to have believed under the provisions of section 5(2)(b)(i) that the property was in immediate need of protection...

There are two aspects to this type of question. The first aspect is to decide what it was that the applicant, in this case Valerie Hill, in her own mind thought. The learned judge assumed, and so do we, for the purposes of this decision, that everything she said about her reasoning was true. I have already perhaps given a sufficient outline of what it was she believed to demonstrate what is meant by that. Up to that point the test was subjective. In other words one is examining what is going on in the applicant's mind. Having done that, the judges in the present cases – and the judge particularly in the case of Valerie Hill – turned to the second aspect of the case, and that is this. He had to decide as a matter of law, which means objectively, whether it could be said that on those facts as believed by the applicant, snipping the strand of the wire, which she intended to do, could amount to something done to protect either the applicant's own home or the homes of her adjacent friends in Pembrokeshire. He decided, again quite rightly in our view, that that proposed act on her part was far too remote from the eventual aim at which she was targeting her actions to satisfy the test. It follows therefore, in our view, that the judges in the present two cases were absolutely right to come to the conclusion that they did so far as this aspect of the case is concerned, and to come to that conclusion as a matter of law, having decided the subjective test as the applicants wished them to be decided. The second half of the question was that of the immediacy of the danger. Here the wording of the Act, one reminds oneself, is as follows: She believed that the property ... was in immediate need of protection. Once again the judge had to determine whether, on the facts as stated by the applicant, there was any evidence on which it could be said that she believed there was a need of protection from immediate danger. In our view that must mean evidence that she believed that immediate action had to be taken to do something which would otherwise be a crime in order to prevent the immediate risk of something worse happening. The answers which I have read in the evidence given by this woman (and the evidence given by the other applicant was very similar) drives this Court to the conclusion, as they drove the respective judges to the conclusion, that there was no evidence on which it could be said that there was that belief.'

Jaggard v *Dickinson* [1981] QB 527 Divisional Court (Donaldson LJ and Mustill J)
Drunkenness as evidence of honest belief in owner's consent to the destruction of property

Facts
The defendant was convicted of criminal damage contrary to s1(1) of the 1971 Act, on facts that showed that she had broken into a house whilst drunk. She had mistaken it for the house of a friend, who she believed would have consented to her causing damage to gain access. She appealed on the ground that the magistrates had erred in refusing to take into account her drunken state as evidence that she had honestly believed she had the consent of the owner to damage the property.

Held
The appeal would be allowed.

Mustill J referred to ss1(1) and 5(2) of the 1971 Act and continued:

'It is convenient to refer to the exculpatory provisions of s5(2) as if they created a defence while recognising that the burden of disproving the facts referred to by the subsection remains on the prosecution. The magistrates held that the appellant was not entitled to rely on s5(2) since the belief relied on was brought about by a state of self-induced intoxication.

In support of the conviction counsel for the respondent advanced an argument which may be summarised as follows (i) where an offence is one of "basic intent", in contrast to one of "specific intent", the fact that the accused was in a state of self-induced intoxication at the time when he did the acts constituting the actus reus does not prevent him from possessing the mens rea necessary to constitute the offence: see *DPP* v *Morgan* [Chapter 32] *DPP* v *Majewski* [Chapter 30]. (ii) Section 1(1) of the 1971 Act creates an offence of basic intent: see *R* v *Stephenson* [1979] QB 695. (iii) Section 5 (3) has no bearing on the present issue. It does not create a separate defence, but is no more than a partial definition of the expression "without lawful excuse" in s1(1). The absence of lawful excuse forms an element in the mens rea: see *R* v *Smith* [1974] QB 354 at 360. Accordingly, since drunkenness does not negative mens rea in crimes of basic intent, it cannot be relied on as part of a defence based on s5(2).

Whilst this is an attractive submission, we consider it to be unsound, for the following reasons. In the first place, the argument transfers the distinction between offences of specific and of basic intent to a context in which it has no place. The distinction is material where the defendant relies on his own drunkenness as a ground for denying that he had the degree of intention or recklessness required in order to constitute the offence. Here, by contrast, the appellant does not rely on her drunkenness to displace an inference of intent or recklessness; indeed she does not rely on it at all. Her defence is founded on the state of belief called for by s5(2). True, the fact of the appellant's intoxication was relevant to the defence under s5(2) for it helped to explain what would otherwise have been inexplicable, and hence lent colour to her evidence about the state of her belief. This is not the same as using drunkenness to rebut an inference of intention or recklessness. Belief, like intention or recklessness, is a state of mind; but they are not the same states of mind.

Can it nevertheless be said that, even if the context is different, the principles established by *Majewski* ought to be applied to this new situation? If the basis of the decision in *Majewski* had been that drunkenness does not prevent a person from having an intent or being reckless, then there would be grounds for saying that it should equally be left out of account when deciding on his state of belief. But this is not in our view what *Majewski* decided. The House of Lords did not conclude that intoxication was irrelevant to the fact of the defendant's state of mind, but rather that, whatever might have been his actual state of mind, he should for reasons of policy be precluded from relying on any alteration in that state brought about by self-induced intoxication. The same considerations of policy apply to the intent or recklessness which is the mens rea of the offence created by s1(1) and that offence is accordingly regarded as one of basic intent (see *R* v *Stephenson*). It is indeed essential that this should be so, for drink so often plays a part in offences of criminal damage, and to admit drunkenness as a potential means of escaping liability would provide much too ready a means of avoiding conviction. But these considerations do not apply to a case where Parliament has specifically required the court to consider the defendant's actual state of belief, not the state of belief which ought to have existed. This seems to us to show that the court is required by s5(3) to focus on the existence of the belief, not its intellectual soundness; and a belief can be just as much honestly held if it is induced by intoxication as if it stems from stupidity, forgetfulness or inattention.

It was however, urged that we could not properly read s5(2) in isolation from s1(1), which forms the context of the words "without lawful excuse" partially defined by s5(2). Once the words are put in context, so it is maintained, it can be seen that the law must treat drunkenness in the same way in relation to lawful excuse (and hence belief) as it does to intention and recklessness, for they are all part of the mens rea of the offence. To fragment the mens rea, so as to treat one part of it as affected by drunkenness in one way and the remainder as affected in a different way, would make the law impossibly complicated to enforce.

If it had been necessary to decide whether, for all purposes, the mens rea of an offence under s1(1) extends as far as the intent (or recklessness) as to the existence of a lawful excuse, I should have wished to consider the observations of James LJ, delivering the judgment of the Court of Appeal in *R v Smith* [1974] QB 354 at 360. I do not however find it necessary to reach a conclusion on this matter and will only say that I am not at present convinced that, when these observations are read in the context of the judgment as a whole, they have the meaning which the respondent has sought to put on them. In my view, however, the answer to the argument lies in the fact that any distinctions which have to be drawn as to the relevance of drunkenness to the two subsections arises from the scheme of the 1971 Act itself. No doubt the mens rea is in general indivisible, with no distinction being possible as regards the effect of drunkenness. But Parliament has specifically isolated one subjective element, in the shape of honest belief, and has given it separate treatment and its own special gloss in s5(3). This being so, there is nothing objectionable in giving it special treatment as regards drunkenness, in accordance with the natural meaning of its words.

In these circumstances, I would hold that the magistrates were in error when they decided that the defence furnished to the appellant by s5(2) was lost because she was drunk at the time. I would therefore allow the appeal.'

R v Smith [1974] QB 354 Court of Appeal (Criminal Division) (Roskill, James, LJJ and Talbot J)

Mens rea of criminal damage

Facts
The defendant was the tenant of a flat. With the landlord's consent he installed some hi-fi equipment and soundproofing. When given notice to quit the flat, the defendant tore down the soundproofing to gain access to some wires that lay behind. Unknown to the defendant the soundproofing had, as a matter of law, become a fixture of the property and therefore property belonging to the landlord. The defendant was convicted of criminal damage contrary to s1(1) of the 1971 Act, and appealed on the ground that he had honestly believed that the property he had destroyed was his own.

Held
The appeal would be allowed and conviction quashed.

James LJ:

'It follows that in our judgment no offence is committed under this section if a person destroys or causes damage to property belonging to another if he does so in the honest though mistaken belief that the property is his own, and provided that the belief is honestly held it is irrelevant to consider whether or not it is a justifiable belief.'

R v Steer [1987] 3 WLR 205 House of Lords (Lords Bridge, Griffiths, Ackner, Oliver and Goff)

Aggravated criminal damage – mens rea as to the endangering of life

Facts
The defendant, who had been in dispute with a business partner, fired an automatic rifle at the bedroom window of his partner's house. The bedroom was occupied at the time. The defendant pleaded guilty to s1(1) criminal damage, and following a ruling by the trial judge, pleaded guilty to a charge under s1(2)(b) of causing criminal damage being reckless as to whether life would be endangered. The defendant appealed against the conviction under s1(2)(b), on the ground that he had not intended that the criminal damage to the window should endanger life, and therefore lacked the mens rea for the aggravated offence. The Court of Appeal allowed the appeal, and the prosecutor appealed to the House of Lords. The question certified for consideration by their Lordships was: whether upon a true construction of s1(2)(b) of the Criminal Damage Act 1971, the prosecution are required to prove that the danger to life resulted from the destruction of or damage to the property, or whether it is sufficient for the prosecution to prove that it resulted from the act of the defendant which caused the destruction or damage.

Held
The appeal would be dismissed.

Lord Bridge:

'Under both limbs of section 1 of the Act of 1971 it is the essence of the offence which the section creates that the defendant has destroyed or damaged property. For the purpose of analysis it may be convenient to omit reference to destruction and to concentrate on the references to damage, which was all that was here involved. To be guilty under subsection (1) the defendant must have intended or been reckless as to the damage to property which he caused. To be guilty under subsection (2) he must additionally have intended to endanger life or been reckless as to whether life would be endangered "by the damage" to property which he caused. This is the context in which the words must be construed and it seems to me impossible to read the words "by the damage" as meaning "by the damage or by the act which caused the damage."...

I can well understand that the prosecution in this case thought it necessary and appropriate that, even if they could not establish the intent to endanger life necessary to support a conviction under section 16 of the [Firearms] Act of 1968 they should include a count in the indictment to mark in some way the additional gravity of an offence of criminal damage to property in which a firearm is used. But they had no need to resort to section 1(2) of the Act of 1971. A person who, at the time of committing an offence under section 1 of the Act of 1971, has in his possession a firearm commits a distinct offence under section 17(2) of the Act of 1968: see Schedule 1 to the Act of 1968, as amended by section 11(7) of the Act of 1971. If the respondent had been charged with that offence in addition to the offence under section 1(1) of the Act of 1971, he must have pleaded guilty to both and, if the prosecution were content to accept that there was no intent to endanger life, this would have been amply sufficient to mark the gravity of the respondent's criminal conduct in the incident at the Gregory bungalow. I would accordingly dismiss the appeal. The certified question should be answered as follows:

> "Upon the true construction of section 1(2)(b) of the Criminal Damage Act 1971 the prosecution are required to prove that the danger to life resulted from the destruction of or damage to property; it is not sufficient for the prosection to prove that it resulted from the act of the defendant which caused the destruction or damage." '

22 Non-Fatal Offences against the Person I

R v *Aitken and Others* [1992] 1 WLR 1066 Courts-Martial Court of Appeal (Farquharson LJ, Alliot and Cazalet JJ)

Section 20 – whether intoxication relevant – mistake by the defendant as to consent

Facts

The appellants and a man named Gibson were all RAF officers attending a party to celebrate the completion of their formal flying training. During the course of the evening the appellants had, in jest, tried to ignite the fire resistant suits of two fellow officers. When Gibson indicated that he was leaving the party to go to bed, the appellants manhandled him and poured white spirit on his fire resistant suit. The white spirit was ignited, and despite the rapid efforts of the appellants to douse the flames, Gibson suffered serious burns. It was accepted that the appellants had not intended to cause injury to Gibson. The appellants were court martialled, and convicted of inflicting grievous bodily harm contrary to s20 of the Offences Against the Person Act 1861, following the judge advocate's direction that the appellants had acted maliciously if they had foreseen harm, or would have done so but for drink, and that their actions were unlawful if they went beyond the type of horseplay to be expected on such occasions.

On appeal.

Held

The appeal would be allowed.

Having confirmed that s20 was an offence requiring foresight of the risk of harm (*R* v *Parmenter*) and that it was to be regarded as an offence of basic intent to which self induced intoxication would afford no defence, Farquharson LJ turned to consider the issue of defences, (p1017G–1020H):

'The appellants have advanced the further ground of appeal that, in the context of the unusual facts of this case, the judge advocate failed to give the court any proper direction as to the meaning of the word "unlawfully" as it appears in section 20.

The judge advocate, in his summing up, sought to deal with the meaning of "unlawfully" as follows:

"Now, what is unlawful? That simply means without lawful justification or excuse – for example, self-defence. Now, you have heard evidence that in the Air Force ethos, various robust games have taken place – perhaps not only in the Air Force – whereby participants accept that a certain degree of risk of injury is likely to be caused. It is an issue for you to decide – and I will perhaps deal with this at a later stage – as to whether or not the incident was unlawful."

Then later the judge advocate continued his summing up:

"There, gentlemen, you really have the evidence. So, where does it take you? First of all, was this merely horseplay? Was there a combined joint enterprise by the three defendants, which involved the setting fire of Flying Officer Gibson's clothes? It is a matter for you from the evidence. Was this no more than horseplay? Looking at it in the light of the Royal Air Force ethos, was this going far beyond normal horseplay, to such an extent that you can say, 'No. This is way beyond those levels. This is not possibly lawful to behave in this manner'? Then you ask yourselves. 'Was this malicious?' within the meaning I have given to you."

It is submitted on behalf of the appellants that the judge advocate failed to give the court a proper direction as to whether the appellants' conduct towards Gibson was, in the particular circumstances, unlawful, and further failed to deal adequately or at all with the relevance of Gibson's consent or the appellants' belief as to his consent in regard to the horseplay in question. Mr Butterfield referred us to this court's decision in *R v Jones (Terence)* (1986) 83 Cr App R 375. It is helpful, we think, to consider that case in some detail. The appellants in that case were convicted of inflicting grievous bodily harm on two schoolboys, aged 14 and 15, who had been tossed high in the air and then allowed to fall to the ground by the appellants. The appellants' evidence was that they regarded this activity as a joke. There was some evidence showing that the victims, likewise, so regarded this. The judge declined to direct the jury that if they thought that the appellants had only been indulging in rough and undisciplined play, not intending to cause harm, and genuinely believing that the victims consented, they should acquit. In the light of this the appellants changed their pleas to guilty. Then, on appeal, their appeals were allowed on the basis that consent to rough and undisciplined horseplay is a defence; and, even if there is no consent, genuine belief, whether reasonably held or not, that it was present, would be a defence.

In giving the judgment of the court, McCowan J recited the facts and continued at p378:

"The second point, which was taken before the learned judge and repeated before us, stemmed from the case of *R v Donovan* (1934) 25 Cr App R 1; [1934] 2 KB 498. It will suffice if we read a part of the judgment of the Court of Criminal Appeal given by Swift J at p11 and p508 respectively, where he said: 'There are, as we have said, well established exceptions to the general rule that an act likely or intended to cause bodily harm is an unlawful act. ... Another exception to the general rule, or, rather, another branch of the same class of exceptions, is to be found in cases of rough and undisciplined sport or play, where there is no anger and no intention to cause bodily harm. An example of this kind may be found in *R v Bruce* (1847) 2 Cox CC 262. In such cases the act is not in itself unlawful, and it becomes unlawful only if the person affected by it is not a consenting party.' The particular words relevant to the present case are 'rough and undisciplined play'. The direction which was sought from the learned judge was that if the jury thought that the appellants had only been indulging in 'rough and undisciplined play', not intending to cause harm, and genuinely believing that the victims were consenting, they were entitled to be acquitted. The learned judge declined so to direct the jury. He said that he proposed to direct them that the causing of an injury resulting in the course of this activity was unlawful. Mr Arlidge [for the appellants] submits, first, that consent to 'rough and undisciplined play' where there is no intention to cause injury, must be a defence. Secondly, he says that even if consent is in fact absent, genuine belief by a defendant that consent was present would be a defence. Thirdly, he says that if the belief is genuinely held, it is irrelevant whether it is reasonably held or not. Those propositions, based on the authority of the cases in *R v Kimber* (1983) 77 Cr App R 225 and *R v Williams* (1984) 78 Cr App R 276, are, in our judgment, correct."

The judge then referred to *Attorney-General's Reference (No 6 of 1980)* [1981] QB 715, where Lord Lane CJ gave the judgment of the court. McCowan J continued, 83 Cr App R 375, 379:

"Mr Mitchell [for the Crown] stresses an absence from the catalogue given by the Lord Chief Justice of any reference to 'rough and undisciplined play'. We note however that the Lord Chief Justice added 'etc' at the end of his list. We do not think that he intended the list to be exhaustive. It may well be that if this jury had been given the opportunity of considering this defence, they would have had little difficulty in rejecting it. But the appellants were entitled to have the defence left to the jury. It was in our judgment wrong for the learned judge to indicate that he would remove it from them. Since it was entirely because of that ruling that the appellants were advised by counsel to plead guilty, it is plain that their convictions cannot stand. They are quashed. Accordingly this appeal is allowed."

The appellants submit that the nature of the horseplay and pranks in which Gibson had been involved that evening before the incident when he sustained his injuries were such that he must be taken to have given his consent to being involved in the sort of boisterous activities which had been taking place throughout much of the evening. The appellants pray in aid the fact that Gibson had been present throughout and had taken part in the various spirited events in the officers' mess at the earlier stage. He had also accompanied the others to Bell's married quarters after the bar had closed when there had been various further jokes and undisciplined pranks, including the two incidents of setting fire to the trousers of Huskisson and Thomas. He then elected to return with the others to the officers' mess where there had been further drinking before the incident in question.

It was submitted that viewed overall in the context of a celebratory evening in the mess such as this, it was clearly arguable that the rough and undisciplined horseplay which the three appellants had perpetrated on Gibson was not per se unlawful. In seeking to restrain him from leaving the room, grappling him to the ground and then, as he was getting up, trying to carry out the same type of burning incident as had happened earlier in the evening the appellants were acting in a manner consistent with what had been going on during much of the time. The fact that Gibson struggled, albeit weakly through drink, to avoid the attentions of the three during the incident in question should not, it was submitted on the appellants' behalf, be taken in isolation. The totality of the circumstances, his knowledge of the course which celebration evenings such as the one in question was likely to take and his continued presence with the others demonstrated an acceptance by him that horseplay of the nature perpetrated upon him might well take place.

It was submitted that the judge advocate had not fully or properly directed the court in regard to this and that, in particular, he had failed to give any direction to the effect that since the Crown accepted that none of the appellants intended to inflict any harm on Gibson, the fact that a much larger quantity of white spirit had been poured on to his clothing than had been the case with Thomas could be viewed as an accident, and thus not unlawful. Additionally, submitted the appellants, given than it was open to the court to find that the horseplay with Gibson was not of itself unlawful, it was incumbent upon the judge advocate, following the decision in *R v Jones (Terence)*, 83 Cr App R 375 to give further directions, first that such conduct, if not unlawful, would only have become unlawful if Gibson had not consented to it, and second that even if Gibson had not consented, the court must consider whether in the circumstances any of the appellants genuinely believed, whether reasonably or not, that Gibson had so consented. ...

However although it must, on the evidence, have been open to the court to find that the incident involving Gibson was per se unlawful, we do not consider, for the reasons submitted to us by Mr Butterfield, that this was so plain that the judge advocate was absolved from a direction that it was in the circumstances open to the court to find that the activities of the appellants were not per se unlawful. In this event the judge advocate should then have directed the court as to the necessity of considering whether Gibson gave his consent as a willing participant to the activities in question, or whether the appellants may have believed this, whether reasonably or not.

In the circumstances we consider that the judge advocate in what was, on any view, a difficult and complex case on the law, failed properly to direct the court on these two important matters as to consent.'

Attorney-General's Reference (No 6 of 1980) [1981] QB 715 Court of Appeal (Criminal Division) (Lord Lane CJ, Phillips and Drake JJ)

Extent of consent as defence to a charge of assault

Facts
See the extract from the judgment of Lord Lane CJ.

The following point of law was referred to the Court of Appeal upon which the court was asked to provide its opinion:

'Where two persons fight (otherwise than in the course of sport) in a public place can it be a defence for one of those persons to a charge of assault arising out of the fight that the other consented to the fight?'

Held
A fight between two persons would be unlawful, whether in public or private, if it involved the infliction of at least actual bodily harm, or if actual bodily harm or worse was intended. This would make most fights between people wishing to 'settle their differences' in this manner unlawful.

Lord Lane CJ:

> 'Our answer to the point of law is No, but not (as the reference implies) because the fight occurred in the public place, but because, wherever it occurred, the participants would have been guilty of assault (subject to self-defence) if (as we understand was the case) they intended to and/or did cause actual bodily harm.
>
> The point of law referred to us by the Attorney-General has revealed itself as having been the subject of much interesting legal and philosophical debate, but it does not seem that the particular uncertainty enshrined in the reference has caused practical inconvenience in the administration of justice during the last few hundred years. We would not wish our judgment on the point to be the signal for unnecessary prosecutions.'

R v Brown [1993] 2 WLR 556 House of Lords (Lord Templeman, Lord Jauncey, Lord Lowry, Lord Mustill and Lord Slynn)

Extent to which victim's consent can negative an assault

Facts
The appellants were members of a group of sado-masochistic homosexuals who carried out acts of violence on each other, from which they derived sexual gratification. The appellants were charged on a number of counts alleging (inter alia) offences under ss47 and 20 of the Offences Against the Person Act 1861. Following the trial judge's ruling that the willing consent of the victim of such assaults did not amount to a defence, the appellants changed their pleas to guilty, and appealed unsuccessfully against conviction. On appeal to the House of Lords;

Held (Lord Mustill and Lord Slynn dissenting)
The appeal would be dismissed.

Lord Templeman:

> 'In some circumstances violence is not punishable under the criminal law. When no actual bodily harm is caused, the consent of the person affected precludes him from complaining. There can be no conviction for the summary offence of common assault if the victim has consented to the assault. Even when violence is intentionally inflicted and results in actual bodily harm, wounding or serious bodily harm the accused is entitled to be acquitted if the injury was a foreseeable incident of a lawful activity in which the person injured was participating. Surgery involves intentional violence resulting in actual or sometimes serious bodily harm but surgery is a lawful activity. Other activities carried on with consent by or on behalf of the injured person have been accepted as lawful notwithstanding that they involve actual bodily harm or may cause serious bodily harm. Ritual circumcision, tattooing, ear-piercing and violent sports including boxing are lawful activities.
>
> In earlier days some other forms of violence were lawful and when they ceased to be lawful they were tolerated until well into the nineteenth century. Duelling and fighting were at first lawful and then tolerated provided the protagonists were voluntary participants. But where the results of these activities was the maiming of one of the participants, the defence of consent never availed the aggressor: see *Hawkins' Pleas of the Crown*, 8th ed (1824), vol 1, ch 15. A maim was bodily harm whereby a man was deprived of the use of any member of his body which he needed to use in order to fight but a bodily injury was not a maim merely because it was a disfigurement. The act of maim was unlawful because the King was deprived of the services of an able-bodied citizen for the defence of the realm. Violence which maimed was unlawful

despite consent to the activity which produced the maiming In these days there is no difference between maiming on the one hand and wounding or causing grievous bodily harm on the other hand except with regard to sentence.

When duelling became unlawful, juries remained unwilling to convict but the judges insisted that persons guilty of causing death or bodily injury should be convicted despite the consent of the victim.

Similarly, in the old days, fighting was unlawful provided the protagonists consented because it was thought that fighting inculcated bravery and skill and physical fitness. The brutality of knuckle fighting however caused the courts to declare that such fights were unlawful even if the protagonists consented. Rightly or wrongly the courts accepted that boxing is a lawful activity ...

The question whether the defence of consent should be extended to the consequences of sado-masochistic encounters can only be decided by consideration of policy and public interest. Parliament can call on the advice of doctors, psychiatrists, criminologists, sociologists and other experts and can also sound and take into account public opinion. But the question must at this stage be decided by this House in its judicial capacity in order to determine whether the convictions of the appellants should be upheld or quashed.

Counsel for some of the appellants argued that the defence of consent should be extended to the offence of occasioning actual bodily harm under s47 of the Act of 1861 but should not be available to charges of serious wounding and the infliction of serious bodily harm under s20. I do not consider that this solution is practicable. Sado-masochistic participants have no way of foretelling the degree of bodily harm which will result from their encounters. The differences between actual bodily harm and serious bodily harm cannot be satisfactorily applied by a jury in order to determine acquittal or conviction.

Counsel for the appellants argued that consent should provide a defence to charges under both s20 and s47 because, it was said, every person has a right to deal with his body as he pleases. I do not consider that this slogan provides a sufficient guide to the policy decision which must now be made. It is an offence for a person to abuse his own body and mind by taking drugs. Although the law is often broken, the criminal law restrains a practice which is regarded as dangerous and injurious to individuals and which if allowed and extended is harmful to society generally. In any event the appellants in this case did not mutilate their own bodies. They inflicted bodily harm on willing victims. Suicide is no longer an offence but a person who assists another to commit suicide is guilty of murder or manslaughter.

The assertion was made on behalf of the appellants that the sexual appetites of sadists and masochists can only be satisfied by the infliction of bodily harm and that the law should not punish the consensual achievement of sexual satisfaction. There was no evidence to support the assertion that sado-masochist activities are essential to the happiness of the appellants or any other participants but the argument would be acceptable if sado-masochism were only concerned with sex, as the appellants contend. In my opinion sado-masochism is not only concerned with sex. Sado-masochism is also concerned with violence. The evidence discloses that the practices of the appellants were unpredictably dangerous and degrading to body and mind and were developed with increasing barbarity and taught to persons whose consents were dubious or worthless ...

In principle there is a difference between violence which is incidental and violence which is inflicted for the indulgence of cruelty. The violence of sado-masochistic encounters involves the indulgence of cruelty by sadists and the degradation of victims. Such violence is injurious to the participants and unpredictably dangerous. I am not prepared to invent a defence of consent for sado-masochistic encounters which breed and glorify cruelty and result in offences under ss47 and 20 of the Act of 1861.'

Lord Jauncey:

'In considering the public interest it would be wrong to look only at the activities of the appellants alone, there being no suggestion that they and their associates are the only practitioners of homosexual sado-masochism in England and Wales. This House must therefore consider the possibility that these activities are practised by others and by others who are not so controlled or responsible as the appellants are claimed to be. Without going into details of all the rather curious activities in which the appellants engaged it would appear to be good luck rather than good judgment which has prevented serious injury from occurring. Wounds can easily become septic if not properly treated, the free flow of blood from a person who is HIV positive or who has Aids can infect another and an inflicter who is carried away by sexual excitement or by drink or drugs could very easily inflict pain and injury beyond the level to which the receiver had consented. Your Lordships have no information as to whether such situations have occurred in relation to other sado-masochistic practitioners. It was no doubt these dangers which caused Lady Mallalieu to restrict her propositions in relation to the public interest to the actual rather than the potential result of the activity. In my view such a restriction is quite unjustified. When considering the public interest potential for harm is just as relevant as actual harm. As Matthew J said in *R v Coney*, 8 QBD 534, 547: "There is, however, abundant authority for saying that no consent can render that innocent which is in fact dangerous." Furthermore, the possibility of proselytisation and corruption of young men is a real danger even in the case of these appellants and the taking of video recordings of such activities suggests that secrecy may not be as strict as the appellants claimed to your Lordships. If the only purpose of the activity is the sexual gratification of one or both of the participants what then is the need of a video recording?

My Lords I have no doubt that it would not be in the public interest that deliberate infliction of actual bodily harm during the course of homosexual sado-masochistic activities should be held to be lawful. In reaching this conclusion I have regard to the information available in these appeals and of such inferences as may be drawn therefrom. I appreciate that there may be a great deal of information relevant to these activities which is not available to your Lordships. When Parliament passed the Sexual Offences Act 1967 which made buggery and acts of gross indecency between consenting males lawful it had available the Wolfenden Report (1957) (Cmnd 247) which was the product of an exhaustive research into the problem. If it is to be decided that such activities as the nailing by A of B's foreskin or scrotum to a board or the insertion of hot wax into C's urethra followed by the burning of his penis with a candle or the incising of D's scrotum with a scalpel to the effusion of blood are injurious neither to B, C and D nor to the public interest then it is for Parliament with its accumulated wisdom and sources of information to declare them to be lawful.'

Lord Lowry:

'What the appellants are obliged to propose is that the deliberate and painful infliction of physical injury should be exempted from the operation of statutory provisions the object of which is to prevent or punish that very thing, the reason for the proposed exemption being that both those who will inflict and those who will suffer the injury wish to satisfy a perverted and depraved sexual desire. Sado-masochistic homosexual activity cannot be regarded as conducive to the enhancement or enjoyment of family life or conducive to the welfare of society. A relaxation of the prohibitions in ss20 and 47 can only encourage the practice of homosexual sado-masochism, with the physical cruelty that it must involve (which can scarcely be regarded as a "manly diversion"), by withdrawing the legal penalty and giving the activity a judicial imprimatur. As well as all this, one cannot overlook the physical danger to those who may indulge in sado-masochism. In this connection, and also generally, it is idle for the appellants to claim that they are educated exponents of "civilised cruelty." A proposed *general* exemption is to be tested by considering the likely *general* effect. This must include the probability that some sado-masochistic activity, under the powerful influence of the sexual instinct, will get out of hand and result in serious physical damage to the participants and that some activity will involve a danger of infection such as these particular exponents do not contemplate for themselves. When considering the danger of infection, with its inevitable threat of Aids, I am not impressed by the argument that this threat can be discounted on the ground that, as long ago as 1967, Parliament, subject to conditions, legalised buggery, now a well-known vehicle for the transmission of Aids.

So far as I can see, the only counter-argument is that to place a restriction on sado-masochism is an unwarranted interference with the private life and activities of persons who are indulging in a lawful pursuit and are doing no harm to anyone except, possibly, themselves. This approach, which has characterised every submission put forward on behalf of the appellants, is derived from the fallacy that what is involved here is the restraint of a lawful activity as opposed to the refusal to relax existing prohibitions in the Act of 1861. If in the course of buggery, as authorised by the Act of 1967, one participant, either with the other participant's consent or not, deliberately causes actual bodily harm to that other, an offence against s47 has been committed. The Act of 1967 provides no shield. The position is as simple as that, and there is no legal right to cause actual bodily harm in the course of sado-masochistic activity.'

Lord Mustill (dissenting):

Having referred to the European Convention on Human Rights he continued:

'I believe that the general tenor of the decisions of the European court does furnish valuable guidance on the approach which the English court should adopt, if free to do so, and I take heart from the fact that the European authorities, balancing the personal considerations invoked by art 8(1) against the public interest considerations called up by art 8(2), clearly favour the right of the appellants to conduct their private lives undisturbed by the criminal law ...

... the decks are clear for the House to tackle completely anew the question whether the public interest requires s47 of the Act of 1861 to be interpreted as penalising an infliction of harm which is at the level of actual bodily harm, but not grievous bodily harm; which is inflicted in private (by which I mean that it is exposed to the view only of those who have chosen to view it); which takes place not only with the consent of the recipient but with his willing and glad co-operation; which is inflicted for the gratification of sexual desire, and not in a spirit of animosity or rage; and which is not engaged in for profit.

My Lords, I have stated the issue in these terms to stress two considerations of cardinal importance. Lawyers will need no reminding of the first, but since this prosecution has been widely noticed it must be emphasised that the issue before the House is not whether the appellants' conduct is morally right, but whether it is properly charged under the Act of 1861. When proposing that the conduct is not rightly so charged I do not invite your Lordships' House to endorse it as morally acceptable. Nor do I pronounce in favour of a libertarian doctrine specifically related top sexual matters. Nor in the least do I suggest that ethical pronouncements are meaningless, that there is no difference between right and wrong, that sadism is praiseworthy, or that new opinions on sexual morality are necessarily superior to the old, or anything else of the same kind. What I do say is that these are questions of private morality; that the standards by which they fall to be judged are not those of the criminal law; and that if these standards are to be upheld the individual must enforce them upon them himself according to his own moral standards, or have them enforced against him by moral pressures exerted by whatever religious or other community to whose ethical ideals he responds. The point from which I invite your Lordships to depart is simply this, that the state should interfere with the rights of an individual to live his or her life as he or she may choose no more than is necessary to ensure a proper balance between the special interests of the individual and the general interests of the individuals who together comprise the populace at large. Thus, whilst acknowledging that very many people, if asked whether the appellants' conduct was wrong, would reply "Yes, repulsively wrong", I would at the same time assert that this does not in itself mean that the prosecution of the appellants under ss20 and 47 of the Offences against the Person Act 1861 is well founded.

This point leads directly to the second. As I have ventured to formulate the crucial question, it asks whether there is good reason to impress upon s47 an interpretation which penalises the relevant level of harm irrespective of consent, ie, to recognise sado-masochistic activities as falling into a special category of acts, such as duelling and prize-fighting, which "the law says shall not be done". This is very important, for if the question were differently stated it might well yield a different answer. In particular, if it were to be held that as a matter of law all infliction of bodily harm above the level of common assault is incapable of being legitimated by consent, except in special circumstances, then we would have to consider whether the public interest required the recognition of private sexual activities as being in a specially exempt category. This would be an altogether more difficult question and one which I would not be prepared to answer in favour of the appellants, not because I do not have my own opinions upon it but because I regard the task as one which the courts are not suited to perform, and which should be carried out, if at all, by Parliament after a thorough review of all the medical, social, moral and political issues, such as was performed by the Wolfenden Committee. Thus, if I had begun from the same point of departure as my noble and learned friend, Lord Jauncey of Tullichettle, I would have arrived at a similar conclusion; but differing from him on the present state of the law, I venture to differ.

Let it be assumed however that we should embark upon this question. I ask myself, not whether as a result of the decision in this appeal, activities such as those of the appellants should *cease* to be criminal, but rather whether the Act of 1861 (a statute which I venture to repeat once again was clearly intended to penalise conduct of a quite different nature) should in this new situation be interpreted so as to *make* it criminal. Why should this step be taken? Leaving aside repugnance and moral objection, both of which are entirely natural but neither of which are in my opinion grounds upon which the court could properly create a new crime, I can visualise only the following reasons.

(1) Some of the practices obviously created a risk of genito-urinary infection, and others of septicaemia. These might indeed have been grave in former times, but the risk of serious harm must surely have been greatly reduced by modern medical science.

(2) The possibility that matters might get out of hand, with grave results. It has been acknowledged throughout the present proceedings that the appellants' activities were performed as a pre-arranged ritual, which at the same time enhanced their excitement and minimised the risk that the infliction of injury would go too far. Of course things might go wrong and really serious injury or death might ensue. If this happened, those responsible would be punished according to the ordinary law, in the same way as those who kill or injure in the course of more ordinary sexual activities are regularly punished. But to penalise the appellants' conduct even if the extreme consequences do not ensue, just because they might have done so, would require an assessment of the degree of risk, and the balancing of this risk against the interests of individual freedom. Such a balancing is in my opinion for Parliament, not the courts; and even if your Lordships' House were to embark upon it the attempt must in my opinion fail at the outset for there is no evidence at all of the seriousness of the hazards to which sado-masochistic conduct of this kind gives rise. This is not surprising, since the impressive argument of [counsel] for the respondents did not seek to persuade your Lordships to bring the matter within the Act of 1861 on the ground of special risks, but rather to establish that the appellants are liable *under the general law* because the level of harm exceeded the critical level marking off criminal from non-criminal consensual violence which he invited your Lordships to endorse.

(3) I would give the same answer to the suggestion that these activities involved a risk of accelerating the spread of auto-immune deficiency syndrome, and that they should be brought within the Act of 1861 in the interests of public health. The consequence would be strange, since what is currently the principal cause for the transmission of this scourge, namely consenting buggery between males, is now legal. Nevertheless, I would have been compelled to give this proposition the most anxious consideration if there had been any evidence to support it. But there is none, since the case for the respondents was advanced on an entirely different ground.

(4) There remains an argument to which I have given much greater weight. As the evidence in the present case has shown, there is a risk that strangers (and especially young strangers) may be drawn into these activities at an early age and will then become established in them for life. This is indeed a disturbing prospect, but I have come to the conclusion that it is not a sufficient ground for declaring these activities to be criminal under the Act of 1861. The element of the corruption of youth is already catered for by the existing legislation; and if there is a gap in it which needs to be filled the remedy surely lies in the hands of Parliament, not in the application of a statute which is aimed at other forms of wrongdoing. As regards proselytisation for adult sado-masochism the argument appears to me circular. For if the activity is not itself so much against the public interest that it ought to be declared criminal under the Act of 1861 then the risk that others will be induced to join in cannot be a ground for making it criminal.

Leaving aside the logic of this answer, which seems to me impregnable, plain humanity demands that a court addressing the criminality of conduct such as that of the present should recognise and respond to the profound dismay which all members of the community share about the apparent increase of cruel and senseless crimes against the defenceless. Whilst doing so I must repeat for the last time that in the answer which I propose I do not advocate the decriminalisation of conduct which has hitherto been a crime; nor do I rebut a submission that a new crime should be created, penalising this conduct, for [counsel for the respondents] has rightly not invited the House to take this course. The only question is whether these consensual private acts are offences against the existing law of violence. To this question I return a negative response.'

Lord Slynn (dissenting):

'I agree that in the end it is a matter of policy. It is a matter of policy in an area where social and moral factors are extremely important and where attitudes can change. In my opinion it is a matter of policy for the legislature to decide. If society takes the view that this kind of behaviour, even though sought after and done in private, is either so new or so extensive or so undesirable that it should be brought now for the first time within the criminal law, then it is for the legislature to decide. It is not for the courts in the interests of "paternalism," as referred to in the passage I have quoted, or in order to protect people from themselves, to introduce, into existing statutory crimes relating to offences *against* the person, concepts which do not properly fit there. If Parliament considers that the behaviour revealed here should be made specifically criminal, then the Offences against the Person Act 1861 or, perhaps more appropriately, the Sexual Offences Act 1967 can be amended specifically to define it. Alternatively, if it is intended that this sort of conduct should be lawful as between two persons but not between more than two persons as falling within the offence of gross indecency, then the limitation period for prosecution can be extended and the penalties increased where sado-masochistic acts are involved. That is obviously a possible course; whether it is a desirable way of changing the law is a different question.

I would therefore answer the question certified on the basis that where a charge is brought in respect of acts done between adults in private under s20 of the Offences against the Person Act 1861 in respect of wounding and under s47 in respect of causing actual bodily harm, it must be proved by the prosecution that the person to whom the act was done did not consent to it.'

R v Chan-Fook [1994] 1 WLR 689 Court of Appeal (Hobhouse LJ, Judge and Bell JJ)

Assault occasioning actual bodily harm – nature of actual bodily harm – whether psychiatric harm sufficient

Facts
The appellant suspected that the victim had stolen a ring belonging to the appellant's girlfriend. The victim's evidence was that the appellant had physically assaulted him whilst interrogating him about the disappearance of the ring. It was not disputed that, following the interrogation, the appellant had dragged the victim upstairs to his room and locked him in. Fearing that the appellant would return to carry out a more serious assault, the victim had tried to escape from the room by tying knotted bed sheets to the curtain rail and climbing out of the window. The curtain rail, unable to take the victim's weight, came away from the wall and he suffered a broken wrist and a dislocated pelvis as a result of his fall to the ground. The trial judge left the charge of assault occasioning actual bodily harm, contrary to s47 of the Offences Against the Person Act 1861, to the jury on the basis that, even if the appellant had not physically assaulted the victim, the nervous hysterical condition induced in the victim by the interrogation, as evidenced by his attempts to escape, could amount to actual bodily harm. The appellant was convicted and appealed.

Held
The appeal was allowed.

Hobhouse LJ:

'[Actual bodily harm] are three words of the English language which require no elaboration and in the ordinary course should not receive any. The word "harm" is a synonym for injury. The word "actual" indicates that the injury (although there is no need for it to be permanent) should not be so trivial as to be wholly insignificant. The purpose of the definition in s47 is to define an element of aggravation in the assault. It must be an assault which besides being an assault (or assault and battery) causes to the victim some injury.

The danger of any elaboration of the words of the statute is that it may have the effect, as was pointed out by the House of Lords, of altering, or at the least distracting the jury from, the ordinary meaning of the words. Further, as can be seen from the summing up in the present case, there may be an elision of the need to show some harm or injury. There will be a risk that language will be used which suggests to the jury that it is sufficient that the assault has interfered with the health or comfort of the victim, whether or not any injury or hurt has been caused. No doubt what is intended by those who have used these words in the past is to indicate that some injury which otherwise might be regarded as wholly trivial is not to be so regarded because it has caused the victim pain. Similarly, an injury can be caused to someone by injuring their health; an assault may have the consequence of infecting the victim with a disease or causing the victim to become ill. The injury may be internal and may not be accompanied by an external injury. A blow may leave no external mark but may cause the victim to lose consciousness.'

Having considered the definition of actual bodily harm provided by Lynskey J in *R v Miller* [1954] 2 QB 282, Hobhouse LJ continued:

'The first question on the present appeal is whether the inclusion of the word "bodily" in the phrase "actual bodily harm" limits harm to harm to the skin, flesh and bones of the victim. Lynskey J rejected this submission. In our judgment he was right to do so. The body of the victim includes all parts of his body, including his organs, his nervous system and his brain. Bodily injury therefore may include injury to any of those parts of his body responsible for his mental and other faculties ...

Accordingly, the phrase "actual bodily harm" is capable of including psychiatric injury. But it does not include mere emotions such as fear or distress nor panic, nor does it include, as such, states of mind that are not themselves evidence of some identifiable clinical condition. The phrase "state of mind" is not a scientific one and should be avoided in considering whether or not a psychiatric injury has been caused; its use is likely to create in the minds of the jury the impression that something which is not more than a strong emotion, such as extreme fear or panic, can amount to actual bodily harm. It cannot. Similarly, juries should not be directed that an assault which causes an hysterical and nervous condition is an assault occasioning actual bodily harm. Where there is evidence that the assault has caused some psychiatric injury, the jury should be directed that the injury is capable of amounting to actual bodily harm; otherwise there should be no reference to the mental state of the victim following the assault unless it be relevant to some other aspect of the case, as it was in *R v Roberts* (1971) 56 Cr App R 95. It is also relevant to have in mind the relationship between the offence of aggravated assault comprised in s47 and simple assault. The latter can include conduct which causes the victim to apprehend immediate and unlawful violence: *Fagan v Metropolitan Police Commissioner* [1969] 1 QB 439. To treat the victim's fear of such unlawful violence, without more, as amounting to actual bodily harm would be to risk rendering the definition of the aggravated offence academic in many cases.

In any case where psychiatric injury is relied upon as the basis for an allegation of bodily harm, and the matter has not been admitted by the defence, expert evidence should be called by the prosecution. It should not be left to be inferred by the jury from the general facts of the case. In the absence of appropriate expert evidence a question whether or not the assault occasioned psychiatric injury should not be left to the jury. Cases where it is necessary to allege that psychiatric injury has been caused by an assault will be very few and far between. It is to be observed that there has been no reported case on the point since 1953 and the present case was not, on a correct assessment, a case where such an allegation should have been made. But, if there should be such a case, the evidential difficulties will be no greater than juries often have to consider in other aspects of the criminal law, for example, an issue of diminished responsibility. There is no reason for refusing to have regard to psychiatric injury as the consequence of an assault if there is properly qualified evidence that it has occurred.'

DPP v *Taylor; DPP* v *Little* [1992] 1 QB 645 Divisional Court (Mann LJ and Hidden J)
Whether assault and battery separate offences – whether now entirely statutory

Facts
Section 39 of the Criminal Justice Act 1988 provided that common assault and battery were to be prosecuted as summary offences. In *Taylor*'s case the justices dismissed the information laid against the defendant by the DPP on the basis that the law required the information to be authorised or laid by the victim, and that s39 did not alter the common law nature of the offence, but merely prescribe a mode of trial.

In *Little*'s case the justices dismissed an information alleging assault and battery on the basis that it was bad for duplicity. The DPP appealed against both rulings.

Held
The appeal in *Taylor*'s case would be allowed, but not in *Little*'s case.

Mann LJ (p650E–655A):

'The two appeals have given rise to a debate upon the question of whether the offences of common assault and battery are statutory offences and of how a charge of common assault should be formulated. These two questions are of general importance in regard to the summary prosecution of assaults: the first because of rule 100(2) of the Rules of 1981 which in a case where the offence charged is a statutory one, requires a reference in the information to the section of the Act of 1988 creating the offence; and the second question because of the inability of justices (special cases apart) to try an information that charges more than one offence: rule 12(1) of the Rules of 1981. ...

My conclusion upon the question of whether the offences of common assault and battery are statutory offences is that they are and have been such since 1861 and accordingly that they should now be charged as being "contrary to section 39 of the Criminal Justice Act 1988". This is not what is currently suggested in the specimen charge in *Stone's Justices' Manual 1991*, 123rd ed, vol 3, p5595, para 9-90 and this now requires amendment.

I turn to the question of how a charge of common assault should be formulated so as to avoid duplicity where the case is one of actual as well as apprehended unlawful force. The form which is hallowed by long use is "did assault and beat" the victim: Stone's Justices' Manual 1991, vol 3, p5595, para 9-90. Mr Godfrey, who appeared for the defendant, Stephen Little, described this form as "lazy 'conventional' language". A proper language, said Mr Godfrey, would be "assault by beating" where force had been used and "assault by threatening" where it had not. He referred us to *Jones* v *Sherwood* [1942] 1 KB 127 where the information was that the appellant "did unlawfully assault or beat" his victim. This court held that a conviction on that information was bad in that the information charged in the alternative. Another decision to which we were referred was *Ware* v *Fox*; *Fox* v *Dingley* [1967] 1 WLR 379. In that case two separate drugs-related offences were joined by the conjunctive "and" rather than the disjunctive "or" but the justices none the less dismissed the information and this court held that they were right to do so.

Although duplicity is a matter of form it is a fundamental matter of form. If an information is duplicitous the prosecutor must elect on which offence he wishes to proceed and if he does not do so the information must be dismissed. In my judgment the unusual allegation of "assault and batter" in the information against Stephen Little was duplicitous. I cannot accept the submission of Mr Collins for the DPP that "and batter" is to be taken as no more than "and beat" expressed in archaic language. I think that in 1990 an informant who uses "batter" must be taken as referring to the offence of battery rather than as employing archaic language. The word "assault" must therefore, by virtue of the contrast with "batter", be taken as used in its pure sense of putting in fear of force. The result is an assertion of two offences. I think the justices were right in their conclusion that the information was duplicitous.

The phrase "assault and beat" by reference to which many thousands of people must have been convicted without objection is not directly before us. The phrase is free of the vice of a contrast with "batter", and the event to which the charge relates is a single occasion, albeit apprehension and receipt of force may be separable by a small unit of time. I think that now may be too late to regard the formulation as objectionable. However, undeniably a more accurate form would avoid a conjunction and use a preposition. Thus "assault by beating" would be immune from argument. Mr Collins accepted that it would be, and I think that in the future prosecutors should avoid conjunctive forms.'

Hills v *Ellis* [1983] QB 680 Divisional Court (Griffiths LJ and McCullough J)
Meaning of 'wilful' in the context of s51(3) Police Act 1964

Facts
The defendant had witnessed a fight outside a football ground. He later saw the innocent party in the fight being arrested by a police officer. He grabbed the officer's elbow and shouted at him in order to alert him to what the defendant feared would be a miscarriage of justice. The policeman told the defendant to desist, but he refused. The defendant was convicted under s51(3) of the Police Act 1964, and appealed to the Divisional Court.

Held
The appeal would be dismissed.

Griffiths LJ:

Lord Parker CJ [considers] the element of wilfulness in the offence, and he says: "The only remaining ingredient, and the one upon which in my judgment this case revolves, is whether the obstructing of which the defendant was guilty was a wilful obstruction. 'Wilful' in this context not only in my judgment means 'intentional' but something which is done without lawful excuse, and that indeed is conceded by counsel."

What is submitted in this case on behalf of the defendant is that his action was not wilful in the sense of being done without lawful excuse, because he had a moral duty to draw to the attention of the officer that he was arresting the wrong man. I cannot accept that submission. Here was an officer, acting in the course of his duty, arresting a man. It would be quite intolerable if citizens, who may genuinely believe the wrong man was arrested, were entitled to lay hands on the police and obstruct them in that arrest because they thought that some other person should be arrested. One has only got to state the proposition to see the enormous abuse to which any such power on the part of the citizen might be put. A private citizen has no lawful excuse to interfere with a lawful arrest by a police officer. Accordingly, he was acting without lawful excuse within the definition as stated by Lord Parker CJ in *Rice* v *Connolly* [below].

The only other authority cited in support of the defendant's submission is *Willmott* v *Atack* [1977] QB 498; [1976] 3 All ER 794. The facts in that case were very different. A police officer was attempting to restrain a man under arrest and to get him into a police car. The defendant intervened, not with the intention of making it more difficult for the police officer to get the man into the police car, but with the intention of helping the officer. But due to the clumsiness of his intervention, the man in fact escaped. There is no doubt that in those circumstances the first part of the definition of "wilfully obstructing" has been fulfilled. The officer had, in fact, been obstructed, but the Court held that it had not been a wilful obstruction. Croom-Johnson J expressed the view of the Court in the following way at pp504 and 800 respectively: "When one looks at the whole context of section 51, dealing as it does with assaults on constables in subsection (1) and concluding in subsection (3) with resistance and wilful obstruction in their execution of their duty, I am of the view that the interpretation of this subsection for which the appellant contends is the right one. It fits the words 'wilfully obstructs' in the context of the subsection, and in my view there must be something in the nature of a criminal intent of the kind which means that it is done with the idea of some form of hostility to the police with the intention of seeing that what is done is to obstruct, and that it is not merely enough to show that he intended to do what he did and that it did, in fact, have the result of the police being obstructed."'

R v Kimber [1983] 1 WLR 1118 Court of Appeal (Criminal Division) (Lawton LJ, Michael Davies and Sheldon J)

Mistake as to the consent of the victim

Facts
The defendant was convicted of indecently assaulting a female patient at a mental hospital contrary to s14 Sexual Offences Act 1956. He appealed on the ground that he had honestly thought she was consenting to his actions.

Held
The appeal would be allowed.

The jury had been misdirected to the extent that the trial judge should have explained to them that if the defendant had honestly believed that the victim was consenting to his actions he would not have had the *mens rea* necessary for the offence. His belief in her consent did not have to be reasonable, merely honest. On the facts, however, it was evident that even if the jury had been properly directed the defendant would still have been convicted, and on that basis the appeal would be dismissed.

R v Venna [1975] 3 WLR 737 Court of Appeal (Criminal Division) (James and Ormrod LJJ and Cusack J)

Mens rea for assault and battery

Facts
The defendant was arrested after being involved in a fracas with police officers during which he had lashed out with his foot, fracturing the hand of an officer who was trying to restrain him. The defendant was convicted of (inter alia) assault occasioning actual bodily harm. He appealed on the ground (inter alia) that recklessness was insufficient mens rea for the offence.

Held
James LJ (having considered the first ground of appeal):

'The second substantial ground of appeal relates to the conviction of assault occasioning actual bodily harm. Having summed up to the jury the issue of self defence in relation to the alleged assault the judge directed them in these terms:

"However, you would still have to consider, on this question of assault by Venna, whether it was an accident. If he is lashing out ... Let me put it this way. Mr Woods on behalf of Venna says 'Well, he is not guilty of an assault because it was neither intentional nor reckless. It was a pure accident that he happened to hit the officer,' and that is quite right. If you hit somebody accidentally, it cannot be a criminal offence so you have got to ask yourselves, 'Was this deliberate, or was it reckless?' If it was, then he is guilty. To do an act deliberately hardly needs explanation. If you see somebody in front of you and you deliberately kick him on the knee, that is a deliberate act and, no two ways about it, that is an assault, but it can equally well be an assault if you are lashing out, knowing that there are people in the neighbourhood or that there are likely to be people in the neighbourhood and, in this case, it is suggested that he had two people by his arms and he knew that he was being restrained so as to lead to arrest. If he lashes out with his feet, knowing that there are officers about him and knowing that by lashing out he will probably or is likely to kick somebody or hurt his hand by banging his heel down on it, then he is equally guilty of the offence. Venna can therefore be guilty of the offence in count 3 in the indictment if he deliberately brought his foot down on Police Constable Spencer's hand or if he lashed out simply reckless as to who was there, not caring an iota as to whether he kicked somebody or brought his heel down on his hands."

Mr Woods argued that the direction is wrong in law because it states that the mental element of recklessness is enough, when coupled with the actus reus of physical contact to constitute the battery involved in assault occasioning actual bodily harm. Recklessness, it is argued, is not enough; there must be intention to do the physical act the subject matter of the charge. Counsel relied on *R v Lamb* [1967] 2 QB 981 and argued that an assault is not established by proof of a deliberate act which gives rise to consequences which are not intended.

In *Fagan v Commissioner of Metropolitan Police* [1969] 1 QB 439, 444, it was said:

"An assault is any act which intentionally – or possibly recklessly – causes another person to apprehend immediate and unlawful personal violence."

In *Fagan* it was not necessary to decide the question whether proof of recklessness is sufficient to establish the mens rea ingredient of assault. That question falls for decision in the present case. Why it was considered necessary for the Crown to put the case forward on the alternative bases of "intention" and "recklessness" is not clear to us. This resulted in the direction given in the summing up.

On the evidence of the defendant himself one would have thought that the inescapable inference was that the defendant intended to make physical contact with whoever might try to restrain him. Be that as it may, in the light of the direction given, the verdict may have been arrived at on the basis of "recklessness." Mr Woods cited *Ackroyd v Barett* (1894) 11 TLR 115 in support of his argument that recklessness, which falls short of intention, is not enough to support a charge of battery, and argued that, there being no authority to the contrary, it is now too late to extend the law by a decision of the courts and that any extension must be by the decision of Parliament.

Mr Woods sought support from the distinction between the offences which are assaults and offences which by statute include the element contained in the word "maliciously," eg unlawful and malicious wounding contrary to section 20 of the Offences Against the Person Act 1861, in which recklessness will suffice to support the charge. See *R v Cunningham* [1957] 2 QB 396. In so far as the editors of text books commit themselves to an opinion on this branch of the law they are favourable to the view that recklessness is or should logically be sufficient to support the charge of assault or battery. See *Glanville Williams Criminal Law*, 2nd ed (1961), para 27 p65; *Kenny's Outlines of the Criminal Law*, 19th ed (1966), para 164 p218; *Russell on Crime*, 12th ed (1964), p656 and *Smith and Hogan Criminal Law*, 3rd ed (1973).

We think that the decision in *Ackroyd v Barett* (supra) is explicable on the basis that the facts of the case did not support a finding of recklessness. The case was not argued for both sides. The case of *Bradshaw* (1878) 14 Cox CC 83 can be read as supporting the view that unlawful physical force applied recklessly constitutes a criminal assault. In our view the element of mens rea in the offence of battery is satisfied by proof that the defendant intentionally or recklessly applied force to the person of another. If it were otherwise the strange consequence would be that an offence of unlawful wounding contrary to section 20 of the Offences Against the Person Act 1861 could be established by proof that the defendant wounded the victim either intentionally or recklessly but, if the victim's skin was not broken and the offence was therefore laid as an assault occasioning actual bodily harm contrary to section 47 of the Act, it would be necessary to prove that the physical force was intentionally applied.

We see no reason in logic or in law why a person who recklessly applies physical force to the person of another should be outside the criminal law of assault. In many cases the dividing line between intention and recklessness is barely distinguishable. This is such a case.'

Commentary

Following *R v Savage*; *R v Parmenter* (extracted in Chapter 23) it would appear that *R v Venna* is still authority for the type of recklessness needed for assault.

23 Non-Fatal Offences against the Person II

R v Blaue [1975] 1 WLR 1411
See Chapter 24.

R v Cato [1976] 1 WLR 110
See Chapter 26.

R v Clarence (1888) 22 QBD 23 Court for Crown Cases Reserved

Whether 'infliction' of grievous bodily harm contrary to s20 of the Offences Against the Person Act 1861 requires proof of an assault

Facts
The defendant had sexual intercourse with his wife whilst suffering from venereal disease. He had been aware of his condition but his wife had not. There was evidence that his wife would not have consented to intercourse if she had known of his condition. The defendant was convicted under both s47 and s20 of the 1861 Act, and appealed against conviction contending that as his wife had consented to intercourse she had not been assaulted, and in the absence of an assault he could not be held to have inflicted any harm upon her.

Held
By a majority of nine to four, both convictions would be quashed.

Stephen J:

> 'I now come to the construction of the precise words of the statute ... is there an "infliction of bodily harm either with or without any weapon or instrument?" I think not for the following reasons.
>
> The words appear to me to mean the direct causing of some grievous injury to the body itself with a weapon, as by a cut with a knife, or without a weapon, as by a blow with the first or by pushing a person down. Indeed, though the word "assault" is not used in the section, I think the words imply an assault and battery of which a wound or grievous bodily harm is the manifest immediate and obvious result. This is supported by ... 14 and 15 Vict c19 s4 of which the present section is a re-enactment. Section 4 of the earlier Act begins with the preamble, "And whereas it is expedient to make further provision for the punishment of aggravated assaults," and then proceeds in the words of the present section, with a trifling and unimportant difference in their arrangement.
>
> Infection by the application of an animal poison appears to me to be of a different character from an assault. The administration of poison is dealt with by section 24, which would be superfluous if poisoning were an "infliction of grievous bodily harm either with or without a weapon or instrument." The one act differs from the other in the immediate and necessary connection between a cut or a blow and the wound

or harm inflicted, and the uncertain and delayed operation of the act by which infection is communicated. If a man by a grasp of the hand infects another with small-pox, it is impossible to trace out in detail the connection between the act and the disease, and it would, I think, be an unnatural use of language to say that man by such an act, "inflicted small-pox on another." It would be wrong in interpreting an Act of Parliament to lay much stress on etymology, but I may just observe that "inflict" is "derived" from "infligo," for which Facciolati's Lexicon three Italian and three Latin equivalents are given, all meaning "to strike" …'

Hawkins J (dissenting):

'In my opinion the legislature, in framing the various sections of the statute already and hereafter referred to, used the words "inflict," "cause" and "occasion" as synonymous terms for the following among other reasons. Let me begin by calling attention to the language of the eighteenth section, which runs thus: "whosoever shall unlawfully and maliciously by any means whatsoever wound or *cause* any grievous bodily harm to any person, etc, with intent, etc, shall be guilty of felony." If the prisoner had been indicted under this section, could anybody doubt that upon proof of his intention to cause the grievous bodily harm he in fact occasioned, he would have fallen within not only the spirit but the precise language of the section according to the strictest interpretation which could be applied to it? I next ask myself what was the object of the 20th section? Clearly it was to provide for cases in which the grievous bodily harm mentioned in section 18, though unlawfully and maliciously caused, was unaccompanied by the felonious intent, which is the aggravating feature of the felony created by that section, and accordingly section 20 made such last-mentioned offence a misdemeanour only, by enacting as follows, "whosoever shall unlawfully or maliciously wound or *inflict* any grievous bodily harm upon any person either with or without any weapon or instrument shall be guilty of a misdemeanour." Surely the object of these two sections could only have been to make the doing of grievous bodily harm with intent a felony, without intent, a mere misdemeanour, and to hold that no man could be convicted under section 20 without proof of an assault would practically amount to holding that maliciously to do grievous bodily harm to another without felonious intent is unpunishable, unless such harm is done through the medium of an assault. It is impossible the legislature could have intended this.'

Commentary

See further *R* v *Wilson*, below.

R v *Cogan and Leak* [1975] 3 WLR 316

See Chapter 27.

R v *Court* [1988] 2 WLR 1071 House of Lords (Lords Keith, Fraser, Griffiths, Ackner and Goff)

Proof of indecency in indecent assault

Facts

The defendant had accused a 12 year old girl of shoplifting in his store, and had spanked her several times on her buttocks, over her clothing. The girl complained to her parents, and the defendant was interviewed by the police. In explaining why he had done it, he made the statement that he might have been motivated by his 'buttock fetish'. The defendant was convicted of indecent assault contrary to s14 of the Sexual Offences Act 1956, following a trial in which the judge had permitted evidence of the defendant's statement to go before the jury. The defendant appealed on the ground that evidence of his secret indecent intent could not convert an act that was not overtly indecent into an indecent assault. The Court of Appeal dismissed the appeal holding that the evidence of his 'buttock fetish' was correctly admitted, and the defendant appealed further to the House of Lords.

Held (Lord Goff dissenting):
The appeal would be dismissed.

Lord Ackner:

> 'It also was common ground before your Lordships, as it was in the Court of Appeal, that if the circumstances of the assault are incapable of being regarded as indecent, then the undisclosed intention of the accused could not make the assault an indecent one. The validity of this proposition is well illustrated by *R v George* [1956] Crim LR 52. The basis of the prosecution's case was that the defendant on a number of occasions removed a shoe from a girl's foot and that he did so, as indeed he admitted, because it gave him a kind of perverted sexual gratification. Counsel for the prosecution submitted that an assault was indecent if it was committed to gratify an indecent motive in the mind of a defendant, even though there was no overt circumstances of indecency. Streatfeild J ruled that an assault became indecent only if it was accompanied by circumstances of indecency towards the person alleged to have been assaulted, and that none of the assaults (the removal or attempted removal of the shoes) could possibly amount to an indecent assault.
>
> Again it was common ground that if, as in this case, the assault involved touching the victim, it was not necessary to prove that she was aware of the circumstances of indecency or apprehended indecency. An indecent assault can clearly be committed by the touching of someone who is asleep or unconscious.
>
> As to the facts of this case, it is important to bear in mind that at the trial, not only did the appellant admit that he was guilty of an assault, but on his behalf his counsel expressly conceded that what had happened *was capable* of amounting to an indecent assault. That concession was repeated in the Court of Appeal and accepted by the court as being a correct concession. Sensibly no attempt was made before your Lordships to withdraw this concession, for the sound reason that the explanation of this unprovoked assault could reveal that the assault was an indecent one, as indeed the girl's father suspected and, as the jury so decided.
>
> The assault which the prosecution seek to establish may be of a kind which is inherently indecent. The defendant removes against her will, a woman's clothing. Such a case, to my mind raises no problem. Those very facts, *devoid of any explanation,* would give rise to the irresistible inference that the defendant intended to assault his victim in a manner which right-minded persons would clearly think was indecent. Whether he did so for his own personal sexual gratification or because, being a misogynist or for some other reason, he wished to embarrass or humiliate his victim, seems to me to be irrelevant. He has failed, ex-hypothesi, to show any lawful justification for his indecent conduct. This, of course, was not such a case. The conduct of the appellant in assaulting the girl by spanking her was only *capable* of being an indecent assault. To decide whether or not right-minded persons might think that assault was indecent, the following factors were clearly relevant – the relationship of the defendant to his victim – were they relatives, friends or virtually complete strangers? How had the defendant come to embark on this conduct and why was he behaving in this way? Aided by such material, a jury would be helped to determine the quality of the act, the true nature of the assault and to answer the vital question – were they sure that the defendant not only intended to commit an assault upon the girl, but an assault which was indecent – was such an inference irresistible? For the defendant to be liable to be convicted of the offence of indecent assault, where the circumstances of the alleged offence can be given an innocent as well as an indecent interpretation, without the prosecution being obliged to establish that the defendant intended to commit both an assault and an indecent one, seems to me quite unacceptable and not what Parliament intended.
>
> Much reliance was placed by counsel for the appellant upon the definition of "indecent assault" in *Beal v Kelley* [1951] 2 All ER 763, 764 as approved by Lord Goddard CJ "an assault, accompanied with circumstances of indecency on the part of the prisoner." It was submitted to your Lordships that an indecent motive can only become "a circumstance of indecency" if it is communicated to the victim by means of words or gestures at the time of the assault. If the motive is not communicated it is not such a

circumstance. However the definition which Lord Goddard CJ accepted has not the force of a statute. It was wholly appropriate to the facts of that case, where the defendant had indecently exposed himself to a young boy and when the boy refused to handle him indecently, he got hold of the boy's arm and pulled him towards himself. In such a case and in many others cited to us, the assault in itself was not indecent. It was the combination of the assault with circumstances of indecency, that established the constituents of the offence. In the instant case, it is the assault itself – its true nature – an assault for sexual gratification, which was capable of amounting to an indecent assault.

The jury in their question to the judge were concerned with the position of a doctor who carried out an intimate examination on a young girl. Mars-Jones J dealt with their point succinctly by saying:

> "In that situation what is vital is whether the examination was necessary or not. If it was not necessary, but indulged in by the medical practitioner, it would be an indecent assault. But if it was necessary, even though he got sexual satisfaction out of it, that would not make it an indecent assault."

I entirely agree. If it could be proved by the doctor's admission that the consent of the parent, or if over 16 the patient, was sought and obtained by the doctor falsely representing that the examination was necessary, then, of course, no true consent to the examination had ever been given. The examination would be an assault and an assault which right-minded persons could well consider was an indecent one. I would not expect that it would make any difference to the jury's decision whether the doctor's false representations were motivated by his desire for the sexual gratification which he might achieve from such an examination, or because he had some other reason, entirely of his own, unconnected with the medical needs or care of the patient, such as private research, which had caused him to act fraudulently. In either case the assault could be, and I expect would be, considered as so offensive to contemporary standards of modesty or privacy as to be indecent. A jury would therefore be entitled to conclude that he in both cases intended to assault the patient and to do so indecently. I can see nothing illogical in such a result. On the contrary, it would indeed be surprising if in such circumstances the only offence that could be properly charged would be that of common assault. No doubt the judge would treat the offence which had been motivated by the indecent motive as the more serious.'

R v George [1956] Crim LR 52

See *R v Court,* above.

R v Khan and Others [1990] 1 WLR 813 Court of Appeal (Criminal Division) (Russell LJ, Rose and Morland JJ)

Facts
The appellants were charged with the attempted rape of a 16-year-old girl. During the course of the trial the judge directed the jury in the following terms: ' ... As in the case of rape, the principles relevant to consent apply in exactly the same way in attempted rape. I do not suppose you need me to go through it again. Apply the same principles as to rape.' Following conviction, the appellants sought to appeal contending that there had been a material misdirection, on the basis that whilst recklessness, as a state of mind on the part of an offender, was relevant to the completed crime of rape, it had no place in the offence of attempted rape.

Held
The appeals would be dismissed.

Russell LJ (having referred to the wording of s1(1) of the Criminal Attempts Act 1981):

'The impact of the words of section 1 of the Act of 1981 and in particular the words "with intent to commit an offence" has been the subject matter of much debate amongst distinguished academic writers. We were referred to and we have read and considered an article by Professor Glanville Williams entitled "The Problem of Reckless Attempts" [1983] Crim LR 365. The argument there advanced is that recklessness can exist within the concept of attempt and support is derived from *R v Pigg* [1982] 1 WLR 762, albeit that authority was concerned with the law prior to the Criminal, Attempts Act 1981. This approach also receives approval from *Smith and Hogan's* Criminal Law, 6th ed (1988), pp287 to 289.

Contrary views, however, have been expressed by Professor Griew and Mr Richard Buxton QC who have both contended that the words "with intent to commit an offence" involve an intent as to every element constituting the crime.

Finally we have had regard to the observations of Mustill LJ giving the judgment of the Court of Appeal (Criminal Division) in *R v Millard and Vernon* [1987] Crim LR 393. That was a case involving a charge of attempting to damage property, the particulars of offence reading:

"Gary Mann Millard and Michael Elliot Vernon, on 11 May 1985 without lawful excuse attempted to damage a wooden wall at the Leeds Road Football Stand belonging to Huddersfield Town Association Football Club intending to damage the said wall or being reckless as to whether the said wall would be damaged."

Mustill LJ said:

"The appellants' case is simple. They submit that in ordinary speech the essence of an attempt is a desire to bring about a particular result, coupled with steps towards that end. The essence of recklessness is either indifference to a known risk or (in some circumstances) failure to advert to an obvious risk. The two states of mind cannot co-exist. Section 1(1) of the Criminal Attempts Act 1981 expressly demands that a person shall have an intent to commit an offence if he is to be guilty of an attempt to commit that offence. The word 'intent' may, it is true, have a specialised meaning in some contexts. But even if this can properly be attributed to the word where it is used in s1(1) there is no warrant for reading it as embracing recklessness, nor for reading into it whatever lesser degree of mens rea will suffice for the particular substantive offence in question. For an attempt nothing but conscious volition will do. Accordingly that part of the particulars of offence which referred to recklessness was meaningless, and the parts of the direction which involved a definition of recklessness, and an implied invitation to convict if the jury found the appellants to have acted recklessly, were misleading. There was thus, so it was contended, a risk that the jury convicted on the wrong basis of the verdict cannot safely be allowed to stand."

At the conclusion of the argument it appeared to us that this argument was logically sound and that it was borne out by the authorities cited to us, especially *R v Whybrow* (1951) 35 Cr App R 141, *Cunliffe v Goodman* [1950] 2 KB 237, 253 and *R v Mohan* [1976] QB 1, and that it was not inconsistent with anything in *Hyam v Director of Public Prosecutions* [1975] AC 55. Our attention had however been drawn to a difference of opinion between commentators about the relationship between the mens rea in an attempt and the ingredients of the substantive offence, and we therefore reserved judgment so as to consider whether the question was not perhaps more difficult than it seemed. In the event we have come to the conclusion that there does exist a problem in this field, and that it is by no means easy to solve; but also that it need not be solved for the purpose of deciding the present appeal. In our judgment two different situations must be distinguished. The first exists where the substantive offence consists simply of the act which constitutes the actus reus (which for present purposes we shall call the "result") coupled with some element of volition, which may or may not amount to a full intent. Here the only question is whether the intent to bring about the result called for by section 1(1) is to be watered down to such a degree, if any, as to make it correspond with the mens rea of the substantive offence. The second situation is more complicated. It exists where the substantive offence does not consist of one result and one mens rea, but rather involves not only the underlying intention to produce the result, but another state of mind directed to some circumstance or act which the prosecution must also establish in addition to proving the result.

The problem may be illustrated by reference to the offence of attempted rape. As regards the substantive offence the "result" takes the shape of sexual intercourse with a woman. But the offence is not established without proof of an additional circumstance (namely that the woman did not consent), and a state of mind relative to that circumstance (namely that the defendant knew she did not consent, or was reckless as to whether she consented).

When one turns to the offence of attempted rape, one thing is obvious, that the result, namely the act of sexual intercourse, must be intended in the full sense. Also obvious is the fact that proof of an intention to have intercourse with a woman, together with an act towards that end, is not enough: the offence must involve proof of something about the woman's consent, and something about the defendant's state of mind in relation to that consent.

The problem is to decide precisely what that something is. Must the prosecution prove not only that the defendant intended the act, but also that he intended it to be non-consensual? Or should the jury be directed to consider two different states of mind, intend as to the act and recklessness as to the circumstances? Here the commentators differ: contrast *Smith & Hogan's Criminal Law*, 5th ed (1983), pp255 et seq., with a note on the Act by Professor Griew in *Current Law Statutes* 1981."

We must now grapple with the very problem that Mustill LJ identifies in the last paragraph of the passage cited.

In our judgment an acceptable analysis of the offence of rape is as follows:

1) the intention of the offender is to have sexual intercourse with a woman;
2) the offence is committed if, but only if, the circumstances are that:
   a) the woman does not consent; *and*
   b) the defendant knows that she is not consenting or is reckless as to whether she consents.

Precisely the same analysis can be made of the offence of attempted rape:

1) the intention of the offender is to have sexual intercourse with a woman;
2) the offence is committed if, but only if, the circumstances are that:
   a) the woman does not consent; *and*
   b) the defendant knows that she is not consenting or is reckless as to whether she consents.

The only difference between the two offences is that in rape sexual intercourse takes place whereas in attempted rape it does not, although there has to be some act which is more than preparatory to sexual intercourse. Considered in that way, the intent of the defendant is precisely the same in rape and in attempted rape and the mens rea is identical, namely, an intention to have intercourse plus a knowledge of or recklessness as to the woman's absence of consent. No question of attempting to achieve a reckless state of mind arises; the attempt relates to the physical activity; the mental state of the defendant is the same. A man does not recklessly have sexual intercourse, nor does he recklessly attempt it. Recklessness in rape and attempted rape arises not in relation to the physical act of the accused but only in his state of mind when engaged in the activity of having or attempting to have sexual intercourse.

If this is the true analysis, as we believe it is, the attempt does not require any different intention on the part of the accused from that for the full offence of rape. We believe this to be a desirable result which in the instant case did not require the jury to be burdened with different directions as to the accused's state of mind, dependent upon whether the individual achieved or failed to achieve sexual intercourse.

We recognise, of course, that our reasoning cannot apply to all offences and all attempts. Where, for example, as in causing death by reckless driving or reckless arson, no state of mind other than recklessness is involved in the offence, there can be no attempt to commit it.

In our judgment, however, the words "with intent to commit an offence" to be found in section 1 of the Act of 1981 mean, when applied to rape, "with intent to have sexual intercourse with a woman in circumstances where she does not consent and the defendant knows or could not care less about her absence of consent." The only "intent", giving that word its natural and ordinary meaning, of the rapist is to have sexual intercourse. He commits the offence because of the circumstances in which he manifests that intent – ie when the woman is not consenting and he either knows it or could not care less about the absence of consent.

Accordingly we take the view that in relation to the four appellants the judge was right to give the directions that he did when inviting the jury to consider the charges of attempted rape.'

R v *Linekar* [1995] 2 WLR 237 Court of Appeal (Criminal Division) (Swinton Thomas LJ, Morland and Steel JJ)

Fraud affecting consent in rape

Facts

The appellant had sexual intercourse with the complainant, who had been working as a prostitute. The complainant alleged that prior to sexual intercourse the appellant had promised to pay her £25, but later refused to do so. The appellant was charged with rape, and convicted following the trial judge's direction to the effect that if the complainant's consent to intercourse had been obtained by fraud she could not properly be regarded as having given her consent. The appellant appealed.

Held

The appeal would be allowed.

Morland J:

> 'An essential ingredient of the offence of rape is the proof that the woman did not consent to the actual act of sexual intercourse with the particular man who penetrated her. If the Crown prove that she did not consent to sexual intercourse, rape is proved. That ingredient is proved in the so called "medical cases". The victim did not agree in those cases to sexual intercourse. In *R* v *Flattery* (1877) 2 QBD 410, she agreed to a surgical procedure which she hoped would cure her fits. In *R* v *Williams* [1923] 1 KB 340, she agreed to a physical manipulation which would provide her with extra air supply to improve her singing.
>
> In our judgment, it is the non-consent to sexual intercourse rather than the fraud of the doctor or choir master that makes the offence rape. Similarly, that ingredient is not proved in the husband impersonation cases because the victim did not consent to sexual intercourse with the particular man who penetrated her. We venture to suggest that at common law it is immaterial whether the penetrator is impersonating a husband, a cohabitee or a lover, as is supported by the Criminal Law Revision Committee in the paragraph that we have quoted.
>
> In the 19th century, English judges got themselves into somewhat of a tangle in impersonation cases. In *R* v *Jackson* (1822) Russ and Ry 487, a court of 12 judges decided by eight to four that carnal knowledge of a woman whilst she was under the belief that the man is her husband was not rape. In *R* v *Barrow* (1868) LR 1 CCR 156, a court of five judges took the same view contrary to the opinion of the trial judge, Kelly CB. In that case Bovill CJ, giving a judgment with which Channell B, Byles J, Blackburn J and Lush J concurred, said, at p158:
>
> > "It does not appear that the woman, upon whom the offence was alleged to have been committed, was asleep or unconscious at the time when the act of connection commenced. It must be taken, therefore, that the act was done with the consent of the prosecutrix, though that consent was obtained by fraud. It falls therefore within the class of cases which decide that, where consent is obtained by fraud, the act done does not amount to rape."
>
> In so far as that case is still good law, it supports the argument of the appellant. In *R* v *Flattery*, 2 QBD 410, a court of five judges expressed dissatisfaction with the decision in *R* v *Barrow* (1868) LR 1 CCR 156. It needed the good sense of the judges in Ireland to resolve the problem in *R* v *Dee* (1884) 14 LRIr 468. The Court of the Crown Cases Reserved of Ireland consisted of six judges including May CJ and Palles CB, May CJ having been the trial judge. The facts of that case are set out shortly in the judgment of May CJ, at pp475–476:

"There is not, I think, any doubt or dispute as to the facts and circumstances of the case. Upon the report of the judge, who was myself, and the findings of the jury, it is, I think, established that Judith Gorman, wife of one J Gorman, who was absent (having gone out to fish), lay down upon a bed in her sleeping-room in the evening, when it was dark; that the prisoner came into the room, personating her husband, lay down upon her and had connexion with her; that she did not at first resist, believing the man to be her husband, but that, on discovering that he was not her husband, which was after the commencement but before the termination of the proceeding, her consent or acquiescence terminated, and she ran downstairs. It appeared, I think, manifestly that the prisoner knew the woman was deceived, as she said to the prisoner in his presence and hearing, when he came into the room, 'You are soon home tonight', to which he made no reply. At the time my own opinion, founded upon well-known cases in England, was that the prisoner was not guilty of rape, but at the request of the counsel for the Crown I left certain questions to the jury, and, upon their findings, directed them to find a verdict of guilty, reserving the case for consideration of the court, which is now called upon to decide the question which arises."

The Chief Justice then went on to consider the various English authorities and then said, at pp478–479:

"Now, rape being defined to be sexual connexion with a woman without her consent, or without, and therefore against, her will, it is essential to consider what is meant and intended by consent. Does it mean an intelligent, positive concurrence of the will of the woman, or is the negative absence of dissent sufficient? In these surgical cases, it is held that the submission to an act believed to be a surgical operation does not constitute consent to a sexual connexion, being of a wholly different character. This is no consensus quoad hoc. In the case of personation there is no consensus quoad hanc personam."

In our judgment, applying those dicta to the facts of the present case, here there was consent by the prostitute to sexual intercourse, consensus quoad hoc. There was consent by the prostitute to sexual intercourse with this particular appellant consensus quoad hanc personam. The so-called "medical cases", such as *R v Flattery* 2 QBD 410 and *R v Williams* [1923] 1 KB 340 are examples of no consensus quoad hoc. The husband impersonation cases are examples of no consensus quoad hanc personam.

Palles CB, in his very learned judgment in *R v Dee* 14 LRIr 468, 488, said:

"I think that it follows that ... an act done under the bona fide belief that it is another act different in its essence is not in law the act of the party. That is the present case – a case which it is hardly necessary to point out is not that of consent in fact sought to be avoided for fraud, but one in which that which took place never amounted to consent. The person by whom the act was to be performed was part of its essence. The consent of the intellect, the only consent known to the law, was the act of the husband only, and of this the prisoner was aware."

In our judgment, the ratio of *R v Dee* is the absence of consent and not the existence of fraud which makes it rape.

R v Dee was followed in 1885 by the Criminal Law Amendment Act 1885 (48 & 49 Vict c 69) which is entitled: "An Act to make further provision for the protection of women and girls, the suppression of brothels and other purposes." Under section 3 of that Act it was enacted:

"Any person who ... (2) By false pretences or false representations procures any woman or girl, not being a common prostitute or of known immoral character, to have unlawful carnal connexion, either within or without the Queen's dominions; ... shall be guilty of a misdemeanor, and being convicted thereof shall be liable at the discretion of the court to be imprisoned for any term not exceeding two years, with or without hard labour. Provided that no person shall be convicted of an offence under this section upon the evidence of one witness only, unless such witness be corroborated in some material particular by evidence implicating the accused."

It should be noted that under that section, in contradistinction to rape where life imprisonment was the sentence, the maximum sentence was one of two years and also, unlike rape, corroboration was required as a matter of law.

It was in section 4 of the same statute that it was enacted in a form that is declaratory of the common law:

"Whereas doubts have been entertained whether a man who induces a married woman to permit him to have connexion with her by personating her husband is or is not guilty of rape, it is hereby enacted and declared that every such offender shall be deemed to be guilty of rape."

Under section 9 of that Act it was enacted that: "If upon the trial of any indictment for rape, ... the jury shall be satisfied that the defendant is guilty of an offence under section 3" – that is procurement of sexual intercourse by false representations – "but are not satisfied that the defendant is guilty of the felony ... the jury may acquit" of rape and find the defendant guilty of the misdemeanour of procuring sexual intercourse by false pretences. Although the wording of the sections is slightly different, they foreshadow similar sections in the Sexual Offences Act 1956, and the offence of procuring sexual intercourse by false representation remains, in the proper case and subject to the appropriate direction for the requirement as a matter of law for corroboration, an alternative verdict that a jury can return.

In 1888 was decided *R* v *Clarence* (1889) 22 QBD 23. This was the well known case of the husband who knew that he was suffering from gonorrhoea and his wife did not, and he quite deliberately had sexual intercourse with her with the result that the disease was communicated to her. He was convicted of an indictment charging him with inflicting grievous bodily harm under section 20, and of an assault occasioning actual bodily harm under section 47 of the Offences Against the Person Act 1861. The court of 13 judges, by a majority of nine to four, decided that Clarence was not guilty under either section.

The importance of *R* v *Clarence*, in our judgment, is that it exposes the fallacy of the submission that there can be rape by fraud or false pretences. Wills J said, at p27:

"That consent obtained by fraud is no consent at all is not true as a general proposition either in fact or in law. If a man meets a woman in the street and knowingly gives her bad money in order to procure her consent to intercourse with him, he obtains her consent by fraud, but it would be childish to say that she did not consent. It only makes it revocable."

Stephen J said, at p43:

"It seems to me that the proposition that fraud vitiates consent in criminal matters is not true if taken to apply the fullest sense of the word, and without qualification. ... Many seductions would be rapes, and so might acts of prostitution procured by fraud, as for instance by promises not intended to be fulfilled."

We interpose to say that that is the situation in this particular appeal, Stephen J continued, at pp43–44:

"These illustrations appear to shew clearly that the maxim that fraud vitiates consent is too general to be applied to these matters as if it were absolutely true. ... The only cases in which fraud indisputably vitiates consent in these matters are cases of fraud as to the nature of the act done. As to fraud as to the identity of the person by whom it is done, the law is not quite clear. In *R* v *Flattery*, in which consent was obtained by representing the act as a surgical operation, the prisoner was held to be guilty of rape. In the case where consent was obtained by the personation of a husband, there was before the passing of the Criminal Law Amendment Act of 1885 a conflict of authority. The last decision in England, *R* v *Barrow*, decided that the act was not rape, and *R* v *Dee*, decided in Ireland in 1884, decided it was. The Criminal Law Amendment Act of 1885 'declared and enacted' that thenceforth it should be deemed to be rape, thus favouring the view taken in *R* v *Dee*. ... they justify the observation that the only sorts of fraud which so far destroy the effect of a woman's consent as to convert a connection consented to in fact into a rape are frauds as to the nature of the act itself, or as to the identity of the person who does the act. There is abundant authority to shew that such frauds as these vitiate consent both in the case of rape and in the case of indecent assault. I should myself prefer to say that consent in such cases does not exist at all, because the act consented to is not the act done."

With that sentence, this court respectfully agrees. Stephen J went on to say, at p44:

"Consent to a surgical operation or examination is not a consent to sexual connection or indecent behaviour. Consent to connection with a husband is not consent to adultery. I do not think that the maxim that fraud vitiates consent can be carried further than this in criminal matters. It is commonly applied to cases of contract, because in all cases of contract the evidence of a consent not procured by force or fraud is essential, but even in these cases care in the application of the maxim is required, because in some instances suppression of the truth operates as fraud, whereas in others at least a suggestion of falsehood is required. The act of intercourse between a man and a woman cannot in any case be regarded as the performance of a contract."

Then at the bottom of p44: "The woman's consent here was as full and conscious as consent could be. It was not obtained by any fraud as to the nature of the act or as to the identity of the agent." Those two last sentences, in our judgment, apply clearly to the facts of this case.

Moving to more recent times, there is the highly persuasive authority of *Papadimitropoulos* v *The Queen* (1956) 98 CLR 249, a decision of the High Court of Australia. The court was presided over by Sir Owen Dixon CJ, and consisted of McTiernan, Webb, Kitto and Taylor JJ. The headnote reads:

"Rape is carnal knowledge of a woman without her consent. Carnal knowledge is the physical act of penetration. It is the consent to such physical act of penetration which is in question upon an indictment for rape. Such a consent demands a perception as to what is about to take place, as to the identity of the man and the character of what he is doing. Once the consent is comprehending and actual, the inducing causes cannot destroy its reality and leave the man guilty of rape. Where a woman consented to sexual intercourse under the belief, fraudulently induced by the man, that she was married to him. *Held*, that the man was not guilty of rape."

The facts of that case were that the complainant believed that she had gone through a marriage with the appellant. In the judgment of the court, the court said, at pp260–261:

"It must be noted that in considering whether an apparent consent is unreal it is the mistake or misapprehension that makes it so. It is not the fraud producing the mistake which is material so much as the mistake itself. But if the mistake or misapprehension is not produced by the fraud of the man, there is logically room for the possibility that he was unaware of the woman's mistake so that a question of his mens rea may arise. So in *R* v *Lambert* (1919) VLR 205, Cussen J says: 'It is plain that, though in these cases the question of consent or non-consent is primarily referable to the mind of the woman, if she has really a mind, yet the mind of the man is also affected by the facts which indicate want of consent or possible want of capacity to consent'. For that reason it is easy to understand why the stress has been on the fraud. But that stress tends to distract the attention from the essential inquiry, namely, whether the consent is no consent because it is not directed to the nature and character of the act. The identity of the man and the character of the physical act that is done or proposed seem now clearly to be regarded as forming part of the nature and character of the act to which the woman's consent is directed. That accords with the principles governing mistake vitiating apparent manifestations of will in other chapters of the law.

In the present case the decision of the majority of the Full Court extends this conception beyond the identity of the physical act and the immediate conditions affecting its nature to an antecedent inducing cause – the existence of a valid marriage. In the history of bigamy that has never been done. The most heartless bigamist has not been considered guilty of rape. Mock marriages are no new thing. Before the Hardwicke Marriage Act it was a fraud easily devised and readily carried out. But there is no reported instance of an indictment for rape based on the fraudulent character of the ceremony. No indictment of rape was founded on such a fraud. Rape, as a capital felony, was defined with exactness, and although there has been some extension over the centuries in the ambit of the crime, it is quite wrong to bring within its operation forms of evil conduct because they wear some analogy to aspects of the crime and deserve punishment. The judgment of the majority of the Full Court of the Supreme Court goes upon the moral differences between marital intercourse and sexual relations without marriage. The difference is indeed so radical that it is apt to draw the mind away from the real question which is carnal knowledge without consent. It may well be true that the woman in the present case never intended to consent to the latter relationship. But, as was said before, the key to such a case as the present lies in remembering that it is the penetration of the woman's body without her consent to such penetration that makes the felony. The capital felony was not directed to fraudulent conduct inducing her consent. Frauds of that kind must be punished under other heads of the criminal law or not at all: they are not rape. To say that in the present case the facts which the jury must be taken to have found amount to wicked and heartless conduct on the part of the applicant is not enough to establish that he committed rape. To say that in having intercourse with him she supposed that she was concerned in a perfectly moral act is not to say that the intercourse was without her consent. To return to the central point; rape is carnal knowledge of a woman without her consent; carnal knowledge is the physical fact of penetration; it is the consent to that which is in question; such a consent demands a perception as to what is about to take place, as to the identity of the man and the character of what he is doing. But once the consent is comprehending and actual the inducing causes cannot destroy its reality and leave the man guilty of rape."

Respectfully applying those dicta to the facts of the present case, the prostitute here consented to sexual intercourse with the appellant. The reality of that consent is not destroyed by being induced by the appellant's false pretence that his intention was to pay the agreed price of £25 for her services. Therefore, he was not guilty of rape.

If anything, the appellant was guilty of an offence under section 3 of the Act of 1956 which was not an alternative that was put to this jury.

In our judgment, the appeal must be allowed, and the conviction and sentence quashed.'

R v Mandair [1994] 2 WLR 700 House of Lords (Lords Mackay, Templeman, Goff, Browne-Wilkinson and Mustill)

Causing grievous bodily harm – whether a lesser included offence available

Facts
The defendant's wife suffered severe facial burns caused by sulphuric acid. The prosecution case was that he had thrown the acid at her. The defendant contended that the burns had been caused accidentally. On a charge of causing grievous bodily harm with intent contrary to s18 of the Offences Against the Person Act 1861, the jury (following guidance from the trial judge) returned a verdict of guilty on an alternative count of '... causing grievous bodily harm contrary to s20 ...' The defendant appealed successfully on the basis that he had been convicted of an offence unknown to law. The Crown appealed.

Held (Lord Mustill dissenting)
The appeal would be allowed as regards the availability of an alternative verdict under s20. The case would be remitted to the Court of Appeal for consideration of the remaining grounds of appeal (which related to the proper direction on mens rea under s20).

Lord Mackay:

'In my view "cause" in section 18 is certainly sufficiently wide to embrace any method by which grievous bodily harm could be inflicted under section 20 and since causing grievous bodily harm in section 18 is an alternative to wounding I regard it as clear that the word "cause" in section 18 is wide enough to include any action that could amount to inflicting grievous bodily harm under section 20 where the word "inflict" appears as an alternative to "wound". For this reason, in my view, following the reasoning of this House in *R v Wilson (Clarence)* [1984] AC 242 an alternative verdict under section 20 was open on the terms of this indictment.

The Court of Appeal in this case, following an earlier decision in *R v Field* (1992) 97 Cr App R 357, held that the jury had found the defendant guilty of an offence unknown to the law.

In my opinion, as I have said, the word "cause" is wider or at least not narrower than the word "inflict". I consider that the verdict of causing grievous bodily harm contrary to section 20 must be construed as a whole ... Since, as I said, causing grievous bodily harm is used in a sense which distinguishes it from wounding, I can read the verdict as a whole only as meaning that the causing of grievous bodily harm was contrary to section 20 in that it consisted of inflicting grievous bodily harm upon another person. Obviously it is highly desirable in matters of this sort involving the liberty of the subject that the precise words of the statute, so far as relevant, should be used in the jury's verdict but where, as here, the jury has actually returned a verdict which to my mind read as a whole is capable of having a clear meaning it is a technicality to decline to give it meaning because the word "cause" is not used in the section and thereby it is said that the defendant was convicted of an offence unknown to the law. A contravention of section 20 is certainly not an offence unknown to the law and I consider that in the circumstances in which the phrase was used "causing grievous bodily harm contrary to section 20" is perfectly comprehensible as meaning that an infliction of grievous bodily harm in what the defendant did in causing grievous bodily harm was a contravention of section 20.'

Lord Mustill:

'The reappearance of section 20 before your Lordships' House barely two years after it was minutely examined in *R v Parmenter* [1992] 1 AC 699 demonstrates once again that this unsatisfactory statute is long overdue for repeal and replacement by legislation which is soundly based in logic and expressed in language which everyone can understand. Meanwhile we must make of sections 18 and 20, those staples of the Crown Court, the best that we can ... The point is very short and I cannot develop it beyond submitting that whereas in the case of both words there must be a causal connection between the defendant's act and the injury, in the case of the "cause" the nature of the connection is immaterial (provided the chain of events is short enough to satisfy the criminal law of causation), but the word "inflict" conveys the idea of a direct and immediate doing of harm. It is true that in *R v Martin* (1881) 8 QBD 54 and *R v Halliday* (1889) 61 LT 701 injuries suffered when the frightened victim was attempting to escape were assumed to bring the case within section 20; but the point was not raised. On the other hand *R v Clarence* (1888) 22 QBD 23, *R v McCready* [1978] 1 WLR 1376 (which on this point I believe to have survived *Wilson*) and *R v Salisbury* [1976] VR 452, an Australian decision which (if correctly read his speech) was approved by Lord Roskill in *Wilson*, support the narrow reading of "inflict". Opinions to the same effect are contained in the 14th Report of the Criminal Law Revision Committee, Offences against the Person (1980) (Cmnd 7844), pp69–70, para 153; the Report of the Law Commission on Offences against the Person (1993) (Law Com No 218), p18, para 12.15, fn 112; *Archbold, Criminal Pleading Evidence & Practice,* 45th ed, vol 2 (1994), p210, para 19–208, *Smith & Hogan, Criminal Law,* 7th ed (1992) pp425–426; and a case note by Professor JC Smith (as he then was) on *R v Snewing* [1972] Crim LR 267. In addition, this reading was taken for granted by the court in *Field*, in the passage already quoted. Thus, although the distinction is undoubtedly very narrow and often of no practical significance I believe that is none the less real, and therefore reject the submission that the words used by the clerk "causing grievous bodily harm" have exactly the same meaning as "inflicting grievous bodily harm", and that the hypothetical verdicts conveyed by the response of guilty to the two versions of the clerk's question will not have exactly the same meaning.'

R v Miller [1954] 2 QB 282 Hampshire Assizes (Lynskey J)

Meaning of actual bodily harm

Facts

The defendant was charged with raping his wife and assault contrary to s47. Lynskey J directed the jury on the assault charge in the following terms:

'The point has been taken that there is no evidence of bodily harm. The bodily harm alleged is said to be the result of the prisoner's actions, and that is, if the jury accept the evidence, that he threw the wife down three times. There is evidence that afterwards she was in a hysterical and nervous condition, but it is said by counsel that that is not actual bodily harm. Actual bodily harm, according to Archbold, 32nd ed, p959, includes "any hurt or injury calculated to interfere with the health or comfort of the prosecutor." There was a time when shock was not regarded as bodily hurt, but the day has gone by when that could be said. It seems to me now that if a person is caused hurt or injury resulting, not in any physical injury, but in an injury to her state of mind for the time being, that is within the definition of actual bodily harm, and on that point I would leave the case to the jury.'

Held
The defendant was acquitted of rape on the basis of his wife's deemed consent, but was convicted of the assault.

R v *Mowatt* [1968] 1 QB 421 Court of Appeal (Criminal Division) (Diplock LJ, Brabin and Waller JJ)

Meaning of 'malicious' under s20 Offences Against the Person Act 1861

Facts
The defendant was convicted under s20 of the Offences Against the Person Act 1861 following an attack he had carried out on a police officer, during which he had rained blows on the officer's face and pushed him roughly to the ground. The defendant appealed on the ground that the trial judge had failed to give an adequate direction to the jury as to the meaning of 'maliciously'.

Held
The appeal would be dismissed.

Diplock LJ:

> 'In the offence under section 20 ... the word "maliciously" does import upon the part of the person who unlawfully inflicts the wound or other grievous bodily harm an awareness that his act may have the consequence of causing some physical harm to some other person. That is what is meant by "the particular kind of harm"; in the citation from Professor Kenny. It is quite unnecessary that the accused should have foreseen that his unlawful act might cause physical harm of the gravity described in the section, ie a wound or serious physical injury. It is enough that he should have foreseen that some physical harm to some person, albeit of a minor character, might result.
>
> In many cases in instructing a jury upon a charge under section 20 ... it may be unnecessary to refer specifically to the word "maliciously".... Where the evidence for the prosecution, if accepted, shows that the physical act of the accused which caused the injury to another person was a direct assault which any ordinary person would be bound to realise was likely to cause some physical harm to the other person (as, for instance, an assault with a weapon or the boot or violence with the hands) and the defence put forward on behalf of the accused is not that the assault was accidental or that he did not realise that it might cause some physical harm to the victim, but is some other defence such as that he did not do the alleged act or that he did it in self-defence, it is unnecessary to deal specifically in the summing-up with what is meant by the word "maliciously" in the section. It can only confuse the jury.'

R v *Olugboja* [1981] 3 WLR 585 (Dunn LJ, Milmo and May JJ)

Rape – consent – direction to the jury

Facts
The appellant was convicted of raping the complainant, J. The point of law raised in the appeal was stated by Dunn LJ as being:

> '... whether to constitute the offence of rape it is necessary for the consent of the victim of sexual intercourse to be vitiated by force, the fear of force, or fraud; or whether it is sufficient to prove that in fact the victim did not consent.'

Held
The appeal would be dismissed.

Dunn LJ (having considered the Report of the Heilbron group (Cmnd 6352), and the CLRC Working Paper on Sexual Offences (1980)):

> 'Although "consent" is [a] common word it covers a wide range of states of mind in the context of intercourse between a man and a woman, ranging from actual desire on the one hand to reluctant acquiescence on the other. We do not think that the issue of consent should be left to a jury without some further direction. What this should be will depend on the circumstances of each case. The jury will have been reminded of the burden and standard of proof required to establish each ingredient, including lack of consent, of the offence. They should be directed that consent, or the absence of it, is to be given its ordinary meaning and if need be, by way of example, that there is a difference between consent and submission; every consent involves a submission, but it by no means follows that a mere submission involves consent: per Coleridge J in *R v Day* 9 C & P 722, 724. In the majority of cases, where the allegation is that the intercourse was had by force or the fear of force, such a direction coupled with specific references to, and comments on, the evidence relevant to the absence of real consent will clearly suffice. In the less common type of case where intercourse takes place after threats not involving violence or the fear of it, as in the examples given by Mrs Trewella [counsel for the appellant] to which we have referred earlier in this judgment, we think that an appropriate direction to a jury will have to be fuller. They should be directed to concentrate on the state of mind of the victim immediately before the act of sexual intercourse, having regard to all the relevant circumstances; and in particular, the events leading up to the act and her reaction to them showing their impact on her mind. Apparent acquiescence after penetration does not necessarily involve consent, which must have occurred before the act takes place. In addition to the general direction about consent which we have outlined, the jury will probably be helped in such cases by being reminded that in this context consent does comprehend the wide spectrum of states of mind to which we earlier referred, and that the dividing line in such circumstances between real consent on the one hand and mere submission on the other may not be easy to draw. Where it is to be drawn in a given case is for the jury to decide, applying their combined good sense, experience and knowledge of human nature and modern behaviour to all the relevant facts of that case.
>
> Looked at in this way we find no misdirection by the judge in this case.'

R v Savage; R v Parmenter [1991] 3 WLR 914 House of Lords (Lord Keith, Lord Brandon, Lord Ackner, Lord Jauncey and Lord Lowry)

Mens rea for s20: mens rea for s47

R v Savage

Facts

The appellant was charged with unlawful wounding contrary to s20 of the Offences Against the Persons Act 1861. The case for the prosecution was that there had been bad feeling between the appellant and another young woman (Miss Beal) that the appellant had approached this other woman and thrown the contents of an almost full pint glass of beer at her, and that she had let go of the glass which broke, with the result that Miss Beal suffered cuts. The appellant admitted that it had been her intention to throw the beer over Miss Beal but denied any intention to cut her with the glass. The trial judge directed the jury that they were entitled to conclude that the appellant had wounded 'maliciously' if they were sure that her unlawful act in throwing the liquid from the glass caused it to slip from her hand and cut Miss Beal. The appellant's appeal against the conviction under s20 was allowed, but a conviction for assault occasioning actual bodily harm contrary to s47 of the Offences Against the Persons Act 1861 was substituted. The following question was certified for consideration by the House of Lords:

> '(1) Whether a verdict of guilty of assault occasioning actual bodily harm is a permissible alternative verdict on a count alleging unlawful wounding contrary to s20 of the Offences against the Persons Act

1861. (2) Whether a verdict of guilty of assault occasioning actual bodily harm can be returned upon proof of an assault and of the fact that actual bodily harm was occasioned by the assault. (3) If it is proved that an assault has been committed and that actual bodily harm has resulted from that assault, whether a verdict of assault occasioning actual bodily harm may be returned in the absence of proof that the defendant intended to cause some actual bodily harm or was reckless as to whether such harm would be caused.'

R v *Parmenter*

Facts
The appellant was charged with four offences of inflicting grievous bodily harm contrary to s20 of the Offences Against the Persons Act 1861 in respect of injuries caused to his three month old son as a result of rough handling on his part. It was contended for the appellant at his trial that he had not had the intent required for the offence, given his lack of experience with small babies. Expert evidence suggested that the handling of the child would not have been inappropriate in the case of a three to four year old child but that it would have been quite inappropriate as regards a new born baby.

On the issue of intent the trial judge directed the jury, inter alia, that it was unnecessary that the accused should have foreseen that his unlawful act might cause physical harm in the form of grievous bodily harm. The jury were directed that it was sufficient that the appellant should have foreseen that some physical harm to some person, albeit of a minor character, might result from his actions. The appellant appealed successfully against his conviction, and the Crown appealed to the House of Lords. The following question was certified for consideration by the House of Lords:

'(1)(a) Whether in order to establish an offence under s20 of the Offences Against the Person Act 1861 the prosecution must prove that the defendant actually foresaw that his act would cause the particular kind of harm which was in fact caused, or whether it is sufficient to prove that (objectively) he ought so to have foreseen. (b) The like question in relation to s47 of the Act. (2)(a) For the purposes of the answer to question (1)(a), whether the particular kind of harm to be foreseen may be any physical harm, or harm of (i) the nature, or (ii) the degree, or (iii) the nature and the degree of the harm which actually occurred? (b) the like question in relation to s47 of the Act.'

R v *Savage*

Held
The appeal would be dismissed.

R v *Parmenter*

Held
The Crown's appeal would be allowed to the extent that a verdict of guilty of assault occasioning actual bodily harm contrary to s47 would be substituted for the conviction under s20.

Lord Ackner:

Given the overlap in the questions certified in both cases, Lord Ackner elected to deal with the issues raised seriatim. His Lordship had observed that in order for the first question certified in the *Savage* appeal to be decided in the appellant's favour, the House would have to depart from its own previous decision in *R* v *Wilson* [1984] AC 242 extracted later in this chapter. Lord Ackner quoted at length from the speech of Lord Roskill in *R* v *Wilson* and concluded:

'Having reviewed the relevant authorities Lord Roskill was content to accept that there can be an infliction of grievous bodily harm contrary to s20 without an assault being committed. For example, grievous bodily harm could be inflicted by creating panic. Another example provided to your Lordships in the course of the argument in the current appeals was interfering with the braking mechanism of a car, so as to cause the driver to be involved in an accident and thus suffer injuries. These are somewhat far-fetched examples. The allegation of inflicting grievous bodily harm or for that matter wounding, as was observed by Glidewell LJ, giving the judgment of the court in the *Savage* case [1991] 2 WLR 418, 421, inevitably imports or includes an allegation of assault, unless there are some quite extraordinary facts.

The critical question remained – do the allegations in a s20 charge "include either expressly or by implication" allegations of assault occasioning actual bodily harm. As to this, Lord Roskill concluded [1984] AC 247, 261:

> "If 'inflicting' can, as the cases show, include 'inflicting by assault,' then even though such a charge may not necessarily do so, I do not for myself see why on a fair reading of s6(3) these allegations do not at least impliedly *include* 'inflicting by assault.' That is sufficient for present purposes though I also regard it as also a possible view that those former allegations *expressly* include the other allegations."

I respectfully agree with this reasoning and accordingly reject the submission that *R v Wilson* was wrongly decided. I would therefore answer the first of the certified questions in the *Savage* case in the affirmative. A verdict of guilty of assault occasioning actual bodily harm is a permissible alternative verdict on a count alleging unlawful wounding contrary to s20 of the Offences Against the Persons Act 1861.

[2] *Can a verdict of assault occasioning actual bodily harm be returned upon proof of an assault together with proof of the fact that actual bodily harm was occasioned by the assault, or must the prosecution also prove that the defendant intended to cause some actual bodily harm or was reckless as to whether such harm would be caused?*

Your Lordships are concerned with the mental element of a particular kind of assault, an assault "occasioning actual bodily harm." It is common ground that the mental element of assault is an intention to cause the victim to apprehend immediate and unlawful violence or recklessness whether such apprehension be caused: see *R v Venna* [1976] QB 421. It is of course common ground that Mrs Savage committed an assault upon Miss Beal when she threw the contents of her glass of beer over her. It is also common ground that however the glass came to be broken and Miss Beal's wrist thereby cut, it was, on the finding of the jury, Mrs Savage's handling of the glass which caused Miss Beal "actual bodily harm." Was the offence thus established or is there a further mental state that has to be established in relation to the bodily harm element of the offence? Clearly the section, by its terms, expressly imposes no such a requirement. Does it do so by necessary implication? It neither uses the word "intentionally" or "maliciously" The words "occasioning actual bodily harm" are descriptive of the word "assault," by reference to a particular kind of consequence.

In neither *Savage*, nor *Spratt*, nor in *Parmenter*, was the court's attention invited to the decision of the Court of Appeal in *R v Roberts* (1971) 56 Cr App R 95. This is perhaps explicable on the basis that this case is not referred to in the index to the current, edition of *Archbold, Criminal Pleading, Evidence and Practice*, 43rd ed (1988). The relevant text, at para 20-117 states: "The mens rea required [for actual bodily harm] is that required for common assault" without any authority being provided for this proposition.

It is in fact *Roberts'* case which provides authority for this proposition.'

Lord Ackner recited the facts of the case and the reasoning of the Court of Appeal (extracted later in this chapter), and concluded:

'Thus once the assault was established, the only remaining question was whether the victim's conduct was the natural consequence of that assault. The words "occasioning" raised solely a question of causation, an objective question which does not involve inquiring into the accused's state of mind. In *R v Spratt* [1990] 1 WLR 1073 McCowan LJ said, at p1082:

> "However, the history of the interpretation of the Act of 1861 shows that, whether or not the word 'maliciously' appears in the section in question, the courts have consistently held that the mens rea of every type of offence against the person covers both actual intent and recklessness, in the sense of taking the risk of harm ensuing with foresight that it might happen."

McCowan LJ then quotes a number of authorities for that proposition. The first is *R v Ward* (1872) LR 1 CCR 356, but that was a case where the prisoner was charged with wounding with intent (s18) and convicted of malicious wounding (s20); next, *R v Bradshaw* (1878) 14 Cox CC 83, but that was a case where the accused was charged with manslaughter, which has nothing to do with a s47 case. Then *R v Cunningham* [1957] 2 QB 396, is quoted, a case under s23 of the Act concerned with unlawfully and maliciously administering, etc, a noxious thing which endangers life. And finally *R v Venna* [1976] QB 421 in which there was no issue as to whether in a s47 case, recklessness had to extend to actual bodily harm. Thus, none of the cases cited were concerned with the mental element required in s47 cases. Nevertheless, the Court of Appeal in *R v Parmenter* [1991] 2 WLR 408, 415, preferred the decision in *R v Spratt* [1990] 1 WLR 1073 to that of *R v Savage (Note)* [1991] 2 WLR 418 because the former was "founded on a line of authority leading directly to the conclusion there expressed."

My Lords, in my respectful view, the Court of Appeal in *Parmenter* were wrong in preferring the decision in *Spratt*'s case. The decision in *Roberts*' case, 56 Cr App R 95 was correct. The verdict of assault occasioning actual bodily harm may be returned upon proof of an assault together with proof of the fact that actual bodily harm was occasioned by the assault. The prosecution are not obliged to prove that the defendant intended to cause some actual bodily harm or was reckless as to whether such harm would be caused.

[3] *In order to establish an offence under s20 of the Act, must the prosecution prove that the defendant actually foresaw that his act would cause harm, or is it sufficient to prove that he ought so to have foreseen?*

Although your Lordships' attention has been invited to a plethora of decided cases, the issue is a narrow one. Is the decision of the Court of Criminal Appeal in *R v Cunningham* [1957] 2 QB 396 still good law, subject only to a gloss placed upon it by the Court of Appeal Criminal Division in *R v Mowatt* [1968] 1 QB 421, or does the later decision of your Lordships' House in *R v Caldwell* [1982] AC 341 provide the answer to this question? These three decisions require detailed consideration.'

Lord Ackner related the salient details of the Court of Appeal's decision in *R v Cunningham* [1957] 2 QB 396, and continued:

'Mr Sedley (counsel for Parmenter) has not invited your Lordships to reconsider the majority decision of your Lordships' House (in *R v Caldwell*). He chose a much less ambitious task. He submits that *R v Cunningham* cannot be bad law, since it is inconceivable that your Lordships' House, in its majority judgement, would have steered such a careful path around it. Your Lordships having power to overrule it, would, so he submits, have felt obliged to do so in order to avoid creating a false double standard of "recklessness." He further submits that it is significant that Lord Diplock, whose speech represented the views of the majority of your Lordships, nowhere suggests that his own judgment in *R v Mowatt* [1968] 1 QB 421 which clarified or modified *Cunningham*, was of doubtful validity.

In the light of these submissions it is necessary to deal in some detail with the *Caldwell* decision [1982] AC 341.'

Lord Ackner then proceeded to detail the facts of the case, and referred at length to the speech of Lord Diplock, and the judgment of Diplock LJ (as he then was in the Court of Appeal in *R v Mowatt* [1968] 1 QB 421. Lord Ackner concluded:

'Mr Sedley submitted that in *Caldwell*'s case your Lordships' House could have followed either of two possible paths to its conclusion as to the meaning of "recklessly" in the Act of 1971. These were: (a) to hold that *Cunningham* (and *Mowatt*) were wrongly decided and to introduce a single test, wherever recklessness was an issue; or (b) to accept that *Cunningham*, (subject to the *Mowatt* "gloss" to which no reference was made), correctly states the law in relation to the Offences Against the Person Act 1861, because the word "maliciously" in that statute was a term of legal art which imported into the concept of recklessness a special restricted meaning, thus distinguishing it from "reckless" or "recklessly" in modern "revising" statutes then before the House, where those words bore their then popular or dictionary meaning.

I agree with Mr Sedley that manifestly it was the latter course which the House followed. Therefore in order to establish an offence under s20 the prosecution must prove either the defendant intended or that he actually foresaw that his act would cause harm.

[4] *In order to establish an offence under s20 is it sufficient to prove that the defendant intended or foresaw the risk of some physical harm or must he intend or foresee either wounding or grievous bodily harm?*

It is convenient to set out once again the relevant part of the judgment of Diplock LJ in *R v Mowatt* [1968] 1 QB 421, 426. Having considered Professor Kenny's statement, which I have quoted above, he then said:

"In the offence under s20 ... for ... which [no] specific intent is required, the word 'maliciously' does import ... an awareness that his act may have the consequence of causing some physical harm to some other person. That is what is meant by 'the particular kind of harm' in the citation from Professor Kenny. It is quite unnecessary that the accused should have foreseen that his unlawful act might cause physical harm of the gravity described in the section, ie, a wound or serious physical injury. *It is enough that he should have foreseen that some physical harm to some person, albeit of a minor character, might result.*" (Emphasis added.)

Mr Sedley submits that this statement of the law is wrong. He contends that properly construed, the section requires foresight of a wounding or grievous bodily harm. He drew your Lordships' attention to criticisms of the *Mowatt* decision made by Professor Glanville-Williams and by Professor JC Smith in their text books and in articles or commentaries. They argue that a person should not be criminally liable for consequences of his conduct unless he foresaw a consequence falling into the same legal category as that set out in the indictment.

Such a general principle runs contrary to the decision in *Roberts'* case, 56 Cr App R 95 which I have already stated to be, in my opinion, correct. The contention is apparently based on the proposition that as the actus reus of a s20 offence is the wounding or the infliction of grievous bodily harm, the mens rea must consist of foreseeing such wounding or grievous bodily harm. But there is no such hard and fast principle. To take but two examples, the actus reus of murder is the killing of the victim, but foresight of grievous bodily harm is sufficient and indeed, such bodily harm, need not be such as to be dangerous to life. Again, in the case of manslaughter, death is frequently the unforeseen consequence of the violence used.

The argument that as s20 and s47 have both the same penalty, this somehow supports the proposition that the foreseen consequences must coincide with the harm actually done, overlooks the oft repeated statement that this is the irrational result of this piecemeal legislation. The Act "is a rag-bag of offences brought together from a wide variety of sources with no attempt, as the draftsman frankly acknowledged, to introduce consistency as to substance or as to form." (Professor Smith in his commentary on *R v Parmenter* [1991] CLR 43.)

If s20 was to be limited to cases where the accused does not desire but does foresee wounding or grievous bodily harm, it would have a very limited scope. The mens rea in a s20 crime is comprised in the word "maliciously." As was pointed out by Lord Lane CJ, giving the judgment of the Court of Appeal in *R v Sullivan* on 27 October 1980 (unreported save in [1981] Crim LR 46) the "particular kind of harm" in the citation from Professor Kenny was directed to "harm to the person" as opposed to "harm to property." Thus it was not concerned with the degree of the harm foreseen. It is accordingly in my judgment wrong to look upon the decision in *Mowatt* [1968] 1 QB 421 as being in any way inconsistent with the decision in *Cunningham* [1957] 2 QB 396.

My Lords, I am satisfied that the decision in *Mowatt* was correct and that it is quite unnecessary that the accused should either have intended or have foreseen that his unlawful act might cause physical harm of the gravity described in s20, ie a wound or serious physical injury. It is enough that he should have foreseen that some physical harm to some person, albeit of a minor character, might result.

In the result I would dismiss the appeal in *Savage's* case, but allow the appeal in *Parmenter's* case, but only to the extent of substituting, in accordance with the provisions of s3(2) of the Criminal Appeal Act 1968, verdicts of guilty of assault occasioning actual bodily harm contrary to s47 of the Act for the four s20 offences of which he was convicted.'

R v Spratt [1990] 1 WLR 1073 Court of Appeal (Criminal Division) (McCowan LJ, Tudor Evans and Brooke JJ)

Mens rea for s47 assault

Facts

The appellant had fired an air pistol from the window of his dwelling into a courtyard below. He claimed that he had been aiming at a sign. A pellet from the gun struck a child playing in the yard. The appellant denied any knowledge that children were in the vicinity of the sign. The appellant was charged with actual bodily harm contrary to s47 of the Offences Against the Persons Act 1861. Following defence counsel's advice that *Caldwell* recklessness now applied to the offence, the appellant pleaded guilty. He had stated in interview, however, that he would not have fired the gun had he known children were playing close by. The appellant appealed initially against the sentence imposed, but in the course of the appeal sought to challenge the conviction on the basis that he had pleaded guilty following erroneous advice from counsel. He contended that the recklessness applicable to s47 was that expounded in *R v Cunningham*, and on that basis he would have pleaded not guilty.

Held

The appeal would be allowed.

McCowan LJ [having referred to ss20 and 47 of the 1861 Act, and the definition of recklessness relied upon by Byrne J in *R v Cunningham* (1957) Cr App R 155 at 159, continued]:

> 'We turn to consider recklessness under section 47. In *R v Bradshaw* (1878) 14 Cox CC 83, the accused was charged with manslaughter arising from what he had done to a member of the opposing team in a game of football. In summing up to the jury Bramwell LJ said, at pp84-85:
>
>> "The question for you to decide is whether the death of the deceased was caused by the unlawful act of the prisoner ... if the prisoner intended to cause serious hurt to the deceased, or if he knew that, in charging as he did, he might produce serious injury and was indifferent and reckless as to whether he would produce serious injury or not, then the act would be unlawful. In either case he would be guilty of a criminal act and you must find him guilty; if you are of a contrary opinion you will acquit him."
>
> "Recklessness" was there defined in a manner consistent with that in the case of *R v Cunningham*. In *R v Venna* [1976] QB 421 the charge was one of assault occasioning actual bodily harm. Police officers called to the scene of a street disturbance had sought to arrest the accused. He resisted violently and in the process went to the ground where two officers held him by the arm. He continued to kick and, in so doing, fractured the hand of one of the officers. The trial judge summed up in these terms (see pp 427–428:
>
>> "If he lashes out with his feet, knowing that there are officers about him and knowing that by lashing out he will probably or is likely to kick somebody or hurt his hand by banging his heel down on it, then he is equally guilty of the offence. Venna can therefore be guilty of the offence in count 3 in the indictment if he deliberately brought his foot down on Police Constable Spencer's hand or if he lashed out simply reckless as to who was there, not caring an iota as to whether he kicked somebody or brought his heel down on his hands."
>
> Giving the judgment of the court, James LJ referred, at p428, to the fact that counsel for Crown had
>
>> "sought support from the distinction between the offences which are assaults and offences which by statute include the element contained in the 'maliciously', eg unlawful and malicious wounding contrary to section 20 of the Offences Against the Person Act 1861, in which recklessness will suffice to support the charge: see *R v Cunningham* [1957] 2 QB 396".
>
> A little later James LJ continued, at pp428–429:

> "*R v Bradshaw* (1878) 14 Cox CC 83 can be read as supporting the view that unlawful physical force applied recklessly constitutes a criminal assault. In our view the element of mens rea in the offence of battery is satisfied by proof that the defendant intentionally or recklessly applied force to the person of another. If it were otherwise the strange consequence would be that an offence of unlawful wounding contrary to section 20 of the Offences Against the Person Act 1861 could be established by proof that the defendant wounded the victim either intentionally or recklessly but, if the victim's skin was not broken and the offence was therefore laid as an assault occasioning actual bodily harm contrary to s47 of the Act, it would be necessary to prove that the physical force was intentionally applied.

We see no reason in logic or in law why a person who recklessly applies physical force to the person of another should be outside the criminal law of assault. In many cases the dividing line between intention and recklessness is barely distinguishable. This is such a case. In our judgment the direction was right in law and this ground of appeal fails."

As Mr Arlidge concedes, if this case is still good law, the *Cunningham* test lies to both section 20 and section 23 type cases on the one hand and to section 47 type cases on the other. He argues that while still applying to section 20 and section 23, it no longer applies to section 47. To adapt the words of James LJ, the strange consequence, if he is right, would be that when directing a jury in a case containing counts both under section 47 and section 20, the judge would have to try to explain the *Caldwell* test to the jury (a notoriously difficult task) under section 47 and then go on to tell the jury that they must apply a completely different test under section 20.

Next we must consider *R v Majewski* [1977] AC 443. In this case the appellant had been charged with assault occasioning actual bodily harm and assault on a police officer in the execution of his duty. His defence was that when the offences were committed he was suffering from the effect of alcohol and drugs. The trial judge directed the jury that self-induced intoxication by drink and drugs could not be a defence and the House of Lords upheld that direction. The importance of this case in the present context is what Lord Elwyn-Jones LC, had to say about *R v Venna* at p474 respectively:

> "If a man of his own volition takes a substance which causes him to cast off the restraints of reason and conscience, no wrong is done to him by holding him answerable criminally for any injury he may do while in that condition. His course of conduct in reducing himself by drugs and drink to that condition in my view supplies the evidence of mens rea, of guilty mind certainly sufficient for crimes of basic intent. It is a reckless course of conduct and recklessness is enough to constitute the necessary mens rea in assault cases: see *R v Venna* [1976] QB 421 per James LJ at p314 and p429. Drunkenness is itself an intrinsic, an integral part of the crime, the other part being the evidence of the unlawful use of force against the victim. Together they add up to criminal recklessness. On this I adopt the conclusion of Stroud in 1920, 36 LQR 273 that: 'it would be contrary to all principle and authority to suppose that drunkenness' (and what is true of drunkenness can equally be true of intoxication by drugs) 'can be a defence for crime in general on the ground that "a person cannot be convicted of a crime unless the mens was rea". By allowing himself to get drunk, and thereby putting himself in such a condition as to be no longer amenable to the law's commands, a man shows such regardlessness as amounts to mens rea for the purpose of all ordinary crimes.' This approach is in line with the American Model Penal Code (s2.08(2)): 'When recklessness establishes an element of the offence, if the actor, due to self-induced intoxication is unaware of a risk of which he would have been aware had he been sober, such unawareness is immaterial.' "

There is no suggestion there or elsewhere in the speeches in the House of criticism of the decision in R v Venna.

That takes us on to *R v Caldwell* [1982] AC 341. [His Lordship referred in detail to Lord Diplock's analysis of *Cunningham* recklessness to be found at pp351–354, and Lord Diplock's analysis, at pp355, of the speech of Lord Elwyn-Jones LC in *DPP v Majewski* (1976) 62 Cr App R 262.]

It is plain from this passage that *R v Venna*, far from having been overruled by the House of Lords in *R v Majewski* or for that matter in *R v Caldwell*, has been approved by it.

In *R v Lawrence* [1982] AC 510, which was a case under a section of the Road Traffic Act 1972, as substituted by s50(1) of the Criminal Law Act 1977, which provided that 'a person who causes the death of another person by driving a motor vehicle on a road recklessly shall be guilty of an offence'. The House of Lords held that an appropriate direction to a jury on what was meant by driving recklessly would be that they had to be satisfied (a) that the defendant was in fact driving the vehicle in such a manner as to create an obvious and serious risk of causing physical injury to some other person who might happen to be using the road or of doing substantial damage to property and (b) that in driving in that manner the defendant did so without having given any thought to the possibility of there being any such risk or, having recognised that there was some risk involved, had nonetheless gone on to take it.

Mr Arlidge founds his argument before us on some words in the speech of Lord Roskill with which their Lordships all agreed in *R v Seymour* [1983] 2 AC 493. There the defendant was prepared to plead guilty to the offence of causing death by reckless driving contrary to section 1 of the Act of 1972, but the prosecution refused to accept that plea, preferring to obtain a jury's verdict upon the only count charged in the indictment, that being manslaughter. The defendant appealed on the ground that the trial judge had misdirected the jury in that where manslaughter was charged, and the charge arose out of the reckless driving of the defendant on the highway, the direction propounded in *R v Lawrence* [1982] AC 510 was inadequate and that in such circumstances the jury should be directed that the prosecution must further prove that the defendant recognised that some risk was involved and had nevertheless proceeded to take that risk. The Court of Appeal (Criminal Division) [1983] RTR 202 and the House of Lords [1983] 2 AC 493 dismissed the defendant's appeals.

The passage relied upon by Mr Arlidge is to be found at where Lord Roskill said, at p506:

"My Lords, I would accept the submision of Mr Hamilton for the Crown that once it is shown that the two offences co-exist it would be quite wrong to give the adjective 'reckless' or the adverb 'recklessly' a different meaning according to whether the statutory or the common law offence is charged. 'Reckless' should today be given the same meaning in relation to all offences which involve 'recklessness' as one of the elements unless Parliament has otherwise ordained."

The words "unless Parliament has otherwise ordained" may well have been intended to refer not only to modern Acts of Parliament which use the word "recklessly" but also to the Act of 1861 where the word "maliciously" is used. However, the history of the interpretation of the Act of 1861 shows that, whether or not the word "maliciously" appears in the section in question, the courts have consistently held that the mens rea of every type of offence against the person covers both actual intent and recklessness, in the sense of taking the risk of harm ensuing with foresight that it might happen: see *R v Ward* (1872) 1 CCR 356; *R v Bradshaw*, 14 Cox CC 83, *R v Cunningham* [1957] 2 QB 396 and *R v Venna* [1976] QB 421. Hence, according to judicial interpretation of the Act of 1861, these are all instances where Parliament "has otherwise ordained".

The sentence: "'Reckless' should today be given the same meaning in relation to all offences which involve 'recklessness' as one of the elements unless Parliament has otherwise ordained" seems to us to be obiter. In any event we cannot believe that by the use of those words their Lordships intended to cast any doubt either upon the decision in *R v Cunningham* [1957] 2 QB 396or, more importantly for present purposes, upon the decision in *R v Venna* [1976] QB 421 which was approved by the House of Lords in both *R v Majewski* [1977] AC 443 and *R v Caldwell* [1982] AC 341.

Finally, Mr Arlidge argues that while *R v Venna* [1976] QB 421 says that *Cunningham* recklessness will amount to guilt under section 47, it does not say that nothing else will do. In other words, it is now possible to add on failure to give thought to the possibility of risk as also qualifying for guilt. We do not accept that interpretation of the decision in *R v Venna*. Moreover, we are not attracted by what would be the consequence of accepting Mr Arlidge's argument, namely that responsibility for the offence of assault occasioning actual bodily harm (in respect of which Parliament used neither the word "maliciously" nor "recklessly") would be wider than for the offence of unlawful wounding (in respect of which Parliament used the word "maliciously").

Accordingly, we consider ourselves bound by the case of *R v Venna*. It follows that the basis upon which the appellant pleaded guilty does not amount to an offence in law. His appeal against conviction on count 2 must, therefore, be allowed and his conviction quashed.

We should, however, mention the case of *Director of Public Prosectuions v K (a minor)* [1990] 1

WLR 1067, in which a boy was charged with assault occasioning actual bodily harm but the justices dismissed the charge. The Divisional Court, applying the *Caldwell* test, allowed the appeal and remitted the case to the magistrates with a direction to convict. However, the point advanced in the present case was never taken before the Divisional Court and they were not referred to *R v Cunningham* or *R v Venna*. In consequence, that case was, in our judgment, wrongly decided.'

Commentary

Note that the court certified under s33(2) of the Criminal Appeal Act 1968, that the following point of law of general public importance was involved in its decision, viz 'When recklessness is relied upon as the mens rea for the offence of assault occasioning actual bodily harm contrary to s47 of the Offences Against the Person Act 1861, should it be defined by the test of (1) foreseeing that the particular kind of harm might be done and yet going on to take the risk of it, not caring about the possible consequences; and/or (2) failing to give any thought to the possibility of there being any such risk: or by some other test?' Leave to appeal to the House of Lords was refused.

See also *R v Savage*, above.

R v Venna [1975] QB 421

See Chapter 22.

R v Wilson [1983] 3 WLR 686 House of Lords (Lords Fraser, Elwyn-Jones, Edmund-Davies, Roskill and Brightman)

Whether 'inflicting' requires proof of an assault.

Facts

The defendant motorist had been involved in an argument with a pedestrian, which culminated in the defendant punching the pedestrian in the face. The defendant was charged under s20 of the 1861 Act, and the jury found him not guilty under this section, but guilty of the lesser offence under s47. The defendant appealed on the ground that it had not been open to the jury, under s6(3) of the Criminal Law Act 1967, to return such a verdict, because s47 was not a lesser included offence within s20 if the defendant's contention, that s20 did not require proof of an assault, was correct. The Court of Appeal quashed his conviction, but certified the following point of law for consideration by the House of Lords:

> 'Whether on a charge of inflicting grievous bodily harm contrary to s20 of the Offences Against the Persons Act 1861 it is open to a jury to return a verdict of not guilty as charged but guilty of assault occasioning actual bodily harm.'

Held

A defendant could be acquitted under s20 and instead be convicted under s47. The s20 charge did not have to 'necessarily' include an allegation of assault for this to be the case. It was sufficient for the purposes of s6(3) of the Criminal Law Act 1967 that the more serious charge against a defendant should expressly, or impliedly, amount to, or include, the lesser offence of which he had actually been convicted.

Lord Roskill:

> 'Stated briefly, the reason [for the Court of Appeal quashing the conviction of Wilson] was that the decision of the Court of Appeal (Criminal Division) in *R v Springfield* (1969) 53 Cr App R 608 made it impossible to justify a conviction for assault occasioning actual bodily harm, contrary to section 47 of the Offences Against the Person Act 1861, since the offence charged of "*inflicting* grievous bodily harm" did not, upon the authorities, *necessarily* include the offence of *assault* occasioning actual bodily harm. The emphasis added to these three words is mine.

'... In the present case, the issue to my mind is not whether the allegations in the section 20 charge, expressly or impliedly, *amount* to an allegation of a section 47 charge, for they plainly do not. The issue is whether they either expressly or impliedly *include* such an allegation. The answer to that question must depend upon what is expressly or impliedly *included* in a charge of "inflicting any grievous bodily harm" ...

What then, are the allegations expressly or impliedly included in a charge of "inflicting grievous bodily harm"? Plainly that allegation must, so far as physical injuries are concerned, at least impliedly if not indeed expressly, include the infliction of "actual harm" because infliction of the more serious injuries must include the infliction of the less serious injuries. But does the allegation of "inflicting" include an allegation of "assault"? The problem arises by reason of the fact that the relevant English case law has proceeded along two different paths. In one group it has, as has already been pointed out, been held that a verdict of assault was a possible alternative verdict of a charge of inflicting grievous bodily harm contrary to section 20. In the other group grievous bodily harm was said to have been inflicted without any assault having taken place, unless of course the offence of assault were to be given a much wider significance than is usually attached to it. This problem has been the subject of recent detailed analysis in the Supreme Court of Victoria in *R* v *Salisbury* [1976] VR 452. In a most valuable judgment – I most gratefully acknowledge the assistance I have derived from that judgment in preparing this speech – the full court drew attention, in relation to comparable legislation in Victoria, to the problems which arose from this divergence in the main stream of English authority. The problem with which your Lordships' House is now faced arose in *Salisbury* in a different way from the present appeals. There, the appellant was convicted of an offence against the Victoria equivalent of section 20. He appealed on the ground that the trial judge had refused to leave to the jury the possibility of convicting him on that single charge of assault occasioning actual bodily harm or of common assault. The full court dismissed the appeal on the ground that at common law these latter offences were not "necessarily included" in the offence of "inflicting grievous bodily harm." The reasoning leading to this conclusion is plain:

> "It may be that the somewhat different wording of section 20 of the English Act has played a part in bringing about the existence of the two lines of authority in England, but, be that as it may, we have come to the conclusion that, although the word "inflicts" ... does not have as wide a meaning as the word "causes" ... the word "inflicts" does have a wider meaning than it would have if it were construed so that inflicting grievous bodily harm always involved assaulting the victim. In our opinion, grievous bodily harm may be inflicted ... either where the accused has directly and violently "inflicted" it by assaulting the victim, or where the accused has "inflicted" it by doing something, intentionally, which, although it is not itself a direct application of force to the body of the victim, does directly result in force being applied violently to the body of the victim, so that he suffers grievous bodily harm. Hence, the lesser misdemeanours of assault occasioning actual bodily harm and common assault ... are not necessarily included in the misdemeanour of inflicting grievous bodily harm ..." (see p461).

This conclusion was reached after careful consideration of English authorities such as *R* v *Taylor*, LR 1 CCR 194; *R* v *Martin* (1881) 8 QBD 54; *R* v *Clarence* (1888) 22 QBD 23 and *R* v *Halliday* (1889) 6 TLR 109. My Lords, it would be idle to pretend that these cases are wholly consistent with each other ...

My Lords, I doubt any useful purpose would be served by further detailed analysis of these and other cases, since to do so would only be to repeat less felicitously what has already been done by the full court of Victoria in *Salisbury* [1976] VR 452. I am content to accept, as did the full court, that there can be an infliction of grievous bodily harm contrary to section 20 without an assault being committed. The critical question is, therefore, whether it being accepted that a charge of inflicting grievous bodily harm contrary to section 20 may not necessarily involve an allegation of assault, but may nonetheless do so, and in very many cases will involve such an allegation, the allegations in a section 20 charge "include either expressly or by implication" allegations of assault occasioning actual bodily harm. If "inflicting" can, as the cases show, *include* "inflicting by assault," then even though such a charge may not necessarily do so, I do not for myself see why these allegations do not at least impliedly include "inflicting by assault". That is sufficient for present purposes though I also regard it as a possible view that those former allegations *expressly* include the other allegations.'

24 Homicide I

R v Blaue [1975] 1 WLR 1411 Court of Appeal (Criminal Division) (Lawton LJ, Thompson and Shaw JJ)

The 'thin skull' rule

Facts

The defendant stabbed the victim, who was a Jehovah's Witness, 13 times. She was rushed to hospital where doctors diagnosed that she would need an immediate blood transfusion if her life was to be saved. The victim refused the necessary transfusion because it was against her religious beliefs. She died from her wounds shortly after. The defendant appealed against his conviction for manslaughter on the ground that the refusal of treatment had broken the chain of causation.

Held

The appeal would be dismissed.

Lawton LJ:

'... Towards the end of the trial and before the summing up started counsel on both sides made submissions as to how the case should be put to the jury. Counsel then appearing for the defendant invited the judge to direct the jury to acquit the defendant generally on the count of murder. His argument was that her refusal to have a blood transfusion had broken the chain of causation between the stabbing and her death. As an alternative he submitted that the jury should be left to decide whether the chain of causation had been broken. Mr Herrod submitted that the judge should direct the jury to convict, because no facts were in issue and when the law was applied to the facts there was only one possible verdict, namely, manslaughter by reason of diminished responsibility.

When the judge came to direct the jury on this issue he did so by telling them that they should apply their common sense. He then went on to tell them they would get some help from the cases to which counsel had referred in their speeches. He reminded them of what Lord Parker CJ had said in *R v Smith* [1959] 2 QB 35, 42 and what Maule J had said 133 years before in *R v Holland* (1841) 2 Mood. & R 351, 352. He placed particular reliance on what Maule J had said. The jury, he said, might find it "most material and most helpful." He continued:

> "This is one of those relatively rare cases, you may think, with very little option open to you but to reach the conclusion that was reached by your predecessors as members of the jury in *R v Holland*, namely, 'yes' to the question of causation that the stab was still, at the time of the girl's death, the operative cause of death – or a substantial cause of death. However, that is a matter for you to determine after you have withdrawn to consider your verdict."

Mr Comyn has criticised that direction on three grounds: first, because *R v Holland* should no longer be considered good law; secondly, because *R v Smith,* when rightly understood, does envisage the possibility of unreasonable conduct on the part of the victim breaking the chain of causation; and thirdly, because the judge in reality directed the jury to find causation proved although he used words which seemed to leave the issue open for them to decide.

In *R v Holland,* 2 Mood. & R 351, the defendant in the course of a violent assault, had injured one of his victim's fingers. A surgeon had advised amputation because of the danger to life through complications developing. The advice was rejected. A fortnight later the victim died of lockjaw. Maule J said at p352: "the real question is, whether in the end the wound inflicted by the prisoner was the cause of death". That distinguished judge left the jury to decide that question as did the judge in this case. They had to decide it as juries always do, by pooling their experience of life and using their common sense. They would not have been handicapped by a lack of training in dialectic or moral theology.

Maule J's direction to the jury reflected the common law's answer to the problem. He who inflicted an injury which resulted in death could not excuse himself by pleading that his victim could have avoided death by taking greater care of himself: see *Hale's Pleas of the Crown* (1800 ed), pp427-428. The common law in Sir Matthew Hale's time probably was in line with contemporary concepts of ethics. A man who did a wrongful act was deemed *morally* responsible for the natural and probable consequence of that act. Mr Comyn asked us to remember that since Sir Matthew Hale's day the rigour of the law relating to homicide has been eased in favour of the accused. It has been – but this has come about through the development of the concepts of intent, not by reason of a different view of causation. Well known practitioner's textbooks, such as *Halsbury's Laws of England*, 3rd ed, vol 10 (1955), p706 and *Russell on Crime,* 12th ed (1964), vol 1, p30 continue to reflect the common law approach. Textbooks intended for students or as studies in jurisprudence have queried the common law rule; see *Hart and Honoré, Causation in Law* (1959), pp320-321 and *Smith and Hogan, Criminal Law*, 3rd ed (1973), p214.

There have been two cases in recent years which have some bearing upon this topic; *R v Jordan* (1956) 40 Cr App R152 and *R v Smith*, [1959] 2 QB 35. In *R v Jordan* the Court of Criminal Appeal, after conviction, admitted some medical evidence which went to prove that the cause of death was not the blow relied upon by the prosecution but abnormal medical treatment after admission to hospital. This case has been criticised but it was probably rightly decided on its facts. Before the abnormal treatment started the injury had almost healed. We share Lord Parker CJ's opinion that *R v Jordan* should be regarded as a case decided on its own special facts and not as an authority relaxing the common law approach to causation. In *R v Smith* [1959] 2 QB 35 the man who had been stabbed would probably not have died but for a series of mishaps. These mishaps were said to have broken the chain of causation. Lord Parker CJ, in the course of his judgment, commented as follows, at p42:

> "It seems to the court that if at the time of death the original wound is still an operating cause and a substantial cause, then the death can properly be said to be the result of the wound, albeit that some other cause of death is also operating. Only if it can be said that the original wounding is merely the setting in which another cause operates can it be said that the death does not flow from the wound. Putting it another way, only if the second cause is so overwhelming as to make the original wound merely part of the history can it be said that the death does not flow from the wound."

The physical cause of death in this case was the bleeding into the pleural cavity arising from the penetration of the lung. This had not been brought about by any decision made by the deceased but by the stab wound.

Mr Comyn tried to overcome this line of reasoning by submitting that the jury should have been directed that if they thought the deceased's decision not to have a blood transfusion was an unreasonable one, then the chain of causation would have been broken. At once the question arises – reasonable by whose standards? Those of Jehovah's Witnesses? Humanists? Roman Catholics? Protestants of Anglo-Saxon descent? The man on the Clapham omnibus? But he might well be an admirer of Eleazar who suffered death rather than eat the flesh of swine (2 Maccabees, ch.6, vv. 18-31) or of Sir Thomas More who, unlike nearly all his contemporaries was unwilling to accept Henry VIII as Head of the Church of England. Those brought up in the Hebraic and Christian traditions would probably be reluctant to accept that these martyrs caused their own deaths.

As was pointed out to Mr Comyn in the course of argument, two cases, each raising the same issue of reasonableness because of religious beliefs, could produce different verdicts depending on where the cases were tried. A jury drawn from Preston, sometimes said to be the most Catholic town in England, might have different views about martyrdom to one drawn from the inner suburbs of London. Mr Comyn accepted that this might be so: it was, he said, inherent in trial by jury. It is not inherent in the common law as expounded by Sir Matthew Hale and Maule J. It has long been the policy of the law that those who use violence on other people must take their victims as they find them. This in our judgment means the whole man, not just the physical man. It does not lie in the mouth of the assailant to say that the victim's religious beliefs which inhibited him from accepting certain kinds of treatment were unreasonable. The question for decision is what caused her death. The answer is the stab wound. The fact that the victim refused to stop this end coming about did not break the causal connection between the act and death.'

R v Cheshire [1991] 1 WLR 844 Court of Appeal (Criminal Division) (Beldam LJ, Boreham and Auld JJ)

Homicide – causation – inadequate medical treatment

Facts

The appellant fired two shots at the deceased (Trevor Jeffrey) during an argument at the 'Ozone' fish and chip shop in Greenwich. The deceased received injuries to his leg and abdomen and died two months later in hospital. The appellant was convicted of murder and appealed on the ground that the trial judge had misdirected the jury on the issue of causation. The cause of the victim's death was given as 'cardio-respiratory arrest due to gunshot wounds', but the appellant had introduced expert evidence to the effect that the death had been caused by a rare complication resulting from the medical treatment he had received, and that the chain of causation had been broken by the negligent medical treatment. The trial judge had directed the jury that the medical treatment could not be regarded as a novus actus interveniens unless the doctors had been reckless in their disregard for the patient's health.

Held

The appeal would be dismissed.

Beldam LJ reviewed the factual background to the case and took, as his basis for the law relating to causation, the judgment of Goff LJ in *R v Pagett* (1983) 76 Cr App R 279. His Lordship continued:

> 'Robert Goff LJ went on to express his indebtedness to the work of Professors Hart and Honoré in *Causation in the Law*, 2nd ed (1985). We too are indebted to section IV of Chapter 12 of that work. Under the heading "Doctor's or Victim's Negligence" the authors deal with cases in which an assault or wounding is followed by improper medical treatment or by refusal of treatment by the victim or failure on his part to take proper care of the wound or injury. The authors trace from Hale's *Pleas of the Crown* (1736) and *Stephen's Digest of the Criminal Law*, 9th ed (1950) the emergence of a standard set by Stephen of common knowledge or skill which they suggest appears to require proof of something more than ordinary negligence in order that one who inflicts a wound may be relieved of liability for homicide. And they refer to most American authorities as requiring at least gross negligence to negative causal connection. English decisions, however, have not echoed these words. In conclusion the authors state, at p362:
>
>> "Our survey of the place of doctor's and victim's negligence in the law of homicide, where differences of policy between civil and criminal law might be expected to make themselves felt, yields a meagre harvest.
>> (i) On Stephen's view, which has some modern support, there is no difference between civil and criminal law as regards the effect of medical negligence: in each case gross negligence ('want of common knowledge or skill') is required to negative responsibility for death."
>
> Whatever may be the differences of policy between the approach of the civil and the criminal law to the question of causation, there are we think reasons for a critical approach when importing the language of the one to the other.
>
> Since the apportionment of responsibility for damage has become commonplace in the civil law,

judges have sought to distinguish the blameworthiness of conduct from its causative effect. Epithets suggestive of degrees of blameworthiness may be of little help in deciding how potent the conduct was in causing the result. A momentary lapse of concentration may lead to more serious consequences than a more glaring neglect of duty. In the criminal law the jury considering the factual question, did the accused's act cause the deceased's death, will we think derive little assistance from figures of speech more appropriate for conveying degrees of fault or blame in questions of apportionment. Unless authority suggests otherwise, we think such figures of speech are to be avoided in giving guidance to a jury on the question of causation. Whilst medical treatment unsuccessfully given to prevent the death of a victim with the care and skill of a competent medical practitioner will not amount to an intervening cause, it does not follow that treatment which falls below that standard of care and skill will amount to such a cause. As Professors Hart and Honoré comment, treatment which falls short of the standard expected of the competent medical practitioner is unfortunately only too frequent in human experience for it to be considered abnormal in the sense of extraordinary. Acts or omissions of a doctor treating the victim for injuries he has received at the heads of an accused may conceivably be so extraordinary as to be capable of being regarded as acts independent of the conduct of the accused but it is most unlikely that they will be.'

His Lordship referred to *R v Jordan* (1956) 40 Cr App R 152 and *R v Smith* [1959] 2 QB 35 and continued:

'Both these cases were considered by this court in of *R v Malcherek and Steel* [1981] 1 WLR 690, in which it had been argued that the act of a doctor in disconnecting a life support machine had intervened to cause the death of the victim to the exclusion of injuries inflicted by the appellants. In rejecting this submission Lord Lane CJ, after considering *R v Jordan*, 40 Cr App R 152 and *R v Smith* [1959] 2 QB 35, said [1981] 1 WLR 690, 696:

"In the view of this Court, if a choice has to be made between the decision in *R v Jordan* 40 Cr App R 152 and that in *Smith* [1959] 2 QB 35, which we do not believe it does (*R v Jordan* being a very exceptional case), then the decision in *R v Smith* is to be preferred."

Later in the same judgment Lord Lane CJ said at pp696-697:

"There may be occasions, although they will be rare, when the original injury has ceased to operate as a cause at all, but in the ordinary case if the treatment is given bona fide by competent and careful medical practitioners, then evidence will not be admissible to show that the treatment would not have been administered in the same way by other medical practitioners. In other words, the fact that the victim has died, despite or because of medical treatment for the initial injury given by careful and skilled medical practitioners, will not exonerate the original assailant from responsibility for the death."

In those two cases it was not suggested that the actions of the doctors in disconnecting the life support machine were other than competent and careful. The court did not have to consider the effect of medical treatment which fell short of the standard of care to be expected of competent medical practitioners.

A case in which the facts bear a close similarity to the case with which we are concerned is the case of *R v Evans and Gardiner (No 2)* [1976] VR 523. In that case the deceased was stabbed in the stomach by the two applicants in April 1974. After operation the victim resumed an apparently healthy life but nearly a year later, after suffering abdominal pain and vomiting and undergoing further medical treatment, he died. The cause of death was a stricture of the small bowel, a not uncommon sequel to the operation carried out to deal with the stab wound inflicted by the applicants. It was contended that the doctors treating the victim for the later symptoms ought to have diagnosed the presence of the stricture, that they had been negligent not to do so and that timely operative treatment would have saved the victim's life.

The Supreme Court of Victoria held that the test to be applied in determining whether a felonious act has caused a death which follows, in spite of an intervening act, is whether the felonious act is still an operating and substantial cause of the death.

The summing up to the jury had been based on the passage already quoted from Lord Parker's judgment in *R v Smith* [1959] 2 QB 35 and the Supreme Court endorsed a direction in those terms. It commented upon the limitations of the decision of *R Jordan* 40 Cr App R 152 and made observations on the difference between the failure to diagnose the consequence of the original injury and cases in which medical treatment has been given which has a positive adverse effect on the victim. It concluded [1976] VR 523, 528:

> "But in the long run the difference between a positive act of commission and an omission to do some particular act is for these purposes ultimately a question of degree. As an event intervening between an act alleged to be felonious and to have resulted in death, and the actual death, a positive act of commission or an act of omission will serve to break the chain of causation only if it can be shown that the act or omission accelerated the death, so that it can be said to have caused the death and thus to have prevented the felonious act which would have caused death from actually doing so."

Later in the judgment the court said, at p534:

> "In these circumstances we agree with the view of the learned trial judge expressed in his report to this court that there was a case to go to the jury. The failure of the medical practitioners to diagnose correctly the victim's condition, however inept or unskillful, was not the cause of death. It was the blockage of the bowel which caused death and the real question for the jury was whether that blockage was due to the stabbing. There was plenty of medical evidence to support such a finding, if the jury chose to accept it."

It seems to us that these two passages demonstrate the difficulties in formulating and explaining a general concept of causation but what we think does emerge from this and the other cases is that when the victim of a criminal attack is treated for wounds or injuries by doctors or other medical staff attempting to repair the harm done, it will only be in the most extraordinary and unusual case that such treatment can be said to be so independent of the acts of the accused that it could be regarded in law as the cause of the victim's death to the exclusion of the accused's acts.

Where the law requires proof of the relationship between an act and its consequences as an element of responsibility, a simple and sufficient explanation of the basis of such relationship has proved notoriously elusive.

In a case in which the jury have to consider whether negligence in the treatment of injuries inflicted by the accused was the cause of death we think it is sufficient for the judge to tell the jury that they must be satisfied that the Crown have proved that the acts of the accused caused the death of the deceased adding that the accused's acts need not be the sole cause or even the main cause of death it being sufficient that his acts contributed significantly to that result. Even though negligence in the treatment of the victim was the immediate cause of his death, the jury should not regard it as excluding the responsibility of the accused unless the negligent treatment was so independent of his acts, and in itself so potent in causing death, that they regard the contribution made by his acts as insignificant.

It is not the function of the jury to evaluate competing causes or to choose which is dominant provided they are satisfied that the accused's acts can fairly be said to have made a significant contribution to the victim's death. We think the word "significant" conveys the necessary substance of a contribution made to the death which is more than negligible.

In the present case the passage in the summing up complained of has to be set in the context of the remainder of the direction given by the learned judge on the issue of causation. He directed the jury that they had to decide whether the two bullets fired into the deceased on 10 December caused his death on 15 February following. Or, he said, put in another way, did the injuries caused cease to operate as a cause of death because something else intervened? He told them that the prosecution did not have to prove that the bullets were the only cause of death but they had to prove that they were one operative and substantial cause of death. He was thus following the words used in *R v Smith* [1959] 2 QB 35. The judge then gave several examples for the jury to consider before reverting to a paraphrase of the alternative formulation used by Lord Parker CJ in *R v Smith*. Finally, he reminded the jury of the evidence which they had heard on this issue. We would remark that on several occasions during this evidence the jury had passed notes to the judge asking for clarification of expressions used by the medical witnesses which showed that they were following closely the factual issues they had to consider. If the passage to which exception has been taken had not been included, no possible criticism could have been levelled at the summing up. Although for reasons we have stated we think that the judge erred when he invited the jury to consider the degree of fault in the medical treatment rather than its consequences, we consider that no miscarriage of justice has actually occurred. Even if more experienced doctors than those who attended the deceased would have recognised the rare complication in time to have prevented the deceased's death, that complication was a direct consequence of the appellant's acts which remained a significant cause of his death. We cannot conceive that, on the evidence given, any jury would have found otherwise.

Accordingly, we dismissed the appeal.'

DPP v *Daley and McGhie* [1980] AC 237 Privy Council (Lord Diplock, Lord Hailsham, Lord Salmon, Lord Edmund-Davies and Lord Keith)

Manslaughter – victim's apprehention of assault

Facts
The defendants chased the deceased, Sydney Smith, and threw stones at him. In attempting to escape he tripped and fell and was subsequently found to be dead.

The defendants were charged with murder and convicted of constructive manslaughter following the trial judge's directions to the jury that:

'... where one person causes in the mind of another by violence or the threat of violence a well-founded sense of danger to life or limb as to cause him to suffer or to try to escape and in the endeavour to escape he is killed, the person creating that state of mind is guilty of at least manslaughter.'

The defendants appealed successfully to the Court of Appeal, and the prosecutor appealed to the Judicial Committee of the Privy Council.

Held
The appeal would be allowed and the convictions restored.

Lord Keith:

'The law regarding manslaughter of the species with which this appeal is concerned was considered by the Court of Appeal (Criminal Division) in *Reg* v *Mackie* (1973) 57 Cr App R 453. It is unnecessary to recite the facts of the case or to quote any passages from the judgment of the court delivered by Stephenson LJ. It is sufficient to paraphrase what in their Lordships' view were there held to constitute the essential ingredients of the prosecution's proof of a charge of manslaughter, laid upon the basis that a person has sustained fatal injuries while trying to escape from assault by the defendant. These are: (1) that the victim immediately before he sustained the injuries was in fear of being hurt physically; (2) that his fear was such that it caused him to try to escape; (3) that whilst he was trying to escape, and because he was trying to escape, he met his death; (4) that his fear of being hurt there and then was reasonable and was caused by the conduct of the defendant; (5) that the defendant's conduct which caused the fear was unlawful; and (6) that his conduct was such as any sober and reasonable person would recognise as likely to subject the victim to at least the risk of some harm resulting from it, albeit not serious harm. Their Lordships have to observe that it is unnecessary to prove the defendant's knowledge that his conduct was unlawful. This was made clear by Lord Salmon speaking with general concurrence in a slightly different but nevertheless relevant context in *Director of Public Prosecutions* v *Newbury* [1977] AC 500, 507. It is sufficient to prove that the defendant's act was intentional, and that it was dangerous on an objective test.

Their Lordships are of opinion at upon the evidence in the present case there was material before the jury upon which, if they did not consider the defendant's guilt of murder to be established beyond reasonable doubt, they were entitled to find them guilty of manslaughter upon the basis which has been described. There was evidence that the defendants threw stones at the deceased. The jury by their verdict showed that they accepted that evidence. There was evidence that the deceased was struck by a stone or stones, but the jury were clearly entitled to regard that evidence as not being of sufficient quality to establish the fact beyond reasonable doubt. There could be no doubt that the deceased in the course of running across the yard sustained injuries which caused his death. If those injuries did not result from his being struck by stones thrown by the defendants, they could only have resulted from his tripping over the ramp and sustaining the injuries in his fall. Did he trip and fall because he was fleeing in haste on account of fear inspired by the defendants' conduct, or, as the defendants suggested, in the course of running to get a gun with which to threaten or attack them? Their Lordships are satisfied that upon a fair view of the evidence as a whole any jury would have been entitled to infer that the former was the true explanation of the deceased's fall, and generally to hold that all the ingredients described above as necessary for a verdict of manslaughter had been proved beyond reasonable doubt. Therefore the issue of manslaughter was a proper one to put before the jury.'

Commentary
See *R v Williams; R v Davis*, below.

R v Dyson [1908] 2 KB 454 Court of Criminal Appeal

Year and a day rule

Facts
The defendant assaulted his own child causing a fractured skull in November 1906. The child died in March 1908, the medical evidence being that the fractured skull was the main cause of death. The defendant was convicted of manslaughter and appealed.

Held
The conviction would be quashed.

Lord Alverstone CJ:

'[The] Appellant had inflicted injuries on the child in November, 1906, and December, 1907 and had suffered imprisonment for both offences. This was an ordinary indictment for manslaughter on March 5, 1908. The misdirection complained of was that Coleridge J had directed the jury that they might find prisoner guilty if the death was caused by the injuries of November, 1906, though the full effect of those injuries was not seen till later. There were no qualifying words in these passages in the summing-up, or they would have given effect to them. It was admitted by counsel for the Crown that this direction was wrong. The cruelty was so clearly established that a somewhat recondite rule of law had been overlooked, viz, that unless deceased dies within a year and a day of the injury a charge of manslaughter cannot be maintained. That rule was stated by Coke, 3 *Institutes*, 47, 53; by Hawkins, 1 *Pleas of the Crown*, c 31, s 9; by East, 1 *Pleas of the Crown*, c5, s112, pp343, 344 and was still the law of England: 3 *Russell on Crimes* (6th ed), p4, where the authorities are collected. What, then ought the Court to do? If he had not been already convicted of the assaults, he might have been convicted under sect. 1 (3) of the Prevention of Cruelty to Children Act, 1904, so that, as it was, this Court could not proceed under sect. 5 (2) of the Criminal Appeal Act. At the same time, *Morris*, LR 1 CCR 90; 36 LJMC 84 (1867), is a clear authority that these two convictions are no bar to an indictment for manslaughter. Can the Court, then, act under the proviso in sect. 4(1) of the Act that they should dismiss the appeal if there was "no substantial miscarriage of justice"? After most careful thought they had come to the conclusion that they could not. For what question should have been left to the jury? Whether appellant accelerated the death by his injury of December, 1907. With a proper direction, as in *Martin*, 5 C & P 128 (1832), deceased's condition having been deteriorated by previous ill-treatment, the jury might and probably would have found appellant guilty of accelerating the death, and he quite accepted the statement of counsel for the Crown that he did so put the case to them. But the reason that they could not use that power was – and it was so very important that it must be stated clearly – that the Court ought not to substitute itself for the jury. It was much to be regretted that Parliament had not given the Court power to order a new trial: such a power might only be wanted in a few instances, but this is one of them. Here, as they could not substitute themselves for the jury, they could not positively say that there would be no miscarriage of justice; they could not say that the jury mus*t* have come to the conclusion that the death was accelerated by the previous assault – probably they would have done so, but there was some evidence – not, indeed, the bulk of the evidence – that death may have been due to a fall: and there was no sign of external injury, and therefore it was not absolutely certain that the death had been accelerated as suggested. It was too serious in such a case to say that the jury must have come to a verdict of guilty. In *Makin v A-G for New South Wales*, 1894 AC at 70, Lord Herschell, C, said: "their Lordships do not think it can properly be said that there has been no substantial wrong or miscarriage of justice, where on a point material to the guilt or innocence of the accused the jury have, notwithstanding objection, been invited by the judge to consider in arriving at their verdict matters which ought not to have been submitted to them." If for "invited .... matters" be read the words "have been told by the judge they might find a verdict of guilty on matters which ought not to have been submitted to them," the cases are very similar.'

R v *Malcherek; R* v *Steel* [1981] 1 WLR 690 Court of Appeal (Criminal Division) (Lord Lane CJ, Ormrod LJ and Smith J)

Medical treatment as a novus actus interveniens

Facts
Both defendants had, in separate incidents, attacked women causing injuries that were so severe, their victims had to be placed on life support machines in hospital. In both cases doctors decided to switch off the machines after determining that the victims were 'brain dead' and that there was no prospect of recovery. Both defendants were convicted of murder. The common ground of appeal in each case was that the doctors had broken the chain of causation between the defendants' attacks and the deaths of the victims by deliberately switching off the life support machines.

Held
The appeals would be dismissed.

Lord Lane CJ:

'The question posed for answer to this Court is simply whether the judge in each case was right in withdrawing from the jury the question of causation. Was he right to rule that there was no evidence on which the jury could come to the conclusion that the assailant did not cause the death of the victim? The way in which the submissions are put by Mr Field-Fisher on the one hand and by Mr Wilfred Steer [counsel for the defendants] on the other is as follows: the doctors, by switching off the ventilator and the life support machine were the cause of death or, to put it more accurately, there was evidence which the jury should have been allowed to consider that the doctors, and not the assailant, in each case may have been the cause of death.

In each case it is clear that the initial assault was the cause of the grave head injuries in the one case and of the massive abdominal haemorrhage in the other. In each case the initial assault was the reason for the medical treatment being necessary. In each case the medical treatment given was normal and conventional. At some stage the doctors must decide if and when treatment has become otiose. This decision was reached, in each of the two cases here, in circumstances which have already been set out in some detail. It is no part of the task of this Court to inquire whether the criteria, the Royal Medical College confirmatory tests, are a satisfactory code of practice. It is not part of the task of this Court to decide whether the doctors were, in either of these two cases, justified in omitting one or more of the so called "confirmatory tests." The doctors are not on trial: the applicant and the appellant respectively were.

There are two comparatively recent cases which are relevant to the consideration of this problem.'

His Lordship considered the first of these, *R v Jordan* (1956) 40 Cr App R 152, and continued:

'The other decision is that of *R v Smith* [1959] 2 QB 35. In that case the appellant had stabbed a fellow soldier with a bayonet. One of the wounds had pierced the victim's lung and had caused bleeding. Whilst being carried to the medical hut or reception centre for treatment, the victim was dropped twice and then, when he reached the treatment centre, he was given treatment which was subsequently shown to have been incorrect. Lord Parker CJ, who gave the judgment of the Court, stressed the fact – if it needed stressing – that *R v Jordan* (1956) 40 Cr App R 152 was a very particular case depending upon its own exact facts, as indeed Hallett J himself in that case had said.

In *R v Smith* (*supra*) counsel for the appellant argued that if there was any other cause, whether resulting from negligence or not, operating; if something happened which impeded the chance of the deceased recovering, then the death did not result from that wound.

A very similar submission to that has been made to this Court by counsel in the instant case. The Court in *R v Smith* (*supra*) was quite unable to accept that contention. Lord Parker CJ said at pp42–43:

"It seems to the court that if at the time of death the original wound is still an operating cause and a substantial cause, then the death can properly be said to be the result of the wound, albeit that some other cause of death is also operating. Only if it can be said that the original wounding is merely the setting in which another cause operates can it be said that the death does not result from the wound. Putting it in another way, only if the second cause is so overwhelming as to make the original wound merely part of the history can it be said that the death does not flow from the wound."

In the view of this Court, if a choice has to be made between the decision in *R v Jordan* (supra) and that in *R v Smith* (supra) which we do not believe it does (*R v Jordan* (supra) being a very exceptional case), then the decision in *Rv Smith* (supra) is to be preferred.

The only other case to which reference has been made, it having been drawn to our attention by Mr Steer, is the case of *R v Blaue* [1975] 1 WLR 1411. That was the case where the victim of a stabbing incident was a Jehovah's Witness who refused to accept a blood transfusion although she had been told that to refuse would mean death for her – a prophecy which was fulfilled. The passage that has been drawn to our attention in that case is the last paragraph of the judgment of Lawton LJ, at p1416:

"The issue of the cause of death in a trial for either murder or manslaughter is one of fact for the jury to decide. But if, as in this case, there is no conflict of evidence and all the jury has to do is to apply the law to the admitted facts, the judge is entitled to tell the jury what the result of that application will be. In this case the judge would have been entitled to have told the jury that the appellant's stab wound was an operative cause of death. The appeal fails."

There is no evidence in the present case here that at the time of conventional death, after the life support machinery was disconnected, the original wound or injury was other than a continuing, operating and indeed substantial cause of the death of the victim, although it need hardly be added that it need not be substantial to render the assailant guilty. There may be occasions, although they will be rare, when the original injury has ceased to operate as a cause at all, but in the ordinary case if the treatment is given bona fide by competent and careful medical practitioners, then evidence will not be admissible to show that the treatment would not have been administered in the same way by other medical practitioners. In other words, the fact that the victim has died, despite or because of medical treatment for the initial injury given by careful and skilled medical practitioners, will not exonerate the original assailant from responsibility for the death. It follows that so far as the ground of appeal in each of these cases relates to the direction given on causation, that ground fails. It also follows that the evidence which it is sought to adduce now, although we are prepared to assume that it is both credible and was not available properly at the trial – and a reasonable explanation for not calling it at the trial has been given – if received could, under no circumstances, afford any ground for allowing the appeal.

The reason is this. Nothing which any of the two or three medical men whose statements are before us could say would alter the fact that in each case the assailant's actions continued to be an operating cause of the death. Nothing the doctors could say would provide any ground for a jury coming to the conclusion that the assailant in either case might not have caused the death. The furthest to which their proposed evidence goes, as already stated, is to suggest, first, that the criteria or the confirmatory tests are not sufficiently stringent and, secondly, that in the present case they were in certain respects inadequately fulfilled or carried out. It is no part of this Court's function in the present circumstances to pronounce upon this matter, nor was it a function of either of the juries at these trials. Where a medical practitioner adopting methods which are generally accepted comes bona fide and conscientiously to the conclusion that the patient is for practical purposes dead, and that such vital functions as exist – for example, circulation – are being maintained solely by mechanical means, and therefore discontinues treatment, that does not prevent the person who inflicted the initial injury from being responsible for the victim's death. Putting it in another way, the discontinuance of treatment in those circumstances does not break the chain of causation between the initial injury and the death.

Although it is unnecessary to go further than that for the purpose of deciding the present point, we wish to add this thought. Whatever the strict logic of the matter may be, it is perhaps somewhat bizarre to suggest, as counsel have impliedly done, that where a doctor tries his conscientious best to save the life of a patient brought to hospital in extremis, skilfully using sophisticated methods, drugs and machinery to do so, but fails in his attempt and therefore discontinues treatment, he can be said to have caused the death of the patient.'

Commentary
See *R* v *Cheshire*, above.

R v *Pagett* (1983) 76 Cr App R 279 Court of Appeal (Criminal Division) (Robert Goff LJ, Cantley and Farquharson JJ)
Chain of causation not broken by reasonably foreseeable actions of third parties

Facts
The defendant armed himself with a shotgun and took a pregnant girl (Gail Kinchen) hostage. The police besieged the flat in which the defendant was holding the girl and called on him to come out. He eventually did so, holding the girl in front of him as a human shield. The defendant fired the shotgun at the police officers who returned fire, striking and killing the girl hostage. The defendant was convicted of her manslaughter and appealed on the ground that the judge had misdirected the jury as to causation.

Held
The appeal would be dismissed.

Robert Goff LJ:

'We turn to the first ground of appeal, which is that the learned judge erred in directing the jury that it was for him to decide *as a matter of law* whether by his unlawful and deliberate acts the appellant caused or was a cause of Gail Kinchen's death. It is right to observe that this direction of the learned judge followed upon a discussion with counsel, in the absence of the jury; though the appellant, having dismissed his own counsel, was for this purpose without legal representation. In the course of this discussion, counsel for the prosecution referred the learned judge to a passage in Professor Smith and Professor Hogan's *Criminal Law* (4th ed (1978), p272), which reads as follows: "Causation is a question of both fact and law. D's act cannot be held to be the cause of an event if the event would have occurred without it. The act, that is, must be a sine qua non of the event and whether it is so is a question of fact. But there are many acts which are sine qua non of a homicide and yet are not either in law, or in ordinary parlance, the cause of it. If I invite P to dinner and he is run over and killed on the way, my invitation may be a sine qua non of his death, but no one would say I killed him and I have not caused his death in law. Whether a particular act which is a sine qua non of an alleged actus reus is also a cause of it is a question of law. Where the facts are admitted the judge may direct the jury that a particular act did, or did not, cause a particular result." There follows a reference to *Jordan* (1956) 40 Cr App R 152.

For the appellant, Lord Gifford criticised the statement of the learned authors that "Whether a particular act which is a sine qua non of an alleged actus reus is also a cause of it is a question of law." He submitted that the question had to be answered by the jury as a question of fact. In our view, with all respect, both the passage in Smith and Hogan's *Criminal Law,* and Lord Gifford's criticism of it, are over-simplifications of a complex matter.

We have no intention of embarking in this judgment on a dissertation on the nature of causation, or indeed of considering any matters other than those which are germane to the decision of the issues now before us. Problems of causation have troubled philosophers and lawyers throughout the ages; and it would be rash in the extreme for us to trespass beyond the boundaries of our immediate problem. Our comments should therefore be understood to be confined not merely to the criminal law, but to cases of homicide (and possibly also other crimes of violence to the person); and it must be emphasised that the problem of causation in the present case is specifically concerned with the intervention of another person (here one of the police officers) whose act was the immediate cause of the death of the victim, Gail Kinchen.

In cases of homicide, it is rarely necessary to give the jury any direction on causation as such. Of course, a necessary ingredient of the crimes of murder and manslaughter is that the accused has by his act caused the victim's death. But how the victim came by his death is usually not in dispute. What is in dispute is more likely to be some other matter: for example, the identity of the person who committed the act which indisputably caused the victim's death; or whether the accused had the necessary intent; or whether the accused acted in self-defence, or was provoked. Even where it is necessary to direct the jury's minds to the question of causation, it is usually enough to direct them simply that in law the accused's act need not be the sole cause, or even the main cause, of the victim's death, it being enough that his act contributed significantly to that result. It is right to observe in passing, however, that even this simple direction is a direction of law relating to causation, on the basis of which the jury are bound to act in concluding whether the prosecution has established, as a matter of fact, that the accused's act did in this sense cause the victim's death. Occasionally, however, a specific issue of causation may arise. One such case is where, although an act of the accused constitutes a causa sine qua non of (or necessary condition for) the death of the victim, nevertheless the intervention of a third person may be regarded as the sole cause of the victim's death, thereby relieving the accused of criminal responsibility. Such intervention, if it has such an effect, has often been described by lawyers as a novus actus interveniens. We are aware that this time-honoured Latin term has been the subject of criticism. We are also aware that attempts have been made to translate it into English, though no simple translation has proved satisfactory, really because the Latin term has become a term of art which conveys to lawyers the crucial feature that there has not merely been an intervening act of another person, but that that act was so independent of the act of the accused that it should be regarded in law as the cause of the victim's death, to the exclusion of the act of the accused. At the risk of scholarly criticism, we shall for the purposes of this judgment continue to use the Latin term ...

... There can, we consider, be no doubt that a reasonable act performed for the purpose of self-preservation, being of course itself an act caused by the accused's own act, does not operate as a novus actus interveniens. If authority is needed for this almost self-evident proposition, it is to be found in such cases as *Pitts* (1842) C & M 284, and *Curley* (1909) 2 Cr App R 96. In both these cases, the act performed for the purpose of self-preservation consisted of an act by the victim in attempting to escape from the violence of the accused, which in fact resulted in the victim's death. In each case it was held as a matter of law that, if the victim acted in a reasonable attempt to escape the violence of the accused, the death of the victim was caused by the act of the accused. Now one form of self-preservation is self-defence; for present purposes, we can see no distinction in principle between an attempt to escape the consequences of the accused's act, and a response which takes the form of self-defence. Furthermore, in our judgment, if a reasonable act of self-defence against the act of the accused causes the death of a third party, we can see no reason in principle why the act of self-defence, being an involuntary act caused by the act of the accused, should relieve the accused from criminal responsibility for the death of the third party. Of course, it does not necessarily follow that the accused will be guilty of the murder, or even of the manslaughter, of the third party; though in the majority of cases he is likely to be guilty at least of manslaughter. Whether he is guilty of murder or manslaughter will depend upon the question whether all the ingredients of the relevant offence have been proved ...

No English authority was cited to us, nor we think to the learned judge, in support of the proposition that an act done in the execution of a legal duty, again of course being an act itself caused by the act of the accused, does not operate as a novus actus interveniens. Before the judge, the cases relied on by the prosecution in support of this proposition were the two Pennsylvanian cases already referred to, *Commonwealth* v *Moyer* (supra) and *Commonwealth* v *Almeida* (supra). However, since the case of *Redline* (supra), neither of these cases can be regarded as authority in the State of Pennsylvania: *Redline* was not cited to the learned judge, we suspect because it is not referred to in Hart and Honoré's *Causation in the Law*, almost certainly because the report of *Redline* was not available to the learned authors when their treatise went to the press. Even so, we agree with the learned judge that the proposition is sound in law, because as a matter of principle such an act cannot be regarded as a voluntary act independent of the wrongful act of the accused. A parallel may be drawn with the so-called "rescue" cases in the law of negligence, where a wrongdoer may be held liable in negligence to a third party who suffers injury in going to the rescue of a person who has been put in danger by the defendant's negligent act. Where, for example, a police officer in the execution of his duty acts to prevent a crime, or to apprehend a person suspected of a crime, the case is surely a fortiori. Of course, it is inherent in the requirement that the police officer, or other person, must be acting in the execution of his duty that his act should be reasonable in all the circumstances: see section 3 of the Criminal Law Act 1967. Furthermore, once again we are only considering the issue of causation. If intervention by a third party in the execution of a legal duty, caused by the act of the accused, results in the death of the victim, the question whether the accused is guilty of the murder or manslaughter of the victim must depend on whether the necessary ingredients of the relevant offence have been proved against the accused, including in particular, in the case of murder, whether the accused had the necessary intent.

The principles which we have stated are principles of law. This is plain from, for example, the case of *Pitts* (1842) C & M 284, to which we have already referred. It follows that where, in any particular case, there is an issue concerned with what we have for convenience called *novus actus interveniens*, it will be appropriate for the judge to direct the jury in accordance with these principles. It does not however follow that it is accurate to state broadly that causation is a question of law. On the contrary, generally speaking causation is a question of fact for the jury. Thus in, for example, *Towers* (1874) 12 Cox CC 530, the accused struck a woman; she screamed loudly, and a child whom she was then nursing turned black in the face, and from that day until it died suffered from convulsions. The question whether the death of the child was caused by the act of the accused was left by the judge to the jury to decide as a question of fact. But that does not mean that there are no principles of law relating to causation, so that no directions on law are ever to be given to a jury on the question of causation. On the contrary, we have already pointed out one familiar direction which is given on causation, which is that the accused's act need not be the sole, or even the main, cause of the victim's death for his act to be held to have caused the death. Similarly, it was held by this Court in the case of *Blaue* [1975] 1 WLR 1411 that "It has long been the policy of the law that those who use violence on other people must take their victims as they find them. This in our judgment means the whole man, not just the physical man. It does not lie in the mouth of the assailant to say that his victim's religious belief which inhibited her from accepting certain kinds of treatment was unreasonable. The question for decision is what caused her death. The answer is the stab wound. The fact that the victim refused to stop this end coming about did not break the causal connection between the act and death" (see at pp274 and 1415, per Lawton LJ delivering the judgment of the Court). This was plainly a statement of a principle of law. Likewise, in cases where there is an issue whether the act of the victim or of a third party constituted a novus actus interveniens, breaking the causal connection between the act of the accused and the death of the victim, it would be appropriate for the judge to direct the jury, of course in the most simple terms, in accordance with the legal principles which they have to apply. It would then fall to the jury to decide the relevant factual issues which, identified with reference to those legal principles, will lead to the conclusion whether or not the prosecution have established the guilt of the accused of the crime of which he is charged.'

R v *Williams; R* v *Davis* [1992] 1 WLR 380 Court of Appeal (Criminal Division) (Stuart-Smith LJ, Waterhouse and Morland JJ)

Homicide – causation – victim's escape

Facts

Williams was the driver of a car who had stopped to give a lift to the deceased, a man called Shephard. Five miles further on, Shephard jumped out of the car whilst it was travelling at 30 miles per hour and suffered fatal head injuries. The evidence indicated that Williams had asked Shephard to make a contribution to the cost of petrol. Davis, also a passenger in the car, alleged that Williams had threatened Shephard with violence if he did not hand over the money, with the result that Shephard had jumped from the car whilst it was moving. Williams contended that Shephard had jumped out following threats made by Davis. In Davis's case, the trial judge had dealt with the issue of causation by directing the jury on the basis of *DPP* v *Daley* (extracted above).

Held

Davis's appeal would be allowed.

Stuart-Smith LJ (his Lordship referred to the speech of Lord Keith in *DPP* v *Daley* at p245, and continued):

'Miss Hare [counsel for the Crown] submits that this direction is sufficient in all cases and is all-embracing. In most cases that is no doubt so, but in some cases, and in our judgment this is one of them, it is necessary to give the jury a direction on causation, and explain the test by which the voluntary act of the deceased may be said to be caused by the defendant's act and is not a novus actus interveniens, breaking the chain of causation between the threat of violence and the death. There must be some proportionality between the gravity of the threat and the action of the deceased in seeking to escape from it. The difficulty in this case was that there was no direct evidence of the nature of the threat ...'

His Lordship then recited extracts from *R* v *Roberts* (1971) 56 Cr App R 95, and *R* v *Mackie* (1973) 57 Cr App R 453:

'It is plain that in fatal cases there are two requirements. The first, as in non-fatal cases, relates to the deceased's conduct which would be something that a reasonable and responsible man in the assailant's shoes would have foreseen. The second, which applies only in fatal cases, relates to the quality of the unlawful act which must be such that all sober and reasonable people would inevitably recognise must subject the other person to some harm resulting therefrom, albeit not serious harm. It should be noted that the headnote is inaccurate and tends to confuse these two limbs.

The harm must be physical harm. Where the unlawful act is a battery, there is no difficulty with the second ingredient. Where, however, the unlawful act is merely a threat unaccompanied and not preceded by any actual violence, the position may be more difficult. In the case of a life-threatening assault, such as pointing a gun or knife at the victim, all sober and reasonable people may well anticipate some physical injury through shock to the victim, as for example in *Reg* v *Dawson* (1985) 81 Cr App R 150 where the victim died of a heart attack following a robbery in which two of the appellants had been masked, armed with a replica gun and pickaxe handles. But the nature of the threat is of importance in considering both the foreseeability of harm to the victim from the threat and the question whether the deceased's conduct was proportionate to the threat: that is to say that it was within the ambit of reasonableness and not so daft as to fake it his own voluntary act which amounted to a novus actus interveniens and consequently broke the chain of causation. It should of course be borne in mind that a victim may in the agony of the moment do the wrong thing.

In this case there was an almost total lack of evidence as to the nature of the threat. The prosecution invited the jury to infer the gravity of the threat from the action of the deceased. The judge put it this way:

> "what was he frightened of was robbery, that this was going to be taken from him by force, and the measure of the force can be taken from his reaction to it. The prosecution suggests that if he is prepared to get out of a moving car, then it was a very serious threat involving him in the risk of, as he saw it, serious injury."

In our judgment that was a wholly impermissible argument and was simply a case of the prosecution pulling itself up by its own bootstraps.

Moreover in a case of robbery the threat of force is made to persuade the victim to hand over money: if the money is handed over actual violence may not eventuate. The jury should consider two questions: first, whether it was reasonably foreseeable that some harm, albeit not serious harm, was likely to result from the threat itself: and, secondly, whether the deceased's reaction in jumping from the moving car was within the range of responses which might be expected from a victim placed in the situation which he was. The jury should bear in mind any particular characteristic of the victim and the fact that in the agony of the moment he may act without thought and deliberation.

In our judgment the direction in *Director of Public Prosecutions* v *Daley* [1980] AC 237 is not sufficient where there is a real issue as to causation. In that case it could hardly be disputed that a reasonable man should foresee that the victim would flee if he was being stoned and that while fleeing he might slip and fall. In the present case the judge did not include this direction as being part of the necessary ingredients of the offence, replying no doubt on *Director of Public Prosecutions* v *Daley*. He referred to the victim's need for a well founded and not a fanciful fear that was out of all proportion to the threat. But that does not relate to his reaction in jumping out of the car. In the last sentence of the passage quoted he refers to the attempt to get out of the car being out of all proportion to the force used. But even here it is put as an alternative and not as an additional requirement and begs the question of what, if any, force was used.

In our judgment the failure of the judge to give any direction on causation was a misdirection and the conviction on this count just be quashed.'

25 Homicide II: Voluntary Manslaughter

Bedder v *DPP* [1954] 2 All ER 801
See *DPP* v *Camplin*, extracted in this chapter.

R v *Byrne* [1960] 2 QB 396 Court of Criminal Appeal (Lord Parker CJ, Hilbery and Diplock JJ)
Abnormality of the mind for the purposes of diminished responsibility

Facts
The defendant had strangled a young woman. There was evidence that he was a sexual psychopath, and could exercise but little control over his actions. The defence of diminished responsibility was rejected by the trial judge, and the defendant was convicted of murder. He appealed on the basis that the defence should have been put to the jury.

Held
The appeal would be allowed, and a conviction for manslaughter substituted for murder, but the sentence of life imprisonment should remain.

Lord Parker CJ:

> 'In his summing-up the learned judge, after summarising the medical evidence, gave to the jury a direction of law on the correctness of which this appeal turns. He told the jury if on the evidence they came to the conclusion that the facts could be fairly summarised as follows: "(1) From an early age he has been subject to these perverted violent desires and in some cases has indulged his desires; (2) the impulse or urge of these desires is stronger than the normal impulse or urge of sex to such an extent that the subject finds it very difficult or perhaps impossible in some cases to resist putting the desire into practice; (3) the act of killing this girl was done under such an impulse or urge; and (4) that setting aside these sexual addictions and practices, this man was normal in every other respect," those facts with nothing more would not bring a case within the section and do not constitute such abnormality of mind as substantially to impair a man's mental responsibility for his acts. "In other words," he went on, "mental affliction is one thing. The section is there to protect them. The section is not there to give protection where there is nothing else than what is vicious and depraved." Taken by themselves, these last words are unobjectionable, but it is contended on behalf of the appellant that the direction taken as a whole involves a misconstruction of the section, and had the effect of withdrawing from the jury an issue of fact, which it was peculiarly their province to decide.'

The Lord Chief Justice then considered the pre-1957 situation, and continued:

> 'It is against that background of the existing law that section 2 (1) of the Homicide Act, 1957, falls to be construed. To satisfy the requirements of the subsection the accused must show: (a) that he was suffering

from an abnormality of mind; and (b) that such abnormality of mind: (i) arose from a condition of arrested or retarded development of mind or any inherent causes or was induced by disease or injury; and (ii) was such as substantially impaired his mental responsibility for his acts in doing or being a party to the killing. "Abnormality of mind," which has to be contrasted with the time-honoured expression in the M'Naughten Rules "defect of reason," means a state of mind so different from that of ordinary human beings that the reasonable man would term it abnormal. It appears to us to be wide enough to cover the mind's activities in all its aspects, not only the perception of physical acts and matters, and the ability to form a rational judgment whether an act is right or wrong, but also the ability to exercise will power to control physical acts in accordance with that rational judgment. The expression "mental responsibility for his acts" points to a consideration of the extent to which the accused's mind is answerable for his physical acts, which must include a consideration of the extent of his ability to exercise will power to control his physical acts.

Whether the accused was at the time of the killing suffering from any "abnormality of mind" in the broad sense which we have indicated above is a question for the jury. On this question medical evidence is, no doubt, of importance, but the jury are entitled to take into consideration all the evidence including the acts or statements of the accused and his demeanour. They are not bound to accept the medical evidence, if there is other material before them which, in their good judgment, conflicts with it and outweighs it. The etiology of the abnormality of mind (namely, whether it arose from a condition of arrested or retarded development of mind or any inherent causes or was induced by disease or injury) does, however, seem to be a matter to be determined on expert evidence.

Assuming that the jury are satisfied on the balance of probabilities that the accused was suffering from "abnormality of mind" from one of the causes specified in the parenthesis of the subsection, the crucial question nevertheless arises: was the abnormality such as substantially impaired his mental responsibility for his acts in doing or being a party to the killing? This is a question of degree and essentially one for the jury. Medical evidence is, of course, relevant, but the question involves a decision not merely whether there was some impairment of the mental responsibility of the accused for his acts, but whether such impairment can properly be called "substantial," a matter upon which juries may quite legitimately differ from doctors.

Furthermore, in a case where the abnormality of mind is one which affects the accused's self-control the step between "he did not resist his impulse" is, as the evidence in this case shows, one which is incapable of scientific proof. *A fortiori* there is no scientific measurement of the degree of difficulty which an abnormal person finds in controlling his impulses. These problems which in the present state of medical knowledge are scientifically insoluble the jury can only approach in a broad, common-sense way. This court has repeatedly approved directions to the jury which have followed directions given in Scots cases where the doctrine of diminished responsibility forms part of the common law. We need not repeat them. They are quoted in *Spriggs* (1958) 42 Cr App R 69; [1958] 1 QB 270. They indicate that such abnormality as "substantially impairs his mental responsibility" involves a mental state which in popular language (not that of the M'Naughten Rules) a jury would regard as amounting to partial insanity or being on the border line of insanity.

It appears to us that the learned judge's direction to the jury that the defence under section 2 of the Act was not available, even though they found the facts set out in numbers 2 and 3 of the learned judge's summary, amounted to a direction that difficulty or even inability of an accused person to exercise will-power to control his physical acts could not amount to such abnormality of mind as substantially impairs his mental responsibility. For the reasons which we have already expressed we think that this construction of the Act is wrong. Inability to exercise will-power to control physical acts, provided that it is due to abnormality of mind from one of the causes specified in the parenthesis in the subsection is, in our view, sufficient to entitle the accused to the benefit of the section; difficulty in controlling his physical acts, depending on the degree of difficulty, may be sufficient. It is for the jury to decide upon the whole of the evidence whether such inability or difficulty has, not as a matter of scientific certainty but on the balance of probabilities, been established and in the case of difficulty whether the difficulty is so great as to amount in their view to a substantial impairment of the accused's mental responsibility for his acts. The direction in the present case thus withdrew from the jury the essential determination of fact which it was their province to decide.

As already indicated, the medical evidence of the appellant's ability to control his physical acts at the time of the killing was all one way. The evidence of the revolting circumstances of the killing and the subsequent mutilations, as of the previous sexual history of the appellant, pointed, we think plainly, to the conclusion that the appellant was what would be described in ordinary language as on the border line of insanity or partially insane. Properly directed, we do not think that the jury could have come to any other conclusion than that the defence under section 2 of the Homicide Act was made out.

The appeal will be allowed and a verdict of manslaughter substituted for the verdict of murder. The only possible sentence, having regard to the tendencies of the appellant, is imprisonment for life. The sentence will, accordingly, not be disturbed.'

DPP v *Camplin* [1978] AC 705 House of Lords (Lords Diplock, Morris, Simon, Fraser and Scarman)

Reasonable man test for provocation

Facts

The defendant was a 15-year-old boy who, having been buggered by the deceased, was then taunted by him. The defendant killed the deceased by hitting him over the head with a chapatti pan. He was convicted of murder following a direction by the trial judge to the jury that they were to judge the defendant by the standard of the reasonable adult, not a reasonable 15 year old boy. The Court of Appeal allowed the appeal on the basis that the more subjective test, which took account of the defendant's age, should have been applied. The Crown appealed to the House of Lords.

Held

The appeal would be dismissed.

Lord Diplock:

'In his address to the jury on the defence of provocation ... counsel for Camplin, had suggested to them that when they addressed their minds to the question whether the provocation relied on was enough to make a reasonable man do as Camplin had done, what they ought to consider was not the reaction of a reasonable adult but the reaction of a reasonable boy of Camplin's age. The judge thought that this was wrong in law. So in his summing-up he took pains to instruct the jury that they must consider whether –

" ... the provocation was sufficient to make a reasonable man in like circumstances act as the defendant did. Not a reasonable boy, as ... (counsel for Camplin) would have it, or a reasonable lad; it is an objective test – a reasonable man."

The jury found Camplin guilty of murder. On appeal the Court of Appeal (Criminal Division) allowed the appeal and substituted a conviction for manslaughter on the ground that the passage I have cited from the summing-up was a misdirection. The court held that –

" ... the proper direction to the jury is to invite the jury to consider whether the provocation was enough to have made a reasonable person of the same age as the appellant in the same circumstances do as he did."

The point of law of general public importance involved in the case has been certified as being:

"Whether, on the prosecution for murder of a boy of 15, where the issue of provocation arises, the jury should be directed to consider the question, under section 3 of the Homicide Act 1957 whether the provocation was enough to make a reasonable man do as he did by reference to a 'reasonable adult' or by reference to a 'reasonable boy of 15' ..."

... [U]ntil the 1957 Act was passed there was a condition precedent which had to be satisfied before any question of applying this dual test could arise. The conduct of the deceased had to be of such a kind as was capable in law of constituting provocation; and whether it was or not was a question for the judge, not for the jury. The House so held in *Mancini v DPP* ([1942] AC 1) where it also laid down a rule of law that the mode of resentment, as for instance the weapon used in the act that caused the death, must bear a reasonable relation to the kind of violence that constituted the provocation.

It is unnecessary for the purposes of the present appeal to spend time on a detailed account of what conduct was or was not capable in law of giving rise to a defence of provocation immediately before the passing of the Act of 1957 ... What, however, is important to note is that this House in *Holmes v DPP* ([1946] AC 588) had recently confirmed that words alone, save perhaps in circumstances of a most extreme and exceptional nature, were incapable in law of constituting provocation.

My Lords, this was the state of law when *Bedder v DPP* ([1959] 1 WLR 1119) fell to be considered by this House. The accused had killed a prostitute. He was sexually impotent. According to his evidence he had tried to have sexual intercourse with her and failed. She taunted him with his failure and tried to get away from his grasp. In the course of her attempts to do so she slapped him in the face, punched him in the stomach and kicked him in the groin, whereupon he took a knife out of his pocket and stabbed her twice and caused her death. The struggle that led to her death thus started because the deceased taunted the accused with his physical infirmity; but in the state of the law as it then was, taunts unaccompanied by any physical violence did not constitute provocation. The taunts were followed by violence on the part of the deceased in the course of her attempt to get away from the accused, and it may be that this subsequent violence would have a greater effect on the self-control of an impotent man already enraged by the taunts than it would have had upon a person conscious of possessing normal physical attributes. So there might have been some justification for the judge to instruct the jury to ignore the fact that the accused was impotent when they were considering whether the deceased's conduct amounted to such provocation as would cause a reasonable or ordinary person to loose his self control. This indeed appears to have been the ground on which the Court of Criminal Appeal had approved the summing-up when they said at p1121:

> "... no distinction is to be made in the case of a person who, though it may not be a matter of temperament is physically impotent, is conscious of the impotence, *and therefore mentally liable to be more excited unduly* if he is 'twitted' or attacked on the subject of that particular infirmity."

This statement, for which I have myself supplied the emphasis, was approved by Lord Simonds LC speaking on behalf of all the members of this House who sat on the appeal; but he also went on to lay down the broader proposition at 1123, that:

> "It would be plainly illogical not to recognise an unusually excitable or pugnacious temperament in the accused as a matter to be taken into account but yet to recognise for that purpose some unusual physical characteristic, be it impotence or another."

... My Lords, ... section [3] ... was intended to mitigate in some degree the harshness of the common law of provocation as it had been developed by recent decisions in this House. It recognises and retains the dual test: the provocation must not only have caused the accused to lose his self-control but also be such as might cause a reasonable man to react to it as the accused did. Nevertheless it brings about two important changes in the law. The first is it abolishes all previous rules of law as to what can or cannot amount to provocation and in particular the rule of law that, save in the two exceptional cases I have mentioned, word unaccompanied by violence could not do so. Secondly it makes clear that if there was any evidence that the accused himself at the time of the act which caused the death in fact lost his self-control in consequence of some provocation however slight it might appear to the judge, he was bound to leave to the jury the question, which is one of opinion not of law, whether a reasonable man might have reacted to that provocation as the accused did.

I agree with my noble and learned friend Lord Simon of Glaisdale that since this question is one for the opinion of the jury the evidence of witnesses as to how they think a reasonable man would react to the provocation is not admissible.

The public policy that underlay the adoption of the "reasonable man" test in the common law doctrine of provocation was to reduce the incidence of fatal violence by preventing a person relying on his own exceptional pugnacity or excitability as an excuse for loss of self-control. The rationale of the test may not be easy to reconcile in logic with more universal propositions as to the mental element in crime. Nevertheless it has been preserved by the Act of 1957 but falls to be applied now in the context of a law of provocation that is significantly different from what it was before the Act was passed.

Although it is now for the jury to apply the "reasonable man" test, it still remains for the judge to direct them what, in the new context of the section, is the meaning of this apparently inapt expression, since powers of ratiocination bear no obvious relationships to powers of self-control. Apart from this the judge is entitled, if he thinks it helpful, to suggest considerations which may influence the jury in forming their own opinions as to whether the test is satisfied; but he should make it clear that these are not instructions which they are required to follow: it is for them and no one else to decide what weight, if any, ought to be given to them.

As I have already pointed out, for the purposes of the law of provocation the "reasonable man" has never been confined to the adult male. It means an ordinary person of either sex, not exceptionally excitable or pugnacious, but possessed of such powers of self-control as everyone is entitled to expect that his fellow citizens will exercise in society as it is today. A crucial factor in the defence of provocation from earliest times has been the relationship between the gravity of provocation and the way in which the accused retaliated, both being judged by the social standards of the day. When Hale was writing in the seventeenth century, pulling a man's nose was thought to justify retaliation with a sword: when *Mancini* v *DPP* ... was decided by this House, a blow with a fist would not justify retaliation with a deadly weapon. But so long as words unaccompanied by violence could not in common law amount to provocation the relevant proportionality between provocation and retaliation was primarily one of the degrees of violence. Words spoken to the accused before the violence started were not normally to be included in the proportion sum. But now that the law has been changed so as to permit of words being treated as provocation, even though unaccompanied by any other acts, the gravity of verbal provocation may well depend on the particular characteristics or circumstances of the person to whom a taunt or insult is addressed. To taunt a person because of his race, his physical infirmities or some shameful incident in his past may well be considered by the jury to be more offensive to the person addressed, however equable his temperament, if the facts on which the taunt is founded are true than it would be if they were not. It would stultify much of the mitigation of the previous harshness of the common law in ruling out verbal provocation as capable of reducing murder to manslaughter if the jury could not take into consideration all those factors which in their opinion would affect the gravity of taunts and insults when applied to the person to whom they are addressed. So to this extent at any rate the unqualified proposition accepted by this House in *Bedder* v *DPP*... that for the purposes of the "reasonable man" test any unusual physical characteristics of the accused must be ignored requires revision as a result of the passing of the Act of 1957.

That he was only 15 years of age at the time of the killing is the relevant characteristic of the accused in the instant case. It is a characteristic which may have its effects on temperament as well as physique. If the jury think that the same power of self-control is not be be expected in an ordinary, average or normal boy of 15 as in an older person, are they to treat the lesser powers of self-control possessed by an ordinary, average or normal boy of 15 as the standard of self-control with which the conduct of the accused is to be compared?

It may be conceded that in strict logic there is a transition between treating age as a characteristic that may be taken into account in assessing the gravity of the provocation addressed to the accused and treating it as a characteristic to be taken into account in determining what is the degree of self-control to be expected of the ordinary person with whom the accused's conduct is to be compared. But to require old heads on young shoulders is inconsistent with the law's compassion of human infirmity to which Sir Michael Foster ascribed the doctrine of provocation more than two centuries ago. The distinction as to the purposes for which it is legitimate to take the age of the accused into account involves considerations of too great nicety to warrant a place in deciding a matter of opinion, which is no longer one to be decided by a judge trained in logical reasoning but by a jury drawing on their experience of how ordinary human beings behave in real life.

There is no direct authority prior to the Act of 1957 that expressly states that the age of the accused could not be taken into account in determining the standard of self-control for the purposes of the reasonable man test – unless this is implicit in the reasoning of Lord Simonds LC in *Bedder* ... The Court of Appeal distinguished the instant case from that of *Bedder* on the ground that what it was there said must be ignored was an unusual characteristic that distinguished the accused from ordinary normal persons, whereas nothing could be more ordinary or normal than to be aged 15. The reasoning in *Bedder* would, I think, permit of this distinction between normal and abnormal characteristics, which may affect the powers of self-control of the accused; but for reasons that I have already mentioned the proposition stated in *Bedder* requires qualification as a consequence of changes in the law affected by the Act of 1957. To try to salve what can remain of it without conflict with the Act could in my view only lead to unnecessary and unsatisfactory complexity in a question which has now become a question for the jury alone. In my view *Bedder*, like *Mancini* ... and *Holmes* ... ought no longer to be treated as an authority on the law of provocation.

In my opinion a proper direction to a jury on the question left to their exclusive determination by section 3 of the Act of 1957 would be on the following lines. The judge should state what the question is using the very terms of the section. He should then explain to them that the reasonable man referred to in the question is a person having the power of self-control to be expected of an ordinary person of the sex and age of the accused, but in other respects sharing such of the accused's characteristics as they think would affect the gravity of the provocation to him; and that the question is not merely whether such a person would in like circumstances be provoked to lose his self-control but also whether he would react to the provocation as the accused did.

I accordingly agree with the Court of Appeal that the judge ought not to have instructed the jury to pay no account to the age of the accused even though they themselves might be of opinion that the degree of self-control to be expected in a boy of that age was less than in an adult. So to direct them was to impose a fetter on the right and duty of the jury which the Act accords to them to act on their own opinion on the matter.'

R v *Johnson* [1989] 1 WLR 740 Court of Appeal (Criminal Division) (Watkins LJ, McCowan and Judge JJ)

Provocation – self induced

Facts
The appellant had made unpleasant comments to the deceased and his female companion. The deceased had retaliated by threatening the appellant with a beer glass. The appellant responded by fatally stabbing the deceased with a flick knife. At his trial the judge, following *Edwards* v *R* [1973] AC 648, refused to leave the defence of provocation to the jury on the basis that it had been self-induced. The appellant was convicted of murder and appealed.

Held
The appeal would be allowed, the conviction for murder would be quashed and a conviction for manslaughter substituted. Section 3 of the Homicide Act 1957 provides that anything can amount to provocation, including actions provoked by the accused. The appellant had been deprived of the opportunity of having his defence considered properly by the jury.

Watkins LJ:

'In the course of the submissions from both counsel for defence and the Crown, the judge raised the matter of "self-induced" provocation. He said: "It is rather difficult to see how a man who excites provocative conduct can in turn rely upon it as provocation in the criminal law."

He was referring there to the unpleasant threatening behaviour by the appellant at the start of the incident. No authority on this point was cited to the judge. The concept of self-induced provocation was not analysed. Counsel for the Crown did not rely on it and, in giving his ruling, the judge did not refer to it. In his conclusion the judge agreed with the submission of the Crown that it would be inappropriate, having regard to the evidence, to leave provocation to the jury. Hence the lack of direction to the jury on this issue.'

His Lordship then referred to s3 of the Homicide Act 1957, *DPP* v *Camplin* [1978] AC 705, and the Privy Council's decision in *Edwards* v *R* [1973] AC 648, and continued:

'On the particular facts of the case Lord Pearson, giving the judgment of the Board, said, at p658:

"On principle it seems reasonable to say that – (1) a blackmailer cannot rely on the predictable results of his own blackmailing conduct as constituting provocation... and the predictable results may include a considerable degree of hostile reaction by the person sought to be blackmailed... (2) but if the hostile reaction by the person sought to be blackmailed goes to extreme lengths it might constitute sufficient provocation even for the blackmailer; (3) there would in many cases be a question of degree to be decided by the jury."

Those words cannot, we think, be understood to mean, as was suggested to us, that provocation which is "self-induced" ceases to be provocation for the purposes of section 3.

The relevant statutory provision being considered by the Privy Council was in similar terms to section 3. In view of the express wording of section 3, as interpreted in *R* v *Camplin* [1978] AC 705 which was decided after *Edwards* v *The Queen* [1973] AC 648, we find it impossible to accept that the mere fact that a defendant caused a reaction in others, which in turn led him to lose his self-control, should result in the issue of provocation being kept outside a jury's consideration. Section 3 clearly provides that the question is whether things done or said or both provoked the defendant to lose his self-control. If there is any evidence that it may have done, the issue must be left to the jury. The jury would then have to consider all the circumstances of the incident, including all the relevant behaviour of the defendant, in deciding (a) whether he was in fact provoked and (b) whether the provocation was enough to make a reasonable man do what the defendant did.

Accordingly, whether or not there were elements in the appellant's conduct which justified the conclusion that he had started the trouble and induced others, including the deceased, to react in the way they did, we are firmly of the view that the defence of provocation should have been left to the jury.

Since it is not possible for us to infer from their verdict that the jury inevitably would have concluded that provocation as well as self-defence had been disproved the verdict of murder will be set aside. A conviction for manslaughter on the basis of provocation will be substituted.'

Commentary

The decision of the Privy Council in *Edwards* v *R*, which is clearly only persuasive, is very difficult to reconcile with the present case. It is submitted that the broader approach of the Court of Appeal represents the more accurate and desirable statement of the law.

R v *Morhall* [1995] 3 WLR 330 House of Lords (Lords Goff, Browne-Wilkinson, Slynn, Nicholls and Steyn)

Provocation – whether glue-sniffing addiction a characteristic of the reasonable man

Facts

The appellant killed another man named Denton following an argument over the appellant's addiction to glue-sniffing. The defence of provocation was put forward on the appellant's behalf at his trial for murder, and following an intervention by counsel for the appellant, the trial judge directed the jury that the characteristic of glue-sniffing was something that they should take into account because it was the issue to which the provocative words were related. The appellant was convicted of murder, and appealed on the ground that the trial judge's direction on this point had been inadequate. The Court of Appeal dismissed his appeal on the basis that the attribution of a characteristic such as an addiction to glue-sniffing was inconsistent with the concept of the reasonable man that had been developed in previous cases, hence the trial judge had been over-generous in his concession to the appellant. The appellant now appealed to the House of Lords for whom the Court of Appeal certified the following point of law: 'When directing a jury on provocation under s3 Homicide Act 1957, and explaining to them in accordance with the model direction of Lord Diplock in *DPP* v *Camplin* ... should the judge exclude from the jury's consideration characteristics and past behaviour of the defendant, at which taunts are directed, which in the judge's view are inconsistent with the concept of a reasonable man?'

Held

The appeal would be allowed, and a conviction for manslaughter substituted.

Lord Goff (having considered the authorities his Lordship considered whether the addiction to glue-sniffing should have been taken into account):

'Judging from the speeches in *R* v *Camplin,* it should indeed have been taken into account. Indeed, it was a characteristic of particular relevance, since the words of the deceased which were said to constitute provocation were directed towards the defendant's shameful addiction to glue-sniffing and his inability to break himself of it. Furthermore, there is nothing in the speeches in *R* v *Camplin* to suggest that a characteristic of this kind should be excluded from consideration. On the contrary, in the passage which I have already quoted from his speech Lord Diplock spoke of the jury taking into consideration "all those factors" which would affect the gravity of the taunts or insults when applied to the defendant. Likewise, Lord Simon of Glaisdale said, at p727D:

"... in determining whether a person of reasonable self-control would lose it in the circumstances, the entire factual situation, which includes the characteristics of the accused, must be considered."

Even so, the Court of Appeal felt that the defendant's addiction to glue-sniffing should be excluded because it was a characteristic which was repugnant to the concept of a reasonable man. It seems to me, with all respect, that this conclusion flows from a misunderstanding of the function of the so-called "reasonable person test" in this context. In truth the expression "reasonable man" or "reasonable person" in this context can lead to misunderstanding. Lord Diplock described it (in *R* v *Camplin* at p716G) as an "apparently inapt expression". This is because the "reasonable person test" is concerned not with ratiocination, nor with the reasonable man whom we know so well in the law of negligence (where we are concerned with reasonable foresight and reasonable care), nor with reasonable conduct generally. The function of the test is only to introduce, as a matter of policy, a standard of self-control which has to be complied with if provocation is to be established in law: see *R* v *Camplin* at p716F, per Lord Diplock, and p726F, per Lord Simon of Glaisdale. Lord Diplock himself spoke of "the reasonable or ordinary person", and indeed to speak of the degree of self-control attributable to the ordinary person is (despite the express words of the statute) perhaps more apt, and certainly less likely to mislead, than to do so with reference to the reasonable person. The word "ordinary" is in fact the adjective used in criminal codes applicable in some other common law jurisdictions (as in New Zealand, as to which see *R* v *McGregor* [1962] NZLR 1069 and *R* v *McCarthy* [1992] 2 NZLR 550, and in Tasmania, as to which see *Stingel* v *The Queen* (1990) 171 CLR 312). Indeed, by exploiting the adjective "reasonable" it is easy to caricature the law as stated in section 3 of the Act of 1957 by talking of the test of, for example, the reasonable blackmailer, or nowadays perhaps, the reasonable glue-sniffer; indeed, the sting of the caricature is derived from the implication that the adjective "reasonable" refers to a person who is guided by reason or who acts in a reasonable manner. This is however misleading. In my opinion it would be entirely consistent with the law as stated in section 3 of the Act of 1957, as properly understood, to direct the jury simply with reference to a hypothetical person having the power of self-control to be expected of an *ordinary* person of the age and sex of the defendant, but in other respects sharing such of the defendant's characteristics as they think would affect the gravity of the provocation to him: see *R* v *Camplin* [1978] AC 705, 718E–F, per Lord Diplock.

I wish however to stress two things. First, it is plain that, in the passage from his speech to which I have just referred, Lord Diplock was not attempting to dictate to judges how they should formulate their directions to juries on provocation. This appears from his statement that "a" proper direction to a jury would be "on the following lines". Provided that trial judges direct juries in accordance with the law, they may do so as they think right, tailoring their direction to the facts of the particular case before them. Second, in an appropriate case, it may be necessary to refer to other circumstances affecting the gravity of the provocation to the defendant which do not strictly fall within the description "characteristics", as for example the defendant's history or the circumstances in which he is placed at the relevant time (see *R* v *Camplin*, at p717C–D, per Lord Diplock, where he referred to "the particular characteristics or circumstances" of the defendant, and at p727D, per Lord Simon of Glaisdale, who referred to "the entire factual situation", including the characteristics of the defendant). At all events in the present case, when the judge turned to the second and objective inquiry, he was entitled to direct the jury that they must take into account the entire factual situation (and in particular the fact that the provocation was directed at a habitual glue-sniffer taunted with his habit) when considering the question whether the provocation was enough to cause a man possessed of an ordinary man's power of self-control to act as the defendant did.

However, the point can be taken further. Among the characteristics stated to be excluded from consideration on the approach favoured by the Court of Appeal is that of being a paedophile. But suppose that a man who has been in prison for a sexual offence, for example rape, has after his release been taunted by another man with reference to that offence. It is difficult to see why, on ordinary principles, his characteristic or history as an offender of that kind should not be taken into account as going to the gravity of the provocation. The point is well made by Professor Smith in his commentary on the present case [1993] Crim LR 957, 958:

> "Suppose that an old lag, now trying to go straight, is taunted with being a 'jailbird'. This might be extremely provoking, especially if it reveals his murky past to new friends or employers unaware of it. It really would not make much sense to ask the jury to consider the effect of such provocation on a man of good character."

In truth, the mere fact that a characteristic of the defendant is discreditable does not exclude it from consideration, as was made plain by Lord Diplock in *R* v *Camplin* when, at p717D, he referred to a shameful incident in a man's past as a relevant characteristic for present purposes. Indeed, even if the defendant's discreditable conduct causes a reaction in another, which in turn causes the defendant to lose his self-control, the reaction may amount to provocation: see *Edwards* v *The Queen* [1973] AC 648, a case concerned with a hostile reaction to his blackmailer by a man whom he was trying to blackmail, and *R* v *Johnson (Christopher)* [1989] 1 WLR 740 in which *Edwards* v *The Queen* was followed and applied by the Court of Appeal in the present case.

Of course glue-sniffing (or solvent abuse), like indulgence in alcohol or the taking of drugs, can give rise to a special problem in the present context, because it may arise in more than one way. First, it is well established that, in considering whether a person having the power of self-control to be expected of an ordinary person would have reacted to the provocation as the defendant did, the fact (if it be the case) that the defendant was the worse for drink at the time should not be taken into account, even though the drink would, if taken by him, have the effect of reducing an ordinary person's power of self-control. It is sometimes suggested that the reason for this exclusion is that drunkenness is transitory and cannot therefore amount to a characteristic. But I doubt whether that is right. Indeed some physical conditions (such as eczema) may be transitory and yet can surely be taken into account if the subject of taunts. In *R* v *Camplin* [1978] AC 705, 726F, Lord Simon of Glaisdale considered that drunkenness should be excluded as inconsistent with the concept of the reasonable man in the sense of a man of ordinary self-control; but it has to be recognised that, in our society, ordinary people do sometimes have too much to drink. I incline therefore to the opinion that the exclusion of drunkenness in this context flows from the established principle that, at common law, intoxication does not of itself excuse a man from committing a criminal offence, but on one or other of these bases it is plainly excluded. At all events it follows that, in a case such as the present, a distinction may have to be drawn between two different situations. The first occurs where the defendant is taunted with his addiction (for example, that he is an alcoholic, or a drug addict, or a glue-sniffer), or even with having been intoxicated (from any cause) on some previous occasion. In such a case, however discreditable such condition may be, it may where relevant be taken into account as going to the gravity of the provocation. The second is the simple fact of the defendant being intoxicated – being drunk, or high with drugs or glue – at the relevant time, which may not be so taken into account, because that, like displaying a lack of ordinary self-control, is excluded as a matter of policy. Although the distinction is a fine one, it will, I suspect, very rarely be necessary to explain it to a jury. Drunkenness itself may be a not unusual feature of cases raising the issue of provocation, as occurred, for example, in *R v Newell* (1980)) 71 Cr App R 331, where the drunkenness of the defendant was rightly excluded as irrelevant. But none of the counsel in the present case had any experience, or indeed knowledge, of a case other than the present in which addiction as such was the subject of verbal taunts or insults said to constitute provocation, with the effect that the addiction was therefore relevant as going to the gravity of the provocation. The present case may therefore be compared with *R v Newell*, in which the defendant's chronic alcoholism was excluded from consideration because "it had nothing to do with the words by which it is said that he was provoked": see p340, per Lord Lane CJ. I only wish to add a warning that the court's strong reliance in that case on the judgment of North J in *R v McGregor* [1962] NZLR 1069 must be regarded with caution, having regard to the reservations expressed with regard to that judgment by the Court of Appeal of New Zealand in *R v McCarthy* [1992] 2 NZLR 550, 557–558, per Cooke P delivering the judgment of the court, part of which is quoted by Professor Smith in his commentary on the present case [1993] Crim LR 957, 958. In particular, I wish to record my concern that the Court of Appeal in *R v Newell* may have placed too exclusive an emphasis on the word "characteristic", as a result of relying on the judgment of North J in *R v McGregor*, where North J was construing a statute in which that word was used.

It follows from what I have said that I am, with all respect, unable to accept the reasoning, or the conclusion, of the Court of Appeal.'

R v Sanders (1991) 93 Cr App R 245 Court of Appeal (Criminal Division) (Watkins LJ, Boreham and Tucker JJ)

Diminished responsibility – weigh to be given to medical evidence

Facts

The appellant had lived with the deceased as his common law wife. He suffered from diabetes, as a result of which he was only partially sighted. He became heavily reliant upon the deceased, and when he was no longer able to work started to suffer from depression. The appellant discovered that the deceased had started a relationship with another man, and as a result formed the intention to kill her, and then take his own life. On the day of her death the deceased visited the appellant, and during the course of the visit he attacked her with a hammer, killing her. He then attempted, unsuccessfully, to take his own life. At his trial for murder the appellant put forward evidence of diminished responsibility. The two expert witnesses both agreed that the appellant was suffering from an abnormality of the mind (caused by a reactive depression) that substantially impaired his responsibility for his actions. The Crown accepted that the appellant suffered from an abnormality of the mind, but did not accept that it affected his responsibility for his actions. Following conviction for murder the appellant appealed to the Court of Appeal on the ground that the trial judge had failed to point out to the jury that the expert testimony as to his state of mind was unanimous in finding that the requirements of s2(1) Homicide Act 1957 were satisfied.

Held

The appeal would be dismissed.

Watkins LJ:

In considering the submission (by Mr Gale, counsel for the appellant) that the trial judge's direction was defective in its failure to remind the jury, that in considering whether the requirements of s2(1) were met, they should note that the medical evidence was 'all one way', Watkins LJ stated the following:

> 'We were referred to the following authorities. *Matheson* [1958] 42 Cr App R 145; [1958] 2 All ER 87, was a five judge court and it was held that where on a charge of murder a defence of diminished responsibility is relied on, and the medical evidence that diminished responsibility exists is uncontradicted and the jury return a verdict of guilty of murder, if there are facts entitling the jury to reject or differ from the opinions of the medical men the Court of Criminal Appeal will not interfere with the verdict unless it can be said that the verdict would amount to a miscarriage of justice. There may be cases where evidence of the conduct of the accused before, at the time of and after the killing may be a relevant consideration for the jury in determining this issue. Where, however, there is unchallenged medical evidence of abnormality of mind and consequent substantial impairments of mental responsibility and no facts or circumstances appear which can displace or throw doubt on that evidence a verdict of guilty of murder is one which cannot be supported having regard to the evidence within the meaning of s4(1) of the Criminal Appeal Act 1907. In the course of the judgment of the Court, which was given by the Lord Goddard CJ, he said at p151 and p89 respectively:

>> "Here it is said there was evidence of premeditation and undoubtedly there was, but an abnormal mind is as capable of forming an intention and desire to kill as one that is normal; it is just what an abnormal mind might do. A desire to kill is quite common in cases of insanity."

> In the holding (42 Cr App R 145) the Court went on:

>> "Where a defence of diminished responsibility is raised, a plea of guilty to manslaughter on this ground should not be accepted; the issue must be left to the jury, as in the case of a defence of insanity."

> It was complained in the perfected grounds in this case if not in the course of submissions to us that the judge had made no reference to premeditation being not necessarily inconsistent with diminished responsibility. That complaint was, we think, quite unjustified for the judge said of it in the green bundle at p4C:

>> "Even if the killing was premeditated, the doctors say that does not exclude or discount diminished responsibility as a defence, or in any way alter their opinions. Although Dr Holland accepted that if the killing was in fact premeditated that would mean that the defendant had not told him the truth. It is for you to assess that evidence and say what you make of it."

> The next case which we were referred to was *Bailey* in 1961; reported in (1978) 66 Cr App R 31 [as a note, following *Walton* v *R*, below]. In that case a 17 year old youth was convicted of murder and sentenced to be detained at Her Majesty's pleasure. The Lord Chief Justice in giving the judgment of the Court said at p32:

>> "This Court has said on many occasions that of course juries are not bound by what the medical witness say, but at the same time they must act on evidence, and if there is nothing before them, no facts and no circumstances shown before them which throw doubt on the medical evidence, then that is all they are left with, and the jury, in those circumstances, must accept it. That was the effect of the decision of this court, sitting as a court of five judges, in the case of *Matheson* and as we understand it, nothing that this court said in the case of *Byrne* (1960) 44 Cr App R 246 throws any doubt upon what was said in *Matheson's* case."

> In *Walton* v *R* (1978) 66 Cr App R 25 [1978] AC 788, a Privy Council case, in the course of giving the opinion of the Board, Lord Keith of Kinkel stated at p30 and p793:

>> "These cases make clear that upon an issue of diminished responsibility the jury are entitled and indeed bound to consider not only the medical evidence but the evidence upon the whole facts and circumstances

of the case. These include the nature of the killing, the conduct of the accused before, at the time of and after it and any history of mental abnormality. It being recognised that the jury on occasion may properly refuse to accept medical evidence, it follows that they must be entitled to consider the quality and weight of that evidence. As was pointed out by Lord Parker CJ in *Byrne* (1960) 44 Cr App R 246, 254 what the jury are essentially seeking to ascertain is whether at the time of the killing the accused was suffering from a state of mind bordering on but not amounting to insanity. That task is to be approached in a broad common sense way."

Finally, we were asked to look at *Kiszko* (1979) 68 Cr App R 62. In that case Bridge LJ, giving the judgment of the Court stated at p69:

> "The most recent pronouncement on this subject, in a judgment of the Privy Council in the case of *Walton v R* (1978) 66 Cr App R 25 seems to us still to encapsulate the law entirely accurately and not to require any modification in the light of the provisions of s2(1)(a) of the Criminal Appeal Act 1968. After referring to earlier authorities, the judgment delivered by Lord Keith of Kinkel is in these terms at page 30. ..."

He then sets out the passage which I have already read. From these cases, in our opinion, two clear principles emerge where the issue is diminished responsibility. The first is that if there are no other circumstances to consider, unequivocal, uncontradicted medical evidence favourable to a defendant should be accepted by a jury and they should be so directed. The second is that where there are other circumstances to be considered the medical evidence, though it be unequivocal and uncontradicted, must be assessed in the light of the other circumstances. Turning again then to the summing up it is right to say that viewed in isolation the judge did not specifically refer to the medical evidence in the main passage of the summing up upon which Mr Gale concentrated his attention. Having dealt faultlessly, it is conceded, with the first two elements, namely abnormality of mind and whether that arose from inherent causes or disease, the judge went on in the orange bundle at p9E:

> "As to the third element, was the abnormality of mind such as substantially impaired the defendant's mental responsibility for his acts? This question is one of degree. It is essentially one for you, the jury. You must approach this question also in a board, common sense way. It means more than some trivial degree of impairment which does not make any appreciable difference to a person's ability to control himself, but it means, equally obviously, something less than total impairment. I can put that in a slightly different way. Substantial does not mean total, that is to say the mental responsibility need not be totally impaired, so to speak, destroyed altogether. It is something in between, and Parliament has left it to you, the jury, to say on the evidence, was the mental responsibility impaired and, if so, was it substantially impaired? The real issue, you may think, remember always that you decide this case, I do not so, is not whether the defendant was suffering from an abnormality of mind arising from inherent causes or induced by disease. The real question, you may think, the real issue is whether that abnormality of mind substantially impaired the defendant's mental responsibility for his acts."

Mr Gale relies heavily on the absence of reference to medical evidence there and in the early stages of the resumed summing up on the final day of the trial. Those passages simply cannot be viewed in isolation. There is, even in the passage relied upon, a reference to the evidence and in the green bundle at p3 the learned judge had this to say:

> "As to diminished responsibility, the defendant relies upon two doctors, whose evidence I will remind you of, who say, in a word, that looking at all the defendant's circumstances namely: his diabetes and its very considerable effect on him; his unemployment over two years, his deteriorating medical condition, particularly affecting his sight, his increasing dependency upon Mrs Sadlier; his deep affection for Mrs Sadlier and his realisation that he was losing her to another man; Mrs Sadlier's final rejection of him; the defendant's entirely genuine and very nearly successful suicide attempt; the defendant's depression and increasing preoccupation with Mrs Sadlier, his appetite, concentration and sleep being affected. Looking at all those matters, the doctors say that the defendant, at the time of the killing, was suffering from abnormality of mind arising from reactive depression which substantially impaired his mental responsibility for his acts in killing Mrs Sadlier. If you find that it is more likely than not that the doctors are right, having looked at all those circumstances, then the defendant will have established diminished responsibility and will thus be entitled to a verdict of manslaughter.

Having regard to that entirely correct direction we are satisfied that there is no substance whatever in the complaint that the judge did not direct the jury properly on the third element. That in our view he clearly did. We are also satisfied that the judge was not called upon to go further than he did with regard to the medical evidence, that is to say beyond reminding them, as he did, that it was so to speak all one way, that it was in the purely medical sense but it did not stand alone for the jury's consideration of the appellant's state of mind. It needs to be said anyway that the medical evidence was challenged upon certain of its assumptions by cross-examination. Regardless of that the jury had to bear in mind, among other matters, the manner of the killing, the contents of the will and the letters, when the last letter was written and certain admissions made by the appellant to the police in interview. We conclude that the summing up, without exception, was a model, to use Mr Gale's words, and therefore cannot in any way be complained of.'

R v Sanderson (1994) 98 Cr App R 325 Court of Appeal (Criminal Division) (Roch LJ, McCullough and Alliot JJ)

Diminished responsibility – nature of abnormality of the mind

Facts
The appellant had killed a woman, and at his trial for murder sought to raise the defence of diminished responsibility based on evidence of his long term use of heroin and cocaine. There was a conflict of expert medical evidence as to the relevance of the drug taking as regards diminished responsibility. For the appellant it was contended that he suffered from an abnormality of the mind, namely paranoid psychosis, that arose from inherent causes, such as the appellant's upbringing, and had been exacerbated by his drug taking. For the Crown it was contended that the appellant did suffer from a form of paranoia that was related to drug use, and that he would not suffer from any paranoia if the drug taking ceased. The appellant was convicted of murder and appealed.

Held
The appeal would be allowed, and a conviction for manslaughter on the grounds of diminished responsibility substituted.

Roch LJ:

"In this case there could not have been any real issue that the appellant, at the time he killed Miss Glasgow, was suffering from an abnormality of mind. He had no reason to want her death apart from his deluded beliefs for weeks. The way in which he inflicted death upon her and his subsequent behaviour all indicated that at the time his judgment and control over his emotions were not those of a normal mind. The first issue which arose on the medical evidence was the nature of that abnormality of mind: was it a paranoid psychosis, that is to say a serious disorder of the mind in which the appellant was suffering from fixed delusions centering around some perverted idea which had some important bearing on his actions, or was he suffering from simple paranoia?

The second issue which arose out of the medical evidence was the cause of the abnormality of mind. Was the abnormality of mind due to inherent causes, the appellant's childhood and upbringing, possibly exacerbated by drug addiction, or simply a side effect or consequence of his drug-taking? It is now well established by authority that for abnormality of the mind to come within the subsection it must be caused by one of the matters listed in the subsection; that is to say it must arise from a condition of arrested or retarded development of mind – of which there is no suggestion in this case – or from inherent causes or be induced by disease or injury.

Dr Bowden's evidence was that the appellant did not have the mental illness of paranoid psychosis and that as far as he was aware medical science showed that the taking of heroin and cocaine could not injure the structures of the brain. Consequently, his evidence was to the effect that the appellant did not and had not had any injury or disease which could have induced the paranoia. Further, his evidence denied that the paranoia arose from inherent cause; it arose simply because the appellant used cocaine. There was no evidence that his use of cocaine was involuntary.

In those circumstances, in our judgment the Common Serjeant was quite correct to direct the jury that if they accepted the evidence of Dr Bowden and rejected that of Dr Coid the defence of diminished responsibility had to fail. In our judgment the jury could not have found that the appellant was suffering from an abnormality of mind within section 2(1) on the evidence of Dr Bowden. Consequently, the first ground of appeal fails.

The Court considers that there is substance in the second and third submissions made by the appellant's counsel, and that for the reasons which we shall give shortly, the jury's verdict in this case is unsafe and unsatisfactory.

Cases of diminished responsibility can become difficult and confusing for a jury, and it is important that the judge in directing the jury should tailor his directions to suit the facts of the particular case. We think it will rarely be helpful to the jury to read to them section 2(1) in its entirety. Further, we consider that Annex F would have been of greater assistance had the words in brackets been confined to "arising from any inherent cause or induced by disease", there being no evidence of arrested or retarded development or of injury.

The judge in his directions to the jury at p9G, which we have already cited, then summarising the defendant's medical evidence and comparing it with the Crown's medical evidence, referred to the abnormality of mind arising from any inherent cause or disease on three occasions. In his final direction to the jury on diminished responsibility at the end of the summing-up, the judge again referred to those two potential causes when he said:

> "Has the defendant proved that he was suffering from an abnormality of mind through inherent cause or induced by disease, that is to say a paranoid psychosis which is a mental illness, whether exacerbated by drugs or not?"

Again the jury were being directed to consider whether the abnormality of mind arose either from inherent cause or was induced by disease. Further, that direction was so worded that the jury could understand the disease to be the mental illness of paranoid psychosis.

However, earlier in the summing up, the judge summarised Dr Coid's opinion in this way:

> "Dr Coid's opinion was this: 'The defendant was at the time of the killing and is now suffering from paranoid psychosis, a mental illness, forming incorrect and abnormal beliefs about other people. This was there already, irrespective of drug abuse. Although paranoid psychosis can be exacerbated by the use of cocaine over the years and much worse, nonetheless, quite apart from the drugs, paranoid psychosis, the mental illness, was there and that amounted to an abnormality of mind,' which is, when you call it inherent or resulting from disease."

We take it the last part should read: "which it is, whether you call it inherent or resulting from disease."

Thus the jury were being told Dr Coid was saying that the abnormality of mind was paranoid psychosis. In our opinion it was those apparently contradictory directions which must have given rise to the jury's questions. Although their questions are not free from ambiguity the jury were probably asking:

> "1. What is meant by induced by disease or injury, that is to say what does induced mean?
> 2. Is paranoid psychosis a disease or injury which can induce an abnormality of mind?"

The judge interpreted the second question as being: "Can a paranoid psychosis be induced by disease or injury?" and told the jury that he did not know; that "nobody speaks of paranoid psychosis arising from disease of injury." That was simply not correct.

The judge had summarised the appellant's doctor's evidence at p9H:

> "It is said for the defence through Dr Coid that there was an underlying paranoid psychosis or mental illness which amounted to an abnormality of mind within the Act. It arose from an inherent cause or disease of long-standing."

Again, at p23E in summarising Dr Coid's evidence the judge told the jury that Dr Coid was saying that paranoid psychosis amounted to an abnormality of mind which it was whether one said it arose from inherent cause or was induced by disease.

The judge should have sought clarification of the jury's questions, and then, if the real difficulty was whether the mental illness or paranoid psychosis was a disease within the meaning of the subsection, he should have directed them that the medical evidence they had was that this abnormality of mind was the mental illness of paranoid psychosis, if Dr Coid was right, and if Dr Coid was correct as to the aetiology of that mental illness, then it came within the words: "arising from any inherent cause" and was therefore within the subsection. In our judgment the answers that the judge gave failed to answer the questions which we believe the jury were asking, and would, in any event have confused them rather than have helped them.

Mr Worsley for the Crown submits that the central issue was left to the jury. The judge finally left to the jury the substantive defence which the appellant was raising. The jury were being told, correctly, that if they accepted Dr Coid's evidence, then the defence, subject to their view on the second question set out in Annex F, would succeed, whereas if they preferred Dr Bowden's evidence, the defence failed. Thus, submits Mr Worsley, even if the questions had been clarified and direct answers given, the jury's verdict would have been the same. He invites us to apply the proviso.

To that submission, Mr Jones replied that the questions themselves showed that the jury were inclined to accept that there was a paranoid psychosis, ie Dr Coid's evidence, rather than Dr Bowden's simple paranoia resulting from the taking of cocaine. The jury's concern was whether the paranoid psychosis came within the subsection. The jury should have been directed that the paranoid psychosis described by Dr Coid could, as a matter of law, come within the subsection. Had that direction been given, the probable verdict would have been one of manslaughter.

We agree with that submission by Mr Jones.

Before concluding this judgment, the Court pays tribute to the arguments of both counsel, and especially to the submissions of Mr Jones, who took us to the legislation on mental deficiency preceding the 1957 Act and two lines of authorities. The first was cases such as *Seers* (1984) 79 Cr App R 261, 264, on the nature and degree of impairment of mental responsibility which is within the section, and the second, cases where the defendant had been abusing drugs or alcohol, such as *Fenton* (1975) 61 Cr App R 261 and *Tandy* (1988) 87 Cr App R 45.

Mr Jones submitted that "disease" in the phrase "disease or injury" in section 2(1) meant "disease of the mind" and was apt to cover mental illnesses which were functional as well as those which were organic. This interesting and difficult question does not, in our view, require an answer in this case. We content ourselves with observing that we did not find the pre-1957 Act authority particularly persuasive in deciding what is meant by "disease or injury" in section 2(1) of the 1957 Act because those authorities were concerned with the meaning of words used by judges to delimit the special defence of insanity which originally resulted in a verdict of guilty by reason of insanity and lead to the defendant being sent to a secure mental institution. We incline to the view that that phrase "induced by disease or injury" must refer to organic or physical injury or disease of the body including the brain, and that that is more probable because Parliament deliberately refrained from referring to the disease of, or injury to, the mind, but included as permissible causes of an abnormality of mind " any inherent cause" which would cover functional mental illness.

For those reasons we allow this appeal, quash the conviction of murder and substitute the conviction of manslaughter.'

R v Seers (1984) 79 Cr App R 261 Court of Appeal (Criminal Division) (Griffiths LJ, Stocker J, and Sir John Thompson)

Diminished responsibility – whether borderline insanity

Homicide II: Voluntary Manslaughter

Facts (as stated by Griffiths J)

'The appellant killed his wife on November 21, 1981, by stabbing her in the chest in the street outside the hostel in which she had been living with their two children after she had left the matrimonial home on October 18. The appellant pleaded guilty to the manslaughter of his wife but raised the defences of provocation and diminished responsibility in answer to the charge of murder.

His defence on the ground of diminished responsibility was supported by the prison medical officer, Dr Rahman, whose evidence was that the appellant was suffering from chronic reactive depression that amounted to a mental illness properly characterised as an abnormality of mind within the meaning of section 2 of the Homicide Act 1957 and that it was of a degree that substantially impaired his mental responsibility at the time of the killing.

The prosecution called a consultant psychiatrist Dr Anton-Stevens who agreed that the appellant was suffering from reactive depression but in his opinion it was not so severe as to amount to an abnormality of mind and did not substantially impair his mental responsibility for killing his wife. Both doctors agreed that a reactive depressive illness could be so severe as to amount to an abnormality of mind and to substantially impair mental responsibility at the time of a killing. The issue between them in this case was the degree of severity of the reactive depression and on which side of the line it fell when applying the test contained in section 2 of the Act.

The prosecution also relied upon the evidence of a number of witnesses who had heard the appellant threaten to kill his wife in the days leading up to the killing which they said indicated a degree of premeditation. The defence, on the other hand, interpreted this evidence as supporting a diagnosis of abnormality of mind on the ground that no normal person intending a murder goes around announcing his intention to commit it.

There was also some lay evidence on which the defence relied indicating a deterioration in the physical appearance and the behaviour of the appellant in the month after his wife left him and before he killed her. The learned judge, no doubt basing himself upon a passage in the judgment of this Court in *Byrne* (1960) 44 Cr App R 246; [1960] 2 QB 396, directed the jury that the test to be applied to determine whether the appellant was suffering from diminished responsibility was whether he could be described in popular language as partially insane or on the borderline of insanity. This was the only test propounded by the judge and he repeated it in various passages of his summing-up.'

The appellant was convicted of the murder of his wife. He appealed against his conviction on the ground that the judge misdirected the jury on the issue of diminished responsibility.

Held

The appeal would be allowed.

Griffiths LJ:

'When first dealing with the defence of diminished responsibility, which is notoriously difficult to explain to a jury, after reading the words of section 2 of the Homicide Act 1957 the judge said:

"Now, that abnormality does not have to go to the extent that the defendant was what could properly be called insane. That would provide a wholly different and separate defence of its own in law, insanity certifiable as such, and no-one suggests that. This defendant falls within that degree of the diminished responsibility test involving his mental state which, in popular language, or ordinary language, would be described as either partial insanity or being on the borderline of insanity, and juries have often been directed that that is a good test for considering whether a man suffers from diminished responsibility and that test has been approved in higher courts than this, and it is for that reason that those very words were put to Dr Rahman to ask if he agreed that this man was not such as could be described as partially insane or being on the borderline of being insane, and he agreed that that description did not apply. That is a test that you can properly take into account." Later he said: "You must consider to what extent you think his condition at that stage, in the circumstances he was in was particularly abnormal, bearing in mind, no doubt, that in our modern age tens of thousands of marriages break up and tens of thousands of marriages result in broken homes in which one parent is deprived of the loss of having the children to live with him or her. Some of them, a large number of them, undoubtedly cause the greatest possible stress of a broken marriage in which children are separated and people become desperately worried and anxious in such circumstances, and the more so if it is against the background of either a business failure or, at the present time, being out of work, but that does not mean that people can be called, in ordinary language, on the borderline of insanity, does it, and that is the issue that you are looking at here." Finally he said: "The just and fair way of putting this, which I have already referred you to in this case, is to ask yourselves the question whether the mental abnormality in this man's case amounts to such a degree that it could be described in popular language as partial insanity or being on the borderline of insanity. When that was put to Dr Rahman he agreed not only that it did not apply to this defendant but he agreed ... anyway the question was put to him that the defendant came nowhere near it, and that is the view of Dr Anton-Stevens from his assessment too."

It is submitted on behalf of the appellant that this was not a case in which the jury would be assisted to determine either the question of mental abnormality or diminution of mental responsibility by reference to borderline or partial insanity.

Although both doctors agreed that a depressive illness could result in an abnormality of mind which would substantially impair a person's mental responsibility, Mr Taylor [for the appellant] submitted that the layman did not readily assimilate a depressive illness with insanity which was associated in the lay mind with such illnesses as schizophrenia or paranoia. Furthermore, says Mr Taylor, the judge virtually withdrew the defence of diminished responsibility from the jury by pointing out to them that both doctors agreed that the appellant was not on the borderline of insanity. It is submitted that the judge should have given a direction in accordance with the substance of the direction in *Byrne* (supra) and in particular should have directed the jury to consider whether the appellant's ability to control his hostility towards his wife had been substantially impaired by a depressive illness, and that this was not an appropriate case to introduce the concept of partial insanity, and still less to give that as the sole test.

The appellant relies upon the decision of the Privy Council in *Rose v The Queen* (1961) 45 Cr App R 102, 106; [1961] AC 496, 507, 508 in which Lord Tucker after citing the judgment of Lord Parker CJ in *Byrne* (1960) 44 Cr App R 246, 252; [1960] 2 QB 396, 403, had this to say of the test of partial insanity:

"Their Lordships respectfully accept this interpretation of the words 'abnormality of mind' and 'mental responsibility' as authoritative and correct. They would not, however, consider that the Court of Criminal Appeal was intending to lay down that in every case the jury must necessarily be directed that the test is always to be the borderline of insanity. There may be cases in which the abnormality of mind relied upon cannot readily be related to any of the generally recognised types of 'insanity'. If, however, insanity is to be taken into consideration, as undoubtedly will usually be the case, the word must be used in its broad popular sense. It cannot too often be emphasised that there is no formula that can safely be used in every case – the direction to the jury must always be related to the particular evidence that has been given and there may be cases where the words 'borderline' and 'insanity' might not be helpful."

We respectfully agree with that passage. It is to be remembered that in *Byrne* (supra) all the doctors agreed that Byrne could be described as partially insane; he was a sexual psychopath who had hideously mutilated a young woman he had killed. In such a case the evidence justifies inviting a jury to determine the defence of impairment of mental responsibility by a test of partial insanity. But it is not a legitimate method of construing an Act of Parliament to substitute for the words of the Act an entirely different phrase and to say that it is to apply in all circumstances. We are sure that this was not the intention of the Court in *Byrne* (supra), and the phrase was, used as one way of assisting the jury to determine the degree of impairment of mental responsibility in an appropriate case, and no doubt to point out that Parliament by the use of the word "substantial" was indicating a serious degree of impairment of mental responsibility. However, we do not think that in a case such as this dealing with a depressive illness it is appropriate to direct a jury solely in terms of partial or borderline insanity. Indeed, we doubt if it is a helpful test at all in such a case. It is interesting to see how Dr Rahman dealt in his evidence with such a test in relation to a reactive depression. "(Q) There are, of course, certain recognised forms of mental illness like schizophrenia? (A) That is insanity. (Q) So far as reactive depression is concerned, how is that termed by the psychiatrist? (A) It is not described as insanity. (Q) Insanity, how is it described? (A) It is a mental state, a psychosis."

We think a jury would be likely to view the matter in the same way, and however seriously depressed they might have thought this appellant, with whatever effect that might have had on his mental state, they would not consider him to be partially insane or on the borderline of insanity. This being so they were bound on the judge's direction to find that the appellant had not made out the defence of diminished responsibility. There was in the view of this Court evidence in this case that would have justified a jury in returning a verdict of manslaughter on grounds of diminished responsibility if directed in accordance with *Byrne* (supra) but leaving out what we consider on the evidence in this case to be the inappropriate test of partial or borderline insanity. For the reasons we have given we are satisfied that the summing-up contained a material misdirection on the issue of diminished responsibility ...'

R v Tandy [1989] 1 WLR 350 Court of Appeal (Criminal Division) 45 (Watkins LJ, Rose J, and Roch J)

Diminished responsibility – relationship with alcoholism

Facts

The defendant, an alcoholic, admitted killing her daughter by strangulation whilst intoxicated. She was convicted following the trial judge's direction to the jury that, as she had chosen to start drinking on the day of the killing, she could not plead that she was suffering from diminished responsibility brought on by the 'disease' of alcoholism. The defendant appealed on the ground that this had been a mis-direction.

Held

The appeal would be dismissed

Watkins LJ:

'The second issue raised at the trial was the defence of diminished responsibility under section 2(1) of the Homicide Act 1957.

It was raised in this way: the appellant was at all material times an alcoholic. According to her first husband she had by 1980 been in that condition. Her own evidence was that she had been drinking heavily for a number of years, her drinking being due to loneliness and two unhappy marriages. She told the doctors who examined her, and the jury, that she normally drank either Barley Wine or Cinzano, but that on Monday, March 3, she had purchased a bottle of vodka. She had not opened this until the morning of the Wednesday, but having opened and started the bottle of vodka, she had consumed 9/10ths of it during the course of that day. She had had her last drink at about 6.30 p.m. She had not previously drunk vodka. Vodka contains more alcohol than Cinzano which the appellant said she had drunk on Monday, 3 March. She could not recall whether or not she had had a drink on the Tuesday.

Scientific evidence showed that her blood-alcohol level at midnight on Wednesday, 5 March, when a sample of blood was taken from her by Dr Stoker, was 240 milligrammes of alcohol per 100 millilitres of blood. The opinion of Dr Wood, a consultant forensic psychiatrist called by the defence, was that at the time of the act of strangulation the level of alcohol in the appellant's blood would have been not less than 330 milligrammes of alcohol per 100 millilitres of blood and could have been anything up to 400 milligrammes of alcohol per 100 millilitres of blood.

Dr Lawson, who gave evidence for the Crown, said that in his view the appellant's blood at the time of the strangulation would have contained approximately 300 milligrammes of alcohol per 100 millilitres of blood. The medical evidence indicated that this level of alcohol would be a lethal intake of intoxicants for a normal person, but that alcoholics, because of their persistent abuse of alcohol, become able to tolerate such levels of alcohol in their blood streams and to dissipate alcohol from their blood streams more quickly than non-alcoholics are able to do. Indeed in this case the evidence of Dr Stoker, who examined the appellant when at midnight he obtained the sample of blood from her, was that her movements were co-ordinated, her speech was all right and the appellant displayed no clinical evidence of intoxication. Dr Stoker had observed her walking up two flights of stairs.

There were three principal areas of conflict between the medical witnesses called at the trial on behalf of the appellant and the medical witness called by the Crown. The first was as to whether alcoholism is or is not a disease. Dr Wood and Dr Milne (a consultant psychiatrist) both expressed the view that alcohol dependence syndrome, or alcoholism in the severity manifested in the appellant's case, constituted a disease. Dr Lawson, who accepted that the appellant was an alcoholic, expressed the opinion that alcoholism, even chronic alcoholism, is not a disease.

In summing up the judge told the jury with regard to that:

"... it is totally unnecessary for you to involve yourselves in that medical controversy about labelling. You have to apply the words of the Act of Parliament in a common sense way and those words are reflected in the wording on that sheet before you." – Here the judge was referring to a document headed, "Questions for the jury" which he had prepared and provided to the jury. – "If you find that a woman is suffering from an abnormality of mind in the form of grossly impaired judgment and emotional responses and if you find that she is so suffering as a direct result of a condition over which she has – and I emphasise the words – *no immediate control*, then you can say that the second element in this defence is proved because her abnormality of mind is induced by disease or injury."

The judge was there telling the jury that the issue they had to decide was not whether alcoholism is or is not a disease, but whether the appellant was suffering from an abnormality of mind, in the form of grossly impaired judgment and emotional responses, as a direct result of her alcoholism, or whether, as the Crown on the evidence of Dr Lawson contended, her abnormal state of mind at the moment of the act of strangulation was due to the fact that she was drunk on vodka.

The second area of conflict between the doctors was whether the appellant's drinking on the Wednesday was voluntary or involuntary. Dr Wood said of this that he thought it would have been very difficult for her to resist the temptation of drink on that day. She was under some pressure to continue drinking to stave off the shakiness and other symptoms of withdrawal affecting her. He also said he would argue that drinking to that extent (that is to say most of a bottle of vodka) was an inherent part of the disease. He considered that compulsion was certainly partly causative of her drinking as she did on that day in that the choice to do so was not a free choice. Compulsion stemmed from her being an alcoholic and her experience that to deny herself drink would lead her to being severely uncomfortable, if not ill. When asked if the appellant in his view at that time had control over her drinking habits, he replied, "No none whatsoever." Dr Milne said that he believed the appellant drank involuntarily, because she was an alcoholic. Dr Lawson agreed that a person who is an alcoholic has a craving for alcohol and a compulsion to drink. His view was that the appellant had control over whether she had the first drink of the day, but once she had had the first drink she was no longer in control.

The third area of conflict in the medical evidence was on the question whether if the appellant had not taken drink that day, she would have strangled her daughter. Dr Lawson put his view in one short answer: "I could not see her killing the child if she were sober." Dr Milne, when asked whether he went as far as to say that if the appellant had not consumed any drink that day she would have still committed this offence, answered "No." Dr Wood agreed that an alcoholic may do something which he or she would not otherwise do but for the intake of alcohol. When asked whether, if the appellant had not consumed any drink that day, she would have still done what she did to her daughter, he said, "I do not know. I think had she not consumed drink on that day she would have been quite seriously ill in another fashion by 8 o'clock that evening." He amplified that answer by saying that the appellant's problem on 5 March, was serious alcoholism and until she had withdrawn from alcohol, whether or not she was intoxicated, she would have suffered from seriously disturbed judgment and emotional control. He thought that her judgment and emotional control would have continued to be severely disturbed on the Wednesday, even had she not drunk the vodka which she drank that day.

The ground of appeal is that there was material misdirection of the jury in regard to the defence of diminished responsibility. The relevant passages in the summing up are where the judge said:

"The choice [of the appellant whether to drink or not to drink on Wednesday March 5 1986] may not have been easy but ... if it was there at all it is fatal to this defence, because the law simply will not allow a drug user, whether the drug be alcohol or any other, to shelter behind the toxic effects of the drug which he or she need not have used."

And where he stated earlier:

"If she had taken no drink on 5 March, 1986, or if you were satisfied that Dr Wood is right in saying that judgment and emotional response would have been grossly impaired even if no drink had been taken, then the answer would be easy, but clearly she did take drink on 5 March, and if she did that as a matter of choice, she cannot say in law or in common sense that the abnormality of mind which resulted was induced by disease."

Mr Stewart, the appellant's counsel, submits that these are misdirections, because: (1) The medical evidence had been unanimous that there might be compulsion to drink at least after the first drink of the day; that it was the cumulative effect of the consumption of 9/10ths of the bottle of vodka which caused her to be in the state of intoxication she was in at the time of the killing. By his directions the judge removed the question of compulsion after the taking of the first drink from the jury's consideration. (2) The directions removed from the jury's consideration Dr Wood's evidence that the alcoholism alone produced an abnormal state of mind which substantially impaired her mental responsibility for her acts. (3) The directions removed from the jury the issue which this Court in *R v Fenton* (1975) 61 Cr App R 261, 263 recognised could arise when an accused person proves such a craving for drink as to produce in itself an abnormality of mind. Lord Widgery CJ's actual words were:

"... cases may arise hereafter where the accused proves such a craving for drink or drugs as to produce in itself an abnormality of mind; but that is not proved in this case. The appellant did not give evidence and we do not see how self-induced intoxication can of itself produce an abnormality of mind due to inherent causes."

(The jury had been rightly told to ignore the effect of alcohol.)

Section 2(1) of the Homicide Act 1957 provides:

"Where a person kills ... he shall not be convicted of murder if he was suffering from such abnormality of mind (whether arising from a condition of arrested or retarded development of mind or any inherent causes or induced by disease or injury) as substantially impaired his mental responsibility for his acts and omissions in doing or being a party to the killing."

The authority of *R v Byrne* [1960] 2 QB 396, 403 established that the phrase "abnormality of mind" was wide enough to cover the mind's activities in all its aspects, including the ability to exercise will power to control physical acts in accordance with rational judgment. But "abnormality of mind" means a state of mind so different from that of ordinary human beings that a reasonable man would term it abnormal.

The defence of diminished responsibility was derived from the law of Scotland, in which one of the colloquial names for the defence was "partial insanity." Normal human beings frequently drink to excess and when drunk do not suffer from abnormality of mind, within the meaning of that phrase in section 2(1) of the Act of 1957.

Whether an accused person was at the time of the act which results in the victim's death suffering from any abnormality of mind is a question for the jury; and as this Court stated in *R v Byrne* (supra), although medical evidence is important on this question, the jury are not bound to accept medical evidence if there is other material before them from which in their judgment a different conclusion may be drawn.

The Court of Appeal in *R v Gittens* [1984] QB 698 said that it was a misdirection to invite the jury to decide whether it was inherent causes on the one hand or drink and pills on the other hand which were the main factor in causing the appellant in that case to act as he did. The correct direction in that case was to tell the jury that they had to decide whether the abnormality arising from the inherent causes substantially impaired the appellant's responsibility for his actions .... In the summing up and in the document headed "Questions for the jury," the judge set out the three matters which the defence had to establish on the balance of probability for the defence of diminished responsibility to succeed. No criticism of that part of the summing up or that part of the "Questions for the Jury" has been made nor could it have been.

So in this case it was for the appellant to show: (l) that she was suffering from an abnormality of mind at the time of the act of strangulation; (2) that that abnormality of mind was induced by disease, namely the disease of alcoholism; and (3) that the abnormality of mind induced by the disease of alcoholism was such as substantially impaired her mental responsibility for her act of strangling her daughter.

The principles involved in seeking answers to these questions are, in our view, as follows. The appellant would not establish the second element of the defence unless the evidence showed that the abnormality of mind at the time of the killing was due to the fact that she was a chronic alcoholic. If the alcoholism had reached the level at which her brain had been injured by the repeated insult from intoxicants so that there was gross impairment of her judgment and emotional responses then the defence of diminished responsibility was available to her, provided that she satisfied the jury that the third element of the defence existed. Further, if the appellant were able to establish that the alcoholism had reached the level where although the brain had not been damaged to the extent just stated, the appellant's drinking had become involuntary, that is to say she was no longer able to resist the impulse to drink, then the defence of diminished responsibility would be available to her, subject to her establishing the first and third elements, because if her drinking was involuntary, then her abnormality of mind at the time of the act of strangulation was induced by her condition of alcoholism.

On the other hand, if the appellant had simply not resisted an impulse to drink and it was the drink taken on the Wednesday which brought about the impairment of judgment and emotional response, then the defence of diminished responsibility was not available to the defendant.

In our judgment the direction which the judge gave the jury accurately reflected these principles. There was evidence on which the jury, directed as they were, could reach their verdict. The appellant had chosen to drink vodka on the Wednesday rather than her customary drink of Cinzano. Her evidence was that she might not have had a drink at all on the Tuesday. She certainly did not tell the jury that she must have taken drink on the Tuesday or Wednesday because she could not help herself. She had been able to stop drinking at 6.30 pm on the Wednesday evening although her supply of Vodka was not exhausted. Thus her own evidence indicated that she was able to exercise some control even after she had taken the first drink, contrary to the view of the doctors. There was the evidence of Dr Lawson that the appellant would have had the ability on that Wednesday to abstain from taking the first drink of the day.

Mr Smith, who appeared for the Crown, pointed out in his submissions that the abnormality of mind described by Dr Wood and Dr Milne was of grossly impaired judgment and emotional responses and it did not include an irresistible craving for alcohol.

The three matters on which the appellant relies in the perfected grounds of appeal for saying that there was a misdirection can be dealt with shortly. As to the first, in our judgment the judge was correct in telling the jury that if the taking of the first drink was not involuntary, then the whole of the drinking on the Wednesday was not involuntary. Further, as we have pointed out, the appellant's own evidence indicated that she still had control over her drinking on that Wednesday after she had taken the first drink.

As to the second, the jury were told correctly that the abnormality of mind with which they were concerned was the abnormality of mind at the time of act of strangulation and as a matter of fact by that time on that Wednesday the appellant had drunk 90 per cent of a bottle of vodka.

On the third point we conclude that for a craving for drinks or drugs in itself to produce an abnormality of mind within the meaning of section 2(1) of the Act of 1957, the craving must be such as to render the accused's use of drink or drugs involuntary. Therefore in our judgment the judge correctly defined how great the craving for drink had to be before it could in itself produce an abnormality of mind. In any event, it was not the evidence of the doctors called, on behalf of the appellant, that her abnormality of mind included, let alone consisted solely, of a craving for alcohol.

For those reasons we find that there was no material misdirection of the jury and we dismiss this appeal.'

26 Homicide III: Involuntary Manslaughter

R v *Adomako* [1994] 3 WLR 288 House of Lords (Lords Mackay, Keith, Goff, Browne-Wilkinson and Woolf)

Killing by gross negligence – fault required

Facts
The defendant was a locum tenens anaesthetist employed at a hospital. He was assisting during an operation on a patient for a detached retina. During the operation the tube from the patient's ventilator became detached. By the time the defendant became aware that something had gone wrong, the damage caused to the patient had become irreversible and he died. The defendant was convicted of manslaughter following a direction from the trial judge, in terms of gross negligence as the basis for liability rather than recklessness. Lord Taylor CJ summarised the ingredients of the offence as follows: proof of the existence of the duty, breach of the duty causing death, and gross negligence. Gross negligence could be any of the following (i) indifference to an obvious risk of injury to health; (ii) foreseeing the risk and determining to run it; (iii) appreciating the risk, intending to avoid it, but displaying a high degree of negligence in the adoption of avoidance techniques; (iv) failure to advert to a serious risk that goes beyond 'mere inadvertence' and which D should have adverted to because of the duty he was under.

Following an unsuccessful appeal the Court of Appeal certified the following point of law of general public importance for consideration by the House of Lords: 'In cases of manslaughter by gross negligence not involving driving but involving a breach of duty is it a sufficient direction to the jury to adopt the gross negligence test set out by the Court of Appeal in the present case following *R* v *Bateman* (1925) 19 Cr App R 8 and *Andrews* v *DPP* [1937] AC 576 without reference to the test of recklessness as defined in *R* v *Lawrence* 1982 AC 510 or as adapted to the circumstances of the case?'

Held
The appeal would be dismissed, the certified question being answered in the affirmative.

Lord Mackay (having referred to *R* v *Bateman* (1925) 19 Cr App R 8 and *Andrews* v *DPP* [1937] AC 576) observed at p295–298):

> 'In my opinion the law as stated in these two authorities is satisfactory as providing a proper basis for describing the crim of involuntary manslaughter. Since the decision in *Andrews* was a decision of your Lordships' House, it remains the most authoritative statement of the present law which I have been able to find and although its relationship to *R* v *Seymour (Edward)* [1983] 2 AC 493 is a matter to which I shall have to return, it is a decision which has not been departed from. On this basis in my opinion the ordinary principles of the law of negligence apply to ascertain whether or not the defendant has been in breach of a duty of care towards the victim who has died. If such breach of duty is established the next question is whether that breach of duty caused the death of the victim. If so, the jury must go on to consider whether that breach of duty should be characterised as gross negligence and therefore as a crime. This will depend

on the seriousness of the breach of duty committed by the defendant in all the circumstances in which the defendant was placed when it occurred. The jury will have to consider whether the extent to which the defendant's conduct departed from the proper standard of care incumbent upon him, involving as it must have done a risk of death to the patient, was such that it should be judged criminal.

It is true that to a certain extent this involves an element of circularity, but in this branch of the law I do not believe that it is fatal to its being correct as a test of how far conduct must depart from accepted standards to be characterised as criminal. This is necessarily a question of degree and an attempt to specify that degree more closely is I think likely to achieve only a spurious precision. The essence of the matter which is supremely a jury question is whether having regard to the risk of death involved, the conduct of the defendant was so bad in all the circumstances as to amount in their judgment to a criminal act or omission.

My Lords, the view which I have stated of the correct basis in law for the crime of involuntary manslaughter accords I consider with the criteria stated by counsel, although I have not reached the degree of precision in definition which he required, but in my opinion it has been reached so far as practicable and with a result which leaves the matter properly stated for a jury's determination.

My Lords in my view the law as stated in *R v Seymour (Edward)* [1983] 2 AC 493 should no longer apply since the underlying statutory provisions on which it rested have now been repealed by the Road Traffic Act 1991. It may be that cases of involuntary motor manslaughter will as a result become rare but I consider it unsatisfactory that there should be any exception to the generality of the statement which I have made, since such exception, in my view, gives rise to unnecessary complexity. For example in *Kong Cheuk Kwan v The Queen* (1985) 82 Cr App R 18 it would give rise to unnecessary differences between the law applicable to those navigating vessels and the lookouts on the vessels.

I consider it perfectly appropriate that the word "reckless" should be used in cases of involuntary manslaughter, but as Lord Atkin put it "in the ordinary connotation of that word". Examples in which this was done, to my mind, with complete accuracy are *R v Stone* [1977] QB 354 and *R v West London Coroner, ex parte Gray* [1988] QB 467.

In my opinion it is quite unnecessary in the context of gross negligence to give the detailed directions with regard to the meaning of the word "reckless" associated with *R v Lawrence (Stephen)* [1982] AC 510. The decision of the Court of Appeal Criminal Division in the other cases with which they were concerned at the same time as they heard the appeal in this case indicates that the circumstances in which involuntary manslaughter has to be considered may make the somewhat elaborate and rather rigid directions inappropriate. I entirely agree with the view that the circumstances to which a charge of involuntary manslaughter may apply are so various that it is unwise to attempt to categorise or detail specimen directions. For my part I would not wish to go beyond the description of the basis in law which I have already given.

In my view the summing up of the judge in the present case was a model of clarity in analysis of the facts and in setting out the law in a manner which was readily comprehensible by the jury. The summing up was criticised in respect of the inclusion of the following passage:

> "Of course you will understand it is not for every humble man of the profession to have all that great skill of the great men in Harley Street but, on the other hand, they are not allowed to practise medicine in this country unless they have acquired a certain amount of skill. They are bound to show a reasonable amount of skill according to the circumstances of the case, and you have to judge them on the basis that they are skilled men, but not necessarily so skilled as more skilful men in the profession, and you can only convict them criminally if, in your judgment, they fall below the standard of skill which is the least qualification which any doctor should have. You should only convict a doctor of causing a death by negligence if you think he did something which no reasonably skilled doctor should have done."

The criticism was particularly of the latter part of this quotation in that it was open to the meaning that if the defendant did what no reasonably skilled doctor should have done it was open to the jury to convict him of causing death by negligence. Strictly speaking this passage is concerned with the statement of a necessary condition for a conviction by preventing a conviction unless that condition is satisfied. It is incorrect to treat it as stating a sufficient condition for conviction. In any event I consider that this passage in the context was making the point forcefully that the defendant in this case was not to be judged by the standard of more skilled doctors but by the standard of a reasonably competent doctor. There were many other passages in the summing up which emphasised the need for a high degree of negligence if the jury were to convict and read in that context I consider that the summing up cannot be faulted.

For these reasons I am of the opinion that this appeal should be dismissed and that the certified question should be answered by saying:

> "In cases of manslaughter by criminal negligence involving a breach of duty, it is a sufficient direction to the jury to adopt the gross negligence test set out by the Court of Appeal in the present case following *R v Bateman* 19 Cr App R and *Andrews v Director of Public Prosecutions* [1937] AC 576 and that it is not necessary to refer to the definition of recklessness in *R v Lawrence* [1982] AC 510, although it is perfectly open to the trial judge to use the word 'reckless' in its ordinary meaning as part of his exposition of the law if he deems it appropriate in the circumstances of the particular case."

We have been referred to the Consultation Paper by the Law Commission on Criminal Law, Involuntary Manslaughter (1994) (Law Com No 135), and we have also been referred to a number of standard textbooks. I have also had the opportunity of considering the note on *R v Prentice* by Sir John Smith [1994] Crim LR 292 since the hearing was completed. Whilst I have not referred to these in detail I have derived considerable help in seeking to formulate my view as a result of studying them.

I have reached the same conclusion on the basic law to be applied in this case as did the Court of Appeal. Personally I would not wish to state the law more elaborately than I have done. In particular I think it is difficult to take expressions used in particular cases out of the context of the cases in which they were used and enunciate them as if applying generally. This can I think lead to ambiguity and perhaps unnecessary complexity. The task of trial judges in setting out for the jury the issues of fact and the relevant law in cases of this class is a difficult and demanding one. I believe that the supreme test that should be satisfied in such directions is that they are comprehensible to an ordinary member of the public who is called to sit on a jury and who has no particular prior acquaintance with the law. To make it obligatory on trial judges to give directions in law which are so elaborate that the ordinary member of the jury will have great difficulty in following them, and even greater difficulty in retaining them in his memory for the purpose of application in the jury room, is no service to the cause of justice. The experienced counsel who assisted your Lordships in this appeal indicated that as a practical matter there was a danger in over elaboration of definition of the word "reckless". While therefore I have said in my view it is perfectly open to a trial judge to use the word "reckless" if it appears appropriate in the circumstances of a particular case as indicating the extent to which a defendant's conduct must deviate from that of a proper standard of care, I do not think it right to require that this should be done and certainly not right that it should incorporate the full detail required in *Lawrence*.'

R v Cato [1976] 1 WLR 110 Court of Appeal (Criminal Division) (Lord Widgery CJ, O'Conner and Jupp JJ)

Nature of unlawful act in constructive manslaughter

Facts
The defendant and the deceased (Farmer), agreed to inject each other with heroin. The deceased had consented to a number of such injections during the course of an evening. The following morning he was found to have died from the effects of the drug taking. The defendant was convicted of maliciously administering a noxious substance contrary to s23 of the Offences Against the Person Act 1861, and of manslaughter, either on the basis that his unlawful act had caused death, or on the basis that he had recklessly caused Farmer's death. The defendant appealed against his convictions on the grounds, inter alia, that there had been no unlawful act since the deceased had consented to the injection of heroin, and

that the consent should have been taken into account in determining whether or not the defendant had acted recklessly.

Held

The appeal would be dismissed.

Lord Widgery CJ:

> 'The next matter, I think, is the unlawful act. Of course, on the first approach to manslaughter in this case it was necessary for the prosecution to prove that Farmer had been killed in the course of an unlawful act. Strangely enough, or it may seem strange to most of us, although the possession or supply of heroin is an offence, it is not an offence to take it, and although supplying it is an offence, it is not an offence to administer it. At least it is not made to be an offence, and so Mr Blom-Cooper [counsel for the defendant] says there was no unlawful act here. That which Cato did – taking Farmer's syringe already charged and injecting the mixture into Farmer as directed – is not an unlawful act, says Mr Blom-Cooper, because there is nothing there which is an offence against the Misuse of Drugs Act 1971, and when he shows us the terms of the section it seems that that is absolutely right.
>
> Of course if the conviction on count 2 remains (that is the charge under section 23 of administering a noxious thing), then that in itself would be an unlawful act. The prohibition in that statute would be enough in itself, and it is probably right to say that, as we are going to uphold the conviction on count 2, as will appear presently, that really answers the problem and destroys the basis of Mr Blom-Cooper's argument.
>
> But since he went to such trouble with the argument, and in respect for it, we think we ought to say that had it not been possible to rely on the charge under section 23 of the Offences against the Person Act 1861, we think there would have been an unlawful act here, and we think the unlawful act would be described as injecting the deceased Farmer with a mixture of heroin and water which at the time of the injection and for the purposes of the injection the accused had unlawfully taken into his possession.'

R v Church [1966] 1 QB 59 Court of Criminal Appeal (Edmund-Davies, Marshall and Widgery JJ)

Nature of the dangerous unlawful act in constructive manslaughter

Facts

The defendant had gone to his van with the deceased, Mrs Nott, for sexual purposes. She had mocked his impotence and he had attacked her, knocking her out. The defendant panicked, and wrongly thinking he had killed her, threw her unconscious body into a river, where she drowned. The defendant appealed against his conviction for manslaughter.

Held

The appeal would be dismissed.

Edmund-Davies LJ:

> 'In the judgment of this court [the trial judge's direction on unlawful manslaughter] ... was a misdirection. It amounted to telling the jury that, whenever any unlawful act is committed in relation to a human being which resulted in death there must be, at least, a conviction for manslaughter. This might at one time have been regarded as good law: ... But it appears to this court that the passage of years has achieved a transformation in this branch of the law and, even in relation to manslaughter, a degree of mens rea has become recognised as essential ... [T]he conclusion of this court is that an unlawful act causing the death of another cannot, simply because it is an unlawful act, render a manslaughter verdict inevitable. For such a verdict inexorably to follow, the unlawful act must be such as all sober and reasonable people

would inevitably recognise must subject the other person to, at least, the risk of some harm resulting therefrom, albeit not serious harm ...'

Commentary
See *R* v *Dawson*, below.

R v *Dalby* [1982] 1 WLR 425 Court of Appeal (Criminal Division) (Waller LJ, Jupp and Waterhouse JJ)

Nature of the unlawful act in constructive manslaughter

Facts
The defendant had been in lawful possession of a controlled drug. He had supplied a quantity of the drug to the deceased (a man named O'Such). The deceased had consumed a large quantity of the drug in one session, and subsequently injected himself with other substances. The following morning the deceased was found to have died of a drug overdose. The defendant was convicted of unlawful act manslaughter, based on his unlawful supply of the controlled drug, and he appealed on the basis that his supply of the drug was not a dangerous act which had operated as the direct cause of death. He contended that the death was due to the deceased's act in consuming such a large dose of the drug in such a short space of time.

Held
The conviction would be quashed.

Waller LJ:

'The difficulty in the present case is that the act of supplying a scheduled drug was not an act which caused direct harm. It was an act which made it possible, or even likely, that harm would occur subsequently, particularly if the drug was supplied to somebody who was on drugs. In all the reported cases, the physical act has been one which inevitably would subject the other person to the risk of some harm from the act itself. In this case, the supply of drugs would itself have caused no harm unless the deceased had subsequently used the drugs in a form and quantity which was dangerous ...

In the judgment of this Court, the unlawful act of supplying drugs was not an act directed against the person of O'Such and the supply did not cause any direct injury to him. The kind of harm envisaged in all the reported cases of involuntary manslaughter was physical injury of some kind as an immediate and inevitable result of the unlawful act, eg, a blow on the chin which knocks the victim against a wall causing a fractured skull and death, or threatening him with a loaded gun which accidentally fires, or dropping a large stone on a train (*DPP* v *Newbury*) or threatening another with an open razor and stumbling with death resulting (*Larkin*).

In the judgment of this Court, where the charge of manslaughter is based on an unlawful and dangerous act, it must be directed at the victim and likely to cause immediate injury, however slight.'

Commentary
See *R* v *Goodfellow*, below.

R v *Dawson* (1985) 81 Cr App R 150 Court of Appeal (Criminal Division) (Watkins LJ, Wood J and Sir John Thompson)

Constructive manslaughter – nature of unlawful act causing death.

318 General Paper I: Criminal Law

Facts

Dawson, accompanied by two other men, Nolan and Walmsley, carried out an attempted robbery at a petrol station. The cashier at the petrol station (Mr Black) was a 60 year old man who, unknown to the appellants, suffered from a heart disease. Dawson had pointed a replica hand gun at the cashier, and Walmsley had banged a pick axe handle on the counter. Money was demanded, but the cashier pressed the alarm button and the appellants fled empty handed. Shortly afterwards the cashier collapsed and died from a heart attack. Following conviction, the appellants sought to appeal on the grounds that the jury had been mis-directed as regards the law relating to the 'dangerous unlawful act' in manslaughter.

Held

As regards the convictions for manslaughter the appeals would be allowed.

Watkins LJ:

His Lordship recited the six perfected grounds of appeal, of which, the second and sixth are of relevance here. The second stated that the judge, wrongly in law, 'directed the jury that putting a person in such terror that he may suffer such emotional or physical disturbance as would be detrimental could for the relevant purpose constitute harm. It is argued that it is not open to a jury to convict if they find merely that an emotional disturbance that was detrimental was suffered by a deceased.'

The sixth stated that the judge, wrongly in law, 'directed the jury that the sane and reasonable people referred to in the test for the creation of the risk of some harm to the person must connote people who know all the facts, including, it is to be inferred, that the deceased suffered from chronic heart disease. There was no evidence that the appellants were aware of that condition. Whilst Walmsley did not include this in his perfected grounds, we shall assume that he seeks to rely on it nevertheless.'

> 'Counts 2 and 6, which can be taken together, have caused us much concern. It has, in our experience, been generally understood that the harm referred to in the second element of the offence of manslaughter, namely, the unlawful act, must be one that all sober and reasonable people would realise was likely to cause some, albeit not serious, harm, means physical harm ... there seems to us to be no sensible reason why shock produced by fright should not come within the definition of harm in this context. From time to time one hears the expression "frightened to death" without thinking that the possibility of such event occurring would be an affront to reason or medical knowledge. Shock can produce devastating and lasting effects, for instance upon the nervous system. That is surely harm, ie injury to the person. Why not harm in this context?
>
> In another context, s1 of the Prevention of Crime Act 1953, this Court in *Rapier* (1980) 70 Cr App R 17, seems to have no difficulty in comprehending that one effect of shock can be to produce injury to the person. At p19 Park J said:
>
>> "The judgment of the Court in that case [ie *Edmonds* (1963) 47 CR App R 114; [1963] 2 QB 142] was delivered by Winn J (as he then was). Towards the end of the judgment, at p121 and pp150, 151 of the respective reports, he said: 'The justification, the court assumes, which the learned commissioner had in mind for the adoption of his own phraseology including reference to intent to frighten is to be found in a decision of the Divisional Court reported in the name of *Woodward v Koessler* [1958] 3 All ER 557; [1958] 1 WLR 1255. That was a case where upon the facts it was plain that a sheath knife had been so brandished with such accompanying threatening behaviour that injury might very well be conclusively assumed to have been done as a result of the shock thereby caused. Whether that case must stand upon its own facts, it seems to the court that it is, to put it at its lowest, unsafe and undesirable that directions to juries based upon s1(4) [of the Prevention of Crime Act 1953] should include any reference to intent to frighten unless it be made clear in the passage in which such reference is made that the frightening must be of a kind for which the term 'intimidation' is far more appropriate and of a sort which is capable of producing injury through the operation of shock ...' This Court in the instant case wishes to emphasise that passage in the judgment of Winn J. In our view, in directing a jury in respect of an offence under this section the use of the word 'intimidate' should be avoided unless the evidence discloses that the intention of the person having with

him the article alleged to be an offensive weapon was to cause injury by shock and hence injury to the person; it would seem that circumstances giving rise to that situation must be exceedingly rare."

We shall assume without deciding the point, although we incline to favour the proposition, that harm in the context of manslaughter includes injury to the person through the operation of shock emanating from fright and examine how the judge dealt with this in the second element of the offence. He said:

"But the second question is, would all reasonable people realise it must inevitably create the risk of some harm to Mr Black? That is to say, all reasonable people who knew the facts that you know, including the fact that the gun was a replica and could not fire and thus knew that actually Mr Black could not be injured by a bullet, in other words, but also knowing that Mr Black did not know that; that he might very well think he was being threatened by a real firearm. He did not know it was not loaded with live ammunition. He did not know that at any minute the trigger might not be pulled. All of them have accepted that they intended to secure the money by putting Mr Black in fright. So fear was both to be expected and was intended. I direct you that if an act puts a person in such terror that he or she may suffer emotional or physical disturbance which is detrimental then that disturbance is harm within the meaning of what you have to consider. If, therefore, you conclude that all sober and reasonable people, which means you, because it is your standards that have got to be applied, could only come to the conclusion that the result of the threats with the pickaxe handle and the firearm in the middle of the night was likely to be that inevitably there was a risk that Mr Black would be put in such terror that he would suffer some such disturbance which would be bad for him, then that can be harm and the second element that you have to find is made out."

These directions have been roundly attacked as being wholly erroneous. It was argued that, contrary to an indication given by him to counsel, the judge in that passage directed the jury that a definition of harm was "emotional disturbance which is detrimental produced by terror". He had, as we have seen from a transcript of discussion between him and counsel, intended to direct the jury that a definition of harm for present purposes was emotional *and* physical disturbance produced by terror. We think it was unfortunate that the judge, probably through inadvertence, used the disjunctive "or". As it was, the jury were left with a choice. Which they chose and acted upon we cannot tell. If they acted upon the basis that emotional disturbance was enough to consititute harm then, in our judgment, they would have done so upon a misdirection. Emotional disturbance does not occur to us as sensibly descriptive of injury or harm to the person through the operation of shock produced by terror or fright; moreover, we do not think the word "detrimental" assists to clarify whatever the expression "emotional disturbance" is meant to convey. The further phrase used, namely, "some such disturbance which would be bad for him" is likewise not helpful.

In his endeavours to give the jury appropriate guidance upon the meaning of harm within the facts of this case the judge was sailing uncharted seas. We have every sympathy with him. Unfortunately we think that what he said, other than the use of the phrase "physical disturbance which is detrimental" (this was, we think, by itself, though easier to understand, inadequate) could have led the jury to contemplate merely a disturbance of the emotions as harm sufficient for the purpose of the second element when clearly, in our view, it is not.

In our judgment, a proper direction would have been that the requisite harm is caused if the unlawful act so shocks the victim as to cause him physical injury.

We look finally at the direction, "That is to say all reasonable people who knew the facts that you know." What the jury knew included, of course, the undisputed fact that the deceased had a very bad heart which at any moment could have ceased to function. It may be the judge did not intend that this fact should be included in the phrase "the facts that you know". If that was so, it is regrettable that he did not make it clear. By saying as he did, it is argued "including the fact that the gun was a replica" and so on, the jury must have taken him to be telling them that all facts known to them, including the heart condition, should be taken into account in performing that is undoubtedly an objective test. We think there was a grave danger of that.

This test can only be undertaken upon the basis of the knowledge gained by a sober and reasonable man as though he were present at the scene of and watched the unlawful act being performed and who knows that, as in the present case, an unloaded replica gun was in use, but that the victim may have thought it was a loaded gun in working order. In other words, he has the same knowledge as the man attempting to rob and no more. It was never suggested that any of these appellants knew that their victim had a bad heart. They knew nothing about him.

A jury must be informed by the judge when trying the offence of manslaughter what facts they may and those which they may not use for the purpose of performing the test in the second element of this offence. The judge's direction here, unlike the bulk of an admirable summing-up, lacked that necessary precision and in the form it was given may, in our view, have given the jury an erroneous impression of what knowledge they could ascribe to the sober and reasonable man.

For these reasons we see no alternative to quashing the convictions for manslaughter as unsafe and unsatisfactory. The appeal against the convictions for manslaughter is therefore allowed.'

Commentary
See *R* v *Watson*, below.

DPP v *Newbury and Jones* [1976] AC 500 House of Lords (Lords Diplock, Simon, Kilbrandon, Salmon, and Edmund-Davies)

Mens rea for unlawful act manslaughter

Facts
The defendants, both teenage boys, had thrown a piece of paving stone from a railway bridge onto a train which had been passing beneath them. The missile struck and killed the guard who had been sitting in the driver's compartment. The defendants were convicted of manslaughter, and appealed on the ground that they had not foreseen that their actions might cause harm to any other person.

Held
The appeals would be dismissed.

Lord Salmon:

'In *R* v *Larkin*, Humphreys J said:

> "Where the act which a person is engaged in performing is unlawful, then if at the same time it is a dangerous act, that is, an act which is likely to injure another person, and quite inadvertently the doer of the act causes the death of that other person by that act, then he is guilty of manslaughter."

I agree entirely ... that that is an admirably clear statement of the law which has been applied many times. It makes it plain (a) that an accused is guilty of manslaughter if it is proved that he intentionally did an act which was unlawful and dangerous and that that act inadvertently caused death and (b) that it is unnecessary to prove that the accused knew that the act was unlawful or dangerous. This is one of the reasons why cases of manslaughter vary so infinitely in their gravity. They may amount to little more than pure inadvertence and sometimes to little less than murder ..."

The test is still the objective test. In judging whether the act was dangerous the test is not did the accused recognise that it was dangerous but would all sober and reasonable people recognise its danger? ...'

Lord Edmund-Davies (after expressing his agreement with Lord Salmon, and having referred to *R* v *Church*):

'I believe that *R* v *Church* accurately applied the law as it then existed. I believe, further, that, since it was decided, nothing has happened to change the law in relation to the constituents of involuntary manslaughter caused by an unlawful act. The Criminal Justice Act 1967 has certainly effected no such change, for, as I sought to show in *R v Majewski* [1977] AC 443, section 8 thereof has nothing to do with *when* intent or foresight or any other mental state has to be established, but simply *how* it is to be determined where such determination is called for.

That is not to say that a change in the law may not be opportune. If I may be permitted to introduce a personal note into a judgment, I have the best reason to know that the forthcoming working paper of the Criminal Law Revision Committee on offences against the person will afford those concerned in such important matters an opportunity to assess the cogency of the argument for a drastic change in the law applicable to such cases as the present. But, unless and until such argument prevails and so leads on to legislation, the existing law has to be applied. I hold that the direction of the learned trial judge, Watkins J, was in strict accordance with the settled law and that these appeals should therefore be refused.'

R v Goodfellow (1986) 83 Cr App R 23 Court of Appeal (Criminal Division) (Lord Lane CJ, Boreham and Taylor JJ)

Nature of the unlawful act in constructive manslaughter

Facts

As related in the judgment of the Lord Chief Justice:

'On August 14, 1984 in the early hours of the morning, the appellant set light to the council house he occupied at 24 Cossock Terrace, Pallion. He poured petrol over the sideboard, chair and walls of the downstairs living room, and then set the house on fire by igniting the petrol. In the ensuing blaze three people died: his wife Sarah aged 22, another young woman named Jillian Stuart with whom the appellant was having a liaison, who was in the house that night, and the appellant's two year old son Darren.

The background to these events was as follows. The appellant had been having difficulties with two men in the locality. One of them had been fined for damaging the front door of No. 24. Hence the appellant wanted to move. He had no chance of exchanging his council house for another because he was some "£300 in arrears with his rent." He therefore conceived the idea of setting No. 24 on fire and making it look as though the fire had been caused by a petrol bomb thrown through the window by one of the men. This story was what he initially told the police when they started to make inquiries.

In fact he had obtained the petrol from the motorbike of a friend of his called Dalzell. Part of it, according to him, he used as an experiment in the garden, when the flames simply ignited in one place. The remainder he used as already described.

According to Dalzell, he, Dalzell, told the appellant it was a stupid idea, and Jillian, who was present at the time, disapproved of the plan saying that she was not going to risk her life and the lives of the bairns for him (the appellant). The appellant however told the jury that the fire was Jillian's own idea and that she talked him into carrying it into effect. Jillian had (wisely) arranged for her three children to sleep elsewhere.

The appellant's three children remained in the house because, as he said, it would have been suspicious if they had not been there. The idea was that once the fire started the adults would take the children from the house and all would therefore escape. However the fire spread very rapidly. The appellant fetched a ladder from a neighbour's house, put it against a bedroom window and took to safety two of his children handed out to him by his wife. The fire by then was too intense for anyone else to be saved. Jillian was asphyxiated inside the house. Sarah and Darren died in hospital from their burns.

The grounds of appeal are that the judge failed to direct the jury on the law of manslaughter in relation to the facts of the case, and in particular directed them on the basis of a passage in *Archbold*, 41st ed, which was the subject of adverse criticism by their Lordships in the Privy Council in *Kong Cheuk Kwan v The Queen* (1985) 82 Cr App R 18.'

Held

The appeal would be dismissed.

Lord Lane CJ:

'We are told that there was some discussion between counsel and the judge during the course of the trial as to whether the jury should be directed on the "*Lawrence*" or the "unlawful acts" basis, and that the judge appeared to favour the former. Whether that is so or not, we have to decide whether the direction he in fact gave was correct.

It seems to us that this was a case which was capable of falling within either or both types of manslaughter. On the *Lawrence* aspect, the jury might well have been satisfied that the appellant was acting in such a manner as to create an obvious and serious risk of causing physical injury to some person, and secondly that he, having recognised that there was some risk involved, had nevertheless gone on to take it.

This was equally, in our view, a case for the "unlawful and dangerous act" direction. Where the defendant does an unlawful act of such a kind as all sober and reasonable people would inevitably recognise must subject another person to, at least, the risk of some harm resulting therefrom, albeit not serious harm and causes death thereby, he is guilty of manslaughter: *Church* (1965) 49 Cr App R 206, [1966] 1 QB 59.

Lord Salmon in *Director of Public Prosecutions* v *Newbury* (1976) 62 Cr App R 291; [1976] 2 All ER 365 approved a dictum of Humphreys J in *Larkin* [1943] 1 All ER 217, 219: "Where the act which a person is engaged in performing is unlawful, then if at the same time it is a dangerous act, that is, an act which is likely to injure another person, and quite inadvertently he causes the death of that other person by that act, then he is guilty of manslaughter." Their Lordships in that case (*Newbury*) expressly disapproved of a passage in the judgment of Lord Denning MR in the civil case of *Gray* v *Barr* [1971] 2 All ER 949, 956, in which he asserted that the unlawful act must be done by the defendant with the intention of frightening or harming someone or with the realisation that it is likely to frighten or harm someone. That decision of the House of Lords is, of course, binding upon us.

It is submitted by Mr Stewart on behalf of the appellant that this was not a case of "unlawful act" manslaughter, because the actions of the appellant were not directed at the victim. The authority for that proposition is said to be *Dalby* (1982) 74 Cr App R 348.

In that case the appellant, a drug addict, supplied a class A drug which he had lawfully obtained to a friend, also an addict. Each injected himself intravenously. After the appellant had left, the friend administered to himself two further injections, the nature of which was unknown. When the appellant returned he was unable to wake up his friend. When medical help eventually arrived, the friend was found to be dead. The appellant was convicted of manslaughter either on the unlawful and dangerous act basis, or alternatively on the basis that he was grossly negligent in not calling an ambulance at an earlier stage.

It was held that since the act of supplying the scheduled drug was not an act which caused direct harm and since the unlawful act of supply of the dangerous drug by Dalby per se did not constitute the actus reus of the offence of manslaughter, the conviction had to be quashed. Waller LJ, at page 352, said: "... where the charge of manslaughter is based on an unlawful and dangerous act, it must be an act directed at the victim and likely to cause immediate injury, however slight."

However we do not think that he was suggesting that there must be an intention on the part of the defendant to harm or frighten or a realisation that his acts were likely to harm or frighten. Indeed it would have been contrary to the dicta of Lord Salmon in *DPP* v *Newbury* (supra) if he was. What he was, we believe, intending to say was that there must be no fresh intervening cause between the act and the death. Indeed at p351 he said this: "... the supply of drugs would itself have caused no harm unless the deceased had subsequently used the drugs in a form and quantity which was dangerous."

If we may say so respectfully, we doubt the assertion in Smith and Hogan, *Criminal Law*, 5th ed, p315, that because the Appellate Committee refused the [prosecutor] leave to appeal, *Dalby* (supra) must then be taken to represent the law.

Mr Bethel for the Crown drew our attention to two further cases, namely, *Pagett* (1983) 76 Cr App R 279 and *Mitchell* (1983) 76 Cr App R 293, both of which seem to support our interpretation of *Dalby* (supra).

The questions which the jury have to decide on the charge of manslaughter of this nature are: (1) Was the act intentional? (2) Was it unlawful? (3) Was it an act which any reasonable person would realise was bound to subject some other human being to the risk of physical harm, albeit not necessarily serious harm? (4) Was that act the cause of death?

Whatever indications the judge may have given earlier as to his intentions, he did in fact direct the jury on this type of manslaughter in the passage which we have already quoted. It is true that he went further and added observations which were more appropriate to the *Lawrence* type of manslaughter. If anything, those passages resulted in a direction which was more favourable to the appellant than if they had been omitted.

We do not consider that the jury may have been confused as Mr Stewart contends. The convictions on counts 1 to 3 were neither unsafe nor unsatisfactory.

Finally, as to count 5, Mr Stewart submits that the judge failed to direct the jury specifically that they must be satisfied that the appellant was reckless as to whether the lives of the people upstairs were in danger.

What he said on this point was as follows: "And recklessness, please note as I have already told you, in fact applies equally to the fifth count in the indictment. Indeed it is the only issue in the fifth count in the indictment. So I repeat in relation to count 5 the recklessness, that Goodfellow would have acted recklessly if the prosecution have proved either that first, when he set fire to the house he gave no thought at all to the possibility that the inmates might be injured in circumstances where, if he had given any thought to the matter, it would have been obvious that there was some risk. Or secondly, that he appreciated the risk of injury but nonetheless went on to take it."

We consider that in the circumstances of this case if there was risk of injury at all to the people upstairs then it must follow that there was risk of death. Even had that not been the case we would have applied the proviso. If the judge, instead of using the words "might be injured" had used the words "might be killed," the result would inevitably have been the same. Accordingly this appeal is dismissed.'

R v Mitchell [1983] 2 WLR 938 Court of Appeal (Criminal Division) (Purchas LJ, Talbot and Staughton JJ)

Constructive manslaughter: whether unlawful act must be the direct cause of death

Facts
The defendant had become involved in an altercation whilst queuing in a busy post office. He pushed an elderly man, causing him to fall accidentally onto the deceased, an elderly woman. She was admitted to hospital where she later died from a pulmonary embolism caused by thrombosis of the veins in her injured leg. The defendant was convicted of manslaughter, and appealed on the grounds that his unlawful act had not been directed at the victim, and that the trial judge had not directed the jury adequately on the mens rea required for the offence.

Held
The appeal would be dismissed.

Staughton J:

'Both counsel were agreed that there are four elements in this class of manslaughter, as follows: first, there must be an act which is unlawful; secondly, it must be a dangerous act, in the sense that a sober and reasonable person would inevitably recognise that it carried some risk of harm, albeit not serious harm (that being an objective test); thirdly, the act must be a substantial cause of death; fourthly, the act itself must be intentional. No question relating to any other class of manslaughter (such as manslaughter by gross negligence) arose in this case.

The main question argued was whether the person at whom the act is aimed must also be the person whose death is caused. On that question, it was suggested, there is no authority directly in point. Counsel for Mitchell also argued that the act must have been directed at the victim in the sense, as we understand the point, that it must have had some immediate impact upon the victim. For that proposition the case of *Dalby* (1982) 74 Cr App R 348; [1982] 1 WLR 425, was said to be authority.

There are cases which apparently support the first part of this argument. Thus in *Larkin* (1942) 29 Cr App R 18, Humphreys J, at p23 referred to – "an act which is likely to injure another person, and quite inadvertently the doer of the act causes the death of *that* other person." Similarly in *Church* (1965) 49 Cr App R 206, 213; [1966] 1 QB 59, 70, Edmund Davies J said: "... the unlawful act must be such as all sober and reasonable people would inevitably recognise must subject *the* other person to, at least, the risk of some harm resulting therefrom, albeit not serious harm." (Emphasis supplied in both cases).

However, in neither case was there any question raised of an act, which carried the risk of harm to A, in fact causing the death of B. We cannot treat either case as authority upon that question. It is possible that such a question could have been raised in *Larkin* (supra), but it was not.

Nor does any such question appear to have been raised in the leading case of *Director of Public Prosecutions* v *Newbury and Jones* (1976) 62 Cr App R 291; [1977] AC 500, although it might have been. There two youths aged 15 were on a railway bridge. One of them pushed part of a paving-stone over the bridge parapet towards an oncoming train. It fell on the driver's cab, killing the guard, who was sitting next to the driver. Both were convicted of manslaughter of the guard. Their convictions were upheld by the House of Lords.

Presumably it could have been said that the act of the two youths was aimed at the driver, if at anyone, or perhaps at the passengers, if there were any; it may be that the guard was the least likely to be injured, unless it were known that he was travelling in the front of the train. However, no argument on those lines appears to have been advanced. The whole contest was as to mens rea. It was argued that the youths themselves had to be proved to have foreseen that they might cause harm to someone. That argument was rejected. Lord Salmon, at pp296 and 506 respectively said: "The learned trial judge did not direct the jury that they should acquit the appellants unless they were satisfied beyond a reasonable doubt that the appellants had foreseen that they might cause harm to someone by pushing the piece of paving stone off the parapet into the path of the approaching train. In my view the learned trial judge was quite right not to give such a direction to the jury. The direction which he gave is completely in accordance with established law, which, possibly with one exception to which I shall presently refer, has never been challenged. In *Larkin* (1942) 29 Cr App R 18, Humphreys J said at p23, "Where the act which a person is engaged in performing is unlawful, then if at the same time it is a dangerous act, that is, an act which is likely to injure another person, and quite inadvertently the doer of the act causes the death of that other person by that act, then he is guilty of manslaughter." I agree entirely with Lawton LJ that that is an admirably clear statement of the law which has been applied many times. It makes it plain (a) that an accused is guilty of manslaughter if it is proved that he intentionally did an act which was unlawful and dangerous and that that act inadvertently caused death and (b) that it is unnecessary to prove that the accused knew that the act was unlawful or dangerous. This is one of the reasons why cases of manslaughter vary so infinitely in their gravity. They may amount to little more than pure inadvertence and sometimes to little less than murder. I am sure that in *Church* (1965) 49 Cr App R 206; [1966] 1 QB 59, Edmund Davies J (as he then was), in giving the judgment of the Court, did not intend to differ from or qualify anything which had been said in *Larkin* (supra). Indeed he was restating the principle laid down in that case by illustrating the sense in which the word "dangerous" should be understood. Edmund Davies J said "For such a verdict" (guilty of manslaughter) "inexorably to follow, the unlawful act must be such as all sober and reasonable people would inevitably recognise must subject the other person to, at least, the risk of some harm resulting therefrom, albeit not serious harm." The test is still the objective test. In judging whether the act was dangerous the test is not did the accused recognise that it was dangerous but would all sober and reasonable people recognise its danger?

He went on to say that juries should continue to be directed in accordance with the law as laid down in *Larkin* (supra) and *Church* (supra).

We do not read Lord Salmon as saying that the unlawful and dangerous act must necessarily be aimed at the same other person whose death is caused. No such limitation was contended for in the House of Lords. If it had been, it was at least open to question, as we have suggested, whether the act of the youths was aimed at the guard; and therefore it would have had to be considered whether on that different ground their convictions should be quashed.

Then there is the case of *Dalby* (1982) 74 Cr App R 348; [1982] 1 WLR 425. [His Lordship considered this authority and continued:] For the present it is enough to say that this case too was not concerned with an act aimed at A which in fact causes the death of B. The Court was there concerned with the quality of the act rather than the identity of the person at whom it was aimed. Again we do not read Waller LJ as saying that the unlawful and dangerous act must be aimed at that very person whose death is caused. If, however, that was what the Court was saying, then we would, with the greatest respect, hold that it was not part of the ratio decidendi of the case.

The only authority (if such it be) which we have found to be directly in point is *Russell on Crime* 12th ed (1964) Vol 1, p588, citing the 1839 HM Commissioners on Criminal Law: "Involuntary homicide, which is not by misadventure, includes all cases where, without intention to kill or do great bodily harm, or wilfully to endanger life, death occurs in any of the following instances: Where death results from any unlawful act or omission done or omitted with intent to hurt the person of another, whether the mischief light on the person intended, or on any other person; where death results from any wrong wilfully occasioned to the person of another; where death results from any unlawful act or unlawful omission, attended with risk of hurt to the person of another; where death results from want of due caution either in doing an act, or neglecting to prevent mischief, which the offender is bound by law to prevent."

We can see no reason of policy for holding that an act calculated to harm A cannot be manslaughter if it in fact kills B. The criminality of the doer of the act is precisely the same whether it is A or B who dies. A person who throws a stone at A is just as guilty if, instead of hitting and killing A, it hits and kills B. Parliament evidently held the same view in relation to the allied offence of unlawful and malicious wounding contrary to section 20 of the Offences Against the Person Act 1861: see *Latimer* (1886) 17 QBD 359. We accordingly reject the argument of counsel for Mitchell that, because Mitchell's acts were aimed at Mr Smith, it cannot have been manslaughter when they caused the death of Mrs Crafts.

The second limb of the argument was based wholly on *Dalby* (1982) 74 Cr App R 348; [1982] 1 WLR 425. It was argued that for manslaughter to be established the act of the defendant must be shown to have caused direct harm to the victim. On that ground, although it would be manslaughter to throw a stone at A which hits and kills B, it was submitted that there was no manslaughter in the present case, because there was no physical contact between Mitchell and Mrs Crafts.

The passage which we have already read from *Dalby* was relied on in support of that argument. In particular, there is this sentence in the judgment of the Court (at pp351 and 429 respectively): "The kind of harm envisaged in all the reported cases of involuntary manslaughter was physical injury of some kind as an immediate and inevitable result of the unlawful act, eg a blow on the chin which knocks the victim against a wall causing a fractured skull and death, or threatening with a loaded gun which accidentally fires, or dropping a large stone on a train or threatening another with an open razor and stumbling with death resulting."

We can well understand, if we may say so, why the Court held that there was no sufficient link between Dalby's wrongful act (supplying the drug) and his friend's death. As Waller LJ said: "the supply of drugs would itself have caused no harm unless the deceased had subsequently used the drugs in a form and quantity which was dangerous ... the supply did not cause any direct injury to him."

Here however the facts were very different. Although there was no direct contact between Mitchell and Mrs Crafts, she was injured as a direct and immediate result of his act. Thereafter her death occurred. The only question was one of causation: whether her death was caused by Mitchell's act. It was open to the jury to conclude that it was so caused; and they evidently reached that conclusion.

Since the conclusion of the argument we have seen a transcript of the judgment of this Court in *Pagett* [see Chapter 24]. This supports the views we have expressed in two respects. At p291 Robert Goff LJ, delivering the judgment of the Court, said: "If, as the jury must have found to have occurred in the present case, the appellant used Gail Kinchen by force and against her will as a shield to protect him from any shots fired by the police, the effect is that he committed not one but two unlawful acts, both of which were dangerous – the act of firing at the police, and the act of holding Gail Kinchen as a shield in front of him when the police might well fire shots in his direction in self-defence. Either act could, in our judgment ... constitute the actus reus of the manslaughter."

In the case of the first act mentioned – firing at the police – it could scarcely be said to have been *aimed* at the ultimate victim, Gail Kinchen; nor could it be said by itself to have caused harm to the victim by direct physical contact. We agree that neither requirement exists for manslaughter. Granted an unlawful and dangerous act, the test is one of causation. That is clear from p287 ante where Robert Goff LJ said: "The question whether an accused person can be guilty of homicide, either murder or manslaughter, of a victim the immediate cause of whose death is the act of another person must be determined on the ordinary principles of causation ... "

As to ground (iii), it was argued that the learned judge failed to direct the jury that Mitchell's act had to be a deliberate act, in the sense that he intended to do it. The direction was as follows: "You have been told, and told perfectly accurately, what this offence of manslaughter is: it is where an act a person is engaged in is unlawful and if, at the same time, it is a dangerous act and another person is injured, and is injured even through inadvertence, and as result of an injury death is caused to that other person, then the offence is one of manslaughter. Even if that act is one which is likely to injure another person and it is done quite inadvertently, the offence is one of manslaughter. Again, you have been told, and told quite properly, that it does not matter whether the accused person knows that the act is an unlawful one, or indeed a dangerous one. It does not depend upon what he believes to be unlawful or dangerous. If you came to a conclusion in this case that what this young man, Mitchell, was doing was unlawful, inasmuch as it constituted an assault upon Mr Smith, then your consideration would have to be on whether or not it was dangerous at the same time. In judging whether the act is a dangerous act, the test which you apply is not whether the accused recognises that it was a dangerous act, but whether all sober and reasonable people would have recognised it to be dangerous in the circumstances which attain in this particular case: in other words, whether you consider it was dangerous in the circumstances of this case."

The learned judge there used the words "inadvertence" and "inadvertently". He was perfectly right to do so, in dealing with the connection between the act and the injury or death. There need not be any intention to injure or kill, or any foresight that injury or death would be caused, provided that all sober and reasonable people would have recognised the act to be dangerous. That is the sense in which Humphreys J used the word "inadvertently" in *Larkin* (supra).

But it is said that the judge may have conveyed to the jury that the act need not itself have been a deliberate act. Whether he did or not is, in the context of this case, wholly immaterial. All of Mitchell's actions, whether hitting, pushing, grabbing or throwing, were obviously and admittedly deliberate actions. There was no suggestion of inadvertence, or even automation, in any part of his conduct. The issues before the jury, on this aspect of the case, were firstly self-defence, and secondly whether he did all the things he was said to have done or only some of them. As we have already observed, there is no appeal against the conviction of assault occasioning actual bodily harm. In many if not most cases the judge should direct the jury that the act relied on for an offence of manslaughter must have been a deliberate or intentional act. Here it was quite unnecessary.'

R v Watson [1989] 1 WLR 684 Court of Appeal (Criminal Division) (Lord Lane CJ, Farquharson and Potts JJ)

Constructive manslaughter – dangerous act

Facts

The appellant had burgled a house occupied by an 87 year old man, Mr Moyler, who suffered from a heart condition. The occupant disturbed the appellant, who abused him verbally, but the appellant made off without stealing anything. The police were called shortly afterwards, and a local council workman arrived to repair the windows broken by the appellant in gaining entry. An hour and a half after the burglary Mr Moyler had a heart attack and died. The appellant was convicted of manslaughter and appealed.

Held

The conviction for manslaughter would be quashed on the ground that the appellant's counsel had been denied a sufficient opportunity to address the jury on the issue of whether the excitement caused by the arrival of the police and the council workman could have taken over as the operating and substantial cause of death.

Lord Lane CJ:

His Lordship considered the nature of the unlawful act required as the basis for constructive manslaughter:

> 'It is accepted that the judge correctly defined the offence of manslaughter as it applied to the circumstances as follows:
>
>> "Manslaughter is the offence committed when one person causes the death of another by an act which is unlawful and which is also dangerous, dangerous in the sense that it is an act which all sober and reasonable people would inevitably realise must subject the victim to the risk of some harm resulting whether the defendant realised that or not."
>
> The first point taken on behalf of the appellant is this. When one is deciding whether the sober and reasonable person (the bystander) would realise the risk of some harm resulting to the victim, how much knowledge of the circumstances does one attribute to the bystander? The appellant contends that the unlawful act here was the burglary as charged in the indictment.
>
> The charge was laid under s9(1)(a) of the Theft Act 1968, the allegation being that the appellant had entered the building as a trespasser with intent to commit theft. Since that offence is committed at the first moment of entry, the bystander's knowledge is confined to that of the defendant at that moment. In the instant case there was no evidence that the appellant, at the moment of entry, knew the age or physical condition of Mr Moyler or even that he lived there alone.
>
> The judge clearly took the view that the jury were entitled to ascribe to the bystander the knowledge which the appellant gained during the whole of his stay in the house and so directed them. Was this a misdirection? In our judgment it was not. The unlawful act in the present circumstances comprised the whole of the burglarious intrusion and did not come to an end upon the appellant's foot crossing the threshold or windowsill. That being so, the appellant (and therefore the bystander) during the course of the unlawful act must have become aware of Mr Moyler's frailty and approximate age, and the judge's directions were accordingly correct. We are supported in this view by the fact that no one at the trial seems to have thought otherwise.'

27 Participation

R v Anderson and Morris [1966] 2 QB 110 Court of Criminal Appeal (Lord Parker CJ, Edmund-Davies, Marshall, Roskill and James JJ)

Deliberate departure from the common design

Facts

Anderson and Morris agreed to beat up a man named Welch. Unknown to Morris, Anderson took a knife with him, and during the attack, he deliberately stabbed the victim to death. Anderson was convicted of murder, and Morris was convicted of manslaughter on the basis that, although he had not contemplated death or serious bodily harm, he had contemplated an attack on Welch. Morris appealed.

Held

Morris' conviction as an accomplice to manslaughter would be quashed.

Lord Parker CJ:

'What is complained of is a passage of the summing-up. It is unnecessary to read the direction on law in full. The material direction is:

"If you think there was a common design to attack Welch but it is not proved, in the case of Morris, that he had any intention to kill or cause grievous bodily harm, but that Anderson, without the knowledge of Morris, had a knife, took it from the flat and at some time formed the intention to kill or cause grievous bodily harm to Welch and did kill him – an act outside the common design to which Morris is proved to have been a party – then you would or could on the evidence find it proved that Anderson committed murder and Morris would be liable to be convicted of manslaughter provided you are satisfied that he took part in the attack or fight with Welch."

Mr Lane [counsel for the appellant] submits that that was a clear misdirection. He would put the principle of law to be invoked in this form: that where two persons embark on a joint enterprise, each is liable for the acts done in pursuance of that joint enterprise, that that includes liability for unusual consequences if they arise from the execution of the agreed joint enterprise but (and this is the crux of the matter) that, if one of the adventurers goes beyond what has been tacitly agreed as part of the common enterprise, his co-adventurer is not liable for the consequences of that unauthorised act. Finally he says it is for the jury in every case to decide whether what was done was part of the joint enterprise, or went beyond it and was in fact an act unauthorised by that joint enterprise.

In support of that, he refers to a number of authorities to which this court finds it unnecessary to refer in detail, which in the opinion of this court shows that at any rate for the last 130 or 140 years that has been the true position ... In *R v Smith (Wesley)* ([1963] 1 WLR 1200) the co-adventurer who in fact killed was known by the defendant to have a knife, and it was clear on the facts of that case that the common design involved an attack on a man, in that case a barman, in which the use of a knife would not be outside the scope of the concerted action. Reference was there made to the fact that the case might have been different if in fact the man using the knife had used a revolver, a weapon which he had, unknown to Smith ...

Mr Caulfield [counsel for the Crown], on the other hand, while recognising that he cannot go beyond this long string of decided cases, has said really that they are all part and parcel of a much wider principle which he would put in this form, that if two or more persons engaged in an unlawful act and one suddenly develops an intention to kill whereby death results, not only he is guilty of murder, but all those who have engaged in the unlawful act are guilty of manslaughter. He recognises that the present trend of authority is against that proposition, but he goes back to *Salisbury*'s case (1 Plow. 100) in 1553. In that case a master had laid in wait to attack a man, and his servants, who had no idea of what his, the master's, idea was, joined in the attack, whereby the man was killed. It was held there that those servants were themselves guilty of manslaughter.

The court is by no means clear on the facts as reported that *Salisbury*'s case is really on all fours, but it is in the opinion of the court quite clear that the principle is wholly out of touch with the position today. It seems to this court that to say that adventurers are guilty of manslaughter when one of them has departed completely from the concerted action of the common design and has suddenly formed an intent to kill and has used a weapon and acted in a way which no party to that common design could suspect is something which would revolt the conscience of people today.

Mr Caulfield, in his attractive argument, points to the fact that it would seem to be illogical that, if two people had formed a common design to do an unlawful act and death resulted by an unforeseen consequence, they should be held, as they would undoubtedly be held, guilty of manslaughter; whereas if one of them in those circumstances had in a moment of passion decided to kill, they would be acquitted altogether. The law, of course, is not completely logical, but there is nothing really illogical in such a result, in that it could well be said as a matter of common sense that in the latter circumstances the death resulted or was caused by the sudden action of the adventurer who decided to kill and killed. Considered as a matter of causation there may well be an overwhelming supervening event which is of such a character that it will relegate into history matters which would otherwise be looked upon as causative factors. Looked at in that way, there is really nothing illogical in the result to which Mr Caulfield points.'

Attorney-General's Reference (No 1 of 1975) [1975] 3 WLR 11 Court of Appeal (Criminal Division) (Lord Widgery CJ, Bristow and May JJ)

Facts
The accused had surreptitiously laced a friend's drinks with double measures of alcohol knowing the friend would shortly afterwards be driving home. The friend was convicted of drunken driving. The accused was charged as an accomplice to this offence, but was acquitted following a successful submission of no case. The trial judge took the view that there had to be evidence of some agreement between the accomplice and the principal. The following question was referred to the court:

'Whether an accused who surreptitiously laced a friend's drinks with double measures of spirits when he knew that his friend would shortly be driving his car home, and in consequence his friend drove with an excess quantity of alcohol in his body and was convicted of the offence under the Road Traffic Act 1972 s 6 (1) is entitled to a ruling of no case to answer on being later charged as an aider and abettor, counsellor and procurer, on the ground that there was no shared intention between the two that the accused did not by accompanying him or otherwise positively encourage the friend to drive, or on any other ground.'

Held
The question posed should be answered in the negative.

Lord Widgery CJ:

'The language in the section which determines whether a "secondary party", as he is sometimes called, is guilty of a criminal offence committed by another embraces the four words "aid, abet, counsel or procure". The origin of those words is to be found in section 8 of the Accessories and Abettors Act 1861 which provides:

"Whosoever shall aid, abet, counsel, or procure the commission of any misdemeanour, whether the same be a misdemeanour at common law or by virtue of any Act passed or to be passed, shall be liable to be tried, indicted, and punished as a principal offender."

Thus, in the past, when the distinction was still drawn between felony and misdemeanour, it was sufficient to make a person guilty of a misdemeanour if he aided, abetted, counselled or procured the offence of another. When the difference between felonies and misdemeanours was abolished in 1967, section 1 of the Criminal Law Act 1967 in effect provided that the same test should apply to make a secondary party guilty either of treason or felony.

Of course it is the fact that in the great majority of instances where a secondary party is sought to be convicted of an offence there has been a contact between the principal offender and the secondary party. Aiding and abetting almost inevitably involves a situation in which the secondary party and the main offender are together at some stage discussing the plans which they may be making in respect of the alleged offence, and are in contact so that each knows what is passing through the mind of the other.

In the same way it seems to us that a person who counsels the commission of a crime by another, almost inevitably comes to a moment when he is in contact with that other, when he is discussing the offence with that other and when, to use the words of the statute, he counsels the other to commit the offence.

The fact that so often the relationship between the secondary party and the principal will be such that there is a meeting of minds between them caused the trial judge in the case from which this reference is derived to think that this was really an essential feature of proving or establishing the guilt of the secondary party and, as we understand his judgment, he took the view that in the absence of some sort of meeting of minds, some sort of mental link between the secondary party and the principal, there could be no aiding, abetting or counselling of the offence within the meaning of the section.

So far as aiding, abetting and counselling is concerned we would go a long way with that conclusion. It may very well be, as I said a moment ago, difficult to think of a case of aiding, abetting or counselling when the parties have not met and have not discussed in some respects the terms of the offence which they have in mind. But we do not see why a similar principle should apply to procuring. We approach section 8 of the Act of 1861 on the basis also that if four words are employed here, "aid, abet, counsel or procure", the probability is that there is a difference between each of those four words and the other three, because, if there were no such difference, then Parliament would be wasting time in using four words where two or three would do. Thus, in deciding whether that which is assumed to be done under our reference was a criminal offence we approach the section on the footing that each word must be given its ordinary meaning.

To procure means to produce by endeavour. You procure a thing by setting out to see that it happens and taking the appropriate steps to produce that happening. We think that there are plenty of instances in which a person may be said to procure the commission of a crime by another even though there is no sort of conspiracy between the two, even thought there is no attempt at agreement or discussion as to the form which the offence should take. In our judgment the offence described in this reference is such a case.

If one looks back at the facts of the reference: the accused surreptitiously laced his friend's drink. This is an important element and, although we are not going to decide today anything other than the problem posed to us, it may well be that in similar cases where the lacing of the drink or the introduction of the extra alcohol is known to the driver quite different considerations may apply. We say that because where the driver has no knowledge of what is happening, in most instances he would have no means of preventing the offence from being committed. If the driver is unaware of what has happened, he will not be taking precautions. He will get into his car seat, switch on the ignition and drive home and, consequently, the conception of another procuring the commission of the offence by the driver is very much stronger where the driver is innocent of all knowledge of what is happening, as in the present case where the lacing of the drink was surreptitious.

The second thing which is important in the facts set out in our reference is that following and in consequence of the introduction of the extra alcohol, the friend drove with an excess quantity of alcohol in his blood. Causation here is important. You cannot procure an offence unless there is a causal link between what you do and the commission of the offence, and here we are told that in consequence of the addition of this alcohol the driver, when he drove home, drove with an excess quantity of alcohol in his body.

Giving the words their ordinary meaning in English, and asking oneself whether in those circumstances the offence has been procured, we are in no doubt that the answer is that it has. It has been procured because, unknown to the driver and without his collaboration, he has been put in a position in which in fact he has committed an offence which he never would have committed otherwise. We think that there was a case to answer and that the trial judge should have directed the jury that an offence is committed if it is shown beyond reasonable doubt that the accused knew that his friend was going to drive, and also knew that the ordinary and natural result of the additional alcohol added to the friend's drink would be to bring him above the recognised limit of 80 milligrammes per 100 millilitres of blood.

It was suggested to us that, if we held that there may be a procuring on the facts of the present case, it would be but a short step to a similar finding for the generous host, with somewhat bibulous friends, when at the end of the day his friends leave him to go to their own homes in circumstances in which they are not fit to drive and in circumstances in which an offence under the Road Traffic Act 1972 is committed. The suggestion has been made that the host may in those circumstances be guilty with his guests on the basis that he has either aided, abetted, counselled or procured the offence.

The first point to notice in regard to the generous host is that that is not a case in which the alcohol is being put surreptitiously into the glass of the driver. That is a case in which the driver knows perfectly well how much he has to drink and where to a large extent it is perfectly right and proper to leave him to make his own decision.

Furthermore, we would say that if such a case arises, the basis on which the case will be put against the host is, we think, bound to be on the footing that he has supplied the tool with which the offence is committed. This of course is a reference back to such cases as those where oxy-acetylene equipment was bought by a man knowing it was to be used by another for a criminal offence see *R* v *Bainbridge* [1960] 1 QB 129. There is ample and clear authority as to the extent to which supplying the tools for the commission of an offence may amount to aiding and abetting for present purposes.

Accordingly, so far as the generous host type of case is concerned we are not concerned at the possibility that difficulties will be created, as long as it is borne in mind that in those circumstances the matter must be approached in accordance with well-known authority governing the provision of the tools for the commission of an offence, and never forgetting that the introduction of the alcohol is not there surreptitious, and that consequently the case for saying that the offence was procured by the supplier of the alcohol is very much more difficult.'

R v *Bainbridge* [1959] 3 WLR 356 Court of Criminal Appeal (Lord Parker CJ, Byrne and Winn JJ)

Mens rea required of accomplices

Facts
The defendant had obtained and supplied some cutting equipment which was subsequently used to break into the Midland Bank in Stoke Newington, London. When charged with being an accessory before the fact, the defendant contended that he had known that something illegal was going to be done with the equipment, for example breaking up stolen goods, but that he had not known that it was going to be used to break into a bank. The jury convicted him after being directed by the trial judge that it was sufficient for the prosecution to prove that the defendant had known what 'type' of crime the principals were going to commit. The defendant appealed.

Held

The appeal would be dismissed.

Lord Parker CJ:

'The complaint here is that Judge Aarvold, who tried the case, gave the jury a wrong direction in regard to what it was necessary for them to be satisfied of in order to hold the appellant guilty of being an accessory before the fact. The passages in question are these:

> "To prove that, the prosecution have to prove these matters; first of all, they have to prove that the felony itself was committed. Of that there is no doubt. That is not contested. Secondly, they have to prove that the [appellant] knew that a felony of that kind was intended and was going to be committed, and with that knowledge he did something to help the felons commit the crime. The knowledge that is required to be proved in the mind of the [appellant] is not the knowledge of the precise crime. In other words, it need not be proved that he knew that the Midland Bank, Stoke Newington branch, was going to be broken and entered, and money stolen from that particular bank, but he must know the type of crime that was in fact committed. In this case it is a breaking and entering of premises and the stealing of property from those premises. It must be proved that he knew that that sort of crime was intended and was going to be committed. It is not enough to show that he either suspected or knew that some crime was going to be committed, some crime which might have been a breaking and entering or might have been disposing of stolen property or anything of that kind. That is not enough. It must be proved that he knew that the type of crime which was in fact committed was intended."

There are other passages to the same effect; in particular when the jury returned for further directions before they came to their verdict, the learned judge said this:

> "If in fact, before it has happened, [the appellant], knowing what is going to happen, with full knowledge that a felony of that kind is going to take place, deliberately and wilfully helps it on its way, he is an accessory ... If he was not present he would not be guilty as a principal, but then you would have to decide whether he helped in purchasing this equipment for Shakeshaft knowing full well the type of offence for which it was going to be used, and, with that knowledge, buying it and helping in that way."

Counsel for the appellant, who argued this case very well, contended that that direction was wrong. As he put it, in order that a person should be convicted of being accessory before the fact, it must be shown that, at the time when he bought the equipment in a case such as this, he knew that a particular crime was going to be committed; and by "a particular crime" counsel meant that the premises in this case which were going to be broken into were known to the appellant and contemplated by him, and not only the premises in question but the date when the crime was going to occur; in other words, that he must have known that on a particular date the Stoke Newington branch of the Midland Bank was intended to be broken into.

The court fully appreciates that it is not enough that it should be shown that a person knew that some illegal venture was intended. To take this case, it would not be enough if the appellant knew – he says that he only suspected – that the equipment was going to be used to dispose of stolen property. That would not be enough. Equally, this court is quite satisfied that it is unnecessary that knowledge of the intention to commit the particular crime which was in fact committed should be shown, and by "particular crime" I am using the words in the same way as that in which counsel for the appellant used them, namely, on a particular date and particular premises.

It is not altogether easy to lay down a precise form of words which will cover every case that can be contemplated. But, having considered the cases and the law, this court is quite clear that the direction of Judge Aarvold in this case cannot be criticised. Indeed, it might well have been made with the passage in Foster's *Crown Cases* (3rd edn) (1792) at p369, in mind, because there the learned author says:

> "If the principal totally and substantially varieth, if being solicited to commit a felony of one kind he *wilfully and knowingly* committeth a felony of another, *he* will stand single in that offence, and the person soliciting will not be involved in his guilt. For on *his* part it was no more than a fruitless ineffectual temptation."

The converse of course is that, if the principal does not totally and substantially vary the advice or the help and does not wilfully and knowingly commit a different form of felony altogether, the man who has advised or helped, aided or abetted, will be guilty as an accessory before the fact.

Judge Aarvold in this case, in the passages to which I have referred, makes it clear that there must be not merely suspicion but knowledge that a crime of the type in question was intended, and that the equipment was bought with that in view. In his reference to the felony of the type intended it was, as he states, the felony of breaking and entering premises and the stealing of property from those premises. The court can see nothing wrong in that direction.'

R v *Baldessare* (1930) 22 Cr App R 70 (Court of Criminal Appeal) (The Lord Chief Justice, Talbot and MacNaghten JJ)

Accomplice's liability for accidental departures from the common design

Facts
The defendant was a passenger in a car that had been taken for the purposes of 'joyriding'. The driver (a man named Chapman) killed another road user and was convicted of manslaughter. The defendant was convicted as an accomplice to the manslaughter, as it was an unforeseen consequence of the common design being carried out. He appealed against conviction.

Held
Appeal dismissed.

The Lord Chief Justice:

> 'The appellant appeals on two grounds – first, that there was no evidence on which the jury could properly convict him of manslaughter, and secondly, as he alleges, that there was misdirection in the summing-up of the learned judge. With reference to a considerable part of the case, there was no real dispute. [After stating the facts, His Lordship continued:] It is undoubtedly a cardinal fact in the case that the jury thought fit to acquit both the appellant and Chapman on the charge of stealing the car. The question, therefore, was whether, nevertheless, the two men were associated together in the driving of the car so that, when death resulted from the collision, each was guilty of manslaughter. With regard to the summing-up, we are all of opinion that this was an excellent summing-up; it stated the law clearly and fairly, and if there was any error in it, the error was in favour of the appellant. After that perfectly fair summing-up, the jury came to the conclusion that the appellant was guilty of manslaughter; in other words, they came to the conclusion that the appellant and Chapman were acting together and joined in responsibility, not merely for the taking away of the car from the owner's possession, but also for the driving of it in the way in which it was in fact driven.
>
> The only question for this Court is whether there was any evidence on which the jury could properly find that community of purpose and action. The matter was very carefully argued before us, and we have very carefully considered it, and our conclusion is that we are not prepared to say that there was not evidence on which the jury were entitled to arrive at their verdict. Here was a clandestine ride – commonly called a "joy-ride" – on a dark night in February, without proper lights, and the two men had taken the car for a purpose, which the jury have found was not felonious, but which had as its object a "joy-ride" without the knowledge and assent of the owner. Looking at these facts, and at the actual speed of the car and its movements before and after the collision, we think that the jury were entitled to find that both the appellant and Chapman were responsible for the way in which the car was being driven at the moment of collision.'

Commentary
See *R* v *Betts and Ridley*, below.

R v Betts and Ridley (1930) 22 Cr App R 148 (Court of Criminal Appeal) (Avory, Swift, and Charles JJ)

Accomplice's liability for accidental departures from the common design

Facts

The defendants agreed that Betts would rob a victim by hitting him to the ground and snatching his property, and that Ridley would wait around the corner at the wheel of the 'getaway' car. The plan was carried out, but Betts struck the victim with such force that the victim died from the blow. They were both convicted of murder and appealed.

Held

The appeals would be dismissed. With regard to Ridley's appeal, the common design was carried out, but with an unforeseen consequence, the death of the victim. Where the principal did not deliberately exceed the common design in causing such a result, the accomplice would be jointly responsible for it.

Avory J:

'Now with regard to the case of Ridley, Mr Marshall [counsel for the appellant] has, in a very able address to the Court, attempted to satisfy us that a distinction ought to have been drawn by the jury in the case of Ridley, and that the learned Commissioner ought in his direction to them, to have told them that, even though they found Betts guilty of murder, they yet might find Ridley guilty only of manslaughter. No suggestion is made that Ridley was guilty of anything less than manslaughter, or that he could properly be acquitted altogether. The only question in his case is, whether there was any misdirection of the jury in regard to his case, and whether on the facts of this case, he ought to have been convicted only of manslaughter.

Now bearing in mind that by his own confession he was a party to the agreement that this deceased man should be robbed, and that by his own admission in his own statement he anticipated that he would, at least, be pushed down, it is necessary to see whether upon the authorities there was any ground for distinguishing his case from that of Betts.

First of all, it is clear that in the circumstances he was a principal in the second degree to the robbery with violence, which in fact took place. It is clear law that it is not necessary that the party, to constitute him a principal in the second degree, should be actually present, an eye-witness or ear-witness, of the transaction. He is, in construction of law, present aiding and abetting if with the intention of giving assistance, he is near enough to afford it, should occasion arise. Thus, if he be outside the house, watching to prevent surprise, whilst his companions are in the house committing a felony, such constructive presence is sufficient to make him a principal in the second degree. It is clear that Ridley was present in that sense, so as to make him a principal in the second degree to this crime of robbery with violence; and although it might be true to say that he had not agreed beforehand that Andrews should be struck on the head in a way likely to cause his death, it is clear upon the authorities that if he was a party to this felonious act of robbery with violence – some violence – and that the other person, the principal in the first degree, in the course of carrying out that common design does an act which causes the death, then the principal in the second degree is equally responsible in law. As was said in East's Pleas of the Crown, at page 256, dealing for the moment again with Betts: "He who voluntarily, knowingly and unlawfully intends hurt to the person of another, though he intend not death, yet if death ensue, is guilty of murder or manslaughter according to the circumstances. As if A intending to beat B happen to kill him, if done from preconceived malice" – if done from preconceived intention to rob with violence, it would be the same thing as if done with malice – "it will be no alleviation that he did not intend all the mischief that followed."

That being the position of Betts, what is the position of the principal in the second degree. He is at least, if not more, responsible than an accessory before the fact, and in Foster's Crown Cases, at page

369, dealing with an accessory before the fact, it is said: "Much has been said by writers who have gone before me, upon cases where a person supposed to commit a felony at the instigation of another hath gone beyond the terms of such instigation, or hath, in the execution varied from them. If the principal totally and substantially varieth, if being solicited to commit a felony of one kind he wilfully and knowingly committeth a felony of another, he will stand single in that offence, and the person soliciting will not be involved in his guilt ... but if the principal in substance complieth with the temptation, varying only in circumstance of time or place, or in the manner of execution, in these cases the person soliciting to the offence will, if absent, be an accessory before the fact, if present a principal." It appears to the Court in this case that the case of Ridley comes precisely within this description. Even if Betts did vary in the manner of execution of this agreed plan to rob, and obviously it must have been a plan to rob with some degree of violence, Ridley being present as a principal in the second degree is equally responsible. Therefore, in any view, if the learned Commissioner had made the distinction which is suggested between the two cases, it is obvious that upon a correct view of the law, Ridley in fact in this case was a principal in the second degree to this crime of murder. As the direction stands, and as it was given to the jury, they must, in finding Ridley guilty of murder, be presumed to have found that he was actually a party and privy to an act which was calculated in the judgment of ordinary people to cause death; and having so found, it is impossible that this Court, upon such evidence as this, can interfere with their verdict.'

R v Calhaem [1985] QB 808 Court of Appeal (Criminal Division) (Parker LJ, Tudor Evans J and Sir John Thompson)

Whether principal's actions a departure from the common design

Facts
The defendant had hired a man named Zajac to kill a woman named Shirley Rendell, who was a rival for the affections of Mr Pigot, with whom the defendant was infatuated. Zajac was paid £5,000 by the defendant to carry out the killing. At his trial for the murder of Mrs Rendell, Zajac testified that after being paid the money by the defendant he had resolved not to carry out the killing, but instead to visit Mrs Rendell's house, carrying an unloaded shotgun and a hammer, to act out a charade that would give the appearance that he had tried to kill her. He claimed that when he had stepped inside the front door of the victim's house, she had screamed and he panicked, hitting her several times with the hammer. On the basis of this evidence, the defendant had contended that she could not be guilty of counselling the victim's murder as the killing had been a direct result of Zajac's panic, not her instructions, which he had in any event decided not to follow.

Held
The appeal would be dismissed.

Parker LJ (his Lordship referred to Lord Widgery CJ's judgment in *Attorney-General's Reference (No 1 of 1975)*, extracted above, and continued):

'We must therefore approach the question raised on the basis that we should give the word "counsel" its ordinary meaning, which is, as the judge said, "advise," "solicit," or something of that sort. There is no implication in the word itself that there should be any causal connection between the offence of incitement at common law, the actual offence must have been committed, and committed by the person counselled. To this extent there must clearly be, first, contact between the parties, and, secondly, a connection between the counselling and the murder. Equally, the act done must, we think, be done within the scope of the authority or advice, and not, for example, accidentally when the mind of the final murderer did not go with his actions. For example, if the principal offender happened to be involved in a football riot in the course of which he laid about him with a weapon of some sort and killed someone who, unknown to him, was the person whom he had been counselled to kill, he would not, in our view, have been acting within the scope of his authority; he would have been acting entirely outside it, albeit what he had done was what he had been counselled to do.

We see, however, no need to import anything further into the meaning of the word, unless authority drives us to do so. It is of course possible, and both counsel took this course, to take examples of cases which appear to be anomalous, whichever construction is put upon the wording. Such anomalies do not, in our view, assist. There will always be cases in which difficulties are raised and they are disposed of in the ordinary way by sensible action on the part of the prosecuting authority. So far as the authorities are concerned, there are in them, we accept, phrases which may appear, at any rate at first sight, to assist the view put forward by Mr Carman. We do not propose to go through all the authorities, but some of them must be mentioned.'

His Lordship considered these, and continued:

'... The natural meaning of the word does not imply the commission of the offence. So long as there is counselling – and there was ample evidence in this case of that fact – so long as the principal offence is committed by the one counselled, and so long as the one counselled is acting within the scope of his authority, and not in the accidental way or some such similar way as I have suggested with regard to an incident in a football riot, we are of the view that the offence is made out.

Accordingly, we reject Mr Carman's first submission and hold that the direction by the judge was correct. We would add on this matter however that had we accepted his submission we should have felt unable to apply the proviso, because of the possibility that the jury might have accepted the view that there was no substantial cause and come to the conclusion that it was merely authority which enabled them to convict.

Mr Carman's other points were that (a) the judge erred in his treatment of Zajac's evidence, (b) the judge should have directed the jury that without Zajac's evidence there was no evidence, and (c) the judge failed to give directions as to the importance of two notes which Zajac had written to a fellow-prisoner, one Gillard. As to these, having considered the passages complained of and also the omissions complained of, in the context of the whole of the summing up we need say very little. As to (a), in our view the judge gave the jury the clearest warnings possible with regard to the unreliability of Zajac, which was common ground, and of the need for corroboration of his evidence. He told them that it was open to them, if they wished to do so, to reject his account of his state of mind immediately preceding and at the time of the murder, whilst at the same time to accept the corroborated parts of his evidence. We see nothing wrong in what the judge did and consider that he gave perfectly adequate directions with regard to Zajac.

With respect to the second point, that the judge should have directed the jury that without Zajac's evidence there was no evidence, in our view such a submission is wholly untenable. If there is evidence to go to the jury it is not for the judge to say. "If you reject this bit or that bit of the evidence there is nothing left." Were it to be so the judge would have the task, as we see it, of eliminating piece by piece each bit of evidence until he came down to nothing. If he were to take such a course he would be usurping the function of the jury. Accordingly, we reject that submission.'

Chan Wing Siu v *R* [1985] AC 168 Privy Council (Lords Keith, Bridge, Brandon, and Templeman, and Sir Robin Cooke)

Mens rea required for accomplices to murder

Facts
The appellants were members of a gang who had gone to the deceased's house to commit a robbery, arming themselves with knives. During the robbery the deceased was stabbed to death by a member of the gang. The appellants were convicted as accomplices to the murder and appealed against their convictions on the ground that the trial judge had misdirected the jury as to the mens rea required.

Held

The appeals would be dismissed. For an accomplice to be guilty of murder it was sufficient for the prosecution to establish that he foresaw death or grievous bodily harm as a possible incident of the common design being carried out.

Sir Robin Cooke (after referring to a number of Commonwealth authorities on the mens rea required for the conviction of accomplices):

'What public policy requires was rightly identified in the submissions of the Crown. Where a man lends himself to a criminal enterprise knowing that potentially murderous weapons are to be carried, and in the event they are in fact used by his partner with an intent sufficient for murder, he should not escape the consequences by reliance on a nuance of prior assessment, only too likely to have been optimistic.

On the other hand, if it was not even contemplated by the particular accused that serious bodily harm would be intentionally inflicted, he is not a party to murder.'

Reference was then made to *Davies* v *DPP* [1954] AC 378, and his Lordship continued:

'The test of mens rea here is subjective. It is what the individual accused in fact contemplated that matters. As in other cases where the state of a person's mind has to be ascertained, this may be inferred from his conduct and any other evidence throwing light on what he foresaw at the material time, including of course any explanation that he gives in evidence or in a statement put in evidence by the prosecution. It is no less elementary that all questions of weight are for the jury. The prosecution must prove the necessary contemplation beyond reasonable doubt, although that may be done by inference as just mentioned. If, at the end of the day and whether as a result of hearing evidence from the accused or for some other reason, the jury conclude that there is a reasonable possibility that the accused did not even contemplate the risk, he is in this type of case not guilty of murder or wounding with intent to cause serious bodily harm.

In some cases in this field it is enough to direct the jury by adapting to the circumstances the simple formula common in a number of jurisdictions. For instance, did the particular accused contemplate that in carrying out a common unlawful purpose one of his partners in the enterprise might use a knife or a loaded gun with the intention of causing really serious bodily harm? ...

In cases where an issue of remoteness does arise it is for the jury (or other tribunal of fact) to decide whether the risk *as recognised by the accused* was sufficient to make him a party to the crime committed by the principal. Various formulae have been suggested, including a substantial risk, a real risk, a risk that something might well happen. No one formula is exclusively preferable; indeed it may be advantageous in a summing up to use more than one. For the question is not one of semantics. What has to be brought home to the jury is that occasionally a risk may have occurred to an accused's mind, fleetingly or even causing him some deliberation, but may genuinely have been dismissed by him as altogether negligible. If they think there is a reasonable possibility that the case is in that class, taking the risk should not make that accused a party to such a crime of intention as murder or wounding with intent to cause grievous bodily harm. The judge is entitled to warn the jury to be cautious before reaching that conclusion; but the law can do no more by way of definition; it can only be for the jury to determine any issue of that kind on the facts of the particular case.

The present case not being in that class, their Lordships agree with the Court of Appeal that the attack on the summing up fails and will humbly advise Her Majesty that the appeals should be dismissed.'

R v *Clarkson* [1971] 1 WLR 1402 Courts-Martial Appeal Court (Megaw LJ, Geoffrey Lane and Kilner Brown JJ)

Inactivity at the scene of a crime: whether sufficient for liability

Facts
Two soldiers (the defendants) had entered a room following the noise from a disturbance therein. They found some other soldiers raping a woman, and remained on the scene to watch what was happening. They were convicted of abetting the rapes and appealed on the basis that their mere presence alone could not have been sufficient for liability.

Held
The appeals would be allowed.

Megaw LJ:

'*Coney* [(1882) 8 QBD 534] decided that non-accidental presence at the scene of the crime is not conclusive of aiding and abetting. The jury has to be told by the judge, or as in this case the court-martial has to be told by the judge-advocate, in clear terms what it is that has to be proved before they can convict of aiding and abetting; what it is of which the jury or the court-martial, as the case may be, must be sure as matters of inference before they can convict of aiding and abetting in such a case where the evidence adduced by the prosecution is limited to non-accidental presence ... It is not enough, then, that the presence of the accused has, in fact, given encouragement. It must be proved that he *wilfully* encouraged. In such a case as the present, more than in many other cases where aiding and abetting is alleged, it was essential that that element should be stressed; for there was here at least the possibility that a drunken man with his self-discipline loosened by drink, being aware that a woman was being raped, might be attracted to the scene and might stay on the scene in the capacity of what is known as a voyeur; and, while his presence and the presence of others might in fact encourage the rapers or discourage the victim, he himself, enjoying the scene or at least standing by assenting, might not intend that his presence should offer encouragement to rapers and would-be rapers or discouragement to the victim; he might not realise that he was giving encouragement; so that, while encouragement there might be, it would not be a case in which ... the accused person wilfully encouraged ... it follows that mere intention is not in itself enough. There must be an intention to encourage; and there must also be encouragement in fact, in cases such as the present case.'

R v Cogan and Leak [1975] 3 WLR 316 Court of Appeal (Criminal Division) (Lawton, James LJJ, and Bristow J)

Accomplice's liability where principal lacks mens rea

Facts
Leak persuaded Cogan to have sexual intercourse with Mrs Leak, telling him that she liked being forced to have sex against her will. Cogan was convicted of rape, but appealed successfully on the ground that he had honestly thought she was consenting. Leak now appealed against his conviction for aiding and abetting the rape, on the ground that he could not be liable where the principal offender was acquitted.

Held
The appeal would be dismissed.

Lawton LJ:

'Leak's appeal against conviction was based on the proposition that he could not be found guilty of aiding and abetting Cogan to rape his wife if Cogan was acquitted of that offence as he was deemed in law to have been when his conviction was quashed ... [Counsel for Leak] conceded, however, that his proposition had some limitations. The law on this topic lacks clarity as a perusal of some of the textbooks shows: ... We do not consider it appropriate to review the law generally because as was said by this court in *R v Quick* [1973] QB 910, 923 when considering this kind of problem:

"The facts of each case ... have to be considered and in particular what is alleged to have been done by way of aiding and abetting."

The only case which counsel for Leak submitted had a direct bearing on the problem of Leak's guilt was *Walters v Lunt* [1951] 2 All ER 645. In that case the respondents had been charged under section 33(11) of the Larceny Act 1916, with receiving from a child aged seven years, certain articles knowing them to have been stolen. In 1951, a child under eight years was deemed in law to be incapable of committing a crime: it followed that at the time of receipt by the respondents the articles had not been stolen and that the charges had not been proved. That case is very different from this because here one fact is clear – the wife had been raped.

Cogan had had sexual intercourse with her without her consent. The fact that Cogan was innocent of rape because he believed that she was consenting does not affect the position that she was raped.

Her ravishment had come about because Leak had wanted it to happen and had taken action to see that it did by persuading Cogan to use his body as the instrument for the necessary physical act. In the language of the law the act of sexual intercourse without the wife's consent was the actus reus; it had been procured by Leak who had the appropriate mens rea, namely his intention that Cogan should have sexual intercourse with her without her consent. In our judgment it is irrelevant that the man whom Leak had procured to do the physical act himself did not intend to have sexual intercourse with the wife without her consent. Leak was using him as a means to procure a criminal purpose.

Before 1861 a case such as this, pleaded as it was in the indictment, might have presented a court with problems arising from the old distinctions between principals and accessories in felony. Most of the old law was swept away by section 8 of the Accessories and Abettors Act 1861 and what remained, by section 1 of the Criminal Law Act 1967. The modern law allowed Leak to be tried and punished as a principal offender. In our judgment he could have been indicted as a principal offender. It would have been no defence for him to submit that if Cogan was an "innocent" agent, he was necessarily in the old terminology of the law a principal in the first degree, which was a legal impossibility as a man cannot rape his own wife during co-habitation. The law no longer concerns itself with niceties of degrees in participation of crime; but even if it did, Leak would still be guilty. The reason a man cannot by his own physical act rape his wife during co-habitation is because the law presumes consent from the marriage ceremony: see *Hale, Pleas of the Crown* (1778), vol. 1, p.629. There is no such presumption when a man procures a drunken friend to do the physical act for him. Hale CJ put this case in one sentence; at p629:

"tho in marriage she hath given up her body to her husband, she is not to be by him prostituted to another."

Had Leak been indicted as a principal offender, the case against him would have been clear beyond argument. Should he be allowed to go free because he was charged with "being aider and abettor to the same offence"? If we are right in our opinion that the wife had been raped (and no one outside a court of law would say that she had not been), then the particulars of offence accurately stated what Leak had done, namely he had procured Cogan to commit the offence. This would suffice to uphold the conviction. We would prefer, however, to uphold it on a wider basis. In our judgment convictions should not be upset because of mere technicalities of pleading in an indictment. Leak knew what the case against him was and the facts in support of that case were proved. But for the fact that the jury thought that Cogan in his intoxicated condition might have mistaken the wife's sobs and distress for expressions of her consent, no question of any kind would have arisen about the form of pleading. By his written statement Leak virtually admitted what he had done. As Judge Chapman said in *R v Humphreys* [1965] 3 All ER 689, 692:

"It would be anomalous if a person who admitted to a substantial part in the perpetration of a misdemeanour as aider and abettor could not be convicted on his own admission merely because the person alleged to have been aided and abetted was not or could not be convicted."

In the circumstances of this case it would be more than anomalous: it would be an affront to justice and to the common sense of ordinary folk. It was for these reasons that we dismissed the appeal against conviction.

The sentence passed on Leak for his part in the rape was severe; but the circumstances were horrible.

We can see nothing wrong with that sentence. The assault on the wife the previous day had been brutal. The doctor found no less than 13 bruises in the middle and lower region on the left hand side of her spine. There were other bruises on her back and multiple bruises on her left hip. These bruises were consistent with punching and kicking. Men who use violence of this kind on their wives must expect severe sentences. The sentence of three years was not too severe.'

R v *Dunnington* [1984] QB 472 Court of Appeal (Criminal Division) (Ackner LJ, Beldam J and Sir John Thompson)

Aiding and abetting an attempt

Facts

The defendant had agreed with two other men, Ryan and Peterson, that they should carry out a robbery on a shop. The defendant stole a car for use in the offence, and waited outside the shop whilst Peterson and Ryan went in and ordered the shopkeeper to hand over money. The shopkeeper resisted, and the defendants fled empty handed. The defendant was convicted of attempted robbery as an accomplice and appealed on the ground that such liability had been abolished by s1(4)(b) of the Criminal Attempts Act 1981.

Held

The appeal would be dismissed.

Beldam J:

'It was conceded by the Crown before the learned judge, as it was before us, that the part played by the appellant was solely that of aider and abettor of the offence of attempted robbery. He had been charged as a principal, pursuant to the provisions of section 8 of the Accessories and Abettors Act 1861, as amended by Schedule 12 to the Criminal Law Act 1977.'

His Lordship referred to ss1(1) and 1(4) of the Criminal Attempts Act 1981 and continued:

For the appeal it was argued that section 1, when read with subsection (4) must mean, "If, with intent to commit any offence other than aiding, abetting, counselling, procuring or suborning the commission of an offence, a person does an act which is more than merely preparatory to the commission of the offence, he is guilty of attempting to commit the offence." Although the appellant's acts were more than merely preparatory to the commission of the offence of aiding and abetting, they were done with intent to aid and abet the commission of an offence and so were excluded from the operation of subsection (1) of section 1.

The learned judge ruled against the appellant's submission in these words: "I think that this means the section does not apply to an attempt to aid and abet, and I think, when one looks at it carefully and puts all the words together, that is the clear meaning of it. You cannot attempt to conspire and you cannot attempt to aid and abet, but here the evidence is, which is accepted on the face of it, that the aiding and abetting was completed. He did all that was required for the aiding and abetting. It was the offence that he was aiding and abetting that, fortunately, was not completed, so I think that the Criminal Attempts Act 1981, section 1, does apply."

Before us the arguments for the parties were expanded. For the appellant it was accepted that the Criminal Attempts Act 1981 was based upon the Criminal Attempts Bill, a draft of which was contained in the report of the Law Commission No. 102 and that the intention of the Law Commission was that, whilst it should remain an offence to aid and abet an attempt to commit a crime, it should be made clear that an attempt to aid and abet a crime was not a criminal offence. Nevertheless, on the true construction of the language used in the Act, because Parliament had chosen to exclude attempts to aid and abet by the particular form of language used in the Act and by reference to the intention of the offender, aiding and abetting an attempt was in fact excluded from the operation of section 1(1) of the Act. Finally, it was urged that a person in the position of the appellant could nevertheless be charged with conspiring to commit robbery.

For the prosecution it was argued that the appellant was not charged with attempting to aid and abet, but with aiding and abetting the attempted robbery. He was in fact an aider and abettor and only charged as a principal for procedural reasons. He had, in fact, completed all the acts necessary for the offence of aiding and abetting Peterson and Ryan in their attempt to rob Mr Boagey. Notwithstanding the language of subsection (4) of section 1 of the Criminal Attempts Act 1981, the appellant could still be charged as a principal under the provisions of the Accessories and Abettors Act 1861. The exception did not apply to acts of aiding and abetting which were completed and this was borne out by the use in subsection (4) of the words, "... which, if it were completed, would be triable ..."

The Criminal Attempts Act 1981, closely follows the wording of the draft Bill contained in the Report of the Law Commission No. 102.

Whilst recourse can be had to that Report, in approaching the interpretation of the section for the background of the law as it was and for the legislative intention, it is not proper or desirable that we should use it as a direct statement of what the proposed Bill was to mean or to take the meaning of the section from its commentary of recommendations. We cannot, therefore, take the meaning of the section from the clear indications in part 2G, paragraph 2.123 in the commentary, or from the recommendation No. 5, 1(9), of the Law Commission Paper.

It is to be observed at the outset that if the construction contended for by the appellant is correct, then section 1 of the Act, which was intended to clarify and define the offence of attempting to commit a crime, has relieved of criminal responsibility all accessories or secondary parties in the commission of crimes which are thwarted, because attempts to commit crime at common law are abolished by section 6(2) of the Act. Thus, for example, persons who participate in an unsuccessful crime, by keeping watch for the perpetrators or driving a getaway car (as in the instant case) would be relieved of criminal liability. It can, therefore, be confidently stated that such a result was not the intention of Parliament and we would only give effect to such a construction if the words permitted of no other sensible meaning. We bear in mind, of course, that this is a penal Statute and that conduct exempted from its operation must be given a wide rather than a narrow construction where both are equally compatible with the language used.

Approaching the construction of the section in this way we begin by reminding ourselves that since section 8 of the Accessories and Abettors Act 1861 became law, any person who aided and abetted, counselled or procured the commission of an offence has been liable to be indicted, tried and punished as a principal offender. Accordingly, any person who actually takes part in the commission of an offence by aiding and abetting another to commit it, is liable in law as a principal. It has been a moot question whether in a case in which no person actually participates in the commission of an offence, an accused person can be guilty of the separate offence of attempting to aid and abet the commission of that offence.

For over 120 years those whose proximate acts are done with the intention of aiding and abetting actual participators in crime have been tried and indicted as principals rather than as secondary participants. In excepting from the application of section 1(1) the offences referred to in section 1(4), the draftsman of the section clearly treated aiding, abetting, counselling, procuring or suborning the commission of an offence as if it were a separate offence.

Therefore, returning to section 1(1), it is clear that the words "the offence," where they appear in the phrase, "he is guilty of attempting to commit the offence," must be taken to refer to the same offence as is referred to in the phrase earlier in section 1(1), "with intent to commit an offence." Thus, rephrasing section 1(1), for the purposes of this case, it would, but for the exception, read: "If, with intent to commit the offence of aiding and abetting an offence, a person does an act which is more than merely preparatory to the offence of aiding and abetting an offence he is guilty of attempting to commit the offence of aiding and abetting an offence."

However, so to provide would have created a new offence. Accordingly, to avoid this situation, section 1(4) provided, inter alia, that the provisions of section 1 should not apply to aiding, abetting, counselling, procuring or suborning the commission of an offence. Thus, the Act prevented the creation of the separate offence of attempting to aid and abet the commission of a crime. It did not remove from criminal responsibility the offence of aiding and abetting an attempt to commit a crime.

We therefore conclude that the submission made on behalf of the appellant was rightly rejected by the learned judge and this appeal is, accordingly, dismissed.'

R v Howe [1987] AC 417 House of Lords (Lords Hailsham LC, Bridge, Brandon, Griffiths and Mackay)

[For the facts see Chapter 31. The following extracts from the speeches in the House of Lords concern the legality of charging an accomplice with a greater offence than that charged against the principal.

The second of the three questions certified for the House of Lords was:

'Can one who incites or procures by duress another to kill or to be a party to a killing be convicted of murder if that other is acquitted by reason of duress?']

Lord Mackay:

'I turn now to the second certified question. In the view that I take on question one the second does not properly arise. However, I am of opinion that the Court of Appeal reached the correct conclusion upon it as a matter of principle.

Giving the judgment of the Court of Appeal Lord Lane CJ said [1986] QB 626, 641–642:

"The judge based himself on a decision of this court in *R v Richards* [1974] QB 776. The facts in that case were that Mrs Richards paid two men to inflict injuries on her husband which she intended should 'put him in hospital for a month.' The two men wounded the husband but not seriously. They were acquitted of wounding with intent but convicted of unlawful wounding. Mrs Richards herself was convicted of wounding with intent, the jury plainly, and not surprisingly, believing that she had the necessary intent, though the two men had not. She appealed against her conviction on the ground that she could not properly be convicted as accessory before the fact to a crime more serious than that committed by the principals in the first degree. The appeal was allowed and the conviction for unlawful wounding was substituted. The court followed a passage from *Hawkins' Pleas of the Crown*, vol. 2. c. 29, para. 15: 'I take it to be an uncontroverted rule that [the offence of the accessory can never rise higher than that of the principal]; it seeming incongruous and absurd that he who is punished only as a partaker of the guilt of another, should be adjudged guilty of a higher crime than the other.'

James LJ delivering the judgment in *R v Richards* [1974] QB 776 said, at p780: 'If there is only one offence committed, and that is the offence of unlawful wounding, then the person who has requested that offence to be committed, or advised that that offence be committed, cannot be guilty of a graver offence than that in fact which was committed.' The decision in *R v Richards* has been the subject of some criticism – see for example *Smith & Hogan, Criminal Law*, 5th ed (1983), p140. Counsel before us posed the situation where A hands a gun to D informing him that it is loaded with blank ammunition only and telling him to go and scare X by discharging it. The ammunition is in fact live, as A knows, and X is killed. D is convicted only of manslaughter, as he might be on those facts. It would seem absurd that A should thereby escape conviction for murder. We take the view that *R v Richards* [1974] QB 776 was incorrectly decided, but it seems to us that it cannot properly be distinguished from the instant case."

I consider that the reasoning of Lord Lane CJ is entirely correct and I would affirm his view that where a person has been killed and that result is the result intended by another participant, the mere fact that the actual killer may be convicted only of the reduced charge of manslaughter for some reason special to himself does not, in my opinion in any way, result in a compulsory reduction for the other participant.'

R v Hyde [1990] 3 WLR 1115 Court of Appeal (Criminal Division) (Lord Lane CJ, Rose and Tucker JJ)

Murder – joint enterprise – correct direction on mens rea of accomplices

Facts (as stated by Lord Lane CJ)

'The incident resulting in the death of Gallagher took place outside the Merlin public house, Andover, at about 10.25 pm on 3 June 1988. There was no dispute that Gallagher sustained a violent blow to the forehead, consistent with a heavy kick from a shod foot, which crushed the front of his skull. He died 73 days later, having never regained consciousness. The prosecution case was that the three appellants carried out a joint attack on the victim and were all equally responsible for his death, even though it was not possible to say who had actually struck the fatal blow or blows; furthermore, that their intention had been to cause serious injury; or that each knew that such was the intention of the others when he took part. By 10.00 pm that evening all three, who were regular customers at the Merlin public house, had probably had too much to drink. Sussex and Collins were both overheard making unspecific threatening remarks. When Gallagher left he was closely followed by Hyde and Sussex, and then Collins. Other customers, in the belief that serious trouble was about to break out, gathered on the balcony to watch events unfold. Gallagher was accompanied by a man called Burkwood, who related how Hyde had said to Gallagher, "Hey, feller, you've got a problem." When Gallagher asked "Why?" he was felled by a blow.

Collins told Burkwood, "Get out if you know what's good for you." Burkwood was then knocked against a car, and when he recovered his breath he saw all three appellants round Gallagher (who was already on the ground) kicking him. Other witnesses saw Hyde kicking Gallagher's legs from under him; Sussex punching Gallagher's head; Hyde kicking him between the legs ... and Collins running back for five yards as they left and kicking Gallagher on the head ... .

Each of the three men was questioned by the police. Hyde agreed that he had hit Gallagher, asserting that no one else was involved. He said that he had had a bad day and Gallagher kept picking on him in the public house. He was asked if Gallagher had remained conscious, to which he replied, "Don't think so, not the way I hit him." He was then asked how he had hit him, and replied "With my fist on his face, square on his face with all my bloody weight behind it." Sussex said he had been drunk and had punched Gallagher a few times. Collins said that there was a fight between Hyde and Gallagher with Sussex present. He, Collins, did not hit Gallagher and accompanied the other two after the incident back to the public house.

All three gave evidence before the jury denying that there was any joint enterprise or any intent to do serious harm to Gallagher. Hyde and Sussex said each had acted on his own with no intention beyond a simple assault. Collins, according to them, was responsible for the fatal blow. His actions and intention were nothing to do with them, nor did they foresee what he might intend to do. Collins for his part maintained that there was no joint attack or, if there was, it involved only Hyde and Sussex. The jury, it was submitted, could not be sure whose act caused the death, and that therefore no one should be convicted as the killer.

As to joint enterprise, the trial judge had directed the jury in the followng terms:

> "As I say, ordinarily speaking, if he does something which is beyond the scope of the agreement, that is as you might say the end of the agreement. But, what if the others anticipated that he might do some such thing – and here we have to apply common sense. Fights do get out of hand and escalate. A man who starts by punching may get excited and decide to kick. If there was a tacit agreement to punch and kick, a man who is kicking may decide to give a kick like that which was allegedly given by Collins and which has been described as a place-kick or a penalty kick, a description which if the basic facts are right is not a bad description of the kick. If either of the other two, and you have to consider the case of each of them separately, foresaw and contemplated a real possibility that one of his fellows might in the excitement of the moment go beyond the actual plan and intend to do and do grievous bodily harm, then you have to consider whether that man, the one who had the foresight, did not in truth intend that result himself."

Having explained to the jury that they should distinguish between intention and foresight, the trial judge concluded:

> "We may summarise it shortly by saying that if all three intended to do grievous bodily harm, then that is that, they are all guilty of murder. If they did not, but one of them decided to do it, then if either of the others can be shown to have had the same intention, inasmuch as he foresaw the real possibility that that might

be the result of the fight which he was putting in train, then he too shares in the responsibility as in commonsense he must."

The defendants were each convicted of murder, and appealed on the grounds that:

1. The judge, in the circumstances of the case, erred in directing the jury upon foreseeability, such a direction being unnecessary and confusing.
2. Alternatively, the judge erred in directing the jury that the defendant's foresight of the state of mind of another defendant was a relevant consideration in determining whether the defendant having that foresight had the intention to do grievous bodily harm.
3. Alternatively, the judge's direction on foreseeability did not sufficiently distinguish between foreseeability and intention and/or did not sufficiently underline the necessity for the prosecution to prove the specific intent required for the offence of murder.'

Held

The appeals would be dismissed. The mental element of an accomplice to murder was established by proof that he foresaw death or serious harm as a consequence that might result from the action of the principal offender.

Lord Lane CJ:

'The judgment of this court in *R v Slack* [1989] QB 775 was not delivered until some four months after the conclusion of the hearing of the instant case. Consequently the judge here did not have before him the distinction which we endeavoured to draw in *Slack's* case between the mental element required to be proved vis a vis the secondary party (hereinafter called "B") and that required in the case of the principal party, the actual killer (hereinafter called "A"). In the passages we have cited from the summing up of which complaint is made, the judge was endeavouring to apply the principles which were, prior to *Slack's* case, thought to apply to cases of joint enterprise. The question is whether the directions in the present case were sufficient to comply with the law as it now stands.

There are, broadly speaking, two main types of joint enterprise cases where death results to the victim. The first is where the primary object of the participants is to do some kind of physical injury to the victim. The second is where the primary object is not to cause physical injury to any victim but, for example, to commit burglary. The victim is assaulted and killed as a possibly unwelcome incident of the burglary. The latter type of case may pose more complicated questions than the former, but the principle in each is the same. A must be proved to have intended to kill or to do serious bodily harm at the time he killed as was pointed out in *R v Slack* [1989] QB 775 at 781. B, to be guilty, must be proved to have lent himself to a criminal enterprise involving the infliction of serious harm or death, or to have had an express or tacit understanding with A that such harm or death should, if necessary, be inflicted.

We were there endeavouring, respectfully, to follow the principles enunciated by Sir Robin Cooke in *Chan Wing Sui v The Queen* [1985] AC 168, at 175:

"The case must depend rather on the wider principle whereby a secondary party is criminally liable for acts by the primary offender of a type which the former foresees but does not necessarily intend. That there is such a principle is not in doubt. It turns on contemplation or, putting the same idea in other words, authorisation, which may be expressed but is more usually implied. It meets the case of a crime foreseen as a possible incident of the common unlawful enterprise. The criminal culpability lies in participating in the venture with that foresight."

It has been pointed out by Professor J C Smith, in his commentary on *R v Wakely* [1990] Crim LR 119, 120–121, that in the judgments of *R v Slack* ... and also in *R v Wakely* ... to both of which I was a party, insufficient attention was paid by the court to the distinction between on the one hand tacit agreement by B that A should use violence, and on the other hand a realisation by B that A, the principal party, may use violence despite B's refusal to authorise or agree to its use. Indeed in *R v Wakely* we went so far as to say:

"The suggestion that a mere foresight of the real or definite possibility of violence being used is sufficient to constitute the mental element of murder is prima facie, academically speaking at least, not sufficient."

On reconsideration, that passage is not in accordance with the principles set out by Sir Robin Cooke which we were endeavouring to follow and was wrong, or at least misleading. If B realises (without agreeing to such conduct being used) that A may kill or intentionally inflict serious injury, but nevertheless continues to participate with A in the venture, that will amount to a sufficient mental element for B to be guilty of murder if A, with the requisite intent, kills in the course of the venture. As Professor Smith points out, B has in those circumstances lent himself to the enterprise and by so doing he has given assistance and encouragement to A in carrying out an enterprise which B realises may involve murder.'

Johnson v *Youden* [1950] 1 KB 544 Divisional Court (Lord Goddard CJ, Humphreys and Lynskey JJ)

Mens rea needed by accomplices to strict liability offences

Facts

The principal offender, a builder, was granted a licence by a local authority permitting him to build a house. The licence was granted subject to a condition limiting the maximum price at which it could be sold to £1,025. It was an offence of strict liability, contrary to s7(1) of the Building Materials and Housing Act 1945 to sell the house in excess of any such condition. The builder induced another to buy it from him for £1,275. The defendants in the present case were the partners in the firm of solicitors who had dealt with the sale of the house, and who had been acquitted of aiding and abetting the builder in committing an offence under the 1945 Act. The prosecution appealed.

Held

The appeal would be dismissed in respect of the two partners who had not known that the house was being sold at a price above the maximum permitted by the licence, but would be allowed in respect of the third partner who had known of the higher price that was being paid.

Lord Goddard CJ:

'In regard to the respondents, the justices found that, until 6 April 1949, none of them knew anything about the extra £250 which the builder was receiving, and that the first two respondents, Mr Henry Wallace Youden and Mr George Henry Youden, did not know about it at any time, as the builder deliberately concealed the fact and even refused to give the purchaser a receipt for that £250. The justices, therefore, were right, in our opinion, in dismissing the information against the first two respondents on the ground that they could not be guilty of aiding and abetting the commission of the offence as they did not know of the matter which constituted the offence. If they had known that the builder was receiving the extra £250 and had continued to ask the purchaser to complete, they would have committed an offence by continuing to assist the builder to offer the property for sale, contrary to the provisions of s 7 (1) of the Act of 1945, and, as ignorance of the law is no defence, they would have been guilty of the offence even if they had not realised that they were committing an offence, but a person cannot be convicted of aiding and abetting the commission of an offence if he does not know of the essential matters which would constitute the offence.

In regard to their partner, Mr Brydone, the third respondent, the facts are different. Until 6 or 7 April 1949, he was as ignorant as were his partners that the builder had insisted on receiving £250 beyond what he was entitled to charge, but on 6 April he received a letter from the purchaser's solicitor saying:

"I duly received your letter of 26 March informing me that you are ready to settle at any time and that the amount payable on completion is £925."

The sum was £925, because the controlled price was £1,025, and £100 had been paid as deposit. The letter continued:

> "I think I ought to let you know the reason why I have not as yet proceeded to completion. It is that I have felt compelled to report to the town clerk what I consider to be a breach by your client of provisions of s 7 of the Building Materials and Housing Act 1945."

This letter naturally put the third respondent, who was dealing with the matter, on inquiry, and he thereupon read the relevant provisions of the Act of 1945 and also spoke to the builder who told him a story which, even if it were true, was on the face of it obviously a colourable evasion of the Act. The builder's story was that he had placed the extra £250 in a separate deposit account and that it was to be spent on payment for work as and when he (the builder) would be lawfully able to execute it in the future on the house on behalf of the purchaser.

It seems impossible to imagine that anyone could believe such a story. Who has ever heard of a purchaser, when buying a house from a builder, putting money into the builder's hands because he may want some work done thereafter? I think that the third respondent could not have read s 7 (5) of the Act as carefully as he should have done, because I cannot believe that any solicitor, or even a layman, would not understand that the bargain which the builder described was just the kind of transaction which the Act prohibits. Section 7 (5) provides:

> "In determining for the purposes of this section the consideration for which a house has been sold or let, the court shall have regard to any transaction with which the sale or letting is associated ..."

If the third respondent had read and appreciated those words he would have seen at once that the extra £250 which the builder was getting was in regard to a transaction with which the sale was associated, and was, therefore, an unlawful payment. Unfortunately, however, he did not realise it, but either misread the Act or did not read it carefully, and on the following day he called on the purchaser to complete. He was, therefore, clearly aiding and abetting the builder in the offence which the builder was committing. The result is that, so far as the first two respondents are concerned, the appeal fails and must be dismissed, but, so far as the third respondent is concerned, the case must go back to the justices with an intimation that an offence has been committed, and there must be a conviction.'

R v Rook [1993] 1 WLR 1005 Court of Appeal (Criminal Division) (Lloyd LJ, Potter and Buckley JJ)

Joint enterprise – steps necessary for effective withdrawal

Facts
The appellant was one of four men accused of murder. He had taken an active part in planning the murder, but then stalled his co-defendants. He did not tell them that he did not want the killing to proceed, nor did he do anything to stop them. On the day appointed for the killing, the appellant failed to turn up at the appointed place. He was convicted of murder and appealed on the grounds that the trial judge had not directed the jury correctly on the mental element to be proved in respect of an accomplice to murder who assists prior to the commission of the offence, rather than at the scene of the crime, and that the trial judge had not directed the jury correctly on the issue of withdrawal from the common design.

Held
The appeal would be dismissed. The appellant's failure to attend at the scene of the crime could not of itself amount to an effective withdrawal from the common design.

Lloyd LJ:

> 'Mr Maxwell [for the Crown] submits that where a person has given assistance, for example by providing a gun, in circumstances which would render him liable as a secondary party if he did not withdraw, then

in order to escape liability he must "neutralise" his assistance. He must, so it is said, break the chain of causation between his act of assistance and the subsequent crime, by recovering the gun, or by warning the victim to stay away, or by going to the police. Mr Hockman [counsel for the defendant] submits, on the other hand, that the Crown must prove that the defendant continued ready to help until the moment the crime was committed; and if there is a doubt as to the defendant's state of mind on the day in question, or his willingness to provide further help if required, then the jury must acquit.

As between these two extreme views, we have no hesitation in rejecting the latter. In *Rex* v *Croft* [1944] KB 295, the surviving party of a suicide pact was held to be guilty of murder. Lawrence J, giving the judgment of the court, said, at p298:

"The authorities, however, such as they are, show, in our opinion, that the appellant, to escape being held guilty as an accessory before the fact, must establish that he expressly countermanded or revoked the advising, counselling, procuring or abetting which he had previously given."

In *Rex* v *Whitehouse* [1941] 1 WWR 112, 115–116, Sloan JA said:

"Can it be said on the facts of this case that a mere change of mental intention and a quitting of the scene of the crime just immediately prior to the striking of the fatal blow will absolve those who participate in the commission of the crime by overt acts up to that moment from all the consequences of its accomplishment by the one who strikes in ignorance of his companions' change of heart? I think not. After a crime has been committed and before a prior abandonment of the common enterprise may be found by a jury there must be, in my view, in the absence of exceptional circumstances, something more than a mere mental change of intention and physical change of place by those associates who wish to dissociate themselves from the consequences attendant upon their willing assistance up to the moment of the actual commission of that crime. I would not attempt to define too closely what must be done in criminal matters involving participation in a common unlawful purpose to break the chain of causation and responsibility. That must depend upon the circumstances of each case but it seems to me that one essential element ought to be established in a case of this kind: where practicable and reasonable there must be timely communication of the intention to abandon the common purpose from those who wish to dissociate themselves from the contemplated crime to those who desire to continue in it. What is 'timely communication' must be determined by the facts of each case but where practicable and reasonable it ought to be such communication, verbal or otherwise, that will serve unequivocal notice upon the other party to the common unlawful cause that if he proceeds upon it he does so without the further aid and assistance of those who withdraw. The unlawful purpose of him who continues alone is then his own and not one in common with those who are no longer parties to it nor liable to its full and final consequences."

In *R* v *Becerra* (1975) 62 Cr App R 212 this court approved that passage as a correct statement of the law. The facts of the *Becerra* case were that the victim was killed in the course of a burglary. The appellant had provided the knife shortly before the murder. The court held that the appellant's sudden departure from the scene of the crime with the words "Come on let's go" was an insufficient communication of withdrawal. So the appellant's conviction as a secondary party to the murder was upheld. In *R* v *Whitefield* (1983) 79 Cr App R 36, 39–40, Dunn LJ stated the law as follows:

"If a person has counselled another to commit a crime, he may escape liability by withdrawal before the crime is committed, but it is not sufficient that he should merely repent or change his mind. If his participation is confined to advice or encouragement, he must at least communicate his change of mind to the other, and the communication must be such as 'will serve unequivocal notice upon the other party to the common unlawful cause that if he proceeds upon it he does so without the aid and assistance of those who withdraw'."

In the present case the appellant never told the others that he was not going ahead with the crime. His absence on the day could not possibly amount to "unequivocal communication" of his withdrawal. In his evidence-in-chief, in a passage already quoted, he said that he made it quite clear to *himself* that he did not want to be there on the day. But he did not make it clear to the others. So the minimum necessary for withdrawal from the crime was not established on the facts. In these circumstances, as in the *Becerra* case, it is unnecessary for us to consider whether communication of his withdrawal would have been enough, or whether he would have had to take steps to "neutralise" the assistance he had already given.

Mr Maxwell rightly drew our attention to a sentence in the judgment of Sloan JA in *Rex* v *Whitehouse* [1941] 1 WWR 112, 116, already quoted, where he refers to the service of notice on the other party that if he proceeds he does so without *further* aid from those who withdraw. This may suggest that aid *already* afforded need not be neutralised. We agree with Mr Maxwell that this attaches too much importance to a single word. But that is as far as we are prepared to go in this case. We are not prepared, as at present advised, to give our approval to his proposition in its extreme form. In his *Criminal Law, The General Part*, 2nd ed (1961), p385, para 127, Professor Glanville Williams quotes a graphic phrase from an American authority *Eldredge* v *United States* (1932) 62 F 2d 449, 451, per McDermott J: "A declared intent to withdraw from a conspiracy to dynamite a building is not enough, if the fuse has been set; he must step on the fuse." It may be that this goes too far. It may be that it is enough that he should have done his best to step on the fuse. Since this is as much a question of policy as a question of law, and since it does not arise on the facts of the present case, we say no more about it.'

R v *Saunders and Archer* (1573) 2 Plowd 473 (Warwick Assizes)

Transferred malice and accomplices

Facts

John Saunders wanted to kill his wife so that he could marry his mistress. Alexander Archer provided him with poison in the form of a roasted apple containing arsenic and roseacre. Saunders gave the poisoned apple to his wife, and stood by as she, finding it not to her taste, passed it on to their three year old daughter Eleanor who died as a result. Saunders was found guilty of the murder on the basis of transferred malice. Archer was found not to be a party to the murder because the principal had wilfully exceeded the common design in allowing the child to eat the apple.

Lord Dyer CJ:

'But the most difficult point in this case ... was, whether or no Archer should be adjudged accessory to the murder. For the offence which Archer committed was the aid and advice which he gave to Saunders, and that was only to kill his wife, and no other, for there was no parol communication between them concerning the daughter, and although by the consequences which followed from the giving of the poison by Saunders the principal, it so happened that the daughter was killed, yet Archer did not precisely procure her death, nor advise him to kill her, and therefore whether or not he should be accessory to this murder which happened by a thing consequential to the first act, seemed to them to be doubtful. For which reason they thought proper to advise and consider of it until the next gaol delivery, and in the meantime to consult with the justices in the term ... [It was agreed] that they ought not to give judgment against the said Alexander Archer, because they took the law to be that he could not be adjudged accessory to the said offence of murder, for that he did not assent that the daughter should be poisoned, but only that the wife should be poisoned, which assent cannot be drawn further than he gave it, for the poisoning of the daughter is a distinct thing from that to which he was privy, and therefore he shall not be adjudged accessory to it; and so they were resolved before this time.'

28 Inchoate Offences I

R v Anderson [1986] AC 27 (House of Lords) (Lords Scarman, Diplock, Keith, Bridge, and Brightman)

Mens rea of statutory conspiracy

Facts

The defendant, whilst sharing a prison cell with another man named Andaloussi, agreed that he would help effect Andaloussi's escape from prison once he himself was released, and that he would received £20,000 in return for his efforts. The defendant was released from prison shortly afterwards and received £2,000 from Andaloussi's brothers as an initial payment for his help. The defendant was then injured in a road accident and took no further part in executing the planned escape. When charged with conspiring to effect the release of Andaloussi from prison, the defendant contended that he had lacked the mens rea for conspiracy because, although he had intended to acquire some diamond cutting wire that could be used to cut through prison bars, he had never intended the escape plan to be carried into effect and had not believed that it could actually succeed. The trial judge ruled that, as a matter of law, there was still evidence that the defendant had mens rea, as a result of which he changed his plea to one of guilty, and appealed unsuccessfully to the Court of Appeal. The defendant renewed his appeal before the House of Lords.

Held

The appeal would be dismissed.

Lord Bridge (his Lordship considered s1(1)(A) of the Criminal Law Act 1977 and continued):

'The Act of 1977, subject to exceptions not presently material, abolished the offence of conspiracy at common law. It follows that the elements of the new statutory offence of conspiracy must be ascertained purely by interpretation of the language of section 1(1) of the Act of 1977. For purposes of analysis it is perhaps convenient to isolate the three clauses each of which must be taken as indicating an essential ingredient of the offence as follows: (1) "if a person agrees with any other person or persons that a course of conduct shall be pursued" (2) "which will necessarily amount to or involve the commission of any offence or offences by one or more of the parties to the agreement" (3) "if the agreement is carried out in accordance with their intentions."

Clause (1) presents, as it seems to me, no difficulty. It means exactly what it says and what it says is crystal clear. To be convicted, the party charged must have agreed with one or more others that "a course of conduct shall be pursued." What is important is to resist the temptation to introduce into this simple concept ideas derived from the civil law of contract. Any number of persons may agree that a course of conduct shall be pursued without undertaking any contractual liability. The agreed course of conduct may be a simple or an elaborate one and may involve the participation of two or any larger number of persons who may have agreed to play a variety of roles in the course of conduct agreed.

Again, clause (2) could hardly use simpler language. Here what is important to note is that it is not necessary that more than one of the participants in the agreed course of conduct shall commit a substantive offence. It is, of course, necessary that any party to the agreement shall have assented to play his part in the agreed course of conduct, however innocent in itself, knowing that the part to be played by one or more of the others will amount to or involve the commission of an offence.

It is only clause (3) which presents any possible ambiguity. The heart of the submission for the appellant is that in order to be convicted of conspiracy to commit a given offence the language of clause (3) requires that the party charged should not only have agreed that a course of conduct shall be pursued which will necessarily amount to or involve the commission of that offence by himself or one or more other parties to the agreement, but must also be proved himself to have intended that that offence should be committed. Thus, it is submitted here that the appellant's case that he never intended that Andaloussi should be enabled to escape from prison raised an issue to be left to the jury, who should have been directed to convict him only if satisfied that he did so intend. I do not find it altogether easy to understand why the draftsman of this provision chose to use the phrase "in accordance with their intentions." But I suspect the answer may be that this seemed a desirable alternative to the phrase "in accordance with its terms" or any similar expression, because it is a matter of common experience in the criminal courts that the "terms" of a criminal conspiracy are hardly ever susceptible of proof. The evidence from which a jury may infer a criminal conspiracy is almost invariably to be found in the conduct of the parties. This was so at common law and remains so under the statute. If the evidence in a given case justifies the inference of an agreement that a course of conduct should be pursued, it is a not inappropriate formulation of the test of the criminality of the inferred agreement to ask whether the further inference can be drawn that a crime would necessarily have been committed if the agreed course of conduct had been pursued in accordance with the several intentions of the parties. Whether that is an accurate analysis or not, I am clearly driven by consideration of the diversity of roles which parties may agree to play in criminal conspiracies to reject any construction of the statutory language which would require the prosecution to prove an intention on the part of each conspirator that the criminal offence or offences which will necessarily be committed by one or more of the conspirators if the agreed course of conduct is fully carried out should in fact be committed. A simple example will illustrate the absurdity to which this construction would lead. The proprietor of a car hire firm agrees for a substantial payment to make available a hire car to a gang for use in a robbery and to make false entries in his books relating to the hiring to which he can point if the number of the car is traced back to him in connection with the robbery. Being fully aware of the circumstances of the robbery in which the car is proposed to be used he is plainly a party to the conspiracy to rob. Making his car available for use in the robbery is as much a part of the relevant agreed course of conduct as the robbery itself. Yet, once he has been paid, it will be a matter of complete indifference to him whether the robbery is in fact committed or not. In these days of highly organised crime the most serious statutory conspiracies will frequently involve an elaborate and complex agreed course of conduct in which many will consent to play necessary but subordinate roles, not involving them in any direct participation in the commission of the offence or offences at the centre of the conspiracy. Parliament cannot have intended that such parties should escape conviction of conspiracy on the basis that it cannot be proved against them that they intended that the relevant offence or offences should be committed.

There remains the important question whether a person who has agreed that a course of conduct will be pursued which, if pursued as agreed, will necessarily amount to or involve the commission of an offence is guilty of statutory conspiracy irrespective of his intention, and, if not, what is the mens rea of the offence. I have no hesitation in answering the first part of the question in the negative. There may be many situations in which perfectly respectable citizens, more particularly those concerned with law enforcement, may enter into agreements that a course of conduct shall be pursued which will involve commission of a crime without the least intention of playing any part in furtherance of the ostensibly agreed criminal objective, but rather with the purpose of exposing and frustrating the criminal purpose of the other parties to the agreement. To say this is in no way to encourage schemes by which police act, directly or through the agency of informers, as agents provocateurs for the purpose of entrapment. That is conduct of which the courts have always strongly disapproved. But it may sometimes happen, as most of us with experience in criminal trials well know, that a criminal enterprise is well advanced in the course of preparation when it comes to the notice either of the police or of some honest citizen in such circumstances that the only prospect of exposing and frustrating the criminals is that some innocent person should play the part of an intending collaborator in the course of criminal conduct proposed to be pursued. The mens rea implicit in the offence of statutory conspiracy must clearly be such as to recognise the innocence of such a person, notwithstanding that he will, in literal terms, be obliged to agree that a course of conduct be pursued involving the commission of an offence.

I have said already, but I repeat to emphasise its importance, that an essential ingredient in the crime of conspiring to commit a specific offence or offences under section 1(1) of the Act of 1977 is that the accused should agree that a course of conduct be pursued which he knows must involve the commission by one or more of the parties to the agreement of that offence or those offences. But, beyond the mere fact of agreement, the necessary mens rea of the crime is, in my opinion, established if, and only if, it is shown that the accused, when he entered into the agreement, intended to play some part in the agreed course of conduct in furtherance of the criminal purpose which the agreed course of conduct was intended to achieve. Nothing less will suffice; nothing more is required.

Applying this test to the facts which, for the purposes of the appeal, we must assume, the appellant, in agreeing that a course of conduct be pursued that would, if successful, necessarily involve the offence of effecting Andaloussi's escape from lawful custody, clearly intended, by providing diamond wire to be smuggled into the prison, to play a part in the agreed course of conduct in furtherance of that criminal objective. Neither the fact that he intended to play no further part in attempting to effect the escape, nor that he believed the escape to be impossible, would, if the jury had supposed they might be true, have afforded him any defence.'

Note: See *R* v *Siracusa* below.

R v *Curr* [1968] 2 QB 944 Court of Appeal (Criminal Division) (Lord Parker CJ, Salmon LJ and Fenton Atkinson J)

Actus reus of incitement

Facts
The defendant ran a loan business whereby he would lend money to women with children in return for their handing over their signed Family Allowance books. The defendant would then use other women to cash the Family Allowance vouchers. He was charged with inciting an offence under s9(b) of the Family Allowance Act 1945, which made it an offence for any person to receive any sum by way of Family Allowance knowing it was not properly payable. The defendant appealed.

Held
The appeal would be allowed and conviction quashed.

Fenton Atkinson J:

'Count 3 was of soliciting the commission of a summary offence contrary to section 9 (*b*) of the Act of 1945, the particulars being that on a day unknown the defendant unlawfully "solicited a woman unknown to obtain on his behalf from HM's Postmaster-General the sum of £2 18s as on account of an allowance knowing that it was not properly receivable by her." Mr Kershaw [counsel for the defendant] took a preliminary point on that count that incitement to commit a summary offence is not in fact an idictable offence, and he referred to some old authorities which might lend some countenance to that view. But it appears to this court that Parliament in the Magistrates' Courts Act 1952, in paragraph 20 of Schedule 1, has in fact recognised incitement of this kind as an indictable offence, and it is not necessary, therefore, to go further into that matter, all the more because Mr Kershaw's main point is this, that the offence the commission of which the defendant is said to have solicited is not an absolute statutory offence, but it is one requiring knowledge on the part of the female agent that she is doing something unlawful in receiving the allowance.

Section 9 is headed "Penalty for obtaining or receiving payment wrongfully," and provides:

> "If any person – ... (b) obtains or receives any such sum as on account of an allowance, either as in that person's own right or as on behalf of another, knowing that it was not properly payable, or not properly receivable by him or her; that person shall be liable on summary conviction to imprisonment for a term not exceeding three months or to a fine not exceeding fifty pounds or to both such imprisonment and such fine."

Mr Kershaw's argument was that if the woman agent in fact has no guilty knowledge, knowing perhaps nothing of the assignment, or supposing that the defendant was merely collecting for the use and benefit of the woman concerned, then she would be an innocent agent, and by using her services in that way the defendant would be committing the summary offence himself, but would not be inciting her to receive money knowing that it was not receivable by her. He contends that it was essential to prove to support this charge, that the woman agent in question in this transaction affecting a Mrs Currie knew that the allowances were not properly receivable by her. Mr Hugill's [counsel for the Crown] answer to that submission was that the woman agent must be presumed to know the law, and if she knew the law, she must have known, he contends, that the allowance was not receivable by her. He refers to section 4 (2) of the Act of 1945, to which reference has already been made, and to the Family Allowances (Making of Claims and Payments) Regulations 1946, reg. 8, which provides:

> "Sums on account of an allowance shall become receivable at the times hereinafter prescribed and shall be paid either – (1) by means of allowance orders payable in respect of every week to a person by whom such sums are receivable" that is to say, the wife or husband under section 4 (2) of the Act of 1945 – "or (2) in such other special manner as the Minister may in any particular case and for any particular period determine."

Provision is made also by regulation 12 that, where any person entitled to an allowance becomes unable to act for the time being, the minister may appoint some person to act on their behalf. Provision is made by administrative direction in the case of sickness by the book holder, and there is an instruction No. 12 on a coloured page at the end of the book:

> "Payment during illness: If you are ill for a short time and cannot go to the Post Office to draw the money and, where there is a second payee, he also cannot go, someone else may cash the orders for you if you fill up and sign" a certain form at the back of the voucher.

The argument is that in no other circumstances may an agent lawfully collect for the use and benefit of the book holder, and Mr Hugill was ready to contend, for example, that if a mother with, say, eight children to look after at home asks a neighbour to go and collect her allowance for her, and the neighbour does so, the neighbour would be committing an offence under section 9 (b) of the Act of 1945, and the mother would be guilty of the offence of soliciting. We are by no means satisfied that any agent who collects with the full authority of the book holder and for her use and benefit would commit an offence under that subsection. There appears to be no express prohibition, certainly we were referred to no express prohibition, in the Family Allowances Act, 1945, or any orders making such collection unlawful. On the evidence, the Post Office in practice appear to allow this to be done in certain cases; in our view there can be situations, or may be situations, in which an agent, however well she may know the statute and regulations, could properly suppose that her action in receiving an allowance of this kind was lawful.

In our view the prosecution argument here gives no effect to the word "knowing" in section 9 (b), and in our view the defendant could only be guilty on count 3 if the woman solicited, that is, the woman agent sent to collect the allowance, knew that the action she was asked to carry out amounted to an offence. As has already been said, the defendant himself clearly knew that his conduct in the matter was illegal and contrary to section 9 (b), but it was essential in our view for the jury to consider the knowledge, if any, of the woman agent. The assistant recorder dealt with this count by referring to soliciting as follows: "Solicited means encouraged or incited another person to go and draw that money which should have been paid, you may think, to Mrs Currie." He later dealt with ignorance of the law being no excuse. He went on to deal with statutory offences, section 4 of the Family Allowances Act, 1945, telling the jury in effect that, apart from the case of sickness, nobody else could legally receive these allowances, and then went on to consider the position of the defendant, asking the rhetorical question whether he could be heard to say with his knowledge of this matter and his trafficking in these books that it was not known to be wrong to employ an agent to go and collect the family allowances. But the assistant recorder never followed that with the question of the knowledge of the women agents, and in the whole of the summing-up dealing with this matter he proceeded on the assumption that either guilty knowledge in the woman agent was irrelevant, or, alternatively, that any woman agent must be taken to have known that she was committing an offence under section 9 (*b*).

If the matter had been left on a proper direction for the jury's consideration, they might well have thought that the women agents, other than Mrs Nicholson, whom they acquitted, must have known very well that they were doing something wrong; some of them were apparently collecting as many as 10 of these weekly payments. But the matter was never left to them for their consideration, and here again, so it seems to this court, there was a vital matter where the defence was not left to the jury at all and there was no sufficient direction; it would be quite impossible to say that on a proper direction the jury must have convicted on this count.'

DPP v *Nock* [1978] AC 979 House of Lords (Lords Diplock, Edmund-Davies, Russell, Keith, and Scarman)

Impossibility as a defence to common law conspiracy

Facts
The defendants were convicted of conspiring to produce cocaine, contrary to s4(2) of the Misuse of Drugs Act 1971. Unknown to the defendants, the chemicals they had agreed to use would not have produced cocaine, and they appealed to the Court of Appeal on the ground that they should have been permitted the defence of impossibility. The appeal was dismissed, on the ground that the conspiracy was committed as soon as the agreement was made, regardless of whether it was capable of execution. The defendants renewed their appeal before the House of Lords.

Held
The appeal would be allowed.

Lord Scarman:

'Upon these facts the appellants submit that the evidence reveals no "conspiracy at large," by which they mean an agreement in general terms to produce cocaine if and when they could find a suitable raw material, but only the limited agreement, to which I have referred. Counsel for the appellants concedes that, if two or more persons decide to go into business as cocaine producers, or, to take another example, as assassins for hire (eg "Murder Incorporated"), the mere fact that in the course of performing their agreement they attempt to produce cocaine from a raw material which could not possibly yield it or (in the second example), stab a corpse, believing it to be the body of a living man, would not avail them as a defence: for the performance of their general agreement would not be rendered impossible by such transient frustrations. But performance of the limited agreement proved in this case could not in any circumstances have involved the commission of the offence created by the statute.

The answer sought to be made by the Crown (and accepted by the Court of Appeal) is that the offence of conspiracy is committed when an agreement to commit, or to try to commit, a crime is reached, whether or not anything is, or can be, done to perform it. It is wrong, upon their view, to treat conspiracy as a "preliminary" or "inchoate" crime: for its criminality depends in no way upon its being a step towards the commission of the substantive offence (or, at common law, the unlawful act). Upon this view of the law the scope of agreement is irrelevant: all that is needed to constitute the crime is the intention to commit the substantive offence and the agreement to try to do so.

If the Court of Appeal is right, *R v Smith* [1975] AC 476 can have no application in cases of conspiracy. But neither history nor principle supports this view of the law. In *Board of Trade v Owen* [1957] AC 602, 623-625 Lord Tucker, quoting with approval some observations from R S Wright J's little classic, *The Law of Criminal Conspiracies and Agreements* (1873) and some passages from Sir William Holdsworth's (somewhat larger) work, *The History of English Law*, accepted that the historical basis of the crime of conspiring to commit a crime (the case with which we are now concerned) was that it developed as an "auxiliary" (R S Wright's word) to the law which creates the crime agreed to be committed. Lord Tucker accepted Holdsworth's comment (at p625) that "It was inevitable therefore, as Stephen has said, that conspiracy should come to be regarded as a form of attempt to commit a wrong." Lord Tucker concluded his survey with these words at p626:

> "Accepting the above as the historical basis of the crime of conspiracy, it seems to me that the whole object of making such agreements punishable is to prevent the commission of the substantive offence before it has even reached the stage of an attempt, ... "

Lord Tucker, in whose opinion the other noble and learned Lords sitting with him concurred, by stressing the "auxiliary" nature of the crime of conspiracy and by explaining its justification as being to prevent the commission of substantive offences, has placed the crime firmly in the same class and category as attempts to commit a crime. Both are criminal because they are steps towards the commission of a substantive offence. The distinction between the two is that, whereas a "proximate" act is that which constitutes the crime of attempt, agreement is the necessary ingredient in conspiracy. The importance of the distinction is that agreement may, and usually will, occur well before the first step which can be said to be an attempt. The law of conspiracy thus makes possible an earlier intervention by the law to prevent the commission of the substantive offence. But the distinction has no relevance in determining whether the impossibility of committing the substantive offence should be a defence. Indeed upon the view of the law authoritatively explained and accepted in *Owen's* case [1957] AC 602, logic and justice would seem to require that the question as to the effect of the impossibility of the substantive offence should be answered in the same way, whether the crime charged be conspiracy or attempt.

It is necessary, therefore, to analyse the decision in *R v Smith* [1975] AC 476 in order to determine whether it can reasonably be applied to cases of conspiracy. The Court of Appeal thought that there were difficulties. But I do not agree.

It was – somewhat half-heartedly – suggested by the Crown that the House might reconsider the decision, which we were told is causing difficulties in some respects. It is, however, a very recent decision; and a unanimous one reached after full argument which brought to the attention of this House the relevant case law and exposed the difficulties. More importantly, the decision is, in my respectful opinion, correct in principle. I would not question the decision, though its proper limits may have to be considered. The House decided the case upon two grounds, either of which would have sufficed, standing alone, to support the decision, but both of which commended themselves to the House. They may be described as the statutory (and narrower) ground and the common law principle.

The statutory ground was provided by sections 22 and 24 (3) of the Theft Act 1968. The offence being considered by the House was one of attempting to handle stolen goods. At the time of the attempted handling, the goods had been (this was conceded) restored to lawful custody. The House ruled that, in the case of a statutory offence:

> "The only possible attempt would be to do what Parliament has forbidden. But Parliament has not forbidden that which the accused did, ie, handling goods which have ceased to be stolen goods ... Here the mens rea was proved but there was no actus reus so the case is not within the scope of the section," per Lord Reid at p498c.

With all respect to the Court of Appeal, there is no difficulty in applying this line of reasoning to a case in which the allegation is not an attempt but a conspiracy to commit a statutory offence. First, there is no logical difficulty in applying a rule that an agreement is a conspiracy to commit a statutory offence only if it is an agreement to do that which Parliament has forbidden. It is no more than the application of the principle that an actus reus as well as mens rea must be established. And in the present case there was no actus reus, because there was no agreement upon a course of conduct forbidden by the statute. Secondly, the application of such a rule is consistent with principle. Unless the law requires the actus reus as well as mens rea to be proved, men, whether they be accused of conspiracy or attempt, will be punished for their guilty intentions alone. I conclude the consideration of this ground of decision with a further quotation from Lord Reid's speech, at p500: "But such a radical change in the principles of our law should not be introduced in this way even if it were desirable."

The second ground of decision – the common law principle – can be summarised in words which commended themselves to all the noble and learned Lords concerned with the case. In *R v Percy Dalton (London) Ltd* Birkett J, giving the judgment of the Court of Criminal Appeal said (1949) 33 Cr App R 102, 110:

> "Steps on the way to the commission of what would be a crime, if the acts were completed, may amount to attempts to commit that crime, to which, unless interrupted, they would have led; but steps on the way to the doing of something, which is thereafter done, and which is no crime, cannot be regarded as attempts to commit a crime."

In his speech Lord Hailsham of St Marylebone LC added the rider (a logical one) to the effect "that equally steps on the way to do something which is thereafter *not* completed, but which if done would not constitute a crime, cannot be indicted as attempts to commit that crime," [1975] AC 476, 496C. As in the case of the statutory ground, there is no logical difficulty in the way of applying this principle to the law relating to conspiracy provided it is recognised that conspiracy is a "preliminary" or "auxiliary" crime. And again, as with the statutory ground, common sense and justice combine to require of the law that no man should be punished criminally for the intention with which he enters an agreement unless it can also be shown that what he has agreed to do is unlawful.

The Crown's argument, as developed before your Lordships, rests, in my judgment, upon a misconception of the nature of the agreement proved. This is a case not of an agreement to commit a crime capable of being committed in the way agreed upon, but frustrated by a supervening event making its completion impossible, which was the Crown's submission, but of an agreement upon a course of conduct which could not in any circumstances result in the statutory offence alleged, ie the offence of producing the controlled drug, cocaine.

I conclude therefore that the two parallel lines of reasoning upon which this House decided *R v Smith* [1975] AC 476 apply equally to criminal conspiracy as they do to attempted crime. We were referred to a recent case in the Court of Appeal, *R v Green (Harry)* [1976] QB 985, in which the contrary view was expressed, but not developed at any length. The court in that case, as also the Court of Appeal in this case, attached importance to some observations of Lord Hailsham of St Marylebone LC in *R v Smith* [1975] AC 476, where the indictment undoubtedly included, as the second count, a charge of conspiracy with persons unknown to handle stolen goods. The Lord Chancellor (p489F) remarked that he was unable to understand why the prosecution did not proceed with this charge. He reverted to the point at p497D, and there is an echo of it in Viscount Dilhorne's speech at p503E. In *Green's* case [1976] QB 985, 993 Ormrod LJ treated these remarks as an indication that *R v Smith* [1975] AC 476 is not applicable in cases of conspiracy. The Court of Appeal in the instant case took the same view. But I do not think that either the Lord Chancellor or Viscount Dilhorne was saying anything of the sort. The conspiracy charged in the second count must have ante-dated the police seizure of the van and the return of the goods to lawful custody. Smith must have agreed to help in the disposal of the goods at a time when they were stolen goods and the agreement could be performed. It was an agreement to commit an offence which, but for the police interruption, would have been committed. There is nothing in *R v Smith* which would prevent such an agreement in such circumstances from being treated as a criminal conspiracy.

Our attention was also drawn to two cases, upon which it may be helpful to comment very briefly. In *R v McDonough* (1962) 47 Cr App R 37 the Court of Criminal Appeal held that an incitement to receive stolen goods was complete on the making of the incitement even though there were no stolen goods – perhaps even, no goods at all. In *Haggard v Mason* [1976] 1 WLR 187 the Divisional Court held that the offence of offering to supply a controlled drug was committed, even though the drug in fact supplied was not a controlled drug. Neither of these cases infringes the principle of *R* v *Smith*: for in each, as Lord Widgery CJ pointed out in *Haggard* v *Mason* (p189), the offence was complete. In *McDonough*, 47 Cr App R 37 the actus reus was the making of the incitement and in *Haggard's* case it was the making of the offer.

For these reasons I would allow the appeal.'

R v *Fitzmaurice* [1983] 2 WLR 227 Court of Appeal (Criminal Division) (Lord Justice O'Connor, Neill and Taylor JJ)

Inciting the impossible

Facts

The defendant, acting on false information given to him by his father, arranged for three men to carry out a wages snatch on a woman delivering money to a bank at Bow in East London. The three men were arrested in a van parked outside the bank by the police who had been tipped off by the defendant's father, whose only motive in all this had been to receive some reward money. As there was, in reality, no woman carrying wages to be robbed, the three men arrested outside the bank were acquitted of attempted robbery on the ground of impossibility (note these events took place before the Criminal Attempts Act 1981 came into effect). The defendant was convicted of inciting the robbery, and he now appealed on the basis that he could not be guilty of inciting the impossible.

Held

The appeal would be dismissed.

Neill J:

'Mr Cocks' [Counsel for the appellant] second submission, however, is at first sight more formidable. Incitement is one of the three inchoate offences – incitement, conspiracy and attempt. Mr Cocks argued that there was no logical basis for treating the three offences differently when considering their application in circumstances where the complete offence would be impossible to commit, and that therefore the court should apply the principles laid down by the House of Lords in the case of attempts in *Haughton* v *Smith* (1973) 58 Cr App R 198; [1975] AC 476 and in the case of conspiracy in *Director of Public Prosecutions* v *Nock* [1978] AC 979; (1978) 67 Cr App R 116.

Mr Cocks pointed to the fact that though the law as laid down by the House of Lords in those two cases had been altered by statute by section 1 (2) and section 5 (1) of the Criminal Attempts Act 1981, there had been no change in the law relating to the offence of incitement. Accordingly, he said, the common law rule as to impossibility should be applied.

It is to be observed that the omission of the crime of incitement from the Criminal Attempts Act 1981 followed the recommendations of the Law Commission in their Report No. 102 and was in accordance with the draft bill set out in Appendix A to that report. The Law Commission explained the omission of incitement from the Draft Bill on the basis that in their view the House of Lords in *DPP* v *Nock* (supra) was prepared to distinguish the law relating to incitement from that relating to attempts: see paragraphs 4.2 to 4.4. We have had to give careful attention to these paragraphs in the Law Commission's Report.

We have also had to consider with care the passage in the speech of Lord Scarman in *DPP* v *Nock* (supra) which appears to have formed the basis for the decision by the Law Commission to exclude incitement from their recommendations for change and from their draft bill.

In *DPP* v *Nock* (1978) 67 Cr App R 116; [1978] AC 979, Lord Scarman at p129 and p999 of the respective reports made reference to two cases which had been cited to their Lordships. He said this: "Our attention was also drawn to two cases, upon which it may be helpful to comment very briefly. In *McDonough* (1962) 47 Cr App R 37, the Court of Criminal Appeal held that an incitement to receive stolen goods was complete on the making of the incitement even though there were no stolen goods – perhaps even, no goods at all. In *Haggard* v *Mason* [1976] 1 WLR 187, the Divisional Court held that the offence of offering to supply a controlled drug was committed, even though the drug in fact supplied was not a controlled drug. Neither of these cases infringes the principle in *Haughton* v *Smith* (supra) for, in each, as Lord Widgery CJ pointed out in *Haggard* v *Mason* (supra, p189), the offence was complete. In *McDonough* (supra) the *actus reus* was the making of the incitement; and in *Haggard* v *Mason* (supra) it was the making of the offer."

We have come to the conclusion that, on analysis, this passage in Lord Scarman's speech does not support the proposition that cases of incitement are to be treated quite differently at common law from cases of attempt or conspiracy.

The decision in *Haggard* v *Mason* (supra) related to the statutory offence of offering to supply a controlled drug and, as Lord Scarman pointed out, the actus reus which the prosecution had to prove was the making of the offer.

The explanation of *McDonough's* case, (supra) as it seems to us, is that though there may have been no stolen goods or no goods at all which were available to be received at the time of the incitement, the offence of incitement to receive stolen goods could nevertheless be proved because it was not impossible that at the relevant time in the future the necessary goods would be there.

In our view, therefore, the right approach in a case of incitement is the same as that which was underlined by Lord Scarman in *DPP* v *Nock* (supra) when he considered the offence of conspiracy. In every case it is necessary to analyse the evidence with care to decide the precise offence which the defendant is alleged to have incited.

In *DPP* v *Nock* (1978) 67 Cr App R 116; [1978] AC 979, Lord Scarman said this at p125 and p995 respectively: "The indictment makes plain that the Crown is alleging in this case a conspiracy to commit a crime: and no one has suggested that the particulars fail to disclose an offence known to the law. But the appellants submit, and it is not disputed by the Crown, that the agreement as proved was narrower in scope than the conspiracy charged. When the case was before the Court of Appeal, counsel on both sides agreed that the evidence went to prove that the appellants agreed together to obtain cocaine by separating it from the other substance or substances contained in a powder which they had obtained from one of their co-defendants, a Mr Mitchell. They believed that the powder was a mixture of cocaine and lignocaine, and that they would be able to produce cocaine from it. In fact the powder was lignocaine hydrochloride, an anaesthetic used in dentistry, which contains no cocaine at all. It is impossible to produce by separation or otherwise, cocaine from lignocaine ... The trial judge in his direction to the jury, and the Court of Appeal in their judgment dismissing the two appeals, treated this impossibility as an irrelevance. In their view the agreement was what mattered: and there was plain evidence of an agreement to produce cocaine, even though unknown to the two conspirators it could not be done. Neither the trial judge nor the Court of Appeal thought it necessary to carry their analysis of the agreement further. The trial judge described it simply as an agreement to produce cocaine. The Court of Appeal thought it enough that the prosecution had proved 'an agreement to do an act which was forbidden by section 4 of the Misuse of Drugs Act 1971.' Both descriptions are accurate, as far as they go. But neither contains any reference to the limited nature of the agreement proved: it was an agreement upon a specific course of conduct with the object of producing cocaine, and limited to that course of conduct. Since it could not result in the production of cocaine, the two appellants by pursuing it could not commit the statutory offence of producing a controlled drug."

In our view these words suggest the correct approach at common law to any inchoate offence. It is necessary in every case to decide on the evidence what was the course of conduct which was (as the case may be) incited or agreed or attempted. In some cases the evidence may establish that the persuasion by the inciter was in quite general terms whereas the subsequent agreement of the conspirators was directed to a specific crime and specific target. In such cases where the committal of the specific offence is shown to be impossible it may be quite logical for the inciter to be convicted even though the alleged conspirators (if not caught by section 5 of the Criminal Attempts Act 1981) may be acquitted. On the other hand, if B and C agree to kill D, and A, standing beside B and C, though not intending to take any active part whatever in the crime, encourages them to do so, we can see no satisfactory reason, if it turns out later that D was already dead, why A should be convicted of incitement to murder whereas B and C at common law would be entitled to an acquittal on a charge of conspiracy. The crucial question is to establish on the evidence the course of conduct which the alleged inciter was encouraging.

We return to the facts of the instant case. Mr Cocks submitted that the "crime" which Bonham and the two Browns were being encouraged to commit was a mere charade. The appellant's father was not planning a real robbery at all and therefore the appellant could not be found guilty of inciting the three men to commit it. In our judgment, however, the answer to Mr Cocks' argument is to be found in the facts which the prosecution proved against the appellant. As was made clear by Mr Purnell on behalf of the Crown, the case against the appellant was based on the steps he took to recruit Bonham. At that stage the appellant believed that there was to be a wage snatch and he was encouraging Bonham to take part in it. As Mr Purnell put it, "The appellant thought he was recruiting for a robbery not for a charade." It is to be remembered that the particulars of offence in the indictment included the words "by robbing a woman at Bow." By no stretch of the imagination was that an impossible offence to carry out and it was that offence which the appellant was inciting Bonham to commit.'

R v Hollinshead [1985] AC 978 House of Lords (Lords Fraser, Diplock, Roskill, Bridge and Brandon)

Scope of common law conspiracy to defraud

Facts

The defendants agreed to supply 'black boxes' (devices which caused electricity meters to under-record the amount of electricity used by a consumer), to a 'middle man' who would then sell them on to customers of various Electricity Boards. The defendants were charged on two counts; count one alleging a statutory conspiracy to aid, abet, counsel or procure an offence under s2(1)(b) of the Theft Act 1978, and count two which alleged a common law conspiracy to defraud. The defendants were convicted on the second count, and appealed successfully to the Court of Appeal on the ground that there could be no conspiracy to defraud where the dishonest conduct contemplated was to be carried out by a third party (the 'middle man') not the conspirators. The Crown now appealed to the House of Lords.

The two questions certified for consideration by their Lordships were:

'1. If parties agree (a) to manufacture devices whose only use is fraudulently to alter electricity meters and (b) to sell those devices to a person who intends merely to re-sell them and not himself to use them, does that agreement constitute a common law conspiracy to defraud?
2. Alternatively, is such an agreement properly charged as a statutory conspiracy to aid, abet, counsel or procure persons unknown to commit offences under section 2 of the Theft Act 1978?'

Held

The appeal would be allowed and the convictions of the defendants on count two [conspiracy to defraud] would be restored.

Lord Roskill (his Lordship referred to ss1(1) and 5(1) of the Criminal Law Act 1977, and the speech of Lord Bridge in *R v Ayres* extracted above, and continued):

'My Lords, junior counsel for the prosecution told your Lordships that when settling the indictment he had thought it right to put in the forefront of the prosecution case the charge of conspiracy to defraud in count 2. But, having regard to what the House had said in *R v Ayres* [1984] AC 447, he had also thought it right, lest his own view were not accepted as correct, to add a charge of statutory conspiracy in the terms of count 1. For my part I think he was entirely right to approach the matter in this way. Indeed the very difficulty he encountered in evolving a satisfactory formulation of a charge of statutory conspiracy, of which I shall say more later, reinforces the correctness of his approach.

I therefore turn to consider whether it was necessary for the prosecution in order to secure a conviction on count 2 to aver and prove a dishonest agreement actually to use the black boxes so as to defraud the intended victims, various electricity boards. It was said, and the Court of Appeal (Criminal Division) accepted, that it was not enough that the agreement charged was only dishonestly to manufacture and sell those boxes in order to defraud the intended victims.

Mr Spokes QC, for the respondents, put in the forefront of his submissions a pleading point, namely, that count 2 was in any event bad because it did not aver an agreement to use but only an agreement to manufacture and sell. In my view it is now much too late to take a point of this kind. It should have been taken, if at all, at the trial when if necessary the count could have been amended. But in any event, the point is without substance as well as without merit. It is obvious from the formulation of count 2 that the fraud upon the intended victims could not be successfully practised without use of the black boxes, and that the manufacture and sale was for the dishonest purpose of enabling those black boxes to be used by persons other than the respondents to the detriment of the intended victim.

The real question, as already stated, is whether in order to secure conviction on count 2 it was necessary to aver and prove a dishonest agreement by the respondents actually to use the black boxes, the submission being that it was not enough to show only an intention that such a dishonest use should follow their dishonest manufacture and sale.

My Lords, in my view, with all respect to those who have taken a different view, this submission is contrary to authority. I start with the decision of this House in *R v Scott* [1975] AC 819. It is to be observed that this case was decided before the passing of the Act of 1977. Scott was charged with two offences. First, he was charged with conspiracy to defraud and secondly, with conspiracy to infringe section 21(1)(*a*) of the Copyright Act 1956. He ultimately pleaded guilty to both and was sentenced on both counts: see p822. In this connection I have the permission of my noble and learned friend, Lord Bridge of Harwich, to say that he was in error in saying in *R v Ayres* [1984] AC 447, 454 that the conspiracy under consideration in *R v Scott* [1975] AC 819 did not involve the commission of any identifiable offence. But the House was not there concerned with what would now be called a statutory conspiracy. Indeed since *R v Ayres* the two counts would be mutually exclusive and Scott could not have been convicted on both. That is, however, of no importance in the present case. The importance of the decision in *R v Scott* lies in the conclusion summarised in the headnote:

"(3) That the common law offence of conspiracy to defraud was not limited to an agreement between two or more persons to deceive the intended victim and by such deceit to defraud him; and accordingly, as deceit was not an essential ingredient of the offence, the count was not bad in law and the appellant had been rightly convicted."

Viscount Dilhorne said, at p839: "One must not confuse the object of a conspiracy with the means by which it is intended to be carried out." My noble and learned friend Lord Diplock said, at p841:

"(2) Where the intended victim of a 'conspiracy to defraud' is a private individual the purpose of the conspirators must be to cause the victim economic loss by depriving him of some property or right, corporeal or incorporeal, to which he is or would or might become entitled. The intended means by which the purpose is to be achieved must be dishonest. They need not involve fraudulent misrepresentation such as is needed to constitute the civil tort of deceit. Dishonesty of any kind is enough."

In *Attorney-General's Reference (No. 1 of 1982)* [1983] QB 751, (the whisky label case), the Court of Appeal (Criminal Division) (Lord Lane CJ and Taylor and McCowan JJ) were primarily concerned with the question of jurisdiction to try persons for conspiracy which had been entered into in England but which was to be carried out abroad though that conspiracy would cause economic damage to persons in England. The court held that there was no such jurisdiction. But it is apparent from a passage in the judgment of that court delivered by Lord Lane CJ, at p757, that, but for the question of jurisdiction, the former defendants would have been guilty of conspiracy to defraud. Lord Lane CJ said:

"In each case to determine the object of the conspiracy, the court must see what the defendants actually agreed to do. Had it not been for the jurisdictional problem, we have no doubt the charge against these conspirators would have been conspiracy to defraud potential purchasers of the whisky, for that was the true object of the agreement."

The dishonest agreement there under consideration was to produce, label and distribute bottles of whisky so as to represent them as containing whisky of a well-known brand which in fact they did not contain. The object as the Lord Chief Justice said was to defraud potential purchasers of the whisky outside this country.

In my view the respondents were liable to be convicted of conspiracy to defraud because they agreed to manufacture and sell and thus put into circulation dishonest devices, the sole purpose of which was to cause loss just as the former defendants in the case just referred to would, apart from the jurisdictional problem, have been liable to be convicted of conspiracy to defraud because they agreed dishonestly to produce, label and distribute bottles of whisky, the sole purpose of the sale of which was to defraud potential purchasers of those bottles.

For these reasons, I think, with great respect, the decision of the Court of Appeal (Criminal Division) cannot be supported and that the trial judge's ruling was correct. The convictions on count 2 should therefore be restored.

I wish to make plain that in inviting your Lordships' House to agree with this conclusion I am not suggesting that the principles applicable to common law conspiracy to defraud should in any way be expanded or extended. On the contrary in my view the present cases fall well within existing principles and authorities. I do not arrive at this conclusion with any regret. On the contrary I am sure that the Court of Appeal (Criminal Division) arrived at their conclusion only because they thought that they were compelled to do so. I think commonsense suggests that what the respondents agreed to do plainly constituted a conspiracy to defraud and that no-one save perhaps the most enthusiastic lawyer would willingly hold otherwise.

I can deal with the question raised in connection with count 1 more briefly. As was pointed out in *R v Ayres* [1984] AC 447, 455, in the passage to which I have already referred, offences of statutory conspiracy and of common law conspiracy to defraud are mutually exclusive. It follows that if your Lordships agree with me that the respondents were properly convicted on count 2 of the conspiracy to defraud, this conclusion presupposes that the respondents could not properly have been convicted on count 1 of the statutory conspiracy there charged. The Court of Appeal (Criminal Division) were of the opinion that they could not have been so convicted for the reason that section 1(1) of the Act of 1977 did not upon its true construction make a charge of conspiracy to aid, abet, counsel or procure possible in law. The foundation for this view is a passage in *Smith and Hogan, Criminal Law*, 5th ed (1983), pp234–235, which is quoted in full in the judgment delivered by Hodgson J and with which the Court of Appeal (Criminal Division) expressed complete agreement.

My Lords, I do not find it necessary to consider whether or not this view is correct for this reason. Even if such a charge of conspiracy to aid, abet, counsel or procure were possible in law, I can see no evidence whatever that the respondents ever agreed so to aid, abet, counsel or procure or indeed did aid, abet, counsel or procure those who as the ultimate purchasers or possessors of the black boxes were destined to be the actual perpetrators of the intended frauds upon electricity boards. It follows that on no view could the respondents have been convicted on count 1 even if that count were sustainable in law. The last question is obviously one of some difficulty and a case in which that question arose for direct decision is likely to be a rarity. I suggest that in any future case in which that question does arise it should be treated as open for consideration de novo, as much may depend on the particular facts of the case in question.

In the result I would allow the appeals, answer certified question 1 "Yes" and certified question 2 "No." I would restore the convictions of the respondents on count 2.'

R v McDonough (1962) 47 Cr App R 37

See *DPP v Nock*, and *R v Fitzmaurice*, both above.

R v Siracusa (1990) 90 Cr App R 340 Court of Appeal (Criminal Division) (O'Connor LJ, Boreham and Ian Kennedy JJ)

Statutory conspiracy – mens rea

Facts (as stated by O'Connor LJ)

'On December 13, 1984, a consignment of 52 packing cases of furniture from India consigned to Elongate Ltd arrived at Felixstowe. Customs officers found in some articles of furniture cannabis with a street value of £0.5 million in England and £3 million in Canada. They repacked and waited and watched. The consignment was cleared by shipping agents and delivered to a warehouse, Unit 5, Batsworth Road, Mitcham. The customs moved in on December 18, 1984, seized the consignment and arrested Siracusa and a man named Gaultieri. Unit 5 is a spacious warehouse. There was nothing in it except the 52 cases of furniture and a fork-lift truck. The work in hand was the painting out of the Indian shipping marks with black paint.

On May 28, 1985, a consignment of 84 packing cases of furniture from Thailand consigned to Ital Provisions Ltd arrived at Southampton. Customs officers found in some articles of furniture heroin with a street value of £15 million in England and £75 million in Canada. They repacked some of the heroin and waited and watched. The consignment was not delivered in this country, but trans-shipped and left for Canada on June 8, 1985. After delivery in Canada on June 21, 1985, enforcement officers moved in, seized the consignment and arrested three men. It was found that they had gone unerringly to the cases containing the pieces in which heroin was concealed. In England, Monteleone, Luciani and Di Carlo were arrested on June 21, 1985. The importation of controlled drugs into this country is prohibited by section 3(1)(a) of the Misuse of Drugs Act 1971. That section does not create any offence. The offence is created by section 170(2)(b) of the Customs and Excise Management Act 1979 which provides:

> "(2) ... if any person is, in relation to any goods, in any way knowingly concerned in any fraudulent evasion or attempt at evasion: ... (b) of any prohibition or restriction for the time being in force with respect to the goods under or by virtue of any enactment ... he shall be guilty of an offence..."

At the relevant time, the effect of section 170(4) and Schedule 1 of the Act was that importation of drugs of Class A or Class B was punishable with up to 14 years' imprisonment.

In cases where controlled drugs are imported into this country and a substantive offence is charged as a contravention of section 170(2)(b), the particulars of the offence identify the drug and the class to which it belongs so that the appropriate penalty is not in doubt. Case law has established that although separate offences are created as a result of the different penalties authorised, the mens rea is the same. The prosecution must prove that the defendant knew that the goods were prohibited goods. They do not have to prove that he knew what the goods in fact were. Thus it is no defence for a man charged with importing a Class A drug to say he believed he was bringing in a Class C drug or indeed any other prohibited goods: *Hussain* (1969) 53 Cr App R448; *Shivpuri* (1986) 83 Cr App R 178; *Ellis* (1987).

The appellants contend that where conspiracy to contravene section 170(2)(b) is charged, the position is different so that in this case the prosecution had to prove against each defendant that he knew that the Kashmir operation involved cannabis and that the Thailand operation involved heroin. If this submission is well-founded, then it is said that the learned judge's direction on conspiracy is flawed and strength is added to the contentions of those appellants who submit that in respect of one, other or both counts, there was no case to go to the jury at the end of the prosecution case.'

Held

The appeals would be dismissed.

O'Connor LJ (his Lordship referred to the facts of *R v Anderson*, and the passages from Lord Bridge's speech, extracted elswhere in this chapter, that end with Lord Bridge's comment):

> '"I have said already, but I repeat to emphasise its importance, that an essential ingredient in the crime of conspiring to commit a specific offence or offences under section 1(1) of the Act of 1977 is that the accused should agree that a course of conduct be pursued which he knows must involve the commission by one or more of the parties to the agreement of that offence or those offences. But, beyond the mere fact of agreement, the necessary mens rea of the crime is, in my opinion, established if, and only if, it is shown that the accused, when he entered into the agreement, intended to play some part in the agreed course of conduct in furtherance of the criminal purpose which the agreed course of conduct was intended to achieve. Nothing less will suffice; nothing more is required."'

He then continued:

> 'The last paragraph above cited must be read in the context of that case. We think it obvious that Lord Bridge cannot have been intending that the organiser of a crime who recruited others to carry it out would not himself be guilty of conspiracy unless it could be proved that he intended to play some active part himself thereafter. Lord Bridge had pointed out ... that in these days of highly organised crime the most serious statutory conspiracies will frequently involve an elaborate and complex agreed course of conduct in which many will consent to play necessary but subordinate roles, not involving them in any direct participation in the commission of the offence or offences at the centre of the conspiracy.
>
> The present case is a classic example of such a conspiracy. It is the hallmark of such crimes that the organisers try to remain in the background and more often than not are not apprehended.
>
> Secondly, the origins of all conspiracies are concealed and it is usually quite impossible to establish when or where the initial agreement was made, or when or where other conspirators were recruited. The very existence of the agreement can only be inferred from overt acts. Participation in a conspiracy is infinitely variable: it can be active or passive. If the majority shareholder and director of a company consents to the company being used for drug smuggling carried out in the company's name by a fellow director and minority shareholder, he is guilty of conspiracy. Consent, that is the agreement or adherence to the agreement, can be inferred if it is proved that he knew what was going on and the intention to participate in the furtherance of the criminal purpose is also established by his failure to stop the unlawful activity. Lord Bridge's dictum does not require anything more.
>
> We return to the first sentence of this paragraph in Lord Bridge's speech. He starts by saying: " I have said already, but I repeat to emphasise its importance.... ". We have cited what he had already said when dealing with his clause 2. It is clear that he was not intending to say anything different. So when he goes on to say:
>
>> " ... an essential ingredient in the crime of conspiring to commit a specific offence or offences under section 1(1) of the Act of 1977 is that the accused should agree that a course of conduct be pursued which he knows must involve the commission by one or more of the parties to the agreement of that offence or those offences,..." he plainly does not mean that the prosecution have to prove that persons who agree to import prohibited drugs into this country know that the offence which will be committed will be a contravention of section 170(2) of the Customs and Excise Act.
>
> He is not to be taken as saying that the prosecution must prove that the accused knew the name of the crime. We are satisfied that Lord Bridge was doing no more than applying the words of section 1 of the Criminal Law Act 1977, namely, that when the accused agreed to the course of conduct, he knew that it involved the commission of an offence. The mens rea sufficient to support the commission of a substantive offence will not necessarily be sufficient to support a charge of conspiracy to commit that offence. An intent to cause grievous bodily harm is sufficient to support the charge of murder, but is not sufficient to support a charge of conspiracy to murder or of attempt to murder.
>
> We have come to the conclusion that if the prosecution charge a conspiracy to contravene section 170(2) of the Customs and Excise Management Act by the importation of heroin, then the prosecution must prove that the agreed course of conduct was the importation of heroin. This is because the essence of the crime of conspiracy is the agreement and in simple terms, you do not prove an agreement to import heroin by proving an agreement to import cannabis.

We are confident that in coming to this conclusion, we are not making the enforcement of the anti-drug laws more difficult. If the facts suggest that the agreement was to import prohibited drugs of more than one class, that can be appropriately laid because section 1(1) of the Criminal Law Act expressly provides for the agreed course of conduct to involve the commission of more than one offence.

We are in no doubt that the learned judge made it quite clear to the jury that count 1 required proof of an agreement to import cannabis and count 2, heroin. The learned judge's main direction to the jury on conspiracy is found at p47 of the summing-up. It is sufficient to cite the following passages:

> "Now, members of the jury, would you please take in your hands your copies of the indictment. You will see that each of the two counts charges a conspiracy to contravene a section of the Customs and Excise Management Act of 1979. In those counts all these defendants are charged, but there are different named conspirators in addition to the defendants in the counts. So, the first thing you will have to consider is: What is a conspiracy?
>
> Now, a conspiracy is an agreement between two or more persons to do an unlawful act – in this case to commit a crime. You will see the crime which is set out. You will appreciate, of course, more than one person would have to be involved, you may think, in the commission of the sort of offences you are dealing with here. The question for you is whether it has been proved that each of the defendants is party to such an agreement.
>
> When you look to see what it is that they are alleged to have agreed to have done, you will see that the offence concerned in count 1 is being knowingly concerned, and I stress the word "knowingly," in the fraudulent evasion of the prohibition on the importation of Class B drugs, namely, cannabis resin. Now, you will realise at once that if you are innocently involved, if you have been duped by others, as the first two defendants claim, then of course you are not committing this offence, because you are not being knowingly concerned in the fraudulent evasion of the prohibition on the importation of drugs. Now, 'knowingly concerned' means that you have to know that the goods are subject to prohibition, and there is no suggestion by any of these defendants that they would not know that, and that what they were concerned in was an agreement to effect, in an operation, the evasion of the prohibition fraudulently. 'Fraudulently' means by dishonest conduct, deliberately intended to evade the prohibition on the importation of controlled drugs. Of course, 'importation' means bringing them into this country. Members of the jury, if you turn to count 2, you will see that a similar offence, the ingredients of which I have just explained to you and are the same, is laid, but in this case in relation to the prohibition on the importation of what are called class A drugs, namely, Diamorphine Hydrocholonde, which is heroin.
>
> Now, members of the jury, so far as conspiracy is concerned, if a defendant agrees with any other defendant or named conspirator that a course of conduct should be pursued which, if carried out in accordance with their intentions, would necessarily amount to the offence of being concerned in the fraudulent evasion of the prohibition either on the importation of cannabis in count 1 or heroin in count 2 by one or more parties to the agreement, then he is guilty of conspiracy."

Thereafter the learned judge frequently used the word "drugs", but in circumstances where the jury must have appreciated that for count 1, drugs meant cannabis and for count 2, heroin. For example, at p13, after reminding the jury that Luciani had resigned his directorship in November 1984 and Siracusa had been arrested in December 1984, that is some six months before the heroin shipment arrived, he said that it did not matter:

> "if you are satisfied from the whole of the evidence that they were parties to the agreement of those importations of drugs and that is something you can only decide from everything that happened before and what their participation in it was, they do not have to be on the scene taking an active part when the drugs actually arrive."

There are numerous other similar examples in the summing-up, but as we have said they cannot in any way have confused the jury.'

R* v *Sirat (1985) 83 Cr App R 41 Court of Appeal (Criminal Division) (Parker LJ, French and Mann JJ)

Inciting incitement

Facts (as stated in the judgment of Parker LJ)

'The facts may be shortly stated. Between Thursday, August 16, 1984, and Monday, August 20, both dates inclusive, the appellant had four meetings with Mr Bashir, the last of which was recorded by the police, to whom Mr Bashir had reported after the first two had taken place. It is unnecessary to set out the details of the conversations. It is sufficient to say that they plainly showed that the appellant desired the death of his wife or, if not that, her serious injury, and that he was urging Bashir to (i) either kill or injure her himself, or (ii) pay a man who was in fact non-existent to do so, or (iii) procure the result, whether by doing the deed himself or by paying someone else, not necessarily the non-existent man, to do so.'

The appellant was convicted of incitement to cause grievous bodily harm and appealed.

Held

The appeal would be allowed.

Parker LJ:

'At the close of the prosecution case it was submitted on behalf of the appellant that (i) there was no such offence in law as inciting a person to counsel or abet a third person to commit an offence, and (ii) there was not sufficient evidence to go to the jury that the appellant had incited Bashir himself to murder or cause grievous bodily harm to the appellant's wife. The judge rightly rejected the second of those two submissions and no complaint is made as to that.

We are now only indirectly concerned with the ruling on the first submission; for what now matters is not the ruling itself but the subsequent direction to the jury which was based on it. Of this complaint is made. In the only ground of appeal which was pursued it is contended that the learned judge erred in law "in directing the jury that if the defendant urged the witness Bashir to incite a third man to cause grievous bodily harm to the defendant's wife the defendant was guilty of the offence charged in count 2 of the indictment and in rejecting a submission by defence counsel that there was no such offence in law as inciting a person to counsel or abet a third person to commit an offence."

There is no doubt that at common law incitement to commit a crime is an offence. This being so, it follows logically that if A incites B to incite C to commit a crime, eg to wound D, A is guilty of incitement to commit a crime, namely, incitement. This however is subject to the qualification that if C is non-existent, being either dead or fictional, A would not be guilty, because he would be inciting the commission of an impossible crime. B cannot incite C, because C does not exist. On the basis of *Fitzmaurice* (1983) 76 Cr App R 17; [1983] QB 1083, the judge rightly so directed the jury. Hence, since the jury convicted on count 2, it follows that they must have concluded that the appellant had not urged Bashir to get the fictional man and no other to do the deed.

With regard to the remaining possibilities, the essence of the learned judge's directions appears from the following passages in his summing-up:

"If a man wants a murder to be committed and he tries to persuade somebody else to commit it or he tries to persuade that second person to get a third person to commit it, then the first man is guilty of the crime of incitement ... incitement to murder."

"If you are sure that in reality the effect of what he was saying to Bashir was this, 'I want you to get her seriously injured, do it yourself or get the white man from Leeds to do it,' then what Sirat was proposing was a possibility because the white man from Leeds was only one way in which he was making his proposal. Another, on the basis that I am putting it to you, was that Bashir might do it himself and that was obviously possible, so in that event he would be guilty of count 2 and, equally, if the effect of what he was saying was this, 'I want you to get her seriously injured, get the white man from Leeds to do it if you like, get somebody else to do it if you like, so long as you get somebody,' if that is the effect of what he was saying, then once again the serious injury which he wanted brought about would be a possibility and he would then be guilty of count 2."

"Similarly with count 2, you have to be sure before you can convict him that he desired his wife to be seriously injured and that he tried to persuade Bashir to bring about her serious injury in a way which was, in fact, possible."

In principle there is nothing wrong with these directions, but complication is introduced by the provisions of the Criminal Law Act 1977. Section 1 of that Act created the statutory offence of conspiracy and section 5(1), subject to exceptions which do not matter, abolished the offence of conspiracy at common law. Section 5(7) then provided: "Incitement and attempt to commit the offence of conspiracy (whether the conspiracy incited or attempted would be an offence at common law or under section 1 above or any other enactment) shall cease to be offences." If, therefore, A incites B to agree with C that C will wound D, A's incitement of B is by statute not an offence.

There is, in our view, no doubt that one possible view of the evidence was that the appellant was inciting Bashir to agree, with either the non-existent man or anyone else who would do it at the right price, that such person should cause grievous bodily harm to the appellant's wife. It is therefore clearly possible that the jury may have convicted him of something which by statute is no longer an offence. Moreover, as was accepted by the prosecution, they may have convicted him of an offence with which he was not charged, namely, incitement to incite to cause grievous bodily harm, whereas the prosecution charged incitement to cause grievous bodily harm.

This being so, we allowed the appeal on two grounds: (a) that the appellant may have been convicted of an offence of which he was not charged, and (b) that he may have been convicted of an offence which does not exist.

Lest there be any doubt, we do not intend to indicate that the common law offence of inciting to incite no longer exists. Where however the facts are that the accused's incitement of B is actually to enter into an agreement with C for the commission of a crime, it would in our judgment be impossible to hold that the accused can be guilty of incitement, on the ground that B must of necessity propose the crime to C on the way to making the agreement. Whether other forms of incitement to incite survive will fall for decision when the question arises. It may appear to be absurd that, where a person is inciting actual agreement to be made for the commission of a crime, he should be guilty of no offence, but that where he does not seek actual agreement but mere encouragement he should be guilty. This however is not necessarily absurd, for there may well be circumstances where there is no question of an agreement being sought but where the particular form of incitement is more effective than any attempt to secure agreement.'

Wai Yu-Tsang v *R* [1991] 3 WLR 1006 Privy Council (Lord Bridge, Lord Griffiths, Lord Goff, Lord Jauncey and Lord Lowry)

Mens rea of conspiracy to defraud

Facts
The defendant was convicted of conspiring to defraud the Hang Lung Bank ('the bank'), of which he was the chief accountant, of US$124M. The allegation had been that he had conspired with the managing director, the general manager and others to dishonestly conceal the dishonouring of certain cheques by not recording them in the bank's account. The defendant contended that he was not guilty as he had been acting on the instructions of the managing director, and had acted in good faith to prevent a run on the bank. The trial judge had directed the jury that for conspiracy to defraud, no desire to cause loss on the part of the defendant need be shown. It was sufficient that he had imperilled the economic or proprietary interests of another party. The defendant appealed unsuccessfully to the Court of Appeal Hong Kong, and now appealed to the Privy Council.

Held

The trial judge's direction on the mens rea of conspiracy to defraud had been correct and the appeal would be dismissed.

Lord Goff (having reviewed the complex factual background):

'Before the Court of Appeal (of Hong Kong) a number of issues were raised by the defendant founded upon criticisms of the summing up of the judge. All of those criticisms were rejected by the Court of Appeal. Before their Lordships, however, the defendant's case was directed solely on the judge's direction on the mental element required for a conspiracy to defraud. The judge explained to the jury that the defendant must have been party to an agreement with one or more of the other named conspirators which had a common intention to defraud one or more of the persons or categories of persons named in the indictment. He explained that such an intention must involve dishonesty on the part of the conspirators, and continued:

> "It is fraud if it is proved that there was the dishonest taking of a risk which there was no right to take which – to [the defendant's] knowledge at least – would cause detriment or prejudice to another, detriment or prejudice to the economic or proprietary rights of another. That detriment or prejudice to somebody else is very often incidental to the purpose of the fraudsman himself. The prime objective of fraudsmen is usually to gain some advantage for themselves, any detriment or prejudice to somebody else is often secondary to that objective but nonetheless is a contemplated or predictable outcome of what they do. If the interests of some other person – the economic or proprietary interests of some other person are imperilled, that is sufficient to constitute fraud even though no loss is actually suffered and even though the fraudsman himself did not desire to bring about any loss."

It is plain that that direction was founded upon the judgment of the Court of Appeal in *R* v *Allsop* (1976) 64 Cr App R 29. It was the contention of the defendant that the direction was erroneous in so far as it stated that, for this purpose, the imperilling of an economic interest or the threat of financial prejudice was sufficient to establish fraud, whatever the motive of the accused may have been; and that in so far as *R* v *Allsop* so decided, it was wrong and should not be followed.

In the course of argument, their Lordships were referred to a number of authorities as well as to *R* v *Allsop* itself. They do not however find it necessary for the present purposes to refer to more than a few of these authorities. The first is *Welham* v *Director of Public Prosecutions* [1961] AC 103. That case was in fact concerned with forgery, and in particular with the meaning of the words "intent to defraud" in s4(1) of the Forgery Act 1913. The case has however since been referred to as providing guidance in cases of conspiracy to defraud: see *R* v *Scott* [1975] AC 819, 838, per Viscount Dilhorne, a proposition with which their Lordships are respectfully in agreement. In *Welham* v *Director of Public Prosecutions* [1961] AC 103, the appellant had witnessed forged hire purchase agreements, on the basis of which finance companies advanced large sums of money. His defence was that he had no intention of depriving the finance companies by deceit of any economic advantage, his belief being that the only function of the agreements was to enable the companies to circumvent certain credit restrictions. His only purpose was to mislead the authority which might inspect the records and whose duty was to prevent contravention of the credit restrictions. The House of Lords held that there was no warrant for confining the words "intent to defraud" to an intent to deprive a person by deceit of an economic advantage or to inflict upon him an economic loss, and further that such an intent could exist where there was no other intention than to deceive a person responsible for a public duty into doing something, or failing to do something, which he would not have done, or failed to have done, but for the deceit. Lord Denning, who delivered the leading speech, rejected the argument that an intention to defraud involves an intention to cause economic loss. He referred to opinions of academic lawyers to that effect, and said, at p131:

> "I cannot agree with them on this. If a drug addict forges a doctor's prescription so as to enable him to get drugs from a chemist, he has, I should have thought, an intent to defraud, even though he intends to pay the chemist the full price and no one is a penny the worse off."

Later, at pp132–133, Lord Denning referred to a passage in *East's Please of the Crown* (1803 ed) vol 2, p852, to the effect that forgery at common law denotes a false making – "a making malo animo" – of any written instrument for the purpose of fraud and deceit. He then said, at p133:

> "That was written in 1803, but it has been always accepted as authoritative. It seems to me to provide the key to the cases decided since it was written, as well as those before. The important thing about this definition is that it is not limited to the idea of economic loss, nor to the idea of depriving someone of something of value. It extends generally to *the purpose of fraud and deceit*. Put shortly, 'with intent to defraud' means 'with intent to practice a fraud' on someone or other. It need not be anyone in particular. Someone in general will suffice. If anyone may be prejudiced in any way by the fraud, that is enough."

Lord Radcliffe agreed with the speech of Lord Denning, but went on to express in his own words his view of the meaning of the words "intent to defraud" in s4(1) of the Act of 1913. He rejected the proposition that in ordinary speech "to defraud" is confined to the idea of depriving a man by deceit of some economic advantage or inflicting upon him some economic loss and continued, at p124:

> "Has the law ever so confined it? In my opinion there is no warrant for saying that it has. What it has looked for in considering the effect of cheating upon another person and so in defining the criminal intent is the prejudice of that person: what Blackstone (*Commentaries*, 18th ed, vol 4, at p247) called 'to the prejudice of another man's right.' *East, Pleas of the Crown* (1803), vol 2, at pp852, 854, makes the same point in the chapter on Forgery: 'in all cases of forgery, properly so called, it is immaterial whether any person be actually injured or not, provided any may be prejudiced by it.'"

He went on to say that the special line of cases where the person deceived is a public authority or a person holding public office, and there is no intention on the part of the deceiver to inflict upon him any pecuniary or economic harm, shows that such an intention is not necessary to convict a man of an intention to defraud. The remainder of the Appellate Committee agreed with both Lord Radcliffe and Lord Denning.

This authority establishes that the expression "intent to defraud" is not to be given a narrow meaning, involving an intention to cause economic loss to another. In broad terms, it means simply an intention to practise a fraud on another, or an intention to act to the prejudice of another man's right.

Their Lordships turn next to *R* v *Scott* [1975] AC 819. That case was concerned with a conspiracy temporarily to abstract films from a cinema to enable the appellant to make and distribute copies of the films on a commercial scale, the operation being carried on without the consent of the owners of the copyright or distribution rights in the films. The appellant's argument was to the effect that he could not be guilty of any conspiracy, because the facts did not disclose an agreement to deceive the persons alleged to have been the object of the conspiracy. This argument was rejected by the House of Lords. The leading speech was delivered by Viscount Dilhorne, with whom the remainder of the Appellate Committee agreed. He reviewed the authorities, including *Welham* v *Director of Public Prosecutions* [1961] AC 103, and said [1975] AC 819, 839:

> "I have not the temerity to attempt an exhaustive definition of the meaning of 'defraud.' As I have said, words take colour from the context in which they are used, but the words 'fraudulently' and 'defraud' must ordinarily have a very similar meaning. If, as I think, and as the Criminal Law Revision Committee appears to have thought, 'fraudulently' means 'dishonestly', then 'to defraud' ordinarily means, in my opinion, to deprive a person dishonestly of something which is his or of something to which he is or would or might but for the perpetration of the fraud be entitled. In *Welham* v *Director of Public Prosecutions* [1961] AC 103, 124, Lord Radcliffe referred to a special line of cases where the person deceived is a person holding public office or a public authority and where the person deceived was not caused any pecuniary or economic loss. Forgery whereby the deceit has been accomplished, had, he pointed out, been in a number of cases treated as having been done with intent to defraud despite the absence of pecuniary or economic loss. In this case it is not necessary to decide that a conspiracy to defraud may exist even though its object was not to secure a financial advantage by inflicting an economic loss on the person at whom the conspiracy was directed. But for myself I see no reason why what was said by Lord Radcliffe in relation to forgery should not equally apply in relation to conspiracy to defraud."

In a brief speech Lord Diplock (although he, like the remainder of the Appellate Committee, agreed with the speech of Viscount Dilhorne) was more specific. He said, at p841:

> "(2) Where the intended victim of a 'conspiracy to defraud' is a private individual the purpose of the conspirators must be to cause the victim economic loss by depriving him of some property or right, corporeal or incorporeal, to which he is or would or might become entitled. ... (3) Where the intended victim of a 'conspiracy to defraud' is a person performing public duties as distinct from a private individual it is sufficient if the purpose is to cause him to act contrary to his public duty ..."

With the greatest respect to Lord Diplock, their Lordships consider this categorisation to be too narrow. In their opinion, in agreement with the approach of Lord Radcliffe in *Welham v Director of Public Prosecutions* [1961] AC 103, the cases concerned with persons performing public duties are not to be regarded as a special category in the manner described by Lord Diplock, but rather as exemplifying the general principle that conspiracies to defraud are not restricted to cases of intention to cause the victim economic loss. On the contrary, they are to be understood in the broad sense described by Lord Radcliffe and Lord Denning in *Welham v Director of Public Prosecutions* – the view which Viscount Dilhorne favoured in *R v Scott* [1975] AC 819, as apparently did the other members of the Appellate Committee who agreed with him in that case (apart, it seems, from Lord Diplock).

With these principles in mind, their Lordships turn to *R v Allsop*, 64 Cr App R 29 itself. In that case the defendant was a sub-broker for a hire-purchase company. Acting in collusion with others, he entered false particulars in forms submitted to the company, to induce it to accept applications for hire-purchase facilities which it might otherwise have rejected, although the defendant both expected and believed that the transactions in question would be completed satisfactorily and that the company would achieve its contemplated profit, as it appears in fact to have done. Examples of the false particulars were that the price of the car concerned would be inflated so as to allow an illusory deposit to be shown as having been paid by the intending hire-purchaser; or the value of the car taken in part exchange would be stated at more than the true figure; or a car dealer would be named as the seller when the transaction was a private one and no established car dealer played any part in it. What the defendant sought to achieve was an increase in the company's business, and therefore of his own commission. The defendant was charged with conspiracy to defraud. The judge directed the jury that they must be sure that the conspirators knew that they were inducing the company to act in circumstances in which they might cause or create the likelihood of economic loss or prejudice. The jury convicted the defendant. He appealed on the ground that the judge's direction was too wide; he should, it was submitted, have directed the jury that they must be sure that the defendant intended to cause economic loss to the company. The Court of Appeal dismissed the appeal. The judgment of the court was delivered by Shaw LJ. The central passage in the judgment reads, at p31:

> "It seemed to this court that Mr Heald's argument traversed the shadowy region between intent and motive. Generally the primary objective of fraudsmen is to advantage themselves. The detriment that results to their victims is secondary to that purpose, and incidental. It is 'intended' only in the sense that it is a contemplated outcome of the fraud that is perpetrated. If the deceit which is employed imperils the economic interest of the person deceived, this is sufficient to constitute fraud even though in the event no actual loss is suffered and notwithstanding that the deceiver did not desire to bring about an actual loss."

In reaching this conclusion, the Court of Appeal found it necessary to reconcile it with the narrow definition of conspiracy to defraud expressed in the speech of Lord Diplock in *R v Scott* [1975] AC 819, 841, to which their Lordships have already referred. This they did on the basis that "economic loss" may be "ephemeral and not lasting, or potential and not actual; but even a threat of financial prejudice while it exists may be measured in terms of money." They continued, at p32:

> "In the present case, the part of the history which is common ground reveals that in this sense [the company] did suffer actual loss for they paid too much for cars worth less than their pretended value; and they relied upon the creditworthiness of hire-purchasers as measured by the deposit stated to have been paid when none had been paid. It matters not that in the end the hire-purchasers concerned paid to [the company] what was due to them ..."

They concluded by praying in aid a passage from the speech of Lord Diplock in *R v Hyam* [1975] AC 55, 86, – a case concerned with the mental element in the crime of murder.

In the context of conspiracy to defraud, it is necessary to bear in mind that such a conspiracy is an agreement to practise a fraud on somebody (cf *Welham* v *Director of Public Prosecutions* [1961] AC 103, 133, per Lord Denning). In *R* v *Allsop,* 64 Cr App R 29 what the defendant agreed to do was to present the company with false particulars, in reliance upon which, as he knew, the company would decide whether to enter into hire purchase transactions. It is then necessary to consider whether that could constitute a conspiracy to defraud, notwithstanding that the defendant's underlying purpose or motive was not to damage any economic interest of the company but to ensure that the transaction went through so that he would earn his commission. Their Lordships can see no reason why such an agreement should not be a conspiracy to defraud the company, substantially for the reasons given by the Court of Appeal. The defendant was, for his own purposes, dishonestly supplying the company with false information which persuaded it to accept risks which it would or might not have accepted if it had known the true facts. Their Lordships cannot see why this was not an agreement to practise a fraud on the company because, as Shaw LJ said, it was a dishonest agreement to employ a deceit which imperilled the economic interests of the company.

The attention of their Lordships was drawn to a critique of *R* v *Allsop* in Smith & Hogan, *Criminal Law*, 6th ed (1988), p273, to which they have given careful consideration. The authors first criticise the reference by the Court of Appeal to *R* v *Hyam* [1975] AC 55. With this criticism, their Lordships are inclined to agree, doubting whether an authority on the mental element in the crime of murder throws much light on the nature of a conspiracy to defraud. However, the Court of Appeal only felt it necessary to pray in aid Lord Diplock's speech in *R* v *Hyam* in order to circumnavigate the dictum of Lord Diplock in *R* v *Scott* [1975] AC 819, an exercise which their Lordships do not need to embark upon since they consider that dictum to be, for the reasons they have explained, too narrowly expressed. Next, the authors suggest that *R* v *Allsop* can be explained on the basis that there was an intention on the part of the defendant to defraud the company, since he intended the company to pay, as indeed it did pay, money for cars which it would not have paid, even though in the outcome it suffered no loss. There is force in this suggestion, as was recognised by the Court of Appeal itself: 64 Cr App R 29, 31. But the Court of Appeal was concerned with the question whether the conviction could stand on the basis of the summing up of the trial judge; and their Lordships are now concerned with the correctness of the reasoning of the Court of Appeal on that question, at p31.

Lastly it is suggested that, on the rationalisation which the authors prefer, the case was not about recklessness, and did not decide that anything less than intention in the strict sense would suffice for conspiracy to defraud. Their Lordships are however reluctant to allow this part of the law to become enmeshed in a distinction, sometimes artificially drawn, between intention and recklessness. The question whether particular facts reveal a conspiracy to defraud depends upon what the conspirators have dishonestly agreed to do, and in particular whether they have agreed to practise a fraud on somebody. for this purpose it is enough for example that, as in *R* v *Allsop* and in the present case, the conspirators have dishonestly agreed to bring about a state of affairs which they realise will or may deceive the victim into so acting, or failing to act, that he will suffer economic loss or his economic interests will be put at risk. It is however important in such a case, as the Court of Appeal stressed in *R* v *Allsop*, to distinguish a conspirator's intention (or immediate purpose) dishonestly to bring about such a state of affairs from his motive (or underlying purpose). The latter may be benign to the extent that he does not wish the victim or potential victim to suffer harm; but the mere fact that it is benign will not of itself prevent the agreement from constituting a conspiracy to defraud. Of course, if the conspirators were not acting dishonestly, there will have been no conspiracy to defraud; and in any event their benign purpose (if it be such) is a matter which, if they prove to be guilty, can be taken into account at the stage of sentence.

In forming this view of the matter, their Lordships draw comfort from the fact that *R* v *Allsop* has been accepted as good authority by the Supreme Court of Canada in *R* v *Olan, Hudson and Hartnett* (1978) 41 CCC (2d) 145, 150, per Dickson J delivering the judgment of the court, in a passage subsequently followed by the Supreme Court of Canada in *Vézina* v *The Queen* (1986) 25 DLR (4th) 82, 96, per Lamer J likewise delivering the judgment of the court.

For these reasons their Lordships, like the Court of Appeal, are satisfied that there was no misdirection by the judge in the present case. Their Lordships will humbly advise Her Majesty that this appeal should be dismissed.'

Yip Chiu-Cheung v *R* [1994] 3 WLR 514 Privy Council (Lords Jauncey, Griffiths, Browne-Wilkinson, Mustill and Slynn)

Conspiracy – whether undercover agent has mens rea

Facts

The appellant had entered into an agreement with N, an undercover police officer, whereby N would fly from Australia to Hong Kong, collect a consignment of heroin from the appellant, and return with it to Australia. N kept the Australian and Hong Kong authorities fully informed of the agreement, and they undertook to allow him free passage from Hong Kong and into Australia. The purpose of N's mission was to identify not only the suppliers of the drug in Hong Kong, but also the dealers in Australia. N in fact missed his flight to Hong Kong and proceeded no further with the plan to meet the appellant.

In due course, however, the appellant was charged with, and convicted of, conspiring to traffic in dangerous drugs. He appealed on the ground that there could be no conspiracy given that his co-conspirator, N, had been acting to promote law enforcement, and that N's purpose had been to expose drug-trafficking. The appeal was dismissed by the Court of Appeal of Hong Kong and renewed before the Privy Council.

Held

The appeal would be dismissed.

Lord Griffiths:

'... it was submitted that the trial judge and the Court of Appeal were wrong to hold that Needham, the undercover agent, could be a conspirator because he lacked the necessary mens rea or guilty mind required for the offence of conspiracy. It was urged upon their Lordships that no moral guilt attached to the undercover agent who was at all times acting courageously and with the best of motives in attempting to infiltrate and bring to justice a gang of criminal drug dealers. In these circumstances it was argued that it would be wrong to treat the agent as having any criminal intent, and reliance was placed upon a passage in the speech of Lord Bridge of Harwich in *R* v *Anderson (William Ronald)* [1986] AC 27, 38–39; but in that case Lord Bridge was dealing with a different situation from that which exists in the present case. There may be many cases in which undercover police officers or other law enforcement agents pretend to join a conspiracy in order to gain information about the plans of the criminals, with no intention of taking any part in the planned crime but rather with the intention of providing information that will frustrate it. It was to this situation that Lord Bridge was referring in *R* v *Anderson*. The crime of conspiracy requires an agreement between two or more persons to commit an unlawful act with the intention of carrying it out. It is the intention to carry out the crime that constitutes the necessary mens rea for th offence. As Lord Bridge pointed out, an undercover agent who has no intention of committing the crime lacks the necessary mens rea to be a conspirator.

The facts of the present case are quite different. Nobody can doubt that Needham was acting courageously and with the best motives; he was trying to break a drug ring. But equally there can be no doubt that the method he chose and in which the police in Hong Kong acquiesced involved the commission of the criminal offence of trafficking in drugs by exporting heroin from Hong Kong without a licence. Needham intended to commit that offence by carrying the heroin through customs and on to the aeroplane bound for Australia.

Neither the police, nor customs, nor any other member of the executive have any power to alter the terms of the Ordinance forbidding the export of heroin, and the fact that they may turn a blind eye when the heroin is exported does not prevent it from being a criminal offence.

The High Court of Australia in *A v Hayden (No 2)* (1984) 156 CLR 532 declared emphatically that there was no place for a general defence of superior orders or of Crown or executive fiat in Australian criminal law. Gibbs CJ said, at p540:

> "It is fundamental to our legal system that the executive has no power to authorise a breach of the law and that it is no excuse for an offender to say that he acted under the orders of a superior officer."

This statement of the law applies with the same force in England and Hong Kong as it does in Australia.

Naturally, Needham never expected to be prosecuted if he carried out the plan as intended. But the fact that in such circumstances the authorities would not prosecute the undercover agent does not mean that he did not commit the crime albeit as part of a wider scheme to combat drug dealing.'

29 Inchoate Offences II

Anderton v *Ryan* [1985] AC 560
See *R* v *Shivpuri*, below.

Attorney-General's Reference (No 1 of 1992) (1993) 96 Cr App R 298 Court of Appeal (Criminal Division) (Woolf LJ and Phil J)
Attempted rape – actus reus – steps more than merely preparatory

Facts
The respondent was charged with attempted rape. The evidence indicated that he had pushed the complainant to the ground, removed some of her undergarments, and lain on top of her. When the police arrived she was partially clothed, and the respondent had his trousers down. A police officer noted that the respondent's penis was flaccid. During the course of the trial the judge directed the jury to acquit, on the basis that there was insufficient evidence of the respondent having attempted to have sexual intercourse. The respondent was acquitted. The question referred for consideration by the Court of Appeal was as follows: 'Whether, on a charge of attempted rape, it is incumbent upon the prosecution, as a matter of law, to prove that the defendant physically attempted to penetrate the woman's vagina with his penis.'

Held
The question posed would be answered in the negative.

Lord Taylor CJ:

'In *R* v *Jones (Kenneth Henry)* [1990] 1 WLR 1057 and again in *R* v *Campbell (Tony)* (1991) 93 Cr App R 350, this court made it clear that the words of the Act were to be applied in their plain and natural meaning, as the judge reminded himself in his first ruling. The words are not to be interpreted so as to reintroduce either of the earlier common law tests. Indeed one of the objects of the Act was to resolve the uncertainty those tests created.

One of those tests was the so-called "last act" test, stated in *R* v *Eagleton* (1855) Dears CC 515 ie, has the defendant with intent to commit the full offence, done the last act in his power towards committing that offence, or, as Lord Diplock put it in *Director of Public Prosecutions* v *Stonehouse* [1978] AC 55, 68D, has he "crossed the Rubicon and burnt his boats"? The other test, derived from *Stephen's Digest of the Criminal Law*, 9th ed (1950), ch IV, art 29 was, did the act done with the intent to commit the full offence form part of a series of acts which would constitute its actual commission if not interrupted?

In *R* v *Gullefer (Note)* [1990] 1 WLR 1063 Lord Lane CJ, after referring to those two approaches, said, at p1066:

"It seems to us that the words of the Act of 1981 seek to steer a midway course. They do not provide, as they might have done, that the *R* v *Eagleton* test is to be followed, or that, as Lord Diplock suggested, the defendant must have reached a point from which it was impossible for him to retreat before the actus reus of an attempt is proved. On the other hand the words give perhaps as clear a guidance as is possible in the circumstances on the point of time at which Stephen's 'series of acts' begin. It begins when the merely preparatory acts come to an end and the defendant embarks upon the crime proper. When that is will depend of course upon the facts in any particular case."

Mr Temple submits that here the test applied by the judge amounted to resurrecting the *R* v *Eagleton* test. It would be equivalent in the case of a charge of attempted murder by the use of a gun to saying that unless the trigger of the gun was actually pulled, there was insufficient evidence to go to the jury on that charge.

In our judgment the judge was correct in the ruling which he gave at first and fell into error in reconsidering it at the end of the case.

It is not, in our judgment, necessary, in order to raise a prima facie case of attempted rape, to prove that the defendant with the requisite intent had necessarily gone as far as to attempt physical penetration of the vagina. It is sufficient if there is evidence from which the intent can be inferred and there are proved acts which a jury could properly regard as more than merely preparatory to the commission of the offence. For example, and merely as an example, in the present case the evidence of the young woman's distress, of the state of her clothing, and the position in which she was seen, together with the respondent's acts of dragging her up the steps, lowering his trousers and interfering with her private parts, and his answers to the police, left it open to the jury to conclude that the respondent had the necessary intent and had done acts which were more than merely preparatory. In short that he had embarked on committing the offence itself.'

Attorney-General's Reference (No 3 of 1992) [1994] 1 WLR 409 Court of Appeal (Criminal Division) (Lord Taylor CJ, Schiemann and Wright JJ)

Attempted arson – whether recklessness as to life being endangered sufficient

Facts
The respondents had thrown a petrol bomb from a moving car towards a stationary car. The stationary car was occupied and there were persons nearby on the pavement. The petrol bomb missed the stationary car and hit a wall behind it. The respondents were charged with attempted aggravated arson, contrary to s1(2) of the Criminal Damage Act 1971, one count alleging recklessness as to whether life would be endangered. The trial judge directed that the respondents be acquitted on the ground that the endangering of life was a consequence of criminal damage under the aggravated offence, and thus recklessness was not sufficient mens rea where the charge was one of attempt.

The following question was referred to the Court of Appeal:

> 'Whether on a charge of attempted arson in the aggravated form contemplated by s1(2) of the Criminal Damage Act 1971, in addition to establishing a specific intent to cause damage by fire, it is sufficient to prove that the defendant was reckless as to whether life would thereby be endangered.'

Held
The certified question was answered in the affirmative.

Lord Taylor CJ:

'... In the present case, what was missing to prevent a conviction for the completed offence was damage to the property referred to in the opening lines of section 1(2) of the Act of 1981, what in the example of a crane, which we gave earlier in this judgment, we referred to as "the first named property". Such damage is essential for the completed offence. If a defendant does not intend to cause such damage he cannot intend to commit the completed offence. At worse he is reckless as to whether the offence is committed. The law of attempt is concerned with those who are intending to commit crimes. If that intent cannot be shown, then there can be no conviction.

However, the crime here consisted of doing certain acts in a certain state of mind in circumstances where the first named property and the second named property were the same, in short where the danger to life arose from the damage to the property which the defendant intended to damage. The substantive crime is committed if the defendant damaged property in a state of mind where he was reckless as to whether the life of another would thereby be endangered. We see no reason why there should not be a conviction for attempt if the prosecution can show that he, in that state of mind, intended to damage the property by throwing a bomb at it. One analysis of this situation is to say that although the defendant was in an appropriate state of mind to render him guilty of the completed offence the prosecution had not proved the physical element of the completed offence, and therefore he is not guilty of the completed offence. If, on a charge of attempting to commit the offence, the prosecution can show not only the state of mind required for the completed offence but also that the defendant intended to supply the missing physical element of the completed offence, that suffices for a conviction. That cannot be done merely by the prosecution showing him to be reckless. The defendant must intend to damage property, but there is no need for a graver mental state than is required for the full offence.

The trial judge in the present case, however, went further than this, and held that not merely must the defendant intend to supply all that was missing from the completed offence – namely, damage to the first named property – but also that recklessness as to the consequences of such damage for the lives of others was not enough to secure a conviction for attempt, although it was sufficient for the completed offence. She held that before a defendant could be convicted of attempting to commit the offence it had to be shown that he intended that the lives of others should be endangered by the damage which he intended.

She gave no policy reasons for so holding, and there is no case which bound her so to hold. The most nearly relevant case is *R v Khan (Mohammed Iqbal)* [1990] 1 WLR 813 ...

... An attempt was made in argument to suggest that *R v Khan (Mohammed Iqbal)* was wrongly decided. No policy reasons were advanced for that view, and we do not share it. The result is one which accords with common sense, and does no violence to the words of the statute.

What was missing in *R v Khan (Mohammed Iqbal)* was the act of sexual intercourse, without which the offence was not completed. What was missing in the present case was damage to the first named property, without which the offence was not complete. The mental state of the defendant in each case contained everything which was required to render him guilty of the full offence. In order to succeed in a prosecution for attempt, it must be shown that the defendant intended to achieve that which was missing from the full offence. Unless that is shown, the prosecution have not proved that the defendant intended to commit the offence. Thus in *R v Khan (Mohammed Iqbal)* [1990] 1 WLR 813 the prosecution had to show an intention to have sexual intercourse, and the remaining state of mind required for the offence of rape. In the present case, the prosecution had to show an intention to damage the first named property, and the remaining state of mind required for the offence of aggravated arson.

The judge in the instant case was faced, as we have been faced, not only with citations of views held by the Law Commission at one time on what should be the law of attempt (Law Commission Report on Criminal Law: Attempt and Impossibility (1980) (Law Com No 102)), but also with various articles in legal journals and books commenting on those views. It is right to say that at one time it was proposed that intention should be required as to all the elements of an offence, thus making it impossible to secure a conviction of attempt in circumstances such as the present. However, this proposal has not prevailed, and has been overtaken by *R v Khan (Mohammed Iqbal)*, and a formulation of the draft code which does not incorporate the proposal.

While the judge in the instant case opined that *R v Khan (Mohammed Iqbal)* was distinguishable she did not indicate any policy reasons for distinguishing it. We see none, and none has been submitted to us directly.'

R v Shivpuri [1986] 2 WLR 988 House of Lords (Lords Hailsham, Elwyn-Jones, Scarman, Bridge, and Mackay)

Impossibility as a defence to attempt

Facts

The defendant, whilst in India, was paid £1,000 to act as a drugs courier. He was required to collect a package containing a consignment of drugs which would be delivered to him in England, and distribute its contents according to instructions which would be given to him. On collecting the package, the defendant was arrested by police officers, and he confessed to them that he believed its contents to be either heroin or cannabis. On further analysis by the police the package was found to contain only a harmless vegetable substance. The defendant was convicted of attempting to be knowingly concerned in dealing with and harbouring a controlled drug, namely heroin, and he appealed unsuccessfully to the Court of Appeal. The defendant renewed his appeal before the House of Lords.

Held

The appeal would be dismissed.

Lord Bridge:

> 'The certified question depends on the true construction of the Criminal Attempts Act 1981. That Act marked an important new departure since, by section 6, it abolished the offence of attempt at common law and substituted a new statutory code governing attempts to commit criminal offences. It was considered by your Lordships' House last year in *Anderton* v *Ryan* [1985] AC 560 after the decision in the Court of Appeal which is the subject of the present appeal. That might seem an appropriate starting point from which to examine the issues arising in this appeal. But your Lordships have been invited to exercise the power under the *Practice Statement (Judicial Precedent)* [1966] 1 WLR 1234 to depart from the reasoning in that decision if it proves necessary to do so in order to affirm the convictions appealed against in the instant case. I was not only a party to the decision in *Anderton* v *Ryan*, I was also the author of one of the two opinions approved by the majority which must be taken to express the House's ratio. That seems to me to afford a sound reason why, on being invited to re-examine the language of the statute in its application to the facts of this appeal, I should initially seek to put out of mind what I said in *Anderton* v *Ryan*. Accordingly I propose to approach the issue in the first place as an exercise in statutory construction, applying the language of the Act to the facts of the case, as if the matter were res integra. If this leads me to the conclusion that the appellant was not guilty of any attempt to commit a relevant offence, that will be the end of the matter. But if this initial exercise inclines me to reach a contrary conclusion, it will then be necessary to consider whether the precedent set by *Anderton* v *Ryan* bars that conclusion or whether it can be surmounted either on the ground that the earlier decision is distinguishable or that it would be appropriate to depart from it under the *Practice Statement*.'

His Lordship then related section 1 of the Criminal Attempts Act 1981 and continued:

> 'Applying this language to the facts of the case, the first question to be asked is whether the appellant intended to commit the offence of being knowingly concerned in dealing with and harbouring drugs of Class A or Class B with intent to evade the prohibition on their importation. Translated into more homely language the question may be rephrased, without in any way altering its legal significance, in the following terms: did the appellant intend to receive and store (harbour) and in due course pass on to third parties (deal with) packages of heroin or cannabis which he knew had been smuggled into England from India? The answer is plainly yes, he did. Next, did he in relation to each offence, do an act which was more than merely preparatory to the commission of the offence? The act relied on in relation to harbouring was the receipt and retention of the packages found in the lining of the suitcase. The act relied on in relation to dealing was the meeting at Southall station with the intended recipient of one of the packages. In each case the act was clearly more than preparatory to the commission of the *intended* offence; it was not and could not be more than merely preparatory to the commission of the *actual* offence, because the facts were such that the commission of the actual offence was impossible. Here then is the nub of the matter. Does the "act which is more than merely preparatory to the commission of the offence" in section 1(1) of the Act of 1981 (the actus reus of the statutory offence of attempt) require any more than an act which is more than

merely preparatory to the commission of the offence which the defendant intended to commit? Section 1(2) must surely indicate a negative answer; if it were otherwise, whenever the facts were such that the commission of the actual offence was impossible, it would be impossible to prove an act more than merely preparatory to the commission of that offence and subsections (1) and (2) would contradict each other.

This very simple, perhaps over simple, analysis leads me to the provisional conclusion that the appellant was rightly convicted of the two offences of attempt with which he was charged. But can this conclusion stand with *Anderton* v *Ryan*? The appellant in that case was charged with an attempt to handle stolen goods. She bought a video recorder believing it to be stolen. On the facts as they were to be assumed it was not stolen. By a majority the House decided that she was entitled to be acquitted. I have re-examined the case with care. If I could extract from the speech of Lord Roskill or from my own speech a clear and coherent principle distinguishing those cases of attempting the impossible which amount to offences under that statute from those which do not, I should have to consider carefully on which side of the line the instant case fell. But I have to confess that I can find no such principle.

Running through Lord Roskill's speech and my own in *Anderton* v *Ryan* [1985] AC 560 is the concept of "objectively innocent" acts which, in my speech certainly, are contrasted with "guilty acts." A few citations will make this clear. Lord Roskill said, at p580:

> "My Lords, it has been strenuously and ably argued for the respondent that these provisions involve that a defendant is liable to conviction for an attempt even where his actions are innocent but he erroneously believes facts which, if true, would make those actions criminal, and further, that he is liable to such conviction whether or not in the event his intended course of action is completed."

He proceeded to reject the argument. At p582 I referred to the appellant's purchase of the video recorder and said: "Objectively considered, therefore, her purchase of the recorder was a perfectly proper commercial transaction." A further passage from my speech proceeded, at pp582-583:

> "The question may be stated in abstract terms as follows. Does section 1 of the Act of 1981 create a new offence of attempt where a person embarks on and completes a course of conduct which is objectively innocent, solely on the ground that the person mistakenly believes facts which, if true, would make that course of conduct a complete crime? If the question must be answered affirmatively it requires convictions in a number of surprising cases: the classic case, put by Bramwell B. in *R* v *Collins* (1864) 9 Cox CC 497, of the man who takes away his own umbrella from a stand, believing it not to be his own and with intent to steal it; the case of the man who has consensual intercourse with a girl over 16 believing her to be under that age; the case of the art dealer who sells a picture which he represents to be and which is in fact a genuine Picasso, but which the dealer mistakenly believes to be a fake. The common feature of all these cases, including that under appeal, is that the mind alone is guilty, the act is innocent."

I then contrasted the case of the man who attempts to pick the empty pocket, saying:

> "Putting the hand in the pocket is the guilty act, the intent to steal is the guilty mind, the offence is appropriately dealt with as an attempt, and the impossibility of committing the full offence for want of anything in the pocket to steal is declared by [subsection (2)] to be no obstacle to conviction."

If we fell into error, it is clear that our concern was to avoid convictions in situations which most people, as a matter of common sense, would not regard as involving criminality. In this connection it is to be regretted that we did not take due note of paragraph 2.97 of the Law Commission's report (Criminal Law: Attempt, and Impossibility in Relation to Attempt, Conspiracy and Incitement (1980) (Law Commission No. 102)) which preceded the enactment of the Act of 1981, which reads:

> "If it is right in principle that an attempt should be chargeable even though the crime which it is sought to commit could not possibly be committed, we do not think that we should be deterred by the consideration that such a change in our law would also cover some extreme and exceptional cases in which a prosecution would be theoretically possible. An example would be where a person is offered goods at such a low price that he believes that they are stolen, when in fact they are not; if he actually purchases them, upon the principles which we have discussed he would be liable for an attempt to handle stolen goods. Another case which has been much debated is that raised in argument by Bramwell B. in *R* v *Collins* (1864) 9 Cox

CC 497. If A takes his own umbrella, mistaking it for one belonging to B and intending to steal B's umbrella, is he guilty of attempted theft? Again, on the principles which we have discussed he would in theory be guilty, but in neither case would it be realistic to suppose that a complaint would be made or that a prosecution would ensue."

The prosecution in *Anderton* v *Ryan* itself falsified the Commission's prognosis in one of the "extreme and exceptional cases." It nevertheless probably holds good for other such cases, particularly that of the young man having sexual intercourse with a girl over 16, mistakenly believing her to be under that age, by which both Lord Roskill and I were much troubled.

However that may be, the distinction between acts which are "objectively innocent" and those which are not is an essential element in the reasoning in *Anderton* v *Ryan* and the decision, unless it can be supported on some other ground, must stand or fall by the validity of this distinction. I am satisfied on further consideration that the concept of "objective innocence" is incapable of sensible application in relation to the law of criminal attempts. The reason for this is that any attempt to commit an offence which involves "an act which is more than merely preparatory to the commission of the offence" but for any reason fails, so that in the event no offence is committed, must ex hypothesi, from the point of view of the criminal law, be "objectively innocent." What turns what would otherwise, from the point of view of the criminal law, be an innocent act into a crime is the intent of the actor to commit an offence. I say "from the point of view of the criminal law" because the law of tort must surely here be quite irrelevant. A puts his hand into B's pocket. Whether or not there is anything in the pocket capable of being stolen, if A intends to steal, his act is a criminal attempt; if he does not so intend, his act is innocent. A plunges a knife into a bolster in a bed. To avoid the complication of an offence of criminal damage, assume it to be A's bolster. If A believes the bolster to be his enemy B and intends to kill him, his act is an attempt to murder B; if he knows the bolster is only a bolster, his act is innocent. These considerations lead me to the conclusion that the distinction sought to be drawn in *Anderton* v *Ryan* between innocent and guilty acts considered "objectively" and independently of the state of mind of the actor cannot be sensibly maintained.

Another conceivable ground of distinction which was to some extent canvassed in argument, both in *Anderton* v *Ryan* and in the instant case, though no trace of it appears in the speeches in *Anderton* v *Ryan*, is a distinction which would make guilt or innocence of the crime of attempt in a case of mistaken belief dependent on what, for want of a better phrase, I will call the defendant's dominant intention. According to the theory necessary to sustain this distinction, the appellant's dominant intention in *Anderton* v *Ryan* was to buy a cheap video recorder; her belief that it was stolen was merely incidental. Likewise in the hypothetical case of attempted unlawful sexual intercourse, the young man's dominant intention was to have intercourse with the particular girl; his mistaken belief that she was under 16 was merely incidental. By contrast, in the instant case the appellant's dominant intention was to receive and distribute illegally imported heroin or cannabis.

Whilst I see the superficial attraction of this suggested ground of distinction, I also see formidable practical difficulties in its application. By what test is a jury to be told that a defendant's dominant intention is to be recognised and distinguished from his incidental but mistaken belief? But there is perhaps a more formidable theoretical difficulty. If this ground of distinction is relied on to support the acquittal of the appellant in *Anderton* v *Ryan*, it can only do so on the basis that her mistaken belief that the video recorder was stolen played no significant part in her decision to buy it and therefore she may be acquitted of the intent to handle stolen goods. But this line of reasoning runs into head-on collision with section 1(3) of the Act of 1981. The theory produces a situation where, apart from the subsection, her intention would not be regarded as having amounted to any intent to commit an offence. Section 1(3)(*b*) then requires one to ask whether, if the video recorder had in fact been stolen, her intention would have been regarded as an intent to handle stolen goods. The answer must clearly be yes, it would. If she had bought the video recorder knowing it to be stolen, when in fact it was, it would have availed her nothing to say that her dominant intention was to buy a video recorder because it was cheap and that her knowledge that it was stolen was merely incidental. This seems to me fatal to the dominant intention theory.

'I am thus led to the conclusion that there is no valid ground on which *Anderton* v *Ryan* can be distinguished. I have made clear my own conviction, which as a party to the decision (and craving the indulgence of my noble and learned friends who agreed in it) I am the readier to express, that the decision was wrong. What then is to be done? If the case is indistinguishable, the application of the strict doctrine of precedent would require that the present appeal be allowed. Is it permissible to depart from precedent under the *Practice Statement (Judicial Precedent)* [1966] 1 WLR 1234 notwithstanding the especial need for certainty in the criminal law? The following considerations lead me to answer that question affirmatively. First, I am undeterred by the consideration that the decision in *Anderton* v *Ryan* was so recent. The *Practice Statement* is an effective abandonment of our pretention to infallibility. If a serious error embodied in a decision of this House has distorted the law, the sooner it is corrected the better. Secondly, I cannot see how, in the very nature of the case, anyone could have acted in reliance on the law as propounded in *Anderton* v *Ryan* in the belief that he was acting innocently and now find that, after all, he is to be held to have committed a criminal offence. Thirdly, to hold the House bound to follow *Anderton* v *Ryan* because it cannot be distinguished and to allow the appeal in this case would, it seems to me, be tantamount to a declaration that the Act of 1981 left the law of criminal attempts unchanged following the decision *R* v *Smith* [1975] AC 476. Finally, if, contrary to my present view, there is a valid ground on which it would be proper to distinguish cases similar to that considered in *Anderton* v *Ryan*, my present opinion on that point would not foreclose the option of making such a distinction in some future case.

I cannot conclude this opinion without disclosing that I have had the advantage, since the conclusion of the argument in this appeal, of reading an article by Professor Glanville Williams entitled "The Lords and Impossible Attempts, or Quis Custodiet Ipsos Custodes?" [1986] CLJ 33. The language in which he criticises the decision in *Anderton* v *Ryan* is not conspicuous for its moderation, but it would be foolish, on that account, not to recognise the force of the criticism and churlish not to acknowledge the assistance I have derived from it.

I would answer the certified question in the affirmative and dismiss the appeal.'

R v *Walker & Hayles* (1990) 90 Cr App R 226 Court of Appeal (Criminal Division) (Lloyd LJ, Gatehouse and Pill JJ)

Attempted murder – mens rea

Facts
The appellants carried out a violent attack upon a man named Royston John, which involved dropping him from a third floor balcony to the ground. The appellants were charged with attempted murder. The jury were directed that they could convict if they were sure that the appellants intended to kill the victim, in the sense that they were sure that the appellants knew that there was a 'very high degree of probability' that the victim would be killed. Following conviction, the appellants appealed on the basis that the trial judge had misdirected the jury as to the mental element required on a charge of attempted murder.

Held
The appeal would be dismissed.

Lloyd LJ:

'We turn to the main ground of appeal, namely the direction on intention. Since the charge was attempted murder, the prosecution had to prove an intention to kill. Intention to cause really serious harm would not have been enough. We were told that this is the first case in which this Court has had to consider the correct direction in a case of attempted murder since *R* v *Moloney* (1985) 81 Cr App R 93, [1985] AC 905, *R* v *Hancock and Shankland* (1986) 82 Cr App R 264, [1986] AC 55, and *Nedrick* (1986) 83 Cr App R 267, [1986] 3 All ER 1.

We have already said that there could be no criticism of the initial direction at the start of the summing-up, and repeated at the conclusion. The recorder was right to keep it short. "Trying to kill" was the expression he used as a paraphrase. That was easy for the jury to understand, and could not on any view of the law be regarded as too favourable to the prosecution. "Trying to kill" is synonymous with purpose. It has never been suggested that a man does not intend what he is trying to achieve. The difficulty only arises when he brings about a result which he is not trying to achieve.

But when the jury returned, the recorder, as we have seen, went further. The first question we have had to consider is whether he was right to go further, or whether he should simply have repeated what he had already said, perhaps adding that the jury should consider all the circumstances and use their commonsense. One of the recorder's difficulties – as it has been a difficulty for us – is that the question is not strictly grammatical. But we think that what the jury probably wanted to know could be paraphrased as follows:

> "If we are satisfied that the appellants threw him over, are we bound to go on to consider the question of intention, ie whether they intended to kill or whether it was done in the heat of the moment without any intent? Or is the fact that they threw him over enough?"

If that was indeed the meaning of the question, then it would have been sufficient for the recorder to repeat the direction he had already given. The constant theme of *Moloney* (supra), *Hancock* (supra) and *Nedrick* (supra) is that it is only in rare and exceptional cases that the judge needs to elaborate. Mr Bevan, on behalf of the prosecution, submitted that this was one of those rare and exceptional cases where the recorder was required to elaborate, since the jury were in terms asking for a foresight direction. We do not accept that submission. If our understanding of the question is correct, the jury would have been content with a repetition of the direction which they had already received. We can, however, understand why the recorder went further, since he had only just given a direction in simple terms, which was as clear as could be. Moreover the position is not quite the same in a case of attempted murder as it is in murder. In the great majority of murder cases, as the Court pointed out in *Nedrick* (supra), the defendant's desire goes hand in hand with his intention. If he desires serious harm, and death results from his action, he is guilty of murder. A simple direction suffices in such cases. The rare and exceptional case is where the defendant does not desire serious harm, or indeed any harm at all. But where a defendant is charged with attempted murder, he may well have desired serious harm, without desiring death. So the desire of serious harm does not provide the answer. It does not go hand in hand with the relevant intention, as it does in the great majority of murder cases, since in attempted murder the relevant intention must be an intention to kill.

Considerations such as these may have led the recorder to give the expanded direction in terms of foresight. But, as we have said, it would have been better if he had not done so. The mere fact that a jury calls for a further direction on intention does not of itself make it a rare and exceptional case requiring a foresight direction. In most cases they will only need to be reminded of the simple direction which they will already have been given, namely that the relevant intention is an intention to kill, and that nothing less will suffice.

But the mere fact that the recorder gave a foresight direction in this case, when he need not have done, does not afford any ground of appeal. And so we turn to the direction itself. The main criticism of the direction is that the recorder should have answered the second half of the question with a resounding "No."

Instead he may have confused the jury. He may have led them to equate the probability of death and the foresight of death with an intention to kill. That was the very error exposed in *R* v *Moloney* (supra) and *Nedrick* (1986) 83 Cr App R 267.

We do not regard this criticism as justified. It ignores the third question which the recorder suggested that the jury should ask themselves. Looking at the further direction as a whole, and not piecemeal, the recorder was following the guidelines in *Nedrick*. We quote from page 270:

> "In *R* v *Hancock* (1986) 82 Cr App R 264, [1986] AC 455, the House decided that the *Moloney* guidelines require a reference to probability. Lord Scarman said at p276 and p473: 'They also require an explanation that the greater the probability of a consequence the more likely it is that the consequence was foreseen and that if that consequence was foreseen the greater the probability is that that consequence was also intended."

When determining whether the defendant had the necessary intent, it may therefore be helpful for a jury to ask themselves two questions:

(1) How probable was the consequence which resulted from the defendant's voluntary act? (2) Did he foresee that consequence? If he did not appreciate that death or really serious harm was likely to result from his act, he cannot have intended to bring it about. If he did, but thought that the risk to which he was exposing the person killed was only slight, then it may be easy for the jury to conclude that he did not intend to bring about that result. On the other hand, if the jury are satisfied that at the material time the defendant recognised that death or serious harm would be virtually certain (barring some unforeseen intervention) to result from his voluntary act, then that is a fact from which they may find it easy to infer that he intended to kill or do serious bodily harm, even though he may not have had any desire to achieve that result."

Questions (1) and (2) in the recorder's further direction correspond precisely with questions (1) and (2) in *Nedrick*. If the answers to (l) and (2) had been no, then no further question would have arisen. But if the answers were to be yes, and the jury were to be sure of it, then the third question would arise. I will read it again:

> "If you are sure of that, the last question is this one: you are entitled to draw the inference that when he joined in chucking John over that balcony wall, he was actually trying to kill him if he could, knowing quite well there was a very high degree of possibility that he would be killed when he hit the ground."

It may be that that could have been better expressed. Few summings-up are perfect. But the message is clear enough. What the recorder was saying was:

> "If you are sure of (l) and (2), you would be entitled to draw the inference that they were intending or trying to kill the victim."

It is important to note that the recorder said that the jury would be entitled to draw the inference: he was not saying that they must draw the inference. By the use of the word "entitled," he was making it sufficiently clear to the jury that the question whether they drew the inference or not was a question for them. This is borne out by the passage which immediately followed in which the recorder said that the jury would be entitled to bear in mind the speed of events on the one hand and the speed at which a man can make up his mind on the other.

So we reject the submission that the recorder was equating foresight with intent, or that he may have given that impression to the jury. He was perfectly properly saying that foresight was something from which the jury could infer intent. He was treating the question as part of the law of evidence, not as part of the substantive law of attempted murder.

The second criticism advanced by both appellants is directed to the use of the expression "very high degree of possibility." We were at once struck by the curious use of the word "possibility" when the recorder had twice referred to "high degree of probability." It occurred to us that "possibility" might be a mistranscription, more especially as degrees of possibility are not easy to understand. A thing is either possible, or it is not. Our view was confirmed when counsel for one of the appellants told us that according to his note of the direction, the recorder did indeed refer to "very high degree of probability," not "possibility." We are greatly obliged to counsel for the very proper assistance thus afforded to the court.

But it does not end there. It was argued that even "very high degree of probability" is a misdirection. The recorder should have used the words "virtual certainty." Counsel relied on the concluding passage from the judgment in *Nedrick* (1986) 83 Cr App R 267, 271, [1986] 3 All ER 1, 4.

> "As Lord Bridge said in *Moloney* (p106 and p925): ' ... the probability of the consequence taken to have been foreseen must be little short of overwhelming before it will suffice to establish the necessary intent.' At p926 he uses the expression 'moral certainty'; at p929 he said, ' ... will lead to a certain consequence unless something unexpected supervenes to prevent it.'

Where the charge is murder and in the rare cases where the simple direction is not enough, the jury should be directed that they are not entitled to infer the necessary intention, unless they feel sure that death or serious bodily harm was a virtual certainty (barring some unforeseen intervention) as a result of the defendant's actions and that the defendant appreciated that such was the case. Where a man realises that it is for all practical purposes inevitable that his actions will result in death or serious harm, the inference may be irresistible that he intended that result, however little he may have desired or wished it to happen. The decision is one for the jury to be reached upon a consideration of all the evidence."

Counsel submitted that virtual certainty is the correct test in all cases where the simple direction is not enough, and that to substitute high degree of probability is to water down that test. We agree with counsel this far, that in the rare cases where an expanded direction is required it is better that the judge should continue to use the term "virtual certainty," which has the authority of this Court in *Nedrick*. We also agree that there is no difference in this respect between the kind of case considered in *Nedrick*, where the question was whether serious harm was intended, even though it was not desired, and the present case, where serious harm was clearly desired and the only question is whether death was intended. In the rare cases where a foresight direction is required, the same language should be used.

But we do not accept that the reference to "very high degree of probability" was a misdirection. The truth is, as Messrs Smith and Hogan point out in Criminal Law 6th ed, at p59, that once one departs from absolute certainty, there is bound to be a question of degree. We do not regard the difference of degree, if there is one, between very high degree of probability on the one hand and virtual certainty on the other as being sufficient to render what the recorder said a misdirection. We note that in Lord Bridge's view no reasonable jury could have acquitted the defendant in *Hyam v DPP* (1974) 59 Cr App R 91, (1975) AC 55 if they had been given the correct direction; yet we would venture to wonder whether serious injury in that case would have been regarded by the jury as more than very highly probable. Whatever the direction we suspect that in practice juries will continue to use their commonsense.

We also note that in the Court of Appeal in *Hancock* (1986) 82 Cr App R 264, this Court chose "highly likely" as the test. Although the House of Lords (ibid [1986] AC 455) did not approve the guideline directions suggested by the Court of Appeal, that was on the ground that juries "are not chosen for their understanding of a logical and phased process leading by question and answer to a conclusion but are expected to exercise practical common sense" (a quotation from Lord Scarman's speech), not because of the use of the term "highly likely." Reading Lord Scarman's speech in *Hancock* at p276 and p473, and the first of the two passages which we have quoted from *Nedrick*, we are not persuaded that it is only when death is a virtual certainty that the jury can infer intention to kill. Providing the dividing line between intention and recklessness is never blurred, and provided it is made clear, as it was here, that it is a question for the jury to infer from the degree of probability in the particular case whether the defendant intended to kill, we would not regard the use of the words "very high degree of probability" as a misdirection. To avoid any misunderstanding, we repeat that in the great majority of cases of attempted murder, as in murder, the simple direction will suffice, without any reference to foresight. In the rare case where an expanded direction is required in terms of foresight, courts should continue to use virtual certainty as the test, rather than high probability.'

30 Defences I

Attorney-General for Northern Ireland* v *Gallagher [1963] AC 349 House of Lords (Lords Reid, Goddard, Tucker, Denning, and Morris)

Premeditated intoxication

Facts

The defendant, who may have been a psychopath, decided to kill his wife. After drinking nearly half a bottle of whisky, he stabbed her to death with a knife. One of the matters for consideration by the House of Lords was whether the defence of intoxication was open to the defendant.

Held

Lord Denning:

'My Lords, this case differs from all others in the books in that the accused man, whilst sane and sober, before he took to the drink, had already made up his mind to kill his wife. This seems to me to be far the worse – and far more deserving of condemnation – than the case of a man who, before getting drunk, has no intention to kill, but afterwards in his cups, whilst drunk, kills another by an act which he would not dream of doing when sober. Yet by the law of England in this latter case his drunkenness is no defence even though it has distorted his reason and his will-power. So why should it be a defence in the present case? And is it made any better by saying that the man is a psychopath?

The answer to the question is, I think, that the case falls to be decided by the general principle of English law that, subject to very limited exceptions, drunkenness is no defence to a criminal charge, nor is a defect of reason produced by drunkenness. This principle was stated by Sir Matthew Hale in his Pleas of the Crown, I, p32, in words which I would repeat here:

> "This vice (drunkenness) doth deprive men of the use of reason, and puts many men into a perfect, but temporary phrenzy ... By the laws of England such a person shall have no privilege by this voluntary contracted madness, but shall have the same judgment as if he were in his right senses".

This general principle can be illustrated by looking at the various ways in which drunkenness may produce a defect of reason:

(a) It may impair a man's powers of perception so that he may not be able to foresee or measure the consequences of his actions as he would if he were sober. Nevertheless he is not allowed to set up his self-induced want of perception as a defence. Even if he did not himself appreciate that what he was doing was dangerous, nevertheless if a reasonable man in his place, who was not befuddled with drink, would have appreciated it, he is guilty: see *R* v *Meade*, [1909] 1 KB 895; 25 TLR 359; 2 Cr App R 54, CCA, as explained in *Director of Public Prosecutions* v *Beard*, [1920] AC 479, 502–504.

(b) It may impair a man's power to judge, between right or wrong, so that he may do a thing when drunk which he would not dream of doing while sober. He does not realise he is doing wrong. Nevertheless he is not allowed to set up his self-induced want of moral sense as a defence. In *Beard's* case Lord Birkenhead LC distinctly ruled that it was not a defence for a drunken man to say he did not know he was doing wrong.

(c) It may impair a man's power of self-control so that he may more readily give way to provocation than if he were sober. Nevertheless he is not allowed to set up his self-induced want of control as a defence. The acts of provocation are to be assessed, not according to their effect on him personally, but according to the effect they would have on a reasonable man in his place. The law on this point was previously in doubt (see the cases considered in *Beard's* case), but it has since been resolved by *R v McCarthy,* [1954] 2 QB 105; [1954] 2 WLR 1044; [1954] 2 All ER 262; 38 Cr App R 74, CCA, *Bedder v Director of Public Prosecutions* [1954] 1 WLR 1119; [1954] 2 All ER 801; 38 Cr App R 133, HL; and section 3 of the Homicide Act, 1957.

The general principle which I have enunciated is subject to two exceptions:

1. If a man is charged with an offence in which a specific intention is essential (as in murder, though not in manslaughter), then evidence of drunkenness, which renders him incapable of forming that intention, is an answer: see *Beard's* case. This degree of drunkenness is reached when the man is rendered so stupid by drink that he does not know what he is doing (see *R v Moore* (1852) 3 Car. & Kir. 319), as where, at a christening, a drunken nurse put the baby behind a large fire, taking it for a log of wood (Gentleman's Magazine, 1748, p570); and where a drunken man thought his friend (lying in his bed) was a theatrical dummy placed there and stabbed him to death (The Times, January 13, 1951). In each of those cases it would not be murder. But it would be manslaughter.

2. If a man by drinking brings on a distinct disease of the mind such as delirium tremens, so that he is temporarily insane within the M'Naughten Rules, that is to say, he does not at the time know what he is doing or that it is wrong, then he has a defence on the ground of insanity: see *R v Davis* (1881) 14 Cox CC 563 and *Beard's* case.

Does the present case come within the general principle or the exceptions to it? It certainly does not come within the first exception. This man was not incapable of forming an intent to kill. Quite the contrary. He knew full well what he was doing. He formed an intent to kill, he carried out his intention and he remembered afterwards what he had done. And the jury, properly directed on the point, have found as much, for they found him guilty of murder. Then does the case come within the second exception? It does not, to my mind, for the simple reason that he was not suffering from a disease of the mind brought on by drink. He was suffering from a different disease altogether. As the Lord Chief Justice observed in his summing up: "If this man was suffering from a disease of the mind, it wasn't a kind that is produced by drink."

So we have here a case of the first impression. The man is a psychopath. That is he has a disease of the mind which is not produced by drink. But it is quiescent. And whilst it is quiescent he forms an intention to kill his wife. He knows it is wrong but still he means to kill her. Then he gets himself so drunk that he has an explosive outburst and kills his wife. At that moment he knows what he is doing but does not know it is wrong. So in that respect – in not knowing it is wrong – he has a defect of reason at the moment of killing. If that defect of reason is due to the drink, it is no defence in law. But if it is due to the disease of the mind, it gives rise to a defence of insanity. No one can say, however, whether it is due to the drink or to the disease. It may well be due to both in combination. What guidance does the law give in this difficulty? That is, as I see it, the question of general public importance which is involved in this case.

My Lords, I think the law on this point should take a clear stand. If a man, whilst sane and sober, forms an intention to kill and makes preparation for it, knowing it is a wrong thing to do, and then gets himself drunk so as to give himself Dutch courage to do the killing, and whilst drunk carries out his intention, he cannot rely on this self-induced drunkenness as a defence to a charge of murder, nor even as reducing it to manslaughter. He cannot say that he got himself into such a stupid state that he was incapable of an intent to kill. So also when he is a psychopath, he cannot by drinking rely on his self-induced defect of reason as a defence of insanity. The wickedness of his mind before he got drunk is enough to condemn him, coupled with the act which he intended to do and did do. A psychopath who goes out intending to kill, knowing it is wrong, and does kill, cannot escape the consequences by making himself drunk before doing it. That is, I believe, the direction which the Lord Chief Justice gave to the jury and which the Court of Criminal Appeal found to be wrong. I think it was right and for this reason I would allow the appeal.

I would agree, of course, that if before the killing he had discarded his intention to kill or reversed it – and then got drunk – it would be a different matter. But when he forms the intention to kill and without interruption proceeds to get drunk and carry out his intention, then his drunkenness is no defence and nonetheless so because it is dressed up as a defence of insanity.'

Attorney-General's Reference (No 2 of 1992) [1993] 3 WLR 982 Court of Appeal (Criminal Division) (Lord Taylor CJ, Judge and Blofeld JJ)

Automatism – whether driving without awareness gives rise to the defence

Facts
The respondent had been involved in a collision on a motorway, having driven his heavy goods vehicle into vehicles parked on the hard shoulder, killing two individuals. The respondent contended that he had not noticed the flashing lights of the parked vehicles, because he had been in a state of automatism, referred to as 'driving without awareness', induced by 'repetitive visual stimulus experienced on long journeys on straight flat roads'. The defence of automatism was left to the jury and the respondent was acquitted. The Attorney-General referred the following question for consideration by the Court of Appeal: 'Whether the state described as "driving without awareness" should, as a matter of law, be capable of founding a defence of authomatism.'

Held
The defence of automatism ought not to have been left to the jury, and the question posed for the court would be answered in the negative.

Lord Taylor CJ:

'It is common ground that, for the purposes of this reference, the court should proceed on the basis of Professor Brown's evidence at it highest. He said that "driving without awareness" is not a scientific term but a provisional, or interim, descriptive phrase coined at a conference he had attended. He said that there are two essential components to the act of driving: collision avoidance and steering within highway lanes. In a state of "driving without awareness", the driver's capacity to avoid a collision ceases to exist. This is because repetitive visual stimuli experienced on long journeys on straight, flat, featureless motorways can induce a trance-like state in which the focal point of forward vision gradually comes nearer and nearer until the driver is focusing just ahead of his windscreen. He therefore fails to see further ahead in the central field of vision. However, peripheral vision continues to send signals which are dealt with subconsciously and enable the driver to steer within highway lanes.

Professor Brown said this condition can occur insidiously without the driver being aware it is happening. However, he also said that usually a driver would "snap out" of the condition in response to major stimuli appearing in front of him. Thus flashing lights would usually cause him to regain full awareness. Professor Brown was unable to explain why that had not happened in the present case. In fact, the respondent told police when interviewed that he had seen the flashing lights some quarter of a mile before reaching them. Professor Brown was also unable to explain why the respondent should have steered, apparently deliberately, on the hard shoulder.

Despite his phrase "driving without awareness", Professor Brown agreed that the driver's body would still be controlling the vehicle, that there would be subconscious motivation to his steering and that although "largely unaware of what was happening ahead" and "largely unaware of steering either" the unawareness was not total. Asked if nothing intrudes into the driver's consciousness when he is in this state, the Professor said: "I would not go so far as to say nothing, but very little." There must, as a matter of common sense, be some awareness if, as Professor Brown accepted, the driver will usually be caused to "snap out" of the condition by strong stimuli noticed by his eyes ...

The extent of the loss of control is crucial in the present case. Mr Jones referred to three other authorities in support of his proposition that automatism requires there to be total destruction of voluntary control and that impairment or reduction of voluntary control is insufficient.

Watmore v *Jenkins* [1962] 2 QB 572 was a decision by a court of five judges in a case where the defendant was a diabetic and sought to raise automatism due to hypoglycaemia as a defence to driving charges. Giving the judgment of the court, Winn J said, at p586:

> "It is ... a question of law what constitutes a state of automatism. It is salutary to recall that this expression is not more than a modern catch-phrase which the courts have not accepted as connoting any wider or looser concept than involuntary movement of the body or limbs of a person."

Later, at p587, he referred to the need for: "such a complete destruction of voluntary control as could constitute in law automatism."

Secondly, Mr Jones relies on *Roberts* v *Ramsbottom* [1980] 1 WLR 823, a civil case in which the defendant driver sought to rely on automatism due to a stroke. Neill LJ said, at p831G: "... I am not concerned with the total loss of consciousness but with a clouding or impairment of consciousness." He then referred, inter alia, to *Watmore* v *Jenkins* [1962] 2 QB 572 and *Hill* v *Baxter* [1958] 1 QB 277 and concluded [1962] 2 QB 572, 832:

> "I am satisfied that in a civil action a similar approach should be adopted. The driver will be able to escape liability if his actions at the relevant time were wholly beyond his control. The most obvious case is sudden unconsciousness. But if he retained some control, albeit imperfect control, and his driving, judged objectively, was below the required standard, he remains liable. His position is the same as a driver who is old or infirm. In my judgment unless the facts establish what the law recognises as automatism the driver cannot avoid liability on the basis that owing to some malfunction of the brain his consciousness was impaired. [Counsel] put the matter accurately, as I see it, when he said: 'One cannot accept as exculpation anything less than total loss of consciousness.'"

The third case relied upon by Mr Jones is *Broome* v *Perkins* [1987] RTR 321, where again a driver charged with careless driving relied on an attack of hypoglycaemia as creating automatism. Glidewell LJ referred to *Bratty*'s case [1963] AC 386 and to *Watmore* v *Jenkins* [1962] 2 QB 572. He said [1987] RTR 321, 330:

> "The question which is posed in the case can be rephrased to ask: 'On the evidence, could the justices properly conclude that the defendant was not conscious of what he was doing and that his actions were involuntary and automatic throughout the whole of the five-mile journey over which the erratic driving was observed?' If, during a part or parts of that journey, they were satisfied his actions were voluntary and not automatic, at those times he was driving ...When driving a motor vehicle, the driver's conscious mind receives signals from eyes and ears, decides on the appropriate course of action as a result of those signals, and gives directions to the limbs to control the vehicle. When a person's actions are involuntary and automatic his mind is not controlling or directing his limbs."

Mr Pert concedes that he can find no authority which runs counter to the principle illustrated by those three cases. Moreover, he conceded that despite Professor Brown's phrase "driving without awareness", the professor's description of the condition showed that it amounts only to reduced or imperfect awareness. There remains the ability to steer the vehicle straight. There is also usually a capacity to react to stimuli appearing in the road ahead. In the present case the respondent admitted he had actually seen the flashing light a quarter of a mile from the scene ...

Here, Mr Pert argues that the precipitating cause of the condition described by Professor Brown was the external factor of motorway conditions. However that may be, the proper approach is that prescribed by Lord Lane CJ in *R* v *Burgess* [1991] 2 QB 92, 96:

> "Where the defence of automatism is raised by a defendant, two questions fall to be decided by the judge before the defence can be left to the jury. The first is whether a proper evidential foundation for the defence of automatism had been laid. The second is whether the evidence shows the case to be one of insane automatism, that is to say, a case which falls within the *M'Naghten* Rules, or one of non-insane automatism."

The first of those questions is the one raised by this reference. In our judgment, the "proper evidential foundation" was not laid in this case by Professor Brown's evidence of "driving without awareness". As the authorities cited above show, the defence of automatism requires that there was a total destruction of voluntary control on the defendant's part. Impaired, reduced or partial control is not enough. Professor Brown accepted that someone "driving without awareness" within his description, retains some control. He would be able to steer the vehicle and usually to react and return to full awareness when confronted by significant stimuli.'

R v Bailey [1983] 1 WLR 760 Court of Appeal (Criminal Division) (Griffiths LJ, Pain and Stuart-Smith JJ)

Self-induced automatism

Facts

The defendant was diabetic. His girlfriend had left him to live with a man named Harrison. The defendant visited Harrison to discuss the situation, and whilst there felt unwell. He took a mixture of sugar and water, but ate nothing. Ten minutes later the defendant struck Harrison on the head with an iron bar. The defendant later claimed to have been unable to control his actions because he had been in a hypoglycaemic state. He was charged, inter alia, under s18 of the Offences Against the Person Act 1861. The trial judge directed the jury that the defence of automatism was not available to the defendant because his automatism had been 'self-induced'. The defendant was convicted under s18, and appealed.

Held

Applying the proviso, the appeal would be dismissed.

Griffiths LJ (having reviewed the facts of the case):

'It was therefore the appellant's case that the attack had taken place during a period of loss of consciousness occurring due to hypoglycaemia caused by his failure to take sufficient food following his last dose of insulin. Accordingly, it was submitted that he had neither the specific intent to cause grievous bodily harm for the purpose of section 18, nor the appropriate mens rea or basic intent for the purpose of the section 20 offence.

But the recorder, in effect, told the jury that this defence was not available to the appellant. He said: "One thing is equally clear, members of the jury, that if that state of malfunctioning was induced by any agency or self-induced incapacity, then the defence of automatism does not apply." It is clear from the rest of the summing-up that "self-induced" in this context meant or included the appellant's failure to take sufficient food after his dose of insulin. The recorder appears to have derived this proposition, which he applied to both counts of the indictment, from *R v Quick* [1973] QB 910. In that case the appellant, a nurse in a mental hospital, had attacked a patient. Quick was a diabetic and his defence was that he was in a state of automatism at the time due to hypoglycaemia. The trial judge had ruled that, if established, this amounted to a disease of the mind and could only be relied upon in support of a defence of insanity. Following this ruling, Quick pleaded guilty to assault occasioning actual bodily harm.

The Court of Appeal held that this ruling was wrong and that the malfunctioning caused by the hypoglycaemia was not a disease of the mind and that the appellant was entitled to have his defence considered by the jury. Lawton LJ said, at p922:

"Such malfunctioning, unlike that caused by a defect of reason from disease of the mind, will always relieve an accused from criminal responsibility. A self-induced incapacity will not excuse (see *R v Lipman* [1970] 1 QB 152) nor will one which could have been reasonably foreseen as a result of either doing, or omitting to do something, as, for example, taking alcohol against medical advice after using certain prescribed drugs, or failing to have regular meals whilst taking insulin. From time to time difficult border line cases are likely to arise. When they do, the test suggested by the New Zealand Court of Appeal in *R v Cottle* [1958] NZLR

999, 1011, is likely to give the correct result, viz, can this mental condition be fairly regarded as amounting to or producing a defect of reason from disease of mind?"

But in that case, the offence, assault occasioning actual bodily harm was an offence of basic intent. No specific intent was required. It is now quite clear that even if the incapacity of mind is self-induced by the voluntary taking of drugs or alcohol, the specific intent to kill or cause grievous bodily harm may be negatived. See *R v Majewski* [1977] AC 443. This being so, as it is conceded on behalf of the Crown, the direction to which we have referred cannot be correct so far as the offence under section 18 is concerned.

But it is also submitted that the direction is wrong or at least in too broad and general terms, so far as the section 20 offence is concerned. If the passage quoted above from *R v Quick* correctly represents the law, then the direction given by the recorder was correct so far as the second count was concerned, even though the appellant may have had no appreciation of the consequences of his failure to take food and even though such failure may not have been due to deliberate abstention, but because of his generally distressed condition. In our judgment, the passage from Lawton LJ's judgment was obiter and we are free to re-examine it.

Automatism resulting from intoxication as a result of a voluntary ingestion of alcohol or dangerous drugs does not negative the mens rea necessary for crimes of basic intent, because the conduct of the accused is reckless and recklessness is enough to constitute the necessary mens rea in assault cases where no specific intents forms part of the charge: see *R v Majewski* [1977] AC 443, 476 in the speech of Lord Elwyn Jones LC and in the speech of Lord Edmund-Davies where he said, at p496, quoting from *Stroud, Mens Rea* (1914), p115:

> "The law therefore establishes a conclusive presumption against the admission of proof of intoxication for the purpose of disproving mens rea in ordinary crimes. Where this presumption applies, it does not make 'drunkenness' itself a crime, but the drunkenness is itself an integral part of the crime, as forming, together with the other unlawful conduct charged against the defendant, a complex act of criminal recklessness."

The same considerations apply where the state of automatism is induced by the voluntary taking of dangerous drugs: see *R v Lipman* [1970] 1 QB 152 where a conviction for manslaughter was upheld, the appellant having taken LSD and killed his mistress in the course of an hallucinatory trip. It was submitted on behalf of the Crown that a similar rule should be applied as a matter of public policy to all cases of self-induced automatism. But it seems to us that there may be material distinctions between a man who consumes alcohol or takes dangerous drugs and one who fails to take sufficient food after insulin to avert hypoglycaemia.

It is common knowledge that those who take alcohol to excess or certain sorts of drugs may become aggressive or do dangerous or unpredictable things, they may be able to foresee the risks of causing harm to others, but nevertheless persist in their conduct. But the same cannot be said without more of a man who fails to take food after an insulin injection. If he does appreciate the risk that such a failure may lead to aggressive, unpredictable and uncontrollable conduct and he nevertheless deliberately runs the risk or otherwise disregards it, this will amount to recklessness. But we certainly do not think that it is common knowledge, even among diabetics, that such is a consequence of a failure to take food and there is no evidence that it was known to this appellant. Doubtless he knew that if he failed to take his insulin or proper food after it, he might lose consciousness, but as such he would only be a danger to himself unless he put himself in charge of some machine such as a motor car, which required his continued conscious control.

In our judgment, self-induced automatism, other than due to intoxication from alcohol or drugs, may provide a defence to crimes of basic intent. The question in each case will be whether the prosecution have proved the necessary element of recklessness. In cases of assault, if the accused knows that his actions or inaction are likely to make him aggressive, unpredictable or uncontrolled with the result that he may cause some injury to others, and he persists in the action or takes no remedial action when he knows it is required, it will be open to the jury to find that he was reckless.

Turning again to *R v Quick* [1973] QB 910, 922 and the passage we have quoted, we think that notwithstanding the unqualified terms in which the proposition is stated, it is possible that the Court may not have intended to lay down such an absolute rule. In the following paragraph Lawton LJ considers a number of questions, which are not necessarily exhaustive, which the jury might have wanted to consider if the issue had been left to them. One such question was whether the accused knew that he was getting into a hypoglycaemia episode and if so, why he did not use the antidote of taking sugar which he had been advised to do. These questions suggest that even if the hypoglycaemia was induced by some action or inaction by the accused his defence will not necessarily fail.

In the present case the recorder never invited the jury to consider what the appellant's knowledge or appreciation was of what would happen if he failed to take food after his insulin or whether he realised that he might become aggressive. Nor were they asked to consider why the appellant had omitted to take food in time. They were given no direction on the elements of recklessness. Accordingly, in our judgment, there was also a misdirection in relation to the second count in the indictment of unlawful wounding.

But we have to consider whether, notwithstanding these misdirections, there has been any miscarriage of justice and whether the jury properly directed could have failed to come to the same conclusion. As Lawton LJ said in *Quick's* case at p922, referring to the defence of automatism, it is a "quagmire of law, seldom entered nowadays save by those in desperate need of some kind of defence." This case is no exception. We think it very doubtful whether the appellant laid a sufficient basis for the defence to be considered by the jury at all. But even if he did, we are in no doubt that the jury properly directed must have rejected it. Although an episode of sudden transient loss of consciousness or awareness was theoretically possible, it was quite inconsistent with the graphic description that the appellant gave to the police both orally and in his written statement. There was abundant evidence that he had armed himself with the iron bar and gone to Harrison's house for the purpose of attacking him, because he wanted to teach him a lesson and because he was in the way.

Moreover, the doctor's evidence to which we have referred showed it was extremely unlikely that such an episode could follow some five minutes after taking sugar and water. For these reasons we are satisfied that no miscarriage of justice occurred and the appeal will be dismissed.'

Commentary
R v *Majewski* appears below, reported as *DPP* v *Majewski*.

Bratty v *Attorney-General for Northern Ireland* [1963] AC 386 House of Lords (Viscount Kilmuir LC, Lords Tucker, Denning, Morris and Hodson)

Automatism and insanity distinguished

Facts
The defendant had killed a girl and was charged with her murder. At his trial, evidence was put forward that he may have been suffering from psychomoter epilepsy at the time of the offence. The trial judge directed the jury on the defence of insanity but ruled that the defence of automatism was not available to the defendant. The jury rejected the defence of insanity, and the defendant appealed unsuccessfully to the Court of Criminal Appeal in Northern Ireland. The defendant appealed further to the House of Lords.

Held
The appeal would be dismissed.

Lord Denning:

'My Lords, in the case of *Woolmington* v *Director of Public Prosecutions* [1935] AC 462, 482. Viscount Sankey LC said that "when dealing with a murder case the Crown must prove (a) death as a result of a voluntary act of the accused and (b) malice of the accused."

The requirement that it should be a voluntary act is essential, not only in a murder case, but also in every criminal case. No act is punishable if it is done involuntarily: and an involuntary act in this context – some people nowadays prefer to speak of it as "automatism" – means an act which is done by the muscles without any control by the mind, such as a spasm, a reflex action or a convulsion; or an act done by a person who is not conscious of what he is doing, such as an act done whilst suffering from concussion or whilst sleep-walking. The point was well put by Stephen J in 1889:

> "Can anyone doubt that a man who, though he might be perfectly sane, committed what would otherwise be a crime in a state of somnambulism, would be entitled to be acquitted? And why is this? Simply because he would not know what he was doing,"

See *R v Tolson* (1889) 23 QBD 168, 187. The term "involuntary act" is, however, capable of wider connotations: and to prevent confusion it is to be observed that in the criminal law an act is not to be regarded as an involuntary act simply because the doer does not remember it. When a man is charged with dangerous driving, it is no defence to him to say "I don't know what happened. I cannot remember a thing," see *Hill v Baxter* [1958] 1 QB 277. Loss of memory afterwards is never a defence in itself, so long as he was conscious at the time, see *Russell* v *H M Advocate* [1946] SC(J) 37; *R v Podola* [1960] 1 QB 325; [1959] 3 WLR 718; [1959] 3 All ER 418; 43 Cr App R 220, CCA. Nor is an act to be regarded as an involuntary act simply because the doer could not control his impulse to do it. When a man is charged with murder, and it appears that he knew what he was doing, but he could not resist it, see *Attorney-General for South Australia v Brown* [1960] AC 432; [1960] 2 WLR 588; [1960] 1 All ER 734, PC: though it may go towards a defence of diminished responsibility, in places where that defence is available, see *R v Byrne* [1960] 2 QB 396; [1960] 3 WLR 440; [1960] 3 All ER 1; 44 Cr App R 246, CCA: but it does not render his act involuntary, so as to entitle him to an unqualified acquittal. Nor is an act to be regarded as an involuntary act simply because it is unintentional or its consequences are unforeseen. When a man is charged with dangerous driving, it is no defence for him to say, however truly, "I did not mean to drive dangerously." There is said to be an absolute prohibition against that offence, whether he had a guilty mind or not, see *Hill v Baxter* [1958] 1 QB 277, 282 by Lord Goddard CJ But even though it is absolutely prohibited, nevertheless he has a defence if he can show that it was an involuntary act in the sense that he was unconscious at the time and did not know what he was doing, see *H M Advocate v Ritchie*, 1926 SC (J) 45. *R v Minor* (1955) 15 WWR (NS) 433 and *Cooper v McKenna, ex parte Cooper* [1960] Qd LR 406.

... [A]gain, if the involuntary act proceeds from a disease of the mind, it gives rise to a defence of insanity, but not to a defence of automatism. Suppose a crime is committed by a man in a state of automatism or clouded consciousness due to a recurrent disease of the mind. Such an act is no doubt involuntary, but it does not give rise to an unqualified acquittal, for that would mean that he would be let at large to do it again. The only proper verdict is one which ensures that the person who suffers from the disease is kept secure in a hospital so as not to be a danger to himself or others. That is, a verdict of guilty but insane.'

His Lordship then referred to *R v Charlson* [1955] 1 WLR 317, and Devlin J's ruling in *R v Kemp* (see below), and continued:

'Upon the other point discussed by Devlin J, namely, what is a "disease of the mind" within the M'Naughten Rules, I would agree with him that this is a question for the judge. The major mental diseases, which the doctors call psychoses, such as schizophrenia, are clearly diseases of the mind. But in *Charlson*'s case, Barry J seems to have assumed that other diseases such as epilepsy or cerebral tumour are not diseases of the mind, even when they are such as to manifest themselves in violence. I do not agree with this. It seems to me that any mental disorder which has manifested itself in violence and is prone to recur is a disease of the mind. At any rate it is the sort of disease for which a person should be detained in hospital rather than be given an unqualified acquittal.

It is to be noticed that in *Charlson*'s case and *Kemp*'s case the defence raised only automatism, not insanity. In the present case the defence raised both automatism and insanity. And herein lies the difficulty because of the burden of proof. If the accused says he did not know what he was doing, then, so far as the defence of automatism is concerned, the Crown must prove that the act was a voluntary act, see *Woolmington*'s case. But so far as the defence of insanity is concerned, the defence must prove that the act was an involuntary act due to disease of the mind, see *M'Naughten's* case. This apparent incongruity was noticed by Sir Owen Dixon, the Chief Justice of Australia, in an address which is to be found in 31 Australian Law Journal, p255, and it needs to be resolved. The defence here say: Even though we have not proved that the act was involuntary, yet the Crown have not proved that it was a voluntary act: and that point at least should have been put to the jury.

My Lords, I think that the difficulty is to be resolved by remembering that, whilst the *ultimate* burden rests on the Crown of proving every element in the crime, nevertheless in order to prove that the act was a voluntary act, the Crown is entitled to rely on the *presumption* that every man has sufficient mental capacity to be responsible for his crimes: and that if the defence wish to displace that presumption they must give some evidence from which the contrary may reasonably be inferred. Thus a drunken man is presumed to have the capacity to form the specific intent necessary to constitute the crime, unless evidence is given from which it can reasonably be inferred that he was incapable of forming it, see the valuable judgment of the Court of Justiciary in *Kennedy* v *H M Advocate* 1944 SC(J) 171, 177 which was delivered by Lord Normand. So also it seems to me that a man's act is presumed to be a voluntary act unless there is evidence from which it can reasonably be inferred that it was involuntary. To use the words of Devlin J, the defence of automatism "ought not to be considered at all until the defence has produced at least prima facie evidence," see *Hill* v *Baxter* [1958] 1 QB 277, 285; and the words of North J in New Zealand "unless a proper foundation is laid," see *R* v *Cottle* [1958] NZLR 999, 1025. The necessity of laying down the proper foundation is on the defence: and if it is not so laid, the defence of automatism need not be left to the jury, any more than the defence of drunkenness (*Kennedy* v *H M Advocate* 1944 SC(J) 171), provocation (*R* v *Gauthier* (1943) 29 Cr App R 113, CCA) or self-defence (*R* v *Lobell* [1957] 1 QB 547; [1957] 2 WLR 524; [1957] 1 All ER 734; 41 Cr App R 100, CCA) need be.

What, then, is a proper foundation? The presumption of mental capacity of which I have spoken is a provisional presumption only. It does not put the legal burden on the defence in the same way as the presumption of sanity does. It leaves the legal burden on the prosecution, but nevertheless, until it is displaced, it enables the prosecution to discharge the ultimate burden of proving that the act was voluntary. Not because the presumption is evidence itself, but because it takes the place of evidence. In order to displace the presumption of mental capacity, the defence must give sufficient evidence from which it may reasonably be inferred that the act was involuntary. The evidence of the man himself will rarely be sufficient unless it is supported by medical evidence which points to the cause of the mental incapacity. It is not sufficient for a man to say "I had a black-out": for "black-out" as Stable J said in *Cooper* v *McKenna, ex parte Cooper* [1960] Qd LR 406 at 419, "is one of the first refuges of a guilty conscience and a popular excuse." The words of Devlin J in *Hill* v *Baxter* should be remembered: "I do not doubt that there are genuine cases of automatism and the like, but I do not see how the layman can safely attempt without the help of some medical or scientific evidence to distinguish the genuine from the fraudulent."

When the only cause that is assigned for an involuntary act is drunkenness, then it is only necessary to leave drunkenness to the jury, with the consequential directions, and not to leave automatism at all. When the only cause that is assigned for it is a disease of the mind, then it is only necessary to leave insanity to the jury, and not automatism. When the cause assigned is concussion or sleep-walking, there should be some evidence from which it can reasonably be inferred before it should be left to the jury. If it is said to be due to concussion, there should be evidence of a severe blow shortly beforehand. If it is said to be sleep-walking, there should be some credible support for it. His mere assertion that he was asleep will not suffice.

Once a proper foundation is thus laid for automatism, the matter becomes at large and must be left to the jury. As the case proceeds, the evidence may weigh first to one side and then to the other: and so the burden may appear to shift to and fro. But at the end of the day the legal burden comes into play and requires that the jury should be satisfied beyond reasonable doubt that the act was a voluntary act.'

R* v *Burgess [1991] 2 WLR 1206 Court of Appeal (Criminal Division) (Lord Lane CJ, Roch and Morland JJ)

Sleep-walking – whether automatism or insanity

Facts
The appellant lived alone but was friendly with the woman, who lived in the flat below his, a Ms Katrina Curtis. On the evening in question he visited her flat to watch a video. During the course of the evening she fell asleep on the sofa. She was awoken by the appellant smashing a bottle over her head. Before she could stop him he had picked up the video recorder and brought it down on her head causing cuts and bruises. The appellant was charged on two counts alleging wounding and wounding with intent. At his trial the appellant adduced expert medical evidence to the effect that he had been sleep-walking at the time of the attack and that the defence of automatism should be put before the jury. The trial judge ruled that the only defence the evidence revealed was that of insanity, and the jury in due course found him not guilty by reason of insanity. The appellant's contention was that the defence of automatism should have been left to the jury.

Held
The appeal would be dismissed.

Lord Lane CJ (after considering the facts of the case, and the meaning given to the concept 'disease of the mind' by Devlin J in *R* v *Kemp* [1957] 1 QB 399):

> 'The appellant plainly suffered from a defect of reason from some sort of failure (for lack of a better term) of the mind causing him to act as he did without conscious motivation. His mind was to some extent controlling his actions which were purposive rather than the result simply of muscular spasm, but without his being consciously aware of what he was doing. Can it be said that that "failure" was a disease of the mind rather than a defect or failure of the mind not due to disease? That is the distinction, by no means always easy to draw, upon which this case depends, as others have depended in the past.
>
> One can perhaps narrow the field of inquiry still further by eliminating what are sometimes called the "external factors" such as concussion caused by a blow on the head. There were no such factors here. Whatever the cause may have been, it was an "internal" cause. The possible disappointment or frustration caused by unrequited love is not to be equated with something such as concussion. On this aspect of the case, we respectfully adopt what was said by Martin J and approved by a majority in the Supreme Court of Canada in *Rabey* v *The Queen* [1980] 2 SCR 513, 519, 520 (where the facts bore a similarity to those in the instant case although the diagnosis was different):
>
>> "Any malfunctioning of the mind or mental disorder having its source primarily in some subjective condition or weakness internal to the accused (whether fully understood or not) may be a 'disease of the mind' if it prevents the accused from knowing what he is doing, but transient disturbances of consciousness due to certain specific external factors do not fall within the concept of disease of the mind ... In my view, the ordinary stresses and disappointments of life which are the common lot of mankind do not constitute an external cause constituting an explanation for a malfunctioning of the mind which takes it out of the category of a 'disease of the mind.' To hold otherwise would deprive the concept of an external factor of any real meaning." '

Lord Lane CJ then referred to the speeches of Lord Diplock in *R* v *Sullivan* [1984] AC 156 (at p172), and Lord Denning in *Bratty* v *Attorney-General for Northern Ireland* [1963] AC 386 (at p412) and continued:

> 'It seems to us that if there is a danger of recurrence that may be an added reason for categorising the condition as a disease of the mind. On the other hand, the absence of the danger of recurrence is not a reason for saying that it cannot be a disease of the mind. Subject to that possible qualification, we respectfully adopt Lord Denning's suggested definition.

There have been several occasions when during the course of judgments in the Court of Appeal and the House of Lords observations have been made, obiter, about the criminal responsibility of sleep walkers, where sleep walking has been used as a self-evident illustration of non-insane automatism. For example in the speech of Lord Denning, from which we have already cited an extract, appears this passage, at p409:

> "No act is punishable if it is done involuntarily: and an involuntary act in this context – some people nowadays prefer to speak of it as 'automatism' – means an act which is done by the muscles without any control by the mind, such as a spasm, a reflex action or a convulsion; or an act done by a person who is not conscious of what he is doing, such as an act done whilst suffering from concussion or whilst sleep-walking. The point was well put by Stephen J in 18889: 'Can anyone doubt that a man who, though he might be perfectly sane, committed what would otherwise be a crime in a state of somnambulism, would be entitled to be acquitted? And why is this? Simply because he would not know what he was doing.'"

We have also been referred to a Canadian decision, *R v Parks* (1990) 56 CCC (3d) 449. In that case the defendant was charged with murder. The undisputed facts were that he had, whilst according to him he was asleep, at night driven his motor car some 23 kilometres to the house of his wife's parents where he had stabbed and beaten both his mother-in-law and his father-in-law. His mother-in-law died as a result and his father-in-law sustained serious injuries. A number of defence witnesses, including experts in sleep disorders, gave evidence to the effect that sleep-walking is not regarded as a disease of the mind, mental illness or mental disorder, and the trial judge directed the jury that if the accused was in a state of somnambulism at the time of the killing, then he was entitled to be acquitted on the basis of non-insane automatism. The defendant was acquitted of the murder of his mother-in-law and subsequently acquitted of the attempted murder of his father-in-law.

The Crown appealed from the accused's acquittal and it was held by the Ontario Court of Appeal that the appeal should be dismissed. The court concluded that sleep is a normal condition and "the impairment of the respondent's faculties of reason, memory and understanding was caused not by any disorder or abnormal condition but by a natural, normal condition – sleep:" pp465-466.

We accept of course that sleep is a normal condition, but the evidence in the instant case indicates that sleep-walking, and particularly violence in sleep, is not normal. We were told that *R v Parks* is to be taken to the Supreme Court of Canada. That case apart, in none of the other cases where sleep-walking has been mentioned, so far as we can discover, has the court had the advantage of the sort of expert medical evidence which was available to the judge here.

One turns then to examine the evidence upon which the judge had to base his decision and for this purpose the two medical experts called by the defence are the obvious principal sources. Dr d'Orban in examination-in-chief said:

> "On the evidence available to me, and subject to the results of the tests when they became available, I came to the same conclusion as Dr Nicholas and Dr Eames whose reports I had read, and that was that Mr Burgess's actions had occurred during the course of a sleep disorder."

He was asked, "Assuming this is a sleep associated automatism, is it an internal or external factor?" Answer: "In this particular case, I think that one would have to see it as an internal factor."

Then in cross-examination: Question: "Would you go so far as to say that it was liable to recur?" Answer: "Is is possible for it to recur, yes." Finally, in answer to a question from the judge, namely, "Is this a case of automatism associated with a pathological condition or not?" Answer: "I think the answer would have to be yes, because it is an abnormality of the brain function, so it would be regarded as a pathological condition."

Dr Eames in cross-examination agreed with Dr d'Orban as to the internal rather than the external factor. He accepted that there is a liability to recurrence of sleep-walking. He could not go so far as to say that there is no liability of recurrence of serious violence but he agreed with the other medical witnesses that there is no recorded case of violence of this sort recurring.

The prosecution, as already indicated, called Dr Fenwick, whose opinion was that this was not a sleep-walking episode at all. If it was a case where the appellant was unconscious of what he was doing, the most likely explanation was that he was in what is described as an hysterical dissociative state. That is a state in which, for psychological reasons, such as being overwhelmed by his emotions, the person's brain works in a different way. He carries out acts of which he has no knowledge and for which he has no memory. It is quite different from sleep-walking. He then went on to describe features of sleep-walking. This is what he said:

> "Firstly, violent acts in sleep-walking are very common. In just an exposure of one day to a sleep-walking clinic, you will hear of how people are kicked in bed, hit in bed, partially strangled – it is usually just arms around the neck, in bed, which is very common. Serious violence fortunately is rare. Serious violence does recur, or certainly the propensity for it to recur is there, although there are very few cases in the literature – in fact I know of none – in which somebody has come to court twice for a sleep-walking offence. This does not mean that sleep-walking violence does not recur; what it does mean is that those who are associated with the sleeper take the necessary precautions. Finally, should a person be detained in hospital? The answer to this is: Yes, because sleep-walking is treatable. Violent night terrors are treatable. There is a lot which can be done for the sleep-walker, so sending them to hospital after a violent act to have their sleep-walking sorted out, makes good sense."

Dr Fenwick was also of the view that in certain circumstances hysterical dissociative states are also subject to treatment.

It seems to us that on this evidence the judge was right to conclude that this was an abnormality or disorder, albeit transitory, due to an internal factor, whether functional or organic, which had manifested itself in violence. It was a disorder or abnormality which might recur, though the possibility of it recurring in the form of serious violence was unlikely. Therefore since this was a legal problem to be decided on legal principles, it seems to us that on those principles the answer was as the judge found it to be. It does however go further than that. Dr d'Orban, as already described, stated it as his view that the condition would be regarded as pathological. Pathology is the science of diseases. It seems therefore that in this respect at least there is some similarity between the law and medicine.'

Commissioner of Police of the Metropolis v *Caldwell* [1982] AC 341 House of Lords (Lords Wilberforce, Diplock, Edmund-Davies, Keith of Kinkel, and Roskill)

Defence of self-induced intoxication

Facts

The defendant, who had been sacked from his employment at an hotel, became drunk and returned at night to the hotel, setting it on fire. There were ten people resident in the hotel at the time, but the fire was discovered and extinguished before any serious harm could be caused. The defendant pleaded guilty to a charge under s1(1) of the Criminal Damage Act 1971, but pleaded not guilty to the charge under s1(2) of the 1971 Act, which alleged criminal damage with intent to endanger life or recklessness as to whether life would be endangered. His contention was that due to his drunken state it had never crossed his mind that people's lives might be endangered by his actions, he had simply set fire to the hotel because of his grudge against his former employer. The trial judge directed the jury that self-induced intoxication was no defence to a charge under s1(2), and the defendant was convicted. On appeal, the Court of Appeal quashed his conviction for the offence under s1(2), but upheld the sentence of three years' imprisonment in respect of the s1(1) charge. The prosecutor appealed to the House of Lords, the following question being certified for the opinion of their Lordships –

> 'Whether evidence of self-induced intoxication can be relevant to the following questions – (a) Whether the defendant intended to endanger the life of another; and (b) Whether the defendant was reckless as to whether the life of another would be endangered, within the meaning of section 1(2)(b) of the Criminal Damage Act 1971.'

Held (Lords Wilberforce and Edmund-Davies dissenting)
Self-induced intoxication can provide a defence under s1(2) of the 1971 Act where the basis of the charge against the defendant is that he intended to endanger life. Self-induced intoxication would not, however, avail a defendant who was alleged to have been reckless as to whether life would be endangered.

Lords Diplock, Roskill and Keith of Kinkel further expressed the view that a defendant was to be regarded as reckless where he created an obvious risk of a particular type of harm occurring, and either went on to take that risk, or failed to give any thought to its existence.

Lord Diplock:

'As respects the charge under section 1 (2) the prosecution did not rely upon an actual intent of the respondent to endanger the lives of the residents but relied upon his having been reckless whether the lives of any of them would be endangered. His act of setting fire to it was one which the jury were entitled to think created an obvious risk that the lives of the residents would be endangered; and the only defence with which your Lordships are concerned is that the respondent had made himself so drunk as to render him oblivious of that risk. If the only mental state capable of constituting the necessary mens rea for an offence under section 1 (2) were that expressed in the words "intending by the destruction or damage to endanger the life of another," it would have been necessary to consider whether the offence was to be classified as one of "specific" intent for the purposes of the rule of law which this House affirmed and applied in *R v Majewski* [1977] AC 443; and this it plainly is. But this is not, in my view, a relevant inquiry where "being reckless as to whether the life of another would be thereby endangered" is an alternative mental state that is capable of constituting the necessary mens rea of the offence with which he is charged.

The speech of Lord Elwyn-Jones LC in *R v Majewski* [1977] AC 443, 475, with which Lord Simon of Glaisdale, Lord Kilbrandon and I agreed, is authority that self-induced intoxication is no defence to a crime in which recklessness is enough to constitute the necessary mens rea. The charge in *Majewski* was of assault occasioning actual bodily harm and it was held by the majority of the House, approving *R v Venna* [1976] QB 421, 428, that recklessness in the use of force was sufficient to satisfy the mental element in the offence of assault. Reducing oneself by drink or drugs to a condition in which the restraints of reason and conscience are cast off was held to be a reckless course of conduct and an integral part of the crime. The Lord Chancellor accepted at p475 as correctly stating English law the provision in section 2.08 (2) of the American Model Penal Code:

"When recklessness establishes an element of the offence, if the actor due to self-induced intoxication, is unaware of a risk of which he would have been aware had he been sober, such awareness is immaterial."

So, in the instant case, the fact that the respondent was unaware of the risk of endangering lives of residents in the hotel owing to his self-induced intoxication, would be no defence if that risk would have been obvious to him had he been sober.

My Lords, the Court of Appeal in the instant case regarded the case as turning upon whether the offence under section 1 (2) was one of "specific" intent or "basic" intent. Following a recent decision of the Court of Appeal by which they were bound, *R v Orpin* [1980] 1 WLR 1050, they held that the offence under section 1 (2) was one of "specific" intent in contrast to the offence under section 1 (1) which was of basic intent. This would be right if the only mens rea capable of constituting the offence were an actual intention to endanger the life of another. For the reasons I have given, however, classification into offences of "specific" and "basic" intent is irrelevant where being reckless as to whether a particular harmful consequence will result from one's act is a sufficient alternative mens rea.

My Lords, the learned recorder's summing up was not a model of clarity. Contrary to the view of the Court of Appeal she was right in telling the jury that in deciding whether the respondent was reckless as to whether the lives of residents in the hotel would be endangered, the fact that, because of his drunkenness, he failed to give any thought to that risk was irrelevant; but there were other criticisms of the summing up made by the Court of Appeal which your Lordships very properly have not been invited to consider, since it makes no practical difference to the respondent whether the appeal is allowed or not. Since it is not worth while spending time on going into these critcisms, I would dismiss the appeal.

I would give the following answers to the certified question: (a) If the charge of an offence under section 1 (2) of the Criminal Damage Act 1971 is framed so as to charge the defendant only with "*intending* by the destruction or damage [of the property] to endanger the life of another," evidence of self-induced intoxication can be relevant to his defence. (b) If the charge is, or includes, a reference to his "being reckless as to whether the life of another would thereby be endangered," evidence of self-induced intoxication is not relevant.'

Lord Edmund-Davies (dissenting):

'... the second error [on the part of the trial judge] lay in directing the jury without qualification that (a) all arson is an offence of basic intent and, consequently, that (b) since *R v Majewski* [1977] AC 443 it matters not if, by reasons of the defendant's self-intoxication, he may not have foreseen the possibility that his admittedly unlawful actions endangered life.

Something more must be said about (b), having regard to the view expressed by my noble and learned friend, Lord Diplock, ante, p355 D–E, that the speech of Lord Elwyn-Jones LC in *R v Majewski* "is authority that self-induced intoxication is no defence to a crime in which recklessness is enough to constitute the necessary mens rea." It is a view which, with respect, I do not share. In common with all the noble and learned Lords hearing that appeal, Lord Elwyn-Jones LC adopted the well-established (though not universally favoured) distinction between basic and specific intents. *R v Majewski* [1977] 443 related solely to charges of assault, undoubtedly an offence of basic intent, and the Lord Chancellor made it clear that his observations were confined to offences of that nature; see pp473B–C and G–H, 474H–475E, and 476A–D. My respectful view is that *Majewski* accordingly supplies no support for the proposition that, in relation to crimes of specific intent (such as section 1 (2) (b) of the Act of 1971) incapacity to appreciate the degree and nature of the risk created by his action which is attributable to the defendant's self-intoxication is an irrelevance. The Lord Chancellor was dealing simply with crimes of basic intent, and in my judgment it was strictly within that framework that he adopted the view expressed in the American Penal Code quoted at p475D, and recklessness as an element in crimes of specific intent was, I am convinced, never within his contemplation.

For the foregoing reasons, the Court of Appeal were in my judgment right in quashing the conviction under section 1 (2) (b) and substituting a finding of guilty of arson contrary to section 1 (1) and (3) of the Act of 1971. It follows, therefore, that I agree with learned counsel for the respondent that the certified point of law should be answered in the following manner:

Yes, evidence of self-induced intoxication can be relevant both to (a) whether the defendant intended to endanger the life of another, and to (b) whether the defendant was *reckless* as to whether the life of another would be endangered, within the meaning of section 1 (2) (b) of the Criminal Damage Act 1971.

My Lords, it was recently predicted that,"There can hardly be any doubt that all crimes of recklessness except murder will now be held to be crimes of basic intent within *Majewski*": see *Glanville Williams, Textbook of Criminal Law*, p431. That prophecy has been promptly fulfilled by the majority of your Lordships, for, with the progressive displacement of "maliciously" by "intentionally" or "recklessly" in statutory crimes, that will surely be the effect of the majority decision in this appeal. That I regret, for the consequence is that, however grave the crime charged, if recklessness can constitute its mens rea the fact that it was committed in drink can afford no defence. It is a very long time since we had so harsh a law in this country. Having revealed in *R v Majewski* [1977] AC 443, 495B–497C my personal conviction that, on grounds of public policy, a plea of drunkenness cannot exculpate crimes of basic intent and so exercise unlimited sway in the criminal law, I am nevertheless unable to occur that your Lordships' decision should now become the law of the land. For, as Eveleigh LJ said in *R v Orpin* [1980] 1 WLR 1050, 1054:

> "There is nothing inconsistent in treating intoxication as irrelevant when considering the liability of a person who has willed himself to do that which the law forbids (for example, to do something which wounds another), and yet to make it relevant when a further mental state is postulated as an aggravating circumstance making the offence even more serious."

By way of a postscript I would add that the majority view demonstrates yet again the folly of totally ignoring the recommendations of the Butler Committee (Report of the Committee on Mentally Abnormal Offenders (1975) (Cmnd 6244), paras 18, 53–58).

My Lords, I would dismiss the appeal.'

DPP v Beard [1920] AC 479

See references made to this authority in the extracts from speeches in *DPP v Majewski* (below).

DPP v Majewski [1977] AC 142 House of Lords (Lords Elwyn-Jones, Diplock, Simon, Kilbrandon, Salmon, Edmund-Davies and Russell)

Self-induced intoxication as a defence to crimes of basic intent

Facts
The defendant had been convicted on various counts alleging actual bodily harm, and assaults upon police officers. The offences had occurred after the defendant had consumed large quantities of alcohol and drugs, but at the trial Judge Petre had directed the jury that self-induced intoxication was not available as a defence to these basic intent crimes. The defendant appealed unsuccessfully to the Court of Appeal, and now appealed to the House of Lords.

Held
The appeal would be dismissed.

Lord Elwyn-Jones LC:

'Self-induced alcoholic intoxication has been a factor in crimes of violence, like assault, throughout the history of crime in this country. But voluntary drug taking with the potential and actual dangers to others it may cause has added a new dimension to the old problem with which the courts have had to deal in their endeavour to maintain order and to keep public and private violence under control. To achieve this is the prime purpose of the criminal law. I have said "the courts," for most of the relevant law has been made by the judges. A good deal of the argument in the hearing of the appeal turned on that judicial history, for the crux of the case for the Crown was that, illogical as the outcome may be said to be, the judges have evolved for the purpose of protecting the community a substantive rule of law that, in crimes of basic intent as distinct from crimes of specific intent, self-induced intoxication provides no defence and is irrelevant to offences of basic intent, such as assault.

Mr Tucker's case for the appellant was that there was no such substantive rule of law and that if there was, it did violence to logic and ethics and to fundamental principles of the criminal law which had been evolved to determine when and where criminal responsibility should arise.'

His Lordship then referred to counsel for the appellant's main propositions on the need for mens rea to be proved before criminal liability would be imposed and continued:

'A great deal of the argument in the hearing of the appeal turned on the application to the established facts of what Cave J in *R v Tolson* (1889) 23 QBD 168, 181 called "the somewhat uncouth maxim 'actus non facit reum, nisi mens sit rea'." The judgment of Stephen J in that case has long been accepted as authoritative. He said, at p185:

"Though this phrase is in common use, I think it most unfortunate, and not only likely to mislead, but actually misleading, on the following grounds. It mutually suggests that, apart from all particular definitions of crimes, such a thing exists as a 'mens rea,' or 'guilty mind,' which is always expressly or by implication involved in every definition. This is obviously not the case, for the mental elements of different crimes differ widely. 'Mens rea' means in the case of murder, malice aforethought; in the case of theft, an intention to steal; in the case of rape, an intention to have forcible connection with a woman without her consent; and in the case of receiving stolen goods, knowledge that the goods were stolen. In some cases it denotes mere inattention. For instance, in the case of manslaughter by negligence it may mean forgetting to notice a signal. It appears confusing to call so many dissimilar states of mind by one name."

Stephen J concluded, at p187:

"the principle involved appears to me, when fully considered, to amount to no more than this. The full definition of every crime contains expressly or by implication a proposition as to a state of mind. Therefore, if the mental element of any conduct alleged to be a crime is proved to have been absent in any given case, the crime so defined is not committed; or, again, if a crime is fully defined, nothing amounts to that crime which does not satisfy that definition."

When then is the mental element required in our law to be established in assault? This question has been most helpfully answered in the speech of Lord Simon of Glaisdale in *R v Morgan* [1976] AC 182, 216:

"By 'crimes of basic intent' I mean those crimes whose definition expresses (or, more often, applies) a mens rea which does not go beyond the actus reus. The actus reas generally consists of an act and some consequence. The consequence may be closely connected with the act or remotely connected with it: but with a crime of basic intent the mens rea does not extend beyond the act and its consequence, however, remote, as defined in the actus reus. I take assault as an example of a crime of basic intent where the consequence is very closely connected with the act. The actus reus of assault is an act which causes another person to apprehend immediate and unlawful violence. The mens rea corresponds exactly. The prosecution must prove that the accused foresaw that his act would probably cause another person to have apprehension of immediate and unlawful violence, or would possibly have that consequence, such being the purpose of the act, or that he was reckless as to whether or not his act caused such apprehension. This foresight (the term of art is 'intention') or recklessness is the mens rea in assault. For an example of a crime of basic intent where the consequence of the act involved in the actus reus as defined in the crime is less immediate, I take the crime of unlawful wounding. The act is say, the squeezing of a trigger. A number of consequences (mechanical, chemical, ballistic and physiological) intervene before the final consequence involved in the defined actus reus – namely, the wounding of another person in circumstances unjustified by law. But again here the mens rea corresponds closely to the actus reus. The prosecution must prove that the accused foresaw that some physical harm would ensure to another person in circumstances unjustified by law as a probable (or possible and desired) consequence of his act, or that he was reckless as to whether or not such consequence ensued."

How does the fact of self-induced intoxication fit into that analysis? If a man consciously and deliberately takes alcohol and drugs not on medical prescription, but in order to escape from reality, to go "on a trip," to become hallucinated, whatever the description may be and thereby disables himself from taking the care he might otherwise take and as a result by his subsequent actions causing injury to another – does our criminal law enable him to say that because he did not know what he was doing he lacked both intention and recklessness and accordingly is entitled to an acquittal?

Originally the common law would not and did not recognise self-induced intoxication as an excuse. Lawton LJ spoke of the "merciful relaxation" to that rule which was introduced by the judges during the 19th century, and he added, at p411:

"Although there was much reforming zeal and activity in the 19th century, Parliament never once considered whether self-induced intoxication should be a defence generally to a criminal charge. It would have been a strange result if the merciful relaxation of a strict rule of law had ended, without any Parliamentary intervention, by whittling it away to such an extent that the more drunk a man became, provided he stopped short of making himself insane, the better chance he had of an acquittal ... The common law rule still applied but there were exceptions to it which Lord Birkenhead LC, tried to define by reference to specific intent."

There are, however, decisions of eminent judges in a number of Commonwealth cases in Australia and New Zealand, (but generally not in Canada nor in the United States) as well as impressive academic comment in this country, to which we have been referred, supporting the view that it is illogical and inconsistent with legal principle to treat a person who of his own choice and volition has taken drugs and drink, even though he thereby creates a state in which he is not conscious of what he is doing, any differently from a person suffering from the various medical conditions like epilepsy or diabetic coma and who is regarded by the law as free from fault. However our courts have for a very long time regarded in quite another light the state of self-induced intoxication. The authority which for the last half century has been relied upon in this context has been the speech of the Earl of Birkenhead LC in *Director of Public Prosecutions* v *Beard* [1920] AC 479, who stated, at p494:

> "Under the law of England as it prevailed until early in the 19th century voluntary drunkenness was never an excuse for criminal misconduct; and indeed the classic authorities broadly assert that voluntary drunkenness must be considered rather an aggravation than a defence. This view was in terms based upon the principle that a man who by his own voluntary act debauches and destroys his will power shall be no better situated in regard to criminal acts than a sober man."

Lord Birkenhead LC made an historical survey of the way the common law from the 16th century on dealt with the effect of self-induced intoxication upon criminal responsibility. This indicates how, from 1819 on, the judges began to mitigate the severity of the attitude of the common law in such cases as murder and serious violent crime when the penalties of death or transportation applied or where there was likely to be sympathy for the accused, as in attempted suicide. Lord Birkenhead LC concluded, at p499, that (except in cases where the insanity is pleaded) the decisions he cited

> "establish that where a specific intent is an essential element in the offence, evidence of a state of drunkenness rendering the accused incapable of forming such an intent should be taken into consideration in order to determine whether he had in fact formed the intent necessary to constitute the particular crime. If he was so drunk that he was incapable of forming the intent required he could not be convicted of a crime which was committed only if the intent was proved ... In a charge of murder based upon intention to kill or to do grievous bodily harm, if the jury are satisfied that the accused was, by reason of his drunken condition, incapable of forming the intent to kill or to do grievous bodily harm ... he cannot be convicted of murder. But nevertheless unlawful homicide has been committed by the accused, and consequently he is guilty of unlawful homicide without malice aforethought, and that is manslaughter: *per* Stephen J, in *R* v *Doherty* (1887) 16 Cox CC 306, 307."

He concludes the passage:

> "the law is plain beyond all question that in cases falling short of insanity a condition of drunkenness at the time of committing an offence causing death can only, when it is available at all, have the effect of reducing the crime from murder to manslaughter."

From this it seemed clear – and this is the interpretation which the judges have placed upon the decision during the ensuing half century – that it is only in the limited class of cases requiring proof of specific intent that drunkenness can exculpate. Otherwise in no case can it exempt completely from criminal liability.

Unhappily what Lord Birkenhead LC described on p500 as "plain beyond all question" becomes less plain in the passage in his speech on p504 upon which Mr Tucker not unnaturally placed great emphasis. It reads

> "I do not think that the proposition of law deduced from these earlier cases is an exceptional rule applicable only to cases in which it is necessary to prove a specific intent in order to constitute the graver crime eg, wounding with intent to do grievous bodily harm or with intent to kill. It is true that in such cases the specific intent must be proved to constitute the particular crime, but this is, on ultimate analysis, only in accordance with the ordinary law applicable to crime, for, speaking generally (and apart from certain special offences), a person cannot be convicted of a crime unless the mens was rea. Drunkenness, rendering a person incapable of the intent, would be an answer, as it is for example in a charge of attempted suicide."

Why then would it not be an answer in a charge of manslaughter, contrary to the earlier pronouncement at p499? In my view these passages are not easy to reconcile, but I do not dissent from the reconciliation suggested by my noble and learned friend Lord Russell of Killowen. Commenting on the passage on p504 in 1920 shortly after it was delivered, however, Stroud wrote (36 LQR 270):

> "The whole of these observations ... suggest an extension of the defence of drunkenness far beyond the limits which have hitherto been assigned to it. The suggestion, put shortly, is that drunkenness may be available as a defence, upon any criminal charge, whenever it can be shown to have affected mens rea. Not only is there no authority for the suggestion: there is abundant authority, both ancient and modern, to the contrary."

It has to be said that it is on the latter footing that the judges have applied the law before and since *Beard*'s case and have taken the view that self-induced intoxication, however gross and even if it has produced a condition akin to automatism, cannot excuse crimes of basic intent such as the charges of assault which have given rise to the present appeal.'

His Lordship then referred to *Attorney-General for Northern Ireland* v *Gallagher* (above), and *Bratty* v *Attorney-General for Northern Ireland* (above), and continued:

'In no case has the general principle of English law as described by Lord Denning in *Gallagher's* case [1963] AC 349 and exposed again in *Bratty's* case [1963] AC 386 been overruled in this House and the question now to be determined is whether it should be.

I do not for my part regard that general principle as either unethical or contrary to the principles of natural justice. If a man of his own volition takes a substance which causes him to cast off the restraints of reason and conscience, no wrong is done to him by holding him answerable criminally for any injury he may do while in that condition. His course of conduct in reducing himself by drugs and drink to that condition in my view supplies the evidence of mens rea, of guilty mind certainly sufficient for crimes of basic intent. It is a reckless course of conduct and recklessness is enough to constitute the necessary mens rea in assault cases: see *R* v *Venna* [1976] QB 421, per James LJ at p429. The drunkenness is itself an intrinsic, an integral part of the crime, the other part being the evidence of the unlawful use of force against the victim. Together they add up to criminal recklessness. On this I adopt the conclusion of Stroud in 1920, 36 LQR 273 that:

> "... it would be contrary to all principle and authority to suppose that drunkenness" (and what is true of drunkenness is equally true of intoxication by drugs) "can be a defence for crime in general on the ground that a 'person cannot be convicted of a crime unless the mens was rea'. By allowing himself to get drunk, and thereby putting himself in such a condition as to be no longer amenable to the law's commands, a man shows such regardlessness as amounts to mens rea for the purpose of all ordinary crimes."

This approach is in line with the American Model Penal Code (S. 2.08 (2)):

> "When recklessness establishes an element of the offence, if the actor, due to self-induced intoxication, is unaware of a risk of which he would have been aware had he been sober, such unawareness is immaterial."

Acceptance generally of intoxication as a defence (as distinct from the exceptional cases where some additional mental element above that of ordinary mens rea has to be proved) would in my view undermine the criminal law and I do not think that it is enough to say, as did Mr Tucker, that we can rely on the good sense of the jury or of magistrates to ensure that the guilty are convicted. It may well be that Parliament will at some future time consider, as I think it should, the recommendation in the Butler Committee Report on Mentally Abnormal Offenders (Cmnd 6244, 1975) that a new offence of "dangerous intoxication" should be created. But in the meantime it would be irresponsible to abandon the common law rule, as "mercifully relaxed," which the courts have followed for a century and a half.

How the court of trial should deal with an offender in the circumstances we are considering is not a problem which arises on this appeal. It would no doubt take full account of the relevant medical evidence and of all mitigating factors and give careful consideration to the various alternatives, custodial and non-custodial, punitive and curative, now available to the courts. There is no minimum punishment for the class of assaults with which this appeal is concerned and the court's discretion as to how to deal with the offender is wide.

The final question that arises is whether section 8 of the Act of 1967 has had the result of abrogating or qualifying the common law rule. That section emanated from the consideration the Law Commission gave to the decision of the House in *Director of Public Prosecutions* v *Smith* [1961] AC 290. Its purpose and effect was to alter the law of evidence about the presumption of intention to produce the reasonable and probable consequences of one's acts. It was not intended to change the common law rule.

In referring to "all the evidence" it mean to all the *relevant* evidence. But if there is a substantive rule of law that in crimes of basic intent, the factor of intoxication is irrelevant (and such I hold to be the substantive law), evidence with regard to it is quite irrelevant. Section 8 does not abrogate the substantive rule and it cannot properly be said that the continued application of that rule contravenes the section. For these reasons, my conclusion it that the certified question should be answered "Yes," that there was no misdirection in this case and that the appeal should be dismissed.

My noble and learned friends and I think it may be helpful if we give the following indication of the general lines on which in our view the jury should be directed as to the effects upon the criminal responsibility of the accused of drink and drugs or both, whenever death or physical injury to another person results from something done by the accused for which there is no legal justification and the offence with which the accused is charged is manslaughter or assault at common law or the statutory offence of unlawful wounding under section 20, or of assault occasioning actual bodily harm under section 47 of the Offences against the Person Act 1861.

In the cases of these offences it is no excuse in law that, because of drink or drugs which the accused himself had taken knowingly and willingly, he had deprived himself of the ability to exercise self-control, to realise the possible consequences of what he was doing, or even to be conscious that he was doing it. As in the instant case, the jury may be properly instructed that they "can ignore the subject of drink or drugs as being in any way a defence" to charges of this character.'

R v *Hardie* [1985] 1 WLR 64 Court of Appeal (Criminal Division) (Parker LJ, McCowan and Stuart-Smith J)

Non-reckless self-induced intoxication

Facts
The defendant had voluntarily consumed up to seven valium tablets (a non-controlled drug having a sedative effect). Whilst under the influence of the drug he had started a fire in the flat in which he had been living, but claimed to have been unable to remember anything about it. The defendant was convicted of causing criminal damage being reckless as to whether life would be endangered, following the trial judge's direction to the jury that self-induced intoxication was not available by way of defence to a basic intent crime. The defendant appealed.

Held
The appeal would be allowed.

Parker LJ:

'We deal first with the second of Mr Slowe's [Counsel for the appellant] two contentions. Mr Slowe appreciated that the argument was difficult to sustain in the light of *R* v *Caldwell* [above] but distinguished that case on the ground that, there, the accused had pleaded guilty to a charge under section 1(1) of the Act of 1971and had himself given evidence that his actual intention was to damage the property in question. The distinction is valid but in our view of no assistance. The argument advanced really stems from Lord Diplock's speech where he says, at pp354-355:

"Where the charge is under section 1(2) the question of the state of mind of the accused must be approached in stages, corresponding to paragraphs (a) and (b). The jury must be satisfied that what the accused did amounted to an offence under section 1(1), either because he actually intended to destroy or damage the property or because he was reckless (in the sense that I have described) as to whether it might be destroyed or damaged. Only if they are so satisfied must the jury go on to consider whether the accused also either actually intended that the destruction or damage of the property should endanger someone's life or was reckless (in a similar sense) as to whether a human life might be endangered."

For the convenience of the jury in their deliberations it is no doubt necessary that they approach the question of the accused's state of mind by stages. They are, however, concerned with the state of mind at one stage only, namely when he does the relevant act. If, when doing that act, he creates an obvious risk both that property will be destroyed and that the life of another will be endangered and gives no thought to the possibility of there being either risk, the requirements of the subsection are in our judgment clearly satisfied. If, for example, a person drops a lighted match at a petrol station into a bin containing oily rag by a pump in use by the attendant to fill a car and he thereby creates an obvious risk both that property will be damaged and that the life of the attendant will be endangered, but has given no thought to either matter, it would be farcical to say that the elements of the offence in subsection (1) had been fulfilled but those of subsection (2) had not. We reject the contention on the second point.

We now revert to the first point. It is clear from *R v Caldwell* [1982] AC 341 that self-induced intoxication can be a defence where the charge is only one of specific intention. It is equally clear that it cannot be a defence where, as here, the charge included recklessness. Hence, if there was self-intoxication in this case the judge's direction was correct. The problem is whether, assuming that the effect of the valium was to deprive the appellant of any appreciation of what he was doing it, should properly be regarded as self-induced intoxication and thus no answer.

In *R v Majewski* [1977] Lord Elwyn-Jones LC said, at p471:

"If a man consciously and deliberately takes alcohol and drugs not on medical prescription, but in order to escape from reality, to go 'on a trip,' to become hallucinated, whatever the description may be and thereby disables himself from taking the care he might otherwise take and as a result by his subsequent actions causes injury to another – does our criminal law enable him to say that because he did not know what he was doing he lacked both intention and recklessness and accordingly is entitled to an acquittal?"

A little later he said at pp474–475:

"If a man of his own volition takes a substance which causes him to cast off the restraints of reason and conscience, no wrong is done to him by holding him answerable criminally for any injury he may do while in that condition. His course of conduct in reducing himself by drugs and drink to that condition in my view supplies the evidence of mens rea, of guilty mind certainly sufficient for crimes of basic intent. It is a reckless course of conduct and recklessness is enough to constitute the necessary mens rea in assault cases: see *R v Venna* [1976] QB 421, per James LJ at page 429. The drunkenness is itself an intrinsic, and integral part of the crime, the other part being the evidence of the unlawful use of force against the victim. Together they add up to criminal recklessness. On this I adopt the conclusion of Stroud in 1920, 36 LQR 273 that: '... it would be contrary to all principle and authority to suppose that drunkenness' (and what is true of drunkenness is equally true of intoxication by drugs) 'can be a defence for crime in general on the ground that "a person cannot be convicted of a crime unless the mens was rea."' By allowing himself to get drunk, and thereby putting himself in such a condition as to be no longer amenable to the law's commands, a man shows such regardlessness as amounts to mens rea for the purpose of all ordinary crimes."

Later, at p476:

"In the case of these offences it is no excuse in law that, because of drink or drugs which the accused himself had taken knowingly and willingly, he had deprived himself of the ability to exercise self-control, to realise the possible consequences of what he was doing, or even to be conscious that he was doing it."

R v Majewski was a case of drunkenness resulting from alcoholic consumption by the accused whilst under the influence of non-medically prescribed drugs. *R v Caldwell* [1982] AC 341 was a case of plain drunkenness. There can be no doubt that the same rule applies both to self-intoxication by alcohol and intoxication by hallucinatory drugs, but this is because the effects of both are well known and there is therefore an element of recklessness in the self administration of the drug. *R v Lipman* [1970] 1 QB 152 is an example of such a case.

"Intoxication" or similar symptoms may, however, arise in other circumstances. In *R v Bailey* [1983] 1 WLR 760 this Court had to consider a case where a diabetic had failed to take sufficient food after taking a normal dose of insulin and struck the victim over the head with an iron bar. The judge directed the jury that the defence of automatism, ie that the mind did not go with the act, was not available because the incapacity was self-induced. It was held that this was wrong on two grounds (a) because on the basis of *R v Majewski* [1977] AC 443 it was clearly available to the offence embodying specific intent and (b) because although self-induced by the omission to take food it was also available to negative the other offence which was of basic intent only.

Having referred to *R v Majewski* and *R v Lipman* Griffiths LJ, giving the considered judgment of the Court, said, at p764–765:

> "It was submitted on behalf of the Crown that a similar rule should be applied as a matter of public policy to all cases of self-induced automatism. But it seems to us that there may be material distinctions between a man who consumes alcohol or takes dangerous drugs and one who fails to take sufficient food after insulin to avert hypoglycaemia. It is common knowledge that those who take alcohol to excess or certain sorts of drugs may become aggressive or do dangerous or unpredictable things; they may be able to foresee the risks of causing harm to others, but nevertheless persist in their conduct. But the same cannot be said, without more, of a man who fails to take food after an insulin injection. If he does appreciate the risk that such a failure may lead to aggressive, unpredictable and uncontrollable conduct and he nevertheless deliberately runs the risk or otherwise disregards it, this will amount to recklessness. But we certainly do not think that it is common knowledge, even among diabetics, that such is a consequence of a failure to take food; and there is no evidence that it was known to this appellant. Doubtless he knew that if he failed to take his insulin or proper food after it he might lose consciousness but as such he would only be a danger to himself unless he put himself in charge of some machine such as a motor car, which required his continued conscious control. In our judgment, self-induced automatism, other than that due to intoxication from alcohol or drugs, may provide a defence to crimes of basic intent. The question in each case will be whether the prosecution has proved the necessary element of recklessness. In cases of assault, if the accused knows that his actions or inaction are likely to make him aggressive, unpredictable or uncontrolled with the result that he may cause some injury to others and he persists in the action or takes no remedial action when he knows it is required, it will be open to the jury to find that he was reckless."

In the present instance the defence was that the valium was taken for the purpose of calming the nerves only, that it was old stock and that the appellant was told it would do him no harm. There was no evidence that it was known to the appellant or even generally known that the taking of valium in the quantity taken would be liable to render a person aggressive or incapable of appreciating risks to others or have other side effects such that its self-administration would itself have an element of recklessness. It is true that valium is a drug and it is true that it was taken deliberately and not taken on medical prescription, but the drug is, in our view, wholly different in kind from drugs which are liable to cause unpredictability or aggressiveness. It may well be that the taking of a sedative or soporific drug will, in certain circumstances, be no answer, for example in a case of reckless driving, but if the effect of a drug is merely soporific or sedative the taking of it, even in some excessive quantity, cannot in the ordinary way raise a *conclusive* presumption against the admission of proof of intoxication for the purpose of disproving mens rea in ordinary crimes, such as would be the case with alcoholic intoxication or incapacity or automatism resulting from the self-administration of dangerous drugs.

In the present case the jury should not, in our judgment, have been directed to disregard any incapacity which resulted or might have resulted from the taking of valium. They should have been directed that if they came to the conclusion that, as a result of the valium, the appellant was, as the time, unable to appreciate the risks to property and persons from his actions they should then consider whether the taking of valium was itself reckless. We are unable to say what would have been the appropriate direction with regard to the elements of recklessness in this case for we have not seen all the relevant evidence, nor are we able to suggest a model direction, for circumstances will vary infinitely and model directions can sometimes lead to more rather than less confusion. It is sufficient to say that the direction that the effects of valium were necessarily irrelevant was wrong.

In *R v Bailey (John)* [1983] 1 WLR 760 the Court upheld the conviction notwithstanding the misdirection, being satisfied that there had been no miscarriage of justice and that the jury properly directed could not have failed to come to the same conclusion. That is not so in the present case. Properly directed the jury might well have come to the same conclusion. There was, for example, evidence that the valium really did not materially effect the appellant at all at the relevant time, but we are quite unable to say that they must have come to the same conclusion.'

R v Hennessy [1989] 1 WLR 287 Court of Appeal (Criminal Division) (Lord Lane CJ, Rose and Pill JJ)

Nature of automatism and insanity

Facts
The appellant was a diabetic who needed a twice daily insulin injection in order to stabilise his metabolism. For several days the appellant had not eaten or taken insulin. He was stopped by police officers whilst driving a stolen car. In evidence to the police the appellant stated that he could not remember taking the car, and there was medical evidence to suggest that the appellant had been in a state of hyperglycaemia (high blood sugar level) at the time the car was taken. The appellant was charged, inter alia, with taking a conveyance contrary to s12 Theft Act 1968. He sought to rely on the defence of automatism, but the trial judge indicated that he would only be prepared to direct the jury on the defence of insanity, as defined by the M'Naghten Rules (1843), whereupon the appellant changed his plea to one of guilty, and now appealed to the Court of Appeal.

Held
The appeal would be dismissed. Since the appellant had put his state of mind in issue at the trial, the judge had been quite entitled to raise the issue of insanity. In the present case, the appellant's loss of awareness had not resulted from the operation of external factors upon his body, such as the injection of insulin (see *R v Quick* [1973] QB 910 – injection of insulin causing hypoglycaemia, or low blood sugar levels), but instead had resulted from an inherent physical defect, ie diabetes. The hyperglycaemia suffered by diabetics, which was not corrected by insulin, was to be regarded as a disease of the body which affected the mind for the purposes of the M'Naghten rules.

Lord Lane CJ (having considered the facts):

'The defence to these charges accordingly was that the appellant had failed to take his proper twice a day dose of insulin for two or three days and at the time the events in question took place he was in a state of automatism and did not know what he was doing. Therefore it is submitted that the guilty mind, which is necessary to be proved by the prosecution, was not proved, and accordingly that he was entitled to be acquitted.

The judge took the view, rightly in our view, that the appellant, having put his state of mind in issue, the preliminary question which he had to decide was whether this was truly a case of automatism or whether it was a case of legal "insanity" within the M'Naghten Rules – *M'Naghten's Case* (1843) 10 Cl & Fin 200. He concluded that it was the latter, and he so ruled, whereupon the appellant changed his plea to guilty and was sentenced to the terms of imprisonment suspended which we have already mentioned. The judge then certified the case fit for appeal in the terms which I have already described.

The M'Naghten Rules in the earlier part of the last century have in many ways lost their importance; they certainly have lost the importance they once had, but they are still relevant in so far as they may affect the defence of automatism. Although the rules deal with what they describe as insanity, it is insanity in the legal sense and not in the medical or psychological sense. The rules were, as is well known, embodied in replies given by the judges of that day to certain abstract questions which were placed before them. The historical reasons for the questions being posed it is not necessary for us to describe, interesting though they are.

The answer to the questions were these: first that

> "every man is presumed to be sane, and to possess a sufficient degree of reason to be responsible for his crimes, until the contrary be proved to the satisfaction of the jury."

The second rule is:

> "to establish a defence on the ground of insanity, it must be clearly proved that, at the time of the committing of the act, the party accused was labouring under such a defect of reason, from disease of the mind, as not to know the nature and quality of the act he was doing, or, if he did know it, that he did not know what he was doing was wrong."

The importance of the rules in the present context, namely, the context of automatism, is this. If the defendant did not know the nature and quality of his act because of something which *did not* amount to defect of reason from disease of the mind, then he will probably be entitled to be acquitted on the basis that the necessary criminal intent which the prosecution has to prove is not proved. But if, on the other hand, his failure to realise the nature and quality of his act was due to a defect of reason from disease of the mind, then in the eyes of the law he is suffering from insanity, albeit M'Naghten insanity.

It should perhaps be added, in order to complete the picture, though it is not relevant to the present situation, that where a defendant's failure to appreciate what he was doing was wrong, (that is, the second part of rule 2 of the M'Naghten Rules) where the failure is due to some reason other than a defect of reason from disease of the mind, he will generally have no valid defence at all.

If one wants any confirmation, it is to be found, if we may respectfully say so, in *Smith and Hogan, Criminal Law,* 6th ed (1988), p186, where these matters are very helpfully and clearly set out. If we may just cite the passage from that page, it runs as follows:

> "When a defendant puts his state of mind in issue, the question whether he has raised the defence of insanity is one of law for the judge. Whether D, or indeed his medical witnesses, would call the condition on which he relies 'insanity,' is immaterial. The expert witnesses may testify as to the factual nature of the condition but it is for the judge to say whether that is evidence of 'a defect of reason, from disease of the mind,' because, as will appear, these are legal, not medical, concepts."

Then section 2 of the Trial of Lunatics Act 1883, as amended, by section 1 of the Criminal Procedure (Insanity) Act 1964 provides:

> "(1) Where in any indictment or information any act or omission is charged against any person as an offence, and it is given in evidence on the trial of such person for that offence that he was insane, so as not to be responsible, according to law, for his actions at the time when the act was done or omission made, then, if it appears to the jury before whom such person is tried that he did the act or made the omission charged, but was insane as aforesaid at the time when he did or made the same, the jury shall return a special verdict that the accused is not guilty by reason of insanity."

In the present case therefore what had to be decided was whether the defendant's condition was properly described as a disease of the mind. That does not mean any disease of the brain. It means a disease which affects the proper functioning of the mind. There have been a series of authorities on that particular subject. One such instance is *R* v *Kemp* [1957] 1 QB 399 and the judgment of Devlin J therein.

The question in many cases, and this is one such case, is whether the function of the mind was disturbed on the one hand by disease or on the other hand by some external factor.'

His Lordship then considered the views of Lord Diplock expressed in *R* v *Sullivan* [1984] AC 156, at p172, and the comments of Lawton LJ in *R* v *Quick* [1973] QB 910, at pp 922–923, and continued:

> 'Thus in *Quick's* case the fact that his condition was, or may have been due to the injections of insulin, meant that the malfunction was due to an external factor and not to the disease. The drug it was that caused

the hypoglycaemia, the low blood sugar. As suggested in another passage of the judgment of Lawton LJ (at p922G-H), hyperglycaemia, high blood sugar, caused by an inherent defect, and not corrected by insulin is a disease, and if, as the defendant was asserting here, it does cause a malfunction of the mind, then the case may fall within M'Naghten Rules.

The burden of Mr Owen's argument to us is this. It is that the appellant's depression and marital troubles were a sufficiently potent external factor in his condition to override, so to speak, the effect of the diabetic shortage of insulin upon him. He refers us not only to the passage which I have already cited in *R v Quick* [1973] QB 910, 922 but also to a further passage in *Hill v Baxter* [1958] 1 QB 277, 285–286, which is part of the judgment of Devlin J, sitting with Lord Goddard CJ and Pearson J, in the Divisional Court:

> "I have drawn attention to the fact that the accused did not set up a defence of insanity. For the purposes of the criminal law there are two categories of mental irresponsibility, one where the disorder is due to disease and the other where it is not. The distinction is not an arbitrary one. If disease is not the cause, if there is some temporary loss of consciousness arising accidentally, it is reasonable to hope that it will not be repeated and that it is safe to let an acquitted man go entirely free. But if disease is present, the same thing may happen again, and therefore, since 1800, the law has provided that persons acquitted on this ground should be subject to restraint."

That is the submission made by Mr Owen as a basis for saying the judge's decision was wrong and that this was a matter which should have been decided by the jury.

In our judgment, stress, anxiety and depression can no doubt be the result of the operation of external factors, but they are not, it seems to us, in themselves separately or together external factors of the kind capable in law of causing or contributing to a state of automatism. They constitute a state of mind which is prone to recur. They lack the feature of novelty or accident, which is the basis of the distinction drawn by Lord Diplock in *R v Sullivan* [1984] AC 156, 172. It is contrary to the observations of Devlin J, to which we have just referred in *Hill v Baxter* [1958] 1 QB 277, 285. It does not, in our judgment, come within the scope of the exception of some external physical factor such as a blow on the head or the administration of an anaesthetic.

For those reasons we reject the arguments, able though they were, of Mr Owen. It is not in those circumstance necessary for us to consider the further arguments which he addressed to us based upon the decision *R v Bailey* [1983] 1 WLR 760.

In our judgment the reasoning and judgment of the circuit judge were correct. Accordingly this appeal must be dismissed.'

Commentary
See *R v Bingham* [1991] Crim LR 43.

R v Kemp [1957] 1 QB 399 Bristol Assizes (Devlin J)

Disease of the mind for the purposes of insanity

Facts
The defendant had attacked his wife with a hammer. The evidence put forward at his trial showed that he had not appreciated the nature and quality of his action because of arteriosclerosis, which caused a congestion of blood in the brain, and manifested itself in the defendant's irrational behaviour. The defence had submitted that the defendant was not insane within the M'Naghten Rules, and Devlin J considered the matter:

Held
The jury returned a verdict of guilty, but insane.

Devlin J (having referred to the fact that the only aspect of the M'Naghten Rules in issue here was whether the defendant had been suffering from a disease of the mind, he continued):

'The law is not concerned with the brain but with the mind, in the sense that "mind" is ordinarily used, the mental faculties of reason, memory and understanding. If one read for "disease of the mind" "disease of the brain", it would follow that in many cases the plea of insanity would not be established because it could not be proved that the brain had been affected in any way, either by degeneration of the cells or in any other way. In my judgment the condition of the brain is irrelevant and so is the question of whether the condition of the mind is curable or incurable, transitory or permanent. There is no warranty for introducing those considerations into the definition in the M'Naghten Rules. Temporary insanity is sufficient to satisfy them. It does not matter whether it is incurable and permanent or not.

I think that the approach of Mr Lee [Counsel for the Crown] to the definition in the Rules is the right one. He points out the order of the words "a defect of reason, from disease of the mind." The primary thing that has to be looked for is the defect of reason. "Disease of the mind" is there for some purpose, obviously, but the prime thing is to determine what is admitted here, namely, whether or not there is a defect of reason. In my judgment, the words "from disease of the mind" are not to be construed as if they were put in for the purpose of distinguishing between diseases which have a mental origin and diseases which have a physical origin, a distinction which in 1843 was probably little considered. They were put in for the purpose of limiting the effect of the words "defect of reason." A defect of reason is by itself enough to make the act irrational and therefore normally to exclude responsibility in law. But the Rule was not intended to apply to defects reason caused simply by brutish stupidity without rational power. It was not intended that the defence should plead "although with a healthy mind he nevertheless had been brought up in such a way that he had never learned to exercise his reason, and therefore he is suffering from a defect of reason." The words ensure that unless the defect is due to a diseased mind and not simply to an untrained one there is insanity within the meaning of the Rules.

Hardening of the arteries is a disease which is shown on the evidence to be capable of affecting the mind in such a way as to cause a defect, temporarily or permanently, of its reasoning, understanding and so on, and so is in my judgment a disease of the mind which comes within the meaning of the Rules.'

R v *Kingston* [1994] 3 WLR 519 House of Lords (Lords Keith, Goff, Browne-Wilkinson, Mustill and Slynn)

Involuntary intoxication – whether a defence

Facts
The respondent, a homosexual paedophile who had committed an indecent assault on a 15-year-old boy, claimed that prior to these acts he had been drugged by his co-defendant, and could not recall the incident. There was a difference of medical opinion as to the extent to which the drugs, believed to have been consumed by the respondent, would have affected his ability to recall the incident. However, there was no evidence to suggest that the drugs would have made the respondent do anything he would not have done under normal circumstances. The trial judge ruled that whilst it was not open to the jury to acquit the respondent if they found that his intent to commit the indecent assault had been induced by the surreptitious administration of drugs by his co-defendant, it was open to them to find that secretly administered drugs could negative the respondent's mens rea. The respondent appealed successfully to the Court of Appeal.

The prosecution appealed to the House of Lords.

Held
The appeal would be allowed.

Lord Mustill (having reviewed the facts, his Lordship continued):

'On these facts there are three grounds on which the respondent might be held free from criminal responsibility. First, that his immunity flows from general principles of the criminal law. Secondly, that this immunity is already established by a solid line of authority. Finally, that the court should, when faced with a new problem acknowledge the justice of the case and boldly create a new common law defence.

It is clear from the passage already quoted that the Court of Appeal adopted the first approach. The decision was explicitly founded on general principle. There can be no doubt what principle the court relied upon, for at the outset the court [1994] QB 81, 87, recorded the submission of counsel for the respondent:

> "the law recognises that, exceptionally, an accused person may be entitled to be acquitted if there is a possibility that although his act was intentional, the intent itself arose out of circumstances for which he bears no blame."

The same proposition is implicit in the assumption by the court that if blame is absent the necessary mens rea must also be absent.

My Lords, with every respect I must suggest that no such principle exists or, until the present case, had ever in modern times been thought to exist. Each offence consists of a prohibited act or omission coupled with whatever state of mind is called for by the statute or rule of the common law which creates the offence. In those offences which are not absolute the state of mind which the prosecution must prove to have underlain the act or omission – the "mental element" – will in the majority of cases be such as to attract disapproval. The mental element will then be the mark of what may properly be called a "guilty mind". The professional burglar is guilty in a moral as well as a legal sense; he intends to break into the house to steal, and most would confidently assert that this is wrong. But this will not always be so. In respect of some offences the mind of the defendant, and still less his moral judgment, may not be engaged at all. In others, although a mental activity must be the motive power for the prohibited act or omission the activity may be of such a kind or degree that society at large could not criticise the defendant's conduct severely or even criticise it at all. Such cases are not uncommon. Yet to assume that contemporary moral judgments affect the criminality of the act, as distinct from the punishment appropriate to the crime once proved, is to be misled by the expression "mens rea", the ambiguity of which has been the subject of complaint for more than a century. Certainly, the "mens" of the defendant must usually be involved in the offence; but the epithet "rea" refers to the criminality of the act in which the mind is engaged, not to its moral character.'

His Lordship referred to the Privy Council decision in *Yip Chiu-Cheung* v *R* [1994] 3 WLR 514, and concluded:

'I would therefore reject that part of the respondent's argument which treats the absence of moral fault on the part of the appellant as sufficient in itself to negative the necessary mental element of the offence.'

Having considered the respondent's arguments based on *Pearson's Case* 2 Lew 144, and *Hale's Historia Placiforum Coronae*, he continued:

'There is, however, another line of authority to be considered, for it is impossible to consider the exceptional case of involuntary intoxication without placing it in the context of intoxication as a whole. This area of the law is controversial, as regards the content of the rules, their intellectual foundations, and their capacity to furnish a practical and just solution. Since the law was not explored in depth during the arguments and since it is relevant only as part of the background it is better not to say any more about it than is strictly necessary. Some consideration of the law laid down in *R* v *Majewski* [1977] AC 443 is however inevitable. As I understand the position it is still the law that in the exceptional case where intoxication causes insanity the M'Naghten Rules (*M'Naghten's* Case (1843) 10 Cl & F 200) apply: see *Director of Public Prosecutions* v *Beard* [1920] AC 479, 501 and *Attorney-General for Northern Ireland* v *Gallagher* [1963] AC 349. Short of this, it is no answer for the defendant to say that he would not have done what he did had he been sober, provided always that whatever element of intent is required by the offence is proved to have been present. As was said in *R v Sheehan* [1975] 1 WLR 739, 744C, "a drunken intent is nevertheless an intent". As to proof of intent, it appears that at least in some instances self-induced intoxication can be taken into account as part of the evidence from which the jury draws its conclusions; but that in others it cannot. I express the matter in this guarded way because it has not yet been decisively established whether for this purpose there is a line to be drawn between offences of "specific" and of "basic" intent. That in at least some cases a defendant cannot say that he was so drunk that he could not form the required intent is however clear enough. Why is this so? The answer must I believe be the same as that given in other common law jurisdictions: namely that such evidence is excluded as a matter of policy ...

... There remains the question by what reasoning the House put this policy into effect. As I understand it two different rationalisations were adopted. First that the absence of the necessary consent is cured by treating the intentional drunkenness (or more accurately, since it is only in the minority of cases that the drinker sets out to make himself drunk, the intentional taking of drink without regard to its possible effects) as a substitute for the mental element ordinarily required by the offence. The intent is transferred from the taking of drink to the commission of the prohibited act. The second rationalisation is that the defendant cannot be heard to rely on the absence of the mental element when it is absent because of his own voluntary acts. Borrowing an expression from a far distant field it may be said that the defendant is estopped from relying on his self-induced incapacity.

Your Lordships are not required to decide how these two explanations stand up to attack, for they are not attacked here. The task is only to place them in the context of an intoxication which is not voluntary. Taking first the concept of transferred intent, if the intoxication was not the result of an act done with an informed will there is no intent which can be transferred to the prohibited act, so as to fill the gap in the offence. As regards the "estoppel" there is no reason why the law should preclude the defendant from relying on a mental condition which he had not deliberately brought about. Thus, once the involuntary nature of the intoxication is added the two theories of *Majewski* fall away, and the position reverts to what it would have been if *Majewski* [1977] AC 443 had not been decided, namely that the offence is not made out if the defendant was so intoxicated that he could not form an intent. Thus, where the intoxication is involuntary *Majewski* does not *subtract* the defence of absence of intent; but there is nothing in *Majewsjki* to suggest that where intent is proved involuntary intoxication *adds* a further defence.

My Lords, in the absence of guidance from English authorities it is useful to inquire how other common law jurisdictions have addressed the same problem.'

His Lordship reviewed the relevant Scottish authorities and continued:

'My Lords, I cannot find in this material any sufficient grounds for holding that the defence relied upon is already established by the common law, any more than it can be derived from general principles. Accordingly, I agree with the analysis of Professor Griew, Archbold News, 28 May 1993, pp4–5:

> "What has happened is that the Court of Appeal has recognised a new *defence* to criminal charges in the nature of an exculpatory excuse. It is precisely because the defendant acted in the prohibited way with the intent (the mens rea) required by the definition of the offence that he needs this defence."

There is thus a crucial difference between the issue raised by the second line of argument and that now under scrutiny. As to the former, the Law Commission aptly said, in Consultation Paper No 127 (1993) on Intoxication and Criminal Liability, pp4–5, para 1.12:

> "The person who commits criminal acts while he is intoxicated, at least when he is voluntarily so intoxicated, does not therefore appeal to excuse; but rather raises the prior question of whether, because of his intoxicated state, he can be proved to have been in the (subjective) state of mind for liability. Issues of intoxication are, thus, intimately bound up with the prosecution's task of proving the primary guilt of the defendant: that he did indeed do the act prohibited by the definition of the offence with the relevant state of mind."

By contrast, the excuse of involuntary intoxication, if it exists, is superimposed on the ordinary law of intent.

To recognise a new defence of this type would be a bold step. The common law defences of duress and necessity (if it exists) and the limited common law defence of provocation are all very old. Since counsel for the appellant was not disposed to emphasise this aspect of the appeal the subject was not explored in argument, but I suspect that the recognition of a new general defence at common law has not happened in modern times. Nevertheless, the criminal law must not stand still, and if it is both practical and just to take this step, and if judicial decision rather than legislation is the proper medium, then the courts should not be deterred simply by the novelty of it. So one must turn to consider just what defence is now to be created. The judgment under appeal implies five characteristics.

1. The defence applies to all offences, except perhaps to absolute offences. It therefore differs from other defences such as provocation and diminished responsibility.

2. The defence is a complete answer to a criminal charge. If not rebutted it leads to an outright acquittal, and unlike provocation and diminished responsibility leaves no room for conviction and punishment for a lesser offence. The underlying assumption must be that the defendant is entirely free from culpability.

3. It may be that the defence applies only where the intoxication is due to the wrongful act of another and therefore affords no excuse when, in circumstances of no greater culpability, the defendant has intoxicated himself by mistake (such as by shortsightedly taking the wrong drug). I say that this may be so, because it is not clear whether, since the doctrine was founded in part of the dictum of Park J in *Pearson's* Case, 2 Lew 144, the "fraud or stratagem of another" is an essential element, or whether this was taken as an example of a wider principle.

4. The burden of disproving the defence is on the prosecution.

5. The defence is subjective in nature. Whereas provocation and self-defence are judged by the reactions of the reasonable person in the situation of the defendant, here the only question is whether this particular defendant's inhibitions were overcome by the effect of the drug. The more susceptible the defendant to the kind of temptation presented, the easier the defence is to establish.

My Lords, since the existence or otherwise of the defence has been treated in argument at all stages as a matter of existing law the Court of Appeal had no occasion to consider the practical and theoretical implications of recognising this new defence at common law, and we do not have the benefit of its views. In their absence, I can only say that the defence appears to run into difficulties at every turn. In point of theory, it would be necessary to reconcile a defence of irresistible impulse derived from a combination of innate drives and external disinhibition with the rule that irresistible impulse of a solely internal origin (not necessarily any more the fault of the offender) does not in itself excuse although it may be a symptom of a disease of the mind: *Attorney-General for South Australia* v *Brown* [1960] AC 432. Equally, the state of mind which founds the defence superficially resembles a state of diminished responsibility, whereas the effect in law is quite different. It may well be that the resemblance is misleading, but these and similar problems must be solved before the bounds of a new defence can be set.

On the practical side there are serious problems. Before the jury could form an opinion on whether the drug might have turned the scale witnesses would have to give a picture of the defendant's personality and susceptibilities, for without it the crucial effect of the drug could not be assessed; pharmacologists would be required to describe the potentially disinhibiting effect of a range of drugs whose identity would, if the present case is anything to go by, be unknown; psychologists and psychiatrists would express opinions, not on the matters of psychopathology familiar to those working within the framework of the Mental Health Acts but on altogether more elusive concepts. No doubt as time passed those concerned could work out techniques to deal with these questions. Much more significant would be the opportunities for a spurious defence. Even in the field of road traffic the "spiked" drink as a special reason for not disqualifying from driving is a regular feature. Transferring this to the entire range of criminal offences is a disturbing prospect. The defendant would only have to assert, and support by the evidence of well-wishers, that he was not the sort of person to have done this kind of thing, and to suggest an occasion when by some means a drug might have been administered to him for the jury to be sent straight to the question of a possible disinhibition. The judge would direct the jurors that if they felt any legitimate doubt on the matter – and by its nature the defence would be one which the prosecution would often have no means to rebut – they must acquit outright, all questions of intent, mental capacity and the like being at this stage irrelevant.

My Lords, the fact that a new doctrine may require adjustment of existing principles to accommodate it, and may require those involved in criminal trials to learn new techniques, is not of course a ground for refusing to adopt it, if that is what the interests of justice require. Here, however, justice makes no such demands, for the interplay between the wrong done to the victim, the individual characteristics and frailties of the defendant, and the pharmacological effects of whatever drug may be potentially involved can be far better recognised by a tailored choice from the continuum of sentences available to the judge than by the application of a single yea-or-nay jury decision. To this, there is one exception. The mandatory life sentence for murder, at least as present administered, leaves no room for the trial judge to put into practice an informed and sympathetic assessment of the kind just described. It is for this reason alone that I have felt any hesitation about rejecting the argument for the respondent. In the end however I have concluded that this is not a sufficient reason to force on the theory and practice of the criminal law an exception which would otherwise be unjustified. For many years mandatory sentences have impelled juries to return merciful but false verdicts, and have stimulated the creation of partial defences such as provocation and diminished responsibility whose lack of a proper foundation has made them hard to apply in practice. I do not think it right that the law should be further distorted simply because of this anomalous relic of the history of the criminal law.

All this being said, I suggest to your Lordships that the existing work of the Law Commission in the field of intoxication could usefully be enlarged to comprise questions of the type raised by this appeal, and to see whether by statute a merciful, realistic and intellectually sustainable solution could be newly created. For the present, however, I consider that no such regime now exists, and that the common law is not a suitable vehicle for creating one.'

R v *Lipman* [1970] 1 QB 152 Court of Appeal (Criminal Division) (Widgery and Fenton Atkinson LJJ, and James J)

Intoxication as a defence to basic intent crimes

Facts
The defendant, having voluntarily consumed a quantity of an hallucenogenic drug, killed a woman whilst under the delusion that he was fighting snakes in the centre of the earth. His defence of intoxication was rejected at his trial. He was convicted of manslaughter, and appealed.

Held
The appeal would be dismissed.

Widgery LJ:

'As to manslaughter, the jury were directed that it would suffice for the Crown to prove that "he must have realised before he got himself into the condition he did by taking the drugs that acts such as those he subsequently performed and which resulted in the death were dangerous." In this court Mr Eastham contends that this was a misdirection, and that the jury should have been directed further that it was necessary for the Crown to prove that the defendant intended to do acts likely to result in harm, or foresaw that harm would result from what he was doing.

For the purposes of criminal responsibility we see no reason to distinguish between the effect of drugs voluntarily taken and drunkenness voluntarily induced. As to the latter there is a great deal of authority.'

After referring, inter alia, to *DPP* v *Beard* [1920] AC 479, *Bratty* v *Attorney-General for Northern Ireland*, above, and *Attorney-General for Northern Ireland* v *Gallagher*, above, his Lordship continued:

We can dispose of the present application by reiterating that when the killing results from an unlawful act of the prisoner no specific intent has to be proved to convict of manslaughter, and self-induced intoxication is accordingly no defence. Since in the present case the acts complained of were obviously likely to cause harm to the victim (and did, in fact, kill her) no acquittal was possible and the verdict of manslaughter, at the least, was inevitable.

If and so far as this matter raises a point of law on which the defendant was entitled to appeal without leave, such appeal is dismissed.'

R v *Quick* [1973] QB 910 Court of Appeal (Criminal Division) (Lawton LJ, Mocatta and Milmo JJ)

Automatism and insanity distinguished

Facts
The defendant, a diabetic, was employed as a nurse in a psychiatric hospital. He was charged with assaulting a patient, but had contended that this had occurred whilst he had been in a hypoglycaemia state (low blood sugar level due to an excess of insulin). Following the trial judge's direction that the evidence did not disclose the defence of automatism, the defendant changed his plea to one of guilty, and appealed.

Held
The appeal would be allowed.

Lawton LJ (having referred, inter alia, to *Bratty* v *Attorney-General for Northern Ireland* (above) and *R* v *Kemp* (above) he continued):

'Applied without qualification of any kind, Devlin J's statement of the law [in *R* v *Kemp*] would have some surprising consequences. Take the not uncommon case of the rugby player who gets a kick on the head early in the game and plays on to the end in a state of automatism. If, whilst he was in that state, he assaulted the referee, it is difficult to envisage any court adjudging that he was not guilty by reason of insanity. Another type of case which could occur is that of the dental patient who kicks out whilst coming round from an anaesthetic. The law would be in a defective state if a patient accused of assaulting a dental nurse by kicking her whilst regaining consciousness could only excuse himself by raising the defence of insanity.

In *Hill* v *Baxter* [1958] 1 QB 277, the problem before the Divisional Court was whether the accused had put forward sufficient evidence on a charge of dangerous driving to justify the justices adjudging that he should be acquitted, there having been no dispute that at the time when his car collided with another one he was at the driving wheel. At the trial the accused had contended that he became unconscious as a result of being overcome by an unidentified illness. The court (Lord Goddard CJ, Devlin and Pearson JJ) allowed an appeal by the prosecution against the verdict of acquittal. In the course of examining the evidence which had been put forward by the accused the judges made some comments of a general nature. Lord Goddard CJ referred to some observations of Humphreys J in *Kay* v *Butterworth* (1945) 173 LT 191 which seemed to indicate that a man who became unconscious whilst driving due to the onset of a sudden illness should not be made liable at criminal law and went on as follows, at 282,

"I agree that there may be cases when the circumstances are such that the accused could not really be said to be driving at all. Suppose he had a stroke or an epileptic fit, both instances of what may properly be called Acts of God; he might well be in the driver's seat even with his hands on the wheel but in such a state of unconsciousness that he could not be said to be driving ... In this case, however, I am content to say that the evidence falls far short of what would justify a court holding that this man was in some automatous state."

Lord Goddard CJ did not equate unconsciousness due to a sudden illness, which must entail the malfunctioning of the mental process of the sufferer, with disease of the mind, and in our judgment no one outside the court of law would. Devlin J in his judgment at 285 accepted that some temporary loss of consciousness arising *accidentally* (the italics are ours) did not call for a verdict based on insanity. It is not clear what he meant by "accidentally". The context suggests that he may have meant "unexpectedly" as can happen with some kind of virus infections. He went on as follows:

> "If, however, disease is present the same thing may happen again and therefore since 1800 the law has provided that persons acquitted on this ground should be subject to restraint."

If this be right anyone suffering from a tooth abscess who knows from past experience that he reacts violently to anaesthetics because of some constitutional bodily disorder which can be attributed to disease might have to go on suffering or take the risk of being found insane unless he could find a dentist who would be prepared to take the risk of being kicked by a recovering patient. It seems to us that the law should not give the words "defect of reason from disease of the mind" a meaning which would be regarded with incredulity outside the court.

The last of the English authorities is *Watmore* v *Jenkins* [1962] 2 QB 572 ... In the course of the argument in that case counsel for the accused is reported as having submitted, on the basis of how Lord Murray had directed the jury in *H M Advocate* v *Ritchie* 1926 JC 45:

> "Automatism is a defence to a charge of dangerous driving provided that a person takes reasonable steps to prevent himself from acting involuntarily in a manner dangerous to the public. It must be caused by some factor which he could not reasonably foresee and not by a self-induced incapacity ... "

Subject to the problem of whether the conduct said to have been in a state of automatism was caused by a disease of the mind, we agree with this submission. In this case, had the jury been left to decide whether the appellant Quick at the material time was insane, or in a state of automatism or just drunk, they probably would not have had any difficulty in making up their minds.'

Having referred to a number of Commonwealth authorities, his Lordship continued:

'In this quagmire of law seldom entered nowadays save by those in desperate need of some kind of defence, *Bratty* v *Attorney-General for Northern Ireland*, (supra), provides the only firm ground. Is there any discernible path? We think there is – judges should follow in a common sense way their sense of fairness. This seems to have been the approach of the New Zealand Court of Appeal in *R* v *Cottle* [1958] NZLR 999, and of Sholl J in *R* v *Carter* [1959] VR 105. In our judgment no help can be obtained by speculating (because that is what we would have to do) as to what the judges who answered the House of Lords' questions in 1843 meant by disease of the mind, still less what Sir Matthew Hale meant in the second half of the 17th century [(1682) Vol J, Ch IV.] A quick backward look at the state of medicine in 1843 will suffice to show how unreal it would be to apply the concepts of that age to the present time. Dr Simpson had not yet started his experiments with chloroform, the future Lord Lister was only 16 and laudanum was used and prescribed like aspirins are today. Our task has been to decide what the law means now by the words "disease of the mind". In our judgment the fundamental concept is of a malfunctioning of the mind caused by disease. A malfunctioning of the mind of transitory effect caused by the application to the body of some external factor such as violence, drugs, including anaesthetics, alcohol and hypnotic influences, cannot fairly be said to be due to disease. Such malfunctioning, unlike that caused by a defect of reason from disease of the mind, will not always relieve an accused from criminal responsibility. A self-induced incapacity will not excuse [see *R* v *Lipman*, [1970] 1 QB 152] nor will one which could have been reasonably foreseen as a result of either doing, or omitting to do something, as, for example, taking alcohol against medical advice after using certain prescribed drugs, or failing to have regular meals whilst taking insulin. From time to time difficult borderline cases are likely to arise. When they do, the test suggested by the New Zealand Court of Appeal in *R* v *Cottle* [1958] NZLR 999 is likely to give the correct result, viz. can this mental condition be fairly regarded as amounting to or producing a defect of reason from disease of the mind?

In this case Quick's alleged mental condition, if it ever existed, was not caused by his diabetes but by his use of the insulin prescribed by his doctor. Such malfunctioning of the mind as there was, was caused by an external factor and not a bodily disorder in the nature of a disease which disturbed the working of his mind. It follows in our judgment that Quick was entitled to have his defence of automatism left to the jury and that Bridge J's ruling as to the effect of the medical evidence called by him was wrong. Had the defence of automatism been left to the jury, a number of questions of fact would have had to be answered. If he was in a confused mental condition, was it due to a hypoglycaemic episode or to too much alcohol? If the former, to what extent had he brought about his condition by not following his doctor's instructions about taking regular meals? Did he know that he was getting into a hypoglycaemic episode? If Yes, why did he not use the antidote of eating a lump of sugar as he had been advised to do? On the evidence which was before the jury Quick might have had difficulty in answering these questions in a manner which would have relieved him of responsibility for this acts. We cannot say, however, with the requisite degree of confidence, that the jury would have convicted him. It follows that this conviction must be quashed on the ground that the verdict was unsatisfactory.'

R v Sullivan [1984] AC 156 House of Lords (Lords Diplock, Scarman, Lowry, Bridge and Brandon)

Automatism and insanity distinguished

Facts
The defendant, whilst suffering from a minor epileptic fit, had kicked another man about the head and body. He was charged under s20 of the Offences Against the Person Act 1861, and sought to rely on the defence of automatism. The trial judge ruled that he would be willing to direct the jury on the defence of insanity, but not automatism, whereupon the defendant changed his plea to one of guilty, and appealed unsuccessfully to the Court of Appeal. On appeal to the House of Lords;

Held
The appeal would be dismissed.

Lord Diplock:

'The evidence as to pathology of a seizure due to psychomotor epilepsy can be sufficiently stated for the purposes of this appeal by saying that after the first stage, the prodram, which precedes the fit itself, there is a second stage, the ictus, lasting a few seconds, during which there are electrical charges into the temporal lobes of the brain of the sufferer. The effect of these discharges is to cause him in the post-ictal stage to make movements which he is not conscious that he is making, including, and this was a characteristic of previous seizures which the appellant had suffered, automatic movements of resistance to anyone trying to come to his aid. These movements of resistance might, though in practice they very rarely would, involve violence.

At the conclusion of the evidence, the judge, in the absence of the jury, was asked to rule whether the jury should be directed that if they accepted this evidence it would not be open to them to bring in a verdict of "not guilty," but they would be bound in law to return a special verdict of "not guilty by reason of insanity." The judge ruled that the jury should be so directed.

After this ruling, the appellant, on the advice of his counsel and with the consent of the prosecution and the judge, changed his plea to guilty of assault occasioning actual bodily harm. The jury, on the direction of the judge, brought in a verdict of guilty of that offence, for which the judge sentenced him to three years' probation subject to the condition that during that period he submitted to treatment under the direction of Dr Fenwick at the Maudsley Hospital.

My Lords, neither the legality nor the propriety of the procedure adopted after the judge's ruling has been canvassed in this House; nor was it canvassed in the Court of Appeal to which an appeal was brought upon the ground that the judge ought to have left to the jury the defence of non-insane automatism which, if accepted by them, would have entitled the appellant to a verdict of "not guilty." In these circumstances the present case does not appear to be one in which it would be appropriate of this House to enter into a consideration of the procedure following in the Central Criminal Court after the judge's ruling; more particularly, as it raises some questions that will shortly come before your Lordships for argument in another appeal.

The Court of Appeal held that Judge Lymbery's ruling had been correct. It dismissed the appeal and certified that a point of law of general public importance was involved in the decision, namely: "Whether a person who is proved to have occasioned, contrary to section 47 of the Offences against the Person Act 1861, actual bodily harm to another, whilst recovering from a seizure due to psychomotor epilepsy and who did not know what he was doing when he caused such harm and has no memory of what he did should be found not guilty by reason of insanity."

My Lords, for centuries up to 1843, the common law relating to the concept of mental disorder as negativing responsibility for crimes was in the course of evolution, but I do not think it necessary for your Lordships to embark upon an examination of the pre-1843 position. In that year, following upon the acquittal of one Daniel McNaghten, for shooting Sir Robert Peel's secretary, in what today would probably be termed a state of paranoia, the question of insanity and criminal responsibility was the subject of debate in the legislative chamber of the House of Lords, the relevant statute then in force being the Criminal Lunatics Act 1800 (39 & 40 Geo 3, c 94) "for the safe custody of Insane Persons charged with Offences," which referred to persons who were "insane" at the time of the commission of the offence, but contained no definition of insanity. The House invited the judges of the courts of common law to answer five abstract questions on the subject of insanity as a defence to criminal charges. The answer to the second and third of these questions combined was given to Tindal CJ on behalf of all the judges, except Maule J, and constituted what became known as the McNaghten Rules. The judge's answer is in the following well-known terms (see *McNaghten's Case* (1843) 10 Cl & Fin 200, 210): "the jurors ought to be told in all cases that every man is to be presumed to be sane, and to possess a sufficient degree of reason to be responsible for his crimes, until the contrary be proved to their satisfaction; and that to establish a defence on the ground of insanity, it must be clearly proved that, at the time of the committing of the act, the party accused was labouring under a defect of reason, from disease of the mind, as not to know the nature and quality of the act he was doing; or, if he did know it, that he did not know he was doing what was wrong."

Although the questions put to the judges by the House of Lords referred to the insane delusions of various kinds, the answer to the second and third question (the McNaghten Rules) is perfectly general in its terms. It is stated to be applicable "in all cases" in which it is sought to "establish a defence on the ground of insanity."

This answer was intended to provide a comprehensive definition of the various matters which had to be proved (on balance of probabilities, as it has since been held) in order to establish that he accused was insane within the meaning of the statute of 1800 which, like its successors of 1883 and 1964, make it incumbent upon a jury, if they find the accused to have been "insane" at the time that he committed the acts with which he is charged, to bring in a verdict neither of "guilty" nor of "not guilty" but a special verdict the terms of which have varied under the three successive statutes, but are currently "not guilty by reason of insanity."

The McNaghten Rules have been used as a comprehensive definition for this purpose by the courts for the past 140 years. Most importantly, they were so used by this House in *Bratty v Att-Gen For Northern Ireland* [above]. That case was in some respects the converse of the instant case. Bratty was charged with murdering a girl by strangulation. He claimed to have been unconscious of what he was doing at the time he strangled the girl and he sought to run as alternative defences non-insane automatism and insanity. The only evidential foundation that he laid for either of these pleas was medical evidence that he might have been suffering from psychomotor epilepsy which, if he were, would account for his having been unconscious of what he was doing. No other pathological explanation of his actions having been carried out in a state of automatism was supported by evidence. The trial judge first put the defence of insanity to the jury. The jury rejected it; they declined to bring in the special verdict. Thereupon, the judge refused to put to the jury the alternative defence of automatism. His refusal was upheld by the Court of Criminal Appeal of Northern Ireland and subsequently by this House.

The question before this House was whether, the jury having rejected the plea of insanity, there was any evidence of non-insane automatism fit to be left to the jury. The ratio decidendi of its dismissal of the appeal was that the jury having negatived the explanation that Bratty might have been acting unconsciously in the course of an attack of psychomotor epilepsy, there was no evidential foundation for the suggestion that he was acting unconsciously from any other cause.

In the instant case, as in *Bratty* (supra), the only evidential foundation that was laid for any finding by the jury that the appellant was acting unconsciously and involuntarily when he was kicking Mr Payne, was that when he did so he was in the post-ictal stage of a seizure of psychomotor epilepsy. The evidential foundation in the case of *Bratty*, that he was suffering from psychomotor epilepsy at the time he did the act with which he was charged, was very weak and was rejected by the jury; the evidence in the appellant's case, that he was so suffering when he was kicking Mr Payne, was very strong and would almost inevitably be accepted by a properly directed jury. It would be the duty of the judge to direct the jury that if they did accept the evidence the law required them to bring in a special verdict and none other. The governing statutory provision is to be found in section 2 of the Trial of Lunatics Act 1883. This says "the jury *shall* return a special verdict."

My Lords, I can deal briefly with the various grounds on which it has been submitted that he instant case can be distinguished from what constituted the ratio decidendi in *Bratty*, and that it falls outside the ambit of the McNaghten Rules.

First, it is submitted the medical evidence in the instant case shows that psychomotor epilepsy is not a disease of the mind, whereas in *Bratty* it was accepted by all the doctors that is was. The only evidential basis for this submission is that Dr Fenwick said that in medical terms to constitute a "disease of the mind" or "mental illness," which he appeared to regard as interchangeable descriptions, a disorder of brain functions (which undoubtedly occurs during a seizure in psychomotor epilepsy) must be prolonged for a period of time, usually more than a day; while Dr Taylor would have it that the disorder must continue for a minimum of a month to qualify for the description "disease of the mind."

The nomenclature adopted by the medical profession may change from time to time; Bratty was tried in 1961. But the meaning of the expression "disease of the mind" as the cause of "defect of reason" remains unchanged for the purposes of the application of the McNaghten Rules. I agree with what was said by Devlin J in *Kemp* (1956) 40 Cr App R 121, 128; [1957] 1 QB 399, 407, that "mind" in the McNaghten Rules is used in the ordinary sense of the mental faculties of reason, memory and understanding. If the effect of a disease is to impair these facilities so severely as to have either of the consequences referred to in the later part of the Rules, it matters not whether the aetiology of the impairment is organic, as in epilepsy, or functional, or whether the impairment itself is permanent or is transient and intermittent, provided that it subsisted at the time of the commission of the act. The purpose of the legislation relating to the defence of insanity, ever since its origin in 1800, has been to protect society against recurrence of the dangerous conduct. The duration of a temporary suspension of the mental faculties of reason, memory and understanding, particularly if, as in the appellant's case, it is recurrent, cannot on any rational ground be relevant to the application by the Courts of the McNaghten Rules, though it may be relevant to the course adopted by the Secretary of State, to whom the responsibility for how the defendant is to be dealt with passes after the return of the special verdict of "not guilty by reason of insanity."

To avoid misunderstanding I ought perhaps to add that in expressing my agreement with what was said by Devlin J in *Kemp* (supra) where the disease that caused the temporary and intermittent impairment of the mental faculties was arteriosclerosis, I do not regard that learned judge as excluding the possibility of non-insane automatism (for which the proper verdict would be a verdict of "not guilty") in cases where temporary impairment (not being self-induced by consuming drink or drugs) results from some external physical factor such as a blow on the head causing concussion or the administration of an anaesthetic for therapeutic purposes. I mention this because in *Quick and Paddison* (1973) 57 Cr App R 722, Lawton LJ appears to have regarded the ruling in *Kemp* as going so far as this. If it had done, it would have been inconsistent with the speeches in this House in *Bratty*, where *Kemp* was alluded to without disapproval by Viscount Kilmuir and received the express approval of Lord Denning. The instant case, however, does not in my view afford an appropriate occasion for exploring possible causes of non-insane automatism.

The only other submission in support of the appellant's appeal which I think it necessary to mention is that, because the expert evidence was to the effect that the appellant's acts in kicking Mr Payne were unconscious and thus "involuntary" in the legal sense of that term, his state of mind was not one dealt with by the McNaghten Rules at all, since it was not covered by the phrase "as not to know the nature and quality of the act he was doing." Quite apart from being contrary to all three speeches in this House in *Bratty* (supra) this submission appears to me, with all respect to counsel, to be quite unarguable. Dr Fenwick himself accepted it as an accurate description of the appellant's mental state in the post-ictal stage of a seizure. The audience to whom the phrase in the McNaghten Rules was addressed consisted of peers of the realm in the 1840s when a certain orotundity of diction had not yet fallen out of fashion. Addressed to an audience of jurors in the 1980s it might more aptly be expressed as "He did not know what he was doing."

My Lords, it is natural to feel reluctant to attach the label of insanity to a sufferer from psychomotor epilepsy of the kind to which the appellant was subject, even though the expression in the context of a special verdict of "not guilty by reason of insanity" is a technical one which includes a purely temporary and intermittent suspension of the mental faculties of reason, memory and understanding resulting from the occurrence of an epileptic fit. But the label is contained in the current statute, it has appeared in this statute's predecessors ever since 1800. It does not lie within the power of the courts to alter it. Only Parliament can do that. It has done so twice; it could do so once again.

Sympathise though I do with the appellant, I see no other course open to your Lordships than to dismiss this appeal.'

R v Windle [1952] 2 QB 826 Court of Criminal Appeal (Lord Goddard CJ, Jones and Parker JJ)

Insanity: defendant's ignorance of illegality

Facts
The defendant had killed his wife by administering an overdose of aspirins to her. When interviewed by the police he indicated that he thought he would be hanged for murder. At his trial the judge had refused to allow the defence of insanity to go to the jury on the ground, inter alia, that he had known his actions were unlawful. The defendant appealed.

Held
The appeal would be dismissed.

Lord Goddard CJ:

'The point we have to decide can be put into a very small compass. We are asked to review – I am not sure we are not asked to make new law – what are known as the M'Naghten Rules which in 1843 the judges agreed were the proper tests to be applied in considering the defence of insanity. All the judges, except Maule J, who differed on small points, gave, through the mouth of Tindall CJ, these answers to questions put by the House of Lords ((1843) 10 Cl & F 200, at p210; 4 St Tr (NS) 847, at p931):

"That the jury ought to be told in all cases that every man is presumed to be sane, and to possess a sufficient degree of reason to be responsible for his crimes, until the contrary be proved to their satisfaction; and that, to establish a defence on the ground of insanity, it must be clearly proved that, at the time of the committing of the act, the party accused was labouring under such a defect of reason, from disease of the mind, as not to know the nature and quality of the act he was doing, or, if he did know it, that he did not know he was doing what was wrong."

The argument in this appeal really has been concerned with what is meant by the word "wrong." The evidence that was given on the issue of insanity was that of the doctor called by the appellant and that of the prison doctor who was called by the prosecution. Both doctors expressed without hesitation the view that when the appellant was administering this poison to his wife he knew that he was doing an act which the law forbade. I need not put it higher than that. It may well be that, in the misery in which he had been living with his nagging and tiresome wife who constantly expressed the desire to commit suicide, he thought she was better out of the world than in it. He may have thought it was a kindly act to put her out of her sufferings or imagined sufferings, but the law does not permit such an act as that. There was some exceedingly vague evidence that the appellant was suffering from a defect of reason owing to this communicated insanity, and if the only question in the case had been whether the appellant was suffering from a disease of the mind, that question must have been left to the jury because there was some evidence of it, but that was not the question. The question, as I endeavoured to point out in giving judgment in *Rivett* (1950) 34 Cr App R 87, in all these cases is one of responsibility. A man may be suffering from a defect of reason, but, if he knows that what he is doing is wrong – and by "wrong" is meant contrary to law – he is responsible. Counsel for the appellant, in his very careful argument, suggested that the word "wrong" as it is used in the McNaghten Rules did not mean contrary to law, but had some qualified meaning, that is to say, morally wrong, and that, if a person was in a state of mind through a defect of reason that he thought that what he was doing, although he knew it was wrong in law, was really beneficial, or kind, or praiseworthy, that would excuse him.

Courts of law, however, can only distinguish between that which is in accordance with law and that which is contrary to law. There are many acts which we all know, to use an expression to be found in some of the old cases, are contrary to the law of God and man. In the Decalogue, are the commandments "Thou shalt not kill" and "Thou shalt not steal." Such acts are contrary to the law of man and they are contrary to the law of God. In regard to the Seventh Commandment, "Thou shalt not commit adultery" it will be found that, so far as the criminal law is concerned, though that act is contrary to the law of God, it is not contrary to the law of man. That does not mean that the law encourages adultery: I only say it is not a criminal offence.

The test must be whether an act is contrary to law. In *Rivett* (supra) I referred to the Trial of Lunatics Act, 1883, section 2 (1) of which provides:

"Where in any indictment or information any act or omission is charged against any person as an offence, and it is given in evidence on the trial of such person for that offence that he was insane, so as not to be responsible, according to law, for his actions at the time when the act was done or omission made, then, if it appears to the jury before whom such person is tried that he did the act or made the omission charged, but was insane as aforesaid at the time when he did or made the same, the jury shall return a special verdict ..."

I emphasise again that the test is responsibility "according to law."

I am reminded by Parker J that counsel for the appellant argued that the M'Naghten Rules only applied to delusions. This court cannot agree with that. It is true that when the judges were summoned by their Lordships the occasion had special reference to *McNaghten's case* (supra) but the M'Naghten Rules have ever since that date been generally applied to all cases of insanity, whatever the nature of the insanity or disease of the mind from which the offender is suffering.

In the opinion of the court, there is no doubt that the word "wrong" in the M'Naghten Rules means contrary to law and does not have some vague meaning which may vary according to the opinion of different persons whether a particular act might not be justified. There seems to have been no doubt in this case that it could not be challenged that the appellant knew that what he was doing was contrary to law. In those circumstances what evidence was there that could be left to the jury to suggest that he was entitled to a verdict of Guilty but insane – ie, insane at the time of the act complained of?

Devlin J was right to withdraw the case from the jury. This appeal fails.'

31 Defences II

Abbott v *R* [1977] AC 755

See reference to this authority in extracts from the speeches in *R* v *Howe*, below.

Beckford v *R* [1987] 3 WLR 611

See Chapter 32.

R v *Bourne* [1939] 1 KB 687

See Chapter 23.

R v *Clegg* [1995] 2 WLR 80 House of Lords (Lords Keith, Browne-Wilkinson, Slynn, Lloyd and Nicholls)

Self-defence – homicide – excessive force – whether reducing liability to manslaughter.

Facts

The appellant, whilst serving as a soldier in Northern Ireland, had opened fire on a car that had driven through a check-point. His first three shots were fired at the windscreen of the car as it approached. His fourth and final shot, which was fired into the back of the car as it sped off, hit and killed one of the occupants. At his trial for murder the appellant's contention that he had used reasonable force by way of self-defence, or defence of a colleague, was accepted in relation to the first three shots, but not in relation to the fatal shot. The appellant appealed unsuccessfully to the Court of Appeal in Northern Ireland, which certified the following point of law for determination by the House of Lords: 'Where a soldier or police officer in the course of his duty kills a person by firing a shot with the intention of killing or seriously wounding that person and the firing is in self-defence or in defence of another person, or in the prevention of crime, or in effecting or assisting in the lawful arrest of offenders or suspected offenders or of persons unlawfully at large, but constitutes force which is excessive and unreasonable in the circumstances, is he guilty of manslaughter and not murder?'

Held

The appeal was dismissed. Where the use of excessive force resulted in death the correct conviction was one for murder. There was no valid distinction to be drawn between death resulting from excessive force used in self-defence and similar force used in the prevention of crime, and no exception could be recognised in the case of soldiers or police officers acting in the course of duty.

Lord Lloyd (having dealt with the substantive points raised on the appeal, his Lordship considered the arguments in favour of altering the law):

> 'I have already mentioned some of the arguments in favour of changing the law when dealing with the third question. They have never been expressed more persuasively, or with greater insight, than they

were by the Court of Appeal in the present case. The ground had already been covered by the Criminal Law Revision Committee in its 14th Report in 1980 (Cmnd 7844), at a time when the Australian law had not yet been brought back into line with *Palmer* v *The Queen* [1971] AC 814. In paragraph 73 of the recommendations we find:

> "Where a person kills in a situation in which it is reasonable for some force to be used in self-defence or in the prevention of crime but the defendant uses excessive force, he should be liable to be convicted of manslaughter not murder if, at the time of the act, he honestly believed that the force he used was reasonable in the circumstances."

In paragraph 59 of the Law Commission's draft criminal code (Criminal Law, A Criminal Code for England and Wales (1989) (Law Com No 177, vol 1)) we find:

> "A person who, but for this section, would be guilty of murder is not guilty of murder if, at the time of his act, he believes the use of the force which causes death to be necessary and reasonable to effect a purpose referred to in section 44 (use of force in public or private defence), but the force exceeds that which is necessary and reasonable in the circumstances which exist or (where there is a difference) in those which he believes to exist."

Finally the House of Lords Report of the Select Committee on Murder and Life Imprisonment (Session 1988–89) (HL 78-I), to which I have already referred, found the argument in favour of a qualified defence of using excessive force in self-defence to be convincing. I would refer in particular to the memorandum prepared by Viscount Colville of Culross, vol III, p542. These recommendations are all one way. They are entitled to great weight. But Parliament has not yet acted on them. The question thus arises whether this House can itself develop the law along the lines recommended, without waiting for the legislature. Encouragement to take such a course is to be found in the majority decision of the House in *DPP for Northern Ireland* v *Lynch* [1975] AC 653. In that case the question was whether duress was available as a defence to a person charged with aiding and abetting murder. The House held, by a majority, that it was. Lord Wilberforce said, at pp684–685:

> "The broad question remains how this House, clearly not bound by any precedent, should now state the law with regard to this defence in relation to the facts of the present case. I have no doubt that it is open to us, on normal judicial principles, to hold the defence admissible. We are here in the domain of the common law: our task is to fit what we can see as principle and authority to the facts before us, and it is no obstacle that these facts are new. The judges have always assumed responsibility for deciding questions of principle relating to criminal liability and guilt, and particularly for setting the standards by which the law expects normal men to act. In all such matters as capacity, sanity, drunkenness, coercion, necessity, provocation, self-defence, the common law, through the judges, accepts and sets the standards of right-thinking men of normal firmness and humanity at a level which people can accept and respect. The House is not inventing a new defence: on the contrary, it would not discharge its judicial duty if it failed to define the law's attitude to this particular defence in particular circumstances."

But there are difficulties in adopting this broad approach in the present case, attractive though it might be. In the first place, *DPP for Northern Ireland* v *Lynch* has since been overruled by this House in *R* v *Howe* [1987] AC 417. The dissenting speech of Lord Simon of Glaisdale in *Lynch's* case has been vindicated.

Secondly, the background is different. The defence of duress was the creation of common law. So also, of course, were the defences of self-defence and the use of force in the prevention of crime. The difference is that in the latter case Parliament has already taken a hand by enacting section 3 of the Act of 1967. Parliament did not, in doing so, see fit to create a qualified defence in cases where the defendant uses excessive force in preventing a crime.

In *R* v *Howe*, one of the reasons given for overruling *DPP for Northern Ireland* v *Lynch* was that Parliament had not acted on a recommendation made by the Law Commission 10 years before (Criminal Law, Report on Defences of General Application (1977) (Law Com No 83)): see per Lord Bridge of Harwich, at p437, and Lord Griffiths, at p443. This reasoning has been criticised with some justice, by

Smith & Hogan, 6th ed, p233; 7th ed, p236. There may be many reasons for a failure to legislate. But the criticism does not have the same force in the present case, where Parliament has indeed acted in the very field which is now in dispute, as well as in closely related fields, such as those covered by sections 2 and 3 of the Homicide Act 1957, section 2 of the Suicide Act 1961 and section 1 of the Abortion Act 1967.

In his dissenting speech in *DPP for Northern Ireland* v *Lynch* Lord Simon of Glaisdale said, at pp695–696:

> "I am all for recognising frankly that judges do make law. And I am all for judges exercising this responsibility boldly at the proper time and place – that is, where they can feel confident of having in mind, and correctly weighed, all the implications of their decision, and where matters of social policy are not involved which the collective wisdom of Parliament is better suited to resolve (see *Launchbury* v *Morgans* [1973] AC 127, 136F–137A, 137G). I can hardly conceive of circumstances less suitable than the instant for five members of an appellate committee of your Lordships' House to arrogate to ourselves so momentous a law-making initiative."

Like Lord Simon, I am not averse to judges developing law, or indeed making new law, when they can see their way clearly, even where questions of social policy are involved. A good recent example would be the affirmation by this House of the decision of the Court of Appeal (Criminal Division) that a man can be guilty of raping his wife (*R* v *R* [1992] 1 AC 599). But in the present case I am in no doubt that your Lordships should abstain from law-making. The reduction of what would otherwise be murder to manslaughter in a particular class of case seems to me essentially a matter for decision by legislature, and not by this House in its judicial capacity. For the point in issue is, in truth, part of the wider issue whether the mandatory life sentence for murder should still be maintained. That wider issue can only be decided by Parliament. I would say the same for the point at issue in this case. Accordingly I would answer the certified question of law as follows. On the facts stated, and assuming no other defence is available, the soldier or police officer will be guilty of murder, and not manslaughter. It follows that the appeal must be dismissed.'

R v *Dudley and Stephens* (1884) 14 QBD 273 Queen's Bench Division (Lord Coleridge CJ, Grove and Denman JJ, Pollock and Huddlestone BB)

Availability of the defence of necessity

Facts
The two defendants, a third man and a cabin boy, were cast adrift in a boat following a shipwreck. They were 1600 miles from land, and had endured seven days without food and water, when the defendants decided to kill the cabin boy, who was in any case close to death, so that they might eat his flesh and drink his blood, in the hope that they might then survive long enough to be rescued. Four days after the killing, the three survivors were picked up by a passing vessel. On returning to England the defendants were charged with the boy's murder. The jury returned a special verdict whereby they found that, although the defendants would probably not have survived had they not killed the boy, and that he was likely to have died first anyway, there was no greater necessity for killing the boy than any of the other survivors. The jury's finding was referred to the judges of the Queen's Bench Division.

Held
The defendants could not raise the defence of necessity to a charge of murder.

Lord Coleridge CJ:

> 'Now, except for the purpose of testing how far the conservation of a man's own life is in all cases and under all circumstances, an absolute, unqualified, and paramount duty, we exclude from our consideration all the incidents of war. We are dealing with a case of private homicide, not one imposed upon men in

the service of their Sovereign and in the defence of their country. Now it is admitted that the deliberate killing of this unoffending and unresisting boy was clearly murder, unless the killing can be justified by some well-recognised excuse admitted by the law. It is further admitted that there was in this case no such excuse, unless the killing was justified by what has been called "necessity." But the temptation to the act which existed here was not what the law has ever called necessity. Nor is this to be regretted. Though law and morality are not the same, and many things may be immoral which are not necessarily illegal, yet the absolute divorce of law from morality would be of fatal consequence; and such divorce would follow if the temptation to murder in this case were to he held by law an absolute defence of it. It is not so. To preserve one's life is generally speaking a duty, but it may be the plainest and the highest duty to sacrifice it. War is full of instances in which it is a man's duty not to live, but to die. The duty, in case of shipwreck, of a captain to his crew, of the crew to the passengers, of soldiers to women and children, as in the noble case of the *Birkenhead*; these duties impose on men the moral necessity, not of the preservation, but of the sacrifice of their lives for others, from which in no country, least of all, it is to be hoped, in England, will men ever shrink, as indeed, they have not shrunk. It is not correct, therefore, to say that there is any absolute or unqualified necessity to preserve one's life. "Necesse est ut eam, non ut vivam," is a saying of a Roman officer quoted by Lord Bacon himself with high eulogy in the very chapter on necessity to which so much reference has been made. It would be a very easy and cheap display of commonplace learning to quote from Greek and Latin authors, from Horace, from Juvenal, from Cicero, from Euripides, passage after passage, in which the duty of dying for others has been laid down in glowing and emphatic language as resulting from the principles of heathen ethics; it is enough in a Christian country to remind ourselves of the Great Example whom we profess to follow. It is not needful to point out the awful danger of admitting the principle which has been contended for. Who is to be the judge of this sort of necessity? By what measure is the comparative value of lives to be measured? Is it to be strength, or intellect, or what? It is plain that the principle leaves to him who is to profit by it to determine the necessity which will justify him in deliberately taking another's life to save his own. In this case the weakest, the youngest, the most unresisting, was chosen. Was it more necessary to kill him than one of the grown men? The answer must be "No" –

"So spake the Friend, and with necessity,
The tyrant's plea, excused his devilish deeds."

It is not suggested that in this particular case the deeds were "devilish" but it is quite plain that such a principle once admitted might be made the legal cloak for unbridled passion and atrocious crime. There is no safe path for judges to tread but to ascertain the law to the best of their ability and to declare it according to their judgment; and if in any case the law appears to be too severe on individuals, to leave it to the Sovereign to exercise that prerogative of mercy which the Constitution has intrusted to the hands fittest to dispense it.

It must not be supposed that in refusing to admit temptation to be an excuse for crime it is forgotten how terrible the temptation was; how awful the suffering; how hard in such trials to keep the judgment straight and the conduct pure. We are often compelled to set up standards we cannot reach ourselves, and to lay down rules which we could not ourselves satisfy. But a man has no right to declare temptation to be an excuse, though he might himself have yielded to it, nor allow compassion for the criminal to change or weaken in any manner the legal definition of the crime. It is therefore our duty to declare that the prisoners' act in this case was wilful murder, that the facts as stated in the verdict are no legal justification of the homicide; and to say that in our unanimous opinion the prisoners are upon this special verdict guilty of murder.'

R v *Fitzpatrick* [1977] NI 20 Court of Criminal Appeal in Northern Ireland (Lowry LCJ and Jones LJ)

Denial of duress to defendants voluntarily joining criminal associations

Facts

The defendant had voluntarily joined the IRA. He was subsequently forced, by other IRA members, to take part in serious offences, involving robbery and murder. At his trial the defendant had sought to rely on the defence of duress, but the trial judge had ruled that it was not available to a defendant who voluntarily joined a violent criminal association, and subsequently found himself forced by other gang members to commit offences. The defendant appealed against his convictions for murder and robbery.

Held

The appeal would be dismissed.

The appeal proceeded on three grounds, inter alia, 1(a), that the trial judge had wrongfully directed himself in deciding that duress was not available to a defendant who voluntarily joined a criminal organisation; and 1(b) if the first ground of appeal should fail, that the trial judge had been wrong in directing himself that the defendant's attempts to dissociate himself from the IRA were of no avail.

Lowry LCJ:

'As to ground 1(a), we consider that the learned trial judge properly directed himself and that he correctly applied the legal principles to the facts.

Counsel on both sides have informed us that the point is devoid of judicial authority and we have not found anything to suggest the contrary. Therefore we have to decide, in the absence of judicial decisions, what is the common law. Assistance may be sought from the opinions of text-writers, judicial dicta and the reports of Commissions and legal committees, and from analogies with legal systems which share our common law heritage, with a view to considering matters of general principle and arriving at the answer.'

His Lordship referred to a number of foreign and Commonwealth penal codes, and the House of Lords' decision in R v *Lynch* (considered in *R v Howe*, below) and continued:

'We recognise that the issue which we have to decide was not before the House in R v *Lynch* and that we cannot seek to extract a binding rule from the passages we have cited, but we believe that their lordships' observations collectively tend towards a rejection of the present appellant's argument.

Lord Edmund-Davies' reference to Lord Diplock's observations in *Hyam's* case helpfully reminds us of the common law approach to a problem when, as here, there is a lack of judicial authority. We are not here dealing with the doctrine of precedent or custom, for none has been established, but with the use of analogy and the observance of what Sir Frederick Pollock in his essay on Judicial Caution and Valour called "the duty of the Court to keep the rules of law in harmony with the enlightened common sense of the nation." This is not a subject which is governed by any doctrines that can be recognised as "rules of the common law," and therefore we must resort to what we believe, within a framework of fairness and justice to the individual, to represent expediency, reasonableness and widely accepted notions of morality. The codes and draft codes to which we have referred and the signs of what is accepted as the common law in the United States furnish, in our opinion, strong indications of the answer to which these criteria should lead us in relation to the questions we have to decide. As Cardozo J pointed out when considering the Nature of the Judicial Process, "The final cause of law is the welfare of society." So far as we may derive assistance from analogy, we have been referred to the law on voluntary drunkenness as affecting criminal responsibility and to the ineffectiveness of pleading the orders of a superior when answering to a criminal charge: *R v Axtell* (1660) Kel 13, where this plea was, not surprisingly, of little avail to one of the regicides. One might also perhaps have regard to the *volenti* principle in relation to tortious liability.

In the Law Commission's Working Paper No. 55 it is stated (correctly, as we respectfully consider) that the defence of duress may be regarded as a concession to human infirmity in the face of an overwhelming evil threatened by another (para 3). In this respect it differs from the doctrine of duress in contract, where the principle is to restore the innocent victim of duress to his rightful position vis-a-vis the other party to the contract who has coerced him into an unfair bargain. Again, returning to the criminal sphere, the defence of duress differs from those of self-defence and provocation, since self-defence exculpates the perpetrator who defends himself against a wrongful attacker and the defence of provocation, which is also concerned with the wrongful behaviour of the victim towards the perpetrator, may mitigate the punishment and can reduce murder to manslaughter. In criminal law, therefore, the defence of duress does not derive from the wrongful conduct of the other party to a contract or of a victim who has himself provoked the criminal act of the accused, but enures for the benefit of a person who has been compelled by the coercion of a third party to commit a crime against society and against an *innocent* victim. Accordingly, it is reasonable to expect that the accused, if he is to benefit from this defence, should himself be morally innocent.

The defence of duress is based on a balance of moral factors. It abandons what may be called the higher morality which adopts the view that death is preferable to dishonour and that man has a paramount duty, at whatever cost to himself, not to inflict unjustified harm on his fellow man. In relation to first degree murder at least, an analogous principle apparently still holds (*R* v *Abbott* [above]) but it is applied more pragmatically than ethically, since a first degree murderer whose only intention was to inflict serious personal injury is morally less culpable than an accomplice in a planned murder, or indeed than a person who attempts to murder. Generally speaking, however, the defence of duress looks to a practical morality. Crime deliberately committed is excusable if the coercive threat to the perpetrator is more than he can be expected to resist. Thus moral excusability erases the criminality of the guilty act and the guilty mind, because the crime was committed, and the conscious intention to commit it was formed, under a compulsion so strong that it is said that the perpetrator ought not to be expected to resist it. Putting the matter thus one can appreciate an argument for saying that duress if proved should merely be reflected in the severity of the punishment and not in exculpation of the crime, but it is now too late to pretend that this approach would reflect the common law. And yet the authorities show that the availability of duress as a defence is quite strictly, and in a sense arbitrarily, limited by reference to the nature of the threats which may be relied on by the accused as constituting duress, even though other kinds of threats might be still more oppressive and effective. This limitation is, incidentally, maintained in the codes and draft codes to which we have referred.

If a person behaves immorally by, for example, committing himself to an unlawful conspiracy, he ought not to be able to take advantage of the pressure exercised on him by his fellow criminals in order to put on when it suits him the breastplate of righteousness. An even more rigorous view which, as we have seen, prevails in the United States, but does not arise for consideration in this case, is that, if a person is culpably negligent or reckless in exposing himself to the risk of being subjected to coercive pressure, he too loses the right to call himself innocent by reason of his succumbing to that pressure.

A practical consideration is that, if some such limit on the defendant's duress does not exist, it would be only too easy for every member of an unlawful conspiracy and for every member of a gang except the leader to obtain an immunity denied to ordinary citizens. Indeed, the better organised the conspiracy and the more brutal its internal discipline, the surer would be the defence of duress for its members. It can hardly be supposed that the common law tolerates such an absurdity.

In making this last observation we are not saying that the ease with which a defence can be put up is a reason for not allowing that defence and impartially considering it when made. Still less do we subscribe to any doctrine that, when society is threatened, the ordinary protection of the common law can, except by statute, be withheld even from those who are alleged to have conspired against it: "Amid the clash of arms the laws are not silent." On the other hand what we are contemplating here is the possibility that any band of criminals could so organise their affairs in advance as to confer mutual immunity in respect of any crime to which duress provides a defence ...

We are continually reminded that the method of the common law is not to draw lines or to attempt exhaustive definitions. It is often enough to say that one knows on which side of the line a case falls without drawing the line itself: *Hobbs* v *L & S W Rly* (1875) LR 10 QB 111, 121, per Blackburn J, *Mayor of Southport* v *Morris* [1893] 1 QB 359, 361, *per* Lord Coleridge CJ. It may be tempting to go further and try to draw up a system, but it is not always wise. This court is satisfied that there are circumstances in which persons who associate with violent criminals and voluntarily expose themselves to the risk of compulsion to commit criminal acts cannot according to the common law avail themselves of the defence of duress. We are further satisfied that, wherever the line should be drawn, this appellant falls on the side of it where that defence is not available to him.

... [W]e guard ourselves against the use of any expression which might tend to confine the application of that principle to illegal, in the narrow sense of proscribed, organisations. A person may become associated with a sinister group of men with criminal objectives and coercive methods of ensuring that their lawless enterprises are carried out and thereby voluntarily expose himself to illegal compulsion, whether or not the group is or becomes a proscribed organisation.

Nor indeed, so far as the facts are concerned, do we consider that the evidence of the nature and activities of the relevant organisations has necessarily to be the same formal and precise character as it apparently was in this case.

As to ground 1(b), which we have set out above but which did not seem to be pressed in this court, here again we agree with the trial judge. To say that the appellant could revive for his own benefit the defence of duress by trying to leave the organisation is no more cogent an argument than saying that he tried unavailingly to resist the order to carry out a robbery. In each case the answer is the same: if a person voluntarily exposes and submits himself, as the appellant did, to illegal compulsion, he cannot rely on the duress to which he has voluntarily exposed himself as an excuse either in respect of the crimes he commits against his will or in respect of his continued but unwilling association with those capable of exercising upon him the duress which he calls in aid.'

R v Gotts [1992] 2 AC 412 House of Lords (Lord Keith, Lord Templeman, Lord Jauncey, Lord Lowry and Lord Browne-Wilkinson)

Duress as a defence to attempted murder

Facts
The appellant, then aged 16, had attacked his mother causing her serious injuries. He was charged with attempted murder and wounding with intent. The appellant contended that he had been ordered to kill his mother by his father, and had been told that he would be shot if he did not carry out the order. The trial judge rejected counsel for the appellant's submissions that duress was available as defence to a charge of attempted murder, whereupon the appellant changed his plea to one of guilty of attempted murder, and was placed on probation for three years. The Court of Appeal upheld the ruling of the trial judge, and the appellant now appealed to the House of Lords.

Held (Lord Keith and Lord Lowry dissenting):
The appeal would be dismissed.

Lord Jauncey (having considered the historical development of duress as a defence at common law, continued (p422 F–G and 423E–426G)):

'My Lords, there is nothing in the writings to which I have referred which leads me to conclude that at common law duress is or is not a defence to attempted murder. In arriving at this conclusion or lack of it I am fortified by the fact that Lord Lane CJ [1991] 1 QB 660, 667 came to a similar view where he said:

"In these circumstances we are not constrained by a common law rule or by authority from considering whether the defence of duress does or does not extend to the offence of attempted murder."

... I consider that the matter is still at large. On appeal (*Director of Public Prosecutions for Northern Ireland* v *Lynch* [1975] AC 653), it was held by a majority of this House that the defence of duress was available to a person charged with murder as a principal in the second degree. In a dissenting judgment Lord Simon of Glaisdale referred, at p687A, to the need for the law to draw a line somewhere and went on to pose the question: "But if an arbitrary line is thus drawn, is not one between murder and traditionally lesser crimes equally justifiable?" It is, in my view, taking too much out of these observations to treat them as recognising the availability of the defence of duress to a charge of attempted murder.

In *Abbott* v *The Queen* [1977] AC 755, the Privy Council by a majority held that on a charge of murder the defence of duress was not available to a principal in the first degree who took part in the actual killing. Mr Farrer relied on a passage from the dissenting judgment of Lord Wilberforce at p772:

"*Director of Public Prosecutions for Northern Ireland* v *Lynch* having been decided as it was, the most striking feature of the present appeal is the lack of any indication, in the judgment of the majority, *why* a flat declaration that in no circumstances whatsoever may the actual killer be absolved by a plea of duress makes for sounder law and better ethics. In truth, the contrary is the case. For example D attempts to kill P but, though injuring him, fails. When charged with attempted murder he may plead duress (*R* v *Fagan* (unreported), 20 September 1974, and several times referred to in *Lynch*). Later P dies and D is charged with his murder; if the majority of their Lordships are right, he now has no such plea available."

The observations as to attempted murder were obiter and I do not consider that *R* v *Fagan*, a Northern Irish case, which proceeded upon a concession by the Crown that the defence was available to a charge of attempted murder, can be treated as authoritative.

The last and most important of the three cases is *R* v *Howe* [1987] AC 417 in which it was held that the defence of duress was available neither to the person who had actually killed the victim nor, overruling *Director of Public Prosecutions of Northern Ireland* v *Lynch*, to those who had been involved in the murder as principals in the second degree. This case "[restored] the law to the condition in which it was almost universally thought not be prior to Lynch": *per* Lord Hailsham of Marylebone LC at p430. Accordingly, duress is no defence to murder in whatever capacity the accused is charged with that crime.

My Lords, I share the view of Lord Griffiths that

"it would have been better had [the development of the defence of duress] not taken place and that duress had been regarded as a factor to be taken into account in mitigation as Stephen suggested in his *History of the Criminal Law of England*, vol II, p108:" *R* v *Howe* [1987] AC 417, 439

– a view which was expressed in not dissimilar terms by Lord Hunter in the Scottish case of *Thomson* v *HM Advocate* (1983) SCCR 368, 372: "I doubt whether – at any rate in the case of very serious crimes – it is sound legal policy ever to admit coercion as a full defence leading, if established, to acquittal." At the time of the earlier writings on duress as a defence, offences against the person were much more likely to have involved only one or two victims. Weapons and substances capable of inflicting mass injury were not readily available to terrorists and other criminals as they are in the reputedly more civilised times in which we now live. While it is not now possible for this House to restrict the availability of defence of duress in those cases where it has been recognised to exist, I feel constrained to express the personal view that given the climate of violence and terrorism which ordinary law-abiding citizens have now to face Parliament might do well to consider whether that defence should continue to be available in the case of all very serious crimes. I am aware that in expressing this personal view I am at odds with the recommendations of the Law Commission Report, Criminal Law Report on Defences of General Application (1977) (Law Com No 83), but I am also aware that during some 14 years since its publication Parliament has, perhaps advisedly, taken no action thereanent.

However, in this appeal there is no question of your Lordships being asked to deny the defence in circumstances where it has previously been held to be available. I have already expressed the opinion that earlier writings leave the matter at large. I do not consider that the obiter dictum of Lord Wilberforce in *Abbott* v *The Queen* [1977] AC 755 to which I have already referred, supported as it is only by *R* v *Fagan*, 20 September 1974, which proceeded upon a concession, can be regarded as authoritative and there are no other observations in any of the three recent cases to a similar effect. There are, however, two obiter dicta in *R* v *Howe* [1987] AC 417 to which I must refer. Lord Hailsham, dealing with a defence argument as to the illogicality of allowing the defence of duress to a charge of attempted murder but not to one of murder, said, at p432:

"More persuasive, perhaps, is the point based on the availability of the defence of duress on a charge of attempted murder, where the actual intent to kill is an essential prerequisite. It may be that we must meet this casus omissus in your Lordships' House when we come to it. It may require reconsideration of the availability of the defence in that case too."

I understand Lord Hailsham there to be accepting that the question was still open for decision by his House and that his use of the word "reconsideration" was not intended to connote a change in established law. Lord Griffiths dealt with the matter more positively, at p445:

"As I can find no fair and certain basis upon which to differentiate between participants to a murder and as I am firmly convinced that the law should not be extended to the killer, I would depart from the decision of this House in *Director of Public Prosecution for Northern Ireland* v *Lynch* [1975] AC 653 and declare the law to be that duress is not available as a defence to a charge of murder, or to attempted murder. I add attempted murder because it is to be remembered that the prosecution have to prove an even more evil intent to convict of attempted murder than in actual murder. Attempted murder requires proof of an intent to kill, whereas in murder it is sufficient to prove an intent to cause really serious injury. It cannot be right to allow the defence to one who may be more intent upon taking a life than the murderer."

As the question is still open for decision by your Lordships it becomes a matter of policy how it should be answered. It is interesting to note that there is no uniformity of practice in other common law countries. The industry of Mr Miskin who appeared with Mr Farrer disclosed that in Queensland, Tasmania, Western Australia, New Zealand and Canada duress is not available as a defence to attempted murder but that it is available in almost all of the states of the United States of America. The reason why duress has for so long been stated not to be available as a defence to a murder charge is that the law regards the sanctity of human life and the protection thereof as of paramount importance. Does that reason apply to attempted murder as well as to murder? As Lord Griffiths pointed out in the passage to which I have just referred, an intent to kill must be proved in the case of attempted murder but not necessarily in the case of murder. Is there logic in affording the defence to one who intends to kill but fails and denying it to one who mistakenly kills intending only to injure? If I may give two examples:

(1a) A stabs B in the chest intending to kill him and leaves him for dead. By good luck B is found whilst still alive and rushed to hospital where surgical skill saves his life.
(1b) C stabs D intending only to injure him and inflicts a near identical wound. Unfortunately D is not found until it is too late to save his life.

I see no justification of logic or morality for affording a defence of duress to A who intended to kill when it is denied to C who did not so intend.

(2a) E plants in a passenger aircraft a bomb timed to go off in mid-flight. Owing to bungling it explodes while the aircraft is still on the ground with the result that some 200 passengers suffer physical and mental injuries of which many are permanently disabling, but no-one is killed.
(2b) F plants a bomb in a light aircraft intending to injure the pilot before it takes off but in fact it goes off in mid-air killing the pilot who is the sole occupant of the airplane.

It would in my view be both offensive to common sense and decency that E, if he established duress, should be acquitted and walk free without a stain on his character notwithstanding the appalling results which he has achieved, whereas F who never intended to kill should, if convicted in the absence of the defence, be sentenced to life imprisonment as a murderer.

It is, of course, true that withholding the defence in any circumstances will create some anomalies but I would agree with Lord Griffiths (*R* v *Howe* [1987] AC 417, 444A) that nothing should be done to undermine in any way the highest duty of the law to protect the freedom and lives of those that live under it. I can therefore see no justification in logic, morality or law in affording to an attempted murderer the defence which is withheld from a murderer. The intent required of an attempted murderer is more evil than that required of a murderer and the line which divides the two offences is seldom, if ever, of the deliberate making of the criminal. A man shooting to kill but missing a vital organ by a hair's breadth can justify his action no more than can the man who hits that organ. It is pure chance that the attempted murderer is not a murderer and I entirely agree with what Lord Lane CJ [1991] 1 QB 660, 667 said: that the fact that the attempt failed to kill should not make any difference.

For the foregoing reasons I have no doubt that the Court of Appeal reached the correct conclusion and that the appeal should be dismissed.'

Lord Lowry (dissenting) (p436B–439D):

'The foundation of the Crown's argument is that, accepting the sanctity of human life as the basis for denying the defence of duress in murder, both logic and morality demand that that defence must be withheld from one who tried (albeit unsuccessfully), and therefore *intended*, to kill, when one considers that in murder the defence is withheld not only from the deliberate killer but also from the killer who intended only to inflict very serious injury and from all principals in the second degree, whatever their mens rea. But the logic and, to some extent, also the morality of this proposition are open to attack, as follows.

1. Treason, too, is an excluded offence and it does not invariably involve killing or attempting or conspiring to kill. It is the ultimate crime against the state (a man-made, as distinct from a divinely ordained, offence).
2. The principle that a person ought to die himself rather than kill an innocent is attractive but does not touch the case in which the killer did not intend to cause death, nor does it touch a principal in the second degree either, if he merely intended the victim to suffer serious personal injury.
3. There is much authority to show that duress can be relevant which involves a threat not to the killer, but to others, in particular his wife and children, which fundamentally alters the moral problem: see *R v Brown and Morley* (1968) SASR 467, 498, *per* Bray CJ; *R v Hurley and Murray* [1967] VR 526; *Abbott v The Queen* [1977] AC 755, 767A and 769F, *per* Lord Salmon; *R v Howe* [1987] AC 417, 433, *per* Lord Hailsham of St Marylebone LC, and at p453, *per* Lord Mackay of Clashfern, and also various statutory codes and the Law Commission's draft Bill on A Criminal Code for England and Wales (vol 1 AppA) (1989) (Law Com No 177), the combined effect of which is to show that threats to harm others can be a basis for the defence of duress.

My Lords, I suggest that the only thing which can reconcile the anomalies that have been a prolific source of comment is the stark fact of death. Murder is a result related crime, as Lord Hailsham of St Marylebone LC and Lord Mackay of Clashfern both observed in *R v Howe* at p430 and 457. Thus, to exclude treason and murder relates the doctrine of duress to serious results (admittedly an unsuccessful *attempt* to subvert the government can itself be treason), namely, danger to the state or a crime committed with guilty intent and resulting in, but not necessarily aimed at, loss of life, and does not specially relate that doctrine to a scale of moral turpitude. It is founded on practical considerations and not on a moral value judgment: the recourse of moral values was found in Hale's explanation (*Pleas of the Crown*, vol 1, p51), which related only to murder (and certainly not to robbery) and which, even in relation to murder, did not serve to justify the law's attitude, since it did not cover the guilty causation of death while intending merely to injure.

Blackstone's explanation that crimes created by the laws of society are in relation to duress distinguished from natural offences, so declared by the law of God (*Commentaries on the Laws of England*, vol IV, p30), equally fails to satisfy, since treason is typically a crime created by the laws of society for its own protection and because the explanation does not contemplate a mere intent to injure.

I sympathise with the proposition that attempted murder should be recognised as an exempted crime. But from the point of view of deterrence this idea holds no special attraction. If one makes the somewhat artificial assumption (without which the principle of deterrence has no meaning) that a potential offender will know when the defence of duress is not available, one then has to realise that, whatever the law may be about *attempted* murder, one who sets out to kill under threat will be guilty of murder if he succeeds. Therefore the deterrent is in theory operative already. The moral position, too, is clouded, because *Director of Public Prosecutions for Northern Ireland* v *Lynch* [1975] AC 653 in this respect alone affirming the majority opinion of the Court of Criminal Appeal in Northern Ireland, affirmed that the offender, even when acting under duress, intends to commit the crime (of murder, not attempted murder). But his guilty intent is of a special kind: "coactus voluit", as the Latin phrase has it. Thus the denial of the duress defence, based on moral principles, is not straightforward. It may not be just a case of the law saying: "Although you did not succeed, you intended to kill. Therefore you cannot rely on duress." The law might equally well say: "As with other offenders who allege duress, your guilty intent was caused by threats. Therefore, since the intended victim did not die, you, like other offenders, can rely on those threats as a defence. If the victim had died in circumstances amounting to murder or if treason had been the crime, it would of course have been different." This emphasises the point that murder is a result-related crime.

The choice is between the two views propounded by Lord Lane CJ [1991] 1 QB 660, 664F–G and 667B: (1) *if* the common law recognised that murder and treason were the only excepted crimes, then we are bound to accept that as the law, whether it seems a desirable conclusion or not; the fact that there is no binding decision on the point does not weaken a rule of the common law which has stood the test of time; or (2) we are not constrained by a common law rule or by authority from considering whether the defence of duress does or does not extend to the offence of attempted murder.

I consider that the view to be preferred is that which is contained in the first of these propositions and that to adopt the second would result in an unjustified judicial change in the law. It is only with diffidence that I would express an opinion on the criminal law which conflicts with that of such highly respected authorities as the present Lord Chief Justice and my noble and learned friend, Lord Griffiths, but on this occasion I feel obliged to do so. I proceed to give my reasons for this conclusion.

Both judges and textwriters have pointed out that the law on the subject is vague and uncertain. In *R v Brown and Morley* (1968) SASR 467, 479 the court mentioned "the defence of duress, as to which there is little direct authority and much theoretical discussion". And, speaking of compulsion, whether by a husband over a wife, by threats of injury or by necessity, Stephen said in his *History of the Criminal Law of England*, vol II, at p105:

> "Of the three forms of compulsion above mentioned, I may observe generally that hardly any branch of the law of England is more meagre or less satisfactory than the law on this subject."

Your Lordships have seen that Professor Kenny expressed himself to the same effect in his *Outlines of Criminal Law*, 13th edition. There have, moreover, been few cases in which the doctrine of duress has been directly in issue either with regard to the offences in relation to which it may provide a defence or as to the kind of threatening conduct which may constitute duress. There has, for all that, been considerable discussion and debate. In such an atmosphere it is easy for the discussion to focus on what the law ought to be rather than on what it is, and that is an unsatisfactory basis for the exercise of criminal jurisdiction. But, in my opinion, this vagueness ought not to encourage innovation which makes a departure from the received wisdom even if that wisdom is imperfect. This is particularly true if the innovation is retrospective in effect, to the prejudice of an accused person.

Hale's philosophical explanation of withholding the duress defence (*Pleas of the Crown*, vol 1, p51) is not a good starting point for putting attempted murder in the category of murder and treason or for saying that it is in that category already. The intention of the offender is evil, but when the attempt has failed the sentence is variable, although someone who kills through compassion or who kills intending only to injure receives a fixed sentence (until recently a capital sentence). That a man who did not mean to kill can be found guilty of murder and will receive a mandatory life sentence is arguably a blot on our legal system but that is the law and this fact sets murder apart. Such a result is consistent with the traditional view that one who causes death when committing a felony (I exclude manslaughter) is guilty of murder. In *R v Stephenson* [1947] NI 110 the accused was charged with the murder of a woman on whom he performed an abortion but, on the verdict of the jury, was convicted of manslaughter. The principle on which Stephenson was charged, although outmoded, is further proof that murder is a result related crime.

Stephen (*History of the Criminal Law of England*, vol II, p108) – and many have agreed with him – thought that duress should not be a defence to *any* crime, but this view does not justify taking the most obvious candidate for exclusion from that defence any more than all the other offences below murder and treason which are listed in the code of 1879 and in relation to which your Lordships can safely say that the duress defence is available. Whatever one may say about the earlier days, attempted murder was a fully established and serious crime in 1861 and has been ever since.

To withhold in respect of *every* crime the defence of duress, leaving it to the court (or, in relation to fixed penalty crimes, the executive) to take mitigating circumstances into account, seems logical. But to withhold that defence only from a selected list of serious crimes (some of which incur variable penalties) is questionable from a sentencing point of view, as indeed the sentence in the present case shows. The defence is withheld on the ground that the crime is so odious that it must not be palliated: and yet, if circumstances are allowed to mitigate the punishment, the principle on which the defence of duress is withheld has been defeated.

The fact that the sentence for attempted murder is at large is, with respect to those who think otherwise, no justification for withholding the defence of duress. Quite the reverse, because it is the theoretical inexcusability of murder and treason which causes those crimes (the fixed penalty for which can be, mitigated only by the executive) to be deprived of the duress defence.'

And further (p441D–G):

'If the common law has had a policy towards duress heretofore, it seems to have been to go by the result and not primarily by the intent and, if a change of policy is needed with regard to criminal liability, it must be made prospectively by Parliament and not retrospectively by a court.

I am not influenced in favour of the appellant by the supposed illogicality of distinguishing between attempted murder on the one hand and conspiracy and incitement to murder on the other and I agree on this point with the view of Lord Lane CJ: short of murder itself, attempted murder is a special crime. But I am not swayed in favour of the Crown by the various examples of the anomalies which are said to result from holding that the duress defence applies to attempted murder. As Lord Lane CJ said, at p668B, it would be possible to suggest anomalies wherever the line is drawn. The real logic would be to grant or withhold the duress defence universally.

Attempted murder, however heinous we consider it, was a misdemeanour. Until 1861 someone who shot and missed could suffer no more than two years' imprisonment and I submit that, when attempted murder became a felony, that crime, like many other serious felonies, continued to have available the defence of duress.'

R v Graham [1982] 1 WLR 294 Court of Appeal (Criminal Division) (Lord Lane CJ, Taylor and McCullough JJ)

Model direction to the jury on the defence of duress

Facts
The defendant, a homosexual, lived with another man named King, with whom he was having a sexual relationship. King was jealous of the defendant's wife and, having tricked her into visiting the defendant, he strangled her to death with an electrical flex. The defendant had been ordered to help King carry out this killing by pulling on one end of the flex. There was evidence that the defendant, who had been drinking and taking valium, was terrified of King, and at his trial for murder he sought to rely on the defence of duress. The jury rejected the defence and convicted the defendant, following the trial judge's direction, detailed in the extract from Lord Lane CJ's judgment (see below). The defendant appealed.

Held
The appeal would be dismissed.

Lord Lane CJ:

'As a matter of public policy, it seems to us essential to limit the defence of duress by means of an objective criterion formulated in terms of reasonableness. Consistency of approach in defences to criminal liability is obviously desirable. Provocation and duress are analogous. In provocation the words or actions of one person break the self-control of another. In duress the words or actions of one person break the will of another. The law requires a defendant to have the self-control reasonably to be expected of the ordinary citizen in his situation. It should likewise require him to have the steadfastness reasonably to be expected of the ordinary citizen in his situation. So too with self-defence, in which the law permits the use of no more force than is reasonable in the circumstances. And in general, if a mistake is to excuse what would otherwise be criminal, the mistake must be a reasonable one.

It follows that we accept Mr Sherrard's [counsel for the Crown] submission that the direction in this case was too favourable to the appellant. The Crown having conceded that the issue of duress was open to the appellant and was raised on the evidence, the correct approach on the facts of this case would have been as follows. (1) Was the defendant, or may he have been, impelled to act as he did because, as a result of what he reasonably believed King had said or done, he had good cause to fear that if he did not so act King would kill him or (if this is to be added) cause him serious physical injury? (2) If so, have the prosecution made the jury sure that a sober person of reasonable firmness, sharing the characteristics of the defendant, would not have responded to whatever he reasonably believed King said or did by taking part in the killing? The fact that a defendant's will to resist has been eroded by the voluntary consumption of drink or drugs or both is not relevant to this test.'

R v Howe [1987] AC 417 House of Lords (Lords Hailsham LC, Bridge, Brandon, Griffiths and Mackay)

Duress as a defence to murder

Facts
The House of Lords had before it two appeals, that of Howe and Bannister, and that of Burke and Clarkson. The points of law certified for consideration by the Law Lords were:

'(1) Is duress available as a defence to a person charged with murder as a principal in the first degree (the actual killer)? (2) Can one who incites or procures by duress another to kill or to be a party to a killing be convicted of murder if that other is acquitted by reason of duress? (3) Does the defence of duress fail if the prosecution prove that a person of reasonable firmness sharing the characteristics of the defendant would not have given way to the threats as did the defendant?'

Held
The certified questions would be answered respectively (1) No; (2) Yes; (3) Yes. The defendants' appeals would be dismissed.

For extracts dealing with the second certified question, see Chapter 27.

Lord Hailsham LC (on the first certified question):

'In my opinion, this must be decided on principle and authority, and the answer must in the end demand a reconsideration of the two authorities of *Director of Public Prosecutions for Northern Ireland* v *Lynch* [1975] AC 653 and *Abbott* v *The Queen* [1977] AC 755. Having been myself a party to *Abbott,* I feel I owe it to the two noble and learned friends then with me in the majority to say that we were very conscious of the fact that our decision would only be of persuasive authority in the English jurisdiction whilst the decision in *Lynch,* though a Northern Irish case, which distinguished for the purposes of duress between principals in the first degree on the one hand, and principals in the second degree and aiders and abettors on the other, being a decision of the House of Lords would be likely to be treated as binding throughout England and Wales as well as Northern Ireland. We did, however, say, at p763:

"Whilst their Lordships feel bound to accept the decision of the House of Lords in *Lynch's* case they find themselves constrained to say that had they considered (which they do not) that the decision is an authority which requires the extension of the doctrine to cover cases like the present they would not have accepted it."

Speaking only for myself, it was precisely because the three noble and learned Lords in the majority in *Lynch* had expressly left open the availability of duress as a defence to the actual participant in a murder that I found it possible to accept the decision in *Lynch* without criticism, and then only because the *Abbott* appeal was solely concerned with the question so expressly left open. One only needs to read the facts in *Abbott* to be aware of exactly what the Board was being asked to do if it extended *Lynch* and allowed the appeal.

The present case, in my opinion, affords an ideal and never to be repeated opportunity to consider as we were invited expressly to do by the respondent, the whole question afresh, if necessary, by applying the *Practice Statement (Judicial Precedent)* [1966] 1 WLR 1234 to the decision in *Lynch*.

I therefore consider the matter first from the point of view of authority. On this I can only say that at the time when *Lynch* was decided the balance of weight in an unbroken tradition of authority dating back to Hale and Blackstone seems to have been accepted to have been that duress was not available to a defendant accused of murder. I quote only from Hale and Blackstone. Thus *Hale's Pleas of the Crown,* (1736) vol 1, p51:

> "if a man be desperately assaulted, and in peril of death, and cannot otherwise escape, unless to satisfy his assailant's fury he will kill an innocent person then present, the fear and actual force will not acquit him of the crime and punishment of murder, if he commit the fact; for he ought rather to die himself, than kill an innocent: …"

Blackstone's Commentaries on the Laws of England, (1857 ed) vol 4, p28 was to the same effect. He wrote that a man under duress: "ought rather to die himself than escape by the murder of an innocent."

I forbear to quote the eloquent and agonised passage in the dissenting speech of Lord Simon of Glaisdale in *Lynch* [1975] AC 653, 695, or the more restrained exposition of Lord Kilbrandon, at p702, on the law as expressed in *R v Dudley and Stephens* (1884) 14 QBD 273. These quotations are unnecessary since it seems to have been accepted both by the majority in *Lynch* and the minority in *Abbott*, that, to say the least, prior to *Lynch* there was a heavy preponderance of authority against the availability of the defence of duress in cases of murder.

I would only add that article 8 of the Charter of the International Military Tribunal, Treaty Series No. 27 of 1946 at Nuremberg (Cmd 6903), which was, at the time, universally accepted, save for its reference to mitigation, as an accurate statement of the common law both in England and the United States of America that:

> "The fact that the defendant acted pursuant to the order of his government or of a superior shall not free him from responsibility, but may be considered in mitigation of punishment if the tribunal determines that justice so requires."

"Superior orders" is not identical with "duress," but, in the circumstances of the Nazi regime, the difference must often have been negligible. I should point out that under article 6, the expression "war crimes" expressly included that of murder; which, of course, does not include the killing of combatants engaged in combat.

What then is said on the other side? I accept, of course, that duress for almost all other crimes had been held to be a completed defence. I need not cite cases. They are carefully reviewed in *Lynch* and establish I believe that the defence is of venerable antiquity and wide extent. I pause only to say that although duress has, in my view, never been defined with adequate precision, two views of its nature can no longer be viewed as correct in the light of reported authority. The first is that of Stephen in his *History of the Criminal Law of England* (1883), of vol 2, p108 who first promulgated the opinion that duress was not a defence at all but, as in the Nuremberg statute, only a matter of mitigation. The fact is that, where it is applicable at all, in a long line of cases duress has been treated as a matter of defence entitling an accused to a complete acquittal. But in almost every instance where duress is so treated a cautionary note has been sounded excluding murder in terms sometimes more, and sometimes less emphatic, from the number of crimes where it can be put forward.

The second unacceptable view is that, possibly owing to a misunderstanding which has been read into some judgments, duress as a defence affects only the existence or absence of mens rea. The true view is stated by Lord Kilbrandon (of the minority) in *Lynch* [1975] AC 653 and by Lord Edmund-Davies (of the majority) in his analysis, at p709.

Lord Kilbrandon said, at p703:

> "the decision of the threatened man whose constancy is overborne so that he yields to the threat, is a *calculated decision to do what he knows to be wrong,* and is therefore that of a man with, perhaps to some exceptionally limited extent, a 'guilty mind.' But he is at the same time a man whose mind is less guilty than is his who acts as he does but under no such constraint." [emphasis mine.]

In coming to the same conclusion Lord Edmund-Davies, at pp709–710 quoted from Professor Glanville Williams' well known treatise Criminal Law, 2nd ed (1961), p751, para 242:

> "True duress is not inconsistent with act and will as a matter of legal definition, the maxim being coactus volui. Fear of violence does not differ in kind from fear of economic ills, fear of displeasing others, or any other determinant of choice, it would be inconvenient to regard a particular type of motive as negativing of will."

After approving a paragraph from Lowry CJ, Lord Edmund-Davies went on to say that two quotations from Lord Goddard CJ in the disgusting case of *Reg* v *Bourne* (1952) 36 Cr App R 125 were subject to criticism on this score: see *Lynch* [1975] AC 653, 710.

Before I leave the question of reported authority I must refer to two other cases. The first is *R* v *Kray (Ronald)* (1969) 53 Cr App R 569 which was, to some extent, relied on by the majority in *Lynch*, on the score of an obiter dictum of Widgery LJ at p578. I do not myself regard this passage as authoritative. It depends on a concession by the Crown regarding a party who was not before the Court of Appeal as his case had been disposed of at first instance in order to found a submission by the appellants. The dictum is also open to the criticism that Widgery LJ appeared to treat duress as making a person otherwise than an "independent actor" which is contrary to the analysis which I have accepted above.

The other reported authority is the famous and important case of *R* v *Dudley and Stephens* (1884) 14 QBD 273. That is generally and, in my view correctly, regarded as an authority on the availability of the supposed defence of necessity rather than duress. But I must say frankly that, if we were to allow this appeal, we should, I think, also have to say that *Dudley and Stephens* was bad law. There is, of course, an obvious distinction between duress and necessity as potential defences; duress arises from the wrongful threats or violence of another human being and necessity arises from any other objective dangers threatening the accused. This, however, is, in my view a distinction without a relevant difference, since on this view duress is only that species of the genus of necessity which is caused by wrongful threats. I cannot see that there is any way in which a person of ordinary fortitude can be excused from the one type of pressure on his will rather than the other.

I shall revert to *Dudley and Stephens* when I come to consider some of the issues of principle involved in our response to the first certified question. But at this stage I feel that I should say that in *Abbott* I would have been prepared to accept a distinction between *Abbott* [1977] AC 755 and *Lynch* [1975] AC 653 on the basis of the argument which appeared to attract Lord Morris of Borth-y-Gest at pp671-672 of *Lynch*. I would not myself have immersed myself in the somewhat arcane terminology of accessory, principal in the second degree, and aiding and abetting. But it did seem to me then, and it seems to me now, that there is a valid distinction to be drawn in ordinary language between a man who actually participates in the irrevocable act of murder to save his own skin or that of his nearest and dearest and a man who simply participates before or after the event in the necessary preparation for it or the escape of the actual offender. It is as well to remember that, in *Abbott* the facts were that Abbott had dug a pit, thrown the victim into it, subjected her in co-operation with others to murderous blows and stab wounds and then buried her alive. It seems to me that those academics who see no difference between that case and the comparatively modest part alleged (falsely as is now known) in *Lynch* to have been played by the defendant under duress have parted company with a full sense of reality. Nevertheless and in spite of this, and in the face of the somewhat intemperate criticism to which this type of distinction has sometimes been subjected since *Abbott* I am somewhat relieved to know that the views of my noble and learned friends on the main issue permit me to escape from such niceties and simply to say that I do not think that the decision in Lynch can be justified on authority and that, exercising to the extent necessary, the freedom given to us by the *Practice Statement (Judicial Precedent)* [1966] 1 WLR 1234 which counsel for the respondent urged us to apply, I consider that the right course in the instant appeal is to restore the law to the condition in which it was almost universally thought to be prior to *Lynch*. It may well be that law was to a certain extent unclear and to some extent gave rise to anomaly. But these anomalies I believe to be due to a number of factors extraneous to the present appeal and to the intrinsic nature of duress. The first is the mandatory nature of the sentence in murder. The second resides in the fact that murder being a "result" crime, only being complete if the victim dies within the traditional period of a year and a day and that, in consequence, a different crime may be charged according to whether or not the victim actually succumbs during the prescribed period. The third lies in the fact (fully discussed amongst many other authorities in *R v Hyam* [1975] AC 55) that, as matters stand, the mens rea in murder consists not simply in an intention to kill, but may include an intent to commit grievous bodily harm. It has always been possible for Parliament to clear up this branch of the law (or indeed to define more closely the nature and extent of the availability of duress as a defence). But Parliament has conspicuously, and perhaps deliberately, declined to do so. In the meantime, I must say that the attempt made in *Lynch* to clear up this situation by judicial legislation has proved to be an excessive and perhaps improvident use of the undoubted power of the courts to create new law by creating precedents in individual cases.

This brings me back to the question of principle. I begin by affirming that, while there can never be a direct correspondence between law and morality, an attempt to divorce the two entirely is and has always proved to be doomed to failure, and, in the present case, the overriding objects of the criminal law must be to protect innocent lives and to set a standard of conduct which ordinary men and women are expected to observe if they are to avoid criminal responsibility

... In general, I must say that I do not at all accept in relation to the defence of murder it is either good morals, good policy or good law to suggest, as did the majority in *Lynch* and the minority in *Abbott* that the ordinary man of reasonable fortitude is not to be supposed to be capable of heroism if he is asked to take an innocent life rather than sacrifice his own. Doubtless in actual practice many will succumb to temptation, as they did in *Dudley and Stephens*. But many will not, and I do not believe that as a "concession to human frailty" the former should be exempt from liability to criminal sanctions if they do. I have known in my own lifetime of too many acts of heroism by ordinary human beings of no more than ordinary fortitude to regard a law as either "just or humane" which withdraws the protection of the criminal law from the innocent victim and casts the cloak of its protection upon the coward and the poltroon in the name of a "concession to human frailty."

I must not, however, underestimate the force of the arguments on the other side, advanced as they have been with such force and such persuasiveness by some of the most eminent legal minds, judicial and academic, in the country.

First, amongst these is, perhaps, the argument from logic and consistency. A long line of cases, it is said, carefully researched and closely analysed, establish duress as an available defence in a wide range of crimes, some at least, like wounding with intent to commit grievous bodily harm, carrying the heaviest penalties commensurate with their gravity. To cap this, it is pointed out that at least in theory, a defendant accused of this crime under section 18 of the Offences against the Person Act 1861, but acquitted on the grounds of duress, will still be liable to a charge of murder if the victim dies within the traditional period of one year and a day. I am not, perhaps, persuaded of this last point as much as I should. It is not simply an anomaly based on the defence of duress. It is a product of the peculiar mens rea allowed on a charge of murder which is not confined to an intent to kill. More persuasive, perhaps, is the point based on the availability of the defence of duress on a charge of attempted murder, where the actual intent to kill is an essential prerequisite. It may be that we must meet this casus omissus in your Lordships' House when we come to it. It may require reconsideration of the availability of the defence in that case too.

I would, however, prefer to meet the case of alleged inconsistency head on. Consistency and logic, though inherently desirable, are not always prime characteristics of a penal code based like the common law on custom and precedent. Law so based is not an exact science. All the same, I feel I am required to give some answer to the question posed. If duress is available as a defence to some crimes of the most grave why, it may legitimately be asked, stop at murder, whether as accessory or principal and whether in the second or the first degree? But surely I am entitled, as in the view of the Common Serjeant in the instant case of Clarkson and Burke, to believe that some degree of proportionality between the threat and the offence must, at least to some extent, be a prerequisite of the defence under existing law. Few would resist threats to the life of a loved one if the alternative were driving across the red lights or in excess of 70 mph. on the motorway. But, to use the Common Serjeant's analogy, it would take rather more than the threat of a slap on the wrist or even moderate pain or injury to discharge the evidential burden even in the case of a fairly serious assault. In such a case the "concession to human frailty" is no more than to say that in such circumstances a reasonable man of average courage is entitled to embrace as a matter of choice the alternative which a reasonable man could regard as the lesser of two evils. Other considerations necessarily arise where the choice is between the threat of death or a fortiori of serious injury and deliberately taking an innocent life. In such a case a reasonable man might reflect that one innocent human life is at least as valuable as his own or that of his loved one. In such a case a man cannot claim that he is choosing the lesser of two evils. Instead he is embracing the cognate but morally disreputable principle that the end justifies the means.

I am not so shocked as some of the judicial opinions have been at the need, if this be the conclusion, to invoke the availability of administrative as distinct from purely judicial remedies for the hardships which might otherwise occur in the most agonising cases. Even in *Dudley and Stephens* in 1884 when the death penalty was mandatory and frequently inflicted, the prerogative was used to reduce a sentence of death by hanging to one of 18 months in prison. In murder cases the available mechanisms are today both more flexible and more sophisticated. The trial judge may make no minimum recommendation. He will always report to the Home Secretary, as he did in the present case of Clarkson and Burke. The Parole Board will always consider a case of this kind with a High Court judge brought into consultation. In the background is always the prerogative and, it may not unreasonably be suggested, that is exactly what the prerogative is for. If the law seems to bear harshly in its operation in the case of a mandatory sentence on any particular offender there has never been a period of time when there were more effective means of mitigating its effect than at the present day. It may well be thought that the loss of a clear right to a defence justifying or excusing the deliberate taking of an innocent life in order to emphasise to all the sanctity of a human life is not an excessive price to pay in the light of these mechanisms. Murder, as every practitioner of the law knows, though often described as one of the utmost heinousness, is not in fact necessarily so, but consists in a whole bundle of offences of vastly differing degrees of culpability, ranging from brutal, cynical and repeated offences like the so called Moors murders to the almost venial, if objectively immoral, "mercy killing" of a beloved partner.

Far less convincing than the argument based on consistency is the belief which appears in some of the judgments that the law must "move with the times" in order to keep pace with the immense political and social changes since what are alleged to have been the bad old days of Blackstone and Hale. I have already dealt with this argument in my respectful criticism of the dissent in *R v Hyam* [1975] AC 55. The argument is based on the false assumption that violence to innocent victims is now less prevalent than in the days of Hale or Blackstone. But I doubt whether this is so. We live in the age of the holocaust of the Jews, of international terrorism on the scale of massacre, of the explosion of aircraft in mid air, and murder sometimes at least as obscene as anything experienced in Blackstone's day. Indeed one of the present appeals may provide an example. I have already mentioned the so-called Moors murders. But within weeks of hearing this appeal a man was convicted at the Central Criminal Court, *R v Hindawi* [(unreported), 24 October 1986; see The Times, 25 October 1986], of sending his pregnant mistress on board an international aircraft at Heathrow, with her suitcase packed with a bomb and with the deliberate intention of sending the 250 occupants, crew, passengers, mistress and all to a horrible death in mid air. I cannot forbear to say that if *Abbott* [1977] AC 755 was wrongly decided, and had the attempt succeeded, the miscreant who did this would have been free to escape scot free had he been in a position to discharge the evidential burden on duress and had the prosecution, on the normal *Woolmington* principles (*Woolmington* v *Director of Public Prosecutions* [1935] AC 462, 482), been unable to exclude beyond reasonable doubt the possibility of his uncorroborated word being true. I must also point out in this context that known terrorists are more and not less vulnerable to threats than the ordinary man and that a plea of duress in such a case may be all the more plausible on that account. To say this is not to cast doubt on the reliability and steadfastness of juries. Counsel for the appellants was able to say with perfect truth that, where duress in fact has been put forward in cases where it was available, juries have been commendably robust as they were in the instant cases in rejecting it where appropriate. The question is not one of the reliability of juries. It is one of principle. Should the offence of duress be available in principle in such a case as that of *R* v *Hindawi* where, of course, it was not put forward? The point which I am at the moment concerned to make is that it is not clear to me that the observations of Blackstone and Hale, and almost every respectable authority, academic or judicial, prior to *Lynch* are necessarily to be regarded in this present age as obsolescent or inhumane or unjust owing to some supposed improvement in the respect for innocent human life since their time which unfortunately I am too blind to be able for myself to perceive. Still less am I able to see that a law which denies such a defence in such a case must be condemned as lacking in justice or humanity rather than as respectable in its concern for the sanctity of innocent lives. I must add that, at least in my view, if *Abbott* were wrongly decided some hundreds who suffered the death penalty at Nuremberg for murders were surely the victims of judicial murder at the hands of their conquerors owing to the operation of article 8. Social change is not always for the better and it ill becomes those of us who have participated in the cruel events of the 20th century to condemn as out of date those who wrote in defence of innocent lives in the 18th century.

During the course of argument it was suggested that there was available to the House some sort of half way house between allowing these appeals and dismissing them. The argument ran that we might treat duress in murder as analogous to provocation, or perhaps diminished responsibility, and say that, in indictments for murder, duress might reduce the crime to one of manslaughter. I find myself quite unable to accept this. The cases show that duress, if available and made out, entitles the accused to a clean acquittal, without, it has been said, the "stigma" of a conviction. Whatever other merits it may have, at least the suggestion makes nonsense of any pretence of logic or consistency in the criminal law. It is also contrary to principle. Unlike the doctrine of provocation, which is based on emotional loss of control, the defence of duress, as I have already shown, is put forward as a "concession to human frailty" whereby a conscious decision, it may be coolly undertaken, to sacrifice an innocent human life is made as an evil lesser than a wrong which might otherwise be suffered by the accused or his loved ones at the hands of a wrong doer. The defence of diminished responsibility (which might well, had it then been available to *Dudley and Stephens,* have prevailed there) is statutory in England though customary in Scotland, the land of its origin. But in England at least it has a conceptual basis defined in the Homicide Act 1957 which is totally distinct from that of duress if duress be properly analysed and understood. Provocation (unique to murder and not extending even to "section 18" offences) is a concession to human frailty due to the extent that even a reasonable man may, under sufficient provocation, temporarily lose his self control towards the person who has provoked him enough. Duress, as I have already pointed out, is a concession to human frailty in that it allows a reasonable man to make a conscious choice between the reality of the immediate threat and what he may reasonably regard as the lesser of two evils. Diminished responsibility as defined in the Homicide Act 1957 depends on abnormality of mind impairing mental responsibility. It may overlap duress or even necessity. But it is not what we are discussing in the instant appeal.

I must add that, had I taken a different view, in the cases of Bannister and Howe and, for rather different reasons, in the case of Burke, I would have gone on to consider the questions whether in any of these appeals the appellants had discharged the evidential burden in duress, or whether, if they had, on the facts described in the judgment of Lord Lane CJ, the proviso should not have been applied in every case. The case of Clarkson is surely beyond dispute on the assumption that the second certified question is not answered in his favour. But whatever may be the characteristics of duress, even on the existing law the ingredients of immediacy and absence of voluntary association: see *R* v *Fitzpatrick* [1977] NI 20, must be essential components of the evidential burden more or less on the lines of the draft bill annexed to the Law Commission Report No. 83, to which I have referred above. Even apart from this and on the assumption that the matter should properly have been left to the jury, I am rather more than doubtful whether any properly instructed jury could have acquitted on the murder charges in either of the instant cases or on the facts of *Abbott*. It is not necessary to express a concluded opinion on this since, for the reasons I have adumbrated above, I consider that these appeals should be dismissed and the certified questions answered respectively (1) no, (2) yes, (3) yes. If so, the questions relating to the proviso and evidential burden do not arise. So far as I have indicated, the decision of this House in *Lynch* [1975] AC 653 should be regarded as unsatisfactory and the law left as it was before *Lynch* came up for decision. The decision in *Abbott* [1977] AC 755 should be followed.'

R v Hudson and Taylor [1971] 2 QB 202 Court of Appeal (Criminal Division) (Lord Parker CJ, Widgery LJ and Cooke J)

Immediacy of threat in duress

Facts
The defendants were two young women who had given evidence against a man named Wright at his trial on a charge of wounding. Wright was subsequently acquitted, and it emerged that the defendants had given perjured evidence, having been threatened with serious physical harm if they told the truth at Wright's trial. At their trial for perjury the defendants sought to rely on the defence of duress, but the trial judge directed the jury that the defence of duress was not available because the threat was not sufficiently immediate. The defendants were convicted and appealed.

Held
Appeals allowed.

Lord Widgery LJ:

'This appeal raises two main questions: first, as to the nature of the necessary threat and, in particular, whether it must be "present and immediate"; secondly, as to the extent to which a right to plead duress may be lost if the accused has failed to take steps to remove the threat as, for example, by seeking police protection.

It is essential to the defence of duress that the threat shall be effective at the moment when the crime is committed. The threat must be a "present" threat in the sense that it is effective to neutralise the will of the accused at that time. Hence an accused who joins a rebellion under the compulsion of threats cannot plead duress if he remains with the rebels after the threats have lost their effect and his own will has had a chance to re-assert itself (*McCrowther's Case* (1746) Fost. 13; and *A-G v Whelan* [1934] IR 518). Similarly a threat of future violence may be so remote as to be insufficient to overpower the will at the moment when the offence was committed, or the accused may have elected to commit the offence in order to rid himself of a threat hanging over him and not because he was driven to act by immediate and unavoidable pressure. In none of these cases is the defence of duress available because a person cannot justify the commission of a crime merely to secure his own peace of mind.

When, however, there is no opportunity for delaying tactics, and the person threatened must make up his mind whether he is to commit the criminal act or not, the existence at that moment of threats sufficient to destroy his will ought to provide him with a defence even though the threatened injury may not follow instantly, but after an interval. This principle is illustrated by *Subramaniam v Public Prosecutor* [1956] 1 WLR 965, when the appellant was charged in Malaya with unlawful possession of ammunition and was held by the Privy Council to have a defence of duress, fit to go to the jury, on his plea that he had been compelled by terrorists to accept the ammunition and feared for his safety if the terrorists returned.

In the present case the threats of Farrell were likely to be no less compelling, because their execution could not be effected in the court room, if they could be carried out in the streets of Salford the same night. Insofar, therefore, as the recorder ruled as a matter of law that the threats were not sufficiently present and immediate to support the defence of duress we think that he was in error. He should have left the jury to decide whether the threats had overborne the will of the appellants at the time when they gave the false evidence.

Counsel for the Crown, however, contends that the recorder's ruling can be supported on another ground, namely, that the appellants should have taken steps to neutralise the threats by seeking police protection either when they came to court to give evidence, or beforehand. He submits on grounds of public policy that an accused should not be able to plead duress if he had the opportunity to ask for protection from the police before committing the offence and failed to do so. The argument does not distinguish cases in which the police would be able to provide effective protection, from those when they would not, and it would, in effect, restrict the defence of duress to cases where the person threatened had been kept in custody by the maker of the threats, or where the time interval between the making of the threats and the commission of the offence had made recourse to the police impossible. We recognise the need to keep the defence of duress within reasonable bounds but cannot accept so severe a restriction on it. The duty, of the person threatened, to take steps to remove the threat does not seem to have arisen in an English case but in a full review of the defence of duress in the Supreme Court of Victoria (*R v Hurley, R v Murray* [1967] VR 525), a condition of raising the defence was said to be that the accused "had no means, with safety to himself, of preventing the execution of the threat."

In the opinion of this court it is always open to the Crown to prove that the accused failed to avail himself of some opportunity which was reasonably open to him to render the threat ineffective, and that on this being established the threat in question can no longer be relied on by the defence. In deciding whether such an opportunity was reasonably open to the accused the jury should have regard to his age and circumstances, and to any risks to him which may be involved in the course of action relied on.

In our judgment the defence of duress should have been left to the jury in the present case, as should any issue raised by the Crown and arising out of the appellants' failure to seek police protection. The appeals will, therefore, be allowed and the convictions quashed.'

R v McInnes [1971] 1 WLR 1600 Court of Appeal (Criminal Division) (Edmund-Davies LJ, Lawton and Forbes JJ)

The nature of self-defence

Facts
The defendant was convicted of stabbing another man, and appealed on the basis that the trial judge had not dealt adequately in his summing-up with the defence of self-defence.

Held
The appeal would be dismissed.

Edmund-Davies LJ:

'The first criticism of the learned judge's treatment of self-defence is that he misdirected the jury in relation to the question of whether an attacked person must do all he reasonably can to retreat before he turns upon his attacker. The direction given was in these terms: "In our law if two men fight and one of them after a while endeavours to avoid any further struggle and retreats as far as he can, and then when he can go no further turns and kills his assailant to avoid being killed himself, that homicide is excusable, but notice that to show that homicide arising from a fight was committed in self-defence it must be shown that the party killing had retreated as far as he could, or as far as the fierceness of the assault would permit him."

One does not have to seek far for the source of this direction. It was clearly quoted from *Archbold's*

Criminal Pleading Evidence & Practice, 37th ed (1969) p780, para 2495, which is in turn based upon a passage in *Hale's Pleas of the Crown,* (1800) vol. 1 pp481, 483. In our judgment, the direction was expressed in too inflexible terms and might, in certain circumstances, be regarded as significantly misleading. We prefer the view expressed by the full court of Australia that a failure to retreat is only an *element* in the considerations upon which the reasonableness of an accused's conduct is to be judged (see *Palmer* v *The Queen*; [1971] 2 WLR 831, 840), or as it is put in *Smith and Hogan Criminal Law* (2nd ed (1969), p231): "… simply a factor to be taken into account in deciding whether it was necessary to use force, and whether the force used was reasonable."

The modern law on the topic was, in our respectful view, accurately set out in *R* v *Julien* [1969] 1 WLR 839, 843 by Widgery LJ, as he then was, in the following terms:

> "It is not, as we understand it, the law that a person threatened must take to his heels and run in the dramatic way suggested by Mr McHale; but what is necessary is that he should demonstrate by his actions that he does not want to fight. He must demonstrate that he is prepared to temporise and disengage and perhaps to make some physical withdrawal; and that that is necessary as a feature of the justification of self-defence is true, in our opinion, whether the charge is a homicide charge or something less serious."

In the light of the foregoing, how stands the direction given in the present case? Viewed in isolation, that is to say, without regard to the evidence adduced, it was expressed in too rigid terms. But the opportunity to retreat remains, as the trial judge said, "an important consideration," and, when regard is had to the evidence as to the circumstances which prevailed, in our view it emerges with clarity that the appellant could have avoided this fatal incident with ease by simply walking or running away – as, indeed, he promptly did as soon as Reilly had been stabbed. It is submitted by the defence that the appellant had manifested an unwillingness to fight, but, in our judgment, the evidence is strongly to the opposite effect. In these circumstances, had the jury been directed on the lines indicated in *R* v *Julien*, we cannot think that they would have come to a different conclusion in relation to the plea of self-defence than that which their verdict demonstrates. Accordingly, no miscarriage of justice occurred as a result of the direction given, and, had it been necessary to do so, we should unhesitatingly have applied the proviso to section 2 (1) of the Criminal Appeal Act 1968.'

R v *Martin* (1989) 88 Cr App R 343 Court of Appeal (Criminal Division) (Lord Lane LCJ, Simon Brown and Roch JJ)

Necessity as a defence to driving whilst disqualified

Facts
The appellant's wife had suicidal tendencies and had in the past attempted to take her own life on a number of occasions. On the day in question, the appellant's son had overslept and was likely to lose his job if he arrived late for work. The appellant's wife became extremely distraught and threatened to kill herself if the appellant did not get the son to work on time. The appellant, who had been disqualified from driving, drove his son to work, in the course of which he was apprehended by the police. The appellant was convicted of driving whilst disqualified following the trial judge's ruling that the defence of necessity was not open to him, and he now appealed against that conviction.

Held
The appeal would be allowed.

Simon Brown J:

> 'Sceptically though one may regard that defence on the facts – and there were, we would observe, striking difficulties about the detailed evidence when it came finally to be given before the judge in mitigation – the sole question before this court is whether those facts, had the jury accepted that they were or might be true, amounted in law to a defence. If they did, then the appellant was entitled to a trial of the issue

before the jury. The jury would of course have had to be directed properly upon the precise scope and nature of the defence, but the decision on the facts would have been for them. As it was, such a defence was pre-empted by the ruling. Should it have been?

In our judgment the answer is plainly not. The authorities are now clear. Their effect is perhaps most conveniently to be found in the judgment of this court in *Conway* (1988) 88 Cr App R 159, [1988] 3 All ER 1025. The decision reviews earlier relevant authorities.

The principles may be summarised thus. First, English law does in extreme circumstances, recognise a defence of necessity. Most commonly this defence arises as duress, that is, pressure upon the accused's will from the wrongful threats or violence of another. Equally, however, it can arise from other objective dangers threatening the accused or others. Arising thus it is conveniently called "duress of circumstances".

Secondly, the defence is available only if, from an objective standpoint, the accused can be said to be acting reasonably and proportionately in order to avoid a threat of death or serious injury.

Thirdly, assuming the defence to be open to the accused on his account of the facts, the issue should be left to the jury, who should be directed to determine these two questions: first, was the accused, or may he have been, impelled to act as he did because as a result of what he reasonably believed to be the situation he had good cause to fear that otherwise death or serious physical injury would result? Secondly, if so, may a sober person of reasonable firmness, sharing the characteristics of the accused, have responded to that situation by acting as the accused acted? If the answer to both those questions was yes, then the jury would acquit: the defence of necessity would have been established.

That the defence is available in cases of reckless driving is established by *Conway (supra)* itself and indeed by an earlier decision of the court in *Willer* (1986) 83 Cr App R 225. *Conway* is authority also for the proposition that the scope of the defence is no wider for reckless driving than for other serious offences. As was pointed out in the judgment, (1988) 88 Cr App R at 164, [1988] 3 All ER at 1029h: "reckless driving can kill".

We see no material distinction between offences of reckless driving and driving whilst disqualified so far as the application of the scope of this defence is concerned. Equally we can see no distinction in principle between various threats of death: it matters not whether the risk of death is by murder or by suicide or, indeed, by accident. One can illustrate the matter by considering a disqualified driver being driven by his wife, she suffering a heart attack in remote countryside and he needing instantly to get her to hospital.

It follows from this that the judge quite clearly did come to a wrong decision on the question of law, and the appellant should have been permitted to raise this defence for what it was worth before the jury.

It is in our judgment a great pity that that course was not taken. It is difficult to believe that any jury would in fact have swallowed the improbably story which this defendant desired to advance. There was, it emerged when evidence was given in mitigation, in the house at the time a brother of the boy who was late for work, who was licensed to drive, and available to do so; the suggestion was that he would not take his brother because of "a lot of aggravation in the house between them". It is a further striking fact that when apprehended by the police the appellant was wholly silent as to why on this occasion he had felt constrained to drive. But those considerations, in our judgment were essentially for the jury, and we have concluded, although not without hesitation that it would be inappropriate here to apply the proviso.'

Palmer v *R* [1971] AC 814 Privy Council (Lords Morris, Donovan and Avonside)

Self-defence

Facts
The defendant appealed against his conviction for murder, contending that where there was evidence that he had acted by way of self-defence, but that the victim's death had been caused by the defendant's use of excessive force, the jury should be directed to return a verdict of manslaughter not murder.

Held

The appeal would be dismissed.

Lord Morris:

'If the jury are satisfied by the prosecution beyond doubt that an accused did not act in self-defence, then it may be that in some cases (of homicide) they will have to consider whether the accused acted under the stress of provocation. (See for example *Mancini v Director of Public Prosecutions* (1941) 28 Cr App R 65; [1942] AC 1 and *Bullard* (1957) 42 Cr App R 1; [1957] AC 635.) If the jury are satisfied by the prosecution that the accused did not act in self-defence and was not provoked, then the jury will have to decide whether the accused had the intent that is necessary if the crime of murder is to be proved. If on the evidence in a case the view is possible that though all questions of self-defence and of provocation are rejected by the jury it would be open to them to conclude that, though the accused acted unjustifiably, he had no intent to kill or to cause serious bodily injury, then manslaughter should be left to the jury. But it is not every fanciful hypothesis that need be presented for their consideration.

On behalf of the appellant it was contended that, if where self-defence is an issue in a case of homicide a jury came to the conclusion that an accused person was intending to defend himself, then an intention to kill or to cause grievous bodily harm would be negatived: so it was contended that, if in such a case the jury came to the conclusion that excessive force had been used, the correct verdict would be one of manslaughter: hence it was argued that in every case where self-defence is left to a jury they must be directed that there are the three possible verdicts, viz Guilty of murder, Guilty of manslaughter, and Not Guilty. But in many cases where someone is intending to defend himself he will have had an intention to cause serious bodily injury or even to kill and, if the prosecution satisfy the jury that he had one of these intentions in circumstances in which or at a time when there was no justification or excuse for having it, then the prosecution will have shown that the question of self-defence is eliminated. All other issues which on the facts may arise will be unaffected.

An issue of self-defence may of course arise in a range and variety of cases and circumstances where no death has resulted. The test as to its rejection or its validity will be just the same as in a case where death has resulted. In its simplest form the question that arises is the question: Was the defendant acting in necessary self-defence? If the prosecution satisfy the jury that he was not, then all other possible issues remain ...

... In their Lordships' view, the defence of self-defence is one which can be and will be readily understood by any jury. It is a straightforward conception. It involves no abstruse legal thought. It requires no set words by way of explanation. No formula need be employed in reference to it. Only common sense is needed for its understanding. It is both good law and good sense that a man who is attacked may defend himself. It is both good law and good sense that he may do, but may only do, what is reasonably necessary. But everything will depend upon the particular facts and circumstances. Of these a jury can decide. It may in some cases be only sensible and clearly possible to take some simple avoiding action. Some attacks may be serious and dangerous. Others may not be. If there is some relatively minor attack, it would not be common sense to permit some action of retaliation which was wholly out of proportion to the necessities of the situation. If an attack is serious so that it puts someone in immediate peril, then immediate defensive action may be necessary. If the moment is one of crisis for someone in imminent danger, he may have to avert the danger by some instant reaction. If the attack is all over and no sort of peril remains, then the employment of force may be by way of revenge or punishment or by way of paying off an old score or may be pure aggression. There may no longer be any link with a necessity of defence. Of all these matters the good sense of a jury will be the arbiter. There are no prescribed words which must be employed in or adopted in a summing-up. All that is needed is a clear exposition, in relation to the particular facts of the case, of the conception of necessary self-defence. If there has been no attack, then clearly there will have been no need for defence. If there has been attack so that defence is reasonably necessary, it will be recognised that a person defending himself cannot weigh to a nicety the exact measure of his necessary defensive action. If a jury thought that in a moment of unexpected anguish a person attacked had only done what he honestly and instinctively thought was necessary, that would be most potent evidence that only reasonable defensive action had been taken. A jury will be told that the defence of self-defence, where the evidence makes its raising possible, will fail only if the prosecution show beyond doubt that what the accused did was not by way of self-defence. But their Lordships consider, in agreement with the approach in the *De Freitas* case [[1960] 2 WIR 523], that if the prosecution have shown that what was done was not done in self-defence, then that issue is eliminated from the case. If the jury consider that an accused acted in self-defence or if the jury are in doubt as to this, then they will acquit. The defence of self-defence either succeeds so as to result in an acquittal or it is disproved, in which case as a defence it is rejected. In a homicide case the circumstances may be such that it will become an issue as to whether there was provocation so that the verdict might be one of manslaughter. Any other possible issues will remain. If in any case the view is possible that the intent necessary to constitute the crime of murder was lacking, then that matter would be left to the jury.'

R v Shepherd (1988) 86 Cr App R 47 Court of Appeal (Criminal Division) (Mustill LJ, Gatehouse J and Rougier J)

Duress – availability to one who voluntarily joins a criminal enterprise

Facts (as stated by Mustill LJ)

'Martin Brian Shepherd, who now appeals by leave of the single judge, was convicted at the Crown Court in Southampton of five counts alleging burglary. Several other offences were taken into consideration when concurrent sentences of nine months' imprisonment were imposed. The offences were all of a similar character. The appellant, in the company of a varying number of other men, would enter retail premises. Some would distract the shopkeeper, whilst others would carry away boxes of goods, usually cigarettes. In this simple way the thieves were able to make off with goods of very considerable value. Ultimately some of them, including the appellant, were caught. In the last of a series of interviews the appellant admitted what he had done, and pointed out to the police the premises concerned. There was reason to believe that another man, whom we shall call P, was also involved in some of the offences, but he was not charged with any of them. P is a man with many convictions for offences of dishonesty and violence. On these facts it would seem that the appellant had no choice but to plead guilty to all the charges. In the event however he sought to raise a defence on the following lines. He had originally been recruited to the joint enterprise by P. The very first of the offences took place during April 1986, and the appellant played a willing part. It was a stroke of great good fortune for the appellant that this offence was on the list of those taken into consideration, and was not the subject of a plea of guilty. But he was unnerved by the experience and wanted to give up. He was however threatened by P with violence to himself and his family and was compelled to carry on with the thefts, and did so until he was caught some weeks later. The story, which was not mentioned in the police records of his interviews, receives some colour from the undoubted fact that P was subsequently sent to prison for an assault on the appellant committed within the precincts of the court whilst the case was awaiting trial, and there was evidence of another assault on him at much the same time. On the appellant's pleas of not guilty the matter came for trial in the Crown Court on January 5, 1987. We mention this date because it was some three months before another division of this Court gave judgment in *Sharp* (1987) 85 Cr App R 207, [1987] 3 WLR 1. If the order of events had been different, and the guidance given in that judgment had been available to counsel and the learned assistant recorder, it may well be that a different course would have been adopted. At all events what happened was this. Counsel for the appellant very properly informed the prosecution that the defence of duress was to be raised, and of the basis for it. Counsel for the prosecution intimated that he would contend that on the authorities the defence was unsound, even if the appellant's story was true, since his original participation in the joint venture had been voluntary. Since the validity of this argument would affect the scope of the evidence and cross-examination, it was thought proper to raise the question of the law at the outset in order to save a possible waste of time and cost. The learned assistant recorder agreed to this proposal, and after argument he ruled in favour of the prosecution. In spite of this the appellant maintained his pleas, and gave evidence on his own behalf. For reasons which we do not follow, he was permitted to give his story of duress, even though the assistant recorder had already ruled that it was immaterial as indeed he was to direct the jury when he reminded them of what the appellant had said. The story was not however tested in any way. The jury retired for only ten minutes before returning verdicts of guilty, having really been left no choice in the matter. The appellant now appeals, contending that the issue of duress should not have been withdrawn from the jury.'

Held

The appeal would be allowed.

Mustill LJ:

'The basis for [the appellant's contention], as it was developed in the course of the appeal, was substantially different from the argument presented at the trial. It was (and still is) accepted on behalf of the prosecution that duress may in appropriate circumstances be available as a defence to a person charged with offences such as the present. It was (and still is) accepted on behalf of the appellant that this defence is not available when the defendant has, to put the matter neutrally, voluntarily brought himself into the situation from which the duress has arisen. The problem concerns the breadth of this exception. At the trial no recourse was had to authority beyond a very compressed account in *Archbold, Criminal Pleading, Evidence and Practice* (42nd ed) paragraph 17-58, of the judgment delivered by the Lord Chief Justice of Northern Ireland in *Fitzpatrick* [1977] NILR 20. This was relied on by counsel for the appellant in support of a submission that the accused forfeits the right to rely on duress only where he has joined an "organisation" possessing some kind of formal, although illicit, structure such as has existed in Northern Ireland and elsewhere. The judge rejected this contention. Any doubts about whether he was right to do so have been laid to rest by *Sharp* (supra), and we need say no more about this point. The exclusion from the defence of duress is undoubtedly capable of operating where the persons with whom the defendant involves himself are simply co-conspirators banded together for a single offence or a group of offences. This was not however the only question of principle which arose on the facts which we have summarised. Does a voluntary participation in any joint criminal act entail that any act of duress thereafter committed by another participant is to be excluded from consideration when the defence is raised? Or is the exception to be more narrowly understood?

The learned assistant recorder did not have the benefit of argument on this point, but evidently understood the passage cited from *Archbold* as supporting the former opinion, for he ruled as follows:

"I read the Lord Chief Justice of Northern Ireland to be saying that those who play with fire cannot complain if they are thereafter burnt. Those who voluntarily associate with others or even only with one other in anticipation of their being led into crime cannot thereafter complain if matters get out of hand and go beyond their contemplation. I see no reason at all to read the judgment as applying only to political organisations or to violent organisation or to large organisations. If it be the case that Mr Shepherd, the defendant in this case, voluntarily went along with the first of those escapades he cannot rely upon threats which arose thereafter to avoid responsibility for his participation in the later escapades."

This ruling, which was in any event debatable, was put seriously in question by the subsequent decision in *Sharp* (supra), and the issue was argued in full before us, with citation from *Hurley and Murray* [1967] VR 526, *Lynch* (1975 61 Cr App R 6, *Fitzpatrick* (supra), *R v Howe* [1987] AC 417 and *Sharp* itself.

At the conclusion of the argument we had arrived at the following opinion:

(1) Although it is not easy to rationalise the existence of duress as a defence rather than a ground of mitigation, it must in some way be founded on concession to human frailty in cases where the defendant has been faced with choice between two evils.

(2) The exception which exists where the defendant has voluntarily allied himself with the person who exercises the duress must be founded on the assumption that, just as he cannot complain if he had the opportunity to escape the duress and failed to take it, equally no concession to frailty is required if the risk of duress is freely undertaken.

(3) Thus, in some instances it will follow inevitably that the defendant has an excuse: for example, if he has joined a group of people dedicated to violence a political end, or one which is overtly ready to use violence for other criminal ends. Members of so called paramilitary illegal groups, or gangs of armed robbers, must be taken to anticipate what may happen to them if their nerve fails, and cannot be heard to complain if violence is indeed threatened.

(4) Other cases will be difficult. There is no need for recourse to extravagant examples. Common sense must recognise that there are certain kinds of criminal enterprises the joining of which, in the absence of any knowledge of propensity to violence on the part of one member, would not lead another to suspect that a decision to think better of the whole affair might lead him into serious trouble. The logic which would appear to underlie the law of duress would suggest that if trouble did unexpectedly materialise, and if it put the defendant into a dilemma in which a reasonable man might have chosen to act as he did, the concession to human frailty should not be denied to him.

Having arrived at these conclusions on the argument addressed to us, it appeared to us plain there had been a question which should properly have been put to the jury and that the appeal must accordingly be allowed. We intimated that this would be so, whilst taking the opportunity to put our reasons in writing.

Naturally a proper scepticism would have been in order when the defence came to be examined at the trial, for there were many aspects on which the appellant could have been pressed. In particular, his prior knowledge of P would require investigation. At the same time the trial would not have been a foregone conclusion since the concerted shoplifting enterprise did not involve violence to the victim either in anticipation or in the way it was actually put into effect. The members of the jury have had to ask themselves whether the appellant could be said to have taken the risk of P's violence simply by joining a shoplifting gang of which he was a member. Of course even if they were prepared to give the appellant the benefit of the doubt in this respect, an acquittal would be far from inevitable. The jury would have then to consider the nature and timing of the threats, and the nature and persistence of the offences, in order to decide whether the defendant was entitled to be exonerated. It may well be that, in the light of the evidence as it emerged, convictions would have followed. But the question was never put to the test. The issues were never investigated. The jury were left with no choice but to convict. In these circumstances we saw no alternative but to hold that the convictions could not stand. The sentences necessarily fell away, leaving the fortunate appellant with no penalty attached to the first offence of which he was undeniably guilty, but which was not the subject of any charge. That was the position at the conclusion of the argument. Since then we have been able to study a transcript of the ruling of the trial judge in *Sharp* (Kenneth Jones J), a ruling which was approved on appeal (see (1987) 85 Cr App R at 212, [1987] AC at 7F). It is sufficiently important in the present context to justify quotation at length:

> "In my judgment there is no authority binding upon me on this point, but there are the strongest and most powerful pointers to what is the correct answer. In my judgment the law does not go so far as to embody that which was submitted by the Crown in the Court of Criminal Appeal in Northern Ireland in *Lynch's* case [1975] Nl 35, namely that the defence of duress is not available to an accused who voluntarily joins in a criminal enterprise and is afterwards subjected to threats of violence, but in my judgment the defence of duress is not available to an accused who voluntarily exposes and submits himself to illegal compulsion.
>
> It is not merely a matter of joining in a criminal enterprise; it is a matter of joining in a criminal enterprise of such a nature that the defendant appreciated the nature of the enterprise itself and the attitudes of those in charge of it, so that when he was in fact subjected to compulsion he could fairly be said by a jury to have voluntarily exposed himself and submitted himself to such compulsion. Therefore on the facts advanced by or which are about to be advanced by Mr Mylne, I hold that duress is not available as a defence to Sharp to the charge of murder, or indeed of manslaughter.
>
> Of course it follows that it would be a question of fact for the jury as to whether Sharp had voluntarily exposed and submitted himself to this illegal compulsion. The facts, as Mr Mylne proposes to advance them, do not necessarily dispose of that matter. It is still a matter for the jury to decide – though as I am sure he will concede, the evidence lies very heavily against him in view of his client's admitted complicity in this offence, and indeed his client's view of the man who was in charge of it, namely Hussey. If the jury can find it possible to say that he, although joining in this criminal enterprise did not voluntarily expose or

submit himself to the possibility of coercion, compulsion by Hussey, then the jury would be putting him then in the position of the innocent bystander, and duress would be available to him as a defence. If the jury took the view on the totality of the evidence it has to be fairly and justly said that he voluntarily disposed and submitted himself to illegal compulsion, then the defence of duress is not open to him. So much for the defence of duress."

This ruling, if we may say so, corresponds exactly with the view which we had independently formed. In the interests of accuracy it must be acknowledged that it was the ruling itself, rather than the whole of the passage in which it was expressed, which was the subject of the approval on appeal. Nevertheless the terms of the judgment delivered by the Lord Chief Justice were such as to make it clear, to our mind, that the approach of the trial judge was correct. In the context of that case, given the facts, such a conclusion was fatal to the appeal. Here, by contrast, it demonstrates that the issue ought to have been left to the jury. In conclusion we should add that we have also examined the provisions of various penal statutes and codes emanating from other common law countries: for example, the Crime Act 1961, section 24 of New Zealand; the Model Penal Code, section 2.09(2) of the United States; and codes of Canada and various states in Australia. These are not identical in their terms, but they are all consistent with the view which we have expressed, as are the opinions set out in Law Commission Working Paper No 83, paragraphs 2.35 to 2.38, and in articles including those by P J Rowe "Duress and Criminal Organisations" (1979), 42 MLR 102, and R S O'Reagan, "Duress and Criminal Conspiracies" [1971 Crim LR 35.

For these reasons therefore we consider that the conviction should be quashed.

R v Williams (Gladstone) (1984) 78 Cr App R 276

See Chapter 32.

32 Defences III

Beckford* v *R [1987] 3 WLR 611 Privy Council (Lords Keith, Elwyn-Jones, Templeman, Griffiths and Oliver)

Mistake as to self-defence

Facts
The defendant was a police officer sent to a house where, so he was told, a man with a gun was terrorising the occupants. On arrival at the house he saw the suspect run out of the back door. The defendant fired at the suspect, killing him. He was charged with murder, and raised the defence of self-defence based on his honest belief that the suspect was armed and that therefore his own life was in imminent danger. The trial judge directed the jury that such a belief had to be reasonably held. The defendant was convicted, and appealed to the Privy Council.

Held
The appeal would be allowed.

Lord Griffiths:

'It is accepted by the prosecution that there is no difference on the law of self-defence between the law of Jamaica and the English common law and it therefore falls to be decided whether it was correctly decided by the Court of Appeal in *R v Williams (Gladstone)* (1983) 78 Cr App R 276 that the defence of self-defence depends upon what the accused "honestly" believed the circumstances to be and not upon the reasonableness of that belief – what the Court of Appeal in Jamaica referred to as the "honest belief" and "reasonable belief" schools of thought.

There can be no doubt that prior to the decision of the House of Lords in *R v Morgan* [1976] AC 182 the whole weight of authority supported the view that it was an essential element of self-defence not only that the accused believed that he was being attacked or in imminent danger of being attacked but also that such belief was based on reasonable grounds. No elaborate citation of authority is necessary but counsel for the Crown rightly drew attention to such 19th century authorities as *Foster's Case* (1825) 1 Lew 187; *R v Weston* (1879) 14 Cox CC 346 and *R v Rose* (1884) 15 Cox CC 540 in which the judges charged the jury that self-defence provided a defence to a charge of murder if the accused honestly and on reasonable grounds believed that his or another's life was in peril. It is however to be remembered that it was not until 1898 that an accused was able to give evidence in his own defence and it is natural that the judges in the absence of any direct statement of his belief from the accused should have focused attention upon the inference that could be drawn from the surrounding circumstances. Nevertheless, even after 1898 the law of self-defence continued to be stated as propounded by the judges in the 19th century; see *R v Chisam* (1963) 47 Cr App R 130 in which Lord Parker CJ, at p133, approved the following statement of the law in *Halsbury's Laws of England*, 3rd ed, vol 10 (1955) (Criminal Law), p723, para. 1382:

"Where a forcible and violent felony is attempted upon the person of another, the party assaulted, or his servant, or any other person present, is entitled to repel force by force, and, if necessary, to kill the aggressor. There must be a reasonable necessity for the killing, or at least an honest belief based upon reasonable grounds that there is such a necessity."

In *R v Fennell* [1971] 1 QB 428, 431, Widgery LJ, who was soon to succeed Lord Parker CJ as Lord Chief of Justice, said:

> "Where a person honestly and reasonably believes that he or his child is in imminent danger of injury it would be unjust if he were deprived of the right to use reasonable force by way of defence merely because he had made some genuine mistake of fact."

The question then is whether the present Lord Chief Justice, Lord Lane, in *R v Williams (Gladstone)*, 78 Cr App R 276 was right to depart from the law as declared by his predecessors in the light of the decision of the House of Lords in *R v Morgan* [1976] AC 182. *R v Morgan* was a case of rape and counsel for the Crown had submitted that the decision of the majority turned solely upon their view of the specific intention required for the commission of that crime and accordingly had no relevance to the law of self-defence. It was further submitted that the question now before their Lordships was settled by an earlier decision of the Privy Council in *Palmer v The Queen* [1971] AC 814. This submission is founded upon the fact that Lord Morris of Borth-y-Gest in giving the judgment of the Board set out a very lengthy passage from the summing up of the judge and commented, at p824:

> "Their Lordships conclude that there is no room for criticism of the summing up or of the conduct of the trial unless there is a rule that in every case where the issue of self-defence is left to the jury they must be directed that if they consider that excessive force was used in defence then they should return a verdict of guilt of manslaughter. For the reasons which they will set out their Lordships consider there is no such rule."

The only question raised for the determination of the Board was that stated by Lord Morris of Borth-y-Gest. It is true that, in the passage quoted from the summing up the judge had stated the ingredients of self-defence in the then conventional form of reasonable belief; but it was not this part of his summing up that was under attack nor did it receive any particular consideration by the Board. Their Lordships are unable to attach greater weight to the approval of the summing up than as indicating that it was in conformity with the practice of directing juries that the accused must have reasonable grounds for believing that self-defence was necessary.

In *R v Morgan* [1976] AC 182 each member of the House of Lords held that the mens rea required to commit rape is the knowledge that the woman is not consenting or recklessness as to whether she is consenting or not. From this premise the majority held that unless the prosecution proved that the man did not believe the woman was consenting or was at least reckless as to the consent they had failed to prove the necessary mens rea which is an essential ingredient of the crime. Lord Edmund-Davies in his dissent, at pp221-235, referred to the large body of distinguished academic support for the view that it is morally indefensible to convict a person of a crime when owing to a genuine mistake as to the facts he believes that he is acting lawfully and has no intention to commit the crime and therefore has no guilty mind. He expressed his preference for this moral approach but felt constrained by the weight of authority, including the cases on self-defence, to hold that the law required the accused's belief should not only be genuine but also based upon reasonable grounds.

In *R v Kimber* [1983] 1 WLR 1118 the Court of Appeal applied the decision in *R v Morgan* to a case of indecent assault and held that a failure to direct the jury that the prosecution had to make them sure that the accused had never believed that the woman was consenting was a misdirection. Lawton LJ in the course of his judgment rejected the submission that the decision in *R v Morgan* was confined to rape and clearly regarded it as of far wider significance. Commenting upon an obiter dictum in *R v Phekoo* [1981] 1 WLR 1117, 1127, he said, at p1123:

> "the court went on, after referring to *R v Morgan*, to say, clearly obiter, per Hollings J at p1127H: 'It seems to us clear that this decision was confined and intended to be confined to the offence of rape.' We do not accept that this was the intention of their Lordships in Morgan's case. Lord Hailsham of St Marylebone started his speech by saying that the issue as to belief was a question of great academic importance in the theory of English criminal law." '

His Lordship then considered *R v Williams (Gladstone)* (below) at some length, and continued:

'Looking back, *R v Morgan* [1976] AC 182 can now be seen as a landmark decision in the development of the common law returning the law to the path upon which it might have developed but for the inability of an accused to give evidence on his own behalf. Their Lordships note that not only has this development the approval of such distinguished criminal lawyers as Professor Glanville Williams and Professor Smith: see *Textbook of Criminal Law*, 2nd ed (1963), pp137-138, and *Smith and Hogan, Criminal Law*, 5th ed (1983), pp329-330; but it also has the support of the Criminal Law Revision Committee: see Fourteenth Report on Offences against the Person (1980) Cmnd 7844) and of the Law Commission: see A Report to the Law Commission on Codification of the Criminal Law (1985) (Law Com No. 143).

There may be a fear that the abandonment of the objective standard demanded by the existence of reasonable grounds for belief will result in the success of too many spurious claims of self-defence. The English experience has not shown this to be the case. The Judicial Studies Board with the approval of the Lord Chief Justice has produced a model direction on self-defence which is now widely used by judges when summing up to juries. The direction contains the following guidance:

> "Whether the plea is self-defence or defence of another, if the defendant may have been labouring under a mistake as to the facts, he must be judged according to his mistaken belief of the facts: that is so whether the mistake was, on an objective view, a reasonable mistake or not."

Their Lordships have heard no suggestion that this form of summing up has resulted in a disquieting number of acquittals. This is hardly surprising for no jury is going to accept a man's assertion that he believed that he was about to be attacked without testing it against all the surrounding circumstances. In assisting the jury to determine whether or not the accused had a genuine belief the judge will of course direct their attention to those features of the evidence that make such a belief more or less probable. Where there are no reasonable grounds to hold a belief it will surely only be in exceptional circumstances that a jury will conclude that such a belief was or might have been held.'

C (A Minor) v *DPP* [1995] 2 WLR 383 House of Lords (Lords Jauncey, Bridge, Ackner, Lowry and Browne-Wilkinson)

Confirmation of doli incapax presumption

Facts
The appellant, a 12-year-old boy, had been convicted by magistrates of interfering with a motor cycle with intent to commit theft, contrary to s9(1) Criminal Attempts Act 1981. The court had found that he had done substantial damage to the motor cycle and had run away when the police arrived, and inferred from this that the appellant had known that he had done something seriously wrong. On appeal against conviction, on the ground that the appellant's actions were merely equivocal, and could simply be evidence that he knew he had been naughty, the Divisional Court held that the rebuttable assumption that a child between the ages of 10 and 14 was incapable of committing a crime should no longer form part of English criminal law. The following question of law was confirmed for consideration by the House of Lords: 'Whether there continues to be a presumption that a child between the ages of 10 and 14 is doli incapax and, if so, whether that presumption can only be rebutted by clear positive evidence that he knew that his act was seriously wrong, such evidence not consisting merely in the evidence of the acts amounting to the offence itself.'

Held
The appeal was allowed. Both parts of the certified question were answered in the affirmative. The prosecution would have to prove that the defendant aged between 10 and 14 had committed the unlawful act, and at the time had known that it was seriously wrong, as opposed to merely naughty or mischievous. Lord Lowry, whilst noting that the view adopted by the Divisional Court was echoed in the 1985 draft

Criminal Code Bill, was persuaded to reject the argument for judicial reform of the existing law by the fact that in its paper 'Crime, Justice and Protecting the Public' (Cm 965) the government had confirmed its support for the retention of the doli incapax rule. Given that the issue involved arguments based on social policy it was, in his Lordship's view, a classic case for parliamentary investigation, deliberation and legislation.

Lord Lowry addressed himself to the specific points raised by Laws J in support of the Divisional Court's decision to abolish the presumption, not, as he explained, to refute them, but to show that they were not conclusive on the matter. He observed (inter alia):

'1. It is true that there is (and has been for a considerable time) compulsory education and, as the judge said, perhaps children now grow up more quickly. But better formal education and earlier sophistication do not guarantee that the child will more readily distinguish right from wrong.
2. The presumption is "out of step with the general law". True enough, but the *general* law was not meant to apply without qualification to children under 14.
3. I agree that the phrase "seriously wrong" is conceptually obscure, and that view is confirmed by the rather loose treatment accorded to the doli incapax doctrine by the textbooks, but, when the phrase is contrasted with "merely naughty or mischievous", I think its meaning is reasonably clear.
4. The rule is said to be illogical because the presumption can be rebutted by proof that the child was of normal mental capacity *for his age*; this leads to the conclusion that every child is initially presumed not to be of normal mental capacity *for his age*; which is absurd. This argument involves a point which I must deal with when considering the second part of the certified question (how to prove that the child is doli capax), but at this stage I will focus on the illogicality. We start with a benevolent presumption of doli incapax, the purpose of which was to protect children between 7 (now by statute 10) and 14 years from the full rigour of the criminal law. The fact that the presumption was rebuttable has led the courts to recognise that the older the child (see *B v R* 44 Cr App R 1, 3) and the more obviously heinous the offence, the easier it is to rebut the presumption. Proof of mental normality has in practice (understandably but perhaps not always logically) been largely accepted as proof that the child can distinguish right from wrong and form a criminal intent. The presumption itself is not, and never has been, completely logical; it provides a benevolent safeguard which evidence can remove. Very little evidence is needed but it must be adduced as part of the prosecution's case, or else there will be no case to answer. ...
6. It has also been said that the rule is divisive because it bears hardly on perhaps isolated acts of wrongdoing done by children from "good homes", and also perverse because it absolves children from "bad homes" who are most likely to commit "criminal" acts. One answer to this observation (not entirely satisfying, I agree) is that the presumption contemplated the conviction and punishment of children who, possibly by virtue of their superior upbringing, bore moral responsibility for their actions and the exoneration of those who did not. The Divisional Court's argument provides support for the modern outlook in favour of prescribing suitable treatment (which may or may not be punitive) for the many children who commit antisocial acts, instead of searching for moral culpability, which should then be visited with retribution.
7. It is then said (with considerable force, I would admit) that the presumption is an outmoded survival from an age in which criminal guilt was inevitably followed by ferocious retribution. But, while times have greatly changed since the days when children of 8 and 10 years were hanged for offences much less heinous than murder, it should be observed that the purpose and effect of the presumption is still to protect children between 10 and 14 from the full force of the criminal law.'

His Lordship summarised the position thus:

'A long and uncontradicted line of authority makes two propositions clear. The first is that the prosecution must prove that the child defendant did the act charged and that when doing that act he knew that it was a wrong act as distinct from an act of mere naughtiness or childish mischief. The criminal standard of proof applies. What is required has been variously expressed, as in *Blackstone*, "strong and clear beyond all doubt or contradiction", or, in *R v Gorrie* (1918) 83 JP 136, "very clear and complete evidence" or, in

B v R (1958) 44 Cr App R 1, 3 per Lord Parker CJ, "It has often been put in this way, that ... 'guilty knowledge must be proved and the evidence to that effect must be clear and beyond all possibility of doubt'." No doubt, the emphatic tone of some of the directions was due to the court's anxiety to prevent merely naughty children from being convicted of crimes and in a sterner age to protect them from the draconian consequences of conviction.

The second clearly established proposition is that evidence to prove the defendant's guilty knowledge, as defined above, must not be the mere proof of the doing of the act charged, however horrifying or obviously wrong that act may be. As Erle J said in *R v Smith (Sidney)* (1845) 1 Cox CC 260:

> "... a guilty knowledge that he was doing wrong – must be proved by the evidence, and cannot be presumed from the mere commission of the act. You are to determine from a review of the evidence whether it is satisfactorily proved that at the time he fired the rick (if you should be of the opinion he did fire it) he had a guilty knowledge that he was committing a crime."

The report of *R v Kershaw* (1902) 18 TLR 357, 358, where a boy of 13 was charged with murder, states:

> "[Bucknill J], in summing up, pointed out that the commission of a crime was in itself no evidence whatever of the guilty state of mind which is essential before a child between the ages of 7 and 14 can be condemned."

In that case the jury found the prisoner guilty of manslaughter and he was sentenced to 10 years' penal servitude.

The cases seem to show, logically enough, that the older the defendant is and the more obviously wrong the act, the easier it will generally be to prove guilty knowledge. The surrounding circumstances are of course relevant and what the defendant said or did before or after the act may go to prove his guilty mind. Running away is usually equivocal, as Laws J rightly said it was in the present case, because flight from the scene can as easily follow a naughty action as a wicked one. There must, however, be a few cases where running away would indicate guilty knowledge, where an act is either wrong or innocent and there is no room for mere naughtiness. An example might be selling drugs at a street corner and fleeing at the sight of a policeman.

The Divisional Court here, assuming that the presumption applied, would have reversed the youth court, rightly, in my opinion, because there was no evidence, outside the commission of the "offence," upon which one could find that the presumption had been rebutted.

In order to obtain that kind of evidence, apart from anything the defendant may have said or done, the prosecution has to rely on interviewing the suspect or having him psychiatrically examined (two methods which depend on receiving co-operation) or on evidence from someone who knows the defendant well, such as a teacher, the involvement of whom adversely to the child is unattractive. Under section 34 of the Criminal Justice and Public Order Act 1994 a child defendant's silence when questioned before trial may be the subject of comment if he fails to mention something which is later relied on in his defence and which he could reasonably have been expected to mention at the earlier stage, but I do not see how that provision could avail the prosecution on the issue of guilty knowledge. Mr Robertson [counsel for the appellant] informed your Lordships that convictions or pleas of guilty occur in a high proportion of cases governed by the presumption. I cannot speak from experience, but perhaps one explanation may be that except in very serious cases the courts, lacking really cogent evidence, often treat the rebuttal of the presumption as a formality. (Indeed its very existence was initially overlooked in *R v Coulburn* (1987) 87 Cr App R 309, where the charge was one of murder.) My speculation, for it is nothing more, is strengthened by the reflection that courts have frequently accepted evidence of normal mental development as proof of mature discernment, although the two are not true equivalents.

My Lords, I have reached without difficulty the conclusion that both parts of the certified question should be answered "Yes". I would therefore allow the appeal and remit the case to the High Court in order that it may be sent back to the youth court with a direction to dismiss the charge against the appellant. But the judges in the court below have achieved their object, at least in part, by drawing renewed attention to serious shortcomings in an important area of our criminal law. Forty years have passed since the article by Professor Glanville Williams and the years between have witnessed many criticisms and suggested remedies, but no vigorous or reasoned defence of the presumption. I believe that the time has come to examine further a doctrine which appears to have been inconsistently applied and which is certainly capable of producing inconsistent results, according to the way in which courts treat the presumption and depending on the evidence to rebut it which is available in each case.

One solution which has already been suggested is to abolish the presumption with or without an increase in the minimum age of criminal responsibility. This, as Mr Robertson pointed out, could expose children to the full criminal process at an earlier age than in most countries of Western Europe. An alternative might be to give a youth court exclusive jurisdiction (save in family matters) over children up to a specified age (say, 14 or 16) applying only civil remedies for anti-social behaviour under 10 (or 12) years and both civil and punitive remedies above that age.

Your Lordships will remember the way in which Harper J began his judgment in *R (A Child) v Whitty* (1993) 66 A Crim R 462, a case decided by the Supreme Court of Victoria:

> " 'No civilised society,' says Professor Colin Howard in his book entitled *Criminal Law*, 4th ed (1982), p343, 'regards children as accountable for their actions to the same extent as adults.' ... The wisdom of protecting young children against the full rigour of the criminal law is beyond argument. The difficulty lies in determining when and under what circumstances that protection should be removed."

The distinction between the treatment and the punishment of child "offenders" has popular and political overtones, a fact which shows that we have been discussing not so much a legal as a social problem, with a dash of politics thrown in, and emphasises that it should be within the exclusive remit of Parliament. There is need to study other systems, including that which holds sway in Scotland, a task for which the courts are not equipped. Whatever change is made, it should come only after collating and considering the evidence and after taking account of the effect which a change would have on the whole law relating to children's anti-social behaviour. This is a classic case for parliamentary investigation, deliberation and legislation.

I believe, my Lords, that we have reached the stage when the author of a lengthy judgment (or a lengthy argument)) needs an excuse for his prolixity. My excuse is that, reviewing a bold and imaginative judgment, I have deemed it not only courteous but also necessary to demonstrate my reasons for saying that the presumption is still part of our law, and not just to assert the fact. Secondly, without suggesting the answer, which I am not qualified to give, I hope that my survey may help to provide the incentive for a much-needed new look at an undoubted problem.'

DPP v *Morgan* [1976] AC 182 House of Lords (Lords Cross, Hailsham, Simon, Edmund-Davies and Fraser)

Honest mistake sufficient to negative mens rea

Facts
The defendants were convicted of rape, and appealed on the ground, inter alia, that they had honestly believed the woman to have been consenting. Their appeals were dismissed by the Court of Appeal. On appeal to the House of Lords:

Held
(Applying the proviso to s2(1) Criminal Appeals Act 1968) the appeals would be dismissed.

Lord Hailsham (reciting the terms of the trial judge's summing up to the jury):

> "'First of all, let me deal with the crime of rape. What are its ingredients? What have the prosecution to prove to your satisfaction before you can find a defendant guilty of rape? The crime of rape consists in having unlawful sexual intercourse with a woman without her consent and by force. By force. Those words

mean exactly what they say. It does not mean there has to be a fight or blows have to be inflicted. It means that there has to be some violence used against the woman to overbear her will or that there has to be a threat of violence as a result of which her will is overborne. You will bear in mind that force or the threat of force carries greater weight when there are four men involved than where there is one man involved. In other words, measure the force in deciding whether force is used. One of the elements to which you will have regard is the number of men involved in the incident.

Further, the prosecution have to prove that each defendant intended to have sexual intercourse with this woman without her consent, not merely that he intended to have intercourse with her but that he intended to have intercourse without her consent. Therefore if the defendant believed or may have believed that Mrs Morgan consented to him having sexual intercourse with her, then there would be no such intent in his mind and he would not be guilty of the offence of rape, but such a belief must be honestly held by the defendant in the first place. He must really believe that. And, secondly, his belief must be a reasonable belief; such a belief as a reasonable man would entertain if he applied his mind and thought about the matter. It is not enough for a defendant to rely upon a belief, even though he honestly held it, if it was completely fanciful; contrary to every indication which could be given which would carry some weight with a reasonable man. And, of course, the belief must be not a belief that the woman would consent at some time in the future, but a belief that at the time when intercourse was taking place or when it began that she was then consenting to it."

No complaint was made of the first paragraph where the learned judge is describing what, to use the common and convenient solecism, is meant by the actus reus in rape. Nor is there any complaint by the appellants of the judge's first proposition describing the mental element.

It is upon the second proposition about the mental element that the appellants concentrate their criticism. An honest belief in consent, they contend, is enough. It matters not whether it be also reasonable. No doubt a defendant will wish to raise argument or lead evidence to show that his belief was reasonable, since this will support its honesty. No doubt the prosecution will seek to cross examine or raise arguments or adduce evidence to undermine the contention that the belief is reasonable, because, in the nature of the case, the fact that a belief cannot reasonably be held is a strong ground for saying that it was not in fact held honestly at all. Nonetheless, the appellants contend, the crux of the matter, the factum probandum, or rather the fact to be refuted by the prosecution, is honesty and not honesty plus reasonableness. In making reasonableness as well as honesty an ingredient in this "defence" the judge, say the appellants, was guilty of a misdirection.

My first comment upon this direction is that the propositions described "in the first place" and "secondly" in the above direction as to the mental ingredient in rape are wholly irreconcileable. In practice this was accepted by both counsel for the appellants and for the respondent, counsel for the appellants embracing that described as "in the first place" and counsel for the respondent embracing the "secondly", and each rejecting the other as not being a correct statement of the law. In this, in my view, they had no alternative.

If it be true, as the learned judge says "in the first place," that the prosecution have to prove that

"each defendant intended to have sexual intercourse without her consent, not merely that he intended to have intercourse with her but that he intended to have intercourse without her consent,"

the defendant must be entitled to an acquittal if the prosecution fail to prove just that. The necessary mental ingredient will be lacking and the only possible verdict is "not guilty." If, on the other hand, as is asserted in the passage beginning "secondly," it is necessary for any belief in the woman's consent to be "a reasonable belief" before the defendant is entitled to an acquittal, it must either be because the mental ingredient in rape is not "to have intercourse and to have it without her consent" but simply "to have intercourse" subject to a special defence of "honest and reasonable belief," or alternatively to have intercourse without a reasonable belief in her consent. Counsel for the Crown argued for each of these alternatives, but in my view each is open to insuperable objections of principle. No doubt it would be possible, by statute, to devise a law by which intercourse, voluntarily entered into, was an absolute offence, subject to a "defence" or belief whether honest or honest and reasonable, of which the "evidential" burden is primarily on the defence and the "probative" burden on the prosecution. But in my opinion such is not the crime of rape as it has hitherto been understood. The prohibited act in rape is to have intercourse without the victim's consent. The minimum mens rea or guilty mind in most common law offences, including rape, is the intention to do the prohibited act, and that is correctly stated in the proposition stated "in the first place" of the judge's direction. In murder the situation is different, because the murder is only complete when the victim dies, and an intention to do really serious bodily harm has been held to be enough if such be the case.

The only qualification I would make to the direction of the learned judge's "in the first place" is the refinement for which, as I shall show, there is both Australian and English authority, that if the intention of the accused is to have intercourse nolens volens, that is recklessly and not caring whether the victim be a consenting party or not, that is equivalent on ordinary principles to an intent to do the prohibited act without the consent of the victim.

The alternative version of the learned judge's direction would read that the accused must do the prohibited act with the intention of doing it without an honest and reasonable belief in the victim's consent. This in effect is the version which took up most of the time in argument, and although I find the Court of Appeal's judgment difficult to understand, I think it the version which ultimately commended itself to that court. At all events I think it the more plausible way in which to state the learned judge's "secondly." In principle, however, I find it unacceptable. I believe that "mens rea" means "guilty or criminal mind", and if it be the case, as seems to be accepted here, that mental element in rape is not knowledge but intent, to insist that a belief must be reasonable to excuse is to insist that either the accused is to be found guilty of intending to do that which in truth he did not intend to do, or that his state of mind, though innocent of evil intent, can convict him if it be honest but not rational ...

I believe the law on this point to have been correctly stated by Lord Goddard CJ in *R v Steane* [1947] KB 997, 1004, when he said:

> "... if on the totality of the evidence there is room for more than one view as to the intent of the prisoner, the jury should be directed that it is for the prosecution to prove the intent to the jury's satisfaction, and if, on a review of the whole evidence, they either think that the intent did not exist or they are left in doubt as to the intent, the prisoner is entitled to be acquitted."

That was indeed, a case which involved a count where a specific, or, as Professor Smith has called it, an ulterior, intent was, and was required to be, charged in the indictment. But, once it be accepted that an intent of whatever description is an ingredient essential to the guilt of the accused I cannot myself see that any other direction can be logically acceptable. Otherwise a jury would in effect be told to find an intent where none existed or where none was proved to have existed. I cannot myself reconcile it with my conscience to sanction as part of the English law what I regard as logical impossibility, and, if there were any authority which, if accepted would compel me to do so, I would feel constrained to declare that it was not to be followed. However for reasons which I will give, I do not see any need in the instant case for such desperate remedies.

The beginning of wisdom in all the "mens rea" cases to which our attention was called is, as was pointed out by Stephen J in *R v Tolson*, 23 QBD 168, 185, that "mens rea" means a number of quite different things in relation to different crimes. Sometimes it means an intention, eg, in murder, "to kill or to inflict really serious injury." Sometimes it means a state of mind or knowledge, eg in receiving or handling goods "knowing them to be stolen." Sometimes it means both an intention and a state of mind, eg "dishonestly and without a claim of right made in good faith with intent permanently to deprive the owner thereof." Sometimes it forms part of the essential ingredients of the crime without proof of which the prosecution, as it were, withers on the bough. Sometimes it is a matter, of which, though the "probative" burden may be on the Crown, normally the "evidential" burden may usually (though not always) rest on the defence, eg, "self-defence" and "provocation" in murder, though it must be noted that if there is material making the issue a live one, the matter must be left to the jury even if the defence do not raise it. Moreover, of course, a statute can, and often does, create an absolute offence without any degree of mens rea at all. It follows from this, surely, that it is logically impermissible, as the Crown sought to do in this case, to draw a necessary inference from decisions in relation to offences where mens rea means one thing, and cases where it means another, and in particular from decisions on the construction of statutes, whether these be related to bigamy, abduction or the possession of drugs, and decisions in relation to common law offences ...

... Once one has accepted, what seems to be abundantly clear, that the prohibited act in rape is non-consensual sexual intercourse, and that the guilty state of mind is an intention to commit it, it seems to me to follow as a matter of inexorable logic that there is no room either for a "defence" of honest belief or mistake, or of a defence of honest and reasonable belief or mistake. Either the prosecution proves that the accused had the requisite intent, or it does not. In the former case it succeeds, and in the latter it fails. Since honest belief clearly negatives intent, the reasonableness or other wise of that belief can only be evidence for or against the view that the belief and therefore the intent was actually held, and it matters not whether, to quote Bridge J in the passage cited above, "the definition of a crime includes no specific element beyond the prohibited act." If the mental element be primarily an intention and not a state of belief it comes within his second proposition and not his third. Any other view, as for insertion of the word "reasonable" can only have the effect of saying that a man intends something which he does not.

By contrast, the appellants invited us to overrule the bigamy cases from *R* v *Tolson* ... onwards and perhaps also *R* v *Prince* ... (the abduction case) as wrongly decided at least in so far as they purport to insist that a mistaken belief must be reasonable. The arguments for this view are assembled, and enthusiastically argued, by Professor Glanville Williams in his treatise on *Criminal Law*, ... and by Smith and Hogan.

Although it is undoubtedly open to this House to reconsider *R* v *Tolson* and the bigamy cases, and perhaps *R* v *Prince* which may stand or fall with them, I must respectfully decline to do so in the present case. Nor is it necessary that I should. I am not prepared to assume that the statutory offences of bigamy or abduction are necessarily on all fours with rape, and before I was prepared to undermine a whole line of cases which have been accepted as law for so long, I would need argument in the context of a case expressly relating to the relevant offences. I am content to rest my view of the instant case on the crime of rape by saying that it is my opinion that the prohibited act is and always has been intercourse without consent of the victim and the mental element is and always has been the intention to commit that act, or the equivalent intention of having intercourse willy-nilly not caring whether the victim consents or no. A failure to prove this involves an acquittal because the intent, an essential ingredient, is lacking. It matters not why it is lacking if only it is not there, and in particular it matters not that the intention is lacking only because of a belief not based on reasonable grounds. I should add that I myself am inclined to view *R* v *Tolson* as a narrow decision based on the construction of a statute, which prima facie seemed to make an absolute statutory offence, with a proviso, related to the seven year period of absence, which created a statutory defence. The judges in *R* v *Tolson* decided that this was not reasonable, and, on general jurisprudential principles, imported into the statutory offence words which created a special "defence" of honest and reasonable belief of which the "evidential" but not the probative burden lay on the defence. I do not think it is necessary to decide this conclusively in the present case. But if this is the true view there is a complete distinction between *Tolson* and the other cases based in statute and the present.'

Jaggard v *Dickinson* [1981] 2 WLR 118

See Chapter 21.

R v *O'Grady* [1987] 3 WLR 321 Court of Appeal (Criminal Division) (Lord Lane CJ, Boreham and McGowan JJ)

Mistake as to self-defence induced by intoxication

Facts

The defendant had spent a day drinking with the deceased, at the end of which they went to the defendant's flat where they fell asleep. The defendant was awoken by blows to his head being administered by the deceased, and retaliated with what he thought were a few mild blows, after which he fell asleep again. When the defendant woke up some time later he found the body of the deceased who had died from blows to the head. The defendant was charged with murder, and claimed at his trial that he was mistaken as to the amount of force that he had needed to use to defend himself because he had been drinking. The trial judge directed the jury that the defendant was entitled to rely on the defence of self-defence, and was to be judged on the facts as he believed them to be, but he was not entitled to go beyond what was reasonable by way of self-defence, and the fact that he might have mistakenly done so due to the effect of drink did not afford him a defence. The defendant appealed against his conviction for manslaughter.

Held

The appeal would be dismissed.

Lord Lane CJ:

'The grounds of appeal advanced by Mr Wadsworth [counsel for the appellant] are as follows. (1) Whilst the judge was correct to refer to mistake induced by drink in connection with self-defence, he was wrong to limit the reference to mistake as to the existence of an attack; he should have included the possibility of mistake as to the severity of an attack which was the most likely possibility on the facts. (2) By leaving the matter to the jury as he did, the judge in effect divorced the reasonableness of the appellant's reaction from the appellant's state of mind at the time. (3) The judge failed when giving his further direction to the jury to remind them that a defendant is never required to judge to a nicety the amount of force which is necessary and that they should give great weight to the view formed by the appellant at the time, even though that view might have been affected by alcohol.

As to the first two grounds, these require an examination of the law as to intoxication in relation to mistake. Counsel have referred us to a number of authorities. It is not necessary for us to refer to all of these. In three of them the jury were invited to take the defendant's drunkenness into account when deciding whether he genuinely apprehended an assault upon himself: *R v Gamlen* (1858) 1 F & F 90; *Marshall's Case* (1830) 1 Lew 76; and *R v Wardrope* [1960] Crim LR 770. However the reports of those cases leave a great deal to be desired and as far as we can discover there is no case directly in point which is binding upon us.

As McCullough J, when granting leave, pointed out helpfully in his observations for the benefit of the court;

> "Given that a man who *mistakenly* believes he is under attack is entitled to use reasonable force to defend himself, it would seem to follow that, if he *is* under attack and mistakenly believes the attack to be more serious than it is, he is entitled to use reasonable force to defend himself against an attack of the severity he believed it to have. If one allows a mistaken belief induced by drink to bring this principle into operation, an act of gross negligence (viewed objectively) may become lawful even though it results in the death of the innocent victim. The drunken man would be guilty of neither murder nor manslaughter."

How should the jury be invited to approach the problem? One starts with the decision of this court in *R v Williams (Gladstone)* (1983) 78 Cr App R 276, namely, that where the defendant might have been labouring under a mistake as to the facts he must be judged according to that mistaken view, whether the mistake was reasonable or not. It is then for the jury to decide whether the defendant's reaction to the threat, real or imaginary, was a reasonable one. The court was not in that case considering what the situation might be where the mistake was due to voluntary intoxication by alcohol or some other drug.

We have come to the conclusion that where the jury are satisfied that the defendant was mistaken in his belief that any force or the force which he in fact used was necessary to defend himself and are further satisfied that the mistake was caused by voluntarily induced intoxication, the defence must fail. We do not consider that any distinction should be drawn on this aspect of the matter between offences involving what is called specific intent, such as murder, and offences of so called basic intent, such as manslaughter. Quite apart from the problem of directing a jury in a case such as the present where manslaughter is an alternative verdict to murder, the question of mistake can and ought to be considered separately from the question of intent. A sober man who mistakenly believes he is in danger of immediate death at the hands of an attacker is entitled to be acquitted of both murder and manslaughter if his reaction in killing his supposed assailant was a reasonable one. What his intent may have been seems to us to be irrelevant to the problem of self-defence or no. Secondly, we respectfully adopt the reasoning of McCullough J already set out.

This brings us to the question of public order. There are two competing interests. On the one hand the interest of the defendant who has only acted according to what he believed to be necessary to protect himself, and on the other hand that of the public in general and the victim in particular who, probably through no fault of his own, has been injured or perhaps killed because of the defendant's drunken mistake. Reason recoils from the conclusion that in such circumstances a defendant is entitled to leave the Court without a stain on his character.

We find support for that view in the decision of the House of Lords in *R v Majewski* [1977] AC 443, and in particular in the speeches of Lord Simon of Glaisdale and Lord Edmund-Davies. We cite a passage from the speech of Lord Simon of Glaisdale, at p476:

"(1) One of the prime purposes of the criminal law, with its penal sanctions, is the protection from certain proscribed conduct of persons who are pursuing their lawful lives. Unprovoked violence has, from time immemorial, been a significant part of such proscribed conduct. To accede to the argument on behalf of the appellant would leave the citizen legally unprotected from unprovoked violence where such violence was the consequence of drink or drugs having obliterated the capacity of the perpetrator to know what he was doing or what were its consequences. (2) Though the problem of violent conduct by intoxicated persons is not new to society, it has been rendered more acute and menacing by the more widespread use of hallucinatory drugs. For example, in *R v Lipman* [1970] 1 QB 152, the accused committed his act of mortal violence under the hallucination (induced by drugs) that he was wrestling with serpents. He was convicted of manslaughter. But, on the logic of the appellant's argument, he was innocent of any crime."

Lord Edmund-Davies said, at p492:

"The criticism by the academics of the law presently administered in this country is of a two-fold nature: (1) It is illogical and therefore inconsistent with legal principle to treat a person who of his own volition has taken drink or drugs any differently from a man suffering from some bodily or mental disorder of the kind earlier mentioned or whose beverage had, without his connivance, been 'laced' with intoxicants; (2) it is unethical to convict a man of a crime requiring a guilty state of mind when ex hypothesi, he lacked it."

Lord Edmund-Davies then demonstrated the fallacy of those criticisms.

Finally we draw attention to the decision of this court in *R v Lipman* [1970] 1 QB 152 itself. The defence in that case was put on the grounds that the defendant, because of the hallucinatory drug which he had taken, had not formed the necessary intent to found a conviction for murder, thus resulting in his conviction for manslaughter. If the appellant's contentions here are correct, Lipman could successfully have escaped conviction altogether by raising the issue that he believed he was defending himself legitimately from an attack by serpents. It is significant that no one seems to have considered that possibility.'

R v Smith [1974] QB 354

See Chapter 21.

R* v *Tolson (1889) 23 QBD 168 Court for Crown Cases Reserved (Lord Coleridge CJ, Denman, Field, Manisty, Hawkins, Stephen, Cave, Day, A L Smith, Wills, Grantham and Charles JJ, Pollock and Huddleston BB)

Mistake as a defence to crimes of strict liability

Facts

The defendant was deserted by her husband in 1881. She was subsequently told by her brother-in-law that he had drowned at sea. In 1887, honestly (although mistakenly) believing herself to be a widow, the defendant remarried. In December 1887 the defendant's husband returned from America, and she was convicted of bigamy contrary to s58 of the Offences Against the Person Act 1861. Her appeal was considered by the Court for Crown Cases Reserved.

Held

(By a majority of nine to five) the conviction would be quashed.

Stephen J:

> 'My view of the subject is based upon a particular application of the doctrine usually, though I think not happily, described by the phrase "non est reus, nisi mens set rea." ... The principle involved appears to me, when fully considered, to amount to no more than this. The full definition of every crime contains expressly or by implication a proposition as to a state of mind. Therefore, if the mental element of any conduct alleged to be a crime is proved to have been absent in any given case, the crime so defined is not committed; or, again if a crime is fully defined, nothing amounts to that crime which does not satisfy that definition. Crimes are in the present day much more accurately defined by statute or otherwise than they formerly were. The mental element of most crimes is marked by one of the words "maliciously," "fraudulently," "negligently," or "knowingly," but it is the general – I might, I think, say, the invariable – practice of the legislature to leave unexpressed some of the mental elements of crime. In all cases whatever, competent age, sanity and some degree of freedom from some kinds of coercion are assumed to be essential to criminality, but I do not believe they are ever introduced into any statute by which any particular crime is defined.
>
> The meaning of the words "malice," "negligence" and "fraud" in relation to particular crimes has been ascertained by numerous cases. Malice means one thing in relation to murder, another in relation to the Malicious Mischief Act, and a third in relation to libel, and so of fraud and negligence.
>
> With regard to knowledge of fact, the law, perhaps, is not quite so clear, but it may, I think, be maintained that in every case knowledge of fact is to some extent an element of criminality as much as competent age and sanity. To take an extreme illustration, can anyone doubt that a man who, though he might be perfectly sane, committed what would otherwise be a crime in a state of somnambulism, would be entitled to be acquitted? And why is this? Simply because he would not know what he was doing. A multitude of illustrations of the same sort might be given. I will mention one or two glaring ones. *Levett's Case*, (1638) Cro Car 538, decides that a man who, making a thrust with a sword at a place where, upon reasonable grounds, he supposed a burglar to be, killed a person who was not a burglar, was held not to be a felon, though he might be (it was not decided that he was) guilty of killing per infortuniam, or possibly, se defendendo, which then involved certain forfeitures. In other words, he was in the same situation as far as regarded the homicide as if he had killed a burglar. In the decision of the judges in *McNaghten's Case*, ... it is stated that if under an insane delusion one man killed another, and if the delusion was such that it would, if true, justify or excuse the killing, the homicide would be justified or excused. This could hardly be if the same were not law as to a sane mistake ...
>
> It is said, first, that the words of 24 & 25 Vict c 100, s57, are absolute, and that the exceptions which that section contains are the only ones which are intended to be admitted, and this it is said is confirmed by the express proviso in the section – an indication which is thought to negative any tacit exception. It is also

supposed that the case of *R v Prince* (1875) LR 2 CCR 154, decided on section 55, confirms this view. I will begin by saying how far I agree with these views. First, I agree that the case turns exclusively upon the construction of section 57 of 24 & 25 Vict c 100. Much was said to us in argument on the old statute, 1 Jac 1, c 11. I cannot see what this has to do with the matter. Of course, it would be competent to the legislature to define a crime in such a way as to make the existence of any state of mind immaterial. The question is solely whether it has actually done so in this case.

In the first place I will observe upon the absolute character of the section. It appears to me to resemble most of the enactments contained in the Consolidation Acts of 1861, in passing over the general mental elements of crime which are presupposed in every case. Age, sanity and more or less freedom from compulsion, are always presumed, and I think it would be impossible to quote any statute which in any case specifies these elements of criminality in the definition of any crime. It will be found that either by using the words wilfully and maliciously, or by specifying some special intent as an element of particular crimes, knowledge of fact is implicitly made part of the statutory definition of most modern definitions of crime, but there are some cases in which this cannot be said. Such are section 55, on which *R v Prince* was decided, section 56, which punishes the stealing of "any child under the age of fourteen years," section 49, as to procuring the defilement of any "woman or girl under the age of twenty-one," in each of which the same question might arise as in *R v Prince*; to these I may add some of the provisions of the Criminal Law Amendment Act of 1885. Reasonable belief that a girl is sixteen or upwards is a defence to the charge of an offence under sections 5, 6 and 7, but this is not provided for as to an offence against section 4, which is meant to protect girls under thirteen.

It seems to me that as to the construction of all these sections the case of *R v Prince* is a direct authority. It was the case of a man who abducted a girl under sixteen, believing, on good grounds, that she was above that age. Lord Esher, then Brett J, was against the conviction. His judgment establishes at much length, and, as it appears to me, unanswerably, the principle above explained, which he states as follows: "That a mistake of facts on reasonable grounds, to the extent that, if the facts were as believed, the acts of the prisoner would make him guilty of no offence at all, is an excuse, and that such an excuse is implied in every criminal charge and every criminal enactment in England."

Lord Blackburn, with whom nine other judges agreed, and Lord Bramwell, with whom seven others agreed, do not appear to me to have dissented from this principle, speaking generally; but they held that it did not apply fully to each part of every section to which I have referred. Some of the prohibited acts they thought the legislature intended to be done at the peril of the person who did them, but not all.

The judgment delivered by Lord Blackburn proceeds upon the principle that the intention of the legislature in section 55 was "to punish the abduction unless the girl was of such an age as to make her consent an excuse."

Lord Bramwell's judgment proceeds upon this principle: "The legislature has enacted that if anyone does this wrong act he does it at the risk of her turning out to be under sixteen. This opinion gives full scope to the doctrine of the mens rea. If the taker believed he had her father's consent, though wrongly, he would have no mens rea; so if he did not know she was in anyone's possession nor in the care or charge of anyone. In those cases he would not know he was doing the act forbidden by statute."

All judges, therefore, in *R v Prince* agreed on the general principle, though they all, except Lord Esher, considered that, the object of the legislature being to prevent a scandalous and wicked invasion of parental rights (whether it was to be regarded as illegal apart from the statute or not), it was to be supposed that they intended that the wrongdoer should act at his peril. As another illustration of the same principle, I may refer to *R v Bishop* (1880) 5 QBD 259. The defendant in that case was tried before me for receiving more than two lunatics into a house not duly licensed, upon an indictment on 8 & 9 Vict c 100, s44. It was proved that the defendant did receive more than two persons, whom the jury found to be lunatics, into her house, believing honestly, and on reasonable grounds, that they were not lunatics. I held that this was immaterial, having regard to the scope of the Act, and the object for which it was apparently passed, and this court upheld that ruling.

The application of this to the present case appears to me to be as follows. The general principle is clearly in favour of the prisoner, but how does the intention of the legislature appear to have been against them?

It could not be the object of Parliament to treat the marriage of widows as an act to be if possible prevented as presumably immoral. The conduct of the [woman] convicted was not in the smallest degree immoral, it was perfectly natural and legitimate. Assuming the facts to be as [she] supposed, the infliction of more than a nominal punishment on [her] would have been a scandal. Why, then, should the legislature be held to have wished to subject [her] to punishment at all ...?

It is argued that the proviso that a remarriage after seven years' separation shall not be punishable, operates as a tacit exclusion of all other exceptions to the penal part of the section. It appears to me that it only supplies a rule of evidence which is useful in many cases, in the absence of explicit proof of death. But it seems to me to show not that belief in the death of one married person excuses the marriage of the other only after seven years' separation, but that mere separation for that period had the effect which reasonable belief of death caused by other evidence would have at any time. It would to my mind be monstrous to say that seven years' separation should have a greater effect in excusing a bigamous marriage than positive evidence of death, sufficient for the purpose of recovering a policy of assurance or obtaining probate of a will, would have ...'

R v Williams (Gladstone) (1984) 78 Cr App R 276 Court of Appeal (Criminal Division) (Lord Lane CJ, Skinner and McGowan JJ)

Mistake as to a defence

Facts
A man named Mason saw a youth trying to rob a woman in the street. He chased the youth and knocked him to the ground. The defendant, who had not witnessed the robbery, then came on the scene. Mason told the defendant that he was a police officer (which was untrue). When Mason proved unable to verify this by producing a warrant card, a struggle ensued, which resulted in the defendant being charged with causing bodily harm. At his trial the defendant raised the defence that he had mistakenly believed Mason to be unlawfully assaulting the youth and had intervened to prevent any further harm. The defendant was convicted following a direction to the jury from the trial judge to the effect that the defendant's mistake had to be both honest and reasonable. The defendant appealed.

Held
The appeal would be allowed.

Lord Lane CJ:

'One starts off with the meaning of the word "assault." "Assault" in the context of this case, that is to say using the word as a convenient abbreviation for assault and battery, is an act by which the defendant, intentionally or recklessly, applies unlawful force to the complainant. There are circumstances in which force may be applied to another lawfully. Taking a few examples: first, where the victim consents, as in lawful sports, the application of force to another will, generally speaking, not be unlawful. Secondly, where the defendant is acting in self-defence: the exercise of any necessary and reasonable force to protect himself from unlawful violence is not unlawful. Thirdly, by virtue of section 3 of the Criminal Law Act 1967, a person may use such force as is reasonable in the circumstances in the prevention of crime or in effecting or assisting in the lawful arrest of an offender or suspected offender or persons unlawfully at large. In each of those cases the defendant will be guilty if the jury are sure that first of all he applied force to the person of another, and secondly that he had the necessary mental element to constitute guilt.

The mental element necessary to constitute guilt is the intent to apply unlawful force to the victim. We do not believe that the mental element can be substantiated by simply showing an intent to apply force and no more.

What then is the situation if the defendant is labouring under a mistake of fact as to the circumstances? What if he believes, but believes mistakenly, that the victim is consenting, or that it is necessary to defend himself, or that a crime is being committed which he intends to prevent? He must then be judged against the mistaken facts as he believes them to be. If judged against those facts or circumstances the prosecution fail to establish his guilt, then he is entitled to be acquitted.

The next question is, does it make any difference if the mistake of the defendant was one which, viewed objectively by a reasonable onlooker, was an unreasonable mistake? In other words should the jury be directed as follows: "Even if the defendant may have genuinely believed that what he was doing to the victim was either with the victim's consent or in reasonable self-defence or to prevent the commission of crime, as the case may be, nevertheless if you, the jury, come to the conclusion that the mistaken belief was unreasonable, that is to say that the defendant as a reasonable man should have realised his mistake, then you should convict him."

It is upon this point that the large volume of historical precedent with which Mr Howard threatened us at an earlier stage is concerned. But in our judgment the answer is provided by the judgment of this Court in *Kimber* (1983) 77 Cr App R 255; [1983] 1 WLR 1118, by which, as already stated, we are bound. There is no need for me to rehearse the facts, save to say that that was a case of an alleged indecent assault upon a woman. Lawton LJ deals first of all with the case of *Albert* v *Lavin* (1981) 72 Cr App R 178; [1982] AC 546; then at p229 and p1122 of the respective reports: "The application of the *Morgan* principle ((1975) 61 Cr App R 136; [1976] AC 182) to offences other than indecent assault on a woman will have to be considered when such offences come before the courts. We do, however, think it necessary to consider two of them because of what was said in the judgment. The first is a decision of the Divisional Court in *Albert* v *Lavin* (1981) 72 Cr App R 178; [1982] AC 546. The offence charged was assaulting a police officer in the execution of his duty, contrary to section 51 of the Police Act 1964. The defendant in his defence contended, inter alia, that he had not believed the police officer to be such and in consequence had resisted arrest. His counsel analysed the offence in the same way as we have done and referred to the reasoning in *Director of Public Prosecutions* v *Morgan*. Hodgson J delivering the leading judgment, rejected this argument and in doing so said, at p190 and p561 of the respective reports: 'In my judgment Mr Walker's ingenious argument fails at an earlier stage. It does not seem to me that the element of unlawfulness can properly be regarded as part of the definitional elements of the offence. In defining a criminal offence the word "unlawful" is surely tautologous and can add nothing to its essential ingredients ... And no matter how strange it may seem that a defendant charged with assault can escape conviction if he shows that he mistakenly but unreasonably thought his victim was consenting but not if he was in the same state of mind as to whether his victim had a right to detain him, that in my judgment is the law.' We have found difficulty in agreeing with this reasoning" – and I interpolate, so have we – "even though the judge seems to be accepting that belief in consent does entitle a defendant to an acquittal on a charge of assault. We cannot accept that the word 'unlawful' when used in a definition of an offence is to be regarded as 'tautologous.' In our judgment the word 'unlawful' does import an essential element into the offence. If it were not there social life would be unbearable, because every touching would amount to a battery unless there was an evidential basis for a defence. This case was considered by the House of Lords. The appeal was dismissed, but their Lordships declined to deal with the issue of belief."

That is the end of the citation from *Kimber* (supra) in so far as it is necessary for the second point. I read a further passage from p230 and p1123 respectively which sets out the proper direction to the jury, and is relevant to the first leg of the appellant's argument in this case. It reads as follows: "In our judgment the learned recorder should have directed the jury that the prosecution had to make them sure that the appellant never had believed that Betty was consenting. As he did not do so, the jury never considered an important aspect of his defence."

We respectfully agree with what Lawton LJ said there with regard both to the way in which the defence should have been put and also with regard to his remarks as to the nature of the defence. The reasonableness or unreasonableness of the defendant's belief is material to the question of whether the belief was held by the defendant at all. If the belief was in fact held, its unreasonableness, so far as guilt or innocence is concerned, is neither here nor there. It is irrelevant. Were it otherwise, the defendant would be convicted because he was negligent in failing to recognise that the victim was not consenting or that a crime was not being committed and so on. In other words the jury should be directed first of all that the prosecution have the burden or duty of proving the unlawfulness of the defendant's actions; secondly, if the defendant may have been labouring under a mistake as to the facts, he must be judged according to his mistaken view of the facts; thirdly, that is so whether the mistake was, on an objective view, a reasonable mistake or not.

In a case of self-defence, where self-defence or the prevention of crime is concerned, if the jury came to the conclusion that the defendant believed, or may have believed, that he was being attacked or that a crime was being committed, and that force was necessary to protect himself or to prevent the crime, then the prosecution have not proved their case. If however the defendant's alleged belief was mistaken and if the mistake was an unreasonable one, that may be a powerful reason for coming to the conclusion that the belief was not honestly held and should be rejected.

Even if the jury come to the conclusion that the mistake was an unreasonable one, if the defendant may genuinely have been labouring under it, he is entitled to rely upon it.

We have read the recommendations of the Criminal Law Revision Committee, Part IX, paragraph 72(a), in which the following passage appears: "The common law defence of self-defence should be replaced by a statutory defence providing that a person may use such force as is reasonable in the circumstances as he believes them to be in the defence of himself or any other person." In the view of this Court that represents the law as expressed in *DPP* v *Morgan* (supra) and in *Kimber* (supra) and we do not think that the decision of the Divisional Court in *Albert* v *Lavin* (supra) from which we have cited can be supported.

For those reasons this appeal must be allowed and the conviction quashed.'

R v *Woods* (1981) 74 Cr App R 312 Court of Appeal (Criminal Division) (Griffiths LJ, May and Hollings JJ)

Rape – intoxicated mistake as to victim's consent

Facts (as stated by Griffiths LJ)

'On July 18, 1980, in the Crown Court at Preston the appellant was convicted of rape and sentenced to three years' imprisonment. He now appeals against that conviction by leave of the single judge. He was indicted, together with three other young men, of a collective rape of one girl. Steven Lyon, one of his co-accused, pleaded guilty and was sentenced to 18 months' imprisonment; another man was acquitted; and the third, John Slater, was also convicted and sentenced to four years' imprisonment.

It arose out of a disgraceful incident on Saturday, September 29, 1979. The victim, who was aged only 19, had been drinking at a club in Blackburn. I can summarise the facts by saying that after she left the club it was alleged that these young men had raped her one after the other.

The appellant made admissions of his part in it to the police. He said he had felt sick ever since it happened and he was disgusted with himself and asked if the girl was all right. When charged with rape he said that he was glad that he had been caught and he admitted that he had been attempting to have intercourse with the girl. He said, and no doubt this is true, it would never have happened if he had not been so drunk. Forensic evidence showed that he had seminal staining on his underpants and there were fragments of grass on the outside of his jacket and a small amount of soil, all consistent with taking part in this rape in the car park.

At his trial he went back on those admissions and said in effect that he had so much to drink that he was not sure what had happened. He did not know whether he had raped her or not and did not realise that she was not consenting to anything that went on. The sole ground of this appeal is that the learned judge wrongly directed the jury that the appellant's self-induced intoxication afforded him no defence to the allegation that he was reckless as to whether the complainant consented to sexual intercourse.'

Held
The appeal would be dismissed.

Griffiths LJ:

'Mr. Bennett [for the appellant] ... founded his submission upon the wording of section 1 of the Sexual Offences (Amendment) Act 1976. Subsection (l) provides: "For the purposes of section 1 of the Sexual Offences Act 1956 (which relates to rape) a man commits rape if (a) he has unlawful sexual intercourse with a woman who at the time of the intercourse does not consent to it; and (b) at the time he knows that she does not consent to the intercourse or he is reckless as to whether she consents to it; and references to rape in other enactments (including the following provisions of this Act) shall be construed accordingly."

Mr Bennett concedes that if the section ended there he could not pursue this appeal in the face of the decision of the House of Lords in *Director of Public Prosecutions* v *Majewski* (1976) 62 Cr App R 262; [1977] AC 443, and in the very recent case of *Caldwell* (1981) 73 Cr App R 13; [1981] 1 All ER 961. To show that he is correct to make his concession at that stage it is only necessary to read a short passage from the speech of Lord Diplock in *Caldwell*. Lord Diplock said, at p21 and p 967g of the respective reports: "The speech of the Lord Chancellor, Lord Elwyn-Jones, in *DPP* v *Majewski* (1976) 62 Cr App R 262, 270; [1977] AC 443, 474, 475, with which Lord Simon, Lord Kilbrandon and I agree, is authority that self-induced intoxication is no defence to a crime in which recklessness is enough to constitute the necessary mens rea. The charge in *DPP* v *Majewski* was of assault occasioning actual bodily harm and it was held by the majority of the House, approving *Venna* (1975) 61 Cr App R 310, 314; [1976] QB 421, 428, that recklessness in the use of force was sufficient to satisfy the mental element in the offence of assault. Reducing oneself by drink or drugs to a condition in which the restraints of reason and conscience are cast off was held to be a reckless course of conduct and an integral part of the crime. The Lord Chancellor accepted as correctly stating English law the provision in paragraph 2.08 (2) of the American Model Penal Code: "When recklessness establishes an element of the offence, if the actor, due to self-induced intoxication, is unaware of a risk of which he would have been aware had he been sober, such awareness is material." "So, in the instant case, the fact that the respondent was unaware of the risk of endangering the lives of residents in the hotel owing to his self-induced intoxication would be no defence if that risk would have been obvious to him had he been sober."

Mr Bennett, however, relies upon the wording of subsection (2) which provides: "It is hereby declared that if at a trial for a rape offence the jury has to consider whether a man believed that a woman was consenting to sexual intercourse, the presence or absence of reasonable grounds for such a belief is a matter to which the jury is to have regard, in conjunction with any other relevant matters in considering whether he so believed."

He submits that the language of this subsection is directing the jury to take into account a defendant's drunken state as a possible reasonable ground for his belief that a woman is consenting to intercourse.

As the law stood immediately before the passing of this Act self-induced intoxication was no defence to a crime of rape (see *DPP* v *Majewski* (supra)). If Parliament had intended to provide in future that a man whose lust was so inflamed by drink that he ravished a woman, should nevertheless be able to pray in aid his drunken state to avoid the consequences we would have expected them to have used the clearest words to excess such a surprising result which we believe would be utterly repugnant to the great majority of people. We are satisfied that Parliament had no such intention and that this is clear from the use of the word "relevant" in the sub-section. Relevant means, in this context, legally relevant. The law, as a matter of social policy, has declared that self-induced intoxication is not a legally relevant matter to be taken into account in deciding as to whether or not a woman consents to intercourse.

Accordingly, the appellant's drunkeness was not a matter that the jury were entitled to take into consideration in deciding whether or not reasonable grounds existed for the appellant's belief that the woman consented to intercourse. The learned judge rightly directed the jury on this issue. In fact we believe that the object of subsection (2) is the very reverse of that contended by the appellant. It was not intended to make it easier for a man who rapes a woman to escape punishment by saying, in spite of the other evidence, that he thought she consented. The subsection directs the jury to look carefully at all the other relevant evidence before making up their minds on this issue. Mr Bennett cited the Divisional

Court decision in *Jaggard* v *Dickinson* (1980) 72 Cr App R 33; [1980] 3 All ER 716, in support of his construction of subsection (2). That was a decision upon the wording of a different statute. We do not find it assists us in the resolution of the construction of this statute and we found it unnecessary to express any view upon whether or not we regard it as correctly decided. For these reasons this appeal is dismissed.'

33 Introduction to Theft – The Actus Reus of Theft

Attorney-General's Reference (No 1 of 1983) [1984] 3 WLR 686 Court of Appeal (Criminal Division) (Lord Lane CJ, Davies and Kennedy JJ)

Property belonging to another – s5(4) Theft Act 1968

Facts
The defendant, a woman police officer, received payment for a day's overtime that she had not in fact worked. The money was credited to her bank account as a result of an error on the part of her employer. Although she received no demand for repayment of the money, there was evidence that she knew it had been paid into her account and intended to allow it to remain there. At her trial for theft of the sum overpaid, the trial judge, at the close of the prosecution case, directed the jury to acquit. The question of whether a charge of theft was possible in such a situation was referred to the Court of Appeal.

Held
Provided there was sufficient evidence of mens rea, a charge of theft could succeed in such a situation.

Lord Lane CJ:

'The question comes up to this court on the Attorney-General's Reference in the following form:

"Whether a person who receives overpayment of a debt due to him or her by way of a credit to his or her bank account through the 'direct debit' system operated by the banks and who knowing of that overpayment intentionally fails to repay the amount of the overpayment may be" – which is an amendment Mr Worsley has asked us to make to the reference – "guilty of theft of the credit to the amount of the overpayment."

In our opinion the question posed in that form does not arise from the wording of the charge as laid in the indictment, which I have just read. It does not seem to us that on any view the respondent stole the sum of £74.74. It seems to us that if she stole anything she stole the chose in action, that is to say, the debt which was owed to her by the bank at which she held her account. However, it has emerged in the course of argument this morning that no one was under any illusion at the trial as to what the true issues were before the court, and no one was under any illusion as to what was sought to be proved by the prosecution. We are, therefore, content to proceed with this opinion as though the indictment was in order and was not – as Mr Worsley concedes – infelicitously worded.

First of all, what is the legal position with regard to the payment of money by one bank to another for the credit of a customer's account? The position was described in clear language by Lord Goddard CJ in *R v Davenport* [1954] 1 WLR 569; [1954] 1 All ER 602, 603:

"although we talk about a person having money in a bank the only person who has money in a bank is the banker. If I pay money into my bank, either by paying cash or a cheque, that money at once becomes the money of the banker. The relationship between banker and customer is that of debtor and creditor. He does not hold my money as an agent or trustee; the leading case of *Foley* v *Hill* (1848) 2 HL Cas 28 exploded that idea. When the banker is paying out, whether in cash over the counter or by crediting the bank account of somebody else, he is paying out his own money, not my money, but he is debiting me in my account. I have a chose in action, that is to say, I have a right to expect that the banker will honour my cheque, but he does it out of his own money."

From that exposition of the true relationship between bank and client, it follows that what the respondent in the present case got was simply the debt due to her from her own bank. That is so unless her account was overdrawn or overdrawn beyond any overdraft limit, in which case she did not even get that right to money. That point is made in a decision of this Court in *R v Kohn* (1979) 69 Cr App R 395. There was no evidence in the present case as to whether the respondent's bank balance was in credit, overdrawn or anything about overdraft limits imposed by the manager of the bank. It was assumed on all hands that the account was in credit.

That brings us to the question of the basic definition of theft, which is to be found in section 1(1) of the Theft Act 1968, which provides: "(1) A person is guilty of theft if he dishonestly appropriates property belonging to another with the intention of permanently depriving the other of it; and 'thief' and 'steal' shall be construed accordingly."

The property in the present case was the debt owed by the bank to the respondent and in order to show that that can be property one turns to section 4(1) of the Act of 1968 which reads: " 'Property' includes money and all other property, real or personal, including things in action and other intangible property." The debt here was a thing in action, therefore the property was capable of being stolen.

It will be apparent that, at first blush, that debt did not belong to anyone except the respondent herself. She was the only person who had the right to go to her bank and demand the handing over of that £74.74. Had there been no statutory provision which altered that particular situation that would have been the end of the case, but if one turns to section 5(4) of the Act, one finds these words: "Where a person gets property by another's mistake, and is under an obligation to make restoration (in whole or in part) of the property or its proceeds or of the value thereof, then to the extent of that obligation the property or proceeds shall be regarded (as against him) as belonging to the person entitled to restoration, and an intention not to make restoration shall be regarded accordingly as an intention to deprive that person of the property or proceeds."

In order to determine the effect of that subsection upon this case one has to take it piece by piece to see what the result is read against the circumstances of this particular prosecution. First of all: "Did the respondent get property?" The word "get" is about as wide a word as could possibly have been adopted by the draftsman of the Act. The answer is "Yes." The respondent in this case did get her chose in action, that is, her right to sue the bank for the debt which they owed her – money which they held in their hands to which she was entitled by virtue of the contract between bank and customer.

Secondly: "Did she get it by another's mistake?" the answer to that is plainly "Yes." The Receiver of the Metropolitan Police made the mistake of thinking she was entitled to £74.74 when she was not entitled to that at all.

"Was she under the obligation to make restoration of either the property or its proceeds or its value?" We take each of those in turn. "Was she under an obligation to make restoration of the property?" – the chose in action. The answer to that is "No." It was something which could not be restored in the ordinary meaning of the word. "Was she under an obligation to make restoration of its proceeds?" The answer to that is "No." There were no proceeds of the chose in action to restore. "Was she under an obligation to make restoration of the value thereof?" – the value of the chose in action. The answer to that seems to us to be "Yes."

I should say here, in parenthesis, that a question was raised during the argument this morning as to whether "restoration" is the same as "making restitution." We think that on the wording of section 5(4) as a whole, the answer to that question is "yes." One therefore turns to see whether, under the general principles of restitution, this respondent was obliged to restore or pay for the benefit which she received. Generally speaking the respondent, in these circumstances, is obliged to pay for a benefit received when the benefit has been given under a mistake on the part of the giver as to a material fact. The mistake must be as to a fundamental or essential fact and the payment must have been due to that fundamental or essential fact. The mistake here was that this police officer had been working on a day when she had been at home and not working at all. The authority for that proposition is to be found in *Norwich Union*

Fire Insurance Society Ltd v *Wm H Price Limited* [1934] AC 455. That sets out the principles we have in precis form endeavoured to describe.

In the present case, applying that principle to the facts of this case, the value of the chose in action – the property – was £74.74 and there was a legal obligation upon the respondent to restore that value to the Receiver when she found that the mistake had been made. One continues to examine the contents of section 5(4). It follows from what has already been said that the extent of that obligation – the chose in action – has to be regarded as belonging to the person entitled to restoration, that is, the Receiver of the Metropolitan Police.

As a result of the provisions of section 5(4) the debt of £74.74 due from the respondent's bank to the respondent notionally belonged to the Receiver of the Metropolitan Police, therefore the prosecution, up to this point, have succeeded in proving – remarkable though it may seem – that the "property" in this case belonged to another within the meaning of section 1 in the Theft Act 1968 from the moment when the respondent because aware that this mistake had been made and that her account had been credited with the £74.74 and she consequently became obliged to restore the value. Furthermore, by the final words of section 5(4) once the prosecution succeed in proving that the respondent intended not to make restoration that is notionally to be regarded as an intention to deprive the Receiver of that property which notionally belongs to him.

That would leave two further matters upon which the prosecution would have to satisfy the jury. First, that there was an appropriation under the wording of section 1, if that is not already established by virtue of the application to the facts of section 3(1) which provides:

> "Any assumption by a person of the rights of an owner amounts to an appropriation, and this includes, where he has come by the property (innocently or not) without stealing it, any later assumption of a right to it by keeping or dealing with it as owner."

The second matter upon which the prosecution would have to satisfy the jury is that the respondent had acted dishonestly. Whether they would have succeeded in proving either of those two matters we do not pause to enquire.

Before parting with the case we would like to say that it should often be possible to resolve this type of situation without resorting to the criminal law. We do, however, accept that there may be occasions – of which this may have been one – where a prosecution is necessary. We do not feel it possible to answer the question posed to us in any more specific form that the form in which this opinion has been delivered and that is our answer to the question posed to us.'

R v *Gilks* [1972] 1 WLR 1341 Court of Appeal (Criminal Division) (Cairns and Stephenson LJJ and Willis J)

Property belonging to another – s5(4) Theft Act 1968

Facts
The defendant entered a betting shop and placed a bet on a horse named 'Fighting Scot'. The horse was not successful, the race in which it had run being won by a horse named 'Fighting Taffy'. Due to a cashier's mistake, however, the defendant was paid £106 winnings. The defendant was subsequently convicted of theft of the money, and appealed.

Held
The appeal would be dismissed.

Cairns LJ:

> 'The gap in the law which section 5(4) was designated to fill was, as the Deputy Chairman rightly held, that which is illustrated by the case of *Moynes* v *Coopper* [1956] 1 QB 439. There a workman received a

paypacket containing £7 more than was due to him, but did not become aware of the overpayment till he opened the envelope some time later. He then kept the £7. This was held not to be theft because there was no animus furandi at the moment of taking, and *R v Middleton* LR 2 CCR 38 was distinguished on that ground. In *Moynes v Coopper* [1956] 1 QB 439, 445, it was observed that the law as laid down in *R v Middleton*, was reproduced and enacted in section 1(2)(i) of the Larceny Act 1916. It would be strange indeed if section 5(4) of the Theft Act 1968, which was designed to bring within the net of theft a type of dishonest behaviour which escaped before, were to be held to have created a loophole for another type of dishonest behaviour which was always within the net.

An alternative ground on which the deputy chairman held that the money should be regarded as belonging to Ladbrokes was that "obligation" in section 5(4) meant an obligation whether a legal one or not. In the opinion of this Court, that was an incorrect ruling. In a criminal statute, where a person's criminal liability is made dependent on his having an obligation, it would be quite wrong to construe that word so as to cover a moral or social obligation as distinct from a legal one. As, however, we consider that the deputy chairman was right in ruling that the prosecution did not need to rely on section 5(4) of the Act of 1968, his ruling on this alternative point does not affect the result.

The other main branch of the defendant's case is the contention that the deputy chairman misdirected the jury on the meaning of "dishonestly" in section 1(1) of the Theft Act 1968. The relevant part of the defendant's evidence is set out in the summing up in a passage of which no complaint is made:

"Now, what this man says is that he did not act dishonestly. He says in his view bookmakers and punters are a race apart and that when you are dealing with your bookmaker different rules apply. He agreed it would be dishonest if his grocer gave him too much change and he knew it and kept the change; he agreed it would be dishonest but he says bookmakers are different and if your bookmaker makes a mistake and pays you too much there is nothing dishonest about keeping it."

The deputy chairman, having referred to this evidence, and to evidence that the defendant had not hurried away from the betting shop after receiving this large sum, said:

"Well, it is a matter for you to consider, members of the jury, but try to place yourselves in that man's position at that time and answer the question whether in your view he thought he was acting honestly or dishonestly."

In our view that was in the circumstances of this case a proper and sufficient direction on the matter of dishonesty. On the face of it the defendant's conduct was dishonest: the only possible basis on which the jury could find that the prosecution had not established dishonesty would be if they thought it possible that the appellant did have the belief which he claimed to have. There is no complaint about the direction as to onus: the deputy chairman expressly said: "The prosecution have to satisfy you that he did appropriate the money dishonestly."

Mr Galpin [counsel for the defendant] thought that the jury should be specifically reminded of the terms of section 2(1)(a) of the Act and suggested this to the deputy chairman. The deputy chairman then summarised that subsection, gave a somewhat irrelevant illustration of a case where it might apply, and then added:

"Nor would somebody be guilty of theft if he believed, even if he was wrong, but nevertheless believed he had some right in law to take the property, and that, you see, is the reason why Mr Galpin puts the case on behalf of the defendant that this defendant believed that when dealing with your bookmaker if he makes a mistake you can take the money and keep it and there is nothing dishonest about it."

The complaint is centred on the word "and." It is contended that the jury may have understood this direction to mean that the defendant would be acting dishonestly unless *(a)* he believed he had the right to take the money and keep it and *(b)* he believed there was nothing dishonest about that conduct. It is said that the jury may have thought that the defendant's state of mind was: "I believe that in law I am entitled to take from my bookmaker anything he is foolish enough to pay me, though of course I know that it would be dishonest to do so," and he pointed out that under the section 2(1)(a) of the Theft Act 1968 this would entitle him to be acquitted, whereas the direction might be taken to mean that he would be guilty.

In our opinion, this is too refined an argument. We think it is clear that in the context the word "and" meant "and therefore" or "and so" and the jury would understand it in that way. A few minutes earlier the deputy chairman had accurately stated the effect of the subsection in words that could not be clearer. The defendant in his evidence had drawn no distinction between what he believed he was in law entitled to do and what he believed it was honest to do. His own words were "there is nothing dishonest about keeping it," not "I think you are entitled in law to keep it." If the two expressions are taken to have different meanings, the defendant had not made out any case under section 2 (1) *(a)*; if they are taken to have the same meaning, then no complaint can be made of the way in which the deputy chairman dealt with the matter.

For these reasons this court is of the opinion that all the grounds of appeal fail; and that the appeal must be dismissed.'

R v *Hall* [1973] 1 QB 126 Court of Appeal (Criminal Division) (Edmund-Davies and Stephenson LJJ and Boreham J)

Property belonging to another – s5(3) Theft Act 1968

Facts
The defendant, a travel agent, had received sums of money from clients as deposits on airline tickets. He was convicted of theft of the money when the tickets failed to materialise. The defendant claimed that the sums received were deposited in the company's trading account and spent on overheads. The defendant appealed to the Court of Appeal.

Held
The appeal would be allowed.

Edmund-Davies LJ (having referred to the terms of s5(3) of the Theft Act 1968):

'Mr Jolly [counsel for the defendant] submitted that in the circumstances arising in these seven cases there arose no such "obligation" upon the accused. He referred us to a passage in the Eighth Report of the Criminal Law Revision Committee (1966) (Cmnd 2977), at p127, which reads:

> "Subsection (3) provides for the special case where property is transferred to a person to retain and deal with for a particular purpose and he misapplies it or its proceeds. An example would be the treasurer of a holiday fund. The person in question is in law the owner of the property; but the subsection treats the property, as against him, as belonging to the persons to whom he owes the duty to retain and deal with the property as agreed. He will therefore be guilty of stealing from them if he misapplies the property or its proceeds."

Mr Jolly submitted that the example there given is, for all practical purposes, identical with the actual facts in *R* v *Pulham* (unreported) June 15, 1971, where, incidentally, section 5 (3) was not discussed, the convictions there being quashed, as we already indicated, owing to the lack of a proper direction as to the accused's state of mind at the time when he appropriated. But he submits that the position of a treasurer of a solitary fund is quite different from that of a person like the defendant, who was in general, and genuine, business as a travel agent, and to whom people pay money in order to achieve a certain object – in the present cases, to obtain charter flights to America. It is true, he concedes, that thereby the travel agent undertakes a contractual obligation in relation to arranging flights and at the proper time paying the airline and any other expenses. Indeed, the defendant throughout acknowledged that this was so, though contending that in some of the seven cases it was the other party who was in breach. But what Mr Jolly resists is that in such circumstances the travel agent "is under an obligation" to the client "to retain and deal with ... in a particular way" sums paid to him in such circumstances.

What cannot of itself be decisive of the matter is the fact that the appellant paid the money into the firm's general trading account. As Widgery J (as he then was) said in *Yule* (1963) 47 Cr App R 229, at p234; [1964] 1 QB 5 decided under section 20 (1) (iv) of the Larceny Act 1916, at p10:

> "The fact that a particular sum is paid into a particular banking account . . . does not affect the right of persons interested in that sum or any duty of the solicitor either towards his client or towards third parties with regard to disposal of that sum."

Nevertheless, when a client goes to a firm carrying on the business of travel agents and pays them money, he expects that in return he will, in due course, receive the tickets and other documents necessary for him to accomplish the trip for which he is paying, and the firm are "under an obligation" to perform their part to fulfil his expectation and are liable to pay him damages if they do not. But, in our judgment, what was not here established was that these clients expected them to "retain and deal with that property or its proceeds in a particular way," and that an "obligation" to do so was undertaken by the appellant.

We must make clear, however, that each case turns on its own facts. Cases could, we suppose, conceivably arise where by some special arrangement (preferably evidenced by documents), the client could impose upon the travel agent an "obligation" falling within section 5 (3). But no such special arrangement was made in any of the seven cases here being considered. It is true that in some of them documents were signed by the parties; thus, in respect of counts 1 and 3 incidents there was a clause to the effect that the "People to People" organisation [the business operated by the defendant] did not guarantee to refund deposits if withdrawals were made later than a certain date; and in respect of counts 6, 7 and 8 the defendant wrote promising "a full refund" after the flights paid for failed to materialise. But neither in those nor in the remaining two cases (in relation to which there was no documentary evidence of any kind) was there, in our judgment, such a special arrangement as would give rise to an "obligation" within section 5 (3).

It follows from this that, despite what on any view must be condemned as scandalous conduct by the appellant, in our judgment, upon this ground alone this appeal must be allowed and the convictions quashed. But as, to the best of our knowledge, this is one of the earliest cases involving section 5 (3), we venture to add some observations:

(A) Although section 5 (3) was not referred to in *R v Pulham* and the case turned on section 2 (1) *(b)* of the Act, it is equally essential for the purposes of the former provision that dishonesty should be present at the time of appropriation. We are alive to the fact that to establish this could present great (and may be insuperable) difficulties when sums are on different dates drawn from a general account. Nevertheless, they must be overcome if the Crown is to succeed.

(B) Where the case turns, wholly or in part, on section 5 (3) a careful exposition of the subsection is called for. Although it was canvassed by counsel in the present case, it was nowhere quoted or even paraphrased by the commissioner in his summing up. Instead he unfortunately ignored it and proceeded upon the assumption that, as the accused acknowledged the purpose for which clients had paid him money, ipso facto there arose an "obligation . . . to retain and deal with" it for that purpose. He therefore told the jury:

> "The sole issue to be determined in each count is this: Has it been proved that the money was stolen in the sense I have described, dishonestly appropriated by him for purposes other than the purpose for which the monies were handed over? Bear in mind that this is not a civil claim to recover money that has been lost."

We have to say respectfully that this will not do, as cases under section 20 (1) (iv) of the Larceny Act 1916 illustrate. Thus in *R v Sheaf* (1927) 19 Cr App 46, it was held that whether money had been "entrusted" to the defendant for and on account of other persons was a question of fact for the jury and must therefore be the subject of an express direction, Avory J said, at p48:

> "It is not sufficient to say that if the question had been left they might have determined it against the appellant. When we once arrive at the conclusion that a vital question of fact has not been left to the jury, the only ground on which we can affirm a conviction is that there has been no miscarriage of justice."

The same point was made in *R v Bryce* (1955) 40 Cr App R 62.

(C) Whether in a particular case the Crown has succeeded in establishing an "obligation" of the kind coming within section 5 (3) of the new Act may be a difficult question. Happily, we are not called upon to anticipate or solve for the purposes of the present case the sort of difficulties that can arise. But, to illustrate what we have in mind, mixed questions of law and fact may call for consideration. For example, if the transaction between the parties is wholly in writing, is it for the judge to direct the jury that, as a matter of law, the defendant had thereby undertaken an "obligation" within section 5 (3)? On the other hand, if it is wholly, or partly, oral, it would appear that it is for the judge to direct them that, if they find certain facts proved, it would be open to them to find that an "obligation" within section 5 (3) had been undertaken – but presumably not that they must so find, for so to direct them would be to invade their territory. In effect, however, the commissioner unhappily did something closely resembling that in the present case by his above-quoted direction that the only issue for their consideration was whether the accused was proved to have been actuated by dishonesty.

We have only to add that Mr Jalland [counsel for the Crown] submitted that, even if the Commissioner's failure to deal with section 5 (3) amounted to a misdirection, this is a fitting case in which to apply the proviso. But point (1), successfully taken by defence counsel, is clearly of such a nature as to render that course impossible. We are only too aware that, in the result, there will be many clients of the defendant who, regarding themselves as cheated out of their money by him, will think little of a law which permits him to go unpunished. But such we believe it to be, and it is for this court to apply it.'

R v Meech [1973] 3 WLR 507 Court of Appeal (Criminal Division) (Roskill LJ, Thompson and Stocker JJ)

Nature of appropriation – whether cheque proceeds property belonging to another

Facts

As stated by Roskill LJ:

'A man named McCord had obtained a cheque for £1,450 from a hire purchase finance company by means of a forged instrument. The cheque itself was a perfectly valid document. McCord, who was an undischarged bankrupt, feared that were he to cash this cheque himself, his crime would be more likely to be discovered than if he persuaded a friend to cash it for him. McCord, therefore, asked Meech (to whom McCord owed £40) to cash the cheque for him and Meech agreed so to do. At the time Meech agreed so to do Meech was wholly unaware of the dishonest means whereby McCord had become possessed of the cheque. Meech paid the cheque into his own account at a branch of Lloyds Bank Ltd at High Wycombe on September 11, 1972. The bank was seemingly unwilling to allow him to cash the cheque until it had been cleared. On September 13, 1972 Meech drew his own cheque for £1,410 on his own account at that branch and that cheque was duly cashed by the bank on that day. The difference between the two sums was represented by McCord's £40 debt to Meech. By the time this cheque was cashed, the original cheque had been cleared. Between the paying in of the original cheque on September 11 and the obtaining of the cash on September 13, Meech became aware that McCord had acquired the original cheque dishonestly.

We were told by counsel that Meech, following legal argument at the end of the evidence, was allowed by the judge to be re-called. Meech then told the jury that not only did he find out about McCord's dishonesty but that he then honestly believed that if he cashed the cheque he would commit an offence. In the view of the direction given by the judge to which we refer later, we think it clear that the jury must be taken to have rejected this story of honest belief on Meech's part.

Before the cheque was cashed but after Meech discovered its dishonest origin, Meech agreed with Parslow and Jolliffe that after the cheque was cashed Meech would take the money to a prearranged destination. The two other men were to join him there. A fake robbery, with Meech as the victim, was to be staged and indeed was staged, the purpose clearly being to provide some explanation to McCord of Meech's inability to hand over the money to McCord.

This was done; Parslow and Jolliffe between them removed the money after leaving Meech as the apparent victim. The bogus robbery was reported to the police, who, being less credulous than the three men imagined McCord might be, investigated the matter and soon became convinced that the robbery story was bogus, as indeed it was soon shown to be. It is clear that Meech was influenced by the thought that even if the bogus nature of the robbery were suspected by McCord, McCord would never dare to go to the police and complain for that would involve revealing his own dishonesty.

All the appellants alleged in evidence that the "robbery" was honest in its purpose in that it was designed to enable the money to be returned to the hire purchase finance company whom McCord had defrauded.'

The defendants were convicted of theft and appealed on the ground that the trial judge had misdirected the jury in stating that the proceeds of the cheque were property belonging to another within s5(3) of the Theft Act 1968, because there had been no legal obligation owed to McCord to deal with the proceeds in any particular way.

Held

Roskill LJ (on the nature of the 'obligation' referred to in s5(3)):

'Counsel for all the defendants relied strongly on the series of recent decisions that "obligation" means "legal obligation". The judge so directed the jury. In giving this direction he no doubt had in mind the successive decisions of this court in *R* v *Hall* [above], *R* v *Gilks* [above] and *R* v *Pearce* [[1973] Crim LR 321]. Reliance was also placed on paragraph 76 of Professor Smith's *The Law of Theft*, 2nd ed (1972) – a passage written just before the decisions referred to.

Since the judge so directed the jury, we do not find it necessary further to consider those decisions beyond observing that the facts of those cases were vastly different from those of the present case.

Starting from this premise – that "obligation" means "legal obligation" – it was argued that even at the time when Meech was ignorant of the dishonest origin of the cheque, as he was at the time when he agreed to cash the cheque and hand the proceeds less the £40 to McCord, McCord could never have enforced that obligation because McCord had acquired the cheque illegally. In our view this submission is unsound in principle. The question has to be looked at from Meech's point of view not McCord's. Meech plainly assumed an "obligation" to McCord which on the facts then known to him he remained obliged to fulfil and, on the facts as found, he must be taken at that time honestly to have intended to fulfil. The fact that on the true facts if known McCord might not and indeed would not subsequently have been permitted to enforce that obligation in a civil court does not prevent that "obligation" on Meech having arisen. The argument confuses the creation of the obligation with the subsequent discharge of that obligation either by performance or otherwise. That the obligation might have become impossible of performance by Meech or of enforcement by McCord on grounds of illegality or for reasons of public policy is irrelevant. The opening words of section 5(3) clearly look to the time of the creation of or the acceptance of the obligation by the bailee and not to the time of performance by him of the obligation so created and accepted by him.

It is further to be observed in this connection that this subsection deems property (including the proceeds of property) which does not belong to the bailor to belong to the bailor so as to render a bailee who has accepted an obligation to deal with the property or to account for it in a particular way but then dishonestly fails to fulfil that obligation, liable to be convicted of theft whereas previously he would have been liable to have been convicted of fraudulent conversion though not of larceny. It was not seriously disputed in argument that before 1968 Meech would have had no defence to a charge of fraudulent conversion.

The first branch of the argument therefore clearly fails. The second argument (as already indicated) was that even if Meech initially became under an obligation to McCord, that obligation ceased to bind Meech once Meech discovered McCord had acquired the cheque by fraud. It was argued that once Meech possessed this knowledge, performance of his pre-existing obligation would have involved him in performing an obligation which he knew to be illegal. Thus, it was said, he was discharged from performance and at the time of his dishonest misappropriation had ceased to be bound by his obligation so that he could not properly be convicted of theft by virtue of section 5(3).

This submission was advanced at considerable length before the judge. It is not necessary to relate those

Introduction to Theft – The Actus Reus of Theft   471

arguments more fully. The judge rejected the arguments and he directed the jury in the following terms so far as relevant. After saying that there were three considerations which Meech said affected his mind and led him not to carry out his agreement with McCord, the judge dealt correctly with the first two of the three matters. He continued as follows:

> "Thirdly, he says that he was worried about being involved in the offence of obtaining money by fraud; that he knew this to be, as he described it, a 'dodgy' cheque – knew not at the time that he was handed it, but knew before he drew the cash; that he alleges that from enquiries made on September 11 and 12 he discovered what was seemingly common knowledge among some motor dealers of High Wycombe, that McCord was involved in a dishonest transaction. His knowledge of this was limited and inaccurate, since he thought that there was a name Harris involved. He is not entitled in law to repudiate his agreement merely on the basis of suspicions about McCord. The only basis on which he was entitled to refuse payment was that he refused because if he had honoured the agreement he, Meech, would have committed a criminal offence, or that was his belief. Only if that was the basis – or if you thought on the evidence that may have been the basis – was there no obligation to pay. Otherwise, although you may well think many people had a better right than McCord, so far as Meech was concerned it was for his obligation to deal with the proceeds of the cheque in the way that he had agreed with McCord that he would."

The judge thus emphasised that the obligation to McCord remained but that Meech would be excused performance if performance would have involved commission of a criminal offence or if Meech genuinely believed that such performance would involve commission of a criminal offence. Of course if Meech acted as he did honestly and had an honest reason for not performing his obligation and for claiming relief from performance of that obligation, this would clearly be the end of any criminal charge against him. But the jury, as already pointed out, clearly negatived any such honest intention or belief on Meech's part. The argument before this court was that even though he was found to have acted dishonestly, he still could not be convicted of theft.

There was considerable discussion whether if he were not guilty of theft, he could have been convicted of any other offence, for example, of conspiracy or of dishonest handling of the proceeds of the cheque which he knew to have been obtained dishonestly. That is not the question. The question is whether he was guilty of theft and not whether if he is not guilty of theft he might have been properly charged with and convicted of some other offence.

The answer to the main contention is that Meech being under the initial obligation already mentioned, the proceeds of the cheque continued as between him and McCord to be deemed to be McCord's property so that if Meech dishonestly misappropriated those proceeds he was by reason of section 5(3) guilty of theft even though McCord could not have enforced performance of that obligation against Meech in a civil action. Some reliance was placed on a passage in Professor Smith's *The Law of Theft*, p31, para 76:

> "Thus there is no redress in civil or criminal law against a client who is accidentally overpaid by a bookmaker. The same principle no doubt governs other cases where the transaction is void or illegal by statute or at common law. If this is a defect in the law, the fault lies with the civil law and not with the Theft Act. If the civil law says that the defendant is the exclusive owner of the money and under no obligation to repay even an equivalent sum, it would be incongruous for the criminal law to say he had stolen it."

It must be observed that that passage was written with reference to section 5(4) of the Theft Act 1968 and not with reference to s5(3) of that Act. It immediately follows a discussion of the Gaming Act cases. We do not think the learned author had a case such as the present in mind. On no view could it be said in the present case that the common law would regard Meech as the "exclusive owner" of the original cheque or of its proceeds. The true owner of the proceeds was the hire-purchase finance company. They could have sued Meech to judgment for the full value of the original cheque. But Meech having received the original cheque from McCord under the obligation we have mentioned, the criminal law provides that as between him and McCord the cheque and its proceeds are to be deemed to be McCord's property so that a subsequent dishonest misappropriation of the cheque or its proceeds makes Meech liable to be convicted of theft. We are therefore clearly of the view that Meech was properly convicted of theft just as under the old law he would have been liable to have been convicted of fraudulent conversion. We therefore think that the judge was quite right in leaving this case to the jury and that the direction which he gave was correct. If it be open to criticism at all, the criticism might be that the direction was arguably too favourable to the defendants.'

Moynes v *Cooper* [1956] 1 QB 439 Divisional Court (Lord Goddard LJ, Hilbery and Stable JJ)

Property belonging to another – s5(4) Theft Act 1968

Facts

The defendant received an overpayment of £6 19s 6d in his wage packet. He was unaware of the overpayment until later he opened the wage packet at home later that day. The defendant spent the money that had been paid to him in error and was charged with stealing it under the Larceny Act 1916.

Held

The defendant was not guilty of stealing the overpayment.

Lord Goddard CJ:

'The problem as to dishonest appropriation in cases where money has been paid under a mistake has been the subject of many cases and much difference of judicial opinion. The appeal committee were of opinion that this case was indistinguishable from *R* v *Prince* (1868) LR 1 CCR 150, decided in 1868. In that case the cashier of a bank, who had authority to pay cheques, was deceived by the presentation of a forged cheque by the prisoner. He paid the amount of the cheque and the prisoner was indicted for stealing the proceeds. It was held that this did not amount to larceny. Blackburn J, lamenting, as we also may, that this was the law, said: "If the owner intended the property to pass, though he would not so have intended had he known the real facts, that is sufficient to prevent the offence of obtaining another's property from amounting to larceny." It was held in that case that the prisoner's offence amounted to obtaining the money by a false pretence, but in the present case no question of false pretences arises as the defendant made no representation of any sort.

The next case which bears on the subject is *R* v *Middleton* (1873) LR 2 CCR 38, and in 1885 there came the much discussed case of *R* v *Ashwell* (1885) 16 QBD 190; 2 TLR 151, in which unfortunately the court was equally divided. We do not propose to discuss these or any subsequent cases on the subject in detail because in our opinion the matter is now concluded by section 1 (2) of the Larceny Act, 1916. It will be remembered that there have been in the last 90 years two codifications of the law of larceny. The first was the Larceny Act of 1861, the long title of which is: "An Act to consolidate and amend the statute law of England and Ireland relating to larceny and other similar offences." While that Act in section 1 defined a considerable number of terms, such as "document of title to goods" and "valuable security" among others, it did not contain a definition of larceny or any of the necessary constituents of that crime. The Larceny Act of 1916, which is now the governing statute, is entitled: "An Act to consolidate and simplify the law relating to larceny triable on indictment and kindred offences," and does contain an elaborate definition of larceny. This Act was not intended to alter the law and, as has often been said, it has not done so; but while the Act of 1861 consolidated, and to some extent amended, the statute law, the later Act consolidates and simplifies the whole law, which includes the common law as expounded by judicial decision. What amounts to a "taking" sufficient to amount to larceny was much discussed in *R* v *Middleton*, and in our opinion it is the effect of that decision which is reproduced and enacted as the law. Section 1 (2) (i) of the Act of 1916 provides: "the expression 'takes' includes obtaining the possession ... (c) under a mistake on the part of the owner with knowledge on the part of the taker that possession has been so obtained." This, in our opinion, is affirming the common law that the taker must have animus furandi at the same time when he takes the property. In *Middleton's* case the wrong amount of money was paid by the post office clerk before the prisoner, who picked it up knowing of the clerk's mistake and so took it animo furandi. In the present case it is found that the defendant did not know of the mistake when he took the money, so the taking was not animo furandi. We prefer to base our decision on this ground, namely, that there was no taking here within the section. The decision in *R* v *Prince* depended on the fact that the bank, acting thorough its authorised clerk, did intend to pass the property in the money though it was induced to do so not by its own or his mistake but by fraud. Where a transfer of property is obtained by fraud, there is no doubt but that the property does pass, subject, however, to the right of the defrauded party on discovering the fraud to disaffirm the transaction and resume his property. In the present case the action would be for money had and received to the company's use as paid under a mistake of fact.'

(See *R* v *Gilks*, above.)

R v *Turner (No 2)* [1971] 1 WLR 901 Court of Appeal (Criminal Division) (Lords Parker CJ, Widgery LJ and Bridge J)

Property belonging to another – s5(1) Theft Act 1968

Facts
The defendant took his car to be repaired at a garage operated by a man named Arthur Brown. Once the repairs were completed, Brown parked the car in the road outside his garage as he was short of space. The defendant, who had retained a spare key, drove the car away that night. Later, when questioned by police, he denied that he had ever put the car in to be repaired at Brown's garage. He appealed against his conviction for theft on the ground that the car could not be regarded as 'property belonging to another' within s5(1) of the Theft Act 1968.

Held
Appeal dismissed.

Lord Parker CJ:

'The trial lasted, six days, in the course of which every conceivable point seems to have been taken and argued. In the result, however, when it comes to this Court two points, and two only, are taken. It is said in the first instance that while Mr Brown may have had possession or control in fact, that is not enough, and that it must be shown, before it can be said that the property "belonged to" Mr Brown, those being the words used in section 1 (1) of the Theft Act, that that possession is, as it is said, a right superior to that in the defendnat. It is argued from that in default of proof of a lien – and the judge in his summing up directed the jury that they were not concerned with the question of whether there was a lien – that Mr Brown was merely a bailee at will and accordingly had no sufficient possession.

The words "belonging to another" are specifically defined in section 5 of the Act, subsection (1) of which provides that: "Property shall be regarded as belonging to any person having possession or control of it, or having in it any proprietary right or interest." The sole question was whether Mr Brown had possession or control.

This Court is quite satisfied that there is no ground whatever for qualifying the words "possession or control" in any way. It is sufficient if it is found that the person from whom the property is taken, or to use the words of the Act, appropriated, was at the time in fact in possession or control. At the trial there was a long argument as to whether that possession or control must be lawful, it being said that, by reason of the fact that this car was subject to a hire-purchase agreement, Mr Brown could never even as against the defendant obtain lawful possession or control. As I have said, this court is quite satisfied that the judge was quite correct in telling the jury they need not bother about lien, and that they need not bother about hire purchase agreements. The only question was whether Mr Brown was in fact in possession or control.'

34 Appropriation

R v Atakpu; *R v Abrahams* [1993] 3 WLR 812 Court of Appeal (Criminal Division) (Stuart-Smith LJ, Ward and May JJ)

Theft Act 1968 s3(1) – appropriation – where committed – whether same property capable of being appropriated more than once by the defendant

Facts

The appellants hired cars in Germany using false documents. They planned to sell the cars on returning with them to the United Kingdom. The appellants were detained at customs on returning to the United Kingdom, and in due course charged with conspiring to steal the cars. Following a direction from the trial judge that an appropriation of the vehicles occurred within the United Kingdom, the appellants were convicted of theft and subsequently appealed.

Held

The appeals would be allowed.

Ward J (his Lordship considered the impact of the House of Lords' decision in *R v Gomez* [1993] AC 442 on the interpretation of appropriation in s3(1) of the Theft Act 1968, and continued):

'So interesting questions arise in this appeal as to (1) whether the theft committed abroad continued within the jurisdiction so that it could be established here by the retention of the car after the hire period had expired, or by ringing the changes or by some other fresh appropriation; (2) whether cars stolen abroad could be stolen again, and again and again, within the jurisdiction each time an appropriation of them is made.

These questions do not admit a clear nor an easy answer ...

In *R v Meech* [1974] QB 549 the Court of Appeal appeared to accept the proposition that if the withdrawal of money from the bank account was an appropriation then it was a misappropriation once and for all and the subsequent dividing up of the money between co-defendants could not be another dishonest misappropriation.

R v Pitham (1976) 65 Cr App R 45 supports the theory that appropriation is an instantaneous act complete at the moment that defendant appropriates the goods by assuming the rights of owner and offering them for sale. On the facts of that case the appropriation was instantaneous for the thief had clearly done all he was going to do in relation to the property. The question had arisen in connection with the charge of dishonest handling against those to whom he sold the property. The words in s22 of the Theft Act 1968 which are there to ensure that stealing and handling are separate offences are "otherwise than in the course of the stealing". It is implicit in those words that the act of stealing may run a longer course than an instant. The court indeed left open for later decision the question which divided Professor Smith (*The Law of Theft*, 3rd ed (1977), para 400) and Professor Griew (*The Theft Act 1968*, 2nd ed (1974), paras 8-18, 8-19) as to how long the course of stealing could be.

A person is guilty of robbery under s8 of the Theft Act 1968 if he steals and immediately before or at the time of doing so he uses force. In *R v Hale (Robert)* (1978) 68 Cr App R 415 the court rejected the argument that the theft was complete at the time of taking the jewellery box and that force used to effect escape was not sufficient to constitute robbery ...

Endeavouring to summarise it would seem that (1) theft can occur in an instant by a single appropriation but it can also involve a course of dealing with property lasting longer and involving several appropriations before the transaction is complete; (2) theft is a finite act – it has a beginning and it has an end; (3) at what point the transaction is complete is a matter for the jury to decide upon the facts of each case; (4) though there may be several appropriations in the course of a single theft or several appropriations of different goods each constituting a separate theft as in *R v Skipp* [1975] Crim LR 114, no case suggests that there can be successive thefts of the same property (assuming of course that possession is constant and not lost or abandoned, later to be assumed again).

Can these conclusions stand in the light of *R v Gomez* [1993] AC 442? Whilst we see the logic of the argument that if there are several appropriations each one can constitute a separate theft, we flinch from reaching that conclusion. Professor Glanville Williams would seem to share our reluctance so to find. He wrote in *Appropriation: A Single or Continuous Act?* [1978] Crim LR 69:

> "A man steals a watch, and two weeks later sells it. In common sense and ordinary language he is not guilty of a second theft when he sells it. Otherwise it would be possible, in theory, to convict a thief of theft of a silver teapot every time he uses it to make the tea."

We agree that the answer lies in s3(1) of the Theft Act 1968 ...'

His Lordship recited the provisions of s3(1) and continued:

> 'If therefore, he has come by the property by stealing it then his later dealing with the property is by implication not included among the assumptions of the right of an owner which amount to an appropriation within the meaning of s3(1). We reject the speculation that he would not have come by the property by stealing it if an indictment for the theft would not lie because the theft occurred abroad. There is no reason to restrict the plain ordinary words of s3(1) in such a narrow legalistic way. We note that one is guilty of handling stolen property under s24 and the provisions of the Act apply whether the stealing occurred in England or Wales or elsewhere. "Stealing" must have the same meaning in s3(1) as it has in s24. In our judgment, if goods have once been stolen, even if stolen abroad, they cannot be stolen again by the same thief exercising the same or other rights of ownership over the property.
>
> We find it more difficult to answer the first question we posed as to whether or not theft is a continuous offence. On a strict reading of *R v Gomez* [1993] AC 442 any dishonest assumption of the rights of the owner made with the necessary intention constitutes theft and that leaves little room for a continuous course of action.
>
> We would not wish that to be the law. Such restriction and rigidity may lead to technical anomalies and injustice. We would prefer to leave it for the common sense of the jury to decide that the appropriation can continue for so long as the thief can sensibly be regarded as in the act of stealing or, in more understandable words, so long as he is "on the job" as the editors of *Smith & Hogan, Criminal Law*, 7th ed (1992), p513, suggest the test should be. Since the matter is not strictly necessary for our decision we, like the court in *R v Pitham* will leave it open for further argument. It is not necessary for us to decide because no jury properly directed could reasonably arrive at a conclusion that the theft of these motor cars was still continuing days after the appellant had first taken them. If the jury had been asked when and where these motor cars were stolen they could only have answered that they were stolen in Frankfurt or Brussels. The theft was completed abroad and the thieves could not steal again in England!'

Chan Man-Sin v R [1988] 1 WLR 196 Privy Council (Lords Brandon, Ackner and Oliver, Sir John Stephenson and Sir Edward Eveleigh)

Appropriation of funds in bank accounts

Facts

As stated by Lord Oliver:

'The defendant was at all material times an accountant for two companies, Hunter Corporation Ltd ("Hunter") and Merit Investment Co Inc ("Merit") which maintained bank accounts in Hong Kong with the Standard Chartered Bank Ltd. Between 26 July 1983, by means of five forged cheques drawn on Merit's account, he withdrew sums totalling HK$2,750,647 and caused them to be deposited in his personal account with the Overseas Trust Bank Ltd. As a result, Merit's account became overdrawn but it had arranged a facility with the bank up to HK$3,000,000 and this limit was not exceeded. Between 31 December 1983 and 30 March 1984, by means of five further forged cheques, the defendant withdrew from Hunter's account sums totalling HK$2,022,392.30 which he caused to be deposited to the credit of the account of a business of which he was the sole proprietor. Hunter had likewise arranged a facility with the bank up to a limit of HK$4,000,000 and these withdrawals, although the account was overdrawn, did not cause the limit to be exceeded. Between 11 April 1984 and 12 May 1984 the defendant, again by the use of forged cheques, caused five further sums amounting in all the HK$2,690,608 to be withdrawn from Hunter's account. This time, however, the authorised overdraft limit of HK$4,000,000 was exceeded on each occasion.

The defendant's defalcations came to light in July 1984 and he was duly charged in the District Court of Hong Kong at Victoria with five charges of theft of choses in action, namely debts owed by the bank to Merit (charges 1 to 5) and 10 charges of theft of choses in action, namely debts owed by the bank to Hunter, charges 11 to 15 being those relating to the last-mentioned series of forgeries. On 9 December 1985 he was convicted of charges 1 to 10 and sentenced to imprisonment for three years concurrent in respect of each conviction. He was acquitted of charges 11 to 15 on the technical ground that, since there was in respect of the sums of the subject matter of those charges neither a debt due from the bank to Hunter nor any subsisting arrangement under which Hunter was entitled to draw from the bank, there was no chose in action of Hunter capable of being stolen. The defendant sought leave to appeal from the Court of Appeal of Hong Kong against his convictions but that application was dismissed on 30 May 1986. On 5 November 1986 special leave was granted by Order in Council to appeal to their Lordships' Board against the judgment of the Court of Appeal.'

Held

The appeal would be dismissed.

Lord Oliver:

'The argument for the defendant is a simple one and is founded upon the proposition that a bank is not entitled in law, as against its customer, to debit the customer's account with the amount of any cheque which the bank has not, in fact, any authority from the customer to honour. Thus, it is said, if the bank honours a forged cheque and debits the customer's account accordingly, the transaction is, quite simply, a nullity as a matter of law so far as the customer is concerned and the customer, on discovering the unauthorised debit to his account, is entitled to insist upon its being reversed. For this proposition reliance is, quite rightly, placed upon the decision of their Lordships' Board in *Tai Hing Cotton Mill Ltd* v *Liu Chong Hing Bank Ltd* [1986] AC 80. Starting out from this foundation, the defendant argues that the presentation of the 10 forged cheques in respect of which the defendant was convicted produced, as a matter of legal reality, no diminution at all of the respective credit balances of the companies. The bank simply made unauthorised debits to their accounts which they were entitled to have reversed upon demand. Thus, it is argued, although the defendant was no doubt guilty of offences of forgery and obtaining a pecuniary advantage by deception with which he was not charged, he could not have been guilty of the offences with which he was charged, namely, theft of Merit's or Hunter's choses in action.

The Theft Ordinance of Hong Kong follows, in all respects material to the instant case, the provisions of the English Theft Act 1968. Section 2 provides: "(1) A person commits theft if he dishonestly appropriates property belonging to another with the intention of permanently depriving the other of it;"

and section 5 includes "things in action and other intangible property" within the statutory definition of "property." It is not disputed that the debt due to the customer from his banker is a chose in action capable of being stolen and this equally applies to the sum which a customer is entitled to overdraw under contractual arrangements which he has made with the bank (see *R v Kohn* (1979) 69 Cr App R 395), though strictly in the latter case the chose in action is the benefit of the contractual arrangement with the bank. What is argued, however, is that, since as between the customer and the bank an unauthorised debit entry in the customer's account is a mere nullity, the customer is deprived of nothing and therefore there has been no appropriation. Equally, it is said that, since the customer whose property is alleged to have been stolen has not in fact been deprived of anything, there cannot have been an intention permanently to deprive him of the property. Thus, it is argued, there were lacking two essential ingredients of the offences with which the defendant was charged and he was entitled to an acquittal.

Their Lordships can deal very briefly with the second submission. The defendant did not elect to give evidence and if there was, as the prosecution contended, an appropriation of the companies' property, there was ample evidence from which the intention permanently to deprive them of it could be inferred. Even if it were possible to infer or assume that the defendant contemplated that the fraud would be discovered and appreciated also that his employers would or might challenge the bank's entitlement to payment of the sums debited, he would fall within the provisions of section 7 of the Ordinance. That section provides:

> "(1) A person appropriating property belonging to another without meaning the other permanently to lose the thing itself is nevertheless to be regarded as having the intention of permanently depriving the other of it if his intention is to treat the thing as his own to dispose of regardless of the other's rights; ..."

Quite clearly here the defendant was purporting to deal with the companies' property without regard to their rights.

Reverting to the defendant's principal ground of appeal, this has an appealing simplicity. The defendant's difficulty, however, is that it entirely ignores the artificial definition of appropriation which is contained in section 4(1) of the Ordinance and reproduces section 3(1) of the Act of 1968 ...

The owner of the chose in action consisting of a credit with his bank or a contractual right to draw on an account has, clearly, the right as owner to draw by means of a properly completed negotiable instrument or order to pay and it is, in their Lordships' view, beyond argument that one who draws, presents and negotiates a cheque on a particular bank account is assuming the rights of the owner of the credit in the account or (as the case may be) of the pre-negotiated right to draw on the account up to the agreed figure. Ownership, of course, consists of a bundle of rights and it may well be that there are other rights which an owner could exert over the chose in action in question which are not trespassed upon by the particular dealing which the thief chooses to assume. In *R v Morris (David)* [1984] AC 320, however, the House of Lords decisively rejected a submission that it was necessary, in order to constitute an appropriation as defined by section 3(1) of the Act of 1968, to demonstrate an assumption by the accused of all the rights of an owner.

Their Lordships are, accordingly, entirely satisfied that the transactions initiated and carried through by the defendant constituted an assumption of the rights of the owner and, consequently, an appropriation. It is unnecessary, for present purposes, to determine whether that occurred on presentation of the forged cheques or when the transactions were completed by the making of consequential entries in the bank accounts of the companies and the defendant or his business respectively. It is, in their Lordships' view, entirely immaterial that the end result of the transaction may be a legal nullity for it is not possible to read into section 4(1) of the Ordinance any requirement that the assumption of rights there envisaged should have a legally efficacious result. Their Lordships are fortified in the view which they have formed by the recent decision of the English Court of Appeal (Criminal Division) in *R v Wille* (unreported), 26 January 1987, of which they have been provided with a transcript and in which the court reached the same conclusion in circumstances not materially dissimilar to those in the instant case. It seems probable that if that decision had been reported at the time when special leave was applied for it would not have been granted. Their Lordships will accordingly humbly advise Her Majesty that the appeal should be dismissed.'

(See *R v Kohn* (1979) 69 Cr App R 395.)

R v Gomez [1992] 3 WLR 1067 House of Lords (Lord Keith, Lord Jauncey, Lord Lowry, Lord Browne-Wilkinson, Lord Slynn)

Theft – appropriation – *Lawrence* or *Morris*

Facts
The defendant was an assistant in a shop specialising in consumer electronics. A man named Ballay, who had come into possession of two stolen building society cheques, approached him asking if he could supply electrical goods in return for the cheques. The defendant was aware that the cheques were stolen and agreed to help. He consulted his manager, a Mr Gilberd, to check whether or not the store would accept such cheques (he did not of course inform Mr Gilberd that they were stolen). Gilberd instructed the defendant to check with the bank, and the defendant later informed him that the cheques were to be treated as if they were cash. Over a period of a few days the defendant provided Ballay with electrical goods to the value of £16,000. The cheques were banked and in due course dishonoured. During the course of his trial the defendant made a submission that he should not be charged with theft as there had been no appropriation of the goods. This submission was based on the proposition that any such appropriation had to be without the consent of the owner, and that the owner in this case, through its agent, had expressly consented to the delivery of the goods. The trial judge rejected this submission, and the defendant changed his plea to guilty. He appealed on the basis that the trial judge should have followed the House of Lords' decision in *R v Morris* (1983) 77 Cr App R 164, and the Court of Appeal allowed his appeal. Lord Lane CJ commenting that since the transfer of the goods to Ballay had been with the consent and express authority of the owner, there was no lack of authorisation and therefore no appropriation. The Crown appealed to the House of Lords.

Held (Lord Lowry dissenting)
The appeal would be allowed.

Lord Keith recited the questions certified for consideration by the House of Lords as being:

'When theft is alleged and that which is alleged to be stolen passes to the defendant with the consent of the owner, but that has been obtained by a false representation, has (a) an appropriation within the meaning of section 1(1) of the Theft Act 1968 taken place, or (b) must such a passing of property necessarily involve an element of adverse inference with or usurpation of some right of the owner?'

Having considered *Lawrence* and *Morris* (extracted at length in this chapter), his Lordship continued (p1076B–1081A):

'In my opinion Lord Roskill [in *Morris*] was undoubtedly right when he said ... that the assumption by the defendant of any of the rights of an owner could amount to an appropriation within the meaning of section 3(1), and that the removal of an article from the shelf and the changing of the price label on it constituted the assumption of one of the rights of the owner and hence an appropriation within the meaning of the subsection. But there are observations in the passage which, with the greatest possible respect to my noble and learned friend Lord Roskill, I must regard as unnecessary for the decision of the case and as being incorrect. In the first place, it seems to me that the switching of price labels on the article is in itself an assumption of one of the rights of the owner, whether or not it is accompanied by some other act such as removing the article from the shelf and placing it in a basket or trolley. No one but the owner has the right to remove a price label from an article or to place a price label upon it. If anyone else does so, he does an act, as Lord Roskill puts it, by way of adverse interference with or usurpation of that right. This is no less so in the case of the practical joker figured by Lord Roskill than in the case of one who makes the switch with dishonest intent. The practical joker, of course, is not guilty of theft because he has not acted dishonestly and does not intend to deprive the owner permanently of the article. So the label switching in itself constitutes an appropriation and so to have held would have been sufficient for the dismissal of both appeals. On the facts of the two cases it was unnecessary to decide whether, as argued by Mr Jeffreys, the mere taking of the article from the shelf and putting it in a trolley or other receptacle amounted to the assumption of one of the rights of the owner, and hence an appropriation. There was much to be said in favour of the view that it did, in respect that doing so gave the shopper control of the article and the capacity to exclude any other shopper from taking it. However, Lord Roskill expressed the opinion, at p332, that it did not, on the ground that the concept of appropriation in the context of section 3(1):

> "involves not an act expressly or impliedly authorised by the owner but an act by way of adverse interference with or usurpation of those rights."

While it is correct to say that appropriation for purposes of section 3(1) includes the latter sort of act, it does not necessarily follow that no other act can amount to an appropriation and in particular that no act expressly or impliedly authorised by the owner can in any circumstances do so. Indeed *R v Lawrence* [1972] AC 626 is a clear decision to the contrary since it laid down unequivocally that an act may be an appropriation notwithstanding that it is done with the consent of the owner. It does not appear to me that any sensible distinction can be made in this context between consent and authorisation.

In the civil case of *Dobson v General Accident Fire and Life Assurance Corporation plc* [1990] 1 QB 274 a Court of Appeal consisting of Parker and Ingham LJJ considered the apparent conflict between *R v Lawrence* and *R v Morris* [1984] AC 320 and applied the former decision. The facts were that the plaintiff had insured property with the defendant company against inter alia "loss or damage caused by theft". He advertised for sale a watch and ring at the total price of £5,950. A rogue telephoned expressing an interest in buying the articles and the plaintiff provisionally agreed with him that the payment would be by a building society cheque in the plaintiff's favour. The rogue called on the plaintiff next day and the watch and the ring were handed over to him in exchange for a building society cheque for the agreed amount. The plaintiff paid the cheque into his bank, which informed him that it was stolen and worthless. The defendant company denied liability under its policy of insurance on the ground that the loss of the watch and ring was not caused by theft within the meaning of the Act of 1968. The plaintiff succeeded in the county court in an action to recover the amount of his loss, and the decision was affirmed by the Court of Appeal. One of the arguments for the defendants was that there had been no theft because the plaintiff had agreed to the transaction with the rogue and reliance was placed on Lord Roskill's statement in *R v Morris* at p332, that appropriation

> "involves not an act expressly or impliedly authorised by the owner but an act by way of adverse interference with or usurpation of those rights."

In dealing with this argument Parker LJ said [1990] 1 QB 274, 281:

> "The difficulties caused by the apparent conflict between the decisions in *R v Lawrence* [1972] AC 626 and *R v Morris (David)* [1984] AC 320 have provided, not surprisingly, a basis for much discussion by textbook writers and contributors of articles to law journals. It is, however, clear that their Lordships in *R v Morris* did not regard anything said in that case as conflicting with *R v Lawrence* for it was specifically referred to in Lord Roskill's speech, with which the other members of the [Appellate] Committee all agreed, without disapproval or qualification. The only comment made was that, in *R v Lawrence*, the House did not have to consider the precise meaning of 'appropriation' in section 3(1) of the Act of 1968. With respect, I find this comment hard to follow in the light of the first of the questions asked in *R v Lawrence* and the answer to it, the passages from Viscount Dilhorne's speech already cited, the fact that it was specifically argued 'appropriates is meant in a pejorative, rather than a neutral sense in that the appropriation is against the will of the owner', and finally that dishonesty was common ground. I would have supposed that *the* question in *R v Lawrence* was whether appropriation necessarily involved an absence of consent."

Parker LJ then said that he found other difficulties in Lord Roskill's speech in *R v Morris*, and after setting out the facts of the case and quoting a long passage from that speech, at p332, and also the answers to the certified question he continued, at pp283–284:

"In the passage at p332 Lord Roskill, as it seems to me, impliedly envisages that mere label switching could be an appropriation and that this is so is confirmed by the answer to the certified question which specifically uses the words 'either by that act alone'. What then is it which would make label switching alone something which adversely affects or usurps the right of the owner? At p332 it appears to be envisaged that it will depend upon the question whether the label switching was dishonest and coupled with the other elements of the offence of theft or was due to a perverted sense of humour. This, however, appears to run together the elements of dishonesty and appropriation when it is clear from *R v Lawrence* [1972] AC 626 that they are separate. That the two elements were indeed, at any rate to some extent, run together is plain from the fact that the answer to the certified question begins with the words 'There is a dishonest appropriation'.

Moreover, on general principles, it would in my judgment be a plain interference with or usurpation of an owner's rights by the customer if he were to remove a label which the owner had placed on goods or put another label on. It would be a trespass to goods and it would be usurping the owner's rights, for only he would have any right to do such an act and no one could contend that there was any implied consent or authority to a customer to do any such thing. There would thus be an appropriation. In the case of the customer with a perverted sense of humour there would however be no theft for there would probably be no dishonesty and certainly no intent permanently to deprive the owner of the goods themselves.

The case of the customer who simply removes goods from the shelves is of course different because the basis on which a supermarket is run is that customers certainly have the consent of the owner to take goods from the shelves and take them to the checkout point there to pay the proper price for them. Suppose, however, that there were no such consent – in, for example, a shop where goods on display were to be taken form the shelves only by the attendant. In such a case a customer who took from the shelves would clearly be usurping the right of the owner. Indeed he would be doing so if he did no more than move an item from one place on a shelf to another. The only difference appears to be that in the one case there is consent and in the other there is not. Since, however, it was held in *R v Lawrence* [1972] AC 626 that consent is not relevant to appropriation there must, one would have supposed, be no difference between the two cases on that aspect of the offence.

There are further matters in *R v Morris* [1984] AC 320 in which I find difficulty. I mention only two. The first is the observations made on *R v McPherson* [1973] Crim LR 191. That was a case in which the defendant took two bottles of whisky from the shelves and put them in her shopping bag. The sole question in issue was whether there had been an appropriation. It was held in the Court of Appeal that there had been. As to this Lord Roskill said, at p333: "That was not, of course, a label switching case, but it is a plain case of appropriation effected by the combination of the acts of removing the goods from the shelf and of concealing them in the shopping bag. *R v McPherson* is to my mind clearly correctly decided as are all the cases which have followed it. It is wholly consistent with the principles which I have endeavoured to state in this speech."

Reference to the transcript of the judgment in that case however reveals that the decision did not turn on concealment in the shopping bag but was expressly upon the ground that the goods were appropriated when they were taken from the shelves. This indeed was recognised in *Anderton v Wish (Note)* (1980) 72 Cr App R 23, 25, where Roskill LJ giving the judgment of the court said: "The Court of Appeal ... held ... they were guilty of theft because when the bottles were taken there was a dishonest appropriation. If that decision is right and, with respect, it seems to me plainly right ..." Furthermore in *R v Morris* [1984] AC 320 Lord Roskill said, at p334: "... I understand all your Lordships to agree that *Anderton v Wish* ... was rightly decided for the reasons given."

Later, at p285 Parker LJ quoted this passage from the speech of Lord Roskill in *R v Morris* [1984] AC 320, 334:

"'without going into further detail I respectfully suggest that it is on any view wrong to introduce into this branch of the criminal law questions whether particular contracts are void or voidable on the ground of mistake or fraud or whether any mistake is sufficiently fundamental to vitiate a contract. These difficult questions should so far as possible be confined to those fields of law to which they are immediately relevant and I do not regard them as relevant questions under the Theft Act 1968.'"

and continued [1990] 1 QB 274, 285:

> "After anxious consideration I have reached the conclusion that whatever *R* v *Morris* did decide it cannot be regarded as having overruled the very plain decision in *R* v *Lawrence* [1972] AC 626 that appropriation can occur even if the owner consents and that *R* v *Morris* itself makes it plain that it is no defence to say that the property passed under a voidable contract."

On this ground Parker LJ dismissed the appeal.

Bingham LJ at p287, plainly took the view that a customer in a supermarket assumes some of the rights of an owner when he takes goods into his possession and exercises control over them by putting them in a basket or trolley, and thus appropriates them. Later, at p289, he mentioned that in Lord Roskill's speech in *Morris* no reference was made to Viscount Dilhorne's ruling in *Lawrence* that appropriation might occur even though the owner has permitted or consented to the property being taken, and continued:

> "I do not find it easy to reconcile this ruling of Viscount Dilhorne, which was as I understand central to the answer which the House gave to the certified question, with the reasoning of the House in *R* v *Morris* [1984] AC 320. Since, however, the House in *R* v *Morris* considered that there had plainly been an appropriation in *R* v *Lawrence* [1972] AC 626, this must (I think) have been because the Italian student, although he had permitted or allowed his money to be taken, had not in truth consented to the taxi driver taking anything in excess of the correct fare. This is not wholly satisfactory reconciliation, since it might be said that a supermarket consents to customers taking goods from its shelves only when they honestly intend to pay and not otherwise. On the facts of the present case, however, it can be said, by analogy with *R* v *Lawrence*, that although the plaintiff permitted and allowed his property to be taken by the third party, he had not in truth consented to the third party becoming owner without giving a valid draft by the building society for the price. On this basis I conclude that the plaintiff is able to show an appropriation sufficient to satisfy section 1(1) of the Theft Act 1968 when the third party accepted delivery of the article."

It was argued for the defendant in the present appeal that *Dobson* v *General Accident Fire and Life Assurance Corporation plc* [1990] 1 QB 274 was wrongly decided. I disagree, and on the contrary find myself in full agreement with those parts of the judgment of Parker LJ to which I have referred. As regards the attempted reconciliation by Bingham LJ of the reasoning in *R* v *Morris* [1984] AC 320 with the ruling in *R* v *Lawrence* [1972] AC 626 it appears to me that the suggested basis of reconciliation, which is essentially speculative, is unsound. The actual decision in *Morris* was correct, but it was erroneous, in addition to being unnecessary for the decision, to indicate that an act expressly or impliedly authorised by the owner could never amount to an appropriation. There is no material distinction between the facts in *Dobson* and those in the present case. In each case the owner of the goods was induced by fraud to part with them to the rogue. *Lawrence* makes it clear that consent to or authorisation by the owner of the taking by the rogue is irrelevant. The taking amounted to an appropriation within the meaning of section 1(1) of the Act of 1968. *Lawrence* also makes it clear that it is no less irrelevant that what happened may also have constituted the offence of obtaining property by deception under section 15(1) of the Act.

In my opinion it serves no useful purpose at the present time to seek to construe the relevant provisions of the Theft Act by reference to the report which preceded it, namely the Eighth Report of the Criminal Law Revision Committee on Theft and Related Offences (1966) (Cmnd 2977). The decision in *Lawrence* was a clear decision of this House upon the construction of the word "appropriate" in section 1(1) of the Act, which had stood for 12 years when doubt was thrown upon it by obiter dicta in *Morris*. *Lawrence* must be regarded as authoritative and correct, and there is no question of it now being right to depart from it.

It is desirable to say a few words about *R* v *Skipp* [1975] Crim LR 114 and *R* v *Fritschy* [1985] Crim LR 745. In the first case the defendant, posing as a haulage contractor, was instructed to collect consignments of goods from three different places and deliver them to a certain destination. He collected the goods and made off with them. The Court of Appeal, on his appeal against his conviction for theft upon one count covering all three consignments, on the ground that the count was bad for duplicity in that there were three separate appropriations, held that there had been no appropriation until the last of the goods were loaded, or probably until the defendant deviated from the route to the proper destination. In the second case the defendant was instructed by the owner to collect a quantity of krugerrands in London and deliver them to a safe deposit in Switzerland. Although the short report is not very clear on the matter, it seems that the defendant, having collected the coins, took them to Switzerland and there made away with them. The trial judge directed the jury if at the time he collected the coins the defendant had formed the dishonest intention of keeping them for himself he was guilty of theft. The Court of Appeal overturned the resultant conviction for theft on the ground, following *Morris*, that there had been no appropriation in England because the defendant had there taken possession of the krugerrands with the owner's authority. In my opinion both these cases were inconsistent with *Lawrence* and were wrongly decided.

There were cited to your Lordships a number of cases involving the abstraction of money from a limited company by a person who was in a position to give the consent of the company to the abstraction. It is sufficient to say that I agree with what my noble and learned friend, Lord Browne-Wilkinson, has to say about these cases in the speech to be delivered by him, and that in my opinion a person who thus procures the company's consent dishonestly and with the intention of permanently depriving the company of the money is guilty of theft contrary to section 1(1) of the Act of 1968.

My Lords, for the reasons which I have given I would answer branch (a) of the certified question in the affirmative and branch (b) in the negative, and allow the appeal.'

Lord Browne-Wilkinson, in the course of a speech in which he expressed his support for the views expressed by Lord Keith, made two observations on the issues raised which are of note, (p1109H–1111E):

'The fact that Parliament used that composite phrase – "dishonest appropriation" – in my judgment casts light on what is meant by the word "appropriation". The views expressed (obiter) by this House in *R v Morris* [1984] AC 320 that "appropriation" involves an act by way of adverse interference with or usurpation of the rights of the owner treats the word appropriation as being tantamount to "misappropriation". The concept of adverse interference with or usurpation of rights introduces into the word appropriation the mental state of both the owner and the accused. So far as concerns the mental state of the owner (did he consent?), the Act of 1968 expressly refers to such consent when it is a material factor: see sections 2(1)(b), 11(1), 1291 and 13. So far as concerns the mental state of the accused, the composite phrase in section 1(1) itself indicates that the requirement is dishonesty.

For myself, therefore, I regard the word "appropriation" in isolation as being an objective description of the act done irrespective of the mental state of either the owner or the accused. It is impossible to reconcile the decision in *Lawrence* (that the question of consent is irrelevant in considering whether there has been an appropriation) with the views expressed in *Morris*, which latter views in my judgment were incorrect.

It is suggested that this conclusion renders section 15 of the Act of 1968 otiose since a person who, by deception, persuades the owner to consent to part with his property will necessarily be guilty of theft within section 1. This may be so though I venture to doubt it. Take for example a man who obtains land by deception. Save as otherwise expressly provided, the definitions in sections 4 and 5 of the Act apply only for the purposes of interpreting section 1 of the Act: see section 1(3). Section 34(1) applies subsection (1) of section 4 and subsection (1) of section 5 generally for the purposes of the Act. Accordingly the other subsections of section 4 and section 5 do not apply to section 15. Suppose that a fraudster has persuaded a victim to part with his house: the fraudster is not guilty of theft of the land since section 4(2) provides that you cannot steal land. The charge could only be laid under section 15 which contains no provisions excluding land from the definition of property. Therefore, although there is a substantial overlap between section 1 and section 15, section 15 is not otiose.

Turning to the company cases, the dictum in *R v Morris* [1984] AC 320 has led to much confusion and complication where those in de facto control of the company have been charged with theft from it. The argument which has found favour in certain of the authorities runs as follows. There can be no theft within section 1 if the owner consents to what is done: Reg v Morris. If the accused, by reason of being the controlling shareholder or otherwise is "the directing mind and will of the company" he is to be treated as having validly consented on behalf of the company to his own appropriation of the company's property. This is apparently so whether or not there has been compliance with the formal requirements of company law applicable to dealings with the property of a company and even to cases where the consent relied on is ultra vires: see *R v Roffel* [1985] VR 511 and *R v McHugh* (1988) 88 Cr App R 385.

In my judgment this approach was wrong in law even if the dictum in *Morris* has been correct. Where a company is accused of a crime the acts and intentions of those who are the directing minds and will of the company are to be attributed to the company. That is not the law where the charge is that those who are the directing minds and will have themselves committed a crime against the company: see *Attorney-General's Reference (No 2 of 1982)* [1984] QB 624 applying *Belmont Finance Corporation Ltd v Williams Furniture Ltd* [1979] Ch 250.

In any event, your Lordships' decision in this case, re-establishing as it does the decision in *R v Lawrence* [1972] AC 626, renders the whole question of consent by the company irrelevant. Whether or not those controlling the company consented or purported to consent to the abstraction of the company's property by the accused, he will have appropriated the property to the company. The question will be whether the other necessary elements are present, viz was such appropriation dishonest and was it done with the intention of permanently depriving the company of such property? In my judgment the decision in *R v Roffel* [1985] VR 511 and the statements of principle in *R v McHugh*, 88 Cr App R 385, 393, are not correct in law and should not be followed. As for *Attorney-General's Reference (No 2 of 1982)*, in my judgment both the concession made by counsel (that there had been an appropriation) and the decision in that case was correct, as was the decision in *R v Philippou*, 89 Cr App R 290.

I am glad to be able to reach this conclusion. The pillaging of companies by those who control them is now all too common. It would offend both common sense and justice to hold that the very control which enables such people to extract the company's assets constitutes a defence to a charge of theft from the company. The question in each case must be whether the extraction of the property from the company was dishonest, not whether the alleged thief has consented to his own wrongdoing.'

Lord Lowry (dissenting) cited extracts from the Criminal Law Revision Committee's Report that presaged the enactment of the Theft Act 1968 to support his assertion that the intention of Parliament had been to maintain a fundamental distinction between theft and obtaining property by deception. Having further considered *Lawrence* and *Dobson*, he continued (p1097H–1098G):

'The report of the argument in this House in *R v Lawrence* [1972] AC 626 shows that the appellant, understandably from his own point of view, again approached the case as one of false pretences. That basis would provide grounds for an acquittal of the charge of theft if the word "appropriates" in section 1(1) connotes an absence of consent by the owner, and the appellant presented his argument on the meaning of that subsection, at p630A, in the same way as in the Court of Appeal and with the same unsuccessful result. But that was not all. Viscount Dilhorne at p631, when reviewing the evidence, expressed the opinion that the facts of the case fell far short of establishing that Mr Occhi, the Italian student who was the victim of the taxi driver, had consented to the acquisition by the appellant of the £6, as argued at p628. On that footing the taxi driver could have been guilty of larceny by a trick (in old-fashioned terms), so as to be guilty of theft under any interpretation of section 1(1). It has to be said, however, that the way in which Mr Occhi left the taxi at the end of the journey without further question seems more consistent with his having accepted that £7 in all was the fare to be charged and that he had been induced by the driver's false representations to part out and out with all the money which he had passively allowed the taxi driver to take from his wallet. It is of no assistance, however, to your Lordships in the present appeal to debate the finer points of *R v Lawrence* with a view to deciding whether the decision in this House (although not that of the Court of Appeal) can be justified on the special facts. What is important is the unequivocal, but in my respectful opinion wrong, statement of the law made by Viscount Dilhorne, at p623A (to which I referred at the outset of my speech), that Parliament by omitting the words "without the consent of the owner" from section 1(1) of the Act of 1968 "has relieved the prosecution of the burden of establishing that the taking was without the owner's consent." He added "That is no longer an ingredient of the offence" (sc "of theft"). The reasoning which follows is based on the opinion, already inseparable from what has been said, that appropriation is a neutral expression and does not convey the sense of taking property for oneself without the owner's authority. As in the Court of Appeal, the defence argument was primarily directed towards implying words into section 1(1), a difficult task at best, and only secondarily towards the meaning of "appropriates": see p631A. But the only speech delivered did not consider this second point and the summary treatment of the appellant's argument is reflected in the opinion expressed, at p633, that the point certified and argued was scarcely worthy of their Lordships' attention. My Lords, I have found nothing in *Lawrence* which affects my view of the present appeal. The crucial statement, apart from what was said at p632A, was at p632E: "[Appropriation] may occur even though the owner has permitted or consented to the property being taken." If "taken" there signifies a permitted change of ownership, I respectfully cannot agree.'

He concluded (p1108D–1109E):

'In my opinion, any attempt to reconcile the statement of principle in *Lawrence* and *Morris* is a complete waste of time. And certainly reconciliation cannot be achieved by the unattractive solution of varying the meaning of "appropriation" in different provisions of the Act of 1968. It is clear that, whether they succeeded or not, both the Criminal Law Revision Committee and the draftsman must have intended to give the word one meaning, which would be the same in the Act as in the committee's report.

To simplify the law, where possible, is a worthy objective but, my Lords, I maintain that the law, as envisaged in the report, is simple enough: there is no problem (and there would have been none in *Lawrence*, *Morris* and the present case) if one prosecutes under section 15 all offenders involving obtaining by deception and prosecutes theft in general under section 1. In that way some thefts will come under section 15, but no "false pretences" will come under section 1.

The defendant can already count himself lucky to have received only a two-year sentence, having regard to the amount involved and to the position of trust which he held. He will be even more fortunate if he has his conviction quashed, since there was against him an open-and-shut case under section 15. But, if I am right in my analysis, one cannot simply be content to say that, if his conviction is restored, the respondent will have suffered no injustice. The right level answer, based on the true meaning of the Act, must be found and applied.

If my submissions are correct, the question finally remains whether your Lordships are bound by the doctrine of precedent to follow and apply the statements in *R v Lawrence* [1972] AC 626, 632 that Parliament, by omitting the words "without the consent of the owner" from section 1(1) of the Act of 1968, has "relieved the prosecution of the burden of establishing that the taking was without the owner's consent" and that "[appropriation] may occur even though the owner has permitted or consented to the property being taken." I suggest not. In the first place, Viscount Dilhorne had already expressed the opinion that the facts of the case fell short of establishing that the victim had consented to the acquisition by the appellant of the money he was alleged to have stolen. This line of reasoning (though not the approach of the Court of Appeal in *Lawrence*) supports a conviction for theft under section 1(1) on any view of the law and enables your Lordships to regard the statements at p632 as obiter dicta. Secondly, it follows that *Dobson v General Accident Fire and Life Assurance Corporation plc* [1990] 1 QB 274, the only case of authority on the point which is at the heart of this appeal (which case in any event is not binding on your Lordships), applied the obiter dicta in Lawrence to reach an erroneous conclusion. Thirdly, Lord Roskill's statement in *R v Morris* [1984] AC 320, while it may be obiter, contradicts Viscount Dilhorne's.

Lastly, let me assume that Viscount Dilhorne's statements have the character of a "decision" as that word is used in the *Practice Statement (Judicial Precedent)* [1966] 1 WLR 1234, which intimated that this House would depart from a previous decision "when it appears right to do so". Your Lordships might then so elect. The *Practice Statement* referred to "the especial need for certainty as to the criminal law", but there is ample proof that both before and after *Morris* certainty has been lacking. The cases on the *Practice Statement* are conveniently found in *Halsbury's Laws of England*, 4th edition vol 26 (1979), p296, para 577. A previous decision should not be departed from merely because the House considers it to be wrong and only rarely should questions of construction be reconsidered. But the precise *meaning* of section 1(1) has not received serious judicial attention before. Furthermore, your Lordships may feel that it is inconvenient and undesirable for the criminal law as enunciated in *Lawrence* and *Dobson* to be in conflict with the law affecting the title to money and other kinds of property.'

R v *Governor of Pentonville Prison, ex parte Osman* [1990] 1 WLR 277 Divisional Court (Lloyd LJ, and French J)

Appropriation – where acts constituting appropriation take place

Facts
The applicant sought habeus corpus. He was alleged to have dishonestly dispatched a telex instructing a New York bank to transfer funds from the bank account belonging to the company of which he was the chairman [BMFL], to the bank account of another unconnected company [one of the 'Carrian' companies], from whom he was to receive corrupt payments. One of the issues before the court was that of where the alleged theft had occurred.

Held
The act of sending the telex amounted to appropriation, therefore the offence was committed in the country from which it was transmitted.

Lloyd LJ:

'Mr Ross-Munro [for the applicant] concedes that there is jurisdiction to try charge 31, which relates to the theft of Hong Kong dollars. But he submits that the United States dollar thefts all took place in the United States, since that is where BMFL's property was appropriated. Mr Nicholls, on the other hand, submits that the property was appropriated in Hong Kong.

In considering Mr Ross-Munro's argument, it is convenient to take method A, since it was the method most frequently adopted, as well as the most straightforward. It will be remembered that under method A BMFL would send a telex to its correspondent bank in New York, instructing it to pay the amount of the United States dollar loan to the payees' correspondent bank in the United States, for the account of one of the Carrian companies. It was common ground that the only property of BMFL capable of being stolen was the chose in action represented by the debt, if any, due to BMFL from its correspondent bank in the United States, or the contractual right, if any, to overdraw on BMFL's account. Mr Ross-Munro argued that the theft of the chose in action took place in the United States when BMFL's account was debited, and not before. That was the moment of appropriation. The dealing ticket, confirmation slip and telex were the means whereby the theft was carried out. The theft was not completed until the account was debited. Mr Nicholls argued to the contrary, that there was an appropriation when the telex instruction was sent, if not before, and that that appropriation took place in Hong Kong.

In support of his argument Mr Ross-Munro referred us to the decision of the Court of Appeal (Criminal Division) in *R v Tomsett* [1985] Crim LR 369 (Note), 19 March 1985, a decision to which, as it happens, both members of the present Court were party. In that case the defendant was a telex operator employed by Credit Suisse in London. He was convicted of conspiracy to steal from the bank by diverting 7 million dollars from an account in New York to an account in Geneva. Fortunately, the dishonest plan was discovered in time. Counsel for the defendant argued that the contemplated theft would have taken place in New York or Geneva. Accordingly, the theft would not have been indictable here. We alerted the prosecution to a possible argument that the defendant appropriated the chose in action in New York, when he sent the telex from London, and that the appropriation therefore took place in England. But counsel for the prosecution declined to support the conviction on that ground. His only argument was that the theft must have taken place in England, because it was Crédit Suisse's money.

We dealt with that argument as follows:

"Mr Hart-Leverton's argument to the contrary was that the contemplated theft would have been a crime committed here. Alternatively, he argued that the underlying object of the conspiracy was to inflict pecuniary loss on Crédit Suisse in London. On one or other or both of those grounds he submitted that the conspiracy was indictable in England. Mr Hart-Leverton did not cite any authority in support of his first argument. His sole submission was that the subject manner of the theft was, as he put it, Crédit Suisse's money. We cannot accept that submission. Prima facie a theft takes place where the property is appropriated; prima facie appropriation takes place where the property is situated. The subject matter of the theft in the present case was either a debt or alternatively cash over the counter. If it was a debt then the debt was unquestionably situated in New York. If it was cash over the counter, the cash was unquestionably situated in Geneva. It might perhaps have been argued that, though the debt was situated in New York, nevertheless, the appropriation took place in England, since this was where the appropriating telex was dispatched. But no such argument was advanced ... in the absence of any argument for the Crown other than the one we have mentioned, we feel bound to accept Mr Stevens' submission that the contemplated theft would have taken place either in New York or Geneva, and would not therefore have been indictable here."

Mr Ross-Munro argued that *R* v *Tomsett* is binding on us, and that we are therefore bound to hold that the sending of the telex from Hong Kong was not an appropriation. We do not, he said, disregard the decision as per incuriam merely because the right point had not been argued. We cannot accept that argument. It would be carrying the doctrine of stare decisis beyond all reason. We could not uphold the conviction in *Tomsett* on a point which the prosecution declined to argue. On the other hand it is quite obvious, even without reading between the lines, that we were leaving the present point open for another day. We said that a theft prima facie takes place where the property is appropriated, and appropriation prima facie takes place where the property is situated. The emphasis is on prima facie. There was no acceptable argument advanced by the Crown to displace the prima facie position. The law of England cannot be made or unmade by the willingness of counsel to argue a point. The ratio of *Tomsett* stands. It was not per incuriam. But the present point was left undecided.

Mr Ross-Munro also relied on *R* v *Kohn* (1979) 69 Cr App R 395. One of the arguments in that case was that the defendant could not be liable for theft when the customer's account was overdrawn, but within the overdraft limits. The Court rejected that argument. Geoffrey Lane LJ said, at p. 407:

"If the account is in credit, as we have seen, there is an obligation to honour the cheque. If the account is within the agreed limits of the overdraft facilities, there is an obligation to meet the cheque. In either case it is an obligation which can only be enforced by action. For purposes of this case it seems to us that that sufficiently constitutes a debt within the meaning of the word as explained by Lord Reid. It is a right of property which can properly be described as a thing in action and therefore potentially a subject of theft under the provisions of the Act of 1968. The cheque is the means by which the theft of this property is achieved. The completion of the theft does not take place until the transaction has gone through to completion."

Mr Ross-Munro relied on the last two sentences of that passage. He submits that it is authority for the proposition that there can be no appropriation until the amount of the cheque has been debited to the account in question. We do not so read the passage. But in any event the observation was obiter. This appears from the subsequent case of *R* v *Navvabi* [1986] 1 WLR 1311. In that case the defendant issued a cheque supported by a cheque guarantee card. The account was overdrawn, and that defendant had no overdraft facility. It was held that he could not be held liable for theft. After quoting the passage from *Kohn*, already cited, Lord Lane CJ said, at p1316:

"The last sentence of this passage did not affect the result in *Kohn* and was to that extent obiter. It suggests (and has been taken by Professor Griew [1986] Crim LR 362 to mean) that theft occurs at the time when the bank transfers the funds."

So it was clear that Lord Lane CJ himself regarded the sentence on which Mr Ross-Munro relies as obiter.

In *Chan Man-sin* v *R* (1988) 86 Cr App R 303, [1988] 1 WLR 196 the appellant was convicted of stealing by drawing forged cheques on a company's bank account. It was argued that he could not be liable for theft, since the bank would be bound to reimburse the company's account when the forgeries came to light. The Privy Council rejected that argument. Lord Oliver of Aylmerton said, at p199:

"The owner of the chose in action consisting of a credit with his bank or a contractual right to draw on an account has, clearly, the right as owner to draw by means of a properly completed negotiable instrument or order to pay and it is, in their Lordships' view, beyond argument that one who draws, presents and negotiates a cheque on a particular bank account is assuming the rights of the owner of the credit in the account or (as the case may be) of the pre-negotiated right to draw on the account up to the agreed figure. Ownership, of course, consists of a bundle of rights and it may well be that there are other rights which an owner could exert over the chose in action in question which are not trespassed on by the particular dealing which the thief chooses to assume. In *R v Morris* [1984] AC 320 however, the House of Lords decisively rejected a submission that it was necessary, in order to constitute an appropriation as defined by section 3(1) of the Act of 1968, to demonstrate an assumption by the accused of all the rights of an owner. Their Lordships are, accordingly, entirely satisfied that the transactions initiated and carried through by the defendant constituted an assumption of the rights of the owner and, consequently an appropriation. It is unnecessary, for present purposes, to determine whether that occurred on presentation of the forged cheques or when the transactions were completed by the making of consequential entries in the bank accounts of the companies and the defendant or his business respectively. It is, in their Lordships' view, entirely immaterial that the end result of the transaction may be a legal nullity for it is not possible to read into section (4)(1) of the ordinance any requirement that the assumption of rights there envisaged should have a legally efficacious result."

Mr Ross-Munro relied on the reference to the transaction being "carried through" to completion. But it is clear from the passage as a whole that Lord Oliver was leaving open the question whether the presentation of the cheque was itself an appropriation.

In the light of *Navvabi* and *Chan Man-sin* it is unnecessary to mention two earlier unreported cases to which we were referred, save to say that in *R v Doole* (unreported), 21 March 1985, it does not appear to have been argued that the defendant's request to transfer the sum standing to the credit of the deposit account in question was an appropriation; and in *R v Wille* (1987) 86 Cr App R 296 the summing up approved by the Court of Appeal certainly suggests that the drawing and issuing of the cheque without authority would itself be an appropriation. We will not read the whole of the relevant passage of the summing up, but it concludes, at p302:

> "So that in this particular case if you are sure in relation to any of the cheques in a count in the indictment, if you are sure that the defendant had no authority to draw that cheque, why then in drawing the cheque and issuing it he appropriated the debt which the bank owed to Ginarco because he assumed in relation to it the rights of an owner by taking it upon himself to direct the bank in effect to pay out money, thus lessening the debt, and it matters not that the bank were acting contrary to the mandate, that is wholly irrelevant for this purpose, it is the drawing and the issuing of the cheque without authority which constitutes the appropriation."

The Court of Appeal said that it was not possible to improve upon the terms in which the judge had summed up. In the *Chan Man-sin* case, [1988] 1 WLR 196, 200, Lord Oliver of Aylmerton said that if *R v Wille* had been reported at the time when the defendant sought special leave to appeal, the probability is that leave would have been refused.

So we would hold, contrary to Mr Ross-Munro's argument, that the question whether the sending of the telex was an appropriation is fully open on the authorities. What should our answer be? We find the views expressed by Professor Smith, *Law of Theft*, 5th ed (1984), p55-56, para 106, and his comments on *R v Tomsett* [1985] Crim LR 369 convincing.

In R v *Morris* [1984] AC 320 the House of Lords made it clear that it is not necessary for an appropriation that the defendant assume all rights of an owner. It is enough that he should assume any of the owner's rights: see *per* Lord Roskill, at p331, and the passage cited above from *Chan Man-sin*. If so, then one of the plainest rights possessed by the owner of the chose in action in the present case must surely have been the right to draw on the account in question. Mr Ross-Munro argues that the right to draw on an account in credit, or within an agreed overdraft limit, is not a right but a liberty or a power. He refers us in that connection to Glanville Williams, *Textbook of Criminal Law*, 2nd ed (1983), p763. We find that hard to understand. So far as the customer is concerned, he has a right as against the bank to have his cheques met. It is that right which the defendant assumes by presenting a cheque, or by sending a telex instruction without authority. The act of sending the telex is therefore the act of theft itself, and not a mere attempt. It is the last act which the defendant has to perform and not a preparatory act. It would matter not if the account were never in fact debited. We can find no way of excluding the sending of the telex in such circumstances from the definition of appropriation contained in section 3(1) of the Theft Act 1968.

Professor Griew suggests that this view may raise practical problems, on the ground that it would be necessary in every case for the prosecution to prove the state of the account at the moment of appropriation, that is to say, when the telex is sent, as distinct from the moment when the account is debited. But we do not understand Professor Griew to doubt the correctness of the view in principle. In any event, proof of the state of the account, either by direct evidence or by proper inference, will normally be available.

Mr Ross-Munro argued that until the account is debited there is no "adverse interference" with any right of the owner, and therefore, on the authority of *R v Morris* [1984] AC 320, no appropriation. The theft of a chose in action is analogous to the theft of a chattel by destruction: see Griew, *The Theft Acts 1968 and 1978*, 3rd ed (1978), para 2-11, a passage approved by the Court of Appeal in *R v Kohn*, 69 Cr App R 395, 405.

Mr Nicholls replies that Lord Roskill's dictum in *R v Morris* at p332 was obiter and inconsistent with the previous decision of the House of Lords in *R v Lawrence (Alan)* [1972] AC 626: obiter, because the specific act of appropriation referred to in the certified question was the switching of price labels on stolen goods, not the removal of the goods from the shelf; inconsistent with *Lawrence* because that case established that absence of consent was not an essential element in the crime of theft.

It is unnecessary for us to consider the relationship between these two cases, on which, as Professor Griew sardonically observes, *The Theft Acts 1968 and 1978*, 5th ed (1986), para 2-70, no two commentators (nor, we would add, any two judges) take the same view. For we regard ourselves as bound, or as good as bound, by the meaning attributed to the word "appropriation" by the unanimous decision of the House of Lords in *R v Morris*. Applying that meaning to the facts of the instant case, we would hold that a defendant "usurps the customer's rights when he, without the customer's authority, dishonestly issues the cheque drawn on the customer's account." If "adverse interference" adds anything to usurpation, then he also thereby adversely interferes with the customer's rights. The theft is complete in law, even though it may be said that it is not complete in fact until the account is debited.

Finally, Mr Ross-Munro argued that even if the sending of the telex was the appropriation, the appropriation takes place where the telex is received, not where it is sent. He relied on the analogy of acceptance of a contractual offer by telex. It is sufficient to say that we can see no real analogy. If we are right that the act of sending the telex was the act of appropriation, then the place where that act was performed, namely, the place where the telex was despatched, is the place where the chose in action was appropriated. We do not rule out the possibility that the place where the telex is received may also be regarded as the place of appropriation, if our courts were ever to adopt the view that a crime may have a dual location. But in the meantime, we would hold that Hong Kong was the place of appropriation under Method A.'

R v Hale (1978) 68 Cr App R 415

See Chapter 36.

Lawrence v Metropolitan Police Commissioner [1972] AC 626 House of Lords (Viscount Dilhorne, Lords Donovan, Pearson, Diplock and Cross)

Appropriation – whether owner's lack of consent a vital ingredient

Facts

As stated by Viscount Dilhorne:

'On September 1, 1969, a Mr Occhi, an Italian who spoke little English, arrived at Victoria Station on his first visit to this country. He went up to a taxi-driver, the appellant, and showed him a piece of paper on which an address in Ladbroke Grove was written. The appellant said that it was very far and very expensive. Mr Occhi got into the taxi, took one pound out of his wallet and gave it to the appellant who then, the wallet being still open, took a further six pounds out of it. He then drove Mr Occhi to Ladbroke Grove. The correct lawful fare for the journey was in the region of 10s 6d.

The appellant was charged with and convicted of the theft of the six pounds. In cross-examination, Mr Occhi, when asked whether he had consented to the money being taken, said that he had "permitted." He gave evidence through an interpreter and it does not appear that he was asked to explain what he meant by the use of that word. He had not objected when the six pounds were taken. He had not asked for the return of any of it. It may well be that when he used the word "permitted," he meant no more than that he had allowed the money to be taken. It certainly was not established at the trial that he had agreed to pay to the appellant a sum far in excess of the legal fare for the journey and so had consented to the acquisition by the appellant of the six pounds. The main contention of the appellant in this House and in the Court of Appeal was that Mr Occhi had consented to the taking of the six pounds and that, consequently, his conviction could not stand.'

The two points of law certified for consideration by the House of Lords were:

'(1) whether Section 1(1) of the Theft Act 1968 is to be construed as though it contained the words "without the consent of the owner" or words to that effect;
(2) whether the provisions of Section 15(1) and of Section 1(1) of the Theft Act 1968, are mutually exclusive in the sense that if the facts proved would justify a conviction under Section 15(1) there cannot lawfully be a conviction under Section 1(1) on those facts.'

Held

Both certified questions would be answered in the negative, and the appeal dismissed.

Viscount Dilhorne (in considering the first certified question):

'I see no ground for concluding that the omission of the words "without the consent of the owner" was inadvertent and not deliberate, and to read the subsection as if they were included is, in my opinion, wholly unwarranted. Parliament by the omission of these words has relieved the prosecution of the burden of establishing that the taking was without the owner's consent.'

As regards the second certified question he continued:

'There is nothing in the Act to suggest that they should be regarded as mutually exclusive and it is by no means uncommon for conduct on the part of the accused to render him liable to conviction for more than one offence. Not infrequently there is some overlapping of offences. In some cases the facts may justify a charge under Section 1(1) and also a charge under Section 15(1). On the other hand, there are cases which only come within Section 1(1) and some which are only within Section 15(1). If in this case the appellant had been charged under Section 15(1) he would, I expect, have contended that there was no deception, that he simply appropriated the money and that he ought to have been charged under Section 1(1). In my view he was rightly charged under that section.'

R v Navvabi [1986] 1 WLR 1311 Court of Appeal (Criminal Division) (Lord Lane CJ, McGowan and Rose JJ)

Unauthorised drawing of cheques – whether appropriation

Facts

The defendant had opened a number of bank accounts using false names, and had subsequently used the cheques and cheque cards with which he had been provided to draw cheques on the accounts in favour of casinos at which he gambled. There were insufficient funds in the accounts to meet the cheques drawn, and the defendant had not arranged any overdraft facilities. He was convicted of theft from the banks in relation to the cheques he had drawn in favour of the casinos, on the basis that the offence occurred when the cheques were delivered to the casinos. The defendant appealed on the ground that either he had not appropriated any property by writing the cheques, or that it did not occur until such cheques were actually honoured by the paying banks.

Held

The appeal would be allowed.

Lord Lane CJ:

'Before the trial judge and again in this court counsel for the appellant submitted that no identifiable property was appropriated, because the contractual obligation imposed on the bank was referable not to any asset which it had at the time the cheque was drawn and delivered to the casino, but to those funds which it had at the time of presentation by the casino. It was further submitted that, if there was identifiable property, its appropriation took place when the bank honoured the cheque and the funds were transferred to the casino by the bank, and not at the time the cheque was drawn and delivered to the casino. Furthermore it was contended that theft in such a way was so academic a concept that only an academically-minded person understanding such niceties would be able to form the necessary intention permanently to deprive the owner. Counsel for the appellant conceded, though this court doubts the correctness of that concession, that if the prosecution case had been presented on the basis that the appropriation took place at the time the funds were transferred by the bank to the casino, the conviction would be unimpeachable.

On behalf of the Crown it was submitted that the sums of £50 and £100 were sufficiently identifiable notwithstanding that they were only part of the bank's assets; that when a cheque backed by a guarantee card is drawn on an account without funds, the drawer assumes the rights of the bank in their money by directing them to do something with their property which they did not want to do, the property in question being either money or other intangible property but not a chose in action; and the elements necessary for theft being dishonesty, misappropriation of the property of another and an intention permanently to deprive, the thief's knowledge of the identity of the owner and whether the drawer believed he was stealing from the bank or the casino was immaterial.

In order to test the validity of these submissions one turns to the Theft Act 1968.'

His Lordship referred to sections 1(1)–6(1) and continued:

'It is common ground between counsel that no authority directly in point is to be found in the several decisions of the Courts which have been cited. No discourtesy is intended to the diligence of counsel if we refer to only two of these decisions: *R v Kohn* (1979) 69 Cr App R 395, on which the appellant relies, and *R v Pitham and Hehl* (1977) 65 Cr App R 45, on which the prosecution rely.

Kohn was a decision of a differently constituted division of this court. The appellant, a director of a limited company, had been convicted of theft from the company in drawing cheques for his own purposes on the company's account in amounts (i) within the credit standing to the account, (ii) within the overdraft limit on the account and (iii) in excess of the overdraft limit. The convictions in relation to situations (i) and (ii) were upheld and in relation to (iii) quashed. In relation to (i) and (ii) it was held that the company's thing in action was stolen, whereas in situation (iii) nothing in action existed.

The following is an extract from the judgment of the Court referring to the debt owed by the bank to the company, at p407:

"It is a right of property which can properly be described as a thing in action and therefore potentially a subject of theft under the provisions of the 1968 Act. The cheque is the means by which the theft of the property is achieved. The completion of the theft does not take place until the transaction has gone through to completion."

The last sentence of this passage did not affect the result in *Kohn* (supra) and was to that extent obiter. It suggests (and has been taken by Professor Griew in his article "Stealing and Obtaining Bank Credits" [1986] Crim LR 356 at 362 to mean) that theft occurs at the time when the bank transfers the funds. But Professor Smith has argued (see [1985] Crim LR 370 and *The Law of Theft*, 5th ed (1983), paragraph 106), that the delivery of the cheque to the payee is "an assumption of the rights of an owner" and therefore the appropriation. There may, however, as Professor Griew points out, be practical difficulties with this approach, for the state of the account may be much more difficult to ascertain when the cheque is delivered to the payee than when it is presented to the bank. Such difficulties, however, do not arise, or call for resolution, in the present case.

In *R* v *Pitham and Hehl* (supra) another division of this Court upheld the appellants' convictions for handling on the basis that a third man, in purporting to sell to them someone else's furniture, had assumed the rights of the owner to the furniture when he showed it to the appellants and invited them to buy what they wanted: at that moment he appropriated the goods to himself.

We note that *Pitham and Hehl* has also been criticised by both Professor Glanville Williams in *The General Part, Criminal Law*, 2nd ed (1983), p764) and Professor Smith in *The Law of Theft*, 5th ed (1983), para 27). It is sufficient for the purposes of the present case to say that despite the submissions of counsel before us, we see no incompatibility between the decisions in *Pitham and Hehl* and *Kohn*.

Neither of these cases however helps us to resolve the present matter which, it seems to this Court, turns essentially on the construction of section 3(1): Was use of the cheque card to guarantee payment of a cheque delivered to the casino and drawn on an account with inadequate funds an assumption of the rights of the bank and thus appropriation? In our judgment it was not. That use of the cheque card and delivery of the cheque did no more than give the casino a contractual right as against the bank to be paid a specified sum from the bank's funds on presentation of the guaranteed cheque. That was not in itself an assumption of the rights of the bank to that part of the bank's funds to which the sum specified in the cheque corresponded: there was therefore no appropriation by the drawer either on delivery of the cheque to the casino or when the funds were ultimately transferred to the casino.'

R v *Pitham and Hehl* (1976) 65 Cr App R 45

See Chapter 40.

35 The Mens Rea of Theft

R v Duru (1973) 58 Cr App R 151
See reference to this authority in *R* v *Lloyd*, below.

R v Ghosh [1982] 3 WLR 110 Court of Appeal (Criminal Division) (Lord Lane CJ, Lloyd and Eastham JJ)
Direction to the jury on dishonesty

Facts

As stated by Lord Lane CJ:

'On April 29, 1981 before the Crown Court in St Albans, the appellant was convicted on four counts of an indictment laid under the Theft Act 1968: on count 1, attempting to procure the execution of a cheque by deception; on count 2, attempting to obtain money by deception; on counts 3 and 4, obtaining money by deception. Count 1 was laid under section 20(2) and the remainder under section 15(1). He was fined the sum of £250 on each count with a term of imprisonment to be served in default of payment.

At all material times the appellant was a surgeon acting as *a locum tenens* consultant at a hospital. The charges alleged that he had falsely represented that he had himself carried out a surgical operation to terminate pregnancy or that money was due to himself or an anaesthetist for such an operation, when in fact the operation had been carried out by someone else, and/or under the National Health Service provisions.

His defence was that there was no deception; that the sums paid to him were due for consultation fees which were legitimately payable under the regulations, or else were the balance of fees properly payable; in other words that there was nothing dishonest about his behaviour on any of the counts.

The effect of the jury's verdict was as follows: as to count 1, that the appellant had falsely represented that he had carried out a surgical operation and had intended dishonestly to obtain money thereby; that as to count 2 he had falsely pretended that an operation had been carried out under the National Health Service; that as to count 3 he had falsely pretended that money was due to an anaesthetist; and as to count 4 that he had obtained money by falsely pretending that an operation had been carried out on a fee-paying basis when in fact it had been conducted under the terms of the National Health Service.

The grounds of appeal are simply that the learned judge misdirected the jury as to the meaning of dishonesty.'

Held

The appeal would be dismissed

Lord Lane CJ:

'What the judge had to say on that topic was as follows: "Now, finally dishonesty. There are, sad to say, infinite categories of dishonesty. It is for you. Jurors in the past and, whilst we have criminal law in the future, jurors in the future have to set the standards of honesty. Now it is your turn today, having heard what you have, to consider contemporary standards of honesty and dishonesty in the context of all that you have heard. I cannot really expand on this too much, but probably it is something rather like getting something for nothing, sharp practice, manipulating systems and many other matters which come to your mind."

The law on this branch of the Theft Act 1968 is in a complicated state and we embark upon an examination of the authorities with great diffidence.

When *Rv McIvor* [1982] 1 WLR 409 came before the Court of Appeal, there were two conflicting lines of authority. On the one hand there were cases which decided that the test of dishonesty for the purposes of the Theft Act 1968 is, what we venture to call, subjective – that is to say the jury should be directed to look into the mind of the defendant and determine whether he knew he was acting dishonestly: see *R v Landy and Others* [1981] 1 WLR 355 where Lawton LJ giving the reserved judgment of the Court of Appeal said: "An assertion by a defendant that throughout a transaction he acted honestly does not have to be accepted but has to be weighed like any other piece of evidence. If that was the defendant's state of mind, or may have been, he is entitled to be acquitted. But if the jury, applying their own notions of what is honest and what is not, conclude that he could not have believed he was acting honestly, then the element of dishonesty will have been established. What a jury must not do is to say to themselves: 'If we had been in his place we would have known we were acting dishonestly so he must have known he was'."

On the other hand there were cases which decided that the test of dishonesty is objective. Thus in *R v Green and Greenstein* [1975] 1 WLR 1353, the judge had directed the jury: "... there is nothing illegal in stagging. The question you have to decide and what this case is all about is whether these defendants, or either of them, carried out their stagging operations in a dishonest way. To that question you apply your own standards of dishonesty. It is no good, you see, applying the standards of anyone accused of dishonesty, otherwise everybody accused of dishonesty, if he were to be tested by his own standards, would be acquitted automatically, you may think. The question is essentially the one for a jury to decide and it is essentially one which the jury must decide by applying its own standards." The Court of Appeal, in a reserved judgment, approved that direction.

In *R v McIvor* (supra) the Court of Appeal sought to reconcile these conflicting lines of authority. They did so on the basis that the subjective test is appropriate where the charge is conspiracy to defraud, but in the case of theft the test should be objective. We quote from the relevant passage in full: "It seems elementary, first, that where the charge is conspiracy to defraud the prosecution must prove actual dishonesty in the minds of the defendants in relation to the agreement concerned, and, second, that where the charge is an offence contrary to section 15 of the Theft Act 1968 the prosecution must prove that the defendant knew or was reckless regarding the representation concerned. The passage in my judgment in *Landy* (supra) to which we have referred should be read in relation to charges of conspiracy to defraud, and not in relation to charges of theft contrary to section 1 of the 1968 Act. Theft is in a different category from conspiracy to defraud, so that dishonesty can be established independently of the knowledge or belief of the defendant, subject to the special cases provided for in section 2 of the Act. Nevertheless, where a defendant has given evidence of his state of mind at the time of the alleged offence, the jury should be told to give that evidence such weight as they consider right, and they may also be directed that they should apply their own standards to the meaning of dishonesty."

The question we have to decide in the present case is, first, whether the distinction suggested in *McIvor* (supra) is justifiable in theory, and secondly, whether it is workable in practice.

In *R v Scott* [1975] AC 819, the House of Lords had to consider whether deceit is a necessary element in the common law crime of conspiracy to defraud. They held that it is not. It is sufficient for the Crown to prove dishonesty. In the course of his speech Viscount Dilhorne traced the meaning of the words "fraud," "fraudulently" and "defraud" in relation to simple larceny, as well as the common law offence of conspiracy to defraud. After referring to *Stephen, History of the Criminal Law of England* (1883), Vol 2, pp121, 122 and *East's Pleas of the Crown* (1803) p553 he continued at p128 and p836 of the respective reports as follows: "The Criminal Law Revision Committee in their Eighth Report on *Theft and Related Offences* (1966) (Cmnd 2977) in paragraph 33 expressed the view that the important element of larceny, embezzlement and fraudulent conversion was 'undoubtedly the dishonest appropriation of another person's property'; in paragraph 35 that the words 'dishonestly appropriates' meant the same as 'fraudulently converts to his own use or benefit, or the use or benefit of any other person,' and in paragraph 39 that 'dishonestly' seemed to them a better word than 'fraudulently.'

Parliament endorsed these views in the Theft Act 1968, which by section 1(1) defined theft as the dishonest appropriation of property belonging to another with the intention of permanently depriving the other of it. Section 17 of that Act replaces section 82 and 83 of the Larceny Act 1861 and the Falsification of Accounts Act 1875. The offences created by those sections and by that Act made it necessary to prove that there had been an 'intent to defraud.' Section 17 of the Theft Act 1968 substitutes the words 'dishonestly with a view to gain for himself or another or with intent to cause loss to another' for the words 'intent to defraud.'

If 'fraudulently' in relation to larceny meant 'dishonestly' and 'intent to defraud' in relation to falsification of accounts is equivalent to the words now contained in section 17 of the Theft Act 1968 which I have quoted, it would indeed be odd if 'defraud' in the phrase 'conspiracy to defraud' has a different meaning and means only a conspiracy which is to be carried out be deceit."

Later on in the same speech Viscount Dilhorne continued as follows at p839: "As I have said, words take colour from the context in which they are used, but the words 'fraudulently' and 'defraud' must ordinarily have a very similar meaning. If, as I think, and as the Criminal Law Revision Committee appears to have thought, 'fraudulently' means 'dishonestly,' then 'to defraud' ordinarily means, in my opinion, to deprive a person dishonestly of something which is his or of something to which he is or would or might but for the perpetration of the fraud be entitled."

In *R v Scott* the House of Lords were only concerned with the question whether deceit is an essential ingredient in cases of conspiracy to defraud; and they held not. As Lord Diplock said at p841B, "dishonesty of any kind is enough." But there is nothing in the case of *R v Scott* which supports the view that, so far as the element of dishonesty is concerned, "theft is in a different category from conspiracy to defraud." On the contrary the analogy drawn by Viscount Dilhorne between the two offences, and indeed the whole tenor of his speech, suggests the precise opposite.

Nor is there anything in *R v Landy* [1981] 1 WLR 355, itself which justifies putting theft and conspiracy to defraud into different categories. Indeed the Court went out of its way to stress that the test for dishonesty, whatever it might be, should be the same whether the offence charged be theft or conspiracy to defraud. This is clear from the reference to *R v Feely* [1973] QB 530, which was a case under section 1 of the Theft Act 1968. Having set out what we have for convenience called the subjective test, the Court in *Rv Landy* continue at p365: "In our judgment this is the way *Rv Feely* [1973] QB 530 should be applied in cases where the issue of dishonesty arises. It is also the way in which the jury should have been directed in this case ..."

In support of the distinction it is said that in conspiracy to defraud the question arises in relation to an agreement. But we cannot see that this makes any difference. If "A" and "B" agree to deprive a person dishonestly of his goods, they are guilty of conspiracy to defraud: see *R v Scott's* case (supra). If they dishonestly and with the necessary intent deprive him of his goods, they are presumably guilty of theft. Why, one asks respectfully, should the test be objective in the case of simple theft, but subjective where they have agreed to commit a theft?

The difficulties do not stop there. The court in *R v McIvor* (supra) evidently regarded cases under section 15 of the Theft Act 1968 as being on the subjective side of the line, at any rate so far as proof of deception is concerned. This was the way they sought to explain *R v Greenstein* [1975] 1 WLR 1353. In that case, after directing the jury in the passage which we have already quoted, the judge continued, at p1360: "Now in considering whether Mr Green or Mr Greenstein had or may have had an honest belief in the truth of their representations, ... the test is a subjective one. That is to say, it is not what you would have believed in similar circumstances. It is what you think they believed and if you think that they, or either of them, had an honest belief to that effect, well then of course there would not be any dishonesty. On the other hand, if there is an absence of reasonable grounds for so believing, you might think that that points to the conclusion that they or either of them, as the case may be, had no genuine belief in the truth of their representations. In this case, applying your own standards, you may think that they acted dishonestly and it would be for you to say whether it has been established by this prosecution that they had no such honest belief ..."

The Court of Appeal in *R v Greenstein* (supra) appear to have approved that passage. At any rate they expressed no disapproval. In *R v McIvor* [1982] 1 WLR 409 the Court reconciled the two passages quoted from the judge's summing up as follows at p415: "It seems clear that these two passages are concerned with different points. The first, which follows and adopts the standards laid down in *R v Feely* (supra) is concerned with the element of dishonesty in section 15 offences. While the second is specifically concerned with the mental element in relation to the false representation the subject matter of the charge. Clearly, if a defendant honestly believes that the representation made was true the prosecution cannot prove that he knew of, or was reckless as to, its falsity."

The difficulty with section 15 of the Theft Act 1968 is that dishonesty comes in twice. If a person knows that he is not telling the truth he is guilty of dishonesty. Indeed deliberate deception is one of the two most obvious forms of dishonesty. One wonders therefore whether "dishonestly" in section 15(1) adds anything, except in the case of reckless deception. But assuming it does, there are two consequences of the distinction drawn in *R v McIvor* (supra). In the first place it would mean that the legislation has gone further than its framers intended. For it is clear from paragraphs 87-88 of the Criminal Law Revision Committee's Eighth Report that "deception" was to replace "false pretence" in the old section 32(1) of the Larceny Act 1916, and "dishonestly" was to replace "with intent to defraud." If the test of dishonesty in conspiracy to defraud cases is subjective, it is difficult to see how it could have been anything other than subjective in considering "intent to defraud." It follows that, if the distinction drawn in *R v McIvor* (supra) is correct, the Criminal Law Revision Committee were recommending an important charge in the law by substituting "dishonestly" for "with intent to defraud"; for they were implicitly substituting an objective for a subjective test.

The second consequence is that in cases of deliberate deception the jury will have to be given two different tests of dishonesty to apply: the subjective test in relation to deception and the objective test in relation to obtaining. This is indeed what seems to have happened in *R v Greenstein* (supra). We cannot regard this as satisfactory from a practical point of view. If it be sought to obviate the difficulty by making the test subjective in relation to both aspects of section 15, but objective in relation to section 1, then that would certainly be contrary to what was intended by the Criminal Law Revision Committee. For in paragraph 88 they say: "The provision in clause 12(1) making a person guilty of criminal deception if he 'dishonestly obtains' the property replaces the provision in the 1916 Act, section 32(1) making a person guilty of obtaining by false pretences if he 'with intent to defraud, obtains' the things there mentioned. The change will correspond to the change from 'fraudulently' to 'dishonestly' in the definition of stealing (contained in section 1)."

We feel, with the greatest respect, that in seeking to reconcile the two lines of authority in the way we have mentioned, the Court of Appeal in *R v McIvor* (supra) was seeking to reconcile the irreconcilable. It therefore falls to us now either to choose between the two lines of authority or to propose some other solution.

In the current supplement to *Archbold Criminal Pleading Evidence and Practice*, 40th ed (1979), paragraph 1460, the editors suggest that the observations on dishonesty by the Court of Appeal in *R v Landy* (supra) can be disregarded "in view of the wealth of authority to the contrary." The matter, we feel, is not as simple as that.

In *R v Waterfall* [1970] 1 QB 148, the defendant was charged under section 16 of the Theft Act 1968 with dishonestly obtaining a pecuniary advantage from a taxi driver. Lord Parker CJ, giving the judgment of the Court of Appeal, said pp150-151: respectively: "The sole question as it seems to me in this case revolves around the third ingredient, namely, whether what was done was done dishonestly. In regard to that the deputy recorder directed the jury in this way: 'If on reflection and deliberation you came to the conclusion that this defendant never did have any genuine belief that Mr Tropp [the accountant] would pay the taxi fare, then you would be entitled to convict him ...' In other words, in that passage the deputy recorder is telling the jury they had to consider what was in this particular defendant's mind: had he a genuine belief that the accountant would provide the money? That, as it seems to this court, is a perfectly proper direction subject to this, that it would be right to tell the jury that they can use as a test, though not a conclusive test, whether there were any reasonable grounds for that belief. Unfortunately, however, just before the jury retired, in two passages the deputy recorder, as it seems to this Court, was saying: you cannot hold that this man had a genuine belief unless he had reasonable grounds for that belief."

Lord Parker then sets out the passages in question and continues at p151: " ... the court is quite satisfied that those directions cannot be justified. The test here is a subjective test, whether the particular man had an honest belief, and of course whereas the absence of reasonable ground may point strongly to the fact that that belief is not genuine, it is at the end of the day for the jury to say whether or not in the case of this particular man he did have that genuine belief."

That decision was criticised by academic writers. But it was followed shortly afterwards in *R v Royle* [1971] 1 WLR 1764, another case under section 16 of the Theft Act 1968. Edmund Davies LJ giving the judgment of the Court said this at p1769: "The charges being that debts had been dishonestly 'evaded' by deception, contrary to section 16(2)(a), it was incumbent on the commissioner to direct the jury on the fundamental ingredient of dishonesty. In accordance with *R v Waterfall* (supra), they should have been told that the test is whether the accused had an honest belief and that, whereas the absence of reasonable ground might point strongly to the conclusion that he entertained no genuine belief in the truth of his representation, it was for them to say whether or not it had been established that the appellant had no such genuine belief."

It is to be noted that the Court in that case treated the "fundamental ingredient of dishonesty" as being the same as whether the defendant had a genuine belief in the truth of the representation.

In *R v Gilks* [1972] 1 WLR 1341, which was decided by the Court of Appeal the following year, the appellant had been convicted of theft contrary to section 1 of the Theft Act 1968. The facts were that he had been overpaid by a book-maker. He knew that the book-maker had made a mistake, and that he was not entitled to the money. But he kept it. The case for the defence was that "book-makers are a race apart." It would be dishonest if your grocer gave you too much change and you kept it, knowing that he had made a mistake. But it was not dishonest in the case of a book-maker.

The judge directed the jury, at p1345: "Well, it is a matter for you to consider, members of the jury, but try and place yourselves in that man's position at that time and answer the question whether in your view he thought he was acting honestly or dishonestly."

Cairns LJ giving the judgment of the Court of Appeal held that that was, in the circumstances of the case, a proper and sufficient direction on the matter of dishonesty. He continued, at p1345: "On the face of it the defendant's conduct was dishonest: the only possible basis on which the jury could find that the prosecution had not established dishonesty would be if they thought it possible that the defendant did have the belief which he claimed to have."

A little later *R v Feely* [1973] QB 530 came before a Court of five judges. The case is often treated as having laid down an objective test of dishonesty for the purpose of section 1 of the Theft Act. But what it actually decided was (i) that it is for the jury to determine whether the defendant acted dishonestly and not for the judge, (ii) that the word "dishonestly" can only relate to the defendant's own state of mind, and (iii) that it is unnecessary and undesirable for judges to define what is meant by "dishonesty."

It is true that the Court said at pp537–538: "Jurors, when deciding whether an appropriation was dishonest can be reasonably expected to, and should, apply the current standards of ordinary decent people."

It is that sentence which is usually taken as laying down the objective test. But the passage goes on: "In their own lives they have to decide what is and what is not dishonest. We can see no reason why, when in a jury box, they should require the help of a judge to tell them what amounts to dishonesty." The sentence requiring the jury to apply current standards leads up to the prohibition on judges from applying *their* standards. That is the context in which the sentence appears. It seems to be reading too much into that sentence to treat it as authority for the view that "dishonesty can be established independently of the knowledge or belief of the defendant." If it could, then any reference to the state of mind of the defendant would be beside the point.

This brings us to the heart of the problem. Is "dishonestly" in section 1 of the Theft Act 1968 intended to characterise a course of conduct? Or is it intended to describe a state of mind? If the former, then we can well understand that it could be established independently of the knowledge or belief of the accused. But if, as we think, it is the latter, then the knowledge and belief of the accused are at the root of the problem.

Take for example a man who comes from a country where public transport is free. On his first day here he travels on a bus. He gets off without paying. He never had any intention of paying. His mind is clearly honest; but his conduct, judged objectively by what he has done, is dishonest. It seems to us that in using the word "dishonestly" in the Theft Act, Parliament cannot have intended to catch dishonest conduct in that sense, that is to say conduct to which no moral obloquy could possibly attach. This is sufficiently established by the partial definition in section 2 of the Theft Act itself. All the matters covered by section 2(1) relate to the belief of the accused. Section 2(2) relates to his willingness to pay. A man's belief and his willingness to pay are things which can only be established subjectively. It is difficult to see how a partially subjective definition can be made to work in harness with the test which in all other respects is wholly objective.

If we are right that dishonesty is something in the mind of the accused (what Professor Glanville Williams calls "a special mental state"), then if the mind of the accused is honest, it cannot be deemed dishonest merely because members of the jury would have regarded it as dishonest to embark on that course of conduct.

So we would reject the simple uncomplicated approach that the test is purely objective, however attractive from the practical point of view that solution may be.

There remains the objection that to adopt a subjective test is to abandon all standards but that of the accused himself, and to bring about a state of affairs in which "Robin Hood would be no robber": *R v Greenstein* (supra). This objection misunderstands the nature of the subjective test. It is no defence for a man to say "I knew that what I was doing is generally regarded as dishonest; but I do not regard it as dishonest myself. Therefore I am not guilty." What he is however entitled to say is "I did not know that anybody would regard what I was doing as dishonest." He may not be believed; just as he may not be believed if he sets up "a claim of right" under section 2(1) of the Theft Act 1968, or asserts that he believed in the truth of a misrepresentation under section 15 of the Theft Act. But if he *is* believed, or raises a real doubt about the matter, the jury cannot be sure that he was dishonest.

In determining whether the prosecution has proved that the defendant was acting dishonestly, a jury must first of all decide whether according to the ordinary standards of reasonable and honest people what was done was dishonest. If it was not dishonest by those standards, that is the end of the matter and the prosecution fails.

If it was dishonest by those standards, then the jury must consider whether the defendant himself must have realised that what he was doing was by those standards dishonest. In most cases, where the actions are obviously dishonest by ordinary standards, there will be no doubt about it. It will be obvious that the defendant himself knew that he was acting dishonestly. It is dishonest for a defendant to act in a way which he knows ordinary people consider to be dishonest, even if he asserts or genuinely believes that he is morally justified in acting as he did. For example, Robin Hood or those ardent anti-vivisectionists who remove animals from vivisection laboratories are acting dishonestly, even though they may consider themselves to be morally justified in doing what they do, because they know that ordinary people would consider these actions to be dishonest.

Cases which might be described as borderline, such as *Boggeln* v *Williams* [1978] 1 WLR 873, will depend upon the view taken by the jury as to whether the defendant may have believed what he was doing was in accordance with the ordinary man's idea of honesty. A jury might have come to the conclusion that the defendant in that case was disobedient or impudent, but not dishonest in what he did.

So far as the present case is concerned, it seems to us that once the jury had rejected the defendant's account in respect of each count in the indictment (as they plainly did), the finding of dishonesty was inevitable, whichever of the tests of dishonesty was applied. If the judge had asked the jury to determine whether the defendant might have believed that what he did was in accordance with the ordinary man's idea of honesty, there could have only been one answer – and that is no, once the jury had rejected the defendant's explanation of what happened.

In so far as there was a misdirection on the meaning of dishonesty, it is plainly a case for the application of the proviso to section 2(1) of the Criminal Appeal Act 1968. This appeal is accordingly dismissed.'

R v *Lloyd* [1985] 3 WLR 30 Court of Appeal (Criminal Division) (Lord Lane CJ, Farquharson and Tudor Price JJ)

Intention to permanently deprive – s6(1) Theft Act 1968

Facts
The defendant was a cinema projectionist who agreed with other defendants, to make private video copies of first run feature films. The plan involved taking the print of a film at the end of an evening's public showing, and returning it after copies had been made, in time for the next day's performance. The defendants were convicted of conspiracy to steal, and appealed on the ground that there had been no intention to permanently deprive the owners of the film.

Held
The appeals would be allowed.

Lord Lane CJ:

'The complaint by the appellants is this, that the judge misdirected the jury first of all in leaving the question for them to decide whether the removal of a film in these circumstances could amount to theft, and secondly, in allowing them to consider section 6(1) of the Theft Act 1968 as being relevant at all in the circumstances of this case.

The point is a short one. It is not a simple one. It is not without wider importance, because if the judge was wrong in leaving the matter in the way in which he did for the jury to consider, it might mean, as we understand it, that the only offence of which a person in these circumstances could be convicted would be a conspiracy to commit a breach of the Copyright Act 1956. At the time when this particular case was being tried, the maximum penalties available for the substantive offence under the Copyright Act were minimal. Those penalties have now been increased by the provisions of the Copyright (Amendment) Act 1983, and in the light of that Act it can be said that although Parliament perhaps has not entirely caught up with this type of prevalent pirating offence, it is at least gaining on it.

We turn now to the provisions of the Theft Act 1968, the conspiracy alleged being a breach of that particular Act. Section 1(1) of that Act provides that "A person is guilty of theft if he dishonestly appropriates property belonging to another with the intention of permanently depriving the other of it; and 'thief' and 'steal' shall be construed accordingly."

On that wording alone these appellants were not guilty of theft or of conspiracy to steal. The success of their scheme and their ability to act with impunity in a similar fashion in the future, depended, as we have already said, upon their ability to return the film to its rightful place in the hands of the Odeon Cinema at Barking as rapidly as possible, so that its absence should not be noticed. Therefore the intention of the appellants could more accurately be described as an intention temporarily to deprive the owner of the film and was indeed the opposite of an intention permanently to deprive.

What then was the basis of the prosecution case and the basis of the judge's direction to the jury? It is said that section 6(1) of the Theft Act brings such actions as the appellants performed here within the provisions of section 1. The learned judge left the matter to the jury on the basis that they had to decide whether the words of section 6(1) were satisfied by the prosecution or not.

Section 6(1) provides: "A person appropriating property belonging to another without meaning the other permanently to lose the thing itself is nevertheless to be regarded as having the intention of permanently depriving the other of it if his intention is to treat the thing as his own to dispose of regardless of the other's rights; and a borrowing or lending of it may amount to so treating it if, but only if, the borrowing or lending is for a period and in circumstances making it equivalent to an outright taking or disposal."

That section has been described by JR Spencer in his article [1977] Crim LR 653, as a section which "sprouts obscurities at every phrase," and we are inclined to agree with him. It is abstruse. But it must mean, if nothing else, that there are circumstances in which a defendant may be deemed to have the intention permanently to deprive, even though he may intend the owner eventually to get back the object which has been taken.

We have had the benefit of submissions by Mr Du Cann in this case. His first submission is that the definition of "property" in section 4 of the Theft Act 1968 does not include value, and he submits that it was on the basis of loss of value or loss of virtue of the films that the prosecution of the case proceeded. In order to substantiate that submission, he referred us to the decision of the House of Lords in *Rank Film Distributors Ltd* v *Video Information Centre* [1982] AC 380. Relying upon that case he sought to demonstrate to us that the provisions of the Theft Act 1968 do not cover the stealing of copyright or kindred matters.

We are indebted to Mr Du Cann for his careful arguments on this point, namely to the effect that copyright is probably not a subject of theft, but we are not concerned with that proposition here, so it seems to us, except perhaps incidentally, because the allegation here was one of conspiracy to steal feature films, not the copyright in them, and the allegation that the defendants conspired together to steal feature films depends upon proof by the prosecution that that is the thing that they were conspiring to steal.

Mr Du Cann next cites to us a series of helpful cases, and they are these. First of all *R* v *Warner (Brian William)* (1970) 55 Cr App R 93. This was a case in which the judgment of the Court was delivered by Edmund Davies LJ Having cited the words in which the chairman directed the jury, Edmund Davies LJ, continued, at pp96-97: "But unfortunately his direction later became confused by his references to section 6, the object of which he may himself have misunderstood. There is no statutory definition of the words 'intention of permanently depriving,' but section 6 seeks to clarify their meaning in certain respects. Its object is in no wise to cut down the definition of 'theft' contained in section 1. It is always dangerous to paraphrase a statutory enactment, but its apparent aim is to prevent specious pleas of a kind which have succeeded in the past by providing, in effect, that it is no excuse for an accused person to plead absence of the necessary intention if it is clear that he appropriated another's property intending to treat it as his own, regardless of the owner's rights. Section 6 thus gives illustrations, as it were, of what can amount to the dishonest intention demanded by section 1(1). But it is a misconception to interpret it as watering down section 1."

Then Mr Du Cann referred us to the case of *R* v *Duru* [1974] 1 WLR 2. That was a case involving cheques. The allegation was that the defendant had obtained certain cheques from the local authority by deception with the intention of permanently depriving the council of them. That was contrary to section 15(1) of the Theft Act 1968, but section 6(1) was equally applicable in that case as it would have been had the allegation been one simply of theft.

Megaw LJ, delivering the judgment of the Court, said, at p8: "So far as the cheque itself is concerned, true it is a piece of paper. But it is a piece of paper which changes its character completely once it is paid, because then it receives a rubber stamp on it saying it has been paid and it ceases to be a thing in action, or at any rate it ceases to be, in its substance, the same as it was before; that is, an instrument on which payment falls to be made. It was the intention of the appellants, dishonestly and by deception, not only that the cheques should be made out and handed over, but also that they should be presented and paid, thereby permanently depriving the Greater London Council of the cheque in its substance as a thing in action. The fact that the mortgagors were under an obligation to repay the mortgage loans does not affect the appellants' intention permanently to deprive the Council of these cheques. If it were necessary to look to section 6(1) of the Theft Act, this Court would have no hesitation in saying that that subsection, brought in by the terms of section 15(3), would also be relevant, since it is plain that the appellants each had the intention of causing the cheque to be treated as the property of the person by whom it was to be obtained, to dispose of, regardless of the rights of the true owner."

Finally Mr Du Cann referred us to the case of *R* v *Downes* (1983) 77 Cr App R 260. That was a case similar in essence to *R* v *Duru* (supra). The judgment in *R* v *Downes* was delivered by Nolan J who said at p266-267: "It is of some interest to note in *Duru* the Court was referred to the earlier case of *Warner*

(1970) 55 Cr App R 93, which Mr Lodge [counsel for the appellant in that case] cited in support of the narrower reading of section 6(1) for which he contended. *Warner* ... does not however appear to us, as evidently it did not appear to this Court in *Duru* ... to have any significant bearing on the point at issue. It follows that, for substantially the same reasons as those given by the learned judge, we consider that the charge of theft is made out, the vouchers having been dishonestly appropriated with the intention of destroying their essential character and thus depriving the owners, the Inland Revenue, of the substance of their property. In our judgment therefore the appeal must be dismissed."

In general we take the same view as Professor Griew in *The Theft Acts 1968 and 1978*, 4th ed (1982), p47 at paragraph 2-73, namely, that section 6 should be referred to in exceptional cases only. In the vast majority of cases it need not be referred to or considered at all.

Deriving assistance from another distinguished academic writer, namely Professor Glanville Williams, we would like to cite with approval the following passage from his *Textbook of Criminal Law*, 2nd ed (1983), p719: "In view of the grave difficulties of interpretation presented by section 6, a trial judge would be well advised not to introduce it to the jury unless he reaches the conclusion that it will assist them, and even then (it may be suggested) the question he leaves to the jury should not be worded in terms of the generalities as applied to the alleged facts. For example, the question might be: 'Did the defendant take the article, intending that the owner should have it back only on making a payment? If so, you would be justified as a matter of law in finding that he intended to deprive the owner permanently of his article, because the taking of the article with that intention is equivalent to an outright taking.' "

Bearing in mind the observations of Edmund Davies LJ in *R v Warner* (supra), we would try to interpret the section in such a way as to ensure that nothing is construed as an intention permanently to deprive which would not prior to the 1968 Act have been so construed. Thus the first part of section 6(1) seems to us to be aimed at the sort of case where a defendant takes things and then offers them back to the owner for the owner to buy if he wishes. If the taker intends to return them to the owner only upon such payment, then, on the wording of section 6(1), that is deemed to amount to the necessary intention permanently to deprive: see for instance *R v Hall* (1848) 1 Den 381, where the defendant took fat from a candlemaker and then offered it for sale to the owner. His conviction for larceny was affirmed. There are other cases of similar intent: for instance, "I have taken your valuable painting. You can have it back on payment to me of £X,000. If you are not prepared to make that payment, then you are not going to get your painting back."

It seems to us that in this case we are concerned with the second part of section 6(1), namely the words after the semi-colon: "and a borrowing or lending of it may amount to so treating it if, but only if, the borrowing or lending is for a period and in circumstances making it equivalent to an outright taking or disposal." These films, it could be said, were borrowed by Lloyd from his employers in order to enable him and the others to carry out their "piracy" exercise.

Borrowing is ex hypothesi not something which is done with an intention permanently to deprive. This half of the subsection, we believe, is intended to make it clear that a mere borrowing is never enough to constitute the necessary guilty mind unless the intention is to return the "thing" in such a changed state that it can truly be said that all its goodness or virtue has gone: for example: *R v Beecham* (1851) 5 Cox CC 181, where the defendant stole railway tickets intending that they should be returned to the railway company in the usual way only after the journeys had been completed. He was convicted of larceny. The learned judge in the present case gave another example, namely the taking of a torch battery with the intention of returning it only when its power is exhausted.

That being the case, we turn to inquire whether the feature films in this case can fall within that category. Our view is that they cannot. The goodness, the virtue, the practical value of the films to the owners has not gone out of the article. The film could still be projected to paying audiences, and, had everything gone according to the conspirators' plans, would have been projected in the ordinary way to audiences at the Odeon Cinema, Barking, who would have paid for their seats. Our view is that those particular films which were the subject of this alleged conspiracy had not themselves diminished in value at all. What had happened was that the borrowed film had been used or was going to be used to perpetrate a copyright swindle on the owners whereby their commercial interests were grossly and adversely affected in the way that we have endeavoured to describe at the outset of this judgment. That borrowing, it seems to us, was not for a period, or in such circumstances, as made it equivalent to an outright taking or disposal. There was still virtue in the film.

For those reasons we think that the submissions of Mr Du Cann on this aspect of the case are well founded. Accordingly the way in which the learned judge directed the jury was mistaken, and accordingly this conviction of conspiracy to steal must be quashed.'

R v McIvor [1982] 1 WLR 409

See references to this authority in *R v Ghosh*, above.

R v Warner (1970) 55 Cr App R 93

See references to this authority in *R v Lloyd*, above.

36 Sections 8 and 9 Theft Act 1968

R v Collins [1972] 3 WLR 243 Court of Appeal (Criminal Division) (Edmund-Davies and Stephenson LJJ and Boreham J)

Burglary – nature of 'entry' – mens rea for trespass

Facts
As stated by Edmund Davies LJ:

'At about 2 o'clock in the early morning of Saturday, July 24, of last year, a young girl of 18 went to bed at her mother's home in Colchester. She had spent the evening with her boyfriend. She had taken a certain amount of drink, and it may be that this fact affords some explanation of her inability to answer satisfactorily certain crucial questions put to her.

She has the habit of sleeping without wearing night apparel in a bed which was very near the lattice-type window of her room. At one stage in her evidence she seemed to be saying that the bed was close up against the window which, in accordance with her practice, was wide open. In the photographs which we have before us, however, there appears to be a gap of some sort between the two, but the bed was clearly quite near the window.

At about 3.30 or 4 am she awoke and she then saw in the moonlight a vague form crouched in the open window. She was unable to remember, and this is important, whether the form was on the outside of the window sill or on that part of the sill which was inside the room, and for reasons which will later become clear, that seemingly narrow point is of crucial importance.

The young lady then realised several things: first of all, that the form in the window was that of a male; secondly, that he was a naked male; and thirdly, that he was a naked male with an erect penis. She also saw in the moonlight that his hair was blond. She thereupon leapt to the conclusion that her boy-friend, with whom for some time she had been on terms of regular and frequent sexual intimacy, was paying her an ardent nocturnal visit. She promptly sat up in bed, and the man descended from the sill and joined her in bed and they had full sexual intercourse. But there was something about him which made her think that things were not as they usually were between her and her boy-friend. The length of his hair, his voice as they had exchanged what was described as "love talk," and other features led her to the conclusion that somehow there was something different. She turned on the bed-side light, saw that her companion was not her boy-friend, and slapped the face of the intruder, who was none other than the appellant. He said to her: "Give me a good time tonight," and got hold of her arm, but she bit him and told him to go. She then went into the bathroom and he promptly vanished. She said that she would not have agreed to intercourse if she had known that the person entering her room was not her boy-friend; but there was no suggestion of any force having been used upon her, and the intercourse which took place was undoubtedly effected with no resistance on her part.'

The defendant was convicted of burglary with intent to rape contrary to section 9(1)(a) of the 1968 Act, and appealed on the ground that he had not entered the young woman's room as a trespasser.'

Held
Appeal allowed.

Edmund-Davies LJ:

'Now, one feature of the case which remained at the conclusion of the evidence in great obscurity is where exactly the appellant was at the moment when, according to him, the girl manifested that she was welcoming him. Was he kneeling on the sill outside the window or was he already inside the room, having climbed through the window frame, and kneeling upon the inner sill? It was a crucial matter, for there were certainly three ingredients which it was incumbent upon the Crown to establish. Under section 9 of the Theft Act 1968, which renders a person guilty of burglary if he enters any building or part of a building as a trespasser and with the intention of committing rape, the entry of the accused into the building must first be proved. Well, there is no doubt about that, for it is common ground that he did enter the girl's bedroom. Secondly, it must be proved that he entered as a trespasser. We will develop that point a little later. Thirdly, it must be proved that he entered as a trespasser with intent at the time of entry to commit rape therein.

The second ingredient of the offence – that the entry must be as a trespasser – is one which has not, to the best of our knowledge, been previously canvassed in the courts. Views as to its ambit have naturally been canvassed by the textbook writers, and it is perhaps not wholly irrelevant to recall that those who were advising the Home Secretary before the Theft Bill was presented to Parliament had it in mind to get rid of some of the frequently absurd technical rules which had been built up in relation to the old requirement in burglary of a "breaking and entering." The cases are legion as to what this did or did not amount to, but happily it is not now necessary for us to consider them. But it was in order to get rid of those technical rules that a new test was introduced, namely, that the entry must be "as a trespasser."

What does that involve? According to the learned editors of Archbold's *Criminal Pleading, Evidence and Practice*, 37th ed (1969), paragraph 1505: "Any intentional, reckless or negligent entry into a building will, it would appear, constitute a trespass if the building is in the possession of another person who does not consent to the entry. Nor will it make any difference that the entry was the result of a reasonable mistake on the part of the defendant, so far as trespass is concerned." If that be right, then it would be no defence for the appellant to say (and even were he believed in saying), "Well, I honestly thought that this girl was welcoming me into the room and I therefore entered, fully believing that I had her consent to go in." If *Archbold* is right, he would nevertheless be a trespasser, since the apparent consent of the girl was unreal, she being mistaken as to who was at her window. We disagree. We hold that, for the purposes of section 9 of the Theft Act, a person entering a building is not guilty of trespass if he enters without knowledge that he is trespassing or at least without acting recklessly as to whether or not he is unlawfully entering.

A view contrary to that of the learned editors of *Archbold* was expressed in Professor Smith's book on *The Law of Theft*, 1st ed (1968), where, having given an illustration of an entry into premises, the author comments at paragraph 462: "It is submitted that ... D should be acquitted on the ground of lack of mens rea. Though under the civil law he entered as a trespasser, it is submitted that he cannot be convicted of the criminal offence unless he knew of the facts which caused him to be a trespasser or, at least, was reckless." The matter has also been dealt with by Professor Griew, who in paragraph 4-05 of his work on the *Theft Act 1968* has this passage: "What if D wrongly believes that he is not trespassing? His belief may rest on facts which, if true, would mean that he was not trespassing: for instance, he may enter a building by mistake, thinking that it is the one he has been invited to enter. Or his belief may be based on a false view of the legal effect of the known facts: for instance, he may misunderstand the effect of a contract granting him a right of passage through a building. Neither kind of mistake will protect him from tort liability for trespass. In either case, then, D satisfies the literal terms of section 9(1): he 'enters ... as a trespasser.' But for the purposes of criminal liability a man should be judged on the basis of the facts as he believed them to be, and this should include making allowances for a mistake as to rights under the civil law. This is another way of saying that a serious offence like burglary should be held to require mens rea in the fullest sense of the phrase: D should be liable for burglary only if he knowingly trespasses or is reckless as to whether he trespasses or not. Unhappily it is common for Parliament to omit to make clear whether mens rea is intended to be an element in a statutory offence. It is also, though not equally, common for the courts to supply the mental element by construction of the statute."

We prefer the view expressed by Professor Smith and Professor Griew to that of the learned editors of *Archbold*. In the judgment of this Court, there cannot be a conviction for entering premises "as a trespasser" within the meaning of section 9 of the Theft Act unless the person entering does so knowing that he is a trespasser and nevertheless deliberately enters, or, at the very least, is reckless as to whether or not he is entering the premises of another without the other party's consent.

Having so held, the pivotal point of this appeal is whether the Crown established that this appellant at the moment when he entered the bedroom knew perfectly well that he was not welcome there or, being reckless as to whether he was welcome or not, was nevertheless determined to enter. That in turn involves consideration as to where he was at the time when the complainant indicated that she was welcoming him into her bedroom. If, to take an example that was put in the course of argument, her bed had not been near the window but was on the other side of the bedroom, and he (being determined to have her sexually even against her will) climbed through the window and crossed the bedroom to reach her bed, then the offence charged would have been established. But in this case, as we have related, the layout of the room was different, and it became a point of nicety which had to be conclusively established by the Crown as to where he was when the girl made welcoming signs, as she unquestionably at some stage did.

How did the learned judge deal with this matter? We have to say regretfully that there was a flaw in his treatment of it. Referring to section 9, the learned judge said: "There are three ingredients. First is the question of entry. Did he enter into that house? Did he enter as a trespasser? That is to say, was the entry, if you are satisfied there was an entry, intentional or reckless? And, finally, and you may think this is the crux of the case as opened to you by Mr Irwin [counsel for the Crown], if you are satisfied that he entered as a trespasser, did he have the intention to rape this girl?" The learned judge then went on to deal in turn with each of these three ingredients. He first explained what was involved in "entry" into a building. He then dealt with the second ingredient. But the learned judge here unfortunately repeated his earlier observation that the question of entry as a trespasser depended on "was the entry intentional or reckless?" We have to say that this was putting the matter inaccurately. This mistake may have been derived from a passage in the speech of Crown counsel when replying to the submission of "No case." Mr Irwin at one stage said: "Therefore, the first thing that the Crown have got to prove, my Lords, is that there has been a trespass which may be an intentional trespass, or it may be reckless trespass." Unfortunately the judge regarded the matter as though the second ingredient in the burglary charged was whether there had been an intentional or reckless entry, and when he came to develop this topic in his summing up that error was unfortunately perpetuated. The judge told the jury: "He had no right to be in that house, as you know, certainly from the point of view of the girl's parent. But if you are satisfied about entry, did he enter intentionally or recklessly? What the prosecution say about that is, you do not really have to consider recklessness because when you consider his own evidence he intended to enter that house, and if you accept the evidence I have just pointed out to you, he in fact did so. So, at least, you may think, it was intentional. At the least, you may think it was reckless because as he told you he did not know whether the girl would accept him."

We are compelled to say that we do not think the learned judge by these observations made sufficiently clear to the jury the nature of the second test about which they had to be satisfied before the defendant could be convicted of the offence charged. There was no doubt that his entry into the bedroom was "intentional." But what the defendant had said was "She knelt on the bed, she put her arms around me and then I went in." If the jury thought he might be truthful in that assertion, they would need to consider whether or not, although entirely surprised by such a reception being accorded to him, the appellant might not have been entitled reasonably to regard her action as amounting to an invitation to him to enter. If she in fact appeared to be welcoming him, the Crown do not suggest that he should have realised or even suspected that she was so behaving because, despite the moonlight, she thought he was someone else. Unless the jury were entirely satisfied that the appellant made an effective and substantial entry into the bedroom without the complainant doing or saying anything to cause him to believe that she was consenting to his entering it, he ought not to be convicted of the offence charged. The point is a narrow one, as narrow maybe as the window sill which is crucial to this case. But this is a criminal charge of gravity and, even though one may suspect that his intention was to commit the offence charged, unless the facts show with clarity that he in fact committed it, he ought not to remain convicted.

Some question arose as to whether or not the appellant can be regarded as a trespasser ab initio. But we are entirely in agreement with the view expressed in *Archbold*, again in para. 1505, that the common law doctrine of trespass ab initio has no application to burglary under the Theft Act 1968. One further matter that was canvassed ought perhaps to be mentioned. The point was raised that, the complainant not being the tenant or occupier of the dwelling-house and her mother being apparently in occupation, this girl herself could not in any event have extended an effective invitation to enter, so that, even if she had expressly and with full knowledge of all material facts invited the appellant in, he would nevertheless be a trespasser. Whatever be the position in the law of tort, to regard such a proposition as acceptable in the criminal law would be unthinkable.

We have to say that this appeal must be allowed on the basis that the jury were never invited to consider the vital question whether the appellant did enter the premises as a trespasser, that is to say knowing perfectly well that he had no invitation to enter or reckless of whether or not his entry was with permission. The certificate of the learned judge, as we have already said, demonstrated that he felt there were points involved calling for further consideration. That consideration we have given to the best of our ability. For the reasons we have stated, the outcome of the appeal is that the appellant must be acquitted of the charge preferred against him. The appeal is accordingly allowed and his conviction quashed.'

R v *Dawson* (1976) 64 Cr App R 170 Court of Appeal (Criminal Division) (Lawton LJ, MacKenna and Swanwick JJ)

Robbery – ingredients

Facts

As stated by Lawton LJ:

'On the night of July 10, 1975, a Blue Jacket in the Royal Navy on *HMS Hampshire* was on shore leave in Liverpool. Shortly before midnight he went to the Liverpool Pier Head to wait for transport to take him across to Birkenhead where his ship was berthed. He was approached by these two appellants and a third man who was never apprehended.

I turn now to the evidence. According to the Blue Jacket, two of the men came alongside him and the third was behind him. This is what he said: "There was one standing on the other side and just nudging me with the shoulder and I lost my balance. Q. Did it distract your attention, or did he stop you from being able to resist? A. I was trying to keep my balance. I was being pushed from side to side and I was trying to keep my balance. I was more interested in keeping my balance than anything else. Q. If you had been able to keep your balance what would you have been able to do when the hand was put to the wallet? A. I think I would have been able to apprehend the person. Q. Why weren't you able to apprehend them? A. I was trying to keep my balance. I was more interested in trying to keep my balance."

One of the men, almost certainly the third man who was not apprehended, managed to get his hand into the sailor's pocket, and extract a wallet which contained a fairly substantial sum of money. Once the wallet had been extracted from the sailor's pocket the three men ran off. The sailor tried to chase them, then realised he had not got a hope of catching them. Fortunately at that moment a police patrol car came along; the sailor told the police officers what had happened and the police patrol car went in pursuit of the three. They managed to apprehend two. Of the two who were apprehended they told a pack of lies as to what they had been doing. When they repeated that story at the trial they were not believed by the jury.

The question posed on their appeal was whether there was enough evidence to go before the jury on the charge of robbery, and the case is reported on the direction to be given to juries on charges under the Theft Act 1968, particularly, in the instant case, under section 8 of that Act.'

Held

The appeals would be dismissed.

Lawton LJ:

'Mr Locke, for the appellants, has been very realistic about the case. He has not sought to criticise the summing-up, although he did put forward some criticisms in his grounds of appeal. He did not pursue them here. The summing-up was a model of fairness. The learned judge was conscious of the difficulty as to whether the sailor had described what a jury would regard as "using force on him for the purposes of stealing."

Mr Locke had submitted at the end of the prosecution's case that what had happened could not in law amount to the use of force. He called the learned judge's attention to some old authorities and to a passage in *Archbold* [see now 39th ed, 1976, paragraph 1483] based on the old authorities, and submitted that because of those old authorities there was not enough evidence to go to the jury. He sought before this Court to refer to the old authorities. He was discouraged from doing so because this Court is of the opinion that in these cases what judges should now direct their attention to is the words of the statute. This has been said in a number of cases since the Theft Act 1968.

The object of that Act was to get rid of all the old technicalities of the law of larceny and to put the law into simple language which juries would understand and which they themselves would use. That is what has happened in section 8 which defines "robbery." That section is in these terms: "A person is guilty of robbery if he steals, and immediately before or at the time of doing so, and in order to do so, he uses force on any person or puts or seeks to put any person in fear of being then and there subjected to force."

The choice of the word "force" is not without interest because under the Larceny Act 1916 the word "violence" had been used, but Parliament deliberately on the advice of the Criminal Law Revision Committee changed that word to "force." Whether there is any difference between "violence" or "force" is not relevant for the purposes of this case; but the word is "force." It is a word in ordinary use. It is a word which juries understand. The learned judge left it to the jury to say whether jostling a man in the way which the victim described to such an extent that he had difficulty in keeping his balance could be said to be the use of force. The learned judge, because of the argument put forward by Mr Locke, went out of his way to explain to the jury that force in these sort of circumstances must be substantial to justify a verdict.

Whether it was right for him to put that objective before the word "force" when Parliament had not done so we will not discuss for the purposes of this case. It was a matter for the jury. They were there to use their common sense and knowledge of the world. We cannot say that their decision as to whether force was used was wrong. They were entitled to the view that force was used.

Other points were discussed in the case as to whether the force had been used for the purpose of distracting the victim's attention or whether it was for the purpose of overcoming resistance. Those sort of refinements may have been relevant under the old law, but so far as the new law is concerned the sole question is whether the accused used force on any person in order to steal. That issue in this case was left to the jury. They found in favour of the Crown.

We cannot say that this verdict was either unsafe or unsatisfactory. Accordingly the appeal is dismissed.'

R v Hale (1978) 68 Cr App R 415 Court of Appeal (Criminal Division) (Waller and Eveleigh LJJ and Tudor Evans J)

Force used at the time of stealing – duration of stealing

Facts

As stated by Eveleigh LJ:

'The prosecution alleged that the appellant and one McGuire went to the house of a Mrs Carrett. When she answered the door they rushed in. Each was wearing a stocking mask. The appellant put his hand over Mrs Carrett's mouth to stop her screaming and McGuire went upstairs to search. The appellant subsequently released his hold on Mrs Carrett and she went to the settee. He undid her dressing gown and touched her. He also exposed himself. McGuire then came downstairs with a jewellery box and asked where the rest was. The telephone rang. It was a next door neighbour who had heard Mrs Carrett scream and wanted to know if everything was all right. Under threat from the appellant she replied everything was all right. All three then went upstairs and Mrs Carrett was asked where her money was. The appellant and McGuire then used the toilet and on their return said that they would tie her up and she was not to telephone the police. They tied her ankles and hands and put socks in her mouth. They went out of the front door warning her not to telephone, saying that they would come back and do something to her little boy if she phoned the police within five minutes.

McGuire failed to appear at the trial, but in March of this year he pleaded guilty to robbery and was sentenced to four years' imprisonment.

Hale's defence was that there was no robbery or theft and no indecent assault. He said that Mrs Carrett had agreed to a mock robbery as part of an insurance fraud.

The learned judge read to the jury the definition of robbery from section 8 of the Theft Act 1968 and also correctly directed them upon the meaning of the word "steals." He also said "A person who goes into somebody else's house with or without a companion and makes the householder fear for her safety or to apprehend violence if she does not co-operate, or who ties her up at the end of the episode in order to make sure that he can get away safely with the plunder, is guilty of robbery. Do you understand that? That is what is said by the prosecution obviously took place here." He continued, "In order to be sure that a person is guilty of robbery, you have to be sure that they were stealing and the definition of stealing is that a person is guilty of stealing if he dishonestly appropriates property belonging to another with the intention of permanently depriving the other of it. Well putting it really in, I hope, equally simple and understandable words, the question for you here is whether you feel sure that this accused, by the use of force, or putting her in fear, got hold of Mrs Carrett's property without her consent, and without believing that he had got her consent, and intending to appropriate it for his own purposes without giving it back to her afterwards."

When the learned judge resumed his summing-up the following morning, he re-capitulated to the jury the matters upon which they had to feel sure before they could find the defendants guilty. He said "First, that Mrs Carrett did not consent to her property being taken; secondly that the defendant knew that; thirdly that the defendant intended to deprive her of the property permanently and, if the matter stopped there, that would be stealing. Fourthly, for robbery, which is an aggravated form of stealing, that the appellant was a party to using or threatening force to enable him and his companion successfully to find and to take and to carry away and so steal and appropriate that property without interruption."

On behalf of the appellant it is submitted that the learned judge misdirected the jury in that the passages quoted above could indicate to them that if an accused used force in order to effect his escape with the stolen goods that would be sufficient to constitute the crime of robbery. In so far as the facts of the present case are concerned, counsel submitted that the theft was completed when the jewellery box was first seized and any force thereafter could not have been "immediately before or at the time of stealing" and certainly not "in order to steal." The essence of the submission was that the theft was completed as soon as the jewellery box was seized.'

Held

The appeal would be dismissed.

Eveleigh LJ:

'In the present case there can be little doubt that if the appellant had been interrupted after the seizure of the jewellery box the jury would have been entitled to find that the appellant and his accomplice were assuming the rights of an owner at the time when the jewellery box was seized. However, the act of appropriation does not suddenly cease. It is a continuous act and it is a matter for the jury to decide whether or not the act of appropriation has finished. Moreover, it is quite clear that the intention to deprive the owner permanently, which accompanied the assumption of the owner's rights was a continuing one at all material times. This Court therefore rejects the contention that the theft had ceased by the time the lady was tied up. As a matter of common-sense the appellant was in the course of committing theft; he was stealing.

There remains the question whether there was robbery. Quite clearly the jury were at liberty to find the appellant guilty of robbery relying upon the force used when he put his hand over Mrs Carrett's mouth to restrain her from calling for help. We also think that they were also entitled to rely upon the act of tying her up provided they were satisfied (and it is difficult to see how they could not be satisfied) that the force so used was to enable them to steal. If they were still engaged in the act of stealing the force was clearly used to enable them to continue to assume the rights of the owner and permanently to deprive Mrs Carrett of her box, which is what they began to do when they first seized it.

Taking the summing-up as a whole, and in relation to the particular facts of this case, the jury could not have thought that they were entitled to convict if the force used was not at the time of the stealing and for the purpose of stealing. The learned judge said "In order to be sure that the person is guilty of robbery you have to be sure they were stealing." While the use of the words complained of would not serve as an alternative definition of robbery and could, if standing alone, be open to the criticism that the learned judge was arriving at a conclusion of fact which the jury had to decide, those words did not stand alone and this Court is satisfied that there was no misdirection. This appeal is accordingly dismissed.'

R v *Jones (John) and Smith (Christopher)* [1976] 1 WLR 672 Court of Appeal (Criminal Division) (James and Geoffrey Lane LJJ, and Cobb J)

Trespass – burglary contrary to section 9(1)(b) Theft Act 1968

Facts
The defendants, Christopher Smith and John Jones, took two television sets from the house of Alfred Smith, the father of one of the defendants, without his knowledge or consent. The defendants were convicted of burglary contrary to section 9(1)(b) of the Theft Act 1968, despite evidence given by Alfred Smith, that his son' ... would never be a trespasser in my house ...' The defendants appealed on the ground that there had been no proof of trespass by them.

Held
The appeals would be dismissed

James LJ:

'Mr Rose [counsel for the appellants] argues that a person who had a general permission to enter premises of another person cannot be a trespasser. His submission is as short and as simple as that. Related to this case he says that a son to whom a father has given permission generally to enter the father's house cannot be a trespasser if he enters it even though he had decided in his mind before making the entry to commit a criminal offence of theft against the father once he had got into the house and had entered the house solely for the purpose of committing that theft. It is a bold submission. Mr Rose frankly accepts that there has been no decision of the Court since this statute was passed which governs particularly this point. He has reminded us of the decision in *Byrne* v *Kinematograph Renters Society Ltd* [1958] 1 WLR

762, which he prays in aid of his argument. In that case persons had entered a cinema by producing tickets not for the purpose of seeing the show, but for an ulterior purpose. It was held in the action, which sought to show that they entered as trespassers pursuant to a conspiracy to trespass, that in fact they were not trespassers. The important words in the judgment of Harman J at p776: are "They did nothing that they were not invited to do, ..." That provides a distinction between that case and what we consider the position to be in this case.

Mr Rose has also referred us to one of the trickery cases, a case of *R v Boyle* [1954] 2 QB 292, and in particular the passage on p295. He accepts that the trickery cases can be distinguished from such a case as the present because in the trickery cases it can be said that that which would otherwise have been consent to enter was negatived by the fact that consent was obtained by a trick. We do not gain any help in the particular case from that decision. We were also referred to *R v Collins* [1973] QB 100 and in particular to the long passage commencing at p104 where Edmund Davies LJ commenced the consideration of what is involved by the words "... the entry must be 'as a trespasser'." It is unnecessary to cite that passage in full; suffice it to say that this Court on that occasion at p104 expressly approved the view expressed in Professor Smith's book, the *Law of Theft* (1968) (1st ed) paragraph 462, and also the view of Professor Griew in his publication, *Theft Act* (1968) (1st ed) para. 4-05, upon this aspect of what is involved in being a trespasser.

In our view the passage there referred to is consonant with the passage in the well-known case, *Hillen and Pettigrew v ICI (Alkali) Ltd* [1936] AC 65, 69 where Lord Atkin said: "My Lords, in my opinion this duty to an invitee only extends so long and so far as the invitee is making what can reasonably be contemplated as an ordinary and reasonable use of the premises by the invitee for the purpose for which he has been invited. He is not invited to use any part of the premises for purposes which he knows are wrongfully dangerous and constitute an improper use. As Scrutton LJ has pointedly said [in *The Calgarth* [1926] P 93 at p110] 'When you invite a person into your house to use the staircase you do not invite him to slide down the banisters.' " That case of course was a civil case in which it was sought to make the defendant liable for a tort.

The decision in *R v Collins* (supra) in this Court, a decision upon the criminal law, added to the concept of trespass as a civil wrong only the mental element of mens rea, which is essential to the criminal offence. Taking the law as expressed in *Hillen and Pettigrew v ICI (Alkali) Ltd* (supra) and *R v Collins* (supra) it is our view that a person is a trespasser for the purpose of section 9(1)(*b*) of the Theft Act 1968, if he enters premises of another knowing that he is entering in excess of the permission that has been given to him, or being reckless as to whether he is entering in excess of the permission that has been given to him to enter, providing the facts are known to the accused which enable him to realise that he is acting in excess of the permission given or that he is acting recklessly as to whether he exceeds that permission, then that is sufficient for the jury to decide that he is in fact a trespasser.

In this particular case it was a matter for the jury to consider whether, on all the facts, it was shown by the prosecution that the defendants entered with the knowledge that entry was being effected against the consent or in excess of the consent that had been given by Mr Smith senior to his son Christopher. The jury were, by their verdict satisfied of that. It was a novel argument that we heard, interesting but one without, in our view, any foundation.'

R v Walkington [1979] 1 WLR 1169 Court of Appeal (Criminal Division) (Geoffrey Lane LJ, Swanwick and Wien JJ)

Entry into part of a building as a trespasser

Facts
Taken from the judgment of Geoffrey Lane LJ:

'On January 20, 1977, shortly before closing time of Debenhams Store in Oxford Street, the appellant was seen in the menswear department of that store. He was kept under observation by Mr Rogers, who was a store detective, and two of his colleagues. The store closed at six o'clock. At about 20 minutes to six the various counter assistants were cashing up their tills. The evidence given by Mr Rogers was that the appellant seemed to be interested primarily, if not solely, in what was going on at the various tills in the store.

In due course he was observed to travel up on the escalator to the first floor. On that floor was an unattached till in the centre of a three-sided counter, the drawer of the till being partially opened. There was some dispute as to the precise dimensions of this three-sided rectangular counter, but what was agreed was that it was a movable counter. It was not static in the sense of being fixed to the floor. One of the descriptions of it showed that what we may call the north side of the counter was about four feet in length, the east side was about 12 feet in length and the west side was about six feet in length, the till being situated on the north side, the four feet length. Other descriptions of the counter gave different dimensions. But in each case it is to be observed that the till was in a corner formed by two of these counters. The evidence was that the area inside that rectangle or partial rectangle was reserved for the staff and it was clear, so it was suggested, that any customer seeing that area would realise that his permission to be in the store did not extend to a permission to be in that area.

The appellant, on the evidence, moved to the opening of the rectangular area described, that is to say to the part thereof which was not filled in by any counter, looked all around him, then bent down and having got to the till pulled the drawer further open. Having looked into the drawer the appellant slammed it to, said something and started making his way out of the shop, when he was stopped by the store detective.

In fact there was nothing in the drawer. The fact that the till drawer was partially open was an indication to anyone in the know that the assistant at that particular counter had cashed that particular till up.

The police were duly called in and the appellant was arrested. He was taken to Marylebone police station where he made a statement in writing, which reads as follows: "I came up the West End to do some shopping and I went into Debenhams for a tie. I walked around the store for a while and looked at some coats. I went up on the first floor to have a look at the shoes. After a while I noticed a till partly open with a drawer beneath it. I thought I might be able to steal something from it so I opened the drawer but there was nothing in it worth stealing which was my intention. I shut the drawer again and walked away. That was when the security bloke stopped me. I don't know why I did it now, it seems so stupid. I would like to take this opportunity of saying how sorry I am and apologise to the store, the police and the court."

His main ground of appeal was that the deputy circuit judge should have allowed the defence submission and withdrawn the case from the jury in that it would be wrong to divide the store artificially into "parts" in the way that would be necessary to make the case of burglary out of the situation presented by the prosecution; thus the appellant could not be said to have trespassed behind the counter.'

Held

The appeal would be dismissed.

Geoffrey Lane LJ (having considered s9 of the Theft Act 1968):

'What the prosecution had to prove here was that the defendant had entered a part of a building as a trespasser with intent to steal anything in that part of the building. Mr Osborne submitted that this could not be said to be a part of a building. It was a submission which we confess we found a little difficult to follow. But it transpired that what Mr Osborne was principally relying upon was a passage in a publication by Professor Griew entitled *The Theft Acts 1968 and 1978*, 3rd ed (1979). He made particular reference to paragraph 4-16 at p68, which reads: "D has the licence that all customers have in a shop to move from counter to counter. He now moves to counter 2, intending to steal at it. If in doing so he is entering a different 'part' of the shop, he may be guilty of burglary, for entry for a purpose other than that for which a licence to enter is granted is a trespassory entry. But it does not seem likely that the courts will be hasty to divide buildings artificially into 'parts' in the way that would be necessary to make a case of burglary out of the situation presented here."

With respect to Mr Osborne it seems to us that that passage is not dealing with the present situation at all. It is dealing with a situation where there is no physical demarcation at all and the only matter which may cause the man to be a trespasser is a change of intention in his own mind. This is not the situation here. Here there is a physical demarcation, and if one turns to the same publication at the passage where Professor Griew is dealing with the situation which exists here, we find this at paragraph 4-07: "A licence to enter a building may extend to part of the building only. If so, the licensee will trespass if he enters some other part not within the scope of the licence. To do so with intent to commit in that other part one of the specified offences, or to do so and then to commit or attempt to commit one of those offences therein, will be burglary." That seems to us precisely to fit the circumstances of the present case and really deals the death blow to this part of Mr Osborne's submission.

If support is required, it is to be found in Professor Smith's publication *The Law of Theft*, 3rd ed (1978), at paragraph 329 (i), where he says: "A customer in a shop who goes behind the counter and takes money from the till during a short absence of the shopkeeper would be guilty of burglary even though he entered the shop with the shopkeeper's permission. The permission did not extend to his going behind the counter."

There are similar passages at paragraphs 331 and 334. Paragraph 331 is the only one to which I need refer: "It would seem that the whole reason for the words 'or part of a building' is that D may enter or be in part of a building without trespass and it is desirable that he should be liable as a burglar if he trespasses in the remainder of the building with the necessary intent. It is submitted that the building need not be physically divided into 'parts.' It ought to be sufficient if a notice in the middle of a hall stated, 'No customers beyond this point.' These considerations suggest that, for the present purposes, a building falls into two parts only; first, that part in which D was lawfully present and, second, the remainder of the building. This interpretation avoids anomalies which arise if physical divisions within a building are held to create 'parts'."

One really gets two extremes, as it seems to us. First of all you have the part of the building which is shut off by a door so far as the general public is concerned, with a notice saying "Staff Only" or "No admittance to customers." At the other end of the scale you have for example a single table in the middle of the store, which it would be difficult for any jury to find properly was a part of the building into which the licensor prohibited customers from moving.

Here, it seems to us, was a physical demarcation. Whether it was sufficient to amount to an area from which the public were plainly excluded was a matter for the jury. It seems to us that there was ample evidence on which they could come to the conclusion (a) that the management had impliedly prohibited customers entering that area and (b) that this particular defendant knew of that prohibition. Whether the jury came to the conclusion that the prosecution made out their case was a matter for them, but there is no dispute that the judge, in those two careful passages which I have read, left the matter fairly and correctly to the jury.'

R v Wilson [1983] 3 WLR 686

See Chapter 23.

37 Sections 21 and 25 Theft Act 1968

R v Bundy [1977] 1 WLR 914 Court of Appeal (Criminal Division) (Lawton LJ, MacKenna and Gibson JJ)

Place of abode – section 25(1) Theft Act 1968

Facts
The defendant appealed against his conviction under section 25(1) of the Theft Act 1968, on the ground that as he lived in his car, the articles that had been found there were 'at his place of abode'.

Held
The appeal would be dismissed.

Lawton LJ:

' ... The phrase, "place of abode", as Mr Zeidman's [counsel for the defendant] researches have shown, has occurred in a number of Acts of Parliament, all dealing with entirely different subject matters. For example, the phrase occurs in section 23 of the Landlord and Tenant Act 1927 and has been construed widely by the courts. It also occurred in the Summary Jurisdiction Act 1848; in that context it was construed narrowly. This Court does not get any help from comparing constructions of the phrase in other Acts of Parliament dealing with other subject matters.

We must construe the phrase in the context in which it appears in section 25(1) of the Theft Act. In that context it is manifest that no offence is committed if a burglar keeps the implements of his criminal trade in his place of abode. He only commits an offence when he takes them from his place of abode. The phrase "place of abode," in our judgment, connotes, first of all, a site. That is the ordinary meaning of the word "place". It is a site at which the occupier intends to abide. So, there are two elements in the phrase "place of abode" – the element of site and the element of intention. When the defendant took the motor car to a site with the intention of abiding there, then his motor car on that site could be said to be his "place of abode", but when he took it from that site to move it to another site where he intended to abide, the motor car could not be said to be his "place of abode" during transit.

When he was arrested by the police he was not intending to abide on the site where he was arrested. It follows that that was not then at his "place of abode". He may have had a "place of abode" the previous night, but he was away from it at the time of his arrest when in possession of articles which could be used for the purpose of theft. It follows, in our judgment, that there is no substance in the point which has been taken on behalf of the defendant. It was contended that the judge did not give an adequate direction to the jury as to what was the meaning of "place of abode". It is obvious why he did not. He was under the impression that there was no dispute about the matter. Mr Zeidman, in circumstances which we understand, did not disabuse the judge. It follows, in our judgment, that the judge cannot be criticised for having failed to direct the jury about a matter which was never in dispute at the trial.

Accordingly, the appeal will be dismissed.'

R v Cooke [1986] AC 909 House of Lords (Lords Bridge, Brandon, Brightman, Mackay and Goff)

Section 25 (1) Theft Act 1968 – nature of a 'cheat'

Facts

The defendant was a British Rail catering steward, who was alleged to have agreed with other employees that they would take their own food onto trains to sell to passengers, with the intention of keeping any monies paid for themselves. The defendant was convicted of common law conspiracy to defraud, but appealed successfully to the Court of Appeal on the ground that he should have been charged with statutory conspiracy under the Criminal Law Act 1977, because the conduct agreed upon, if carried out, would have resulted in the commission of substantive offences such as going equipped, contrary to s25 of the Theft Act 1968, and false accounting, contrary to s17 of the same Act. The Crown now appealed to the House of Lords, the following question being certified for their Lordships' consideration:

'Whether conspiracy to defraud at common law may or may not be charged where the evidence discloses a conspiracy to defraud one alleged victim and in addition discloses a conspiracy to commit a substantive offence and/or discloses a substantive offence against a different alleged victim having regard to ss1 and 5 of the Criminal Law Act 1977.'

Held

The appeal was allowed. Conspiracy to commit a substantive offence could only be charged as a statutory conspiracy, but where the evidence disclosed both common law and statutory conspiracies, the prosecution could proceed with charges in respect of both, provided they were brought as separate counts, or indeed could proceed with the common law offence alone.

The following extracts deal with the question of whether the defendants would have committed offences contrary to s25 (1) Theft Act 1968 if their agreement had been carried out.

Lord Bridge:

'… the appeal also succeeds, in my opinion, on the narrower ground that there was no material before the Court of Appeal or your Lordships to justify the inference that the defendant and his fellow conspirators agreed on a course of conduct which necessarily involved the commission of offences under sections 25 and 15 of the Theft Act 1968. The nub of the matter is that, to succeed in this argument, the defendant must be in a position to say: "I could not have practised this fraud on my employers without first obtaining money by deception from passengers on the train." This issue was never raised at the trial. What would have happened if it had been is mere speculation. Upright citizens as the ordinary run of British Rail passengers may be presumed to be, I am not prepared to assume that they would necessarily refuse to take and pay for refreshments even if they knew perfectly well that the buffet staff were practising the kind of "fiddle" here involved.'

Lord Mackay:

'I turn now to consider the second submission. The defendant maintained that the evidence in this case disclosed the statutory conspiracy to commit the offence of going equipped for cheat contrary to section 25(1) of the Theft Act 1968 whereas the Crown maintained the contrary. Certain decisions of the Court of Appeal were referred to as relevant to this submission. In the first of these *R v Rashid* [1977] 1 WLR 298, Rashid, who was a British Rail steward, was stopped when about to board his train carrying with him two sliced loaves of bread and a bag of tomatoes. He was charged with an offence against section 25(1) of the Theft Act 1968 on the ground that he had intended to use his own materials to make sandwiches to sell to passengers for his own profit.'

His Lordship referred to ss25(1), 25(3) and 15(1) of the Theft Act 1968, and continued:

'Rashid was convicted and appealed on the ground that the verdict of the jury was unsafe and unsatisfactory in that they had been misdirected by the trial judge saying that in effect section 25(3) of the Theft Act 1968 applied, the judge not referring specifically to section 25(5) or giving a direction as to the precise offence or offences under section 15 of the Act of 1968 which the appellant could have committed with his bread and tomatoes.

Bridge LJ, having held that the directions given were inadequate, went on, at p302:

"The only basis on which this offence could possibly be proved was on the basis that it was intended by the defendant to use his bread and tomatoes to practise an effective and operative deception upon railway passengers without which the railway passengers would not have purchased the sandwiches. The court is inclined to think, though it is unnecessary for present purposes so to decide, that this whole prosecution was really misconceived and that on a proper direction no jury would have convicted in these circumstances."'

His Lordship then considered Geoffrey Lane LJ's judgment in *R v Doukas*, (below):

'Finally, on this aspect of the appeal we were referred to *R v Corboz* (unreported), 2 July 1984. Corboz was a chief steward with British Rail who had with him at his work a small quantity of coffee which he sold, or intended to sell, to British Rail's passengers, retaining for himself the proceeds of sale. He was convicted of an offence under section 25(1) of the Theft Act 1968 and appealed against his conviction on the ground of misdirection of the jury by the trial judge. The court tested the correctness of the summing up by considering whether it accorded with the guidance given in *R v Doukas* [1978] 1 WLR 372. Having concluded that the summing up did meet this standard the appeal was dismissed, the court indicating that in future it would be well if in directing juries with regard to an offence of this kind judges should use a direction strictly in accordance with the terms of the judgment of the court in *Doukas*.

I respectfully agree, that the elements necessary to establish the offence are correctly described in the judgment of Geoffrey Lane LJ in *R v Doukas*. I do not, however, agree with the prosecution's way of putting their case on the element of dishonesty as described in the judgment. The dishonesty in question is the lying to or misleading the guests so that there is a deception of the guests.

Although the court in *R v Rashid* [1977] 1 WLR 298 indicated doubt whether in the circumstances of that case a jury could properly have convicted, the only question to be decided by the Court of Appeal in that case was whether there had been a misdirection by the trial judge and the court held that there had. Therefore the conviction was set aside. In my opinion the question whether the necessary ingredients for the offence have been established in any particular case is one for the jury, and whether they have been will depend on the detail of the evidence particularly that relating to the attitude and understanding of those receiving the supplies.

I consider it quite impossible to say that the evidence led in the present case, and we do not have a full record of it before us, would inevitably have produced, had the jury been required to consider the matter, a verdict that the defendant was guilty of a conspiracy to breach section 25, and indeed this was the reason that the Court of Appeal did not substitute a conviction of a statutory conspiracy to breach that section for the verdict of guilty of conspiracy to defraud which the jury actually returned.

The final submission for the defendant, if it were correct, would give him an answer to the conviction for conspiracy to defraud in the present case for the same reason as led to the decision in *Ayres* [1984] AC 447. The submission is that the conduct by which it was agreed that British Rail should be defrauded was theft of British Rail money contrary to section 1 of the Theft Act 1968 or was false accounting contrary to section 17 of the Theft Act 1968. As I have already said this submission was not put in the Court of Appeal and we do not have the transcript of evidence available to us, but on the basis of the information which has been put before your Lordships I am of opinion that this submission of the defendant has not been made out. *Attorney-General's Reference (No. 1 of 1985)* [1986] QB 491 negatives the contention that the conduct here in question could amount to theft. As to false accounting, your Lordships were informed that the method of accounting required by British Rail from an employee in the position of the defendant is that all British Rail stock on the restaurant car at the beginning of the journey is detailed and then the stock which remains after the journey is detailed and the difference between these discloses the transactions, the proceeds of which have to be accounted for to British Rail by the employee. On what we know of the position in the present case that account that the defendant intended to make to British Rail would be perfectly in order since the fraud alleged is based upon using not British Rail supplies which would show up in the account, but private supplies which do not show up in the accounts.

While this submission might well require reconsideration in a case where a full record of the evidence was available, on the basis of the information put before your Lordships in the present appeal, I am of opinion that it fails. Even if it were to succeed it would be difficult to avoid the conclusion that the proviso should be applied.'

R v Doukas [1978] 1 WLR 372 Court of Appeal (Criminal Division) (Geoffrey Lane LJ, Milmo and Watkins JJ)

Section 25(1) Theft Act 1968 – nature of a 'cheat'

Facts
The defendant was a wine waiter at an hotel. He was arrested whilst bringing his own wine into the hotel intending to sell it to customers as the hotel's, and keep the proceeds. He was convicted under section 25(1) Theft Act 1968, and appealed on the ground that had the customers purchased his wine there would have been no 'cheat' as required by section 25(1), since they were indifferent as to whose wine they were buying.

Held
The appeal would be dismissed.

Geoffrey Lane LJ:

'Combining those two sections of the Theft Act – section 25 and section 15 – which are apposite, one reaches this result: a person shall be guilty of an offence if, when not in his place of abode, he has with him any article for use in the course of or in connection with, any deception, whether deliberate or reckless, by words or conduct, as to fact or as to law, for purposes of dishonestly obtaining property belonging to another with the intention of permanently depriving the other of it.

If one analyses that combined provision, one reaches the situation that the following items have to be proved. First of all, that there was an article for use in connection with the deception: here the bottles. Secondly, that there was a proposed deception: here the deception of the guests into believing that the proffered wine was hotel wine and not the waiter's. Thirdly, an intention to obtain property by means of deception, and the property here is the money of the guests which he proposes to obtain and keep. Fourthly, dishonesty. There is twofold dishonesty in the way the prosecution put the case. First of all the dishonesty in respect of his employers, namely putting into his pocket the money which really should go to the hotel and, more important, the second dishonesty vis-à-vis the guests, the lying or misleading the guests into believing that the wine which had been proffered was the hotel wine and not the waiter's wine. Fifthly, there must be proof that the obtaining would have been, wholly or partially, by virtue of the deception. The prosecution must prove that nexus between the deception and obtaining. It is this last and final ingredient which, as we see it in the present case, is the only point which raises any difficulty. Assuming, as we must, and as was obviously the case, that the jury accepted the version of the police interviews and accepted that the defendant had made the confession to which I have referred, then the only question was, would this obtaining have in fact been caused by the deception practised by the defendant?

We have, as in the notice of appeal, been referred to the decision in *Rashid* [1977] 1 WLR 298, which was a decision by another division of this Court. That case concerned not a waiter in a hotel, but a British Rail waiter who substituted not bottles of wine for the railway wine but his own tomato sandwiches for the railway tomato sandwiches; and it is to be observed that the basis of the decision in that case was that the summing up of the judge to the jury was inadequate. On that basis the appeal was allowed. But the Court went on to express its views obiter on the question whether in those circumstances it could be said that the obtaining was by virtue of deception and it came to the conclusion, as I say obiter, that the answer was probably no.

Of course each case of this type may produce different results according to the circumstances of the case and according, in particular, to the commodity which is being proffered. But, as we see it, the question has to be asked of the hypothetical customer, "Why did you buy this wine?" or "If you had been told the truth, would you or would you not have bought the commodity?" It is, at least in theory, for the jury in the end to decide that question.

Here, as the ground of appeal is simply the judge's action in allowing the case to go to the jury, we are answering that question, so to speak, on behalf of the judge rather than the jury. Was there evidence of the necessary nexus fit to go to the jury? Certainly so far as the wine is concerned, we have no doubt at all that the hypothetical customer, faced with the waiter saying to him: "This of course is not hotel wine, this is stuff which I imported into the hotel myself and I am going to put the proceeds of the wine, if you pay, into my own pocket," would certainly answer, so far as we can see, "I do not want your wine, kindly bring me the hotel carafe wine." Indeed it would be a strange jury that came to any other conclusion, and a stranger guest who gave any other answer, for several reasons. First of all the guest would not know what was in the bottle which the waiter was proffering. True he may not know what was in the carafe which the hotel was proffering, but he would at least be able to have recourse to the hotel if something was wrong with the carafe wine, but he would have no such recourse with the waiter; if he did, it would be worthless.

It seems to us that the matter can be answered on a much simpler basis. The hypothetical customer must be reasonably honest as well as being reasonably intelligent and it seems to us incredible that any customer, to whom the true situation was made clear, would willingly make himself a party to what was obviously a fraud by the waiter upon his employers. If that conclusion is contrary to the obiter dicta in *R v Rashid* (supra), then we must respectfully disagree with those dicta.

It is not necessary to examine the question any further as to whether we are differing from *R v Rashid* (supra) or not. But it seems to us, beyond argument, that the learned judge was right in the conclusion he reached and was right to allow the matter to go to the jury on the basis which he did.

There are two other matters which are raised on behalf of the appellant. The first is the question of the gin, whisky, brandy and Cointreau which was found in the appellant's car, which was also included in the indictment as being part of the articles which were being used for cheating. The jury were invited, if they wished, to come to a separate conclusion on the spirits from that which they reached on the wine. They did not make any distinction and Mr Adams [counsel for the defendant] suggests that they must have been wrong so far as the spirits were concerned on the basis that any customer who was proffered a sealed bottle of a proprietary brand of spirits, either brandy, whisky or gin, would be certain, or might reasonably be expected to say "Yes" to the waiter's offer, although he may have said "No" so far as the wine was concerned. We think that the same reasoning can be applied to that. No reasonable customer would lend himself to such a swindle, whether the basis of the swindle was wine or spirits.'

R v Ellames [1974] 1 WLR 1391 Court of Appeal (Criminal Division) (Megaw LJ, Browne and Wien JJ)

Section 25(1) Theft Act 1968 – no liability where offence already committed

Facts
The defendant was convicted under section 25(1) Theft Act 1968, and appealed on the ground that the articles in question had been used in the commission of offences, but were not intended for use in the immediate future.

Held
The appeal would be allowed.

Browne J:

'In our judgment, the words in subsection (1) "has with him any article for use" means "has with him for the purpose" (or "with the intention") "that they will be used." The effect of subsection (3) is that if the article is one "made or adapted for use in committing a burglary, theft or cheat" that is evidence of the necessary intention, though not of course conclusive evidence. If the article is not one "made or adapted" for such use, the intention must be proved on the whole of the evidence, as it must be in the case of an article which is so made or adapted, if the defendant produces some innocent explanation. We agree with the editors of Smith and Hogan, *Criminal Law*, 3rd ed (1973), pp484-485, that section 25 is directed against acts preparatory to burglary, theft or cheat: "questions as to D's knowledge of the nature of the thing can hardly arise here, since it must be proved that he intended to use it in the course of or in connection with" burglary, theft or cheat; and that the mens rea for this offence includes "an intention to use the article in the course of or in connection with any of the specified crimes."

An intention to use must necessarily relate to use in the future. If any support is needed for this view, we think it is found in the recent decision of this Court in *R v Allamby and Medford* [1974] 3 All ER 126, decided under the Prevention of Crime Act 1953. It seems to us impossible to interpret section 25(1) as if it read "has with him any article for use or *which has been used* in the course of or in connection with any burglary, theft or cheat." Equally, it is impossible to read subsection (3) as if it said "had it with him for *or after* such use."

In our judgment, the words "for use" govern the whole of the words which follow. The object and effect of the words "in connection with" is to add something to "in the course of." It is easy to think of cases where an article could be intended for use "in connection with" though not "in the course of" a burglary etc, eg articles intended to be used while doing preparatory acts or while escaping after the crime (see Smith and Hogan, 3rd ed (1973), pp485-486).

In our view, to establish an offence under section 25(1) the prosecution must prove that the defendant was in possession of the article, and intended the article to be used in the course of or in connection with some future burglary, theft or cheat. But it is not necessary to prove that he intended it to be used in the course of or in connection with any specific burglary, theft or cheat; it is enough to prove a general intention to use it for *some* burglary, theft or cheat; we think that this view is supported by the use of the word "any" in section 25(1). Nor, in our view, is it necessary to prove that the defendant intended to use it himself; it will be enough to prove that he had it with him with the intention that it should be used by someone else. For example, if in the present case it had been proved that the defendant was hiding away these articles, which had already been used for one robbery, with the intention that they should later be used by someone for some other robbery, he would be guilty of an offence under section 25(1).'

R v Garwood [1987] 1 WLR 319 Court of Appeal (Criminal Division) (Lord Lane CJ, Caulfield and McGowan JJ)

Section 21(1) Theft Act 1968 – meaning of menaces

Facts

As stated by Lord Lane CJ:

'On 12 September 1986 in the Crown Court at Acton the appellant, Patrick Augustus Garwood, was convicted of blackmail and was sentenced to $2^1/_2$ years' imprisonment. In addition a suspended sentence of four months' imprisonment, imposed at Willesden Magistrates' Court on 22 May 1986 for theft, was activated in full and ordered to run consecutively, making a total of 34 months' imprisonment.

He now appeals against conviction and sentence by leave of the single judge.

The charge arose out of events on 3 June 1986. On that date a conversation took place between the appellant and the victim, an Indian youth called Sayed, aged 18, as a result of which Sayed went home and fetched £10 which he gave to the appellant. So much was not in dispute.

Sayed gave evidence that, as he was passing through the flats where he lived on the way to the library, carrying a bag full of books, the appellant – whom he knew by sight – called out to him from behind. The appellant then indicated to Sayed that he should follow him into a secluded area in the vicinity of the flats. Having arrived there the appellant accused Sayed of having "done over" his house. He asked Sayed if he or his family had a television or jewellery; he asked where they were kept; he stated that he wanted something "to make it quits" for what he alleged Sayed had done.

He then became aggressive, seizing Sayed by the shirt and pushing him up against a girder. He eventually demanded £10 and some jewellery saying that if the victim had been white he would have beaten him up by then. At that Sayed went home and got £10 which he gave to the appellant. He told the appellant that he could not get any jewellery. The appellant then said to him, "Don't tell the police or your parents or I'll get you." He demanded that Sayed should give him a further £20 three days later; if he did this, he would be protected. On 7 June the appellant met Sayed at a bus stop and reminded him that the £20 had not been forthcoming.

When the appellant was interviewed by the police, he denied any threats or aggression towards Sayed. He denied asking Sayed anything about the television or jewellery. He said that the two of them had had a conversation about sport and that he had asked Sayed if he could lend him £5. Sayed agreed and brought back £10. So he asked if he could borrow the £10, to which Sayed had agreed. He admitted that he had seen Sayed on 7 June. He was then simply apologising for not having paid back the money. The appellant gave evidence along the lines of his statement to the police, except that he said he only ever asked the victim for £10; the mention of £5 was a mistake.'

The defendant appealed against conviction, contending that the trial judge had misdirected the jury as to the meaning of 'menaces', under s21(1).

Held

The appeal would be dismissed.

Lord Lane CJ:

'In our judgment it is only rarely that a judge will need to enter upon a definition of the word menaces. It is an ordinary word of which the meaning will be clear to any jury. As Cairns LJ said in *R v Lawrence (Rodney)* (1971) 57 Cr App R 64, 72:

> "In exceptional cases where because of special knowledge in special circumstances what would be a menace to an ordinary person is not a menace to the person to whom it is addressed, or where the converse may be true, it is no doubt necessary to spell out the meaning of the word."

It seems to us that there are two possible occasions upon which a further direction on the meaning of the word menaces may be required. The first is where the threats might affect the mind of an ordinary person of normal stability but did not affect the person actually addressed. In such circumstances that would amount to a sufficient menace: see *R v Clear* [1968] 1 QB 670.

The second situation is where the threats in fact affected the mind of the victim, although they would not have affected the mind of a person of normal stability. In that case, in our judgment, the existence of menaces is proved providing that the accused man was aware of the likely effect of his actions upon the victim.

If the recorder had told the jury that Sayed's undue timidity did not prevent them from finding "menaces" proved, providing that the appellant realised the effect his actions were having on Sayed, all would have been well. The issue before the jury was clear-cut. If they felt sure that Sayed's version of events was true, there were plainly menaces. If they thought that the appellant's version might be true, there were equally plainly no menaces. There was no need for the recorder to have embarked upon any definition of the word. It only served to confuse, as the jury's question showed.

However, if he had given a proper and full answer to the jury's question in the terms which we suggested earlier, the jury could have been in no doubt at all that if Sayed's version was correct – which they must

R v Harvey and Others (1980) 72 Cr App R 139 Court of Appeal (Criminal Division) (Shaw LJ, Wien and Bingham JJ)

Section 21(1) Theft Act 1968 – whether demand 'unwarranted'

Facts
The defendants had paid a man named Scott £20,000 for a consignment of cannabis. When delivery took place it was discovered that the consignment contained rubbish, not cannabis. The defendants made threats to Scott and his family indicating that they would be killed or injured if the £20,000 was not returned. The defendants were convicted, inter alia, of blackmail, and appealed on the ground that the demands made to Scott and his family had been warranted for the purposes of s21(1) Theft Act 1968.

Held
The appeals would be dismissed.

Bingham J:

> 'For the appellants it was submitted that the learned judge's direction, and in particular the earlier of the passages quoted, was incorrect in law because it took away from the jury a question properly falling within their province of decision, namely, what the accused in fact believed. He was wrong to rule as a matter of law that a threat to perform a serious criminal act could never be thought by the person making it to be a proper means. While free to comment on the unlikelihood of a defendant believing threats such as were made in this case to be a proper means, the judge should nonetheless (it was submitted) have left the question to the jury. For the Crown it was submitted that a threat to perform a criminal act can never as a matter of law be a proper means within the subsection, and that the learned judge's direction was accordingly correct. Support for both these approaches is to be found in academic works helpfully brought to the attention of the Court.
>
> The answer to this problem must be found in the language of the subsection, from which in our judgment two points emerge with clarity: (1) The subsection is concerned with the belief of the individual defendant in the particular case: "... a demand with menaces is unwarranted unless *the person making it does so in the belief* ..." (added emphasis). It matters not what the reasonable man, or any man other than the defendant, would believe save in so far as that may throw light on what the defendant in fact believed. Thus the factual question of the defendant's belief should be left to the jury. To that extent the subsection is subjective in approach, as is generally desirable in a criminal statute. (2) In order to exonerate a defendant from liability his belief must be that the use of the menaces is a "proper" means of reinforcing the demand. "Proper" is an unusual expression to find in a criminal statute. It is not defined in the Act, and no definition need be attempted here. It is, however, plainly a word of wide meaning, certainly wider than (for example) "lawful." But the greater includes the less and no act which was not believed to be lawful could be believed to be proper within the meaning of the subsection. Thus no assistance is given to any defendant, even a fanatic or a deranged idealist, who knows or suspects that his threat, or the act threatened, is criminal, but believes it to be justified by his end or his peculiar circumstances. The test is not what he regards as justified, but what he believes to be proper. And where, as here, the threats were to do acts which any sane man knows to be against the laws of every civilised country no jury would hesitate long before dismissing the contention that the defendant genuinely believed the threats to be a proper means of reinforcing even a legitimate demand.
>
> It is accordingly our conclusion that the direction of the learned judge was not strictly correct. If it was necessary to give a direction on this aspect of the case at all (and in the absence of any evidence by the defendants as to their belief we cannot think that there was in reality any live issue concerning it) the

jury should have been directed that the demand with menaces was not be to regarded as unwarranted unless the Crown satisfied them in respect of each defendant that the defendant did not make the demand with menaces in the genuine belief both – (a) that he had had reasonable grounds for making the demand; and (b) that the use of menaces was in the circumstances a proper (meaning for present purposes a lawful, and not a criminal) means of reinforcing the demand.

The learned judge could, of course, make appropriate comment on the unlikelihood of the defendants believing murder and rape or threats to commit those acts to be lawful or other than criminal.

On the facts of this case we are quite satisfied that the misdirection to which we have drawn attention could have caused no possible prejudice to any of the appellants. Accordingly, in our judgment, it is appropriate to apply the proviso to section 2(1) of the Criminal Appeal Act 1968, and the appeals are dismissed.'

38 Sections 15 and 16 Theft Act 1968

R v *Callender* [1992] 3 WLR 501 Court of Appeal (Criminal Division) (Russell LJ, Roch and Wright JJ)

Section 16(1) Theft Act 1968 – meaning of employment

Facts
The appellant agreed to prepare accounts for a number of small businessmen, having falsely held himself out as being professionally qualified to do so. He was convicted of obtaining a pecuniary advantage by deception, and appealed on the ground that he had not obtained an opportunity to earn remuneration in an office or employment, as he had offered his services as an independent contractor, and thus fell outside the wording of the subsection.

Held
The appeal would be dismissed.

Wright J (pp504G–505B):

'The words "office" and "employment" are not further defined anywhere in the Act, and, somewhat surprisingly, appear rarely to have fallen for consideration by this court. Nevertheless, it is accepted that, appearing as they do in a penal statute, they fall to be construed narrowly rather than widely.

The only occasion upon which they appear to have been considered by this court was in *R* v *McNiff* [1986] Crim LR 57, in respect of which we have been helpfully provided with a transcript of the judgment. It is plain, we think, that that case falls to be considered in the light of its own particular facts, and does not purport to give any general guidance as to the meaning of the words under consideration.

In that case, the opportunity to earn remuneration arose when the appellant obtained the grant of a tenancy of a public house owned by and tied to a large brewery company. He did not, it is to be noted, obtain employment as a manager. This court held that the tenant or prospective tenant of a tied public house, whatever else he may have been, was not in the "employment" of the brewery. It was contended by the Crown that the holder of a justice's licence, which by virtue of his appointment as tenant the appellant might have been able to obtain, was the holder of an "office" within the meaning of the Act; but this court did not find it necessary to decide that point on the facts of the case.'

His Lordship then referred to the views expressed by academics on this matter, and continued, (pp506C–507A):

'We have come to the clear conclusion that Parliament, in adopting the phrase "office or employment", intended section 16(1) of the Acts of 1968 to have a wider impact than one confined to the narrow limits of a contract of service. A small indication is the use of the word "remuneration", which is a wide term, and the absence of any reference to salary or wages. We take the view that the interpretation of the words in question involves the consideration of their meaning as a matter of ordinary language. That meaning, in our judgment, is not to be arrived at by reference to the more limited and technical interpretations given to these words in the context of the law of master and servant, as in *Mersey Docks and Harbour Board* v *Coggins & Griffith (Liverpool) Ltd* [1947] AC 1, or in the context of pensions and National Insurance law, as in *Ready Mixed Concrete (South East) Ltd* v *Minister of Pensions and National Insurance* [1968] 2

QB 497, or in the context of income tax, as in *Edwards v Clinch* [1982] AC 845. In this last named authority, relied upon by Mr Reynolds in support of his contentions as to the true interpretation of the word "office", it is noteworthy that Lord Wilberforce, at p860, commented that over the years words of ordinary meaning had acquired, in the context of tax legislation, a signification coloured by legal construction in a technical context, and that return to the pure source of common parlance was no longer possible.

There can, we think, be no doubt whatever that the ordinary dictionary meaning of "employed" and "employment" is considerably wider than that enshrined in the various authorities that we have referred to. The *Shorter Oxford English Dictionary* defines "employ" as "To find work or occupation for" and in the passive sense "often merely to be occupied". "Employment" is defined as "That on which (one) is employed; business; occupation; a commission". It seems to us that it is a perfectly proper use of ordinary language and as such to be readily understood by ordinary literate men and women to say of a person in this appellant's position that his services as an accountant were "employed" by his customers, and that this state of affairs is properly to be described by the word "employment". As such the facts in this case fall within the ambit of section 16(2).

We cannot close our eyes to the fact that if the arguments advanced on behalf of the appellant in relation to this ground of appeal are soundly based, then there is, not a small lacuna, but a yawning gap in the protection for the public afforded by section 16 of the Act of 1968 through which a large number of dishonest people can – by arranging matters so that they come within the definition of "self-employed" – escape conviction and punishment for the kind of deceitful conduct of which the jury, by their verdicts in the instant case, found this appellant to be guilty. That is a conclusion to which we would be reluctant to come unless we were constrained to do so by higher authority directly in point, of which we are satisfied there is none. In such circumstances we reject the contentions advanced on behalf of the appellant on this first ground of appeal.'

Commissioner of the Police for the Metropolis v *Charles* [1977] AC 177 House of Lords (Lords Diplock, Salmon, Edmund-Davies and Fraser and Viscount Dilhorne)

Unauthorised use of cheque card – whether an offence contrary to s16(1) Theft Act 1968

Facts
The defendant drew cheques on his current account for amounts in excess of his agreed overdraft. The cheques had been supported by the cheque guarantee card provided by the defendant's bank. The defendant was convicted on a number of counts alleging that he had obtained a pecuniary advantage (being allowed to borrow by way of overdraft) by deception, contrary to s16(1) of the Theft Act 1968. The defendant's conviction was upheld by the Court of Appeal, and he appealed further to the House of Lords.

Held
The appeal would be dismissed.

Lord Edmund-Davies:

'What representation, if any, did the accused make when he cashed each of those cheques? It was against the background of his knowledge of his limited overdraft facilities that he drew each for £30 in favour of Mr Cersell, the club manager, and on each occasion produced his cheque card so that its number could be endorsed on the back of each cheque. The essence of the defence consists in Mr Comyn's [counsel for the defendant] submissions that by such conduct the only representation made was that "This cheque, backed by the card, will be honoured without question"; that such representation was true; that there was accordingly no deception of the club staff; and that therefore no offence was committed even though as a result the accused's account became overdrawn substantially beyond the permitted limit in consequence of his bank doing precisely what he had represented they would do on presentation of each of the cheques.

Both in the Court of Appeal and before your Lordships there was considerable discussion as to what representation is to be implied by the simple act of drawing a cheque. Reference was made to *R v Page (Note)* [1971] 2 QB 330, where the Court of Appeal (Criminal Division) adopted with apparent approval the following passage which (citing *R v Hazelton* (1874) LR 2 CCR 134 in support) has appeared in *Kenny, Outlines of Criminal Law* ever since the 1st edition appeared in 1902, see pp246-247:

"Similarly the familiar act of drawing a cheque – a document which on the fact of it is only a command of a future act – is held to imply at least three statements about the present: (1) That the drawer has an account with that bank; (2) That he has authority to draw on it for that amount; (3) That the cheque, as drawn, is a valid order for the payment of that amount (ie that the present state of affairs is such that, in the ordinary course of events, the cheque will on its future presentment be duly honoured). It may be well to point out, however, that it does not imply any representation that the drawer now has money in this bank to the amount drawn for; inasmuch as he may well have authority to overdraw, or may intend to pay in (before the cheque can be presented) sufficient money to meet it."

My noble and learned friend, Lord Fraser of Tullybelton, rightly pointed out that representations (1) and (2) were supererogatory in the light of representation (3), which embraced both of them. My noble and learned friend, Lord Diplock, also criticised representation (2) on the ground that the representation made by the simple act of drawing a cheque does not relate to or rest upon "authority" but is rather a representation that the drawer had contracted with his bank to honour his cheques. Notwithstanding the antiquity of the quoted passage, it accordingly appears right to restrict the representation made by the act of drawing and handing over a cheque to that which has been conveniently labelled "Page (3)." The legal position created by such an act was even more laconically described by Pollock B in *R v Hazelton*, LR 2 CCR 134, 140 in this way:

"I think the real representation made is that the cheque will be paid. It may be said that that is a representation as to a future event. But that is not really so. It means that the existing state of facts is such that in ordinary course the cheque will be met."

With understandable enthusiasm, Mr Comyn submitted that this was correct and that such representation was manifestly true when made, as was demonstrated by the later honouring of all the accused's cheques. But it has to be remembered that we are presently concerned to inquire what was the *totality* of the representations; with whether they were true or false to the accused's knowledge; whether they deceived; and whether they induced the party to whom they were addressed to act in such a manner as led to the accused obtaining "increased borrowing by way of overdraft." What of the production and use of the cheque card when each of the 25 cheques in the new cheque book was drawn on the night of January 2-3, 1973? Is Mr Comyn right in submitting that the only representation made by its production was the perfectly correct one that, "This cheque, backed by this card, will be honoured without question"? In my judgment, he is not. The accused knew perfectly well that he would not be able to get more chips at the club simply by drawing a cheque. The cheque alone would not have been accepted; it had to be backed by a cheque card. The card played a vital part, for (as my noble and learned friend, Lord Diplock, put it during counsel's submission) in order to make the bank liable to the payee there must be knowledge on the payee's part that the drawer has the bank's authority to bind it, for in the absence of such knowledge the all-important contract between payee and bank is not created; and it is the representation by the drawer's production of the card that he has that authority that creates such contractual relationship and estops the bank from refusing to honour the cheque. By drawing the cheque the accused represented that it would be met, and by producing the card so that the number thereon could be endorsed on the cheque he in effect represented, "I am authorised by the bank to show this to you and so create a direct contractual relationship between the bank and you that they will honour this cheque." The production of the card was the badge of the accused's ostensible authority to make such a representation on the bank's behalf. And this emerges with clarity from the evidence of the club manager, Mr Cersell, who repeatedly stressed during his lengthy testimony that the accused's cheque would not have been accepted unless accompanied by a cheque card the signature on which corresponded with that of the accused when making out the cheque.

If, indeed, such was the representation made by the production of the cheque card, I did not understand

Mr Comyn to dispute that it was false, and, though he withdrew (as he was perfectly entitled to do) an earlier concession that it was false to the knowledge of the accused, that must inevitably have been his state of mind. For by the time he drew the twentieth cheque (count 9) he had already drawn 19 cheques, each for £30 and totalling £570, and when he drew the twenty-fifth cheque (count 10) he had previously drawn 24 cheques, each for a like amount and totalling £720. He therefore clearly knew that he was using the cheque card in circumstances and for a purpose for which it was wholly unwarranted.

There remains to be considered the vitally important question of whether it was established that it was as a result of such dishonest deception that the club's staff were induced to give chips for cheques and so, in due course, caused the accused's bank account to become improperly overdrawn. This point exercised the Court of Appeal, though they were not troubled by the fact that, whereas the deception alleged was said to have induced the club servants to accept the cheques, the pecuniary advantage was obtained from and damnified only the bank. In that they were, in my judgment, right, for *R v Kovacks* [1974] 1 WLR 370 correctly decided (as, indeed, appellant's counsel accepted) that, in the words of Lawton LJ, at p373:

> "Section 16(1) does not provide either expressly or by implication that the person deceived must suffer any loss arising from the deception. What does have to be proved is that the accused by deception obtained for himself or another a pecuniary advantage. What there must be is a causal connection between the deception used and the pecuniary advantage obtained."

What had troubled the Court of Appeal, however, was the question of inducement, and this after hearing Mr Tabachnik, learned counsel for the accused, submit that in a cheque card case there is no such implied representation as that conveniently labelled "Page (2)":

> "for the simple reason that the payee is not, in the slightest degree, concerned with the question of the drawer's credit-worthiness. The state of the drawer's account at the bank, the state of the contractual relationship between the bank and the drawer is ... a matter of complete indifference to the payee of the cheque; it is a matter to which he never needs to apply his mind ... where the recipient of the cheque has the bank's express undertaking held out in the form of a cheque card to rely on, there is no necessity, in order to give business efficacy to the transaction, that there should be any collateral representation implied on the part of the drawer of the cheque as to the state of his account with the bank or the state of his authority to draw on that account. Still less is there any basis for an inference that any such representation operates on the mind of the recipient of the cheque as an inducement persuading him to accept it. He relies, ... and relies exclusively, on the bank's undertaking embodied in the cheque card." (per Bridge LJ [1976] 1 WLR 248, 255C–F).

Whether a party was induced to act as he did because of the deception to which he was dishonestly subjected is a question of fact to be decided on the evidence adduced in each case. In the present case the Court of Appeal were apparently led to reject – with some reluctance – the foregoing trenchant submissions on behalf of the accused because in what the court regarded as the virtually indistinguishable case of *R v Kovacks* [1974] 1 WLR 370, 373 Lawton LJ had said:

> "The railway booking clerk and the pet shop owner had been deceived because the appellant in presenting the cheque card with her cheque had represented that she was entitled to be in possession of it and to use it ... The next question is: how did she obtain this pecuniary advantage? On the facts the answer is clear, namely, by inducing the railway booking clerk and the pet shop owner to believe that she was entitled to use the cheque card when she was not."

Then is there room for coming to a different conclusion on the similar, though not identical, facts of the present case? In my judgment, it again emerges clearly from the evidence of Mr Cersell that there is not. He accepted that:

> "with a cheque card, so long as the conditions on the back are met, the bank will honour the card irrespective of the state of the drawer's account or the authority, or lack of it, which he has in drawing on the account,"

and that "All those matters, in fact, once there is a cheque card, are totally irrelevant." But in this context it has again to be borne in mind that the witness made clear that the accused's cheques were accepted *only* because he produced a cheque card, and he repeatedly stressed that, had he been aware that the accused was using his cheque book and cheque card "in a way in which he was not allowed or entitled to use [them]" no cheque would have been accepted. The evidence of that witness, taken as a whole, points irresistibly to the conclusions (a) that by this dishonest conduct the accused deceived Mr Cersell in the manner averred in the particulars of the charges and (b) that Mr Cersell was thereby induced to accept the cheques because of his belief that the representations as to both cheque and card were true. These and all other relevant matters were fully and fairly dealt with in the admirable summing up of His Honour Judge Finestein QC, the jury showed by their verdicts that they were fully alive to the nature of the issues involved, and in my judgment there was ample evidence to entitle them to arrive at their "guilty" verdicts on the two charges with which we are concerned in this appeal. I would therefore dismiss it.

Something finally needs to be said about the point of law of public importance certified as fit to be considered by this House. It was expressed in this way [1976] 1 WLR 248, 259:

> "When the holder of a cheque card presents a cheque in accordance with the conditions of the card which is accepted in exchange for goods, services or cash, does this transaction provide evidence of itself from which it can or should be inferred (a) that the drawer represented that he then had authority, as between himself and the bank, to draw a cheque for that amount, and (b) that the recipient of the cheque was induced by that representation to accept the cheque?"

I have to say that (b) is not a point of law at all. It raises a question of pure fact. As such, it is unanswerable in general terms (which is the object of certifying points for consideration by this House), for whether people were induced must depend on all the circumstances and, above all, upon what the recipient of cheques in those circumstances has to say. In the vase majority of cases the recipient will be a witness, and it becomes a question for the jury who have seen and heard him to determine whether inducement has been established.

The underlying aim of (a), too, is capable of being more accurately expressed, albeit by the change of only a few words in the certified question. The preferable form is that suggested by my noble and learned friend, Viscount Dilhorne, viz:

> "When the holder of a cheque card presents it together with a cheque made out in accordance with the conditions of the card, which cheque is accepted in exchange for goods, services or cash, does this transaction provide evidence of itself from which it can be inferred that the drawer represented that he then had authority as between himself and the bank to use the card in order to oblige the bank to honour the cheque?"

In my judgment, the proper answer to that revised question is "Yes." '

Lord Diplock:

> 'When a cheque card is brought into the transaction, it still remains the fact that all the payee is concerned with is that the cheque should be honoured by the bank. I do not think that the fact that a cheque card is used necessarily displaces the representation to be implied from the act of drawing the cheque which has just been mentioned. It is, however, likely to displace that representation at any rate as the main inducement to the payee to take the cheque, since the use of the cheque card in connection with the transaction gives to the payee a direct contractual right against the bank itself to payment on presentment, provided that the use of the card by the drawer to bind the bank to pay the cheque was within the actual or ostensible authority conferred upon him by the bank.
>
> By exhibiting to the payee a cheque card containing the undertaking by the bank to honour cheques drawn in compliance with the conditions indorsed on the back, and drawing the cheque accordingly, the drawer represents to the payee that he has actual authority from the bank to make a contract with the payee on the bank's behalf that it will honour the cheque on presentment for payment.
>
> It was submitted on behalf of the accused that there is no need to imply a representation that the drawer's authority to bind the bank was actual and not merely ostensible, since ostensible authority alone would suffice to create a contract with the payee that was binding on the bank; and the drawer's

possession of the cheque card and the cheque book with the bank's consent would be enough to constitute his ostensible authority. So, the submission goes, the only representation needed to give business efficacy to the transaction would be true. This argument stands the doctrine of ostensible authority on its head. What creates ostensible authority in a person who purports to enter into a contract as agent for a principal is a representation made to the other party that he has the actual authority of the principal for whom he claims to be acting to enter into the contract on that person's behalf. If (1) the other party has believed the representation and on the faith of that belief has acted upon it and (2) the person represented to be his principal has so conducted himself towards that other party as to be estopped from denying the truth of the representation, then, and only then, is he bound by the contract purportedly made on his behalf. The whole foundation of liability under the doctrine of ostensible authority is a representation, believed by the person to whom it is made, that the person claiming to contract as agent for a principal has the actual authority of the principal to enter into the contract on his behalf.'

R v *Doukas* [1978] 1 All ER 1061

See Chapter 37.

DPP v *Ray* [1974] AC 370 House of Lords (Lords Reid, MacDermott, Morris, Hodson and Pearson)

Deception by conduct

Facts

The defendant was one of a number of men who had entered a restaurant and ordered a meal. At the end of the meal they decided not to pay, and ran out of the restaurant whilst the attention of the waiters was distracted. The defendant's conviction under s16(1) of the Theft Act 1968 was quashed on appeal to the Divisional Court. The prosecution now appealed to the House of Lords.

Held (Lords Reid and Hodson dissenting)

The appeal would be allowed.

Lord MacDermott:

'To prove the charge against the respondent the prosecution had to show that he (i) by a deception (ii) had dishonestly (iii) obtained for himself (iv) a pecuniary advantage. The last of these ingredients no longer raises, on the facts of this appeal, the problems of interpretation which were recently considered by this House in *R* v *Turner* [1974] AC 357. By that decision a debt is "evaded" even if the evasion falls short of being final or permanent and is only for the time being; and a pecuniary advantage has not to be proved in fact as it is enough if the case is brought within section 16(2)(*a*) or (*b*) or (*c*).

On the facts here, this means that the respondent's debt for the meal he had eaten was evaded for the purposes of subsection (2)(*a*); and that in consequence he obtained a pecuniary advantage within the meaning of subsection (1). No issue therefore arises on the ingredients I have numbered (iii) and (iv). Nor is there any controversy about ingredient (ii). If the respondent obtained a pecuniary advantage as described he undoubtedly did so dishonestly. The case is thus narrowed to ingredient (i) and that leaves two questions for consideration. First, do the facts justify a finding that the respondent practised a deception? And secondly, if he did, was his evasion of the debt obtained by that deception?

The first of these questions involves nothing in the way of words spoken or written. If there was deception on the part of the respondent it was by his conduct in the course of an extremely common form of transaction which, because of its nature, leaves much to be implied from conduct. Another circumstance affecting the ambit of this question lies in the fact that, looking only to the period *after* the meal had been eaten and the respondent and his companions had decided to evade payment, there is nothing that I can find in the discernible conduct of the respondent which would suffice in itself to show that he was then practising a deception. No doubt he and the others stayed in their seats until the waiter went into the kitchen and while doing so gave all the appearance of ordinary customers. But, in my opinion, nothing in this or in anything else which occurred *after* the change of intention went far enough to afford proof of deception. The picture, as I see it, presented by this last stage of the entire transaction, is simply that of a group which had decided to evade payment and were awaiting the opportunity to do so.

There is, however, no sound reason that I can see for restricting the inquiry to this final phase. One cannot, so to speak, draw a line through the transaction at the point where the intention changed and search for evidence of deception only in what happened before that or only in what happened after that. In my opinion the transaction must for this purpose be regarded in its entirety, beginning with the respondent entering the restaurant and ordering his meal and ending with his running out without paying. The different stages of the transaction are all linked and it would be quite unrealistic to treat them in isolation.

Starting, then, at the beginning one finds in the conduct of the respondent in entering and ordering his meal evidence that he impliedly represented that he had the means and the intention of paying for it before he left. That the respondent did make such a representation was not in dispute and in the absence of evidence to the contrary it would be difficult to reach a different conclusion. If this representation had then been false and matters had proceeded thereafter as they did (but without any change of intention) a conviction for the offence charged would, in my view, have had ample material to support it. But as the representation when originally made in this case was not false there was therefore no deception at that point. Then the meal is served and eaten and the intention to evade the debt replaced the intention to pay. Did this change of mind produce a deception?

My Lords, in my opinion it did. I do not base this conclusion merely on the change of mind that had occurred for that in itself was not manifest at the time and did not amount to "conduct" on the part of the respondent. But it did falsify the representation which had already been made because that initial representation must, in my view, be regarded not as something then spent and past but as a continuing representation which remained alive and operative and had already resulted in the respondent and his defaulting companions being taken on trust and treated as ordinary, honest customers. It covered the whole transaction up to and including payment and must therefore, in my opinion, be considered as continuing and still active at the time of the change of mind. When that happened, with the respondent taking (as might be expected) no step to bring the change to notice, he practised, to my way of thinking, a deception just as real and just as dishonest as would have been the case if his intention all along had been to go without paying.

Holding for these reasons that the respondent practised a deception, I turn to what I have referred to as the second question. Was the respondent's evasion of the debt obtained by that deception?

I think the material before the justices was enough to show that it was. The obvious effect of the deception was that the respondent and his associates were treated as they had been previously, that is to say as ordinary, honest customers whose conduct did not excite suspicion or call for precautions. In consequence the waiter was off his guard and vanished into the kitchen. That gave the respondent the opportunity of running out without hindrance and he took it. I would therefore answer this second question in the affirmative.'

Lord Morris:

'It is clear that the respondent went into the restaurant in the capacity of an ordinary customer. Such a person by his conduct in ordering food impliedly says: "If you will properly provide me with that which I order, I will pay you the amount for which I will become liable." In some restaurants a customer might have a special arrangement as to payment. A customer might on occasion make a special arrangement. Had there been any basis for suggesting that the respondent was not under obligation to discharge his debt before he left the restaurant that would have been recorded in the case stated. All the facts as found make it unlikely that it would have been possible even to contend that in this case the debt incurred was other than one which was to be discharged by a cash payment made before leaving.

If someone goes to a restaurant and, having no means whatsoever to pay and no credit arrangement, obtains a meal for which he knows he cannot pay and for which he has no intention of paying he will be guilty of an offence under section 15 of the Theft Act. Such a person would obtain the meal by deception. By his conduct in ordering the meal he would be representing to the restaurant that he had the intention of paying whereas he would not have had any such intention. In the present case when the respondent ordered his meal he impliedly made to the waiter the ordinary representation of the ordinary customer that it was his intention to pay. He induced the waiter to believe that that was his intention. Furthermore, on the facts as found it is clear that all concerned (the waiter, the respondent and his companions) proceeded on the basis that an ordinary customer would pay his bill before leaving. The waiter would not have accepted the order or served the meal had there not been the implied representation.

The situation may perhaps be unusual where a customer honestly orders a meal and therefore indicates his honest intention to pay but thereafter forms a dishonest intention of running away without paying if he can. Inherent in an original honest representation of an intention to pay there must surely be a representation that such intention will continue.

In the present case it is found as a fact that when the respondent ordered his meal he believed that he would be able to pay. One of his companions had agreed to lend him money. He therefore intended to pay. So far as the waiter was concerned the original implied representation made to him by the respondent must have been a continuing representation so long as he (the respondent) remained in the restaurant. There was nothing to alter the representation. Just as the waiter was led at the start to believe that he was dealing with a customer who by all that he did in the restaurant was indicating his intention to pay in the ordinary way, so the waiter was led to believe that that state of affairs continued. But the moment came when the respondent decided and therefore knew that he was not going to pay: but he also knew that the waiter still thought that he was going to pay. By ordering his meal and by his conduct in assuming the role of an ordinary customer the respondent had previously shown that it was his intention to pay. By continuing in the same role and behaving just as before he was representing that his previous intention continued. That was a deception because his intention, unknown to the waiter, had become quite otherwise. The dishonest change of intention was not likely to produce the result that the waiter would be told of it. The essence of the deception was that the waiter should not know of it or be given any sort of clue that it (the change of intention) had come about. Had the waiter suspected that by a change of intention a secret exodus was being planned, it is obvious that he would have taken action to prevent its being achieved.

It was said in the Divisional Court that a deception under section 16 should not be found unless an accused has actively made a representation by words or conduct which representation is found to be false. But if there was an original representation (as, in my view, there was when the meal was ordered) it was a representation that was intended to be and was a continuing representation. It continued to operate on the mind of the waiter. It became false and it became a deliberate deception. The prosecution do not say that the deception consisted in not informing the waiter of the change of mind; they say that the deception consisted in continuing to represent to the waiter that there was an intention to pay before leaving.

On behalf of the respondent it was contended that no deception had been practised. It was accepted that when the meal was ordered there was a representation by the respondent that he would pay but it was contended that once the meal was served there was no longer any representation but that there was merely an obligation to pay a debt: it was further argued that thereafter there was no deception because there was no obligation in the debtor to inform his creditor that payment was not to be made. I cannot accept these contentions. They ignore the circumstance that the representation that was made was a continuing one: its essence was that an intention to pay would continue until payment was made: by its very nature it could not cease to operate as a representation unless some new arrangement was made.

A further contention on behalf of the respondent was that the debt was not in whole or in part evaded. It was said that on the facts as found there was an evasion of the payment of a debt but no evasion of the debt and that a debt (which denotes an obligation to pay) is not evaded unless it is released or unless there is a discharge of it which is void or voidable. I cannot accept this contention. Though a "debt," as referred to in the section does denote an obligation to pay, the obligation of the respondent was to pay for his meal before he left the restaurant. When he left without paying he had, in my view, evaded his obligation to pay before leaving. He dodged his obligation. Accordingly he obtained a "pecuniary advantage."

The final question which arises is whether, if there was deception and if there was pecuniary advantage, it was by the deception that the respondent obtained the pecuniary advantage. In my view, this must be a question of fact and the magistrates have found that it was by his deception that the respondent dishonestly evaded payment. It would seem to be clear that if the waiter had thought that if he left the restaurant to go to the kitchen the respondent would at once run out, he (the waiter) would not have left the restaurant and would have taken suitable action. The waiter proceeded on the basis that the implied representation made to him (ie of an honest intention to pay) was effective. The waiter was caused to refrain from taking certain courses of action which but for the representation he would have taken. In my view, the respondent during the whole time that he was in the restaurant made and by his continuing conduct continued to make a representation of his intention to pay before leaving. When in place of his original intention he substituted the dishonest intention of running away as soon as the waiter's back was turned, he was continuing to lead the waiter to believe that he intended to pay. He practised a deception on the waiter and by so doing he obtained for himself the pecuniary advantage of evading his obligation to pay before leaving. That he did so dishonestly was found by the magistrates who, in my opinion, rightly convicted him.'

Lord Reid (dissenting):

'If a person induces a supplier to accept an order for goods or services by a representation of fact, that representation must be held to be a continuing representation lasting until the goods or services are supplied. Normally it would not last any longer. A restaurant supplies both goods and services: it supplies food and drink and the facilities for consuming them. Customers normally remain for a short time after consuming their meal, and I think that it can properly be held that any representation express or implied made with a view of obtaining a meal lasts until the departure of the customers in the normal course.

In my view, where a new customer orders a meal in a restaurant, he must be held to make an implied representation that he can and will pay for it before he leaves. In the present case the accused must be held to have made such a representation. But when he made it it was not dishonest: he thought he would be able to borrow money from one of his companions.

After the meal had been consumed the accused changed his mind. He decided to evade payment. So he and his companions remained seated where they were for a short time until the waiter left the room and then ran out of the restaurant.

Did he thereby commit an offence against section 16 of the Theft Act 1968? It is admitted, and rightly admitted, that if the waiter had not been in the room when he changed his mind and he had immediately run out he would not have committed an offence. Why does his sitting still for a short time in the presence of the waiter make all the difference?

The section requires evasion of his obligation to pay. That is clearly established by his running out without paying. Secondly, it requires dishonesty: that is admitted. There would have been both evasion and dishonesty if he had changed his mind and run out while the waiter was absent.

The crucial question in this case is whether there was evasion "by any deception." Clearly there could be no deception until the accused changed his mind. I agree with the following quotation from the judgment of Buckley J in *In re London and Globe Finance Corporation Ltd* [1903] 1 Ch 728, 732:

> "To deceive is, I apprehend, to induce a man to believe that a thing is true which is false, and which the person practising the deceit knows or believes to be false."

So the accused, after he changed his mind, must have done something intended to induce the waiter to believe that he still intended to pay before he left. Deception, to my mind, implies something positive. It is quite true that a man intending to deceive can build up a situation in which his silence is as eloquent as an express statement. But what did the accused do here to create such a situation? He merely sat still.

It is, I think apparent from the case stated that the magistrates accepted the prosecution contention that:

"... as soon as the intent to evade payment was formed and the appellant still posed as an ordinary customer the deception had been made."

The magistrates stated that they were of opinion that:

"... having changed his mind as regards payment, by remaining in the restaurant for a further 10 minutes as an ordinary customer who was likely to order a sweet or coffee, the appellant practised a deception."

I cannot read that as finding that after he changed his mind he intended to deceive the waiter into believing that he still intended to pay. And there is no finding that the waiter was in fact induced to believe that by anything the accused did after he changed his mind. I would infer from the case that all that he intended to do was to take advantage of the first opportunity to escape and evade his obligation to pay.

Deception is an essential ingredient of the offence. Dishonest evasion of an obligation to pay is not enough. I cannot see that there was, in fact, any more than that in this case.

I agree with the Divisional Court [1973] 1 WLR 317, 323:

"His plan was totally lacking in the subtlety of deception and to argue that his remaining in the room until the coast was clear amounted to a representation to the waiter is to introduce an artificiality which should have no place in the Act."

I would therefore dismiss this appeal.'

Halstead v *Patel* [1972] 1 WLR 661 Divisional Court (The Lord Chief Justice, Melford Stevenson and Forbes JJ)

Section 15(1) Theft Act 1968 – cheque drawn without authority

Facts

As stated by the Lord Chief Justice:

'The respondent was employed by the Post Office for some time, and on October 30, 1970, he opened a National Giro Account, the National Giro Headquarters being at Bootle, which was not where he was serving at that time. The account was duly opened; he arranged to have his wages paid into the account, and so they were paid until, unhappily for him, there was a strike of Post Office employees, which meant that he received no wage for a substantial period, and the money being fed into the account was cut off for that reason. He knew that he was not allowed to overdraw. The justices find that he read and understood a booklet issued to him when the account was opened, which told him that he could not overdraw. The money coming into the account consisted of his wages when they were paid, and the money going out of the account was always withdrawn by him in the form of cheques payable to cash which he presented at a Post Office, the Giro system allowing the account holder to withdraw a sum not exceeding £20 in cash on demand at any Post Office, and this was the way in which the respondent operated his account.

On January 14, 1971, his account was overdrawn by a small sum, £7 6s 11d, and he was sent a letter which the justices find he received, pointing out this overdraft, and asking him to clear the account immediately. However, despite the receipt of that letter, he went on drawing cheques. There was a credit in respect of wages which momentarily brought his account into credit to the tune of about £21, but during January and early February, when no further credits were coming into the account, he proceeded to draw cheques. By January 30 his account was overdrawn to the extent of £48; on February 4 he cashed a further cheque, raising the overdraft to £68. The same thing happened again on February 17. In due course the respondent was interviewed by representatives of the Giro Office, if I may so describe it, and his explanation of what happened became perfectly clear. He was receiving no wages because of the strike; he had to have money to live, so he knowingly and quite deliberately overdrew his account, knowing that the money was not there to meet these cheques, and knowing that he had no business to overdraw. His explanation was that he needed the money to live, and that he intended to make good to the National

Giro the amount which he had overdrawn as soon as the Post Office strike was over and as soon as he was in funds to achieve that.'

The justices dismissed the charges against the defendant on the basis that there was insufficient evidence of his intention to permanently deprive the Post Office of the sums involved. The prosecutor appealed by way of case stated.

Held

The appeal would be allowed.

The Lord Chief Justice (having referred to s15):

'Taking the essentials of that section separately, it is necessary to show that the obtaining was by deception. One goes back to authority on the earlier law to remind oneself of what representation is made by someone who presents a cheque for payment at a bank other than the bank or branch upon which the cheque is drawn. We find that conveniently in *R v Page* [1971] 2 QB 330, 333 where the extract from *Kenny's Outlines of Criminal Law*, 15th ed (1936), p284 adopted by the court on that occasion is set out. The extract is this: "... the familiar act of drawing a cheque (a document which on the face of it is only a command of a future act) is held to imply at least three statements about the present: (1) that the drawer has an account with that bank; (2) that he has authority to draw on it for that amount; (3) that the cheque, as drawn, is a valid order for the payment of that amount (ie that the present state of affairs is such that, in the ordinary course of events, the cheque will on its future presentment be duly honoured)." There was here clearly a deception within the meaning of that definition.

When the defendant drew these cheques he knew there was no money in the account; he knew he had no business to draw them, yet he made what on *Kenny's* interpretation of the law was a false representation to the effect that the cheque would be duly honoured in the ordinary course of events. So much for the deception.

The next question is whether it was done with the intention of permanently depriving the Post Office of the money. It is here, I think, with deference to the justices, that they went wrong. There can be no doubt in this case that the actual notes or coins which were handed over the counter to the defendant were leaving the control of the Post Office for ever. There was no doubt at all of an intention permanently to deprive the Post Office of the actual coins or notes which were transferred. Accordingly, the only remaining feature of the offence which justified consideration is the requirement of dishonesty.

So far as dishonesty is concerned, it is quite clearly established on authority that a man who passes a cheque in respect of an account in which there are no immediate funds to meet the cheque does not necessarily act dishonestly if he genuinely believes on reasonable grounds that when the cheque is presented to the paying bank there will be funds to meet it. For example the man who, overdrawn on Saturday, draws a cheque in favour of a third party in the honest and well-founded belief that funds will be put into his bank on the Monday, is a man who many juries would undoubtedly acquit of any dishonesty, because he has a genuine and honest belief that the cheque will be met in the ordinary course of events. But that is not this case; this case is the more common case in which there is no suggestion that the drawer of the cheque thought that funds would be available when the cheque in the ordinary course reached Bootle for payment. This is a case of a man who knows perfectly well that there are no funds and that there will not be funds to meet the cheque on presentation, but who has the hope, and as the justices find, honest intention of repaying the money another day when he acquires funds for the purpose.

What is the situation in regard to that defence in the context of the requirement of section 15 that the action shall be dishonest? For this I go to *R v Cockburn* (1968) 52 Cr App R 134, where the headnote reads: "If money belonging to another person is dishonestly taken by the defendant against the will of the owner and without claim of right and with intention at the time of taking permanently to deprive the owner of the property in the notes and coins concerned, the defendant is guilty of larceny. The fact that he intended soon to replace the money taken with its currency equivalent and reasonably expected to be able to do so may be a matter of strong mitigation, but it does not constitute a defence to the charge." That headnote is fully justified by the reference by Winn LJ, at p138; [1968] 1 WLR 281, 285, to a dictum of Lord Goddard CJ in *R* v *Williams* [1953] 1 QB 660, 688: "... it seems to the Court in this case that, by taking the coins and notes and using them for their own purposes, the appellants intended to deprive the Postmaster-General of the property in those notes and coins, and in so doing they acted without a claim of right and they acted fraudulently because they knew what they were doing. The knew they had no right to take the money which they knew was not their money. The fact that they may have had a hope or expectation in the future of repaying that money is a matter which at most can go to mitigation and does not amount to a defence."

To my mind those authorities make the whole situation in this case crystal clear. When the cheques were presented for payment, the defendant knew that he had no right to overdraw, he knew he had no funds in the Giro account to meet these cheques, and that he had no prospect of providing such funds before the cheques were presented in the ordinary course. He had at best the pious hope of repaying this money at some uncertain future date when the Post Office strike was over, and that, as Lord Goddard CJ pointed out (supra), although it may be a matter in mitigation, is no defence to this charge. The element of dishonesty is satisfied on proof that he had no belief based on reasonable grounds that the money would be there when the cheque was presented. It is not enough to meet the allegation of dishonesty to say: I honestly meant to pay the money back some day.'

R v *King; R* v *Stockwell* [1987] 2 WLR 746 Court of Appeal (Criminal Division) (Neill LJ, Waterhouse and Saville JJ)

Operative deception for s15(1) Theft Act 1968

Facts

As stated by Neill LJ:

'On 5 March 1985 the appellants went to the house of Mrs Mitchell, in New Milton. Mrs Mitchell, who had lived in the house all her life, was a widow of 68 years of age. The appellants told her that they were from Streets, a firm of tree surgeons. She knew of the firm, and in answer to her question one of the appellants claimed to be Mr Street. They told her that a sycamore tree in her garden was likely to cause damage. They purported to carry out a test, with a plastic strip placed against the tree, and one of the appellants then said that the tree was dangerous.

They told her that the roots of the tree were growing into the gas main and could cause thousands of pounds in damage. They told her that it would cost £150 to fell the tree, which Mrs Mitchell agreed to pay. They then looked at other trees and told her that another sycamore was dangerous as well as one of her conifers. In addition they told her that the roots of her bay tree were causing damage to the foundations of the house. Mrs Mitchell asked the appellants about the cost of doing all the work, and they told her that to remove the four trees including the bay tree would cost about £500. When Mrs Mitchell told them that she was going to telephone her brother, one of the appellants informed her that they would do the work for £470 if paid in cash. Mrs Mitchell then said that she would have to go and get the money from the bank. In fact, she decided to draw some money from her two building society accounts. From one account she withdrew £100, and she was in the process of withdrawing £200 from her account with a second building society, intending at that stage to go to her bank to draw the balance, when the cashier at the second building society noticed that she seemed very distressed.

Following a conversation between Mrs Mitchell and the cashier, the police were informed. Police officers then went to Mrs Mitchell's house and found the appellants there. The appellants were arrested, and on 17 February 1986 they appeared at the Crown Court at Southampton on an indictment charging them with attempting to obtain property by deception, contrary to section 1(1) of the Criminal Attempts Act 1981.'

The defendants were convicted of attempting to obtain property by deception, contrary to s1(1) of the

Criminal Attempts Act 1981, and s15(1) of the Theft Act 1968, and appealed on the ground that there was no operative deception on their part.

Held
The appeals would be dismissed.

Neill LJ:

'In support of the appeal against conviction counsel for the appellants argued that the judge erred in rejecting the motion to quash the indictment, or alternatively the submission that there was no case to answer. The argument was developed on the following lines: (1) that, as the appellants were charged with an attempt, it was incumbent on the prosecution to prove that if the relevant conduct had been completed it would have constituted a criminal offence. (2) That if the appellants had received £470 for cutting down the trees they would have been paid by reason of the work they had done, and not by reason of any representation they had made to secure the work. (3) That since the decision in *R* v *Lewis* (unreported), Somerset Assizes January 1922 it had been generally recognised that conduct of the kind complained of in the present case did not constitute the criminal offence of obtaining property by false pretences or by deception because, as a matter of causation, the relevant property was obtained by reason of the work carried out rather than by reason of any representation or deception. Our attention was directed to statements on the subject in some leading textbooks. (4) That the offence of obtaining a pecuniary advantage by deception contrary to section 16 of the Theft Act 1968 had no relevance in the present case: (*a*) because the appellants were not given the opportunity to earn the remuneration "in an office or employment"; on the facts of this case the appellants were independent contractors; and (*b*) because during the course of the argument at the trial the prosecution stated in terms that they were not relying on the provisions of section 16.

In order to examine these arguments it is necessary to start by setting out the particulars of offence as stated in the indictment, as amended. The particulars read:

> "David King and Jimmy Stockwell on 5 March 1985 in Hampshire, dishonestly attempted to obtain from Nora Anne Mitchell, £470 in money with the intention of permanently depriving the said Nora Anne Mitchell thereof by deception, namely by false oral representations that they were from J. F. Street, Tree Specialists, Pennington, that essential work necessary to remove trees in order to prevent damage to the gas supply and house foundations would then have to be carried out."

It will be remembered that the word "then" towards the end of the particulars was added by way of amendment on 18 February.

The argument advanced on behalf of the appellants on causation or remoteness was founded on the decision in *R* v *Lewis*, and on commentaries on that decision by academic writers. The report of the decision in *R* v *Lewis* is scanty and, as far as we are aware, is contained only in a footnote in *Russell on Crime*, 12th ed (1964), vol 2, p1186, note 66. In that case (which was a decision at Somerset Assizes in January 1922) a schoolmistress obtained her appointment by falsely stating that she possessed a teacher's certificate. She was held to be not guilty of obtaining her salary by false pretences, on the ground that she was paid because of the services she rendered, and not because of the false representation.

It was submitted on behalf of the appellants that the principle underlying the decision in *R* v *Lewis* could be applied in the present case. It was further submitted that the authority of *R* v *Lewis* was implicitly recognised by the enactment of section 16(2)(*c*) of the Theft Act 1968. Section 16 is concerned with the obtaining of a pecuniary advantage by deception; section 16(2) provides:

> "a pecuniary advantage is to be regarded as obtained for a person ... where ... (*c*) he is given the opportunity to earn remuneration or greater remuneration in an office or employment ..."

It is to be observed, however, that Professor Glanville Williams in his *Textbook of Criminal Law*, 1st ed (1978), p751 has this to say of the decision in *R* v *Lewis*:

> "Yet Lewis would not have got the job, and consequently her salary, if it had not been for the pretence.

Her object in making the pretence was to get the salary. Assuming, as is likely, that the employer would not have made her any payment of salary if the lie had not been operating on his mind, there was certainly a factual causal connection between the lie and the obtaining of salary. Why should it not be a causal connection in law? We have seen that when the defendant produces a consequence intentionally, this is generally regarded as imputable to him. Why should it not be so here?"

Furthermore, the author of *Russell on Crime*, p1187 (immediately after footnote 66 already referred to) states:

"But it is submitted that cases of this kind could be placed beyond doubt if the indictment were worded carefully. The essential point in this crime is that in making the transfer of goods the prosecutor must have been influenced by the false pretence as set out in the indictment."

We have given careful consideration to the argument based on causation or remoteness and have taken account of the fact that some support for the argument may be provided by the writings of a number of distinguished academic lawyers. Nevertheless, we have come to the conclusion that on the facts of the present case the argument is fallacious.

In our view, the question in each case is: was the deception an operative cause of the obtaining of the property? This question falls to be answered as a question of fact by the jury applying their common sense.

Moreover, this approach is in accordance with the decision of the Court for Crown Cases Reserved in *R v Martin* (1867) LR 1 CCR 56, where it was held that a conviction for obtaining a chattel by false pretences was good, although the chattel was not in existence at the time that the pretence was made, provided the subsequent delivery of the chattel was directly connected with the false pretence. Bovill CJ said, at p60:

"What is the test? Surely this, that there must be a direct connection between the pretence and the delivery – that there must be a continuing pretence. Whether there is such a connection or not is a question for the jury."

The decision in *R v Martin* was referred to with approval in *R v Moreton* (1913) 8 Cr App R 214, where Lord Coleridge J said, at p217:

"*Martin* leaves the law in no doubt; it was held there that the fact that the goods are obtained under a contract does not make the goods so obtained goods not obtained by a false pretence, if the false pretence is a continuing one and operates on the mind of the person supplying the goods."

In the present case there was, in our judgment, ample evidence upon which the jury could come to the conclusion that had the attempt succeeded the money would have been paid over by the victim as a result of the lies told to her by the appellants. We consider that the judge was correct to reject both the motion to quash the indictment and the submission that there was no case to answer.'

R v Lambie [1982] AC 449 House of Lords (Lords Diplock, Fraser, Russell, Keith and Roskill)

Unauthorised use of credit card – whether deception

Facts
As stated by Lord Roskill:

'... on April 20, 1977, the respondent was issued by Barclays Bank Ltd ("the bank") with a Barclaycard ("the card"). That card was what today is commonly known as a credit card. It was issued subject to the Barclaycard current conditions of use, and it was an express condition of its issue that it should be used only within the respondent's credit limit. That credit limit was £200 as the respondent well knew, since that figure had been notified to her in writing when the card was issued. The then current conditions of use included an undertaking by the respondent, as its holder, to return the card to the bank on request. No complaint was, or indeed could be, made of the respondent's use of the card until November 18, 1977.

Between that date and December 5, 1977, she used the card for at least 24 separate transaction, thereby incurring a debt of some £533. The bank became aware of this debt and thereupon sought to recover the card. On December 6, 1977, the respondent agreed to return the card on December 7, 1977. She did not, however, do so. By December 15, 1977, she had used the card for at least 43 further transactions, incurring a total debt to the bank of £1,005.26.

My Lords, on December 15, 1977, the respondent entered into the transaction out of which this appeal arises. She visited a Mothercare shop in Luton. She produced the card to a departmental manager at Mothercare named Miss Rounding. She selected goods worth £10.35. Miss Rounding completed the voucher and checked that the card was current in date, that it was not on the current stop list and that the respondent's signature on the voucher corresponded with her signature on the card. Thereupon, the respondent took away the goods which she had selected. In due course, Mothercare sent the voucher to the bank and were paid £10.35 less the appropriate commission charged by the bank. On December 19, 1977, the respondent returned the card to the bank.

My Lords, at her trial at Bedford Crown Court, on August 1 and 2, 1979, before Judge Counsell and a jury, the respondent faced two charges of obtaining a pecuniary advantage by deception contrary to section 16(1) of the Theft Act 1968. These were specimen charges. The first related to an alleged offence on December 5, 1977, and the second to the events which took place at the Mothercare shop at Luton which I have just related.'

The defendant was convicted of the second charge, obtaining a pecuniary advantage contrary to s16(1) Theft Act 1968, and appealed successfully to the Court of Appeal where it was held that the use of the credit card by the defendant had not involved any operative deception. The prosecution appealed.

Held

The appeal would be allowed.

Lord Roskill:

'My Lords, at the close of the case for the prosecution, learned counsel for the respondent invited the learned judge to withdraw both counts from the jury on, it seems from reading the learned judge's clear ruling upon this submission, two grounds, first, that as a matter of law there was no evidence from which a jury might properly draw the inference that the presentation of the card in the circumstances I have described was a representation by the respondent that she was authorised by the bank to use the card to create a contract to which the bank would be a party, and secondly, that as a matter of law there was no evidence from which a jury might properly infer that Miss Rounding was induced by any representation which the respondent might have made to allow the transaction to be completed and the respondent to obtain the goods. The foundation for this latter submission was that it was the existence of the agreement between Mothercare and the bank that was the reason for Miss Rounding allowing the transaction to be completed and the goods to be taken by the respondent, since Miss Rounding knew of the arrangement with the bank, so that Mothercare was in any event certain of payment. It was not, it was suggested, any representation by the respondent which induced Miss Rounding to complete the transaction and to allow the respondent to take the goods.

My Lords, the learned judge rejected these submissions. He was clearly right to do so, as indeed was conceded in argument before your Lordships' House, if the decision of this House in *R v Charles* [1977] AC 177 is of direct application. In that appeal this House was concerned with the dishonest use, not as in the present appeal of a credit card, but of a cheque card. The appellant defendant was charged and convicted on two counts of obtaining a pecuniary advantage by deception, contrary to section 16 of the Act of 1968. The Court of Appeal (Criminal Division) and your Lordships' House both upheld those convictions. Your Lordships unanimously held that where a drawer of a cheque which is accepted in return for goods, services or cash uses a cheque card he represents to the payee that he has the actual authority of the bank to enter on its behalf into the contract expressed on the card that it would honour the cheque on presentation for payment.

'My Lords, I quote in their entirety three paragraphs from the speech of my noble and learned friend, Lord Diplock [1977] AC 177, 182-183, which, as I venture to think, encapsulate the reasoning of all those members of your Lordships' House who delivered speeches ...'

His Lordship referred to passages from Lord Diplock's speech which are set out above under *Commissioner of the Police for the Metropolis* v *Charles*, and continued:

'If one substitutes ... the words "to honour the voucher" for the words "to pay the cheque," it is not easy to see why mutatis mutandis the entire passages are not equally applicable to the dishonest misuse of credit cards as to the dishonest misuse of cheque cards.

But the Court of Appeal in the long and careful judgment delivered by Cumming-Bruce LJ felt reluctantly impelled to reach a different conclusion. The crucial passage in the judgment which the learned Lord Justice delivered reads thus [1981] 1 WLR 78, 86-87:

"We would pay tribute to the lucidity with which the judge presented to the jury the law which the House of Lords had declared in relation to deception in a cheque card transaction. If that analysis can be applied to this credit card deception, the summing up is faultless. But, in our view, there is a relevant distinction between the situation described in *R* v *Charles* [1977] AC 177 and the situation devised by Barclays Bank for transactions involving use of their credit cards. By their contract with the bank, Mothercare had bought from the bank the right to sell goods to Barclaycard holders without regard to the question whether the customer was complying with the terms of the contract between the customer and the bank. By her evidence Miss Rounding made it perfectly plain that she made no assumption about the defendant's credit standing at the bank. As she said, 'the company rules exist because of the company's agreement with Barclaycard.' The flaw in the logic is, in our view, demonstrated by the way in which the judge put the question of the inducement of Miss Rounding to the jury: 'Is that a reliance by her, Miss Rounding of Mothercare, upon the presentation of the card as being due authority *within the limits as at that time* as with count one?' In our view, the evidence of Miss Rounding could not found a verdict that necessarily involved a finding of fact that Miss Rounding was induced by a false representation that the defendant's credit standing at the bank gave her authority to use the card."

I should perhaps mention, for the sake of clarity, that the person referred to as the appellant in that judgment is the present respondent.

It was for that reason that the Court of Appeal (Criminal Division) allowed the appeal, albeit with hesitation and reluctance. That court accordingly certified the following point of law as of general public importance, namely:

"In view of the proved differences between a cheque card transaction and a credit card transaction, were we right in distinguishing this case from that of *R* v *Charles* [1977] AC 177 upon the issue of inducement?"

My Lords, as the appellant says in paragraph 9 of his printed case, the Court of Appeal (Criminal Division) laid too much emphasis upon the undoubted, but to my mind irrelevant, fact that Miss Rounding said she made no assumption about the respondent's credit standing with the bank. They reasoned from the absence of assumption that there was no evidence from which the jury could conclude that she was "induced by a false representation that the defendant's credit standing at the bank gave her authority to use the card." But, my Lords, with profound respect to the learned Lord Justice, that is not the relevant question. Following the decision of this House in *R* v *Charles*, it is in my view clear that the representation arising from the presentation of a credit card has nothing to do with the respondent's credit standing at the bank but is a representation of actual authority to make the contract with, in this case, Mothercare on the bank's behalf that the bank will honour the voucher upon presentation. Upon that view, the existence and terms of the agreement between the bank and Mothercare are irrelevant, as is the fact that Mothercare, because of that agreement, would look to the bank for payment. That being the representation to be implied from the respondent's actions and use of the credit card, the only remaining question is whether Miss Rounding was induced by that representation to complete the transaction and allow the respondent to take away the goods. My Lords, if she had been asked whether, had she known the respondent was acting dishonestly and, in truth, had no authority whatever from the bank to use the credit card in this way, she (Miss Rounding) would have completed the transaction, only one answer is possible – no. Had an affirmative answer been given to this question, Miss Rounding would, of course, have become a participant in furtherance of the respondent's fraud and a conspirator with her to defraud both Mothercare and the bank. Leading counsel for the respondent was ultimately constrained, rightly as I think, to admit that had that question been asked of Miss Rounding and answered, as it must have been, in the negative, this appeal must succeed. But both he and his learned junior strenuously argued that, as my noble and learned friend, Lord Edmund-Davies, pointed out in his speech in *R* v *Charles* [1977] AC 177, 192-193, the question whether a person is or is not induced to act in a particular way by a dishonest representation is a question of fact, and since what they claimed to be the crucial question had not been asked of Miss Rounding, there was no adequate proof of the requisite inducement. In her deposition, Miss Rounding stated, no doubt with complete truth, that she only remembered this particular transaction with the respondent because some one subsequently came and asked her about it after it had taken place. My Lords, credit card frauds are all too frequently perpetrated, and if conviction of offenders for offences against sections 15 or 16 of the Act of 1968 can only be obtained if the prosecution are able in each case to call upon the person upon whom the fraud was immediately perpetrated to say that he or she positively remembered the particular transaction and, had the truth been known, would never have entered into that supposedly well-remembered transaction, the guilty would often escape conviction. In some cases, of course, it may be possible to adduce such evidence if the particular transaction is well remembered. But where as in the present case no one could reasonably be expected to remember a particular transaction in detail, and the inference of inducement may well be in all the circumstances quite irresistible, I see no reason in principle why it should not be left to the jury to decide, upon the evidence in the case as a whole, whether that inference is in truth irresistible as to my mind it is in the present case. In this connection it is to be noted that the respondent did not go into the witness box to give evidence from which that inference might conceivably have been rebutted.

My Lords, in this respect I find myself in agreement with what was said by Humphreys J giving the judgment of the Court of Criminal Appeal in *R* v *Sullivan* (1945) 30 Cr App R 132, 136:

"It is, we think, undoubtedly good law that the question of the inducement acting upon the mind of the person who may be described as the prosecutor is not a matter which can only be proved by the direct evidence of the witness. It can be, and very often is, proved by the witness being asked some question which brings the answer: 'I believed that statement and that is why I parted with my money'; but it is not necessary that there should be that question and answer if the facts are such that it is patent that there was only one reason which anybody could suggest for the person alleged to have been defrauded parting with his money, and that is the false pretence, if it was a false pretence."

It is true that in *R* v *Laverty* (1970) 54 Cr App R 495, Lord Parker CJ said, at p498, that the Court of Appeal (Criminal Division) was anxious not to extend the principle in *R* v *Sullivan* further than was necessary. Of course, the Crown must always prove its case and one element which will always be required to be proved in these cases is the effect of the dishonest representation upon the mind of the person to whom it is made. But I see no reason why in cases such as the present, where what Humphreys J called the direct evidence of the witness is not and cannot reasonably be expected to be available, reliance upon a dishonest representation cannot be sufficiently established by proof of facts from which an irresistible inference of such reliance can be drawn.

My Lords, I would answer the certified question in the negative and would allow the appeal and restore the conviction of the respondent upon the second count in the indictment which she faced at Bedford Crown Court.'

R v *Thompson* [1984] 1 WLR 962 Court of Appeal (Criminal Division) (May LJ, Bristow and MacPherson JJ)

Theft Act 1968 section 15 – where obtaining takes place

Facts

The defendant was employed as a computer operator at a bank in Kuwait. He opened a number of savings accounts there, and programmed his employer's computer to re-direct funds intended for clients' accounts into his own savings accounts. On his return to England, he telexed the Kuwait bank to transfer the funds from his savings accounts there to accounts in England. The defendant was convicted of obtaining property by deception contrary to section 15(1) of the Theft Act 1968, and he appealed on the ground that the English courts lacked jurisdiction since, in his view, the obtaining of property occurred in Kuwait.

Held

The appeal would be dismissed.

May LJ:

'It will thus be apparent, and it has been the Crown's case throughout, that the *obtaining* in the six offences under section 15 of the Theft Act 1968 alleged against the appellant in this case occurred in England, within the jurisdiction, at the time when in each instance he received into a particular bank account the sterling equivalent of the credit balance in an account in Kuwait, which he had fraudulently created and which the bank transferred by telex as the result of the request in the appellant's letters. One might have thought that any other contention about the place where the relevant obtaining in each of the six offences in this case occurred was unarguable. However, Mr Caplan [counsel for the defendant] has attractively argued before us that the relevant obtaining in each of the six instances occurred as the result of fraud committed by this appellant, and occurred in Kuwait on each occasion when the corresponding debit and credit entries in the respective savings accounts were made as the result of his dishonest manipulation of the bank's computer.

Mr Caplan has submitted that section 15 is not concerned with questions of lawful title to any relevant property but, as the section itself specifically provides, with the ownership, possession or control of such property. He submits that when one asks the question whether at any material time – that is to say at any time before the bank in Kuwait was asked to remit to England – the appellant had control of what seemed to be his credit balance, the answer must be "Yes, he did" – at least until the bank discovered the fraud. Until they were so put on inquiry it would not have been possible for them to have said that this appellant had no such credit balance. Mr Caplan went on to argue that the proof of the pudding was in the eating because the bank in Kuwait in fact acted upon the letters which the appellant wrote asking for the transfers of his credit balances; it is thus difficult to say, Mr Caplan contends, that the appellant did not have control of a credit balance when the bank acted upon the basis that he did. In this connection he referred us to the case of *R v Kohn* (1979) 69 Cr App R 395. That was a case in which the defendant had been an accountant for various companies and in that capacity had used company cheques to draw sums of money from the bank accounts of the companies concerned, which he thereafter pocketed and used for himself. He was charged with nine counts of theft. It was contended that the property which he had stolen by the company cheques used in that way were choses in action, the property of the bank's customer, his employer, and that in those circumstances, having regard to the definition of "property" in section 4 of the Theft Act 1968, the indictment was properly drawn and the offences properly charged.

When *Kohn*'s case came before this Court on appeal, it held that in respect of those accounts from which he had drawn money where the defendant's employer was in credit, the bank had owed the employer a debt, and therefore by obtaining the money in that way the defendant had obtained a chose in action or property and the conviction could be sustained. A similar situation obtained, so it was held, where the account of the relevant employing company was in overdraft, but in overdraft within the extent of a facility which had previously been granted by the bank. There was however one count in respect of which Kohn was charged where the company's account was overdrawn to an extent in excess of any facility which had been granted by the bank. In those circumstances, as the employer/customer would not have been in a position to sue the bank for any debt, and no money was legitimately owed by the bank on the cheque as drawn – because all that was needed was for the bank to return it marked "return to drawer" – there was no chose in action, there was thus no theft by Kohn, and consequently that count could not be substantiated. In relation to that count the only passage in the judgment of the court, which was delivered by Geoffrey Lane LJ (as he then was), to which we think it is necessary to refer is where, in considering the submissions by Mr Tyrrell on behalf of the appellant in that case the Court said at p405:

> "It seems to us that the argument is quite untenable. First of all, is there a thing in action, and the answer is undoubtedly yes. Secondly, has the appellant appropriated it? The answer is yes. Was the intention permanently to deprive the owner, and again there was ample evidence upon which the jury properly directed could come to the conclusion that it was. Was it dishonest? Again there was ample evidence on which the jury could come to that conclusion. A submission was made at the close of the prosecution case similar to that made to us, which the judge rejected. We think he was right to reject it. Mr Tyrrell has frankly said that his researches have brought to light no authorities which give any support to his proposition. In so far as there is authority it is against his contentions. It is contained in the writings of two eminent academic lawyers: first of all Professor Griew in his book *The Theft Acts 1968 and 1978*, 3rd ed (1978), paras. 2-11, where one finds this: 'The case of an employee (D) who has authority to draw on his employer's (P's) bank account and who dishonestly draws on it for unauthorised purposes seems also to be theft (assuming the account to be in credit). D has in some manner appropriated the debt owed by the bank to P. Although nothing in the transaction operates as an assignment of that debt to D, it would seem that D has appropriated the debt or part of it by causing P's credit balance to be diminished, or at the very least taking the risk of such diminution. The case is analogous to the theft of a chattel by destruction.' The whole of that passage, and particularly the last sentence, if it is correct, as we think it is, sounds the death knell to this particular submission on behalf of the appellant."

Death knell it may have been in the case of *Kohn case*: in the instant appeal Mr Caplan fastens upon the last part of the approved passage from Professor Griew's book where he wrote: "... or at the very least taking the risk of such diminution." He submits that when the appellant acted as he did in programming the computer in Kuwait with the result that in addition to it appearing to give him credit on his savings accounts it also diminished the amounts standing to the credit of the other five substantial but dormant accounts, there was at the very least the risk of the diminution in the credit balances on those accounts. Consequently he submitted that we ought to hold that for the purposes of the relevant provisions of the Theft Act 1968 the obtaining of the property, the chose in action, occurred in Kuwait at the time that the computer went into action as the appellant's plane was in the air over the Mediterranean.

We think, however, that one may legitimately ask: of what property did this appellant in that way obtain control in Kuwait? What was the nature of that property? Mr Caplan's reply, as we understand it, was that the appellant obtained the control of those credit balances on his savings accounts, which were effectively choses in action, and were such until the bank discovered his fraud. With all respect to Mr Caplan's persuasive argument, we think that when it is examined it is untenable. We do not think that one can describe as a chose in action a liability which has been brought about by fraud, one where the action to enforce that liability is capable of immediate defeasance as soon as the fraud is pleaded. It is neither here nor there, we think, that the person defrauded, in this case the bank, may not have been aware that one of its employees had been fraudulent in this way until a later time. The ignorance of the bank in no way, in our view, breathes life into what is otherwise a defunct situation brought about entirely by fraud. One has only to take a simple example. Discard for the moment the modern sophistication of computers and programs and consider the old days when bank books were kept in manuscript in large ledgers. In effect all that was done by the appellant through the modern computer in the present case was to take a pen and debit each of the five accounts in the ledger with the relevant sums and then credit each of his own five savings accounts in the ledger with corresponding amounts. On the face of it his savings accounts would then have appeared to have in them substantially more than in truth they did have as the result of his forgeries; but we do not think that by those forgeries any bank clerk in the days before computers would in law have thus brought into being a chose in action capable either of being stolen or of being obtained by deception contrary to section 15 of the Theft Act 1968.

In so far as the customers whose accounts had been fraudulently debited and who had to be reimbursed by the bank, as Mr Caplan submitted, are concerned, we prefer the approach of Mr Walsh. He submitted that properly considered it was not a question of reimbursement: it was merely a question of correcting forged documents, forged records, to the condition in which they ought to have been but for the fraud.

In those circumstances and for those reasons we agree with the learned judge in the court below that the only realistic view of the undisputed facts in this case is that the six instances of obtaining charged in the indictment each occurred when the relevant sums of money were received by the appellant's banks in England. Further it seems to us quite clear (as it was to the learned judge below) that those sums of money were obtained as the result of the letters which the appellant wrote to the bank in Kuwait. The only proper construction to be put upon those letters is that they contain the representations pleaded in the particulars of offences in the indictment. Those representations were the effective cause of each and every one of the obtainings. However, Mr Caplan submits and we agree that each of those matters, that is to say where did the obtaining take place and of what did it consist, were the representations made, and were they the effective cause of each of the particular obtainings, were matters of fact to be determined by the jury. It may be, Mr Caplan accepts, that in the circumstances of the instant case any verdict on any of the counts by a jury other than one of guilty would have been perverse. Nevertheless he contends that the appellant was on those issues of fact entitled to have the jury's verdict.'

39 The Theft Act 1978

R v Allen [1985] AC 1029 House of Lords (Lord Hailsham LC, Lords Scarman, Diplock, Bridge and Brightman)

Section 3(1) Theft Act 1978 – intent to avoid payment

Facts
The defendant had stayed at an hotel for nearly a month and left without paying the bill outstanding of £1,286. He contacted the hotel a few days later and explained he was in financial difficulties but would return to the hotel to collect his belongings and leave his passport as security. When he did so he was arrested and charged with an offence contrary to s3(1) of the Theft Act 1978. The defendant claimed that he was not acting dishonestly and he had genuinely expected to be able to pay the bill from the proceeds of various business ventures. The trial judge directed the jury that the intent to avoid payment merely referred to the time when payment should have been made 'on the spot'. The jury returned a guilty verdict. The Court of Appeal quashed the conviction and allowed the accused's appeal.

The Crown appealed to the House of Lords.

Held
The appeal would be dismissed.

Lord Hailsham LC:

'After a fairly lengthy summing up by the trial judge to which, in the light of what happened, I need make no special reference, the jury retired at 1 pm and came back at 2.18 pm with a note containing the following specific question for guidance by the judge:

"Regarding count 2 of the indictment, the words 'and with intent to avoid payment of the £1,286.94', do you refer to permanent intention or one applying only to the dates mentioned in the charge?"

To this question the judge gave the following explicit answer:

"The answer is: one applying to 8 and 11 February 1983. You see it says in count 2: 'knowing that payment on the spot for goods supplied and services done was required or expected from him …' 'On the spot' means the day you leave. There was no payment on the spot when he should have paid. It contrasts sharply with count 1 where the intent there is permanent; that is not so in count 2 where he was required to pay on the spot; and there has been a failure to do that. Will you please, once more, retire to consider your verdict?"

The original summing up had contained the same direction, but in view of what happened there is no need to refer to it separately, for the effect on the jury of this specific reply was immediate and decisive. Within five minutes they returned the verdict of guilty.

Despite some (though not unanimous) textbook opinions in an opposite sense (see Smith *The Law of Theft* (5th ed, 1984) para. 250, p130, Griew *The Theft Acts 1968 and 1978* (4th ed, 1982) para. 11-14, p155 and, less strongly, Glanville Williams *Textbook of Criminal Law* (2nd ed, 1983) p878), I consider this answer to be clearly erroneous.'

His Lordship referred to s3 of the Theft Act 1978, and continued:

'The Crown's contention was that the effect of this section is to catch not only those who intend permanently to avoid payment of the amount due, but also those whose intention is to avoid payment on the spot, which, after all, is the time at which, ex hypothesi, payment has been "expected or required", and the time, therefore, when the "amount" became "due".

The judgment of the Court of Appeal, with which I agree, was delivered by Boreham J. He said ([1985] 1 All ER 148 at 154, [1985] 1 WLR 50 at 57):

> "To secure a conviction under s3 of the 1978 Act the following must be proved: (1) that the defendant in fact made off without making payment on the spot; (2) the following mental elements: (a) knowledge that payment on the spot was required or expected of him; and (b) dishonesty; and (c) intent to avoid payment [sc 'of the amount due']."

I agree with this analysis. To this the judge adds the following comment:

> "If (c) means, or is taken to include, no more than an intention to delay or defer payment of the amount due, it is difficult to see what it adds to the other elements. Anyone who knows that payment on the spot is expected or required of him and who then dishonestly makes off without paying as required or expected must have at least the intention to delay or defer payment. It follows, therefore, that the conjoined phrase 'and with intent to avoid payment of the amount due' adds a further ingredient: an intention to do more than delay or defer, an intention to evade payment altogether."

My own view, for what it is worth, is that the section thus analysed is capable only of this meaning. But counsel for the Crown very properly conceded that, even if it were equivocal and capable of either meaning, in a penal section of this kind any ambiguity must be resolved in favour of the subject and against the Crown. Accordingly, the appeal falls to be dismissed either if on its true construction it means unambiguously that the intention must be permanently to avoid payment, or if the clause is ambiguous and capable of either meaning. Even on the assumption that, in the context, the word "avoid" without the addition of the word "permanently" is capable of either meaning, which Boreham J was inclined to concede, I find myself convinced by his final paragraph, which reads:

> "Finally, we can see no reason why, if the intention of Parliament was to provide, in effect, that an intention to delay or defer payment might suffice, Parliament should not have said so in explicit terms. This *might* have been achieved by the insertion of the word 'such' before payment in the phrase in question. It *would* have been achieved by a grammatical reconstruction of the material part of s3(1) thus, 'dishonestly makes off without having paid and with intent to avoid payment of the amount due as required or expected'. To accede to the Crown's submission would be to read the section as if it were constructed in that way. That we cannot do. Had it been intended to relate the intention to avoid 'payment' to 'payment as required or expected' it would have been easy to say so. The section does not say so. At the very least it contains an equivocation which should be resolved in favour of [the respondent]."

There is really no escape from this argument. There may well be something to be said for the creation of a criminal offence designed to protect, for instance, cab drivers and restaurant keepers against persons who dishonestly abscond without paying on the spot and without any need for the prosecution to exclude an intention to pay later, so long as the original act of "making off" could be described as dishonest. Unlike that in the present section, such an offence might very well as with the railway ticket offence, be triable summarily, and counsel for the Crown was able to call in aid the remarks of Cumming-Bruce LJ in *Corbyn* v *Saunders* [1978] 2 All ER 697 at 699, [1978] 1 WLR 400 at 403 which go a long way to support such as view. But, as the Court of Appeal remarked, that decision was under a different statute and a differently worded section which did not contain both the reference to "dishonestly" and the specific intention "to avoid payment" as two separate elements in the mens rea of the offence. In order to give the section now under consideration the effect required the section would have to be remodelled in the way suggested by Boreham J in the passage quoted above, or the word "and" in the ultimate phrase would have to be read as if it meant "that is to say" so that the required intent would be equated with "dishonestly" in the early part of the subsection.

Apart from the minor matter not relevant to the judgment there is nothing really to be added to the judgment delivered by Boreham J.

The minor matter to which I have just referred was the disinclination of the Court of Appeal to consider the Criminal Law Revision Committee's Thirteenth Report (Section 16 of the Theft Act 1968) (Cmnd 6733 (1977)) which led to the passing of the 1978 Act. In accordance with the present practice, this, for the purpose of defining the mischief of the Act but not to construe it, their Lordships in fact have done. The "mischief" is covered by paras. 18 to 21 of the report and it is significant that the report was accompanied by a draft Bill, 3 of which is in terms identical with s3 of the Act, save that the proposed penalty was three years instead of two. Though we did not use it as an aid to construction, for the purpose of defining the mischief to be dealt with by the section, I consider it to be relevant. The discussion had originated from the decision in *DPP* v *Ray* [1973] 3 All ER 131, [1974] AC 370 and the committee defined the mischief in the following terms (para. 18):

> "... there was general support for our suggestion that where the customer knows that he is expected to pay on the spot for goods supplied to him or services done for him it should be an offence for him dishonestly to go away without having paid *and intending never to pay*." (My emphasis.)

From this it is plain beyond doubt that the mischief aimed at by the authors of the report was precisely that which the Court of Appeal, construing the section without reference to the report, attributed to the section by the mere force of grammatical construction.

In the result I agree with the judgment of the Court of Appeal and apart from my reference to the Criminal Law Revision Committee report can add nothing usefully to it ...'

R v *Firth* (1990) 91 Cr App R 217 Court of Appeal (Criminal Division) (The Lord Chief Justice, Mr Justice Rose and Mr Justice Morland)

Evasion of a liability by deception – s2(1)(a) Theft Act 1978

Facts

The appellant was a consultant gynaecologist/obstetrician who dealt with both National Health Service and private patients. The prosecution alleged that he had failed to inform the hospital treating several of his patients that they were receiving private medical treatment, and hence he had not been billed for the treatment that they had received. He was charged, inter alia, with four counts (hereinafter referred to as counts 4 to 7) of evading a liability by deception contrary to s2(1)(c) of the Theft Act 1978. The appellant was convicted and appealed (inter alia), on the following ground:

> 'That the learned recorder erred in not acceding to the submission made by the defence at the close of the Crown's case that counts 4, 5, 6 and 7 were wrongly laid in law in that the allegations to be proved required proof of acts of commission whereas the evidence disclosed only acts of omission.'

Held

The appeal would be dismissed.

Lord Lane CJ:

> 'It is not altogether clear what [ground 1 of the ground of appeal] means. We take it to mean that the counts laid under section 2(1)(c) of the Theft Act cannot be brought home against the defendant unless the prosecution prove that the dishonest obtaining was achieved by acts of commission, that is to say the deception must be by commission, and not by omission.
>
> One turns to the Act itself to see what the draftsman of the statute in fact says. Section 2 reads as follows ...'

His Lordship recited sections 2(1)(c) and 2(2) of the 1978 Act and continued:

> 'That would cover, for instance, if it were the case, this appellant obtaining an exemption on behalf of a patient whom he was treating.

The prosecution allegation in these various counts was that the appellant, by failing dishonestly to inform the hospital of the private patient status of the women ... had caused either them or himself not to be billed for services which should have been charged against them.

If, as was alleged, it was incumbent upon him to give the information to the hospital and he deliberately and dishonestly refrained from doing so, with the result that no charge was levied either upon the patients or upon himself, in our judgment the wording of the section and subsection which I have just read is satisfied. It matters not whether it was an act of commission or an act of omission. Providing those matters were substantiated the prosecution had made out their case. That means, in brief, that the recorder was right to reject any submission to the contrary.

But before us Mr Rogers [counsel for the appellant] enlarged upon that ground of appeal and the second limb of the argument was this. He submitted to us that the words "legally enforceable" in the section mean that in order to proceed under that subsection the prosecution has to establish an existing liability at the time when the alleged deception is made. I hope I do his submission justice: I think that is the proposition which he advanced. If, accordingly, goes on the submission, the defendant is asking for a service to be performed, the liability only arises when the service has been performed. Consequently, goes the submission, one must find the liability and then go on to prove that the deception was practised when the liability had arisen. In the present case, he submits, if the deception was practised before the liability to pay had come into existence, then no offence was committed.

It seems to us that that overlooks the wording not only of section 2(1)(c), but also the wording of the two previous paragraphs, because both in 2(1)(a) and 2(1)(b) the words "existing liability" are to be found. Let me read paragraph (a): "... where a person by any deception – (a) dishonestly secures the remission of the whole or any part of any existing liability to make a payment, whether his own or another's." There is similar wording in (b).

It is immediately to be remarked that in paragraph (c) the word "existing" is omitted. It seems to us that that is indicative of what the draftsman of the Act really meant. The argument put forward by Mr Rogers might very well have something to command it if section 2(1)(c) had contained the word "existing", but the word in that paragraph is conspicuous by its absence. The words as they stand are apt to cover an expected liability or future liability, even if the deception alleged is not in truth a continuing deception. The omission of the word "existing" was, it seems clear to us, purposeful and not a matter of chance.

Consequently in our judgment the second limb to ground 1 of the notice of appeal fails and that part of the appeal cannot be successful.'

R v *Holt and Lee* [1981] 1 WLR 1000 Court of Appeal (Criminal Division) (Griffiths LJ, Lawson and Balcombe JJ)

Section 2(1)(b) Theft Act 1978 – forgoing payment of a liability

Facts

As stated by Lawson J:

'... in the evening of December 9, 1979, the appellants consumed meals costing £3.65 in the Pizzaland Restaurant in Southport. There was a police officer off-duty also feeding in the restaurant and he overheard the appellants planning to evade payment for their meals by the device of pretending that a waitress had removed a £5 note which they had placed on the table. When presented with their bill, the appellants advanced this deception and declined payment. The police officer concerned prevented them from leaving the restaurant and they were shortly afterwards arrested and charged.'

The defendants were convicted of attempting to commit an offence contrary to section 2(1)(b) of the Theft Act 1978, and appealed on the basis that if they had not been apprehended they would in fact have committed an offence contrary to section 2(1)(a) of the 1978 Act.

Held
The appeals would be dismissed.

Lawson J:

'At the close of the prosecution case in the Crown Court, Mr Reid [counsel for the defendant], who has also conducted this appeal, made a submission which was overruled, the main point of which was that assuming the facts as we have recounted them to be correct, the attempt to evade thus emerging was an attempt to commit an offence not under section 2(1)(b) as charged but under section 2(1)(a) of the Act of 1978 since, he submitted, had the attempt succeeded, the defendants' liability to pay for their meals would have been "remitted" and not just "forgone," to use the contrasting terms contained in the respective subsections.

Mr Reid further developed his submission before us. As we understand it, he submits that the vital differences between the two offences defined in the first two paragraphs of section 2(1) of the Act of 1978 are that "remission" involves that, first, the creditor who "remits" the debtor's existing liability must communicate his decision to the debtor and, secondly, the legal consequence of the "remission" is to extinguish the debt, whereas the "forgoing of an existing liability," to use the words of section 2(1)(b), need not be communicated to the debtor and has not the consequence in law of extinguishing such liability. We find great difficulty in introducing these concepts into the construction of the subsection. We will later return to the matter.

Mr Reid further submitted that the effect of section 2(1) of the Act of 1978 was to create three different offences but conceded that there could be situations in which the conduct of the debtor or his agent could fall under more than one of the three paragraphs of section 2(1).

The elements of the offence defined by section 2(1)(b) of the Act relevant to the present case are clearly these: first, the defendant must be proved to have the intent to make permanent default on the whole or part of an existing liability. This element is unique to section 2(1)(b); it has no application to the offences defined in section 2(1)(a) or (c). Secondly, given such intent, he must use deception. Thirdly, his deception must be practised dishonestly to induce the creditor to forgo payment.

It must always be remembered that in the present case, whatever offence was being attempted, the attempt failed. The creditor was not induced by the dishonest deception and did not forgo payment. It is clear on the evidence that the appellants' conduct constituted an attempt to evade liability be deception, and the jury, who were properly directed, clearly concluded that the appellants' conduct was motivated by the intent to make permanent default on their supper bill. Thus, all the elements needed to enable an attempt to commit the offence defined in section 2(1)(b) were found to be present, so that the appellants were rightly convicted and charged.

Reverting to the construction of section 2(1) of the Act, as to which the commentators are not at one, we are not sure whether the choice of expressions describing the consequences of deception employed in each of it s paragraphs, namely, in paragraph (a) "secures the remission of an existing liability," in paragraph (b) "induces a creditor ... to forgo payment" and in paragraph (c) "obtains any exemption from ... liability" are simply different ways of describing the same end result or represent conceptual differences.

Whilst it is plain that there are substantial differences in the elements of the three offences defined in section 2(1), they show these common features: first, the use of deception to a creditor in relation to a liability, secondly, dishonesty in the use of deception, and thirdly, the use of deception to gain some advantage in time or money. Thus the differences between the offences relate principally to the different situations in which the debtor-creditor relationship has arisen.

The practical difficulty which Mr Reid's submission failed to confront is strikingly illustrated by cases of attempting to commit an offence under section 2(1)(a) or section 2(1)(b). If, as he submits, section 2(1)(a) requires communication of remission to the debtor, whereas section 2(1)(b) does not require communication of the "forgoing of payment" but, as the case is a mere attempt, the matter does not *end* in remission of liability or forgoing of payment, then the prosecution would be in a dilemma since it would either be impossible to charge such an attempt or the prosecution would be obliged to charge attempts in the alternative in which case, since any attempt failed, it would be quite uncertain which of the alternatives it was.'

R v Lambie [1982] AC 449
See Chapter 38.

40 Handling Stolen Goods

R v Bloxham [1983] 1 AC 109 House of Lords (Lords Diplock, Scarman, Bridge and Brandon)

Innocent receipt of stolen goods – subsequent disposal with mens rea

Facts

As stated by Lord Bridge:

'... in January 1977 the appellant purchased a motor car for £1,300. He paid the seller £500 in cash and was to pay the balance when the seller produced the car's registration document, but in the event this never happened. The car had in fact been stolen. It is accepted by the Crown that the appellant did not know or believe this when he acquired the car. In December 1977 he sold the car for £200 to an unidentified third party who was prepared to take the car without any registration document.

The appellant was charged under section 22(1) of the Theft Act 1968 with handling stolen goods, the particulars of the relevant count in the indictment alleging that he

"dishonestly undertook or assisted in the disposal or realisation of certain stolen goods, namely a Ford Cortina motor car registered number SJH 606M, by or for the benefit of another, namely the unknown purchaser knowing or believing the same to be stolen goods."

At the trial it was submitted that the count disclosed no offence in that the disposal or realisation of the car had been for the appellant's own benefit, not for the benefit of the unknown purchaser, and that in any event the purchaser was not within the ambit of the categories of "other person" contemplated by section 22(1). The judge ruled that the purchaser derived a benefit from the transaction, in that, although he got no title, he had the use of the car; that there was no reason to give any restricted construction to the words "another person" in the subsection; that, accordingly, on the undisputed facts, the appellant had undertaken the disposal or realisation of the car for the benefit of another person within the meaning of section 22(1). In face of this ruling the appellant entered a plea of guilty, thereby, it may be noted, confessing both his guilty knowledge and his dishonesty in relation to the December transaction.

On appeal against conviction to the Court of Appeal, the court affirmed the trial judge's ruling and dismissed the appeal. The court certified the following point of law of general public importance as involved in their decision:

"Does a bona fide purchaser for value commit an offence dishonestly undertaking the disposal or realisation of stolen property for the benefit of another if when he sells the goods on he knows or believes them to be stolen?"

The present appeal is brought by leave of your Lordships' House.'

Held

The appeal would be allowed.

Lord Bridge (having referred to s22(1) of the Theft Act 1968):

'It is, I think, now well settled that this subsection creates two distinct offences, but no more than two. The first is equivalent to the old offence of receiving under section 33 of the Larceny Act 1916. The second is a new offence designed to remedy defects in the old law and can be committed in any of the various ways indicated by the words from "undertakes" to the end of the subsection. It follows that the new offence may and should be charged in a single count embodying in the particulars as much of the relevant language of the subsection, including alternatives, as may be appropriate to the circumstances of the particular case, and that such a count will not be bad for duplicity. It was so held by Geoffrey Lane J delivering the judgment of the Court of Appeal in *R v Willis* [1972] 1 WLR 1605, and approved by the Court of Appeal in *R v Deakin* [1972] 1 WLR 1618. So far as I am aware, this practice has been generally followed ever since.

The critical words to be construed are "undertakes ... their ... disposal or realisation ... for the benefit of another person." Considering these words first in isolation, it seems to me that, if A sells his own goods to B, it is a somewhat strained use of language to describe this as a disposal or realisation of the goods for the benefit of B. True it is that B obtains a benefit from the transaction, but it is surely more natural to say that the disposal or realisation is for A's benefit than for B's. It is the purchase, not the sale, that is for the benefit of B. It is only when A is selling as agent for a third party C that it would be entirely natural to describe the sale as a disposal or realisation for the benefit of another person.

But the words cannot, of course, be construed in isolation. They must be construed in their context, bearing in mind, as I have pointed out, that the second half of the subsection creates a single offence which can be committed in various ways. I can ignore for present purposes the concluding words "or if he arranges to do so," which throw no light on the point at issue. The preceding words contemplate four activities (retention, removal, disposal, realisation). The offence can be committed in relation to any one of these activities in one or other of two ways. First, the offender may himself undertake the activity *for the benefit of* another person. Secondly, the activity may be undertaken *by* another person and the offender may assist him. Of course, if the thief or an original receiver and his friend act together in, say, removing the stolen goods, the friend may be committing the offence in both ways. But this does not invalidate the analysis and if the analysis holds good, it must follow, I think, that the category of other persons contemplated by the subsection is subject to the same limitations in whichever way the offence is committed. Accordingly, a purchaser, as such, of stolen goods, cannot, in my opinion, be "another person" within the subsection, since his act of purchase could not sensibly be described as a disposal or realisation of the stolen goods *by* him. Equally, therefore, even if the sale to him could be described as a disposal or realisation for his benefit, the transaction is not, in my view, within the ambit of the subsection. In forming this opinion I have not overlooked that in *R v Deakin* [1972] 1 WLR 1618, 1624, Phillimore LJ said of the appellant, a purchaser of stolen goods who was clearly guilty of an offence under the first half of section 22(1) but had only been charged under the second half, that he was "involved in the realisation." If he meant to say that a purchase of goods is a realisation of those goods by the purchaser, I must express my respectful disagreement.

If the foregoing considerations do not resolve the issue of construction in favour of the appellant, at least they are, I believe, sufficient to demonstrate that there is an ambiguity. Conversely it is no doubt right to recognise that the words to be construed are capable of the meaning which commended itself to the learned trial judge and to the Court of Appeal. In these circumstances, it is proper to test the question whether the opinion I have expressed in favour of a limited construction of the phrase "for the benefit of another person" is to be preferred to the broader meaning adopted by the courts below, by any available aids to construction apt for the resolution of statutory ambiguities.

As a general rule, ambiguities in a criminal statute are to be resolved in favour of the subject, sc in favour of the narrower rather than the wider operation of an ambiguous penal provision. But here there are, in my opinion, more specific and weightier indications which point in the same direction as the general rule.

First, it is significant that the Theft Act 1968, notwithstanding the wide ambit of the definition of theft provided by sections 1 and 3(1), specifically protects the innocent purchaser of goods who subsequently discovers that they were stolen, by section 3(2) which provides:

> "Where property or a right to interest in property is or purports to be transferred for value to a person acting in good faith, no later assumption by him of rights which he believed himself to be acquiring shall, by reason of any defect in the transferor's title, amount to theft of the property."

It follows that, though some might think that in this situation honesty would require the purchaser, once he knew the goods were stolen, to seek out the true owner and return them, the criminal law allows him to retain them with impunity for his own benefit. It hardly seems consistent with this that, if he deals with them for the benefit of a third party in some way that falls within the ambit of the activities referred to in the second half of section 22(1), he risks prosecution for handling which carries a heavier maximum penalty (14 years) than theft (10 years). The force of this consideration is not, in my view, significantly weakened by the possibility that the innocent purchaser of stolen goods who sells them after learning they were stolen may commit the quite distinct offences of obtaining by deception (if he represents that he has a good title) or, conceivably, of aiding and abetting the commission by the purchaser of the offence of handling by receiving (if both know the goods were stolen).

Secondly, it is clear that the words in parenthesis in section 22(1) "otherwise than in the course of the stealing" were designed to avoid subjecting thieves, in the ordinary course, to the heavier penalty provided for handlers. But most thieves realise the goods they have stolen by disposing of them to third parties. If the judge and the Court of Appeal were right, all such thieves are liable to prosecution as principals both for theft and for handling under the second half of section 22(1).

Finally, we have the benefit of the report of the Criminal Law Revision Committee, 8th Report, Theft and Related Offences (1966) (Cmnd 2977), which led to the passing of the Theft Act 1968 including the provisions presently under consideration in the same form as they appeared in the draft Bill annexed to the report, to assist us in ascertaining what was the mischief which the Act, and in particular the new offence created by section 22(1), was intended to cure. We are entitled to consider the report for this purpose to assist us in resolving any ambiguity, though we are not, of course, entitled to take account of what the committee thought their draft Bill meant: *Black-Clawson International Ltd v Papierwerke Waldhof-Aschaffenburg AG* [1975] AC 591.

There is a long section in the report headed "Handling stolen goods, etc" from paragraphs 126 to 144. The committee, after drawing attention to the limitations of the existing offence of receiving, say in paragraph 127:

> "... we are in favour of extending the scope of the offence to certain other kinds of meddling with stolen property. This is because the object should be to combat theft by making it more difficult and less profitable to dispose of stolen property. Since thieves may be helped not only by buying the property but also in other ways such as facilitating its disposal, it seems right that the offence should extend to these kinds of assistance."

This gives a general indication of the mischief aimed at. The ensuing paragraphs, after setting out the proposed new provision in the terms which now appear in section 22(1) of the Act, give numerous illustrations of the activities contemplated as proper to attract the same criminal sanction as that previously attaching to the old offence of receiving. Throughout these paragraphs there is no hint that a situation in any way approximating to the circumstances of the instant case lay within the target area of the mischief which the committee intended their new provision to hit.

For these reasons I have reached the conclusion that any ambiguity in the relevant language of section 22(1) should be resolved in favour of the narrower meaning suggested earlier in this opinion.'

R v Brown [1970] 1 QB 105 Court of Appeal (Criminal Division) (Lord Parker CJ, Winn LJ and Eveleigh J)

Assisting in the retention of stolen goods – failure to inform the police

Facts

As stated by Lord Parker CJ:

'The short facts were that on a night in January a café at Weymouth was broken into and a quantity of cigarettes and foodstuff was stolen. The next morning, January 19, police went to the flat of which the defendant was the tenant and found him in bed, and in that flat they found a quantity of the stolen goods. He was asked if he knew anything about the theft, and he said that he did not. He did not impede a search and some of the stolen goods, namely ham, bacon and other perishable foodstuffs were found in a refrigerator. The police did not find any quantity of the cigarettes which had been stolen. When he was about to be arrested, or indeed had been arrested, the defendant said to the officer "Get lost" and he was thereupon taken to the police station. It was only later that the cigarettes were found; they had been taken out of their packets, put into a plastic bag and were in fact at the foot of a wardrobe in which some of the defendant's clothes were hanging.'

The defendant was subsequently convicted of handling stolen goods contrary to s22(1) of the Theft Act 1968, by dishonestly assisting in their retention, and appealed.

Held

The appeal would be dismissed.

Lord Parker CJ:

'The point of law arises on a direction given by the chairman in regard to the handling of stolen goods. In fact the defendant had been charged on three counts; the first was the breaking in. The prosecution did not pursue that and the jury at the direction of the chairman acquitted him. The second and third counts both alleged offences of handling the goods, but they were divided into two parts, count 2 relating to a handling by way of receiving, getting the goods into his possession or control, and on that likewise he was acquitted. But the third count alleged a handling of goods by dishonestly assisting in the retention of the stolen goods. It is in regard to the direction on that count upon which he was convicted that this appeal arises.

This conviction must clearly have been on the basis that the jury were satisfied that, at some stage before the police arrived, the defendant knew that these cigarettes had been stolen, and indeed that the rest of the property had been stolen. It was on the assumption that the jury were so satisfied that the chairman gave this direction:

"So far as the other count of dishonestly assisting in the retention of the goods is concerned, it appears to me that the matter for you to consider is whether, assuming that you are satisfied that Brown knew that these stolen cigarettes were in the wardrobe when Detective Constable Chatterley came, he was dishonestly assisting in their retention by not telling the constable that they were there."

He goes on to embroider that:

"Remember that when Constable Chatterley went there, having found the perishable goods but not the cigarettes, he went and spoke to the defendant whose reply merely was, "Get lost!" The defendant was thereupon arrested. Well, instead of saying "Get lost!," it would have been open to the defendant, assuming that he knew all about it, to have said to the constable, "You will find that the rest of the goods, which are cigarettes, are hidden behind the drawer in that wardrobe there."

Later he said much the same:

"The matters to which you ought to apply your minds are the hiding of the cigarettes behind the drawer of the wardrobe and assisting in their retention, if you think he did, by not telling Detective Constable Chatterley that the cigarettes were there."

Finally, just before the jury retired he said:

"Well, members of the jury, it may well be that if Brown had kept his mouth completely shut it might on that be possible to say he was not guilty, but he did not keep his mouth completely shut, he told the police constable to get lost, and it is for you, members of the jury, to consider whether in saying 'Get lost' instead of helping the police constable he was dishonestly assisting in the retention of stolen goods."

It is urged here that the mere failure to reveal the presence of the cigarettes, with or without the addition of the spoken words "Get lost," was incapable in itself of amounting to an assisting in the retention of the goods within the meaning of section 22(1). The court has come to the conclusion that that is right. It does not seem to this court that the mere failure to tell the police, coupled if you like with the words "Get lost," amounts in itself to an assisting in their retention. On the other hand, those matters did afford strong evidence of what was the real basis of the charge here, namely that, knowing that they had been stolen, he permitted them to remain there or, as it has been put, provided accommodation for these stolen goods in order to assist Holden to retain them. To that extent, it seems to this court, that the direction was incomplete. The chairman should have gone on to say:

> "But the fact that he did not tell the constable that they were there and said 'Get lost' is evidence from which you can infer if you think right that this man was permitting the goods to remain in his flat, and to that extent assisting in their retention by Holden."

It may be thought to be a matter of words, but in the opinion of the court some further direction was needed. On the other hand it is a plain case in which the proviso should be applied. It seems to the court that the only possible inference in these circumstances, once Holden was believed, is that the defendant was assisting in their retention by housing the goods and providing accommodation for them, by permitting them to remain there. In those circumstances the court is satisfied that the appeal fails and should be dismissed.'

R v Grainge [1974] 1 WLR 619 Court of Appeal (Criminal Division) (Scarman LJ, Chapman and Eveleigh JJ)

Handling stolen goods – mens rea

Facts

As stated by Eveleigh J:

> 'On March 7, 1973, the appellant, his co-defendant a man named O'Connor, and a third man entered a shop in Sheffield which sold office machinery and stationery. During the course of the visit O'Connor stole a pocket calculating machine valued at £59. The loss of the machine was soon noticed and the salesman went out of the shop into the street to search for the three men. Having seen them, he noticed that one of the men passed the calculator to the appellant. Eventually the salesman reported the matter to a police officer, who then cautioned and arrested all three men and told them that he was taking them to the offices of the Criminal Investigation Department. On the way the officer noticed the appellant pass the calculator across towards the direction of O'Connor's pocket. In evidence the appellant said, "I never gave it a second thought. He is a friend of mine. I have known him two or three years. He has never been dishonest. I never even asked him about it. I just put it in my pocket. I thought it was a radio."'

The defendant was convicted of handling stolen goods, and appealed on the ground that the trial judge had misdirected the jury as to the mens rea required.

Held

The appeal would be allowed.

Eveleigh J:

> 'The appeal against conviction is based upon grounds which may be summarised as follows. A. The recorder misdirected the jury to the effect that suspicion that the goods were stolen was an alternative to knowledge or belief as an essential mental element, and failed to direct them that the test thereof was

subjective and not objective. B. The recorder failed to direct the jury that knowledge or belief must be proved at the time when the goods were received.

The recorder said, "... you have got to decide whether there was any element of dishonesty about it and that ... he handled it dishonestly, that at the time he knew or believed or suspected that the article had been stolen. That is what is referred to as guilty knowledge." He then referred to the circumstances from which knowledge could be inferred and continued, "... so those are the three elements, the theft, the dishonest handling and the guilty knowledge, the knowledge or belief or suspicion that the property was stolen when it was handled."

In our judgment this passage in its reference to suspicion was a misdirection. Before the Theft Act 1968 it was necessary for the prosecution to prove that the accused knew that the goods were "stolen or obtained in any way whatsoever under circumstances which amount to felony or misdemeanour": see section 33(1) of the Larceny Act 1916. It is understandable that members of the jury might have different views as to the degree of certainty in the mind of an accused necessary to constitute knowledge. Furthermore, they might well have had difficulty in evaluating the evidence upon which proof of knowledge rested, and have asked, "How can I know what was in the accused's mind?"

These two considerations naturally led to directions being given with a view to indicating that absolute certainty was not necessary, *R* v *White* (1859) 1 F & F 665, and to indicating the appropriate facts in a given case which might lead to an inference of knowledge.

Negligence or even recklessness did not amount to knowledge: see *R* v *Havard* (1914) 11 Cr App R 2. Knowledge might be inferred from evidence that the accused wilfully shut his eyes to facts from which ordinary men would realise that the goods were stolen, but the inference is a process of reasoning based on the circumstances of the case and not a presumption of law.

Section 22 of the Theft Act 1968 has clarified the law. It provides, inter alia, that if "knowing or believing" goods to be stolen a person dishonestly receives them he is guilty of the offence of handling stolen goods. The section does not say that suspicion is enough.

Atwal v *Massey* [1971] 3 All ER 881 illustrates the scope of the section. Lord Widgery CJ said in relation to the facts of the Case stated at p882: "Of course the whole case reeked with suspicion ... but it was for the justices to decide as a matter of fact whether the appellant at the time when he received the kettle knew that it was stolen or believed it to be stolen and took it dishonestly under the terms of the section."

At the close of the summing-up counsel for the prosecution drew the recorder's attention to the direction he had given the jury as to the relevance of suspicion. He then sought to put the matter right in the following way: "What counsel wishes me to clarify to you if I misled you was if a man suspects that property is stolen he then cannot shut his eyes to the suspicion but must be put on inquiry as to whether or not it was stolen. It is not enough to have suspicion. He cannot say 'I am going to forget it.' He has got to do something about it. In other words, when he suspects property is stolen he is on inquiry, he must be on his guard. He cannot shut his eyes to the fact that it may be stolen."

The recorder had previously dealt with the question of guilty knowledge when he dealt with the elements of the offence using the words set out at the beginning of this judgment. He said: "... you can infer guilty knowledge from the surrounding circumstances of the transaction, or if a man shuts his eyes and does not make an inquiry. A person is not entitled to shut his eyes if circumstances look suspicious and from suspicion such as that you can infer guilty knowledge."

The various expressions used by the recorder went some way to eradicating the error introduced when he had spoken of suspicion as an actual ingredient in the offence. In all the circumstances, however, this court does not think that he completely succeeded. The summing up as a whole could well have left the jury with the impression that suspicious circumstances, irrespective of whether the accused himself appreciated they were suspicious, imposed a duty as a matter of law to act and inquire and that a failure so to do was to be treated as knowledge or belief.

In *Atwal* v *Massey* (supra) the justices had asked: "... whether the fact that the appellant ought to have known that the kettle was stolen is sufficient to render him guilty of an offence under section 22 [of the] Theft Act 1968." Lord Widgery CJ said, at p882: "If when the justices say that the appellant ought to have known that the kettle was stolen they mean that any reasonable man would have realised that it was stolen, then that is not the right test. It is not sufficient to establish an offence under section 22 that the goods were received in circumstances which would have put a reasonable man on his inquiry. The question is a subjective one: was the appellant aware of the theft or did he, suspecting the goods to be stolen, deliberately shut his eyes to the consequences? It may be that the justices meant the word 'ought' to have the second meaning, namely that he suspected but closed his eyes, but we do not think that we ought to speculate on such a possibility, but rather that we ought to deal with this matter on the words used by the justices in the case." Lord Widgery CJ was not seeking to introduce another definition of the offence, but was examining the possible approaches made by the justices to the question which they had to decide and he was emphasising at the same time that the mental element was subjective.

No doubt the recorder was seeking to explain the position to the jury along the lines indicated by Lord Widgery CJ. It is, however, impossible to be satisfied that the jury did interpret the words in a manner consistent with the definition of the offence as laid down by section 22 of the Act.

In an appellate court's judgment there are frequently found possible alternative expressions which accurately embrace the definition of a criminal offence. The danger of treating them as alternative definitions lies in the fact that they are often formulated to deal with the particular facts before the court and to meet the arguments in the case. There is the further risk that repetition will not be precise – as happened in this case.

Where the words of a statute are in simple language in common use it is better to adhere to those words when actually defining the case to the jury: see *R* v *Feely* [1973] QB 530.

As to the second ground of appeal the recorder used the word "handled" and not the word "received" when he said it was "at that time," ie when it was handled, that knowledge had to be proved. Counsel for the defence submitted that the jury were not clearly directed that upon an indictment, as in this case, which charged a receiving, guilty knowledge had to be shown to exist at the time of the receipt. We think there is substance in the point.

In the judgment of this court the recorder ought to have made plain that it was at that moment of receipt and not at any time during the handling thereafter that guilty knowledge had to be proved.

For those reasons the appeal is allowed.'

R v *Griffiths* (1974) 60 Cr App R 14 Court of Appeal (Criminal Division) (James and Ormrod LJJ and Waller J)

Handling stolen goods – mens rea

Facts

As stated by James LJ:

'On October 3, 1973, at the Crown Court at Gloucester, Leslie George Griffiths, the appellant, was convicted of an offence of handling a pair of stolen candlesticks. On a second indictment he was convicted of an offence of burglary committed on April 28, 1973. He was sentenced to consecutive terms of two years' imprisonment. He appeals against the conviction of handling by way of certificate granted by the Recorder under section 1(1) of the Criminal Appeal Act 1968. He also applies for leave to appeal against the sentences.

The candlesticks were stolen from a church in Cheltenham on May 31, 1973. The appellant, who lived in Cheltenham, was arrested on June 4 in Cirencester. He had tried to sell the candlesticks that afternoon to two dealers to whom he admittedly told lies as to how he came into possession of the candlesticks. He first told the police that he had bought them that afternoon from a dealer. He later said he had purchased them from a man he could not describe in the High Street in Cheltenham that morning. When asked if he had asked the man where they came from, he replied, "You don't ask questions like that, do you?" When it was suggested that he must have realised they were stolen he replied, "Yes, I suppose so." In a written statement he repeated the story of buying the candlesticks from the man in the High Street and said, "I did not ask him where he got them, you don't do things like that, do you?" The defence was the same as the account in his written statement. He denied making answer to the police in terms that he knew the candlesticks were stolen. He said in evidence that he might have had suspicions, but the suspicions were not related to any criminal offence.'

Held

The appeal would be dismissed.

James LJ (after stating the facts):

'There was no evidence tending to show that the appellant was the thief. It was not suggested to or by any witness, including the appellant, that the appellant was the thief or that the candlesticks were in his possession, to use the words of section 22(1) of the Theft Act, "in the course of the stealing." But at the close of the evidence, in the absence of the jury, Mr Keane – who appeared for the appellant at the trial and who has conducted the appeal in this Court – submitted to the Recorder that the burden lay on the Crown to prove the positive factor that the candlesticks were in the appellant's possession otherwise than in the course of the stealing, and that on the evidence the Crown had not established that the appellant was not the thief. Mr Keane indicated that he proposed to address the jury on those lines and the Recorder, in rejecting the submission, said he proposed to direct the jury that there was no evidence that the appellant was the thief.

Mr Keane also raised at this stage of the trial a question as to what the Crown must establish to prove an offence under section 22(1) of the Theft Act 1968 in relation to "knowing or believing" the goods to be stolen goods. He invited the Recorder's attention to *Atwal* v *Massey* (1972) 56 Cr App R 6. It is significant to observe that the Recorder in discussion with counsel expressed the view that "The jury have to get inside the mind and they can decide, taking into account the circumstances, whether the man did know or believe."

In this appeal Mr Keane takes the same two points, the first alone being the subject of the Recorder's certificate. Upon the first point the argument is that, in the state of the evidence, the Recorder should have directed the jury that they should first decide whether they believed or rejected the appellant's version as to the receipt of the goods, and, if they rejected his version as to receipt, they should convict only if they were sure that the Crown had established that his receipt was otherwise than in the course of the stealing. Mr Keane relied on *Stapylton* v *O'Callaghan* [1973] 2 All ER 782. In that case the magistrate dismissed both informations, one alleging dishonestly receiving a stolen driving licence and the other alleging theft of the same licence, because he found the evidence inconclusive as to how the defendant came into possession of the licence and the prosecution had failed to satisfy him which offence had been committed. The facts found by the magistrate were that the defendant dishonestly possessed himself of the licence, which was a stolen licence, and intended to keep that licence. On the appeal by case stated to the Divisional Court, Lord Widgery CJ pointed out, at p784, that on those findings the defendant was one who had appropriated property belonging to another within the definition of "appropriated" in section 3(1) of the Theft Act 1968 and therefore the offence of theft was committed. The judgment continued: "Of course, if one looks on to section 22, which is the section charging handling, one finds that activities such as described here if committed otherwise than in the course of stealing may be caught by section 22, and understandably attract a more severe penalty, but if the facts justify the conclusion that the offence of stealing was committed, the right course in my judgment is to convict of stealing and not to go on to consider the possible additional hazard of convicting the accused of handling with the added penalty which might arise." Mr Keane also referred to *Seymour* (1954) 1 WLR 678 but we derive no assistance in the present matter from that authority which is concerned with the circumstances in which an indictment should contain counts for theft and receiving (under the old law) and the procedure appropriate to the return of the jury's verdict where that is done.

The Recorder directed the jury in terms which made no reference to "otherwise than in the course of the stealing" in relation to the ingredients of the offence charged. He did not give the direction which Mr

Keane has argued should have been given. In the judgment of this Court the Recorder was absolutely right to deal with this aspect of the case as he did. There was no issue as to whether the receipt of the candlesticks was otherwise than in the course of the stealing. In a case in which there is, on the evidence, an issue as to whether the receipt of stolen goods was in the course of the stealing or otherwise a direction would be necessary. To give such a direction in this case, in which there was no issue to which counsel's submission could relate, would have been both confusing and wrong.

The second point taken has caused us more difficulty. Mr Keane argues that the Recorder misdirected the jury in that he told them that they could convict if they were satisfied that the appellant was in one of three states of mind as to the stolen nature of the candlesticks, (i) that he knew, (ii) that he believed, or (iii) that he suspected and deliberately chose not to ask any questions as to the circumstances. The passage in the summing-up upon which Mr Keane particularly relies is, "there is a third possibility which you may think is a matter of common sense although it is a matter of good law, and that is this, that a man suspects that goods are stolen and then deliberately shuts his eyes to the circumstances and doesn't want to know. You may have in those circumstances a man with real suspicion – not grounds for suspicion, but really suspecting – who really closes his eyes to the circumstances – a man in law in those circumstances knows or believes the goods were stolen." Taken in isolation, those words are capable of being construed as directing the jury that *as a matter of law* they must find that the appellant knew or believed the goods to be stolen if they found that he suspected they were stolen and he deliberately shut his eyes to the circumstances. Such a direction would be wrong in that it removes from the jury's consideration the essential ingredient which it is for the jury to decide. Whether the jury seized upon this particular part of the summing-up and construed it in that way is a matter for speculation. But if it is open to that construction and there is a possibility that the jury approached their task on the basis of a misdirection, then we should have to consider the application of the proviso to Section 2(1) of the Criminal Appeal Act 1968. The passage cited is not to be read in isolation. It follows the direction which commences earlier: "At the time when he acquired possession of the candlesticks, what was his state of mind? Now, you have got here a difficult task, and every jury has to do it. You have got to enter into the mind of this particular man. It is no use saying, 'Well, we think a reasonable man would be suspicious in these circumstances.' That is something which arises in the civil court, it does not arise in the criminal court at all. You convict a man on what he thought, and not on what somebody else thought. It is because you cannot naturally open his skull and look inside and see what he is thinking, and you have got to do the best you can, in accordance with your oath, on the evidence you have got. What you have got to say is, 'In the circumstances of what we are given on the evidence, are we sure, are we satisfied that Mr Griffiths dishonestly received these goods? Has he dishonestly received them knowing or believing the same to have been stolen?' Now what is meant by knowing or believing is not all that difficult, and would you please be very careful about this. You can, in law, know or believe something to have been stolen in three different ways. The first is that you know about the theft – either because you saw the theft or you know about the theft, or the thief told you and you believed it. The second is that without actually knowing anything about the theft instinctively you can believe that they were stolen, and there may be plenty of circumstances in which way that things come (into) your possession you know and could not help but believe that they were stolen. Although it is not the charge as laid ..." then follow the words already cited and the Recorder continues: "That is the way you have got to approach Mr Griffiths in this case. Did he know? Perhaps there is no evidence at all that he knew the goods were actually stolen, but did he believe? You will have to consider the circumstances of how he said the goods came into his possession, and if he knew they were stolen. Did he know they were stolen? Did he know they were stolen or did he have the real suspicion that they were stolen and shut his eyes to the circumstances of the case, and that they were stolen, and the way the things came into his possession?"

Then later there is another passage, "It is a matter for you whether you think it is an indication that he either knew the goods were stolen or believed they were stolen, or was closing his eyes to circumstances where he was really suspicious about it. It is a matter for you entirely to judge ..." And later: "It is a matter for you, but he said that 'If I said that I bought them off a chap in the High Street, then that is so suspicious that I wouldn't expect them to pay over money,' if that is what Mr Griffiths suspected that the shopkeepers might think, does it now follow that he himself has also thought that buying off someone in the High Street was a bit suspicious? It is a matter for you."

Finally the Recorder said: "... what do you believe about what Mr Griffiths thought about where these candlesticks came from really? Do you suppose that Mr Griffiths thought about it? If you decided that he did not think about it at all, then you decide things in his favour. But if you do decide that he did think about it on this basis, that it was a stranger coming up to him in the market place and offering him goods at half price, members of the jury, it is a matter for you whether you decide that Mr Griffiths came at that moment into the category of someone who did have real suspicion that the goods were stolen and deliberately shut his eyes to the circumstances. It is a matter for you to decide what you think."

It appears to this Court that the Recorder in giving his directions on this aspect of the case was seeking to follow what was said by Lord Widgery, the Lord Chief Justice, in *Atwal* v *Massey* (supra). In that case the justices convicted the appellant of an offence of handling a stolen kettle. The facts found by the justices were that the appellant received the stolen kettle and obtained possession of it after it had been stolen by one Mott, who had left it by a gate to be collected by the appellant. The appellant paid Mott for it. The justices found that the appellant, from the circumstances in which he had collected the kettle, ought to have known that it was stolen. The question for the Divisional Court was whether the fact that the appellant ought to have known it was stolen was sufficient to render him guilty of an offence under section 22. In his judgment, with which O'Connor and Lawson JJ agreed, the Lord Chief Justice said at (p7): "It was for the justices to decide as a matter of fact whether the appellant at the time he received the kettle knew it was stolen or believed it to have been stolen and took it dishonestly under the terms of the section," and having pointed out that the test was not whether the circumstances in which the goods received would have put a reasonable man on inquiry, he continued: "The question is a subjective one, was the appellant aware of the theft or did he believe the goods to be stolen or did he, suspecting the goods to be stolen, deliberately shut his eyes to the consequences?" The conviction was quashed on the basis that, on the words of the justices in the case "ought to have known", the justices applied the wrong test.

Mr Keane argues that the words in the judgment "or did he suspecting that the goods were stolen deliberately shut his eyes to the consequences," if they are to be taken as adding a third state of mind to those of knowing or believing, are an extension of the definition of the offences contained in the statute. In *Grainge* (1973) 59 Cr App R 3; [1974] 1 WLR 619, the appellant was convicted of handling a stolen calculating machine after a direction of the Recorder that the requirement of guilty knowledge in the offence was satisfied by proof of "knowledge or belief or suspicion that the property was stolen when it was handled." On appeal this was held to be a misdirection which was not wholly corrected in other passages of the summing-up. The relevance of the judgment to the present matter is that Eveleigh J, giving the judgment of the Court, said at pp5 and 623 of the respective reports, after citing the judgment in *Atwal* v *Massey* (supra): "Lord Widgery CJ was not seeking to introduce another definition of the offence but was examining the possible approaches made by the justices to the question they had to decide and he was emphasising at the same time that the mental element was subjective." We understand the judgment in *Atwal* v *Massey* (supra) in the same way. It is inconceivable that the Lord Chief Justice would have sought to introduce an additional alternative mental element into the statutory definition which is restricted to "knowing or believing." *Atwal* v *Massey* (supra) is to be read as the judgment of the Divisional Court dealing with the approach which justices, as judges of fact, may adopt in order to arrive at their decision as to the knowledge or belief of the defendant.

There is a danger in the adoption of the passage cited from the judgment in *Atwal* v *Massey* (supra) as the direction to a jury unless great care is taken to avoid confusion between the mental element of knowledge or belief and the approach by which the jury may arrive at a conclusion as to knowledge or belief. To direct the jury that the offence is committed if the defendant, suspecting that the goods were stolen, deliberately shut his eyes to the circumstances as an alternative to knowing or believing the goods were stolen is a misdirection. To direct the jury that, in common sense and in law, they may find that the defendant knew or believed the goods to be stolen, because he deliberately closed his eyes to the circumstances, is a perfectly proper direction.

Taking this summing up as a whole, we are satisfied that the jury were left in the understanding that it was their province to decide the state of mind of the appellant at the time when he received the candlesticks and that that issue was not removed from their consideration. Further, although the direction at page 10 could have been better expressed than in the words "a man in law in those circumstances knows or believes," we are satisfied that the direction read in its entirety is that the jury had to be satisfied of either knowledge or belief and that one approach to that issue on the facts was to decide whether the appellant suspected the candlesticks were stolen and adopted an attitude of wilful blindness to the circumstances of receipt. We, therefore, conclude, after some doubt, that there was no misdirection and that the appeal fails on this point as it does upon the first point raised. We would add that had we decided that there was in this respect a misdirection, we would have had no hesitation in applying the proviso. The evidence was overwhelming and no reasonable jury on this evidence could have arrived at a conclusion other than that the appellant believed the goods were stolen.'

R v Kanwar [1982] 1 WLR 845 Court of Appeal (Criminal Division) (Dunn LJ, Cantley and Sheldon JJ)

Assisting in the retention of stolen property

Facts

As stated by Cantley J:

'In counts 7 and 9 of an indictment on which she was tried with others, the appellant was charged with dishonestly assisting in the retention of stolen goods for the benefit of Maninder Singh Kanwar, who was her husband. She was convicted and by way of sentence was given a conditional discharge. She now appeals against her conviction.

Her husband had brought the stolen goods to their house where the goods were used in the home. It was conceded that the appellant was not present when the goods were brought to the house. She was in hospital at the time. On November 2, 1978, police officers, armed with a search warrant, came to the house to look for and take away any goods which they found there which corresponded with a list of stolen goods in their possession. The appellant arrived during the search and was told of the object of the search. She replied: "There's no stolen property here."

She was subsequently asked a number of questions with regard to specific articles which were in the house and in reply to those questions, she gave answers which were lies. It is sufficient for present purposes to take two examples. She was asked about a painting which was in the living room and she replied: "I bought it from a shop. I have a receipt." The officer said: "That's not true." She said: "Yes, I have." He said: "If you can find a receipt, please have a look." She made some pretence of looking for the receipt but none was produced and ultimately she at least tacitly admitted there was none. The painting is one of the articles in the particulars to count 9.

She was also asked about a mirror which was in the kitchen. This is one of the articles in the particulars to count 7. The officer said: "What about the mirror?" She said: "I bought it from the market." The officer asked: "When?" She said: "Sometime last year." There is no dispute that that answer was a lie as was the answer about the painting. Later on, she was warned that she was telling lies and that the property was stolen. She said: "No, it isn't. We're trying to build up a nice home." Ultimately, although the officer had had no intention of arresting her when he came to the house, he did arrest her and she was subsequently charged.

The appellant did not give evidence and the evidence of the police officer stood uncontradicted.'

The defendant was convicted on two counts of handling stolen goods contrary to s22(1) Theft Act 1968, by assisting in their retention, and appealed.

Held

The appeal would be dismissed.

Cantley J:

'In *R* v *Thornhill* (unreported), May 15, 1981, and *R* v *Sanders*, The Times, March 1, 1982, decided in this court on February 25, 1982, it was held that merely using stolen goods in the possession of another does not constitute the offence of assisting in their retention. To constitute the offence, something must be done by the offender, and done intentionally and dishonestly, for the purpose of enabling the goods to be retained. Examples of such conduct are concealing or helping to conceal the goods, or doing something to make them more difficult to find or to identify. Such conduct must be done knowing or believing the goods to be stolen and done dishonestly and for the benefit of another.

We see no reason why the requisite assistance should be restricted to physical acts. Verbal representations, whether oral or in writing, for the purpose of concealing the identity of stolen goods may, if made dishonestly and for the benefit of another, amount to handling stolen goods by assisting in their retention within the meaning of section 22(1) of the Theft Act 1968.

The requisite assistance need not be successful in its object. It would be absurd if a person dishonestly concealing stolen goods for the benefit of a receiver could establish a defence by showing that he was caught in the act. In the present case, if, while the police were in one part of the house, the appellant, in order to conceal the painting had put it under a mattress in the bedroom, it would not alter the nature of her conduct that the police subsequently looked under the mattress and found the picture because they expected to find it there or that they caught her in the act of putting it there.

The appellant told these lies to the police to persuade them that the picture and the mirror were not the stolen property which they had come to take away but were her lawful property which she had bought. If that was true, the articles should be left in the house. She was, of course, telling these lies to protect her husband, who had dishonestly brought the articles there but, in our view, she was nonetheless, at the time, dishonestly assisting in the retention of the stolen articles.

In his summing up, the judge directed the jury:

"It would be quite wrong for you to convict this lady if all she did was to watch her husband bring goods into the house, even if she knew or believed that they were stolen because, no doubt, you would say to yourselves: What would she be expected to do about it? Well, what the Crown say is that she knew or believed them to be stolen and that she was a knowing and willing party to their being kept in the house in those circumstances. The reason the Crown say that – and we shall be coming to the evidence – is that when questioned about a certain number of items, Mrs Kanwar gave answers which the Crown say were not true and that she could not possibly have believed to be true and that she knew perfectly well were untruthful. So, say the prosecution, she was not just an acquiescent wife who could not do much about it, she was, by her conduct in trying to put the police officers as best she could off the scent, demonstrating that she was a willing and knowing party to those things being there and that she was trying to account for them. Well, it will be for you to say, but you must be satisfied, before you can convict her on either of these counts, not only that she knew or believed the goods to be stolen, but that she actively assisted her husband in keeping them there; not by just passive acquiescence in the sense of saying: 'What can I do about it?,' but in the sense of saying: 'How nice to have these things in our home, although they are stolen goods.' "

In so far as this direction suggests that the appellant would be guilty of the offence if she was merely willing for the goods to be kept and used in the house and was thinking that it was nice to have them there, although they were stolen goods, it is a misdirection. We have considered whether on that account the conviction ought to be quashed. However, the offence was established by the uncontradicted evidence of the police officer which, looked at in full, clearly shows that in order to mislead the officer who had come to take away stolen goods, she misrepresented the identity of the goods which she knew or believed to be stolen. We are satisfied that no miscarriage of justice has occurred and the appeal is accordingly dismissed.'

R v Pitchley (1973) 57 Cr App R 30 Court of Appeal (Criminal Division) (Cairns LJ, Nield and Croom-Johnson JJ)

Assisting in the retention of stolen property

Facts

The defendant was asked by his son to look after £150, which he did by placing the money in his own Post Office savings account. The defendant subsequently discovered that his son had stolen the money, but allowed the money to remain in his account until questioned by the police. The defendant was convicted of assisting in the retention of stolen property contrary to s22(1) of the Theft Act 1968, and appealed.

Held

The appeal would be dismissed.

Cairns LJ:

> 'The main point that has been taken by Mr Kalisher, who is appearing for the appellant in this Court, is that, assuming that the jury were not satisfied that the appellant received the money knowing it to have been stolen, and that is an assumption which clearly it is right to make, then there was no evidence after that, that from the time when the money was put into the savings bank, that the appellant had done any act in relation to it. His evidence was, and there is no reason to suppose that the jury did not believe it, that at the time when he put the money into the savings bank he still did not know or believe that the money had been stolen – it was only at a later stage that he did. That was on the Saturday according to his evidence, and the position was that the money had simply remained in the savings bank from the Saturday, to the Wednesday when the police approached the appellant. It is fair to say that from the moment when he was approached he displayed the utmost frankness to the extent of correcting them when they said it was £100 to £150 and telling them where the post office savings book was so that the money could be got out again and restored to its rightful owner.
>
> But the question is: Did the conduct of the appellant between the Saturday and the Wednesday amount to an assisting in the retention of his money for the benefit of his son Brian? The Court has been referred to the case of *Brown* (1969) 53 Cr App R 527, [1970] 1 QB 105 [see above].
>
> In this present case there was no question on the evidence of the appellant himself, that he was permitting the money to remain under his control in his savings bank book, and it is clear that this Court in the case of *Brown* (supra) regarded such permitting as sufficient to constitute retention within the meaning of retention. That is clear from the passage I have already read, emphasised in the next paragraph, the final paragraph of the judgment, where the Lord Chief Justice said (at p531): "It is a plain case in which the proviso should be applied. It seems to this Court that the only possible inference in these circumstances, once Holden was believed is that this man was assisting in their retention by housing the goods and providing accommodation for them, by permitting them to remain there." It is important to realise that that language was in relation to a situation where there was no evidence that anything active had been done by the appellant in relation to the goods.
>
> In the course of the argument, Nield J cited the dictionary meaning of the word "retain" – keep possession of, not lose, continue to have. In the view of this Court, that is the meaning of the word "retain" in this section. It was submitted by Mr Kalisher that, at any rate, it was ultimately for the jury to decide whether there was retention or not and that even assuming that what the appellant did was of such a character that it could constitute retention, the jury ought to have been directed that it was for them to determine as a matter of fact, whether that was so or not. The Court cannot agree with that submission. The meaning of the word "retention" in this section is a matter of law in so far as the construction of the word is necessary. It is hardly a difficult question of construction because it is an ordinary English word and in the view of this Court, it was no more necessary for the Deputy Chairman to leave to the jury the question

of whether or not what was done amounted to retention, than it would be necessary for a judge in a case where goods had been handed to a person who knew that they had been stolen for him to direct the jury it was for them to decide whether or not that constituted receiving.

We are satisfied that no complaint of the summing-up which was made can be sustained and that there is no other ground on which this verdict could be said to be unsafe or unsatisfactory. The appeal is therefore dismissed.'

R v *Pitham and Hehl* (1976) 65 Cr App R 45 Court of Appeal (Criminal Division) (Lawton and Waller LJJ and Bristow J)

Handling otherwise than in the course of stealing

Facts

The defendants had met a man named Millman at the house of another man, named McGregor, who was in prison. Millman told the defendants that McGregor's furniture was for sale, and the defendants agreed to buy it from him. Millman was convicted of theft of McGregor's furniture, and the defendants were convicted of handling stolen goods by agreeing to buy it. The defendants appealed against their convictions on the ground that the handling alleged against them had not taken place 'otherwise than in the course of stealing'.

Held

The appeal would be dismissed.

Lawton LJ:

'The third way [in which the prosecution put its case] and the one the jury in the end accepted, was that Millman was the man who had stolen the property and these two had bought from the thief Millman, knowing it to have been stolen. This third way was reflected in counts 4 and 5. Now, stated in that way, the issues would appear to be easy for a jury to understand. Mr Murray, with much ingenuity and persistence, for which he is to be congratulated, has urged upon the Court that this simple case goes to the very heart of what seems to be an academic difference of opinion between the professor of law at Nottingham University, Professor Smith, and the professor of law at Leicester University, Professor Griew, as to the construction of a few words in section 22 of the Theft Act 1968.

Section 22(1) of the Theft Act provides: "A person handles stolen goods if (otherwise than in the course of the stealing)" – I emphasise the words "otherwise than in the course of the stealing" – "knowing or believing them to be stolen goods he dishonestly receives the goods, or dishonestly undertakes or assists in their retention, removal, disposal, or realisation by or for the benefit of another person, or if he arranges to do so." Now, the two conflicting academic views can be summarised in this way. Professor Smith's view in his book on *The Theft Act 1968* (2nd ed, 1974), para. 400, seems to be that "in the course of the stealing" can be a very short time or it can be a very long period of time. Professor Griew in his book *The Law of Theft* (3rd ed, 1977) paras. 8-18, 8-19, seems to be of the opinion that, "in the course of the stealing," embraces not only the act of stealing as defined by section 1 of the Theft Act 1968, but in addition making away with the goods. In the course of expounding their differing views in their books on the Theft Act the two professors have both referred to ancient authorities. Both are of the opinion that the object of the words, "otherwise than in the course of the stealing," was to deal with the situation where two men are engaged in different capacities in a joint enterprise. In those circumstances, unless some such limiting words as those to which I have referred were included in the definition of handling, a thief could be guilty of both stealing and receiving. An illustration of the sort of problem which arises is provided by Professor Smith's reference to the old case of *Coggins* (1873) 12 Cox CC 517. In his book on the Theft Act at paragraph 400, he summarises the facts of *Coggins* (supra) in these terms: "If a servant stole money from his master's till and handed it to an accomplice in his master's shop, the accomplice was guilty of larceny and not guilty of receiving." He added another example. It was the case of *Perkins* (1852) 5 Cox CC 554. He summarises that case as follows: "Similarly, if a man committed larceny in the room in which he lodged and threw a bundle of stolen goods to an accomplice in the street, the accomplice was guilty of larceny and not guilty of receiving."

In our judgment the words to which I have referred in section 22(1), were designed to make it clear that in those sorts of situations a man could not be guilty under the Theft Act of both theft and handling. As was pointed out to Mr Murray by my brother, Bristow J, in the course of argument, the Theft Act in section 1 defines theft. It has been said in this Court more than once that the object of that definition was to make a fresh start so as to get rid of all the subtle distinctions which had arisen in the past under the old law of larceny. Subsection (1) of section 1 has a side heading, "Basic definition of theft." That definition is in these terms: "A person is guilty of theft if he dishonestly appropriates property belonging to another with the intention of permanently depriving the other of it; and 'thief' and 'steal' shall be construed accordingly." What Parliament meant by "appropriate" was defined in section 3(1): "Any assumption by a person of the rights of an owner amounts to an appropriation, and this includes, where he has come by the property (innocently or not) without stealing it, any later assumption of a right to it by keeping or dealing with it as owner."

Mr Murray's submission – a very bold one – was that the general words with which section 3(1) opens, namely, "Any assumption by a person of the rights of an owner amounts to an appropriation," are limited by the words beginning "and this includes." He submitted that those additional words bring back into the law of theft something akin to the concept of asportation, which was one of the aspects of the law of larceny which the Theft Act 1968 was intended to get rid of. According to Mr Murray, unless there is something which amounts to "coming by" the property there cannot be an appropriation. We disagree. The final words of section 3(1) are words of inclusion. The general words at the beginning of section 3(1) are wide enough to cover *any* assumption by a person of the rights of an owner.

What was the appropriation in this case? The jury found that the two appellants had handled the property *after* Millman had stolen it. That is clear from their acquittal of these two appellants on count 3 of the indictment which had charged them jointly with Millman. What had Millman done? He had assumed the rights of the owner. He had done that when he took the two appellants to 20 Parry Road, showed them the property and invited them to buy what they wanted. He was then acting as the owner. He was then, in the words of the statute, "assuming the rights of the owner." The moment he did that he appropriated McGregor's goods to himself. The appropriation was complete. After this appropriation had been completed there was no question of these two appellants taking part, in the words of section 22, in dealing with the goods "in the course of the stealing."

It follows that no problem arises in this case. It may well be that some of the situations which the two learned professors envisage and discuss in their books may have to be dealt with at some future date, but not in this case. The facts are too clear.

Mr Murray suggested the learned judge should have directed the jury in some detail about the possibility that the appropriation had not been an instantaneous appropriation, but had been one which had gone on for some time. He submitted that it might have gone on until such time as the furniture was loaded into the appellant's van. For reasons we have already given that was not a real possibility in this case. It is not part of a judge's duty to give the jury the kind of lecture on the law which may be appropriate for a professor to give a class of undergraduates. We commend the judge for not having involved himself in a detailed academic analysis of the law relating to this case when on the facts it was as clear as anything could be that either these appellants had helped Millman to steal the goods, or Millman had stolen them and got rid of them by sale to these two appellants. We can see nothing wrong in the learned judge's approach to this case and on that particular ground we affirm what he did and said.'

41 Accomplices

R v Anderson and Morris [1966] 2 QB 110 Court of Criminal Appeal (Lord Parker CJ, Edmund-Davies, Marshall, Roskill and James JJ)

Joint enterprise

Facts

Anderson and Morris agreed to attack another man. Unknown to Morris Anderson took a knife with him and stabbed the victim to death. Morris was merely standing by and did nothing at the time the victim was killed. Anderson was convicted of murder and Morris of manslaughter. Both appealed.

Held

In the light of fresh evidence a new trial was ordered for Anderson. The court accepted the submission by Counsel for the applicant that where two persons embark on a joint enterprise, each is liable for the acts done in pursuance of that joint enterprise. That liability includes liability for uncontemplated consequences that may arise from the execution of the agreed joint enterprise but where one of the parties goes beyond what has expressly or impliedly been agreed between the parties, the other party is not liable for the consequences of that unauthorized act as the chain of causation that links him to the consequences has been broken by the other party's deliberate departure from the agreement.

Conviction for manslaughter quashed.

Attorney-General's Reference (No 1 of 1975) [1975] 3 WLR 11 Court of Appeal (Criminal Division) (Lord Widgery CJ, Bristow and May JJ)

Aiding and abetting – procuring – whether motorist's offence procured by defendant

Facts

The question referred to the court was as follows:

'Whether an accused who surreptitiously laced a friend's drinks with double measures of spirits when he knew that his friend would shortly be driving his car home, as in consequence his friend drove with an excess quantity of alcohol in his body and was convicted of the offence under the Road Traffic Act 1972 s6(1) is entitled to a ruling of no case to answer on being later charged as an aider and abettor, counsellor and procurer, on the grounds that there was no shared intention between the two, that the accused did not by accompanying him or otherwise positively encourage the friend to drive, or on any other ground.'

Held

The Court of Appeal considered that there was a difference in meaning between the four words 'aid, abet, counsel or procure'. Aiding and abetting and also counselling almost inevitably involved a situation where the secondary party and the main offender are together at some stage discussing the offence which they are planning. However, the court considers that this was not necessary for the offence of procuring. To procure means to produce by endeavour. It was possible for a person to procure the commission of an offence by another even though there was no sort of conspiracy between them or even any attempt at agreement or discussion as to what form the offence should take. There had to be shown to be a cause or link between the procuring and the commission of the offence, a link which the Court of Appeal felt was satisfied on the facts of the case before them. The court therefore considered that there was a case to answer and that the accused had procured an offence contrary to s6(1) of the Road Traffic Act 1972 by supplying the alcohol.

R v *Bainbridge* [1959] 3 WLR 656 Court of Criminal Appeal (Lord Parker CJ, Byrne and Winn JJ)

Mens rea required of an accomplice

Facts
Cutting equipment left at the scene of a burglary was found to have been purchased by the appellant six weeks before the burglary took place. The appellant was charged of being an accessory before the fact to the burglary. The prosecution had contended that the appellant had bought the equipment on behalf of the burglars with full knowledge that it was to be used, if not for the particular burglary, at any rate for the purpose of breaking and entering generally. The appellant contended that although he was suspicious and thought the equipment would be used for some illegal purpose he did not know it would be used for the purpose it actually was used for. The appellant was convicted and appealed to the Court of Appeal on point of law.

Held
The court held that it was not enough to show merely that some illegal venture was intended. For example, it would not have been enough if the appellant had only known, or been suspicious, that the cutting equipment was to be used to dispose of stolen property as it was not the type of offence contemplated. However, it was unnecessary to show knowledge of the intention of others to commit that particular crime which did in fact take place.

The appeal was dismissed.

Aiding and abetting requires proof of mens rea, a positive act of assistance voluntarily done. An indifference as to the result of the crime does not automatically negative abetting.

Appeal dismissed.

R v *Bourne* (1952) 36 Cr App R 125 Court of Criminal Appeal (Lord Goddard CJ, Hilbery and Slade JJ)

Abetting without a principal offender

Facts
Bourne was charged and convicted of aiding and abetting his wife to commit buggery with a dog. The wife was not charged as a principal and it was assumed that she was forced to commit the offence and could have pleaded duress if charged. Bourne appealed against conviction.

Held
The court rejected Bourne's argument that as his wife could not have been convicted as a principal as she was acting under the duress of her husband therefore there was no crime to aid and abet. The jury accepted that the wife did not consent and assuming that she would have pleaded duress if charged the effect of such a plea would be that the wife had admitted the commission of the crime but pleaded to be

excused from punishment by reason of duress. Undoubtedly a court would have allowed a verdict of 'not guilty' to be entered. However, the effect of the plea was not to show that no offence had been committed but merely that she should be excused from punishment.

The court also rejected Bourne's argument that as there was no finding that he was present when the act was done there could be no aiding and abetting. The charge was 'you being present aided and abetted, counselled and procured ...' The jury had accepted the evidence that he caused his wife to have connection with the dog, therefore he was guilty, whether you called him an aider and abettor or an accessory or a principal in the second degree.

R v Calhaem [1985] Crim LR 303 Court of Appeal (Criminal Division) (Parker LJ, Tudor Evans J and Sir John Thompson)

Counselling – whether causal connection to offence required

Facts
The appellant was charged with murder. A third party called Zajac who had pleaded guilty to murder claimed that the appellant had hired him to kill the victim because she was jealous of the victim. Zajac claimed that he had gone to the victim's house only to act out a charade, pretending to try to kill the victim. However, when the victim had screamed Zajac had lost control and killed her. The judge directed the jury that to counsel a crime was to incite, instruct or authorise and if the killing was within the instruction or authorisation the appellant would be guilty. She was convicted and appealed on the ground that the judge had misdirected the jury.

Held
The Court of Appeal rejected the appeal and the appellant's contention that there should be a substantial link between the counselling and the death that occurred. Citing *A-G's Reference (No 1 of 1975)* the Court considered the word 'counsel' in its ordinary meaning. There was no implication that there had to be a substantial link between the instruction or authorisation and the crime. All that was required was that the offence was committed by the one counselled acting within the scope of what had been authorised.

Chan Wing-Siu & Others v *R* [1984] 3 WLR 677 Privy Council (Lords Keith, Bridge, Brandon and Templeman and Sir Robin Cooke)

Mens rea – unlawful joint enterprise – contemplation of risk of serious injury

Facts
The appellants entered the victim's house. Each apparently knew that at least one of the others carried a knife and might well use it. One stood guard over the victim's wife, the others stabbed the victim.

Held
On appeal to the Privy Council concerning the appropriate direction as to the liability of the one or ones who did not do the actual stabbing, the Privy Council held that where a person embarks upon an unlawful joint enterprise he will be liable for murder if he foresaw that there was a possible risk that it would result in the infliction of really serious bodily harm, unless that risk was so remote that it would be disregarded. Since the carrying of knives did not make the risk so remote, each was guilty of murder even though it could not be proved which did the stabbing.

R v *Clarkson* [1971] 1 WLR 1402 Courts-Martial Appeal Court (Megaw LJ, Geoffrey Lane and Kilner-Brown JJ)

Aiding and abetting – presence insufficient

Facts
The appellants, who were soldiers, heard a disturbance from an adjoining room. They went to look in the room and found a girl being raped by at least three soldiers. The appellants remained there while the girl was raped but there was no evidence that the appellants had done any positive act to assist. They were charged with aiding and abetting rape. They appealed to the Court-Martial Appeal Court.

Held
It is not enough that the continuing, non-accidental presence of the accused has in fact given encouragement to the principal offenders. It must be shown that the accused intended to give encouragement and also did give encouragement in fact.

Appeals allowed.

R v *Cogan and Leak* [1976] QB 217 Court of Appeal (Criminal Division) (Lawton and James LJJ and Bristow J)

Aiding and abetting – whether procurer committing an offence

Facts
Leak invited Cogan to have sexual intercourse with his wife. Cogan gave evidence that he thought the wife had consented even though the jury found that she had not. Cogan was charged and convicted of rape, the trial judge having directed the jury that Cogan's mistake had to be reasonable. However, the jury stated that Cogan had believed the wife was consenting even though he had no evidence for such a belief. Leak was charged and convicted of aiding and abetting the rape by Cogan.

They appealed to the Court of Appeal.

Held
The Court of Appeal allowed Cogan's appeal applying the principle stated by the House of Lords in *Director of Public Prosecutions* v *Morgan* that an honest albeit unreasonable mistake afforded a defence. However, Leak's appeal against conviction was dismissed. Leak's counsel contended that as Cogan had been acquitted of rape there was no offence that Leak could have aided and abetted.

Lawton LJ:

> 'The only case which Counsel for Leak submitted had a direct bearing on the problem of Leak's guilt was *Walters* v *Lunt*. In that case the respondent had been charged under the Larceny Act 1916 s33 (1) with receiving from a child aged 7 years certain articles knowing them to have been stolen. In 1951 a child under 8 years was deemed in law to be incapable of committing a crime; it followed that at the time of receipt by the respondents the articles had not been stolen and that the charge had not been proved. The case is very different from this because here one fact is clear – the wife had been raped. Cogan had had sexual intercourse with her without her consent. The fact that Cogan was innocent of rape because he believed that she was consenting does not affect the position that she was raped ...
>
> In the language of the law the act of sexual intercourse without the wife's consent was the actus reus; it had been procured by Leak who had the appropriate mens rea, namely his intention that Cogan should have sexual intercourse with her without her consent. In our judgment it is irrelevant that the man whom

Leak had procured to do the physical act itself did not intend to have sexual intercourse with the wife without her consent. Leak was using him as a means to procure a criminal purpose ...

In our judgment he could have been indicted as a principal offender. It would have been no defence for him to submit that if Cogan was an "innocent" agent he was necessarily in the old terminology of the law a "principal in the first degree", which was legally impossible as a man cannot rape his own wife during cohabitation. The law no longer concerns itself with niceties of degrees in participation in crime; but even if it did, Leak would still be guilty. The reason a man cannot by his own physical act rape his wife during cohabitation is because the law presumes a consent from the marriage ceremony: see Hale (Pleas of the Crown). There is no such presumption when a man procures a drunken friend to do the physical act for him ...

Had Leak been indicted as a principal offender the case against him would have been clear beyond argument. Should he be allowed to go free because he was charged with "being aider and abettor to the same offence"? If we are right in our opinion that the wife had been raped (and no one outside a court of law would say that she had not been), then the particulars of the offence accurately stated what Leak had done, namely he had procured Cogan to commit the offence. This would suffice to uphold the conviction. We would prefer, however, to uphold it on a wider basis. In our judgment conviction should not be upset because of mere technicalities of pleading in an indictment. Leak knew what the case against him was and the facts in support of that case were proved ...'

By his written statement Leak virtually admitted what he had done. As Judge Chapman said in *R v Humphreys & Turner*

'It would be anomalous if a person who admitted to a substantial part of the perpetration of a misdemeanour as aider and abettor could not be convicted on his own admission merely because the person alleged to have been aided and abetted was not or could not be convicted.'

Cogan's appeal against conviction allowed.

Leak's appeal against conviction dismissed.

R v Coney (1882) 8 QBD 534 Court for Crown Cases Reserved (Cave J)

Actus reus of the offence

Facts
The defendant, with one other, stood by and watched an illegal prize fight. He was charged with aiding and abetting. He was convicted but the Chairman of the Berkshire Quarter Sessions reserved a case for the opinion of the Court for Crown Cases Reserved.

Held
That although intentional presence is prima facie evidence of aiding and abetting there has to be some participation in the act. A person does not become an aider and abettor merely because he does not try to prevent the felony.

Appeal allowed.

Director of Public Prosecutions for Northern Ireland v *Maxwell* [1978] 1 WLR 1350 House of Lords (Viscount Dilhorne, Lords Hailsham, Edmund-Davies, Fraser and Scarman)

Aiding and abetting – mens rea – no knowledge of form of attack

Facts
The appellant was involved in a terrorist operation as the driver of a car which was used by others to get to a place where they planted a bomb. The appellant was charged as a principal offender with offences contrary to the Explosive Substances Act 1883. He was charged as a principal even though there was no attempt by the prosecution to show that he was actually present when the bomb was placed or that he ever had it in his possession or under his control. The appellant was convicted at first instance and his appeal to the Court of Appeal of Northern Ireland was dismissed. He appealed to the House of Lords.

Held
There was nothing wrong with the form of the indictment against the accused since by statute aiders and abettors can be charged as principals. However, where there was a case of aiding and abetting the particulars of the indictment should make very clear the real nature of the case alleged against the accused. However, the fact that the accused did not know the particular crime intended was immaterial providing that the defendant had within his contemplation crimes of the type which were committed by the principal.

Hui Chi-ming v *R* [1991] 3 WLR 495 Privy Council (Lord Bridge of Harwich, Lord Oliver of Aylmerton, Lord Goff of Chieveley, Lord Jauncey of Tullichettle and Lord Lowry)

Joint unlawful enterprise – joint attack

Facts
After hearing from his girlfriend that, at her brother's instigation, Ah Hung had tried to intimidate her into giving him up, Ah Po told his friends that his girlfriend had been bullied and he asked them to go to a certain estate to look for Ah Hung and 'for someone to hit'. Ah Po, carrying a length of waterpipe, and two other youths, set off in one taxi; the appellant and two other friends followed in another. The group (or some of them) attacked someone other than Ah Hung and the man died from his injuries. No witness saw the appellant speak to anyone or strike a blow, or play any particular part in the assault. Although Ah Po had been acquitted of murder and convicted of manslaughter, the appellant was convicted of murder and he appealed against that decision on the ground, inter alia, that the trial judge had misdirected the jury as to the participation of an accomplice in a common unlawful enterprise. He had told the jury, inter alia: '(10) The accused would also be guilty if he lent himself to a criminal enterprise knowing that a potentially lethal weapon was being carried by one of his companions, and in the event it is in fact used by one of his partners with an intent sufficient for murder. Then he too will be guilty of that offence if your are sure beyond reasonable doubt that the accused contemplated that in the carrying out of the common unlawful purpose, one of his partners in the enterprise might use a lethal weapon with the intention of at least causing really serious bodily harm. it is what the accused in fact contemplated that matters.'

Held
The appeal would be dismissed.

Lord Lowry:

'The principle enunciated in [*Chan Wing-siu* v *R* [1984] 3 All ER 877] has since been clearly stated by Lord Lane CJ in the Court of Appeal, Criminal Division, in *R* v *Ward* (1987) 85 Cr App R 71 and *R* v *Slack* [1989] 3 All ER 90, in both of which *Chan*'s case was expressly approved and applied, and most recently in *R v Hyde* [1990] 3 All ER 892, which also applied *Chan*'s case. Having referred to *R v Slack* Lord Lane CJ said in *R v Hyde* [1990] 3 All ER 892 at 895–896: [see *R v Hyde*, above].

That passage from the judgment in *R v Hyde* correctly states, in their Lordships' opinion, the law applicable to a joint enterprise of the kind described, which results in the commission of murder by the principal as an incident of the joint enterprise.

Against that background their Lordships consider the [appellant's] two arguments ... The first can be readily disposed of on the facts by pointing out that Ah Po's arming himself with the waterpipe before setting out showed unequivocally what he *did* contemplate at that stage, since the connection between the argument and the facts to which it was directed was tenuous, to say the least.

Counsel's submission, however, was based on the passage ... from *Johns v R* (1980) 143 CLR 108 at 130–131. The issue in that case was whether an accessory before the fact is, like a principal in the second degree, responsible for an act constituting the offence charged if such act was contemplated as a *possible* incident of the common purpose, or whether it has to be established as a *likely* or *probable* consequence of the way in which the crime was to be committed. The court unanimously accepted the former alternative. But, in the course of their judgment, Mason, Murphy and Wilson JJ stated the law in the manner already quoted, requiring the act to have been within the contemplation of both the principal and the accessory as an act which might be done in the course of carrying out the primary criminal intention. It is on the basis of that passage that the appellant contends that the secondary party cannot be liable unless the relevant act was within the contemplation of both the principal and the secondary party.

Johns v R is a leading case on the law relating to accessories. It was specifically relied on by Sir Robin Cooke in *Chan*'s case, in which the same central issue fell to be considered. It is, however, plain that, in the passage upon which the appellant relies, attention was being concentrated on those cases in which the question is whether the act of the principal falls within the common purpose of the parties ...

In such a case the contemplation of both parties will be relevant. But, as appears from Sir Robin Cooke's judgment in *Chan*'s case (and as was recognised by Lord Lane CJ in *R v Hyde*, departing in this respect from some of the observations contained in the earlier judgments in the *Slack* and *Wakely* cases), the secondary party may be liable simply by reason of his participating in the joint enterprise with foresight that the principal may commit the relevant act as part of the joint enterprise ...

In practice, of course, in most cases the contemplation of both the primary and the secondary party is likely to be the same; if there is an alleged difference, it will arise where the secondary party asserts in his defence that he did not have in contemplation the act which was in the contemplation of the principal. But their Lordships are unable to accept that in every case the relevant act must be shown to have been in the contemplation of *both* parties before the secondary party can be proved guilty.

Let it be supposed that two men embark on a robbery. One (the principal) to the knowledge of the other (the accessory) is carrying a gun. The accessory contemplates that the principal may use the gun to wound or kill if resistance is met with or the pair are detected at their work but, although the gun is loaded, the only use initially contemplated by the principal is for the purpose of causing fear, by pointing the gun or even by discharging it, with a view to overcoming resistance or evading capture. Then at the scene the principal changes his mind, perhaps through panic or because to fire for effect offers the only chance of escape, and shoots the victim dead. His act is clearly an incident of the unlawful enterprise and the possibility of its occurrence as such was contemplated by the accomplice. According to what was said in *Chan*'s case the accomplice, as well as the principal, would be guilty of murder. Their Lordships have to say that, having regard to what is said in *Chan*'s case and the cases which applied it, they do not consider the prior contemplation of the principal to be a necessary additional ingredient. In their opinion the judge had no duty to direct the jury to that effect ... in his summing up.

In none of the cases reviewed, including the case under appeal, was the prior contemplation of the principal a live issue. But it must be recognised that to hold the accomplice to be guilty in the example their Lordships have posed is consistent with the *Chan* and *Hyde* cases.

Their Lordships appreciate that the hypothetical example they have given is largely theoretical. Rarely, if ever, will a case arise in which the accessory, but not the principal, contemplates the possibility of a further relevant offence and, if the facts appeared to support such a hypothesis, the defence would no doubt seize the opportunity to contend that the accomplice himself had not been proved to have contemplated something which was not in the mind of the principal. Alternatively, he might contend that the principal's further act had gone beyond the contemplated area of guilty conduct, with the result that the accessory to the planned offence was not criminally liable for the new offence. In truth, the point taken by the appellant was academic; but, for the reasons they have given, their Lordships reject it as unsound.

The appellant's second point relies on Sir Robin Cooke's use of the word "authorisation" as a synonym for contemplation in the passage already cited from his judgment. Their Lordships consider that Sir Robin Cooke used this word – and in that regard they do not differ from counsel – to emphasise the fact that mere foresight is not enough: the accessory, in order to be guilty, must have foreseen the relevant offence which the principal may commit as a possible incident of the common unlawful enterprise and must, with such foresight, still have participated in the enterprise. The word "authorisation" explains what is meant by contemplation, but does not add a new ingredient. That this is so is manifest from Sir Robin Cooke's pithy conclusion …:"The criminal culpability lies in participating in the venture with that foresight."

Their Lordships are satisfied that the trial judge accurately conveyed that idea to the jury by para (10) of his directions.

This was a strong case of at least tacit agreement that Ah Hung should be attacked accompanied by foresight, as admitted by the appellant, that a very serious assault might occur, even if that very serious assault had not been planned from the beginning. It is, moreover, easier to prove against an accomplice that he contemplated and by his participation accepted the use of extra force in the execution of the planned assault than it normally would be to show contemplation and acceptance of a new offence, such as murder added to burglary.

Their Lordships therefore reject all the criticisms of the judge's directions to the jury on joint enterprise.'

R v *Hyde* [1990] 3 WLR 1115 Court of Appeal (Lord Lane CJ, Rose and Tucker JJ)

Joint unlawful enterprise – direction to jury

Facts
Outside a public house, a man sustained a violent blow to the forehead and he died 73 days later. The three appellants were charged with murder and the prosecution alleged that they had carried out a joint attack on the victim and were all equally responsible for his death, even though it was not possible to say who had actually struck the fatal blow or blows; furthermore, that their intention had been to cause serious injury, or that each knew that such was the intention of the others when he took part. All three appellants gave evidence denying that there was any joint enterprise or any intent to do the victim serious harm, but they were convicted of murder and against those convictions they now appealed contending, inter alia, that the judge had misdirected the jury on the law of joint enterprise.

Held
The appeals would be dismissed.

Lord Lane CJ:

'The passages in the summing up of which complaint is made are these:

"As I say ordinarily speaking if he does something which is beyond the scope of the agreement, that is as you might say the end of the agreement. But, what if the others anticipated that he might do some such thing? and here we have to apply common sense. Fights do get out of hand and escalate. A man who starts by punching may get excited and decide to kick. If there was a tacit agreement to punch and kick, a man who is kicking may decide to give a kick like that which was allegedly given by Collins and which has been described as a place-kick or a penalty kick, a description which if the basic facts are right is not a bad description of the kick. If either of the other two, and you have to consider the case of each of them separately, foresaw and contemplated a real possibility that one of his fellows might in the excitement of the moment go beyond the actual plan and intend to do and do grievous bodily harm, then you have to consider whether that man, the one who had the foresight, did not in truth intend that result himself."

The judge then went on to explain to the jury the distinction which may, in some cases, exist between what a man desires should happen and what a man intends should happen. He explained to the jury that foresight that something will happen is not necessarily the same as an intention that it should happen, though it may be powerful evidence of such intention. The judge concluded this part of his summing up with the following words:

> "We may summarise it shortly by saying that if all three intended to do grievous bodily harm, then that is that, they are all guilty of murder. If they did not but one of them decided to do it, then if either of the others can be shown to have had the same intention, inasmuch as he foresaw the real possibility that that might be the result of the fight which he was putting in train, then he too shares in the responsibility as in common sense he must."

The specific complaints as set out in the notice of appeal are as follows. (1) The judge, in the circumstances of the case, erred in directing the jury on foreseeability, such a direction being unnecessary and confusing. (2) Alternatively, the judge erred in directing the jury that the defendant's foresight of the state of mind of another defendant was a relevant consideration in determining whether the defendant having that foresight had the intention to do grievous bodily harm. (3) Alternatively, the judge's direction on foreseeability did not sufficiently distinguish between foreseeability and intention and/or did not sufficiently underline the necessity for the prosecution to prove the specific intent required for the offence of murder.

The judgment of this court in *R v Slack* [1989] 2 WLR 513 was not delivered until some four months after the conclusion of the hearing of the instant case. Consequently the judge here did not have before him the distinction which we endeavoured to draw in *R v Slack* between the mental element required to be proved vis-à-vis the secondary party (hereinafter called 'B') and that required in the case of the principal party, the actual killer (hereinafter called 'A'). In the passages we have cited from the summing up of which complaint is made, the judge was endeavouring to apply the principles which were, prior to *R v Slack*, thought to apply to cases of joint enterprise.

The question is whether the directions in the present case were insufficient to comply with the law as it now stands.

There are, broadly speaking, two main types of joint enterprise cases where death results to the victim. The first is where the primary object of the participants is to do some kind of physical injury to the victim. The second is where the primary object is not to cause physical injury to any victim but, for example, to commit burglary. The latter type of case may pose more complicated questions than the former, but the principle in each is the same. A must be proved to have intended to kill or to do serious bodily harm at the time he killed. As was pointed out in *R v Slack*, B, to be guilty, must be proved to have lent himself to a criminal enterprise involving the infliction of serious harm or death, or to have had an express or tacit understanding with A that such harm or death should, if necessary, be inflicted.

We were there endeavouring, respectfully, to follow the principles enunciated by Sir Robin Cooke in *Chan Wing-siu v R* [1984] 3 WLR 677.

> "The case must depend rather on the wider principle whereby a second party is criminally liable for acts by the primary offender of a type which the former foresees but does not necessarily intend. That there is such a principle is not in doubt. It turns on contemplation or, putting the same idea in other words, authorisation, which may be express but is more usually implied. It meets the case of a crime foreseen as a possible incident of the common unlawful enterprise. The criminal culpability lies in participating in the venture with that foresight."

It has been pointed out by Professor Smith, in his commentary on *R v Wakely* [1990] Crim LR 119 at 120–121, that in the judgments in *R v Slack* and also in *R v Wakely* itself, to both of which I was a party, insufficient attention was paid by the court to the distinction between on the one hand tacit agreement by B that A should use violence, and on the other hand a realisation by B that A, the principal party, may use violence despite B's refusal to authorise or agree to its use. Indeed in *R* v *Wakely* we went so far as to say:

> "The suggestion that a mere foresight of the real or definite possibility of violence being used is sufficient to constitute the mental element of murder is prima facie, academically speaking at least, not sufficient."

On reconsideration, that passage is not in accordance with the principles set out by Sir Robin Cooke which we were endeavouring to follow and was wrong, or at least misleading. If B realises (without agreeing to such conduct being used) that A may kill or intentionally inflict serious injury, but nevertheless continues to participate with A in the venture, that will amount to a sufficient mental element for B to be guilty of murder if A, with the requisite intent, kills in the course of the venture. As Professor Smith points out, B has in those circumstances lent himself to the enterprise and by so doing he has given assistance and encouragement to A in carrying out an enterprise which B realises may involve murder.

That being the case it seems to us that the judge was correct when he directed the jury in the terms of those passages of the summing up which we have already quoted. It may be that a simple direction on the basis of *R* v *Anderson and Morris* [1966] 2 WLR 1195 would, in the circumstances of this case, have been enough, but the direction given was sufficiently clear and the outcome scarcely surprising.'

R v *Jefferson* [1994] 1 All ER 270 Court of Appeal (Watkins LJ, Auld and Scott Baker JJ)

Aiding and abetting a possibility?

Facts
Following widespread disorder after a televised football match, charges were brought under ss1 (riot) and 2 (violent disorder) of the Public Order Act 1986. The question arose, amongst others, as to whether aiding and abetting by encouragement of such an offence could itself be an offence under that Act.

Held
The answer was in the affirmative.

Auld J:

> 'In our judgment, the offences created by the 1986 Act may be committed by aiders and abettors as well as by principals. As counsel for the Crown pointed out, the question is not whether s6 of the 1986 Act excludes s8 of the [Accessories and Abettors Act] 1861, and it is only in part one of construction. An aider and abettor of an offence is a common law notion, not a creation of statute. It is of general application to all offences, whether at common law or of statutory creation, unless expressly excluded by statute. Section 8 of the 1861 Act is merely a deeming provision as to how aiders and abettors are to be dealt with at trial. The proper approach is to consider whether there is anything in the 1986 Act which excludes, in relation to the public order offences created by it, the general common law principle of aiding and abetting.
>
> In our view, s6 is concerned only with identifying, in statutory form, the requisite mens rea for each of the offences provided for in ss1 to 5. It does not exclude or cut down in relation to any of those offences the liability of an aider and abettor who is aware of and party to the requisite intent of the principal offender.'

Johnson v *Youden* [1950] 1 KB 544 King's Bench Division (Lord Goddard CJ, Humphreys and Lynskey JJ)

Mens rea needed by accomplices to strict liability offences

Facts
The respondents who were all partners in a firm of solicitors were charged with aiding and abetting a builder with an offence under s7(1) of the Building Materials and Housing Act 1945 which provided that it would be an offence for a builder to sell a house in excess of a price fixed by the local authority. The Justices dismissed the information against the respondents. The Prosecutor appealed by way of a case stated.

Held
The justices had found that two of the respondents had never known of the receipt by the builder of the extra money and therefore the Justices had been correct in dismissing the information against those two. However, the third respondent had known the builder was getting the extra payment even though he did not recognize it to be an illegal payment and therefore, as ignorance of the law is no defence, he was clearly aiding and abetting the builder. The appeal of the prosecutor was allowed in relation to the third respondent.

National Coal Board v *Gamble* [1958] 3 WLR 434 Queen's Bench Division (Gamble J)

Aiding and abetting – mens rea

Facts
The National Coal Board had sold a bulk quantity of coal. A lorry which had come to fetch the coal was found by the weighbridge operator to be overloaded. The operator's task was merely to hand over a ticket and record the amount of coal taken and he allowed the lorry to leave. The lorry driver drove an overweight lorry on the public road, an offence contrary to the Motor Vehicles (Construction and Use) Regulations 1955 and the National Coal Board was charged with aiding and abetting the offence. They were convicted at first instance and appealed to the Divisional Court.

Held
The court drew a distinction between a situation where property in the coal had passed to the purchasers before the offence was committed, in which case there was nothing that the Coal Board could have done, and the situation where property had not passed in which case they sold the coal with knowledge that an offence was going to be committed. On the facts before them the court found that the property had not passed until after the goods were weighed and therefore it was open to the operator to refuse to transfer the load.

R v *Richards* [1973] 3 WLR 888 Court of Appeal (Criminal Division) (James LJ, Kilner Brown and Boreham JJ)

Aiding and abetting – counselling and procuring – procurer cannot be guilty of graver offence than that committed

Facts
The appellant had arranged with the two co-accused that they should attack her husband, the appellant hoping that if he were injured the care she could give him would improve their deteriorating marriage. The plan was carried out and the husband sustained injuries to his head. The appellant and the co-accused were charged with offences contrary to s18 and s20 of the Offences Against the Person Act 1861. The appellant was convicted of the more serious offence under s18 and the co-accused were convicted under s20 but acquitted under s18.

The appellant appealed.

Held

James LJ:

'The appellant was not present at the time when the offence occurred and therefore she was not what could be described as an abettor of those who actually did the acts. It was not correct to say that "that which was done with the intention of the appellant who was not present at the time". Only one offence was committed and that was the offence of unlawful wounding under s20 Offences Against the Person Act 1861 and any person who requested that offence to be committed cannot be guilty of a graver offence than that which was in fact committed.'

Conviction quashed and a verdict of guilty of unlawful wounding substituted.

R v *Roberts* [1993] 1 All ER 583 Court of Appeal (Criminal Division) (Lord Taylor of Gosforth CJ, Hutchinson and Holland JJ)

Murder – joint unlawful enterprise

Facts

The appellant and one Gray had gone to the home of an elderly recluse, intending to rob him. In the course of the robbery the recluse was beaten to death. The appellant and Gray blamed each other. Both were convicted of robbery and murder: the appellant appealed against his conviction of murder.

Held

The appeal would be dismissed.

Lord Taylor of Gosforth CJ:

'Reference was made to *Chan Wing-siu* v *R* [1984] 3 All ER 877 in *R* v *Slack* [1989] 3 All ER 90. There the appellant and B burgled a house. B stabbed the elderly householder with a knife carried and handed to him by the appellant. The trial judge posed the question to the jury concerning the appellant:

"Did [he] contemplate and foresee that Buick *might* kill or cause grievous bodily harm to Mrs Crowder as part of their joint enterprise and did she die as a result of such conduct by Buick? If so it is open to you to find that he so intended and that he is guilty of murder." (The judge's emphasis.)

That direction was approved by this court. In *R* v *Hyde* [1990] 3 All ER 892, the three appellants were convicted of murder. They had not carried weapons, but they had jointly set out to attack the victim, who died from injuries inflicted by kicking. In dismissing the appeals Lord Lane CJ said ([1990] 3 All ER 892 at 895):

"There are, broadly speaking, two main types of joint enterprise cases where death results to the victim. The first is where the primary object of the participants is to do some kind of physical injury to the victim. The second is where the primary object is not to cause physical injury to any victim but, for example, to commit burglary. The victim is assaulted and killed as a (possibly unwelcome) incident of the burglary. The latter type of case may pose more complicated questions than the former, but the principle in each is the same."

After referring to *Chan Wing-siu* v *R*, *R* v *Slack*, *R* v *Wakely* [1990] Crim LR 119 and observations by Professor Smith on the latter two cases, Lord Lane CJ went on to state the law in the passage read and repeated to the jury by the trial judge in the present case …

In *Hui Chi-ming* v *R* [1991] 3 All ER 897, another case from Hong Kong concerning joint enterprise, Lord Lowry giving the advice of the Privy Council, quoted with approval an extensive part of Lord Lane CJ's judgment in *R* v *Hyde*, culminating with the passage cited by the trial judge in the present case. Lord Lowry went on:

"That passage from the judgment in *R* v *Hyde* correctly states, in their Lordships' opinion, the law applicable to a joint enterprise of the kind described, which results in the commission of murder by the principal as an incident of the joint enterprise."

In our judgment the principle stated by Lord Lane CJ in *R* v *Hyde* is of general application, whether weapons are carried or not and (as Lord Lane CJ expressly said) whether the object of the enterprise be to cause physical injury or to do some other unlawful act, eg burglary or robbery. True, it will be easier for the Crown to prove that B participated in the venture realising that A might wound with murderous intent if weapons are carried or if the object is to attack the victim or both. But that is purely an evidential difference, not a difference in principle.

With regard to the passage relied upon in *Chan Wing-siu* v *R* we are doubtful whether the defendant B, who fleetingly thinks of the risk of A using violence with murderous intent in the course of a joint enterprise only to dismiss it from his mind and goes on to lend himself to the venture, can truly be said, at the time when he so lends himself, to "foresee" or "realise" that A might commit murder. In such a case B can hardly have such foresight or realisation at the time he lends himself to the venture because he has banished the risk from his mind. The words "realise" and "realisation" used by Lord Lane CJ and by the trial judge here aptly described the test, because to realise something may happen is surely to contemplate it as a real not fanciful possibility. Accordingly, we are inclined to the view that seeking to distinguish between a fleeting but rejected consideration of a risk and a continuing realisation of a real risk will, in most cases, be unnecessary. It would also over-complicate directions to juries and possibly lead to confusion.

However, even accepting that it may be necessary or desirable in some cases, due to possible remoteness of the risk, for the judge to give the jury more help, we do not think the present case fell into that category. This was not, to take an extreme example, a case of burglars entering in the erroneous belief that the householder was on holiday and one of them encountering and killing the householder. Here, the appellant knew the plan was to rob an old man in his cottage. He consistently conceded in evidence that he knew the victim was unlikely to yield up his money or goods without resistance. The nub of the case was therefore not whether the appellant realised force might be used but whether he realised only that some physical harm might be done or that really serious injury might be inflicted. As to that, the learned judge gave the clearest possible directions of law to the jury both at the beginning of his summing up and after their question.'

R v *Rook* [1993] 1 WLR 1005 Court of Appeal (Criminal Division) (Lloyd LJ, Potter and Buckley JJ)

Joint enterprise – steps necessary for effective withdrawal

Facts
The appellant was one of four men accused of murder. He had taken an active part in planning the murder, but then stalled his co-defendants. He did not tell them that he did not want the killing to proceed, nor did he do anything to stop them. On the day appointed for the killing, the appellant failed to turn up at the appointed place. He was convicted of murder and appealed on the grounds that the trial judge had not directed the jury correctly on the mental element to be proved in respect of an accomplice to murder who assists prior to the commission of the offence, rather than at the scene of the crime, and that the trial judge had not directed the jury correctly on the issue of withdrawal from the common design.

Held
The appeal would be dismissed. On the issue of the mental element of those who assist in murder, otherwise than at the scene of the crime, Lloyd LJ observed:

'... it is not necessary for the prosecution to show that the secondary party intended the victim to be killed, or to suffer serious injury. It is enough that he should have foreseen the event, as a real or substantial risk

'... We see no reason why the same reasoning should not apply in the case of a secondary party who lends assistance or encouragement before the commission of the crime ... It follows that it is no defence to a secondary party to say that he did not intend the victim to be killed, or suffer serious harm, if he contemplated or foresaw the event as a real or serious risk.'

The appellant's failure to attend at the scene of the crime could not of itself amount to an effective withdrawal from the common design. As a minimum he must communicate his intention to withdraw to the other parties. Citing McDermott J in *Eldredge* v *United States* (1932) 62 F 2d 449, 451, Lloyd LJ agreed with the view that 'A declared intent to withdraw from a conspiracy to dynamite a building is not enough, if the fuse has been set; D must step on the fuse', save only that his Lordship thought that it would be enough that the defendant should have done his best to step on the fuse.

R v *Slack* [1989] 3 WLR 513 Court of Appeal (Criminal Division) (Lord Lane CJ, Kennedy and Hutchison JJ)

Murder – joint enterprise – offence in contemplation

Facts
Believing that she (Mrs Crowder) kept money in her flat and intending to rob her, the appellant and one Buick went to the elderly widow's home. The evidence indicated that the women's throat had been cut in the course of the enterprise and that the appellant had told the police that he had responded to Buick's request to 'pass us a knife'. In relation to a charge of murder, the judge had given the jury written directions, one of which was: 'Did the accused contemplate and foresee that Buick might kill or cause grievous bodily harm to Mrs Crowder as part of their joint enterprise and did she die as a result of such conduct by Buick? If so it is open to you to find that he so intended and that he is guilty of murder.' On appeal against conviction of murder, the appellant contended that this direction wrongly equated foresight and contemplation with intent.

Held
The appeal would be dismissed.

Lord Lane CJ:

'Some confusion has arisen as to the proper direction to be given to a jury in these circumstances. That seems to be partly due to some of the observations of the Judicial Committee of the Privy Council in *Chan Wing-Siu* v *R* [1984] 3 WLR 677. There three assailants armed with knives burst into the flat of a prostitute, intent it seems on robbery. One of them murdered the prostitute's husband. It could scarcely be doubted that there was a joint agreement to kill or inflict serious injury if necessary. The trial judge's direction in that case, so far as it is relevant, was as follows:

"You may convict ... of murder if you come to the conclusion ... that the accused contemplated that either of his companions might use a knife to cause bodily harm on one ... of the occupants ..."

In upholding the conviction Sir Robin Cooke, in the course of delivering the judgment of the Board, said:

"The case must depend rather on the wider principle whereby a secondary party is criminally liable for acts by the primary offender of a type which the former foresees but does not necessarily intend. That there is such a principle is not in doubt. It turns on contemplation or, putting the same idea in other words, authorisation, which may be express but is more usually implied. It meets the case of a crime foreseen as a possible incident of the common unlawful enterprise. The criminal culpability lies in participating in the venture with that foresight."

Their Lordships expressly adopted the principle enunciated by the five-judge court in *R v Anderson and Morris* [1966] 2 WLR 1195 where Lord Parker CJ, delivering the judgment of the court, said:

" ... where two persons embark on a joint enterprise ... that includes liability for unusual consequences if they arise from the execution of the agreed joint enterprise but (and this is the crux of the matter) ... if one of the adventurers goes beyond what has been tacitly agreed as part of the common enterprise, his co-adventurer is not liable for the consequences of that unauthorised act. Finally ... it is for the jury in every case to decide whether what was done was part of the joint enterprise, or went beyond it and was in fact an act unauthorised by that joint enterprise."

The Judicial Committee seems primarily to have been concerned with the problem posed by a conditional agreement, eg "We do not want to kill or seriously injure, but if necessary we will."

Chan Wing-Siu v R was considered and approved by this court in *R v Ward* (1986) 85 Cr App R 71 ... This court in *R v Ward* reiterated the passage from *R v Anderson and Morris* cited above ...

As appears from the cases we have cited, the direction may be in a variety of different forms. Provided that it is made clear to the jury that for B to be guilty he must be proved to have lent himself to a criminal enterprise involving the infliction, if necessary, of serious harm or death or to have had an express or tacit understanding with A that such harm or death should, if necessary, be inflicted, the precise form of words in which the jury are directed is not important. As Sir Robin Cooke observed in *Chan Wing-siu v R*:

"No one formula is exclusively preferable; indeed it may be advantageous in a summing up to use more than one. For the question is not of semantics."

The principle was expressed authoritatively by the House of Lords in *DPP for Northern Ireland v Maxwell* [1978] 1 WLR 1350 ...

Lowry LCJ, whose judgment in the Northern Ireland Court of Criminal Appeal was upheld by the House of Lords, said:

"The relevant crime must be within the contemplation of the accomplice and only exceptionally would evidence be found to support the allegation that the accomplice had given the principal a completely blank cheque."

Lord Scarman, having cited with approval that final sentence, went on:

"The principle thus formulated has great merit. It directs attention to the state of mind of the accused: not what he ought to have in contemplation, but what he did have. It avoids definition and classification, while ensuring that a man will not be convicted of aiding and abetting any offence his principal may commit, but only one which is within his contemplation. He may have in contemplation only one offence, or several; and the several which he contemplates he may see as alternatives. An accessory who leaves it to his principal to choose is liable, provided always the choice is made from the range of offences from which the accessory contemplates the choice will be made."

In our judgment the ... question posed by the judge in the instant case in his written directions to the jury was in accordance with the principles we have endeavoured to express. The question made it clear to the jury that the appellant must have at least tacitly agreed that, if necessary, serious harm should be done to Mrs Crowder, or that he lent himself to the infliction of such harm. There was ample evidence before the jury on which they could come to the conclusion that the prosecution had satisfied them so as to feel sure on these matters so far as the appellant was concerned.'

R v Smith [1988] Crim LR 616 Court of Appeal (Criminal Division) (Russell LJ, Leonard and Pill JJ)

Causing grievous bodily harm with intent – joint enterprise

Facts
The victim (who died after the appellant's trial) and his friend were attacked – twice – by the appellant

and his co-defendants because they believed them to be rival football supporters. During the second attack they were kicked as they lay on the ground. The appellant admitted to the police that he had kicked a man lying on the ground and his description of that man matched the victim. At the trial, the prosecution relied upon the appellant's involvement in a joint enterprise with his co-defendants rather than upon direct evidence of physical violence by the appellant. The judge directed the jury that if two persons agree to do some harm but it was no part of the agreement to do really serious bodily harm and one person attacks the victim intending and causing really serious bodily harm, the second person is guilty of causing grievous bodily harm with intent even though he did not himself intend that his partner should cause the victim really serious bodily harm, if he could and did foresee that in the course of the agreed attack there was a real risk that his partner might attack one of the victims viciously with the intention of causing him really serious bodily harm. The appellant appealed against conviction of causing grievous bodily harm with intent on the ground that the judge's directions erred in that (1) it was left open to the jury to convict even if the co-defendant acted outside the scope of the agreement; (2) the concept of foresight was equated with the concept of intent; (3) the jury could have convicted even though there was no intent demonstrated on the part of the appellant; (4) the case was regarded as one which could be equated with the Privy Council decision in *Chang Wing-siu* [1984] 3 WLR 677.

Held
The appeal would be allowed and the conviction quashed.

The court bore in mind, inter alia, the decision in *Anderson* v *Morris* [1966] 50 Cr App R 216. The present case concerned a specific intent and it was incumbent upon the judge to direct in the plainest terms that the appellant could only be convicted if the jury were sure that he had the requisite intent to cause grievous bodily harm and that the foresight the judge referred to was not of itself to be regarded as an intent, though it could properly be regarded as evidence supporting the existence of the intent necessary to establish the offence. The Court agreed that the present case was not to be equated with *Chang Wing Siu*, above. The court regarded it as impossible to substitute a verdict on the lesser count of inflicting grievous bodily harm because of the judge's direction that the appellant could be convicted of that offence even though he did not personally intend that the victim should suffer any physical injury whatsoever, provided that he foresaw a real risk of the co-defendant causing some physical harm in the course of carrying out their agreement to attack the victim.

R v *Whitefield* [1984] Crim LR 97 Court of Appeal (Criminal Division) (Dunn LJ, Bristow J and Sir John Thompson)

Agreement to take part in burglary – whether notice of withdrawal sufficient

Facts
The appellant admitted discussing the possibility of committing a burglary of a flat with a third party. He later decided not to take part and informed the other of his withdrawal. The burglary took place and the defendant who admitted his original involvement was charged with burglary. He was convicted after the trial judge ruled that the appellant's communication of withdrawal was not enough to provide a defence.

Held
Applying *Becerra* [1975] and *Grundy* [1977] it would be sufficient if the appellant communicated his withdrawal from the common enterprise by indicating that if the other party decided to proceed it would be without his aid and assistance.

Appeal allowed.